9/09

Fodor's

D0959396

PACII
NORT

17th Edition

**Where to Stay and Eat
for All Budgets**

**Must-See Sights
and Local Secrets**

Ratings You Can Trust

Fodor's Travel Publications   New York, Toronto, London, Sydney, Auckland
www.fodors.com

FODOR'S PACIFIC NORTHWEST
Editor: Eric B. Wechter

Editorial Production: Linda Schmidt
Editorial Contributors: Shelley Arenas, Carissa Bluestone, Kimberly Gadette, Janna Mock-Lopez, Deston Nokes, Rob Phillips, Holly S. Smith, Alison Appelbe, Gina Bacon, Erica Duecy, Carolyn B. Heller, Satu Hummasti, Sue Kernaghan, Vanessa Lazo Greaves, Chris McBeath, Jennifer Snarski, Carolyn Trefler, Jessamyn Westbarker
Maps & Illustrations: David Lindroth, Ed Jacobus, and Mark Stroud, *cartographers* Bob Blake, Rebecca Baer, and William Wu, *map editors*
Design: Fabrizio LaRocca, *creative director*; Guido Caroti, Siobhan O'Hare, *art directors*; Tina Malaney, Chie Ushio, Ann McBride, *designers*; Melanie Marin, *senior picture editor*; Moon Sun Kim, *cover designer*
Cover Photo (Ruby Beach, Olympic National Park, Washington): Digital Vision/Media Bakery
Production/Manufacturing: Angela McLean

17th Edition

ISBN 978–1–4000–0733–2

ISSN 1098–6774

SPECIAL SALES

This book is available at special discounts for bulk purchases for sales promotions or premiums. Special editions, including personalized covers, excerpts of existing books, and corporate imprints, can be created in large quantities for special needs. For more information, write to Special Markets/Premium Sales, 1745 Broadway, MD 6-2, New York, New York 10019, or e-mail specialmarkets@randomhouse.com.

AN IMPORTANT TIP & AN INVITATION

Although all prices, opening times, and other details in this book are based on information supplied to us at press time, changes occur all the time in the travel world, and Fodor's cannot accept responsibility for facts that become outdated or for inadvertent errors or omissions. So **always confirm information when it matters,** especially if you're making a detour to visit a specific place. Your experiences—positive and negative—matter to us. If we have missed or misstated something, **please write to us.** We follow up on all suggestions. Contact the Pacific Northwest editor at editors@fodors.com or c/o Fodor's at 1745 Broadway, New York, NY 10019.

PRINTED IN THE UNITED STATES OF AMERICA
10 9 8 7 6 5 4 3 2 1

Be a Fodor's Correspondent

Your opinion matters. It matters to us. It matters to your fellow Fodor's travelers, too. And we'd like to hear it. In fact, we need to hear it.

When you share your experiences and opinions, you become an active member of the Fodor's community. That means we'll not only use your feedback to make our books better, but we'll publish your names and comments whenever possible. Throughout our guides, look for "Word of Mouth," excerpts of your unvarnished feedback.

Here's how you can help improve Fodor's for all of us.

Tell us when we're right. We rely on local writers to give you an insider's perspective. But our writers and staff editors—who are the best in the business—depend on you. Your positive feedback is a vote to renew our recommendations for the next edition.

Tell us when we're wrong. We're proud that we update most of our guides every year. But we're not perfect. Things change. Hotels cut services. Museums change hours. Charming cafés lose charm. If our writer didn't quite capture the essence of a place, tell us how you'd do it differently. If any of our descriptions are inaccurate or inadequate, we'll incorporate your changes in the next edition and will correct factual errors at fodors.com immediately.

Tell us what to include. You probably have had fantastic travel experiences that aren't yet in Fodor's. Why not share them with a community of like-minded travelers? Maybe you chanced upon a beach or bistro or B&B that you don't want to keep to yourself. Tell us why we should include it. And share your discoveries and experiences with everyone directly at fodors.com. Your input may lead us to add a new listing or highlight a place we cover with a "Highly Recommended" star or with our highest rating, "Fodor's Choice."

Give us your opinion instantly at our feedback center at www.fodors.com/feedback. You may also e-mail editors@fodors.com with the subject line "Pacific Northwest Editor." Or send your nominations, comments, and complaints by mail to Pacific Northwest Editor, Fodor's, 1745 Broadway, New York, NY 10019.

You and travelers like you are the heart of the Fodor's community. Make our community richer by sharing your experiences. Be a Fodor's correspondent.

Happy traveling!

Tim Jarrell, Publisher

CONTENTS

MAPS

ABOUT THIS BOOK

Our Ratings

Sometimes you find terrific travel experiences, and sometimes they just find you. But usually the burden is on you to select the right combination of experiences. That's where our ratings come in.

Sometimes a place is so unique that superlatives don't do it justice: you just have to be there to know. These sights, properties, and experiences get our highest rating, **Fodor's Choice** indicated by orange stars throughout this book.

Black stars highlight sights and properties we deem **Highly Recommended** places that our writers, editors, and readers praise again and again for consistency and excellence.

By default, there's another category: any place we include in this book is by definition worth your time, unless we say otherwise. And we will.

Disagree with any of our choices? Care to nominate a place or suggest that we rate one more highly? Visit our feedback center at www.fodors.com/feedback.

Budget Well

Hotel and restaurant price categories from ¢ to $$$$

are defined in the opening pages of each chapter. For attractions, we always give standard adult admission fees; reductions are usually available for children, students, and senior citizens. Want to pay with plastic? **AE, D, DC, MC, V** following restaurant and hotel listings indicate whether American Express, Discover, Diners Club, MasterCard, and Visa are accepted.

Restaurants

Unless we state otherwise, restaurants are open for lunch and dinner daily. We mention dress only when there's a specific requirement and reservations only when they're essential or not accepted—it's always best to book ahead.

Hotels

Hotels have private bath, phone, TV, and air-conditioning and operate on the European Plan (aka EP, meaning without meals), unless we specify that they use the Continental Plan (CP, with a continental breakfast), Breakfast Plan (BP, with a full breakfast), or Modified American Plan (MAP, with breakfast and dinner), or are all-inclusive (AI, including all meals and most activities). We always list facilities but not whether you'll

be charged an extra fee to use them, so when pricing accommodations, find out what's included.

Many Listings

★	Fodor's Choice
★	Highly recommended
✉	Physical address
↔	Directions
⬥	Mailing address
☎	Telephone
🖷	Fax
⊕	On the Web
✆	E-mail
🖃	Admission fee
☉	Open/closed times
Ⓜ	Metro stations
▭	Credit cards

Hotels & Restaurants

🏨	Hotel
⇥	Number of rooms
⚴	Facilities
⑩	Meal plans
✗	Restaurant
⌂	Reservations
↘	Smoking
⚏	BYOB
✗🏨	Hotel with restaurant that warrants a visit

Outdoors

⚐	Golf
⚠	Camping

Other

☾	Family-friendly
⇨	See also
⊠	Branch address
☞	Take note

WHAT'S WHERE

PORTLAND

Oregon's largest city is among the nation's most livable—not surprising given its progressive policies, excellent public transportation, proximity to nature, and burgeoning music, arts, and restaurant scenes. The city is divided in half by the Willamette River, which runs north–south through the center of Portland. West of the river is Downtown, as well as the trendy neighborhoods of Nob Hill and the Pearl District, and the city's largest parks, Washington Park and Forest Park. On the east side, a different city presents itself. Several popular neighborhoods, including the Hawthorne District, the Alberta Art District, and Sellwood's antiques district, are in the middle of large residential neighborhoods. Some of these areas on the east side feel like small towns in and of themselves, with a main street of shopping and restaurants surrounded by quiet residential areas. On the east side there are also many small neighborhood parks that provide a respite from sightseeing.

OREGON

Although the climate and landscape of Oregon vary dramatically from place to place, much of the state enjoys a constant level of natural splendor. The Pacific coast is a wild and rocky 300-mi stretch with many small towns; driving down the twisting, coastline-hugging U.S. 101 is a right of passage for residents and a highlight of many vacations. In the north are the Columbia River Gorge and Mount Hood, dramatic examples of the power of earth and water, and home to some of the best rafting and hiking in the region. On the gentler side, the Willamette Valley is a lush wine-producing region and home to Eugene and other laid-back cities. Eastern Oregon is little-visited but full of odd surprises like fossil beds and miles of bleak high-country desert.

SEATTLE

Seattle is a sprawling city shaped by many beautiful bodies of water. On the west is Puget Sound; on the east is massive Lake Washington. The city sits in the middle, bisected by highway I–5 and further divvied up by more lakes and canals. As a reminder that real wilderness is not too far away, the city also has amazing views of two major mountain ranges, the Olympics and the Cascades, and on clear days Mt. Rainier looms over the southern side so impressively that even lifelong Seattleites never cease to be amazed by it.

Its attractive downtown with a skyline of business and governmental buildings is punctuated by tourist favorites like Pike Place Farmers Market and the Space Needle. Beyond

this core the city is an amalgam of residential neighborhoods. Each posseses a distinct personality—from the hip, artsy, anything-goes Capitol Hill to quiet, moneyed Queen Anne area perched atop one of the city's steepest hills. The laid-back neighborhoods above the Lake Washington Ship Canal, like Fremont and Ballard, have recently found their way onto most itineraries thanks to their growing shopping, dining, and nightlife scenes.

Washington presents hundreds of opportunities to appreciate the great outdoors. Watch whales from coastal lighthouses, dine on fresh seafood in waterside towns, tramp through dripping rain forests, kayak along rocky beaches, and hike high mountains—and do it all in one trip.

A few hours on the road to the north or south of Seattle delivers you to the unspoiled trails of North Cascades and Mt. Rainier National Parks, as well as along scenic drives over mountain passes and through farmland where there's always fresh produce for sale on the side of the road. The Olympic Peninsula, to the west of Seattle, with its combination of deserted beaches, rain-forest walks, and craggy Olympic Mountain trails draws the majority of Washington's visitors. Much of the southern part of the state is wine country, with the Yakima and Walla Walla valleys side by side. Eastern Washington and its major city Spokane may be far from Seattle (nearly 300 mi), but there are a few sights of note, both man-made, like the Grand Coulee Dam, and natural, like the Palouse, a range of rolling, verdant (in summer) hills formed from silt dunes.

The modern skyscrapers of cosmopolitan Vancouver enjoy a spectacular setting. Tall fir trees and rock spires tower close by, the ocean is at your doorstep, and residents who have come from every corner of the earth create a young and vibrant atmosphere. Worth the trip for the ferry ride alone, Anglophile Victoria, on Vancouver Island, is a stunner. The capital of British Columbia, it is full of stately Victorian structures outlined at night with thousands of starry lights. Many people see Victoria as part of a Vancouver trip, but it is easily reached by ferry from Seattle as well.

QUINTESSENTIAL PACIFIC NORTHWEST

The Pacific Northwest's natural diversity is staggering, both in and out of cities. You can easily get up close and personal with this amazingly varied landscape and explore gardens, forests, lakes, rivers, mountains, beaches, and just about any other kind of ecological zone. Even if your idea of a nature experience is sitting on a rock outdoors, you don't have to miss out: from many beaches and bluffs you can glimpse migrating whales in season.

Out on the Land

The mountains of the Pacific Northwest have given many an adventurer quite a challenge. It is no coincidence that many members of the U.S. expedition teams to Mount Everest come from this region, where the challenges include Washington's Mt. Baker, Mt. Adams, and Mt. Rainier, as well as Oregon's Mt. Hood. Most Oregon downhillers congregate around Mt. Hood and Mt. Bachelor, but there is also skiing to the south at Willamette Pass and Mt. Ashland. Resort and lift-ticket prices tend to be less expensive here than at the internationally known ski destinations, but the slopes, especially on weekends, can be crowded. In the forests and along coastal rivers and estuaries deer, bald eagles, herons, and egrets are commonly seen. Forests in western Washington are dense and overgrown with ferns, mosses, and other vegetation. This is true of the rain forests of the southwest coast and the Olympic Peninsula as well as the forests on the western slopes of the Cascades. Trees in the alpine areas are often gnarled and bent by snow and wind into fascinating shapes. Forests east of the Cascades are sunny and contain stands of ponderosa pine. In spring the forest floor is covered with wildflowers, as are the steppes of the Columbia Plateau.

Residents of the Pacific Northwest are surrounded by a spectacular landscape, which you can delve into by exploring as the natives do.

Beaches

The coasts of Oregon, Washington, and British Columbia have long, sandy beaches that run for miles at a stretch. Though the waters are generally too cold or treacherous for swimming (even in summertime, beachgoers must be prepared to dress warmly), these beaches dazzle visitors in other ways. Often backed by cliffs topped with towering trees or dotted with enormous boulders, they are some of the most beautiful and iconic in the world. Digging for clams and huddling around a bonfire (rain or shine) are two local favorites. The most accessible ocean beaches in the Pacific Northwest are in Oregon, southern Washington, around the Olympic Peninsula, and tucked into Puget Sound. U.S. 101, which meanders down the coasts of Washington and Oregon, provides easily accessed views from windswept promontories.

Out on the Water

Sea lions, seals, dolphins, and whales are a few of the marine mammals that can be observed in bays, near headlands, and along the coast. In spring and summer thousands of gray whales pass by the British Columbia, Washington, and Oregon coasts on their seasonal migration from Alaska to Baja California in Mexico. One of the easiest and most exciting ways to see them is by taking a whale-watching boat excursion. Oregon's swift rivers provide challenges to boaters, canoeists, kayakers, and rafters. Washington's turbulent mountain streams and rivers are also popular with rafters and white-water kayakers. It's best to visit eastern Washington's lakes and coulees between April and mid-October, when the weather is at its best. Lake Chelan, Moses Lake, and the Columbia River Gorge are very popular during the height of the travel season.

IF YOU LIKE

Music

As Seattle continues to shake off the yoke of grunge with an ever-evolving music scene that has grown to include everything from alt-country to hip-hop, Portland beats its drum louder and louder—every indie rocker knows the Rose City is the place to be these days. Independent coffeehouses spin the best of the underground, and intimate clubs with great acoustics inspire soulful jam sessions, while the glittering concert halls of the hub cities host world-class classical performances.

■ **Benaroya Hall, Seattle, WA.** Superior acoustics and an appropriately grand lobby with Elliott Bay views help the Seattle Symphony tackle the master composers.

■ **Northwest Folklife Festival, Seattle, WA.** Sometimes it's hard to spot the remaining hippies in a sea of hipsters, but they reach critical mass at this fun celebration of roots and ethnic folk music.

■ **The Crystal Ballroom, Portland, OR.** A grand historic space with a long history of great live shows, the Crystal Ballroom hosts everything from local indie rockers like the Decemberists to special events of the Portland Jazz Festival.

■ **The Cellar Restaurant and Jazz Club, Vancouver, BC.** One of the best jazz clubs in the world, the Cellar presents Canadian and international players, with two sets per night.

Museums

Although you'll discover a plethora of art and history museums, the Pacific Northwest continues to fascinate visitors with its diverse selection of museums, all of which complement the region's equally diverse culture.

■ **Columbia River Maritime Museum, Astoria, OR.** The observation tower of a World War II submarine and the personal belongings of the passengers of area shipwrecks are among the exhibits here.

■ **Evergreen Aviation Museum, McMinnville, OR.** Engrossing facts about aviation complement an awesome assortment of flying machines at this expansive repository best known as the address of Howard Hughes's "flying boat," the *Spruce Goose*, which has wingspan longer than a football field and its end zones.

■ **High Desert Museum, Bend, OR.** Evocative and intricate walk-through dioramas and an indoor-outdoor zoo with creatures great and tiny convey the High Desert's past and present in a delightfully airy and family-friendly space.

■ **Poulsbo Marine Science Center, Poulsbo, WA.** The creatures of Puget Sound squirm, swim, and squirt. You can have a first-hand experience (excuse the pun) with some of them thanks to the center's touch tanks.

■ **Seattle Asian Art Museum.** Pick an Asian country—any Asian country—and you're likely to find art or artifacts from it here.

■ **Wing Luke Museum, Seattle, WA.** Costumes, crafts, and photographs of immigrants from Asia and the Pacific islands all under one roof.

Distinctive Lodging

In the Pacific Northwest you can stay in hip, urban neighborhoods, along the beach, in the woods, or atop snow-covered mountains. Accommodations include elegant, full-service boutique hotels, simple chain hotels in the suburbs, luxury mountain retreats, ski chalets, national park cabins, and local motels. Bed-and-breakfasts are especially popular and are found throughout the region, with rooms in quaint, historic homes, farmhouses surrounded by grazing horses and llamas, sprawling log cabins amid the rain forest, and weathered cedar mansions beside the lake or bay.

- **Hotel 1000, Seattle, WA.** The pride of the city's recent hotel boom, this chic beauty offers plenty of high-tech sensors and gadgets to fiddle with, along with the city's only state-of-the-art virtual driving range.

- **Heceta House, Heceta Head, OR.** Occupying the same dramatic promontory as a working lighthouse, this Queen Anne–style B&B has views of the Pacific that inspire many a marriage proposal.

- **Salish Lodge, Snoqualmie, WA.** Stare at the Snoqualmie River from a window-seat in your room. Contemplate a dinner of sea bass or beef tenderloin while shaking off the sleepiness that has set in after that late-afternoon massage.

- **Sunriver Resort, Sunriver, OR.** A former military base near Bend has transformed into an almost self-contained resort village. Golf, great food, luxury rooms, and, above all, the high desert's sweeping sense of splendid isolation are the main draws here.

- **Birchfield Manor, Yakima, WA.** A stay here puts you on a plateau in the middle of wine country. The restaurant is one of the region's best: all the entrées come with an exotic homemade bread of the day.

- **Opus, Vancouver.** At this boutique hotel, room designs bear a made-up character's name—Dede's room, Bob & Carole's place—and range from kitschy to glitzy to understated. With eclectic decors, offbeat amenities (complimentary oxygen canisters), and floor to ceiling windows, personality abounds at this Yaletown hotspot.

FLAVORS OF THE PACIFIC NORTHWEST

Pacific Northwest cuisine highlights regional seafood, locally grown produce, and locally raised meats, often prepared in styles that borrow from Pan-Asian, French, and Italian influences. All the region's major cities have top-rated, nationally renowned dining spots, as well as funky, inexpensive little eateries that also pride themselves on serving seasonal and often organic ingredients.

Seafood

The Northwest's dining scene is forever eclectic because of the combined abundance of fresh seafood and the imaginative ways it's cooked. Many restaurants such as **McCormick & Schmick's** print menus daily and feature a "fresh list" with more than 30 types of seafood represented, most of which are caught from local waters. And since Dungeness crab, salmon, tuna, sole, oysters, spotted prawns, scallops, and swordfish are all within pole's reach, chefs take serious and artful pleasure in discovering ways to fry, grill, bake, stir-fry, sear, poach, barbecue, and sauté the latest catch in new, inventive ways.

■ **Elliott's Oyster House, Seattle, WA.** Brave the touristy waterfront to belly up to the shellfish bar—you won't find better oysters or Dungeness crab in Seattle

■ **Matt's in the Market, Seattle, WA.** Right next to Seattle's prime source of fresh fish, Pike Place Market, Matt's serves a must-try oyster po'boy and Penn Cove mussels with chorizo or Dungeness crab bisque, and pan-roasted fillets of wild salmon and ling cod served with light vinaigrettes.

■ **Jake's Famous Crawfish, Portland, OR.** For more than 100 years Portlander's have come to Jake's. You should,

too, especially during crawfish season (May–September).

■ **Blue Water Café, Vancouver, BC.** Ask the staff to recommend wine-pairings from the BC-focused list, and enjoy exquisitely prepared seafood, which may include overlooked varieties such as mackerel, sardines, and herring.

Foraged Foods

Pacific Northwest chefs are fanatical, in a delicious way, about sustainability, which entails presenting dishes with ingredients raised, grown, or foraged within 100 mi. Northwest chefs are so determined to maintain an unwavering connection to the land that many have become obsessed with foraged foods, either hiring professional foragers or on occasion tromping off into the woods themselves. Bounties of morels, chanterelles, and bolete mushrooms (fall), stinging nettles and fiddlehead ferns (spring), and huckleberries and blackberries (summer) now dictate the menus of many restaurants. From both Portland and Seattle, farmland is in immediate distance of urban boundaries, therefore everyday deliveries of fruits and vegetables—like asparagus, eggplant, pears, and cherries—is achievable.

■ **Sitka & Spruce, Seattle, WA.** Wild greens and edible flowers always show up in salads or as garnishes alongside fresh seafood or free-range chicken from Vashon Island farms at Chef Matt Dillon's tiny temple to the Northwest.

■ **Lark, Seattle, WA.** Naturally raised veal sweetbreads come with a sunchoke puree, and spring nettles are stuffed into spinach ravioli at Lark, where the small menu names every local farm that contributes to its dishes.

- **The Herbfarm, Woodinville, WA.** Every year the Herbfarm honors mushroom season with the Mycologist's Dream menu, which sees the fungi go into everything from ravioli to flan. The rest of the year blackberries may mingle with rose geranium in ice cream or caviar may be accompanied by a jelly flavored with wild ginger and local rhizomes.

- **clarklewis, Portland, OR.** Regional vegetables, seafood, and meat cultivated from local suppliers appear on a daily changing menu of pastas, entrées, and sides

Wineries

Thanks to a mild climate with soil, air, water, and temperature conditions comparable to regions of France, the Northwest is recognized for producing prime varieties of wine. Aptly compared to Napa, in Oregon and Washington alone there are more than 43,000-plus acres of vineyards. In charming, rural settings, some just outside of larger cities such as Portland and Seattle, petite to larger vineyards offer behind-the-scenes tours and have quaint wine-tasting rooms where sampling the merchandise is encouraged. Another trend putting this winemaking region in the spotlight is the production of organic wine. In keeping with the sustainable food and farm movement in the Northwest, vineyards are trying their hand in developing fertilization, production, harvesting, and fermentation techniques that produce delicious, flavorful, ecofriendly varieties that set the standard in the wine world.

Artisanal Cocktails

The artisan drinks of the region are thoughtful and high-quality, often following the same principles as Pacific Northwest cuisine by only using local and seasonal ingredients, including fresh juices and herbs garnered from farmers' markets. Bourbon lovers never had it so good, as the drink seems to be at the base of most creations; for the rest, there are plenty of obscure lavender-infused liqueurs to choose from. If the idea of fresh honey, rhubarb, or ginger beer corrupting a fine liquor makes you queasy, rest assured that classic drinks are making a comeback, too. In Seattle, for example, several bartenders are single-handedly restoring the dignity of the martini, the Manhattan, and the French 75.

- **Mint/820, Portland, OR.** Bartender and owner Lucy Brennan wrote the book on creative cocktails—literally; she's the author of *Hip Sips*, which features more than 60 recipes.

- **Zig Zag, Seattle, WA.** Zig Zag pours the best martinis in Seattle, along with more exotic fare like the Trident (cynar, aquavit, dry sherry, and peach bitters) and improvised cocktails for residents who know to ask for them.

- **Roux, Portland, OR.** The bartenders at Roux are known throughout Portland as masters of New-Orleans/Southern–inspired cocktails.

- **Licorous, Seattle, WA.** Licorous customizes its nibbles to complement the drink list. Parmigiano-and-chorizo palmiers may be suggested to temper the sweet-and-sour Playa Rosa, made with tequila infused with hibiscus, and fresh lime and pineapple juices.

WHEN TO GO

The Pacific Northwest's mild climate is best from June through September. Hotels in the major tourist destinations are often filled in July and August, so it's important to book reservations in advance. Spring and fall are also excellent times to visit. The weather usually remains quite good, and the prices for accommodations, transportation, and tours can be lower (and the crowds much smaller!) in the most popular destinations. In winter, snow is uncommon in the lowland areas but abundant in the nearby mountains, making the region a skier's dream.

Climate

Average daytime summer highs are in the 70s; winter temperatures are generally in the 40s. Rainfall varies greatly from one locale to another. In the coastal mountains, for example, 160 inches of rain falls annually, creating temperate rain forests. In eastern Oregon, Washington, and British Columbia, near-desert conditions prevail, with rainfall as low as 6 inches per year. Seattle has an average of only 36 inches of rainfall a year—less than New York, Chicago, or Miami—however, in winter the rain may never seem to end. More than 75% of Seattle's annual precipitation occurs from October through March. Portland is equally gray and drizzly in winter.

Forecasts **National Weather Service** (⊕ www.wrh.noaa.gov). **Weather Channel** (⊕ www.weather.com).

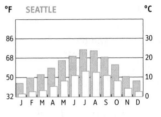

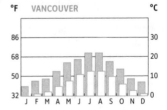

PACIFIC NORTHWEST DRIVING TOUR

NORTH CASCADES NATIONAL PARK
Days 1 & 2

From Seattle, drive 71 mi (1½ hours) up I–5 to Route 20 and ❶ **Sedro-Woolley,** where you can pick up information about ❷ **North Cascades National Park** at the park headquarters. From Sedro-Woolley, it's at least an hour's drive on Route 20 to the park entrance. Take your first stroll through an old-growth forest from the visitor center in Newhalem, then devote the rest of the day to driving through the **Cascades** on Route 20, stopping at various overlooks. Exit the park and continue through the **Methow Valley** to ❸ **Winthrop** (1¾ hour from Newhalem) to stay the night.

Spend the morning of Day 2 at the park, hiking and exploring. In the afternoon head south on Route 20, then Route 153, then U.S. 97, then I–82 (just over 300 mi total, 4½ hours) to ❹ **Yakima** to stay the night. Alternatively, head down to Yakima straight after breakfast and spend the late afternoon in wine country exploring one or two of the vineyards along I–82.

MOUNT RAINIER NATIONAL PARK
Days 3 & 4

On the morning of Day 3, take U.S. 12 west from Yakima 102 mi (about 2 hours) to Ohanapecosh, the southern entrance to ❺ **Mount Rainier National Park.** When you arrive, take the 35-mi three-hour drive on Sunrise Road, which reveals the "back" (northeast) side of Rainier. A room at the **Paradise Inn** is your base for the next two nights. On Day 4, energetic hikers will want to tackle one of the four- to six-hour trails that lead up among the park's many peaks. Or try one of the ranger-led walks through wildflower meadows. Another option is to hike to Panorama Point near the foot of the **Muir Snowfield** for breathtaking views of the glaciers and high ridges of Rainier overhead. After dinner at the inn, watch the sunset's alpenglow on the peak from the back porch.

OLYMPIC NATIONAL PARK
Days 5, 6 & 7

From Rainier take Route 7 to Route 510 to I–5 south. About two hours into your drive, and shortly after getting on I–5 south, you'll have the option of stopping in Olympia, Washington's capital, for a leg-stretch (there's a pleasant loop trail around the lake by the domed Capitol Building), and lunch in one of the city's cute cafés or coffeehouses. In Olympia you can pick up U.S. 101 north. The highway winds through scenic Puget Sound countryside, skirting the Olympic foothills and periodically dipping down to the waterfront. Another 2½ hours (and about 119 mi) of driving will bring you to ❻ **Port Angeles,** a great place to wind down, have dinner, and spend the night.

The next morning, launch into a full day at ❼ **Olympic National Park.** Explore the

THE PLAN

DISTANCE: 1,800 mi

TIME: 10 days

BREAKS: Overnight in Winthrop, Yakima, Mount Rainier National Park, Port Angeles, and Lake Quinault, WA; and Florence, Crater Lake National Park, and Ashland, OR.

Pacific Northwest Driving Tour

BRITISH COLUMBIA

Vancouver

VANCOUVER ISLAND

CANADA
USA

Bellingham

Oroville

North Cascades National Park

97

Victoria

Cape Flattery

Neah Bay

Juan de Fuca Strait

Sedro-Woolley ①

Rockport

②

Winthrop ③

20

Brewster

Port Angeles ⑥

Port Townsend

WASHINGTON

Wenatchee

La Push ⑧

⑦

Olympic National Park

101

16

Seattle

90

RANGE

2

97

90

Ellensburg

Tacoma

Auburn

101

Aberdeen

Willapa Bay

OLYMPIA

Elbe

Mount Rainier National Park ⑤

Ohanapecosh

12

Yakima ④

82

Kennewick

Chehalis

Morton

Long Beach

YAKIMA VALLEY

5

Kelso

Mount St. Helens National Volcanic Monument

CASCADE

84

Arlington

Umatilla

Astoria

Cannon Beach

26

Columbia

14

14

Portland

The Dalles

97

Tillamook

Oceanside ⑩

SALEM

WILLAMETTE VALLEY

Deschutes

Madras

26

Newport

Albany

20

Prineville

OREGON

Florence ⑪

Oregon Dunes National Recreation Area

101

Eugene

Bend

20

Riley

58

Coos Bay

138

Crater Lake National Park

Summer Lake

Summer Lake

Roseburg

⑫

97

Gold Beach

5

Grants Pass

62

Upper Klamath Lake

Paisley

46

Ashland ⑬

Klamath Falls

Lake View

Oregon Caves National Park

CALIFORNIA

0 ___ 50 mi
0 ___ 50 km

Hoh Rain Forest and **Hurricane Ridge** before heading back to Port Angeles for the evening.

Start Day 7 with a drive west on U.S. 101 through Forks (remember to fill up the tanks and get snacks here before you hit a lonely stretch of road) and on to ❽ **La Push** via Route 110, a total of about 68 mi. Here, an hour-long lunchtime stroll to **Second or Third Beach** will offer a taste of the wild Pacific coastline. Back on U.S. 101, head south two hours to **Lake Quinault,** which is about 83 mi from La Push. Check into the Lake Quinault Lodge, then drive up the river 6 mi to one of the rain-forest trails through the lush Quinault Valley.

THE PACIFIC COAST
Day 8

Leave Lake Quinault early on Day 8 for the long but scenic drive south on U.S. 101. Here the road winds through coastal spruce forests, periodically rising on headlands to offer Pacific Ocean panoramas. Once you're in Oregon, small seaside resort towns beckon with cafés, shops, and inns. **Astoria** (121 mi from Lake Quinault) or **Cannon Beach** (22 mi from Astoria) are both great places to take a breather and grab some lunch; there are some lovely beaches and coastal trails in the Cannon Beach area, too. In ❾ **Tillamook** (famous for its cheese and not much else), take a detour onto the Three Capes Loop, a stunning 35-mi byway off U.S. 101, which takes about an hour to complete. If you need another break, stop at ❿ **Oceanside,** which is along the loop, for a snack. Once you're back on U.S. 101, continue south. Your final stop is the charming village of ⓫ **Florence,** 290

mi from Lake Quinault, where you can spend the night.

CRATER LAKE NATIONAL PARK
Day 9

From Florence, take U.S. 101 south to Reedsport, routes 38 and 138 east to Sutherlin, I–5 south to Roseburg, and Route 138 east again to ⓬ **Crater Lake National Park,** 180 mi total (about 4½ hours). Once inside the park, you can continue along Rim Drive for another half hour for excellent views of the lake.

In the afternoon, head south on Route 62 to I–5, and on to ⓭ **Ashland,** 83 mi (about two hours) from Crater Lake. Plan to stay the night in one of Ashland's many superb B&Bs. Have dinner and attend one of the **Oregon Shakespeare Festival** productions (mid-February through early November).

If you shave a day off the Washington portion of the trip by only spending two days on the Olympic Peninsula, you can add a day here. The following morning, take the lake boat tour and a hike through the surrounding forest before heading down to Ashland and spending the second night there.

PORTLAND
Day 10

Head back north on I–5 from Ashland to ⓮ **Portland.** The drive is 284 mi and takes about 4½ hours. With a reasonably early start, you'll arrive in time to explore a few neighborhoods and enjoy a good meal and a comfortable hotel stay.

Portland

WORD OF MOUTH

"If your style is to wander on foot, Portland is good for that, as it is a very walkable, not-too-large city with plenty of opportunities to take breaks.shopping, drinking , eating, parks etc."

—Scarlett

"One nice thing about Portland is that if you stay in Downtown you can walk to many locations. If you are into music, check out a concert at the Crystal Ballroom."

—bkropf

Updated by
Janna Mock-
Lopez

Portland's proximity to mountains, ocean, and desert adds an element of natural grandeur to its urban character. Majestic Mt. Hood, about 55 mi to the east, acts as a kind of mascot, and on a clear day several peaks of the Cascade Range are visible, including Mt. St. Helens. The west side of town is built on a series of forested hills that descend to the downtown area, the Willamette River, and the flatter east side. Filled with stately late-19th-century and modern architecture, linked by an effective transit system, and home to a vital arts scene, Portland is a place where there's much to do day or night, rain or shine.

The quality of life remains a constant priority here. As far back as 1852, Portland began setting aside city land as parks. Included among Portland's 250 parks, public gardens, and greenways are the nation's largest urban wilderness, the world's smallest park, and the only extinct volcano within a city's limits in the lower 48 states. A temperate climate and plenty of precipitation keep Portland green year-round. The City of Roses, as it's known, celebrates its favorite flower with a monthlong Rose Festival in June, but the floral spectacle really starts three months earlier, when streets and gardens bloom with the colors of flowering trees, camellias, rhododendrons, and azaleas.

Within Portland's 145-square-mi borders are 90 diverse and distinct neighborhoods. You'll find creative works on street corners, as well as in police stations, jails, transit stations, parks, and civic buildings. The MAX light-rail line along North Interstate Avenue is virtually an outdoor gallery of installations and sculptures. As for the performing arts, Portland has several high-level professional theater companies, the Oregon Symphony, the Portland Opera, and Chamber Music Northwest, to name a few. Those into nightlife will also find some of the best live-band and club action in the country. Families have plenty of kid-friendly attractions to enjoy, including the Oregon Zoo and adjacent Portland Children's Museum, Oaks Amusement Park, and the Oregon Museum of Science and Industry.

Architectural preservation is a major preoccupation in Portland, particularly when it comes to the 1860s brick buildings with cast-iron columns and the 1890s ornate terra-cotta designs that grace areas like the Skidmore, Old Town, and Yamhill national historic districts. In the Pearl District, older industrial buildings are being given new life as residential lofts, restaurants, office space, galleries, and boutiques. An extension of the MAX light-rail line to Portland International Airport and the Portland Streetcar have made the city easy to get around in without a car, connecting Portland State University, downtown, and the Pearl District and Nob Hill neighborhood. The city's farsighted approach to growth and its pitfalls means it reaps all of the benefits and few of the problems of its boom. As a result, Portland is more dynamic than ever, cultivating a new level of sophistication, building on enhanced prosperity, and bursting with fresh energy.

TOP 5

1. Being one of the hottest foodie destinations on the planet, experience an amazingly textured and full culinary range of global delights created with fresh, locally grown or harvested ingredients.

2. Beer "hop-ping" (no pun intended) between among more than 40 microbrews sampling offbeat-named varieties such as Hallucinator, Doggie Claws, and Sock Knocker.

3. Get up close and personal with Portland's true quirky nature by staying at, or visiting one of the many beautifully restored McMenamins properties in and around town.

4. Spend the day at Washington Park where you can absorb recreation and inspiration. Stroll through the International Rose Test Garden, the Japanese Garden, the Oregon Zoo, World Forrestry Center, and the Children's Museum all within a short distance of one another.

5. Peruse the infinite aisles of more than a million new and used books at Powell's City of Books in the Pearl. Top off hours of literary wander-lust with a fresh mocha or Ginseng tea downstairs at World Cup Coffee and Tea House.

EXPLORING PORTLAND

The Willamette River is Portland's east–west dividing line. Burnside Street separates north from south. The city's 200-foot-long blocks make them easy to walk, but you can also explore the downtown core and Nob Hill by MAX light rail, the Portland Streetcar, or Tri-Met buses (⇨ *Portland Essentials*). Closer to the downtown core are the Pearl District and Old Town/Chinatown. Both the Pearl District and Nob Hill have a plethora of restaurants, specialty shops, and nightspots.

DOWNTOWN

Portland has one of the most attractive, inviting downtown urban cores in the United States. It's clean, compact, and filled with parks, plazas, and fountains. With a mix of new and historic buildings, architecture aficionados will find plenty to admire. Hotels, shops, museums, restaurants, and entertainment can all be found here, and the entire downtown area is part of the TriMet transit system's Fareless Square, within which you can ride MAX, the Portland Streetcar, or any bus for free.

Numbers in the margin correspond to the Downtown, the Pearl District & Old Town/Chinatown map.

WHAT TO SEE

❷ **Central Library.** The elegant, etched-graphite central staircase and elaborate ceiling ornamentation make this no ordinary library. With a gallery space on the second floor and famous literary names engraved on the walls, this building is well worth a walk around. ⊠ *801 S.W. 10th Ave., Downtown* ☎ *503/988–5123* ▭ *Free* ☉ *Mon. and Thurs.–Sat. 10–6, Tues. and Wed. 10–8, Sun. noon–5.*

GREAT ITINERARIES

IF YOU HAVE 1 DAY

Spend the morning exploring downtown. Visit the Portland Art Museum or the Oregon History Center, stop by the historic First Congregational Church and Pioneer Courthouse Square, and take a stroll along the Park Blocks or Waterfront Park. Eat lunch and do a little shopping along Northwest 23rd Avenue in the early afternoon, and be sure to walk down a few side streets to get a look at the beautiful historic homes in Nob Hill. From there, drive up into the northwest hills by the Pittock Mansion, and finish off the afternoon at the Japanese Garden and the International Test Rose Garden in Washington Park. If you still have energy, head across the river for dinner on Hawthorne Boulevard; then drive up to Mt. Tabor Park for Portland's best view of the sunset.

IF YOU HAVE 3 DAYS

On your first day, follow the one-day itinerary above, exploring downtown, Nob Hill, and Washington Park, but stay on the west side for dinner, and take your evening stroll in Waterfront Park. On your second morning, visit the Portland Classical Chinese Garden in Old Town, and then head across the river to the Sellwood District for lunch and antiquing. Stop by the Crystal Springs Rhododendron Garden; then head up to Hawthorne District in the afternoon. Wander through the Hawthorne and Belmont neighborhoods for a couple of hours, stop by Laurelhurst Park, and take a picnic dinner up to Mt. Tabor Park. In the evening, catch a movie at the Bagdad Theatre, or get a beer at one of the east-side brewpubs. On Day 3, take a morning hike in Hoyt Arboretum or Forest Park; then spend your afternoon exploring shops and galleries in the Pearl District and on northeast Alberta Street. Drive out to the Grotto, and then eat dinner at the Kennedy School or one of the other McMenamins brewpubs.

❿ City Hall. Portland's four-story, granite-faced City Hall, which was completed in 1895, is an example of the Renaissance Revival style popular in the late 19th century. Italian influences can be seen in the porch, the pink scagliola columns, the cornice embellishments, and other details. Much beauty was restored when the building was renovated in the late 1990s. The ornate interior—with intricate scrollwork, decorative tile, sunny atrium, and art exhibits—provides a fine shortcut between Southwest 4th and 5th avenues. ✉ *1220 S.W. 5th Ave., Downtown* ☎ *503/823–4000* ⊗ *Weekdays 8–5.*

❽ Governor Tom McCall Waterfront Park. The park named for a former governor of Oregon revered for his statewide land-use planning initiatives stretches north along the Willamette River for about a mile to Burnside Street. Broad and grassy, it yields a fine ground-level view of downtown Portland's bridges and skyline. The park, on the site of a former expressway, hosts many events, among them the Rose Festival, classical and blues concerts, and the Oregon Brewers Festival. The four-day **Cinco de Mayo Festival** in early May celebrates Portland's sister-city relationship with Guadalajara, Mexico. Next to the Rose Festival, this is one of Portland's biggest get-togethers. Food and arts-

IF YOU LIKE

BIKING

Portland has been called the best city in the country for biking, and with bike lanes galore, mild weather year-round, and a beautiful waterfront to ride along, it's no wonder. Not only does cycling provide an excellent form of transportation around here, it also has evolved into a medium of progressive politics and public service. Riders gather at least once every month to ride en masse through the streets of the city in an event called Critical Mass to show solidarity as a powerful alternative to an auto-society, and they have been known to gather force for the purpose of political protest. In addition, several bike co-ops have sprung up throughout the city in the past several years, devoted to providing used bikes at decent prices to members of the community, as well as to teaching bike maintenance and the economic and environmental benefits of becoming a commuter on two wheels.

PUB THEATERS

Everyone knows that Oregon loves its microbrews, and sipping a pint of local brew is one of Oregon's favorite pastimes, but Portlanders have taken this a step further, creating a recreational venue fondly called the pub theater; that is, a movie theater showing second-run, classic, or cult films for $2 or $3, where you can buy a pitcher of good locally brewed beer and a slice of pizza to enjoy while watching. The McMenamins brothers are largely to thank for this phenomenon, being the masterminds behind such popular spots as the Bagdad Theatre, the Mission Theatre, and the St. John's Pub, but unaffiliated establishments like the Laurelhurst Theatre and the Clinton Street Theater manage to edge in on the action as well.

BRIDGES

With a river running through the center of the city, Portland has one of the most interesting urban landscapes in the country, due in no small part to the several unique bridges that span the width of the Willamette River. Five of the city's 10 bridges are drawbridges, frequently raised to let barges go through, and there is something awe-inspiring and anachronistic in watching a portion of a city's traffic and hubbub stand still for several minutes as a slow-moving vessel floats through still water. Each bridge is beautiful and different: the St. John's Bridge has elegant 400-foot towers, the Broadway Bridge is a rich red hue, the arches of the huge two-level Fremont Bridge span the river gracefully, and the Steel Bridge has a pedestrian walkway just 30 feet above the water, allowing walkers and bikers to get a fabulous view of the river.

and-crafts booths, stages with mariachi bands, and a carnival complete with a Ferris wheel line the riverfront for the event. Bikers and joggers enjoy the area year-round. The arching jets of water at the **Salmon Street Fountain** change configuration every few hours and are a favorite cooling-off spot during the dog days of summer. ⊠ *S. W. Naito Pkwy. (Front Ave.) from south of Hawthorne Bridge to Burnside Bridge, Downtown.*

Downtown, The Pearl District & Old Town/Chinatown

N.W. Glisan St.
N.W. Flanders St.
N.W. Everett St.
N.W. Davis St. CHINATOWN DISTRICT
N.W. Couch St.
W. Burnside St.

SKIDMORE OLD TOWN NATIONAL HISTORIC DISTRICT

Ankeny St.
S.W. Ash St.
S.W. Pine St.
S.W. Oak St.
S.W. Stark St.

Burnside Bridge

N.W. 19th Ave.
N.W. 18th Ave.
N.W. 17th Ave.
N.W. 16th Ave.
N.W. 14th Ave.
N.W. 10th Ave.
N.W. 9th Ave.
N.W. 6th Ave.
N.W. 4th Ave.
N.W. 3rd Ave.

MAX LIGHT RAIL

CENTRAL CITY STREETCAR

405

S.W. 13th Ave.
S.W. 12th Ave.
S.W. 11th Ave.
S.W. 10th Ave.
S.W. 9th Ave.
S.W. Park Ave.

S.W. Washington St.
S.W. Alder St.
6th Ave./Transit Mall St.
S.W. Morrison St.

S.W. Yamhill St.
S.W. Taylor St.
S.W. Salmon St.
S.W. Main St.
S.W. Madison St.
S.W. Columbia St.
S.W. Clay St.
S.W. Market St.
S.W. Mill St.

S.W. Jefferson St.

5th Ave./Transit Mall
S.W. 4th Ave.
S.W. 3rd Ave.
S.W. 2nd Ave.
S.W. 1st Ave.

MAX LIGHT RAIL

GOVERNOR (TOM McCALL) WATERFRONT PARK

S.W. Naito Pkwy. (Front Ave.)

Morrison Bridge

Willamette River

Hawthorne Bridge

5

TO CHILDREN'S MUSEUM ↓

26

0   1/4 mile
0   1/4 kilometer

South Park Blocks

S.W. Broadway

26

26

KEY

—O— *Max Light Rail*
—←— *Sreetcar*

⑨ Mark O. Hatfield U.S. Courthouse. This skyscraper's sophisticated exterior is clad in Indiana limestone, and the courtroom lobbies have expansive glass walls. Whimsical bronze critters make light of the justice system in a piece titled *Law of Nature*, the centerpiece of a ninth-floor sculpture garden that has grand city views. Visitors must pass through a security screening and show photo ID. ⊠ *S.W. 3rd Ave. between Main and Salmon Sts., Downtown* ⌨ *Free* ⊙ *Weekdays.*

⑥ Old Church. This building erected in 1882 is a prime example of Carpenter Gothic architecture. Tall spires and original stained-glass windows enhance its exterior of rough-cut lumber. The acoustically resonant church hosts free classical concerts at noon each Wednesday. If you're lucky you'll get to hear one of the few operating Hook and Hastings tracker pipe organs. ⊠ *1422 S.W. 11th Ave., Downtown* ☎ *503/222–2031* ⊕ *www.oldchurch.org* ⌨ *Free* ⊙ *Weekdays 11–3.*

④ Oregon Historical Society. Impressive eight-story-high trompe-l'oeil
★ murals of Lewis and Clark and the Oregon Trail (the route the two pioneers took from the Midwest to the Oregon Territory) cover two sides of this downtown museum, which follows the state's story from prehistoric times to the present. A pair of 9,000-year-old sagebrush sandals, a covered wagon, and an early chainsaw are displayed inside "Oregon My Oregon," a permanent exhibit that provides a comprehensive overview of the state's past. Other spaces host large traveling exhibits and changing regional shows. The center's research library is open to the public; its bookstore is a good source for maps and publications on Pacific Northwest history. ⊠ *1200 S.W. Park Ave., Downtown* ☎ *503/222–1741* ⊕ *www.ohs.org* ⌨ *$10* ⊙ *Mon.–Sat. 10–5, Sun. noon–5.*

❶ Pioneer Courthouse Square. Considered by most to be the living room, public heart, and commercial soul of Downtown Portland, Pioneer Square is not entirely square but rather centered in this amphitheatrical brick piazza. Special seasonal, charitable, and festival-oriented events often take place in this premier people-watching space. On Sunday, **vintage trolley** (☎ *503/323–7363*) cars run from the MAX station here to Lloyd Center, with free service every half hour between noon and 6 PM. Call to check on the current schedule. You can pick up maps and literature about the city and the state here at the **Portland/Oregon Information Center** (☎ *503/275–8355* ⊕ *www.pova.com* ⊙ *Weekdays 8:30–5:30, Sat. 10–4, Sun. 10–2 Mar.–Oct.*). Directly across the street is one of downtown Portland's most familiar landmarks, the classically sedate **Pioneer Courthouse.** Built in 1869, it's the oldest public building in the Pacific Northwest. ⊠ *701 S.W. 6th Ave., Downtown.*

❺ Portland Art Museum. The treasures at the Pacific Northwest's oldest
★ visual- and media-arts facility span 35 centuries of Asian, European, and American art. A high point is the Center for Native American Art, with regional and contemporary art from more than 200 tribes. **The Jubitz Center for Modern and Contemporary Art** contains six floors devoted entirely to modern art, which rotates and has more than 400 works of art from the Museum's permanent collection. The film cen-

ter presents the annual Portland International Film Festival in February and the Northwest Film Festival in early November. Also take a moment to linger in the peaceful outdoor sculpture garden. ⊠*1219 S.W. Park Ave., Downtown* ☎*503/226–2811, 503/221–1156 film schedule* ⊕*www.pam.org* ☎*$10* ☉*Tues., Wed., and Sat. 10–5, Thurs. and Fri. 10–8, Sun. noon–5.*

⓫ Portland Building. *Portlandia,* the second-largest hammered-copper statue in the world, surpassed only by the Statue of Liberty, kneels on the second-story balcony of one of the first postmodern buildings in the United States. The design of the building itself was considered controversial. As architect Michael Graves's first major design commission, it's buff-color, with brown-and-blue trim and exterior decorative touches. A huge fiberglass mold of Portlandia's face is exhibited in the second-floor Public Art Gallery, which provides a good overview of Portland's 1% for Art Program, and the hundreds of works on display throughout the city. ⊠*1120 S.W. 5th Ave., Downtown* ☎*Free* ☉*Weekdays 8–6.*

❸ Portland Center for the Performing Arts. The "old building" and the hub of activity here is the **Arlene Schnitzer Concert Hall,** host to the Oregon Symphony, musical events of many genres, and lectures. Across Main Street, but still part of the center, is the 292-seat **Delores Winningstad Theater,** used for plays and special performances. Its stage design and dimensions are based on those of an Elizabethan-era stage. The 916-seat **Newmark Theater,** is also part of the complex. ⊠*S.W. Broadway and S.W. Main St., Downtown* ☎*503/274–6560* ⊕*www.pcpa.com* ☉*Free tours Wed. at 11* AM, *Sat. every ½ hr 11–1, and 1st Thurs. of month at 6* PM.

❼ Portland Farmer's Market. On Saturday from April through mid-December, local farmers, bakers, chefs, and entertainers converge at the South Park Blocks near the PSU campus for Oregon's largest open-air farmer's market. It's a great place to sample the regional bounty of seasonal and organic produce, and to witness an obsession for local food that's revolutionizing Portland's culinary scene. There's also a Wednesday market. ⊠*South Park Blocks at S.W. Park Ave. and Montgomery St., Downtown* ☎*503/241–0032* ⊕*www.portlandfarmersmarket.org* ☉*Apr.–mid-Dec., Sat. 8:30–2; May–Oct., Wed. 10–2.*

PEARL DISTRICT & OLD TOWN/CHINATOWN

The Pearl District is the fastest-growing part of Portland. Mid-rise residential lofts have sprouted on almost every block, and boutiques, outdoor retailers, galleries, and trendy restaurants border the streets. The Portland streetcar line passes through here with stops at two new, ecologically themed city parks.

Old Town/Chinatown is where Portland was born. The 20-square-block section includes buildings of varying ages and architectural designs. MAX serves the area with a stop at the Old Town/Chinatown station.

Numbers in the margin correspond to the Downtown, the Pearl District & Old Town/Chinatown map.

WHAT TO SEE

⑯ Chinatown Gate. Recognizable by its five roofs, 64 dragons, and two huge lions, the Chinatown Gate is the official entrance to the **Chinatown District**. During the 1890s, Portland had the second-largest Chinese community in the United States. Today's Chinatown is compressed into a handful of blocks with a few restaurants (many prefer Chinese eateries outside the district), shops, and grocery stores. ⊠ *N.W. 4th Ave. and Burnside St., Old Town/Chinatown.*

⑱ Jamison Square Park. This gently terraced park surrounded by tony Pearl District lofts contains a soothing fountain that mimics nature. Rising water gushes over a stack of basalt blocks, gradually fills the open plaza, and then subsides. Colorful 30-foot tiki totems by pop artist Kenny Scharf stand along the park's west edge. Take the streetcar to Jamison Square. ⊠ *N.W. 10th Ave. and Lovejoy St., Pearl District.*

⑭ Japanese-American Historical Plaza. Take a moment to study the evocative figures cast into the bronze columns at the plaza's entrance; they show Japanese-Americans before, during, and after World War II—living daily life, fighting in battle for the United States, and marching off to internment camps. Simple blocks of granite carved with haiku poems describing the war experience powerfully evoke this dark episode in American history. ⊠ *N.W. Naito Pkwy. and Davis St., in Waterfront Park. Old Town/Chinatown.*

⑰ Jean Vollum Natural Capital Center. Known to most locals as the Ecotrust Building, this building has a handful of organic and environment-friendly businesses and retail, including Hot Lips Pizza, World Cup Coffee, and Patagonia (outdoor clothes). Built in 1895 and purchased by Ecotrust in 1998, the building has been significantly adapted to serve as a landmark in sustainable, "green" building practices. Grab a "field guide" in the lobby and take the self-guided tour of the building, which begins with the original "remnant wall" on the west side of the parking lot; proceeds throughout the building; and ends on the "eco-roof," a grassy rooftop with a great view of the Pearl District. ⊠ *721 N.W. 9th Ave., Pearl District* ☎ *503/227–6225* ⊕ *www.ecotrust.org* 🖼 *Free* ☉ *Weekdays 7–6; ground-floor businesses also evenings and weekends.*

⑬ Oregon Maritime Center and Museum. Local model makers created most of this museum's models of ships that plied the Columbia River. Contained entirely within the stern-wheeler steamship *Portland*, docked at the foot of Southwest Pine Street on the seawall in Tom McCall Waterfront Park, this small museum provides an excellent overview of Oregon's maritime history. Starting spring 2008 visitors will benefit by the museum's extensive remodels. ⊠ *On steamship at end of S.W. Pine St., in Waterfront Park, Skidmore District* ☎ *503/224–7724* ⊕ *www. oregonmaritimemuseum.org* 🖼 *$5* ☉ *Wed–Sun. 11–4.*

15 **Portland Classical Chinese Garden.** In a twist on the Joni Mitchell song,
Fodor'sChoice the city of Portland and private donors took down a parking lot and
★ unpaved paradise, as it were, when they created this wonderland
neighboring the Pearl District and Old Town/Chinatown. It's the largest Suzhou-style garden outside China, with a large lake, bridged and
covered walkways, koi- and water lily–filled ponds, rocks, bamboo,
statues, waterfalls, and courtyards. A team of 60 artisans and designers from China literally left no stone unturned—500 tons of stone
were brought here from Suzhou—in their efforts to give the windows,
roof tiles, gateways, including a "moongate," and other architectural
aspects of the garden some specific meaning or purpose. Also on the
premises are a gift shop and a two-story teahouse overlooking the lake
and garden. ⊠ *N.W. 3rd Ave. and Everett St., Old Town/Chinatown*
☎ *503/228–8131* ⊕ *www.portlandchinesegarden.org* ⊒ *$7* ☉ *Nov.–
Mar., daily 10–5; Apr.–Oct., daily 9–6. Tours daily at noon and 1.*

12 **Portland Saturday Market.** On weekends from March to Christmas, the
Fodor'sChoice west side of the Burnside Bridge and the Skidmore Fountain environs
★ has North America's largest open-air handicraft market. If you're looking for a diverse blend of jewelry, yard art, housewares, and decorative
goods made from every material under the sun, you'll enjoy perusing
an amazing collection of talent in a favorite local pastime. Entertainers
and food and produce booths add to the festive feel. ⊠ *Under west end
of Burnside Bridge, from S.W. Naito Pkwy. to Ankeny Sq., Skidmore
District* ☎ *503/222–6072* ⊕ *www.saturdaymarket.org* ☉ *Mar.–Dec.,
Sat. 10–5, Sun. 11–4:30.*

19 **Powell's City of Books.** The largest independent bookstore in the world,
Fodor'sChoice with more than 1.5 million new and used books, Powell's is a Portland
★ landmark that can easily consume several hours. It's so big it has its
own map, and rooms are color-coded according to the types of books,
so you can find your way out again. Be sure to espy the pillar bearing
signatures of prominent sci-fi authors who have passed through the
store—the scrawls are protected by a jagged length of Plexiglas. At the
very least, stop into Powell's for a peek or grab a cup of coffee at the
adjoining branch of World Cup Coffee. ⊠ *1005 W. Burnside St., Pearl
District* ☎ *503/228–4651* ⊕ *www.powells.com* ☉ *Daily 9* AM–11 PM.

NOB HILL & VICINITY

The showiest example of Portland's urban chic is Northwest 23rd
Avenue—sometimes referred to with varying degrees of affection
as "trendy-third"—a 20-block thoroughfare that cuts north–south
through the neighborhood known as Nob Hill. Fashionable since the
1880s and still filled with Victorian residential architecture, the neighborhood is a mixed-use cornucopia of Old Portland charm and New
Portland hip. With its cafés, restaurants, galleries, and boutiques, it's
a delightful place to stroll, shop, and people-watch. More restaurants,
shops, and nightspots can be found on Northwest 21st Avenue, a few
blocks away. The Portland Streetcar runs from Legacy Good Samaritan Hospital in Nob Hill, through the Pearl District on 10th and 11th

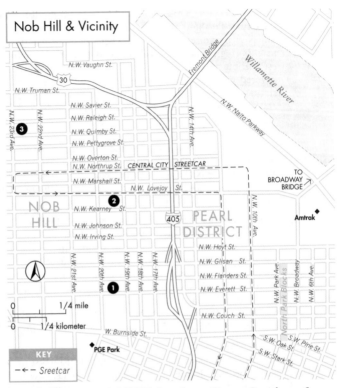

avenues, connects with MAX light rail near Pioneer Courthouse Square downtown, and then continues on to Portland State University and RiverPlace on the Willamette River.

Numbers in the margin correspond to the Nob Hill & Vicinity map.

WHAT TO SEE

❸ Clear Creek Distillery. The distillery keeps such a low profile that it's practically invisible. But ring the bell and someone will unlock the wrought-iron gate and let you into a dim, quiet tasting room where you can sample Clear Creek's world-famous Oregon apple and pear brandies and grappas. ✉ *1430 N.W. 23rd Ave., near Quimby St., Nob Hill* ☎ *503/248–9470* ⊕ *www.clearcreekdistillery.com* ⊘ *Weekdays 9–5, Sat. noon–5.*

❶ Temple Beth Israel. The imposing sandstone, brick, and stone structure with a massive domed roof and Byzantine styling was completed in 1928 and still serves a congregation first organized in 1858. ✉ *1972 N.W. Flanders St., Nob Hill.*

❷ The 3D Center of Art and Photography. Half gallery and half museum, this center devoted to three-dimensional imagery exhibits photographs best viewed through red-and-blue glasses, in addition to artifacts on the history of stereoscopic art. A collection of rare Nazi-era stereo-cards is displayed next to Viewmasters and 3-D snapshot cameras. A three-dimensional rendering of famous classical paintings is one of many changing 3-D slide shows you might see in the backroom Stereo Theatre. ✉*1928 N.W. Lovejoy St., Nob Hill* ☎*503/227–6667* ⊕*www.3dcenter.us* ✉*$4* ⊘*Thurs.–Sat. 11–5, Sun 1–5; also 1st Thurs. of month* 6 PM–9 PM.

WASHINGTON PARK & FOREST PARK

The best way to get to Washington Park is via MAX light rail, which travels through a tunnel deep beneath the city's West Hills. Be sure to check out the Washington Park station, the deepest (260 feet) transit station in North America. Graphics on the walls depict life in the Portland area during the past 16.5 million years. There's also a core sample of the bedrock taken from the mountain displayed along the walls. Elevators to the surface put visitors in the parking lot for the Oregon Zoo, the World Forestry Center Discovery Museum, and the Children's Museum.

Numbers in the margin correspond to the Washington Park & Forest Park map.

WHAT TO SEE

❸ **Children's Museum.** Colorful sights and sounds offer a feast of sensations
☾ for kids of all ages where hands-on play is the order of the day. Visit nationally touring exhibits, catch a storytime, a sing-along, or a puppet show in the Play It Again theater, create sculptures in the clay studio, splash hands in the water works display, or make a creation from junk in the Garage. ✉*4015 S.W. Canyon Rd., Washington Park* ⊕*U.S. 26, Zoo exit* ☎*503/223–6500* ✉*$6* ⊘*Tues.–Sat. 9–5, Sun. 11–5.*

❽ **Forest Park.** The nation's largest (5,000 acres) urban wilderness, this city-owned park, with more than 50 species of birds and mammals, has more than 70 mi of trails. Running the length of the park is the 24½-mi Wildwood Trail, which extends into Washington Park. The 11-mi Leif Erikson Drive, which picks up from the end of Northwest Thurman Street, is a popular place to jog or ride a mountain bike. The **Portland Audubon Society** (✉*5151 N.W. Cornell Rd.* ☎*503/292–9453*) supplies free maps and sponsors a bevy of bird-related activities including guided bird-watching events. There's a hospital for injured and orphaned birds as well as a gift shop stocked with books and feeders. ✉*Past Nob Hill in Northwest district. Take N.W. Lovejoy St. west to where it becomes Cornell Rd. and follow to park* ☎*503/823–7529* ✉*Free* ⊘*Daily dawn–dusk.*

❹ **Hoyt Arboretum.** Ten miles of trails wind through the arboretum, which has more than 1,000 species of plants and one of the nation's largest collections of coniferous trees; pick up trail maps at the visitor center. Also here are the Winter Garden and a memorial to veterans of the Vietnam War. ✉*4000 S.W. Fairview Blvd., Washington Park* ☎*503/228–8733* ⊕*www.hoytarboretum.org* ✉*Free* ⊘*Arboretum daily dawn–dusk, visitor center daily 9–4.*

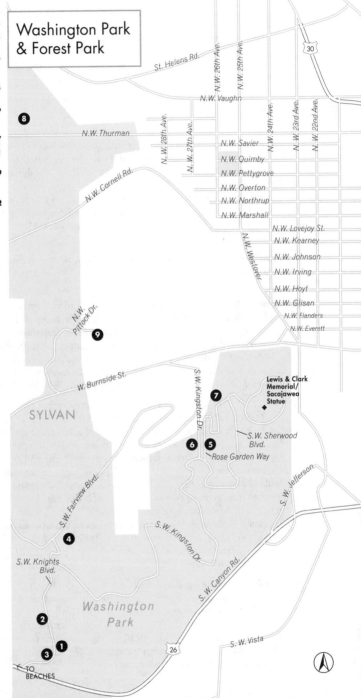

Washington Park & Forest Park

St. Helens Rd.

N.W. Vaughn

N.W. Thurman

N.W. 26th Ave.

N.W. 25th Ave.

N.W. 24th Ave.

N.W. 23rd Ave.

N.W. 22nd Ave.

30

N.W. 28th Ave.

N.W. 27th Ave.

N.W. Savier

N.W. Quimby

N.W. Pettygrove

N.W. Overton

N.W. Northrup

N.W. Marshall

N.W. Cornell Rd.

N.W. Lovejoy St.

N.W. Kearney

N.W. Johnson

N.W. Irving

N.W. Hoyt

N.W. Glisan

N.W. Flanders

N.W. Everett

N.W. Westover

N.W. Pittock Dr.

W. Burnside St.

SYLVAN

S.W. Kingston Dr.

Lewis & Clark
Memorial/
Sacajawea
Statue

S.W. Sherwood
Blvd.

Rose Garden Way

S.W. Jefferson

S.W. Fairview Blvd.

S.W. Kingston Dr.

S.W. Knights
Blvd.

Washington
Park

S.W. Canyon Rd.

26

S.W. Vista

← TO
BEACHES

5 **International Rose Test Garden.** Despite the name, these grounds are not ★ an experimental greenhouse laboratory but three terraced gardens, set on 4 acres, where 10,000 bushes and 400 varieties of roses grow. The flowers, many of them new varieties, are at their peak in June, July, September, and October. From the gardens you can see highly photogenic views of the downtown skyline and, on fine days, the Fuji-shape slopes of Mt. Hood, 50 mi to the east. Summer concerts take place in the garden's amphitheater. Take MAX light rail to Washington Park station and transfer to Bus No. 63. ⊠ *400 S.W. Kingston Ave., Washington Park* ☎ *503/823–3636* ⊕ *www.portlandonline.com* ⊠ *Free* ⊘ *Daily dawn–dusk.*

6 **Japanese Garden.** The most authentic Japanese garden outside Japan is Fodor'sChoice nestled among 5½ acres of Washington Park above the International ★ Rose Test Garden. This serene spot, designed by a Japanese landscape master represents five separate garden styles: Strolling Pond Garden, Tea Garden, Natural Garden, Sand and Stone Garden, and Flat Garden. The Tea House was built in Japan and reconstructed here. The west side of the Pavilion has a majestic view of Portland and Mt. Hood. Take MAX light rail to Washington Park station and transfer to Bus No. 63. ⊠ *611 S.W. Kingston Ave., Washington Park* ☎ *503/223–1321* ⊕ *www.japanesegarden.com* ⊠ *$6.75* ⊘ *Oct.–Mar., Mon. noon–4, Tues.–Sun. 10–4; Apr.–Sept., Mon. noon–7, Tues.–Sun. 10–7.*

7 **Oregon Holocaust Memorial.** This memorial to those who perished during the Holocaust bears the names of surviving families who live in Oregon and Southwest Washington. A bronzed baby shoe, a doll, broken spectacles, and other strewn possessions await notice on the cobbled courtyard. Soil and ash from six Nazi concentration camps is interred beneath the black granite wall. Take MAX light rail to Washington Park station, and transfer to Bus No. 63. ⊠ *S.W. Wright Ave. and Park Pl., Washington Park* ☎ *503/352–2930* ⊕ *http://ohrc.pacificu. edu* ⊠ *Free* ⊘ *Daily dawn–dusk.*

1 **Oregon Zoo.** This beautiful animal park in the West Hills is famous for ☺ its Asian elephants. Major exhibits include an African section with ★ rhinos, hippos, zebras, and giraffes. Steller Cove, a state-of-the-art aquatic exhibit, has two Steller sea lions and a family of sea otters. Other exhibits include polar bears, chimpanzees, an Alaska Tundra exhibit with wolves and grizzly bears, a penguinarium, and habitats for beavers, otters, and reptiles native to the west side of the Cascade Range. In summer a 4-mi round-trip narrow-gauge train operates from the zoo, chugging through the woods to a station near the International Rose Test Garden and the Japanese Garden. Take the MAX light rail to the Washington Park station. ⊠ *4001 S.W. Canyon Rd., Washington Park* ☎ *503/226–1561* ⊕ *www.oregonzoo.org* ⊠ *$9.75, $2 2nd Tues. of month* ⊘ *Mid-Apr.–mid-Sept., daily 9–6; mid-Sept.–mid Apr., daily 9–4.*

9 **Pittock Mansion.** Henry Pittock, the founder and publisher of the *Orego-* ★ *nian* newspaper, built this 22-room, castlelike mansion, which combines French Renaissance and Victorian styles. The opulent manor, built in 1914, is filled with art and antiques. The 46-acre grounds, north of Washington Park and 1,000 feet above the city, have superb views of the skyline, rivers, and the Cascade Range. There's a teahouse and a small hiking trail. ✉3229 N.W. Pittock Dr. (from W. Burnside St. heading west, turn right on N.W. Barnes Rd. and follow signs), north of Washington Park ☎503/823–3623 ⊕www.pittockmansion. com ☜$7 ⊙June–Aug, daily 11–4; Sept.–Dec. and Feb.–May, daily noon–4.

❷ World Forestry Discovery Center Museum. Visitors will find interactive and multimedia exhibits that teach forest sustainability. A white-water raft ride, smoke-jumper training simulator, and Timberjack tree harvester all provide different perspectives on Pacific Northwest forests. On the second floor the forests of the world are explored in various travel settings. A canopy lift ride hoists visitors to the 50-foot ceiling to look at a Douglas fir. A $1 parking fee is collected upon entry. Or take MAX light rail to the Washington Park station. ✉4033 S.W. Canyon Rd., Washington Park ☎503/228–1367 ⊕www.worldforestry.org ☜$7 ⊙Daily 10–5.

EAST OF THE WILLAMETTE RIVER

Portland is known as the City of Roses, but the 10 distinctive bridges spanning the Willamette River have also earned it the name Bridgetown. The older drawbridges, near downtown, open several times a day to allow passage of large cargo ships and freighters. You can easily spend a couple of days exploring the attractions and areas on the east side of the river.

Numbers in the margin correspond to the East of the Willamette River map.

WHAT TO SEE

NEED A BREAK?

At the Bagdad Theatre and Pub (✉3702 S.E. Hawthorne Blvd., Hawthorne District ☎503/236–9234) you can buy a pint of beer and a slice of pizza and watch a movie.

❸ Hawthorne District. This neighborhood stretching from the foot of Mt. Tabor to 30th Avenue tends to attract a more college-age, "bohemian," crowd than downtown or Nob Hill. With many bookstores, coffeehouses, taverns, restaurants, antiques stores, used-CD shops, and boutiques filling the streetfront, it is easy to spend a few hours wandering the street. ✉S.E. Hawthorne Blvd. between 30th and 42nd Aves., Hawthorne District .

❹ Mt. Tabor Park. Dirt trails and asphalt roads wind through forested hillsides and past good picnic areas to the top of Mt. Tabor, an extinct volcano with a panoramic view of Portland's West Hills and Cascade mountains. This butte and the conical hills east of the park are evidence of the gigantic eruptions that formed the Cascade Range millions of years ago. One of the best places in the city to watch the sunset, the park is also a popular place to bike, hike, picnic, or just throw a Fris-

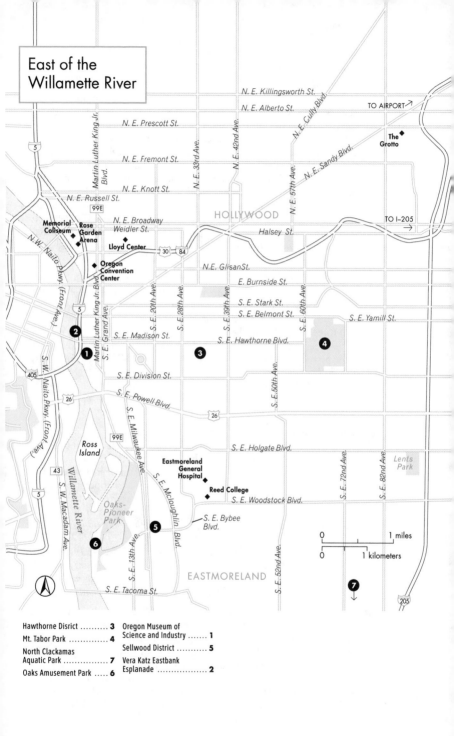

East of the
Willamette River

N. E. Killingsworth St.

N. E. Alberto St.

N. E. Cully Blvd.

TO AIRPORT →

N. E. Prescott St.

N. E. Sandy Blvd.

The
Grotto

N. E. Fremont St.

N. E. 33rd Ave.

N. E. 42nd Ave.

N. E. 57th Ave.

N. E. Knott St.

N. E. Russell St.

99E

HOLLYWOOD

Memorial
Coliseum

Rose
Garden
Arena

N. E. Broadway

Weidler St.

N. W. Naito Pkwy. (Front Ave.)

Lloyd Center

30 84

Halsey   St.

TO I-205
→

Oregon
Convention
Center

N.E. Glisan St.

Martin Luther King Jr. Blvd.

5

S. E. Grand Ave.

S. E. 20th Ave.

S. E. 28th Ave.

S. E. 39th Ave.

S. E. 60th Ave.

E. Burnside St.

S. E. Stark St.

S. E. Belmont St.

S. E. Yamill St.

2

S. E. Madison St.

1

3

S. E. Hawthorne Blvd.

4

S. W. Naito Pkwy. (Front Ave.)

405

S. E. Division St.

S. E. 50th Ave.

26

S. E. Powell Blvd.

26

99E

S. E. Milwaukee Ave.

S. E. Holgate Blvd.

S. E. 72nd Ave.

S. E. 82nd Ave.

Lents
Park

Ross
Island

Eastmoreland
General
Hospital

43

Willamette River

Reed College

S. E. McLoughlin Blvd.

S. E. Woodstock Blvd.

Oaks-
Pioneer
Park

5

S. E. Bybee
Blvd.

0   1 miles

S. W. Macadam Ave.

6

S. E. 13th Ave.

0   1 kilometers

S. E. 52nd Ave.

EASTMORELAND

7
↓

S. E. Tacoma St.

205

bee. ⊠*S.E. 60th Ave. and Salmon St., just east of Hawthorne District* ⊕*www.portlandonline.com* ⊙*Daily dawn–dusk.*

The Grotto. Owned by the Catholic Church, the National Sanctuary of Our Sorrowful Mother, as it's officially known, displays more than 100 statues and shrines in 62 acres of woods. The grotto was carved into the base of a 110-foot cliff and has a replica of Michelangelo's *Pietà.* The real treat is found after ascending the cliff face via elevator, as you enter a wonderland of gardens, sculptures, and shrines, and a glass-walled cathedral with an awe-inspiring view of the Columbia River and the Cascades. There's a dazzling Festival of Lights at Christmastime (late November and December), with 250,000 lights, and holiday concerts in the 600-seat chapel. Sunday masses are held here, too. ⊠*Sandy Blvd. at N.E. 85th Ave., near airport* ☎*503/254–7371* ⊕*www. thegrotto.org* ☞*Plaza level free; elevator to upper level $3* ⊙*Mid-May–Labor Day, daily 9–7:30; Labor Day–late Nov. and Feb.–mid-May, daily 9–6:30; late Nov.–Jan., daily 9–4.*

❼ North Clackamas Aquatic Park. If you're visiting Portland with kids any time of the year and are looking for a great way to cool off—especially on one of Portland's hot July or August days—check out this 45,000-square-foot, all-indoor attraction, whose main pool has 4-foot waves and three super slides. There's also a 25-yard-long lap pool, a wading pool, an adults-only hot whirlpool, and a café. Children under age 8 must be accompanied by someone 13 or older. ⊠*7300 S.E. Harmony Rd., Milwaukie* ☎*503/557–7873* ⊕*www.clackamas.us/ncprd/aquatic* ☞*$9.99* ⊙*Open swim mid-June–Labor Day, weekdays noon–4 and 7–9, weekends 11–3 and 4–8; Labor Day–mid-June, Sat. noon–7, Sun. noon–5.*

❻ Oaks Amusement Park. There's a small-town charm to this park, with bumper cars, thrill rides, and roller-skating year-round. A 360-degree loop roller coaster and other high-velocity, gravity-defying contraptions border the midway, along with a carousel and Ferris wheel. The skating rink, built in 1905, is the oldest continuously operating one in the United States, and features a working Wurlitzer organ. There are outdoor concerts in summer. ⊠*S.E. Spokane St. east of Willamette River; from S.E. Tacoma St. on east side of Sellwood Bridge, take S.E. 6th Ave. north and Spokane west, Sellwood* ☎*503/233–5777* ⊕*www. oakspark.com* ☞*Park free, multiride bracelets $11.25–$14, individual-ride tickets $2.25* ⊙*Mid-June–Labor Day, Tues.–Thurs. noon–9, Fri. and Sat. noon–10, Sun. noon–7; late-Apr.–mid-June and Labor Day–Oct., weekends noon–7; late-Mar.–late-Apr., weekends noon–5.*

❶ Oregon Museum of Science and Industry *(OMSI).* Hundreds of hands-on exhibits draw families to this interactive science museum, which also has an Omnimax theater and the Northwest's largest planetarium. The many permanent and touring exhibits are loaded with enough hands-on play for kids to fill a whole day exploring robotics, ecology, rockets, computers, animation, and outer space. Moored in the Willamette as part of the museum is a 240-foot submarine, the USS *Blueback,* which can be toured for an extra charge. ⊠*1945 S.E. Water Ave.,* *south of Morrison Bridge, under Hawthorne Bridge ☎503/797–6674 or 800/955–6674 ⊕www.omsi.edu ☎Full package $19, museum $9, planetarium $5.50, Omnimax $8.50, submarine $3.50 ⊗Mid-June–Labor Day, daily 9:30–7; Labor Day–mid-June, daily 9:30–5.*

⑤ Sellwood District. The browseable neighborhood that begins east of the Sellwood Bridge was once a separate town. Annexed by Portland in the 1890s, it retains a modest charm. On weekends the antiques stores along 13th Avenue do a brisk business. Each store is identified by a plaque that tells the date of construction and the original purpose of the building. More antiques stores, specialty shops, and restaurants are near the intersection of Milwaukie and Bybee. ⊠*S.E. 13th Ave. between Malden and Clatsop Sts., Sellwood.*

❷ Vera Katz Eastbank Esplanade. A stroll along this 1½-mi pedestrian and ★ cycling path across from downtown is one of the best ways to experience the Willamette River and Portland's bridges close-up. Built in 2001, the esplanade runs along the east bank of the Willamette River between the Hawthorne and Steele bridges, and features a 1,200-foot walkway that floats atop the river, a boat dock, and public art. Pedestrian crossings on both bridges link the esplanade to Waterfront Park, making a 3-mi loop. Take MAX light rail to the Rose Quarter station. ⊠*Parking at east end of Hawthorne Bridge, between Madison and Salmon Sts.*

WHERE TO EAT

Portland's abundance of amazing choices makes it is easy to stumble upon some great food. True food enthusiasts will also be well rewarded by doing a little research to find some of the out-of-the-way places that have much to offer. Many of the city's trendier restaurants are in Nob Hill and the Pearl District, and downtown is filled with many diverse, quality menus at some of the city's long-running reliables. But an incredible smattering of cuisines can be found on the east side of town as well, near Hawthorne Boulevard and Alberta Street and tucked away in myriad neighborhoods in between.

Restaurants are arranged first by neighborhood and then by type of cuisine served.

WHAT IT COSTS				
¢	$	$$	$$$	$$$$
AT DINNER under $10	$10–$20	$20–$30	$30–$40	over $40

Restaurant prices are per person for a main course at dinner.

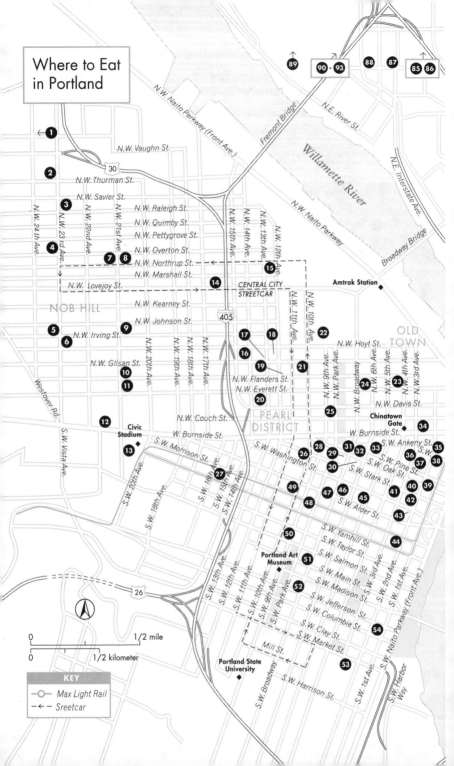

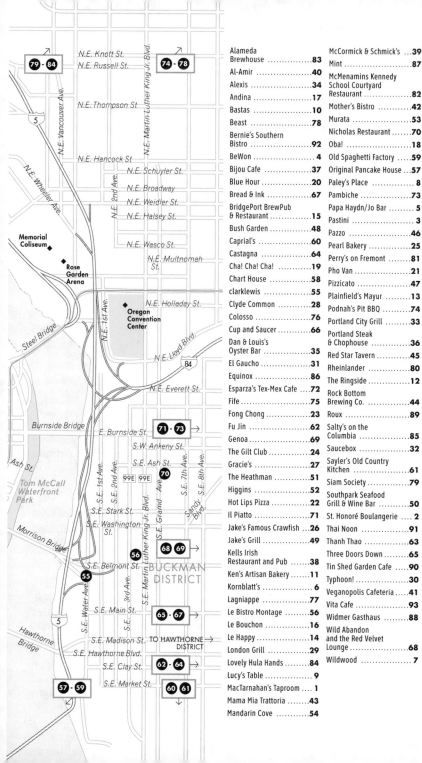

DOWNTOWN

AMERICAN

$–$$ ✕ **Jake's Grill.** Not to be confused with the Jake's of seafood fame, this eatery in the Governor Hotel has more turf than surf. Steaks and the Sunday brunch are popular draws. Private booths with green velvet curtains make for a cozy, intimate dinner. The bar is famous for its Bloody Marys. ✉ *611 S.W. 10th Ave., Downtown* ☎ *503/220–1850* ▭ *AE, D, DC, MC, V.*

$–$$ ✕ **Red Star Tavern & Roast House.** Cooked in a wood-burning oven, smoker, rotisserie, or grill, the cuisine at Red Star can best be described as American comfort food inspired by the bounty of the Pacific Northwest. Spit-roasted chicken, maple-fired baby back ribs with a brown-ale glaze, charred salmon, and crayfish étouffée are some of the better entrées. The wine list includes regional and international vintages, and 10 microbrews are on tap. The spacious restaurant, in the 5th Avenue Suites Hotel, has tufted leather booths, murals, and copper accents. ✉ *503 S.W. Alder St., Downtown* ☎ *503/222–0005* ▭ *AE, D, DC, MC, V.*

¢–$ ✕ **Mother's Bistro.** The menu is loaded with home-style favorites—macaroni and cheese with extra ingredients of the day, soups, pierogi, matzo-ball soup, pot roast, and meat loaf. For vegetarians there's a couscous stew. The high ceilings in the well-lit dining room lend an air of spaciousness, but the tables are a bit close together. The bar is open late Friday and Saturday. ✉ *409 S.W. 2nd Ave., Downtown* ☎ *503/464–1122* ▭ *AE, D, MC, V* ◷ *Closed Mon. No dinner Sun.*

¢–$ ✕ **Rock Bottom Brewing Co.** Some locals might balk at the idea of a corporate brewpub in a city that prides itself on its outstanding local microbrews, but this slightly upscale establishment manages to do just fine and serves some tasty dinner options, including burgers, pasta, and salads. With a full bar, pool upstairs, and rustic decor, there is plenty to please the after-work crowd. Brewery tours are available. ✉ *210 S.W. Morrison St.,* ☎ *503/796–2739* ▭ *AE, D, MC, V.*

CHINESE

$–$$$ ✕ **Mandarin Cove.** One of Portland's better Chinese restaurants has Hunan- and Szechuan-style beef, chicken, pork, seafood, and vegetarian dishes. There are almost two-dozen seafood choices. Try the sautéed scallops simmered in spicy tomato sauce. ✉ *111 S.W. Columbia St.,* ☎ *503/222–0006* ▭ *AE, DC, MC, V* ◷ *No lunch.*

CONTEMPORARY

$$$ ✕ **The Gilt Club.** Cascading gold curtains, ornate show-piece chandeliers, and all-encompassing high-back booths complement a swanky rich-red dining room. The food is equally lush, with buttercup pumpkin gnocchi topped with an Oregon venison ragu or truffle, red quinoa, and goat cheese custard with roasted autumn baby vegetables. Topping off the swank is the drink menu loaded with flavor embellished drinks such as Tracy's First Love, with house-infused cucumber vodka, muddled cucumber, basil, and fresh lime. ✉ *306 N.W. Broadway, Downtown* ☎ *503/222–4458* ▭ *AE, MC, V* ◷ *Closed Sun.*

$$$ ✕**Gracie's.** Stepping into this dining room is like stepping into a swanky,
FodorśChoice prestigious supper club in the 1940s. Dazzling chandeliers, beautifully
★ rich floor to ceiling draperies, velvet couches and marble-topped tables
emulate class. Gracie's is inside the Hotel DeLuxe, a 1940s movie-
time starlet-theme hotel. Serving breakfast, lunch and dinner, meals
are prepared with fresh ingredients, interesting interpretations and
expert preparation. Dishes like grilled swordfish and stuffed pork loin
are perfectly seasoned and served with seasonal grilled vegetables. The
brunch serves a delicious blend of fruits, eggs, meats, waffles, crepes,
and more. Memorable service, swanky setting, and enticing menu selec-
tion make this a must do in Portland. ⊠ 729 S.W. 15th Ave., Down-
town ☎503/222–2171 ⊟ AE, D, MC, V

$$–$$$ ✕**Fife.** To really appreciate how good food gets made, visit welcom-
ing and comfortable Fife. The open kitchen allows diners to capture
glimpses of sizzling chef Marco Shaw in action, cooking up what-
ever seasonal ingredients dictate. From smoked chili-rubbed cast-iron
chicken with potatoes and wilted greens to lamb rack chops with black
lentils, carrots and pecan-mint puree, guests enjoy a straight-forward
blend of menu items prepared to perfection. Don't miss the coconut
cream pie with bittersweet chocolate sauce for dessert. ⊠ 4440 N.E.
Fremont St., Downtown ☎971/222–3433 ⊟ MC, V ☺Closed Sun.
and Mon. No lunch

$–$$$ ✕**Portland City Grill.** On the 30th
floor of the US Bank Tower, Port-
land City Grill has one of the best
views in town. You can sit at a
windowside table and enjoy the
Portland skyline while eating fine
steak and seafood with an Asian
flair; it's no wonder that this restaurant is a favorite hot spot for
the city's jet set. The adjoining bar
and lounge has comfortable arm
chairs all along its windowed walls,
which are the first to get snatched

> **WORD OF MOUTH·**
>
> "Our new fave is the Portland City
> Grill, you will have excellent views
> here. If you like Sushi, they do a
> great Dragon Roll here. We had a
> nice 2 hour lunch here this sum-
> mer with 3 of the kids and had a
> great time!"
>
> –kimamom

up during the extremely popular happy hour each day. ⊠111 S.W.
5th Ave., Downtown ☎503/450–0030 ⊟AE, D, MC, V ☺No lunch
weekends.

$–$$ ✕ **Clyde Common.** If you want to experience "community" than this
bustling, contemporary spot is for you. From politicians, quasi-celebri-
ties, socialites, to hip, trendy, straight, and gay visitors from all walks
of life frequent this newer establishment. Big community tables dominate this restaurant, which means you'll never know who you'll end
up sitting next to and the interesting conversations you may have. The
kitchen is equally accessible and open, allowing you to see what's going
on from any vantage point. There is a smaller mezzanine with regular
seating. The menu leans toward the edge. From frogs' legs, chicken
livers, and sardines that have been baked, roasted, and fried accompanied by a host of interesting ingredients including horseradish, nettles,
and refried peanuts, there's no shortage of invention. Even the drinks

surprise like the Ace Gibson with Medoyeff vodka and house pickled onion, or the Anemic Mary with serrano chili and sun-dried tomato vodka, celery juice, and sour mix. ⊠ *1014 S.W. Stark St., Downtown* ☎ *503/228–3333* ▭ *AE, D, MC, V.*

$–$$ **★** ✕ **The Heathman.** Chef Philippe Boulot revels in fresh ingredients of the Pacific Northwest. His menu changes with the season, and includes entrées made with grilled and braised fish, fowl, veal, lamb, and beef. Among the chef's Northwest specialties are a delightful Dungeness crab, mango, and avocado salad and a seafood paella made with mussels, clams, shrimp, scallops, and chorizo. Equally creative choices are available for breakfast and lunch. The dining room, scented with wood smoke and adorned with Andy Warhol prints, is a favorite for special occasions. ⊠ *Heathman Hotel, 1001 S.W. Broadway, Downtown* ☎ *503/790–7752* ▭ *AE, D, DC, MC, V.*

$–$$ **Fodor's**Choice **★** ✕ **Higgins.** Chef Greg Higgins, former executive chef at the Heathman Hotel, focuses on ingredients from the Pacific Northwest and on organically grown herbs and produce while incorporating traditional French cooking styles and other international influences into his menu. Start with a salad of warm beets, asparagus, and artichokes or the country-style terrine of venison, chicken, and pork with dried sour cherries and a roasted-garlic mustard. Main courses change seasonally and might include dishes made with Alaskan spot prawns, halibut, duck, or pork loin. Vegetarian items are available. A bistro menu is available in the adjoining bar, where comfortable leather booths and tables provide an alternative to the main dining room. ⊠ *1239 S.W. Broadway, Downtown* ☎ *503/222–9070* ▭ *AE, D, DC, MC, V* ☉ *No lunch weekends.*

¢–$ ✕ **Bijou Cafe.** This spacious, sunny, high-ceiling restaurant has some of the best breakfasts in town: French-style crepes and oyster hash are a few popular favorites, along with fabulous pancakes and French toast. Breakfast is served all day, and at lunch there are burgers, sandwiches, and soups, as well as delectable daily specials. ⊠ *132 S.W. 3rd Ave., Downtown* ☎ *503/222–3187* ▭ *MC, V* ☉ *No dinner.*

CONTINENTAL

$$–$$$$ ✕ **London Grill.** The plush, dimly lit dining room in the historic Benson Hotel serves classic dishes made with fresh, seasonal local ingredients. Try the cedar-smoked salmon with juniper-berry sauce. With one of the longest wine lists around and a good chance of live jazz guitar or piano music, this is a place to truly indulge. Breakfast is also available. Jackets are encouraged, but not required, for men. ⊠ *309 S.W. Broadway,* ☎ *503/295–4110* ▭ *AE, D, DC, MC, V.*

IRISH

¢–$$ ✕ **Kells Irish Restaurant and Pub.** Step into cool, dark Kells for a pint of Guinness and such authentic pub fare as fish-and-chips, Guinness stew, shepherd's pie, and Irish soda bread. Burgers and vegetarian sandwiches round out the bar menu, and there's breakfast on weekends. Live Irish music plays every night of the week. Be sure and ask the bartender how all those folded-up dollar bills got stuck to the ceiling. ⊠ *112 S.W. 2nd Ave.,* ☎ *503/227–4057* ▭ *AE, D, MC, V.*

ITALIAN

¢–$$ ✕**Pazzo.** The aromas of roasted garlic and wood smoke greet patrons of the bustling, street-level dining room of the Hotel Vintage Plaza. Pazzo's menu relies on deceptively simple new Italian cuisine—creative pastas, risottos, and grilled meats, fish, and poultry, as well as antipasti and appetizers. All the baked goods are made in the Pazzoria Bakery & Cafe next door. The decor is a mix of dark wood, terra-cotta, and dangling garlands of garlic. Breakfast is served daily. ⊠*627 S.W. Washington St., Downtown* ☎*503/228–1515* ▭*AE, D, DC, MC, V.*

$–$$ ✕**Mama Mia Trattoria.** Warmth and comfort are the specialties of Mama's, which is the place to come to if you're in the mood for spaghetti with meatballs, lasagna, or potato gnocchi. Don't let the sultry red interior, sparkly chandeliers, and starched tablecloths fool you. This mildly boisterous place allows you to be more casual than it is (just like mom), and the bar is open late into the night. ⊠*439 S.W. 2nd Ave.,* ☎*503/295–6464* ▭*AE, D, DC, MC, V* ⊗*No lunch.*

JAPANESE

$$–$$$$ ✕**Murata.** Slip off your shoes and step inside one of the tatami rooms at Murata, Portland's best Japanese restaurant. You can also pull up a chair at the corner sushi bar. So ordinary-looking it barely stands out among the office towers near Keller Auditorium, the restaurant draws a crowd of locals, celebrities, and Japanese businesspeople who savor the sushi, sashimi, tempura, hamachi, and teriyaki. Grilled salmon cheeks stand out among many seafood specialties. ⊠*200 S.W. Market St.,* ☎*503/227–0080* ▭*AE, MC, V* ⊗*Closed Sun. No lunch Sat.*

$–$$ ✕**Bush Garden.** This authentic Japanese restaurant, which opened in 1960, is known for its sashimi and sukiyaki but also offers traditional favorites such as udon noodles, bento, tempura, and teriyaki. There is karaoke singing Monday–Saturday. ⊠*900 S.W. Morrison St.,* ☎*503/226–7181* ▭*AE, D, DC, MC, V* ⊗*Closed Sun.*

LEBANESE

$ ✕**Al-Amir.** Upon entering the restaurant and moving beyond the small bar in the front, through the elaborately large and ornate Middle Eastern gateway into a dark, stylish dining room, choose between excellent broiled kebabs, falafel, hummus, tabbouleh, and baba ghanoush. There's live music and belly dancing on Friday and Saturday. ⊠*223 S.W. Stark St.* ☎*503/274–0010* ▭*AE, D, MC, V* ⊗*No lunch weekends.*

PAN-ASIAN

$ ✕**Saucebox.** Creative pan-Asian cuisine and many creative cocktails draw the crowds to this popular restaurant and nightspot near the big downtown hotels. Inside the long and narrow space with closely spaced tables draped with white cloths, Alexis Rockman's impressive and colorful 24-foot painting *Evolution* spans the wall over your head, and mirrored walls meet your gaze at eye level. The menu includes Korean baby back ribs, Vietnamese pork tenderloin, and Indonesian roasted Javanese salmon. An excellent late-night menu is served after 10 PM. ⊠*214 S.W. Broadway, Downtown* ☎*503/241–3393* ▭*AE, DC, MC, V* ⊗*Closed Sun. and Mon. No lunch.*

PIZZA

¢ ✕ **Pizzicato.** This local chain serves pies and slices topped by inventive combinations such as chanterelles, shiitakes, and portobellos, or andouille sausage, shrimp, and smoked mozzarella. The menu includes large salads to share, antipasti, and panini. The restaurant interiors are clean, bright, and modern. Beer and wine are available. ⊠705 S.W. Alder St., Downtown ☎503/226–1007 ⊠505 N.W. 23rd Ave., Nob Hill ☎503/242–0023 ▭AE, D, DC, MC, V.

SEAFOOD

❻ ✕ **Jake's Famous Crawfish.** Diners have been enjoying fresh Pacific Northwest seafood in Jake's warren of wood-panel dining rooms for more
$–$$ than a century. The back bar came around Cape Horn during the 1880s, and the chandeliers hanging from the high ceilings date from 1881. The restaurant gained a national reputation in 1920 when crawfish was added to the menu. White-coat waiters take your order from an almost endless sheet of daily seafood specials year-round, but try to come during crawfish season (May–September), when you can sample the tasty crustacean in pie, cooked Creole style, or in a Cajun-style stew over rice. ⊠401 S.W. 12th Ave., Downtown ☎503/226–1419 ▭AE, D, DC, MC, V ☉No lunch Sun.

❻ ✕ **McCormick & Schmick's.** The seafood is flawless at this lively restaurant, where you can dine in a cozy, private wooden booth downstairs
$–$$ or upstairs overlooking the bar. Fresh Pacific Northwest oysters and Alaskan halibut are favorites; specialties include Dungeness crab cakes with roasted red-pepper sauce. A new menu is printed daily with a list of more than two-dozen fresh seasonal choices. Oregon and California vineyards take center stage on the wine list. The popular bar has bargain happy-hour appetizers and a wide selection of top-shelf, single-malt scotches. ⊠235 S.W. 1st Ave., Downtown ☎503/224–7522 ▭AE, D, DC, MC, V ☉No lunch.

$ ✕ **Southpark Seafood Grill & Wine Bar.** Wood-fired seafood is served in this comfortable, art deco–tinged room with two bars. Chef Ronnie Mac-Quarrie's Mediterranean-influenced menu includes grilled grape-leaf-wrapped salmon with pomegranate and sherry glaze as well as tuna au poivre with mashed potatoes and red-wine demi-glace. There's a wide selection of fresh Pacific Northwest oysters and fine regional wines available by the glass. Some of the desserts are baked to order. ⊠901 S.W. Salmon St., Downtown ☎503/326–1300 ▭AE, D, MC, V.

¢–$ ✕ **Dan & Louis's Oyster Bar.** Oysters at this Portland landmark near the river come fried, stewed, or on the half shell. The clam chowder is tasty, but the crab stew is a rare treat. Combination dinners let you mix your fried favorites. The collection of steins, plates, and marine art has grown since the restaurant opened in 1907 to fill beams, nooks, crannies, and nearly every inch of wall. ⊠208 S.W. Ankeny St., Downtown ☎503/227–5906 ▭AE, D, DC, MC, V.

STEAK

$$–$$$$ ✕ **El Gaucho.** Three dimly lit dining rooms with blue walls and striped
FodorśChoice upholstery invite those with healthy pocketbooks. The specialty here
★ is 28-day, dry-aged, certified Angus beef, but chops, ribs, and chicken

entrées are also cooked in the open kitchen. The chateaubriand for two is carved tableside. Seafood lovers might want to try the tomato fennel bouillabaisse. Service is impeccable at this Seattle transplant in the elegant Benson Hotel. Each night live Latin guitar music serenades the dinner guests. ⊠*319 S.W. Broadway, Downtown* ☎*503/227–8794* ▤*AE, DC, MC, V* ☯*No lunch.*

¢–$$$ ✕**Portland Steak & Chophouse.** Expensive cuts of steak and prime rib are the draw at this steak house in the Embassy Suites hotel. The menu includes wood-fired pizzas, pasta, and café meals. Surf lovers can choose the Hawaiian ahi, cioppino, or seafood linguine. The bar menu draws a loyal happy-hour crowd. ⊠*121 S.W. 3rd Ave., Downtown* ☎*503/223–6200* ▤*AE, D, MC, V.*

THAI

$–$$ ✕**Typhoon!** A Buddha statue with burning incense watches over diners at this popular restaurant in the Lucia Hotel. Come enjoy the excellent food in a large, modern dining room filled with colorful art and sleek red booths. The spicy chicken or shrimp with crispy basil, the curry and noodle dishes, and the vegetarian spring and salad rolls are standouts. If tea is your thing, 145 varieties are available, from $2 a pot to $55 for some of the world's rarest. ⊠*400 S.W. Broadway, Downtown* ☎*503/224–8285* ▤*AE, D, DC, MC, V.*

VEGETARIAN

¢ ✕**Veganopolis Cafeteria.** Everything on the menu here is meat-, dairy-, and egg-free, right down to house-made cheeses (made from nuts), baked goods, and organic beer and wine. Chill music swirls through the sleek, airy interior, filled at lunchtime with office workers queued up for such sophisticated sandwiches as quinoa burgers, corned seitan Reubens, and vegan BLTs. It also has soups, salads, hot dishes, and fair-trade coffee. In the evening there's a dinner buffet, and breakfast Saturday mornings. ⊠*412 S.W. 4th Ave.,* ☎*503/226-3400* ▤*AE, D, DC, MC, V* ☯*Closed Sun.*

PEARL DISTRICT & OLD TOWN/CHINATOWN

AMERICAN

¢ ✕**BridgePort BrewPub & Restaurant.** The hops- and ivy-covered, century-old industrial building seems out of place among its neighbors, but once inside you'll be clear about the business here: frothy pints of BridgePort's ale, brewed on the premises. The India Pale Ale is a specialty, but a treat for the indecisive is the seven-glass sampler that might also include "Old Knucklehead," the brewery's barley wine–style ale. Seafood, chicken, steak, pasta, salads, and small plates are served for lunch and dinner, as well as pub favorites. In summer the flower-festooned loading dock is transformed into a beer garden. ⊠*1313 N.W. Marshall St., Pearl District* ☎*503/241–3612* ▤*MC, V.*

CAFÉS

¢ ✕**Pearl Bakery.** A light breakfast or lunch can be had at this popular spot known for its excellent fresh breads, pastries, cakes, and sandwiches. The cakes, cookies, croissants, and Danish are some of the best in the city. ✉*102 N.W. 9th Ave., Pearl District* ☎*503/827–0910* ⊘*No dinner* ⊟*MC, V.*

CHINESE

¢–$ ✕**Fong Chong.** Although it looks run-down, Fong Chong is considered by some to serve the best dim sum in town. The family-style eatery has dumplings filled with shrimp, pork, or vegetables, accompanied by plenty of different sauces. If you haven't eaten dim sum before, just take a seat: the food is brought to you on carts and you pick what you want as it comes by. ✉*301 N.W. 4th Ave., Chinatown* ☎*503/228–6868* ⊟*AE, MC, V.*

FRENCH

$$$ ✕**Le Bouchon.** A warm, jovial waitstaff make Francophiles feel right at home at this French bistro in the Pearl District, which serves classic French cuisine for lunch and dinner. Duck confit, truffle chicken, bouillabaisse, and escargots are all cooked to perfection by chef Claude Musquin. And for dessert, chocolate mousse is a must-try. ✉*517 N.W. 14th Ave. Pearl District* ☎*503/248–2193* ⊟*AE, MC, V* ⊘*Closed Sun. and Mon.*

¢–$ ✕**Le Happy.** This tiny creperie just outside of the hubbub of the Pearl District can serve as a romantic dinner-date spot or just a cozy place to enjoy a drink and a snack. You can get sweet crepes with fruit, cheese, and cream or savory ones with meats and cheeses; in addition, the dinner menu is rounded out with steaks and salads. It's a classy joint, but not without a sense of humor: Le Trash Blanc is a bacon and cheddar crepe, served with a can of Pabst. ✉*1011 N.W. 16th Ave., Pearl District* ☎*503/226–1258* ⊟*MC, V* ⊘*Closed Sun. No lunch.*

GREEK

$ ✕**Alexis.** The Mediterranean furnishings here consist only of white walls and basic furnishings, but the authentic Greek flavor keeps the crowds coming for *kalamarakia* (deep-fried squid served with *tzatziki,* a yogurt dip), *horiatiki* (a Greek salad combination with feta cheese and kalamata olives), and other traditional dishes. If you have trouble making up your mind, the gigantic Alexis platter includes a little of everything. ✉*215 W. Burnside St., Old Town* ☎*503/224–8577* ⊟*AE, D, MC, V* ⊘*Closed Sun. No lunch Sat.*

LATIN

$–$$ ✕**Oba!** Many come to Oba! for the upscale bar scene, but this Pearl District salsa hangout also serves excellent Latin American cuisine, including coconut prawns, roasted vegetable enchiladas and tamales, and other seafood, chicken, pork, and duck dishes. The bar is open late Friday and Saturday. ✉*555 N.W. 12th Ave., Pearl District* ☎*503/228–6161* ⊟*AE, D, DC, MC, V* ⊘*No lunch.*

MEDITERRANEAN

$$$–$$$$ ✕**Blue Hour.** Recognized as perhaps one of Portland's sweetest spots for chic, this vastly open space features towering ceilings and flowing floor-to-ceiling curtains throughout the restaurant. The waitstaff are as sophisticated as the white tablecloths and fancy selection of entrées, which change daily based on available ingredients, and to their own

credit, the chef's whims. Four-course prix-fixe menus are available for lunch and dinner. Ongoing appetizers to try are the "20 greens" salad and sea scallops wrapped in applewood smoked bacon with celery root puree and caper dressing. Top the meal off with a bittersweet chocolate chestnut torte with honey cream. ⊠*250 N.W. 13th Ave., Pearl District* ☎*503/226–3394* ⊟*AE, D, MC, V.*

MEXICAN

¢ ✕ **Cha! Cha! Cha!** Burritos and tacos are so tasty at this lively taqueria that if it weren't always shoehorned with customers, patrons would probably get up and dance. Part of a local chain, Cha! Cha! Cha! takes cuisine you'd expect to find on a taco truck in southern Mexico and puts it on a plate in the Pearl. The extensive menu includes *machaca* (a burrito with shredded beef, sautéed vegetables, scrambled eggs, and Spanish rice) and fish tacos filled with fresh pollack. ⊠*1208 N.W. Glisan St., Pearl District* ☎*503/221–2111* ⊟*AE, D, MC, V.*

PERUVIAN

$$–$$$ ✕ **Andina.** Portland's sleekest, trendiest, and most brightly colored restaurant gives an artful presentation to designer and traditional Peruvian cuisine. Asian and Spanish flavors are the main influences on this cuisine, evident in an extensive seafood menu that includes five kinds of ceviche, grilled octopus, and pan-seared scallops with black quinoa. There are also entrées with poultry, beef, and lamb. A late-night bar swills with sangria, small plates, and cocktails, and a shrinelike wine shop hosts private multicourse meals downstairs. ⊠*1314 N.W. Glisan St., Pearl District* ☎*503/228–9535* ⊟*AE, D, MC, V* ⊗*No lunch Sun.*

PIZZA

¢ ✕ **Hot Lips Pizza.** A favorite of Portland's pizza lovers, Hot Lips bakes organic and regional ingredients into creative pizzas, available whole or by the slice. Seasonal variations might feature apples, squash, wild mushrooms, and blue cheese. It also has soups, salads, and sandwiches. Beverages include house-made berry sodas, a large rack of wines, and microbrew six-packs. Dine inside the Ecotrust building, outside on the eco-roof, or take it all across the street for an impromptu picnic in Jamison Square. ⊠*721 N.W. 9th Ave., Pearl District* ☎*503/595–2342* ⊟*AE, D, MC, V.*

VIETNAMESE

¢–$ ✕ **Pho Van.** This spacious, minimalist restaurant is the newer and trendier of the two Pho Van locations in Portland—the less expensive twin is on the far east side, on 82nd Avenue. A big bowl of pho noodle soup is delicious, enough to fill you up, and costs only $8 or $9. The friendly waitstaff will help you work your way through the menu and will make suggestions to give you the best sampling of Vietnamese cuisine. ⊠*1012 N.W. Glisan St., Pearl District* ☎*503/248–2172* ⊟*AE, D, MC, V* ⊗*Closed Sun.* ⊠*1919 S.E. 82nd Ave.* ☎*503/788–5244.*

NOB HILL & VICINITY

AMERICAN

$–$$$$ ✕**The Ringside.** This Portland institution has been famous for its beef for more than 50 years. Dine in cozy booths on rib eye, prime rib, and New York strip, which come in regular- or king-size cuts. Seafood lovers will find plenty of choices: a chilled seafood platter with an 8-ounce lobster tail, Dungeness crab, oysters, jumbo prawns, and Oregon bay shrimp. The onion rings, made with Walla Walla sweets, are equally renowned. ⊠*2165 N.W. Burnside St.,* ☎*503/223–1513* ⊟*AE, D, MC, V* ⊘*No lunch.*

¢–$$ ✕**Papa Haydn/Jo Bar.** Many patrons come to this bistro just for the luscious desserts or for the popular Sunday brunch (reservations essential). Favorite dinner items include pan-seared scallops, dinner salads, and grilled flatiron steak. Wood-fired, rotisserie-cooked meat, fish, and poultry dishes plus pasta and pizza are available next door at the jazzy **Jo Bar.** ⊠*701 N.W. 23rd Ave., Nob Hill* ☎*503/228–7317 Papa Haydn, 503/222–0048 Jo Bar* ⊟*AE, MC, V.*

CAFÉS

¢   ✕**Ken's Artisan Bakery.** Golden crusts are the trademark of Ken's rustic breads, croissants, tarts, and puff pastries, good for breakfast, lunch, and light evening meals. Sandwiches, barbecue pulled pork, and croque monsieur are served on thick slabs of freshly baked bread, and local berries fill the flaky pastries. And if the dozen tables inside the vibrant blue bakery are always crammed, sit outside at one of the sidewalk café tables. On Monday nights they serve pizza, and the bakery stays open to 9 PM. ⊠*338 N.W. 21st Ave.,* ☎*503/248–2202* ⊟*MC, V* ⊘*No dinner Tues.–Sun.*

¢   ✕**St. Honoré Boulangerie.** Light meals and pastries are available at this
★   authentic French bakery, named for the patron saint of bakers. Start the day off with plain or chocolate croissant, or café au lait. For lunch and dinner there's quiche, savory puff pastries and tarts, croque monsieur, and a variety of fresh salads. Or simply unwind from shopping with a glass of wine and a luscious dessert at one of the sidewalk café tables. ⊠*2335 N.W. Thurman St.* ☎*503/445–4342* ⊟*MC, V.*

CONTEMPORARY

$–$$$ ✕**Wildwood.** The busy center bar, stainless-steel open kitchen, and blond-wood chairs set the tone at this restaurant serving fresh Pacific Northwest cuisine. Chef Dustin Clark's entrées include dishes made with lamb, pork loin, chicken, steak, and seafood. There's also a vegetarian selection. Wildwood also has a family-style Sunday supper menu with selections for two or more people. ⊠*1221 N.W. 21st Ave., Nob Hill* ☎*503/248–9663* ⊟*AE, MC, V.*

$–$$ ✕**Lucy's Table.** Amid this corner bistro's regal purple and gold interior, chef Michael Conklin creates Northwest cuisine with a mix of Italian and French accents. The seasonal menu includes lamb, steak, pork, and seafood dishes. For dessert try the *boca negra,* chocolate cake with Frangelico whipped cream and cherries poached with port and walnut Florentine. Valet parking is available Wednesday–Saturday.

⌧706 N.W. 21st Ave., Nob Hill ☎503/226–6126 ▭AE, DC, MC, V ⊘Closed Sun. No lunch.

¢–$ ✕**MacTarnahan's Taproom.** The copper beer-making equipment at the door tips you off to the specialty of the house—beer. This restaurant in the northwest industrial district is part of a 27,000-square-foot Mac-Tarnahan's brewery complex. Start with a tasting platter featuring seven different beers. The haystack back ribs with garlic rosemary fries are popular, and the fish-and-chips use a batter made with Mac's signature ale. Asparagus-artichoke lasagna is a good vegetarian option. Eat it all on the patio overlooking the landscaped grounds. ⌧2730 N.W. 31st Ave., off N.W. Yeon St., ☎503/228–5269 ▭AE, DC, MC, V.

DELICATESSEN

¢ ✕**Kornblatt's.** This kosher deli and bagel bakery evokes a 1950s diner. Thick sandwiches are made with fresh bread and lean fresh-cooked meats, and the tender home-smoked salmon and pickled herring are simply mouthwatering. For breakfast, try the poached eggs with spicy corned-beef hash, blintzes, or potato latkes. ⌧628 N.W. 23rd Ave., Nob Hill ☎503/242–0055 ▭AE, MC, V.

FRENCH

$–$$ ✕**Paley's Place.** This charming bistro serves French cuisine Pacific
Fodor'sChoice Northwest–style. Among the entrées are dishes with duck, New York
★ steak, chicken, pork tenderloin, and halibut. A vegetarian selection is also available. There are two dining rooms and a classy bar. In warmer months there's outdoor seating on the front porch and back patio. ⌧1204 N.W. 21st Ave., Nob Hill ☎503/243–2403 ▭AE, MC, V ⊘No lunch.

INDIAN

$–$$ ✕**Plainfield's Mayur.** Portland's finest Indian cuisine is served in an elegant Victorian house. The tomato-coconut soup with fried curry leaves and the vegetarian and vegan dishes are highlights. Appetizers include the authentic Bombay *bhel* salad with tamarind dressing and the *dahi wadi* (crispy fried lentil croquettes in a spicy yogurt sauce). Meat and seafood specialties include lobster in brown onion sauce and tandoori lamb. ⌧852 S.W. 21st Ave., one block south of Burnside, ☎503/223–2995 ▭AE, D, DC, MC, V ⊘No lunch.

ITALIAN

$ ✕**Bastas.** In a converted Tastee-Freez, this arty bistro serves dishes from all over Italy. The walls are painted with Italian earth tones, and a small side garden provides alfresco dining in good weather. The menu includes scaloppine, grilled lamb, and creative seafood and pasta dishes. ⌧410 N.W. 21st Ave., Nob Hill ☎503/274–1572 ▭AE, MC, V ⊘No lunch.

¢ ✕**Pastini.** It's hard to go wrong with anything at this classy Italian bistro, which has more than two dozen pasta dishes under $10. Rigatoni *zuccati* comes in a light cream sauce with butternut squash, wild mushrooms, and spinach; *linguini misto mare* is a seafood linguine in white wine. It also has panini sandwiches, antipasti, and dinner salads. Open for lunch and dinner, Pastini is part of a local chain. There's often a crowd, but from this location you can browse the shops while waiting for a table. ⊠ *1506 N.W. 23rd Ave.,* ☏ *503/595–1205* ✍ *Reservations not accepted* ⊟ *AE, DC, MC, V* ☺ *No lunch Sun.*

KOREAN

$–$$ ✕ **BeWon.** Named for the favorite secret garden of ancient Korean royalty, BeWon prepares a tasty Korean feast. An array of traditional Korean side dishes, presented in an elegant assembly of little white bowls, accompanies such entrées as stir-fried seafood, simmered meat and fish, rice and soup dishes, and fermented vegetables (kimchi). To really experience a dynasty there's *han jung shik,* a traditional seven-course prix-fixe dinner available with or without wine pairings. ⊠ *1203 N.W. 23rd Ave.,* ☏ *503/464–9222* ⊟ *AE, D, MC, V* ☺ *No lunch weekends.*

EAST OF THE WILLAMETTE

AMERICAN–CASUAL

¢–$ ✕ **Alameda Brewhouse.** A spacious dining room and bar in a high-ceiling room with light wood and stainless steel gives this brewhouse a feeling of urban chic while still managing to remain friendly and casual. Many people come for the excellent microbrews made on premises, but the food must not be overlooked; this is no pub grub. With creative pasta dishes such as mushroom-artichoke linguine, salmon gyros, ahi tacos, and delicious burgers, it is clear that this restaurant has as much thought going into its menu and ingredients as it does into its brewing. ⊠ *4675 N.E. Fremont St., Alameda* ☏ *503/460–9025* ⊟ *AE, DC, MC, V.*

¢–$ ✕ **McMenamins Kennedy School Courtyard Restaurant.** Whether you are coming to the Kennedy School to stay overnight at the hotel, to watch a movie, or just to enjoy dinner and drinks, the Courtyard Restaurant can add to your evening. The food, ranging from burgers, salads, and pizzas to fish-and-chips, pasta, prime rib, and beef stew, can satisfy most any appetite. Several standard McMenamins microbrews are always available, in addition to seasonal specialty brews. ⊠ *5736 N.E. 33rd Ave., near Alberta District* ☏ *503/288–2192* ⊟ *AE, D, MC, V.*

ASIAN

$$–$$$ ✕ **Lovely Hula Hands.** Sisters and co-owners have spent a great deal of effort to create a warm, contemporary environment to enjoy the freshest possible ingredients in carefully selected dishes. The menu changes daily so depending upon the season you can expect a roasted winter vegetable stew of squash, carrots, fennel, parsnips, broccoli, and chickpeas, served with saffron rice and minted yogurt, or in summer, a creamy soufflé made with chanterelles, sweet corn, spinach, and cippolini onions. Year-round count on their authentic 1920s cocktails such as the Pegu Club, a blend of Bombay Sapphire, Cointreau, fresh lime juice and bitters. Seating here is limited and they don't take reservations, so aside from the romantic ambiance, expect a wait and perhaps one of the best burgers in town. ⊠ *4057 N Mississippi Ave., North Mississippi* ☏ *503/445–9910* ⊟ *MC, V .*

$–$$ ✕**Siam Society.** Entering through oversize red-shutter doors, beautiful outdoor patio surrounded by full plants and flowers and lush upstairs lounge create an inviting ambience to mirror the diverse dining experience. Expect large portions of menu highlights such as Cascade natural char-grilled steak with a red wine reduction sauce and sweet potato fries lightly sprinkled with white truffle oil, and banana roasted pork, which consists of slow-cooking pork shoulder for five days while wrapped in banana leaves, then served with grilled pineapple. Drinks not to be missed are ginger lime Cosmo and jalapeno-pear kamikaze. ⊠ *2703 N.E. Alberta St., Alberta District* ☎*503/922–3675* ▤ *MC, V* ✆ *Closed Mon.*

CAFÉS

¢   ✕**Cup and Saucer.** This casual diner-style restaurant is extremely popular with hip young locals and is always packed on weekends, especially for breakfast and lunch. The long menu includes all-day breakfast, quiches, burgers, sandwiches, soups, and salads, with plenty of vegetarian and vegan options. ⊠*3566 S.E. Hawthorne Blvd., Hawthorne District* ☎*503/236–6001* ⬫*Reservations not accepted* ▤*MC, V.*

¢   ✕**Tin Shed Garden Cafe.** This small restaurant is a popular breakfast spot, known for its shredded potato cakes, biscuits and gravy, sweet-potato cinnamon French toast, creative egg and tofu scrambles, and breakfast burritos. The lunch and dinner menu has creative items like a creamy artichoke sandwich, and a chicken sandwich with bacon, Gorgonzola, and apple, in addition to burgers, salads, and soups. A comfortable outdoor patio doubles as a beer garden on warm spring and summer evenings, and the adjacent community garden rounds off the property with a peaceful sitting area. ⊠*1438 N.E. Alberta St., Alberta District* ☎*503/288–6966* ⬫*Reservations not accepted* ▤*MC, V* ✆*No dinner Mon. and Tues.*

CAJUN–CREOLE

¢–$ ✕**Le Bistro Montage.** Spicy Cajun is the jumping-off point for the chef at this sassy bistro under the Morrison Bridge on Portland's east side. Jambalayas, blackened pork, chicken, catfish, linguine, and old-fashioned macaroni dishes are served up from around noon until the wee hours in a spot that's loud, crowded, and casually hip. The wine list includes more than 100 varieties. ⊠*301 S.E. Morrison St., off Martin Luther King Jr. Blvd. beneath Morrison Bridge* ☎*503/234–1324* ⬫*Reservations not accepted* ▤*No credit cards* ✆*No lunch weekends.*

CHINESE

¢   ✕**Fu Jin.** Although the place looks a bit tattered, this family-run neighborhood restaurant consistently serves good wok-cooked favorites at reasonable prices. The fried tofu dishes and sesame-crusted shrimp are tasty. ⊠*3549 S.E. Hawthorne Blvd., Hawthorne District* ☎*503/231–3753* ▤*D, MC, V* ✆*Closed Thurs.*

CONTEMPORARY

$$$$ ✕**Beast.** This restaurant is a quintessential example of Portland's creative cuisine. An unidentified red building leads you inside where there are two large communal tables, which seat 8 and 16 respectively.

Another major portion of the dining room is actually a very open, very accessible in-the-mix kitchen. Diners have the option of three or five prix-fixe courses from a menu that constantly changes. Vegetarians will indeed struggle as they kindly decline substitutions and courses live up to the restaurant's namesake with dishes such as chicken and duck liver mousse, wine and truffle braised beef, and steak tartare with quail egg toast. ⊠ *5425 N.E. 30th Ave., Alberta District* ☎*503/841–6968* ▭ *MC, V*

$$ ⨯ **Castagna.** Enjoy the bouillabaisse or one of the inventive Mediterranean seafood entrées at this tranquil Hawthorne restaurant. The pan-seared scallops with mushrooms are the signature dish. Next door is the more casual **Cafe Castagna** (☎*503/231–9959*), a bistro and bar open nightly serving pizzas and other slightly less expensive, lighter fare. ⊠*1752 S.E. Hawthorne Blvd., Hawthorne District* ☎*503/231–7373* ▭*AE, D, DC, MC, V* ⊗*Closed Mon. and Tues. No lunch.*

$–$$ ⨯ **Caprial's.** PBS cooking-show star Caprial Pence serves Northwest-inspired creations at her bustling, brightly lit bistro with an open kitchen, full bar, and velvet armchairs. The dinner menu changes monthly and is limited to four or five choices, which have included pan-roasted salmon as well as smoked and grilled pork loin chop. The wine "wall" (you pick the bottle) has more than 200 varieties. ⊠*7015 S.E. Milwaukie Ave., Sellwood* ☎*503/236–6457* ▭*AE, MC, V* ⊗*Closed Sun. and Mon.*

★ ⨯ **clarklewis.** This cutting-edge restaurant, aka "darklewis" for imprac-**$–$$$** tical lighting, is making big waves for inventive farm-fresh meals served inside a converted warehouse loading dock. Regional vegetables, seafood, and meat cultivated from local suppliers appear on a daily changing menu of pastas, entrées, and sides. Diners can order small, large, and family-style sizes, or let the chef decide with the fixed-price meal. Although the food is flawless, a lack of signage and proper reception can make your first visit feel a little like arriving at a party uninvited. ⊠*1001 S.E. Water Ave., Produce Row* ☎*503/235–2294* ⊗*Closed Sun. No lunch weekends* ▭*AE, MC, V.*

$–$$$ ⨯ **Equinox.** Locally grown organic produce, free-range meats, wild seafood, and cage-free chickens come to the table as many world cuisines at this eclectic neighborhood restaurant on North Mississippi Street. Renovated-garage chic and a pleasant outdoor patio create a casual atmosphere for enjoying an unusual combination of ingredients. Spicy *togorashi* chicken is roasted with sesame seeds, chilies, and orange peel, and topped with a ginger demi-glace. Vegetarian entrées might be tofu, spinach, and coconut-tomato-basil curry. An almond flan dessert is served in a towering martini glass. ⊠*830 N. Shaver St., at N. Mississippi St., Albina* ☎*503/460–3333* ⊗*Closed Mon. No dinner Sun.*

$–$$$ ⨯ **Mint.** The owner of this cool, romantic restaurant happens also to be a top-notch bartender. Drinks made with maple syrup, nutmeg, and avocados are commonplace—and just as her drinks selections are hard to categorize, so too are the menu items. Global flavors influence anevolving choice of interesting items like opah poached in coconut lemongrass sakeand sautéed rabbit loin with garlic mashed potatoes andwild boar bacon. When you're done, slip next door to 820, the sister lounge to this suave establishment. ⊠*816 N. Russell St.,* ☎*503/284–5518* ▤*AE, MC, V* ⊘*Closed Sun. No lunch.*

$–$$ ╳**Perry's on Fremont.** This diner, still famous for burgers, chicken pot-pies, and fish-and-chips, has gone a bit more upscale with the addition of pricier menu items such as steak and salmon. Eat outside on the large patio among the flowers, and don't pass up one of the desserts. ⊠*2401 N.E. Fremont St.,* ☎*503/287–3655* ▤*AE, D, MC, V* ⊘*Closed Sun. and Mon. No lunch weekdays.*

¢–$ ╳**Bread and Ink.** The old-fashioned elegance will strike you as soon as you walk in, but the high-ceiling dining room, done in cream and forest green, is not trendy in any way, and it is partly this earnest dedication to quality food that has helped it gain its name as a neighborhood landmark. Breakfast is a specialty and might include brioche French toast, smoked fish, and legendary blintzes. Lunch and dinner yield good choices, including burgers, poached salmon, and crab cakes. ⊠*3610 S.E. Hawthorne Blvd., Hawthorne District* ☎*503/239–4756* ▤*AE, D, MC, V.*

¢–$ ╳**Wild Abandon and the Red Velvet Lounge.** Inside this small, bohemian-looking building, owner Michael Cox creates an inventive Mediterranean-influenced menu that includes fresh seafood, pork, beef, and pasta entrées. Vegetarian selections might be ziti, panfried tofu, or polenta lasagna made with roasted eggplant, squash, and spinach. The popular Sunday brunch includes omelets, Benedict dishes, breakfast burritos, and vegan French toast. ⊠*2411 S.E. Belmont St., near Hawthorne District* ☎*503/232–4458* ▤*AE, D, DC, MC, V* ⊘*Closed Tues. No lunch weekdays.*

CUBAN

¢–$ ╳**Pambiche.** Locals know that you can drive by Pambiche any night
★ of the week and find it packed. With traditional Cuban fare including plantains, roast pork, mojitos, and Cuban espresso, it is no surprise why. If you have some time to wait for a table, you should stop by and make an evening of it at this hopping neighborhood hot spot. Don't miss out on the incredible dessert here; it is the sole reason why some people make the trip. ⊠*2811 N.E. Glisan St., near Laurelhurst* ☎*503/233–0511* ✍*Reservations not accepted* ▤*D, MC, V.*

GERMAN

$ ╳**Rheinlander.** A strolling accordionist and singing servers entertain as patrons dine on authentic traditional German food, including sauerbraten, hasenpfeffer, schnitzel, sausage, and rotisserie chicken. **Gustav's,** the adjoining pub and grill, serves slightly less expensive entrées, including sausages, cabbage rolls, and German meatballs, in an equally festive, if slightly more raucous, environment. ⊠*5035 N.E. Sandy Blvd.,* ☎*503/288–5503* ▤*AE, MC, V.*

¢–$ ✕**Widmer Gasthaus.** This old-world–style brewpub, part of the adjacent Widmer Brothers Brewery, is just steps away from the MAX light-rail station on North Interstate Avenue. Ale-dunked sausages, schnitzel, and sauerbraten are well matched to the signature Hefeweizen and other German-style beers, tapped from the handsome hardwood-and-brass bar. Chicken potpie, steak, pasta, and burgers are also served, in addition to the Widmer brothers' beloved beer cheese soup. ✉*955 N. Russell St., at N. Interstate Ave. Albina* ☎*503/281–3333* ⚲*Reservations not accepted* ▭*AE, D, MC, V.*

ITALIAN

$$$$ ✕**Genoa.** Widely regarded as the finest restaurant in Portland, Genoa
★   serves a seven-course prix-fixe menu focusing on authentic Italian cuisine, that changes every two weeks. Although the dining room is a bit drab, seating is limited to a few dozen diners, so service is excellent. Smoking is permitted in a separate sitting room. ✉*2822 S.E. Belmont St., near Hawthorne District* ☎*503/238–1464* ⚲*Reservations essential* ▭*AE, D, DC, MC, V* ⊗*No lunch.*

$–$$ ✕**Three Doors Down.** Down a side street in the busy Hawthorne shop-
★   ping district, this small Italian restaurant is known for quality Italian food, with exquisite seafood dishes, skillful pasta concoctions, and decadent desserts. The intimate restaurant's reputation brings people coming back again and again, even though they might have to wait on the sidewalk for close to an hour. ✉*1429 S.E. 37th Ave., Hawthorne District* ☎*503/236–6886* ▭*AE, D, MC, V* ⊗*Closed Mon. No lunch.*

$ ✕**Il Piatto.** On a quiet residential street, this laid-back trattoria and espresso house turns out inventive dishes and classic Italian favorites. A tasty sun-dried-tomato–pesto spread instead of butter accompanies the bread. Entrées include smoked salmon ravioli in a lemon cream sauce with capers and leeks. The vegetarian lasagna with grilled eggplant and zucchini, topped with pine nuts, is rich and satisfying. The extensive wine selection focuses on varieties from Tuscany. ✉*2348 Ankeny St., near Laurelhurst* ☎*503/236–4997* ▭*DC, MC, V* ⊗*No lunch Sat.–Mon.*

LEBANESE

¢   ✕**Nicholas Restaurant.** In a small streetfront along an unimpressive
★   stretch of Grand Avenue, this hidden gem serves some of the best Lebanese food in Portland, for prices that can't be beat. Everything from the fresh homemade pita to the hummus, falafel, baba ghanoush, and kebabs is delicious and comes in enormous portions. No alcohol is served here. ✉*318 S.E. Grand Ave., near Burnside Bridge* ☎*503/235–5123* ▭*No credit cards.*

SEAFOOD

$–$$$ ✕**Salty's on the Columbia.** Pacific Northwest salmon (choose blackened or grilled, a half or full pound) is what this comfortable restaurant overlooking the Columbia River is known for. Blackberry-barbecue-glazed salmon highlights local ingredients. Loaded with prawns, oysters, crab, mussels, and clams, the seafood platter offers plenty of variety. The menu also includes chicken and steak. There is a heated, covered deck and an uncovered deck for open-air dining. ☒*3839 N.E. Marine Dr.,* ☎*503/288–4444* ▭*AE, D, DC, MC, V.*

SOUTHERN

$–$$ ✕**Bernie's Southern Bistro.** You definitely won't find finer soul food in Portland. At first glance, Bernie's may seem fairly expensive for the cuisine, but then, this food is in a different realm from that of your garden-variety fried chicken. Restaurant specialties include crisp fried green tomatoes, crawfish, and catfish, in addition to delectable fried chicken, collard greens, and black-eyed peas. The inside of the restaurant is painted in warm oranges, and the lush outdoor patio is a Portland favorite. ☒*2904 N.E. Alberta St.,* ☎*503/282–9864* ▭*AE, D, MC, V* ☉*Closed Sun. and Mon. No lunch.*

$ ✕**Podnah's Pit BBQ.** Nondescript in appearance, this little storefront diner hardly even declares itself with outdoor signage. But the Texas and Carolina-style dishes inside are the stuff big boy barbecue's are made of. Melt-in-your-mouth pulled pork, ribs, chicken and lamb are all served up in a sassy vinegar-based sauce. ☒ *1469 N.E. Prescott St., Alberta District* ☎*503/281–3700* ▭ *MC, V*

¢   ✕**Lagniappe.** Catfish, oysters, shrimp, and crawfish tails are served up as jambalaya and po'boys at this New Orleans–style soul-food diner. Lagniappe (pronounced "lan-yap") also makes sandwiches from smoked pulled pork and beef brisket. Black-eyed peas, hush puppies, and collard greens round out the menu of sides. Dining is informal and extends to an outside patio in good weather. ☒*1934 N.E. Alberta St., 97211 Alberta District* ☎*503/249–7675* ⌖*Reservations not accepted* ▭*AE, D, MC, V* ☉*Closed Mon. and Tues.*

SOUTHWESTERN

¢–$ ✕**Esparza's Tex-Mex Cafe.** Be prepared for south-of-the-border craziness at this beloved local eatery. Wild West kitsch festoons the walls, but it isn't any wilder than some of the entrées that emerge from chef-owner Joe Esparza's kitchen. Look for such creations as lean smoked-sirloin tacos—Esparza's is renowned for its smoked meats—and, for the truly adventurous diner, ostrich enchiladas. ☒*2725 S.E. Ankeny St., at S.E. 28th Ave., near Laurelhurst* ☎*503/234–7909* ⌖*Reservations not accepted* ▭*AE, D, MC, V* ☉*Closed Sun.*

SPANISH

¢–$ ✕**Colosso.** A dimly lit tapas bar and restaurant, casual Colosso is one of the most romantic places to dine in northeast Portland. The best way to get the full experience of the place is to order a pitcher of sangria and split a few of the small tapas plates between you and your companions. In the evening the restaurant is usually crowded with folks drinking cocktails late into the night. ☒*1932 N.E. Broadway, Broadway District* ☎*503/288–3333* ▭*D, MC, V* ☉*No lunch.*

STEAK

$–$$ ✕**Sayler's Old Country Kitchen.** Home of the massive 72-ounce steak (free if you can eat it in an hour—and some do), Sayler's complements its steak-focused menu with a few seafood and chicken dinners. With no pretense of being trendy or hip, this large family-style restaurant and lounge near Gresham has been around since 1946, and relies today on the same old-fashioned menu and quality it did back then. ✉10519 S.E. Stark St., ☎503/252–4171 ⊟AE, D, MC, V ⊘No lunch.

THAI

¢–$ ✕**Thai Noon.** Thai Noon is a popular spot that serves excellent traditional dishes including red, green, and yellow curry; stir fries; and noodle dishes in a vibrant orange dining room with only about 12 tables. You can choose the spiciness of your meal, but beware that although "medium" may be milder than "hot," it is still quite spicy. Thai iced tea is also available as a boozy cocktail from the adjoining bar and lounge. Try the fried banana split or the mango ice cream for dessert. ✉2635 N.E. Alberta St., Alberta District ☎503/282–2021 ⊟MC, V.

VEGETARIAN

¢ ✕**Vita Cafe.** Vegan mac and cheese and vegetarian biscuits and gravy are but a few of the old favorites with a new spin. This hip restaurant along Alberta Street has a large menu with American, Mexican, Asian, and Middle Eastern–inspired entrées, and both herbivores and carnivores are sure to find something. There is plenty of free-range, organic meat to go around, in addition to the vegan and vegetarian options. Finish off your meal with a piece of decadent German chocolate cake or a peanut-butter fudge bar. ✉3024 N.E. Alberta St., Alberta District ☎503/335–8233 ⊟MC, V.

VIETNAMESE

¢–$ ✕**Thanh Thao.** This busy Asian diner in the heart of Portland's bohemian Hawthorne neighborhood has an extensive menu of Vietnamese stir-fries, noodles, soups, and Thai favorites. Be prepared to wait for *and* at your table: the place is often packed, and service is famously slow. But the food and generous portions are worth the wait. ✉4005 S.E. Hawthorne Blvd., Hawthorne District ☎503/238–6232 ⊟D, MC, V ⊘Closed Tues.

WEST OF DOWNTOWN

AMERICAN–CASUAL

¢ ✕**Original Pancake House.** Not to be confused with any chain imitations, this pancake house is the real deal. Faithful customers have been coming for close to 50 years to wait for a table at this bustling, cabin-like local landmark, and you can expect to find a contented crowd of locals and tourists alike from the time the place opens at 7 AM until afternoon. With pancakes starting at $7.25, it's not the cheapest place to get a stack, but with 20 varieties and some of the best waffles and crepes around, it's worth the trip. ✉8601 S.W. Barbur Blvd., Burlingame, ☎503/246–9007 ✍Reservations not accepted ⊟No credit cards ⊘Closed Mon. and Tues. No dinner.

CONTEMPORARY

$–$$ ✕**Chart House.** On a hill high above the Willamette River, the Chart House has a stunning view of the city and the surrounding mountains from almost all of its tables. Prime rib is a specialty, but the seafood dishes, including coconut-crunchy shrimp deep-fried in tempura batter and the Cajun spiced yellowfin ahi are just as tempting. ⊠*5700 S.W. Terwilliger Blvd.,* ☎*503/246–6963* ☐*AE, D, DC, MC, V* ⊘*No lunch weekends.*

ITALIAN

¢ ✕**Old Spaghetti Factory.** An old trolley car, oversize velvet chairs, dark wood, and fun antiques fill this huge restaurant overlooking the Willamette River. With a lounge upstairs, room for 500 diners, and a great view of the river, the flagship location of this nationwide restaurant chain is a great place for families, with basic pasta dishes and a kids' menu. ⊠*0715 S.W. Bancroft St.* ☎*503/222–5375* ⚓*Reservations not accepted* ☐*AE, D, DC, MC, V.*

WHERE TO STAY

Many of the elegant hotels near the city center or on the riverfront appeal because of their proximity to the city's attractions. MAX light rail is within easy walking distance of most properties. Many downtown hotels cater to business travelers and offer special discounts on weekends. Additional accommodations clustered near the Convention Center and the airport are almost exclusively chain hotels, and tend to be slightly less expensive than those found downtown. An alternative to the standard hotels in the city are the several beautiful B&Bs spread throughout residential neighborhoods in the northwest and northeast, where there are lovely homes, unique and luxurious guest rooms, deluxe home-cooked breakfasts, and friendly and knowledgeable innkeepers.

WHAT IT COSTS					
	¢	$	$$	$$$	$$$$
FOR 2 PEOPLE	under $100	$100–$150	$150–$200	$200–$250	over $250

Hotel prices are for a standard double room, excluding room tax, which varies 6%–9½% depending on location.

DOWNTOWN

$$$–$$$$ 🖵**Heathman Hotel.** Superior service, a renowned restaurant, a central
Fodor'sChoice downtown location (adjoining the Performing Arts Center), and swank
★ public areas have earned the Heathman its reputation for quality. From the teak-panel lobby hung with Warhol prints to the rosewood elevators and marble fireplaces, this hotel exudes refinement. The guest rooms provide the latest in customized comfort: a bed menu allows you to choose from orthopedic, European pillowtop, or European featherbed mattresses for your resting pleasure, and the bathrooms have plenty of marble and mirrors. The second-floor mezzanine, with a small art gallery with works changing every several weeks and a

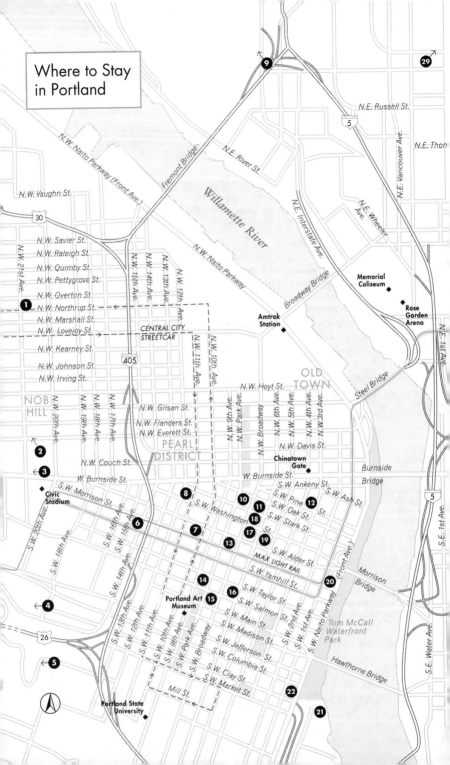

1

small library (primarily filled with the works of notable Heathman guests), overlooks the high-ceiling Tea Court, a popular gathering spot in the evening. **Pros:** Beauty, location and service. **Cons:** Small rooms and expensive parking. ⊠*1001 S.W. Broadway, Downtown, 97205* ☎*503/241–4100 or 800/551–0011* ▤*503/790–7110* ⊕*www.heath manhotel.com* ⇗*117 rooms, 33 suites* ⓖ*In-room: Ethernet, minibar. In-hotel: Wi-Fi, restaurant, room service, bar, gym, concierge, laundry service, parking (fee), no-smoking rooms, some pets allowed* ▤*AE, D, DC, MC, V.*

$$–$$$
★
 Governor Hotel. With its mahogany walls and mural of Pacific Northwest Indians fishing in Celilo Falls, the clubby lobby of the distinctive Governor sets the overall tone for the hotel's 1920s Arts and Crafts style. Painted in soothing earth tones, the tastefully appointed guest rooms have large windows, honor bars, and bathrobes. Some have whirlpool tubs, fireplaces, and balconies. Jake's Grill is on the property, the streetcar runs right out front, and the hotel is one block from MAX. **Pros:** Large rooms, beautiful historic property, excellent on-site restaurant. **Cons:** Some have said there's inconsistency with the attention to detailed cleanliness. ⊠*614 S.W. 10th Ave., Downtown, 97205* ☎*503/224–3400 or 800/554–3456* ▤*503/241–2122* ⊕*www. govhotel.com* ⇗*68 rooms, 32 suites* ⓖ*In-room: dial-up. In-hotel: restaurant, room service, bar, concierge, laundry service, parking (fee), no-smoking rooms* ▤*AE, D, DC, MC, V.*

$$–$$$ **Hotel Lucia.** Modern track lighting, black-and-white David Kennerly celebrity photos, and comfy leather chairs adorn this eight-story boutique hotel in the heart of downtown—walking distance to Nordstrom, Powell's, and the MAX line. The hotel's goal to "deliver calm" is accomplished in part through such conveniences as a pillow "menu" offering seven choices in pillows, stored customer profiles (so you automatically receive that same pillow next time), and Aveda soaps and lotions. The Pet Package caters to the small, furry members of your family with a special bed, set of dishes, treats, and even Fiji water. **Pros:** Very upscale and beautiful decor. **Cons:** Small rooms and limited shelf and storage space in the bathrooms. ⊠*400 S.W. Broadway St., Downtown, 97205* ☎*503/225–1717 or 877/225–1717* ▤*503/225–1919* ⊕*www. hotellucia.com* ⇗*127 rooms, 33 suites* ⓖ*In-room: Wi-Fi. In-hotel: restaurant, room service, gym, concierge, laundry service, parking (fee), no-smoking rooms, some pets allowed* ▤*AE, D, DC, MC, V.*

$$–$$$ **Hotel Vintage Plaza.** This historic landmark takes its theme from the area's vineyards. Guests can fall asleep counting stars in top-floor rooms, where skylights and wall-to-wall conservatory-style windows rate highly among the special details. Hospitality suites have extra-large rooms with a full living area, and the deluxe rooms have a bar. All are appointed in warm colors and have cherrywood furnishings; some rooms have hot tubs. Complimentary wine is served in the evening, and an extensive collection of Oregon vintages is displayed in the tasting room. Two-story town-house suites are named after local wineries. **Pros:** Beautiful decor and nice complimentary wine selections. **Cons:** Since it is pet-friendly, some allergic people may be affected by the allowance of pets. ⊠*422 S.W. Broadway, Downtown, 97205* ☎*503/228–1212* *or 800/243–0555* ≜*503/228–3598* ⊕*www.vintageplaza.com* ↩*107 rooms, 21 suites* ☐*In-room: dial-up. In-hotel: Wi-Fi, restaurant, room service, bar, gym, concierge, parking (fee), some pets allowed* ☐*AE, D, DC, MC, V.*

$$–$$$ 🏨**Portland Marriott Downtown.** The large rooms at Marriott's 16-floor corporate-focused waterfront property are decorated in off-whites; the best ones face east with a view of the Willamette and the Cascades. All rooms have work desks, high-speed Internet access, and voice mail. Champions Lounge, filled with sports memorabilia, is a singles' hot spot on weekends. It's six blocks from MAX light rail. **Pros:** Excellent location near the waterfront. **Cons:** No refrigerators or minibars ✉*1401 S.W. Naito Pkwy., Downtown, 97201* ☎*503/226–7600 or 800/228–9290* ≜*503/221–1789* ⊕*www.marriott.com* ↩*503 rooms, 6 suites* ☐*In-room: dial-up. In-hotel: restaurant, room service, bar, pool, gym, concierge, laundry facilities, laundry service, airport shuttle (fee), parking (fee), no-smoking rooms* ☐*AE, D, DC, MC, V.*

$$–$$$ 🏨**RiverPlace Hotel.** This hotel is adorned with muted color schemes, Craftsman-style desks, and ergonomic chairs in all guest rooms. It has one of the best views in Portland, overlooking the river, the marina, and skyline as well as a landscaped courtyard. Extras include bathrobes, afternoon tea and cookies, and rooms stocked with Starbucks coffee and Tazo tea. **Pros:** Wide selection of room options, awesome location and great beds. **Cons:** No pool. ✉*1510 S.W. Harbor Way, Downtown, 97201* ☎*503/228–3233 or 800/227–1333* ≜*503/295–6161* ⊕*www. riverplacehotel.com* ↩*39 rooms, 45 suites* ☐*In-room: DVD. In-hotel: Wi-Fi, restaurant, room service, concierge, parking (fee), no-smoking rooms* ☐*AE, D, DC, MC, V.*

$–$$$ 🏨**Benson Hotel.** Portland's grandest hotel was built in 1912. The hand-
★   carved Russian Circassian walnut paneling and the Italian white-marble staircase are among the noteworthy design touches in the public areas. In the guest rooms expect to find small crystal chandeliers and inlaid mahogany doors. Some even have the original ceilings. Extra touches include fully stocked private bars and bathrobes in every room. **Pros:** Beautiful lobby and excellent location. **Cons:** Room and hall interiors could use updating. ✉*309 S.W. Broadway, Downtown, 97205* ☎*503/228–2000 or 888/523–6766* ≜*503/471–3920* ⊕*www.bensonhotel.com* ↩*287 rooms* ☐*In-room: dial-up. In-hotel: Wi-Fi, 2 restaurants, room service, bar, gym, concierge, laundry service, parking (fee), Internet* ☐*AE, D, DC, MC, V.*

$$ 🏨**Embassy Suites.** The grand lobby welcomes you at this property in the historic Multnomah Hotel building. The spacious, two-room suites have large windows, sofa beds, and wet bars. The indoor pool curves around the lower level of the hotel. A complimentary shuttle will take you within a 2-mi radius, based on availability. A cooked-to-order full breakfast and cocktail reception with light snacks are included in the rate. **Pros:** Beautiful historic building. **Cons:** Poor snack reception and no in and out privileges in self-park garage across the street. ✉*319 S.W. Pine St., Downtown, 97204* ☎*503/279–9000 or 800/642–7892* ≜*503/497–9051* ⊕*www.embassyportland.com* ↩*276 suites* ☐*In-*

room: refrigerator. In-hotel: Wi-Fi, restaurant, bar, pool, gym, spa, concierge, laundry service, parking (fee) ▭AE, D, DC, MC, V ⍟BP.

$$ ⌂ **Hilton Portland & Executive Tower.** Together, two buildings comprise a gargantuan complex of luxuriously contemporary bedrooms, meeting rooms, restaurants, and athletic facilities, including two indoor swimming pools. The property is within walking distance of the Performing Arts Center, Pioneer Courthouse Square, the Portland Art Museum, and MAX light rail. More than 60 restaurants are within a few blocks. **Pros:** Nice workout facilities and indoor pools. **Cons:** Lots of construction going on downtown for the next several years along where this property is located. ✉ *921 S.W. 6th Ave., Downtown, 97204* ☎ *503/226–1611 or 800/445–8667* ⎙ *503/220–2565* ⊕ *www. hilton.com* ⇨ *773 rooms, 9 suites* ⌂ *In-room: dial-up. In-hotel: 2 restaurants, bars, pools, gym, parking (fee), no-smoking rooms, Internet* ▭AE, D, DC, MC, V.

$$ ⌂ **Hotel Monaco.** The 1912 Lipman Wolfe Department Store reopened as this boutique hotel in 1997. A tall vestibule with a marble mosaic floor leads to the art-filled lobby, where guests gather by the fireplace for an early-evening glass of wine or a morning cup of coffee. Warm fall colors, stripes, and floral prints adorn the 10-story property's 550-square-foot suites, divided by curtained sliding doors. Upholstered chairs, fringed ottomans, and other appointments in the sitting areas will make you feel right at home (or wish you had one like this). The large bathrooms are stocked with every amenity. Downstairs in the lobby is the Dosha Spa. **Pros:** Large comfortable rooms, accommodating staff, free Starbuck's coffee in the morning. **Cons:** Rooms can get chilly at night because of drafty windows. ✉ *506 S.W. Washington St., Downtown, 97204* ☎ *503/222–0001 or 888/207–2201* ⎙ *503/222–0004* ⊕ *www.portland-monaco. com* ⇨ *82 rooms, 137 suites* ⌂ *In-room: dial-up. In-hotel: Wi-Fi, restaurant, room service, gym, laundry service, parking (fee), no-smoking rooms, some pets allowed* ▭AE, D, DC, MC, V.

$$ ⌂ **Marriott City Center.** The lobby of this 20-story boutique property, in the heart of the downtown arts and dining area, is accented with a grand staircase, maple paneling, and marble floors. The plush rooms have voice mail, large work desks, and coffeemakers. The MAX light rail is two blocks away. **Pros:** Spacious nicely decorated rooms. **Cons:** No refrigerators in rooms, however, they are available upon request. ✉ *520 S.W. Broadway, Downtown, 97205* ☎ *503/226–6300 or 800/228–9290* ⎙ *503/227–7515* ⊕ *www.marriott.com* ⇨ *249 rooms, 10 suites* ⌂ *In-room: dial-up. In-hotel: Wi-Fi, restaurant, room service, bar, gym, concierge, laundry service, parking (fee)* ▭AE, D, DC, MC, V.

$$ ☷**Paramount.** Inside this 15-story boutique-style property—two blocks from Pioneer Square, MAX, and the Portland Art Museum—earth tones, plush dark-wood furnishings, dried flowers, honor bars, and granite baths adorn the cozy rooms. Some have outdoor balconies and whirlpool tubs. The grand suites also have wet bars and gas fireplaces. **Pros:** Beautiful spacious showers and bathtubs. **Cons:** Small workout/fitness facilities. ✉ *808 S.W. Taylor St., Downtown, 97205* ☎ *503/223–9900* ☏ *503/223–7900 or 800/663–1144* ⊕ *www.port landparamount.com* ⇋ *154 rooms* ⟁ *In-room: refrigerator. In-hotel: dial-up, Wi-Fi, restaurant, room service, gym, concierge, laundry service, parking (fee), no-smoking rooms* ▭ *AE, D, DC, MC, V.*

$$ ☷**Westin.** This European-style boutique property combines luxury with convenience. Its tastefully appointed rooms include entertainment-center armoires, work desks, plush beds covered with layers of down, and granite bathrooms with separate showers and tubs. Pioneer Square and MAX are two blocks away. The Daily Grill features traditional American fare in an upscale, casual atmosphere. **Pros:** Prime downtown location. **Cons:** No spas or saunas. ✉ *750 S.W. Alder St., Downtown, 97205* ☎ *503/294–9000 or 888/625–5144* ☏ *503/241–9565* ⊕ *www. westin.com* ⇋ *205 rooms* ⟁ *In-room: Wi-Fi, safe. In-hotel: dial-up, Wi-Fi, restaurant, room service, bar, gym, concierge, laundry service, parking (fee)* ▭ *AE, D, DC, MC, V.*

$–$$ ☷**Four Points Sheraton.** If you're concerned about location, consider this five-story hotel on the MAX light-rail line. Some of the rooms have balconies; east-facing rooms offer views of the Willamette River and the Governor Tom McCall Waterfront Park. Guests have privileges at Bally's Total Fitness nearby. ✉ *50 S.W. Morrison St., Downtown, 97204* ☎ *503/221–0711 or 800/368–7764* ☏ *503/484–1417* ⊕ *www. fourpoints.com* ⇋ *140 rooms* ⟁ *In-hotel: restaurant, room service, bar, gym, laundry service, parking (fee), no-smoking rooms, some pets allowed* ▭ *AE, D, DC, MC, V.*

$–$$ ☷**Hotel deLuxe.** If you long to be transported back to the era of 1940s Hollywood glamour, this vintage hotel is perfect for your time travel itinerary. More than 400 black-and-white photographs adorn corridor walls, with each of the eight floors cast into a cinematic theme such as Music Masters, Rebels, Exiles, and Immigrants. Complementing the vintage and dramatic decor are rooms decked out with high-tech amenities such as flat-screen HDTV's and MP3 docking stations. If the standard King James Bible in the drawer doesn't ignite your spiritual flame, then choose from a selection of texts including Buddhist, Taoist, Catholic, or even Scientologist offerings. **Pros:** Swanky, sophisticated ambience and extras such as a "pillow" menu. **Cons:** Older building means older windows, which can feel drafty at night. ✉ *729 S.W. 15th Ave., Downtown, 97205* ☎ *503/219–2094 or 866/895–2094* ☏ *503/219–2095* ⊕ *www.hoteldeluxeportland.com* ⇋ *130 rooms* ⟁ *In-room: refrigerator. In-hotel: public Wi-Fi., restaurant, room service, bar, parking (fee), no-smoking rooms, some pets allowed* ▭ *AE, D, DC, MC, V* ⦿*CP.*

$–$$ ☷**Mark Spencer.** Near Portland's gay-bar district and Powell's City of Books, the Mark Spencer has one of the best values in town. The rooms are clean and comfortable, and all have full kitchens, plus a rooftop garden deck open to all guests. Breakfast is included, as well as afternoon tea and cookies. The hotel is a major supporter of local arts and offers special packages that include theater tickets to performances by the Artists Repertory Theatre, Portland Opera, and Center Stage. **Pros:** In-room kitchens with stove top and full refrigerator are a great bonus. **Cons:** Older property absent of contemporary updates compared to other downtown properties. ✉ *409 S.W. 11th Ave., 97205* ☎ *503/224–3293 or 800/548–3934* 🖨 *503/223–7848* ⊕ *www.mark spencer.com* ⟿ *102 rooms* ♿ *In-room: kitchen. In-hotel: public Wi-Fi., laundry facilities, laundry service, no-smoking rooms, some pets allowed* ▤ *AE, D, DC, MC, V* ⦿ *CP.*

¢–$ ★ 🏨 **The Jupiter Hotel.** The hip and adventurous, looking for a place to dock their iPods for the night, flock to this contemporary hotel, which provides easy access to downtown, the nearby Rock Gym, and more on-site amenities than any other hotel in town. Rooms feature iPod docking stations, Blu-dot furniture, down comforters and colorful shag pillows, and chalkboard doors. Also on-site are a hair salon, a spa, a clothing and gift boutique, and a rock club (the Doug Fir, ⇨ *Dancing*). **Pros:** If you want to party, it's next to a fun hot spot. **Cons:** If you want a quieter experience, it's near a loud hot spot. ✉ *800 E. Burnside, near Downtown, 97214* ☎ *503/230–9200 or 877/800–0004* 🖨 *503/230–9300* ⊕ *www.jupiterhotel.com* ⟿ *78 rooms, 1 suite* ♿ *In-room: DVD. In-hotel: Wi-Fi, restaurant, room service, bar, spa, parking (fee), no-smoking rooms, some pets allowed* ▤ *AE, D, DC, MC, V.*

EAST OF THE WILLAMETTE

$$–$$$ ★ 🏨 **Portland's White House.** Hardwood floors with Oriental rugs, chandeliers, antiques, and fountains create a warm and romantic mood at this elegant bed-and-breakfast inn in a Greek Revival mansion in the historic Irvington District. The mansion was built in 1911 and is on the National Register of Historic Landmarks. Rooms have private baths, flat-screen TVs, and mahogany canopy or four-poster queen- and king-size beds. A full breakfast is included in the room rate, and the owners offer vegetarian or vegan options. Smoking and pets are not permitted. **Pros:** A beautiful, authentic historical Portland experience, excellent service. **Cons:** It's in a residential neighborhood so shops and restaurants are several blocks away. ✉ *1914 N.E. 22nd Ave., Irvington, 97212* ☎ *503/287–7131 or 800/272–7131* 🖨 *503/249–1641* ⊕ *www.portlandswhitehouse.com* ⟿ *8 suites* ♿ *In-room: dial-up. In-hotel: Wi-Fi, parking (no fee), no-smoking rooms* ▤ *AE, D, MC, V* ⦿ *BP.*

$–$$ 🏨 **Doubletree Hotel.** This bustling, business-oriented hotel maintains a huge traffic in meetings and special events. The public areas are a tasteful mix of marble, rose-and-green carpet, and antique-style furnishings. The large rooms, many with balconies, have views of the mountains or the city center. Lloyd Center and the MAX light-rail line are across the street; the Oregon Convention Center is a five-minute walk away. **Pros:** Location and access to shops. **Cons:** Pool is outdoors. ✉ *1000 N.E. Multnomah St., Lloyd District, 97232* ☎ *503/281–6111 or 800/222–*

8733 🖷*503/284–8553* ⊕*www.doubletree.com* ⇖*476 rooms* ♿*In-room: dial-up. In-hotel: 2 restaurants, room service, bar, pool, gym, concierge, laundry service, parking (fee)* ⊟*AE, D, DC, MC, V.*

$–$$
Fodor'sChoice
★
🏨 **Lion and the Rose.** This 1906 Queen Anne–style mansion is one of Portland's premier B&Bs and the city's only Victorian one. Oak and mahogany floors, original light fixtures, antique silver, and the coffered dining-room ceiling set a tone of formal elegance, while the wonderfully friendly, accommodating, and knowledgeable innkeepers make sure that you feel perfectly at home. A two-course breakfast and evening snacks are served daily, and afternoon tea is available upon request. In a beautiful residential neighborhood, you are just a block from the shops and restaurants that fill northeast Broadway and within an easy walk of a free MAX ride downtown. **Pros:** Gorgeous home, top-notch service. **Cons:** Kids under 10 not allowed. ⊠*1810 N.E. 15th Ave., Irvington, 97212* 🕾*503/287–9245 or 800/955–1647* 🖷*503/287–9247* ⊕*www. lionrose.com* ⇖*7 rooms* ♿*In-room: dial-up In-hotel: Wi-Fi, parking (no fee), no kids under 7, no-smoking rooms* ⊟*AE, D, DC, MC, V.*

$–$$
🏨 **Marriott Residence Inn—Lloyd Center.** With large, fully equipped suites and only a short walk from both the Lloyd Center and a MAX stop within Fareless Square, this three-level apartment-style complex is perfect for extended-stay visitors or for tourists. Rooms come equipped with full kitchens and ample seating space, and many have wood-burning fireplaces. There's a large complimentary breakfast buffet each morning, and an hors-d'oeuvres reception on weekday evenings. ⊠*1710 N.E. Multnomah St., Lloyd District, 97232* 🕾*503/288–1400 or 800/331–3131* 🖷*503/288–0241* ⊕*www.marriott.com* ⇖*168 rooms* ♿*In-room: kitchen. In-hotel: Wi-Fi, bar, pool, gym, laundry facilities, parking (no fee), no-smoking rooms, some pets allowed* ⦿❘*BP.*

$
🏨 **Holiday Inn Portland.** This sleek, modern hotel is very close to the Rose Quarter, the Coliseum, and the Convention Center and is within easy walking distance of Lloyd Center, the MAX line, and the Broadway Bridge leading to downtown. Between its attractive rooms and its ample facilities, it provides a reliable and convenient option for both business travelers and tourists. **Pros:** Indoor pool, convenient location. **Cons:** In-room refrigerators are based upon request and not guaranteed. ⊠*1441 N.E. 2nd Ave., Lloyd District/Convention Center, 97232* 🕾*503/233–2401 or 877/777–2704* 🖷*503/238–7016* ⊕*www.hiport land.com* ⇖*240 rooms* ♿*In-room: Wi-Fi. In-hotel: restaurant, bar, pool, gym* ⊟*AE, D, DC, MC, V.*

¢–$
🏨 **Georgian House.** This redbrick Georgian Colonial–style house with neoclassical columns is on a quiet, tree-lined street in the Irvington neighborhood. The gardens in back can be enjoyed from one of the guest verandas or from the gazebo. The largest and sunniest of the guest rooms is the Lovejoy Suite, with a tile fireplace and brass canopy bed. **Pros:** Hospitality and intimate environment. **Cons:** For those who want bustle, it's in a residential neighborhood. ⊠*1828 N.E. Siskiyou St., Irvington, 97212* 🕾*503/281–2250 or 888/282–2250* 🖷*503/281–3301* ⊕*www.thegeorgianhouse.com* ⇖*2 rooms with shared bath;*

2 suites ♿*In-room: no phone. In-hotel: no TV (some), no-smoking rooms* ▭*MC, V* ⓘⓄⓘ*BP.*

¢–$ ▦**Inn at the Convention Center.** This independently run hotel is directly across the street from the Convention Center, four blocks from Lloyd Center, and right along the MAX line. This no-frills hotel offers convenience as its main asset. Many of the simple and comfortable rooms at the six-story facility have refrigerators and/or minibars. **Pros:** Right next to convention center. **Cons:** According to past visitors, it's not wheelchair friendly and is in need of updates. ✉*420 N.E. Holladay St., Lloyd District/Convention Center, 97232* ☎*503/233–6331* 🖷*503/233–2677* ⊕*www.innatcc.com* ↩*97 rooms* ♿*In-room: refrigerator (some), Wi-Fi. In-hotel: laundry facilities, laundry service, parking (no fee), no-smoking rooms, Ethernet* ▭*AE, D, DC, MC, V.*

¢–$ ▦**McMenamins Kennedy School.** In a renovated elementary school in ★   northeast Portland, the Kennedy School may well be one of the most unusual hotels you'll ever encounter. With all of the guest rooms occupying former classrooms, complete with the original chalkboards and cloakrooms, and with small bars known as Detention Bar (with cigars and one of the only two TVs on site) and Honors Bar (with classical music and cocktails), the McMenamins brothers have created a multiuse facility that is both luxurious and fantastical. Room rates include movie admission and use of the outdoor soaking pool. **Pros:** Funky, authentic Portland experience. **Cons:** No bathtubs in bathrooms. ✉*5736 N.E. 33rd Ave., near Alberta District, 97211* ☎*503/249–3983* ⊕*www.kennedyschool.com* ↩*35 rooms* ♿*In-room: no TV. In-hotel: Wi-Fi , restaurant, bars, parking (no fee), no-smoking rooms* ▭*AE, D, DC, MC, V* ⓘⓄⓘ*BP.*

¢–$ ▦**Red Lion Hotel Convention Center.** Across the street from the Convention Center and adjacent to the MAX, this hotel is as convenient as can be for both business travelers and tourists. It provides a few more on-site amenities than some of the other hotels right by the Convention Center (Shilo Inn and Inn at the Convention Center are right across the street), which is reflected in its slightly higher rates. **Pros:** Right next to convention center. **Cons:** They do accept pets so if you're allergic, be sure to ask for a no-pet room. ✉*1021 N.E. Grand Ave., Lloyd District/Convention Center, 97232* ☎*503/235–2100 or 800/343–1822* 🖷*503/238–0132* ⊕*www.redlion.com* ↩*174 rooms* ♿*In-room: refrigerator. In-hotel: Wi-Fi, restaurant, room service, bar, gym, parking (fee), no-smoking rooms, some pets allowed.*

WEST OF DOWNTOWN

$–$$$$ ▦**Heron Haus.** This lovely, bright B&B is inside a stately, 100-year-old three-floor Tudor-style mansion near Forest Park. Special features include a tulip-shape bathtub in one room and a tiled, seven-head antique shower in another. You can enjoy a relaxing afternoon in the secluded sitting garden. All rooms have phones, work desks, and fireplaces. Breakfast, included in the room rate, is a fancy continental affair. **Pros:** Nice modern amenities. **Cons:** In a residential neighborhood and not immediately near public transportation. ✉*2545 N.W.*

Westover Rd., Nob Hill, 97210 ☎*503/274–1846* 🖷*503/248–4055*
⊕*www.heronhaus.com* ➪*6 rooms* ♿*In-room: Wi-Fi. In-hotel: Wi-Fi,
parking (no fee), no-smoking rooms* ⊟*MC, V* ⍐*CP.*

$–$$ 🏨**Hillsboro Courtyard by Marriott.** This hotel provides easy access to
shopping and restaurants in Hillsboro, as well as quick access onto
U.S. 26 toward Portland. With large, comfortable rooms, it is perfect for business travelers, or for tourists who don't mind being several miles from downtown Portland. **Pros:** Nice indoor pool and free
shuttle service. **Cons:** For those interested in being near Portland, this
is a distance, especially with traffic. ⊠*3050 N.W. Stucki Pl., Hillsboro
97124* ☎*503/690–1800 or 800/321–2211* 🖷*503/690–0236* ⊕*www.
marriott.com* ➪*149 rooms, 6 suites* ♿*In-room: Wi-Fi. In-hotel: Wi-
Fi, restaurant, room service, bar, pool, gym, laundry facilities, laundry
service, no-smoking rooms, Internet* ⊟*AE, D, DC, MC, V.*

$–$$ 🏨**Inn @ Northrup Station.** Bright colors, original artwork, retro designs,
★ and extremely luxurious suites fill this hotel in Nob Hill. Just moments
from the shopping and dining on Northwest 21st Avenue, the inn looks
like a stylish apartment building from the outside, with patios or balconies adjoining most of the suites, and a garden terrace for all guests
to use. The striking colors and bold patterns found on bedspreads,
armchairs, pillows, and throughout the halls and lobby manage to be
charming, elegant, and fun, never falling into the kitsch that plagues
many places that strive for "retro" decor. All rooms have full kitchens,
two TVs, three phones, and large sitting areas. **Pros:** Full kitchens and
great location. **Cons:** Past guests have commented on the lack of noise
insulation. ⊠*2025 N.W. Northrup St., Nob Hill, 97209* ☎*503/224–
0543 or 800/224–1180* 🖷*503/273–2102* ⊕*www.northrupstation.
com* ➪*70 suites* ♿*In-room: kitchen. In-hotel: Wi-Fi, parking (no fee),
no-smoking rooms* ⊟*AE, D, DC, MC, V* ⍐*CP.*

$–$$ 🏨**MacMaster House.** On King's Hill, next to Washington Park's Japa-
★ nese and rose gardens, this 17-room Colonial Revival mansion built
in the 1890s is comfortable and fascinating. A hybrid assortment of
Victorian furniture and antiques fills the parlors, and the guest rooms
on the second and third floors are charming without being too cute.
The two suites with large, private, old-fashioned baths are the ones
to choose, especially the spacious Artist's Studio, tucked garretlike
under the dormers, with a high brass bed and fireplace. A two-night
minimum stay is required on weekends. Full breakfast and complimentary evening glass of wine, beer, or soft drink is included. **Pros:**
Wonderful decor and ambience. **Cons:** No children under 14 allowed.
⊠*1041 S.W. Vista Ave., near Nob Hill, 97205* ☎*503/223–7362 or
800/774–9523* 🖷*503/224–8808* ⊕*www.macmaster.com* ➪*5 rooms
with shared bath, 2 suites* ♿*In-room: VCR. In-Room: Wi-Fi* ⊟*AE,
MC, V* ⍐*BP.*

¢–$$ 🏨**Hilton Garden Inn Beaverton.** This four-level Hilton in suburban Bea-
verton brings a much-needed lodging option to Portland's west side.
The property offers bright rooms with plush carpeting, work desks,
and microwaves. It's right off U.S. 26. **Pros:** Reliable amenities for the
money. **Cons:** Not immediately near public transportation. ⊠*15520
N.W. Gateway Ct., Beaverton 97006* ☎*503/439–1717 or 800/445–*

8667 🖨️*503/439–1818* 🌐*www.hilton.com* 📠*150 rooms* 🛏️*In-room: refrigerator. In-hotel: Wi-Fi, restaurant, room service, bar, pool, parking (no fee), no-smoking rooms* ▭*AE, D, DC, MC, V.*

PORTLAND INTERNATIONAL AIRPORT AREA

$–$$$ **Embassy Suites Portland Airport.** Suites in this eight-story atrium hotel have beige walls and blond-wood furnishings. The lobby has a waterfall and pond with koi. All suites come with separate bedrooms and living areas with sleeper sofas. A full breakfast is included, and cocktails are free at happy hour. It's on the MAX airport light-rail line. **Pros:** Reliable service and amenities. **Cons:** The airport area is still being developed so there are not yet a lot of shops or restaurants in the vicinity. ✉️*7900 N.E. 82nd Ave., Airport, 97220* 🖨️*503/460–3000* 🖨️*503/460–3030* 🌐*www.portlandairport.embassysuites.com* 📠*251 suites* 🛏️*In-room: refrigerator. In-hotel: Wi-Fi, restaurant, room service, pool, gym, concierge, laundry service, airport shuttle, parking (no fee)* ▭*AE, D, DC, MC, V* ⦿*BP.*

$$ **Shilo Suites Airport.** Each room in this large, four-level all-suites inn is bright, with floral-print bedspreads and drapes, and has a microwave, wet bar, and two oversize beds. The indoor pool and hot tub are open 24 hours. Local calls are free. **Pros:** Large indoor pool and spacious rooms: **Cons:** The airport area is still being developed so there are not yet a lot of shops or restaurants in the vicinity. ✉️*11707 N.E. Airport Way, Airport, 97220* 🖨️*503/252–7500 or 800/222–2244* 🖨️*503/254–0794* 🌐*www.shiloinns.com* 📠*200 rooms* 🛏️*In-room: refrigerator. In-hotel: Wi-Fi, restaurant, room service, bar, pool, gym, laundry facilities, laundry service, airport shuttle, parking (no fee), no-smoking rooms* ▭*AE, D, DC, MC, V* ⦿*CP.*

$–$$ **Red Lion Hotel on the River.** The rooms in this four-story hotel on the Columbia River have balconies and good views of the river and Vancouver, Washington. Public areas glitter with brass and bright lights that accentuate the greenery and the burgundy, green, and rose color scheme. **Pros:** River location and right near the Jantzen Beach shopping center. and views. **Cons:** Pool is outdoors. ✉️*909 N. Hayden Island Dr., east of I–5's Jantzen Beach exit, Jantzen Beach, 97217* 🖨️*503/283–4466 or 800/733–5466* 🖨️*503/283–4743* 🌐*www.redlion.com* 📠*320 rooms* 🛏️*In-room: Wi-Fi. In-hotel: Wi-Fi, 2 restaurants, room service, bar, tennis court, pool, gym, laundry facilities, laundry service, parking (no fee), no-smoking rooms* ▭*AE, D, DC, MC, V.*

¢–$ **Courtyard Airport.** This six-story Marriott inn is designed for business travelers. Rooms are brightly decorated in royal blue and gold tones and have sitting areas and work desks. It's ¾ mi east of I–205 and 3 mi east of the airport. **Pros:** Reliable service and amenities. **Cons:** The airport area is still being developed so there's not yet a lot of shops or restaurants in the vicinity ✉️*11550 N.E. Airport Way, Airport, 97220* 🖨️*503/252–3200 or 800/321–2211* 🖨️*503/252–8921* 🌐*www.courtyard.com* 📠*150 rooms, 10 suites* 🛏️*In-room: Wi-Fi. In-hotel: Wi-Fi, restaurant, room service, bar, pool, gym, laundry facilities, laundry service, parking (no fee), no-smoking rooms* ▭*AE, D, DC, MC, V.*

NIGHTLIFE & THE ARTS

NIGHTLIFE

Portland's flourishing music scene encompasses everything from classical concerts to the latest permutations of rock and roll and hip-hop. The city has become something of a base for young rock bands, which perform in dance clubs scattered throughout the metropolitan area. Good jazz groups perform nightly in clubs and bars. Top-name musicians and performers in every genre regularly appear at the city's larger venues.

BARS & LOUNGES

DOWNTOWN Many of the best bars and lounges in Portland are found in its restaurants.

At the elegant **Heathman Hotel** (⊠*1001 S.W. Broadway* ☎*503/241–4100*) you can sit in the marble bar or the wood-paneled Tea Court. **Huber's Café** (⊠*411 S.W. 3rd Ave.* ☎*503/228–5686*), the city's oldest restaurant, is noted for its Spanish coffee and old-fashioned feel. The young and eclectic crowd at the **Lotus Cardroom and Café** (⊠*932 S.W. 3rd Ave.* ☎*503/227–6185*) comes to drink, and play pool or foosball. The **Rialto** (⊠*529 S.W. 4th Ave.* ☎*503/228–7605*) is a large, dark bar with several pool tables and enthusiastic pool players as well as some of the best Bloody Marys in town. **Saucebox** (⊠*214 S.W. Broadway* ☎*503/241–3393*) attracts a sophisticated crowd who enjoy colorful cocktails and trendy DJ music Wednesday–Saturday evenings. With more than 120 choices, **Southpark** (⊠*901 S.W. Salmon St.* ☎*503/326–1300*) is a perfect spot for a post-symphony glass of wine. At **Veritable Quandary** (⊠*1220 S.W. 1st Ave.* ☎*503/227–7342*), along the river, you can sit in the cozy tree-filled outdoor patio or in the glass atrium.

NORTHWEST The modern bar at **Bluehour** (⊠*250 N.W. 13th Ave., Pearl District* ☎*503/226–3394*) draws a chic crowd for specialty cocktails such as the Bluehour Breeze (house-infused grapefruit vodka with a splash of cranberry). Close to the trendy restaurants and shops of Northwest 21st and 23rd streets, the **Brazen Bean** (⊠*2075 N.W. Glisan St., Pearl District* ☎*503/294–0636*) is a house-turned-cocktail-and-cigar bar, and has wraparound porch seating where you can enjoy one of two-dozen-odd specialty martinis. Boisterous **Gypsy** (⊠*625 N.W. 21st Ave., Nob Hill* ☎*503/796–1859*) has 1950s-like furnishings. **Henry's 12th Street Tavern** (⊠*10 N.W. 12th Ave., Pearl District* ☎*503/227–5320*) has 100 beers and hard ciders on draft, plasma-screen TVs, and a billiards room in a historic building, formerly the Henry Weinhard's brewery. Young hipsters pack **Muu-Muus** (⊠*612 N.W. 21st Ave., Nob Hill* ☎*503/223–8169*) on weekend nights. At **Oba!** (⊠*555 N.W. 12th Ave., Pearl District* ☎*503/228–6161*), plush tans and reds with lime-green backlit walls set a backdrop for South American salsa. **21st Avenue Bar & Grill** (⊠*721 N.W. 21st Ave., Nob Hill* ☎*503/222–4121*) is open until 2:30 AM and has a patio and outdoor bar. The upscale martini set chills at **Wildwood** (⊠*1221 N.W. 21st Ave., Nob Hill* ☎*503/248–9663*).

EAST
PORTLAND

An artsy, hip, east-side crowd, not to be mistaken for the downtown jet-setters, hangs and drinks martinis and wine at the minimalist **Aalto Lounge** (⊠ *3356 S.E. Belmont St.* ☎ *503/235–6041*). One of few bars on northeast Alberta Street, **Bink's** (⊠ *2715 N.E. Alberta St.* ☎ *503/493–4430*) is a small, friendly neighborhood spot with cozy seats around a fireplace, a pool table, and a good jukebox. It serves only beer and wine. **Colosso** (⊠ *1932 N.E. Broadway* ☎ *503/288–3333*), a popular tapas bar, draws a cocktail-sipping crowd of hipsters at night. Green lanterns glow on the curvy bar and hip patrons sip Mojitos or other mixed drinks at the no-smoking hot spot **820** (⊠ *820 N. Russell St.* ☎ *503/460–0820*). A laid-back beer-drinking crowd fills the **Horse Brass Pub** (⊠ *4534 S.E. Belmont St.* ☎ *503/232–2202*), as good an English-style pub as you will find this side of the Atlantic, with more than 50 beers on tap and air thick with smoke. The open, airy **Imbibe** (⊠ *2229 S.E. Hawthorne Blvd.* ☎ *503/239–4002*) serves up creative cocktails, such as its namesake, the Imbibe Infusion—a thyme-and-ginger-infused vodka and strawberry martini with a touch of lemon. **Noble Rot** (⊠ *2724 S.E. Ankeny St.* ☎ *503/233–1999*) is a chic east-side wine bar with excellent food and red-leather booths.

BREWPUBS, BREW THEATERS & MICROBREWERIES

Dozens of small breweries operating in the metropolitan area produce pale ales, bitters, bocks, barley wines, and stouts. Some have attached pub operations, where you can sample a foaming pint of house ale. "Brew theaters," former neighborhood movie houses whose patrons enjoy food, suds, and recent theatrical releases, are part of the microbrewery phenomenon.

The **Bagdad Theatre and Pub** (⊠ *3702 S.E. Hawthorne Blvd., Hawthorne District* ☎ *503/236–9234*) screens recent Hollywood films and serves McMenamins ales and Pizzacato Pizza.

The first McMenamins brewpub, the **Barley Mill Pub** (⊠ *1629 S.E. Hawthorne Blvd., Hawthorne District* ☎ *503/231–1492*), is filled with Grateful Dead memorabilia and concert posters and is a fun place for families. **BridgePort BrewPub & Restaurant** (⊠ *1313 N.W. Marshall St., Pearl District* ☎ *503/241–7179*), Portland's oldest microbrewery, prepares hand-tossed pizza (⇨ *Where to Eat*) to accompany its ales. Inside an old warehouse with high ceilings and rustic wood tables, the **Lucky Labrador Brew Pub** (⊠ *915 S.E. Hawthorne Blvd.* ☎ *503/236–3555*) serves handcrafted ales and pub food both in the brewery and on the patio, where your four-legged friends are welcome to join you.

The **Mission Theatre** (⊠ *1624 N.W. Glisan St., Nob Hill* ☎ *503/223–4527*) was the first brew theater to show recent Hollywood offerings and serve locally brewed McMenamins ales.

Tugboat Brewery (⊠ *711 S.W. Ankeny St., Downtown* ☎ *503/226–2508*) is a small, cozy brewpub with books and games, picnic tables, and experimental jazz several nights a week.

The McMenamins chain of microbreweries includes some pubs in restored historic buildings. **Ringlers** (⊠ *1332 W. Burnside St., Down-*

town ☎*503/225–0627*) occupies the first floor of the building that houses the famous Crystal Ballroom. **Ringlers Annex** (✉*1223 S.W. Stark St., Downtown* ☎*503/525–0520*), one block away from Ringlers, is a pie-shape corner pub where you can puff a cigar while drinking beer, port, or a single-malt scotch. **Widmer Brewing and Gasthaus** (✉*955 N. Russell St., North Portland, near Fremont Bridge* ☎*503/281–3333*) brews German-style beers and has a full menu; you can tour the adjacent brewery Friday and Saturday.

COFFEEHOUSES & TEAHOUSES

DOWNTOWN   Quite possibly the best coffee around, **Stumptown Coffee Roasters** (✉*128 S.W. 3rd Ave., Downtown* ☎*503/295–6144*) has three local cafés, where its beans are roasted daily on vintage cast-iron equipment for a consistent, fresh flavor. **Three Lions Bakery** (✉*1138 S.W. Morrison St., Downtown* ☎*503/224–3429*) turns out excellent pastries as well as strong java; sandwiches, fresh-made quiches, and salads are also served.

NOB HILL &   **Anna Bannanas** (✉*1214 N.W. 21st Ave., Nob Hill* ☎*503/274–2559*)
VICINITY   serves great espresso and coffee, veggie sandwiches, soup, and smoothies; there's outdoor seating out front. One of the newer additions to the Portland coffee scene, **World Cup Coffee and Tea** (✉*1740 N.W. Glisan St.* ☎*503/228–4152*) sells excellent organic coffee and espresso in Nob Hill, as well as at its store in the Pearl District at the Ecotrust Building and at Powell's City of Books on Burnside.

EAST   **Common Grounds** (✉*4321 S.E. Hawthorne Blvd., East Portland* ☎*503/*
PORTLAND   *236–4835*) has plush couches and serves desserts plus sandwiches and soup. **Palio Coffee and Dessert House** (✉*1996 S.E. Ladd St., Ladd's Addition, near Hawthorne District* ☎*503/232–9412*), in the middle of peaceful residential Ladd's Addition, has delicious desserts and espresso, and is open later than many coffee shops in the area. Twentysomething sippers lounge on sofas and overstuffed chairs at **Pied Cow** (✉*3244 S.E. Belmont St., East Portland* ☎*503/230–4866*), a laid-back alternative to more yuppified establishments. **Stumptown Coffee Roasters** (✉*4525 S.E. Division St.* ☎*503/230–7702* ✉*3356 S.E. Belmont St.* ☎*503/232–8889*) has two cafés on the East Side: the original site, where organic beans are still roasted daily, and the newest site, next door to the Stumptown Annex, where patrons can participate in "cuppings" (tastings) daily at 3 PM. **Rimsky Korsakoffee House** (✉*707 S.E. 12th Ave., East Portland* ☎*503/232–2640*), one of the city's first coffeehouses, is still one of the best, especially when it comes to desserts. With soft music and the sound of running water in the background, the **Tao of Tea** (✉*3430 S.E. Belmont St., East Portland* ☎*503/736–0119*) serves vegetarian snacks and sweets as well as more than 80 loose-leaf teas.

GAY & LESBIAN CLUBS

Scandals (✉*1125 S.W. Stark St., Downtown* ☎*503/227–5887*) is low-key and has plate-glass windows with a view of Stark Street and the city's streetcars. The new location, as of December 2005, has a small dance floor, video poker, and a pool table, and the bar serves light food noon to close.

LIVE MUSIC

BLUES, FOLK & ROCK — The **Aladdin Theater** (✉ *3017 S.E. Milwaukie Ave.* ☎ *503/233–1994*), in an old movie theater, is one of the best music venues in town, and serves microbrews and pizza.

Berbati's Pan (✉ *10 S.W. 3rd Ave., Old Town* ☎ *503/226–2122*), on the edge of Old Town, has dancing and presents live music, everything from big band and swing to acid jazz, rock, and R&B.

Candlelight Room (✉ *2032 S.W. 5th Ave., Downtown* ☎ *503/222–3378*) presents blues nightly.

Dublin Pub (✉ *6821 S.W. Beaverton–Hillsdale Hwy., Beaverton* ☎ *503/ 297–2889*), on the west side, pours more than 50 beers on tap and hosts Irish bands and rock groups.

Kell's Irish Restaurant & Pub (✉ *112 S.W. 2nd Ave., Old Town* ☎ *503/227– 4057*) serves terrific Irish food and presents Celtic music nightly. Locals crowd the **Laurelthirst Public House** (✉ *2958 N.E. Glisan St., Laurelhurst* ☎ *503/232–1504*) to eat tasty food, sit in cozy red booths, and listen to folk, jazz, country, or bluegrass music on its tiny stage. There are pool tables in an adjoining room. **Produce Row Cafe** (✉ *204 S.E. Oak St., east side, near Burnside Bridge and I–5* ☎ *503/232–8355*) has a huge beer list, a great beer garden, a down-to-earth flavor, and live bluegrass, folk, and acoustic music most nights of the week.

JAZZ — Upstairs at the **Blue Monk** (✉ *3341 S.E. Belmont St., East Portland* ☎ *503/595–0575*) local artists' works are on display and patrons nosh on large plates of pasta and salads; the live-jazz venue downstairs displays jazz memorabilia and photos. Dubbed one of the world's Top 100 Places to Hear Jazz by *DownBeat*, **Jimmy Mak's** (✉ *300 S.W. 10th, Pearl District* ☎ *503/295–6542*) also serves Greek and Middle Eastern dishes and has a basement lounge outfitted with two pool tables and an Internet jukebox.

THE ARTS

For tickets to most events, call **Ticketmaster** (☎ *503/224–4400* ⊕ *www. ticketmaster.com*) or **TicketsWest** (☎ *503/224–8499* ⊕ *www.tickets west.com*). In summer, half-price tickets for almost any event are available the day of the show at Ticket Central in the **Visitor Information and Services Center** (✉ *Pioneer Courthouse Sq., Downtown* ☎ *503/275– 8358 after 10* AM), open Monday–Saturday 9–4:30. This is an outlet for tickets from Ticketmaster and TicketsWest. Credit cards are accepted, but you must buy tickets in person.

CLASSICAL MUSIC

CHAMBER MUSIC — **Chamber Music Northwest** (✉ *522 S.W. 5th Ave., Suite 725, Downtown* ☎ *503/294–6400* ⊕ *www.cnmw.org/*) presents some of the most sought-after soloists, chamber musicians, and recording artists from the Portland area and abroad for a five-week summer concert series; performances take place at Reed College and Catlin Gabel School.

OPERA **Portland Opera** (⊠222 S.W. Clay St. ☎503/241–1802 or 866/739–6737 ⊕www.portlandopera.org) and its orchestra and chorus stage five productions annually at the Keller Auditorium.

ORCHESTRAS The **Oregon Symphony** (⊠923 S.W. Washington ☎503/228–1353 or 800/228–7343 ⊕www.orsymphony.org) presents more than 40 classical, pop, children's, and family concerts each year at the Arlene Schnitzer Concert Hall.

☺ The **Metropolitan Youth Symphony** (⊠1133 S.W. Market St., Suite 210 ☎503/239–4566 ⊕www.metroyouthsymphony.org), a talented collective of youth musicians, performs family-friendly concerts throughout the year at various Portland venues including the Arlene Schnitzer Concert Hall.

The **Portland Baroque Orchestra** (☎503/222–6000 ⊕www.pbo.org) performs works on period instruments in a season that runs October–April. Performances are held at **Reed College's Kaul Auditorium** (⊠3203 S.E. Woodstock Blvd., Reed/Woodstock), the **Agnes Flanagan Chapel at Lewis & Clark College** (⊠615 S.W. Palatine Hill Rd., Southwest Portland), and downtown at **First Baptist Church** (⊠1425 S.W. 20th Ave., Downtown).

DANCE

Body Vox (☎503/229–0627 ⊕www.bodyvox.com) performs energetic contemporary dance–theater works at several locations in Portland.**Do Jump! Extremely Physical Theatre** (⊠1515 S.E. 37th Ave. ☎503/231–1232 ⊕www.dojump.org) showcases its creative acrobatic work at the Echo Theatre near Hawthorne.

Oregon Ballet Theatre (⊠818 S.E. 6th Ave. ☎503/222–5538 or 888/922–5538 ⊕www.obt.org) produces five classical and contemporary works a year, including a much-loved holiday *Nutcracker*. Most performances are at Keller Auditorium.

FILM

★ Not-to-be-missed Portland landmarks when it comes to movie-viewing, the **McMenamins theaters and brewpubs** offer beer, pizza, and inexpensive tickets to second-run blockbusters in uniquely renovated buildings that avoid any hint of corporate streamlining. Local favorites include the **Bagdad Theatre** (⊠3702 S.E. Hawthorne Blvd. ☎503/236–9234), the **Mission Theatre** (⊠1624 N.W. Glisan ☎503/223–4527), and the **Kennedy School** (⊠5736 N.E. 33rd St. ☎503/249–3983), found in a renovated elementary school along with a bed-and-breakfast and a restaurant.

The **Northwest Film Center** (⊠1219 S.W. Park Ave., Downtown ☎503/221–1156 ⊕www.nwfilm.org), a branch of the Portland Art Museum, screens all manner of art films, documentaries, and independent features, and presents the three-week Portland International Film Festival in February and March. Films are shown at the Whitsell Auditorium, next to the museum, and at the **Guild Theatre** (✉ *879 S.W. Park Ave.*).

THEATER

Imago Theatre (✉ *17 S.E. 8th Ave.* ☎ *503/231–9581* ⊕ *www.imago theatre.com*) is considered by some to be Portland's most outstanding innovative theater company, specializing in movement-based work for both young and old.

☾ **Oregon Children's Theatre** (☎ *503/228–9571* ⊕ *www.octc.org*) puts on three or four shows a year at major venues throughout the city for school groups and families.

Portland Center Stage (✉ *The Gerding Theater at the Armory, at 128 N.W. 11th Ave., Downtown* ☎ *503/274–6588* ⊕ *www.pcs.org*) produces six contemporary and classical works between October and April in the 800-seat Newmark Theater.

SPORTS & THE OUTDOORS

Portlanders are definitely oriented to the outdoors. Hikers, joggers, and mountain bikers take to the city's hundreds of miles of parks, paths, and trails. The Willamette and Columbia rivers are used for boating and water sports; however, it's not easy to rent any kind of boat for casual use. Big-sports fervor is reserved for Trail Blazer games, held at the Rose Quarter arena on the east side. The Portland/Oregon Visitors Association *(⇨ Visitor Information in Portland Essentials)* provides information on sports events and outdoor activities in the city.

PARTICIPANT SPORTS

BICYCLING

Bicycling has become a cultural phenomenom in Portland—possibly the most beloved mode of transportation in the city. *Bicycling* magazine has named Portland the Number One cycling city in the United States. Aside from the sheer numbers of cyclists you see on every road and pathway, notable bike-friendly aspects of this city include well-marked bike lanes on many major streets, bike paths meandering through parks and along the banks of the Willamette River, street signs reminding motorists to yield to cyclists at many intersections, and bike racks on the front of TriMet buses.

Despite the occasionally daunting hills and frequent wintertime rain, cycling remains one of the best ways to see what Portland offers. Bike paths on both the east and west sides of the Willamette River continue south of downtown, and you can easily make a several-mile loop by crossing bridges to get from one side to the other. (Most bridges, including the Broadway Bridge, the Steel Bridge, the Hawthorne Bridge, and the Sellwood Bridge, are accessible to cyclists.)

Forest Park's Leif Erikson Drive is an 11-mi ride through Northwest Portland's Forest Park, accessible from the west end of Northwest

Thurman Street. Parts of this ride and other Forest Park trails are recommended only for mountain bikes. Bicycling on Sauvie Island is a rare treat, with a 12-mi loop around the island with plenty of spots for exploring. To get to Sauvie Island from Portland, you can brave the 10-mi ride in the bike lane of U.S. 30, or you can shuttle your bike there via TriMet Bus 17. The Springwater Corridor, when combined with the Esplanade ride on the east side of the Willamette, can take you all the way from downtown to the far reaches of southeast Portland along a former railroad line. The trail heads east beginning near Sellwood, close to Johnson Creek Boulevard.

For more information on bike routes and resources in and around Portland, visit the **Department of Transportation** (⊕ *www.portlandonline. com/transportation*) Web page. Here you can download maps, or order "Bike There," a glossy detailed bicycle map of the metropolitan area. Bikes can be rented at several places in the city. Rentals can run anywhere from $20 to $50 per day and are commonly available for cheaper weekly rates, running from $75 to $150 per week. Bike helmets are generally included in the cost of rental. Good hybrid bikes for city riding are available at **CityBikes Workers Cooperative** (⊠*734 S.E. Ankeny St., near Burnside and Martin Luther King Jr. Blvd.* ☎*503/239–6951*) on the east side. For treks in Forest Park, mountain bikes can be rented at **Fat Tire Farm** (⊠*2714 N.W. Thurman St., near Forest Park* ☎*503/222–3276*). For jaunts along the Willamette, try **Waterfront Bicycle Rentals** (⊠*0315 S.W. Montgomery St., Suite 3, Downtown* ☎*503/227–1719*).

GOLF

Broadmoor Golf Course (⊠*3509 N.E. Columbia Blvd., near airport,* ☎*503/281–1337*) is an 18-hole, par-72 course where the greens fee runs $22 and an optional cart costs $22.At the 18-hole, par-72 **Colwood National Golf Club** (⊠*7313 N.E. Columbia Blvd., near airport,* ☎*503/254–5515*), the greens fee is $20–$24, plus $26 for an optional cart.**Eastmoreland Golf Course** (⊠*2425 S.E. Bybee Blvd., Sellwood,* ☎*503/775–2900*) has a highly regarded 18-hole, 72-par course close to the Rhododendron Gardens, Crystal Springs Lake, and Reed College. The greens fee is $15–$32, plus $28 for an optional cart. **Glendoveer Golf Course** (⊠*14015 N.E. Glisan St., near Gresham,* ☎*503/253–7507*) has two 18-hole courses, one par-71 and one par-73, and a covered driving range. The greens fee runs $16–$30; carts are $13 for 9 holes, $26 for 18 holes. **Heron Lakes Golf Course** (⊠*3500 N. Victory Blvd., west of airport, off N. Marine Dr.,* ☎*503/289–1818*) consists of two 18-hole, par-72 courses: the less-challenging Greenback and the Great Blue, generally acknowledged to be the most difficult links in the greater Portland area. The greens fee at the Green, as it is locally known, is $26–$30, while the fee at the Blue runs $37–$40. An optional cart at either course costs $26. **Pumpkin Ridge Golf Club** (⊠*12930 N.W. Old Pumpkin Ridge Rd., North Plains* ☎*503/647– 4747 or 888/594–4653* ⊕*www.pumpkinridge.com*) has 36 holes, with the 18-hole Ghost Creek par-71 course open to the public. According to *Golf Digest,* Ghost Creek is one of the best public courses in the nation. Pumpkin Ridge hosted the U.S. Women's Open in 1997 and in 2003. The greens fee is $135; the cart fee is $15. **Rose City Golf Course** (✉*2200 N.E. 71st Ave., east of Hollywood District,* ☎*503/253–4744*) has one 18-hole, par-72 course. Greens fees are $28–$32; carts are $26 for 18 holes.

SKIING

Mountain Shop (✉*628 N.E. Broadway, Lloyd District/Irvington* ☎*503/288–6768* ⊕*www.mountainshop.net*) rents skis and equipment. **REI** (✉*1405 N.W. Johnson St., Pearl District* ☎*503/221–1938*) can fill all your ski-equipment rental needs.

SPECTATOR SPORTS

BASEBALL

The **Portland Beavers** (☎*503/553–5555*), Portland's Triple-A team, play at the downtown **PGE Park** (✉*1844 S.W. Morrison St., Downtown* ☎*503/553–5400*) April–September.

BASKETBALL

The **Portland Trail Blazers** (✉*1 Center Ct., Rose Quarter* ☎*503/797–9617*) of the National Basketball Association play in the Rose Garden.

HORSE RACING

Thoroughbred and quarter horses race, rain or shine, October–May, at **Portland Meadows** (✉*1001 N. Schmeer Rd., between I-5 and Martin Luther King Jr. Blvd., along Columbia Slough* ☎*503/285–9144 or 800/944–3127*).

SOCCER

The **Portland Timbers** (☎*503/553–5400*), Portland's United Soccer League First Division team, play at the downtown **PGE Park** (✉*1844 S.W. Morrison St., Downtown* ☎*503/553–5400*) April–September.

SHOPPING

Portland's main shopping area is **Downtown,** between Southwest 2nd and 10th avenues and between Southwest Stark and Morrison streets. The major department stores are scattered over several blocks near Pioneer Courthouse Square. Northeast **Broadway** between 10th and 21st avenues is lined with boutiques and specialty shops. **Nob Hill,** north of downtown along Northwest 21st and 23rd avenues, is home to eclectic clothing, gift, book, and food shops. Most of the city's fine-art galleries are concentrated in the booming **Pearl District. Sellwood** has more than 50 antiques and collectibles shops along southeast 13th Avenue, plus specialty shops and outlet stores for sporting goods. **Hawthorne Boulevard** between 30th and 42nd avenues has an often countercultural grouping of bookstores, coffeehouses, antiques stores, and boutiques.

The open-air **Portland Saturday Market** (✉*Burnside Bridge, underneath west end, Old Town* ☎*503/222–6072*), open on weekends, is a favorite place to not only experience the people of Portland but also find one of a kind, unique handcrafted home, garden, and gift items. *(See Old Town/Chinatown in Exploring Portland.)*

MALLS & DEPARTMENT STORES

DOWNTOWN/CITY CENTER

Macy's at Meier & Frank Square (✉*621 S.W. 5th Ave., Downtown* ☎*503/223–0512*), a Portland department store that dates from 1857, has five floors of general merchandise at its main location downtown. Seattle-based **Nordstrom** (✉*701 S.W. Broadway, Downtown* ☎*503/224–6666*) sells fine-quality apparel and accessories and has a large footwear department. Bargain lovers should head for the **Nordstrom Rack** (✉*245 S.W. Morrison St., Downtown* ☎*503/299–1815*) outlet across from Pioneer Place mall. **Pioneer Place** (✉*700 S.W. 5th Ave., Downtown* ☎*503/228–5800*) has more than 80 upscale specialty shops (including April Cornell, Coach, J. Crew, Godiva, and Fossil) in a three-story, glass-roof atrium setting. You'll find good, inexpensive ethnic foods from more than a dozen vendors in the Cascades Food Court in the basement. **Saks Fifth Avenue** (✉*850 S.W. 5th Ave., Downtown* ☎*503/226–3200*).

BEYOND DOWNTOWN

NORTHEAST PORTLAND **Lloyd Center** (✉*N.E. Multnomah St. at N.E. 9th Ave., Northeast Portland* ☎*503/282–2511*), which is on the MAX light-rail line, has more than 170 shops (including Nordstrom, Sears Roebuck, and Macy's), an international food court, a multiscreen cinema, and an ice-skating pavilion. The mall is within walking distance of Northeast Broadway, which has many specialty shops, boutiques, and restaurants.

SOUTHEAST PORTLAND **Clackamas Town Center** (✉*Sunnyside Rd. at I–205's Exit 14, Southeast Portland* ☎*503/653–6913*) has four major department stores, including Nordstrom and Macy's, as well as more than 180 shops. Discount stores are nearby.

SOUTHWEST PORTLAND **Washington Square** (✉*9585 S.W. Washington Square Rd., at S.W. Hall Blvd. and Hwy. 217, Tigard* ☎*503/639–8860*) contains five major department stores, including Macy's and Sears Roebuck; a food court; and more than 140 specialty shops. Discount and electronics stores are nearby. A little farther south of Portland, the **Streets of Tanasbourne** (✉*N.W. 194th at Cornell Rd., off U.S. 26, Hillsboro* ☎*503/533–0561*) has 52 choices of high-end specialty shops, including Clogs n' More, Abercrombie & Fitch, and White House/Black Market.

SPECIALTY STORES

ART DEALERS & GALLERIES

Portland's art galleries, once concentrated downtown, are spreading throughout the city to northeast and southeast Portland. **First Thursday** gives art appreciators a chance to check out new exhibits while enjoying music and wine. Typically, the galleries are open in the evening, but hours vary depending on the gallery. Find out what galleries are participating **Downtown** (☎ *503/295–4979* ⊕ *www.firstthursdayportland. com*) and in the **Pearl District** (⊕ *www.firstthursday.org*). The Alberta Arts District hosts a **Last Thursday Arts Walk** (☎ *503/972–2206* ⊕ *www. artonalberta.org*) each month.

Photographic Image Gallery (⊠ *79 S.W. Oak St., Old Town* ☎ *503/224– 3543*) carries prints by nationally known nature photographers Christopher Burkett and Joseph Holmes, among others, and has a large supply of photography posters.

Quintana's Galleries of Native American Art (⊠ *120 N.W. 9th Ave., Pearl District* ☎ *503/223–1729 or 800/321–1729*) focuses on Pacific Northwest coast, Navajo, and Hopi art and jewelry, along with photogravures by Edward Curtis.

Talisman Gallery (⊠ *1476 N.E. Alberta St., Alberta District* ☎ *503/284– 8800*) is a cooperative gallery formed in 1999 that showcases two artists each month, including local painters and sculptors.

Twist (⊠ *30 N.W. 23rd Pl., Nob Hill* ☎ *503/224–0334* ⊠ *Pioneer Pl.* ☎ *503/222–3137*) has a huge space in Nob Hill and a smaller shop downtown. In Nob Hill are contemporary American ceramics, glass, furniture, sculpture, and handcrafted jewelry; downtown carries an assortment of objects, often with a pop, whimsical touch.

BOOKS

Annie Bloom's (⊠ *7834 S.W. Capital Hwy., Multnomah Village* ☎ *503/ 246–0053*), a local favorite, has a friendly, knowledgeable staff and great selections of children's books, remainders, Judaica, and fun greeting cards.

Broadway Books (⊠ *1714 N.E. Broadway, Broadway District* ☎ *503/284–1726*) is a fabulous independent bookstore with books on all subjects, including the Pacific Northwest and Judaica.

In Other Words (⊠ *3734 S.E. Hawthorne Blvd., Hawthorne District* ☎ *503/232–6003*) is a nonprofit bookstore that carries feminist literature and hosts feminist events and readings.

New Renaissance Bookshop (⊠ *1338 N.W. 23rd Ave., Nob Hill* ☎ *503/224–4929*), between Overton and Pettygrove, is dedicated to New Age and metaphysical books and tapes.

★ **Powell's City of Books** (⊠ *1005 W. Burnside St., Downtown* ☎ *503/228– 4651*), the largest retail store of used and new books in the world (with more than 1.5 million volumes), covers an entire city block on the edge of the Pearl District. It also carries rare hard-to-find editions.

Powell's for Cooks and Gardeners (⊠ *3747 Hawthorne Blvd., Hawthorne District* ☎ *503/235–3802*) on the east side has a small adjoining grocery. There's also a small store in the Portland International Airport.

Twentythird Ave. Books (⊠ *1015 N.W. 23rd Ave., Nob Hill* ☎ *503/224– 5097*) is a cozy independent bookstore that makes for great browsing if you want to escape the bustle of 23rd Avenue.

CLOTHING

Clogs 'n' More (⊠ *717 S.W. Alder St., Downtown* ☎ *503/279–9358* ⊠ *3439 S.E. Hawthorne, Hawthorne District* ☎ *503/232–7007*), with locations both on the west and east sides of the city, carries quality clogs and other shoes.

Eight Women (✉ *3614 S.E. Hawthorne Blvd., Hawthorne District* ☎ *503/236–8878*) is a tiny boutique "for mother and child," with baby clothes, women's nightgowns, jewelry, and handbags.

Elizabeth Street and Zelda's Shoe Bar (✉ *635 N.W. 23rd Ave., Nob Hill* ☎ *503/243–2456*), two connected boutiques in Nob Hill, carry a sophisticated, highly eclectic line of women's clothes, accessories, and shoes.

Hanna Andersson sells high-quality, comfortable clothing for children and families from their **retail store** (✉ *327 N.W. 10th Ave.* ☎ *503/321–5275*), next to the company's corporate office, as well as through their **outlet store** (✉ *7 Monroe Pkwy., Lake Oswego* ☎ *503/697–1953*) in Lake Oswego's Oswego Towne Square, south of Portland.

Imelda's Designer Shoes (✉ *3426 S.E. Hawthorne Blvd., Hawthorne District* ☎ *503/233–7476*) is an upscale boutique with funky, fun shoes for women with flair.

Mario's (✉ *833 S.W. Morrison St., Downtown* ☎ *503/227–3477*), Portland's best store for fine men's and women's clothing, carries designer lines by Prada, Dolce & Gabbana, Etro, and Loro Piana—among others.

Mimi and Lena (✉ *1914 N.E. Broadway, Broadway District* ☎ *503/224–7736*) is a small boutique with expensive but beautifully feminine and unique designer clothing.

Niketown (✉ *930 S.W. 6th Ave., Downtown* ☎ *503/221–6453*), Nike's flagship retail store, has the latest and greatest in Nike products. **Portland Nike Factory Store** (✉ *2650 N.E. Martin Luther King Jr. Blvd., Northeast Portland* ☎ *503/281–5901*) sells products that have been on the market six months or more.

Nob Hill Shoes and Repair (✉ *921 N.W. 23rd Ave., Nob Hill* ☎ *503/224–8682*), a tiny spot, sells men's and women's shoes from Keen and Earth Shoes, as well as Dansko clogs.

Norm Thompson Outfitters (✉ *1805 N.W. Thurman St., Nob Hill* ☎ *503/221–0764*) carries classic fashions for men and women, innovative footwear, and one-of-a-kind gifts.

Portland Outdoor Store (✉ *304 S.W. 3rd Ave., Downtown* ☎ *503/222–1051*) stubbornly resists all that is trendy, both in clothes and decor, but if you want authentic Western gear—saddles, Stetsons, boots, or cowboy shirts—head here.

Portland Pendleton Shop (✉ *S.W. 4th Ave. and Salmon St., Downtown* ☎ *503/242–0037*) stocks clothing by the famous local apparel maker.

Tumbleweed (✉ *1804 N.E. Alberta St., Alberta District* ☎ *503/335–3100*) carries fun and stylish designer clothing you might describe as "country chic," for the woman who likes to wear flirty feminine dresses with cowboy boots. There is also unique baby and toddler clothing in their children's shop next door.

MUSIC

Artichoke Music (✉ *3130 S.E. Hawthorne Blvd., Hawthorne District* ☎ *503/232–8845*) is a friendly family-owned business that sells guitars, banjos, mandolins, and other instruments that might come in handy for a bluegrass band. Music lessons are given in two soundproof practice rooms, and music performances and song circles are held in the café in the back.

Music Millennium Northwest (⊠*3158 E. Burnside.St., Laurelhurst* ☎*503/ 231–8926*) stocks a huge selection of CDs and tapes in every possible musical category, from local punk to classical.

OUTDOOR SUPPLIES

Andy and Bax (⊠*324 S.E. Grand Ave., near Morrison Bridge* ☎*503/ 234–7538*) is an army-navy/outdoors store, with good prices on everything from camo gear to rafting supplies.

Next Adventure Sports (⊠*426 S.E. Grand Ave., near Morrison Bridge* ☎*503/ 233–0706*) carries new and used sporting goods, including camping gear, snowboards, kayaks, and mountaineering supplies.

TOYS

Finnegan's Toys and Gifts (⊠*922 S.W. Yamhill St., Downtown* ☎*503/ 221–0306*), downtown Portland's largest toy store, stocks artistic, creative, educational, and other types of toys.

Kids at Heart (⊠*3445 S.E. Hawthorne Blvd., Hawthorne District* ☎*503/231–2954*) is a small, colorful toy store on Hawthorne with toys, models, and stuffed animals for kids of all ages.

PORTLAND ESSENTIALS

To research prices, get advice from other travelers, and book travel arrangements, visit www.fodors.com.

BY AIR

Portland International Airport (PDX) is a sleek, modern airport with service to many national and international destinations. It is easily accessible from downtown Portland. Even if your final destination is in another city in Oregon, you may choose to fly into Portland and rent a car to get there, because all other airports in the state are small regional airports with limited service. It is possible, however, to get a connecting flight from Portland airport to smaller cities in Oregon. Portland Airport is served by all major airlines as well as by several smaller regional carriers. ⇨ *See Pacific Northwest Essentials for carrier phone numbers.*

Contacts Portland International Airport (⊠*N.E. Airport Way at I–205* ☎*877/ 739–4636* ⊕*www.flypdx.com/*).

AIRPORT
TRANSFERS

TriMet trains and buses serve the airport *(*⇨*By Bus)*.

BY BUS

GETTING
AROUND

TriMet operates an extensive system of buses, streetcars, and light-rail trains. The Central City streetcar line runs between Legacy Good Samaritan hospital in Nob Hill, the Pearl District, downtown, and Portland State University. To Nob Hill it travels along 10th Avenue and then on Northwest Northrup; from Nob Hill it runs along Northwest Lovejoy and then on 11th Avenue. Trains stop every few blocks. MAX light-rail trains run between downtown, the airport, and the western and eastern suburbs and stop at the zoo, the Rose Garden arena, PGE Park, and Lloyd Center.

A 5½-mi extension of the MAX light-rail system runs from the Gateway Transit Center (at the intersection of I–84 and I–205) directly to and from the airport. Trains arrive at and depart from inside the passenger terminal near the south baggage-claim area. The trip takes about 35 minutes from downtown. TriMet Bus 12, which runs about every 15 minutes, also serves the airport. The fare to or from the airport on MAX or the bus is $1.75.

Contacts **Greyhound Terminal** (⊠ *550 N.W. 6th Ave., Old Town* ☎ *503/243–2310, 800/231–2222, 503/243–2337 baggage, 503/243–2361 customer service).* **TriMet/MAX** (⊠ *6th Ave. and Morrison St., Downtown* ☎ *503/238–7433* ⊕ *www. trimet.org).*

BY CAR

I–5 enters Portland from the north and south. I–84, the city's major eastern corridor, terminates in Portland. U.S. 26 and U.S. 30 are primary east–west thoroughfares. Bypass routes are I–205, which links I–5 and I–84 before crossing the Columbia River into Washington, and I–405, which arcs around western downtown. Most city-center streets are one-way only, and Southwest 5th and 6th avenues between Burnside and Southwest Madison streets are limited to bus traffic.

From the airport to downtown, take I–205 south to westbound I–84. Drive west over the Willamette River and take the City Center exit. If going to the airport, take I–84 east to I–205 north; follow I–205 to the airport exit.

Traffic on I–5 north and south of downtown and on I–84 and I–205 east of downtown is heavy between 6 AM and 9 AM and between 4 and 8 PM. Four-lane U.S. 26 west of downtown can be bumper-to-bumper any time of the day going to or from downtown.

BY TAXI

Taxi fare is $2.50 at flag drop plus $2.10 per mile. The first person pays by the meter, and each additional passenger pays $1. Cabs cruise the city streets, but it's better to phone for one. The major companies are Broadway Cab, New Rose City Cab, Portland Taxi Company, and Radio Cab. The trip between downtown Portland and the airport takes about 30 minutes by taxi. The fare is about $30.

Taxi Companies **Broadway Cab** (☎ *503/227–1234).* **New Rose City Cab** (☎ *503/282–7707).* **Portland Taxi Company** (☎ *503/256–5400).* **Radio Cab** (☎ *503/227–1212).*

BY TRAIN

Amtrak serves Union Station. The *Coast Starlight* operates daily between Seattle, Portland, and Los Angeles. The *Empire Builder* travels between Portland and Chicago via Spokane and Minneapolis. The *Cascades,* with modern European train cars, operates daily between Eugene, Portland, Seattle, and Vancouver, BC.

Metropolitan Area Express, or MAX, links the eastern and western Portland suburbs with downtown, Washington Park and the Oregon Zoo, the Lloyd Center district, the Convention Center, and the Rose Quarter. From downtown, trains operate daily 5:30 AM–1 AM, with a fare of $1.75 for travel through one or two zones, $2.05 for three zones, and $4.25 for an unlimited all-day ticket.

Train Information & Reservations **Amtrak** (⊠ *800 N.W. 6th Ave., Old Town* ☎ *800/ 872–7245).* **MAX** (☎ *503/238–7433).*

EMERGENCIES

Emergency Services **Ambulance, fire, police** (☎ *911).*

Hospitals **Legacy Emanuel Hospital and Health Center** (⊠ *2801 N. Gantenbein Ave., North Portland, near Fremont Bridge* ☎ *503/413–2200).* **Legacy Good Samaritan Hospital & Medical Center** (⊠ *1015 N.W. 22nd Ave., Nob Hill* ☎ *503/413–7711).* **Providence Portland Medical Center** (⊠ *4805 N.E. Glisan St., near Laurelhurst* ☎ *503/215–1111).* **Providence St. Vincent Hospital** (⊠ *9205 S.W. Barnes Rd., west of Downtown* ☎ *503/216–1234).*

24-Hour Pharmacy **Walgreens** (⊠ *940 S.E. 39th Ave., East Portland* ☎ *503/238– 6053).*

TOUR OPTIONS

BOAT TOURS Sternwheeler Riverboat Tours' *Columbia Gorge* departs year-round from Tom McCall Waterfront Park on two-hour excursions of the Willamette River; there are also Friday-night dinner cruises. During the summer the sternwheeler travels up the Columbia River. For the more adventurous, Willamette Jetboat Excursions offers whirling, swirling one- and two-hour tours along the Willamette River that include an up-close visit with Willamette Falls.

Tour Operator **Sternwheeler Riverboat Tours** (⊠ *S.W. Naito Pkwy. and Stark St., Riverfront Park* ☎ *503/223–3928).* **Willamette Jetboat Excursions** (⊠ *S.E. Marion St.* ☎ *888/538–2628).*

BUS TOURS Gray Line operates City of Portland and Pacific Northwest sightseeing tours, including service to Chinook Winds Casino in Lincoln City, from April through October; call for departure times and tours.

Tour Operator **Gray Line** (☎ *503/684–3322 Ext. 2* ⊕ *www.grayline.com).*

TROLLEY TOURS The Willamette Shore Trolley company operates vintage double-decker electric trolleys that provide scenic round-trips between suburban Lake Oswego and downtown, along the west shore of the Willamette River. The 7-mi route, which the trolley traverses in 45 minutes, passes over trestles and through Elk Rock tunnel along one of the most scenic stretches of the river. The line, which opened in 1885, was electrified in 1914, and Southern Pacific Railway operated dozens of trips daily along this route in the 1920s. Passenger service ended in 1929, and the line was taken over by the Oregon Electric Railway Historical Society. Reservations are recommended. The trolley ($8 round-trip) departs from Lake Oswego at noon and 2:30 PM and Portland at 1 and 3:15 on weekends from May through October. Charters are available year-round.

Contacts **Willamette Shore Trolley** (✉ *311 N. State St., Lake Oswego* ⬛ *South of RiverPlace Marina, at Sheridan and Moody Sts., Portland* ☎ *503/697–7436*).

WALKING
TOURS
The Portland Oregon Visitors Association *(⇨ Visitor Information)*, which is open weekdays 9–5 and Saturday 9–4, has brochures, maps, and guides to art galleries and select neighborhoods.

VISITOR INFORMATION

Tourist Information **Portland Oregon Visitors Association** (✉ *1000 S.W. Broadway, Suite 2300, 97205* ☎ *800/962–3700* ⊕ *www.travelportland.com*).

Portland Oregon Visitors Association Information Center (✉ *Pioneer Courthouse Sq.* ☎ *503/275–8355 or 877/678–5263*).

Oregon

WORD OF MOUTH

"Most visitors are satisfied with one day each in the Gorge and at Crater Lake, but I've never heard anyone say they spent too much time on the coast. You could spice up the trip with stops at points of interest—wineries or whatever—along the way, but I'd suggest building your itinerary around those three major attractions."

—beachbum

No matter what you're looking for in a vacation, few states offer more than Oregon. Within a 90-minute drive from Portland or Eugene you can lose yourself in the recreational landscape of your choice: uncrowded ocean beaches, snow-silvered mountain wilderness, or a monolith-studded desert that has served as the backdrop for many a Hollywood Western. In the Willamette Valley wine country scores of tasting rooms offer up the fruit of the vine. Food lovers find that Oregon produces some of the nation's best fruits, vegetables, and seafood, all of which can be enjoyed in fine restaurants throughout the state. Plenty of attractions keep the kids busy, too, from the Enchanted Forest near Salem to the exceptional Oregon Coast Aquarium in Newport. And shoppers take note—there's no sales tax in Oregon.

Although Oregon is notorious for rain, and winters can indeed be wet and dreary, the rest of the year more than makes up for it. Much of the state is actually a desert, and most of the precipitation falls west of the Cascades. At its eastern end, Oregon begins in a high, sage-scented desert plateau that covers nearly two-thirds of the state's 96,000 square mi. As you move west, the landscape rises to 11,000-foot-high alpine peaks, meadows, and lakes; plunges to fertile farmland and forest; and ends at the cold, tumultuous Pacific.

EXPLORING OREGON

Oregon's coastline stretches south from Astoria to the California border. Inland a bit, the fertile Willamette River valley also runs north–south. The mighty Columbia River travels west of the Cascade Range past the Mount Hood Wilderness Area to Astoria. The resort towns of Bend and Sisters are in Central Oregon, and the sparsely populated desert region is east of the Cascades.

Oregon tourist-information centers are marked with blue "I" signs from main roads. Opening and closing times vary, depending on the season and the individual office; call ahead for hours (⇨ *Visitor Information in Essentials*).

ABOUT THE RESTAURANTS

Fresh foods grown, caught, and harvested in the Northwest are standard fare in gourmet restaurants throughout Oregon. Outside urban areas and resorts, most restaurants tend to be low-key and unpretentious, both in ambience and cuisine. On the coast, look for regional specialties—clam chowder, fresh fish (particularly salmon), sweet Dungeness crab, mussels, shrimp, and oysters. Elsewhere in the state fresh river fish, local lamb, and beef, and seasonal game dishes appear on many menus, supplemented by Oregon hazelnuts and wines. Desserts made with local fruits such as huckleberries, raspberries, and marionberries are always worth trying.

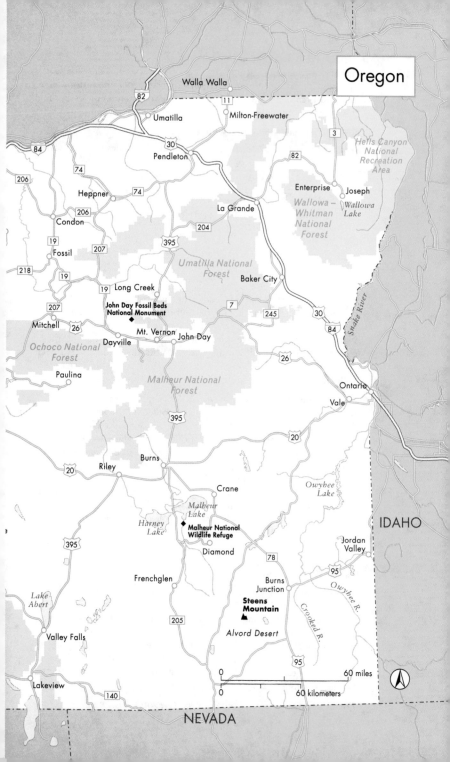

ABOUT THE HOTELS

Luxury hotels, sophisticated resorts, historic lodges, Old West hotels, and rustic inns are among Oregon's diverse accommodations. Cozy bed-and-breakfasts, many of them in Victorian-era houses in small towns, are often real finds.

WHAT IT COSTS				
¢	$	$$	$$$	$$$$
Restaurants	under $10	$10–$20	$20–$30	$30–$40	over $40
Hotels	under $100	$100–$150	$150–$200	$200–$250	over $250

Restaurant prices are per person for a main course at dinner. Hotel prices are for a standard double room, excluding room tax, which varies 6%–9½% depending on location.

TIMING

Winters in western Oregon are usually mild, but they can be relentlessly rainy. To the east of the Cascade Range winters are clearer, drier, and colder. December–April are the best months for whale-watching along the coast, and February–May are best for bird-watching at the Malheur National Wildlife Refuge in southeastern Oregon. Spring weather is changeable on both sides of the Cascades, but the landscape is a Technicolor wonder of wildflowers, flowering fruit trees (in the Hood River valley), and gardens bursting with rhododendrons and azaleas.

Jacksonville and Eugene host world-class summer music festivals, and the theater season in Ashland lasts from February to October. July and August are the prime months for visiting Crater Lake National Park, which is often snowed in for the rest of the year. Those months are predictably dry east of the Cascades, where it can get downright hot, but you can make a quick escape to the coast, where even summer weather can be cool and foggy. If you're looking for clear days along the coast, however, late summer and early fall are your best bets; these are also the best times to visit the many wineries in the Willamette Valley. Fall is spectacular throughout the state, with leaves at their colorful peak in late October.

THE OREGON COAST

Updated by Deston S. Nokes

Oregon has 300 mi of white-sand beaches, not a grain of which is privately owned. U.S. 101, called Highway 101 by most Oregonians, parallels the coast along the length of the state. It winds past sea-tortured rocks, brooding headlands, hidden beaches, historic lighthouses, and tiny ports, with the gleaming gunmetal-gray Pacific Ocean always in view. With its seaside hamlets, outstanding fresh seafood eateries, and small hotels and resorts, the Oregon Coast epitomizes the finest in Pacific Northwest living.

Points of interest can be found on the Oregon Coast map.

ASTORIA

96 mi northwest of Portland on U.S. 30.

The mighty Columbia River meets the Pacific at Astoria, the oldest city west of the Rockies. In its early days Astoria was a placid amalgamation of small town and hardworking port city. Settlers built sprawling Victorian houses on the flanks of **Coxcomb Hill.** Many of the homes have since been restored and are no less splendid as bed-and-breakfast inns. In recent years the city itself has awakened with a greater variety of trendy dining and lodging options, staking its claim as a destination resort town.

> **TOP 5**
>
> 1. Riding the Oregon Dunes National Recreation Area, more thrills than an amusement park.
>
> 2. U.S. 101 between Port Orford and Brookings is one of the most scenic drives on the West Coast.
>
> 3. Tu Tu' Tun Lodge is a tranquil oasis of scenic beauty and warm commaraderie.
>
> 4. Cannon Beach will charm you with intimate hotels, gourmet restaurants, and the best coffee.
>
> 5. Oregon Coast Aquarium has earned its reputation as one of the best aquariums in the country.

The **Columbia River Maritime Museum,** on the downtown waterfront, explores the maritime history of the Pacific Northwest and is one of the two most interesting man-made tourist attractions on the Oregon coast (Newport's aquarium is the other). Beguiling exhibits include the personal belongings of some of the ill-fated passengers of the 2,000 ships that have foundered here since 1811. Also here are a bridge from the World War II destroyer USS *Knapp* (which can be viewed from the inside), the fully operational U.S. Coast Guard Lightship *Columbia,* and a 44-foot Coast Guard motor lifeboat. ☒ *1792 Marine Dr., at 17th St.* ☎ *503/325–2323* ⊕ *www.crmm.org* ☏ *$8* ⊙ *Daily 9:30–5.*

The **Astoria Column,** a 125-foot monolith atop Coxcomb Hill that was patterned after Trajan's Column in Rome, rewards your 164-step, spiral-stair climb with views over Astoria, the Columbia River, the Coast Range, and the Pacific. Or if you don't want to climb, the column's artwork, depicting important Pacific Northwest historical milestones, is stunning. ☒ *From U.S. 30 downtown take 16th St. south 1 mi to top of Coxcomb Hill* ☏ *Free* ⊙ *Daily 9–dusk.*

☉ ★ "Ocean in view! O! The joy!" recorded William Clark, standing on a spit of land south of present-day Astoria in the fall of 1805. **Fort Clatsop National Memorial** is a faithful replica of the log stockade depicted in Clark's journal. Park rangers, who dress in period garb during the summer and perform such early-19th-century tasks as making fire with flint and steel, lend an air of authenticity, as does the damp and lonely feel of the fort itself. ☒ *Fort Clatsop Loop Rd. 5 mi south of Astoria; from U.S. 101, cross Youngs Bay Bridge, turn east on Alt. U.S. 101, and follow signs* ☎ *503/861–2471* ⊕ *www.nps.gov/focl* ☏ *$3* ⊙ *Daily 9–5.*

☉ The earthworks of 37-acre **Fort Stevens,** at Oregon's northwestern tip, were mounded up during the Civil War to guard the Columbia against

Oregon Coast

WASHINGTON

Columbia River

Ft. Stevens
State Park
Ft. Clatstop
National Memorial
Astoria
26
101
30

Seaside

Tillamook Head
Ecola State Park
Cannon Beach

Oswald West
State Park
53

Nehalem Bay
Manzanita
Tillamook Bay
Garibaldi

*TILLAMOOK
STATE FOREST*
26

Forest
Grove

Yamhill

Portland

Hood
River

84

Cape Meares
State Park
6
Tillamook

Mt. Hood ▲

26

Cape Lookout
State Park
**Three Capes
Loop**

Dundee

Newberg
Champoeg
State Park

Government
Camp

Cape Kiwanda
State Natural Area
Pacific City

McMinnville

Aurora

*MT. HOOD
NATIONAL
FOREST*

Robert Straub
State Park
18

Willamette
Mission
State Park

The Oregon
Garden

Gleneden Beach
Lincoln City

Salem

Silver Falls
State Park

Depoe Bay

Sublimity

**Mt.
Jefferson** ▲

Yaquina Head
Newport

214

22

101

Albany

20

PACIFIC OCEAN

*WILLAMETTE
NATIONAL
FOREST*

Waldport

34

Corvallis

Brownsville

20

Sisters

Yachats

99E

McKenzie
Bridge
126

242
(closed in winter)

**Cape
Perpetua**

*SIUSLAW
NATIONAL
FOREST*

36

Springfield
126

McKenzie Pass ◆

Heceta Head

126

Eugene

Mt. Bachelor ▲

*DESCHUTES
NATIONAL
FOREST*

Florence

Cottage
Grove

5

58

Waldo
Lake

Willamette Pass ◆

Winchester
Bay

Oakridge

58

97

*OREGON DUNES
NATL. REC. AREA*

Reedsport

38

**Umpqua
Lighthouse Park**

Oakland

Steamboat

*UMPQUA
NATIONAL
FOREST*

Charleston
Shore Acres
State Park
**Coos Bay
& North Bend**

138

Roseburg

Cape Arago
State Park

Myrtle
Point

Winston

*UMPQUA
VALLEY*

*CRATER LAKE
NATIONAL PARK*

Bandon

42

Wildlife
Safari

Canyonville

Crater
Lake

**Cape Blanco
State Park**

97

Port Orford

Rogue River

Prospect

*ROGUE
RIVER
NATIONAL
FOREST*

Prehistoric
Gardens

Agness

Grants
Pass

*Upper
Klamath
Lake*

**Gold
Beach**

5

Pistol River
101

*SISKIYOU
NATIONAL
FOREST*

199

238

Medford

Klamath
Falls

Samuel H.
Boardman
State Park
Brookings

Loeb
State Park

Cave
Junction

46

Jacksonville
Oregon Caves
Nat'l. Monument

Ashland

**Mt.
Ashland** ▲

0   30 miles

Harbor

0   30 kilometers

CALIFORNIA

2

a Confederate attack. No such event occurred, but during World War II Fort Stevens became the only mainland U.S. military installation to come under enemy (Japanese submarine) fire since the War of 1812. The fort's abandoned gun mounts and eerie subterranean bunkers are a memorable destination. The corroded skeleton of the *Peter Iredale*, a century-old English four-master ship, protrudes from the sand just west of the campground, a stark testament to the temperamental nature of the Pacific. ⊠ *Fort Stevens Hwy. (from Fort Clatsop, take Alt. U.S. 101 west past U.S. 101, turn north onto Main St.–Fort Stevens Hwy., and follow signs)* ☎ *503/861–2000* ⊕ *www.visitfortstevens.com* ⊠ *$3 per vehicle* ⊘ *Mid-May–Sept., daily 10–6; Oct.–mid-May, daily 10–4.*

★ One of the Oregon coast's oldest commercial smokehouses, **Josephson's** uses alderwood for all processing and specializes in Pacific Northwest chinook and coho salmon. You can choose mouthwatering selections of fish smoked on the premises, including hot smoked pepper or wine-maple salmon, as well as smoked halibut, sturgeon, tuna, oysters, mussels, scallops, and prawns by the pound or in sealed gift packs. ⊠ *106 Marine Dr.,* ☎ *503/325–2190* 🖷 *503/325–4075* ⊕ *www.josephsons. com* ⊠ *Free* ⊘ *Mon.–Sat. 9–6, Sun. 9–5:30.*

The **Astoria Riverfront Trolley,** also known as "Old 300," is a beautifully restored 1913 streetcar that travels for 4 mi along Astoria's historic riverfront. Get a close-up look at the waterfront, from the Port of Astoria to the East Morring Basin; the Columbia River; and points of interest in between while reliving the past through guided and narrated historical tours. ⊠ *1095 Dwayne St.* ☎ *503/325–6311* ⊕ *www.oldoregon. com/Pages/AstoriaRiverfrontTrolley.htm* ⊠ *$1 per boarding, $2 all-day pass* ⊘ *Memorial Day–Labor Day, Mon.–Thurs. 3–9, Fri.–Sun. noon–9; fall, winter, and spring—check trolley shelters.*

WHERE TO EAT

¢–$$ ✕ **Bridgewater Bistro.** Astoria's new fine-dining entry has a broad range
★ of selections, whether you want meat, fish, or vegetarian fare. Located next to the new Columbia Pier Hotel, the restaurant serves inexpensive bistro fare (such as burgers and fish-and-chips) as well as more refined dishes such as Moroccan chicken and duck breast. It also offers a prix-fixe four-course meal and a large selection of fine wines. ⊠ *20 Basin St.* ☎ *503/325–6777* ⊕ *www.bridgewaterbistro.com* ▤ *AE, D, MC, V.*

¢–$$ ✕ **Cannery Cafe.** Original fir floors, windows, and hardware combine with expansive views of the Columbia River to give this restaurant in a renovated 1879 cannery an authentic, nautical feel. Homemade breakfast fare, often with crab or salmon, comes with potato pancakes and buttermilk biscuits. Fresh salads, large specialty sandwiches, clam chowder, and crab cakes are lunch staples. The dinner menu emphasizes seafood, including cioppino, an Italian fish stew, and Dungeness crab alfredo. ⊠ *1 6th St.* ☎ *503/325–8642* ▤ *AE, D, DC, MC, V.*

¢–$ ✕ **Clemente's.** Serving possibly the best seafood on the Oregon Coast,
Fodor'sChoice chefs Gordon and Lisa Clement are making a significant critical and
★ popular splash in Astoria. Grounded in Mediterranean cuisine from Italy and the Adriatic Coast, Clemente's inventive specials feature the freshest catches of that day. From succulent sea-bass salad to a hearty

sturgeon sandwich—meals are dished up for reasonable prices. Dungeness crab cakes stuffed with crab rather than breading, and wild scallop fish-and-chips liven up a varied menu. Not interested in fish? Try the spaghetti with authentic meatballs. ⊠*1335 Marine Dr.* ☎*503/325–1067* ⊟*AE, D, MC, V.*

WHERE TO STAY

$$$$
Fodor'sChoice
★
▥ Cannery Pier Hotel. Every room has a gorgeous river view with tugboats shepherding barges to and fro. Built upon century-old pilings right where the Columbia River meets the Pacific Ocean, the hotel is in the restored Union Fisherman's Cooperative Packing Company building, an integral part of the town's history. The interior, however, is modern and bright, with a liberal use of glass and polished wood, including hardwood floors in the rooms. The property sits on the Astoria Riverwalk and on the Trolley Line, and gourmet dining is within walking distance. **Pros:** Amazing river views, great in-room amenities, next to fine-dining. **Cons:** Everything looks sparkling new, in contrast to a town with rustic charm. ⊠*10 Basin St., 97103* ☎*503/325–4996 or 888/325–4996* 🖷*503/325–8350* ⊕*www.cannerypierhotel.com* ➦*46 rooms, 8 suites* ♿*In-room: refrigerator, DVD, Ethernet, no a/c. In-hotel: Some pets allowed* ⊟*AE, D, MC, V* ⦿*CP.*

$$–$$$$
★
▥ Hotel Elliott. This upscale, five-story downtown hotel is located in the heart of Astoria's historic district. The property retains the elegance of yesteryear updated with modern comforts. On the rooftop you can relax in the garden and enjoy views of the Columbia River and the Victorian homes dotting the hillside. In your room you can warm your feet on the heated stone floors in the bathroom. And downstairs you can sample fine wines in the Cabernet Room or guiltlessly enjoy a cigar in the tucked-away Havana Room. **Pros:** Captures the city's historical ambience beautifully. Every effort made to infuse the rooms with upscale amenities. A place for cigar smokers to enjoy a stogie. **Cons:** A place for cigar smokers to enjoy a stogie. ⊠*357 12th St., 97103* ☎*877/378–1924* ⊕*www.hotelelliott.com* ➦*32 rooms* ♿*In-room: Ethernet, no a/c. In-hotel: some pets allowed* ⊟*AE, D, MC, V.*

$–$$
▥ Benjamin Young Inn. On the National Register of Historic Places, this handsome 5,500-square-foot Queen Anne inn is surrounded by century-old gardens. Among the ornate original details are faux graining on frames and molding, shutter-blinds in windows, and Povey stained glass. The spacious guest rooms mix antiques with contemporary pieces and have views of the Columbia River from their tall windows. City tennis courts are right next door. There's a two-night minimum on holiday and July, August, and September weekends. **Pros:** Property has great character, large rooms and personable owner. **Cons:** Located in a neighborhood instead of on the water. ⊠*3652 Duane St., 97103* ☎*503/325–6172 or 800/201–1286* ⊕*www.benjaminyounginn.com* ➦*3 rooms, 1 2-bedroom suite* ♿*In-room: no a/c. In-hotel: no-smoking rooms, no elevator* ⊟*AE, D, MC, V* ⦿*BP.*

SEASIDE

12 mi south of Astoria on U.S. 101.

As a resort town Seaside has brushed off its former garish, arcade-filled reputation and now supports a bustling tourist trade, with hotels, condominiums, and restaurants surrounding a long beach. It still has fun games and noise to appeal to young people, but it has added plenty of classy getaways for adults. Only 90 mi from Portland, Seaside is often crowded, so it's not the place to come if you crave solitude. Peak times include February, during the Trail's End Marathon; mid-March, when hordes of teenagers descend on the town during spring break; and July, when the annual Miss Oregon Pageant is in full swing.

Just south of town, waves draw surfers to the Cove, a spot jealously guarded by locals.

It's a 2½-mi hike from the parking lot of **Saddle Mountain State Park** to the summit of Saddle Mountain. It's much cooler at that elevation. The campground, 14 mi north of Seaside, has 10 primitive sites. ✉*Off U.S. 26* ☎*800/551-6949* 🔖*$9 for overnight camping, first-come, first-served. Hiking is free* 🕐*Mar.–Nov., daily.*

WHERE TO EAT

$–$$ ✕**Guido & Vito's Italian Eatery.** In a sea of family-oriented fish restaurants
★ sits this pleasant, quiet restaurant cooking Italian food right. Be it a zesty Ceaser, sausage and beef meatballs, or a belly-warming, mushroom-slathered veal marsala, diners won't be disappointed. ✉*604 Broadway* ☎*503/717–1229* ▭*D, MC, V* 🕐*No Lunch.*

$–$$ ✕**Girtle's Seafood & Steaks.** Huge portions at reasonable prices is the motto of this family-oriented restaurant. Here you'll find juicy steaks, fresh local seafood, and plenty of home-spun selections for kids. It also lays out a substantial, classic breakfast spread. ✉*604 Broadway* ☎*503/738–8417* ⊕*www.girtles.com* ▭*AE, D, MC, V.*

$–$$ ✕**Yummy Wine Bar & Bistro.** Despite the name, this is a warm, fun wine bar for adults. Owner Corey R. Albert serves inventive dishes such as paninis and fresh seafood that blend well with fine Pacific Northwest wines. No children admitted. ✉*831 Broadway* ☎*503/738–3100* ⊕*www.yummywinebarbistro.com* ▭*AE, MC, V* 🕐*Closed Tues. and Wed.*

WHERE TO STAY

$$$$ 🏨**Rivertide Suites.** Seaside's new hotel may not be right on the beach,
🕐 but its splendid accommodations are within walking distance of the
★ town's best cuisine, shopping, and beach activities. Offering one- and two-bedroom suites and studios, Rivertide gives guests options of different packages to appeal to golfers, whale-whatchers, or romantic couples. Breakfast is complimentary. **Pros:** New, clean, and near plenty of shopping and boardwalk activities. **Cons:** The view of a still, city river is unfortunate. Request a higher-floor room if you can. ✉*102 N. Holladay, 97138* ☎*503/436–2241 or 888/777–4047* 🖨*503/436–2159* ⊕*www.rivertidesuites.com* 🛏*45 rooms* 🔑*In-room: no a/c*

(some). In-hotel: Pool, Wi-Fi, laundry, some pets allowed ⊟*AE, D, MC, V* ⦿❙*BP.*

¢–$$ 🏨 **Hillcrest Inn.** Friendliness, cleanliness, and convenience are bywords of the Hillcrest, which is only one block from both the beach and the convention center, and three blocks from the downtown area's restaurants and shops. You're welcome to use the picnic tables, lawn chairs, and even the barbecue on the grounds. **Pros:** Simple, affordable and near Seaside's beach and essentials. **Cons:** No frills except for Wi-Fi and laundry. ⊠*118 N. Columbia St., 97138* ☎*503/738–6273 or 800/270–7659* 🖷*503/717–0266* ⟋*19 rooms, 4 suites, 3 2-bedroom cottages, 1 6-bedroom house* ⚲*In-room: no a/c (some). In-hotel: kitchen (some), refrigerator, Wi-Fi, laundry facilities* ⊟*AE, D, MC, V.*

¢ 🏨 **Royale.** This small motel right in the center of downtown is on the Necanicum River, 3½ blocks from the beach, and within very close walking distance to shopping and restaurants. Some rooms have river views. There's ample off-street parking. **Pros:** Simple and cheap. **Cons:** No views. ⊠*531 Ave. A, 97138* ☎*503/738–9541* ⟋*26 rooms* ⚲*In-room: no a/c, no elevator* ⊟*D, DC, MC, V.*

EN ROUTE   A brisk 2-mi hike from U.S. 101 south of Seaside leads to the 1,100-foot-high viewing point atop **Tillamook Head.** The view from here takes in the **Tillamook Rock Light Station,** which stands a mile or so out to sea. The lonely beacon, built in 1881 on a straight-sided rock, towers 41 feet above the surrounding ocean. In 1957 the lighthouse was abandoned; it is now a columbarium.

Eight miles south of Seaside, U.S. 101 passes the entrance to **Ecola State Park,** a playground of sea-sculpted rocks, sandy shoreline, green headlands, and panoramic views. The park's main beach can be crowded in summer, but the **Indian Beach** area contains an often-deserted cove and explorable tidal pools. ☎*503/436–2844 or 800/551–6949* ⊠*$3 per vehicle* ⊙*Daily dawn–dusk.*

CANNON BEACH

10 mi south of Seaside on U.S. 101, 80 mi west of Portland on U.S. 26.

Cannon Beach is a mellow and trendy place to enjoy art, wine, and fine dining and take in the sea air. One of the most charming hamlets on the coast, the town has beachfront homes and hotels, and a weathered-cedar downtown shopping district. On the downside, the Carmel of the Oregon coast can be more expensive and crowded than other towns along Highway 101's shoreline.

Towering over the broad, sandy beach is **Haystack Rock,** a 235-foot-high monolith that is one of the most-photographed natural wonders on the Oregon coast. ⚠ **The rock is temptingly accessible during some low tides, but the Coast Guard regularly airlifts stranded climbers from its precipitous sides, and falls have claimed numerous lives over the years.** Every May the town hosts the Cannon Beach Sandcastle Contest, for which thousands throng the beach to view imaginative and often startling works in this most transient of art forms.

Shops and galleries selling kites, upscale clothing, local art, wine, coffee, and food line **Hemlock Street,** Cannon Beach's main thoroughfare.

WHERE TO STAY & EAT

$–$$ ✕**The Bistro.** Flowers, candlelight, and classical music convey romance at this 11-table restaurant. The menu includes imaginative continental-influenced renditions of local seafood and pasta dishes as well as specialty salads. The signature dish is the fresh seafood stew. ⊠*263 N. Hemlock St.* ☎*503/436–2661* ▤*MC, V* ☉*Closed Tues. and Wed. Nov.–Jan. No lunch.*

¢–$ ✕**Sleepy Monk.** In a region famous for its gourmet coffee, one small
★ roaster brews a cup more memorable than any chain. Sleepy Monk attracts java aficionados on caffeine prilgimages from all over the Pacific Northwest; and it's not unusual to see a line outside the door. Its certified organic and fair trade beans are roasted without adding water, which adds unnecessary weight. There's a variety of teas too. Local, fresh pastries are stacked high and deep. If you're a coffee fan, this is your Shangri-la. ⊠*1235 South Hemlock* ☎*503/436–2796* ⊕*www. sleepymonkcoffee.com* ▤*MC, V* ☉*Closed Mon. –Thurs.*

$$$–$$$$ ✕▦**Stephanie Inn.** One of the most beautiful views on the coast deserves
Fodor'sChoice one of the most splendid hotels. With a stunning view of Haystack
★ Rock, the Stephanie Inn keeps its focus on romance, superior service, and luxurious rooms. Impeccably maintained, with country-style furnishings, fireplaces, large bathrooms with whirlpool tubs, and balconies, the rooms are so comfortable you may never want to leave—except perhaps to enjoy the four-course prix-fixe dinners of innovative Pacific Northwest cuisine. The restaurant serves the most delectable rack of lamb in the state. Generous country breakfasts are included in the room price, as are evening wine and hors d'oeuvres. **Pros:** One of the finest romantic getaways in Oregon; terrific fine dining and attentive service. **Cons:** It's better to go with someone than solo. Not many single travelers here. Expensive. ⊠*2740 S. Pacific St., 97110* ☎*503/436– 2221 or 800/633–3466* ⊟*503/436–9711* ⊕*www.stephanie-inn.com* ⇆*50 rooms* ⧉*In-room: DVD, refrigerator. In-hotel: no kids under 12* ▤*AE, D, DC, MC, V* ⊚❘*BP.*

$$$–$$$$ ▦**Ocean Lodge.** To celebrate special occasions, create new memories,
★ or enjoy first-rate service, this is the destination. Designed to capture the feel of a 1940s beach resort, this lodge is right on the beach. Most rooms have oceanfront views, and all have open wood beams, simple but sophisticated furnishings, gas fireplaces, and balconies or decks. The lobby floor is reclaimed spruce wood, while stairs were fashioned from old stadium bleachers. A massive rock fireplace anchors the lobby, and there is a second fireplace in the second-floor library, with a large selection of games for the whole family at your disposal. Other extras include an extensive book collection and complimentary DVDs. Bungalows across the street do not have ocean views but are large and private. ⊠*2864 S. Pacific St., 97110* ☎*503/436-2241 or 888/777–4047*

🖃*503/436–2159* ⊕*www.theoceanlodge.com* 🖅*45 rooms* ⌂*In-room: no a/c (some). In-hotel some pets allowed* ▤*AE, D, MC, V.*

EN ROUTE

South of Cannon Beach, U.S. 101 climbs 700 feet above the Pacific, providing dramatic views and often hair-raising curves as it winds along the flank of **Neahkahnie Mountain.** Cryptic carvings on beach rocks near here and centuries-old Native American legends of shipwrecked Europeans gave rise to a tale that the survivors of a sunken Spanish galleon buried a fortune in doubloons somewhere on the side of the 1,661-foot-high mountain.

OSWALD WEST STATE PARK

10 mi south of Cannon Beach on U.S. 101.

Adventurous travelers will enjoy a sojourn at one of the best-kept secrets on the Pacific coast, **Oswald West State Park,** at the base of Neah-kahnie Mountain. Park in one of the two lots on U.S. 101 and use a park-provided wheelbarrow to trundle your camping gear down a ½-mi trail. An old-growth forest surrounds the 36 primitive campsites (reservations not accepted), and the spectacular beach contains caves and tidal pools.

The trail to the summit, on the left about 2 mi south of the parking lots for Oswald West State Park (marked only by a HIKERS sign), rewards the intrepid with unobstructed views over surf, sand, forest, and mountain. Come in December or March and you might spot pods of gray whales. Campsites are first-come, first-served, with 30 walk-in tent sites. ⊠*Ecola Park Rd.* 🕾*503/368–5943 or 800/551–6949* ⊕*www. oregonstateparks.org* 🖃*Day use free, tent site $14* ⊗*Day use daily dawn–dusk; camping Mar.–Oct.*

MANZANITA

20 mi south of Cannon Beach on U.S. 101.

Manzanita is a secluded seaside community with only a little more than 500 full-time residents. It's on a sandy peninsula peppered with tufts of grass on the northwestern side of Nehalem Bay. It is a tranquil small town, but its restaurants, galleries, and 18-hole golf course have increased its appeal to tourists. Manzanita and Nehalem Bay both have become popular windsurfing destinations.

Established in 1974, **Nehalem Bay Winery** is known for its pinot noir, chardonnay, blackberry, and plum fruit wines. The winery also has a busy schedule of events, with concerts, barbecues, an occasional pig roast, children's activities, performances at the Theatre Au Vin, and a bluegrass festival the third week of August. ⊠*34965 Hwy. 53, Nehalem* 🕾*503/368–9463 or 888/368–9463* 🖷*503/368–5300* ⊕*www.nehalembaywinery.com* ⊗*Daily 9–6.*

2

WHERE TO STAY

$$$ Ⓣ **Inn at Manzanita.** This 1987 Scandinavian structure, filled with light-color woods, beams, and glass, is half a block from the beach. Shore pines on the property give upper-floor patios a treehouse feel, all rooms have decks, and two have skylights. A nearby café serves breakfast, and area restaurants are nearby. In winter the inn is a great place for storm-watching. There's a two-day minimum stay on weekends. The inn now offers three child-friendly rooms and a new penthouse suite. 20-day cancellation notice required. ⊠*67 Laneda Ave., Box 243, 97130* ☎*503/368–6754* 📠*503/368–5941* ⊕*www.innatmanzanita. com* ➪*13 rooms, penthouse* ♿*In-room: no a/c. In-hotel: no phone (some), kitchen (some), refrigerator. No pets, no elevator* ⊟*AE, D, MC, V.*

CAMPING 🏕**Nehalem Bay State Park.** Close enough to the ocean that you'll poten-tially be lulled to sleep by the waves, the park is on the edge of Nehalem Bay, which is popular for kayaking, crabbing, and fishing. ⊠*Off U.S. 101, 3 mi south of Manzanita Junction* ☎*800/452–5687 reservations, 800/551–6949 information* ⊕*www.oregonstateparks.org.* ⌂*Reserva-tions essential* ♿*Flush toilets, partial hookups, dump station, drinking water, showers, fire pits, picnic tables, electricity, swimming (ocean)* ➪*265 electrical sites, 18 yurts, 17 sites with corrals* ⊟*MC, V*

TILLAMOOK

30 mi south of Oswald West State Park and Neahkahnie Mountain on U.S. 101.

More than 100 inches of annual rainfall and the confluence of three rivers contribute to the lush green pastures around Tillamook, prob-ably best known for its thriving dairy industry and cheese factory. The Tillamook County Cheese Factory ships about 40 million pounds of cheese around the world every year.

Just south of town is the largest wooden structure in the world, one of two gigantic buildings constructed in 1942 by the U.S. Navy to shelter blimps that patrolled the Pacific Coast during World War II. Hangar A was destroyed by fire in 1992, and Hangar B was subsequently con-verted to the Tillamook Naval Air Station Museum.

The **Three Capes Loop** over Cape Meares, Cape Lookout, and Cape Kiwanda offers spectacular views of the ocean and coastline (⇨ below).

Ⓒ The **Pioneer Museum** in Tillamook's 1905 county courthouse has an intriguing if old-fashioned hodgepodge of Native American, pioneer, logging, and natural-history exhibits, along with antique vehicles and military artifacts. ⊠*2106 2nd St.* ☎*503/842–4553* 🎟*$3* 🕐*Tues.– Sun. 9–5.*

More than 750,000 visitors annually journey through the **Tillamook County Creamery,** the largest cheese-making plant on the West Coast. Here the rich milk from the area's thousands of Holstein and brown Swiss cows becomes ice cream, butter, and cheddar and Monterey Jack cheeses. There is a self-guided cheesemaking tour and an extensive shop where tasty cheeses and smoked meats can be purchased; and you'll definitely want a waffle cone full of your favorite ice-cream flavor. Try the marionberry. ⊠*4175 U.S. 101 N, 2 mi north of Tillamook* ☎*503/815–1300* ⊕*www.tillamookcheese.com* ⊠*Free* ☉*Mid-Sept.– May, daily 8–6; June–mid-Sept., daily 8–8.*

☾ The **Blue Heron French Cheese Company** specializes in French-style cheeses—Camembert, Brie, and others. There's a free petting zoo for kids, a sit-down deli, wine and cheese tastings, and a gift shop that carries wines and jams, mustards, and other products from Oregon. ⊠*2001 Blue Heron Dr., watch for signs from U.S. 101* ☎*503/842– 8281* ⊕*www.blueheronoregon.com* ⊠*Free* ☉*Memorial Day–Labor Day, daily 8–8; Labor Day–Memorial Day, daily 8–6.*

In the world's largest wooden structure, a former blimp hangar south of town, the **Tillamook Naval Air Station Museum** displays one of the finest private collections of vintage aircraft from World War II, including a B-25 Mitchell and an ME-109 Messerschmidt. The 20-story building is big enough to hold half a dozen football fields. ⊠*6030 Hangar Rd., ½ mi south of Tillamook; head east from U.S. 101 on Long Prairie Rd. and follow signs* ☎*503/842–1130* ⊕*www.tillamookair.com* ⊠*$11* ☉*Daily 9–5.*

WHERE TO STAY & EAT

$–$$ ✕ **Roseanna's.** Nine miles west of Tillamook in Oceanside, Roseanna's is in a rustic 1915 building on the beach opposite Three Arch Rock, so you might be able to watch sea lions and puffins while you eat. The calm of the beach is complemented in the evening by candlelight and fresh flowers. Have halibut or salmon half a dozen ways, or try the baked oysters or Gorgonzola seafood pasta. ⊠*1490 Pacific Ave., Oceanside* ☎*503/842–7351* ⚐*Reservations not accepted* ▱*MC, V.*

¢–$ ✕ **Artspace.** You'll be surrounded by artwork as you enjoy homemade creations at Artspace in Bay City, 6 mi north of Tillamook. The menu may include garlic-grilled oysters, vegetarian dishes, and other specials, all beautifully presented, often with edible flowers. ⊠*9120 5th St., Bay City* ☎*503/377–2782* ▱*No credit cards* ☉*Closed Mon.*

$–$$ ▦ **Sandlake Country Inn.** Tucked into a bower of old roses on 2 acres, this intimate bed-and-breakfast is in a farmhouse built of timbers that washed ashore from a shipwreck in 1890. It is listed on the Oregon Historic Registry and filled with antiques. The Timbers Suite has a massive, king-size wood canopy bed, wood-burning fireplace, and two-person jetted tub; the Starlight Suite occupies four rooms on the second floor and includes a canopy queen bed and double-sided fireplace. A four-course breakfast is delivered to the door. **Pros:** A very pretty, comfortable stay. **Cons:** Probably not a great place to bring the kids. ⊠*8505 Galloway Rd., Pacific City 97112* ☎*503/965–6745 or 877/726–3525* ⊕*www.sandlakecountryinn.com* ⚐*1 room, 2 suites, 1 cottage* ⚐*In-room: no a/c. In-hotel: no phone (some), no elevator* ▱*D, MC, V* ⍉*BP.*

THREE CAPES LOOP

Starts south of downtown Tillamook off 3rd St.

★ The Three Capes Loop, a 35-mi byway off U.S. 101, is one of the coast's most thrilling driving experiences. The loop winds along the coast between Tillamook and Pacific City, passing three distinctive headlands—Cape Meares, Cape Lookout, and Cape Kiwanda. Bay-ocean Road heading west from Tillamook passes what was the thriving resort town of Bay Ocean. More than 30 years ago, Bay Ocean washed into the sea—houses, a bowling alley, everything—during a raging Pacific storm.

Nine miles west of Tillamook, trails from the parking lot at the end of Bay Ocean Spit lead through the dunes to a usually uncrowded and highly walkable white-sand beach.

Cape Meares State Park is on the northern tip of the Three Capes Loop. Cape Meares was named for English navigator John Meares, who voyaged along this coast in 1788. The restored **Cape Meares Lighthouse**, built in 1890 and open to the public May–September, provides a sweeping view over the cliff to the caves and sea-lion rookery on the rocks below. A many-trunked Sitka spruce known as the Octopus Tree grows near the lighthouse parking lot. ⊠ *Three Capes Loop 10 mi west of Tillamook* ☎ *800/551–6949* ⊕ *www.oregonstateparks.org* 🖼 *Free* ☾ *Park daily dawn–dusk. Lighthouse Apr.–Oct., daily 11–4.*

Cape Lookout State Park lies south of the beach towns of Oceanside and Netarts. A fairly easy 2-mi trail—marked on the highway as WILDLIFE VIEWING AREA—leads through giant spruces, western red cedars, and hemlocks to views of Cascade Head to the south and Cape Meares to the north. Wildflowers, more than 150 species of birds, and migrating whales passing by in early April make this trail a favorite with nature lovers. The park has a picnic area overlooking the sea and a year-round campground. ⊠ *Three Capes Loop 8 mi south of Cape Meares* ☎ *800/551–6949* ⊕ *www.oregonstateparks.org* 🖼 *Day use $3:38 full hookup $20, 1 electric $20, 173 tent (maximum site 60 feet) $16; 13 yurts $27; group tent (2 areas); hiker/biker camp $4; 3 deluxe cabins (with bathrooms, kitchen, TV/VCR) $66* ☾ *Daily dawn–dusk.*

Huge waves pound the jagged sandstone cliffs and caves at **Cape Kiwanda State Natural Area.** The much-photographed, 235-foot-high **Haystack Rock** juts out of Nestucca Bay just south of here. Surfers ride some of the longest waves on the coast, hang gliders soar above the shore, and beachcombers explore tidal pools and take in unparalleled ocean views. ⊠ *Three Capes Loop 15 mi south of Cape Lookout* ☎ *800/551–6949* 🖼 *Free* ⊕ *www.oregonstateparks.org* ☾ *Daily sunrise–sunset.*

PACIFIC CITY

1½ mi south of Cape Kiwanda on Three Capes Loop.

The beach at Pacific City, the town visible from Cape Kiwanda, is one of the few places in the state where fishing dories (flat-bottom boats with high, flaring sides) are launched directly into the surf instead of from harbors or docks. During the commercial salmon season in late summer it's possible to buy salmon directly from the fishermen.

A walk along the flat white-sand beach at **Robert Straub State Park** leads down to the mouth of the Nestucca River, considered by many to be the best fishing river on the north coast. ⊠ *West from main intersection in downtown Pacific City across Nestucca River, follow signs* ☎*800/551–6949* ⊠*Free* ⊙*Daily 7* AM*–dusk.*

OFF THE BEATEN PATH

Nature Conservancy Cascade Head Trail. The trail at one of the most unusual headlands on the Oregon coast winds through a rain forest where 250-year-old Sitka spruces and a dense green undergrowth of mosses and ferns is nourished by 100-inch annual rainfalls. After the forest comes grassy and treeless Cascade Head, a rare example of a maritime prairie. Magnificent views down to the Salmon River and east to the Coast Range open up as you continue along the headland, where black-tailed deer often graze and turkey vultures soar in the strong winds. You need to be in fairly good shape for the first and steepest part of the hike, which can be done in about an hour. The 270-acre area has been named a United Nations Biosphere Reserve. Coastal bluffs make this a popular hang-gliding and kite-flying area. ⊠*Savage Rd., 6 mi south of Neskowin off U.S. 101; turn west on Three Rocks Rd. and north on Savage* ☎*503/230–1221* ⊕*www.nature.org* ⊠*Free* ⊙*The upper trail is closed by the Forest Service from Jan. to mid July.*

WHERE TO EAT

$–$$ ✕ **Riverhouse.** Fresh seafood, sandwiches, and home-baked desserts are the specialties at this casual dining spot overlooking the Nestucca River. Original, all-natural salad dressings are a big hit with guests and available for sale in gift packs. ⊠*34450 Brooten Rd.* ☎*503/965–6722* ▤*MC, V.*

LINCOLN CITY

16 mi south of Pacific City on U.S. 101, 78 mi west of Portland on Hwy. 99 W and Hwy. 18.

Once a series of small villages, Lincoln City is a sprawling, suburbanish town without a center. But the endless tourist amenities make up for the coastal charm it lacks. Clustered like barnacles on the offshore reefs are fast-food restaurants, gift shops, supermarkets, candy stores, antiques markets, dozens of motels and hotels, a factory-outlet mall, and a busy casino. Lincoln City is the most popular destination city on the Oregon coast, but its only real geographic claim to fame is the 445-foot-long **D River**, stretching from its source in Devil's Lake to the Pacific; *Guinness World Records* lists the D as the world's shortest river.

The only casino built directly on the beach in Oregon, **Chinook Winds** has slot machines, blackjack, poker, keno, and off-track betting. The entry atrium is accented with a two-story waterfall and natural rocks, trees, and plants to replicate the fishing ground of the Confederated Tribes of the Siletz, who own the casino. The Siletz Room has good food, and there is an all-you-can-eat buffet, a snack bar, and a lounge. An arcade will keep the kids busy while you are on the gambling floor. Big-name entertainers perform in the showroom. ⊠*1777 N.W. 44th St.,* ☎*541/996–5825 or 888/244–6665.*

The imaginative craftspeople at the **Alder House II** studio turn molten glass into vases and bowls, which are available for sale. It is the oldest glass-blowing studio in the state. ⊠*611 Immonen Rd.* ☎*541/996–2483* ⊕*www.alderhouse.com* ⊡*Free* ☉*Mid-Mar.–Nov., daily 10–5.*

Canoeing and kayaking are popular on the small lake at **Devil's Lake State Park,** which is in turn popular with coots, loons, ducks, cormorants, bald eagles, and grebes. It's the only Oregon-coast campground within the environs of a city. There are 28 full hookups $23, 5 electric with cable $23, 54 tent sites $17, hiker/biker camp $4, and 10 yurts $29. ⊠*1452 N.E. 6th St.* ☎*541/994–2002 or 800/551–6949* ⊕*www.oregonstateparks.org/* ⊡*Free* ☉*Daily.*

WHERE TO STAY & EAT

$$$–$$$$ ✕ **Bay House.** Inside a charming bungalow, this restaurant serves meals to linger over while you enjoy views across sunset-gilded Siletz Bay. The seasonal Pacific Northwest cuisine includes Dungeness crab cakes with roasted-chili chutney, fresh halibut Parmesan, and roast duckling with cranberry compote. The wine list is extensive, the service impeccable. ⊠*5911 S.W. U.S. 101, about 5 mi south of Lincoln City* ☎*541/996–3222* ⊟*AE, D, MC, V.*

$–$$ ✕ **Kyllo's.** Light-filled Kyllo's rests on stilts beside the D River. It's one of the best places in Lincoln City to enjoy casual but well-prepared seafood, pasta, and meat dishes. ⊠*1110 N.W. 1st Ct.* ☎*541/994–3179* ⊟*AE, D, MC, V.*

$$–$$$$ ⚇ **Inn at Spanish Head.** You'll find tidal pools right outside your door at this condominium resort set on a bluff. All of the bright, contemporary units have ocean views. Choose from one-bedroom suites, deluxe studios, or deluxe rooms. **Pros:** Sweeping views of the ocean through floor-to-ceiling windows. **Cons:** Pretty pricey. ⊠*4009 S. U.S. 101, 93767* ☎*541/996–2161 or 800/452–8127* ⊟*541/996–4089* ⊕*www.spanishhead.com* ⊷*127 rooms, incl. 49 suites* ⌂*In-hotel: restaurant, room service, bar, pool* ⊟*AE, D, DC, MC, V.*

GLENEDEN BEACH

7 mi south of Lincoln City on U.S. 101.

Salishan, the most famous resort on the Oregon coast, perches high above placid Siletz Bay. This expensive collection of guest rooms, vacation homes, condominiums, restaurants, golf fairways, tennis courts, and covered walkways blends into a forest preserve; if not for the signs, you'd scarcely be able to find it.

The well-respected **Lawrence Gallery at Salishan** has a well-informed staff that will guide you through the collections of work by Northwest artists, including paintings (pastels, oils, and watercolors), glassworks, bronze and metal, furniture, and ceramics and porcelain. ⊠*7755 N.*

U.S. 101, ☎541/764–2318 or 800/764–2318 ⊕*www.lawrencegallery. net* ☯ *Weekdays 10–5, weekends 10–6.*

WHERE TO STAY & EAT

$$–$$$$ ✕**Dining Room at Salishan.** The Salishan resort's main dining room, a
★   multilevel expanse of hushed waiters, hillside ocean views, and snow-white linen, serves Pacific Northwest cuisine. House specialties include fresh local fish, game, beef, and lamb. By all means make a selection from the wine cellar, which has more than 17,000 bottles. ☒*7760 N. U.S. 101* ☎*541/764–2371* ⚒*Reservations essential* ▤*AE, D, DC, MC, V* ☯*No lunch.*

$$ ✕**Sidedoor Café.** This dining room with a high ceiling, exposed beams, a fireplace, and many windows just under the eaves shares a former tile factory with the Eden Hall performance space. The menu changes constantly—fresh preparations have included mushroom-crusted rack of lamb and broiled swordfish with citrus-raspberry vinaigrette over coconut-ginger basmati rice. ☒*6675 Gleneden Beach Loop Rd.,* ☎*541/764–3825* ▤*AE, D, MC, V* ☯*Closed Tues.*

$$$–$$$$ ▦**Salishan Lodge and Golf Resort.** From the soothing, silvered cedar of
★   its rooms, divided among eight units in a hillside forest preserve, to its wood-burning fireplaces, Salishan embodies a uniquely Oregonian elegance. Each of the quiet rooms has a balcony, and original works by Northwest artists. A nice little touch is the MP3-compatible clock radios in each room. Given all this, plus fine food and a recently redesigned par-71 golf course, you'll understand why the timeless lodge is one of the premier resorts on the coast. **Pros:** Very elegant resort with plenty of activites on the property. **Cons:** A shuttle takes you to your room. Lots of corporate guests. ☒*7760 N. U.S. 101, 97388* ☎*541/764–3600 or 800/452–2300* ▤*541/764–3681* ⊕*www.salishan.com* ⤷*205 rooms* ⚒*In-room: refrigerator, Wi-Fi. In-hotel: 2 restaurants, room service, bar, golf course, tennis courts, pool, gym, beachfront, concierge, laundry service* ▤*AE, D, DC, MC, V.*

DEPOE BAY

12 mi south of Lincoln City on U.S. 101.

Depoe Bay calls itself the whale-watching capital of the world. The small town was founded in the 1920s and named in honor of Charles DePoe, of the Siletz tribe, who in turn was named for his employment at a U.S. Army depot in the late 1800s. With a narrow channel and deep water, its tiny harbor is also one of the most protected on the coast. It supports a thriving fleet of commercial- and charter-fishing boats. The Spouting Horn, a natural cleft in the basalt cliffs on the waterfront, blasts seawater skyward during heavy weather. ☒*Depoe Bay Chamber of Commerce* ☎*541/765–2889* ⊕*www.depoebaychamber.org.*

Fogarty Creek State Park. Bird-watching and viewing the tidal pools are the key draws here, but hiking and picnicking are also popular at this park 4 mi north of Depoe Bay on U.S. 101. Wooden footbridges arch through the forest. The beach is rimmed with cliffs. ☒*U.S. 101* ☎*541/265–9278 or 800/551–6949* ⊕*www.oregonstateparks.org* ▤*Free* ☯*Daily.*

NEWPORT

12 mi south of Depoe Bay on U.S. 101, 114 mi from Portland, south on I–5 and west on Hwy. 34 and U.S. 20.

Thanks to an easily accessible beach, outstanding aquarium, a lively performing-arts center, and the local laid-back attitude, Newport remains a favorite both with regional travelers looking for a weekend escape and those who come for longer stays.

Newport exists on two levels: the highway above, threading its way through the community's main business district, and the old **Bayfront** along Yaquina Bay below (watch for signs on U.S. 101). With its high-masted fishing fleet, well-worn buildings, seafood markets, and art galleries and shops, Newport's Bayfront is an ideal place for an afternoon stroll. So many male sea lions in Yaquina Bay loiter near crab pots and bark from the waterfront piers that locals call the area the Bachelor Club. Visit the docks to buy fresh seafood or rent a small boat or kayak to explore Yaquina Bay.

The **Oregon Coast Aquarium,** a 4½-acre complex, has re-creations of offshore and near-shore Pacific marine habitats, all teeming with life: playful sea otters, comical puffins, fragile jellyfish, and even a 60-pound octopus. There's a hands-on interactive area for children and one of North America's largest seabird aviaries. Permanent exhibits include Passages of the Deep, a trio of tanks linked by a 200-foot underwater tunnel with 360-degree views of sharks, wolf eels, halibut, and other sea life. Large coho salmon and sturgeon can be viewed in a naturalistic setting through a window wall 9 feet high and 20 feet wide. ⊠ *2820 S.E. Ferry Slip Rd. Heading south from Newport, turn right at southern end of Yaquina Bay Bridge and follow signs* ☎ *541/867–3474* ⊕ *www.aquarium.org* ⊠ *$13.25* ⊙ *Summer, daily 9–6; winter, daily 10–5.*

Interactive and interpretive exhibits are at Oregon State University's **Hatfield Marine Science Center.** The star of the show is a large octopus in a touch tank near the entrance. She seems as interested in human visitors as they are in her; guided by a staff volunteer, you can sometimes reach in to stroke her suction-tipped tentacles. ⊠ *2030 S. Marine Science Dr. Heading south from Newport, cross Yaquina Bay Bridge on U.S. 101 S and follow signs* ☎ *541/867–0100* ⊕ *hmsc.oregonstate.edu* ⊠ *Donation* ⊙ *Memorial Day–Labor Day, daily 10–5; Labor Day–Memorial Day, Thurs.–Mon. 10–4.*

Marine Discovery Tours conducts a Sea Life Cruise. The 65-foot excursion boat *Discovery,* with inside seating for 49 and two viewing levels, departs throughout the day. Its public cruise season is March–October, while reserved group tours are welcome throughout the year. *Discovery* is wheelchair accessible. ⊠ *345 S.W. Bay Blvd., Newport* ☎ *800/903–2628* ⊠ *$33* ▭ *D, MC, V.*

Seven miles north of Newport, beachfront **Beverly Beach State Park** extends from Yaquina Head to the headlands of Otter Rock. It has a campground with 53 full hookups $21, 75 electrical $21, 128 tent sites $17, hiker/biker camp, and 21 yurts $29. ⊠ *U.S. 101* ☎ *541/265–9278 or 800/551–6949* ⊕ *www.oregonstateparks.org/* ✑ *Free* ◷ *Daily.*

A rocky shoreline separates the day-use **Devil's Punch Bowl State Natural Area** from the surf. It's a popular whale-watching site just 9 mi north of Newport and has excellent tidal pools. ⊠ *U.S. 101* ☎ *541/265–9278* ✑ *Free* ◷ *Daily.*

Fishing, crabbing, boating, windsurfing, hiking, and beachcombing are popular at **South Beach State Park.** A campground has 228 electrical hookups $22, 27 yurts $30, group tent sites $66, and hiker/biker camp $4. Wi-Fi access. ⊠ *U.S. 101 S* ☎ *541/867–4715 or 541/867–7451* ◷ *Daily.*

☾ The tallest lighthouse on the Oregon Coast is the 93-foot **Yaquina Head**
★ **Lighthouse,** which recently underwent a $1 million restoration. Tours are self-guided. ⊠ *4 mi north of bridge in Newport* ☎ *541/574–3100* ✑ *Call for prices* ◷ *Mid-June–mid-Sept., daily noon–4; in winter, call ahead.*

★ At the **Yaquina Head Outstanding Natural Area,** thousands of birds—cormorants, gulls, common murres, pigeon guillemots—make their home just beyond shore on Pinnacle and Colony rocks, and nature trails wind through fields of sea grass and wildflowers, leading to spectacular views. There is also an interpretive center. ⊠ *750 N.W. Lighthouse Dr.* ☎ *541/574–3100* ⊕ *www.blm.gov* ✑ *$5 per vehicle, 9 passengers or fewer* ◷ *Daily dawn–dusk.*

WHERE TO EAT

$$ ✕ **Tables of Content.** The well-plotted prix-fixe menu at the restaurant of the outstanding Sylvia Beach Hotel changes nightly. Chances are the main dish will be fresh local seafood, perhaps a moist grilled salmon fillet in a sauce Dijonnaise, served with sautéed vegetables, fresh-baked breads, and rice pilaf; a decadent dessert is also included. The interior is functional and unadorned, with family-size tables, but be forewarned, dinners can be long, so young children may get restless. ⊠ *267 N.W. Cliff St., from U.S. 101 head west on 3rd St.* ☎ *541/265–5428* ⌀ *Reservations essential* ⊟ *AE, MC, V* ◷ *No lunch.*

$–$$ ✕ **Canyon Way Restaurant and Bookstore.** Cod, Dungeness crab cakes, bouillabaisse, and Yaquina Bay oysters are among the specialties of this Newport dining spot up the hill from the center of the Bayfront. There's also a deli counter for takeout. The restaurant, which has an outdoor patio, is to one side of a well-stocked bookstore. Fast Eddie's Bar serves lighter fare and lunch sandwiches as well as light dinners. ⊠ *S.W. Canyon Way off Bay Front Blvd.* ☎ *541/265–8319* ⊟ *AE, MC, V* ◷ *Closed Sun.*

¢ ✕ **Panini Bakery.** The owner, who operates this local favorite bakery
★ and espresso bar, prides himself on hearty and home-roasted meats, hand-cut breads, and friendly service. The coffee's organic, the eggs free range, the orange juice fresh squeezed, and just about everything

GREAT ITINERARY

NORTHWEST OREGON IN 3 DAYS

After enjoying the Columbia River Maritime Museum, Astoria Column, and lunch at Clemente's in Astoria, take U.S. 101 to the coastal resort town of Cannon Beach, enjoying a masterful cup of coffee at Sleepy Monks. After a peaceful beach stroll by Haystack Rock, continue south to Newport and visit the Oregon Coast Aquarium. On Day 2, backtrack north 30 miles on Hwy. 101 and drive east on Hwy. 18 at Otis. Drive 45 miles to McMinnville and tour the Evergreen Aviation Museum. From there you can branch out and tour the famous Yamhill Valley wine country, driving northeast on Hwy. 99 and stopping

at vineyards in Amity, Dundee, and Newberg. On Day 3 take Highway 99 W north toward Portland, where you can stop at the upscale Bridgeport Village Shopping Mall in Tigard. There it connects with I–5 heading north into Portland. If you wish, continue through the city to I–84. The interstate winds eastward to the Columbia Gorge. At Troutdale, get on the Historic Columbia River Highway, which passes Multnomah Falls before rejoining I–84. Continue east to the Bonneville Dam and The Dalles. If you'll be staying in the area four days, spend the third night in Hood River and swing down to Mount Hood the next morning.

is made from scratch. Take a seat inside, or, in good weather, streetside tables are a great place to view the Nye Beach scene. ⊠ *232 N.W. Coast Hwy.* ☎ *541/265–5033* ▬*No credit cards.*

WHERE TO STAY

¢–$$ ⚏**Sylvia Beach Hotel.** Make reservations far in advance for this 1913-vintage beachfront hotel, where reading, writing, and old conversation ecplise technological hotel-room isolation. Its antiques-filled rooms are named for famous writers. A pendulum swings over the bed in the Poe room. The Christie, Twain, Tolkein, Woolf, and Colette rooms each are notable; all have fireplaces, decks, and great ocean views. A well-stocked split-level upstairs library has decks, a fireplace, slumbering cats, and too-comfortable chairs. Complimentary mulled wine is served here nightly at 10. **Pros:** Great place to write home about. No TV. **Cons:** No Internet access. ⊠ *267 N.W. Cliff St., 97365* ☎ *541/265–5428 or 888/795–8422* ⊕ *www.sylviabeachhotel.com* ➭*20 rooms* ⚐ *In-room: no phone. In-hotel: restaurant no Internet* ▬*AE, MC, V* ⎥⓪⎢*BP.*

WALDPORT

15 mi south of Newport on U.S. 101, 67 mi west of Corvallis on Hwy. 34 and U.S. 20.

Long ago the base of the Alsi Indians, Waldport later became a gold-rush town and a logging center. In the 1980s it garnered national attention when local residents fought the timber industry and stopped the spraying of dioxin-based defoliants in the Coast Range forests. Waldport attracts many retirees and those seeking an alternative to the expensive beach resorts nearby.

The **Drift Creek Wilderness** east of Waldport holds some of the rare old-growth forest that have triggered battles between the timber industry and environmentalists. Hemlocks hundreds of years old grow in parts of this 9-square-mi area. The 2-mi **Harris Ranch Trail** winds through these ancient giants—you may even spot a spotted owl. The Siuslaw National Forest–Waldport Ranger Station provides directions and maps. No motorized vehicles are permitted in the wilderness. ✉ *Risely Creek Rd. From Waldport, take Hwy. 34 east for 7 mi to Alsea River crossing* ☎ *541/563–3211* ☉ *Ranger Station open weekdays 8–4.*

WHERE TO STAY

$$ 🖼️**Cliff House Bed-and-Breakfast.** The view from Yaquina John Point, on which this B&B sits, is magnificent. The house, which in livelier days was a bordello, is done in a mix of classic American antiques and comfortable overstuffed furniture. Plush rooms all have ocean views; three have balconies and wood-burning stoves. A glass-front terrace looking out over 8 mi of white-sand beach leads down to the garden. ✉ *1450 Adahi Rd., 1 block west of U.S. 101, 97394* ☎ *541/563–2506* 🖨 *541/563–3903* ⊕ *www.cliffhouseoregon.com* 🛏 *4 rooms* ♿ *In-room: VCR. In-hotel: No elevator* ▤ *MC, V* 🍴 *BP.*

YACHATS

8 mi south of Waldport on U.S. 101.

The small town of Yachats (pronounced "yah-*hots*") is at the mouth of the Yachats River, and from its rocky shoreline, which includes the highest point on the Oregon coast, trails lead to beaches and dozens of tidal pools. A relaxed alternative to the more touristy communities to the north, Yachats has all the coastal pleasures: B&Bs, good restaurants, deserted beaches, tidal pools, surf-pounded crags, fishing, and crabbing.

The oceanside **Tillicum Beach Campground** 3½ mi north of Yachats is so popular there is a 10-day-stay limit. Many of the campsites have beachfront views. Open year-round, there are 59 sites, $22 for electric and water hookups. ✉ *U.S. 101* ☎ *541/563–3211* 🎫 *Day use free* ☉ *Daily.*

The Yachats River meets the Pacific Ocean at **Yachats Ocean Road State Recreation Area**, 1 mi from Yachats. Whale-watching is a popular activity. ✉ *U.S. 101 to Yachats Ocean Rd.* ☎ *541/997–3851 or 800/551–6949* ⊕ *www.oregonstateparks.org* 🎫 *Free* ☉ *Daily.*

WHERE TO STAY & EAT

$-$$ ✕**Adobe Restaurant.** The extraordinary ocean views sometimes upstage the meal, but if you stick to the seafood, you'll come away satisfied. The Baked Crab Pot is a rich, bubbling casserole filled with Dungeness crab and cheese in a shallot cream sauce; best of all is the Captain's Seafood Platter, heaped with prawns, scallops, grilled oysters, and razor clams. Breakfast, lunch, and dinner daily, 8 AM–9 PM. Reservations for dinner only. ✉ *1555 U.S. 101* ☎ *541/547–3141* ▤ *AE, D, DC, MC, V.*

¢–$ ✕**The Drift Inn.** Affordable, family-friendly, and lively, the Drift Inn serves breakfast, lunch, and dinner featuring fresh seafood, all-natural steaks, and other Pacific Northwest ingredients. It has live music every night, and serves Oregon beers and wines. It's also known for its ginger dressing. The restaurant offers a view of the Yachats River where it meets the ocean. Open 8 AM–9:30 PM. ✉*124 Hwy. 101 N* ☎*541/547–4477* ⊕*www.the-drift-inn.com*▤*MC, V.*

$$–$$$$ 🏨**Overleaf Lodge.** Located on a rocky shoreline at the north end Yachats, the Overleaf Lodge is the perfect place to enjoy a spectacular sunset in splendid comfort. Renowned for well-kept, spacious rooms and impeccable views. Continental breakfast provided, no dining otherwise. **Pros:** Best hotel in one of the Coast's best communities. **Cons:** No dining, exercise room is small. ✉*280 Overleaf Lodge La., 97498* ☎*541/547–4880* ⊕*www.overleaflodge.com* ↩*54 rooms and suites* ⚬*Day spa includes soaking pool, hot tub, steam rooms, and saunas. Massages and facials available. Small exercise room. Conference room holds up to 25.* ▤*AE, D, MC, V* ⧉*BP.*

CAPE PERPETUA

9 mi south of Yachats town on U.S. 101.

With the highest lookout point on the Oregon coast, Cape Perpetua towers 800 feet above the rocky shoreline. Named by Captain Cook on St. Perpetua's Day in 1778, the cape is part of a 2,700-acre scenic area popular with hikers, campers, beachcombers, and naturalists. General information and a map of 10 trails are available at the **Cape Perpetua Visitors Center,** on the east side of the highway, 2 mi south of Devil's Churn. The easy 1-mi **Giant Spruce Trail** passes through a fern-filled rain forest to an enormous 500-year-old Sitka spruce. Easier still is the marked Auto Tour; it begins about 2 mi north of the visitor center and winds through Siuslaw National Forest to the ¼-mi **Whispering Spruce Trail.** Views from the rustic rock shelter here extend 150 mi north and south and 37 mi out to sea. The **Cape Perpetua Interpretive Center,** in the visitor center, has educational movies and exhibits about the natural forces that shaped Cape Perpetua. ✉*U.S. 101* ☎*541/547–3289* 🚗*Parking fee $5* ☉*Daily 10–4.*

HECETA HEAD

10 mi south of Cape Perpetua on U.S. 101, 65 mi from Eugene, west on Hwy. 126 and north on U.S. 101.

A ½-mi trail from the beachside parking lot at **Devil's Elbow State Park** leads to **Heceta Head Lighthouse,** whose beacon, visible for more than 21 mi, is the most powerful on the Oregon coast. ✉*U.S. 101* ☎*541/997–3851* 🚗*Day use $3, lighthouse tours free* ☉*Lighthouse May–Sept., daily 11–5; Mar., Apr. and Oct., daily 11–3; Nov.–Feb. call for times. Park daily dawn–dusk.*

In 1880 a sea captain named Cox rowed a small skiff into a fissure in a 300-foot-high sea cliff. Inside, he was startled to discover a vaulted chamber in the rock, 125 feet high and 2 acres in area. Hundreds of massive sea lions—the largest bulls weighing 2,000 pounds or more—covered every available horizontal surface. Cox had no way of knowing it, but his discovery would eventually become one of the Oregon coast's premier tourist attractions, **Sea Lion Caves.** An elevator near the cliff-top ticket office descends to the floor of the cavern, near sea level, where Steller's and California sea lions and their fuzzy pups can be viewed from behind a wire fence. This is the only known hauling-out area and rookery for wild sea lions on the mainland in the Lower 48, and it's an awesome sight and sound—and aroma! In spring and summer the mammals usually stay on the rocky ledges outside the cave; in fall and winter they move inside. You'll also see several species of seabirds here, including migratory pigeon guillemots, cormorants, and three varieties of gulls. Gray whales are visible during their northern and southern migrations, October–December and March–May. ✉91560 U.S. 101, 1 mi south of Heceta Head ☎541/547–3111 ⌑$9 ⏱Daily 9–5 ▭MC, V.

WHERE TO STAY

$$–$$$$ ⊞**Heceta House.** On a windswept promontory, this unusual late-Victorian B&B surrounded by a white-picket fence is one of Oregon's most remarkable bed-and-breakfasts. Now owned by the U.S. Forest Service, it is managed by Mike and Carol Korgan, certified executive chefs who prepare a seven-course breakfast (included in the room rate) each morning. The menu changes according to the season. Meals include herbs and produce out of the Lightstation garden and highlight the best of Oregon: artisan cheeses, sausages, produce, and Carol's pastries. The nicest of the simply furnished rooms is the Mariner's, with a private bath and an awe-inspiring view. Filled with period detailing and antiques, the common areas are warm and inviting. If you're lucky, you may hear Rue, the resident ghost, in the middle of the night. ✉92072 U.S. 101 S, Yachats 97498 ☎541/547–3696 ⊕www.hecetalighthouse. com ⌑6 rooms, 4 with bath ▭D, MC, V ⎮○⎮BP.

FLORENCE

12 mi south of Heceta Head on U.S. 101, 63 mi west of Eugene on Hwy. 126.

Tourists and retirees have been flocking to Florence in ever greater numbers in recent years. Its restored waterfront Old Town has restaurants, antiques stores, fish markets, and other diversions. But what really makes the town so appealing is its proximity to remarkable stretches of coastline. Seventy-five creeks and rivers empty into the Pacific Ocean in and around Florence, and the Siuslaw River flows right through town. When the numerous nearby lakes are added to the mix, it makes for one of the richest fishing areas in Oregon. Salmon, rainbow trout, bass, perch, crabs, and clams are among the water's treasures. Fishing boats and pleasure craft moor in Florence's harbor, forming a pleasant backdrop for the town's restored buildings. South of town, miles of white-sand dunes lend themselves to everything from solitary hikes to rides aboard all-terrain vehicles.

☾ Florence is the gateway to the **Oregon Dunes National Recreation Area,** a
★ 41-mi-long swath of undulating camel-color sand. The dunes, formed by eroded sandstone pushed up from the sea floor millions of years ago, have forests growing on them, water running through them, and rivers that have been dammed by them to form lakes. **Honeyman Memorial State Park,** 522 acres within the recreation area, is a base camp for dune-buggy enthusiasts, mountain bikers, hikers, boaters, horseback riders, and dogsledders (the sandy hills are an excellent training ground). The dunes are a vast and exuberant playground for children, particularly the slopes surrounding cool **Cleawox Lake.** ✉ *Oregon Dunes National Recreation Area office, 855 U.S. 101, Reedsport* ☎ *541/271–6000* ⛵ *Day use $5* ☉ *Daily dawn–dusk.*

Ride year-round along the Oregon Dunes National Recreation Area at **C & M Stables,** spotting not only marine life—sea lions, whales, and all manner of coastal birds—but also bald eagles, red-tailed fox, and deer. Rides range from hour-long trots to half-day adventures. Children must be at least eight years old for the beach ride or six years old for the dune trail rides. Please review the Web site for other restrictions and policies: www.oregonhorsebackriding.com. There are also six overnight RV spaces. ✉ *90241 U.S. 101 N* ☎ *541/997–7540* ⛵ *$35–$100* ▤ *AE, D, MC, V* ☉ *Daily 10–5.*

A trail from **Carl G. Washburne Memorial** park connects you to the Heceta Head Trail, which you can use to reach the Heceta Head lighthouse. The campground has 56 full hookups $22, 7 tent sites $17, hiker/biker sites $4, and 2 yurts $29. ✉ *93111 U.S. 101 N* ☎ *541/547–3416* ⊕ *www.oregonstateparks.org* ☉ *Daily.*

★ Beginning at Siltcoos Lake, where cottages float on the water, the **Siltcoos River Canoe Trail** winds through thick rain forest, past towering sand dunes, emerging some 4 mi later at white-sand beaches and the blue waters of the Pacific, where seals and snowy plovers rest. The river is a Class I with no rapids, but there are a few trees to navigate and one very short portage around a small dam.

WHERE TO EAT

$–$$ ✕ **Bridgewater Seafood Restaurant.** Freshly caught seafood—20 to 25 choices nightly—is the mainstay of this creaky-floored Victorian-era restaurant in Florence's Old Town. Whether you opt for patio dining during summer or lounge seating in winter, the varied menu of pastas, burgers, and soups offers something for everyone. A live jazz band provides some foot-tapping fun. ✉ *1297 Bay St.* ☎ *541/997–9405* ▤ *AE, D, MC, V.*

¢–$ ✕ **Mo's.** Two things you'll always find at Mo's are clear bayfront views and a creamy bowl of clam chowder. This coastal coffeeshop-esque institution has been around for more than 40 years, consistently providing fresh seafood and down-home service. ✉ *1436 Bay St.* ☎ *541/997–2185* ▤ *AE, D, MC, V.*

REEDSPORT

20 mi south of Florence on U.S. 101, 90 mi southwest of Eugene via I–5 and Hwy. 38.

The small town of Reedsport owes its existence to the Umpqua River, one of the state's great steelhead-fishing streams.

Exhibits at the **Umpqua Discovery Center** in the waterfront area give a good introduction to the Lower Umpqua estuary and surrounding region. One of the two state-of-the-art wings focuses on cultural history; the other, on natural history, has an indoor simulated walking trail, which whisks you through four seasons. *409 Riverfront Way* *541/271–4816* *www.umpquadiscoverycenter.com* *Museum $8* *June–Sept., daily 9–5; Oct.–May, daily 10–4.*

The natural forces that created the towering sand dunes along this section of the Oregon coast are explained in interpretive exhibits at the Reedsport **Oregon Dunes National Recreation Area Visitors Center.** The center, which also sells maps, books, and gifts, is a good place to pick up free literature on the area. *855 Highway Ave., south side of Umpqua River Bridge* *541/271–3611* *Free* *Mid-May–mid-Sept., daily 8–4:30; mid-Sept.–mid-May, weekdays 8–4:30.*

A herd of wild Roosevelt elk, Oregon's largest land mammal, roams within sight of the **Dean Creek Elk Viewing Area.** Abundant forage and a mild winter climate enable the elk to remain at Dean Creek year-round. The best viewing times are early morning and just before dusk. *Hwy. 38, 3 mi east of Reedsport, watch for signs* *Free* *Daily dawn–dusk.*

On Eel Lake near the town of Lakeside, the little-known **William M. Tugman State Park** is surrounded by a dense forest of spruce, cedar, fir, and alder. Recreational activities include fishing, swimming, canoeing, and sailing. A campground has 94 electrical sites $16, hiker/biker camp $4, and 16 yurts $27. *U.S. 101 S* *541/888–4902 or 800/551–6949* *www.oregonstateparks.org* *$3 per vehicle day-use fee* *Daily.*

EN ROUTE

A public pier at **Winchester Bay's Salmon Harbor,** 3¼ mi south of Reedsport, juts out over the bay and yields excellent results for crabbers and fishermen (especially those after rockfish). There's also a full-service marina with a fish market, **the Sportsmen's Cannery,** which serves a fresh seafood barbecue on weekends (from Memorial Day to Labor Day) is a must for locals in the know.

WHERE TO STAY & EAT

★ $ ✕**Pizza Ray's.** Outstanding pizza, sandwiches, and fresh fish-and-chips highlight this casual local restaurant on Winchester Bay's Salmon Harbor. Be sure and try the halibut fish-and-chips. Local delivery. It also serves breakfast and a weekend brunch *105 Coho Point Loop* *541/271–2431* *MC, V.*

¢ **Anchor Bay Inn.** In the center of Reedsport, this clean, inexpensive motel has hospitable service and easy access to the dunes. **Pros:** Frugal choice. **Cons:** Road noise. *1821 Winchester Ave., 97467* *541/271–*

2149 or 800/767–1821 ⊟541/271–1802 ⊕*www.u-s-history.com/or/
a/anchobin.htm* ⇌*21 rooms* ⚲*In-hotel: pool, laundry facilities, some
pets allowed, no elevator* ⊟*AE, D, MC, V* ⎃*CP.*

UMPQUA LIGHTHOUSE PARK

6 mi south of Reedsport on U.S. 101.

Some of the highest sand dunes in the country are found in the 50-acre
Umpqua Lighthouse Park. The first **Umpqua River Lighthouse,** built
on the dunes at the mouth of the Umpqua River in 1857, lasted only
four years before it toppled over in a storm. It took local residents 33
years to build another one. The "new" lighthouse, built on a bluff
overlooking the south side of Winchester Bay and operated by the U.S.
Coast Guard, is still going strong, flashing a warning beacon out to sea
every five seconds. The **Douglas County Coastal Visitors Center** adjacent to the lighthouse has a museum and can arrange lighthouse tours.
⊠*Umpqua Hwy., west side of U.S. 101* ☎*541/271–4118* ⎘*Donations suggested* ⊘*Lighthouse May–Sept., Wed.–Sat. 10–4, Sun. 1–4.*

COOS BAY & NORTH BEND

*27 mi south of Reedsport on U.S. 101, 116 mi southwest of Eugene,
I–5 to Hwy. 38 to U.S. 101.*

The Coos Bay–Charleston–North Bend metropolitan area, collectively
known as the Bay Area (population 25,000), is the gateway to rewarding recreational experiences. The town of Coos Bay lies next to the
largest natural harbor between San Francisco Bay and Seattle's Puget
Sound. A century ago, vast quantities of lumber cut from the Coast
Range were milled in Coos Bay and shipped around the world. Coos
Bay still has a reputation as a rough-and-ready port city, but with mill
closures and dwindling lumber reserves it has begun to look in other
directions, such as tourism, for economic prosperity.

To see the best of the Bay Area head west from Coos Bay on Newmark
Avenue for about 7 mi to **Charleston.** Though it's a Bay Area community,
this quiet fishing village at the mouth of Coos Bay is a world unto itself.
As it loops into town the road becomes the Cape Arago Highway and
leads to several oceanfront parks.

The highlight here at **Coos County Historical Society Museum** is a 1922
steam locomotive used in Coos County logging. On display are a formal 1900 parlor, a pioneer kitchen, and exhibits on Native American
history, agriculture, and industry such as logging, shipping, and mining.
⊠*1220 Sherman St., North Bend* ☎*541/756–6320 or 541/756–4847*
⎘*Free* ⊘*Tues.–Sat. 10–4.*

A placid semicircular lagoon protected from the sea by overlapping
fingers of rock and surrounded by reefs, **Sunset Bay State Park** is one
of the few places along the Oregon coast where you can swim without worrying about the currents and undertows. Only the hardiest
souls will want to brave the chilly water, however. ⊠*2 mi south of*

Charleston off Cape Arago Hwy.
☎866/888–6100 ⊕*www.oregon-
stateparks.org* ⌑*29 full hookup
$20, 34 electrical $20, 66 tent $16,
8 yurts $27, and hiker/biker camp
$4 ⊗ Daily dawn–dusk.*

At **Shore Acres State Park** an observation building on a grassy bluff
overlooking the Pacific marks
the site that held the mansion of
lumber baron Louis J. Simpson.
The view over the rugged wave-
smashed cliffs is splendid, but the
real glory of Shore Acres lies a few
hundred yards to the south, where

an entrance gate leads into what was Simpson's private garden. Beautifully landscaped and meticulously maintained, the gardens incorporate
formal English and Japanese designs. From March to mid-October the
grounds are ablaze with blossoming daffodils, rhododendrons, azaleas,
roses, and dahlias. In December the entire garden is decked out with
a dazzling display of holiday lights. ⊠*10965 Cape Arago Hwy., 1 mi
south of Sunset Bay State Park* ☎*866/888–6100* ⌑*$3 per vehicle
day-use fee* ⊗ *Daily 8–dusk.*

The distant barking of sea lions echoes in the air at **Cape Arago State
Park.** A trio of coves connected by short but steep trails, the park overlooks the **Oregon Islands National Wildlife Refuge,** where offshore
rocks, beaches, islands, and reefs provide breeding grounds for seabirds
and marine mammals. ⊠*End of Cape Arago Hwy., 1 mi south of
Shore Acres State Park* ☎*866/888–6100* ⌑*Free* ⊗ *Daily dawn–dusk*
⊕ *www.oregonstateparks.org.*

On a rock island just 12 mi offshore south of Coos Bay, **Cape Arago
Lighthouse** has had several iterations; the first lighthouse was built here
in 1866, but it was destroyed by storms and erosion. A second, built in
1908, suffered the same fate. The current white tower, built in 1934,
is 44 feet tall and towers 100 feet above the ocean. If you're here on a
foggy day, listen for its unique foghorn. The lighthouse is connected to
the mainland by a bridge. Neither is open to the public, but there's an
excellent spot to view this lonely guardian and much of the coastline.
From U.S. 101, take Cape Arago Highway to Gregory Point, where it
ends at a turnaround, and follow the short trail.

· The fragile ecosystem at **South Slough National Estuarine Research Reserve**
supports everything from algae to bald eagles and black bears. More
than 300 species of birds have been sighted at the reserve, which has
an interpretive center, guided walks (summer only), and nature trails
that give you a chance to see things up close. ⊠*Seven Devils Rd., 4 mi
south of Charleston* ☎*541/888–5558* ⌑*Free* ⊗ *Trails daily dawn–
dusk, interpretive center Memorial Day–Labor Day, daily 8:30–4:30;
Labor Day–Memorial Day, Mon.–Sat. 10–4:30.*

2

WHERE TO STAY & EAT

$–$$ ✕**Portside Restaurant.** The fish at this gem of a restaurant overlooking the Charleston boat basin comes straight to the kitchen from the dock outside. Try the steamed Dungeness crab with drawn butter. On Friday night come for the all-you-can-eat seafood buffet. The nautical furnishings—vintage bayside photos, boat lamps, navigational aids, coiled rope—reinforce the view of the harbor through the restaurant's picture windows. ⊠*8001 Kingfisher Rd. Follow Cape Arago Hwy. from Coos Bay* ☎*541/888–5544* ☐*AE, MC, V.*

$ ✕**Blue Heron Bistro.** You'll find subtle preparations of local seafood, chicken, and homemade pasta at this busy bistro. There are no flat spots on the far-ranging menu; even the innovative soups and desserts are excellent. The skylit tile-floor dining room seats about 70 amid natural wood and blue linen. The seating area outside has blue awnings and colorful Bavarian window boxes that add a festive touch. Espresso and 18 microbrewery beers are available. ⊠*100 W. Commercial St.* ☎*541/267–3933* ☐*MC, V* ☉*Closed Sun. Oct.–May.*

$$ ⌂**Coos Bay Manor.** Built in 1912 on a quiet residential street in Coos Bay, this 15-room Colonial Revival manor is listed on the National Register of Historic Places. Hardwood floors, detailed woodwork, high ceilings, and antiques and period reproductions offset the red-and-gold-flecked wallpaper. An unusual open balcony on the second floor leads to the large rooms. Innkeeper Pam Bate serves a full breakfast (included in the rates) in the wainscoted dining room. Kids are welcome. **Pros:** Very nicely kept and decorated. **Cons:** Located in town, instead of the beach. ⊠*955 S. 5th St., 97420* ☎*541/269–1224 or 800/269–1224* ⊕*www.coosbaymanor.com* ⬐*5 rooms, 3 with bath* ☐*AE, MC, V* ⦿|*BP.*

BANDON

25 mi south of Coos Bay on U.S. 101.

Referred to by some who cherish its romantic lure as Bandon-by-the-Sea, Bandon is both a harbor town and a popular vacation spot. Bandon is famous for its cranberry products, its cheese factory, as well as its artists' colony, complete with galleries and shops. Two National Wildlife Refuges, Oregon Islands and Bandon Marsh, are within the city limits.

The Bandon Dunes links-style course is a worldwide attraction, often ranked in the top three golf courses in the U.S.

It may seem odd that tiny Bandon bills itself as the cranberry capital of Oregon. But 10 mi north of town lie acres of bogs and irrigated fields where tons of the tart berries are harvested every year. Each October a Cranberry Festival, complete with a parade and a fair, takes place.

The **Bandon Historical Society Museum,** in the old City Hall building, documents the town's past through dioramas, historic photos, and artifacts, such as marine and logging equipment. ⊠*270 Fillmore St.* ☎*541/347–2164* ▱*$2* ☉*Mon.–Sat. 10–4.*

The octagonal **Coquille Lighthouse** at **Bullards Beach State Park,** built in 1896 and no longer in use, stands lonely sentinel at the mouth of the Coquille River. From the highway the 2-mi drive to reach it passes through the Bandon Marsh, a prime bird-watching and picnicking area. The beach beside the lighthouse is a good place to search for jasper, agate, and driftwood. Note: 104 full hookups, 81 electrical $20; 13 yurts $27; horse camp $16; hiker/biker camp $4. B and C camp loops are closed October 1, 2007–May 15, 2008, while construction crews add 50-amp electric service and new water and sewer connections. The A loop and Yurt Village remain open. ⊠*U.S. 101, 2 mi north of Bandon* ☎*800/551–6949, 541/347–3501 lighthouse* ⊡*Free* ⊙*Daily dawn–dusk.*

The "walk-through safari" on 21 acres of **West Coast Game Park** has free-roaming wildlife: 450 animals and 75 species including lions, tigers, snow leopards, bears, chimps, cougars, and camels, make it one of the largest wild-animal petting parks in the United States. The big attractions here are the young animals: bear cubs, tiger cubs, whatever is suitable for actual handling. It is 7 mi south of Bandon on U.S. 101. ⊠*U.S. 101* ☎*541/347–3106* ⊕*www.gameparksafari.com* ⊡*$13* ⊙*Mid-June–Labor Day, daily 9–7; spring and early fall, daily 9–5.*

WHERE TO STAY & EAT

$–$$
★
✕**Lord Bennett's.** His lordship has a lot going for him: a cliff-top setting, a comfortable and spacious dining area, sunsets visible through picture windows overlooking Face Rock Beach, and musical performers on weekends. The rich dishes include prawns sautéed with sherry and garlic and steaks topped with shiitake mushrooms. A Sunday brunch is served. ⊠*1695 Beach Loop Rd.* ☎*541/347–3663* ▭*AE, D, MC, V.*

$$$–$$$$
★
▥**Bandon Dunes Golf Resort.** This playland for the nation's golfing elite is no stranger to well-heeled athletes flying in to North Bend on private jets to play on the resort's three distinct courses. Its lodge provides a luxurious place to relax after a day on the links, with single rooms and four-bedroom suites, many with beautiful views of the famous Bandon Dunes Golf Course. There are cottages available that are designed for a quartet of golfers. Each unit includes a gathering room with fireplace, outdoor patio area, and four separate bedrooms with a king bed and private bath. There are also other lodging options available throughout the vast resort property and five different restaurant and lounge choices. Greens fees range, according to season and other factors, $210–$265 a round from May to October, $75–$220 other months. **Pros:** Great place for a foursome to get away from it all for a special golfing vacation. **Cons:** Very expensive and set apart from coastal communities. ⊠*57744 Round Lake Dr., 97411* ☎*541/347–4380 or 800/345–6008* ⊕*www.bandondunesgolf.com* ⮑*Call or consult Web site for different room descriptions* ▭*AE, DC, MC, V.*

CAPE BLANCO STATE PARK

27 mi south of Bandon on U.S. 101.

2

Cape Blanco is the westernmost point in Oregon and perhaps the windiest—gusts clocked at speeds as high as 184 mph have twisted and battered the Sitka spruces along the 6-mi road from U.S. 101 to the **Cape Blanco Lighthouse.** The lighthouse, atop a 245-foot headland, has been in continuous use since 1870, longer than any other in Oregon. No one knows why the Spaniards sailing past these reddish bluffs in 1603 called them *blanco* (white). One theory is that the name refers to the fossilized shells that glint in the cliff face. Campsites at the 1,880-acre **Cape Blanco State Park** are available on a first-come, first-served basis. Saturday-evening tours are available in summer, with a donation suggested. ⊠*Cape Blanco Rd., follow signs from U.S. 101* ☎*541/332–6774 state park* ⊕*www.oregonstateparks.org* ✉*Lighthouse tour $2. Day use free, campsites 53 electrical hookups $16; 4 cabins $35; horse camp (8 sites, 4 double corrals) $14; group tent (4 areas) $61; hiker/biker camp $4.* ⊙*Park daily dawn–dusk; lighthouse Apr.–Oct. 31, Tues.–Sun. 10–3:30.*

EN ROUTE

U.S. 101 between Port Orford and Brookings, often referred to as the "fabulous 50 miles," soars up green headlands, some of them hundreds of feet high, and past a seascape of cliffs and sea stacks. The ocean is bluer and clearer—though not appreciably warmer—than it is farther north, and the coastal countryside is dotted with farms, grazing cattle, and small rural communities. As you round a bend between Port Orford and Gold Beach you'll see one of those sights that make grown-ups groan and kids squeal with delight: a huge, open-jawed Tyrannosaurus rex, with a green brontosaurus peering out from the forest beside it.

The kids are hollering at the giant, razor-toothed Tyrannasaurus Rex by the side of the road, so you might as well pull the car over and run them through the **Prehistoric Gardens** (⊠*36848 U.S. 101* ☎*541/332–4463*), which are filled with 23 life-size replicas of these primeval giants. The complex is open daily 9 AM–dusk. Admission is $8.

PORT ORFORD

30 mi south of Bandon on U.S. 101.

The westernmost incorporated city in the contiguous United States, Port Orford is surrounded by forests, rivers, lakes, and beaches of the Pacific Ocean. The jetty at Port Orford offers little protection from storms, so every night the fishing boats are lifted out and stored on the docks. Commercial fishing boats search for crab, tuna, snapper, and salmon in the waters out of Port Orford, and diving boats gather sea urchins for Japanese markets. The area is a favorite spot for sport divers because of the near-shore, protected reef and for whale watchers in fall and early spring.

Six miles south of Port Orford, **Humbug Mountain State Park** is especially popular with campers. The park usually has warm weather, thanks to the nearby mountains, which block the ocean breezes. Windsurfing and scuba diving are popular here. Hiking trails lead to the top of Humbug Mountain. The campground has 32 electrical ($16) and 62 tent sites ($14), and a hiker/biker camp ($4). ⊠ *U.S. 101* ☎ *541/332–6774 or 800/551–6949* ⊕ *www.oregonstateparks.org* ☉ *Daily.*

WHERE TO STAY

$–$$ 🏨 **Floras Lake House by the Sea.** This cedar home rests beside freshwater Floras Lake, spring-fed and separated from the ocean by only a sand spit. It's a bit tricky to find. The owners run a windsurfing school on the lake. The interior of the house is light, airy, and comfortable, with picture windows, exposed beams, contemporary couches, and a wood-stove. Two rooms have fireplaces, and all have private deck entrances. Outside, there's a garden, with a sauna beside the lake. ⊠ *92870 Boice Cope Rd., Langlois 97450* ☎ *541/348–2573* 🖶 *541/348–9912* ⊕ *www.floraslake.com* ⇆ *4 rooms* ⚘ *In-room: no phone. In-hotel: no TV, Wi-Fi, no elevator* ⊟ *MC, V* ☉ *Closed Nov.–mid-Feb.* �𐃷 *BP.*

$ 🏨 **Home by the Sea.** One of the oldest B&Bs in Oregon, this three-story shingle house is on a headland jutting into the Pacific. A nearby path leads down to the beach. Both guest rooms have views of the ocean, as does the lower-level solarium and breakfast room, a great spot for watching whales (October–May is the best time) and winter storms. ⊠ *444 Jackson St., 97465* ☎ *541/332–2855* ⊕ *www.homebythesea. com* ⇆ *2 rooms* ⚘ *In-room: no a/c. In-hotel: laundry facilities, no-smoking rooms, Wi-Fi, no elevator* ⊟ *MC, V* �𐃷 *BP.*

GOLD BEACH

35 mi south of Cape Blanco on U.S. 101.

The fabled **Rogue River** is one of the few U.S. rivers to merit Wild and Scenic status from the federal government.

From spring to late fall an estimated 50,000 visitors descend on the town to take one of the daily jet-boat excursions that roar upstream from Wedderburn, Gold Beach's sister city across the bay, into the Rogue River Wilderness Area. Black bears, otters, beavers, ospreys, egrets, and bald eagles are seen regularly on these trips.

Gold Beach is very much a seasonal town, thriving in summer and nearly deserted the rest of the year. It marks the entrance to Oregon's banana belt, where mild, California-like temperatures take the sting out of winter and encourage a blossoming trade in lilies and daffodils.

The parking lots at **Cape Sebastian State Park** are more than 200 feet above sea level. At the south parking vista you can see up to 43 mi north to Humbug Mountain. Looking south, you can see nearly 50 mi toward Crescent City, California, and the Point Saint George Lighthouse. A deep forest of Sitka spruce covers most of the park. There's a 1½-mi walking trail. No drinking water. ⊠ *U.S. 101* ☎ *541/469–2021 or 800/551–6949* ⊕ *www.oregonstateparks.org* ✉ *Free* ☉ *Daily.*

2

WHERE TO STAY & EAT

$ ✕**Rollin 'n Dough Bakery & Bistro.** Patti Joyce greets people like family in
★ her kitchen. Not only does she create exquisite pastries, cheesecakes, and breads, but her Rollin 'n Dough Deli also carries imported cheeses, ethnic meats, and gourmet lunches. The Bistro has table service for soups, salads, pasta dishes, specialty sandwiches, and desserts. It's a little tough to find, but worth seeking out: it's on the north bank of the Rogue River, across the street from Lex's Landing. Closed at times during the winter months. ✉*94257 N. Bank Rogue* ☎*541/247–4438* ▤*MC, V* ☉*Lunch only Tues.–Sat. 10:30–3.*

$$$$ ⌂**Tu Tu' Tun Lodge.** Pronounced "too-*too*-tin," this well-known fish-
FodorśChoice ing resort is a slice of heaven on the Rogue River, 7 mi upriver from
★ Gold Beach. Owners Dirk and Laurie Van Zante believe that love is in the details, and do whatever is needed to provide the guest with a singular Northwest experience. All the units in this small establishment present rustic elegance. Some have hot tubs, others have fireplaces, and a few have both; private decks overlook the river. Two deluxe rooms feature outdoor soaking tubs with river views. Guided fishing trips and river activities here are popular, and nearby jet-boat excursions and world-class golf at Bandon Dunes are also draws. The restaurant (closed November–April) serves breakfast, lunch, and dinner; the last, open to nonguests (though reservations are hard to come by), consists of a five-course prix-fixe meal that changes nightly. **Pros:** Warm, personable, beautiful and luxurious. Delicious gourmet dining and wine tasting. Activities to suit every taste. **Cons:** No TV, not well suited for young kids. ✉*96550 N. Bank Rogue, 97444* ☎*541/247–6664* ⊟*541/247–0672* ⊕*www.tututun.com* ⇆*18 rooms, 3-bedroom house* ⌂*In-room: Wi-Fi, no TV. In-hotel: restaurant, bar, golf course* ▤*D, MC, V.*

▌**EN ROUTE** Between Gold Beach and Brookings you'll cross Thomas Creek Bridge, the highest span in Oregon. Take advantage of the off-road coastal viewing points along the 10-mi-long **Samuel H. Boardman State Park**—especially in summer, when highway traffic becomes heavy and rubbernecking can be dangerous.

BROOKINGS

27 mi south of Gold Beach on U.S. 101.

A startling 90% of the pot lilies grown in the United States come from a 500-acre area inland from Brookings. Mild temperatures along this coastal plain provide ideal conditions for flowering plants of all kinds—even a few palm trees, a rare sight in Oregon.

The town is equally famous as a commercial and sportfishing port at the mouth of the turquoise-blue **Chetco River.** Salmon and steelhead weighing 20 pounds or more swim here.

The **Chetco Valley Historical Museum,** inside a mid-19th-century stagecoach stop and trading post, has some unusual items and is worth a brief visit. An iron casting that bears a likeness to Queen Elizabeth I has led to speculation that it was left during an undocumented landing on the Oregon coast by Sir Francis Drake. On a hill near the museum stands the **World Champion Cypress Tree,** 99 feet tall and with a 27-foot circumference. ✉*5461 Museum Rd.* ☎*541/469–6651* 💲*$1 donation* ⊙*Memorial Day–Labor Day, Sat. and Sun. noon–4.*

Loeb State Park contains 53 riverside campsites and some fine hiking trails, including one that leads to a hidden redwood grove. There's also a grove of myrtlewood trees, which you'll find only in southwest Oregon and northern California. ✉*North bank of Chetco River, 10 mi east of Brookings (follow signs from U.S. 101)* ☎*541/469–2021 or 800/551–6949* ⟵*Reservations not accepted* 💲*Day use free, 48 electrical sites $16, 3 rustic cabins $35* ⊙*Daily dawn–dusk* ⊕ *www. oregonstateparks.org.*

There is plenty to see and do at **Harris Beach State Park,** where you can watch the gray whales migrate in spring and winter. Bird Island, also called Goat Island, is a National Wildlife Sanctuary and a breeding site for rare birds. There is a campground with 36 full hookups, 50 electrical $21; 63 tent $17 (cable TV hookups in selected campsites); 6 yurts $29; hiker/biker camp $4; and Wi-Fi. ✉*U.S. 101* ☎*541/469–2021 or 800/551–6949* ⊕*www.oregonstateparks.org* 💲*Free* ⊙*Daily.*

WHERE TO STAY & EAT

$–$$ ✕**Smuggler's Cove.** Fishing vessels docked in the adjacent boat basin and picture windows looking out to the sea lend a salty feel to this low-key restaurant. The daily seafood specials—usually halibut and salmon—are the best bets. For lunch try the fish-and-chips or the crab melt, and for a real dinner treat, dive into the steak and lobster for $60. ✉*16011 Boat Basin Rd.* ☎*541/469–6006* ☐*AE, D, MC, V.*

$–$$ 🏨**Chetco River Inn.** Forty acres of private forest surround this remote ★ inn 17 mi from Brookings up the North Bank Road along the Chetco River. The house stands only 100 feet from one of the cleanest rivers in the country, so you can swim in summer and fish in fall and winter. Guests also come here to hike, hunt wild mushrooms, and relax in the library or in front of the fireplace. There's a lavender and herb garden, as well. The host cooks delicious dinners that sometimes star a nickelbright salmon fresh from the stream. Rooms have thick comforters and panoramic river and forest views. ✉*21202 High Prairie Rd., 97415* ☎*541/251–0087* 🖶*541/469–4341* ⊕*www.chetcoriverinn.com* ⟿*5 rooms, 1 cottage* ♿*In-room: no a/c. In-hotel: no phone, no elevator, laundry* ☐*No credit cards* ⊙|*BP.*

$–$$ 🏨**Portside Suites.** This all-suite hotel offers spacious rooms for business or relaxing and gazing at harbor ships. Although the Portside's local charm is somewhat diminished by the asphalt parking lot it sits in the middle of, it has pleasant harbor, ocean, or river views, and fireplaces and hot tubs in some rooms. There are meeting facilities for corporate guests. ✉*16219 Lower Harbor Rd., 97415* ☎*541/469–7100 or 866/767-8111* 🖶*541/469-6022* ⊕*www.destinationbrookings.com/* ⟿*12 rooms* ♿*In-room: Wi-Fi. In-hotel: laundry facilities, no elevator* ☐*AE, D, MC, V.*

THE OREGON COAST ESSENTIALS

BY AIR

The North Bend Municipal Airport (OTH) is the only airport on the coast serviced by a major carrier; Horizon Air flies into North Bend from Portland four times daily.

Contacts **Horizon Air** (☎*800/547-9308*). **Newport Municipal Airport** (☎*800/424-3655 or 541/867-7422*). **North Bend Municipal Airport** (☎*541/756-8531*).

BY CAR

U.S. 101 runs the length of the coast, sometimes turning inland for a few miles. The highway enters coastal Oregon from Washington State at Astoria and from California near Brookings. U.S. 30 heads west from Portland to Astoria. U.S. 20 travels west from Corvallis to Newport. Highway 126 winds west to the coast from Eugene. Highway 42 leads west from Roseburg toward Coos Bay.

VISITOR INFORMATION

Contacts **Astoria–Warrenton Area Chamber of Commerce** (✉*111 W. Marine Dr., Astoria 97103* ☎*503/325-6311 or 800/875-6807* ⊕*www.oldoregon. com*). **Bay Area Chamber of Commerce** (✉*145 Central Ave., Coos Bay 97420* ☎*541/266-0868* ⊕*www.oregonsbayareachamber.com*). **Brookings Harbor Chamber of Commerce** (✉*16330 Lower Harbor Rd., 97415* ☎*541/469-3181 or 800/535-9469* ⊕*www.brookingsor.com*). **Cannon Beach Chamber of Commerce** (✉*207 N. Spruce St., 97110* ☎*503/436-2623* ⊕*www.cannonbeach.org*). **Florence Area Chamber of Commerce** (✉*290 U.S. 101, 97439* ☎*541/997-3128* ⊕*www.florencechamber.com*). **Greater Newport Chamber of Commerce** (✉*555 S.W. Coast Hwy., 97365* ☎*503/265-8801 or 800/262-7844* ⊕*www. newportchamber.org*). **Lincoln City Visitors Center** (✉*801 S.W. U.S. 101, Suite 1 97367* ☎*541/996-1274 or 800/452-2151* ⊕*www.oregoncoast.org*). **Seaside Visitors Bureau** (✉*7 N. Roosevelt Ave., 97138* ☎*503/738-3097 or 888/306-2326* ⊕*www.seasideor.com*). **Tillamook Chamber of Commerce** (✉*3705 U.S. 101 N, 97141* ☎*503/842-7525* ⊕*www.tillamookchamber.org*). **Yachats Area Chamber of Commerce** (✉*241 Hwy. 101, 97498* ☎*541/547-3530 or 800/929-0477* ⊕*www.yachats.org*).

THE WILLAMETTE VALLEY & WINE COUNTRY

During the 1940s and 1950s, researchers at Oregon State University concluded that the Willamette Valley—the wet, temperate trough between the Coast Range to the west and the Cascade Range to the east—had an unsuitable climate for the propagation of varietal wine grapes. Evidently, they were wrong.

The faultiness of the researchers' techniques has been proven by the success of Oregon's burgeoning wine industry. More than 100 wineries dot the Willamette (pronounced "wil-*lam*-it") Valley, the bulk of them in Yamhill County in the northern part of the state. Two-dozen more wineries are scattered between the Umpqua and Rogue valleys (near Roseburg and Ashland, respectively) to the south. Their products—mainly cool-climate varietals like pinot noir, chardonnay, and Johannesberg Riesling—have won gold medals in blind tastings against the best wines of California and Europe.

Points of interest can be found on the Willamette Valley & Wine Country and Salem maps.

FOREST GROVE

24 mi west of Portland on Hwy. 8.

Forest Grove is surrounded by stands of Douglas firs and giant sequoia, including the largest giant sequoia in the state. To head to the wineries from here, head south from Forest Grove on Highway 47 and watch for the blue road signs between Forest Grove, Gaston, and Yamhill.

With 1,800 students, **Pacific University** is on a shady campus that provides a respite from sightseeing. It was founded in 1849, making it one of the oldest educational institutions in the western United States. Concerts and special events are held in McCready Hall in the Taylor-Meade Performing Arts Center. The school also has a College of Optometry. ⊠*2043 College Way* ☎*503/357–6151* ⊕*www. pacificu.edu* ☎*Free* ⊙*Daily.*

> **TOP 5**
>
> 1. Siuslaw National Forest—the breathtaking greenery is about as Oregon as it gets.
>
> 2. Evergreen Aviation Museum—a mecca for airplane enthusiasts.
>
> 3. Yamhill County wineries—it's impossible to select one, so the fun is in the seeking.
>
> 4. C'est la Vie Inn—witness the special care and detail placed into restoring this landmark property.
>
> 5. Silver Falls State Park—the falls, surrounding hikes, and recreation for every season makes this a special Willamette Valley destination.

A beautiful area in the Coast Range foothills, **Scoggin Valley Park and Henry Hagg Lake** has a 15-mi-long hiking trail that surrounds the lake. Bird-watching is best in spring. Recreational activities include fishing, boating, waterskiing, and picnicking, and a 10½-mi, well-marked bicycle lane parallels the park's perimeter road. ⊠*Scoggin Valley Rd.* ☎*503/846–8715* ⊕*www.co.washington.or.us* ☎*$5* ⊙*Daily dawn–dusk; open Mar.–Nov.*

WHERE TO STAY

$$ ▦ **McMenamins Grand Lodge.** On 13 acres of pastoral countryside, this converted Masonic rest home has accommodations that run from bunk-bed rooms to a three-room fireplace suite. The lodge's sturdy 1922 brick buildings also include pubs that serve several McMenamins draft beers. Rooms are furnished with period antiques such as oak night stands and porcelain sinks. For those not staying in the bunkhouse, rates include use of the European-style soaking pool, continental breakfast during the week, and a full breakfast on weekends. At the Compass Room Theater, feature films are screened nightly; kids accompanied by a guardian are permitted at the early show. ⊠*3505 Pacific Ave., 97116*

Willamette Valley & Wine Country

WASHINGTON

Columbia River

PACIFIC OCEAN

CALIFORNIA

Ft. Stevens State Park
Astoria
Ft. Clatstop National Memorial
26 101
Tillamook Head
Seaside
Ecola State Park
Cannon Beach
Oswald West State Park
53
26
TILLAMOOK STATE FOREST
Nehalem Bay
Manzanita
Garibaldi
Hood River
84
Tillamook Bay
Cape Meares State Park
Forest Grove
6
Tillamook
Lake Oswego
Portland
Mt. Hood
Cape Lookout State Park
Dundee & Yamhill
Tigard
26
Government Camp
Cape Kiwanda State Natural Area
McMinnville
Oregon City
Pacific City
5
Aurora
MT. HOOD NATIONAL FOREST
Lincoln City
Grand Ronde
Willamette Mission State Park
Silverton
Depoe Bay
Silver Falls State Park
Mt. Jefferson
Yaquina Head
Salem see detail map
22
Newport
Albany
20
WILLAMETTE NATIONAL FOREST
Waldport
Corvallis
20
Yachats
34
Sisters
Cape Perpetua
99E
126
242 (closed in winter)
Heceta Head
SIUSLAW NATIONAL FOREST
36
McKenzie Bridge
Florence
126
Springfield
McKenzie River Highway
McKenzie Pass
Mt. Bachelor
Eugene
Cottage Grove
DESCHUTES NATIONAL FOREST
Winchester Bay
58
Oakridge
Waldo Lake
OREGON DUNES NAT'L. REC. AREA
Reedsport
38
Willamette Pass
Umpqua Lighthouse Park
58
97
North Bend
Oakland
Charleston
Steamboat
UMPQUA NATIONAL FOREST
Coos Bay
Cape Arago State Park
Roseburg
138
Bandon
Winston
UMPQUA VALLEY
CRATER LAKE NATIONAL PARK
Myrtle Point
Wildlife Safari
42
Canyonville
Crater Lake
Port Orford
Rogue River
Prospect
97
ROGUE RIVER NATIONAL FOREST
Agness
Gold Beach
Grants Pass
Upper Klamath Lake
SISKIYOU NATIONAL FOREST
199
5
Medford
101
Klamath Falls
Pistol River
238
Cave Junction
Jacksonville
Loeb State Park
46
Ashland
Oregon Caves Nat'l. Monument
Mt. Ashland
Harbor

0   30 miles

0   30 kilometers

☎503/992–9533 or 877/992–9533 ⊕www.thegrandlodge.com ⟿77 rooms ♿In-hotel: bars, spa ▭AE, D, DC, MC, V.

LAKE OSWEGO

9 mi south of Portland.

Contrary to the intentions of its early founders, who built iron smelters in an effort to turn the area into "the Pittsburgh of the West," Lake Oswego is an affluent residential community immediately south of Portland, between the Willamette and Tualatin rivers. The Willamette Shore Trolley, operated by the Oregon Electric Railway Historical Society, carries passengers along the Willamette between downtown Lake Oswego and the Riverplace area at the south end of Portland's downtown.

Framed by an open fireplace on one end and a reflecting pond on the other, **Millennium Plaza Park** is the site of many community events as well as a Saturday farmer's market. ✉200 1st St., ☎503/675–2549 ⊗Mid-May–mid-Oct., Sat. 8–1.

Originally built in 1887, the **Willamette Shore Trolley**—one standard and one double-decker trolley, both of museum quality—carries passengers on a 45-minute ride to Portland along a scenic 7-mi route, which you can travel one-way or round-trip; you'll take in Mt. Hood and the wooded banks of the Willamette River. In summer there are four departures daily from Lake Oswego. Reservations are recommended. In December there are special Lights Along the River excursions. ✉311 State St., ☎503/697–7436 ⊕www.trainweb.org/oerhs/wst.htm ⊡$10 round-trip ⊗Early May–Memorial Day, weekends; Memorial Day–Labor Day, Thurs.–Sun.; Labor Day–end of Sept., Fri.–Sun.; Oct., Sat.

WHERE TO EAT

$$–$$$ ✗ **Tucci.** This small, intimate Italian dining sanctuary serves succulent, fresh scallops and tasty local meats dressed with tantalizing sauces. A full-service lounge offers a bounty of wines and spirits, and the warm chocolate polenta cake's silky decadence is incomparable. Reserve a table overlooking the river, select a bottle of wine, and settle in for a memorable experience. ✉220 A Ave. ☎503/697–3383 ⊕www.tucci.biz ⊗ Closed weekends ▭AE, D, DC, MC, V.

TIGARD

10 mi southwest of Portland on Interstate 5.

This Portland suburb has made great strides in attracting visitors with its festivals and shopping options. Its old downtown Main Street is enjoying a rebirth with antique shops, espresso bars, and fashionable eateries.

On the banks of the Tualatin River, 79-acre **Cook Park** is where suburbanites gather to enjoy a variety of team sports. The park also has

2

hoseshoe pits, a fishing dock, small boat ramp, picnic shelters, and several walking trails and bike paths. Wildlife includes great blue herons and river otters. Cook Park is located south of Durham Road at the end of 92nd Avenue near Tigard High School ⊠*17005 S.W. 92nd Ave.* Each June, activity at Cook Park reaches a fever pitch with the three-day **Tigard Festival of Balloons** (⊕www.tigardballoon.org), which draws more than 20,000 people to enjoy dozens of hot-air ballons and other events morning, noon and night.

WHERE TO EAT

$ ✕ **Café Allegro.** Located in the heart of Old Town Tigard, Café Allegro serves authentic Italian cuisine in a cozy bistro setting. The rustic decor provides a funky backdrop to tasty fresh salads, hearty pasta dishes and pizzas, and a variety of desserts. The Greek fettuccine is a tantalizing choice, and the small-football-size meat calzone is a mighty plunge into decadence. ⊠*12386 S.W. Main St.,* ☎*503/684–0130* ⊕*www.cafeallegrotigard.com* ▤*AE, D, MC, V* ◌*No lunch Sun.*

¢ ✕ **Sanchez Taqueria.** It may not look like much from the outside, but the Mexican food at this simple family restaurant has no peer. From its mole and crispy sopes to its carnita enchiladas, the food is fresh and sumptuously authentic. Wash it all down with a cup of orchata, a drink made of rice, milk, and cinnamon. ⊠*13050 S.W. Pacific Hwy.,* ☎*503/684–2838* ▤*MC, V.*

SHOPPING

Bridgeport Village has diverted more cars off of Interstate 5 than any other site in the Willamette Valley. With 500,000 square feet of upscale shops, boutiques, eateries, and a luxury spa, the outdoor mall is a magnet for residents and visitors. It also has the largest multiscreen cinema in the state, including an IMAX theater. Take Interstate 5 to exit 290 and go west. The mall is on the corner of S.W. 72nd and Boones Ferry Rd. ⊠*7455 S.W. Bridgeport Rd.,* ☎*503/968–8940* ⊕*www.bridgeport-village.com* ◌*Mon–Sat., 10–9, Sun. 11–6.*

OREGON CITY

19 mi southeast of Portland.

Historic Oregon City was the destination for thousands of pioneer families, who traveled the Oregon Trail from St. Louis, Missouri, to the promised land on the western frontier. Several of Oregon's prominent early residents built homes in Oregon City on the Willamette River's east bank, where the river plunges 40 feet over a basaltic ridge at Willamette Falls. The End of the Oregon Trail Interpretive Center debuted in 1993 to commemorate the Trail's 150th anniversary. Dozens of historic homes, churches, and other buildings have been restored and now offer tours into times past. More than 26,000 people live here today; the city is the seat of Clackamas County, one of three counties that make up the Portland metropolitan area.

Resembling three large covered wagons, the **End of the Oregon Trail Interpretive Center,** 19 mi south of Portland, is hard to miss. The history of the Oregon Trail is brought to life through theatrical shows, exhibits, and hands-on activities. Maps and guidebooks are available if you're charting a trip along the Oregon Trail from one end to the other. ⊠*1726 Washington St.* ☎*503/657–9336* ⊕*www.endoftheoregontrail.org* ⌖*Store free, show $7* ⊗*Tues.–Sat. 11–4, Sun. noon–4.*

An officer for a fur-trading company, Dr. John McLoughlin lost his job when he forwarded supplies to needy Oregon Trail pioneers, but his presence and deeds in the area are remembered at **McLoughlin House National Historic Site**, the mansion he moved to with his family in 1846. The site is perhaps the key historic home in the city. ⊠*713 Center St.* ☎*503/656–5146* ⊕*www.mcloughlinhouse.org* ⌖*Free* ⊗*Wed.–Sat. 10–4, Sun. 1–4.*

Along the Clackamas River and only 45 minutes from Portland, **Milo McIver State Park** is a popular rafting, canoeing, and kayaking area. There's also a 27-hole disc golf course. An annual Civil War reenactment is staged here in April; 300 actors participate. Camping permitted: 44 electrical $17; 9 walk-in tent $15. ⊠*Hwy. 213 N to Hwy. 212 and Hwy. 211 SE* ☎*503/630–7150 or 800/551–6949* ⊕*www.oregonstateparks.org* ⌖*Day use $3 per vehicle* ⊗*Mar.–Nov., daily.*

The Willamette Falls are created when the Willamette River at Oregon City spills 40 feet over a basaltic ridge. The **Willamette Falls Locks** were built in the early 1870s to move river traffic around the falls. ⊠*On Willamette River, in West Linn* ☎*503/656–3381* ⊗*Daily; information center June–Oct., daily 9:30–4.*

WHERE TO EAT

¢ ✕**McMenamins Pub.** At this bustling family favorite you can order a Communication Breakdown Burger—Tillamook cheddar, onions, mushrooms, and peppers—among others, including a few meatless options. Couple your burger or sandwich with a creative ale such as chocolaty Black Rabbit Porter or raspberry Ruby Ale. Kid-pleasing comfort foods include grilled cheese, corn dogs, and peanut butter and jelly. The pub becomes more of a bar scene after 10 PM. ⊠*102 9th St.,* ☎*503/655–8032* ▭*AE, D, MC, V.*

DUNDEE & YAMHILL

31 mi southwest of Portland on Hwy. 99 W.

The lion's share (more than 90%) of the U.S. hazelnut crop is grown in Dundee, a haven of produce stands and wine-tasting rooms. The 25 mi of Highway 18 between Dundee and Grande Ronde, in the Coast Range, roll through the heart of the Yamhill Valley wine country. What used to be a pleasant drive through quaint Dundee is now a traffic bottleneck nightmare, as the one road is the main artery from Lincoln City to suburban Portland. Until the Dundee bypass is built, weekday visits are best.

WINERIES

★ Pinot noir, chardonnay, and sparkling wines are among the specialties vintaged at **Argyle Winery** (✉ *691 Hwy. 99 W,* ☎ *503/538–8520 or 888/427–4953* ⊕ *www.argylewinery.com*). The winery is open daily

ⓒ 11–5.**Sokol Blosser** (✉ *5000 Sokol Blosser La., 3 mi west of Dundee off*

Fodor'sChoice *Hwy. 99 W* ☎ *503/864–2282 or 800/582–6668* ⊕ *www.sokolblosser.*

★ *com*), one of Oregon's oldest and largest wineries, has a tasting room and walk-through vineyard with a self-guided tour that explains the grape varieties—pinot noir and chardonnay, among others. Open daily 10–4.

WHERE TO EAT

$$ ✕ **Tina's.** Chef–proprietors Tina and David Bergen bring a powerful

Fodor'sChoice one-two punch to this Dundee favorite that often lures Portlanders

★ away from their own restaurant scene. The couple shares cooking duties—Tina does the baking and is often on hand to greet you—and David brings his experience as a former caterer and employee of nearby Sokol Blosser Winery to the table, ensuring that you have the right glass of wine—and there are many—to match your course. Fish and game vie for attention on the country French menu—entrées might include grilled Oregon salmon or Alaskan halibut, or a braised rabbit, local lamb, or tenderloin. Avail yourself of any special soups, particularly if there's corn chowder in the house. A lunch menu includes soup, sandwiches, and Tina's grilled hamburger, made with free-range beef. Service is as intimate and laid-back as the interior. A double fireplace divides the dining room, with heavy glass brick shrouded by bushes on the highway side, so you're not bothered by the traffic on Highway 99. ✉ *760 Hwy. 99 W,* ☎ *503/538–8880* ⊕ *www.tinasdundee.com* ▭ *AE, D, MC, V.*

$–$$ ✕ **Dundee Bistro.** This highly regarded, 80-seat restaurant run by the Ponzi wine family uses Northwest organic foods such as Draper Valley chicken and local foods such as locally produced wines, fruits, vegetables, nuts, mushrooms, fish, and meats. Vaulted ceilings provide an open feeling inside, warmed by abundant fresh flowers and the works of local Oregon artists. ✉ *100-A S.W. 7th St., Dundee* ☎ *503/554–1650* ▭ *AE, DC, MC, V.*

MCMINNVILLE

39 mi southwest of Portland on Hwy. 99 W.

The Yamhill County seat, McMinnville lies at the center of Oregon's burgeoning wine industry. There is a larger concentration of wineries in Yamhill County than in any other area of the state, and the vineyards in the McMinnville area, including some in the town of Dayton to the east, also produce the most award-winning wines. Among the varieties are chardonnay, pinot noir, and pinot gris. Most of the wineries in the area offer tours and tastings. McMinnville's downtown area, with a pleasantly disproportionate number of bookstores and art galleries for its size, is well worth exploring; many of the historic district buildings, erected 1890–1915, are still standing and are remarkably well maintained.

Fodor'sChoice   The claim to fame of the **Evergreen Aviation Museum** is the Howard
★   Hughes' *Spruce Goose,* on permanent display here. If you can take your eyes off the *Spruce Goose* there are also more than 45 historic planes and replicas here from the early years of flight and World War II, as well as the postwar and modern eras. There's a museum store and café—the Spruce Goose Café, of course—and there are ongoing educational programs and special events. ✉*500 N.E. Michael King Smith Way,* ☎*503/434–4180* ⊕*www.sprucegoose.org* ⬚*$13* ⊙*Daily 9–5, closed holidays.*

A perennial football powerhouse in NCAA Division III, **Linfield College** is an outpost of brick and ivy amid McMinnville's farmers'-market bustle. The college, founded in 1849 and the second oldest in Oregon, hosts the **International Pinot Noir Celebration** (☎*503–883–2200*) at the end of July and beginning of August (⊕*www.ipnc.org/*) ✉*900 S.E. Baker St* ⊕*www.linfield.edu.*

NEED A BREAK?   Try Tillamook ice cream on a waffle cone at **Serendipity Ice Cream** (✉ **502 N.E. 3rd St.** ☎ *503/474–9189*), an old-fashioned ice-cream parlor in the former Cook's Hotel; the building was constructed in 1886.

WINERIES

★   Its original tasting area was the back of a 1952 Ford pick-up. Its Gamay noir label notes that the wine gives "more enjoyment to hamburgers [and] fried chicken." And the winery's current architecture still includes a trailer affectionately referred to as the "mobile chateau," already on the property when winemaker Myron Redford purchased the winery in 1974. These modest and whimsical touches underscore what seems to be Redford's philosophy for **Amity Vineyards** (✉*18150 Amity Vineyards Rd. SE, Amity* ☎*503/835–2362* ⊕*www.amityvineyards.com*): take your winemaking a lot more seriously than you take yourself. Taste the pinot blanc for Redford's take on the grape, and also linger in the tasting room to sample the pinot noir and the gewürztraminer, among other varieties. Chocolates made with Amity's pinot noir and other products are available for sale. Hours are daily, October–May noon–5 and June–September 11–5.

In Dundee's Red Hills, **Domaine Serene** (✉*6555 N.E. Hilltop La., Dayton* ☎*503/864–4600* ⊕*www.domaineserene.com*) is a world-class five-level winery and a well-regarded producer of Oregon pinot noir, as well as chardonnay and syrah. It's open Wednesday–Sunday 11–4.

If Oregon presents the problem of so many wines, so little time, the **Oregon Wine Tasting Room and The Bellevue Market** (✉*19690 S.W. Hwy. 18,* ☎*503/843–3787* ⊙*Daily 11–5:45*) provides a handy one-stop tasting venue, with 150 wines from 70 Oregon wineries, some of which rarely open to the public. There's also a gallery and deli on the premises.

WHERE TO STAY & EAT

$–$$$ ✕ **Joel Palmer House.** Joel Palmer was an Oregon pioneer, and his 1857 home in Dayton is now on the National Register of Historic Places. There are three small dining rooms, each seating about 15 people. The chef specializes in wild-mushroom dishes; a popular starter is Heidi's three-mushroom tart. Entrées include rib eye au poivre, rack of lamb, breast of duckling, and coq au vin; desserts include apricot-walnut bread pudding and crème brûlée. Or, if you really, really like mushrooms, have your entire table order Jack's Mushroom Madness Menu, a five-course extravaganza for $75.00 per person. ⊠ *600 Ferry St., Dayton* ☎ *503/864–2995* ⊕ *www.joelpalmerhouse.com* ▭ *AE, D, DC, MC, V* ☾ *Closed Sun. and Mon. No Lunch.*

$$ ✕ **Nick's Italian Cafe.** Modestly furnished but with a voluminous wine ★ cellar, Nick's is a favorite of area wine makers. The food is spirited and simple, reflecting the owner's northern Italian heritage. A five-course prix-fixe menu changes nightly for $45. À la carte options are also available. ⊠ *521 N.E. 3rd St.* ☎ *503/434–4471* 🖶 *503/472–0440* ⌖ *Reservations essential* ▭ *AE, MC, V* ☾ *Closed Sun., Mon. No lunch.*

$ 🏠 **Mattey House Bed & Breakfast.** Built in 1982 by English immigrant
Fodor's Choice Joseph Mattey, a local butcher, this Queen Anne Victorian mansion—
★ on the National Register of Historic Places—has several cheerful areas that define it. Downstairs is a cozy living room jammed with antiques, dual dining areas—a parlor with white wicker and a dining room with elegant furniture—and a porch with a swing. The four upstairs rooms are whimsically named after locally grown grape varieties—riesling, chardonnay, pinot noir, and Blanc de Blanc—and are decorated in keeping with the character of those wines: the chardonnay room, for instance, has tall windows and crisp white furnishings, and the pinot noir has dark-wood pieces and reddish wine accents. A small balcony off the upstairs landing is perfect for sipping a glass of wine on a cool Yamhill Valley evening. Proprietors Jack and Denise will ensure you're comfortably ensconced, familiar with the local history, surrounding vineyards, and the antiquing scene, and holding that glass of wine: in case you don't remember where you are, the house, on 10 acres, is bound by an orchard and its own vineyard, which the couple maintains. If your imprudent enough to duck out before the fine full breakfast, which might include poached pears with raspberry sauce, frittatas, and Dutch-apple pancakes, Denise or Jack will have pastry and hot coffee available before you set off. A rule barring children under 10 is waived if you're renting the entire house. ⊠ *10221 N.E. Mattey La., off Hwy. 99 W, ¼ mi south of Lafayette, 97128* ☎ *503/434–5058* 🖶 *503/434–6667* ⊕ *www.matteyhouse.com* 📷 *4 rooms* 🅰 *In-room: no phone. In-hotel: no-smoking rooms* ▭ *AE, MC, V* ⍜ *BP.*

¢–$ 🏠 **Hotel Oregon.** Built in 1905, this historic facility—the former Elberton Hotel—was rescued from decay by the McMenamins chain, renovated in 1998, and reopened the following year. It's four stories of brick; rooms have tall ceilings and high windows. The hotel is outfitted in late Victorian furnishings, but its defining design element is its art. The hotel is whimsically decorated by McMenamins' half-dozen staff artists: around every corner, even in the elevator, you'll find art—sometimes serene, often times bizarre and haunting—as well as photos and sayings scribbled on the walls. The Oregon has a first-floor pub serving three meals a day, a rooftop bar with an impressive view of Yamhill County, and a cellar wine bar, resembling a dark speakeasy, that serves only area vintages. ⊠*310 N.E. Evans St., 97128* ☎*503/472–8427 or 888/472–8427* ⊕*www.mcmenamins.com* ☞*42 rooms* ⚐*In-hotel: bars* ▭*AE, D, DC, MC, V.*

GRAND RONDE

24 mi southwest of McMinnville on Hwy. 18.

Grand Ronde is mostly a stopping place for people en route to the coast who want to spend time at the town's Indian-operated casino. In July and August the Confederated Tribes of Grand Ronde hold powwows; the August event draws 12,000 to 15,000 people.

On the campus of the Confederated Tribes of Grand Ronde, the **West Valley Veterans Memorial** pays tribute to all war veterans, but in particular is a marker for the 190,000 Native American veterans. ⊠*9615 Grand Ronde Rd.,* ☎*503/879–5211 or 800/422–0232* ⊕*www.grandronde.org.*

WHERE TO STAY

$ ▦ **Spirit Mountain Casino and Lodge.** Its location on Highway 18, one of the main routes from Portland to the ocean, makes this casino (owned and operated by the Confederated Tribes of the Grande Ronde Community of Oregon) a popular stop. Only 90 minutes from Portland and 45 minutes from Salem, this is the biggest casino resort in Oregon. The 90,000-square-foot casino has more than a thousand slots, as well as poker and blackjack tables, roulette, craps, Pai Gow poker, keno, bingo, and off-track betting. Big-name comedians and rock and country musicians perform in the 1,700-seat concert hall, and there's an arcade for the kids. There's complimentary shuttle service from Portland and Salem. Dining options include an all-you-can-eat buffet, a deli, and a café. Rooms have Pacific Northwest and Native American themes, with carved wooden headboards and Pendleton Woolen Mills bedding. ⊠*27100 S.W. Hwy. 18, Grande Ronde 97396* ☎*503/879–3764 or 888/668–7366* ⊟*503/879–3938* ⊕*www.spirit-mountain.com* ☞*254 rooms* ⚐*In-hotel: 5 restaurants, room service, bar* ▭*D, MC, V.*

SILVER FALLS STATE PARK

★ *26 mi east of Salem, Hwy. 22 to Hwy. 214.*

Hidden amid old-growth Douglas firs in the foothills of the Cascades, Silver Falls is the largest state park in Oregon (8,700 acres). South Falls, roaring over the lip of a mossy basalt bowl into a deep pool 177 feet below, is the main attraction here, but 13 other waterfalls—half of them more than 100 feet high—are accessible to hikers. The best time to visit is in the fall, when vine maples blaze with brilliant color, or early spring, when the forest floor is carpeted with trilliums and yellow violets. There are picnic facilities and a day lodge; in winter you can cross-country ski. Camping facilities include 52 year-round electrical $20; 45 tent (tent sites closed Oct. 31–Apr. 1) $16; group tent (3 areas) $61; horse camp $16–$48; 14 cabins $35. ⊠ *20024 Silver Falls Hwy. SE, Sublimity* ☎ *503/873–8681 or 800/551–6949* ⊕ *www. oregonstateparks.org.* ⊠ *$3 per vehicle* ⊙ *Daily dawn–dusk*

SALEM

❶–❾ *24 mi from McMinnville, south on Hwy. 99 W and east on Hwy. 22, 45 mi south of Portland on I–5.*

Salem has a rich pioneer history, but before that it was the home of the Calapooia Indians, who called it Chemeketa, which means "place of rest." Salem is said to have been renamed by missionaries. According to one story, the name is an Anglicized form of the Hebrew "shalom," or peace, while another story suggests it was named specifically for Salem, Massachusetts. Although trappers and farmers preceded them in the Willamette Valley, the Methodist missionaries had come in 1834 to minister to Native Americans, and they are credited with the founding of Salem. In 1842 they established the first academic institution west of the Rockies, which is now known as Willamette University.

Salem became the capital when Oregon achieved statehood in 1859 (Oregon City was the capital of the Oregon Territory). Today, with a population of more than 135,000, Salem serves as the seat to Marion County as well as the home of the state fairgrounds. Government ranks as a major industry here, while the city's setting in the heart of the fertile Willamette Valley stimulates rich agricultural and food-processing industries. Extensive nearby farmlands are devoted to the cultivation of vegetables, berries, hops, and flowers, and more than a dozen wineries are in or near Salem. The main attractions in Salem are west of I–5 in and around the Capitol Mall.

Numbers in the margin correspond to the Salem map.

WHAT TO SEE

❶ A. C. Gilbert's Discovery Village. This is a different kind of kids' museum, celebrating the life and the inventions of A. C. Gilbert, including Erector sets and American Flyer trains. The first floor and grounds are wheelchair accessible. ⊠ *116 Marion St.,* ☎ *503/371–3631* ⊕ *www. acgilbert.org* ⊠ *$5.50* ⊙ *Mon.–Sat. 10–5, Sun. noon–5.*

❼ Bush's Pasture Park. These 105 acres of rolling lawn and formal English gardens include the remarkably well preserved **Bush House,** an 1878 Italianate mansion at the park's far western boundary. It has 10 marble fireplaces and virtually all of its original furnishings. The house and gardens are on the National Register of Historic Places. **Bush Barn Art Center,** behind the house, exhibits the work of Northwest artists and has a sales gallery. ⊠ *600 Mission St. SE* ☎ *503/363–4714* ⊕ *www. salemart.org* ⊠ *$4* ⊙ *Mar. and Apr., Tues.–Sun. 1–4; May–Sept., Tues.–Sun. 1–5; Oct.–Dec., Tues.–Sun. 1–4; Jan., Feb. call for times.*

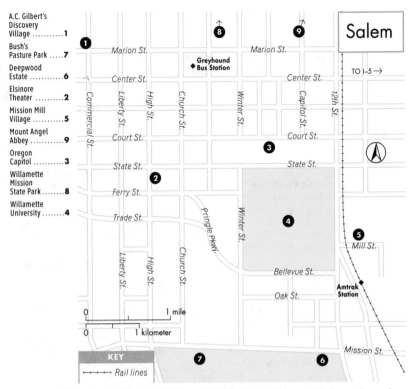

Salem

6 **Deepwood Estate.** This fanciful 1894 Queen Anne–style house has splendid interior woodwork and original Povey stained glass. The ornate, multigabled home was designed by prominent northwest architect W.C. Knighton, and the fine gardens were created in 1929 by landscape designers Elizabeth Lord and Edith Schryver. The estate is on the National Register of Historic Places. ✉*1116 Mission St. SE* ☎*503/363–1825* 💵*$4* ⏰*May–Sept., Sun.–Fri. noon–5; Oct.–Apr., Tues.–Sat. noon–5.*

2 **Elsinore Theatre.** This flamboyant Tudor Gothic vaudeville house opened on May 28, 1926, with Edgar Bergen in attendance. Clark Gable (who lived in Silverton) and Gregory Peck performed on stage. The theater was designed to look like a castle, with a false stone front, chandeliers, ironwork, and stained-glass windows. It's now a lively performing arts center with a busy schedule of bookings, and there are concerts on its Wurlitzer pipe organ. Group Tours for $3.00 per person can be arranged. ✉*170 High St. SE,* ☎*503/375–3574* 🖷*503/375–0284* ⊕*www.elsinoretheatre.com.*

5 **Mission Mill Village.** The **Thomas Kay Woolen Mill Museum** complex (circa 1889), complete with working water wheels and millstream, looks as if the workers have just stepped away for a lunch break. Teasel gigging, napper flock bins, and the patented Furber double-acting napper are but a few of the machines and processes on display. The **Jason Lee House,** the **John D. Boon Home,** and the **Methodist Parsonage** are also part of the village. There is nothing grandiose about these early pioneer homes, the oldest frame structures in the Northwest, but they reveal a great deal about domestic life in the wilds of Oregon in the 1840s. The adjacent **Marion County Historical Society Museum** (☎ *503/364–2128*) displays pioneer and Calapooia Indian artifacts. ⌧ *Museum complex, 1313 Mill St. SE* ☎ *503/585–7012* ⊕ *www. missionmill.org* ⌑ *$8, includes tour* ☉ *Daily 10–5* ☞ *Guided tours of houses and woolen mill museum are given when possible.*

❾ **Mount Angel Abbey.** On a 300-foot-high butte, this Benedictine monastery was founded in 1882. It's the site of one of two American buildings designed by Finnish architect Alvar Aalto. A masterpiece of serene and thoughtful design, Aalto's library opened its doors in 1970, and has become a place of pilgrimage for students and aficionados of modern architecture. ⌧ *18 mi from Salem, east on Hwy. 213 and north on Hwy. 214* ☎ *503/845–3030* ⊕ *www.mtangel.edu* ⌑ *Free.*

❸ **Oregon Capitol.** A brightly gilded bronze statue of the *Oregon Pioneer* stands atop the 140-foot-high Capitol dome, looking north across the Capitol Mall. Built in 1939 with blocks of gray Vermont marble, Oregon's Capitol has an elegant yet austere neoclassical feel. East and west wings were added in 1978. Relief sculptures and deft historical murals soften the interior. Tours of the rotunda, the House and Senate chambers, and the governor's office leave from the information center under the dome. ⌧ *900 Court St.* ☎ *503/986–1388* ⊕ *www.leg.state. or.us* ⌑ *Free* ☉ *Weekdays 8–5.*

❽ **Willamette Mission State Park.** Along pastoral lowlands by the Willamette River, this serene park holds the largest black cottonwood tree in the United States. A thick-barked behemoth by a small pond, the 265-year-old tree has upraised arms that bring to mind J. R. R. Tolkien's fictional Ents. Site of Reverend Jason Lee's 1834 pioneer mission, the park also offers quiet strolling and picnicking amid an old orchard and along the river. The Wheatland Ferry, at the north end of the park, began carrying covered wagons across the Willamette in 1844, using pulleys. ⌧ *Wheatland Rd., 8 mi north of Salem, I-5 Exit 263* ☎ *503/393–1172 or 800/551–6949* ⊕ *www.oregonstateparks.org* ⌑ *Day use $3* ☉ *Daily 8* AM–*dusk.*

❹ **Willamette University.** Behind the Capitol, across State Street but half a world away, are the brick buildings and grounds of Willamette University, the oldest college in the West. Founded in 1842, Willamette has long been a breeding ground for aspiring politicians (former Oregon senators Mark O. Hatfield and Robert Packwood are alumni). **Hatfield Library,** built in 1986 on the banks of Mill Stream, is a handsome brick-and-glass building with a striking campanile; tall, prim **Waller Hall,** built in 1841, is one of the oldest buildings in the Pacific Northwest. ⌧ *Information desk, Putnam University Center, Mill St.* ☎ *503/370–6300* ⊕ *www.willamette.edu* ☉ *Weekdays 8–5.*

**OFF THE
BEATEN
PATH**

Schreiner's Iris Gardens. Some call the Willamette Valley near Salem the "Bulb Basket of the Nation." Irises and tulips create fields of brilliant color in near-perfect growing conditions. Schreiner's Iris Gardens, established in 1925, ships bulbs all over the world; during the short spring growing season (mid-May–early June), the 10-acre display gardens blaze with fancifully named varieties such as Hello Darkness, Well Endowed, and Ringo. ⊠ *3625 Quinaby Rd. NE, north from Salem take I–5 to Exit 263, head west on Brooklake Rd., south on River Rd., and east on Quinaby* ☎ *503/393–3232* ⊕ *www.schreinersgarden.com* ☜ *Free* ☼ *Dawn–dusk during blooming season; the height is May.*

WHERE TO STAY & EAT

¢–$$ ✕ **DaVinci.** Salem politicos flock to this two-story downtown restaurant for Italian-inspired dishes cooked in a wood-burning oven. No shortcuts are taken in the preparation, so don't come if you're in a rush. But if you're in the mood to linger over seafood and fresh pasta that's made on the premises, this may be your place. The wine list is one of the most extensive in the Northwest; the staff is courteous and extremely professional. Wine tasting and live jazz Thursday at 6 PM. ⊠ *180 High St.* ☎ *503/399–1413* ▤ *AE, DC, MC, V* ☼ *No lunch.*

$$ ⊞ **A Creekside Garden Inn.** Nine blocks from the center of town, the Creekside is on ½ acre of flower gardens bordering Mill Creek, beautifully on display from the spacious porch out back. The garden theme spills into each of the guest rooms in this 1938 Mt. Vernon–inspired Colonial, which are decorated with lovely garden themes. Some nice personal and business touches include movies and popcorn in the evenings, a fax and copy machine, and meeting space. Willamette University and the Capitol are within walking distance. There's a two-night minimum during holidays and events at Willamette University. ⊠ *333 Wyatt Ct. NE, 97301* ☎ *503/391–0837 or 800/949–0837* ⊟ *503/391–1713* ⊕ *www.salembandb.com* ☜ *5 rooms* ☖ *In-room: no phone (some). In-hotel: Wi-Fi, no elevator* ▤ *MC, V* ⎖ *BP.*

ALBANY

20 mi from Salem, south on I–5 and west on U.S. 20.

Known as the grass-seed capital of the world, Albany is believed to be home to one of the largest and most varied collections of historic buildings in Oregon. Some 700 historic buildings, scattered over a 100-block area in three districts, include every major architectural style in the United States since 1850. The area is listed on the National Register of Historic Places. Eight covered bridges can also be seen on a half-hour drive from Albany.

Pamphlets and maps for self-guided walking and driving tours are available from the **Albany Visitors Association.** (⊠ *250 Broadalbin SW #110* ☎ *541/928–0911 or 800/526–2256* ⊕ *www.albanyvisitors.com*).

The first frame house in Albany was Monteith House, built in 1849. Now the **Monteith House Museum,** restored and filled with period furnishings and historic photos, it is widely thought to be the most authentic restoration of a Pacific Northwest pioneer-era home. ⊠*518 2nd Ave. SW,* ☎*800/526–2256* ⊕*www.albanyvisitors.com* 🏷*Donation* ⊘*Mid-June–mid-Sept., Wed.–Sat. noon–4; mid-Sept.–mid-June, by appointment.*

WHERE TO EAT

$–$$ **Sybaris.** This fine bistro in Albany's historic downtown is receiving

FodorsChoice   enthusiastic reviews. Owners Matt and Janel Bennett strive to ensure

★   that most of their menu's ingredients, including the lamb, eggs, and vegetables, are raised within 10 mi. Even the huckleberries to make the ice cream are gathered in secret locations by their mushroom picker. With a monthly rotating menu, it serves upscale, flavorful cuisine at reasonable prices. ⊠*442 1st Ave. W,* ☎*541/928–8157* ⊕*www.sybarisbistro.com* ⊘ *Tues.–Thurs. 5–9, Fri. and Sat. 5–10. Reservations advised* ⊘*Closed Sun. and Mon.* ⊟*AE, D, DC, MC, V.*

CORVALLIS

10 mi southwest of Albany on U.S. 20, 35 mi from Salem, south on I–5 and west on Hwy. 34.

To some, Corvallis is a brief stopping place along the way to Salem or Portland. To others, it's a small town that gives you a chance to escape from the bigger cities. Driving the area's economy are a growing engineering and high-tech industry, a burgeoning wine industry, and more traditional local agricultural crops, such as grass and legume seeds. Corvallis is home to the Beavers and Oregon State University. It offers plenty of outdoor activities as well as scenic attractions, from covered bridges to wineries and gardens.

The **Osborn Aquatic Center** is not the site of your ordinary lap pool. There are water slides, a water channel, water cannons, and floor geysers. ⊠*1940 N.W. Highland Dr.* ☎*541/766–7946* 🏷*$4* ⊘*June–Sept.*

The pace quickens in Corvallis around the 400-acre campus of **Oregon State University,** west of the city center. Established as a land-grant institution in 1868, OSU has more than 19,000 students, many of them studying the agricultural sciences and engineering. ⊠*15th and Jefferson Sts.* ☎*541/737–1000* ⊕*oregonstate.edu.*

There are more than 20,000 pioneer and Native American artifacts on display at **Benton County Historical Museum.** There are also a cut-glass and porcelain collection, the reconstruction of a Victorian parlor, and a costume exhibit. ⊠*1101 Main St., Philomath* ☎*541/929–6230* ⊕*www.bentoncountymuseum.org* 🏷*Free* ⊘*Tues.–Sat. 10–4:30.*

★   The highest point in the Coast Range, at 4,097 feet, Mary's Peak, within **Siuslaw National Forest,** offers panoramic views of the Cascades, the Willamette Valley, and the rest of the Coast Range. On a clear day you can see as far as the Pacific Ocean. There are several picnicking areas, more than 10 mi of hiking trails, and a small campground. There are stands of noble fir and alpine meadows. The forest, which is 2 mi from Corvallis, includes the Oregon Dunes National Recreation Area, and the Cape Perpetua Interpretive Center. People usually access the Forest using one of several major highways: highways 26, 6, and 18 all access the North Central Coast, highways 20 and 34 access Newport and the Central Coast, Highway 126 accesses Florence and the north part of the Oregon Dunes, and Highway 38 accesses Reedsport and the southern section of the Oregon Dunes. ⊠4077 S.W. Research Way, ☎541/750–7000 ⊕www.fs.fed.us/r6/siuslaw ☑Free ⊙Daily dawn–dusk.

WHERE TO EAT

$–$$ ✕**Michael's Landing.** In a former railroad depot overlooking the Willamette River, this restaurant is known for its large menu of steak, seafood, chicken, and pasta dishes. Try the Northwest salmon baked in a wine and butter sauce. Sunday brunch includes omelets, quiche, and pancakes; and there's a good kids' menu. ⊠603 N.W. 2nd St., ☎541/754–6141 ☰AE, D, DC, MC, V.

MCKENZIE BRIDGE

58 mi east of Eugene on Hwy. 126.

On the beautiful McKenzie River, the town of McKenzie Bridge is surrounded by lakes, waterfalls, covered bridges, and wilderness trails in the Cascades. Fishing, skiing, backpacking, and rafting are among the most popular activities in the area.

A 1,240-acre reservoir in the Willamette National Forest, **Blue River Dam and Lake** has miles of forested shoreline. From May through September, boats are launched from ramps at Saddle Dam and Lookout Creek. Recreational activities include fishing, swimming, waterskiing, and camping at Mona Campground. ⊠Forest Rd. 15 in Willamette National Forest ☎541/822–3381 ☑Free ⊙June–Sept., daily.

Four miles outside of McKenzie Bridge is **Cougar Dam and Lake,** the highest embankment dam ever built by the Army Corps of Engineers—452 feet above the stream bed. The resulting reservoir, on the South Fork McKenzie River, covers 1,280 acres. The public recreation areas are in the Willamette National Forest. A fish hatchery is in the vicinity. You can visit the dam year-round, but the campgrounds are open only from May to September. ⊠Forest Rd. 19 in Willamette National Forest ☎541/822–3381 ☑Free ⊙June–Sept., daily; most areas closed rest of yr.

MCKENZIE RIVER HIGHWAY

East of Eugene on Hwy. 126.

Highway 126, as it heads east from Eugene, is known as the McKenzie River Highway. Following the curves of the river, it passes grazing lands, fruit and nut orchards, and the small riverside hamlets of the McKenzie Valley. From the highway you can glimpse the bouncing, bubbling, blue-green McKenzie River, one of Oregon's top fishing, boating, and white-water rafting spots, against a backdrop of densely forested mountains, splashing waterfalls, and jet-black lava beds. The small town of McKenzie Bridge marks the end of the McKenzie River Highway and the beginning of the 26-mi McKenzie River National Recreation Trail, which heads north through the Willamette National Forest along portions of the Old Santiam Wagon Road.

OFF THE
BEATEN
PATH

McKenzie Pass. Just beyond McKenzie Bridge, Highway 242 begins a steep, 22-mi eastward climb to McKenzie Pass in the Cascade Range. The scenic highway, which passes through the Mt. Washington Wilderness Area and continues to the town of Sisters (⇨ *Central Oregon*), is generally closed October–June because of heavy snow. Novice motorists take note, this is not a drive for the timid: it's a challenging exercise in negotiating tight curves at quickly fluctuating, often slow speeds— the skid marks on virtually every turn attest to hasty braking—so take it slow, and don't be intimidated by cars on your tail itching to take the turns more quickly.

EUGENE

63 mi south of Corvallis on I–5.

Eugene was founded in 1846 when Eugene Skinner staked the first federal land-grant claim for pioneers. Back then it was called Skinner's Mudhole. Wedged between two landmark buttes—Skinner and Spencer—along the Willamette River, Eugene is the culinary, cultural, sports, and intellectual hub of the central Willamette Valley. The home of the University of Oregon is consistently given high marks for its "livability." A large student and former-student population lends Eugene a youthful vitality and countercultural edge. Full of parks and oriented to the outdoors, Eugene is a place where bike paths are used, pedestrians *always* have the right-of-way, and joggers are so plentiful that the city is known as the Running Capital of the World.

Shopping and commercial streets surround the Eugene Hilton and the Hult Center for the Performing Arts, the two most prominent downtown buildings.

WHAT TO SEE

Alton Baker Park. Named after the community newspaper's publisher, the Alton Baker Park is a place of many community events. Live music is performed in summer. There's fine hiking and biking at Alton Baker on the banks of the Willamette River. A footpath along the river runs the length of the park. Also worth seeing is the Whilamut Natural Area, an open space with 13 "talking stones," each with an inscription. Also there is a very nice dog section. ⊠ *Centennial Blvd. east of Ferry St. Bridge* ☎ *541/484–5307 or 541/682–2000* ☉ *Daily 6* AM*–11* PM.

Eugene Saturday Market. Every Saturday between April and November, local craftspeople, farmers, and chefs provide cheap eats and nifty arts and crafts at this outdoor market. No pets. ⊠ *8th Ave. and Oak St.*

☎ *541/686–8885* ⊕*www.eugenesaturdaymarket.org* ⊠*Free* ⊙*Apr. 7–Nov. 10, Sat. 10–5.*

★ **5th Street Public Market.** A former chicken-processing plant is the site of this popular shopping mall, filled with small crafts, art, and gifts stores. Dining includes sit-down restaurants, decadent bakeries, and the international diversity of the second-floor food esplanade. ⊠*5th Ave. and High St.* ☎*541/484–0383* ⊕*www.5stmarket.com* ⊙*Shops Mon.–Sat. 10–7, Sun. 10–6.*

George E. Owen Memorial Rose Garden. Three thousand roses bloom June–September at this 9-acre garden west of Skinner Butte Park, along the Willamette River. Magnolia, cherry, and oak trees dot the grounds. ⊠*300 N. Jefferson St.* ☎*541/682–4833* ⊠*Free* ⊙*Daily 6 AM–11 PM.*

Hendricks Park. This quiet park east of the University of Oregon is at its most glorious in May, when its towering rhododendrons and azaleas blossom in shades of pink, yellow, red, and purple. From the university's Franklin Boulevard gate, head south on Agate Street, east on 19th Avenue, south on Fairmont Boulevard, and east on Summit Avenue. ⊠*Summit and Skyline Aves.* ⊕*www.friendsofhendrickspark.org.*

Lane County Historical Museum. Collections dating from the 1840s to the present are in a 14,000-square-foot building. Exhibits include period rooms, vehicles, early trades, Oregon Trail and early settlement, historic photographs, and memorabilia from the 1920s and 1930s. ⊠*740 W. 13th Ave.* ☎*541/682–4242* ⊕*www.lanecountyhistoricalsociety.org* ⊠*$2* ⊙*Tues.–Sat. 10–4.*

Maude Kerns Art Center. The oldest church in Eugene, two blocks east of the University of Oregon, is the site of this arts facility, which exhibits contemporary fine art and crafts. ⊠*1910 E. 15th Ave.* ☎*541/345–1571* ⊠*Suggested donation $3* ⊙*Weekdays 10–5:30, Sat. noon–4.*

☼ **Science Factory.** Formerly the Willamette Science and Technology Center (WISTEC) and still known to locals by its former name, Eugene's imaginative, hands-on museum assembles rotating exhibits designed for curious young minds. The adjacent **planetarium,** one of the largest in the Pacific Northwest, presents star shows and entertainment events. ⊠*2300 Leo Harris Pkwy.* ☎*541/682–7888 museum, 541/461–8227 planetarium* ⊕*www.sciencefactory.org* ⊠*$7 for both Science Hall and Planetarium, $4 each* ⊙*Wed.–Sun. noon–4* ⊙*Closed Oregon Duck home football games and major holidays.*

Skinner Butte Park. Skinner Butte Park, rising from the south bank of the Willamette River, provides the best views of any of the city's parks; it also has the greatest historic cachet, since it was here that Eugene Skinner staked the claim that put Eugene on the map. Skinner Butte Loop leads to the top of Skinner Butte, from which **Spencer Butte,** 4 mi to the south, can be seen. The two main trails to the top of Skinner Butte traverse a sometimes difficult terrain through a mixed-conifer forest. ⊠*2nd Ave. and High St.* ☎*541/682–5521* ⊠*Free* ⊙*Daily 10 AM–midnight.*

University of Oregon. The true heart of Eugene lies southeast of the city center at its university (⊕www.uoregon.edu). Several fine old buildings can be seen on the 250-acre campus; **Deady Hall,** built in 1876, is the oldest. More than 400 varieties of trees grace the bucolic grounds, along with outdoor sculptures that include *The Pioneer* and *The Pioneer Mother.* The two bronze figures by Alexander Phimster Proctor were dedicated to the men and women who settled the Oregon Territory and less than a generation later founded the university.

Eugene's two best museums are affiliated with the university. The **Jordan Schnitzer Museum of Art** next to the library, underwent a major renovation and expansion, nearly doubling its size. It includes galleries featuring American, European, Korean, Chinese, and Japanese art. (⊠*1430 Johnson La.* ☎*541/346–3027* ⊕*www.uoma.uoregon.edu* 🖃*$5*). Relics of a more local nature are on display at the **University of Oregon Museum of Natural History** (⊠*1680 E. 15th Ave.* ☎*541/346–3024* ⊕*www.natural-history.uoregon.edu* 🖃*$3*), devoted to Pacific Northwest anthropology and the natural sciences. Its highlights include the fossil collection of Thomas Condon, Oregon's first geologist, and a pair of 9,000-year-old sagebrush sandals.

University of Oregon main entrance ⊠*Agate St. and Franklin Blvd.* 🖃*$3 suggested donation for both museums* ☉*Art museum Wed. noon–8, Thurs.–Sun. noon–5; natural history museum Wed.–Fri. noon–5, weekends 11–5.*

OFF THE BEATEN PATH

Waldo Lake. Nestled in old-growth forest, Waldo Lake is famed as a remarkably clean and pristine body of water. The lake is accessible only after a short hike, so bring comfortable shoes. ⊠*From Eugene take Hwy. 58 to Oakridge and continue toward Willamette Pass; follow signs north to Waldo Lake.*

WHERE TO EAT

$$–$$$

★ ✕**Marché.** The name translates into "market," meaning that this renowned Eugene restaurant works with a dozen local farmers to bring the freshest, most organic local food to the table. Specialties include salmon, halibut, sturgeon, and beef tenderloin, braised pork shoulders, and outstanding local oysters. Reservations recommended. ⊠*296 E. 5th Ave.,* ☎*541/342–3612* ▤*AE, D, MC, V.*

$$–$$$

✕**Sweetwaters.** The dining room at the Valley River Inn, which overlooks the Willamette at water level, specializes in Pacific Northwest cuisine. Try the salmon with Szechuan peppercorn crust and cranberry vinaigrette or the grilled beef fillet with Oregon blue-cheese crust. There is a bar area outside as well as a deck for open-air dining. There's a kids' menu and a Sunday brunch. Reservations recommended. ⊠*1000 Valley River Way* ☎*541/687–0123* ▤*AE, D, DC, MC, V.*

$–$$

Fodor'sChoice

★ ✕**Red Agave.** Two local women managed to establish this cozy romantic restaurant in an old building that at one point was a refuse dump, and the result is a hard-to-categorize winner that has Mexican and Latino influences. Menu items might include sesame-crusted salmon with chipotle barbecue glaze, which you can consider washing down with a tamarind margarita. Flans, like much of the menu, are seasonal;

try the Kahlua flan or the orange flan with chocolate in the middle. ⊠*454 Willamette St.* ☎*541/683–2206* ▭*DC, MC, V* ⊘*Closed Sun. No lunch.*

¢–$
★ ✕**Excelsior Café.** The expert cuisine enhances the appealing European elegance of this restaurant, bar, and bistro-style café across from the University of Oregon. The chef uses only fresh local produce, but Excelsior is best known for its meats, such as a delectable osso bucco Milanese. The menu changes according to the season, but staples include delicious salads and soups, gnocchi, grilled chicken, broiled salmon, and sandwiches. The dining room, shaded by blossoming cherry trees in the spring, has a quiet, understated feel. There's outdoor seating on the patio. Serves breakfast, lunch, dinner, bistro lounge and Sunday brunch. ⊠*754 E. 13th Ave.* ☎*541/342–6963 or 800/321–6963* ⊕*www.excelsiorinn.com.* ▭*AE, D, DC, MC, V.*

¢–$
★ ✕**Turtles Bar & Grill.** Parking around this spot is scarce, and there aren't enough tables, but the food is worth the obstacles. The barbecue entrées, particularly the pulled-pork sandwich, are tasty, and the staff is quite friendly. ⊠*2692 Willamette St.* ☎*541/465–9038* ▭*AE, D, DC, MC, V.*

WHERE TO STAY

$$$ ▤**Campbell House.** Built in 1892 on the east side of Skinner Butte, Campbell House is one of the oldest structures in Eugene. Restored with fastidious care, the luxurious B&B is surrounded by an acre of landscaped grounds. The parlor, library, and dining rooms have their original hardwood floors and curved-glass windows. Differing architectural details, building angles, and furnishings (a mixture of century-old antiques and reproductions) lend each of the rooms a distinctive personality. One suite has a whirlpool. The room rates include a full breakfast including fresh-baked pastries. The house now serves dinner seven nights a week, with a prix-fixe offering or à la carte. ⊠*252 Pearl St., 97401* ☎*541/343–1119 or 800/264–2519* ⊟*541/343–2258* ⊕*www. campbellhouse.com* ⟿*12 rooms, 7 suites, 1 cottage* ⌂*In-room: DVD or VCR. In-hotel: Wi-Fi, no elevator* ▭*AE, D, MC, V.*

$$$ ▤**Valley River Inn.** At this inn on the banks of the Willamette River, some rooms have an outdoor patio or balcony, some have river or pool views, and concierge rooms have access to a private lounge. The location is splendid, and current renovation should elevate the hotel's appearance to match its surroundings. The inn's restaurant is the popular Sweetwaters *(see review above).* ⊠*1000 Valley River Way, 97401* ☎*541/687–0123 or 800/543–8266* ⊟*541/682–0289* ⊕*www. valleyriverinn.com* ⟿*257 rooms* ⌂*In-hotel: restaurant, bar, pool, gym, bicycles, concierge, laundry service, airport shuttle, free parking* ▭*AE, D, DC, MC, V.*

$$
Fodor'sChoice
★ ▤**C est la Vie Inn.** Listed on the National Register of Historic Places, the restored 1891 Queen Anne Victorian bed and breakfast has been updated to provide old-world comfort with modern-day amenities. The inn serves as an excellent hub for enjoying Eugene, as it is close to downtown shops, restaurants, galleries, and bicycle paths. The Hult Center for the Performing Arts and the University of Oregon campus are also within walking distance. Each guestroom is luxurious and romantic,

with private bath and individual cooling/heating controls. The parlor and dining rooms are ornately decorated in period furnishings, and the inn offers concierge services for dry cleaning, theater tickets, and restaurant reservations. ✉*1006 Taylor St., 97402* ☎*866/302–3014 or 541/302–3014* ⊕*www.cestlavieinn.com* ⇆*3 rooms, 1 suite* ♿*In-room: DVD, Wi-Fi. In-hotel: no elevator, no-smoking rooms* ▭*AE, D, MC, V.*

$$ ⊡**Excelsior Inn.** This small hotel in a former fraternity house manifests a
★ quiet sophistication commensurate with lodgings found in quaint European villages. Crisply detailed, with cherrywood doors and moldings, it has rooms furnished in a refreshingly understated manner, each with a marble-and-tile bath and some with fireplaces. The rates include a delicious breakfast. The ground-level Excelsior Café is one of Eugene's best restaurants. ✉*754 E. 13th Ave., 97401* ☎*541/342–6963 or 800/321–6963* 🖷*541/342–1417* ⊕*www.excelsiorinn.com* ⇆*14 rooms* ♿*In-hotel: Wi-Fi., restaurant, bar, parking* ▭*AE, D, DC, MC, V.*

NIGHTLIFE & THE ARTS

Hult Center for the Performing Arts. This is the locus of Eugene's cultural life. Renowned for the quality of its acoustics, the center has two theaters that are home to Eugene's symphony and opera. ✉*1 Eugene Center, at 7th Ave. and Willamette St.* ☎*541/682–5087, 541/682–5000 tickets, 541/682–5746 24-hr event recording* ☉*Call for hrs.*

Conductor Helmuth Rilling leads the internationally known **Oregon Bach Festival** (☎*541/682–5000 for tickets, 800/457–1486 for information* ⊕*www.bachfest.uoregon.edu*) every summer. Concerts, chamber music, and social events—held mainly in Eugene at the Hult Center and the University of Oregon School of Music but also in Corvallis and Florence—are part of this 17-day event.

In May and August the **the John G. Shedd Institute for the Arts** (☎*541/434–7000 tickets, 541/687–6526* ⊕*www.ofam.org*) presents concerts at the Hult Center and in parks around Eugene

SPORTS & THE OUTDOORS

BIKING & JOGGING The **River Bank Bike Path,** originating in Alton Baker Park on the Willamette's north bank, is a level and leisurely introduction to Eugene's topography. It's one of 120 mi of trails in the area. **Prefontaine Trail,** used by area runners, travels through level fields and forests for 1½ mi.

SKIING **Willamette Pass** (✉*Hwy. 58, 69 mi southeast of Eugene* ☎*541/345–7669 or 800/444–5030*), 6,666 feet high in the Cascade Range, packs an annual average snowfall of 300 inches atop 29 runs. The vertical drop is 1,563 feet. Four triple chairs and one double chair service the downhill ski areas, and 13 mi of Nordic trails lace the pass. Facilities here include a ski shop; day care; a bar and restaurant; and Nordic and downhill rentals, repairs, and instruction.

SHOPPING

Tourists coming to the Willamette Valley, especially to Eugene, can't escape without experiencing the 5th Street Public Market in downtown Eugene. There are plenty of small crafts shops, and the food mall yields many cuisines, including vegetarian, pizza, and seafood. **Smith Family Bookstore** (⊠ *768 E. 13th* ☎ *541/345–1651* ⊠ *525 Willamette St.* ☎ *541/343–4717*) is a wonderful resource for used books. **Valley River Center** (⊠ *Delta Hwy. and Valley River Dr.,* ☎ *541/683–5511*) is the largest shopping center between Portland and San Francisco. There are five department stores, including Meier & Frank and JCPenney, plus 130 specialty shops and a food court.

COTTAGE GROVE

20 mi south of Eugene on I–5.

With more than a half dozen historic "creek covers" close by, Cottage Grove's self-proclaimed title as the Covered Bridge Capital of Oregon is well deserved. Of particular note is the Chambers Railroad Bridge, the only one of its kind west of the Mississippi River, built in 1925 to carry logs to mill. Cottage Grove's historic downtown, through which the Willamette River flows, has attracted moviemakers and light-industrial developers alike.

Formerly a mining area, **Brice Creek Trail** has been transformed into a path for hikers and bikers, though it is recommended for only intermediate and advanced riders. ⊠ *Trailhead is 25 mi southeast of Cottage Grove. From Cottage Grove, I–5's Exit 174, go right on Brice Creek Rd. No. 2470 (19 mi)* ☎ *541/942–5591* ☉ *Daily.*

A mile outside Cottage Grove in the Coast Range foothills, **Chateau Lorane Winery** produces some unusual varieties, including Grignolino, Durif, pinot meunier, and Baco noir. A 25-acre lake and picnic area make this a popular spot for picnics and large events. ⊠ *27415 Siuslaw River Rd., Lorane* ☎ *541/942–8028* ⊕ *www.chateaulorane.com* ☉ *June–Sept., daily noon–5; Oct–May, Sat. and Sun noon–5; also by appointment.*

Oregon has the largest collection of **covered bridges** in the western United States. The Willamette Valley has more than 34 of the wooden structures. There are six bridges on a loop drive just outside Cottage Grove. The widest bridge in the state is off Highway 58 near Lowell. Four others are nearby. ☎ *503/986–3514* ⊕ *www.cottagegrove.net* ▣ *Free* ☉ *Daily.*

WILLAMETTE VALLEY & WINE COUNTRY ESSENTIALS

BY AIR

You can fly into Portland's International Airport and begin your travels at the northern part of the Willamette Valley, or explore the southern end first by flying into Eugene's Mahlon Sweet Airport. The latter is served by America West, Horizon, Skywest, and United/United Express. Another option is to mix your itineraries and use both airports, as the flight from Portland to Eugene is a mere 40 minutes. There are also smaller airports scattered throughout the valley.

2

BY CAR

I–5 runs north–south the length of the Willamette. Many Willamette Valley attractions lie not too far east or west of I–5. Highway 22 travels west from the Willamette National Forest through Salem to the coast. Highway 99 travels parallel to I–5 through much of the Willamette Valley. Highway 34 leaves I–5 just south of Albany and heads west, past Corvallis and into the Coast Range, where it follows the Alsea River. Highway 126 heads east from Eugene toward the Willamette National Forest; it travels west from town to the coast.

VISITOR INFORMATION

Contacts **Chehalem Valley Chamber of Commerce (Newberg, Dundee and St. Paul)** (⊠ *415 E. Sheridan, 97132* ☎ *503/538–2014* 🖷 *503/538–2463* ⊕ *www. newberg.org*). **Corvallis Convention and Visitors Bureau** (⊠ *553 N.W. Harrison, 97330* ☎ *541/757–1544 or 800/334–8118* ⊕ *www.visitcorvallis.com*). **Cottage Grove Chamber of Commerce** (⊠ *700 E. Gibbs, Suite C, 97424* ☎ *541/942–2411* ⊕ *www.cgchamber.com*). **Forest Grove Chamber of Commerce** (⊠ *2417 Pacific Ave., 97116* ☎ *503/357–3006* ⊕ *www.fgchamber.org*). **Lake Oswego Chamber of Commerce and Visitor's Center** (⊠ *242 B St., 97034* ☎ *503/636-3634* ⊕ *www. lake-oswego.org*). **Lane County Convention and Visitors Association (Eugene)** (⊠ *754 Olive St., Eugene 97401* ☎ *541/343–6335 or 800/547–5445* ⊕ *www. visitlanecounty.org*). **McMinnville Chamber of Commerce** (⊠ *417 N.W. Adams St., 97128* ☎ *503/472–6196* ⊕ *www.mcminnville.org*). **North Plains Area Chamber of Commerce** (ᗑ *Box 152, North Plains 97133* ☎ *503/647–2207* ⊕ *www.north-plainschamberofcommerce.org*). **Oregon City Chamber of Commerce** (⊠ *1201 Washington St., 97045* ☎ *503/656–1619 or 800/424–3002* ⊕ *www.oregoncity. org*). **Oregon Wine Country/ Willamette Valley Visitors Association** (⊠ *553 N.W. Harrison Blvd., Corvallis 97330* ☎ *866/548–5018* ⊕ *www.oregonwinecountry. org*). **Philomath Area Chamber of Commerce** (ᗑ *Box 606, Philomath 97370* ☎ *541/929–2454* 🖷 *541/929–4420* ⊕ *www.philomathchamber.org*). **Salem Convention & Visitors Center** (⊠ *1313 Mill St. SE, 97301* ☎ *503/581–4325 or 800/874–7012* ⊕ *www.travelsalem.com*). **Tigard Area Chamber of Commerce** (⊠ *12345 SW Main St., 97223* ☎ *503/639–1656* ⊕ *www.tigardchamber. org*). **Yamhill Valley Visitors Association** (ᗑ *Box 774, McMinnville 97128* ☎ *503/883–7770* ⊕ *www.yamhillvalley.org*).

THE COLUMBIA GORGE & MT. HOOD AREA

Updated
by Kimberly
Gadette

Volcanoes, lava flows, Ice Age floodwaters, and glaciers were Nature's tools of choice to carve a breathtaking 80-mi landscape now called the Columbia River Gorge. Proof of human civilization here reaches back 31,000 years, and excavations near the Dalles have uncovered evidence that salmon fishing is a 10,000-year-old tradition in these parts.

In 1805 Lewis and Clark discovered the Columbia River to be the only waterway that led to the Pacific. Their first expedition was a treacherous route through wild, plunging rapids, but their successful navigation set a new exodus in motion. By the 1850s almost 12,000 new settlers had arrived in the Oregon Territory.

Sightseers, hikers, and skiers have long found contentment in this robust region, officially labeled a national scenic area in 1986. Highlights of the Columbia River Gorge include Multnomah Falls, Bonneville Dam, and the rich orchard land of Hood River—a windsurfing hub. To the south of Hood River are all the alpine attractions of the 11,245-foot-high Mt. Hood. From Portland, the Columbia Gorge–Mt. Hood Scenic Loop is the easiest way to see the gorge and the mountain. Take I–84 east to Troutdale and follow U.S. 26 to Bennett Pass (near Timberline), where Highway 35 heads north to Hood River; then follow I–84 back to Portland. Or make the loop in reverse

Winter weather in the Columbia Gorge and the Mt. Hood area is

> **TOP 5**
>
> 1. Lakecliff Bed & Breakfast: perched on a cliff amid ferns and fir trees overlooking the Gorge.
>
> 2. Stonehedge Gardens restaurant: luxuriant garden terraces and amazing food.
>
> 3. Timberline Lodge: Play peek-a-boo with Mt. Hood on the ascending 6-mi approach; stand under the 96-foot stone chimney in the lobby.
>
> 4. Bonneville Hot Springs Resort & Spa: for its dramatic lobby and redwood-paneled lap pool.
>
> 5. Multomah Falls: Easy to climb for a close-up inspection.

much more severe than in Portland and western Oregon. At times I–84 may be closed because of snow and ice. If you're planning a winter visit, be sure to carry plenty of warm clothes. Note that chains are a requirement for traveling over mountain passes. In spring the gorge's 77 waterfalls, including 11 that cascade over 100 feet, are especially energetic—and photogenic. In early fall look for maple, tamarack, and aspen trees fairly bursting with brilliant red and gold color. But no matter the season, the basalt cliffs, the acres of lush forest, and that glorious expanse of water make the gorge worth visiting time and again.

GRESHAM

10 mi east of Portland off I–84.

Gresham was founded in the mid-1800s by westward-bound pioneers who cut a trail in the wilderness as they descended Mt. Hood. Today it remains a well-traveled passageway between the Columbia River Gorge and the Mt. Hood recreation areas.

With a population of about 97,745, Gresham is Oregon's fourth-largest city and is recognized as Portland's largest suburb to the east, with light manufacturing, technology, and agriculture forming its employment infrastructure. Gresham calls itself the "city of music" for the festivals that have flourished there. The first and most notable is the annual Mt. Hood Jazz Festival (⊕ *www.mthoodjazz.org*) hosted by Gresham and Mt. Hood Community College in early August.

Learn about this city's logging and agricultural roots at **Gresham History Museum,** in the beautiful former Carnegie Library building built

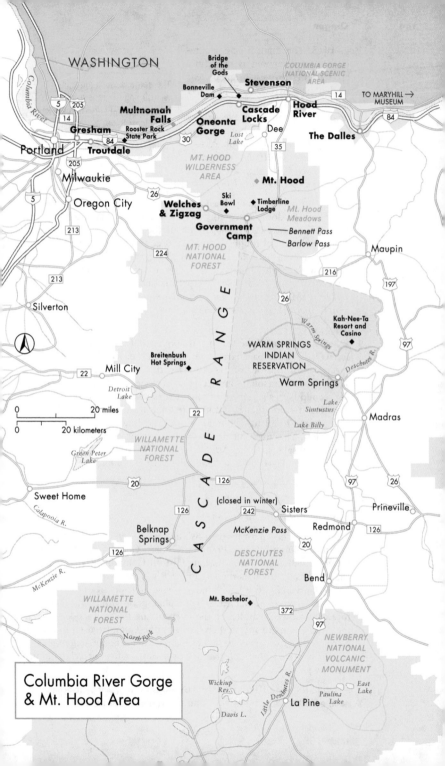

Columbia River Gorge
& Mt. Hood Area

in 1913. The English Tudor exterior is complemented by an artfully crafted interior with original clear leaded-glass windows and finely finished wood and trim. Authentic artifacts and an extensive gallery of more than 3,000 photos are on display. Even the bathroom has its own gallery. ⊠*410 N. Main Ave.* ☎*503/661–0347* ⊒*Donation suggested* ☉*Tues.–Sat. 10–4.*

In downtown Gresham, **Main City Park** has more than 17 acres of tree-filled outdoor space for picnics, basketball, and other recreational activities. A 4½-mi stretch of the **Springwater Trail Corridor,** which runs through the park and connects to a regional 40-mi loop, is a multi-use site for walking, jogging, and biking, and can accommodate wheelchairs. East of the I–205, a soft-surface path is set aside for equestrian use. The park is open from sunrise to sunset. ⊠*219 S. Main Ave.* ⊕*www.portlandonline.com/parks/finder/index. cfm?PropertyID=679&action=ViewPark.*

WHERE TO EAT

$ ✕**Rose's Tea Room.** Take tea in this converted 1928 home while being serenaded in three-part harmony by Rose and her two daughters. Rose's specialty is a four-tier royal high tea with some contemporary twists. The first tier is seasonal soup served with scones and Devonshire cream; the second is fresh fruit, traditional tea sandwiches, and savories; the third has desserts that might include English sticky toffee pudding or tarts. Leave room for the final tier, a chocolate course, with truffles and cakes. The lunch menu also has a selection of other sandwiches, soups, and salads. ⊠*155 S.E. Vista Ave.* ☎*503/665–7215* ⊒*MC, V* ☉*Tues.–Sat. 11–4* ☉*Closed Sun. and Mon. No dinner.*

TROUTDALE

13 mi east of Portland on I–84.

Troutdale is known for its great fishing spots, as well as antiques stores and the Columbia Gorge Premium Outlets. Continuing eastward, as the gorge widens, is the 22-mi-long **Historic Columbia River Highway,** U.S. 30 (also known as the Columbia River Scenic Highway and the Scenic Gorge Highway). The oldest scenic highway in the U.S., it is a construction marvel that integrates asphalt path with cliff, ocean, and forest landscapes. Paralleling the interstate on the south side of I–84, the road climbs to forested riverside bluffs. Completed in 1922, the serpentine highway was the first paved road in the gorge built expressly for automotive sightseers. (Keep an eye out for five waterfalls along the way.)

A few miles east of Troutdale on U.S. 30 is **Crown Point State Scenic Corridor,** a 730-foot-high bluff with an unparalleled 30-mi view down the

2

Columbia River Gorge. **Vista House,** the two-tier octagonal structure on the side of the cliff, opened its doors to visitors in 1916; the rotunda has displays about the gorge and the highway. Vista House's architect Edgar Lazarus was the brother of Emma Lazarus, author of the poem displayed at the base of the Statue of Liberty. ⊠ *U.S. 30* ☎ *503/695– 2261 or 800/551-6949* ⊕ *www.oregonstateparks.org* ▱ *Free* ⊗ *Daily* ⚲ *ADA accessible.*

About 4 mi east of the Troutdale bridge, **Dabney State Park** has boating, hiking, and fishing. There's also a popular summer swimming hole and an 18-hole disc golf course. A boat ramp is open year-round. ⊠ *U.S. 30, 4 mi east of Troutdale* ☎ *800/551-6949* ⊕ *www.oregonstateparks. org* ▱ *Day use $3 per vehicle* ⊗ *Daily dawn–dusk.*

The most famous beach lining the Columbia River, **Rooster Rock State Park** is below Crown Point; access is from the interstate only. Three miles of sandy beaches, panoramic cascades, and a large swimming area makes this a popular spot. True naturists appreciate that one of Oregon's two designated nude beaches is at the east end of Rooster Rock, and that it's not visible to conventional sunbathers. ⊠ *I–84, 7 mi east of Troutdale* ☎ *503/695–2261* ⊕ *www.oregonstateparks.org* ▱ *Day use $3 per vehicle* ⊗ *Daily 7–dusk.*

WHERE TO STAY & EAT

$–$$$ ✕ **Black Rabbit Restaurant & Bar.** Chef John Zenger's grilled rib-eye steak, old-fashioned roasted chicken, and sesame-crusted salmon are popular entrées at this McMenamins Hotel restaurant. Vivid murals depicting the gorge's history enrich your view as you linger over dinner in a high-backed wooden booth. Enjoy an Edgefield wine or any one of five McMenamins brews (made on-site, approximately 50 yards away!). Patio seating is available, with plenty of heaters to handle the unpredictable Oregon weather. Top off your meal with a homemade dessert and, wouldn't you know?, a McMenamins' home-roasted cup of coffee. ⊠ *2126 S.W. Halsey St.,* ☎ *503/492–3086* ⊕ *www.mcmenamins. com/index.php?loc=114* ▤ *AE, D, DC, MC, V.*

¢–$ 🛏 **McMenamins Edgefield.** As you explore the grounds of this Georgian Revival manor, you'll feel like you've entered a European village filled with activity and beauty. Wander through 38 acres of gardens, orchards, and vineyards with a drink in your hand. Enjoy complimentary movies in the Edgefield Theater, live music in the winery, and golf at the 17-hole course. There are three restaurants and six bars to choose from, as well as a pool hall and distillery. Ruby's Spa offers an amplitude of body treatments. Be sure to make reservations ahead of time for the Black Rabbit restaurant and Ruby's Spa. **Pros:** Plenty of choices for eating and drinking. A large variety of rooms and prices to choose from. **Cons:** Crowds can get large at this busy place. ⊠ *2126 S.W. Halsey St., 97060* ☎ *503/669–8610 or 800/669–8610* ⊕ *www. mcmenamins.com* ⇄ *114 rooms, 24 beds in men's/women's hostels* ⚲ *In-room: some a/c, no phone, no TV. In-hotel: no TV, 3 restaurants, 6 bars, 17-hole golf course, spa, public Wi-Fi, parking (no fee)* ▤ *AE, D, DC, MC, V.*

Fodor's Choice ★

MULTNOMAH FALLS

20 mi east of Troutdale on I–84 or Historic Columbia River Hwy. (U.S. 30).

Multnomah Falls, a 620-foot-high double-decker torrent, the second-highest year-round waterfall in the nation, is by far the most spectacular of the cataracts east of Troutdale. The scenic highway leads down to a parking lot; from there, a paved path winds to a bridge over the lower falls. A much steeper trail climbs to a viewing point overlooking the upper falls.

WHERE TO EAT

$–$$ ✕ **Multnomah Falls Lodge.** Vaulted ceilings, stone fireplaces, and exquisite
★   views of Multnomah Falls are complemented by wonderful service and an extensive menu at this restaurant, which is listed on the National Register of Historic places. Consider the halibut fish-and-chips, the lemon- and herb-roasted wild salmon, or ancho chile and espresso-cured flat iron steak. Breakfast favorites include blueberry, buttermilk, or huckleberry pancakes. A particular pleaser for out-of-town guests, the champagne Sunday brunch is held 8–2. For a treat during warmer months, sit on the patio and get close to the falls without feeling a drop. ✉*Exit 31 off I–84, 50000 Historic Columbia River Hwy., Bridal Veil* ☎*503/695–2376* ⊕*www.multnomahfallslodge.com* ▤*AE, D, MC, V* ⊗*Daily 8* AM–9 PM.

ONEONTA GORGE

2 mi east of Multnomah Falls on Historic Columbia River Hwy.

Following the old highway east from Multnomah Falls, you come to a narrow, mossy cleft with walls hundreds of feet high. Oneonta Gorge is most enjoyable in summer, when you can walk up the streambed through the cool green canyon, where hundreds of plant species—some found nowhere else—flourish under the perennially moist conditions. At other times of the year, take the trail along the west side of the canyon. The clearly marked trailhead is 100 yards west of the gorge, on the south side of the road. The trail ends at Oneonta Falls, about ½ mi up the stream. Bring boots or submersible sneakers—plus a strong pair of ankles—because the rocks are slippery. East of Oneonta Gorge, the scenic highway returns to I–84.

CASCADE LOCKS

7 mi east of Oneonta Gorge on Historic Columbia River Hwy. and I–84, 30 mi east of Troutdale on I–84.

In pioneer days, boats needing to pass the bedeviling rapids near the town of Cascade Locks had to portage around them. The locks that gave the town its name were completed in 1896, allowing waterborne passage for the first time. Native Americans still use the locks for their traditional dip-net fishing.

2

The first federal dam to span the Columbia, **Bonneville Dam** was dedicated by President Franklin D. Roosevelt in 1937. Its generators (visible from a balcony during self-guided powerhouse tours) have a capacity of nearly a million kilowatts, enough to supply power to more than 200,000 single-family homes. There is a modern visitor center on Bradford Island, complete with underwater windows for viewing migrating salmon and steelhead as they struggle up fish ladders. The best viewing times are between April and October. In recent years the dwindling runs of wild Columbia salmon have made the dam a subject of much environmental controversy. ⊠ *Bonneville Lock and Dam, U.S. Army Corps of Engineers, from I–84 take Exit 40, head northeast, and follow signs 1 mi to visitor center,Cascade Locks* ⊕ *www.nwp.usace.army.mil/ op/b/home.asp* ☎ *541/374–8820* ⊡ *Free* ☉ *Visitor center daily 9–5.*

Below Bonneville Dam, the ponds at the **Bonneville Fish Hatchery** teem with fingerling salmon, fat rainbow trout, and 6-foot-long sturgeon. The hatchery raises chinook and coho salmon; from mid-October to late November you can watch as staff members spawn the fish, beginning a new hatching cycle, or feed the trout with food pellets from a coin-operated machine. ⊠ *From I–84 take Exit 40 and follow signs northeast 1 mi to Hatchery 70543 N.E. Herman Loop* ☎ *541/374– 8393* ⊡ *Free* ☉ *Hatchery grounds daily dawn–dusk, spawning room daily. Winter hrs are 7:30–4:30, summer hrs are 7:30–7:30.*

Cascade Locks is the home port of the 600-passenger stern-wheeler *Columbia Gorge.* Between mid-June and early October the relic ship churns upriver, then back again, on two-hour excursions through some of the Columbia River Gorge's most impressive scenery. The ship's captain will talk about the gorge's fascinating 40-million-year geology and about pioneering spirits and legends, such as Lewis and Clark, who once triumphed over this very same river. Group bookings and private rentals available. Call sales department at 800/224–3901 for rates. ⊠ *Cruises leave from Marine Park in Cascade Locks. Marine Park, 355 Wanapa St.* ☎ *541/374–8427 or 800/224–3901* ⊕ *www.sternwheeler. com* ⚓ *Reservations essential* ⊡ *Prices vary, depending on choice of excursion: sightseeing, brunch, dinner, or Landmarks of the Gorge cruises, $25–$80.* ☉ *Varying hrs, generally May–Oct.* ☐ *AE, MC, V.*

WHERE TO EAT

$–$$ ✕ **Pacific Crest Pub.** A woodsy tavern with cedar-shake walls, historical photos, and a stone fireplace provides hearty servings of starters, salads, and main courses, including on-site-smoked salmon chowder and oven-roasted chicken accompanied by house-specialty horseradish. If you like feta cheese with your pizzas, try the house favorite, the Greek "Pizza of the Gods." During warmer months, sit outside in the adjacent courtyard and take in mountain and river views while sipping one of 13 featured microbrews, including Full Sail and Walking Man. ⊠ *500 Wanapa St.* ☎ *541/374–9310* ☐ *D, MC, V* ☉ *Closed Mon.*

STEVENSON, WASHINGTON

Across the river from Cascade Locks via the Bridge of the Gods and 4 mi east on Hwy. 14.

For a magnificent vista 135 feet above the Columbia, as well as a speedy route between Oregon and Washington, $1 will pay your way over the grandly named **Bridge of the Gods.** Slightly west of the bridge, hikers gain access to the Oregon-Washington link of the Mexico-to-Canada **Pacific Crest Trail.** Travel east on Highway 14 for about 10 minutes to reach the small town of Stevenson, with several antiques shops and good places to grab a bite. ⊕*www.portofcascadelocks.org/bridge.htm.*

★ For several hundred years, 848-foot **Beacon Rock** was a landmark for river travelers, including Native Americans, who recognized this point as the last rapids of the Columbia River. Lewis and Clark are thought to have been the first white men to see the volcanic remnant. Picnic atop old lava flows after hiking a 1-mi trail, steep but safe, which leads to tremendous views of the Columbia Gorge and the river. A round-trip hike takes 45–60 minutes. The site is a few miles west of the Bridge of the Gods.

NEED A BREAK? Funky and fun, '60s Haight-Ashbury meets Native American art, **Bahma Coffee Bar** is the place in Stevenson for Wi-Fi (with purchase) and, of course, coffee. Or choose from grilled panini sandwiches, soups, fresh carrot juice, wine, sake, tea and tasty homemade pastries. Scrabble tournaments, games aplenty, reading material, and live music on some weekends. All this, and a super staff. ⊠*256 S.W. 2nd St., Hwy. 14,* ☎*509/427–8700* ⊕*www.bahmacoffeebar.com* ☾*Daily 8:30–5* ▭*MC, V.*

☾ A petroglyph whose eyes seem to look straight at you, "She Who Watches" or "Tsagaglalal" is the logo for the **Columbia Gorge Interpretive Center.** Sitting among the dramatic basaltic cliffs on the north bank of the Columbia River Gorge, the museum explores the life of the gorge: its history, culture, architecture, legends, and much more. The younger crowd may enjoy the reenactment of the gorge in the Creation Theatre. Or a 37-foot high fishwheel from the 19th century. Historians will appreciate studying the water route of the Lewis & Clark Expedition. There's also an eye-opening exhibit that examines current environmental impacts on the area. ⊠*990 S.W. Rock Creek Dr., Stevenson, WA* ✛*1 mi east of Bridge of the Gods on Hwy. 14* ☎*509/427–8211 or 800/991–2338* ⊕*www.columbiagorge.org* ☜*$7* ☾*Daily 10–5* ☞*Wheelchair accessible.*

WHERE TO STAY & EAT

$–$$ ✕**Pacific Crest Dining Room.** After a rejuvenating spa treatment or hike, ★ the fresh healthy cuisine is a special treat. You can dine in the low light of the muted main room (metal pine-tree light fixtures are custom made) or in the adjoining lounge, its 12-foot high glass wall overlooking the manicured courtyard and the forest beyond. The pastry chef works through the night, ensuring fresh-baked breads and pastries by sunrise. Healthy never tasted so good, with crisp salads, Pacific Northwest fish (amazing ahi tuna!), Cascade-area beef, and gourmet vegetarian fare. Late afternoons, the lounge serves goodies such as hazelnut-crusted brie and Walking Man beer-battered halibut and chips. ✉ *1252 E. Cascade Dr., North Bonneville, WA* ☎ *509/427–9711* ⊕ *www.bonnevilleresort.com* 🖃 *AE, D, MC, V.*

$$–$$$$ ☷ **Bonneville Hot Springs Resort and Spa.** Enter an architectural wonder-
★   land of wood, iron, rock, and water ... water everywhere. Owner Pete Cam and his five sons built the resort to share their love of these historic mineral springs with the public, especially those seeking physical renewal. The three-story lobby, with its suspended black iron trestle, Paul Bunyan-size river-rock fireplace, and floor-to-ceiling arched windows, is magnificent to behold. The unique redwood-paneled, 25-meter indoor lap pool is adjacent to an immaculate European spa, offering over 40 candlelit treatments (mineral baths, body wraps, massages). Rooms are spacious, with upscale furnishings. **Pros:** Glorious grounds, amazing architectural detail, attentive and knowledgeable spa staff. **Cons:** Must reserve spa appointments separately from room reservations. The dull, boxy exterior belies what's inside. ✉ *1252 E. Cascade Dr., North Bonneville, WA 98639* ✛ *3 mi west of Bridge of the Gods on Hwy. 14, right on Hot Springs Way, right on E. Cascade Dr. follow for ½ mi* ☎ *509/427–7767 or 866/459–1678* 🖶 *509/427–7733* ⊕ *www.bonnevilleresort.com* ⮐ *78 rooms* ♿ *ADA-compliant rooms, elevator, restaurant, bar, pool, spa, concierge, business/event facilities, Internet, parking.* 🖃 *AE, D, MC, V.*

$$–$$$$ ☷ **Skamania Lodge.** "Skamania," the Chinook word for "swift water," overlooks exactly that with its 175 acres sitting to the north of the Columbia River Gorge. So big you need a map to get around, the Lodge impresses with its multitude of windows that take in the surrounding forests and Gorge, Montana slate tiling, Native American artwork, and an immense word-burning fireplace. Outstanding recreational facilities include an 18-hole, par-70 golf course, 3 hiking trails, large indoor pool, and even a sand volleyball court. The accommodating staff will pack you a box lunch if you're going out to explore for the day. **Pros:** Addresses the active guest as well as the kids, U.S. Forest Service has a kiosk in the lobby, well-suited to handle large events, conferences, weddings. **Cons:** Costs can quickly multiply for a large family, can get crowded, sometimes there's a wait for table seating in the dining room. ✉ *Skamania Lodge Way north of Hwy. 14, 1½ mi east of the Bridge of the Gods, 1131 S.W. Skamania Lodge Way 98648* ☎ *509/427–7700 or 800/221–7117* 🖶 *509/427–2547* ⊕ *www.skamania.com* ⮐ *254 rooms* ♿ *In-room: Wi-fi. In-hotel: restaurants, bars, golf course, tennis courts, pool, gym, spa, bicycles, concierge, executive floor, public Wi-Fi, parking (no fee), some pets allowed* 🖃 *AE, D, DC, MC, V.*

HOOD RIVER

17 mi east of Cascade Locks on I-84.

For years, the incessant easterly winds blowing through the town of Hood River were nothing more than a nuisance. Then somebody bolted a sail to a surfboard, waded into the fat part of the gorge, and a new recreational craze was born. A fortuitous combination of factors—mainly the reliable gale-force winds blowing against the current—has made Hood River the self-proclaimed boardsailing capital of the world. Especially in summer, this once-somnolent town swarms with colorful "board-heads" from as far away as Europe and Australia. Not just content to surf the water, others are boosting their hangtime with another craze, the kiteboard. In winter, many of these same athletes stay in town, but turn south to ski on mountain slopes that are only a short drive away. Other outdoor enthusiasts find the area's fishing, boating, swimming, and hiking venues the best in the region.

> **GRAPE EXPECTATIONS?**
>
> The Columbia Gorge Winemakers Association is credited with the catchy slogan, "A World of Wine in 40 Miles." Representing 3 different regions, there's a 40-mi area within the gorge that varies in soil and climate, supporting more than 22 wineries. Though vintners state that in Europe a similar variety of wines would encompass 1,200 mi, they swear that the gorge can do it all, from rieslings to nebbiolos, from pinot noirs to pinot gris. Meaning that whatever the weather . . . the weather's just "vine."

Hood River's rich pioneer past is reflected in its downtown historic district. The City of Hood River publishes a free self-guided walking tour (available through the City of Hood River government office or the Hood River Chamber of Commerce) that will take you on a tour of more than 40 civic and commercial buildings dating from 1893 to the 1930s, some of which are listed in the National Register of Historic Places.

Either by car or bicycle, tour Hood River valley's **Fruit Loop,** whose vast orchards surround the Hood River. You'll see apples, pears, cherries, and peaches fertilized by volcanic soil, pure glacier water, and a conducive harvesting climate. Along the 35 mi of farms are a host of delicious baked goods, wines, flowers, and nuts. Festive farm activities from April to November also give a taste of the agricultural life. While on the loop, consider stopping at the town of **Parkdale** to lunch, shop, and snap a photo of Mt. Hood's north face. There are well-marked signs on the entire 35-mi loop. ✉ *Rte. begins on Hwy. 35* ⊕ *www. hoodriverfruitloop.com.*

An efficient and relaxing way to survey Mt. Hood and the Hood River, the **Mt. Hood Scenic Railroad and Dinner Train** was established in 1906 as a passenger and freight line. Chug alongside the Hood River through vast fruit orchards before climbing up steep forested canyons, glimpsing Mt. Hood along the way. There are four trip options: a four-hour excursion (serves light concessions with two daily departures, morning and afternoon), dinner, brunch, and a themed murder-mystery dinner. Choose from brunch fare such as raspberry crepes, omelets, and eggs Benedict. Favorite dinner selections include huckleberry-sauced salmon, sun-dried tomato ravioli, and chicken picatta. Exceptional service is as impressive as the scenery. ✉ *110 Railroad Ave.* ☎ *541/386–3556* *or 800/872–4661* ⊕*www.mthoodrr.com* ▭*AE, D, V* ▧*$25–$80* ⊙*Apr.–Dec., call for schedule.*

2

NEED A BREAK?

A glass-walled microbrewery with a windswept deck overlooking the Columbia, the **Full Sail Tasting Room and Pub** (⊠*506 Columbia St.* ☎*541/386–2247*) has won major awards at the Great American Beer Festival. Savory snack foods complement fresh ales. The Taster Tray, seven 4-ounce samples for $5, is a great way to explore the many varieties of Full Sail brews. On-site brewery tours available.

Awarded the Oregon Winery of the Year in 2007 by the Northwest Wine Press, **Cathedral Ridge Winery** has a 6-acre vineyard. Popular varietals include riesling, pinot gris, and syrah. The tasting room is open 11–5 daily. ⊠*4200 Post Canyon Dr.,* ☎*800/516–8710* ⊕*www.cathedralridgewinery.com* ▧*Free* ⊙*Daily 11–5.*

Sauvignon blanc, cabernet sauvignon, and merlot are among the varieties produced at the 12-acre, family-owned **Hood River Vineyards,** which overlook the Columbia River Gorge and the Hood River valley. Bottles are sold individually; best sellers are the pinot noir and chardonnay. ⊠*4693 Westwood Dr.* ☎*541/386–3772* ⊕*www.hoodrivervineyards. us* ▧*Free* ⊙*Apr.–Oct., daily 11–5; Nov.–Mar., Wed.–Sun. 11–5.*

OFF THE BEATEN PATH

Lost Lake. One of the most-photographed sights in the Pacific Northwest, this lake's waters reflect towering Mt. Hood and the thick forests that line its shore. Cabins are available for overnight stays, and because no motorboats are allowed on Lost Lake, the area is blissfully quiet. ⊠*Lost Lake Rd., take Hood River Hwy. south from Hood River to town of Dee and follow signs. Also accessible from Lolo Pass.* ☎*541/386–6366* ▧*Day use $5.*

WHERE TO STAY & EAT

$$ ✕**Stonehedge Gardens.** It's not just the cuisine that's out of this world—
Fodor'sChoice Stonehedge is of another time and place, surrounding you with 7 acres
★ of lush English gardens that gracefully frame its multitude of stone terraces and trickling fountains. Each of the four dining rooms in the restored 1898 home has a distinct personality, from cozy to verdant to elegant. The curry shiitake mushroom soup is a Bite of the Gorge favorite. The fresher-than-fresh seafood and meat are melded with sauces and spices that heighten rather than smother. Just when you think your meal is complete, along comes the Flaming Bread Pudding. ⊠*3405 Cascade Ave.* ☎*541/386–3940* ▭*AE, MC, V* ⊙*No lunch.*

$$ ☷**Lakecliff Bed & Breakfast.** Perched on a cliff overlooking the Colum-
★ bia Gorge, this beautiful 1908 summer home has long been a favorite spot for weddings. Designed by architect A.E. Doyle (who also created the Multnomah Falls Lodge), this 3-acre magical land of ferns, fir trees, and water is a stunner. There's a deck at the back of the house, fireplaces and river views in three of the rooms, and top-notch service, including hot coffee right outside your door in the morning. "Large, spoiling breakfasts" says the owner, referring to her poached pears, blueberry pancakes, and butterscotch pecan rolls. For summer, make reservations as far ahead as possible. **Pros:** Glorious views, friendly and

accommodating staff. **Cons:** No king-size beds, need to book months in advance. ✉ *3820 Westcliff Dr., head east from I–84 Exit 62, 97031* ☎ *541/386–7000* 🖷 *541/386–1803* ⊕ *www.lakecliffbnb.com* ⇆4 *rooms* 🖒 *In-room: no phone, no TV. In-hotel: no elevator* ☰*MC, V.*

THE DALLES

20 mi east of Hood River on I–84.

The Dalles lies on a crescent bend of the Columbia River where the river narrows and once spilled over a series of rapids, creating a flagstone effect. French voyagers christened it *dalle,* or "flagstone." The Dalles is the seat of Wasco County and the trading hub of north–central Oregon. It gained fame early in the region's history as the town where the Oregon Trail branched, with some pioneers departing to travel over Mt. Hood on Barlow Road and the others continuing down the Columbia River. This may account for the small-town, Old West feeling that still permeates the area. Several historical Oregon moments as they relate to the Dalles' past are magnificently illustrated on eight murals painted by renowned Northwest artists, located downtown within short walking distance of one another.

The 1856-vintage Fort Dalles Surgeon's Quarters is the site of the **Fort Dalles Museum,** the oldest history museum in Oregon. The museum's first visitors came through the doors in 1905. On display in authentic hand-hewn log buildings, originally part of a military base, are the personal effects of some of the region's settlers and a collection of early automobiles. The entrance fee gains you admission to the **Anderson House** museum across the street, which also has pioneer artifacts. ✉ *500 W. 15th St., at Garrison* ☎ *541/296–4547* ⊕ *www.historicthedalles.org* ☞*$3* 🕑 *Thurs.–Mon. 11–4* 🕑 *Closed Nov.–Mar.*

♻ Exhibits at the **Columbia Gorge Discovery Center–Wasco County Historical Museum** highlight the geological history of the Columbia Gorge, back 40 million years when volcanoes, landslides, and floods carved out the area. The museum focuses on 10,000 years of Native American life and exploration of the region by white settlers. ✉ *5000 Discovery Dr.* ☎ *541/296–8600* ⊕ *www.gorgediscovery.org* ☞*$8* 🕑 *Daily 9–5.*

At **the Dalles Lock and Dam,** a hydroelectric dam just east of the Bonneville Dam, you can ride the free Dalles Dam Tour Train to the fish ladder and powerhouse. There's also a sturgeon pond at the visitor center. ✉*Exit 87 (in summer) or Exit 88 other times off I–84 2 mi east of the Dalles at Lake Celilo* ☎*541/296–1181* ⊕*www.nwp.usace.army. mil/op/d/thedalles.asp* ☞*Free* 🕑 *Varied hrs throughout the year—call ahead.*

Built in 1897, **Old St. Peter's Landmark** is a Gothic brick church with brilliant stained glass, hand-carved pews, marble altars, and an immense pipe organ. Steamboat captains once used the 176-foot steeple as a navigational benchmark. The landmark now functions as a nondenominational, nonprofit organization that is available for tours, weddings, and other private functions. ✉*3rd and Lincoln Sts.* ☎*541/296–5686*

⊕www.oldstpeterslandmark.org ✉*Free, donation suggested* ☉*Feb.– Dec., Tues.–Fri. 11–3, weekends 1–3.*

WHERE TO EAT

$ ✕**Cousin's Restaurant.** Home cooking rules the roost at this family restaurant with a frontier motif. Try the home-style pot roast, old-fashioned meat loaf, or Tom Turkey supper with all the trimmings. Goofy but catchy, all the waitstaff goes by the name "Cousin." The ample menu includes plenty of vegetarian choices, all-day breakfast, and plenty of kids' choices. ✉*2114 W. 6th St.,* ☎*541/298–2771* ⊕*www. cousinsthedalles.com* ▭*AE, D, DC, MC, V.*

¢–$ ✕**Petite Provence.** The new cream puff in town, this bistro/bakery/dessertery serves eggs, crepes, and croissants for breakfast; hot and cold sandwiches and salads for lunch, and fresh-baked pastries and breads (you can take a loaf home). The sparkling display case tempts with a goodly selection of napoleons, éclairs, tarts, mousses. A spinoff from the main site in the Portland suburb of Lake Oswego (La Provence), this branch successfully retains the charms of its big sister. ✉*408 E. 2nd St.,* ☎*541/506–0037* ▭*AE, D, MC, V .*

MT. HOOD

About 60 mi east of Portland on I–84 and U.S. 26, 65 mi from the Dalles, west on I–84 and south on Hwy. 35 and U.S. 26.

Majestically towering 11,245 feet above sea level, Mt. Hood is what remains of the original north wall and rim of a volatile crater. Although the peak no longer spews ash or fire, active steam vents can be spotted high on the mountain. Native Americans in the area named it Wy'east, after a great chief who mystically became the mountain. In anger, Wy'east spouted flames and threw rocks toward the sky. The name was changed in 1792 when a crew of the British Royal Navy, the first recorded Caucasians sailing up the Columbia River, spotted the mountain and named it after a famed British naval officer by the name of–you guessed it–Hood.

Mt. Hood offers the only year-round skiing in the lower 48 states, with three major ski areas and 26 lifts, as well as extensive areas for cross-country skiing and snowboarding. Many of the ski runs turn into mountain-bike trails in summer. The mountain is also popular with climbers and hikers. In fact, some hikes follow parts of the Oregon Trail, and signs of the pioneers' passing are still evident.

★   The highest mountain in Oregon and the fourth-highest peak in the Cascades, "the Mountain" is a focal point of the 1.1-million-acre **Mt. Hood National Forest,** an all-season playground attracting more than 7 million visitors annually. Twenty miles southeast of Portland, it extends south from the Columbia River Gorge for more than 60 mi and includes 189,200 acres of designated wilderness. These woods are perfect for hikers, horseback riders, mountain climbers, and cyclists. Within the forest are more than 80 campgrounds and 50 lakes stocked with brown, rainbow, cutthroat, brook, and steelhead trout. The Sandy,

Salmon, and other rivers are known for their fishing, rafting, canoeing, and swimming. Both forest and mountain are crossed by an extensive trail system for hikers, cyclists, and horseback riders. The **Pacific Crest Trail,** which begins in British Columbia and ends in Mexico, crosses at the 4,157-foot-high Barlow Pass. As with most other mountain destinations within Oregon, weather can be temperamental, and snow and ice may affect driving conditions as early as October and as late as May. Bring tire chains and warm clothes as a precaution.

For a glimpse into the area's vivid history, stop at the **Mt. Hood Information Center** (⊠*24403 E. Welches Rd., Welches* ☎*503/622–4822 or 888/622–4822*) and pick up a copy of the *Barlow Road.* This is a great navigational map of the first emigrant road over the Cascades, where pioneers traveled west via ancient Indian trails to avoid the dangers of the mighty Columbia River. Since this forest is close to the Portland metro area, campgrounds and trails are potentially crowded over the summer months, especially on weekends. If camping, contact the forest service desk while you're at the Mt. Hood Information Center. Prepare yourself by gathering information about the more than 80 campgrounds, including a string of neighboring campgrounds that rest on the south side of Mt. Hood: Trillium Lake, Still Creek, Timothy Lake, Little Crater Lake, Clackamas Lake, Summit Lake, Clear Lake, and Frog Lake. Each varies in what it offers and in price. The mountain is overflowing with day-use areas, and passes can be obtained for $5. There are also Mt. Hood National Forest maps with details about well-marked trails. ⊠*24403 E. Welches Rd.* ⊕*www.mthood.info* ✉*Day use free–$5, campsites $12–$14* ☾*Information center weekdays 9–5, weekends 9–4, most campgrounds open year-round.*

WHERE TO STAY & EAT

$$–$$$ ✕**Cascade Dining Room.** If the wall of windows isn't coated with snow, ★ you may get a good look at some of the neighboring peaks. Vaulted wooden beams and a wood-plank floor, handcrafted furniture, hand-woven drapes, and a lion-size stone fireplace set the scene. Executive Chef Leif Benson has been going strong since 1979, incorporating Mt. Hood–grown morels in his "campfire spice" wild salmon, pistachios in his basmati rice, and truffles with his pheasant. A four-course tasting menu (including the house favorite, crème brûlée) is always a delightful option. Open for breakfast, lunch, and dinner; look for the clever mix of lobster with macaroni and cheese at the noon hour. Sunday brunch buffet, an all-you-can-eat affair, is almost as big as the fireplace. ⊠*Timberline Rd., Timberline* ☎*503/622–0700 or 800/547–1406* ⊕*www.timberlinelodge.com* ▤*AE, D, MC, V.*

$$ ▦**Timberline Lodge.** The approach alone, an unforgettable 6-mi ascent ☾ that circles Mt. Hood, is reason enough to visit the magnificent Tim-★ berline Lodge. Now you see it, now you don't: Mt. Hood teases you the whole way up, then quite unexpectedly, the Lodge materializes out of the mist ... and you momentarily forget about the snow-capped peak. It's no wonder that Stanley Kubrick used shots of the Lodge's exterior for the film *The Shining.* Built to complement the size and majesty of Mt. Hood, the massive structure was erected from timber and rock

2

donated by the forests of the mountain itself. From 1936 to1937 more than 500 men and women toiled, forging metal for furniture and fixtures, sculpting old telephone poles into beams and banisters, weaving, looming, sawing. But for once, the historical artifacts are not displayed behind a glass wall—they are the chairs you sit on, the doors you walk through, the floors you step on. Enjoy the restaurants, the snow sports, the hiking paths; relax by the lobby's massive fireplace with a 96-foot stone chimney. But also take in the marvelously detailed 22-minute film (located on the lower level) to learn about the building's genesis–it'll help you appreciate Timberline all the more! **Pros:** A thrill to stay on the mountain itself, great proximity to all snow activity, plush featherbeds, amazing architecture throughout, fun dining places. **Cons:** Rooms are very small, no a/c in summer, prepare yourself for carloads of tourists. ⊠ *Timberline, Timberline Lodge, OR 97028* ☎ *503/231–5400 or 800/547–1406* 🖷 *503/727–3710* ⊕ *www.timberlinelodge.com* 🛏 *60 rooms* ⌂ *In-room: no a/c. In-hotel: restaurant, bar, pool, gym, elevator, concierge, parking (no fee)* ▭ *AE, D, MC, V.*

SPORTS & THE OUTDOORS

SKIING One of the longest ski seasons in North America unfolds at **Timberline Lodge Ski Area** (⊠ *Off U.S. 26, Timberline* ☎ *503/272–3311*). The U.S. ski team conducts summer training at this full-service ski area. It's the only ski area in the lower 48 states that's open year-round (except for two weeks in late September), and that also welcomes snowboarders. Timberline is famous for its Palmer chairlift, which takes skiers to a high glacier for summer skiing. There are five double chairs and two high-speed quad chairs. The top elevation is 8,500 feet, with a 3,600-foot vertical drop, and the longest run is 3 mi. Facilities include a day lodge with fast food and a ski shop; lessons and equipment rental and repair are available. Parking requires a Sno-Park permit. Lift tickets per day are $54 peak, $49 regular. The area is open Sunday–Tuesday 9–5 and Wednesday–Saturday 9 AM–10 PM; the lift is also open June–August, daily 7–1:30.

GOVERNMENT CAMP

45 mi from the Dalles, south on Hwy. 35 and west on U.S. 26, 54 mi east of Portland on I–84 and U.S. 26.

Government Camp, an alpine resort village, has a fair number of hotels and restaurants. It's a convenient drive from here to Mt. Hood's five ski resorts or to Welches, which has restaurants and a resort.

WHERE TO STAY & EAT

¢–$ ✕**Charlie's Mountain View.** Old and new skis plaster the walls, lift chairs function as furniture, and photos of famous skiers and other memorabilia are as abundant as the menu selections. Open flame–grilled steaks and hamburgers are worthy here, and house specialties include creamy mushroom soup and chicken Caesar salad with dressing made from scratch. When they're in season, try the apple dumplings. There's also a full bar, with live music on Saturday nights from 9 to 1 AM. ⊠ *88462 E. Government Camp Loop* ☎ *503/272–3333* ⊕ *www.charliesmountainview.com* ▤ *AE, D, DC, MC, V.*

¢–$ ✕**Huckleberry Inn.** Whether it's 2 AM or 2 PM, Huckleberry Inn welcomes you 24 hours a day with soups, milk shakes, burgers, sandwiches, and omelets. Well-known treats are made with huckleberries, and include pie, pancakes, tea, jelly, and vinaigrette salad dressing. ⊠ *88611 E. Government Camp Loop* ☎ *503/272–3325* ⊕ *www.huckleberry-inn.com* ▤ *MC, V.*

$$$ 🏠**Thunderhead Lodge.** Within walking distance of the Mt. Hood Ski Bowl (its night lights visible from your cabin), the Lodge is a jump-off site for many activities in the area: hiking, mountain biking, fishing, white-water rafting, and in winter, snowboarding, sledding, and cross-county and downhill skiing. Room sizes and capacities vary according to your needs, and there's a rec room with foosball, a pool table, wet bar, and fireplace. A special treat: no matter how cold, the outdoor pool is geothermally heated from underground. Note: this particular rental company, All Seasons Property Management, has many other properties as well, including pet-friendly facilities. Check out *www.mthoodrent.com* to find your ideal cabin. ⊠ *87577 E. Government Camp Loop 97028* ☎ *503/622–1142* ⊕ *www.mthoodrent.com/proppages/thunderhead.html* ⏍ *10 units* △ *In-room: no phone, full kitchens. In-hotel: no elevator, pool, laundry facilities* ▤ *MC, V.*

SPORTS & THE OUTDOORS

DOWNHILL SKIING On the eastern slope of Mt. Hood, **Cooper Spur Ski and Recreation Area** (⊠ *Follow signs from Hwy. 35 for 3½ mi to ski area* ☎ *541/352–7803*) caters to families and has two rope tows and a T-bar. The longest run is 2/3 mi, with a 500-foot vertical drop. Facilities and services include rentals, instruction, repairs, and a ski shop, day lodge, snack bar, and restaurant. Call for hours. Mt. Hood's largest resort, **Mt. Hood Meadows Ski Resort** (⊠ *10 mi east of Government Camp on Hwy. 35* ☎ *503/337–2222 or 800/754–4663* ⊕ *www.skihood.com*) has more than 2,000 skiable acres, dozens of runs, seven double chairs, one triple chair, one quad chair, a top elevation of 7,300 feet, a vertical drop of 2,777 feet, and a longest run of 3 mi. Facilities include a day lodge, seven restaurants, two lounges, a ski school, and a ski shop; equipment rental and repair are also available. The ski area closest to Portland, **Mt. Hood Ski Bowl** (⊠ *53 mi east of Portland, across U.S. 26 from Government Camp* ☎ *503/272–3206 or 800/SKIBOWL* ⊕ *www.skibowl.com*) is called "America's largest night ski area." It has 63 trails serviced by four double chairs and five surface tows, a top elevation of 5,050 feet, a vertical drop of 1,500 feet, and a longest run of 3½ mi. You can take advantage of two day lodges, a mid-mountain warming hut, three restaurants, and two lounges. Sleigh rides are conducted, weather permitting. In 2006 the new Summer Tube Hill was installed on the eastern side of Skibowl. The longest run at the **Summit Ski Area** (✉ *Government Camp Loop Hwy., east end, Government Camp* ☎ *503/272–0256*) is ½ mi, with a 400-foot vertical drop; there's one chairlift and one rope tow. Facilities include instruction, a ski shop, a cafeteria, and a day lodge. Bike rentals are available in summer.

2

WELCHES & ZIGZAG

14 mi west of Government Camp on U.S. 26, 40 mi east of Portland, I–84 to U.S. 26.

Welches' claim to fame is that it was the site of Oregon's first golf course, built at the base of Mt. Hood in 1928. And another golf course is still going strong today. *See the Resort at the Mountains.*

Find restaurants, gas stations, and other services in these two small towns at the base of Mt. Hood.

Drop by the **Mt. Hood Information Center** in Welches for detailed information on all the Mt. Hood area attractions. (✉ *24403 E. Welches Rd.,* ☎ *503/622–4822* 🌐 *mthood.info*).

WHERE TO STAY & EAT

$$–$$$ ✕ **Tartans Pub and Steakhouse.** With a name like "Tartans," you'd better have an impressive assortment of single-malt Scotches—happily, they do. Pictures of golf courses abound in the two fireplace anterooms. You can choose to dine in the Tartans Room, with views of the lush, green golf course, or the 18-chair Cellar Room for a more intimate setting. This classy-casual dining spot specializes in wild game (venison, buffalo), Oregon salmon, and crab. There's an inexpensive kids' menu, and breakfast is also available. ✉ *68010 E. Fairway Ave., Welches* ☎ *503/622–3101 or 800/669–7666* ▭ *AE, D, DC, MC, V* ⊗ *Closed Nov.–April.*

$$$ ★ **Cascade Property Management - Mt. Hood Vacation Rentals.** Doggedly determined to ensure a great time for the two and four-pawed vacationer alike, 20 of the 27 vacation homes/cabins/condos welcome the family pet as a "bone-a-fide" member of the family. Yet it's still all on the upscale side, with fireplaces/woodburning stoves, hot tubs, river views, full kitchens. Cascade Property Management has been accommodating Mt. Hood visitors since 1991, carefully choosing properties that offer a true representation of a mountain home vacation spot with beauty as well as privacy. For families and groups, a majority of the places can accommodate 8–10 guests. **Pros:** Knowledgeable, hospitable staff, gorgeous homes nestled throughout the Mt. Hood area, family and pet friendly. **Cons:** Bring your own shampoo and hair dryer. Rules need to be followed upon leaving home in appropriate manner. ✉ *24403 E. Welches Rd, Suite 104, 97067* ☎ *503/622–5688 or 800/635–5417* 🌐 *www.mthoodrentals.com* *In-room: kitchens, DVD/VCR, Ethernet, Wi-Fi. In-hotel: no elevator, laundry facilities, parking (no fee),* ▭ *MC, V.*

$–$$ 🏔 **The Resort at the Mountains.** Here in the highlands of Mt. Hood, the Cascades are seemingly close enough for golfers to hit with a long drive. You can croquet on the only court and lawn-bowling green in the Northwest or choose from plenty of nearby outdoor activities such as fly-fishing on the Salmon River, horseback riding, white-water rafting, and all snow-related sports. Golf and skiing packages are offered, as well as comprehensive meeting and event facilities. Accommodations run from double rooms to two-bedroom condos. Each of the tastefully decorated rooms has a deck or patio overlooking the forest, courtyard, or fairway. Self-contained, the resort has its own golf shop (pros available for lessons), tennis courts, pool/Jacuzzi, gym, restaurants, bars, etc. **Pros:** Every sport available, clean rooms, plenty of choices in size. **Cons:** There will be crowds, may not appeal if a guest isn't a fan of golf. ✉ *68010 E. Fairway Ave.; follow signs south from U.S. 26 in Welches, 97067* ☎ *503/622–3101 or 800/669–7666* 🖷 *503/622–2222* ⊕ *www.theresort.com* ⮐ *160 rooms* ☦ *In-room: a/c (most), kitchen (some), Wi-Fi. In-hotel: no elevator2 restaurants, bars, 27-hole golf course, 4 tennis courts, pool, gym, bicycles, laundry facilities, concierge, public Wi-Fi,parking, some pets allowed (fee)* ▱*AE, D, MC, V.*

¢–$ 🏔 **The Cabins Creekside at Welches.** Affordability, accessibility to rec-
★   reational activities, and wonderful hosts make this a great lodging choice in the Mt. Hood area. Comfortable, large studio units that each accommodate from one to four people have knotty-pine vaulted ceilings and log furnishings. As a bonus, full-size kitchens make cooking "at home" a breeze. Surrounding woods offer privacy. Patios on each unit face the seasonal creek, and each cabin has lock-storage units large enough to hold bikes, skis, or snowboards. ✉ *25086 E. Welches Rd., 97067* ☎ *503/622–4275* ⊕ *www.mthoodcabins.com* ⮐ *10 cabins* ☦ *In-room: kitchen, VCR, DVD, Wi-Fi. In-hotel: laundry facilities* ▱*AE, D, MC, V.*

THE COLUMBIA GORGE & MT. HOOD ESSENTIALS

BY CAR

I–84 is the main east–west route into the Columbia River Gorge. U.S. 26, heading east from Portland and northwest from Prineville, is the main route into the Mt. Hood area. Portions of I–84 and U.S. 26 that pass through the mountains pose winter-travel difficulties, though the state plows these roadways regularly. The gorge is closed frequently during harsh winters due to ice and mud slides. Extreme winds can also make driving hazardous and potentially result in highway closures.

The Historic Columbia River Highway (U.S. 30) from Troutdale, to just east of Oneonta Gorge, passes Crown Point State Park and Multnomah Falls. I–84/U.S. 30 continues on to The Dalles. Highway 35 heads south from The Dalles to the Mt. Hood area, intersecting with U.S. 26 at Government Camp.

2

VISITOR INFORMATION

Contacts **Columbia River Gorge Visitors Association** (✉ *404 W. 2nd St., The Dalles 97058* ☎ *800/984–6743* ⊕ *www.crgva.org*). **Hood River County Chamber of Commerce** (✉ *405 Portway Ave., 97031* ☎ *541/386–2000 or 800/366–3530* ⊕ *www.hoodriver.org*). **Mt. Hood Chamber of Commerce** (✉ *24403 E. Welches Rd., Welches 97067* ☎ *503/622–3017* ⊕ *www.mthood.org*). **Mt. Hood Information Center** (✉ *24403 E. Welches Rd., Welches 97067* ☎ *503/622–4822* ⊕ *mthood. info*). **Mt. Hood National Forest Ranger Stations** (✉ *6780 Hwy. 35, Mt. Hood 97041* ☎ *541/352–6002* ✉ *Superintendent, 16400 Champion Way, off U.S. 26, Sandy 97055* ☎ *503/668–1700*). **Oregon Tourism Commission** (✉ *775 Summer St. NE, Salem 97301-1282* ☎ *503/986–0000 or 800/547–7842* ⊕ *www. traveloregon.com*).

CENTRAL OREGON

Updated by Kimberly Gadette

The arid landscape east of the Cascades differs dramatically from that on the lush, wet western side. Crossing the mountains, you enter a high-desert plateau with scrubby buttes, forests of ponderosa pine, and mile after mile of sun-bleached earth. The booming resort town of Bend is the most prominent playground in central Oregon, but within the region are dozens of other outdoor recreational hubs, many of them blissfully uncrowded.

Ponts of interest can be found on the Central Oregon map. Numbers in the margin correspond to the Bend map.

WARM SPRINGS

115 mi southeast of Portland on U.S. 26.

If, like the many visitors who begin their journey in Portland, you enter the Warm Springs Indian Reservation after traversing the frosty alpine skirt of Mt. Hood, you may feel you've been teleported from *The Sound of Music* into *A Fistful of Dollars*. This austere desert landscape is nothing short of stunning—a country of brooding solitary buttes, lonely pines, and untamed ravines, lorded over by the snowcapped spires of Mt. Jefferson and Mt. Hood. For a crash course in Oregon's thrilling contrasts, you could do no better. A singular museum and the popular desert resort of Kah-Nee-Ta provide cultural and economic bases for the three confederated tribes who live here.

TOP 5

1. Cork (restaurant): Amazing food and squares of block glass as design motif.

2. Drake Park/Mirror Pond: Watch the mallards from the old wooden bridge above.

3. Kokanee Café: for delectable vermicelli crab cakes and the hand-cranked ice cream.

4. The Lodge at Suttle Lake has a glorious view of the lake and a forested, 3½ mile rolling walk around the perimeter.

5. Pilot Butte, for its stupendous views of the nine surrounding mountain peaks.

The Confederated Tribes of the Warm Springs Reservation created the ★ **Museum at Warm Springs** south of town to preserve their traditions and keep their legacy alive. On display are tribal heirlooms, beaded artifacts, baskets, historic photographs, ceramics, and traditional dwellings. This haul is the product of years of carefully planned collecting and curating and is seen as a model tribal-run cultural resource. The museum's buildings, with such unmistakable nods to tribal history as conical, tepee-like atriums and sleek modernist lines, received an award from the American Institute of Architects. The museum's gift shop sells Native American crafts. ⊠*2189 U.S. 26,* ☎*541/553–3331* ⊕*www. warmsprings.biz/museum/* ⊠*$6* ◷*Mar.–Nov., daily 9–5; Nov.–Mar., Wed.–Sun. 9–5.*

WHERE TO STAY & EAT

¢–$ ✕**Deschutes Crossing.** Even if you're just passing through, this classic diner on the banks of the verdant Deschutes is a worthy stop. Breakfast, served all day, includes basic eggs, hash browns, and toast configurations, along with pork chops, steak and eggs, and the acclaimed Cowboy Breakfast of ground beef, eggs, hash browns, and toast. While you're waiting for that coffee refill, check out the vintage photos. ⊠*U. S. 26 at Deschutes River 2198 N. Hwy. 26,* ☎*541/553–1300* ▭*MC, V.*

$$$ ▦**Kah-Nee-Ta Resort and Casino.** Kah-Nee-Ta means "root digger" in one of the reservation's native tongues, but this modern destination resort doesn't really match that humble moniker. Built around hot mineral springs that feed huge open-air swimming pools, Kah-Nee-Ta has an isolated, exclusive feel that makes a tempting escape from bustling Portland or Bend. The casino, straight out of third-tier Vegas, strikes a depressing and tacky note with its windowless, stifling atmosphere. But the rooms are comfortable, and the staff is friendly and helpful. Best of all are the sweeping, sparse desert panoramas; restorative mineral pools; and pristine juniper-scented air, a form of aromatherapy in itself. Speaking of aromatherapy, Spa Wanapine has massage, reflexology, facials, and other New Age treatments. The Juniper Room serves decent food with a distinct regional inflection; a more affordable seafood buffet is also available. The upscale suites have tile fireplaces and hot tubs, big-screen TVs, and king-size beds. An RV park and wood-frame, canvas-covered tepees (bring your own bedroll) form the "village" around the hot springs below the main lodge. Kah-Nee-Ta also has a water slide, kayak rentals, and maps to nearby hiking trails. ⊠*6823 Hwy. 8, 11 mi north of Warm Springs, Hwy. 3 north of U.S. 26, follow signs, 97761* ☎*541/553–6123 or 800/554-4786* ⊟*541/553–6119* ⊕*www.kah-nee-taresort.com* ⬫*139 rooms, 21 tepees* ⌕*In-room: Wi-Fi. In-hotel: 2 restaurants, bar, golf course, tennis court, pools, gym, spa, bicycles concierge, executive floor, public Wi-Fi, parking (no fee)* ▭*AE, D, MC, V.*

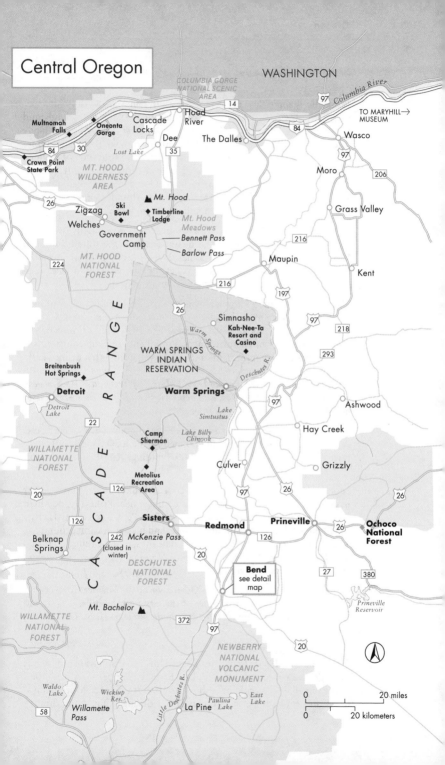

Central Oregon

WASHINGTON

COLUMBIA GORGE
NATIONAL SCENIC
AREA

Columbia River

14

97

TO MARYHILL →
MUSEUM

Multnomah
Falls

Oneonta
Gorge

Cascade
Locks

Hood
River

Dee

The Dalles

Wasco

84

30

Lost Lake

35

84

97

Crown Point
State Park

Moro

MT. HOOD
WILDERNESS
AREA

206

26

Zigzag

Ski
Bowl

▲ Mt. Hood

Grass Valley

Welches

Timberline
Lodge

Mt. Hood
Meadows

Government
Camp

— Bennett Pass

216

— Barlow Pass

MT. HOOD
NATIONAL
FOREST

Maupin

Kent

224

216

197

26

Simnasho

97

218

Warm Springs

Kah-Nee-Ta
Resort and
Casino

293

WARM SPRINGS
INDIAN
RESERVATION

Deschutes R.

Breitenbush
Hot Springs

Warm Springs

Ashwood

Detroit

97

Detroit
Lake

Lake
Simtustus

22

Hay Creek

Camp
Sherman

Lake Billy
Chinook

WILLAMETTE
NATIONAL
FOREST

Culver

Grizzly

Metolius
Recreation
Area

126

26

20

Sisters

126

Redmond

Prineville

Ochoco
National
Forest

126

242
McKenzie Pass
(closed in
winter)

Belknap
Springs

20

DESCHUTES
NATIONAL
FOREST

27

380

Bend
see detail
map

Prineville
Reservoir

Mt. Bachelor ▲

372

WILLAMETTE
NATIONAL
FOREST

97

NEWBERRY
NATIONAL
VOLCANIC
MONUMENT

20

Waldo
Lake

Wickiup
Res.

Paulina
Lake

East
Lake

58

Willamette
Pass

La Pine

0   20 miles

0   20 kilometers

CASCADE RANGE

PRINEVILLE

52 mi east of Sisters on Hwy. 126, 35 mi northeast of Bend on Hwy. 126 and U.S. 97.

Prineville is the oldest town in central Oregon and the only incorporated city in Crook County. Surrounded by verdant ranch lands and the purplish hills of the Ochoco National Forest, Prineville will likely interest you chiefly as a jumping-off point for some of the region's more secluded outdoor adventures. The area attracts thousands of anglers, boaters, sightseers, and rock hounds to its nearby streams, reservoirs, and mountains. Rimrocks nearly encircle Prineville, and geology nuts dig for free agates, limb casts, jasper, and thunder eggs on mining claims provided by the local chamber of commerce.

The town itself is dominated by a tire-distribution company owned by local magnate Les Schwab. The dusty streets of the state's unofficial "cowboy capital" have seen woollier days—the city grew up around a disreputable saloon, and range wars between cattlemen and sheep men claimed casualties among all involved species a century ago.

A tough little stone building (it was a bank once, and banks out here needed to be tough) is the site of the museum of the Crook County Historical Society, the **Bowman Museum.** The 1911 edifice is now on the National Register of Historic Places. Prominent are pioneer artifacts—chiefly agricultural implements and deadly weapons—that defined early Prineville. ⊠*246 N. Main St.* ☎*541/447–3715* ⊕*www.bowmanmuseum.org* ⊠*Free* ⊙*Memorial Day–Labor Day, weekdays 10–5, weekends 11–4; Labor Day–Dec. and Feb.–Memorial Day, Tues.–Fri. 10–5, Sat. 11–4.* ⊙*Closed Jan.*

Three stolid stories of gray stone anchor the **Crook County Courthouse.** A perpetual memorial flame maintained by the local American Legion burns in front of this stately 1909 building. ⊠*300 N.E. 3rd St.* ☎*541/447–6553.*

Mountain streams flow out of the Ochoco Mountains and join together to create the Crooked River, which is dammed near Prineville. Bowman Dam on the river forms **Prineville Reservoir State Park.** Recreational activities include boating, swimming, fishing, and hiking. A campground has 22 full hookups, 23 electrical and 23 tent sites, and 5 cabins. ⊠*19020 S.E. Parkland Dr.* ☎*541/447–4363 or 800/452–5687* ⊕*www.oregon stateparks.org* ⊠*Day use $3 per vehicle* ⊙*Daily.*

About ½ mi west of Prineville, **Ochoco Viewpoint** is a scenic overlook that commands a sweeping view of the city and the hills, ridges, and buttes beyond. ⊠*½ mi west of Prineville on U.S. Hwy. 126* ⊠*Free* ⊙*Daily.*

WHERE TO STAY & EAT

$$$$ ✕**Crooked River Dinner Train.** Dine aboard this excursion train as it winds through the rimrock-lined Crooked River valley between Redmond and Prineville. The ride and show are the draw here. Murder mysteries and train robberies are played out during dinners and Sunday

brunches, as well as on special holidays. There are no set hours and times, so be sure to call the office for reservations and departure times. ✉495 N.E. O'Neil Way, Redmond ☎541/548–8630 ⊕*www.crooke-driverdinnertrain.com* ▤*AE, D, MC, V* ⊗ *No events months of Nov., Jan., and Feb.*

¢ 🏨**Rustlers Inn.** From the old-style covered walkways to the large, antiques-furnished rooms, this motel is Old West all the way. Each room is decorated differently—if you call in advance, the managers will attempt to match your room furnishings to your personality. Some rooms have kitchenettes. The Rustlers allows pets to stay for a one-time fee. ✉960 N.W. 3rd St. (U.S. 26), 97754 ☎541/447–4185 ⊕*www.rustlersinn.com* ⇆*19 rooms* ♿*In-room: Wi-Fi. In-hotel: no elevator, public Wi-Fi, parking, some pets allowed* ▤*AE, D, DC, MC, V.*

REDMOND

40 mi east of Sisters on Hwy. 126, 15 mi northeast of Bend on U.S. 97.

Redmond sits at the western end of Oregon's high desert, 4 mi from the Deschutes River and within minutes of several lakes. As with Deschutes County, Redmond has experienced some of the most rapid growth in the state during the past 10 years, largely owing to a dry and mild climate and year-round downhill and cross-country skiing, fishing, hiking, mountain biking, and rock hounding. Still, this is no gentrified resort town à la Bend, as a stroll through downtown will attest. Smith Rock State Park, north of Redmond, attracts die-hard rock climbers from around the world with its hundreds of climbing routes and hiking trails. Wildlife is abundant in the park, which is a nesting area for birds of prey.

Picnicking and fishing are popular at **Cline Falls State Park,** a rest area commanding scenic views on the Deschutes River 5 mi west of Redmond. ✉*Hwy. 126, west of Redmond* ☎*800/551–6949* ⊕*www.oregonstateparks.org* ▤*Free* ⊗*Daily.*

During trout season, **Firemen's Pond** is jumping with fish. Only children and adults with disabilities are permitted to fish here. ✉*Lake Rd. and Sisters Ave.* ☎*541/548–6068* ▤*Free* ⊗*Daily.*

A local farmer created the 4-acre **Petersen's Rock Gardens** near Bend. All of the petrified wood, agate, jasper, lava, and obsidian came from within an 85-mi radius of the garden, and was used to make miniature buildings and bridges, terraces and towers. Among the structures are a micro–Statue of Liberty and five little castles up to 6 feet tall. The attraction includes a small museum and picnic tables. ✉*7930 S.W. 77th St.,* ☎*541/382–5574* ▤*$3 suggested* ⊗*Daily 9–5.*

★ A small, scenic viewpoint about 30 minutes north of Bend, the **Peter Skene Ogden Wayside** is at the top of a dizzyingly severe 300-foot-deep river canyon 10 mi north of Redmond. ✉*U.S. 97 N* ☎*541/548–7501* ▤*Free* ⊗*Daily.*

Fodor's Choice   Eight miles north of Redmond, **Smith Rock State Park** is world famous
★   for rock climbing. You might spot golden eagles, prairie falcons, mule
deer, river otters, and beavers. Due to the environmental sensitivity
of the region, the animal leash law is strongly enforced. ⊠ *Off U.S.
97 9241 N.E. Crooked River Dr., Terrebonne* ☎ *541/548–7501 or
800/551–6949* ⊕ *www.oregonstateparks.org* ⊠ *Day use $3 per vehicle*
⊙ *Daily.*

WHERE TO STAY & EAT

$ ✕ **Sully's Italian Restaurant.** This home-style Italian restaurant is a Red-
mond favorite. With a redbrick interior and candles on every table,
Sully's is proud to serve its take on the always-classic spaghetti and
meatballs, manicotti, and eggplant Parmesan. ⊠ *314 S.W. 5th St.,*
☎ *541/548–5483* ⊟ *D, MC, V.*

$ ⬚ **Eagle Crest Resort.** Eagle Crest is 5 mi west of Redmond, above the
canyon of the Deschutes River. In this high-desert area the grounds are
covered with juniper and sagebrush. The rooms are in a single building
on the landscaped grounds, and some of the suites have gas fireplaces.
The resort is on nearly 1,700 acres. There are 10 mi of bike trails and
a 2-mi hiking trail where you can fish in the river. **Pros:** A full-service
resort, great for kids, pet friendly. **Cons:** There can be crowds, kids, and
pets ⊠ *1522 Cline Falls Hwy., 97756* ☎ *541/923–2453 or 800/682–
4786* ⊟ *541/923–1720* ⊕ *www.eagle-crest.com* ⬚ *100 rooms, 45
suites, 75 town houses* ⬚ *In-room: DVD, kitchen (some), refrigerator, Wi-Fi. In-hotel: 4 restaurants, bar, golf courses, tennis court, pool,
gym, bicycles, children's programs (ages 3–12), laundry facilities, public Wi-Fi, airport shuttle, pets allowed* ⊟ *AE, DC, MC, V.*

OCHOCO NATIONAL FOREST

25 mi east of Prineville off U.S. 26.

East of the flat, juniper-dotted countryside around Prineville the landscape changes to forested ridges covered with tall ponderosa pines
and Douglas firs. Sheltered by the diminutive Ochoco Mountains and
with only about a foot of rain each year, the **Ochoco National Forest,**
established in 1906 by President Theodore Roosevelt, manages to lay
a blanket of green across the dry, high desert of central Oregon. This
arid landscape—marked by deep canyons, towering volcanic plugs,
and sharp ridges—goes largely unnoticed except for the annual influx
of hunters during the fall. The Ochoco, part of the old Blue Mountain Forest Reserve, is a great place for camping, hiking, biking, and
fishing in relative solitude. In its three wilderness areas—Mill Creek,
Bridge Creek, and Black Canyon—it's possible to see elk, wild horses,
eagles, and even cougars. The **Ochoco National Forest Headquarters/Prin-
evine Ranger Station,** ⊠ *3160 N.E. 3rd St., U.S. 26,* ☎ *541/416–6500*
⊙ *Forest year-round, some sections closed during bad weather, ranger
station weekdays 7:30–4:30.*

A 43-mi scenic route, the **Summit Prairie Loop** winds past Lookout Mountain, Round Mountain, Walton Lake, and Big Summit Prairie. The prairie abounds with trout-filled creeks and has one of the finest stands of

ponderosa pines in the state; wild mustangs roam the area. The prairie can be glorious between late May and June, when wildflowers with evocative names like mules ear, wyethia, biscuit root, and yellow bells burst into bloom. Call Ochoco/Prineville Ranger Station for more info at 541/416–6500. ⊠*Forest Service Rd. 22 east to Forest Service Rd. 30, which turns into Forest Service Rd. 3010, south, to Forest Service Rd. 42 heading west, which loops back to Forest Service Rd. 22.*

SPORTS & THE OUTDOORS

HIKING Pick up maps at the Ochoco/Prineville Ranger Station for the trails through the 5,400-acre **Bridge Creek Wilderness** and the demanding **Black Canyon Trail** (24 mi round-trip) in the Black Canyon Wilderness. The 1½-mi **Ponderosa Loop Trail** follows an old logging road through ponderosa pines growing on hills. In early summer wildflowers take over the open meadows. The trailhead begins at Bandit Springs Rest Area, 22 mi east of Prineville on U.S. 26. A 2½-mi, one-way trail winds through old-growth forest and mountain meadows to **Steins Pillar,** a giant lava column with panoramic views; be prepared for a workout on the trail's poorly maintained second half, and allow at least three hours for the hike. To get to the trailhead, drive east 9 mi from Prineville on U.S. 26, head north (to the left) for 6½ mi on Mill Creek Road (also signed as Forest Service Road 33), and head east (to the right) on Forest Service Road 500.

SKIING Two loops for cross-country skiers start at Bandit Springs Rest Area, 29 mi east of Prineville on U.S. 26. One loop is designed for beginners and the other for intermediate to advanced skiers. Both traverse the area near the Ochoco Divide and have great views. Ochoco National Forest headquarters has a handout on skiing trails and can provide the required Sno-Park permits, which are also available from the **Department of Motor Vehicles** (⊠*Ochoco Plaza, 1595 E. 3rd St., Suite A-3, Prineville* ☎*541/447–7855*).

BEND

58 mi south of Warm Springs, U.S. 26 to U.S. 97, 160 mi from Portland, east and south on U.S. 26 and south on U.S. 97.

Bend, Oregon's largest city east of the Cascades, is a modern-day boomtown; in the '90s it was the state's fastest-growing city. The fuel for this bonanza isn't oil, gold, or timber—instead, Bend swells on the strength of its enviable climate, proximity to skiing, and its growing reputation as a playground and recreational escape. Sadly, the growth has also propelled a soulless spread of chain stores and fast-food slingers along U.S. 20 outside of town, camouflaging Bend's attractiveness. On the other hand, stylish, walkable downtown Bend retains a small-city charm.

The neighboring Mt. Bachelor, though hardly a giant among the Cascades at 9,065 feet, has one singular advantage over all its taller relatives—by virtue of its location, it's the first to get snowfall, and the last to see it go. Inland air collides with the Pacific's damp influence,

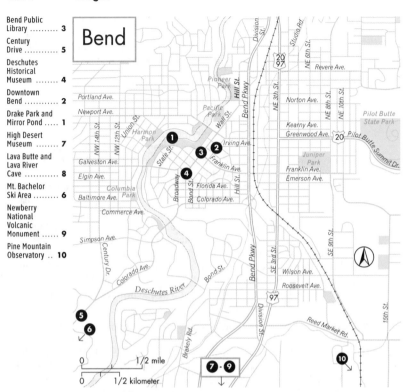

creating skiing conditions immortalized in songs by local rock bands, by raves from the ski press, and in recommendations from popular resort facilities. Like most great ski hills, "the Batch" is a way of life for some, infusing Bend with a ski-bum ethos and healthy dose of what some would describe as a hormonal, postcollegiate buzz.

Alongside this outdoorsy counterculture, Bend has boutique shopping and upscale dining/lodging on par with other urban centers in the state, if not beyond. Despite Oregon's overall economic doldrums, in recent years downtown Bend has undergone a serious makeover, with trend-setting new restaurants and bars taking over one street corner after another. It'll be interesting to see what the future holds for the once sleepy little mill town of Bend.

WHAT TO SEE

③ **Bend Public Library.** Inspirational quotes such as Christa McAuliffe's
🕐 "What are we doing here? We're reaching for the stars," adorn the outer walls of this 40,000 square-foot structure. You may feel like you're reaching for the stars yourself when you ascend the main stair-case—Scandinavian-style blond wood and sharp modernist architec-tural lines abound, and light pours through a wall-size glass window by sculptor Maya Radoczy. Upstairs, the library's fine collection, national and international periodicals, and dozens of public Internet terminals

bask in a light-flooded, vaulted space. Downstairs, to the left of the lobby, find the extensive Children Services section. ⊠ *601 N.W. Wall St.* ☎ *541/617–7040* ⊕ *www.dpls.lib.or.us/SectionIndex.asp?SectionID=6* ⊙ *Mon.–Thurs. 10–8, Fri. 10–6, Sat. 10–5, Sun. 1–5.*

⑤ Century Drive. For 100 mi, this forest-highway loop beginning and ending in Bend meanders past dozens of high mountain lakes good for fishing, hiking, waterskiing, and camping. To find it, take Highway 46 for the first two-thirds of the trip, and then take U.S. 97 at LaPine to return to Bend.

④ Deschutes Historical Museum. A striking 1914 building constructed from locally quarried volcanic tuff has Indian artifacts, historical photos of the region, and a pioneer schoolroom from 1915. ⊠ *129 N.W. Idaho Ave.,* ☎ *541/389–1813* ⊕ *www.deschuteshistory.org* ⊠ *$5* ⊙ *Tues.– Sat. 10–4:30.*

Deschutes National Forest. This 1.6-million-acre forest has 20 peaks higher than 7,000 feet, including three of Oregon's five highest mountains, more than 150 lakes, and 500 mi of streams. A pass is required for all day and overnight use of the trailhead facilities in 13 national forests in Oregon and Washington. ⊠ *1001 S.W. Emkay Dr.* ☎ *541/383–5300* 🖷 *541/383–5531* ⊕ *www.fs.fed.us/r6/centraloregon/* ⊠ *Park pass required: day-use pass $5* ⊙ *Daily.*

★ Downtown Bend. Bend's heart is an area of about six blocks, centered on Wall and Bond streets. Here you'll find boutique shops, fine restaurants, and lively nightlife establishments, as well as a few old-time pharmacies, taverns, and hardware stores keeping it real. ⊠ *Bend Visitor Center: 917 N.W. Harriman* ⊕ *www.visitbend.com* ⊙ *Center hrs: weekdays 9–5, Sat. 10–4.*

① Drake Park and Mirror Pond. Bend's first city park is also its most prominent and lovely. Eleven acres of exactingly manicured greensward and trees snake along the banks of the Deschutes just a few blocks west of downtown. At the far western end of Bend's favorite greenspace, you'll see the High Wheel, a salute to antique logging equipment. It's big . . . but not as big as Drake Park's "Munch n' Music" free summer concert series. Running and walking trails lead to footbridges that will take you out to beautifully renovated, early-20-century neighborhoods. ⊠ *N.W. Riverside Blvd., west of downtown* ⊕ *www.fs.fed.us/r6/centraloregon/wildlife/sites/11-drakepark.shtml* ♿ *Renovated restrooms, including ADA-compliant.*

NEED A BREAK? A sleekly designed coffee shop with modernist blond-wood furnishings, **Bellatazza** starts with morning jolts and pastries in the heart of downtown Bend, and continues serving into the night. Wireless Internet access is available with purchase. (⊠ *869 N.W. Wall St.,* ☎ *541/318–0606* ⊙ *Mon.–Sat. 6 AM–9 PM, Sun. 7–7* ▭ *MC, V*)

⑦ High Desert Museum. The West was truly wild, and this combo museum/ zoo proves it. Kids will love the up close and personal encounters with gila monsters, snakes, lizards, Ochoco the bobcat, and Snowshoe the

FodorsChoice ★

synx. Actors in costume take part in the "Living History" series, where you can chat with stagecoach drivers, boomtown widows, pioneers, and homesteaders. With 53,000 indoor square feet, a quarter-mile trail, and an additional 32,000 square feet of outdoor exhibits and live animal habitats, it's no wonder that the museum sells admission tickets that cover a two-day visit. ⊠ *59800 S. Hwy. 97, , 7 mi south of Downtown Bend* ☎ *541/382–4754* ⊕ *www.highdesertmuseum.org* ⊠ *$15* ⊙ *Daily 9–5* ♿ *Stroller rental $3, wheelchair rentalrestaurant on-site.*

IF YOU'RE FEELING "PEAKED" . . .

If scaling mountains with ropes and pitons doesn't appeal, there's always the option of a horsepower-aided ascent. From downtown Bend, drive east on Greenwood Avenue all of 1.1 mi, turn left (north) at N.E. Pilot Butte Summit Drive and let the gas pedal do the walking all the way up to **Pilot Butte**. Three-hundred-sixty-degree views await you, as well as a bird's-eye view of Bend below. A bronze sundial-type gizmo at the center will finally end the guessing as to which of the nine surrounding mountains is which.

❾ **Newberry National Volcanic Monument.** The last time Newberry Volcano blew its top was about 13 centuries ago. Paulina Peak, which is on an unpaved road at the south end of the national monument, has the best view into the crater and its two lakes, Paulina and East. Lava Butte and Lava River Cave are at the north end of the monument near the visitor center. *Note: visitor center may still be under renovation; these hours are subject to change, call first.* ⊠ *Visitor center: U.S. 97, 10 mi south of Bend, 58201 S. Hwy. 97* ☎ *541/593–2421* ⊕ *www.fs.fed.us/r6/centraloregon/newberrynvm/index.shtml* ⊠ *$5 per vehicle* ⊙ *Late Apr.–mid-Oct., daily 9–5; Labor Day–Memorial Day, Wed.–Sun. 9:30–5.*

❽ On the north end of the Newberry National Volcanic Monument, you'll find **Lava Butte and Lava River Cave.** The Lava Butte area has several large basalt lava flows as well as the 500-foot Lava Butte cinder cone. Lava River Cave is a 1-mi-long lava tube. Enter by the visitor center. *Note: visitor center may still be under renovation; these hours are subject to change, call first.* ⊠ *58201 S. Hwy. 97,* ☎ *541/593–2421* ⊕ *Lava Butte: www.fs.fed.us/r6/centraloregon/newberrynvm/interest-lavabutte.shtml* ⊕ *Lava River Cave: www.fs.fed.us/r6/centraloregon/newberrynvm/interest-lavariver.shtml* ⊠ *$5 per vehicle* ⊙ *May–Oct., daily 9–5.*

❿ **Pine Mountain Observatory.** Three reflecting telescopes, with apertures of 15-inch-, 24-inch-, and 32-inch-diameters, each in its own domed building, monitor the universe from atop 6,500-foot Pine Mountain. Take a peek, 26 mi southeast of Bend. ⊠ *U.S. 20, near Millican* ☎ *541/382–8331* ⊕ *http://pmo-sun.uoregon.edu* ⊠ *$3 donation requested* ⊙ *May–Sept., Fri. and Sat. evenings.*

2

WHERE TO EAT

$$ **✗Cork.** Like the most popular girl in high school, Cork gives off an
Fodor'sChoice air of confidence, knowing it's literally at the top of the Bend foodie
★ chain. And like that girl, Cork is pretty, with its block glass used as
room dividers (a separate wine bar is off to the left), soft lighting,
cocoa-color linens, and metal sculptures. Winning "best of" awards
since its inception in 2001, Cork owes its success to the genius of Chef
Greg Unruh, still working his own hot line. His presentation is art on
a plate ... with a flower on top. Whether you choose fish (ahi and scal-
lops are supreme), beef, or chicken, the textures melt in your mouth,
the adventurous mix of ingredients blending exquisitely. Lavender pork
with figs, tequila-treated prawns with chile pancetta ... you can't go
wrong. ⊠*150 N.W. Oregon Ave.* ☎*541/382–6881* ⊕*www.corkbend.
com* ⌖*Reservations essential* ▤*MC, V* ⊘*Closed Sun. and Mon. No
lunch.*

$–$$ **✗Merenda.** With its menu forever in flux, Merenda chef Jody Denton
Fodor'sChoice is constantly exploring new ways to bring Bend the very best. The
★ showroom kitchen with a tiled wood-burning rotisserie, polished hardwood floors, and large bustling bar is almost as hip as the dining room
with its 20-foot redbrick walls covered with modern art. Whether you
want lunch, light appetizers, a late-afternoon happy hour, or full dinner, Merenda is at your beck and call with French/Italian influences.
Nightly wood-fired specials are offered as well as handmade pastas,
vegetarian dishes, and seafood complemented by a wine list critics call
"the best in Central Oregon." Note: If you love sushi, Chef Denton
has recently opened the nearby Deep, which is getting as many raves as
Merenda. ⊠*900 N.W. Wall St.* ☎*541/330–2304* ⊕*www.merendares-
taurant.com* ⌖*Reservations essential* ▤*AE, D, DC, MC, V.*

¢–$ **✗Deschutes Brewery & Public House.** Bendites are fiercely loyal to their
★ city's first original brewpub, established in 1988. Not only does the
Brewery bake its own bread and pizza dough (adding in its own malt),
it makes its sausages, sauces, mustards, dressings, soups, etc. House
favorites include sweet-and-spicy mac and cheese and fish-and-chips.
Though the always-popular Black Butte Porter is a Public House classic, don't overlook the new seasonal choices. Or order a sampler of
six different tastes for $5.25. Monday nights are especially big, with
$1-discounted beers and burgers. It is almost always hopping, and you
may find yourself waiting to be seated, as there are no reservations.
However, time flies as you admire the quasi-medieval murals of peas-
ants downing ale, watch the four TVs broadcasting sports, or people-watch the boisterous crowd while you wait. ⊠*1044 N.W. Bond
St.,* ☎*541/382–9242* ⊕*www.deschutesbrewery.com* ▤*AE, MC, V*
⊘*Daily 11–10 or midnight.*

¢–$ **✗La Rosa.** Come for the Red Cactus Margarita—stay for the food.
Voted Best Mexican Restaurant in Bend time and again, La Rosa offers
classic Mexican combination plates, as well as gourmet lobster-tail
enchiladas, grilled prawns wrapped in apple-smoked bacon, and pork
loin baked in banana leaves. There are plenty of vegetarian entrées
offered as well. As one fan puts it, "La Rosa es la bomba!" Choose to

dine indoors or on the heated patio. ⊠*1114 N.W. College Way, #104,* ☎*541/318–7210* ⊕*www.larosabend.com* ▭*AE, MC, V.*

$$$$
Fodor's Choice
★

Lara House Lodge. Fully refurbished in pure Craftsman style, this six-suite B&B promises plenty of luxury. The kitchen positively gleams with modern appliances, and exposed dark-wood beams and wrought-iron appointments adorn the common rooms. An inviting fireplace is framed by artful tiles and large-paned windows overlook Drake Park's Mirror Pond. From the Bachelor Suite on the main floor with private entrance to the spacious Summit Suite at the top, each of the six rooms exudes high style and warmth. The gourmet breakfast, served on the front porch or in the sun room or great dining room, may consist of a crustless salmon rice torte, shortbread waffles, or herb-filled crepes. Try to arrive by 5 PM to enjoy the Northwest wine reception. Upscale eateries are also just two blocks away. **Pros:** Clean lines and uncluttered feel make a relaxing environment, park and town are pleasant, accessible walks. **Cons:** No pets or kids. ⊠*640 N.W. Congress St. NW, 97701* ☎*541/388–4064 or 800/766–4064* ⊕*www.larahouse. com* ⤢*6 rooms* ♿*In room: no phones, Internet. In-hotel: no elevator, public Internet, no kids.* ▭*D, MC, V* ❍|*BP.*

$$$$
Fodor's Choice
★

Sunriver Resort. The pine-scented desert that this premier outdoor resort calls home provides a redolent landscape for you and your family to enjoy. The Deschutes River flows directly through the complex, providing Class III white-water rafting trips, canoeing, and kayaking. There are three golf courses, including the renowned Crosswater, seven tennis courts, and skiing at nearby Mt. Bachelor. If indoor fitness is more your style, check out Sage Springs Spa. Lodging choices vary from vacation rentals to Sunriver guestrooms. For families, kids' programs are held at Fort Funnigan, with activities designed for ages 3 through 12. From Bend: 15 mi south on US 97, exit at Sunriver Resort Lodging sign/Century Dr., drive 2 mi to the lodge. **Pros:** Huge variety of activities close togehter, much pampering, dog friendly. **Con:** Although self-contained, it has the feel of a busy town. ⊠*17600 Center Dr.Sunriver 97707* ☎*541/593–1000 or 800/547–3922* ☐*541/593–5458* ⊕*www. sunriver-resort.com* ⤢*205 units; over 400 additional vacation rental properties* ♿*In-room: VCR, Ethernet, some kitchens. In-hotel: 3–6 restaurants, bar, golf courses, tennis courts, 3 pools, gym, spa, bicycles, no elevator, children's programs (ages 3–12), concierge, public Internet, shuttle service, parking (no fee), some pets allowed (fee)* ▭*AE, D, DC, MC, V.*

$$$

Pine Ridge Inn. This immaculate two-floor B&B is surrounded by ponderosa pines and junipers. The friendly staff goes out of its way to accommodate—if you can't make it to the 5 pm wine social, they'll be happy to bring a glass to your room upon request. All rooms have fireplaces, with either decks or patios. The suites have full sitting areas, seven with Jacuzzis. Hot breakfasts come with a choice of entrées, as well as the usual continental buffet spread of juices, pastries, and cereals. The turndown service comes with a special homemade goodie on the pillow. **Pros:** Clean spacious rooms, separate bathing and vanity areas, nightlight imbedded on the stairs in the suites. **Cons:** The river view is also the highway view; with 20 rooms, it has a less intimate feel than expected from a B&B. ✉ *1200 S.W. Century Dr., 97702* ☎ *541/389–6137 or 800/600–4095* 🖳 *541/385–5669* ⊕ *www.pineridgeinn.com* ➬ *20 rooms* ⚲ *In-room: refrigerator, VCR, Wi-Fi. In-hotel: elevator, public Wi-Fi, parking (no fee)* ☰ *AE, D, MC, V* ⎮○⎮ *BP.*

OFF THE BEATEN PATH

Cowboy Dinner Tree Steakhouse. Seventy miles south of Sunriver you'll find an authentic campfire cook, and he's firing up a genuine taste of the Old West. Oregonians will tell you that the 30-ounce steak or whole chicken over an open flame, plus all the fixings, is more than worth the trip. Serving the "true cowboy cut," the Dinnertree ensures leftovers will be enjoyed for days. If you journey from afar, lodging is available in the rustic buckaroo bunkhouse. Plates are $23.50 per adult, $10.25 for kids 7–13; kids 6 and under free. Lodging in the bunkhouse is $100 for two, dinner included. Call for exact directions: off Hwy. 31, 4½ mi south on East Bay Road. ✉ County Rd. 4-12/Forest Service Rd. 28, Silver Lake 97638 ☎ *541/576–2426* ⊕ *www.cowboydinnertree.homestead.com* ⊙ *June–Oct., Thurs.–Sun. 4 PM–8:30. Nov.–May, Fri.–Sun. 4 PM–8:30.*

$–$$$ **Seventh Mountain Resort.** Proud of the fact that it's "the closest accommodation to Mt. Bachelor" (approximately 14 mi away), this resort has been a host to Central Oregon's year-round outdoor activities since 1972. It's on the banks of the Deschutes River, so white-water rafting and fishing are right outside the door. Among the recreational facilities there's an outdoor roller rink that converts to an ice-skating rink in winter. For the younger guests, Camp Ranger Kids Camp has activities for ages 4 to 11. Accommodations include standard bedrooms with a queen-size bed, deluxe bedrooms with private deck, and studios with fireplaces and full kitchens, as well as private 2 and 3-bedroom homes. Consider Seasons Restaurant, the resort's latest upscale dining spot, specializing in Pacific Northwest cuisine. **Pros:** Kid friendly, varied accommodations, some moderately priced. **Cons:** Golf course is not on-site, but ½ mi away, under different ownership; no spa facilities. ✉ *18575 S.W. Century Dr., Deschutes National Forest, Bend 97702* ☎ *541/382–8711 or 800/452–6810* 🖳 *541/382–3517* ⊕ *www.seventh mountain.com* ➬ *170 rooms* ⚲ *In-room: Wi-Fi, kitchens (some). In-hotel: 3 restaurants, bar, tennis courts, pools, water sports, bicycles, no elevator, children's programs (ages 4–11), concierge, public Wi-Fi, parking (no fee)* ☰ *AE, D, MC, V.*

NIGHTLIFE & THE ARTS

Bend's take on a space-age cocktail haven, **Astrolounge** (✉ *147 N.W. Minnesota Ave.,* ☎ *541/388–0116*) comes complete with matte-black-and-chrome industrial furnishings, a loft-style layout, and 25 specialty martinis. There's an "Astrodiasiac" martini for two—'nuff said. The bar connects to a bistro sharing the out-of-this-world motif. Oregon may be synonymous with microbrew ale and pinot noir, but then along came the **Bendistillery Sampling Room and Martini Bar** (✉ *850 N.W. Brooks St.,* ☎ *541/388–6868*). The hard stuff produced in-state usually ended up on the bottom shelves of low-end taverns, but Bendistillery changed that, handcrafting small batches of spirits flavored with local herbs. Bend sits in the middle of one of the world's great juniper forests, making the gin a particular treat. This slick little tasting room stirs up bracing martinis and highballs incorporating Bendistillery's products, resulting in a perfect bar-crawl kickoff or classy nightcap. Named for the Prineville tire tycoon, the **Les Schwab Amphitheater** (⊠*344 S.W. Selvin Hixon Dr.* ☎*541/312–8510 or 541/318–5457* ⊕*www.bendconcerts.com*), an open-air venue in the Old Mill District, brings national music tours to Bend.

SPORTS & THE OUTDOORS

BICYCLING **U.S. 97** north to the Crooked River Gorge and Smith Rock provides bikers with memorable scenery and a good workout. **Sunriver** has 26 mi of paved bike paths.

SKIING Many Nordic trails—more than 165 mi of them—wind through the **Deschutes National Forest** (☎*541/383–5300*). Call for information about conditions.

☾ **Mt. Bachelor Ski Area** is one of the best resort areas in the U.S.—60% of the downhill runs are rated expert. One of the 11 lifts takes skiers all the way to the mountain's 9,065-foot summit. The vertical drop is 3,265 feet; the longest of the 70 runs is 2 mi. Facilities and services include equipment rental and repair, a ski school, ski shop, Nordic skiing, weekly races, and day care; you can enjoy restaurants, bars, and six lodges. Other activities include cross-country skiing, a tubing park, sled dog rides, snowshoeing, and in summer hiking and chair-lift rides. The 36 mi of trails at the **Mount Bachelor Nordic Center,** most of them near the base of the mountain, are by and large intermediate. ⊠*Cascade Lakes Hwy.* ☎*541/382–2442 or 800/829–2442* ⊕*www. mtbachelor.com* ⊡*Lift tickets $56–$66 per day* ☉*Nov.–July, daily 8–4, or as weather allows.*

SHOPPING

Carrying high-end Asian furniture and whimsical keepsakes from around the world, **Azila Nora** is a visual treat. It's also the only Oregon distributor of a highly-specialized line of handmade pottery from Zimbabwe called "Penzo." (⊠*605 N.W. Newport Ave.,* ☎*541/389–6552*). A fun, flashy shop, **Hot Box Betty** (⊠*903 N.W. Wall St.* ☎*541/383–0050*) sells high fashion for women and men, carrying DVF, Burning Torch, Frye Boots, and Isabelle Fiore bags. Visit the Hot Box if only to meet the delightful ladies running the store. An enthusiastic husband-and-wife team presides over **Millette's Kitchen Store** (⊠*1052 N.W. Newport Ave., Suite 103* ☎*541/617–0312*), crammed to the

---

WANDERLUST

See Bend a whole new way with **Wanderlust Tours,** (☎541/389–8359 ⊕www.wanderlusttours.com)an interpretive guide and touring company that takes small groups on canoeing, caving, or snowshoeing tours, sightseeing in remote areas. Offering trips for all ability levels and ages, Wanderlust gives full service (you don't have to worry about bringing a thing, not even food).Tours vary by season and price. Rates for the moonlight canoe rides are $60–$65 per person, and range from $42–$47 for most of the other trips. .

2

ceiling with fine foods. Bend was once the site of one of the world's largest sawmill operations, a sprawling industrial complex along the banks of the Deschutes. In recent years, the abandoned shells of the old factory buildings of the **Old Mill District** (⊠ *545 S.W. Powerhouse Dr.,* ☎ *541/312–0131* ⊕ *www.theoldmill.com*) have been transformed into an attractive shopping center, the Shops at the Old Mill District, a project honored with national environmental awards. Bend's main concentration of national chain retailers can be found here, including Gap/Gap Kids, Banana Republic, and Victoria's Secret, along with the Central Oregon Visitors Association, a 16-screen multiplex movie house, and the Les Schwab Amphitheater. A friendly and attentive staff sells sleek modern outdoor gear and clothing at **Pandora's Backpack** (⊠ *920 N.W. Bond St., Suite 101,* ☎ *541/382–6694*). Renovated in 2003 to mix office, retail, and loft space, **St. Clair Place** (⊠ *920 N.W. Bond St.*) houses a spa (the ZantéAveda Lifestyle Salon), antiques shops, galleries, a flower shop (Wildflowers) and a casual tapas and cocktail bistro (**"28"**) ☎ *541/385–0828.* The word for "treasure" in Japanese is "takara." And that's just what Takara carries in its home and garden specialty shop, representing artists who sell their one-of-a-kind works exclusively to this oasis of calm at ⊠ *2754 N.W. Crossing Dr.,* ☎ *541/385–1144.*

SISTERS

18 mi northwest of Bend on U.S. 20.

Sisters derived its name from a group of three Cascade peaks (Faith, Hope, and Charity) that rise to the southwest. If you enter the central Oregon high desert area from Santiam Pass or the McKenzie River Highway, Sisters appears to be a town out of the Old West. The town fathers–or perhaps we should say "sisters"–strictly enforce an 1800s-style architecture. Rustic cabins border a llama ranch on the edge of town. Western storefronts give way to galleries. A bakery occupies the former general store, and the town blacksmith's home now has a flower shop. Although its population remains under 1,800, Sisters increasingly attracts visitors as well as urban runaways who appreciate its tranquillity and charm. The Metolius River area to the west is a special find for fly-fisherman as well as springtime wildflower lovers.

Three and a half miles east of Sisters, **Hinterland Ranch** has been breeding llamas and Polish Arabian horses since 1965, owning one of the largest and oldest llama herds in North America. This is a working ranch where you can observe the llamas and purchase llama fleece, yarn and gifts. ⊠ *67750 U.S. Hwy. 20 W,* ☎ *541/549–1215* 📠 *541/549–5262* 🕑 *Mon.–Sat. 7:30–5.*

NEED A BREAK?

In a rustic-looking former general store, **Sisters Bakery** (⊠ *251 E. Cascade St.* ☎ *541/549–0361*) turns out high-quality pastries, coffee, and doughnuts. If you're an early riser, this place is ideal. Sunday through Thursday they open at 5 ᴀᴍ to start their day, as well as yours. Sunday–Thursday 5–5, Friday and Saturday 6–6. Cash or check only.

WHERE TO EAT

$$$$ ✕**Jen's Garden.** This "Garden" has grown to become the first award-
★ winning, upscale restaurant Sisters could claim in years. The little ox-
blood-red cottage swung open its doors in February of 2006—and by
the following year it was garnering praise faster than you could say
"Best of." In keeping with the European custom of small servings, the
five courses are deliberately integrated so that the flavors complement
each other. And every two weeks the menu is new, from soup to nuts.
Or rather, in Jen-Garden speak, from appetizer to fish course to entrée
to salad to dessert. For each course there are a few choices: chantrelle
and butternut squash ravioli or New Zealand cockles/fennel/tomato/
sausage broth; osso buco or berry-bread-pudding-stuffed roasted quail.
If you prefer, you can always order à la carte. But since this is Jen's Garden, Jen probably knows best. ⊠*403 E. Hood Ave.,* ☎*541/549–2699*
⌂*Reservations essential* ⊟*MC, V* ⊗ *No lunch.*

$–$$ ✕**Bronco Billy's.** Rustle up some good grub at this outrageous tip of the
cowboy hat to the wild and woolly West. Look up and find corral fences
swinging from the ceiling. Look for the kitchen and instead you'll find
the "Ranch Grill." Look for the gift shop and instead you'll find the
"Bronco Boot-Teek." Whether you go for American (burgers, steaks,
BBQ ribs), south-of-the-border (quesadillas, tacos), or even a Caesar
salad, the portions are hefty and tasty to boot. Rooms in this original
1912 hotel are decorated in different themes, and are available for
private parties. Kids are welcome, but management requests you leave
your horse outside. ⊠*190 E. Cascade St.* ☎*541/549–7427* ⊕*www.
broncobillysranchgrill.com* ⊟*D, MC, V* ⊗*Daily 11:30–close.*

¢ ✕**Depot Deli & Cafe.** A railroad theme prevails at this main-street deli. A
miniature train circles above as the kitchen dishes out excellent, inexpensive sandwiches and burgers. Sit inside next to the rough-wood
walls, or out back on the deck. ⊠*250 W. Cascade St.,* ☎*541/549–
2572* ⊟*MC, V*

¢ ✕**Sisters Harvest Basket.** Healthy snacks, sandwiches, and ready-to-go
meals can be found at this friendly spot, which also doubles as a natural
and organic-foods grocery. Favorite requests include halibut Parmesan,
fish tacos, and organically-made pizza. In warmer months there are
tables out back. ⊠*110 S. Spruce St.,* ☎*541/549–0598* ⊟*MC, V .*

WHERE TO STAY

$$ ▧**Black Butte Ranch.** Eight miles west of Sisters, Black Butte Ranch is a
resort with gorgeous mountain views and landscaping to match, with
biking and hiking paths meandering for miles around golf courses,
ponds, and meadows. Window views throughout keep you in perpetual
contact with the snowcapped mountains and pine forests that envelop
the property. Horseback riding, swimming, and golf are dominant
sports here. The Ranch is also convenient to Smith Rock State Park,
the Deschutes River, Mt. Bachelor, and the Hoodoo Ski Bowl. **Pros:**
Great for people who want to avoid a "big hotel" venue, all the ameni-
ties of a resort, yet with individual properties. **Cons:** Since Black Butte
only provides cabin, condo, and house rentals, if you're looking for
hotel rooms, Black Butte isn't for you. Most properties don't have a/c.
⊠*12930 Hawks Beard, 97759* ☎*541/595–6211 or 866/901–2961*

🖩*541/595–1299* ⊕*www.blackbutteranch.com* ⇱*126 properties*
⚲*In-room: no a/c, kitchen (some). In-hotel: 2–4 restaurants, bar, golf
courses, tennis courts, pools, gym, spa, bicycles, children's programs
(10 years and younger), concierge, public Internet (some), some pets
(fee) allowed* ▭*AE, D, DC, MC, V.*

SHOPPING

More than a dozen central Oregon artists are showcased at the **High
Desert Gallery,** "the art and soul of Central Oregon," a repository of
affordable contemporary art that includes precious metal jewelry,
clay jewelry, oil paintings, vases, and stained glass. (⊠*281 W. Cascade Ave.* 🖩*541/549–6250 or 866/549–6250*). Sisters is the site of the
lavishly stocked **Lonesome Water Books** (⊠*221 W. Cascade Ave., Suite
C* 🖩*541/549–2203*), one of Oregon's great independent bookstores.
You can find everything from $1 paperbacks to premium first editions
here.

THE OREGON CASCADES

Oregon's segment of the Cascade Range begins with Mt. Hood and
pushes on south, covering millions of wilderness acres stretching to
Mt. McLoughlin in southern Oregon. Slightly below Mt. Hood in the
Cascade Range are hundreds of tranquil campgrounds as well as trails
friendly to all levels of hikers. In a relatively short west-to-east route
over the range (which encompasses large pieces of two scenic byways,
McKenzie-Santiam Pass and West Cascades Scenic Byways), you'll get
a geographical sampling of the state. Just 47 mi east of Salem along
the North Santiam River is the Detroit Lake Recreation Area, controlled by the Detroit Dam. Only 10 mi north of Detroit Lake, but a
secluded world apart, is Breitenbush Hot Springs Retreat and Conference Center, a spiritual healing and renewal community surrounded by
old-growth forest.

Other popular spots within this region are Hoodoo Ski Bowl near the
crest of the Cascades at Santiam Pass, and over on the eastern slope
within Deschutes National Forest the serenity of Suttle Lake. If you're
looking to fly-fish or relax by listening to stands of ponderosa pine
whisper on a warm, lazy afternoon, consider the Metolius Recreation
Area. The Metolius River, flowing through the small town of Camp
Sherman, has biking and walking trails along its banks in addition to
cabins and several other lodgings.

DETROIT

40 mi east of Salem on Hwy. 22.

A small town with fewer than 300 residents, Detroit was founded in the
late 1800s during construction of the Oregon Pacific Railroad. Its name
was chosen because many of the earlier settlers were from Detroit,
Michigan. Because Detroit Lake is surrounded by tree-laden mountains
and national and state forests, the town will not grow much beyond
its current size. It's also near a wealth of trails and creeks, many of
which are more secluded and tranquil than those in the Mt. Hood area.

Detroit's elevation is 1,573 feet, so getting here through winter snow likely won't be a problem.

One waterway influencing the water level of Detroit Lake is **Detroit Dam** (☎ *503/897–2385 tours*), which rises 463 feet above its foundation in the steep, narrow slopes of North Santiam Canyon. The dam creates 33 mi of shoreline along Detroit Lake conducive to boating, fishing, camping, and picnicking. Guided tours of the lake are available, though in winter the lake is lowered, so depending on snow pack, lake activities may be suspended.

> **HOW MUCH DID BEKINS CHARGE FOR THAT?**
>
> In the summer of 1952, after the Corps of Engineers put their final touches on the Detroit Dam, the entire town flooded. It had to be relocated one half mile to the northwest.

Three miles downstream from Detroit Dam, **Big Cliff Dam** rises 191 feet above its foundation into the canyon and also feeds Detroit Lake.

WHERE TO
STAY & EAT

¢–$ ✕**The Cedars Restaurant and Lounge.** A wacky bear and fish motif greets you as you enter the third-generation-owned Cedars. For 56 years the Layman family has been serving up breakfast, lunch, and dinner to locals and tourists alike. The chicken-fried steak combo is a break-fast standby, and out of eight different burgers, including a vegetarian Gardenburger, the Logger Burger (loaded with bacon, ham, egg, mushrooms, and cheese) is the favorite. Big-screen TVs and pool tables dominate the lumberjack-themed lounge at the back. If you're thinking about cheese and chips, the hefty Cedars Nachos Supreme (2 sizes, vegetarian on request) is the way to go. ⊠ *200 Detroit Ave.,* ☎ *503/854–3636* ▤*MC, V.*

$–$$ 🏠**Breitenbush Hot Springs Retreat and Conference Center.** A cooperative community, tucked away on 150 acres that went uninhabited for 11,000 years, bonds to protect the forest, heal the soul, and provide solitude. Power sources throughout the facility are geo- and hydrother-mal. Retreat prices include modest cabins (lower-price tents and dorms also available), three vegetarian meals per day, well-being programs—including yoga, ancient-forest walks, and meditation—and the use of 45 naturally occurring hot-springs pools, open 24 hours a day. Bathing in the hot springs is clothing-optional. Day use options. Massage thera-pies at additional cost. Just east of Detroit, turn north on Hwy. 46 off Hwy. 22; 10 mi past Cleator Bend Campground turn right onto single-lane bridge crossing Breitenbush River. Road is gravel after bridge and has three forks in its 1½-mi course. Go left at every fork until parking lot. ⚠ **Do not take alternate route Highway 224 from Estacada; it is often dangerous or impassable due to snow, ice, landslides, and fallen trees from early fall through late spring. Pros:** Perfect for getting away from it all, wonderfully inexpensive. **Cons:** Breitenbush is "off the grid," so decide if this for you ⊠*Forest Service Rd. 46, Milepost 10, Detroit 97342* ☎*503/854–3320* 📠*503/854–3819* ⊕*www.breitenbush.com* ⇱*42 cabins* ⌂*No phones* ▤*D, MC, V* ❘❙*FAP.*

METOLIUS RECREATION AREA
9 mi northwest of Sisters, off Hwy. 22.

On the eastern slope of the Cascades and within the 1.6-million-acre Deschutes National Forest, this bounty of recreational wilderness is drier and sunnier than the western side of the mountains, giving way to bountiful natural history, outdoor activities, and wildlife. Spectacular views of jagged, 10,000-foot snowcapped Cascade peaks—including Broken Top, the Three Sisters, and Mt. Jefferson, the second-highest peak in Oregon—sprawl high above the basin of an expansive evergreen valley carpeted by pine.

Within the Deschutes National Forest, 5 mi south of Camp Sherman, the dark cinder cone of **Black Butte** rises 6,400 feet. At its base the **Metolius River** springs forth. Witness the birth of this "instant" river by walking a paved ¼-mi path embedded in ponderosa forest, eventually reaching a viewpoint with the dramatic snow-covered peak of **Mt. Jefferson** on the horizon. At this point, water gurgles to the ground's surface and pours into a wide-trickling creek cascading over a cloister of moss-covered rocks. Within feet it funnels outward, expanding its northerly flow; becomes a full-size river; and meanders east alongside grassy banks and a dense pine forest to join the Deschutes River 35 mi downstream. Because the river is spring fed, the 48°F flow of the water remains constant. In 1988 the 4,600-acre corridor of the Metolius was designated a National Wild and Scenic River. Within the area and along the river, there are ample resources for camping, hiking, biking, swimming, and boating. Enjoy fly-fishing for rainbow, brown, and bull trout in perhaps the best spot within the Cascades.

WHERE TO
STAY & EAT
$–$$
★

✕**The Boathouse.** From a simple marina tackle shop comes a woodsy boathouse, replete with pine, Mexican tiling, Native American art, and water as far as the eye can see. Frequent wine and dessert tastings, summer Sunday BBQ's on the lawn, live-music Friday, mini-banquets on the boat out back ("Camp Run-A-Muk"), and inspired mixology (Blue Green Algae Martini, anyone?) by manager Jason make the Boathouse feel like a party boat. The food is creative and fresh, a well-balanced variety for all tastes. It's upscale at dinner (coconut curry pasta, polenta-crusted halibut, duck with blood-orange raspberry sauce), and casual at lunch (salads, burgers, cheeseboards). Lovely food and the management's genuine joie de vivre give the Boathouse its unique flavor. Fourteen miles west of Sisters on Highway 20, look for the sign for Suttle Lake Resort on the south side of the highway. ✉*13300 U.S. Hwy. 20, Sisters* ☎*541/595–2628* ⊕*www.thelodgeatsuttlelake.com* ⊟*AE, MC, V* ⊗*Thurs.–Mon. 11–9. Limited hrs for breakfast primarily for lodge guests 8:30–10* AM.

$$
Fodor'sChoice
★

⛺**The Lodge at Suttle Lake.** Built in the Grand Cascadian style, the 10,000 square-foot lodge presides over the eastern side of Suttle Lake. Supersized wooden architecture and whimsical charm characterize the main Great Room, which is often flooded with light beneath a sky-high ceiling. Fanciful touches abound—a tepee chandelier, an enormous bison head sporting a fedora, and a stuffed moose with skis posing near the stone fireplace are just a few examples. But management takes its guests seriously; the 10 new lodge rooms are big on luxury, with fireplaces and glorious lake or forest views. The six exterior cabins vary in modern conveniences and size, from the "Rustic" (bring/rent linens) to the "Pointe" that sleeps eight, situated right on the lake. For biking, hiking, boating, or just relaxing, beautiful Suttle Lake is at the center of it all, inviting quiet contemplation and pleasurable recreation. **Pros:** The setting, the accessibility to varied sports in all seasons, the grand look of the place and friendly staff, the variation in choice and price. **Cons:** No a/c in summer. ⊠*13300 U.S. Hwy. 20, 97759* ☎*541/595–2628* ⊕*www.thelodgeatsuttlelake.com* ⇆*10 interior lodge rooms, 6 individual cabins* ⚒*In-room: no a/c, Wi-Fi (some), kitchen (some). In-hotel: elevator, bar, , public Wi-Fi, parking (no fee), some pets allowed (fee)* ⊟*AE, MC, V.*

SKIING On a 5,711-foot summit, **Hoodoo Ski Area** (⊠*U.S. 20, 20 mi west of Sisters* ☎*541/822–3799* ⊕*www.hoodoo.com*) has 806 acres of ski-able terrain. With three quad lifts, one triple lift, one double lift, and 30 downhill runs, skiers of all levels will find suitable thrills. For tranquillity, upper and lower Nordic trails are surrounded by silence. At a 60,000-square-foot lodge at the mountain's base you can take in the view, grab bait, shop, or relax your weary feet. The ski area has kids' activities and child-care services available.

CAMP SHERMAN
10 mi northwest of Sisters on U.S. 20, 5 mi north on Hwy. 14.

Surrounded by groves of whispering yellow-bellied ponderosa pines, larch, fir, and cedars and miles of streamside forest trails, this small, peaceful resort community of 250 residents is part of a designated 86,000-acre conservation area. The area's beauty and natural resources are the big draw: the spring-fed Metolius River prominently glides through town. In the early 1900s Sherman County wheat farmers escaped the dry summer heat by migrating here to fish and rest in the cool river environment. To help guide fellow farmers to the spot, devotees nailed a shoe-box top with the name CAMP SHERMAN to a tree at a fork in the road. Several original buildings still stand from the homesteader days, including some cabins, a schoolhouse, and a tiny chapel.

WHERE TO
STAY & EAT
$$–$$$
Fodor'sChoice
★

✕ **Kokanee Cafe.** Chef Steven Draheim's bold, inventive style has gourmands from nearby cities flocking to this homey hideaway on the banks of the Metolius. With a subtle touch, Draheim often finds a way to introduce a daring ingredient to wonderful effect. Crab cakes, rolled into smallish balls buried inside a crisscross of crisped vermicelli, are crunchy-succulent. Roast duck is enhanced by a sprinkling of organic chocolate bits; and wild salmon is just that when brushed with creamy potato and then heaped with calamari-corn salsa. As if brilliant appetizers, entrées and a fine wine list weren't enough, chef Steven hand-cranks his own ice cream daily, inventing new flavors for different themes. Witness his Skittles and Red Hots creation for candy theme. ⊠*25545 S.W. Forest Service Rd. 1419, Camp Sherman* ☎*541/595–6420* ⊕*www.kokaneecafe.com* ⊟*MC, V* ⊗*Closed Nov.–Apr. No lunch.*

$$$$ ⬚Metolius River Resort. Each of the individually owned cabins at this
Fodor'sChoice resort has splendid views of the sparkling Metolius River, decks fur-
★ nished with Adirondack chairs, full kitchens, fireplaces—and are all
in immaculate condition. Children are allowed, but management asks
that they respect the resort's request to maintain a "peaceful and quiet
area." And therein lies its beauty: the genuine get-away-from-it-all feel
of a private residence nestled in ponderosa pines and aspen. Not to
mention that one of the best fly-fishing rivers in the Cascades flows
right outside your window, and a gourmet restaurant is mere steps
away. ⚠ Make sure to drive in north from Hwy. 20—other routes are dangerous or ill-advised. Pros: Privacy, full view of the river, cabins that feel
like home. Cons: No parties, loud music, loud children, no additional
people (even visitors) allowed. ⊕ Off U.S. 20, northeast 10 mi from
Sisters, turn north on Camp Sherman Rd, stay to left at fork (1419),
and then right at only stop sign. ⊠25551 S.W. Forest Service Rd.
1419, Camp Sherman97730 ☎800/818–7688 ⊕www.metoliusriver-
resort.com ⊄11 cabin homes ☖In-room: VCR/DVD (some), Ethernet, kitchen, parking (no fee). ▤MC, V.

CENTRAL OREGON ESSENTIALS

BY CAR

U.S. 20 heads west from Idaho and east from the coastal town of Newport into central Oregon. U.S. 26 goes southeast from Portland to Prineville, where it heads northeast into the Ochoco National Forest. U.S.
97 heads north from California and south from Washington to Bend.
Highway 126 travels east from Eugene to Prineville; it connects with
U.S. 20 heading south (to Bend) at Sisters. Roads throughout central
Oregon are well maintained and open throughout the winter season,
although it's always advisable to have tire chains in the car.

Rapid population growth in the Bend area has created traffic problems
out of scale with the city's size. If you're trying to head out of or into
town on a major highway during the morning or 5 PM rush, especially
on U.S. 97 between Bend and Redmond, be advised that you may hit
congestion. Parking in downtown Bend is free for the first two hours,
or you can park for free in the historic residential neighborhood just
west of downtown. Free on-street parking is plentiful in all of central
Oregon's other towns and cities.

VISITOR INFORMATION

The best one-stop source for information is the Central Oregon Visitors
Association, a thorough umbrella agency serving the entire area.

Contacts **Bend Chamber of Commerce** (⊠777 N.W. Wall St., 97701 ☎541/382–
3221 ⊕www.bendchamber.org). **Bend Visitor & Convention Bureau** (⊠917
N.W. Harriman, 97701 ☎541/382–8048 or 877/245–8484 ⊕www.visitbend.com).
Central Oregon Visitors Association (⊠661 S.W. Powerhouse Dr., Suite 1301,
Bend 97702 ☎541/389–8799 or 800/800–8334 ⊕www.covisitors.com). **Con-
federated Tribes of Warm Springs** (⊠1233 Veterans St. Warm Springs 97761
☎541/553–1161 ⊕www.warmsprings.com). **Deschutes National Forest** (⊠1001
S.W. Emkay Dr., Bend 97702 ☎541/383–5300 ⊕www.fs.fed.us/r6/centraloregon).

Detroit Lake Recreation Area Business Association (🗁 *Box 574, Detroit 97342* ⊕ *www.detroitlakeoregon.org.*). **Hoodoo Recreation Services** (✉ *U.S. 20, Sisters 97759* ☎ *541/822-3799* ⊕ *www.hoodoo.com*). **Metolius Recreation Area** (🗁 *Box 64, Camp Sherman 97730* ⊕ *www.metoliusriver.com*). **Ochoco National Forest Headquarters and Prineville Ranger Station** (✉ *3160 N.E. 3rd St., Prineville 07754* ☎ *541/416-6500* ⊕ *www.fs.fed.us/r6/centraloregon*). **Prineville-Crook County Chamber of Commerce** (✉ *390 N. Fairview St., 97754* ☎ *541/447-6304* ⊕ *www.visitprineville.com*). **Sisters Chamber of Commerce** (🗁 *Box 430, 97759* ☎ *541/549-0251* ⊕ *www.sisterschamber.com*)..

SOUTHERN OREGON

Updated by
Deston Nokes

Approached from the north, southern Oregon begins where the verdant lowlands of the Willamette Valley give way to a complex collision of mountains, rivers, and ravines. The intricate geography of the "Land of Umpqua," as the area around Roseburg is somewhat romantically known, signals that this is territory very distinct from neighboring regions to the north, east, and west. Wild rivers—the Rogue and the Umpqua are legendary for fishing and boating—and twisting mountain roads venture through the landscape that saw Oregon's most violent Indian wars and became the territory of a self-reliant breed. Don't-Tread-on-Me southern Oregonians see themselves as markedly different from fellow citizens of the Pacific Wonderland. In fact, several early-20th-century attempts to secede from Oregon and proclaim a "state of Jefferson" survive in local folklore and culture—the region's beloved public radio affiliate, for instance, is Jefferson Public Radio.

Some locals refer to this sun-kissed, sometimes blistering-hot landscape as the Mediterranean; others call it Oregon's banana belt. It's a climate built for slow-paced pursuits and a leisurely outlook on life. Folks like to chat down here, and the big cultural draws are Ashland's Oregon Shakespeare Festival and Jacksonville's open-air, picnic-friendly Britt Festivals concert series.

The centerpiece of the region is actually at the region's eastern edge: Crater Lake, created by the violent eruption of Mt. Mazama, is the deepest lake in the United States. Its dark blue clarity is mesmerizing on sunny days but equally stunning in winter, when its rim is covered with snow.

KLAMATH FALLS

60 mi south of Crater Lake National Park on U.S. 97.

Often overlooked by visitors to the region, the Klamath Falls area is one of the most beautiful parts of Oregon. The city of Klamath Falls stands at an elevation of 4,100 feet, on the southern shore of Upper Klamath Lake. The highest elevation in Klamath County is the peak of Mt. Scott, at 8,926 feet. The Klamath Basin, with its six national wildlife refuges, hosts the largest wintering concentration of bald eagles in the contiguous United States. Each February nature enthusiasts from around the world flock to Klamath Falls for the Bald Eagle Conference, the nation's oldest birding festival. There are more than 82 lakes and streams in Klamath County, including Upper Klamath Lake, which covers 133 square mi.

Many species of migratory birds congregate in the Klamath Basin, including the largest concentration of migratory waterfowl on the continent. The Nature Conservancy has called the basin a western Everglades because it is the largest wetland area west of the Mississippi. Humans have significantly damaged the ecosystem through farming and development. More

> **TOP FIVE**
>
> 1. Jacksonville, no other Oregon town preserves the old west so well.
>
> 2. Oregon Shakespeare Festival's presentations are outstanding.
>
> 3. Running Y Ranch in the high-desert country has an amazing assortment of family activities.
>
> 4. Mt. Ashland Ski Area is steep, deep, and thrilling.
>
> 5. Crater Lake. Simply too beautiful to be missed.

than 25% of vertebrate species in the area are now endangered or threatened. Where 30 years ago about 6 million birds used the area every year, today that number is down to 2 to 3 million. Environmental organizations are working to reverse some of the damage. In 2000 and 2001, severe droughts led to bitter feuds over water use among Native Americans, farmers, environmentalists, and federal officials; it's worth keeping in mind that feelings inflamed by the issue linger.

A frontier military post was established in 1863 at the site of what is now **Fort Klamath Museum and Park** to protect pioneers from Indian attack. In 1973, 8 acres of the original post, including the original buildings, were dedicated as Klamath County Park. In 2001 the museum's main log-cabin building burned to the ground, taking some larger exhibits with it. The bulk of the museum's collection survived, however, and is now in a replica of the fort's original guard post. Actors in period military duds lead interpretive tours of the grounds. ⊠ *44 mi north of Klamath Falls on Hwy. 62* ☎ *541/381–2230* ✉ *Donation requested* ⊙ *June–Sept., Thurs.–Mon. 10–6.*

Almost 1 million waterfowl use the **Lower Klamath National Wildlife Refuge** during fall migration. In summer white pelicans, cormorants, herons, egrets, terns, white-faced ibis, grebes, and gulls congregate in the area. But the refuge's star is the bald eagle, some 1,000 of which winter here—the largest concentration in the lower 48 states. ⊠ *8 mi south of Klamath Falls on U.S. 97* ☎ *530/667–2231.*

The anthropology, history, geology, and wildlife of the Klamath Basin are explained at **Klamath County Museum,** with special attention given to the hardships faced by early white settlers. ⊠ *1451 Main St., 97601* ☎ *541/883–4208* ✉ *$3* ⊙ *Tues.–Sat. 9–5.*

Thirty miles north of Klamath Falls, **Collier Memorial State Park and Logging Museum** sits on land given to the State of Oregon by the locally born Collier brothers in honor of their parents. A historic log-cabin exhibit and antique logging equipment dating to the 1880s are among the displays. The park also has picnic areas and a campground. ✉*46000 U.S. 97, Chiloquin 97624* ☎*541/783–2471* ✆*Free* ☉*May–Oct., daily 8–8; Nov.–Apr., daily 8–4.*

More than 100,000 Native American artifacts, the works of 300 major contemporary Western artists, and the largest miniature-gun collection in the world are on display at **Favell Museum of Western Art and Native American Artifacts** in a building made from local volcanic rock. ✉*125 W. Main St., 97601* ☎*541/882–9996* ✆*$7* ☉*Mon.-Sat. 9:30–5:30.*

The history of the region is the focus of a guided tour and exhibits at **Senator George Baldwin Hotel Museum,** a former hotel that the turn-of-the-20th-century politico Baldwin ran and where President Theodore Roosevelt once stayed. Some of the photographs on display were part of Senator Baldwin's daughter Maud's collection. In summer you can take a replica street trolley from here to the Klamath County Museum. ✉*31 Main St., 97601* ☎*541/883–4207* ⊕*www.co.klamath.or.us* ✆*$6 full tour, $4 half hour* ☉*June–Sept., Tues.–Sat. 10–4.*

Twelve miles north of Klamath Falls, **Winema National Forest** covers 1.1 million acres on the eastern slopes of the Cascades. It borders Crater Lake National Park. Hiking, camping, fishing, and boating are popular. In winter snowmobiling and cross-country skiing are available. ✉*U. S. 97* ☎*541/883–6714* ⊕*www.fs.fed.us/r6/frewin* ☉*Daily; campgrounds and picnic areas Memorial Day–Labor Day.*

WHERE TO STAY & EAT

$–$$ ✕**Mr. B.'s Steakhouse.** The dark-wood dining room in this 1920 house suggests more formal pleasures but maintains a relaxed mood. A thoughtful French chef prepares duck in orange sauce, chateaubriand, veal dishes, and the house specialty, rack of lamb. Fresh strawberry shortcake often appears on the menu, and there's a good wine list. ✉*3927 S. 6th St., 97603* ☎*541/883–8719* 🖷*541/883–3996* ▭*AE, D, DC, MC, V* ☉*Closed Sun. and Mon. and all holidays. No lunch.*

$$–$$$ ▦**Running Y Ranch Resort.** Golfers rave about the Arnold Palmer–
☾   designed course here, which wends its way through a juniper-and-pon-
★   derosa–shaded canyon overlooking Upper Klamath Lake. The resort consists of a main lodge and several town house complexes, with hiking, biking, ATV rentals, outdoor ice skating, swimming, horseback riding, sailing, fishing, and wildlife watching the prime activities. A concierge can help arrange a variety of excusions. Rooms in the lodge are spacious and modern; the two- to three-bedroom town houses have numerous amenities. The property has three restaurants, including a fine-dining steak house and lounge with bar food. **Pros:** An immense, family-focused resort with an array of activities **Cons:** Once you're there, it's a long way from anywhere else. ✉*5115 Running Y Rd., 5 mi north of Klamath Falls, 97601* ☎*541/850–5500 or 888/850–0275* 🖷*541/850–5593* ⊕*www.runningy.com* ➟*82 rooms* ☖*In-hotel: golf course, tennis courts, laundry service* ▭*AE, D, DC, MC, V.*

Continued on page 195

Crater Lake National Park

The pure, untrammeled blue of Crater Lake never fails to astound at first sight. The 21-square-mi lake was created 7,700 years ago after the eruption of Mt. Mazama. Days after the eruption, the mountain collapsed on an underground chamber emptied of lava. Rain and snowmelt filled the caldera, creating a sapphire-blue lake so clear that sunlight penetrates to a depth of 400 feet (the lake's depth is 1,943 feet). Today it's both the clearest and deepest lake in the United States—seventh deepest in the world.

WELCOME TO CRATER LAKE

TOP REASONS TO GO

★ **The lake:** Experience the extraordinary rich, sapphire blue of the country's deepest lake close-up as you cruise inside a caldera basin.

★ **Native land:** Enjoy the rare luxury of interacting with totally unspoiled terrain.

★ **The night sky:** Billions of stars glisten in the pitch-black darkness of an unpolluted sky.

★ **Splendid hikes:** Accessible trails wind past colorful bursts of wildflowers gently swaying in the summer breeze.

★ **Camping at its best:** Pitch a tent or pull up a motor home at Mazama Campground, a beautifully situated, guest-friendly, and well-maintained campground.

1 Crater Lake. The focal point of the park, this non-recreational, scenic destination is known for its deep blue hue.

2 Wizard Island. Visitors can take boat rides to this protruding land mass rising from the western section of Crater Lake; it's a great place for a hike or a picnic.

3 Mazama Village. This is your best bet for stocking up on snacks, beverages, and fuel in the park; it's about five miles from Rim Drive.

4 Cleetwood Cove Trail. The only safe, designated trail to hike down the caldera and reach the lake's edge is on the rim's north side off Rim Drive.

GETTING ORIENTED

Crater Lake National Park covers 183,224 acres. Located in Southern Oregon less than 100 mi from the California border, it's surrounded by several Cascade Range forests, including the Winema and Rogue River National Forests. The closest neighboring towns are each approximately 60 mi from the lake, with Roseburg to the Northwest, and Medford and Klamath Falls to the South.

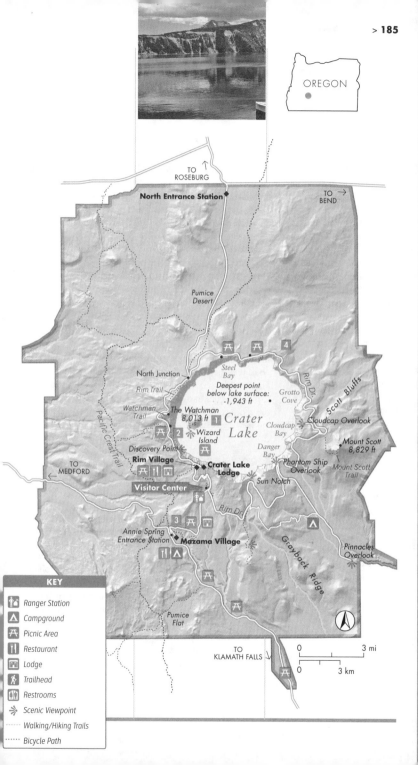

OREGON

TO
ROSEBURG

TO
BEND

North Entrance Station

*Pumice
Desert*

4

North Junction

*Steel
Bay*

Deepest point
below lake surface:
-1,943 ft

*Grotto
Cove*

Rim Trail

Rim Dr.

Scott Bluffs

*Watchman
Trail*

The Watchman
8,013 ft 1

*Crater
Lake*

Cloudcap Overlook

2 *Wizard
Island*

*Cloudcap
Bay*

Mount Scott
8,829 ft

Discovery Point

*Danger
Bay*

*Mount Scott
Trail*

Rim Village

Phantom Ship
Overlook

TO
MEDFORD

Crater Lake
Lodge

Sun Notch

Pacific Crest Trail

Visitor Center

3

Rim Dr.

Annie Spring
Entrance Station

Mazama Village

Grayback Ridge

Pinnacles
Overlook

*Pumice
Flat*

TO
KLAMATH FALLS

| 0 | 3 mi |
| 0 | 3 km |

KEY

Ranger Station
Campground
Picnic Area
Restaurant
Lodge
Trailhead
Restrooms
Scenic Viewpoint
Walking/Hiking Trails
Bicycle Path

CRATER LAKE NATIONAL PARK PLANNER

When to Go

Most of the park is only accessible in late June–early July through mid-October. The rest of the year, snow blocks all park roadways and entrances except Highway 62 and the access road to Rim Village from Mazama Village. Rim Drive is typically closed because of heavy snowfall from mid-October to mid-July, and you could encounter icy conditions any month of the year, particularly in early morning. Crater Lake receives more snowfall—an annual average of 44 feet—than any other national park except for Mount Rainier. For a real-time view of weather conditions at the rim, log onto the Crater Lake Lodge crater cam at ⊕ *www.craterlakelodges. com/cratercam.htm.*

The park's high season is July and August. September and early October—which can be delightful—tend to draw smaller crowds. From October through June, the entire park virtually closes due to heavy snowfall and freezing temperatures. The road is kept open just to the rim in winter, except during severe weather.

Flora & Fauna

Two primary types of fish swim beneath the surface of Crater Lake: kokanee salmon and rainbow trout. It's estimated that hundreds of thousands of kokanee inhabit the lake, but since boating and recreational access is so limited they elude many would-be sportsmen. Kokanees average about 8 to 10 inches in length, but they can grow to nearly 20 inches. Rainbow trout are larger than the kokanee, reaching nearly a foot, but are less abundant in Crater Lake. Trout—including bull, Eastern brook, rainbow, and German brown—also swim in the park's many streams and rivers; but they usually remain elusive because these waterways flow near inaccessibly steep canyons.

Remote canyons also shelter the park's elk and deer populations, which can sometimes be seen at dusk and dawn feeding at forest's edge. Black bears and pine martens—cousins of the short-tailed weasel—also call Crater Lake home. Birds such as three-toed–and hairy woodpeckers, California gulls, red-tailed hawks, and great horned owls are more commonly seen in the summer in forests below the lake.

Good Reads

Crater Lake National Park: A Global Treasure, by former park rangers Ann and Myron Sutton, celebrates the park's first 100 years with stunning photography, charts, and drawings. Ron Warfield's *A Guide to Crater Lake National Park and The Mountain That Used to Be* gives a useful and lushly illustrated overview of Crater Lake's history and physical features. The National Park Service uses Stephen Harris's *Fire Mountains of the West* in its ranger training; the detailed handbook covers Cascade Range geology. *Wildflowers of the Olympics and Cascades,* by Charles Stewart, is an easy-to-use guide to the area's flora and fauna. Also, be sure to pick up a copy of the park newspaper, *Reflections,* upon arrival.

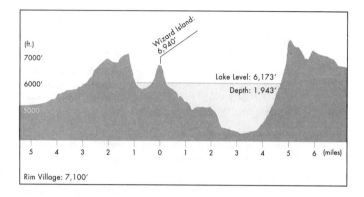

(ft.)
7000'
6000'
5000'

Wizard Island: 6,940'

Lake Level: 6,173'
Depth: 1,943'

5 4 3 2 1 0 1 2 3 4 5 6 (miles)

Rim Village: 7,100'

SCENIC DRIVE

By Janna
Mock-Lopez

★ **Rim Drive.** The 33-mi loop around the lake is the main scenic route, affording views of the lake and its cliffs from every conceivable angle. The drive alone takes up to two hours; frequent stops at overlooks and short hikes can easily stretch this to a half day. Be aware that Rim Drive is typically closed due to heavy snowfall from mid-October to mid-June, and icy conditions can be encountered any month of the year, particularly in early morning. ⊠ *Rim Dr. leads from Annie Spring entrance station to Rim Village, where the drive circles around the rim; it's about 4½ mi from the entrance station to Rim Village. To get to Rim Drive from the park's north entrance at Rte. 230, follow the North Crater Lake access road for about 10 mi.*

WHAT TO SEE

For most visitors, the star attractions of Crater Lake are the lake itself and the breathtakingly situated Crater Lake Lodge. Other park highlights include the natural, unspoiled beauty of the forest and the geological marvels that you can access along the 33-mi Rim Drive.

HISTORIC SITE

Fodor's Choice

★ **Crater Lake Lodge.** First built in 1915, this classic log-and-stone structure still boasts the original lodgepole pine pillars, beams, and stone fireplaces. The lobby, fondly referred to as the Great Hall, serves as a warm, welcoming gathering place where you can play games, socialize with a cocktail, or gaze out of the many windows to view spectacular sunrises and sunsets by a crackling fire. ⊠ *Rim Village just east of Rim Visitor Center.*

SCENIC STOPS

Cloudcap Overlook. The highest road-access overlook on the Crater Lake rim, Cloudcap has a westward view across the lake to Wizard Island and an eastward view of Mt. Scott, the volcanic cone that is the park's highest point, 2 mi away. ✉ *2 mi off Rim Dr., 13 mi northeast of Steel Information Center.*

Discovery Point. This overlook marks the spot at which prospectors first spied the lake in 1853. Wizard Island is just northeast, close to shore. ✉ *Rim Dr., 1½ mi north of Rim Village.*

Mazama Village. In summer a campground, motor inn, amphitheater, gas station, post office, and small store are open here. ✉ *Mazama Village Rd. near Annie Spring entrance station* ☎ *541/830–8700* ⊕ *www. nps.gov/crla* ☉ *June–Sept., daily 8–6.*

Phantom Ship Overlook. From this point you can get a close look at Phantom Ship, a rock formation that resembles a small boat. ✉ *Rim Dr., 7 mi northeast of Steel Information Center.*

Pinnacles Overlook. Ascending from the banks of Sand and Wheeler creeks, unearthly spires of eroded ash resemble the peaks of fairy-tale castles. Once upon a time, the road continued east to a former entrance. A path now replaces the old road and follows the rim of Sand Creek (affording more views of pinnacles) to where the entrance arch still stands. ✉ *5 mi northeast of Steel Information Center.*

Sun Notch. It's a moderate ¼-mi hike through wildflowers and dry meadow to this overlook, which has views of Crater Lake and Phantom Ship. Mind the steep edges. ✉ *E. Rim Dr., 4 mi northeast of Steel Information Center.*

★ **Wizard Island.** To get here you've got to hike down Cleetwood Cove Trail (and back up upon your return) and board the tour boat for a 1¾-hour ride. Definitely bring a picnic. ✉ *Cleetwood Cove Trail, Wizard Island dock* ☎ *541/830–8700* ☉ *Late June–mid-Sept., daily.*

VISITOR CENTERS

Rim Visitor Center. In summer you can obtain park information here, take a ranger-led tour, or stop into the nearby Sinnott Memorial, with a small museum and a 900-foot view down to the lake's surface. In winter, snowshoe walks are offered on weekends and holidays. The Rim Village Gift Store and cafeteria are the only services open in winter. ✉ *Rim Dr. on south side of lake, 7 mi north of Annie Spring entrance station* ☎ *541/594–3090* ⊕ *www.nps.gov/crla* ☉ *Late June–Sept., daily 9:30–5.*

Steel Information Center. The information center is part of the park's headquarters; you'll find restrooms and a first-aid station here. There's also a small post office and a shop that sells books, maps, and postcards. In the auditorium, an ongoing 18-minute film, *The Crater Lake Story,* describes Crater Lake's formation. ✉ *Rim Dr., 4 mi north of Annie Spring entrance station* ☎ *541/594–3100* ⊕ *www.nps.gov/crla* ☉ *Mid-Apr.–early Nov., daily 9–5; early Nov.–mid-Apr., daily 10–4.*

CRATER LAKE IN ONE DAY

Begin your tour at **Steel Information Center,** where interpretive displays and a short video introduce you to the story of the lake's formation and its unique characteristics. Then begin your circumnavigation of the crater's rim by heading northeast on **Rim Drive,** allowing an hour to stop at overlooks—check out the Phantom Ship rock formation in the lake below—before you reach **Cleetwood Cove Trail** trailhead, the only safe and legal access to the lake. Hike down the trail to reach the dock, and hop aboard one of the concessionaire **tour boats** for an almost-two-hour tour around the lake. If you have time, add on a trip to **Wizard Island** for a picnic lunch.

Back on Rim Drive, continue around the lake, stopping at **the Watchman** for a short but steep hike to this peak above the rim, which affords not only a splendid view of the lake, but a broad vista of the surrounding southern Cascades. Wind up your visit at **Crater Lake Lodge**—allow an hour just to wander the lobby of the 1915 structure perched on the rim. Dinner at the lodge restaurant, overlooking the lake and the Cascade sunset, caps the day.

SPORTS & THE OUTDOORS

FISHING

Fishing is allowed in the lake, but you may find the experience frustrating—in such a massive body of water, the problem is finding the fish. Try your luck near the Cleetwood Cove boat dock, or take poles on the boat tour and fish off Wizard Island. Rainbow trout and kokanee salmon lurk in Crater Lake's aquamarine depths, and some grow to enormous sizes. You don't need a state fishing license, but help protect the lake's pristine waters by only using artificial bait as opposed to live worms.

HIKING

EASY **Castle Crest Wildflower Trail.** The 1-mi creek-side loop in the upper part of Munson Valley is one of the park's flatter and less demanding hikes. Wildflowers burst into full bloom here in July. ⊠*Across street from Steel Information Center parking lot, Rim Dr..*

Godfrey Glen Trail. Head down from the rim through Munson Valley to reach the parking area for this 2-mi loop that runs between Steel Information Center and the Castle Crest Wildflower Trail. It'll take you through an excellent example of what geologists term a hanging valley—the place where one valley hangs over a lower valley, with a cliff and a waterfall between them. Deer are frequently seen here, and flowers are abundant. ⊠*2 mi off Rim Dr., 2 4/10 mi south of Steel Information Center.*

MODERATE **Annie Creek Canyon Trail.** Annie Creek is strenuous but still easy compared to some of the steep rim hikes, such as the Cleetwood Trail. The 2-mi loop threads through Annie Creek Canyon, providing views of the narrow cleft scarred by volcanic activity. This is a good spot to look for flowers and deer.   ⊠*Mazama Campground, Mazama Village Rd., near Annie Spring entrance station.*

Cleetwood Cove Trail. This 1-mi strenuous hike descends 700 feet down nearly vertical cliffs along the lake to the boat dock.   ⊠*Cleetwood Cove trailhead, N. Rim Dr., 11 mi north of Rim Village.*

The Watchman Trail. This is the best short hike in the park. Though it's less than a mile each way, the trail climbs more than 400 feet—not

counting the steps up to the actual lookout, which has great views of Wizard Island and the lake.   ⊠*Watchman Overlook, 37/10 mi northwest of Rim Village on W. Rim Dr..*

DIFFICULT   **Boundary Springs Trail.** If you're up for a challenge, consider a trip along this 8-mi trail. Easing down the gradually sloping northwestern shoulders of old Mt. Mazama, the path angles toward Pumice Desert and ends up at Boundary Springs, one of the sources of the Rogue River. To avoid the return trip, many hikers arrange to be picked up at Lake West, a campground outside the park that is easily accessible via Route 230.   ⊠*Pacific Crest Trail parking lot, north access road 2 mi north of Rim Dr., 8 mi south of park's north entrance station.*

Fodor'sChoice   **Mt. Scott Trail.** This 2½-mi trail takes you to the park's highest point— ★   the top of Mt. Scott, the oldest volcanic cone of Mt. Mazama, at 8,929 feet. It will take the average hiker 90 minutes to make the steep uphill trek—and about 45 minutes to get down. The trail starts at an elevation of about 7,450 feet, so the climb is not extreme but does get steep in spots. Views of the lake and the broad Klamath Basin are spectacular.   ⊠*14 mi east of Steel Information Center, across E. Rim Dr. from road to Cloudcap Overlook.*

Pacific Crest Trail. You can hike a portion of the Pacific Crest Trail, which extends from Mexico to Canada and winds through the park for more than 30 mi. For this prime backcountry experience, catch the trail about a mile east of the north entrance road, where it shadows the road along the west rim of the lake for about 6 mi, then descends down Dutton Creek to the Mazama Village area. An online brochure offers further details.   ⊠*Pacific Crest Trail parking lot, north access road 2 mi north of Rim Dr., 8 mi south of park's north entrance station* ⊕*www.nps.gov/crla/brochures/pct.htm.*

2

EDUCATIONAL OFFERINGS

RANGER PROGRAMS

Boat Tours. The most extensively used guided tours in Crater Lake are on the water, aboard launches that carry 49 passengers on a one-hour, 45-minute tour accompanied by a ranger. The boats circle the lake and make a brief stop at Wizard Island, where you can get off if you like. The first of seven tours leaves the dock at 10 AM; the last departs at 4 PM. After Labor Day, the schedule is reduced. To get to the dock you must hike down Cleetwood Cove Trail, a 1-mi walk that drops 700 feet; restrooms are available at the top and bottom of the trail. ⊠ *Cleetwood Cove Trail, off north Rim Dr., 10 mi north of Rim Village* ☎ *541/830–8700* ☜ *$30.50* ☼ *July–mid-Sept., daily.*

Junior Ranger Program. Junior Ranger booklets and badges are available at Steel Information Center and Rim Visitor Center. ☎ *541/594–3090.*

NEARBY TOWNS & ATTRACTIONS

Three small cities serve as gateways to Crater Lake—each a 1½- to 2-hour drive to the park. Klamath Lake, the largest freshwater lake in Oregon, is anchored at its south end by the city of **Klamath Falls.** With year-round sunshine, Klamath Falls is home to acres of parks and marinas from which to enjoy water sports and bird-watching. **Roseburg**'s location at the west edge of the southern Cascades led to its status as a timber-industry center—still the heart of the town's economy—but its site along the Umpqua River has also drawn fishermen here for years. **Ashland** is a charming small city set in the foothills of the Siskiyou Mountains with dozens of fine small inns, shops, and restaurants.

The marble caves, large calcite formations, and huge underground rooms of the **Oregon Caves National Monument** are quite rare in the West. Sometimes as many as 1,000 bald eagles make **Lower Klamath National Wildlife Refuge Complex** their rest stop, amounting to the largest wintering concentration of these birds in the contiguous United States. For more information on nearby towns and attractions, *see* town listings in this chapter.

WHERE TO EAT

There are several casual eateries and a few convenience stores within the park. For fantastic upscale dining on the caldera's rim, head to the Crater Lake Lodge.

$–$$$ ✕**Dining Room at Crater Lake Lodge.** Virtually the only place where you
Fodor'sChoice can dine well once you're in the park, the culinary emphasis here is
★ on fresh, regional Northwest cuisine. The dining room is magnificent, with a large stone fireplace and views out over the clear blue waters of Crater Lake. The evening menu is the main attraction, with tempting delights such as wildflower Alaskan salmon or hazelnut-crusted halibut fillets. Meat lovers can enjoy choices like citrus duck, grilled venison, or conventional flatiron steak. An extensive wine list tops off

the gourmet experience. ⊠*Crater Lake Lodge, Rim Village 97604* ☎*541/594–2255* ⚠*Reservations essential* ▭*AE, D, MC, V* ⊘*Closed mid-Oct.–mid-May.*

$-$$ ✕ **Annie Creek Restaurant.** It's family-style buffet dining here, and pizza and pasta are the main features. The outdoor seating area is surrounded by towering pine trees. ⊠*Mazama Village Rd., near Annie Spring entrance station* ☎*541/594–2255 Ext. 4533* ▭*AE, D, MC, V* ⊘*Closed mid-Sept.–June.*

PICNIC AREAS **Godfrey Glen Trail.** Located in a small canyon abuzz with songbirds, squirrels, and chipmunks, this picnic area has a south-facing, protected location. The half-dozen picnic tables here are in a small meadow; there are also a few fire grills and a pit toilet. ⊠*On Rim Dr., 1 mi east of Annie Spring entrance station.*

Rim Drive. About a half dozen picnic-area turnouts encircle the lake; all have good views, but they can get very windy. Most have pit toilets, and a few have fire grills, but none have running water. ⊠*Rim Dr..*

Rim Village. This is the only park picnic area with running water. The tables are set behind the visitor center, and most have a view of the lake below. There are flush toilets inside the visitor center. ⊠*Rim Dr. on south side of lake, 7 mi north of Annie Spring entrance station.*

Route 62. Set in the fir, spruce, and pine forests of the Cascades' dry side, the three picnic areas along this route have tables, some fire grills, and pit toilets, but no drinking water. Picnickers who mind traffic noise should head farther into the park. ⊠*Rte. 62; 2, 4, and 7 mi southeast of Annie Spring entrance station.*

Vidae Falls. In the upper reaches of Sun Creek, the four picnic tables here enjoy the sound of the small but close-by falls across the road. There is a vault toilet, and a couple of fire grills. ⊠*Rim Dr., 2½ mi east of Steel Information Center, between turnoffs for Crater Peak and Lost Creek.*

Wizard Island. The park's best picnic venue is on Wizard Island; pack a picnic lunch and book yourself on one of the early morning boat tour departures, reserving space on an afternoon return. There are no formal picnic areas and just pit toilets, but there are plenty of sunny, protected spots where you can have a quiet meal and appreciate the astounding scene that surrounds you.

WHERE TO STAY

Crater Lake's summer season is brief, and the park's main lodge is generally booked with guest reservations a year in advance. If you don't snag one, check availability as your trip approaches—cancellations are always possible. Outside the park are options in Prospect, Klamath, Roseburg, or Ashland.

Both tent campers and RV enthusiasts will enjoy the heavily wooded and well-equipped setting of Mazama Campground. Drinking water, showers, and laundry facilities help ensure that you don't have to rough it too much. Lost Creek Campground is much smaller, with fewer provisions and a more "rustic" Crater Lake experience.

2

$$–$$$$ ▨ **Crater Lake Lodge.** The period feel of this 1915 lodge on the caldera's rim is reflected in its lodgepole pine columns, gleaming wood floors, and stone fireplaces in the common areas. With magnificent lake views—and the all-too-brief tourist season at Crater Lake—rooms at this popular spot are often booked a year in advance. Plan ahead, as this is the only "in-park" place to stay by the lake. ⊠ *Rim Village, east of Rim Visitor Center* ☎ *541/830–8700* 🖷 *541/830–8514* ⊕ *www.craterlakelodges.com* ⥰ *71 rooms* ♿ *In-room: no phone, no TV. In-hotel: restaurant* 🖃 *AE, D, MC, V* ⊗ *Closed mid-Oct.–mid-May.*

$$ ▨ **The Cabins at Mazama Village.** In a wooded area 7 mi south of the lake, this complex is made up of several A-frame buildings. All of the modest rooms have two queen beds and a private bath. These rooms fill up fast, so book early. A convenience store and gas station are nearby in the village. ⊠ *Mazama Village, near Annie Spring entrance station* ☎ *541/830–8700* 🖷 *541/830–8514* ⥰ *40 rooms* ♿ *In-room: no phone, no TV* 🖃 *AE, D, MC, V* ⊗ *Closed mid-Oct.–May.*

CAMPGROUNDS   ⛰ **Mazama Campground.** Crater Lake National Park's major visitor
$$ accommodation, aside from the famed lodge on the rim, is set well below the lake caldera in the pine and fir forest of the Cascades. Not far from the main access road (Hwy. 62), it offers convenience more than outdoor serenity—although adjacent hiking trails lead away from the roadside bustle. About half the spaces are pull-throughs, some with electricity, but no hookups are available. The best tent spots are on some of the outer loops above Annie Creek Canyon. ⊠ *Mazama Village, near Annie Spring entrance station* ☎ *541/830–8700* ⥰ *211 sites* ♿ *Flush toilets, dump station, drinking water, guest laundry, showers, fire grates, public telephone* 🖃 *AE, D, MC, V* ⊗ *Mid-June–mid-Oct.*

$ ⛰ **Lost Creek Campground.** The small, remote sites here are usually available on a daily basis. In July and August arrive early to secure a spot. Lost Creek is for tent campers only; RVs must stay at Mazama. ⊠ *Grayback Dr. and Pinnacles Rd.* ☎ *541/594–3090* ⥰ *16 sites* ♿ *Flush toilets, drinking water, fire grates* ⬳ *Reservations not accepted* ⊗ *July–mid-Sept.*

CRATER LAKE ESSENTIALS

ACCESSIBILITY
All the overlooks along Rim Drive are accessible to those with impaired mobility, as are Crater Lake Lodge, the facilities at Rim Village, and Steel Information Center. A half-dozen accessible campsites are available at Mazama Campground.

ADMISSION FEES
Admission to the park is $10 per vehicle, good for seven days.

ADMISSION HOURS
Crater Lake National Park is open 24 hours a day year-round; however, snow closes most park roadways October through June. The park is in the Pacific Time Zone.

EMERGENCIES

Dial 911 for all emergencies in the park. Park police are based at park headquarters, next to Steel Information Center.

PERMITS

Backcountry campers and hikers must obtain a free wilderness permit at Rim Visitor Center or Steel Information Center for all overnight trips.

PUBLIC TELEPHONES AND RESTROOMS

There are public telephones and restrooms at Steel Information Center, Rim Village, Crater Lake Lodge, and the Mazama Village complex. There are also restrooms at the top and bottom of Cleetwood Cove Trail and at many of the park's picnic areas.

SHOPS & GROCERS

Contacts **Diamond Lake Resort** (⊠ *Rte. 138, 25 mi north of Crater Lake* ☎ *541/793–3333 or 800/733–7593*). **Mazama Camper Store** (⊠ *Mazama Village Rd., near Annie Spring entrance station* ☎ *541/830–8700* ⊙ *Closed Oct.–May*).

VISITOR INFORMATION

Contacts **Crater Lake National Park** ⌂ *Box 7, Crater Lake, OR 97604* ☎ *541/594–3090* ⊕ *www.nps.gov/crla.*

MEDFORD

88 mi south of Roseburg on I–5.

Medford is the professional, retail, trade, and service center for eight counties in southern Oregon and northern California. As such, it offers more professional and cultural venues than might be expected for a city of its size. The town has four major shopping centers and the fruit marketing company Harry and David. Lodging and dining tend to be much cheaper in Medford than in nearby (and easily accessible) Ashland and Jacksonville. Near two major rivers and more than 30 lakes and streams, Medford is 71 mi southwest of Crater Lake and 80 mi northeast of the Oregon Caves.

An 1872 water-powered flour grist mill, **Butte Creek Mill** is listed in the National Historic Register and still produces whole-grain food products, which you can buy at the country store here. There's also a modest display of antiques. ⊠*402 Royal Ave. N, Eagle Point* ☎*541/826–3531* ⊕*www.buttecreekmill.com* ✆*Free* ☉*Mon.–Sat. 9–5, Sun. 11–5.*

★ The late Hollywood star Ginger Rogers retired to this area, and the restored vaudeville house **Craterian Ginger Rogers Theater** presents concerts, ballets, theatrical works, and touring shows like the Vienna Boys Choir and Brazil Night. Check the Web for the latest performances and showtimes. ⊠*23 S. Central Ave., 97501* ☎*541/779–3000* ✆*541/779–8175* ⊕*www.craterian.org.*

Jackson County's natural history and collections of the Roxy Ann Gem and Mineral Society are on display at **Crater Rock Museum.** ⊠*2002 Scenic Ave., Central Point* ☎*541/664–6081* ✆*$4* ☉*Tues.–Sat. 10–4.*

Covering 630,000 acres, **Rogue River National Forest** has fishing, swimming, hiking, and skiing. Motorized vehicles and equipment—even bicycles—are prohibited in the 113,000-acre Sky Lakes Wilderness, south of Crater Lake National Park. Its highest point is the 9,495-foot Mt. McLoughlin. Summers here are warm and dry, while winters are bitterly cold, with lots of snow. ⊠*I–5 to Exit 39, Hwy. 62 to Hwy. 140* ☎*541/858–2200* ⊕*www.fs.fed.us/r6/rogue* ✆*Free for most of forest, some trailheads have fees, call for details* ☉*Daily.*

RoxyAnn Winery produces world-class wines while cultivating the vineyards under sustainable land-management practices. The winery was founded in 2002 at the historic Hillcrest Orchard in east Medford, which has been bearing fruit for over 100 years. The property's soil and location are ideally suited to producing cabernet sauvignon, malbec, merlot, cabernet franc, grenache, tempranillo, viognier, and syrah. Visitors are welcome daily between 11 AM and 6 PM at the Tasting Room, located minutes from Interstate 5 in Medford. ⊠*3285 Hillcrest Rd.* ☎*541/776–2315* ✆*541/245–1840* ⊕*www.roxyann.com.*

The focus at **Southern Oregon History Center** is on the Rogue Valley's past, with a research library augmenting rotating exhibits on pioneer history. ⊠*106 N. Central Ave.* ☎*541/773–6536* ⊕*www.sohs.org* ✆*$5* ☉*Wed.–Sat. 1–4.*

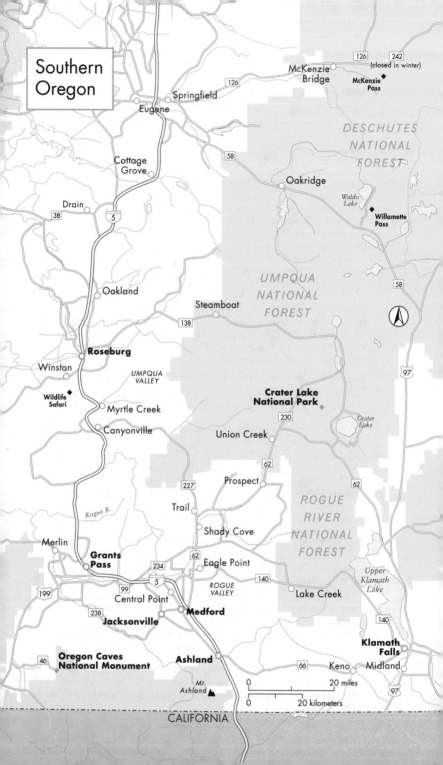

A popular spot for weddings and picnics, **TouVelle State Park** is a day-use park with beautiful hiking trails that wind through a wildlife-viewing area. ⊠ *Off I–5 to Table Rock Rd.* ☎ *541/582–1118 or 800/551–6949* ⊕ *www.prd.state.or.us* ⊠ *Day use $3 per vehicle* ⊙ *Daily.*

WHERE TO STAY & EAT

2

$–$$$ ✕ **Porters Dining at the Depot.** Medford's residents gravitate to this fine din-

★ ing eatery in a restored 1910 train station for aged beef and chops, fresh seafood, seasonal specials, and local wines and produce. Leave room for the hearty desserts. ⊠ *147 N. Front St. 97501* ☎ *541/4857–1910* ⊕ *www.porterstrainstation.com* ⊟ *AE, D, MC, V* ⊙ *No lunch.*

$ ▦ **Under the Greenwood Tree.** Regulars at this B&B between Medford

Fodor'sChoice and Ashland find themselves hard-pressed to decide what they like

★ most: the luxurious and romantic rooms, the stunning 10-acre farm, or the hearty country-style breakfasts cooked by the owner. Gigantic old oaks hung with hammocks shade the inn, a 130-year-old farmhouse exuding genteel charm. There's a manicured 2-acre lawn and a creaky three-story barn for exploring; an outbuilding holds the buckboard wagon that brought the property's original homesteaders westward on the Oregon Trail. The interior is decorated in Renaissance splendor and all rooms have private baths. Afternoon tea is served. ⊠ *3045 Bellinger La., 97501* ⊹ *Head west from I–5 Exit 27 on Barnett Rd., south briefly on Hwy. 99, west on Stewart Ave., south briefly on Hull Rd., and west on Bellinger* ☎ *541/776–0000* ⊕ *www.greenwoodtree. com* ➳ *4 rooms* ⚫ *Wi-Fi, no elevator* ⊟ *AE, D, MC, V.*

JACKSONVILLE

5 mi west of Medford on Hwy. 238.

This perfectly preserved town founded in the frenzy of the 1851 gold rush has served as the backdrop to several Western flicks. It's easy to see why. Jacksonville is one of only eight towns corralled into the National Register of Historic Places lock, stock, and barrel. These days, living-history exhibits offering a glimpse of pioneer life and the world-renowned Britt Festivals of classical, jazz, and pop music are the draw, rather than gold. Trails winding up from the town's center lead to the festival amphitheater, 150-year-old gardens, exotic madrona groves, and an intriguing pioneer cemetery.

For free maps and guides to Jacksonville's many historic structures, stop by the **Jacksonville Chamber of Commerce & Visitor Center** (⊠ *185 N. Oregon St.* ☎ *541/899–8118*).

⟳ In the 1920 Jackson County Jail, the **Children's Museum** has hands-on exhibits of pioneer life and a collection of antique toys. There's an Indian tepee and an old-fashioned store in which to play. A special display highlights local resident Pinto Colvig, the original Bozo the Clown, who co-composed "Who's Afraid of the Big Bad Wolf" and was the voice of a Munchkin, Goofy, both Sleepy and Grumpy, and many other animated film characters. The adjacent **Jacksonville Museum,** inside the old Jackson County Courthouse, has intriguing gold-rush-era artifacts. The "Jacksonville! Boomtown to Home Town" exhibit lays out the area's history. ⊠*206 N. 5th St., 97530* ☎*541/773–6536* 🖷*541/776–7994* ⊕*www.sohs.org* 🖃*$5 for both museums* ☉*Wed.–Sun. 10–4.*

Perched on a bench in the scenic Applegate Valley, **Valley View Vineyard** enjoys one of the best settings in all Oregon. The valley's especially sunny, warm climate produces rich chardonnay, merlot, and cabernet sauvignon vintages. Founded in the 1850s by pioneer Peter Britt, the vineyard was reestablished in 1972. A restored pole barn houses the winery and tasting room. ⊠*1000 Upper Applegate Rd., 10 mi southwest of Jacksonville, 97530* ☎*541/899–8468 or 800/781–9463* ⊕*www.valleyviewwinery.com* ☉*Daily 11–5.*

Fodor'sChoice
★

A trip up the winding road—or, better yet, a hike via the old cart-track marked "Catholic access"—leads to the **Jacksonville Cemetery,** resting place of the clans (the Britts, the Beekmans, and the Orths) that built Jacksonville. You'll also get a fascinating, if sometimes unattractive, view of the social dynamics of the Old West: older graves (the cemetery is still in use) are strictly segregated, Irish Catholics from Jews from Protestants. A somber granite plinth marks the pauper's field, where those who found themselves on the losing end of gold-rush economics entered eternity anonymously. The cemetery closes at sundown. ⊠*Oregon St.; follow posted direction signs from downtown.*

WHERE TO STAY & EAT

$–$$
★

✕ **Jacksonville Inn Restaurant.** The continental fare and 2,000-label wine cellar at this dining room in a gold-rush-era bed-and-breakfast are among the best in southern Oregon. Book well in advance, particularly for stays between late June and August, during the Britt Festival. Try the fresh razor clams, wild salmon, or organic beef dishes. There are tables on the patio for dining alfresco. Breakfast and a Sunday brunch, which tends to highlight seasonal and regional fruits, are also offered. ⊠*175 E. California St.* ☎*541/899–1900* ⌃*Reservations essential* ⊟*AE, D, DC, MC, V* ☉*No lunch Mon.*

$$–$$$$
★

🏨 **Jacksonville Inn.** The spotless period antiques and the host of well-chosen amenities at this 1861-vintage inn evoke what the Wild West might have been had Martha Stewart been in charge. In addition to the main building, the inn includes three larger and more luxurious cottages with fireplaces and saunas. The room rates include a full breakfast. One of the eight rooms in the main inn is named in honor of ubiquitous Jacksonville founding father Peter Britt, while another, the Blanchet Room, honors one of the area's earliest Catholic priests. Both have meticulous pioneer-period furnishings. One room has a whirlpool tub and another a steam shower. The inn's continental restaurant is among the best places to eat in the region. ⊠*175 E. California St., 97530* ☎*541/899–1900 or 800/321–9344* 🖷*541/899–1373* ⊕*www.jacksonvilleinn.com* 🛏*8 rooms, 4 cottages* ⌂*In-room: a/c, refrigerator. In-hotel: restaurant, no elevator* ⊟*AE, D, DC, MC, V* ⊺O⊺*BP.*

$$$

🏨 **The McCully House Inn.** One of Jacksonville's six original homes, a gleaming white Gothic Revival mansion built in 1860, McCully House sits in the midst of a fragrant rose garden. The period-decorated rooms, one with a fireplace and all of them filled with antiques, are on the second floor and have private baths. One upstairs bedroom is furnished with its original bedstead, which was shipped around Cape Horn. ⊠*240 E. California St., 97530* ☎*541/899–1942 or 800/367–1942* 🖷*541/899–1560* ⌨*3 rooms, 1 suite* ⌂*In-hotel: restaurant, no elevator* ▭*MC, V* ⏩*BP.*

NIGHTLIFE & THE ARTS

★ Every summer some of the finest musicians in the world gather for the **Britt Festivals** (☎*541/773–6077 or 800/882–7488* ⊕*www.brittfest. org*), outdoor concerts and theater presentations lasting from mid-June to mid-September. Folk, country, pop, and classical performances are staged in an outdoor amphitheater on the estate of 19th-century photographer and painter Peter Britt. Tickets must be obtained well in advance for most performances, and those who wish the best spaces on the lawn near the stage should show up early.

ASHLAND

20 mi from Jacksonville, east on Hwy. 238 and southeast on I–5.

As you walk Ashland's twisting hillside streets, it seems like every house is a restored Victorian operating as an upscale B&B, though that's not quite all that there is to this town: the Oregon Shakespeare Festival attracts about a quarter of a million theater lovers to the Rogue Valley every year, from mid-February to early November (though tourists don't start showing up en masse until June or so). That influx means Ashland is more geared toward the arts, more eccentric, and more expensive than its size might suggest. The mix of well-heeled theater tourists, bohemian students from Southern Oregon University, and dramatic show folk imbues the town with some one-of-a-kind cultural frissons. The stage isn't the only show in town—skiing at Mt. Ashland and the town's reputation as a secluded getaway keep things hopping year-round.

The Elizabethan Theatre overlooks **Lithia Park,** a 93-acre jewel that is Ashland's physical and psychological anchor. Whether thronged with colorful hippie folk and picnickers on a summer evening or buzzing with joggers and dog walkers in the morning, Lithia is a well-used, well-loved, and well-tended spot. An old-fashioned band shell, a duck pond, a children's playground, nature trails, and Ashland Creek make this a perfect spot for a pretheater picnic. On summer weekend mornings the park plays host to a '60s-ish artisans' market. Each June the festival opens its outdoor season by hosting the Feast of Will in the park, with music, dancing, bagpipes, and food. Tickets (about $12) are available through the festival box office.

The **Schneider Museum of Art,** at the edge of the Southern Oregon University campus, includes a light-filled gallery devoted to special exhibits by Oregon, West Coast, and international artists. Hallways and galleries throughout the rest of the 66,000-square-foot complex display many works by students and faculty. ✉ *250 Siskiyou Blvd.* ☎ *541/552-6245* ⊕ *www.sou.edu/sma* ◷ *Tues.–Sat. 10–4; extended hrs 1st Fri. of month. Closed Sun. and Mon.* ✏ *$3 suggested donation.*

The Oregon Shakespeare Festival has stimulated one of the most extensive networks of B&Bs in the country—more than 50 in all. High season for Ashland-area bed-and-breakfasts is between June and October. Expect to pay $150–$250 per night, which includes breakfast for two; during the off-season the rates are between $90 and $150. The **Ashland B&B Network** (☎ *800/944–0329* ⊕ *www.abbnet.com*) provides referrals to local inns.

WHERE TO EAT

$$ ✕ **Amuse.** This locally celebrated restaurant features Northwest/French
★ cuisine, infused with seasonal, organic meat and produce. Chef–owners Erik Brown and Jamie North prepare a menu daily. Try the slow-roasted wild salmon or any dish featuring Rogue Creamery Crater Lake Blue Cheese. ✉ *15 N. 1st St.* ◷ *Hrs change seasonally, call for information* ☎ *541/488–9000* ⊕ *www.amuserestaurant.com* ▭ *AE, D, MC, V* ◷ *Closed Mon. and Tues.*

$$ ✕ **Chateaulin.** One of southern Oregon's most romantic restaurants is
★ in an ivy-covered storefront a block from the Oregon Shakespeare Festival exhibit center, where it dispenses French food, local wine, and friendly, impeccable service with equal facility. This might be Ashland's most iconic restaurant, the fixed point in a hopping dining scene, where Shakespeare pilgrims return religiously year after year. A prix-fixe menu changes every two weeks. Mainstays include the pan-roasted rack of lamb with a white-wine demi-glace sauce of roasted garlic, fresh basil, black olives, and sun-dried tomatoes, accompanied by a bottle of Oregon pinot noir. But you have to begin with the French Burgundy escargots. ✉ *50 E. Main St., 97520* ☎ *541/482–2264* ⟶ *Reservations essential* ▭ *AE, D, MC, V* ◷ *Closed Mon. Nov.–May. No lunch.*

$$ ✕ **Larks.** In this restaurant off the lobby of the historic Ashland Springs
★ Hotel, owners Doug and Becky Neuman are putting their "farm to table" philosophy into practice. Larks pairs the freshest foods from local farms with great wines, artisan chocolate desserts, and drinks in a relaxing and soothing atmosphere. Comfort food is the order of the day, with servings such as homemade meatloaf, Anniebelle's fried chicken, and maple-glazed pork chops with organic-apple compote. Dessert offerings include Dagoba chocolate sundaes, s'mores, and cheesecake of the day. ✉ *212 E. Main St., 97520* ☎ *541/488–5558* ▭ *AE, D, MC, V.*

¢–$ ✕ **Morning Glory.** Breakfast reaches new heights at this distinctive café across the street from Southern Oregon University. In a blue Craftsman-style bungalow, the café has eclectic furnishings and an attractive patio space bounded by arbors, that complement the food—omelets bursting with fillings such as mushrooms, apple-wood-smoked bacon, toasted walnuts, and fontina cheese; gingerbread waffles; and sourdough blueberry pancakes. No reservations; first-come, first-served. ✉*1149 Siskiyou Blvd.* ☎*541/488–8636* ▭*MC, V* ◷*No dinner*

WHERE TO STAY

$$–$$$$ 🔲**Ashland Springs Hotel.** Ashland's new landmark hotel is a totally ★ restored version of the old, 1925 landmark hotel. Its 70 rooms soothe with a preponderance of gentle fall colors. The unconventional furniture throughout makes for fascinating conversation in itself. The hotel offers theater, sports, and romance packages. It is just steps from the renowned Oregon Shakespeare Festival. Other nearby attractions include Lithia Park, winery and gallery tours, skiing and snow boarding, golf, fishing, tax-free shopping, dining, and pampering at the Waterstone Spa across the street. ✉*212 E. Main St., 97520* ☎*541/488–1700 or 888/795–4545* 🖷*541/488–1701* ⊕*www.ashlandspringshotel.com* ⌂*In-room: Wi-Fi, refrigerator* ▭*AE, D, DC, MC, V* ▮◉▮*CP.*

NIGHTLIFE & THE ARTS

Fodor'sChoice From mid-February to early November, more than 100,000 Bard-loving ★ fans descend on Ashland for the **Oregon Shakespeare Festival** (✉*15 S. Pioneer St., 97520* ☎*541/482–4331* 🖷*541/482–8045* ⊕*www. osfashland.org*), presented in three theaters. Its accomplished repertory company mounts some of the finest Shakespearean productions you're likely to see on this side of Stratford-upon-Avon—plus works by Ibsen, Williams, and contemporary playwrights. Between June and October, plays are staged in the 1,200-seat Elizabethan Theatre, an atmospheric re-creation of the Fortune Theatre in London; the 600-seat Angus Bowmer Theatre, a state-of-the-art facility typically used for five different productions in a single season; and the 350-seat New Theater, which mostly hosts productions of new or experimental work. The festival generally operates close to capacity, so it's important to book ahead.

SPORTS & THE OUTDOORS

The **Adventure Center** (✉*40 N. Main St., Ashland 97520* ☎*541/488– 2819 or 800/444–2819*) books outdoor expeditions in the Ashland region, including white-water raft trips, fishing outings, and bike excursions.

SKIING **Mt. Ashland Ski Area.** This winter sports playground in the Siskiyou Mountains is halfway between San Francisco and Portland. The ski runs get more than 300 inches of snow each year. There are 23 trails in addition to chute skiing in a glacial cirque called the bowl. Two triple and two double chairlifts accommodate a vertical drop of 1,150 feet; the longest of the 22 runs is 1 mi. Facilities include rentals, repairs, instruction, a ski shop, a restaurant, and a bar. ✉*Mt. Ashland Access Rd., 18 mi southwest of downtown Ashland; follow signs 9 mi from I–5 Exit 6* ☎*541/482–2897* ⊕*www.mtashland.com* 🎫*Lift ticket $39* ◷*Nov.–Apr., daily 9–4.* >

GRANTS PASS

30 mi northwest of Medford on I–5.

"It's the Climate!" So says a confident neon sign of 1950s vintage presiding over the downtown of Josephine County's seat. Grants Pass bills itself as Oregon's white-water capital. The Rogue River, preserved by Congress in 1968 as a National Wild and Scenic River, runs right through town. Downtown Grants Pass is a National Historic District, a stately little enclave of 19th-century brick storefronts housing folksy businesses harking back to the 1950s. It's all that white water, however, that compels most visitors—and not a few moviemakers. If the river alone doesn't serve up enough natural drama, the sheer rock walls of nearby Hellgate Canyon rise 250 feet.

A city museum, **Grants Pass Museum of Art** in Riverside Park, displays classic and contemporary art, including the works of local artists. Sculpture and painting dominate, and the focus is on American and regional work. A first-Friday art night is a community rallying point. ⊠*229 S.W. G St.* ☎*541/479–3290* ⊕*www.gpmusuem.com* ⊠*Free* ⊗*Tues.–Sat. noon–4.*

You'll see some of Oregon's most magnificent scenery on a tour of Hellgate Canyon via **Hellgate Jetboat Excursions,** which depart from the Riverside Inn. The 36-mi round-trip from Grants Pass through Hellgate Canyon takes 2 hours. There is also a 5-hour, 75-mi round-trip from Grants Pass to Grave Creek with a stop for a meal on an open-air deck (cost of meal not included). ⊠*966 S.W. 6th* ☎*541/479–7204 or 800/648–4874* ⊕*www.hellgate.com* ⊠*2-hr trip $33; 5-hr trip $58; brunch cruises $47; lunch excursion $44; supper cruises $52* ⊗*May–Sept., daily; brunch cruises May–Sept., weekends 9:15; supper cruises May–Aug., 4:15 daily, 3:15 in Sept.*

In the Klamath Mountains and the Coast Range of southwestern Oregon, the 1.1-million-acre **Siskiyou National Forest** contains the 35-mi-long Wild and Scenic section of the Rogue River, which races through the Wild Rogue Wilderness Area, and the Illinois and Chetco Wild and Scenic Rivers, which run through the 180,000-acre Kalmiopsis Wilderness Area. Activities include white-water rafting, camping, and hiking, but many hiking areas require trail-park passes. ⊠*Off U.S. 199* ☎*541/858–2200* ⊕*www.fs.fed.us/r6/rogue-siskiyou/* ⊠*Park pass required* ⊗*Daily.*

Fodor'sChoice **Valley of the Rogue State Park** has a 1¼-mi hiking trail that follows the
★ Rogue River bank. This is the river made famous by novelist and fisherman Zane Grey. A campground along 3 mi of shoreline has 88 full hookups $20, 59 electrical $20, and 21 tent sites $16, and 6 yurts $27. There are picnic tables, walking trails, playgrounds, and restrooms. ⊠*Exit 45B off I–5* ☎*541/582–1118 or 800/551–6949* ⊕*www.oregonstateparks.org* ⊗*Daily.*

WHERE TO STAY & EAT

$ ✕**The Brewery.** No beer has been brewed in this 1886 building since Prohibition, but the name sounds good anyway. You can order Australian lobster tails (at the market price, more expensive than most of the entrées), steak, grilled salmon, and other surf-and-turf dishes from the extensive menu. Dine under exposed beams between the original brick walls, which surround three dining rooms filled with booths and oak tables. ⊠*509 S.W. G St., 97526* ☎*541/479–9850* ▭*AE, D, DC, MC, V.*

¢ ⊞**Ivy House.** In the Historic District, this 1908 English Arts and Crafts–style brick home was originally a restaurant and tearoom. The restored interior is unfussy, but the guest rooms have eiderdown quilts and antiques, and there are two sitting rooms. From the porch you can enjoy the rose bushes, which were planted in 1908. Restaurants, theaters, galleries, and the river are all within walking distance. The charming English owner observes a fine old tradition: you can have morning tea and biscuits in bed before your full English breakfast. There's a piano and TV in the common area. ⊠*139 S.W. I St., 97526* ☎*541/474–7363* 🖷*541/474–7363* ➥*5 rooms* ⟐*In-hotel: Wi-Fi, no elevator* ▭*No credit cards* ⟐|*BP.*

OREGON CAVES NATIONAL MONUMENT

★ *90 mi from Jacksonville, west on Hwy. 238, south on U.S. 199, and east on Hwy. 46.*

The town of Cave Junction is the turnoff point for the Oregon Caves National Monument. The "Marble Halls of Oregon," high in the verdant Siskiyou Mountains, have enchanted visitors since local hunter Elijah Davidson chased a bear into them in 1874. Huge stalagmites and stalactites, the Ghost Room, Paradise Lost, and the River Styx are part of a ½-mi subterranean tour that lasts about 90 minutes. The tour includes more than 200 stairs and is not recommended for anyone who experiences difficulty in walking or has respiratory or coronary problems. The temperature inside the cave is 44F (7C) year round. Be sure to wear warm clothing and comfortable closed-toe walking shoes. Children over six must be at least 42 inches tall and pass a safety and ability test, because they cannot be carried. ⊠*Hwy. 46, 20 mi southeast of Cave Junction* ☎*541/592–2100* ⊕*www.nps.gov/orca/* 🖻*$8.50* ⊘*Tours: Mar. 24–May 25, hourly 10–4; May 26–June 22, hourly 9–5; June 23–Sept. 3, every 30 min 9–6; Sept. 4–Oct. 8, hourly 9–5; Oct. 9–Oct. 21, hourly 10–4; Oct. 22–Nov. 25, every 2 hrs 10–4; no tours in winter.*

In the pine-oak foothills of the Siskiyou Mountains, **Foris Vineyards,** where coastal and inland climates mingle, has earned a reputation for richly flavored varietal wines such as pinot noir, merlot, and cabernet sauvignon. ⊠*654 Kendall Rd., 97523* ☎*800/843–6747* ⊕*www.foriswine.com* ⊘*Daily 11–5, except some holidays.*

Documenting area Native American and pioneer history, **Kerbyville Museum** is centered in an 1871 home on the National Register of Historic Places. You can investigate your pioneer and mining ancestors in the research library and see exhibits of taxidermy and antique dolls, as well as local Native American artifacts. ⊠*24195 Redwood Hwy., 97531* ☎*541/592–5252* ⊠*$4* ⊙*Apr.–Oct., Thurs.–Mon. 11–3; other times by appointment only.*

WHERE TO STAY & EAT

¢–$ ✕**Wild River Pizza Company & Brewery.** Cool your heels at the communal redwood picnic tables in this pizza parlor on the north end of Cave Junction. If you aren't in the mood for pizza, choose from fish-and-chips, chicken dishes, and sandwiches. There is also an all-you-can-eat buffet, and the restaurant's own seasonal brews are on tap. ⊠*249 N. Redwood Hwy.* ☎*541/592–3556* ☐*D, MC, V.*

$–$$$ 🏠**Out 'n' About.** You sleep among the leaves in the tree houses of this
★   extraordinary resort—the highest is 37 feet from the ground. One has an antique, claw-foot bath; another has separate kids' quarters connected to the main room by a swinging bridge. There is also an earthbound cabin with a view of the old-growth forest. Memorial Day–Labor Day: 2-night minimum during week, 3-night minimum weekends. ⊠*300 Page Creek Rd.* ☎*541/592–2208* ⊕*www.treehouses.com* ⤺*10 tree houses, 1 cabin* ⌂*In-room: no a/c, no phone, kitchenette in two rooms, no TV. In-hotel: no elevator, lodge has Wi-Fi* ☐*MC, V* ��*BP.*

ROSEBURG

73 mi south of Eugene on I–5.

Fishermen the world over hold the name Roseburg sacred. The timber town on the Umpqua River attracts anglers in search of a dozen popular fish species, including bass, brown and brook trout, and chinook, coho, and sockeye salmon. The native steelhead, which makes its run to the sea in the summer, is king of them all.

The north and south branches of the Umpqua River meet up just north of Roseburg. The roads that run parallel to this river give spectacular views of the falls, and the North Umpqua route also provides access to trails, hot springs, and the Winchester fish ladder. White-water rafting, riverside hiking, horseback riding, mountain biking, snowmobiling, and skiing are available in the area.

Sixty miles due west of the northern gateway to Crater Lake National Park and in the Hundred Valleys of the Umpqua, Roseburg produces innovative, well-regarded wines. Wineries are sprouting up throughout the mild, gorgeous farm country around town, mostly within easy reach of I–5.

One of the best county museums in the state, **Douglas County Museum** surveys 8,000 years of human activity in the region. Its fossil collection is worth a stop. ⊠*123 Museum Dr.* ☎*541/957–7007* ⊕*www. co.douglas.or.us/museum* ⊠*$4* ⊙*Mar.–Oct., weekdays 9–5, Sat. 10–5, Sun. noon–5; Nov.–Feb., Tues.–Fri. 9–5, closed Sun. and Mon.*

⏱ ★ Come face to face with free-roaming animals at the 600-acre **Wildlife Safari**, a drive-through wildlife park. There's also a petting zoo, a miniature train, and elephant rides. The admission price includes two drive-throughs in the same day. From I–5 take Exit 119, follow Highway 42 west 3 mi to Lookingglass Road, and take a right on Safari Road. *Box 1600, Winston 97496* ☎*541/679–6761* ⊕*www.wildlifesafari. org* 🖃*$17.50* ⊗*Apr.–Sept., daily 9–5; Oct.–Mar., daily 10–4.*

★ **Abacela Vineyards and Winery** (✉*12500 Lookingglass Rd., Roseburg* ✛*From I–5 Exit 119, head into Winston, take a right on Hwy. 42, a right on Brockway Rd., and a left on Lookingglass Rd.* ☎*541/679–6642* ⊕*www.abacela.com*) derives its name from an archaic Spanish word meaning "to plant grapevines," and that's exactly what this winery's husband-wife team did not so very long ago. Abacela released its first wine in 1999, and quickly established itself as an innovator in the region. Hot-blooded Spanish tempranillo is this place's pride and joy, though inky malbec and torrid sangiovese also highlight a repertoire heavy on Mediterranean varietals. Admission $5 tasting fee. Hours are 11–5 daily.

WHERE TO STAY & EAT

¢–$$ ★ ✗**Tolly's.** You can go formal or informal at this restaurant in Oakland, 18 mi north of Roseburg. Have an old-fashioned soda or malt downstairs in the Victorian ice-cream parlor, or head upstairs to the oak- and antiques-filled dining room for expertly prepared beef, chicken, seafood, and lamb. Try the grilled salmon or the grilled flank steak marinated and served with fiery chipotle chiles. Even wine to go. ✉*115 Locust St. Take I–5's Exit 138 and follow road north from exit for 4 mi, cross railroad tracks, and turn west on Locust* ☎*541/459–3796* ⊕*www.tollys-restaurant.com* ▤*AE, D, MC, V.*

$$–$$$$ 🛏**The Steamboat Inn.** Every fall a Who's Who of the world's top fly-fishermen converges here, high in the Cascades above the emerald North Umpqua River, in search of the 20-pound steelhead that haunt these waters; guide services are available, as are equipment rentals and sales. Others come simply to relax in the reading nooks or on the broad decks of the riverside guest cabins. Lodging choices include riverside cabins, forest bungalows, and riverside suites; the bungalows and suites have kitchens. Make reservations well in advance, especially for a stay between July and October, the prime fishing months. Nearby massage services available. ✉*42705 N. Umpqua Hwy., 38 mi east of Roseburg on Hwy. 138, near Steamboat Creek, Steamboat 97447* ☎*541/498–2230* 🖷*541/498–2411* ⊕*www.thesteamboatinn.com* ✍*8 cabins, 5 cottages, 2 suites, 5 houses* ♿*In-hotel: restaurant no elevator* ▤*MC, V.*

SOUTHERN OREGON ESSENTIALS

BY CAR

I–5 runs north–south the length of the Umpqua and Rogue River valleys, linking Roseburg, Grants Pass, Medford, and Ashland. Many regional attractions lie not too far east or west of I–5. Jacksonville is a short drive due west from Medford. Highway 138 winds along the Umpqua River east of Roseburg to the back door of Crater Lake National Park. Highway 140 passes through Klamath Falls.

VISITOR INFORMATION

Contacts **Ashland Chamber of Commerce and Visitors Information Center** (⊠ *110 E. Main St., 97520* ☎ *541/482–3486* ⊕ *www.ashlandchamber.com*). **Grants Pass Visitors & Convention Bureau** (⊠ *1995 N.W. Vine St., 97526* ☎ *541/476– 7717* ⊕ *www.visitgrantspass.org*). **Illinois Valley Chamber of Commerce (Cave Junction and Oregon Caves National Monument)** (⊠ *Visitor center: 201 Caves Hwy.* ⌂ *Box 312, Cave Junction 97523* ☎ *541/592–3326* ⊕ *www.cavejunction. com*). **Jacksonville Chamber of Commerce** (⊠ *185 N. Oregon St.* ⌂ *Box 33, 97530* ☎ *541/899–8118* ⊕ *www.jacksonvilleoregon.org*). **Klamath County Chamber of Commerce** (⊠ *706 Main St., 97601* ☎ *541/884–5193 or 877/552–6284* ⊕ *www.klamath.org*). **Medford Visitors & Convention Bureau** (⊠ *101 E. 8th St., 97501* ☎ *800/469–6307 or 541/779–4847* ⊕ *www.visitmedford.org*). **Roseburg Visitors & Convention Bureau** (⊠ *410 S.E. Spruce St., 97470* ☎ *541/672–9731 or 800/444–9584* ⊕ *www.visitroseburg.com*). **Southern Oregon Visitors Association** (⊠ *332 W. 6th St., Medford 97501* ☎ *541/779–4691* ⊕ *www.sova.org*).

EASTERN OREGON

Updated by Kimberly Gadette

Travel east from The Dalles, Bend, or any of the foothill communities blossoming in the shade of the Cascades, and a very different side of Oregon makes its appearance. The air is drier, clearer, often pungent with the smell of juniper. The vast landscape of sharply folded hills, wheat fields, and mountains shimmering in the distance evokes the Old West. There is a lonely grandeur in eastern Oregon, a plain-spoken, independent spirit that can startle, surprise, and enthrall.

Much of eastern Oregon consists of national forest and wilderness, and the people who live here lead very down-to-earth lives. This is a world of ranches and rodeos, pickup trucks and country-western music. Some of the most important moments in Oregon's history took place in the towns of northeastern Oregon. The Oregon Trail passed through this corner of the state, winding through the Grande Ronde Valley between the Wallowa and Blue mountain ranges. The discovery of gold in the region in the 1860s sparked a second invasion of settlers, eventually leading to the displacement of the Native American Nez Perce and Paiute tribes. Pendleton, La Grande, and Baker City were all beneficiaries of that gold fever that swept through the area. Yet signs of even earlier times have survived, from the John Day Fossil Beds, with fragments of saber-toothed tigers, giant pigs, and three-toed horses, to Native American writings and artifacts hidden within canyon walls in Malheur County's Leslie Gulch.

Points of interest can be found on the Eastern Oregon map.

UMATILLA

185 mi east of Portland on I–84 and Hwy. 730; 36 mi northwest of Pendleton.

Umatilla is at the confluence of the Umatilla and Columbia rivers. It was founded in the mid-1800s as a trade and shipping center during the Gold Rush, and today is a center for fishing activities. Just east of Umatilla, Hat Rock State Park contains the unusual geological formation from which it gets its name. Farther upstream, McNary Dam generates extensive hydroelectric power and impounds a lake that extends from Umatilla to Richland, Washington, some 70 mi away.

TOP 5

1. Stange Manor (at La Grande): particularly the first glimpse of the mansion, and that sunroom.

2. Driving through the Umatilla National Forest on the winding path on Hwy. 7 going eastward from John Day to Baker City.

3. The Union Hotel with its historic exterior and lobby.

4. The stained-glass ceiling at the Geiser Grand.

5. The Underground Tour at Pendleton.

On the south shore of Lake Wallula, **Hat Rock State Park** shows off a 70-foot basalt rock, the first major landmark that Lewis and Clark passed on their expedition down the Columbia. In his notations, William Clark called it "Hat Rock" … and the name stuck. Standing tall amid rolling sagebrush hills, it overlooks Lake Wallula, a popular spot for jet skiing, swimming, boating, and fishing for rainbow trout, walleye, and sturgeon. In addition to water sports, the park provides scenic picnic spots and expansive views of the stark, desertlike landscape. But because it abuts an upscale lakeside housing development that's visible from some portions of the park, it might be a challenge to pretend you're back in the days of Lewis and Clark. ☒ U.S. 730, 9 mi. east of Umatilla 82375 C St., Hermiston 97838 ☎ 800/551–6949 ⊕ www.oregonstateparks.org ☒ Free, unless reserving picnic area ☉ Dawn–dusk, year-round ♿ ADA accessible restrooms.

The 23,555-acre **Umatilla National Wildlife Refuge** includes marsh, woodland, and wetland habitats that make it vital to migrating waterfowl and bald eagles, in addition to myriad species of resident wildlife. Although there are numerous routes to access portions of the refuge, the best and easiest way to view wildlife in ponds and wetlands is to drive along the McCormick Auto Tour Route, accessible from Paterson Ferry Road, off Route 730, 9 mi west of Umatilla. ☒ Stretches from Boardman, 20 mi west of Umatilla, to Irrigon, 9 mi west of Umatilla, north of I–84 along Columbia River ☎ 509/371–1801 ⊕ www.fws.gov/midcolumbiariver/Umatillapage.htm ☒ Free ☉ Daily dawn–dusk on designated roadways only ♿ No drinking fountains; 1 ADA-compliant pit toilet on Paterson Ferry Rd.

WHERE TO EAT

$ ✕**Desert River Inn Restaurant.** "Homemade clam chowder every day" is the claim of this casual and family-friendly spot serving breakfast, lunch, and dinner daily. Prime rib is a favorite at night. Though not veg-

Eastern Oregon

WASHINGTON

IDAHO

Walla Walla

Umatilla — Hat Rock State Park

82

Milton-Freewater

11

Umatilla National Wildlife Refuge

Hells Canyon

Hermiston

84

Echo

Pendleton

204

3

Wallowa

Imnaha

82

Elgin

Lostine

Joseph

74

Heppner

74

Island City

MOUNTAINS

BLUE

Enterprise

Wallowa-Whitman National Forest

206

206

Condon

La Grande

244

203

North Powder

39

Kent

19

207

395

Elkhorn Dr.

30

Halfway

97

Fossil

Umatilla National Forest

Baker City

86

218

Antelope

Long Creek

Granite

Sumpter

7

Painted Hills

207

19

Prairie City

245

Mitchell

26

Dayville

John Day R.

Mt. Vernon

John Day

Snake River

IDAHO

Ochoco National Forest

←TO PRINEVILLE

380

Paulina

Malheur National Forest

26

Vale

84

395

Ochoco National Forest

20

20

Riley

Burns

Crane

Lake Owyhee

Malheur Lake

New Princeton

78

Turnbull Lake Bed

Jordan Valley

395

Harney Lake

Malheur National Wildlife Refuge

95

Summer Lake

31

Lake Abert

Frenchglen

Steens Loop Road

Burns Junction

Owyhee R.

Valley Falls

205

Steens Mtn.

Alvord Desert

Andrews

95

Fremont-Winema National Forest

0   40 miles

0   40 kilometers

140

CALIFORNIA

NEVADA

etarian-specific, there's plenty of alternatives (e.g., pastas, fish). Replete with large booths and pastel walls, a meal here is a satisfying addition to a day of exploring, boating, or golfing at the course right next door. ⊠*705 Willamette Ave., 97882* ☎*541/922–1000 or 877/922–1500* ⊟*AE, D, DC, MC, V.*

HERMISTON

188 mi east of Portland on I–84, 28 mi northwest of Pendleton.

Watermelon, watermelon everywhere—it's even the town's official logo! Although its population is just over 15,000, Hermiston is the urban service center for nearly three times that many people in the expansive and productive agricultural industry that surrounds it. Irrigated farmlands and ranch lands produce livestock and crops, including alfalfa, potatoes, corn, wheat. As for the watermelons: the confluence of sandy loam soil, dry days, and cool nights creates the sugary magic that makes for the Hermiston brand of extraordinarily tasty fruit. Named for Robert Louis Stevenson's unfinished novel, *The Weir of Hermiston,* the city has more than 75 acres of parks, with the Columbia River just 6 mi to the north and the Umatilla River and Blue Mountains nearby.

The railroad came to Hermiston in 1883, and some of the original tracks are still at **Maxwell Siding Railroad Display,** an outdoor exhibit of railroad cars and memorabilia. There is a 1910 rotary snowplow, a 1913 diner from the Oregon Short Line, a 1912 passenger car, a 1949 steam-powered snowplow (the last of its kind used in the United States), and two cabooses; if you like, you can arrange to get married in one of them. There are some unusual automobiles too, including a rare 1922 Buda. ⊠*200 W. Highland Ave., across from Hermiston High School* ☎*541/567–8532 or 541/567–3759* ⊠*Donation* ☉*Sat. and by appointment.*

★ Ten miles south of Hermiston, just off I–84, lies the tiny jewel of a town called **Echo.** Named for founder J. H. Koontz's then 3-year-old daughter, Echo sits at the intersection of the Oregon Trail and the transcontinental railroad. A 2007 contender for the international LIVCOM award (most liveable city with a population of up to 20,000), Echo has been an annual Tree City USA award winner since 1989. (With a population of 705, it continues to be the smallest Tree City in Oregon.) As you take a short walking tour of the city, approximately an hour, you'll see buildings from prior centuries, including the Chinese House/ON&R Railroad Museum (now filled with railroad artifacts), and 10 sites that are on the National Register of Historic Places. ⊠*1 mi south of I–84 at Exit 188* ☎*541/376–8411 Echo City Hall* ⊕*www.echo-oregon.com.*

WHERE TO STAY & EAT

$–$$ ✕**Hale's Restaurant.** Rodeo artifacts covering the walls, country music, menus bound in soft brown suede, and dark red leather booths, all blend together to give Hale's an upscale feel with a down home, Old West flair. A Hermiston institution since 1906, Hale's is a dependable choice for prime rib, baby back ribs, steak, and pork chops. Open from

10 AM daily, it serves breakfast all day, including some of the weightiest omelets around (using 6 to 7 eggs!). A separate lounge is in the back. ✉174 E. Main St., 97838 ☎541/567–7975 ▤MC, V.

$–$$ 🏨**Oxford Suites Hermiston.** Perhaps Hermiston's most luxurious hotel, this two-building facility has spacious rooms, all with large sitting areas with work desks and sofas. A comped hot breakfast, as well as an evening reception with appetizers and drinks "on the house" makes the Oxford Suites extra special. **Pros:** Spacious rooms, comp food and drink twice a day. **Cons:** Term "suites" is misleading—not all of them have 2 rooms, "spa" refers to in-room tub, not in-hotel facility. ✉1050 N. 1st St., 97838 ☎541/564–8000 or 888/545–7848 🖷514/564–0633 ⊕www.oxfordsuiteshermiston.com ⇥126 rooms, some of them suites with Jacuzzis, 6 rooms are ADA-compliant ⚿ In-room: refrigerator, VCR, DVD, Wi-Fi. In-hotel: pool, gym, laundry facilities, concierge, parking (no fee), some pets allowed (fee) ▤AE, D, DC, MC, V ⚮BP.

PENDLETON

211 mi east of Portland, 129 mi east of the Dalles on I–84.

At the foot of the Blue Mountains amid waving wheat fields and cattle ranches, Pendleton is a quintessential western town with a rip-snorting history. Originally acquired in a swap for a couple of horses, the town's history of wild behavior was evident from the first city ordinance, which outlawed public drunkenness, fights, and shooting off one's guns within the city limits. But Pendleton is also the land of the Umatilla Tribe—the herds of wild horses that once thundered across this rolling landscape were at the center of the area's early Native American cultures. Later, Pendleton became an important pioneer junction and home to a sizable Chinese community. Today's cityscape still carries the vestiges of yesteryear, with many of its century-old homes still standing, from simple farmhouses to stately Queen Annes.

Given its raucous past teeming with cattle rustlers, saloons, and bordellos, the largest city in eastern Oregon (population 17,310), looks unusually sedate. But all that changes in September when the **Pendleton Round-Up** (⇨*Sports & the Outdoors*) draws thousands for a rodeo and related events. Motels fill up, schools close down, and everybody goes hog, er, horse wild for a few days.

Perhaps Pendleton's main source of name-recognition in the country today comes from the **Pendleton Woolen Mills**, home of the trademark wool plaid shirts and colorful woolen Indian blankets that are sold nationwide. Pendleton also produces a full line of men's and women's clothing, and although the main headquarters have moved to Portland, the local mill is still operating, as well as holding tours.

☾ The collection at the **Round-Up Hall of Fame Museum** spans the rodeo's history since 1910 with photographs—including glamorous glossies of prior Rodeo Queens and the Happy Canyon Princesses (all Native American)—as well as saddles, guns, costumes, and even a stuffed championship bronco named War Paint. ✉*1114 S.W. Court Ave., 97801, across from Round-Up grounds* ☎*541/278–0815* ⊕*www. pendletonroundup.com* 🎫*$5* ⊙*Mon.–Sat. 10–4.*

Fodor's Choice ★ **Pendleton Underground Tours.** This 90-minute tour transports you below ground and back through Pendleton's history of gambling, girls, and gold. Originating in 1989, the Underground Tours depict town life from more than a century ago (when 32 saloons and 18 brothels were operating in full swing) to the 1953 closure of the "Cozy Rooms," the best-known bordello in town. The Underground Tour eventually resurfaces, climbing the "31 Steps to Heaven" to those Cozy Rooms, where madam Stella Darby reigned. (From miners to cowboys to servicemen, Miss Stella always knew how to make a feller feel welcome.) The secret gambling lairs, opium dens, and bathhouses that lie directly below the pavement, will give you a whole new perspective of the streets of Pendleton. ✉*37 S.W. Emigrant Ave.* ☎*541/276–0730 or 800/226–6398* ⊕*www. pendletonundergroundtours.com* 🎫*$10* ⊙*Tours operate year-round, with a shorter schedule in winter. Reservations are necessary; call for tour availability and times.*

Inspired by Native American designs, the three Bishop brothers reopened an inactive mill in 1909 with the town's blessing. Still going strong, the **Pendleton Woolen Mills** continue to produce high-quality Indian blankets, Pendleton shirts and sportswear, all famous for their colors, warmth and durability. If you want to know more about the weaving process, the company gives 20-minute tours, 4 times daily. The mill's retail store stocks blankets and clothing; note that there are also some good bargains available on factory seconds. ✉*1307 S.E. Court Pl., 97801* ☎*541/276–6911 or 800/568–3156* ⊕*www.pendleton-usa.com* ⊙*Mon.–Sat. 8–6, Sun. 9–5; tours weekdays at 9, 11, 1:30, and 3.*

☾ Per the **Tamástslikt Cultural Institute,** its mission is "to document and preserve traditions and practices that distinguish the Confederated Tribes from any other peoples." Located at the Wildhorse Casino Resort, the 45,000-square-foot building depicts history from the perspective of the Cayuse, Umatilla, and Walla Walla tribes. (Tamástslikt means "interpret" in the Walla Walla native language.) An art gallery showcases art of local and regional tribal artists. There's also a museum gift shop, theater, and café. School groups are invited to tour. ✉*72789 Hwy. 331, north of I–84 at Exit 216, 97801* ☎*541/966–9748 or 800/654–9453* ⊕*www.tamastslikt.com* 🎫*$6* ⊙*Daily 9–5, except closed Sun. Nov–Mar.* ♿*Meeting facilities, school.*

Near the summit of the Blue Mountains, **Emigrant Springs State Heritage Area,** a park in an old-growth forest, is the site of a popular pioneer stopover along the Oregon Trail. The park has picnic areas, hiking trails, historical information, and gathering spaces for special events. At the campground, in addition to 18 full hookups and 32 tent sites, there are seven rustic cabins, including two totem cabins. There's also a seven-site horse camp. ✉*Off I–84 at Exit 234, 65068, Old Oregon Trail, Meacham* ☎*541/983–2277 or 800/551–6949* ⊕*www.oregon stateparks.org* 🎫*Day use free; camping fees are per day at $16 for*

RV site; $14 for tent site; $20–$35 for cabins, and $14 for horse camp
⊙ Apr–Nov., daily.

Five miles south of Pendleton, the 1,837-acre **McKay Creek National Wildlife Refuge,** next to McKay Reservoir, provides a home for Canadian geese, ducks, pheasants, waterfowl, and plant life. You can drive along gravel roads for several miles through the enchantingly stark expanse of wild grass and sage. ⊠ *Along U.S. 395, 5 mi south of Pendleton on U.S. 395, then turn left at "refuge" sign* ☎ *509/371–1801* ⊕ *www. fws.gov/midcolumbiariver* ☒ *Free* ⊙ *Mar.–Sept., daily dawn—dusk, designated areas only.*

Near the summit of Battle Mountain, **Battle Mountain Scenic Corridor** is a state park filled with fir trees and flowers, and if you've packed a lunch there are picnic facilities at the edge of the Umatilla National Forest. The park makes a good place to relax (as long as it's not snowing), but the real treat is getting here. The drive from Pendleton winds through hills of farmland as it ascends into the mountains and, near the top, affords jaw-dropping views of the green mountains and valleys around each turn. Beware of difficult road conditions through the winter and much of the spring, and remember that the park is bound to be much colder than temperate Pendleton. ⊠ *U.S. 395, 9 mi north of Ukiah; about 40 mi south of Pendleton* ☎ *541/983–2277 or 800/551–6949* ⊕ *www.oregonstateparks.org* ☒ *Free* ⊙ *Mid-Apr.–mid-Oct.*

The 1.4-million-acre **Umatilla National Forest** has three wilderness areas: the Wenaha-Tucannon, the North Fork Umatilla, and the North Fork John Day, as well as the Blue Mountain Scenic Byway and 22 campgrounds. "Umatilla" is the Indian word for "water rippling over sand." In the Blue Mountains of northeastern Oregon and southeastern Washington, the diverse forest land is found both east and south of Pendleton and extends south almost as far as John Day, where it borders the Malheur National Forest. To the east, it is bordered by the Wallowa-Whitman National Forest. Major thoroughfares, including I–84, U.S. 395, and routes 204 and 244, pass through portions of the forest. In the summer months, the Blue Mountain Scenic Byway provides a beautiful way to travel to Baker City from Ukiah or points farther west. ⊠ *2517 S.W. Hailey Ave., 97801* ☎ *541/278–3716* ⊕ *www.fs.fed.us/r6/uma/* ☒ *Parking pass required at trailheads, $5/day or $30 annual.*

WHERE TO STAY & EAT

$$ ✗ **Raphael's.** Is it a restaurant—or a millionaire's seven-gabled home?
★ It's both! The 1904 Raley House was sold and converted in 1991 to its current gastronomic glory, where art deco meets Native American cultural sensibilities. Husband/co-owner/chef Rob Hoffman is crazy for huckleberries—you might find them integrated in the Indian salmon, the pastas, chicken, or wild game (elk, pheasant, buffalo), as well as the crème brûlée. If you'd rather drink your berries, consider Raphael's signature huckleberry martinis and daiquiris. When chef Rob's not using huckleberries, he might mingle apples in his smoked prime rib, or apricots in a pork loin sauce. In sunnier months, consider dining alfresco in the garden out back. Catering services are available, both

in-house and off-site. ⌧*233 S.E. 4th St., 97801* ☎*541/276–8500 or 888/944–CHEF* ⊕*www.raphaelsrestaurant.com* ▭*AE, D, DC, MC, V Closed Sun. and Mon.* No lunch.

¢ ✕**Main Street Diner.** A four-foot statue of Betty Boop poses on the sidewalk directly outside, welcoming all hungry comers. Inside there's a mix of framed pictures of NY Yankee baseball greats, Elvis, movie posters, and '50s records hanging at jaunty angles from exposed brick walls. Plop into a leather teal booth with the retro formica tabletop and order up what locals say is "the best breakfast in town"—including 9 different omelets. After 11, lunch is served until 2 (burgers, Parmesan-baked tacos, shakes, and malts). A highlight is co-owner Marilyn's melt-in-your-mouth bread pudding—she suggests heating it up, though husband/co-owner Larry loves it cold. Either way, Daddy-O, you'll dig it. There's also a kids' menu. ⌧*349 S. Main St., 97801* ☎*541/278–1952* ▭*MC, V.*

¢–$ ▦**The Pendleton House Bed & Breakfast** (formerly Parker House). Aside from the name, this 1917, 6,000 square-foot pink stucco home is unchanged. The Chinese wallpaper, custom fittings, woodwork—all original in this blend of French neoclassical and Italianate architecture. Located in Pendleton's North Hill neighborhood, the B&B is a grand reminder that the Old West had its share of wealth and worldly sophistication. Furnished with period furniture, the rooms are quiet and comfortable. Four of them share one bathroom, but designed by Pittock Mansion architect Edward T. Foulkes, and according to the owner, it's so stunning that guests don't seem to mind the inconvenience. Gourmet breakfasts might include eggs Benedict with proscuitto, toasted pecan-and-cranberry-stuffed French toast, or soufflé frittata ramekins. A complimentary wine and cheese hour is held daily 5–6. **Pros:** Glorious home; small pets allowed, comp wine and cheese hour. **Cons:** One shared bathroom for 4 rooms. ⌧*311 N. Main St., 97801* ☎*541/276–8581 or 800/700–8581* ⊕*www.parkerhousebnb.com* ⇆*5 rooms, 1 with 1/2 bath* ⌨*In-room: no phone, no TV, Wi-Fi (some). In-hotel: elevator, parking (no fee), small pets allowed (fee), kids 14 and up* ▭*AE, MC, V* ⍾*BP.*

¢ ▦**Working Girls Hotel.** From boarding house to bordello to hotel, the refurbished 1890s edifice advertises it's "Old West Comfort" with a large vertical sign hanging from the top of the building. A redheaded lass looks down from the top of the sign, as if wanting to call to potential customers passing by. Exposed brick walls and 18-foot ceilings run throughout, but the individual Victorian antiques that decorate the rooms give them all their own personalities. Owned and operated by the Underground Tours, the inn has a full kitchen and dining room available to guests. **Pros:** Centrally located in downtown Pendleton, fun decor, great prices. **Cons:** Bathrooms in the hall instead of the room, difficult to make contact via phone, no voice mail for taking messages. ⌧*17 S.W. Emigrant Ave., 97801* ☎*541/276–0730 or 800/226–6398* 🖷*541/276–0665* ⊕*www.pendletonundergroundtours.com* ⇆*4 rooms with 2 shared baths, 1 suite* ⌨*In room: no phones, no TV. In-hotel: no children, no elevator* ▭*MC, V.*

SPORTS & THE OUTDOORS

RODEO   More than 50,000 people roll into town during the second full week in September for the **Pendleton Round-Up,** one of the oldest and most prominent rodeos in the United States. With its famous slogan of "Let 'Er Buck," the Round-Up attracts rodeo performers and fans for eight days of parades, races, beauty contests, and children's rodeos, culminating in four days of rodeo events. Vendors line the length of Court Avenue and Main Street, selling beadwork and curios, while country bands twang in the background. Tickets for the events, including the Happy Canyon Night Show and Dance, cost between $14 and $18. Reservations must be made far in advance. ⊠ *Rodeo grounds: 1205 S.W. Court Ave., at S.W. 12th St.* ⊠ *Office, open year-round: 1114 S.W. Court Ave., 97801* ☐ *Box 609, Pendleton 97801* ☎ *541/276–2553 or 800/457–6336* ⊕ *www.pendletonroundup.com.*

SHOPPING

The **Collector's Gallery** (⊠ *223 S.E. Court Ave.* ☎ *541/276–6697*) is a large, disorganized antiques store where you get the feeling there are always more fun treasures to be unearthed around the next corner. On-site craftspeople fashion hand-tooled saddles that are considered the best in the world at **Hamley & Co. Western Store & Custom Saddlery** (⊠ *30 S.E. Court Ave.* ☎ *541/278–1100 or 877/342–6539*), which carries authentic cowboy/cowgirl gear and quality leather products, as well as gifts, art, and their famous saddles. An additional bonus: in 2007 Hamley's opened Hamley's Steakhouse on-site, for lunch and dinner (⊕ *www.hamley.com*). Inside the Center for the Arts, **Riverfront Crafts** (⊠ *214 N. Main St.* ☎ *541/278–9201*) sells the original artwork and crafts of approximately 40 local artists. **Picket Fences** (⊠ *239 S.E. Court Ave.* ☎ *541/276–9515*) is a country store selling home and garden gifts, as well as some antiques.

LA GRANDE

56 mi southeast of Pendleton on I–84 at Hwy. 82.

La Grande started life in the late 1800s as a farming community. It grew slowly while most towns along the Blue Mountains were booming or busting in the violent throes of gold-fueled stampedes. When the railroad companies were deciding where to lay their tracks through the valley, a clever local farmer donated 150 acres to ensure that the Iron Horse would run through La Grande. With steampower fueling a new boom, the town quickly outgrew its neighbors, took the title of county seat from fading Union City (Union City claims it "was robbed"), and with its current population of 12,540 sits at the urban center of the Grand Ronde Valley. La Grande is also the site of the only four-year college in the region, Eastern Oregon State College. Though you can appreciate it for its own charms, La Grande is a convenient stop if you're heading to the nearby Wallowa Mountains.

The **Wallowa Mountains** form a rugged U-shape fortress between Hells Canyon on the Idaho border and the Blue Mountains, west of the Grande Ronde Valley. Sometimes called the American Alps or Little

Switzerland, the granite peaks in this range are between 5,000 and 9,000 feet in height. Dotted with crystalline alpine lakes and meadows, rushing rivers, and thickly forested valleys that fall between the mountain ridges, the Wallowas have a grandeur that can take your breath away. Bighorn sheep, elk, deer, and mountain goats populate the area. Nearly all the trails in the Wallowa Mountains are at least partially contained within the Eagle Cap Wilderness. The offices and visitor center for the mountains are in Enterprise. ⊠ *From La Grande, Rtes. 82, 203, and 237 all lead to parts of Wallowa Mountains. Wallowa Mountains Visitor Center, 88401 Hwy. 82, Enterprise 97828* ☎ *541/426–4978* ⊕ *www.fs.fed. us/r6/w-w/.*

> **KNOW BEFORE YOU GO**
>
> For road closures, weather watches, and warnings, a great resource is Oregon Department of Transportation's Trip Check, www. tripcheck.com. Within Oregon, call 511. If outside the state, 800/977–ODOT.

The 361,446-acre **Eagle Cap Wilderness,** the largest wilderness in Oregon, encompasses most of the Wallowa range and has 534 mi of trails for hard-core backpackers and horseback riders. Most of the popular trailheads are along Eagle Cap's northern edge, most accessible from Enterprise or Joseph, but you also can find several trailheads 20 to 30 mi southeast of La Grande along Route 203. For wilderness information, contact the Wallowa Mountains Visitor Center in Enterprise. (Some areas of the wilderness are accessible year-round, while the high-elevation areas are accessible only for a few months in summer.) To park at most trailheads, you must purchase a Northwest Forest Pass for $5 per day, or $30 per year. To hike into the wilderness, you also need to get a free permit that will alert rangers of your plans. ⊠ *East of La Grande, via Hwy. 82 and Hwy. 203, Wallowa Mountains Visitor Center 88401 Hwy. 82, Enterprise 97828* ☎ *541/426–4978.*

Fourteen miles southeast of La Grande, **Union's National Historic District** is a Victorian-era town that's working to restore many of its historic buildings along the several-block stretch of Main Street. In addition to the picturesque buildings lining Main Street, the main attractions are the **Union Hotel** (⊠ *326 N. Main St., 97883* ☎ *541/562–6135* ⊕ *www. theunionhotel.com*) ⇨ *Where to Stay & Eat),* a beautifully restored hotel with a restaurant and parlor, and the **Union County Museum** (⊠ *11 mi southeast of La Grande via Hwy. 203. 333 S. Main St., Union 97883* ☎ *541/562–6003* 🖾 *$4* ⊘ *May–mid-Oct., Mon.–Sat. 10–4, or by appointment.*), exhibiting the Cowboys Then and Now Collection.

WHERE TO STAY & EAT

$$$ ✕ **Foley Station.** This local favorite has an antique pressed-tin ceiling, an open kitchen, exposed-brick walls and high-backed, rich wood-paneled booths. Primarily a dinner place, there's a happy hour or two, namely "Martinis & Munchies In The Lounge" 3–5 and 9–closing. The seasonal menu wanders from inexpensive burgers to high-end lobsters and steaks, incorporating Northwest ingredients as well as a pronounced Southwestern flair, and hush puppies with jalapeno jelly keep company

with Vietnamese spring rolls. There's a full bar, with wines, micro-brews, and a decent selection of after-dinner ports. ⊠ *1114 Adams Ave.* ☎ *541/963–7473* ▭ *D, MC, V* ⊙ *Daily 3–10*

$ 🏠 **Stange Manor Inn.** A buttercream-color, Georgian Colonial, the
Fodor'sChoice   immaculate Stange Manor impresses in many ways. Gourmet break-
★   fasts are created by owner/hostess Carolyn (a graduate of San Fran-cisco's California Culinary Academy), then cheerily served up in the rose-toned formal dining room. Light bounces merrily off a stained-glass indoor fountain in the white wicker–furnished Sun Room, and as you ascend the great, sweeping staircase leading to the guest rooms you'll feel like Scarlet or Rhett. There are three grand common rooms and a sizeable wood-burning fireplace. The guest rooms have plush, crisp-linen beds, and each room is individually decorated in a manner befitting royalty, which is just how the hosts treat their guests. Quot-ing owner/host Ron Jensen, "This 1924 mansion may have been built by a lumber baron—but I'm the slumber baron!" **Pros:** Great hosts who welcome rather than hover; staying at a mansion is an unusual treat, amazing food; **Cons:** No elevators; no king-size beds. ⊠ *1612 Walnut St., 97850* ☎ *541/963–2400 or 888/2UN–WIND* ⊕ *www.stangemanor.com* ⇆ *2 rooms, 2 suites* ♿ *In-room: no phones, Wi-Fi. In-hotel: no elevator, public Wi-Fi, parking (free), no kids under 12* ▭ *MC, V.*

¢–$ 🏠 **The Historic Union Hotel.** Cast-iron Victorian lampposts frame the
★   entrance to this three-story, redbrick building, its white trim standing out against the red like icing on a cake. The Union Hotel, about 14 mi south of La Grande, offers 16 elegant individually themed rooms. The forest-green Northwest Room has a kitchenette and a jetted tub for two; the Davis Bros.' Room comes with a wood-paneled shower with double showerheads; and for large parties up to 6, the Huffman Suite has a full kitchen. Per owners Dave and Rob, the best part of the hotel is "the guests." **Pros:** Great prices, visual/historical treat, owners go out of their way to accommodate, RV spots. **Cons:** No TV-phones-Internet, a/c isn't central, not ADA-compliant. ⊠ *326 N. Main St., Union 97883* ☎ *541/562–6135 or 888/441–8928* ⊕ *www.theunionhotel.com* ⇆ *16 rooms* ♿ *In-room: no phone, no TV. In-hotel: restaurant, no elevator, parking (no fee), some pets allowed (fee), kids 9 and older; RV accom-modations, 8 spaces, for $20/night* ▭ *AE, D, MC, V.*

ENTERPRISE

6 mi north of Joseph on Hwy. 82.

The seat of Oregon's northeasternmost county, Enterprise is sur-rounded by some of the region's most rugged natural beauty, and is a locus for rugged outdoor activities in winter and summer. To the west lie the Eagle Cap Wilderness, the alpine Wallowa Mountains, and pristine Wallowa Lake, and to the east is the Hells Canyon National Recreation Area.

At the **Wallowa Valley Ranger District headquarters,** (⊠ *88401 Hwy. 82, 97828* ☎ *541/426–4978*) you can find detailed information about the Wallowa-Whitman National Forest and its recreational possibilities.

WHERE TO STAY & EAT

¢–$ ✕ **Terminal Gravity Brew Pub.** Beer connoisseurs from across the state, ★ and just about all the locals, rave about the India Pale Ale at this tiny microbrewery that resides in a canary-yellow house on the outskirts of downtown. (The name "Terminal Gravity" is a brewers' term for the specific gravity that occurs to beer after fermentation is done.) Aspens wave in a front yard dotted with picnic tables, kids and dogs lounging on the wooden front porch. Between the customers both outside and in, both downstairs and up, it can't just be about the hops in this friendly local hangout. The menu is short and simple, with creative sandwiches and burgers. There's a rotating selection of the brews on tap, but it seems that the IPA continues to be the all-around favorite. For further confirmation, check with those dogs on the porch. ⊠ *803 School St., 97828* ☎ *541/426–0158* ▭ *MC, V* ☾ *Wed.–Sat. 4–10, Sun. 4–9* ☾ *Closed Tues.*

¢ ▦ **Cherokee Mingo Motel.** About 16 mi west of Enterprise, the tiny town of Wallowa has a main street, a couple of restaurants and a few stores, as well as this small, friendly motel. Each room has a different theme, ranging from celestial bodies to sea life. Bedspreads, borders and shower curtains all share a colorful pattern that gives each large room a unique flair; the furnishings aren't subtle, but they're fun, and the rooms stand out from the run-of-the-mill units to be found in other motels in the same price range. If you are headed into the Wallowa-Whitman National Forest, or are just seeking to avoid some of the summertime crowds in Enterprise and Joseph, consider spending a night at this remote outpost of civilization. ⊠ *102 N. Alder, Wallowa 97885* ☎ *541/886–2021* ▭ *11 rooms* ♦ *In-room: phone, refrigerator* ▭ *MC, V.*

JOSEPH

80 mi east of La Grande on Hwy. 82.

The area around Wallowa Lake was the traditional home of the Nez Perce Indians—the town of Joseph is named for Chief Joseph, their famous leader. The peaks of the Wallowa Mountains, snow-covered until July, tower 5,000 feet above the regional tourist hubs of the town and Wallowa Lake.

To tour the **Valley Bronze of Oregon** foundry facility, head to its showroom, the **Valley Bronze Gallery** (⊠ *18 S. Main St., Joseph 97846* ☎ *541/ 432–7445*), which displays sculptures by many artists whose works are cast at the foundry, in addition to the work of other artists from around the world. Generally, the gallery is open March–October, daily 10–5. As winter settles in, however, it's recommended to call ahead, because hours often vary. The foundry itself is ½ mi away, and your tour guide will lead you there after the group has gathered at the showroom. ⊠ *Foundry address: 307 W. Alder St.* ☎ *541/432–7551*

⊕*www.valleybronze.com* ✉*$15* ⊘*One tour daily: Mon.–Thurs. at 4, weekends at noon.*

The **Wallowa County Museum** in Joseph has a small but poignant collection of artifacts and photographs chronicling the Nez Perce Wars, a series of battles against the U.S. Army that took place in the late 1870s. Built as a bank in 1888, the building was robbed in 1896, an event that is reenacted with full pageantry every Wednesday at 1 PM in summer, complete with music, dancing girls, gunshots and, as one would expect, much yelping. ✉*110 S. Main St., 97846* ☎*541/432–6095* ⊕*www. co.wallowa.or.us/museum* ✉*Free* ⊘*Memorial Day–3rd weekend in Sept., daily 10–5.*

From Joseph, Highway 82 continues south and ends at sparkling, blue-green **Wallowa Lake** (✉*Wallowa Lake Hwy.*), the highest body of water in eastern Oregon (elevation 5,000 feet). Call the **Joseph Chamber of Commerce** (✉*102 E. 1st St., 97846* ☎*541/432–1015*) for information about Wallowa Lake and its facilities.

Six miles south of Joseph, **Wallowa Lake State Recreation Park** is a campground surrounded on three sides by 9,000-foot-tall snowcapped mountains. It also serves as a gateway to Hells Canyon. It has 121 full hookups, 89 tent sites, 1 2-story cabin (sleeps 8), and 2 yurts. Popular activities include fishing and boating as well as hiking on wilderness trails, horseback riding, and canoeing. There are also bumper boats and miniature golf. You can ride a tramway to the top of one of the mountains. ✉*Off Hwy. 82, 6 mi south of Joseph, 72214 Marina La., 97846* ☎*541/432–4185 or 800/551–6949* ⊕*www.oregonstateparks. org* ✉*Day use $3 per vehicle* ⊘*Daily.*

★ The **Wallowa Lake Tramway,** the steepest gondola in North America, rises 4,000 feet in 15 minutes, rushing you up to the top of 8,150-foot Mt. Howard. Vistas of mountain peaks, forest, and Wallowa Lake far below will dazzle you, both on the way up and at the summit. Two and a half miles of cross-country skiing trails await you at the top. Enjoy lunch at the Summit Grill and Alpine Patio *Where to Eat* before making your return trip back down to earth. ✉*59919 Wallowa Lake Hwy., 97846* ☎*541/432–5331* ⊕*www.wallowalaketramway.com/winter.htm* ✉*$20* ⊘*May, June, and Sept., daily 10–4; July and Aug., daily 10–5.*

WHERE TO EAT

$ ✕**Stubborn Mule Saloon and Steakhouse.** Burgers come in a suprising variety of choices and size at this sports bar with the old saloon feel. Nothing lighter than half a pound goes between the enormous buns here. Seat yourself at one of the wooden tables in the small, no-frills dining room and order the "Piper Pirate Burger," a burger with ham and egg, named after the owner's one-eyed dog. Or cozy up to the Mule's renowned slow-smoked prime rib. The tavern's in the back— shoot a game of pool and have a beer. Many microbrews are on hand, including the local favorite, Terminal Gravity. ✉*104 S. Main St.97846* ☎*541/432–6853* ▭*MC, V* ⊘*Closed Mon. No lunch Tues.–Sun.*

¢–$ ✕ **Summit Grill and Alpine Patio.** Called "The Northwest's Highest Res-
★ taurant," the Summit Grill perches on Mt. Howard, 8,150 feet up. No
worries, you won't have to take the stairs: there's a 15-minute speed
ride via the Wallow Lake Tramway. Though the view usually gets more
attention than the menu, the grill serves a variety of gourmet burgers,
"a mountain of fries," sandwiches, burritos, salads, nachos supreme,
chili, soups, and Oregon beers and wines. On a clear day the chance
to peer at portions of four bordering states is definitely a highlight.
⊠ *59919 Wallowa Lake Hwy.* ☎ *541/432–5331* ▭ *MC, V* ⊗ *Closed
Oct.–Memorial Day.*

**EN
ROUTE**
The **Wallowa Mountain Loop** is a relatively easy way to take in the natural splendor of the Eagle Cap Wilderness and reach Baker City without backtracking to La Grande. The 3½-hour trip from Joseph to
Baker City, designated the Hells Canyon Scenic Byway, winds through
the national forest and part of Hells Canyon Recreation Area, passing over forested mountains, creeks, and rivers. Before you travel
the loop, check with the Joseph Chamber of Commerce about road
conditions; in winter always carry chains. ⊠ *From Joseph, take Little Sheep Creek Hwy. east for 8 mi, turn south onto Forest Service
Rd. 39, and continue until it meets Hwy. 86, which winds past town
of Halfway to Baker City. Further information found at www.fs.fed.
us/r6/w-w/recreation/byway/byway-hc.shtml.*

HELLS CANYON

★ *30 mi northeast of Joseph on Wallowa Mountain Loop.*

This remote place along the **Snake River** is the deepest river-carved gorge
in North America (7,900 feet), with many rare and endangered animal
species. There are three different routes from which to view and experience the canyon, though only one is accessible year-round.

Most travelers take a scenic peek from the overlook on the 45-mi **Wallowa Mountain Loop,** which follows Route 39 from just east of Halfway
on Route 86 to just east of Joseph on Route 350. At the junction of
Route 39 and Forest Road 3965, take the 6-mi round-trip loop to
the 5,400-foot-high rim at Hells Canyon Overlook. This is the easiest way to get a glimpse of the canyon, but be aware that Route 39 is
open only during summer and early fall. During the late fall, winter,
and spring the best way to experience Hells Canyon is to follow a
slightly more out-of-the-way route along the **Snake River Segment** of the
Wallowa Mountain Loop. Following Highway 86 north from Copper-
field, the 60-mi round-trip route winds along the edge of Hells Canyon Reservoir, crosses the Snake River to Hells Canyon Dam on the
Oregon-Idaho border, and continues on to the Hells Canyon National
Recreation Site, with a visitor center and hiking trails. The canyon is
10 mi wide in places. The trip is a memorable one, but be sure you
have a full tank before starting out, since there are no gas stations anywhere along the route. If you're starting from Joseph, you also have the
option of heading to the **Hat Point Overlook.** From Joseph, take Route
350 northeast to Imnaha, a tiny town along the Imnaha River. From

there, Forest Road 4240 leads southeast to Route 315, which in turn heads northeast up a steep gravel road to the overlook. This route is also open only during the summer. Carry plenty of water.

The **Hells Canyon National Recreation Area** is the site of one of the largest elk herds in the United States, plus 422 other species, including bald eagles, bighorn sheep, mule deer, white-tailed deer, black bears, bobcats, cougars, beavers, otters, and rattlesnakes. The peregrine falcon has also been reintroduced here. Part of the area was designated as Hells Canyon Wilderness, in parts of Oregon and Idaho, with the establishment of the Hells Canyon National Recreation Area in 1975. Additional acres were added as part of the Oregon Wilderness Act of 1984, with a current total of 219,006. Nine hundred miles of trails wind through the wilderness area, closed to all mechanized travel. If you want to visit the wilderness it must be on foot, mountain bike, or horseback. Three of its rivers, the Snake, Imnaha, and Rapid have all been designated as Wild and Scenic. Environmental groups have proposed the creation of Hells Canyon National Park to better manage the area's critical habitat. A wildlife-viewing guide is available from the Idaho Department of Fish and Game. ⊠ *Oregon contact: 88401 Hwy. 82, Enterprise, OR 97828* ☎ *541/426–4978 or 541/426–5546* ⊕ *www.fs.fed.us/hellscanyon* ⊠ *Idaho contact: 600 S. WalnutBoise, ID 83712* 🖰 *Idaho Department of Fish and Game, Box 25, Boise, ID 83707* ☎ *208/334–3700* ⊕ *www.fishandgame.idaho.gov.*

The **Wild and Scenic Snake River Corridor** consists of 67½ mi of river federally designated as part of the National Wild and Scenic Rivers System. Extending ¼ mi back from the high-water mark on each shore, the corridor is available for managed public use. Since the corridor itself is not designated as "wilderness," and wilderness area regulations do not therefore apply, there are developed campsites and man-made structures, and some motorized equipment is allowed. In season, both powerboaters and rafters must make reservations and obtain permits for access to the river corridor. ☎ *509/758–0616 general information, 509/758–1957 noncommercial float reservations, 509/758–0270 powerboat reservations* ⊙ *Daily Memorial Day–early Sept.*

HALFWAY

63 mi south of Joseph on Wallowa Mountain Loop.

Halfway, the closest town to Hells Canyon, got its name because it was midway between the town of Pine and the gold mines of Cornucopia. On the southern flanks of the Wallowas, the city is a straightforward, unpretentious community with a Main Street and a quiet rural flavor.

WHERE TO STAY

¢–$$ ⚏ **Pine Valley Lodge.** From the outside, this lodge on Main Street is con-
★   structed like many others built in eastern Oregon during the timber boom of the late 1920s, using wood from the original mines' construction. Inside, the wood mingles with walls of deep blues and reds, reflecting a clean, homespun beauty. Eight assorted rooms of varying decor

and size are available. You can "rock out" in high-backed wicker rocking chairs on the porch, or take a swing on the hammock. Rather than an alarm clock, Pine Valley's wake-up call alerts the nose instead of the ears with homemade blueberry and cranberry/orange scones. What a way to awake! **Pros:** Newly renovated, pets and kids okay. **Cons:** Right on Main Street. ⊠*163 N. Main St., 97834* ☎*541/742–2027* ⊕*www. pvlodge.com* ⇨*8 rooms* ♨*In-room: no phone, some TV. In-hotel: no elevator, public Internet, some pets allowed* ☐*MC, V* ⏺*BP.*

¢–$ 🏠 **The Inn at Clear Creek Farm.** Amid 160 acres of orchards, ponds, woods, and fields on the southeastern flank of the Wallowa Mountains, this 1880s Craftsman-style farmhouse is a comfortable rural retreat. The main house has six rooms, several of which have a lake view. With a wraparound front porch, there are sweeping views of Pine Valley and the Wallowa Mountains. The owners are happy to accommodate family-style meals upon request. **Pros:** Glorious views, many sports activities in area: snowmobiling, hiking, apple/berry picking, rafting. **Cons:** Not exactly on the beaten path. ⊠*48212 Clear Creek Rd., off Fish Lake Rd., 5½ mi north of Halfway, 97834* ☎*541/742–2238 or 866/430–6003* ⊕*www.clearcreekinn.com* ⇨*5 rooms 1 suite* ♨*In room: no phone, Internet. In hotel: parking, some pets allowed* ☐*MC, V.*

BAKER CITY

53 mi west of Halfway on Hwy. 86, 44 mi south of La Grande on U.S. 30 off I–84.

During the Gold Rush, Baker City was the hub. The Big Apple, or rather, the Big Nugget. After gold was discovered in 1861, the rush was on, and Baker City kept on booming. Many smaller towns dried up after the Gold Rush, but Baker City transformed itself into the logging and ranching town that it still is today. Remnants of its turn-of-the-century opulence, when it was the largest city between Salt Lake and Portland, are still visible in the many restored Victorian houses and downtown shops.

Baker City may not have that much gold left in its surrounding hills—but what hills they are. The Wallowas and Eagle Cap, the Elkhorn Ridge of the Blue Mountains, the Umatilla National Forest, the Wallowa-Whitman, Hells Canyon, Monument Rock—the panorama almost completes a full circle. Outdoor enthusiasts flock here for the climbing, fishing, hunting, waterskiing, canoeing, hiking, cycling, and skiing. Baker City's gold rush has been supplanted by the "green rush."

The **Oregon Trail Regional Museum** may seem rather staid after a turn through the National Historic Oregon Trail Interpretive Center, but the museum has one of the most impressive rock collections in the West, the Cavin-Warfel Collection, including thunder eggs, glowing phosphorescent rocks, and a 950-pound hunk of quartz. Other exhibits highlight pioneering, ranching, mining, and antique furniture. ⊠*2480 Grove St., at Campbell St.* ☎*541/523–9308* 💲*$5* 🕐*Mid-Mar.–Oct., daily 9–5.*

★ The **National Historic Oregon Trail Interpretive Center,** 5 mi east of Baker City, does a superb job of re-creating pioneer life in the mid-1800s. From 1841 to 1861 about 300,000 people made the 2,000-mi journey from western Missouri to the Columbia River and the Oregon coast, looking for agricultural land in the West. A simulated section of the Oregon Trail will give you a feel for camp life, the toll the trip took on marriages and families, and the settlers' impact on Native Americans; an indoor theater presents movies and plays. A 4-mi round-trip trail winds from the center to the actual ruts left by the wagons. ✉*Hwy. 86 E, east of I–84 22267 Oregon Highway 8697814* ☎*541/523–1843* ⊕*www.blm.gov/or/oregontrail* ☒*$5* ☉*Apr.–Oct., daily 9–6; Nov.– Mar., daily 9–4.*

NEED A BREAK? Signage overhead depicts a wacky lady with blue hair and purple gown holding a steaming cup. It's **Mad Matilda's Coffee House,** serving all manner of coffees, teas, chais, and for particularly brisk Baker City days, hot chocolate. They also have a no-fee computer with hi-speed Internet. While sipping, take a peek next door at their vintage gift shop, Sane Jane's. ✉*1917 Main St., 97814* ☎*541/523-4588* ⊟*AE, D, DC, MC, V* ☉*Mon.–Sat., starting at 7:30* AM.

In the Wallowa-Whitman National Forest, **Anthony Lakes Ski Area** has a vertical drop of 900 feet and a top elevation of 8,000 feet. There are 21 trails, two lifts, and a 13-km cross-country route. Snowboards are permitted. ✉*Exit 285 off I–84 to Anthony Lakes Rd., 19 mi west of North Powder 47500 Anthony Lake Hwy., North Powder 97867* ☎*541/856–3277* ⊕*www.anthonylakes.com* ☒*Lift tickets: $35* ☉*Nov.–Apr., Thurs.–Sun. 9–4.*

The scenic 106-mi loop of **Elkhorn Drive** winds from Baker City through the Elkhorn Range of the Blue Mountains. Only white-bark pine can survive on the range's sharp ridges and peaks, which top 8,000 feet; spruce, larch, Douglas fir, and ponderosa pine thrive on the lower slopes. The route is well marked; start on Highway 7 west of Baker City, turn onto County Road 24 toward Sumpter, pass Granite on Forest Service Road 73, and then return to Baker City along U.S. 30.

Wallowa-Whitman National Forest. The 2.3-million-acre forest, found both east and west of Baker City, ranges in elevation from 875 feet in the Hells Canyon Wilderness to 9,845 feet in the Eagle Cap Wilderness. There are two other wilderness areas: Monument Rock and North Fork John Day. ✉*Roads leading into and through forest accessible via Hwys. 7 and 237, west of Baker City, as well as Hwys. 86 and 203 on east side Forest HQ at 1550 Dewey Ave., 97814* ☎*541/523–6391* ⊕*www.fs.fed.us/r6/w-w/* ☒*$5 day pass* ☉*Daily.*

WHERE TO STAY & EAT

¢–$ ✕**Barley Brown's.** It's the "Cheers" of Baker City–and everyone knows owner Tyler's name. With on-site brewmaster Shawn Kelso, their "Tumble Off" Pale Ale recently won the gold medal at the Great American Beer Festival. You can watch the process behind glass windows as they brew eight different beers (e.g., "Hot Blonde," "Sled Wreck").

Barley Brown's also makes tasty grub, from burgers and quesadillas to spicy pastas and the occasional alligator. Tyler is committed to using local produce (the hand-cut fries are Baker County potatoes) and hormone-free beef. If you think that Baker City has no nightlife–drop in at the oak and brick-walled Barley Brown's, where there's usually a crowd eating, drinking, jawing, or cheering for their teams on any one of three TVs. ⊠*2190 Main St., 97814* ☎*541/523–4266* ▭*AE, MC, V* ⊗*Closed Sun. No lunch.*

$–$$ 🏨**Geiser Grand Hotel.** She sits like the dowager duchess of Main Street, her cupola clock tower still cutting a sharp figure against a wide Baker City sky. It's the Geiser Grand, built in 1889, the Italianate Renaissance Revival that was once known as the finest hotel between Portland and Salt Lake City. Reopened in 1998 after an $8 million restoration, the rooms still have those 14-foot ceilings, old-fashioned transoms above the doorway, and 10-foot tall windows. But of all the fascinating features, it's the custom-built stained-glass ceiling in hues of green, blue, purple, and red that takes center stage. The fact that it was created from photographs and an oldtimer's memory makes it even more astounding. **Pros:** Fascinating history; if possible, take the complimentary hotel tour. **Cons:** Hotel pipes run loudly at night, disturbing sleep, smoke from bar permeates into Palm Court. ⊠*1996 Main St., 97814* ☎*541/523–1889 or 888/434–7374* 🖷*541/523–1800* ⊕*www.geisergrand.com* ⇥*30 rooms* 🛎*In-room: VCR, Wi-Fi. In-hotel: restaurant, bar, elevator, concierge, public Wi-Fi, parking (no fee), some pets allowed* ▭*AE, MC, V.*

¢ 🏨**Bridge Street Inn.** Right off Main Street, Bridge Street Inn is one of the least-expensive motels in town. With rooms that are clean and reliable, it is an excellent option if you're short on funds. All rooms have microwaves and refrigerators, new sinks, and double-pane windows. A continental breakfast is included. **Pros:** inexpensive, well-insulated, comp breakfast. **Cons:** with 42 ground units, neighbors may be noisy. 1 block away from the more attractive main drag. ⊠*134 Bridge St.97814* ☎*541/523–6571 or 800/932–9220* 🖷*541/523–9424* ⊕*www.bridgestreetinn.net* ⇥*42 rooms* 🛎*In room: Internet. In-hotel: 2 ADA-compliant rooms, Internet, parking (no fee), some pets allowed* ▭*MC, V* ⏏*CP.*

JOHN DAY

80 mi west of Baker City on U.S. 26.

More than $26 million in gold was mined in the John Day area. The town was founded shortly after gold was discovered there in 1862. Yet John Day is better known to contemporaries for the plentiful outdoor recreation it offers and for the nearby John Day Fossil Beds. The town is also a central location for trips to the Malheur National Wildlife Refuge and the towns of Burns, Frenchglen, and Diamond to the south.

As you drive west through the dry, shimmering heat of the John Day Valley on U.S. 26, it may be hard to imagine this area as a humid subtropical forest filled with lumbering 50-ton brontosauruses and 50-

foot-long crocodiles. But so it was, and the eroded hills and sharp, barren-looking ridges contain the richest concentration of prehistoric plant and animal fossils in the world.

Two miles south of John Day, Canyon City is a small town that feels like it hasn't changed much since the Old West days. Memorabilia from the Gold Rush is on display at the small **Grant County Historical Museum**, along with Native American artifacts and antique musical instruments. ⊠ *101 S. Canyon City Blvd., 2 mi south of John Day, Canyon City 97820* ☎ *541/575–0362, 541/575–0509 off-season* ⊕ *www.ortelco. net/~museum* 🖾 *$4* ⊙ *Mid-May–Sept., Mon.–Sat. 9–4:30.*

★ The **Kam Wah Chung & Co. Museum** was a trading post on the Dalles Military Road in 1866 and 1867. It later served as a general store, a Chinese labor exchange for the area's mines, a doctor's shop, and an opium den. Having been listed on the National Register of Historic Places in 1973, the museum is an extraordinary testament to the early Chinese community in Oregon. Tours are on the hour with groups limited to 10 people; if you miss it, you can always catch the 19-minute video lecture given by the curator. ⊠ *Ing-Hay Way off Canton St., adjacent to City Park, 125 N.W. Canton* ☎ *541/575–2800* 🖾 *Free; donations accepted* ⊙ *May–Oct., daily 9–5.*

★ The geological formations that compose the **John Day Fossil Beds National Monument** cover hundreds of square miles and preserve a diverse record of plant and animal life spanning more than 40 million years of the Age of Mammals. The national monument itself is divided into three "units"–Sheep Rock, Painted Hills, and Clarno—each of which looks vastly different and tells a different part of the story of Oregon's history. Each unit has picnic areas, restrooms, visitor information, and hiking trails. The main visitor center is in the Sheep Rock Unit, though bear in mind that it's almost 40 mi northwest of John Day; and Painted Hills and Clarno are about 70 and 115 mi northwest of John Day, respectively. ☎ *541/987–2333 Sheep Rock, 541/462–3961 Painted Hills, 541/763–2203 Clarno* 🖾 *Free.*

WHERE TO EAT

¢–$$ ✕ **The Grubsteak Mining Co.** With old mining equipment hanging from the walls and a large painted mural of miners from the 1860s, this eatery is representative of its name. The neighborhood joint does its job, cooking up good, simple food for breakfast, lunch and dinner. The house dinner favorites include the "Fergus Burger" (2/3 pound of sirloin) and a Jack Daniels flatiron steak. Locals can be found playing pool in the bar at the back of the house long after the sun goes down—until 2 AM, to be exact. ⊠ *149 E. Main St.* ☎ *541/575–1970* ▭ *AE, D, DC, MC, V.*

PAINTED HILLS

9 mi from the town of Mitchell, head west on U.S. 26 and follow signs north.

The fossils at Painted Hills, another unit of the John Day Fossil Beds National Monument, date back about 33 million years and reveal a climate that has become noticeably drier than that of Sheep Rock's era. The eroded buff-color hills reveal striking red and green striations created by minerals in the clay. Come at dusk or just after it rains, when the colors are most vivid. If traveling in spring, the desert wildflowers are most intense between late April and early May. Take the steep ¾-mi **Carroll Rim Trail** for a commanding view of the hills or sneak a peek from the parking lot at the trailhead, about 2 mi beyond the picnic area. The unit is open daily and admission is free. ☎541/462–3961 ⊕*www.nps.gov/joda/planyourvisit/painted_hills_unit.htm*.

BURNS

76 mi south of the town of John Day on U.S. 395.

Named after poet Robert Burns, this town was the unofficial capital of the 19th-century cattle empires that staked claims to these southeastern Oregon high-plateau grasslands. Today Burns is a working-class town of 3,000 residents, surrounded by the 10,185 square mi of sagebrush, rimrock, and grassy plains that compose Harney County, the ninth-largest county in the United States. As the only place in the county with basic tourist amenities, Burns serves as a convenient stopover for many travelers. However, its usefulness as a source of modern convenience goes hand in hand with the sense that, unlike many of the region's smaller outposts, its Old West flavor has largely been lost. Rather than a final destination, think of Burns as a jumping-off point for exploring the poetry of the Malheur National Wildlife Refuge, Steens Mountain, and the Alvord Desert. Outdoor recreation at this gateway to the Steens Mountains includes fishing, backpacking, camping, boating, and hiking.

Note: The Harney County Chamber of Commerce and the Bureau of Land Management office in Hines are good places to obtain information about the area.

You can cut through the 1.4-million-acre **Malheur National Forest** in the Blue Mountains as you drive from John Day to Burns on U.S. 395. It has alpine lakes, meadows, creeks, and grasslands. Black bears, bighorn sheep, elk, and wolverines inhabit dense stands of pine, fir, and cedar. Near Burns the trees dwindle in number and the landscape changes from mountainous forest to open areas covered with sagebrush and dotted with junipers. ⊠*Between U.S. 26 and U.S. 20, accessible via U.S. 395* ☎*541/416–6700 Information from Bureau of Land Management Office for John Day in Prineville* ⊡*Free* ☉*Daily.*

On the site of a former brewery, the **Harney County Historical Museum** keeps a photo collection documenting the area's history. There's also a display of handmade quilts and a turn-of-the-20th-century kitchen exhibit. ⊠*18 W. D St., 97720* ☎*541/573–5618 or 541/573–7225* ⊕*www.burnsmuseum.com* ✉*$4* ⊗*Apr.–Sept., Tues.–Fri. 10–4, Sat. 10–3. Closed other months, however tours may be arranged.*

NEED A BREAK? Sip an espresso and browse through cards, gifts, and books at the **Book Parlor** (⊠**433 N. Broadway** ☎**541/573–2665** ⊗**Tues.–Fri. 9–5:30, Sat. 10–5.** ⊗*Closed Sun. and Mon.*) in the center of town.

MALHEUR NATIONAL WILDLIFE REFUGE

32 mi southeast of Burns on Hwy. 205.

Highway 205 slices south from Burns through one of the most unusual desert environments in the West. The squat, snow-covered summit of Steens Mountain is the only landmark in this area of alkali playas, buttes, scrubby meadows, and, most surprising of all, marshy lakes.

The **Malheur National Wildlife Refuge,** bounded on the north by Malheur and Harney lakes, covers 187,000 acres. It's arid and scorchingly hot in summer, but in the spring and early summer more than 320 species of migrating birds descend on the refuge's wetlands for their annual nesting and mating rituals. Following an ancient migratory flyway, they've been coming here for nearly a million years. The species include sandhill cranes, snowy white egrets, trumpeter swans, numerous hawks, golden and bald eagles, and white-faced ibis. The number of bird-watchers who turn up for this annual display sometimes rivals the number of birds.

The 30-mi Central Patrol Road, which runs through the heart of the refuge, is your best bet for viewing birds. But first stop at the **Malheur National Wildlife Refuge Headquarters,** where you can pick up leaflets and a free map. The staff will tell you where you're most likely to see the refuge's winged inhabitants. The refuge is a short way from local petroglyphs (ask at the headquarters); a remarkable pioneer structure called the **Round Barn** (head east from the headquarters on Narrows–Princeton Road for 9 mi; road turns to gravel and then runs into Diamond Highway, a paved road that leads south 12 mi to the barn); and **Diamond Craters,** a series of volcanic domes, craters, and lava tubes (continue south from the barn 6 mi on Diamond Highway). *Malheur National Wildlife Refuge Headquarters* ⊠*32 mi southeast of Burns on Hwy. 205; follow signs 26 mi south of Burns, 3691 Sodhouse La., Princeton 97721* ☎*541/493–2612* ⊕*www.fws.gov/malheur* ✉*Free* ⊗*Park daily dawn–dusk; headquarters Mon.–Thurs. 8–4, Fri. 8–3, also 8–4 weekends mid-Mar.–Oct.*

FRENCHGLEN

61 mi south of Burns on Hwy. 205.

Frenchglen, the tiny town near the base of Steens Mountain, has no more than a handful of residents, and in the off-season offers no basic services to travelers. In other words: eat first.

Frenchglen is the gateway to **Steens Mountain.** Amid the flat landscape of eastern Oregon, the mountain is hard to miss, but the sight of its 9,700-foot summit is more remarkable from the east, where its sheer face rises from the flat basin of the desolate Alvord Desert, which stretches into Idaho and Nevada. On the western side, Steens Mountain slopes gently upward over a distance of about 20 mi and is less astonishing. Steens is not your average mountain—it's a huge fault block created when the ancient lava that covered this area fractured. Except for groves of aspen, juniper, and a few mountain mahogany, Steens is almost entirely devoid of trees and resembles alpine tundra. But starting in June the wildflower displays are nothing short of breathtaking, as are the views: on Steens you'll encounter some of the grandest scenery in the West.

The mountain is a great spot for hiking over untrammeled and unpopulated ground, but you can also see it by car (preferably one with four-wheel drive) on the rough but passable 52-mi **Steens Loop Road,** open mid-July–October. You need to take reasonable precautions; storms can whip up out of the blue, creating hazardous conditions.

On the drive up you might spot golden eagles, bighorn sheep, and deer. The view out over **Kiger Gorge,** on the southeastern rim of the mountain, includes a dramatic U-shape path carved out by a glacier. A few miles farther along the loop road, the equally stunning **East Rim viewpoint** is more than 5,000 feet above the valley floor. The view on a clear day takes in Alvord Desert. ⊠*Northern entrance to Steens Loop Rd. leaves Hwy. 205 at south end of Frenchglen and returns to Hwy. 205 about 9 mi south of Frenchglen.*

Frenchglen's Mercantile, Frenchglen's only store, is packed with intriguing high-quality Western merchandise, including Stetson hats, horsehair belts, antique housewares, and horse bits, fossilized shark's teeth, silver and turquoise Native American jewelry, Navajo rugs, books, postcards and maps. Cold drinks, film, sunscreen, good coffee, snacks and canned goods are also for sale. The store is only open in the summer, and the dates may change each year; be sure to call ahead to make sure it's open. ⊠*Hwy. 205* ☎*541/493–2738.*

WHERE TO STAY & EAT

¢ 🏨 **Frenchglen Hotel.** A historical example of the 1895–1930 architecture called "American Foursquare," the 1920 Frenchglen Hotel is a simple white wooden house with a porch—Americana at its renovated best. State-owned, managed by John Ross, the hotel serves up a family-style dinner (reservations essential) to guests and the public at the long wooden tables in the combination lobby-dining room; breakfast and lunch are also served. The small bedrooms, upstairs off a single hallway, share two bathrooms. Five new units with queen beds and private baths, at $90 per room, have been added in the back. Though still a part of the Frenchglen Hotel, the new addition is called "Drover's Inn." **Pros:** Historical "round barn" is on-site, close to Steens Mountain and Malheur Refuge; stay overnight in an authentic 1920s, rural American home. **Cons:** Shared bathrooms, not much else in Frenchglen, no phones or TV. ⊠*39184 Hwy. 205, 97736* ☎*541/493–2825* ⇄*8 rooms* ⚐*In-room: no phone, no TV. In-hotel: restaurant, no elevator* ⊟*D, MC, V* ☼*Closed mid-Nov.–mid-Mar.*

OFF THE BEATEN PATH

Alvord Desert. With the eastern face of Steens Mountain in the background, the Alvord Desert conjures up Western movie scenes of parched cowboys riding through the desert—though today you're more likely to see wind sailors scooting across these hard-packed alkali flats and glider pilots using the basin as a runway. But once they go home, this desert is deserted. Snowmelt from Steens Mountain can turn it into a shallow lake until as late as mid-July. ⊠*From Frenchglen take Hwy. 205 south for about 33 mi until road ends at T-junction near town of Fields; go left (north) to Alvord Desert and the tiny settlement of Andrews.*

EASTERN OREGON ESSENTIALS

BY CAR

I–84 runs east along the Columbia River and dips down to Pendleton, La Grande, and Baker City. U.S. 26 heads east from Prineville through the Ochoco National Forest, passing the three units of the John Day Fossil Beds. U.S. 20 travels southeast from Bend in central Oregon to Burns. U.S. 20 and U.S. 26 both head west into Oregon from Idaho.

To reach Joseph take Highway 82 east from La Grande. Highway 86 loops down from Joseph to Baker City. From Baker City, Highway 7 heading west connects to U.S. 26 and leads to John Day. U.S. 395 runs south from John Day to Burns. Highway 205 heads south from Burns through the Malheur National Wildlife Refuge to Frenchglen, Steens Mountain, and the Alvord Desert (all accessed by local roads). In all these areas, equip yourself with chains for winter driving.

VISITOR INFORMATION

Visitor centers and chambers of commerce are always eager to furnish you with information on area attractions, dining, lodging, and shopping. They are generally open from 9 to 5 during the week, sometimes with slightly reduced hours on weekends and in the off-season. In addition, eastern Oregon has several visitor centers and ranger stations geared toward the forests, wildlife areas, and recreation areas in the region.

Contacts Baker County Visitors and Convention Bureau (⊠*490 Campbell St., Baker City 97814* ☎*541/523–3356 or 800/523–1235* ⊕*www.visitbaker.com*) .**Bureau of Land Management** (⊠*U.S. 20 W, Burns 97220* ☎*541/573–4400*) .**Harney County Chamber of Commerce** (⊠*76 E. Washington St., Burns 97720* ☎*541/573–2636* ⊕*www.harneycounty.com*) .**La Grande Chamber of Commerce** (⊠*102 Elm St., 97850* ☎*541/963–8588 or 800/848–9969* ⊕*www.unioncoun-*

tychamber.org). **La Grande Visitors Center** (✉ *102 Elm St.* ☏ *541/963–8588 or 800/848–9969* ⊕ *www.visitlagrande.com*). **Pendleton Chamber of Commerce** (✉ *501 S. Main St., 97801* ☏ *541/276–7411 or 800/547–8911* ⊕ *www.pendletonchamber.com*).

OREGON ESSENTIALS

2

BY AIR

The major airports in Oregon are Portland International Airport and Eugene Airport, also known as Mahlon Sweet Field.

Contacts **Eugene Airport (EUG)** (*Mahlon Sweet Field* ✉ *28855 Lockheed Dr.* ☏ *541/682–5430* ⊕ *www.eugeneairport.com*).

Portland International Airport (PDX) (✉ *7000 N.E. Airport Way* ☏ *877/739–4636* ⊕ *www.flypdx.com*)..

BY BUS

Eugene's Experience Oregon and Portland's Gray Line operate charter bus services and scheduled sightseeing tours that last from a few hours to several days. Greyhound Lines services Oregon with routes from elsewhere on the West Coast and from points east. People Mover travels on U.S. 26 between Bend and John Day.

Contacts **Experience Oregon** (✉ *1574 Coburg Rd., No. 123, Eugene* ☏ *541/342–2662 or 800/342–2662* ⊕ *www.experienceoregon.com*). **Gray Line** (☏ *503/285–9845, 800/422–7042 in Portland* ⊕ *www.grayline.com*). **Greyhound** (☏ *800/231–2222* ⊕ *www.greyhound.com*). **People Mover** (✉ *229 N.E. Dayton St., John Day* ☏ *541/575–2370 or 800/527–2370*)..

BY CAR

I–5 and U.S. 101 enter Oregon heading north from California and south from Washington. I–84 and U.S. 26 head west from the Idaho border to Portland.

ROAD CONDITIONS. Tire chains, studs, or snow tires are essential equipment for winter travel in mountain areas. If you're planning to drive into high elevations, be sure to check the weather forecast beforehand. Even the main-highway mountain passes can be forced to close because of snow conditions. During the winter months state and provincial highway departments operate snow-advisory telephone lines that give pass conditions.

Contacts **Road Conditions hotline** (☏ *503/588–2941, 800/977–6368 in Oregon*).

EMERGENCIES

Contacts For **police, ambulance,** or **other emergencies** in Oregon, dial 911.

Oregon State Police (☏ *503/378–3720 or 800/452–7888*).

BY TRAIN

Amtrak, the U.S. passenger rail system, has daily service to the Pacific Northwest from the Midwest and California. The *Empire Builder* takes a northern route through Minnesota and Montana from Chicago to Spokane, whence separate legs continue to Seattle and Portland. Part of the route to Portland runs through the Columbia River Gorge. The *Cascades* train travels once daily between Seattle and Vancouver and several times a day between Seattle, Portland, and Eugene. The *Coast Starlight,* which runs between Seattle and Los Angeles, passes through the Willamette Valley, serving Portland, Salem, Albany (near Corvallis), Eugene, and Klamath Falls.

Train Information **Amtrak** (☎ *800/872–7245* ⊕ *www.amtrak.com*).

VISITOR INFORMATION

Oregon tourist-information centers are marked with blue "i" signs on main roads. Opening and closing times vary, depending on the season and the individual office; call ahead for hours.

Tourist Information **Central Oregon Visitors Association** (✉ *661 S.W. Powerhouse Dr., Suite 1301, Bend 97702* ☎ *800/800–8334* ⊕ *www.visitcentraloregon. org*). **National Park Service Pacific West Regional Office** (☎ *510/817–1300* ⊕ *www.nps.gov*). **Oregon State Park Information Center** (☎ *800/551–6949* ⊕ *www.oregon.gov/OPRD/PARKS/index.shtml*).

★ **Oregon Tourism Commission** (✉ *775 Summer St. NE, Salem 97310* ☎ *503/986–0000 or 800/547–7842* ⊕ *www.traveloregon.com*). **U.S. Forest Service Recreation Information Center** (☎ *503/872–2750, 877/444–6777 campground reservations*).

Seattle

WORD OF MOUTH

"Seattle has the Pike Market, excellent museums, and its own share of great places to hang out in foul weather. However, it also has great short excursion opportunities—ferries across the Sound, great neighborhood hangouts, shopping and galleries, so it's really hard not to find something of interest to do."

–Gardyloo

Updated
by Carissa
Bluestone

Seattle is defined by water. There's no use denying the city's damp weather, or the fact that its skies are cloudy for much of the year. Seattleites don't tan, goes the joke, they rust. But Seattle is also defined by the rivers, lakes, and canals that bisect its steep green hills, creating distinctive microlandscapes along the water's edge. Fishing boats, floating homes, swank yacht clubs, and waterfront restaurants exist side by side.

Seattle's climate fosters an easygoing lifestyle. Overcast days and long winter nights have made the city a haven for moviegoers and book readers. Hollywood often tests new films here, and residents' per-capita book purchases are among North America's highest. Seattle has all the trappings of a metropolitan hub—two daily newspapers; a state-of-the-art convention center; professional sports teams; a diverse music club scene; and top-notch ballet, opera, symphony, and theater companies. A major seaport, the city is a vital link in Pacific Rim trade.

EXPLORING SEATTLE

To know Seattle is to know its distinctive neighborhoods. Because of the hills, comfortable walking shoes are a must. But before you go charging off, ready to pack each day full of activities, remember that to know Seattle is also to know when to relax. The city has much to see, but make sure you pencil in time to kick back with a cup of coffee or organic herbal tea and enjoy the beauty around you, whether you're gazing at the peaks of the Olympics or Cascades or at an artistically landscaped garden in front of a classic Northwest bungalow.

DOWNTOWN & BELLTOWN

The Elliott Bay waterfront is the heart and soul of Downtown. Stretching along its waters is historic Pike Place Market, the city's biggest (and most crowded) tourist attraction and the source of the fresh, local ingredients used by so many of the city's restaurants. The Seattle Aquarium and the Maritime Discovery Center are on the docks here, close to the ferries that take commuters and tourists to the islands of the Puget Sound.

Downtown is notable for providing the most "urban" atmosphere the city has to offer, as well as many of the check-em-off-the-list sights. Just north and slightly west of Downtown is Belltown. Most of Belltown's action happens between 1st and 4th avenues and between Bell and Virginia streets. Not too long ago, Belltown was home to some of the most unwanted real estate in the city; the only scenesters around were starving artists. Today, Belltown is yuppie heaven, with many luxury condos, trendy restaurants, an ever-increasing number of boutiques, and bars where people actually dress up. ■ TIP➔ **Both Downtown and Belltown are very easy to get around on foot—walking from one neighborhood to the other is easy, too—but if you head down to the waterfront, be prepared for some killer hills on the way back east toward your hotel.**

WHAT TO SEE

★ ❻ **BLVD/Roq La Rue.** If you get tired of looking at totem poles, glass sculptures, and austere black-and-white photos, swing by these sister galleries for a different take on contemporary Northwest art. Cheeky surrealist pop art hangs in Roq La Rue, which is not solely Northwest focused; urban street art from the region populates BLVD. Kirsten Anderson, the owner of both galleries, is well known for injecting some much-needed life into the city's gallery scene by exhibiting work that often gets ignored by traditional venues in spaces that are as professional as all the rest. ⊠*BLVD, 2316 2nd Ave., Belltown* ⊕*www.blvdart.com* ⊠*Roq La Rue, 2312 2nd Ave., Belltown* ☎*206/374–8977* ⊕*www. roqlarue.com* ⊠*Free* ☾ *Wed., Thurs., and Sat. 1–6, Fri. 1–7.*

☾ ❺ **Odyssey Maritime Discovery Center.** Cultural and educational exhibits on Puget Sound and ocean trade are the focus of this waterfront attraction. Learn all about the Northwest's fishing traditions with hands-on exhibits that include kayaking over computer-generated waters, loading a container ship, and listening in on boats radioing one another on Elliott Bay just outside. You can also shop the on-site fish market, dine on the catch of the day at the seafood restaurant, or spy on boaters docking at the marina or cruise ships putting into port. ⊠*2205 Alaskan Way, Pier 66, Belltown* ☎*206/374–4000* ⊕*www.ody.org* ⊠*$7* ☾ *Wed. and Thurs. 10–3, Fri. 10–4, weekends 11–5.*

❼ **Olympic Sculpture Park.** The 9-acre open-air expanse nestled between Belltown and Elliott Bay is a scenic outdoor branch of the Seattle Art Museum. Follow a zigzag path through a variety of natural settings dotted with waterfalls and fishponds. Around the grasses, blossoms, and water features are scattered an amazing variety of oversize, handmade pieces from some of the Northwest's notable visual artists. Though some of the pieces are very interesting, they're all completely upstaged by the views from the upper tier of the park. On clear days, you'll get near-perfect views of the water with the jagged, snowcapped Olympic Mountains in the background. The PACCAR Pavilion has a gift shop, café, and more information about the park. ⊠*Western Ave. between Broad and Bay Sts., Belltown* ☎*206/645–3100* ⊕ *www.seattleartmuseum. org* ⊠*Free* ☾*Park daily dawn–dusk. PACCAR Pavilion May–Sept., Tues.–Sun. 10–5, Fri. until 9; Oct.–Apr., Tues.–Sun. 10–4.*

☾ ❶ **Pike Place Market.** Like many historical sites whose importance is taken for granted, this institution started small. It dates from 1907, when the city issued permits allowing farmers to sell produce from wagons parked at Pike Place. Later the city built permanent stalls. At one time the market was a madhouse of vendors hawking their produce and haggling with customers over prices. Some fishmongers still carry on this kind of frenzied banter, but chances are you won't get them to waver on their prices. Urban renewal almost killed the market, but a group of residents, led by the late architect Victor Steinbrueck, rallied and voted it a historical asset in 1973. Many buildings have been restored, and the complex is connected to the waterfront by stairs and elevators. Booths sell seafood—which can be packed in dry ice for your flight home—produce, cheese, wine, spices, tea, coffee, and crafts. There are

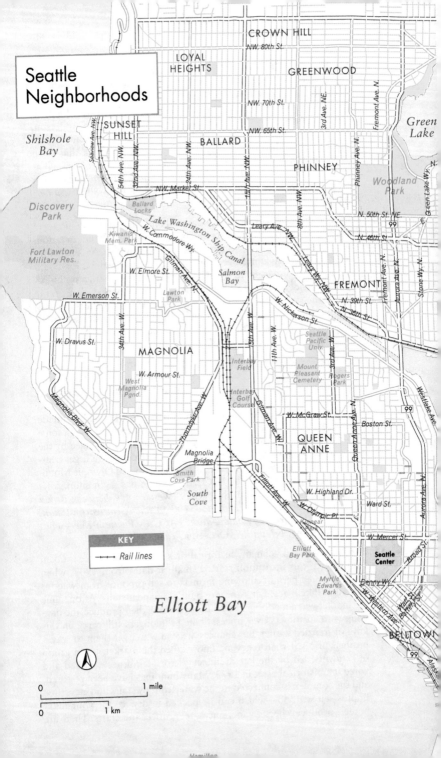

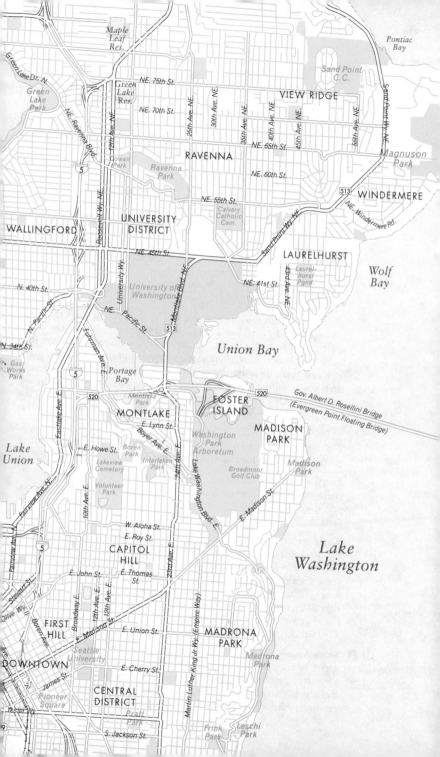

also several restaurants. The flower market is a must-see.

Free maps, available at several locations throughout the market, distinguish among the various types of shops and stalls. Farmers, who come to the market from as far away as the Yakima Valley, east of the Cascade Mountains, have first dibs on the tables, known as "farmers' tables," where they display and sell their own vegetables, fruits, or flowers. Vendors in the so-called high stalls often have fruits and vegetables or crafts that they've purchased locally to sell here. The superb quality of the high-stall produce helps to set Seattle's dining standards.

The shopkeepers who rent stores in the market sell such things as packaged food items, art, curios, pets, and more. Most of the shops are nothing special, catering to the massive number of tourists that make their way through here in high season, but there are a few gems here and there. Because the market is along a bluff, the main arcade stretches down the cliff face for several stories; many shops are below street level. Other shops and restaurants are in buildings east of Pike Place and west of Western Avenue. The information booth is at 1st and Pike.

Tours of the market are given daily and cost $8. Note that you must make reservations for tours at least a day in advance.

Everyone visits the market, which means it is often infuriatingly crowded, especially when cruise ships are in port. During high season, you might never find a quiet corner, but getting to the market early (around 8 AM) is probably your best bet.

There are numerous garages in the area, including one affiliated with the market itself (the Public Market Parking Garage at 1531 Western Avenue), at which you can get validated parking from many merchants; some restaurants offer free parking at this garage after 5 PM. You'll also find several pay lots farther south on Western Avenue. ⊠*Pike Pl. at Pike St., west of 1st Ave., Downtown* ☎*206/682–7453* ⊕*www.pike placemarket.org* ☉*Stall hrs vary: 1st-level shops Mon.–Sat. 10–6, Sun. 11–5; underground shops daily 11–5.*

⟳ ❸ **Seattle Aquarium.** The aquarium should call itself Otters R Us—you could
Fodor's Choice spend hours just watching the delightful antics of the sea otters and
★ their river cousins. The partially open-air Marine Mammal section also includes harbor seals and fur seals, and, unlike at some aquariums, you get unimpeded, close-up views of the animals from two levels—you can

see them sleeping on the rocks or gliding around the water's surface and then go down a floor to watch them as they dive to the bottoms of their pools. If that weren't enough entertainment for one day, the Underwater Dome surrounds you with colorful schools of fish. The tide pool room, usually the most anticlimactic part of an aquarium, is spectacular—tanks and touch pools are bursting with neon-color anemones and starfish. ■ TIP➡ Spend a few minutes in front of the octopus tank even if you don't detect any movement. Your patience will be rewarded if you get to see this amazing creature shimmy up the side of the tank. If you're visiting in fall or winter, dress warmly—the Marine Mammal area is on the waterfront and catches all of those chilly Puget Sound breezes. ✉*Pier 59 off Alaskan Way, Downtown* ☎*206/386–4300* ⊕*www.seattleaquarium.org* ✉*$12.50* ⊙*Daily 9:30–5.*

★ ❷ **Seattle Art Museum.** Long the pride of the city's art scene, SAM is now better than ever after a massive expansion that connects the iconic old building on University Street (where sculptor Jonathan Borofsky's several-stories-high *Hammering Man* still pounds away) to a sleek, light-filled high-rise space around the corner on 1st Avenue and Union Street. As you enter, you'll have the option of wandering around two floors of free public space. The first floor includes the museum's shop; a café that focuses on local, fresh ingredients; and drop-in workshops where the whole family can get creative. The second floor features free exhibitions, including awe-inspiring large-scale installations. The third and fourth floors are dedicated to the museum's extensive permanent collection—surveying Asian, Native American, African, Oceanic, and pre-Columbian art—and special exhibitions; admission is charged for these floors. Among the highlights are the anonymous 14th-century Buddhist masterwork *Monk at the Moment of Enlightenment* and Jackson Pollock's *Sea Change.* The expansion also brought some exciting new pieces to the permanent collection from such artists as Georgia O'Keeffe, John Singer Sargent, Mary Cassatt, and Jasper Johns. Murals, interactive video installations, and unimpeded views of the city thread the galleries together, meaning there's more to gawk at than the collections. ✉*1300 1st Ave., Downtown* ☎*206/654–3100* ⊕*www. seattleartmuseum.org* ✉*$13, free 1st Thurs. of month* ⊙*Tues., Wed., and weekends 10–5, Thurs. and Fri. 10–9, 1st Thurs. until midnight.*

❹ **William Traver Gallery.** A classic gallery space with white walls and creaky, uneven wood floors, William Traver is like a little slice of Soho in Seattle—without the attitude. Light pours in from large picture windows. The focus is on high-price (tens of thousands of dollars) glass art from local and international artists. Pieces are exquisite—never too whimsical or gaudy—and the staff is extremely courteous to those of us who can only enjoy this place as a museum and not a shop. After you're done tiptoeing around the gallery, head back downstairs and around the corner to Vetri, which sells glass art and objects from emerging artists at steep but much-more-reasonable prices. ✉*110 Union St., Downtown* ☎*206/587–6501* ⊕*www.travergallery.com* ✉*Free* ⊙*Tues.–Fri. 10–6, Sat. 10–5, Sun. noon–5.*

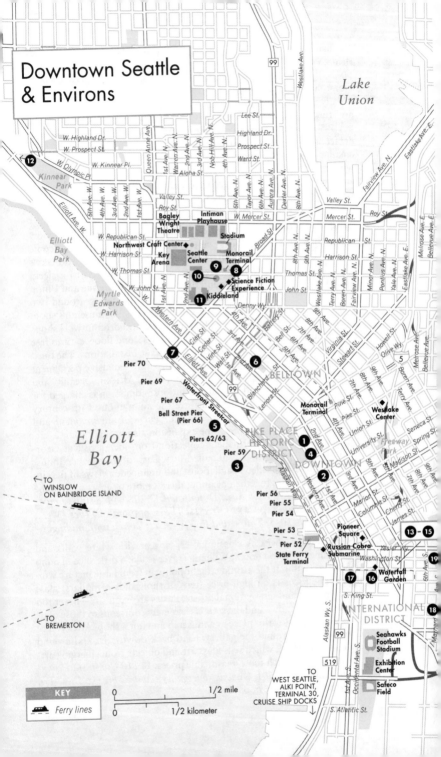

3

E. Blaine St.

E. Garfield St.

E. Howe St.

11th Ave. E.

Boren
Park

Interlaken
Park

Boyer St. E.

Lakeview
Cemetery

E. Garfield St.

Interlaken Pl. E.

26

Lakeview Blvd. E.

E. Highland St.

Grandview Pl. E.

Auburn Pl. E.

E. Galer St.

24th Ave. E.

E. Highland St.

25

Asian Art
Museum

E. Prospect St.

E. Prospect St.

Belmont Ave. E.

Harvard Ave. E.

Federal Ave. E.

E. Ward St.

E. Aloha St.

18th Ave. E.

19th Ave. E.

20th Ave. E.

21st Ave. E.

22nd Ave. E.

E. Roy St.

E. Mercer St.

E. Republican St.

23rd Ave.

24th Ave.

Summit Ave. E.

Boylston Ave. E.

Broadway E.

10th Ave. E.

11th Ave. E.

12th Ave. E.

13th Ave. E.

14th Ave. E.

15th Ave. E.

16th Ave. E.

17th Ave. E.

CAPITOL
HILL

23

E. Thomas St.

E. Thomas St.

E. John St.

E. John St.

Seattle
Central
Community
College

Broadway
Playfield

E. Denny Wy.

E. Howell St.

E. Olive St.

E. Madison St.

E. Olive St.

Belmont Ave. E.

Boylston Ave. E.

Harvard Ave. E.

Broadway E.

Nagle Pl.

12th Ave. E.

E. Pine St.

22

24

10th Ave. E.

11th Ave. E.

E. Pike St.

E. Union St.

23rd Ave.

Seattle
University

13th Ave.

14th Ave.

15th Ave.

16th Ave.

E. Spring St.

E. Marion St.

20th Ave.

21st Ave.

22nd Ave.

24th Ave.

25th Ave.

E. Columbia St.

E. Cherry St.

21

FIRST
HILL

Minor Ave.

E. James St.

E. Jefferson St.

Jefferson St.

Terrace St.

Alder St.

Spruce St.

10th Ave.

11th Ave.

14th Ave.

15th Ave.

16th Ave.

17th Ave.

18th Ave.

19th Ave.

E. Terrace St.

E. Alder St.

E. Spruce St.

E. Fir St.

Yesler Wy.

CENTRAL
DISTRICT

Pratt
Park

S. Main St.

S. Jackson St.

S. Jackson St.

S. King St.

S. Weller St.

S. Lane St.

23rd Ave. S.

S. Rainier St.

S. Dearborn St.

Rainier Ave. S.

S. Davis Pl.

Hiawatha Pl. S.

90

12th Ave. S.

14th Ave. S.

24th Ave. S.

25th Ave. S.

26th Ave. S.

TO
MUSEUM
OF FLIGHT
↓

SEATTLE CENTER & QUEEN ANNE

You're certainly in no danger of driving right past the Seattle Center. Not only is the area home to Seattle's version of the Eiffel tower, the Space Needle, but it is anchored by Frank Gehry's wild Experience Music Project building. Almost all visitors make their way here at least once, whether to visit the museums, catch a concert or show at one of the many performing arts venues, or cheer on the Sonics at the Key Arena.

Just west of the Seattle Center is the intersection of Queen Anne Avenue N and Denny Way. This marks the start of the Queen Anne neighborhood, which stretches all the way up formidable Queen Anne Hill to the ship canal. With the exception of the Seattle Center, Queen Anne doesn't have many sights, but the residential streets west of Queen Anne Avenue in Upper Queen Anne are fun to tool around in if you want to get a look at some of Seattle's most expensive real estate. The wealth extends to the Magnolia neighborhood, the northwest corner of the hill west of 15th Avenue NW. There's only one sight to see in Magnolia, but it's a terrific one—gorgeous Discovery Park.

WHAT TO SEE

The Children's Museum. Enter this colorful, spacious museum off the Seattle Center food court through a Northwest wilderness setting, with winding trails, hollow logs, and a waterfall. From here you can explore a global village where rooms with kid-friendly props show everyday life in Ghana, the Philippines, and Japan. Another neighborhood contains an American post office, a fire station, and a grocery store. Cog City is a giant game of pipes, pulleys, and balls; and kids can test their talent in a mock recording studio. There's a small play area for toddlers, and lots of crafts to help kids learn more about the exhibits. ⊠ *Seattle Center House, 305 Harrison St., Queen Anne* ☎ *206/441–1768* ⊕ *www.thechildrensmuseum.org* ☞ *$7.50* ⊙ *Weekdays 10–5, weekends 10–6.*

Discovery Park. Discovery Park is Seattle's largest park, and it has an Fodor's Choice amazing variety of terrain: cool forest trails that can feel as secluded as mountain hikes lead to meadows, saltwater beaches, sand dunes, a lighthouse, and views that include Puget Sound, the Cascades, and the Olympics. There are 2.8 mi of trails through this urban wilderness, but the North Beach Trail, which takes you along the shore to the lighthouse, is a must-see. Head to the South Bluff Trail to get a view of Mt. Rainier and the skyline. The park has several entrances—if you want to stop at the visitor center to pick up a trail map before exploring, use the main entrance at Government Way. The North Parking Lot is much closer to the North Beach Trail and to Ballard and Fremont, if you're coming from that direction. To get to here from Downtown take 15th Avenue NW and get off at the Emerson Street exit onto W. Emerson. Make a right onto 23rd Avenue W, then a left onto Commodore Way, which will lead you to the park's north entrance. ■ TIP➔ Note that the park is easily reached from Ballard and Fremont. It's sometimes easier to combine a park day with an exploration of those neighborhoods than with a busy Downtown itinerary. ✉*3801 W. Government Way, Magnolia ✛From Downtown Seattle to main entrance: Take Elliott Ave. north until it becomes 15th Ave. NW. Take Dravus St. exit and turn left on Dravus at stoplight. Turn right on 20th Ave. W, which becomes Gilman Ave. W. Gilman eventually becomes W. Government Way; follow road into park* ☎*206/386–4236* ⊕*www.cityof seattle.net/parks* ✉*Free* ⊙*Park daily 6* AM*–11* PM*, visitor center Tues.–Sun. 8:30–5.*

MONORAIL MINUTES

Seattle Center is in an awkward part of the city, but the monorail that runs from Westlake Center (5th Avenue and Pine Street) makes getting here easy from Downtown. The monorail runs daily from 9 AM to 11 PM, with departures every 10 minutes. The ride takes about two minutes.

☝ ❽ **Experience Music Project.** Seattle's most controversial architectural statement is the 140,000-square-foot interactive museum celebrating American popular music. Architect Frank Gehry drew inspiration from electric guitars to achieve the building's curvy design, though it looks more like open-heart surgery than a musical instrument. Regardless, it stands out among the city's cookie-cutter high-rises and therefore it's a fitting backdrop for the world's largest collection of Jimi Hendrix memorabilia, which is flanked by a gallery of guitars once owned by Bob Dylan, Hank Williams, Kurt Cobain, and the bands Pearl Jam, Soundgarden, and the Kingsmen. Experiment with instruments and recording equipment in the interactive Sound Lab, or attend performances or workshops. ✉*5th Ave. between Broad and Thomas Sts., Queen Anne* ☎*206/367–5483* ⊕*www.emplive.org* ✉*$15* ⊙*May 23–Sept. 4, daily 10–5; rest of yr, daily 10–8.*

☝ ⓫ **Pacific Science Center.** With about 200 indoor and outdoor hands-on exhibits and a state-of-the-art planetarium, this is a great place for both kids and grown-ups. The startling dinosaur exhibit is complete with moving robotic creatures, while Tech Zones has robots and virtual-reality games. Machines analyze human physiology in Body Works. The tropical butterfly house is stocked with farm-raised chrysalides weekly; other creatures live in the woodland and tide pool areas. Next door, IMAX movies and laser rock shows run daily. ✉*200 2nd Ave. N, Queen Anne* ☎*206/443–2844* ⊕*www.pacsci.org* ✉*Center $11, IMAX $8, light shows $5–$8* ⊙*Weekdays 10–5, weekends 10–6.*

☝ ★ ❿ **Space Needle.** The distinctive exterior of the 520-foot-high Space Needle is visible throughout much of the city—but the view from the inside out is even better. A 42-second elevator ride up to the circular observation deck yields 360-degree vistas of Elliott Bay, Queen Anne Hill, the University of Washington campus, and the Cascade Range. The Needle was built just in time for the World's Fair in 1962, but has since been refurbished with educational signs, interactive trivia game stations for kids, and the glass-enclosed SpaceBase store and Pavilion spiraling around the base of the tower. Don't waste your money dining at the top-floor SkyCity revolving restaurant; though eating there gets you free admission to the observation deck, the food is overpriced and often mediocre. ■TIP→ **And don't bother doing the trip at all on rainy days.** Note that if you can't decide whether you want the daytime or nighttime view, for $20 you can buy a ticket that allows you to visit twice in one day. ⊠ *5th Ave. and Broad St., Queen Anne* ☎ *206/905–2100* ⊕ *www.spaceneedle.com* ⊠ *$16* ⊙ *Sun.–Thurs. 9 AM–11 PM, Fri. and Sat. 9 AM–midnight.*

PIONEER SQUARE

The Pioneer Square district, directly south of Downtown, is Seattle's oldest neighborhood, and it pushes its historical cache hard in every brochure and guidebook. It certainly attracts visitors because of its elegantly renovated (or in many cases replica) turn-of-the-20th-century redbrick buildings. The district's most unique structure, the 42-story Smith Tower on 2nd Avenue and Yesler Way, was the tallest building west of the Mississippi when it was completed in 1914; today, its observation deck is a great place to get views of the city if you don't want to deal with the Space Needle.

> **A MUST-STOP PHOTO OP**
>
> Kerry Park on W. Highland Drive between 2nd and 3rd Avenues West has outstanding views of the city and the water. It's an all-time favorite spot for snapshots—be prepared to share the view with bus and van tours. If you're heading north on Queen Anne Avenue N, turn left onto W. Highland Drive.

Though its history is pretty clear, the role Pioneer Square plays in the city today is harder to define. It's undeniably the center of the arts scene—there are more galleries in this small neighborhood then we have room to list, and they make up the majority of the neighborhood's sights. ■TIP→ **First Thursday art walks are perhaps the best time to see Pioneer Square, when animated crowds walk from gallery to gallery, viewing the new exhibitions.** That said, the neighborhood is no longer a center for artists per se, as rents have risen in a way that doesn't reflect the value of the neighborhood; only established gallery owners have the cash to rent lofty spaces in heavily trafficked areas.

Nowadays, when Seattleites speak of Pioneer Square they usually speak of the love they have for certain unique neighborhood institutions— Elliott Bay Books, Bud's Jazz Records, Zeitgeist coffeehouse, a certain gallery, a friend's loft apartment—than the love they have for the neighborhood as a whole. Pioneer Square is always worth a visit, but reactions vary. Most people combine Pioneer Square with a trip to the International District, which together would make a full day of touring.

WHAT TO SEE

🔟 **Klondike Gold Rush National Historical Park.** A redbrick building with wooden floors and soaring ceilings contains a small museum illustrating Seattle's role in the 1897–98 gold rush in northwestern Canada's Klondike region. Displays show antique mining equipment, and the walls are lined with photos of gold diggers, explorers, and the hopeful families who followed them. Film presentations, gold-panning demonstrations, and rotating exhibits are scheduled throughout the year. Other sectors of this park are in southeast Alaska. ✉*117 S. Main St., Pioneer Square* 📞*206/553–7220* ⊕*www.nps.gov/klse/* ✉*Free* ⊙*Daily 9–5.*

Foster/White Gallery. One of the Seattle art scene's heaviest hitters, Foster/White has digs as impressive as the works it shows: a century-old building with high ceilings and 7,000 square feet of exhibition space. Internationally acclaimed glass artist Dale Chihuly, and paintings, sculpture, and drawings by Northwest masters Kenneth Callahan, Mark Tobey, and George Tsutakawa are on permanent display. There's another equally impressive branch in Rainier Square at 5th Avenue and Union Street. ✉*220 3rd Ave. S, Pioneer Square* 📞*206/622–2833* ⊕*www.fosterwhite.com* ✉*Free* ⊙*Tues.–Sat. 10–6.*

VISITOR INFO

At a kiosk on Occidental between Main and Jackson streets, you can pick up a booklet that outlines three walking tours around the historic buildings of Pioneer Square and provides facts about each and stories about the characters who inhabited them.

14 G. Gibson Gallery. Vintage and contemporary photography is always on exhibit here, including retrospectives from major artists like Walker Evans, but G. Gibson also shows contemporary paintings, sculpture, and mixed-media pieces. This is another institution of the Seattle art scene, and the gallery's taste is always impeccable. ✉*300 S. Washington St., Pioneer Square* 📞*206/587–4033* ⊕*www.ggibsongallery.com* ✉*Free* ⊙*Tues.–Fri. 11–5:30, Sat. 11–5.*

Fodor'sChoice
★ **15 Greg Kucera Gallery.** One of the most important destinations on the First Thursday gallery walk, this gorgeous space is a top venue for national and regional artists. Be sure to check out the outdoor sculpture deck on the second level. If you can only stomach one gallery visit, this is the place to go. You'll see big names that you might recognize along with newer artists and the thematic group shows are consistently well thought out and well presented. ✉*212 3rd Ave. S, Pioneer Square* 📞*206/624–0770* ⊕*www.gregkucera.com* ✉*Free* ⊙*Tues.–Sat. 10:30–5:30.*

★ **17 Stonington Gallery.** You'll see plenty of cheesy tribal art knockoffs in tourist-trap shops, but this elegant gallery will give you a real look at the best contemporary work of Northwest Coast and Alaska tribal members (and artists from these regions working in the native style). Three floors exhibit wood carvings, paintings, sculpture, and mixed-media pieces. ✉*119 S. Jackson St., Pioneer Square* 📞*206/405–4040* ⊕*www.stoningtongallery.com* ✉*Free* ⊙*Weekdays 10–6, Sat. 10–5:30, Sun. noon–5.*

INTERNATIONAL DISTRICT

The I.D., as it's locally known, began as a haven for Chinese workers who came to the United States to work on the transcontinental railroad. The community has remained largely intact despite anti-

Chinese riots and the forced eviction of Chinese residents during the 1880s and the internment of Japanese-Americans during World War II. About one-third of the residents are Chinese, one-third are Filipino, and another third come from elsewhere in Asia or the Pacific islands. The I.D. stretches from 4th Avenue to 12th Avenue and between Yesler Way and S. Dearborn Street. Although today the main business anchor is the Uwajimaya Japanese superstore, there are also many small Asian restaurants, herbalists, acupuncturists, antiques shops, and private clubs for gambling and socializing. The I.D. is a very popular lunchtime spot with Downtown office workers and a popular dinner spot with many Seattleites. ■TIP➜ **You should definitely make a meal here part of your visit.** Look for the diamond-shape dragon signs in store windows—these establishments will give you a free-parking token. Check out ⊕ *www.cidbia.org* for information on events and festivals in the neighborhood.

WHAT TO SEE

❶⑨ Kobe Terrace. Seattle's sister city of Kobe, Japan, donated a 200-year-old stone lantern to adorn this small hillside park. Despite being so close to I–5, the terrace is a peaceful place to stroll through and enjoy views of the city, the water, and, if you're lucky, Mt. Rainier; a few benches line the gravel paths. The herb gardens you see are part of the Danny Woo Community Gardens, tended to by the neighborhood's residents. ⊠ *Main St. between 6th Ave. S and 7th Ave. S, International District* ☜ *Free* ◷ *Daily dawn–dusk.*

★ **❶⑧ Uwajimaya.** Everyone makes a stop at this fantastic Japanese supermarket. A 30-foot-long red Chinese dragon stretches above colorful mounds of fresh produce and aisles of exotic packaged goods from countries throughout Asia. A busy food court serves sushi, Japanese bento-box meals, Chinese stir-fry combos, Korean barbecue, Hawaiian plates, Vietnamese spring rolls, and an assortment of teas and tapioca drinks. This is a great place to pick up all sorts of snacks; dessert lovers won't know which way to turn first. The housewares section is well stocked with dishes, cookware, appliances, textiles, and gifts. There's also a card section, a Hello Kitty corner, and Yuriko's cosmetics, where you can find Shiseido products that are usually available only in Japan. Last but not least, there's a small branch of the famous Kinokuniya bookstore chain. The large parking lot is free for one hour with a minimum $5 purchase (which will be no problem) or two hours with a minimum $10 purchase—don't forget to have your ticket validated by the cashiers. ⊠ *600 5th Ave. S, International District* ☎ *206/624–6248* ⊕ *www.uwajimaya.com* ◷ *Mon.–Sat. 9 AM–10 PM, Sun. 9–9.*

♺ **❷⓪ Wing Luke Asian Museum.** Named for the Northwest's first Asian-American elected official, this small, well-organized museum surveys the history and cultures of people from Asia and the Pacific islands who settled in the Pacific Northwest. Alongside the costumes, fabrics, crafts, and photographs that kids will love, the museum also provides sophisticated looks at how immigrants and their descendants have transformed and been transformed by American culture. The most poignant and sobering part of the museum is an excellent multimedia exhibit deal-

Fodor's Choice
★

ing with the internment of Japanese-American citizens in camps during World War II. ■TIP→ **The museum is a great place to start your tour of the I.D., as it will provide a context to the neighborhood and the communities living here that you won't get by simply wandering around.** ⊠ *407 7th Ave. S, International District* ☎ *206/623–5124* ⊕ *www.wingluke. org* ☜ *$4, free 1st Thurs. and 3rd Sat. of month* ☉ *Tues.–Fri. 11–4:30, weekends noon–4.*

FIRST HILL

3

Smack between Downtown and Capitol Hill, First Hill is an odd mix of sterile-looking medical facility buildings (earning it the nickname "Pill Hill"), old brick buildings that look like they belong on a college campus, newer residential towers, and a few tree-lined streets. The main draw of the neighborhood is the Frye Art Museum, which is well worth a detour.

WHAT TO SEE

㉑
Fodor'sChoice
★

Frye Art Museum. The Frye was a forgotten museum for a while, haunted only by Seattleites who would come to visit their favorite paintings from the permanent collection—mostly 19th- and 20th-century representational pieces depicting pastoral scenes. But a new curator shook the Frye out of its stupor and now in addition to its beloved permanent collection, this elegant building plays host to eclectic and often avant-garde rotating exhibits. Recent shows have included morbid pencil drawings from Robyn O'Neil; a large collection of pieces from illustrator Henry Darger's mad-genius, 15,000-page, unpublished manuscript; and a retrospective of works from the Leipzeig Art Academy. No matter what's going on in the stark, brightly lighted back galleries, it always seems to blend well with the permanent collection, which occupies two hushed and elegant galleries with velvet couches and dark-blue and purple walls—the latter usually serving as either an amuse-bouche or after-dinner mint to the featured exhibits. The museum is small enough that you can move through it in an hour, but you could easily spend more time here, too. The café has a small courtyard and real entrées in addition to sandwiches and sweets. ⊠ *704 Terry Ave., First Hill* ☎ *206/622–9250* ⊕ *www.fryeart.org* ☜ *Free* ☉ *Tues.–Sat. 10–5 (Thurs. until 8), Sun. noon–5.*

CAPITOL HILL

With its mix of theaters and churches, coffeehouses and nightclubs, stately homes and student apartments, Capitol Hill still deserves its reputation as Seattle's most eclectic neighborhood. Though new money is starting to change the neighborhood—several luxury condo developments will strip part of the Pike–Pine corridor of its most beloved institutions and much of its personality—Capitol Hill has very loyal residents, and it will still take some time to turn the artsy, hip neighborhood into a string of cell phone stores and FedEx/Kinko's branches.

■TIP→ Nothing gets going here too early, so unless you want to check out the parks in the morning, save your visit for the afternoon. After some strolling and shopping, stick around for dinner and barhopping.

Note that trying to find street parking here can be maddening, and many streets are zoned (i.e., only residents with the proper permits can park there). There are, however, quite a few pay lots, and though the ones closest to Seattle University tend to fill up on weekdays, you should be able to find something.

WHAT TO SEE

㉓ Broadway Shopping District. Seattle's youth culture, old money, gay scene, and everything in between all converge on this lively, if somewhat scuzzy stretch of Broadway E between E. Denny Way and E. Roy Street. It's a cluttered stretch of cheap restaurants (with a one or two more-upscale-looking cafés thrown into the mix), even cheaper clothing stores, a few interesting books and records shops, and a few bars. Most of the good shopping, eating, and drinking is along the Pike–Pine corridor or on side streets, and it's a real stretch to claim as some guidebooks do that Broadway is the epicenter of Seattle's counterculture (whatever that means), but a lot of people still find the area compelling because of its human parade. It's also one of the few areas in Seattle that can claim to have a consistently lively street life, and despite some aggressive panhandlers and the occasional twitchy meth-head, the avenue is generally safe at all hours. If you really want to see Seattle in all its quirky glory, head to Dick's Drive-In around 1 AM on a weekend night (or around 11:30 AM the next morning). Between Pine and Roy streets artist Jack Mackie inlaid seven sets of bronze dancing footprints demonstrating the steps for the tango, the waltz, the fox-trot, and others. Look closely at the steps near Roy Street to see coffee beans in the concrete, a nod to the region's love affair with java. Near Pine Street is a bronze effigy of one of the city's most worshiped rock-and-roll icons, Jimi Hendrix. You might see someone leave an offering—a flower, a cigarette, or even a joint—in his outstretched fingers.

㉒ Martin-Zambito Fine Art. If you're interested in Northwest regional art, this gallery is a must. But don't expect a "greatest hits" collection here—David Martin and Dominic Zambito are well known in Seattle's art scene for expanding the study of regional Northwest art namely by uncovering little-known, unknown, or long-forgotten artists, many of them women. Their research has extended the history of the genre to the late 1800s (before they started digging, most collections started in the 1940s). Their exhibits consist of mostly paintings and photographs and tend to focus on WPA and Depression-era works. ⊠721 E. Pike St., Capitol Hill ☎206/726–9509 ⊕www.martin-zambito.com ⊠Free ⊗Tues.–Sat. 11–6.

㉔ Pike–Pine Corridor. Nowadays, more people consider this, not Broadway, the heart of the Hill. The so-called corridor begins at the corners of Pike and Pine streets (which run parallel) and Melrose Avenue. You'll find a bunch of interesting businesses as soon as you enter the area, including the Baguette Box and Bauhaus coffee shop; Faire, another great coffee shop, is just a few blocks north on E. Olive Way. So, if you need some sustenance, grab a coffee and a sandwich and head east on either Pike or Pine. Pine is a slightly more-pleasant walk, but Pike has more stores—and unless you're here in the evening, it's the stores that will be the main draw. The architecture along both streets is a mix of older buildings with small storefronts, a few taller buildings that have loft office spaces, and garages and warehouses (some converted, some not). The best plan of attack is to follow either street to 11th Avenue, which skirts Cal Anderson Park—a small, pleasant park with a unusual conic fountain and reflecting pool, and a great place to take a break after walking and shopping. The park can be either very quiet or filled with all kinds of activities from softball games to impromptu concerts from a neighborhood marching band. If you want a coffee or a snack, cross the park to its northeastern corner, across the street from which is Vivace Roasteria.

25 Volunteer Park. High above the mansions of North Capitol Hill sits 45-acre Volunteer Park, a grassy expanse perfect for picnicking, sunbathing, reading, and strolling. You can tell this is one of the city's older parks by the size of the trees and the rhododendrons, many of which were planted more than a hundred years ago. The Olmsted Brothers, the premier landscape architects of the day, helped with the final design in 1904, and the park has changed surprisingly little since then. The manicured look of the park is a sharp contrast to the wilds of Discovery Park or the Washington Park Arboretum, but the design suits the needs of the densely populated neighborhood well—after all, Capitol Hill residents need someplace to set up Ultimate Frisbee games. A small wading pool by the water tower is extremely popular with families on hot summer days.

Beside the lake in the center of the park is the **Seattle Asian Art Museum** (☎206/654–3100 ⊕www.seattleartmuseum.org ✉$5, free 1st Thurs. and Sat. of month ۞Tues.–Sun. 10–5, Thurs. until 9; call for tour schedule). This 1933 art moderne edifice fits surprisingly well with the stark plaza stretching from the front door to the edge of a bluff, and with the lush plants of Volunteer Park. The museum's collections include thousands of paintings, sculptures, pottery, and textiles from China, Japan, India, Korea, and several Southeast Asian countries. It's a small place, and doesn't take long to move through, but it usually has one or two surprises to keep you around a bit longer, such as the enigmatic short films shown in its theater. Children's crafts tables provide activities related to current exhibits, and free gallery tours are available by appointment. Across from the museum is the **Volunteer Park Conservatory** (☎206/684–4743). This Victorian-style greenhouse has a magnificent (if cramped) collection of tropical plants. The Anna Clise Orchid Collection, begun in 1919, is at its most spectacular in late fall and early winter, when most of the flowers are in full bloom. The conservatory also has some splendid palm trees, a well-stocked koi pond, and, almost incongruously, a collection of cacti and other succulents. Climbing the 108 steps of the old water tower yields some decent views of the city over the park's tree line as well as some old photos and maps of the park. A focal point of the park, at the western edge of the 445-foot-high hill and in front of the Asian Art Museum, is Isamu Noguchi's sculpture *Black Sun,* carved from a 30-ton block of black granite. Many seem to enjoy taking photos of the Space Needle framed in the 9-foot, 9-inch hole of the "sun." ⊠*Park entrance: 14th Ave. E at Prospect St., Capitol Hill* ⊕*www. ci.seattle.wa.us/seattle/parks/park spaces/volpark.htm* ⊠*Free* ⊙*Park daily dawn–dusk; conservatory May–mid-Sept., daily 10–7, otherwise 10–4.*

☺ ★ ㉖ **Washington Park Arboretum.** As far as the area's green spaces go, Volunteer Park gets all the attention, but this 230-acre arboretum is far more

> ### THE SWEETEST STRETCH
>
> Roy Street between Broadway E and Harvard Avenue is a quiet and quaint little street that looks more Europe than Seattle. In addition to some nice shops, you'll find a great coffee shop, Joe Bar, which is a good place to get a crepe in the morning on your way to Volunteer Park. The Massage Sanctuary around the corner on Broadway is excellent. Just strolling down Roy and then heading north on Harvard or Boylston to Prospect and hooking back around down Broadway E past the Bacon Mansion is also pleasurable.

beautiful. On calm weekdays, the place feels really secluded; though there are trails, you feel like you're freer to roam here than at Discovery Park. The seasons are always on full display: in warm winters, flowering cherries and plums bloom in its protected valleys as early as late February, while the flowering shrubs in Rhododendron Glen and Azalea Way are in full bloom March through June. In autumn, trees and shrubs glow in hues of crimson, pumpkin, and lemon; in winter, plantings chosen specially for their stark and colorful branches dominate the landscape. From March through October, visit the peaceful **Japanese Garden** (☎*206/684–4725* ⊠*$5*), a compressed world of mountains, forests, rivers, lakes, and tablelands, open daily from 10 AM until sunset. The pond, lined with blooming water irises in spring, has turtles and brightly colored koi. An authentic Japanese teahouse is reserved for tea ceremonies and instruction on the art of serving tea. The Graham Visitors Center at the park's north end has descriptions of the arboretum's flora and fauna, which include 130 endangered plants, as well as brochures, a garden gift shop, and walking-tour maps. ⊠*2300 Arboretum Dr. E, Capitol Hill* ☎*206/543–8800 arboretum, 206/684–4725 Japanese garden* ⊕*http://depts.washington.edu/wpa* ⊠*Free* ⊙*Park daily 7 AM–dusk, visitor center daily 10–4.*

FREMONT & BALLARD

If you ever wondered where the center of the universe is, look no further—the self-styled "Republic of Fremont" was declared just this by its residents in the 1960s. For many years, Fremont enjoyed its reputation as Seattle's most eccentric neighborhood, home to hippies, starving artists, bikers, and rat-race dropouts. But Fremont has lost a lot of its artist cache as the stores along its main strip turn more upscale, luxury condos and town houses appear above the neighborhood's warren of small houses, and rising rents send many longtime residents reluctantly packing (many to nearby Ballard). During the week, however, this pretty neighborhood is peaceful, friendly, and still very much embodies that accepting, laid-back attitude that made it famous. There are a few quintessential sights—mostly works of public art—as well as a few nice boutiques and vintage stores.

Ballard, directly to the west of Fremont, is everyone's sweetheart. Seattle residents of all stripes can't help but hold some affection for this neighborhood, even as it enters a new, less-humble phase of existence. Ballard used to be almost exclusively Scandinavian and working-class; it was the logical home for the Swedish and Norwegian immigrants who worked in the area's fishing, shipbuilding, and lumber industries. Reminders of its origins still exist—most literally in the Nordic Heritage Museum—but the neighborhood is undergoing inevitable changes as the number of artists, hipsters, and young professionals (many of whom have been priced out of Fremont and Capitol Hill) increases. Trendy restaurants, upscale furniture stores, and boutiques have popped up all along N.W. Market Street and Ballard Avenue, the neighborhood's main commercial strips.

WHAT TO SEE

27 **Fremont Center.** The neighborhood's small center is comprised of two short strips: Fremont Avenue heading north from the Fremont Bridge to N. 39th Street, and a few blocks of N. 36th Street as it veers west off Fremont Avenue toward Ballard. Both streets have an eclectic bunch of shops, cafés, bars, and small businesses. The area also contains most of Fremont's sights.

Beneath the Aurora Bridge at N. 36th Street lurks the 18-foot-tall *Fremont Troll,* clutching a Volkswagen Beetle in his massive left hand. The giant watches over the neighborhood, and even allows people to crawl up onto his shoulders for the obligatory photo. The troll appeared in 1991, commissioned by the Fremont Arts Council. Like all of Fremont's sculptures, he can't escape a little playful decoration—around Halloween, he's given a bicycle-wheel rim as a nose ring and a giant spider crawls on his shoulder.

When Russian counterrevolutionaries knocked over a 7-ton **statue of Lenin** in 1989, they couldn't have known it would end up in Fremont. A man named Lewis Carpenter toted the statue from Slovakia to Seattle in 1989, and when he died in 1994, it made its way to the neighborhood's Sunday flea market. Soon ousted from this den of capitalism, the bronze Bolshevik now stands proudly in front of a burrito joint on N. 36th Street, between Fremont and Evanston avenues. During Gay Pride Weekend, the commissar is sometimes decked out in pink (skirt, hat, lipstick, and pasties) from head to toe.

Fremont's signature statue, *Waiting for the Interurban,* is a cast aluminum sculpture of five figures, one holding a small child. The Interurban was a light-rail system that operated in the '40s. Residents enjoy dressing and ornamenting the figures for just about any joyful occasion, from retirements to birthdays to declarations of love. Look closely at

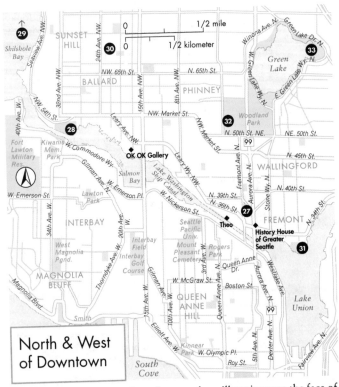

North & West of Downtown

the dog circling the legs of one figure and you'll see it wears the face of a bearded, ornery-looking man. As the story goes, the onetime honorary mayor of Fremont, Armen Stepanian, was upset with Richard Beyer for choosing himself as the artist to create the statue when no one else applied to the Fremont Arts Council for the job. Beyer had the final word in the brouhaha by putting Stepanian's face on the canine. The sculpture's home is on N. 34th Street, just over the Fremont Bridge at Fremont Avenue.

On the corner of N. 35th Street and Evanston Avenue, look up to spot the 53-foot, Russian-built **Fremont Rocket**, which marks the official center of the center of the universe.

There's a lovely stretch of the **Burke-Gilman Trail** along the canal on the west side of the Fremont Bridge. Watch kayakers and small craft float down the river; several benches along the path make it easy to linger for hours.

🖐 ★ **28** **Ballard Locks.** You don't have to be an engineering buff to enjoy watching this fascinating system in action. In addition to boat traffic, the locks see an estimated half million salmon and trout make the journey from saltwater to fresh each year with the help of a nearby fish ladder. Finally, a trip to the locks isn't complete without a stroll around the 7-acre Carl English Jr. Botanic Garden. Guided tours of the locks are available; however, the brochure from the visitor center and the plaques by the locks will give you plenty of information if you don't have time for a tour. ✉ *3015 N.W. 54th St., Ballard* ✛ *From Fremont, head north on Leary Way NW, west on NW Market St., and south on 54th St.* ☎ *206/783–7059* 🌫 *Free* ☉ *Locks daily 7 AM–9 PM; visitor center May–Sept., daily 10–6; Oct.–Apr., Thurs.–Mon. 11–4; call for tour information.*

㉙ Golden Gardens Park. There are 3 mi of forest trails in this 87-acre park, but most people come here to sunbathe, brave the cold waters of Puget Sound for a swim, or just sit on the beach. The stretch of sand closest to the parking lot has a snack bar, picnic tables, and restrooms—and the greatest concentration of people. As you walk farther north, the crowds thin out considerably and you'll have no problem finding a peaceful spot or empty bench. And with the Shilshole Bay Marina so close by, you can bet there will be a lot of white sails in the water to make the view of the sound and the Olympic Mountains in the distance that much more enjoyable. Though there is a large parking lot, finding parking here can be challenging, especially on sunny weekends. Be prepared to circle. ✉ *8498 Seaview Pl. NW, Ballard* ☎ *206/684–4075* 🌫 *Free* ☉ *Daily 6 AM–11:30 PM.*

☾ ㉚ Nordic Heritage Museum. The only educational institute in the country to focus solely on Nordic cultures, this museum in a massive 1900s schoolhouse traces Scandinavian art, artifacts, and heritage all the way from Viking times. Behind the redbrick walls, nine permanent galleries on three floors give an in-depth look at how immigrants from Denmark, Finland, Iceland, Norway, and Sweden came to America and settled in the Pacific Northwest. Among the finds are textiles, china, books, tools, and photographs. Delve into Nordic history in the library; learn a few phrases at the on-site Scandinavian Language Institute; or join in a class or children's program on Nordic arts and crafts. The temporary galleries display paintings, sculpture, and photography by contemporary artists. ✉ *3014 N.W. 67th St., Ballard* ☎ *206/789–5707* ⊕ *www.nordicmuseum.org* 🌫 *$6* ☉ *Tues.–Sat. 10–4, Sun. noon–4.*

WALLINGFORD & GREEN LAKE

Directly east of Fremont is Wallingford, a low-key residential neighborhood with lovely Craftsman houses. Its main commercial drag is N.E. 45th Street from Stone Way to I–5, with most of its notable shops and restaurants clustered within a six-block strip. Wallingford's even more laid-back and low profile than Fremont or Ballard, and outside of a few parks, it has no sights per se. But 45th has an eclectic group of shops, from a gourmet beer store to an erotic bakery to a Hawaiiana merchant, along with a great coffee shop.

WHAT TO SEE

☾ ★ ㉛ Gasworks Park. Though technically in Wallingford, this lovely park can be easily reached from Fremont Center by strolling along the waterfront Burke-Gilman Trail—remember to stay in the clearly designated

Can You Say "Geoduck"?

So you packed Gore-Tex, khakis, and sensible shoes, and you've mastered the art of ordering complicated espresso drinks with urbane insouciance. Now if only you could pronounce Puyallup without raising local eyebrows. Here's a guide to a few of the Northwest's tongue-twisters.

Alki (AL-ki). Rhymes with high; the point where settlers first landed in this area.

Geoduck (GOOEY-duck). Gigantic clam grown in Puget (PEW-jet) Sound, sometimes weighing in at more than 20 pounds. Often surrounded by gaping tourists at Pike Place Market.

Kalaloch (KLAY-lock). Popular scenic stretch on the wild Pacific side of the Olympic Peninsula.

Poulsbo (PAULS-bo). Charming Scandinavian town on Bainbridge Island treasured for its Norwegian bakeries.

Puyallup (pew-AL-up). Home of the Western Washington Fair, a monthlong shindig held each September. Key phrase: "Do the Puyallup."

Sequim (skwim). Rhymes with swim. Between the Olympic Mountains and the Strait of Juan de Fuca (FEW-kah). Famous for Dungeness (dun-jen-NESS) crabs.

Tacoma (Tah-CO-mah). Growing city 30 mi south of Seattle.

Yakima Valley (YAK-him-uh). South-central Washington's picturesque wine country.

For the record, Washington's neighbor to the south is Oregon (OR-eh-gun), Spokane (spo-KAN) is eastern Washington's largest city, Lake Chelan (sha-LAN) is a spectacular body of water southwest of the Methow (MET-how) Valley, and that snowcapped volcano to the south is Mt. Rainier (ray-NEAR).

pedestrian lane, as you'll be sharing the trail with many other walkers, joggers, and speed-demon bicyclists. The park gets its name from the hulking remains of an old gas plant, which, far from being an eyesore, actually lends some character to the otherwise open, hilly, 20-acre park. Get a good view of Downtown Seattle from the zodiac sculpture at the top of the hill, or feed the ducks on the lake. The sand-bottom playground has monkey bars, wooden platforms, and a spinning metal merry-go-round. Crowds throng to picnic and enjoy outdoor summer concerts, movies, and the July 4 fireworks display over Lake Union. ✉ *North end of Lake Union, N. Northlake Way and Meridian Ave. N, Wallingford* ⊘ *Daily 4 AM–11:30 PM.*

🌀 ③ **Green Lake.** This beautiful 342-acre park is a favorite of Seattleites, who jog, blade, bike, and walk their dogs along the 2.8-mi paved path that surrounds the lake. Beaches on both the east and west sides (around 72nd Street) have lifeguards and swimming rafts. Boats, canoes, kayaks, and paddleboats can be rented at Greenlake Boat Rental on the eastern side of the lake. There are also basketball and tennis courts and baseball and soccer fields. A first-rate play area includes a giant sandbox, swings, slides, and all the climbing equipment a child could ever dream of—plus lots of grassy areas and benches where adults can take a break. The park is generally packed, especially on weekends. And you'd better love dogs: the canine-to-human ratio here is just about even. Surrounding the park are lovely middle- and upper-class homes, plus a compact commercial district where you can grab some snacks after your walk. ⊠ *E. Green Lake Dr. N and W. Green Lake Dr. N, Green Lake* ☎ *206/684–4075 general info, 206/527–0171 Greenlake Boat Rental* ⊕ *www.seattle.gov/parks.*

☺ ★ ㉜ **Woodland Park Zoo.** Many of the 300 species of animals in this 92-acre botanical garden roam freely in habitat areas. A jaguar exhibit is the center of the Tropical Rain Forest area, where rare cats, frogs, and birds evoke South American jungles. The Butterflies & Blooms exhibit ($1) shows off the amazing beauty and variety of the winged creatures and describes their relationship with local flora. With authentic thatch-roof buildings, the African Village has a replica schoolroom overlooking animals roaming the savanna; the Asian Elephant Forest Trail takes you through a Thai village; and the Northern Trail winds past rocky habitats where brown bears, wolves, mountain goats, and otters scramble and play. The terrain is mostly flat, making it easy for wheelchairs and strollers (which can be rented) to negotiate. The zoo has parking for $4; it's a small price to pay to avoid the headache of searching for a space on the street. ⊠ *5500 Phinney Ave. N, Phinney Ridge* ☎ *206/684–4800* ⊕ *www.zoo.org* ☑ *Oct.–Apr. $10.50, May–Sept. $15* ☉ *Oct.–Apr., daily 9:30–4; May–Sept., daily 9:30–6.*

WHERE TO EAT

Seattle has a little bit of everything—well, almost everything—but the city is particularly strong on the following cuisines: its own regional take on American cooking, French, Japanese, and Thai. It's hard to say where the scene will go next as celebrity chefs continue to try to outdo each other, but one thing's for sure: they'll all continue using the high-quality ingredients that makes Pacific Northwest cooking famous, meaning that even their missteps are far more palatable than the successes of restaurants in other food towns.

Although dining well in Seattle isn't cheap, you'll still pay far less for a fancy meal here than in Los Angeles, San Francisco, or New York. What's more, ■ TIP→ **most of Seattle's finest restaurants have bar menus from which you can create a respectable meal out of small plates for half the price of a sit-down dinner.**

WHAT IT COSTS					
	¢	$	$$	$$$	$$$$
AT DINNER	under $10	$10–$20	$20–$30	$30–$40	over $40

Prices are per person for a main course, excluding tax and tip.

COFFEEHOUSES

BELLTOWN

Macrina Bakery. Though not a coffee shop in the strictest sense—it's a bakery with a small café that's very popular for breakfast and brunch—Macrina deserves a mention because a) it serves great coffee, and b) it has the best baked goods in Belltown. Though it's usually too frenzied to invite the hours of idleness that other coffee shops may inspire, Macrina is a great place to take a break on your way to or from the Olympic Sculpture Park—get an iced latte and a piece of ridiculously rich cake. ✉ *2408 1st Ave., Belltown* ☎ *206/448–4032* ⊕ *www.macrinabakery. com.*

PIONEER SQUARE & THE INTERNATIONAL DISTRICT

Panama Hotel Tea and Coffee Shop. On the ground floor of the historic Panama Hotel is a serene teahouse with tons of personality and a subtle Asian flair that reflects its former life as a Japanese bathhouse. The space is lovely, with exposed-brick walls, shiny, hardwood floors, and black-and-white photos of old Seattle (many of them relating to the history of the city's Japanese immigrants). Kick back with an individual pot of tea—there are dozens of varieties—or an espresso. This is a good place to bring a book, as it's usually calm and quiet. No credit cards. ✉ *605½ S. Main St., International District* ☎ *206/223–9242* ⊕ *www. panamahotel.net.*

★ **Zeitgeist Coffee.** Not only is Zeitgeist one of the few decent coffee shops in the southern part of the city core, it is also a local favorite. Even Seattleites who don't particularly like Pioneer Square will happily hunt for parking to spend a few hours here, maybe stopping by Elliott Bay Book Company first, which is around the corner on First Avenue. Housed in one of Pioneer Square's great brick buildings, with high ceilings and a few artfully exposed ducts and pipes, Zeitgeist has a simple, classy look that's the perfect backdrop for the frequent art shows held here. You'll feel smarter just sitting in here. ✉ *171 S. Jackson St., Pioneer Square* ☎ *206/583–0497* ⊕ *http://zeitgeistcoffee.com.*

QUEEN ANNE & SEATTLE CENTER

★ **Caffe Fiore.** Blissfully removed from the hubbub of Queen Anne Avenue, the Queen Anne branch of this minichain (the other branches are in Ballard) is in the bottom floor of a house that's been painted and decorated to match the brand's deep-cocoa-and-burnt-orange logo—it's a very cozy spot to spend a few hours. The coffee is some of the best in the city—in fact, you'll see Caffe Fiore roasts used in other shops. ✉ *224 W. Galer St., Queen Anne* ☎ *206/282–1441* ⊕ *www.caffefiore. com.*

El Diablo. El Diablo is a Latin coffeehouse that serves Cuban-style coffee and delicious, authentic Mexican hot chocolate. If you don't want coffee, you can also get a *batido,* a Cuban shake made with real fruit. The interior is splashed with bright yellows, reds, blues, and purples, and most surfaces are covered with murals. It's a bit loud, both in appearance and in noise level—it seems like customers should be sitting around piles of chips and guacamole and giant margaritas, not mugs of coffee—but it's fun and certainly unique among Seattle's java stops. El

Diablo is open late (until midnight on Friday and Saturday and until 11 all other days) and has live music several nights a week. At night, they serve sangria and beer, too. ⊠*1811 Queen Anne Ave. N, Queen Anne* ☎*206/285–0693* ⊕*www.eldiablocoffee.com.*

CAPITOL HILL

B&O Espresso. A cute, cozy neighborhood favorite that looks like a funky, shabby-chic version of a Victorian tearoom, B&O was one of Seattle's earliest purveyors of the latte, and the drinks are still great. The on-site bakery turns out great desserts. The place is always packed for weekend brunch. It's less of a hipster scene than some of the Hill's coffeehouses. ⊠*204 Belmont Ave. E, Capitol Hill* ☎*206/322–5028.*

Joe Bar. Tiny Joe Bar is one of the most charming coffee shops in the city, partly thanks to its location on a serene side street and partly thanks to its intimate yet cheery space. Light pours in through the storefront, which is made up almost entirely of leaded glass panels. A few café tables are perched in front of lime-green walls; a small mezzanine and a few outdoor tables provide some additional seating. Joe Bar serves savory crepes in the morning and beer and wine in the evening, making it more than a place to get your caffeine fix. The coffee isn't the best in the city, but it's pretty good. ⊠*810 E. Roy St., Capitol Hill* ☎*206/324–0407* ⊕*www.joebar.org.*

★ **Victrola Coffee & Art.** Victrola is probably the most loved of Capitol Hill's many coffeehouses, and it's easy to see why. The space is lovely, the coffee and pastries are fantastic, the baristas are skillful, and everyone, from soccer moms to indie rockers, is made to feel like this neighborhood spot exists just for them. Unfortunately, it can be hard to score a table here, especially if you have a big group. If 15th Avenue is too far off the beaten path for you, there's a new branch on Pike between Melrose and Bellevue. ⊠*411 15th Ave. E, Capitol Hill* ☎*206/325–6520* ⊕*www.victrolacoffee.net.*

Fodor's Choice **Vivace Roasteria.** Vivace is considered by many to be the home of Seattle's finest espresso. In fact, they're so dedicated to serving espresso, they don't even offer drip coffee. A long, curving bar and checkerboard floor add some character to a space that might otherwise look like a diner. The place has got a great energy—lively and

bustling, where Hill residents tap on laptops and students from the nearby colleges hold study groups—but it's not necessarily a good spot for a quiet read. There's another branch right across the way from REI on Yale Avenue. ⊠*901 E. Denny Way, Capitol Hill* ☎*206/860–5869* ⊕*www.espressovivace.com.*

FREMONT

★ **Fremont Coffee Company.** This is a second home (and office) to many writers, freelancers, students, and assorted Fremont residents. It helps that the coffeehouse is actually a small house with a wonderful wraparound porch, and that the baristas are some of the friendliest in the city. The coffee's great, too. Inside seating is less comfortable, so save this one for a sunny day. ⊠ *459 N. 36th St., Fremont* ☎ *206/632–3633* ⊕ *www.fremontcoffee.net.*

RESTAURANTS

DOWNTOWN

AMERICAN

$$–$$$$ ✕ **13 Coins.** 13 Coins is a wonderful oddity. One of the few restaurants open 24 hours a day, the place nearly defies description. To say it seems stuck in time, circa 1967, would be true, but it's really stuck in another universe altogether. Maybe it's those ridiculously out-of-proportion, high-back booths, but the place reminds us of Alice's mad tea party presided over by waiters who stumbled into a wormhole somewhere in Brooklyn, New York. Service is downright entertaining—half the fun of coming here, especially late at night, is listening to the waiters and cooks banter as dishes are whisked around. The food is upscale diner fare, consistently good but a bit overpriced. Though the menu does include some standbys like a good cheesesteak and huge frittatas—don't expect hamburgers, fries, and mozzarella sticks here. Menu benchmarks include liver and onions, jumbo shrimp on ice, and platters of steak and pasta big enough to stuff a logger. Seafood dishes aren't quite up to Seattle's high standards, but the steamed clams and the baked king salmon fillet are decent. ⊠ *1125 Boren Ave. N, Downtown* ☎ *206/682–2513* ⊕ *www.13coins.com* ⌂ *Reservations not accepted* ⊟ *AE, D, MC, V.*

$$–$$$ ✕ **Matt's in the Market.** Your first dinner at Matt's is like a first date you
Fodor's Choice   hope will never end. The crown jewel of the Market-area restaurants,
★   Matt's redefined intimate dining and personal service when it opened its 23-seat spot on the second floor of the Corner Market Building. A recent expansion nearly doubled the amount of seats, but the space is still tiny, and the basics remain: a lunch counter perfect for grabbing a delicious po'boy or cup of gumbo, an inviting space with simple adornments like clear glass vases filled with flowers from the market, a seasonal menu that synthesizes the best picks from the restaurant's neighbors, and an excellent wine list. At dinner, starters might include such delectable items as Manila clams steamed in beer, herbs, and chilies; entrées always include at least one catch of the day. And yes, there is a Matt—he's a hell of a nice guy and is often in the restaurant chatting with regulars. ⊠ *94 Pike St., Suite 32, Downtown* ☎ *206/467–7909* ⊕ *www.mattsinthemarket.com* ⌂ *Reservations essential* ⊟ *MC, V* ⊙ *Closed Sun.*

$–$$ ✕ **Marazul.** Does the world really need another "fusion tapas" place? Probably not, but Marazul has added something positive to Seattle's dining scene. The tapas are literally all over the map—Cuban, Caribbean, and pan-Asian influences are responsible for items like miso ceviche and Jamaican jerk salmon sushi, most of which are very successful experiments. A vague island theme (and gallons of premium and hard-to-find rums) holds everything together, but don't expect steel-drum music and giant drinks with umbrellas—Marazul is hip and sexy, with its mix of exotic woods, its gorgeous copper-accented rum bar, and its separate tatami room. Even the gimmicky touches like mah-jongg and dominos games at the bar and world music on the sound system are fun and tastefully executed. Patio seating is available in summer. Breakfast and lunch are served daily, a novel concept for a trendy spot. ⊠*2200 Westlake Ave., South Lake Union* ☎*206/654–8170* ⊕*www. marazulrestaurant.com* ▤*MC, V.*

¢–$ ✕ **Three Girls Bakery.** Pike Place Market is such a tourist trap that the selection of quick and cheap lunch options is pretty dismal. Rest assured that Three Girls Bakery knows how to make a sandwich and they don't skimp on the fillings. Soups are also very good and of course the baked goods are outstanding. This isn't a place to enjoy a sit-down meal, and service can be a bit brusque, so plan on taking your meat-loaf sandwich and macaroons elsewhere. ⊠*1514 Pike Pl., Downtown* ☎*206/622–1045* ▤*No credit cards.*

FRENCH

$$–$$$ ✕ **Campagne.** The white walls, picture windows, snowy linens, fresh flowers, and candles at this urbane restaurant overlooking Pike Place Market and Elliott Bay evoke Provence. So does the robust French country fare, with starters such as seafood sausage, and calamari fillets with ground almonds. Main plates include panfried scallops with a green-peppercorn-and-tarragon sauce, cinnamon-roasted quail served with carrot and orange essence, and Oregon rabbit with an apricot-cider-and-green-peppercorn sauce. ▪TIP➜ **Campagne is open only for dinner, but the adjacent Café Campagne serves breakfast, lunch, and dinner daily.** ⊠*Inn at the Market, 86 Pine St., Downtown* ☎*206/728–2800* ⊕*www.campagnerestaurant.com* ⌖*Reservations essential* ▤*AE, DC, MC, V* ⊗*No lunch.*

$–$$ ✕ **Le Pichet.** Slate tabletops, tile floor, and rolled-zinc bar transport you out of Downtown Seattle and into Paris, 1934. Blackboards spell out the specials. Wines are served from the earthenware *pichets* that inspired the brasserie's name. The menu is heartbreakingly French: at lunch there are rustic pâtés and *jambon et fromage* (ham-and-cheese) sandwiches on crusty baguettes; dinner sees homemade sausages, daily fish specials, and steak tartare. The roast chicken (for two) takes an hour to prepare and is worth every second you'll wait. It's enough to make you think the French invented soul food. Dinner reservations are essential. ⊠*1933 1st Ave., Downtown* ☎*206/256–1499* ⊕*www. lepichetseattle.com* ▤*MC, V.*

Fodor'sChoice
★

MEXICAN

¢–$ ✕ **El Puerco Lloron.** This funky, cafeteria-style diner has some open-air terrace seating on the Pike Place Market Hill Climb, offering views of Elliott Bay on sunny days. It's also got some of Seattle's best and most authentic Mexican cooking—simple, tasty, and inexpensive. More-ambitious highlights include perfect *chiles rellenos* (mild green peppers that are breaded, stuffed with cheese, and fried) and a particularly fla-vorful guacamole. ⊠*501 Western Ave., Downtown* ☎*206/624–0541* ▤*AE, MC, V.* C

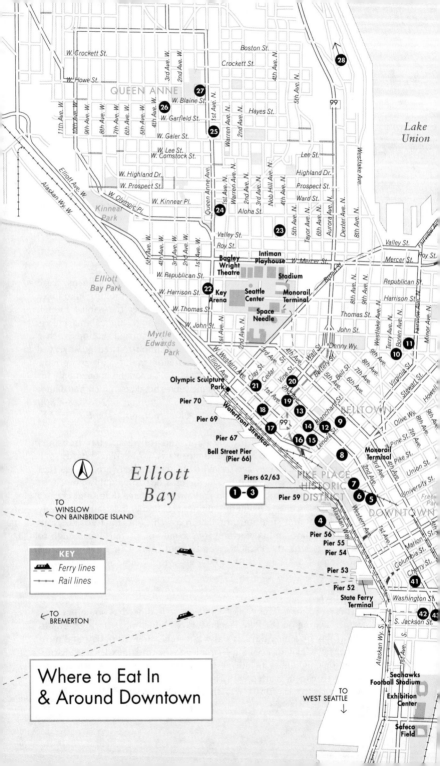

Where to Eat In & Around Downtown

Queen Anne

W. Crockett St.
W. Howe St.
QUEEN ANNE
W. Blaine St.
W. Garfield St.
W. Galer St.
W. Lee St.
W. Comstock St.
W. Highland Dr.
W. Prospect St.
W. Kinnear Pl.
W. Olympic Pl.
Kinnear Park
W. Republican St.
W. Harrison St.
W. Thomas St.
W. John St.

Boston St.
Crockett St.
Hayes St.
Lee St.
Highland Dr.
Prospect St.
Ward St.
Aloha St.
Valley St.
Roy St.

11th Ave. W.
9th Ave. W.
8th Ave. W.
7th Ave. W.
6th Ave. W.
5th Ave. W.
4th Ave. W.
3rd Ave. W.
2nd Ave. W.
1st Ave. W.
3rd Ave. N.
2nd Ave. N.
1st Ave. N.
Queen Anne Ave.
Warren Ave. N.
1st Ave. N.
Warren Ave. N.
2nd Ave. N.
3rd Ave. N.
Nob Hill Ave. N.
4th Ave. N.
5th Ave. N.

Lake Union

5th Ave. N.
99
Westlake Ave.

Elliott Ave. W.
Alaskan Wy. W.

Elliott Bay Park

Myrtle Edwards Park

Bagley Wright Theatre
Intiman Playhouse
W. Mercer St.
Stadium
Key Arena
Seattle Center
Monorail Terminal
Space Needle

Valley St.
Mercer St.
Roy St.
Republican St.
Harrison St.
Thomas St.
John St.
Denny Wy.

8th Ave. N.
9th Ave. N.
Taylor Ave. N.
Aurora Ave. N.
Dexter Ave. N.
8th Ave. N.
Westlake Ave. N.
Terry Ave. N.
Boren Ave. N.
Fairview Ave. N.
Minor Ave. N.

22 Key Arena

Olympic Sculpture Park
Pier 70
Pier 69
Pier 67
Bell Street Pier (Pier 66)
Waterfront Streetcar

W. Western Ave.
W. Clay St.
Cedar St.
Vine St.
Wall St.
Battery St.
Bell St.
Blanchard St.
Lenora St.

3rd Ave.
1st Ave.
2nd Ave.
4th Ave.
5th Ave.
6th Ave.
7th Ave.
8th Ave.
9th Ave.
Virginia St.
Stewart St.
Howell St.
Olive Wy.
Pine St.
Pike St.

BELLTOWN
Monorail Terminal

Elliott Bay

TO WINSLOW ON BAINBRIDGE ISLAND

Piers 62/63
Pier 59
1-3
PIKE PLACE HISTORIC DISTRICT
DOWNTOWN
University St.
Union St.
Seneca St.

Pier 56
Pier 55
Pier 54
Pier 53
Pier 52
State Ferry Terminal
4

Marion St.
Columbia St.
Cherry St.
Washington St.
S. Jackson St.

KEY
⛴ Ferry lines
╫ Rail lines

TO BREMERTON

Alaskan Wy. S.
1st Ave. S.

Seahawks Football Stadium
Exhibition Center
Safeco Field

TO WEST SEATTLE
↓

3

PACIFIC NORTHWEST

$$$–$$$$ ✕**Dahlia Lounge.** Romantic Dahlia started the valentine-red walls trend and it's still working its magic on Seattle couples. It's cozy and then some, but the food plays its part, too. Crab cakes, served as an entrée or an appetizer, lead an ever-changing regionally oriented menu. Other standouts are seared ahi tuna, near-perfect gnocchi, and such desserts as coconut-cream pie and fresh fruit cobblers. Seattle's most energetic restaurateur, chef-owner Tom Douglas also owns Etta's Seafood in Pike Place Market, and the excellent Palace Kitchen on Fifth Avenue. But Dahlia is the one that makes your heart go pitter-patter. ⊠*2001 4th Ave., Downtown* ☎*206/682–4142* ⊕*www.tomdouglas.com/ dahlia* ⌕*Reservations essential* ▤*AE, D, DC, MC, V* ✸*No lunch weekends.*

★ $$$ ✕**Union.** Don't expect to be overwhelmed by wacky design elements or mystified by culinary acrobatics. Do expect to be filled with an inexplicable feeling of well-being when you look back on your meal weeks or even months later. Dining at Union is a special experience, but everything about the place is so understated, the experience may take a while to process. Though from the street the restaurant looks very sleek and a little standoffish (yes, there are an awful lot of red and gray accents), the space becomes very cozy once you settle in; everyone seems like they're either regulars or want to be regulars, and you'll be free to relax here and savor every bite. Fresh ingredients come from Pike Place Market and the menu changes daily to accommodate what's available. Seafood is the strong point—no one cooks a scallop better than Union—but selections always include some type of pork dish, as well as fowl. Entrées are outstanding and reasonably priced, but you might opt to concoct a meal out of starters, which are more fun and inventive. The Dungeness crab salad with avocado and basil oil is always on the menu and it's a must. The wine list is excellent and servers are great at giving advice on which bottle to select. ⊠*1400 1st Ave., Downtown* ☎*206/838–8000* ⊕*www.unionseattle.com* ▤*AE, MC, V* ✸*No lunch.*

SEAFOOD

$–$$$ ✕**Elliott's Oyster House.** No place in Seattle serves better Dungeness crab or oysters than Elliott's, which has gotten the presentation of fresh seafood down to a fine art. You can't go wrong with the local rock-fish or salmon. The dining room is bright, and there's a great view of Elliott Bay and of the harbor tour boats next door. On sunny days the place is packed with diners from all over the country who have come to learn what Seattle is all about. That said, the crowd is usually split fifty-fifty between tourists and locals, as Seattleites still fully embrace this place, especially the raw-bar happy hour. ⊠*Pier 56 off Alaskan Way, Downtown* ☎*206/623–4340* ⊕*http://elliottsoysterhouse.com* ▤*AE, DC, MC, V.*

★ ¢–$ ✕**Emmett Watson's Oyster Bar.** This unpretentious spot can be hard to find—it's in the back of Pike Place Market's Soames-Dunn Building, facing a small flower-bedecked courtyard. But for those who know their oysters, finding this place is worth the effort. Not only are the oysters very fresh and the beer icy cold, but both are inexpensive and available in any number of varieties. If you don't like oysters, try the salmon soup or the fish-and-chips—flaky pieces of fish with very little grease. ⊠ *1916 Pike Pl., Downtown* ☎ *206/448–7721* ⚑ *Reservations not accepted* ☐ *No credit cards* ⊗ *No dinner Sun.*

BELLTOWN

AMERICAN

★ **$$-$$$** ✕**Restaurant Zoë.** Reservations are sought after at this chic eatery on a high-trafficked corner. Its tall windows, lively bar scene, and charming waitstaff add to the popularity, which comes mainly from its inspired kitchen. The talents of chef-owner Scott Staples can be seen in his house-smoked hanger steak served with mashed potatoes, parsnips, and veal jus and his pan-seared sea scallops served over asparagus herb risotto with smoked bacon and blood-orange vinaigrette. Zoë is a great representative of the kind of fine dining experience that Seattle excels at, wherein a sleek, urban space, upscale cooking, and a hip crowd that enjoys people-watching come together to create not a pretentious, overblown, and overpriced spectacle, but a place that is unfailingly laid-back, comfortable, and satisfying. Reservations are recommended. ⊠ *2137 2nd Ave., Belltown* ☎ *206/256–2060* ⊕ *www.restaurantzoe. com* ☐ *AE, D, MC, V* ⊗ *No lunch.*

¢ ✕**Mike's East Coast Sandwiches.** Okay, so the name's a little obnoxious, but we can forgive Mike (who hails from Philadelphia) since he's offering office workers and hungry wanderers hearty grilled sandwiches that are the polar opposite of the polite panini. There is a sandwich called the East Coast, which is exactly the kind of cholesterol-bomb Italian sub that might make East Coasters homesick. However, unlike most East Coast delis, this one also has decent selections for vegetarians, and the bread used for all sandwiches is top-notch. There are a few simple tables inside, but good luck snagging one during the lunch rush. Mike's opens at 8 AM for breakfast. ⊠ *113 Cedar St., Belltown* ☎ *206/818–1744* ☐ *No credit cards* ⊗ *Closed Sun. No dinner.*

JAPANESE

$-$$$ ✕**Saito's Japanese Café and Bar.** Fusion won't fly at this Belltown restaurant, sushi bar, and lounge. Traditional appetizers include *kaarage* (marinated, breaded, and deep-fried chicken), *gyoza* (steamed pork dumplings), and *kakifry* (panfried oysters). Aside from the gorgeous sushi and sashimi, there are many other items to consider, including the *unajyu* (broiled freshwater eel with a tangy sweet sauce) and *salmon misozuke* (brushed with red miso, baked slowly, and served with caramelized turnips). The full bar stocks more than 30 different sakes. Saito's is a tad fancier than the average sushi joint—the skylight's a nice touch—but it's tame compared to Belltown's trendy spots. There are a variety of seating options, but sushi buffs should plant themselves at the bar, where they can merely point to whatever looks good and perhaps even ask the chefs to improvise on a roll or two. ⊠ *2122 2nd Ave., Belltown* ☎ *206/728–1333* ⊕ *www.saitos-cafe.com* ☐ *AE, D, DC, MC, V* ⊗ *Closed Sun. and Mon. No lunch Sat.*

$-$$$ ✕**Shiro's.** Shiro Kashiba is the most famous sushi chef in Seattle; he's been in town for going on 40 years and he still takes the time to helm the sushi bar at his popular restaurant. If you get a seat in front of Shiro, don't be shy—this is one place where ordering *omakase* (chef's choice) is almost a must. Willfully unconcerned with atmosphere, this simple spot is a real curiosity amid Belltown's chic establishments, though it does seem to be charging Belltown prices for simpler pleasures like teriyaki and tempura dinners. Be forewarned that the place has a reputation for spotty table service. ⊠ *2401 2nd Ave., Belltown* ☎ *206/443–9844* ⊕ *www.shiros.com* ☐ *AE, MC, V* ☽ *No lunch.*

PACIFIC NORTHWEST

$$$–$$$$ ✕ **Cascadia.** Water flows over the "rain window," a 9-foot-long panel of glass, etched with a design of the Cascade mountain range, that separates the kitchen and the cherrywood-paneled dining room at this elegant restaurant. Chef Kerry Sear uses fresh regional produce, seafood, meat, and game to create memorable meals, which might include smoked Oregon Muscovy duck with pears and creamed collard greens, marinated sea bass with roasted potatoes and caviar dressing, or crab steak with chanterelles. Seven-course tasting menus ($55–$90) showcase the Northwest's culinary best. That said, most locals swing by Cascadia to snarf down delicious miniburgers at the bar or on the patio; happy hour is extremely popular. Sear occasionally offers tours of Pike Place Market followed by lunch at Cascadia, as well as one-day cooking classes. ⊠ *2328 1st Ave., Belltown* ☎ *206/448–8884* ⊕ *www.cascadiarestaurant.com* ⌂ *Reservations essential* ☐ *AE, DC, MC, V* ☽ *Closed Sun. No lunch.*

SEAFOOD

$$$–$$$$ ✕ **Six Seven.** Like the hotel that houses it, Six Seven would be noteworthy for its views alone—Elliott Bay and the Puget Sound are laid out before you, especially if you opt to dine at the café tables lining the deck (note that it can get windy out there). But it's not just sparkling blue water that brings

> ### WORD OF MOUTH
>
> "I really enjoyed Six Seven in the Edgewater Hotel. Fantastic food and service and a gorgeous view."
>
>   wyatt92

people in for pricey Asian-influenced seafood and chops. The dining room is done in the same country-cabin chic as the hotel, complete with natural-stone fireplaces and fake trees the likes of which you've never seen (the restaurant's central columns are wrapped in bark and have branches sticking out of them). The quality of the food is pretty consistent, and if you want views and seafood in a setting that's a little more elegant and serene than the touristy spots farther downtown, this is a good place to splurge. Lunch is a good deal—and you won't lose that view to the setting sun. If you're not a big spender, the restaurant also has a comfortable bar area with its own "snack" menu (roasted prawns, calamari, crab cakes, Waygu hamburgers, and the like) and well-poured specialty drinks that really pack a wallop. Though you won't necessarily be right up against the glass, you'll be able to see the water from the bar. ⊠ *In Edgewater Hotel, 2411 Alaskan Way, Pier*

67, Belltown ☎*206/728–7000* ⊕*www.edgewaterhotel.com* ▤*AE, DC, MC, V.*

\$\$–\$\$\$ ✕**Etta's Seafood.** Tom Douglas's restaurant near Pike Place Market has a slightly whimsical design and views of Victor Steinbrueck Park. Etta's is the happy medium between the pricey, sleek Downtown restaurants and the cheap yet lovable holes-in-the-wall like Emmett Watson's. The Dungeness crab cakes have always been one of Douglas's signatures and they are a must, as are the various Washington oysters on the half shell. Brunch, served weekends, is the best meal here—it always includes zesty seafood omelets, but the chef also does justice to French toast, eggs and bacon, and Mexican-influenced breakfast dishes. ⊠*2020 Western Ave., Belltown* ☎*206/443–6000* ⊕*www.tomdoug-las.com/ettas* ▤*AE, D, DC, MC, V.*

★ **\$\$–\$\$\$** ✕**Flying Fish.** Chef-owner Christine Keff got the idea for Flying Fish on a trip to Thailand; she was impressed by the simplicity and quality of the seafood dishes grilled up in beachside restaurants. Even after a decade, the Flying Fish has stayed true to its inspiration: the fish is some of the freshest you'll find in Seattle, every ingredient is organic, and the dishes, while inventive, never get too busy. The menu changes daily, but you'll often find seafood and shellfish prepared with Thai curries and seasonings, and you'll always have the option of the delicious no-nonsense fried chicken. This joint is always jumping; dinner reservations are strongly recommended. ⊠*2234 1st Ave., Belltown* ☎*206/728–8595* ⊕*http://flyingfish.com* ▤*AE, DC, MC, V* ☻*No lunch weekends.*

STEAK HOUSE

\$\$\$–\$\$\$\$ ✕**El Gaucho.** Dress to impress here—you don't want to be outclassed by the waistcoated waitstaff that coolly navigates the packed floor of this retro steak house. El Gaucho serves some of the city's most basic, most satisfying fare in a swanky, expansive room. For the complete show, order the items prepared tableside. From the flaming lamb shish kebab to the cool Caesar salad (possibly the city's best), the virtuoso presentation seems to make everything taste better. Ritzy yet comfortable, El Gaucho makes you relax no matter how stressful your day. Of course, you may get heart palpitations once again when you get the bill—by virtue of its entrée sticker shock alone it's likely the most expensive restaurant in Seattle (the smallest steak on the menu is \$39). ⊠*2505 1st Ave., Belltown* ☎*206/728–1337* ⊕*www.elgaucho.com* ⌨*Reservations essential* ▤*AE, MC, V* ☻*No lunch.*

QUEEN ANNE

AMERICAN

★ **\$\$\$–\$\$\$\$** ✕**Canlis.** Canlis has been setting the standard for fancy living since the 1950s. And although there are no longer kimono-clad waitresses, the food and the views overlooking Lake Union are still remarkable. Besides the famous steaks, there are equally famous Quilcene Bay oysters and fresh fish in season. Every year since 1997 Canlis has been the recipient of *Wine Spectator* magazine's Grand Award for its wine list and service. Note that if you want a table on a Friday or Saturday, you should make your reservation at least three weeks in advance.

✉ *2576 Aurora Ave. N, Queen Anne* ☎ *206/283–3313* ⊕ *www.can-lis.com* ⌂ *Reservations essential. Jacket required* ⊟ *AE, DC, MC, V* ⊘ *Closed Sun. No lunch.*

★ **$$–$$$** ✕ **Veil.** Everything in Veil is white, from the leather banquettes to the curtains. It's not the most inspired design choice—didn't this trend come and go in New York about five years ago?—but different textures and little pink lights keep the place from looking too washed out. It's also very different for Seattle, which has managed to bring out the inner curmudgeon in every Seattleite, many of whom seem willing to ignore how outstanding the food is to decry Veil's attempts to be chic and trendy. But Chef Shannon Galusha is an alumni of French Laundry and her restrained menu has allowed Veil to survive both its own hype and the barbs thrown by locals. The braised short rib, for example, comes lightly sauced and punctuated by two perfectly round, crispy, buttery croquettes; the presentation is lovely, but nothing distracts you from the meat, which is so tender you could eat it with a spoon. Desserts are slightly more whimsical than entrées (for example, a banana-and-Nutella crepe with red banana ice cream) and are an absolute must. Don't be disappointed by the small portions—every bite will be good (and extremely rich). Dine midweek if you want quiet and the full attention of your server. Reservations are essential on Friday and Saturday. There is a separate lounge that offers a small-plates menu. ✉ *555 Aloha St., Queen Anne* ☎ *206/216–0600* ⊕ *www.veilrestaurant.com* ⊟ *AE, MC, V* ⊘ *Closed Mon. No lunch.*

$–$$ ✕ **Crow.** It's easy to dismiss Crow as an amalgam of too many recent trends: it's got the converted warehouse space complete with artfully exposed ductwork, the modern comfort food menu, and a list of shareable small plates. But this bistro has proved it has staying power and is fast becoming a neighborhood institution. The food is the main component of locals' loyalty; share some appetizers and then move on to the pan-roasted chicken wrapped in prosciutto or the wonderful house lasagna with Italian sausage. ✉ *823 5th Ave. N, Queen Anne* ☎ *206/283–8800* ⊟ *MC, V* ⊘ *No lunch.*

$–$$ ✕ **Five Spot.** Up the hill from Seattle Center, the unpretentious Five Spot has a regional American menu that makes a new stop every four months or so—Key West, Little Italy, New Orleans, Santa Fe, and the fictitious "Springfield" from The Simpsons are just a few. At the restaurant's cousins, the Coastal Kitchen in Capitol Hill, and Endolyne Joe's in West Seattle, the same rotating menu strategy applies, with more-international flavor but equally satisfying results. This is a popular spot for Sunday brunch. ✉ *1502 Queen Anne Ave. N, Queen Anne* ☎ *206/285–7768* ⊕ *www.chowfoods.com/five* ⊟ *MC, V.*

INTERNATIONAL DISTRICT & PIONEER SQUARE

CHINESE

$ ✕ **Hing Loon.** Food magic happens in this eatery with bright fluorescent lighting, shiny linoleum floors, and large, round, laminate tables. Although many Chinese chefs may head to Linyen after hours, this is where they purportedly come for noodles. The walls are covered with menu specials handwritten (in Cantonese and English) on paper place mats. Employ the friendly waitstaff to help make your selections.

Dishes of particular note are the stuffed eggplant, crispy fried chicken, *Funn* noodles, and any of the seafood offerings. ⊠*628 S. Weller St., International District* ☎*206/682–2828* ☐*DC, MC, V.*

$ ✕**Linyen.** If it weren't in the International District, you'd consider this elegant restaurant an upscale American cafe. But don't let the interior decoration fool you: the first-rate food is authentically Asian. This is the place where Chinese chefs come to eat late at night after they've closed their own kitchens. Favorite dishes include the honey walnut prawns and the Peking duck. ⊠*424 7th Ave. S, International District* ☎*206/622–8181* ☐*AE, MC, V.*

ITALIAN

¢–$ ✕**Salumi.** The kind chef-owner Armandino Batali (father of famed New
Fodor'sChoice York chef Mario Batali) doles out samples of his fabulous house-cured
★ meats while you wait for a table (which you must be willing to share) at this postage-stamp of a place. Order a meatball, oxtail, sausage, or lamb sandwich. The house wine served at lunch is strong, inexpensive, and good. Most people do opt for takeout, though, the line for which goes out the door. Note that Salumi is only open from 11 to 4. ⊠*309 3rd Ave. S, Pioneer Square* ☎*206/621–8772* ☐*AE, D, DC, MC, V* ☉*Closed Sat.–Mon.*

JAPANESE

¢–$ ✕**Maneki.** Maneki has been in its current location since the 1940s and although it's no longer a hidden gem that caters to in-the-know locals and chefs from other Japanese restaurants in the area, the food isn't any less authentic. The sushi is very good, but just as popular are the small plates meant to lay a foundation for lots of sake consumption. Rice-paper lamps and screens add a little bit of old Japan to the otherwise uninspiring space. Larger parties can reserve a tatami room. This place is a mob scene on weekends—don't even think about coming here without a reservation. ⊠*304 6th Ave. S, International District* ☎*622–2631* ⊕*www.manekirestaurant.com* ☐*V* ☉*Closed Mon. No lunch.*

PAN-ASIAN

★ ¢–$ ✕**Uwajimaya Village Food Court.** Not only an outstanding grocery and gift shop, Uwajimaya also has a hoppin' food court offering a quick tour of Asian cuisines at lunch-counter prices. For Japanese or Chinese, the deli offers sushi, teriyaki, and barbecued duck. For Vietnamese food, try the fresh spring rolls, served with hot chili sauce, at Saigon Bistro. Shilla has Korean grilled beef and kim chee stew, and there are Filipino *lumpia* (spring rolls) to be found at Inay's Kitchen. The Honeymoon Tea Shop sells pearl tea, a cold drink served with a fat straw for sucking up the tapioca balls at the bottom of the cup. ⊠*600 5th Ave. S, International District* ☎*206/624–6248* ☐*MC, V.*

VIETNAMESE

★ ¢–$ ✕**Green Leaf.** Locals pack this friendly, cute cafe for an expansive menu of fresh, well-prepared Vietnamese staples. The quality of the food—the *pho*, spring rolls, *bahn xeo* (the Vietnamese version of an omelet), and lemongrass chicken are just a few standouts—and reasonable prices would be enough to make it an instant I.D. favorite, but Green Leaf also proves you don't have to sacrifice ambience to get cheap, authentic Asian food in Seattle. The walls are painted a soft yellow; you'll find bamboo embellishments on lighting fixtures, tables, and chairs; and instead of glaring fluorescents, you'll get dim mood lighting in the evening. The staff greets everyone as though they're regulars. And there are plenty of regulars, enough to fill the tiny 10-table eatery, so reservations for dinner are recommended. ✉ *418 8th Ave. S, International District* ☎ *206/340–1388* ▤ *MC, V.*

CAPITOL HILL & ENVIRONS

AMERICAN

★ **$$–$$$** ✕ **Crush.** Crush could describe the feeling many people have for this pretty restaurant, but it could also describe the state of the tiny foyer on a Saturday night. It's in a converted two-story house (there are dining rooms on both levels), but that's rarely apparent—the beige-and-brown palette and the anachronistic '60s space-age white chairs look like they belong in a Downtown space. The food is very tasty, but it is also very heavy, and therefore not always appropriate for hot summer days. The braised short ribs are Crush's signature dish, and they're so good that as far as we're concerned, the menu could begin and end right there. However, seafood dishes are also quite competent, if not as outstanding as at Union. Some of the desserts are overly ambitious, but others are as out of this world as those strange chairs. The place doesn't seem to have one particular demographic—you'll see cranky gourmands, couples, Belltown girls in beaded halter tops, Madison Park families, Capitol Hill hipsters, and so on. Despite the clamor for a table on the weekend, servers remain serene and you'll never be rushed out the door. ✉ *2319 E. Madison St., Madison Park* ☎ *206/302–7874* ⊕ *www.chefjasonwilson.com* ⌂ *Reservations essential* ▤ *AE, MC, V* ☾ *Closed Sun. and Mon. No lunch.*

★ **$** ✕ **Crave.** Upscale comfort food is almost as popular in this city as Asian fusion, and Crave gets the gold star for its wonderful takes on American standards, its cool industrial-chic space, and its espresso bar that opens at 7 AM. Grilled cheese is made with sharp cheddar, apple slices, and sourdough bread. Mac and cheese has fontina cheese and shiitake mushrooms; the smoked paprika chicken comes with a spring pea–and–hominy succotash. On weekends, brunch replaces lunch service; try a pomegranate mimosa with your French toast or omelet. The dining room is tiny and fills up fast; service suffers a bit when it gets busy. One note of warning: though dining here is usually a pleasant experience, don't expect any of your fellow customers to be in a good mood—the crowd is mixed, but is often heavy with angst-ridden hipsters discussing their relationship problems. ✉ *1621 12th Ave., Capitol Hill* ☎ *206/388–0526* ⊕ *www.cravefood.com* ▤ *MC, V.*

¢ ✕ **Dick's Drive-In.** This local chain of orange hamburger stands has changed little since the 1950s. The fries are hand-cut, the shakes are hand-dipped (i.e., made with hard ice cream), and the burgers are just great. The top-of-the-line burger, Dick's Deluxe ($2.20), has two beef patties, American cheese, lettuce, and onions, and is slathered in their special tartar sauce, but most folks swear by the frill-free plain cheeseburger ($1.30). Open until 2 AM daily, these drive-ins are as popular with families and students as they are with folks girding themselves against hangovers after a night out on the town. The original Dick's is the Wallingford branch, but the Capitol Hill one is more of a local landmark, thanks to its visibility and to the freak show it becomes after the bars let out on weekends. ✉*1115 Broadway E, Capitol Hill* ☎*206/323–1300* ▭*No credit cards* ✉*111 N.E. 45th St., Wallingford* ☎*206/632–5125* ✉*500 Queen Anne Ave. N, Queen Anne* ☎*206/285–5155* ▭*No credit cards.*

ECLECTIC

$–$$ ✕**Dinette.** For Dinette only, we will abandon our skepticism regarding gimmicks: their main claim to fame is fancy toast and we love them dearly for it. Granted, the clams with chorizo, the gnocchi, and the daily seafood specials are all very good, but it's memories of toast that linger. A focus on seasonal ingredients means that the toppings on said toast change regularly but they're always mouthwatering: broccoli rabe with red peppers and fontina; anchovies with arugula and Serrano ham; or Gorgonzola and walnuts. The space couldn't be cozier. Dimly lighted but not dark and brooding, Dinette is all soft blues and creams and gold-foil details. ✉*1514 E. Olive Way, Capitol Hill* ☎*206/328–2282* ⊕*www.dinetteseattle.com* ▭*MC, V* ⊘*Closed Sun. and Mon. No lunch.*

FRENCH

$$ ✕**Crémant.** Chef-owner Scott Emerick's homage to traditional French

FodorsChoice country cooking is, interestingly enough, a modern, almost spare
★ conglomerate of grays and whites—much of the gray coming from unadorned concrete walls. The menu, on the other hand, is made up almost entirely of the classics. It'll be mighty difficult to resist ordering the steak frites as you watch piles of golden fries being whisked to other tables, but nothing tops the savory bouillabaisse. The roasted marrow bones appetizer, a rarity in Seattle, may be hard to stomach visually, but it makes such a wonderfully tender and salty spread that it'll be hard to go back to simply buttering your bread. Rich desserts and an excellent cheese selection ensure that you'll linger even longer. Dining at Crémant can be either be romantic or casual and jovial, depending on the night and the company you're with. The crowd is fairly mixed, with graying foodies in dress shirts sitting next to denim-clad guys who look like they just finished their barista shifts. ✉*1423 34th Ave., Madrona* ☎*206/322–4600* ⊕*www.cremantseattle.com* ⌁*Reservations essential* ▭ *MC, V* ⊘*No lunch.*

★ ¢–$ ✕**Café Presse.** The owners of Le Pichet (see above) have brought their casual French bistro food to the Hill, bestowing the city with a restaurant that is at once trendy and laid-back, immensely satisfying and surprisingly affordable. From the breakfast rush to the wee hours (it's open until 2 am daily), Presse serves up a simple menu of sandwiches (grilled or on baguettes), pomme frites, soups, and salads; there are a few entrées, such as Penn Cove mussels, roasted half chicken, and smoked pork chops for anyone seeking a more complex sit-down meal. The space is Parisian hip via the Northwest (check out the impressive wood-beam ceiling), with the Hill's creative crowd adding to its indie cred. There's a casual dining room with lime-color café tables and exposed brick walls in back, but the front of the house, with its bustling bar area, and floor-to-ceiling windows, is where the action is. ⊠ *1117 12th Ave., Capitol Hill* ☎206/709–7674 ▤ *MC, V.*

PACIFIC NORTHWEST

★ $$$–$$$$ ✕ **Lark.** A barnlike wood-beam ceiling and a few white tablecloths thrown over dark wood create a rustic-elegant venue for 2007 James Beard Award-winning chef John Sundstrom's regional cuisine. Along with Northwest seasonal favorites (sautéed wild mushrooms, local oysters), you'll find French-inflected fare (mussels with bacon, apple cider, and cream; seared foie gras with quince) among the more than 30 selections on the small-plates menu. The wine list is notable, too, both for its variety and quality. The cozy vibe and impress-by-paying prices have made this a favorite date spot for years. ⊠ *926 12th Ave., Capitol Hill* ☎206/323–5275 w *www.larkseattle.com* ⌧*No reservations* ▤*MC, V* ⊗*Closed Mon. No lunch.*

★ ✕ **Sitka & Spruce.** Unceremoniously plunked in a strip mall in the decid-
$–$$ edly nontrendy Eastlake neighborhood is one of the city's best ambassadors of regional cuisine. The menu changes daily, but of one thing you can be sure—whatever's on your plate either came from Washington State or the Pacific Ocean next door. Seasonal treats like morels and fiddlehead ferns are given lots of attention when available. Entrées, which can range from fluke ceviche to organic tri-tip served with piles of fresh greens, can be ordered as small plates to keep costs low and sampling at a maximum. The dining room is simple—bright green walls and bookshelves stacked behind a bar that looks like it was constructed out of wine boxes and a bit of slate are about the only adornment. It's also tiny, so waits can be long, and if you don't score one of the five individual tables, you might end up making new friends at the communal table. ⊠ *2238 Eastlake Ave E, Eastlake* ☎206/324–0662 ⊕ *www.sitkaandspruce.com* ⌧*Reservations not accepted* ▤*MC, V* ⊗*Closed Sun. No dinner Mon. and Tues.*

SEAFOOD

$–$$ ✕ **Coastal Kitchen.** Local restaurant gurus Jeremy Hardy and Peter Levy hit on a surefire formula with their hearty seafood meals prepared according to a rotating menu that highlights the cuisines of such far-flung coastal places as Oaxaca, Vietnam, and Barcelona, to name just a few. The focus changes quarterly, and experiments don't always work, but you can't knock their adventurous spirit. Besides, you always have the option to forgo the specials and order perfectly prepared fish fillets—lightly seasoned and either grilled or pan-seared—and there are never complaints about the roast chicken with creamy mashed potatoes or the marinated pork chop. Nice enough for a date but laid-back enough to bring the kids, Coastal Kitchen has many loyal regulars and it anchors the 15th Avenue strip. ⊠*429 15th Ave. E, Capitol Hill* ☎206/322–1145 ⊕*www.chowfoods.com/coastal* ▤*MC, V.*

THAI

¢–$ ✗**Jamjuree.** Jamjuree has become the Hill's go-to spot for tasty Thai food in a place that is casual without being a hole in the wall. It's a basic but well-coordinated restaurant with wooden booths and tables; a counter with retro-looking bar stools and a few parasols and statues adds a tiny bit of flair to an otherwise restrained space. You'll find all the standard curries and noodle dishes here, but before you automatically order pad thai, consider the daily specials, which are more inventive and usually good. ⊠*509 15th Ave. E, Capitol Hill* ☎*206/323–4255* ⊕*www.jamjuree.com* ▭*AE, MC, V.*

VEGETARIAN

$–$$ ✗**Cafe Flora.** This sweet restaurant off the beaten path in the leafy Madison Park neighborhood offers vegetarian and vegan food for grownups who want more than grilled tofu but don't want to splurge at Carmelita in Greenwood. The menu changes frequently, though the chefs tend to keep things simple, offering dishes like black-bean burgers with spicy aioli, polenta with leeks and spinach, and the very popular "Oaxaca tacos" (corn tortillas filled with potatoes and four types of cheese) at both lunch and dinner. Make sure you sit in the "Atrium," which has a stone fountain, skylight, slate floors, and garden-style café tables and chairs—the other dining room is nice, too, but it's more generic and reminiscent of the kind of upscale coffeeshop you'd find on the ground floor of a mid-range chain hotel. Brunch is very popular—great waffles made with fresh seasonal fruits—but the hectic scene kind of mars the serenity of the place, which is an important part of the equation. ⊠*2901 E. Madison St., Madison Park* ☎*206/325–9100* ⊕*www.cafeflora.com* ⌲*Reservations not accepted* ▭*MC, V.*

FREMONT

AMERICAN

$$ ✗**35th Street Bistro.** The 35th Street Bistro replaced the vaunted Still Life Cafe, which was the epitome of all things Fremont back when the hood was more hippie than yuppie. Although the white tablecloths, good wine list, and the generic bistro-ness of the place suggest that Downtown has moved in uptown, the ghosts of the Still Life must still linger—this place is as casual as some of Fremont's less-flashy eateries, service goes beyond warm into personable, and organic foods populate the menu. The menu is seasonal, but roasted chicken, lamb porterhouse, and fresh seafood are usually on it. ⊠*709 N. 35th St., Fremont* ☎*206/547–9850* ⊕*www.35bistro.com* ▭*V* ☽*No lunch Mon.*

CUBAN

$ ✗**Paseo.** The centerpiece of Lorenzo Lorenzo's slim Cuban-influenced Fodor'sChoice menu is the mouthwatering Midnight Cuban sandwich. The marinated ★ pork sandwich, topped with sautéed onions and served on a chewy baguette, is doused with an amazing sauce (the ingredients of which are known only by Lorenzo) that keeps folks coming back for more. The entrées are also delicious, from scallops with cilantro to prawns in a spicy red sauce. This place is so small, it's more like a glorified lunch truck than a sit-down eatery. There are a few tables, but don't count on

Where to Eat North & West of Downtown

3

getting a seat—Paseo gets so busy the line usually snakes way out the door, and most people opt for takeout. ⊠ *4225 Fremont Ave. N, Fremont* ☎ *206/545–7440* ⊟ *No credit cards* ⊙ *Closed Sun and Mon.*

SUSHI

¢ ✕**Blue C Sushi.** Black banquettes, young sushi chefs, and a giant projection screen showing quirky Japanese TV shows and music videos make Blue C suitable for discerning hipsters, but it has become a true neighborhood haunt, attracting families, friends, and first dates. Despite its trendy interior, this place is lots of fun—just try suppressing a grin as colorful plates of nigiri, sashimi, sushi rolls, and tempura dishes chug past you on a conveyor belt. Simply grab whatever looks good. The color of the plate indicates the price of the dish; your server tallies your bill when you're done. This place gets packed on weekends, but there's an upstairs bar to wait in or you can opt for takeout. The daily happy hour (4–6) is one of the best deals in town—you can get $1 sushi in the bar, with the purchase of one beverage. ⊠ *3411 Fremont Ave. N, Fremont* ☎ *206/633–3411* ⊠ *University Village, 4601 26th Ave. NE, University District* ☎ *206/525–4601* ⊕ *www.bluecsushi.com* ⌦ *Reservations not accepted* ⊟ *MC, V.*

BALLARD

AMERICAN

★ $–$$$ ✕**Wild Mountain Café.** For both an off-the-beaten-path experience and a healthy dose of the West Coast approach to life, take a detour to this adorable purple house. You won't get more of a "like dining in a friend's living room" feeling anywhere else—no rooms were gutted in the house's remodel, so you actually are dining in the living room . . . and the den . . . and the guest room. As for the food, Wild Mountain may never be one of the city's top restaurants, but it serves consistently good and simple American fare made with fresh, organic ingredients, including comfort-food favorites like mac and cheese and a version of chicken Parmesan with panko as breading. Breakfast includes a variety of scrambles, tahini-stuffed French toast, and, of course, homemade granola. **This may be the most sustainable restaurant in Seattle—almost all materials used to create the space (including the kitchen wares) are salvaged, secondhand, or reclaimed, and kitchen scraps go into a compost bin that in turn feeds the restaurant's garden.** ⊠ *1408 N.W. 85th St., Ballard* ☎ *206/297–9453* ⊕ *www.wildmtncafe. com* ⊟ *MC, V.*

¢–$ ✕**Hi-Life.** The Hi-Life is the most versatile restaurant in Ballard. In a converted firehouse, the echoey space has the familiar feeling of a TGI Friday's, which makes it a safe bet for families, but it also has personality enough to appeal to everyone from yuppies sending messages on their Blackberrys to tattooed hipsters nursing hangovers with heaping portions of rich French toast. From morning until night, the Hi-Life has something to satisfy—you can get small plates, full entrées, wood-fired pizzas, breakfast until 3 PM, and so on. The standards are done very well—salads and burgers never disappoint—but the kitchen can also handle more-creative dishes like chorizo-and-shrimp empanadas and breaded oxtail with marscarpone polenta. Note that Hi-Life does close for two hours between lunch and dinner from 3 PM to 5 PM. ⊠ *5425*

Russell Ave. NW, Ballard ☎*206/784–7272* ⊕*www.chowfoods.com/ hilife* ⊟*MC, V.*

FRENCH

★ $$$$ ✕**Le Gourmand.** On an unattractive corner somewhere halfway between Ballard and Fremont is one of the city's definitive French restaurants. The intimate, rustic-chic spot doesn't quite know if it's an unassuming bistro or a romantic, special-occasion dining room, but it sure knows how to charge for the experience. This will be one of the most expensive meals you'll have in the city, but if chef-owner Bruce Naftaly and staff are on their game, it will also be one of the best. Naftaly uses classic French techniques and locally grown ingredients to create stunning dishes such as his roast duckling with black currant sauce (using homemade cassis); or king salmon poached in champagne and gooseberry sauce. Pastry chef Sara Naftaly's dessert menu might include a flourless chocolate cake with raspberries and almond crème anglaise. Though the tasting menus seem like a good deal, patrons seem to prefer ordering à la carte. ■ TIP→If you don't want to pay sky-high prices for the full experience, go next door to Sambar and order from an abbreviated bar menu. ⊠*425 N.W. Market St., Ballard* ☎*206/784–3463* ⌐*Reservations essential* ⊟*AE, MC, V.*

ITALIAN

$$ ✕**Volterra.** For those who favor Italian cooking over French, Volterra has eclipsed Le Gourmand as Ballard's special-occasion restaurant. It's another victim of the deep-red-walls syndrome that Seattle can't seem to rid itself of, but with its black-and-white accents, skylight, and large framed photos of Italy, it's very attractive nonetheless. The restaurant gets the most attention for dishes like wild boar tenderloin and fresh seafood baked in parchment, but it's not too taken with itself to offer something as simple as linguine in clam sauce. The long wine list features many Tuscan wines, as well as selections from other Italian regions. ⊠*5411 Ballard Ave. NW, Ballard* ☎*206/789–5100* ⊕*www. volterrarestaurant.com* ⊟*AE, DC, MC, V* ⊟*No lunch.*

MEXICAN

★ ¢–$ ✕**La Carta de Oaxaca.** True to its name, this restaurant serves traditional Mexican cooking, with Oaxacan accents. The mole negro is a must, served over chicken or pork; another standout is the *albondigas* (a spicy vegetable soup with meatballs). The menu is small plates, which works out to your advantage because you won't have to choose just one savory dish. The small space is sleek: the open kitchen is enclosed by a stainless-steel bar, the walls are covered in gorgeous black-and-white photos wedged together like puzzle pieces, and the light wood tables and black chairs and banquettes look more Scandinavian than Mexican. The place gets very crowded on weekends, and stays busy until late, though if you have a small party you usually don't have to wait too long for a table. ☎*206/782–8722* ⊕*www.lacartadeoaxaca. com* ⊟*AE, DC, MC, V* ◷*Closed Sun. No lunch Mon.*

¢–$ ✕**Senor Moose.** Before you resign yourself to waiting in line for brunch at the Dish Café (the most obvious choice for brunch in the area), head a little farther down Leary Way into Ballard to Senor Moose. Looking like a cross between a truck-stop diner and a Tex-Mex restaurant, this tiny café has outstanding breakfast options, including traditional favorites from every region of Mexico. Wait for a space in the tiny dining room or belly up to the counter and read the paper (someone will have one to share) or just watch the frenetic activity as everything from soup to salsa is made from scratch. Lunch and dinner are just as good as *desayunos,* with delectable pork *carnitas* and chorizo from the state of Michoacan being favorites. ⊠ *5242 Leary Ave. NW, Ballard* ☎ *206/784–5568* ▤ *AE, MC, V* ⊘ *No dinner Sun. and Mon.*

SEAFOOD

$$–$$$$ ✕ **Ray's Boathouse.** The view of Shilshole Bay might be the big draw here, but the seafood is also impeccably fresh and well prepared. Perennial favorites include broiled salmon, Kasu sake–marinated cod, Dungeness crab, and regional oysters on the half shell. Ray's has a split personality: there's a fancy dining room downstairs (reservations essential) and a casual café and bar upstairs (reservations not accepted). In warm weather you can sit on the deck outside the café and watch the parade of fishing boats, tugs, and pleasure craft floating past, almost right below your table. Be forewarned that during happy hour (or early-bird special time) in high season the café feels extremely touristy—jam-packed with sour-faced retirees and frazzled parents dragging kids around by the elbows—and service suffers greatly because of the crowds. ⊠ *6049 Seaview Ave. NW, Ballard* ☎ *206/789–3770* ⊕ *www.rays.com* ▤ *AE, DC, MC, V.*

WALLINGFORD

KOREAN

$$ ✕ **Joule.** Joule injects some life into Seattle's saturated fusion-cooking scene by tempering savory Korean staples with French and American influences. Some dishes, like whole fish on the bone with sweet and sour soy glaze, are predominantly Asian; others, like salty prawns in charmoula butter, are more European. But most exciting are those that tow the line—a Korean version of chili dresses up black beans and pork with soy paste and pickled ginger. The small space, with its chocolate, mustard, and cream tones, and delicate bird paintings, is both cheerful and chic—flickering candles on dark wood tables draw in whispering couples, while solo diners sit at the bar to watch the husband-and-wife chef team at work in the open kitchen. ⊠ *1913 N. 45th St., Wallingford* ☎ *206/632–1913* ⊕ *www.joulerestaurant.com* ▤ *MC, V* ⊘ *Closed Mon. No lunch.*

PACIFIC NORTHWEST

★ $–$$$ ✕ **Tilth.** The city was so excited about Tilth, it made *Seattle Metropolitan Magazine*'s annual "Best Restaurants" issue mere weeks after opening. A certified organic restaurant (a real rarity; it's incredibly difficult for a restaurant to get certification), Tilth serves up wonderful, inventive dishes that can be had as small plates or full entrées—the mini–duck burgers and pork belly deserve special mentions. It's not the sort of place you'd expect to find on Wallingford's busy commercial strip: a Craftsman house, painted a leafy green, has been lovingly spruced up. The tiny dining room—backed by an open kitchen—occupies the ground floor and has an accidental elegance. Though overall dining here is a wonderful experience, Tilth has two notable drawbacks: the service can be a bit snotty—a big no-no in laid-back Wallingford—and the acoustics are terrible (be prepared to shout across your tiny table if you dine during peak hours). Tilth serves brunch on the weekends. ⊠ *1411 N. 45th St., Wallingford* ☎ *206/633–0801* ⊕ *www.tilthrestaurant.com* ⌕ *Reservations essential* ═MC, V ⊘ *Closed Mon. No lunch.*

PIZZA

☾ $ ✕**Tutta Bella.** It's very hard to find good pizza in Seattle—even those spots deemed the best in the city serve sad approximations of the classic slice. So, better to abandon the search for the cheap slice and go the gourmet route. Tutta Bella serves authentic Neopolitan-style pizzas that are made with organic local and imported ingredients and baked in a wood-fired oven. Crusts are thin but wonderfully chewy and sauces are light and tangy. They go easy on the cheese, so be sure to order extra cheese if that's what you're craving. The salads are excellent, too. Takeout is available, but many people opt to sit down in the spacious dining room, which has more of a café vibe than that of a typical pizza house. Tutta Bella is very family friendly, but it's also nice enough to serve as a first-date spot, and as the evening progresses you'll see plenty of couples and groups of friends sipping wine and beer as they enjoy their pies. The place gets packed on weekends, and although there is a small lot adjacent to the building, finding parking can be a problem when it fills up. ⊠ *4411 Stone Way N, Wallingford* ☎ *206/633–3800* ⊕ *www.tuttabellapizza.com* ═*AE, DC, MC, V.*

THAI

$–$$ ✕**May Thai.** May (named after the owner) is in a reconstructed tradi-
Fodor'sChoice tional teak home, which sticks out like a sore thumb (or a wonderful
★ beacon) on an otherwise uninspiring strip in Wallingford. The bar on the lower floor is downright sexy—dim, painted in reds and purples, with comfortable booths and candlelit corners. But to really focus on the food, head up the curving staircase to the elegant dining room. Though many people are quick to dismiss upscale or expensive Thai food as "inauthentic," that charge is completely unfounded here (when they say spicy, they mean spicy) and it's a pleasure to get a menu that is much more concise than at cheaper places, and food that is much more artfully prepared. The pad thai, usually a glutinous, flavorless mess at most places, is complex and comes with some of its ingredients laid out in a banana leaf; you mix them in as you see fit. The *grapao kaidow* (meat sautéed in a garlic basil sauce accompanied by a fried egg over rice) is excellent; and the tart, spicy *tom ka* soups, whether made with shrimp or chicken, are the best in the city. Don't miss the specialty cocktails made with fresh juices. ⊠ *1612 N. 45th St., Wallingford* ☎ *206/675–0037* ═*AE, DC, MC, V*

AMERICAN

$ ✕ **Portage Bay Cafe.** This lovely breakfast and lunch spot is a great alternative if you want to avoid busy University Avenue. Everything's organic here, from the produce piled on the breakfast bar to the breads used to make amazing French toast. At lunch, you'll find sandwiches, salads, and burgers, as well as a few fancier dishes like crab cakes, catfish and ahi fillets, and pork chops. ⊠*4130 Roosevelt Ave. NE, University District* ☎*206/547–8230* ⊕*www.portagebaycafe.com* ▭*AE, DC, MC, V* ☾*No dinner.*

INDIAN

$ ✕ **Bengal Tiger.** Though the immensely popular Taste of India (down the street at the corner of 55th) has a much better ambience—no thought has been put into decor at this no-frills restaurant—Bengal Tiger has become the new neighborhood favorite thanks to its authentic (which often means very spicy) dishes. Most of the menu will yield familiar words—naan, tandoor, vindaloo, tikka masala—but there are a few East Indian items not normally found in curry houses dominated by northern Indian specialties. The lunch buffet is $8. A few specialty dishes require 2- to 24-hour advance notice; check the Web site for details. ⊠*6510 Roosevelt Way, University District* ☎*206/985–0041* ⊕*www.bengaltigerwa.com* ▭*MC, V.*

THAI

¢–$ ✕ **Thai Tom.** This might be the cheapest Thai restaurant in town, but rock-bottom prices aren't the only reason this place is always packed—the food is delicious, authentic, and spicy (two stars is usually pretty hot). The garlic chicken is one of the chef's favorite dishes, so it's not surprising that it rates high among the customers. Pad thai is rich and flavorful instead of oily. Tables can be hard to come by during the dinner rush, but there's usually space at the counter that lines the open kitchen. ⊠*4543 University Ave., University District* ☎*206/548–9548* ▭*No credit cards.*

ITALIAN

$$–$$$ ✕ **Cafe Juanita.** There are so many ways for an expensive, "destination" restaurant to go overboard, making itself nothing more than a special-occasion spectacle, but Cafe Juanita manages to get everything just right. The space is refined without being too designy or too posh, and the food, much of which has a northern Italian influence, is also perfectly balanced: you won't find needlessly flashy fusion cooking or heavy sauces that obliterate subtle flavors. If you've ever had a bad experience with lamb, you must order it here; one bite of the tender saddle of Oregon lamb will expunge all memories of tough wedding entrées or greasy falafel-stand horrors. The daily fish specials are also worth the plunge, especially when the menu's featuring whole fish. Even the "seasonal fruit" offering—so often the most boring item on a dessert menu—is finally done some justice here: instead of being smothered in too-sweet creams or syrups, local strawberries are marinated in

Fodor'sChoice
★

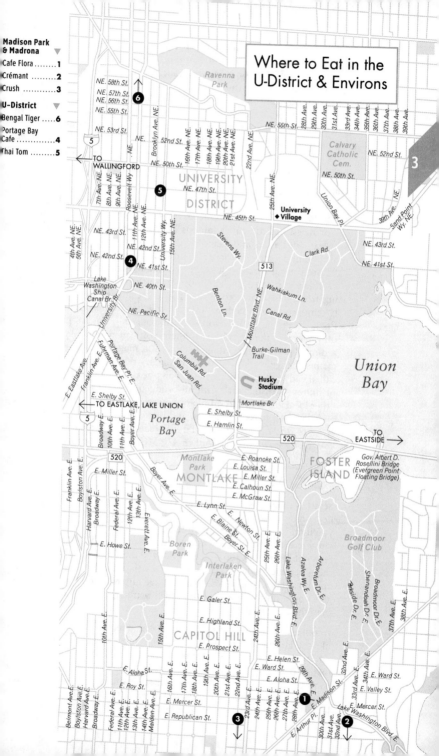

Where to Eat in the U-District & Environs

Ravenna Park

NE. 58th St.
NE. 57th St.
NE. 56th St.
NE. 55th St.

NE. 53rd St.

NE. 55th St.

Calvary Catholic Cem.

NE. 52nd St.

TO WALLINGFORD

NE. 50th St.

NE. 50th St.

UNIVERSITY

NE. 47th St.

DISTRICT

University Village

NE. 45th St.

NE. 43rd St.

NE. 43rd St.

NE. 42nd St.

Stevens Wy.

Clark Rd.

NE. 41st St.

NE. 41st St.

Lake Washington Ship Canal Br. Br.

NE. 40th St.

513

Benton Ln.

Wahkiakum Ln.

NE. Pacific St.

Canal Rd.

Columbia Rd.

Burke-Gilman Trail

San Juan Rd.

Husky Stadium

Union Bay

TO EASTLAKE, LAKE UNION

E. Shelby St.

E. Shelby St.

Mortlake Br.

E. Hamlin St.

Portage Bay

520

TO EASTSIDE

Montlake Park

E. Roanoke St.

FOSTER ISLAND

Gov. Albert D. Rosellini Bridge (Evergreen Point Floating Bridge)

520

E. Miller St.

E. Louisa St.

MONTLAKE

E. Miller St.

E. Calhoun St.

E. McGraw St.

E. Lynn St.

E. Newton St.

Boren Park

E. Blaine St.

E. Howe St.

Interlaken Park

Broadmoor Golf Club

E. Galer St.

E. Highland St.

CAPITOL HILL

E. Prospect St.

E. Aloha St.

E. Helen St.

E. Ward St.

E. Roy St.

E. Aloha St.

E. Ward St.

E. Valley St.

E. Mercer St.

E. Mercer St.

E. Republican St.

Lake Washington Blvd.

E. Arthur Pl.

E. Madison St.

balsamic vinegar, sprinkled with black pepper, and topped with a mild gelato. To top it all off, the restaurant has an excellent wine list. Cafe Juanita prides itself on using fresh, local, and organic ingredients; this is hardly a unique feature among Seattle restaurants, but if you need to convince someone (or yourself) that local and organic foods taste (and look) better, this should be your first stop. ⚠ **Avoid trying to drive here during rush hour—dealing with traffic on the 520 bridge is not an auspicious start to such a great meal.** ⊠ *9702 N.E. 120th Pl., Kirkland* ☎ *425/823–1505* ⊕ *www.cafejuanita.com* ⊟ *MC, V* ☉ *Closed Mon. No lunch.*

PACIFIC NORTHWEST

★ $$$$ ✕ **The Herbfarm.** You may want to fast before dining at the Herbfarm. You'll get no fewer than nine courses here—it's the closest thing the Northwest has to Spain's famous El Bulli restaurant. "Dinner" takes at least four hours and includes five fine Northwest wines, so you may also want to arrange for transportation to and from the restaurant. Before you tuck in, you'll be treated to a tour of the garden, so you'll be able to see exactly where most of your meal's ingredients are coming from. The dining room itself is in a century-old farmhouse and is reminiscent of a country estate—whether said estate is in France, England, or the Pacific Northwest is your call, but it's probably the only place in the Seattle area where you can imagine being part of a dinner party at the summer home of a magnate or baron. The set menus change weekly; if you have dietary restrictions, it's essential to call ahead to make sure that you won't be confronted with a menu full of things you can't eat. With all products coming from the farm, or other local growers and suppliers, you can always expect fresh seafood and shellfish, artisanal cheeses, and luscious seasonal fruits. ⊠ *14590 N.E. 145th St., Woodinville* ☎ *425/485–5300* ⊕ *www.theherbfarm. com* ⌣ *Reservations essential* ⊟ *AE, MC, V* ☉ *No lunch.*

WHERE TO STAY

Seattle's lodging scene can offer endless joys or endless frustrations, depending on your budget and tastes. If you've got money to burn, you'll find plenty of ritzy, high-tech, designer hotels, all of which are clustered in the Downtown area, and some of which have amazing views of Elliott Bay, the Puget Sound, and the Olympic Mountains. On the other end of the price spectrum, Seattle has a few wonderful bed-and-breakfasts, most of which are tucked into residential areas that will give you a much different (and much better) picture of Seattle living than the Downtown core.

Another definite plus of Seattle's scene is that although the major chains like the Hilton and the Westin are well represented, many of the newest, hippest, and most interesting properties are boutique hotels or are owned by smaller, less-corporate chains. You won't find many boring rooms here—each hotel has its own style and great pains are taken to come up with unique motifs and amenities. Unfortunately, the city has very few interesting or cool budget spots—in high season, good luck finding a room for under $100 that has any style, especially if you haven't booked in advance. Most of the reliable, utilitarian chain motels are in awkward (and often downright ugly and unsafe) parts of town. As for the mid-range properties ... well, what mid-range properties? (On the flip side, rates drop so dramatically in low season, high-end properties become reasonably affordable.)

WHAT IT COSTS					
	¢	$	$$	$$$	$$$$
FOR 2 PEOPLE	under $100	$100–$150	$150–$200	$200–$250	over $250

Price categories are assigned based on the range between the least and most expensive standard double rooms in high season. Tax (17%) is extra.

$$$$
★ **Alexis Hotel.** The Alexis occupies two historic buildings near the waterfront. A 2007 refurbishment turned a worn-around-the-edges property into one of the shining stars of the Downtown hotel scene. Using slate grays, soft blues, taupes, and whites, the Alexis has updated its look while maintaining a classic feel—the palette may be modern, but the leather wing chairs in front of the wood-burning fireplaces recall a different era. The Alexis has always had a focus on art (including a rotating collection of paintings selected by a Seattle Art Museum curator in the corridor between wings) and that tradition continues in the rooms as well—all have unique works of art, and several of the suites have further embellishments like shadowboxes containing artists' tools. Be forewarned that making a reservation here can lend to choice fatigue, as the property has 10 different types of specialty rooms in addition to themed suites. The Alexis Suite is hard to ignore: it's a full-blown two-bedroom apartment with wood floors and exposed-brick walls. Downstairs, the Library bistro is one of the city's favorite lunchtime hideaways and bars. **Pros:** Beautifully refurbished rooms, in-room spa services, specialty suites aren't prohibitively expensive. **Cons:** Small lobby, some rooms can be a bit dark. ⊠ *1007 1st Ave., Downtown, 98104* ☎ *206/624–4844 or 888/850–1155* ⊕ *www.alexishotel.com* ⬧ *88 rooms, 33 suites* ⭖ *In-room: refrigerator, Wi-Fi. In-hotel: restaurant, room service, bar, gym, spa, laundry service, concierge, public Wi-Fi, parking (fee), some pets allowed, no-smoking rooms* 🟰 *AE, D, DC, MC, V.*

$$$$
Fodor's Choice
★ **Fairmont Olympic Hotel.** The grande dame of Seattle hotels seems to occupy its own corner of the universe, one that feels more old New York or European than Pacific Northwest. The lobby of the elegant Renaissance Revival–style historic property has intricately carved wood paneling, graceful staircases that lead to mezzanine lounge areas, and plush couches occupied by men in suits and well-dressed older ladies—not a fleece jacket or pair of Birkenstocks in sight. Guest rooms, though lovely, are not quite as impressive as the lobby; however, major renovations, to be completed in late 2008, will change that—everything from fabrics to TVs is being replaced. Ask if any of the renovated rooms are

HOTEL KNOW-HOW

PRICES

Seattle's peak season is May through September, with August at the pinnacle, and prices throughout the city skyrocket then; some are nearly double what they are in low season.

The lodgings listed are the cream of the crop in each price category. Prices are based on the best high-season rates offered directly from the property; they do not take into account discounts or package deals you may find on consolidator Web sites. We always list the facilities that are available—but don't specify whether they cost extra.

Assume that hotels operate on the European Plan (EP, with no meals) unless specified that they use the All-inclusive (all meals and some drinks and activities), Continental Plan (CP, with a Continental breakfast), Modified American Plan (MAP, with breakfast and dinner), or the Full American Plan (FAP, with all meals).

BOOKING TIPS

It is imperative to book in advance for July and August, especially if you want to stay in one of the in-demand budget properties or at any bed-and-breakfast. Some B&Bs start to fill up their summer slots by March or April. The best water-view rooms in Downtown luxury hotels are often gone by mid-February. You aren't likely to have trouble booking a room the rest of the year as long as your visit doesn't coincide with major conventions, or arts or sporting events.

B&Bs fill up quickly, but it's always worth giving them a call to see what's available. Because they encourage longer stays, you may be able to get a last-minute room for a night or two to bridge the gaps that pop up as long-term guests turn over. In this case, you're doing the B&B a favor and may get a discounted rate. All hotels listed have private bath, heat, air-conditioning, TV, and phone unless otherwise noted.

HOW TO SAVE

The best way to save? Travel off-season. Amazing deals at the hottest properties can be had in spring (and sometimes even in early June). Weather is more hit or miss this time of year than in July or August, but there are often many beautiful dry days. Rates drop dramatically again once October rolls around. Mild, picture-perfect fall days are a well-kept secret here—hiking's often good until the end of the month and the Cascades get some beautiful fall colors.

But you probably want to see the city in its late-summer glory. In that case, good luck to you. There isn't much of an upside to Seattle's high season—the best you can do is book as far in advance as possible. Midweek prices may be lower than weekend rates, but don't count on it. You'll always save more with multinight stays, particularly at B&Bs, which often have unofficial policies of giving discounts to long-term guests. The best collection of good deals is on Capitol Hill because most of its properties are B&Bs; the Queen Anne and Lake Union neighborhoods also turn up some good deals and are much closer to Downtown than the U-District, which is the other neighborhood that has a decent selection of mid-range properties.

available when booking, as the hotel's tackling a few floors at a time. Note that executive suites are kind of small for suites; deluxe rooms are nearly the same and slightly cheaper. The well-heeled traveler will find everything he or she needs here: elegant dining at the Georgian, afternoon tea in the lobby, in-room massage and spa services, and a shopping arcade that includes tux rental and couture women's wear. Though it's hard to imagine kids being truly comfortable here, the hotel does its best to accommodate families. **Pros:** Elegant and spacious lobby, renovating all rooms, swimming pool. **Cons:** Rooms are a bit small for the price, may be a little too old-school for style-conscious travelers. ⊠ *411 University St., Downtown, 98101* ☎ *206/621–1700 or 800/441–1414* ⊕ *www.fairmont.com/seattle* ⊅ *232 rooms, 218 suites* △ *In-room: safe, refrigerator, DVD (some), Wi-Fi. In-hotel: 3 restaurants, room service, bar, pool, gym, laundry service, concierge, public Wi-Fi, parking (fee)* ☰ *AE, D, DC, MC, V.*

★ $$$$ ▦ **Hotel Monaco.** The Hotel Monaco is the pet-friendliest hotel in town: not only are pets catered to with special events like canine fashion shows, but anyone who had to leave the pets at home can opt to have a goldfish (who comes with an adorable "hello my name is" introduction card) keep them company. The hotel is full of other fun touches, like bright raspberry-and-cream striped wallpaper, gold sunburst decorations, and animal prints. The bright lobby is a little less whimsical, with hand-painted nautical murals inspired by the fresco at the Palace of Knossos in Crete. There's a nightly wine reception in the lobby, which sometimes includes chair massage or fortune-telling services. Amazingly, none of this fun feels forced or contrived, and guests wishing to have a more low-key experience will be able to do so; they, however, should opt for a room with blue-and-white walls—the eclectic decor is a little easier on the eye in these than in the ones with the raspberry striped wallpaper. **Pros:** Inviting lobby, fun and quirky decor and amenities, great staff. **Cons:** Room decor may be too quirky for some, rooms are a bit pricey for what you get, on-site restaurant is not notable. ⊠ *1101 4th Ave., Downtown, 98101* ☎ *206/621–1770 or 800/945–2240* ⊕ *www.monaco-seattle.com* ⊅ *144 rooms, 45 suites* △ *In-room: refrigerator, DVD, Ethernet, Wi-Fi. In-hotel: restaurant, room service, bar, gym, spa, laundry service, concierge, public Wi-Fi, airport shuttle, parking (fee), some pets allowed, no-smoking rooms* ☰ *AE, D, DC, MC, V.*

★ $$$$ ▦ **W Seattle.** The W set the bar for Seattle's trendy hotels, and although its cool has been recently eclipsed by newer properties like Hotel Max and Hotel 1000, it's still an outstanding choice for hip yet reliable luxury. Candlelight and custom-designed board games encourage lingering around the lobby fireplace on deep couches strewn with throw pillows, and the hotel's bar is popular with guests and locals alike. Decorated in black, brown, and French blue, guest rooms would almost be austere if they didn't have the occasional geometric print to lighten things up a bit. The beds are exceptionally comfortable with pillow-top mattresses and 100% goose-down pillows and comforters. **Pros:** Great bar and restaurant, great beds, extensive concierge services. **Cons:** Unattractive location, self-consciously trendy, readers complain about snotty staff members. ✉*1112 4th Ave., Downtown, 98101* ☎*206/264–6000 or 877/946–8357* ⊕*www.whotels.com* ⇆*419 rooms, 16 suites* ⚷*In-room: safe, refrigerator, DVD, Ethernet. In-hotel: restaurant, room service, bar, gym, laundry service, concierge, public Internet, public Wi-Fi , parking (fee), some pets allowed, no-smoking rooms* ⊟*AE, D, DC, MC, V.*

$$$–$$$$
Fodor'sChoice
★
⌂**Hotel 1000.** Hotel 1000 is new to the scene, but all new luxury properties will have to answer to it. The centerpiece of the small lobby is a dramatically backlighted staircase (don't worry, there's an elevator) and glass sculpture that looks like crystallized stalks of bamboo. The small sitting room off the lobby, with its elegant fire pit surrounded by mid-century modern swiveling leather stools, looks as though it's been designed for leggy Scandinavian beauties and the men in black turtlenecks who love them. The designers wanted the hotel to have a distinctly Pacific Northwest feel and they've succeeded greatly without being campy. The whole hotel is done in dark woods and deep earth tones with an occasional blue accent to represent the water. Materials like rain forest marble connect the urban space to the outdoors as much as possible. Elegant raw silk throws and fabrics in the guest rooms aren't local per se, but they could be seen as a nod to the city's sizable Thai community. Rooms are full of surprising touches, including large tubs that fill from the ceiling, and Hotel 1000 is without a doubt the most high-tech hotel in the city. Your phone will do everything from check the weather and airline schedules to give you restaurant suggestions; your TV doubles as an art gallery, displaying the greatest hits from the period of your choice; and MP3 player and iPod docking stations are standard amenities. If you ever get tired of fiddling with the gadgets in your room, there's a state-of-the-art virtual driving range programmed with some of the world's most challenging courses. **Pros:** Lots of high-tech perks, great restaurant, hip without being alienating. **Cons:** Rooms are dark. ✉*1000 1st Ave., Downtown, 98104* ☎*206/932–3102* ⊕*www.hotel1000seattle.com* ⇆*101 rooms, 19 suites* ⚷*In-room: safe, refrigerator, DVD, Wi-Fi. In-hotel: restaurant, room service, bar, gym, spa, laundry service, concierge, public Wi-Fi, parking (fee), some pets allowed, no-smoking rooms* ⊟*AE, MC, V.*

$$$–$$$$
Fodor'sChoice
★
⌂**Inn at the Market.** For its views alone, the Inn at the Market would be worthy of a Fodor's Choice. But views alone don't make a hotel great—this one has all the pieces of the puzzle from friendly service to a great location (in the north end of Pike Place Market, but tucked away from the bustle of 1st Avenue) to simple, sophisticated guest rooms with Tempur-Pedic beds and bright, spacious bathrooms. Although the decor is nowhere as unique as at the Edgewater (the hotel's only direct competitor), if you book far enough in advance, you can get a far better deal on a water-view room here. All rooms have essentially the same decor and amenities; they're differentiated only by the types of views they offer. You certainly won't be disappointed with the Partial Water View rooms—some have small sitting areas arranged in front of the windows. The four Deluxe Water View rooms are really spectacular, though—708 and 710 are the ones to shoot for, as they share a large private sundeck. Even if you have to settle for a City Side room (a good

deal even in high season), you can enjoy uninterrupted water views from the fifth-floor garden deck. The lobby is small but sweet; you won't see the water from here, but the view of a courtyard with a fountain and ivy-covered balconies is very pleasant. It's worth mentioning that room service is from Campagne, one of the city's best restaurants. The hotel has a complimentary town-car service for Downtown locations. **Pros:** Outstanding views from most rooms and roof deck, steps away from Pike Place Market, small and serene. **Cons:** Little common space, room decor is a little bland. ⊠ *86 Pine St., Downtown, 98101* ☎ *206/443–3600* or *800/446–4484* ⊕ *www.innatthemarket.com* ↘ *60 rooms, 10 suites* ⌂ *In-room: safe, refrigerator, Wi-Fi. In-hotel: 3 restaurants, room service, laundry service, concierge, public Wi-Fi, parking (fee), no-smoking rooms* ⊟ *AE, D, DC, MC, V.*

$$$ ☷ **Westin Hotel.** The flagship of the Westin chain often hosts U.S. presidents and other visiting dignitaries. Northeast of Pike Place Market, Seattle's largest hotel is easily recognizable by its twin cylindrical towers. The innovative design gives all rooms terrific views of Puget Sound, Lake Union, the Space Needle, or the city. Airy guest rooms are furnished in a simple, high-quality style. **Pros:** Great views, reliable chain experience. **Cons:** Rooms lack personality, small bathrooms, pricey for an aging hotel. ⊠ *1900 5th Ave., Downtown, 98101* ☎ *206/728–1000* or *800/228–3000* ⊕ *www.starwoodhotels.com/westin/seattle* ↘ *822 rooms, 43 suites* ⌂ *In-room: safe, refrigerator, Ethernet. In-hotel: 3 restaurants, room service, bars, pool, gym, laundry service, concierge, public Wi-Fi, parking (fee), some pets allowed, no-smoking rooms* ⊟ *AE, D, DC, MC, V.*

★ **$$–$$$** ☷ **Hotel Max.** Fans of minimalism, travelers interested in cutting-edge local artists, and anyone who wants to feel like a rock star will be very happy with the Max, a superstylish hotel that swears it has created a new design esthetic, "Maximalism." The hallway of each floor is dedicated to a different local photographer and giant black-and-white photos cover each door; scenes range from Americana to live concert shots from Seattle's grunge heyday (fifth floor). A few paintings from local artists (different in each room) are all that decorate the gray walls of the guest rooms; a few carefully placed accent colors like an orange bedspread or a red cushion on a stool save the rooms from being drab. The beds are huge and heavenly—a surprising bit of substance from a hotel that prides itself on appearance. The only downside to the Max is that some of the rooms are on the small side—owing more to the constraints of being in a historic building than to tenets of minimalism—and bathrooms have very little counter space. A few rooms, however, are large enough to include black leather couches. **Pros:** Amazing beds, cool artwork, late check-out time available. **Cons:** Small rooms, no views, older travelers may not be comfortable here. ⊠ *620 Stewart St., Downtown, 98101* ☎ *206/728–6299* or *866/833–6299* ⊕ *www. hotelmaxseattle.com* ↘ *163 rooms* ⌂ *In-room: safe, refrigerator, Wi-Fi. In-hotel: restaurant, room service, gym, laundry service, concierge, public Wi-Fi, parking (fee), no-smoking rooms* ⊟ *AE, D, DC, MC, V* ⌾ *CP.*

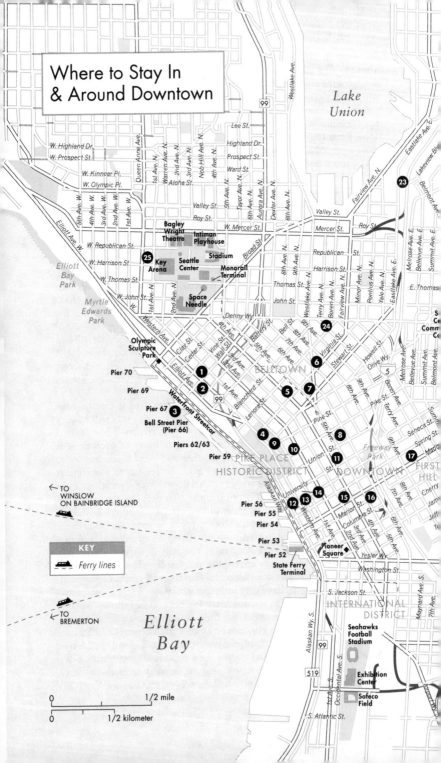

3

$$–$$$ **Inn at Harbor Steps.** Although it's on the lower floors of a modern high-rise residential building, this inn has a country quaint theme, with lots of florals in the guest rooms, country manor–looking plaid armchairs in the lobby, and wicker furniture in the library. Guest rooms are large, with high ceilings, gas fireplaces, and tidy kitchenettes. Bathrooms have large tubs (some of them whirlpools) and oversize glass-enclosed shower stalls. A breakfast buffet is served in the dining room. Complimentary hors d'oeuvres, wine, and tea are served each afternoon in the library. **Pros:** Good price for the location, spacious rooms, comfortable for families. **Cons:** In a condo complex so it lacks the full "hotel experience," not romantic or hip, no valet parking. ⊠ *1221 1st Ave., Downtown, 98101* ☎ *206/748–0973 or 888/728–8910* ⊕ *www. innatharborsteps.com* ⬎ *30 rooms* ⚷ *In-room: refrigerator, Ethernet. In-hotel: pool, gym, laundry service, concierge, parking (fee)* ▭ *AE, MC, V* ⦿*BP.*

$$–$$$ **Red Lion Hotel on 5th Avenue.** In the heart of Downtown, this former bank headquarters is a comfortable business-oriented hotel convenient to the shopping and financial districts. Service is warm and professional; the public spaces have high ceilings, tall windows, and dark-wood paneling. Lining the lobby are sitting areas with couches and overstuffed chairs upholstered in olive green and aubergine velvets and brocades. Guest rooms are midsize and are attractive enough, though decor in standard rooms is only a small step above standard chain motel; they do, however, have pillow-top mattresses, something you won't find in every chain. Rooms on the executive floors, 17–20, have exquisite views of Puget Sound or the city skyline. **Pros:** Location, great water views from some rooms, helpful staff. **Cons:** Boutique prices for a chain hotel, some rooms need updating, readers complain about poor sound insulation between rooms. ⊠ *1415 5th Ave., Downtown, 98101* ☎ *206/971–8000 or 800/733–5466* ⊕ *www.redlion.com* ⬎ *287 rooms, 10 suites* ⚷ *In-room: refrigerator, Wi-Fi. In-hotel: restaurant, room service, gym, laundry service, concierge, public Wi-Fi, parking (fee), some pets allowed, no-smoking rooms* ▭ *AE, D, DC, MC, V.*

¢–$ **Pensione Nichols.** One of the few affordable options Downtown is also a unique and endearing place. Proprietor Lindsey Nichols attends to her guests with great enthusiasm and humor—this is a place where you can just kick back, relax, and be yourself. It's kind of like a hostel for grown-ups, or one for young people who want more privacy and style than a hostel can provide. The bed-and-breakfast is in a historic building, so the rooms are a mixed bag of sizes and layouts, but most have wrought-iron furnishings and all have new beds. Some rooms have shared bathrooms (which are clean and spacious), and most of the rooms on the third floor have skylights instead of windows (because of the building's historic status, Nichols can't renovate to add windows). Second-floor suites have their own bathrooms, as well as full kitchens and large living rooms; one suite has an enclosed balcony, the other has an accessible fire escape. Breakfast is served in the light-filled common area overlooking Elliott Bay. **Pros:** Unique layout, very different from typical hotel experience, great value for location. **Cons:** Shared bathrooms, limited amenities. ✉ *1923 1st Ave., Downtown, 98101* ☎ *206/441–7125* ⊕ *www.pensionenichols.com* ⤶ *8 rooms without bath, 2 suites* ⚘ *In-room: no phone, no TV, Wi-Fi. In-hotel: no elevator, public Wi-Fi, some pets allowed* ⊟ *AE, D, DC, MC, V* ⦿ *CP.*

★ ¢   ⊞ **Green Tortoise Backpacker's Hotel.** The Green Tortoise recently moved into spiffier digs and the new facilities and the impressive cleanliness of the place make this a viable option for all sorts of travelers who don't mind sacrificing a little comfort and privacy for the best deal in town. Sure, the majority of guests are in their early twenties, but the Green Tortoise does get its share of thirty- and even fortysomething travelers. Though singles and couples can rent some of the smaller dorm-style rooms as private accommodations, all rooms here share bathrooms. Bathrooms, however, are spacious, clean, and nicely tiled stand-alone units, so you don't have to worry about showering next to strangers. Each bunk bed has its own locker (bring your own lock), light, and fan. The rate includes a breakfast buffet, with waffle fixings and "unlimited eggs." Security cameras in all the halls and public spaces help to keep guests safe. **Pros:** Cheapest digs in town, great place to socialize with other travelers, across the street from Pike Place Market. **Cons:** Most guests are in their early twenties, no frills rooms with shared bathrooms. ✉ *105 Pike St., Downtown, 98101* ☎ *206/340–1222* ⊕ *www. greentortoise.net* ⤶ *38 rooms without bath* ⚘ *In-room: no phone, no TV, Wi-Fi. In-hotel: no elevator, laundry facilities, public Internet, public Wi-Fi* ⊟ *MC, V* ⦿ *CP.*

BELLTOWN

★ $$$$ ⊞ **Edgewater.** Raised high on stilts above Elliott Bay—with the waves lapping right underneath it—Seattle's only hotel on the water affords spectacular west-facing views of ferries and sailboats, seals and seabirds, and the distant Olympic Mountains. The whole hotel has a rustic-chic, elegant hunting lodge look, with plaid rugs and fabrics and peeled-log furnishings. Many rooms have gas fireplaces. Note that there is a significant price jump between the waterfront rooms and the waterfront premium rooms and the upgrade is not necessarily worth it unless you want a little more space. City-view rooms are very expensive, considering, but if you prefer the hotel's unique take on lodge decor to the sleek, modern look of most Downtown hotels, the expense might be justified, especially if you really like looking at the Space Needle. Some suites have full views, overstuffed chairs, and spa tubs; or just go all-out for the enormous, party-style Beatles Suite (Room 272), where the famous Brits stayed in 1964. The elegant Six Seven restaurant, with its timber-and-river-stone setting and crystal chandeliers, has indoor-outdoor seating with a bay vista. **Pros:** Amazing views, great upscale seafood restaurant, great public lounge area. **Cons:** Best rooms sell out quickly and city view rooms are not worth the expense, standard rooms are small, the chic hunting lodge decor may seem a little forced to some. ✉ *Pier 67, 2411 Alaskan Way, Pier 67, Belltown, 98121* ☎ *206/728– 7000 or 800/624–0670* ⊕ *www.edgewaterhotel.com* ⤶ *213 rooms, 10 suites* ⚘ *In-room: refrigerator, Wi-Fi. In-hotel: restaurant, room* *service, bar, gym, bicycles, laundry service, concierge, public Wi-Fi, parking (fee), no-smoking rooms* ☐*AE, D, DC, MC, V.*

$$$–$$$$ 🖼 **Hotel Ändra.** Scandinavian sensibility and clean, modern lines define this sophisticated Belltown hotel, which is a great, less-pricey alternative to the W. The lobby is fantastic, with armchairs and couches arranged in front of a fireplace that's flanked by floor-to-ceiling bookcases. It also has a loft area, where you can retreat to if Lola, the restaurant right off the lobby, gets too boisterous. Rooms (most of which are suites) have khaki color walls and dark fabrics and woods, with a few bright accents and geometric prints here and there. Alpaca headboards and large wood-framed mirrors are interesting touches, and all the linens, towels (from Frette), and toiletries are high quality. The Ändra's clientele includes people in the creative fields and the music industry, along with Microsoft and biotech moguls in the making. **Pros:** Great lobby lounge, as hip but less expensive than the W, spacious rooms, upscale bathroom amenities. **Cons:** Unattractive part of Belltown, very pricey valet parking, readers complain that staff is not always on the ball. ✉*2000 4th Ave., Belltown, 98101* ☎*206/448–8600 or 877/448–8600* ⊕*www.hotelandra.com* 🛏*4 studios, 23 rooms, 92 suites* ⚅*In-room: safe, refrigerator, Ethernet, Wi-Fi. In-hotel: restaurant, room service, bar, gym, laundry service, concierge, public Wi-Fi* ☐*AE, D, MC, V.*

$$–$$$
Fodor'sChoice
★   🖼 **Inn at El Gaucho.** Dark, swank, and sophisticated, this luxury retro-style 1950s property tops Belltown's beloved El Gaucho steak house. Eighteen ultrachic suites have pale yellow walls, chocolate-color wood, workstations cleverly concealed in closets, and buttery leather furniture. They're filled with such goodies as feather beds, Egyptian linens, Reidel stemware, fresh flowers from Pike Place Market, and large-screen plasma TVs. The sleek bathrooms have rain-style showers and high-end bath and body products. Rooms face either Puget Sound, the city, or the hotel's atrium; atrium rooms are quieter than those that face the street. Room 9 has the best view of the sound. Additional perks include room service from El Gaucho and in-room massages and spa services from the Hyatt's spa team. The one drawback: the flight of stairs you'll have to climb to get to the inn—there's no passenger elevator and because it's in a historic property, there won't be one anytime soon. **Pros:** Beautiful rooms with upscale amenities, great for many occasions from romantic weekend to business travel, great staff. **Cons:** Set of steep stairs and no elevator, you have to go off-site for some amenities (fitness center). ✉*2505 1st Ave., Belltown, 98121* ☎*206/728–1133 or 866/354–2824* ⊕*http://inn.elgaucho.com/inn.elgaucho* 🛏*18 suites* ⚅*In-room: Wi-Fi. In-hotel: restaurant, room service, bar, no elevator, concierge, public Wi-Fi, parking (fee), no-smoking rooms* ☐*AE, MC, V* ⦿*BP.*

★ ¢–$$ 🖼 **Ace Hotel.** The Ace is a dream come true for both penny-pinching hipsters and creative folks who appreciate the chic minimalist decor. Almost everything is white—even wood and brick elements of the original building have been painted over in some places—except for the army surplus blankets on the beds and a few pieces of art on the walls (which include murals from überhip street art luminary Shepard Fairey). The cheapest rooms share bathrooms, which are clean, stand-alone units with enormous showers. Suites are larger (some have leather couches) and have full private bathrooms hidden behind rotating walls. A small dining room hosts a continental breakfast and has a vending machine with unusual items like Japanese snacks. The Ace has guests of all ages, but understand that this is a very specific experience and aesthetic: if you're not soothed (or stimulated) by the stripped-down, almost austere quality of the rooms or not amused by finding a copy of the *Kama Sutra* where the Bible would be, you won't enjoy this place, no matter how much money you're saving. **Pros:** Ultratrendy spot at some of the cheapest rates in town, cool art selection in rooms, good spot to meet other travelers. **Cons:** Most rooms have shared bathrooms, not good for people who want pampering—a lot of amenities are self-serve. ⊠ *2423 1st Ave., Belltown, 98121* ☎ *206/448–4721* ⊕ *www. theacehotel.com* ⇆ *28 rooms* ☍ *In-room: no a/c (some), refrigerator, Wi-Fi. In-hotel: laundry facilities, public Wi-Fi, parking (fee), some pets allowed, no-smoking rooms* ▤ *AE, D, DC, MC, V.*

LAKE UNION

$$$$ ⚏ **Pan Pacific Seattle.** This is a stunning hotel, with views that often
Fodor's Choice   times eclipse the coveted Elliott Bay waterfront ones. The lobby fea-
★   tures a dramatic "floating" staircase (it leads up to meeting spaces and another small lounge), a fireplace, and plush brown suede and leather couches. The Pan Pacific went with a different color palette than most of its competitors—blond and light woods, tan marble, cinnamon accents—and the result is that every corner of the hotel feels full of light even during the gray Seattle winter. In the rooms large tubs are shielded by shoji doors, and Hypnos beds and ergonomic Herman Miller chairs at the desks ensure further comfort. All corner Executive King rooms have terrific views of the Space Needle and the mountains to the west and Lake Union to the north. Of the junior suites, Rooms 10 and 11 have the best views of Lake Union—something to note if you're in town for the July 4 fireworks. The Pan Pacific is part of a luxury condo development that includes a large fitness center (open to hotel guests), a spa, a courtyard of high-end specialty shops, and an enormous Whole Foods, which makes up for the fact that with the exception of the excellent Marazul, the immediate area has few dining options. **Pros:** Beautiful brand-new property, great beds, away from the tourist throngs. **Cons:** Long walk to downtown sights, not many free amenities, shoji doors are pretty but cut down on bathroom privacy in smaller standard rooms. ⊠ *2125 Terry Ave., South Lake Union, 98121* ☎ *206/264–8111* ⊕ *http://seattle.panpacific.com* ⇆ *160 rooms, 1 suite* ☍ *In-room: safe, refrigerator, DVD (some), Wi-Fi. In-hotel: restaurant, room service, bar, gym, spa, laundry service, concierge, public Wi-Fi, parking (fee)* ▤ *AE, DC, MC, V.*

$$–$$$ ⚏ **Silver Cloud Inn Lake Union.** Though not as attractive as its sister property on Capitol Hill, this Silver Cloud branch has something the other doesn't: views of Lake Union from many of its guest rooms as well as from a third-floor lounge. Rooms are simply and adequately furnished; some of the larger water-view rooms have nice love seats and glass doors that give them some extra light. The hotel is on the southeast corner of the lake and dining options within easy walking distance are a bit better here than on the west side. The hotel has a complimentary shuttle service to Downtown sights. Prices are reasonable considering the location, and therefore weekends in August fill up quickly. **Pros:** Pool, great value with free parking and internet, great breakfast. **Cons:** Not within walking distance of major sights, more of a business hotel feel. ☒*1150 Fairview Ave. N, Lake Union, 98109* 🕾*206/447–9500 or 800/330–5812* ⊕*www.scinns.com* ⊲*184 rooms* ⅃*In-room: refrigerator, Ethernet, Wi-Fi. In-hotel: 2 pools, gym, concierge, public Wi-Fi, parking (fee)* ▤*AE, D, DC, MC, V* ⎮◎⎮*CP.*

QUEEN ANNE

$ 🖫**Mediterranean Inn.** The Mediterranean Inn is a welcome addition to Queen Anne and to the Seattle lodging scene in general. It's a relatively new property, which means it's in good condition, and it's one of the best deals in town—you'll get comfortable (though not terribly spacious) studio apartments with small kitchenettes for surprisingly low prices even in high season. Sometimes, you can snag a room here for less than at the neighborhood's reigning budget spot, the Inn at Queen Anne, which isn't as new or nice as the Mediterranean. Furnishings are nothing special, though the rooms here are nicer than at some chain properties that charge more. Some rooms have views of the Space Needle and the Downtown skyline; the rooftop deck has outstanding views of both for all to enjoy. There are two supermarkets very close by to help you stock your kitchenette, and there are numerous bars and restaurants in the area. **Pros:** Great value for location close to Seattle Center, great roof deck. **Cons:** Rooms have kitchenettes but some don't have adequate dining space, beds aren't the greatest, opening windows in non-a/c rooms lets in street noise. ☒*425 Queen Anne Ave. N, Queen Anne, 98109* 🕾*206/428–4700 or 866/525–4700* ⊕*www.mediterranean-inn.com* ⊲*180 studios* ⅃*In-room: no a/c (some), kitchen, Ethernet. In-hotel: gym, laundry facilities, public Internet, parking (fee), some pets allowed, no-smoking rooms* ▤*AE, D, DC, MC, V.*

FIRST HILL

★ $$$$ 🖫**Sorrento Hotel.** Built in 1909, the Sorrento was designed to look like an Italian villa, with a dramatic circular driveway surrounding a palm-fringed fountain. The hotel is in between Downtown and Capitol Hill and convenient to both. Though its immediate area is not terribly attractive (a lot of hospital buildings and clinics nearby), walking a few blocks north toward the excellent Frye Art Museum along tree-lined streets is a very pleasant experience. The wood-paneled lobby and adjacent Fireside Room are explosions of different fabrics: stripes, checks, chenilles, gold brocading, vividly patterned rugs, and so on. This turn-of-the-20th-century private club look certainly isn't everyone's taste, but the dark Fireside Room is undeniably cozy and tranquil. Guest rooms, on the other hand, are light, airy, and more contemporary, with only a few tasseled pillows and a few antique furnishings to tie them to the decor downstairs. The largest are the corner suites; junior suites are only marginally more expensive than the standard rooms and have a bit more space. This place is impeccable: the Italian marble bathrooms gleam, and day-of-the-week rugs in the elevators show that even those oft-neglected spaces get a daily once-over. The Hunt Club serves excellent Pacific Northwest dishes. Town-car service within the Downtown area is complimentary. **Pros:** Serene and classy, great restaurant, great beds with luxurious linens. **Cons:** Odd location, won't appeal to younger travelers or cool-hunters. ✉ *900 Madison St., First Hill, 98104* ☎ *206/622–6400 or 800/426–1265* ⊕ *www.hotelsorrento. com* ↷ *34 rooms, 42 suites* ♿ *In-room: safe, refrigerator, Ethernet. In-hotel: restaurant, room service, bar, gym, laundry service, concierge, public Wi-Fi, parking (fee)* ▤ *AE, D, DC, MC, V.*

CAPITOL HILL

★ $$–$$$ 🖼 **Silver Cloud Inn Broadway.** If you want to stay on Capitol Hill and don't like B&Bs, this is your only option—and a good one it is. Though it doesn't look like much from the outside, the Silver Cloud is full of surprises. The hotel's on a noisy intersection, but you could hear a pin drop in the spacious lobby, which is so comfortable and nicely styled in modern tans, greens, and purples that it looks like it should belong in an independent hotel, not a mid-range chain. Guest rooms are smallish and have no views to speak of due to the property's location, but they have nice furnishings like tall wooden headboards and faux granite–top desks; king rooms have plush plum-color love seats with large ottomans. King Jacuzzi rooms have large tubs and faux fireplaces (which can be set to give off just light or light and heat), but unless you really want that tub, they're not worth the extra cost as the layout is kind of odd—the tub is in what would have been a sitting area only a few feet from the bed, making the room feel cramped. Suites are well laid out and have bay windows—even though the views aren't great, the extra light is a plus. All rooms have microwaves, refrigerators, and wet bars; a shop in the lobby sells snacks and drinks. You're just steps from the Pike–Pine corridor; the hotel provides a free shuttle service to points Downtown. **Pros:** Close to Capitol Hill sights; only non-B&B lodging on the Hill, pool, clean and modern rooms. **Cons:** Immediate location is uninspiring, some rooms are a bit dark, not a great value when high season prices spike. ✉ *1100 Broadway, Capitol Hill, 98122* ☎ *206/325–1400 or 800/590–1801* ⊕ *www.scinns.com* ↷ *179 rooms* ♿ *In-room: refrigerator, Ethernet, Wi-Fi. In-hotel: restaurant, room service, bar, pool, gym, laundry service, concierge, public Wi-Fi, parking (fee), no-smoking rooms* ▤ *AE, D, DC, MC, V* ⋈*CP.*

★ $–$$ 🖼 **11th Avenue Inn.** If your mind's-eye picture of a classic bed-and-breakfast includes antique daybeds, Oriental rugs, and a grand dining room table draped in a lace-edged tablecloth, look no further. The 11th Avenue Inn plays this role perfectly. There are Victorian touches at every turn, but there's nothing chockablock or cluttered about the place: owner David Williams has impeccable taste, and even the small den that holds two public computers and stacks of travel guides, brochures, and laminated menus from the best local restaurants is thoughtfully arranged and appointed. Modestly sized guest rooms are on two floors. The second floor has five rooms; the Citrine is our favorite for its regal antique headboard, but the Opal is a very close second because of the amount of light it gets. The Emerald and Ruby rooms share a bathroom that has a cute green claw-foot tub. The third floor has three rooms, which are closer together but bigger than those on the second floor. They have skylights, and the Garnet and Topaz rooms have window seats from which you can get glimpses of the skyline. A full breakfast is served in the elegant dining room, which is the showpiece of the house. Don't worry about using the wrong fork, though—despite its formal appearance, the inn is a warm and laid-back place, a great ambassador of Seattle hospitality. **Pros:** Unpretentious take on classic B&B, has amenities not found in many B&Bs, friendly staff. **Cons:** No a/c, although most guests are courteous sound does carry in old houses. ⊠ *121 11th Ave. E, Capitol Hill, 98102* ☎ *206/720–7161 or 800/720–7161* ⊕ *www.11thavenueinn.com* ➟ *8 rooms, 6 with bath* ⚬ *In-room: Wi-Fi. In-hotel: no elevator, public Internet, public Wi-Fi, parking (no fee), no kids under 12, no-smoking rooms* ⊟ *AE, D, DC, MC, V* ⏇ *BP.*

¢–$$

Fodor'sChoice
★

Gaslight Inn. Rooms here range from a crow's nest with peeled-log furniture and Navajo-print fabrics to suites with gas fireplaces and antique carved beds. The large common areas evoke a gentlemen's club, with oak wainscoting, high ceilings, and hunter-green carpet. One owner's past career as a professional painter is evident in the impeccable custom-mixed finishes throughout the inn. The Gaslight is more contemporary than many of its competitors and free of the cluttered feeling that most B&Bs have. That's not to say that it doesn't have any decoration—exquisite artwork on display ranges from glass art to ceramic sculptures to mixed-media pieces. There's room to move around in here, including a lovely backyard, and the Gaslight has something no other B&B can claim: a heated pool. **Pros:** Great art collection, house and rooms are more spacious than at other B&Bs, pool. **Cons:** Breakfast is unimpressive, some readers find staff standoffish. ⊠ *1727 15th Ave., Capitol Hill, 98122* ☎ *206/325–3654* ⊕ *www.gaslight-inn.com* ➟ *8 rooms* ⚬ *In-room: no a/c, no phone, refrigerator, Wi-Fi. In-hotel: pool, no elevator, laundry facilities, public Wi-Fi, no-smoking rooms* ⊟ *AE, MC, V* ⏇ *CP.*

¢–$$

Salisbury House. Built in 1904, this Craftsman house sits on a wide, tree-lined street. The spacious rooms contain an eclectic collection of furniture, including some antiques. The decor isn't as eye-popping as at some of its competitors, but travelers who prefer a simpler, more-contemporary look will appreciate the B&B's restraint. The basement suite has a private entrance and phone line, a fireplace, and a whirlpool bath. The Blue Room is the best of the rest: it has a private deck overlooking the garden. The Rose Room is the most traditional looking, with a canopy bed, antique armoire, and floral bed linens. One of the common areas is a sunporch with wicker furniture. The location is not as central as the other B&Bs—it's closer to Volunteer Park than to shops and restaurants—but this can be seen as a plus not a minus. After all, the farther away from the bustle of Broadway and Pike–Pine, the leafier and quieter the neighborhood. Note that the owner has two cats. **Pros:** Close to Volunteer Park, friendly innkeeper can help you plan your stay, porches to relax on. **Cons:** A bit far from Pike-Pine Corridor, some street noise. ⊠ *750 16th Ave. E, Capitol Hill, 98112* ☎ *206/328–8682* ⊕ *www.salisburyhouse.com* ⊷ *4 rooms, 1 suite* ⬡ *In-room: no a/c, no TV, Ethernet, Wi-Fi. In-hotel: no elevator, public Wi-Fi, no kids under 12, no-smoking rooms* ⊟ *AE, DC, MC, V* ⊚| *BP.*

GREEN LAKE

★ **$–$$** 🏨 **Greenlake Guesthouse.** With the demise of the Chelsea Station in Fremont, the Greenlake Guesthouse is the lone representative of the residential neighborhoods north of the canal and west of the University District. Thankfully, it's outstanding in every way. The house (which actually feels like a house instead of a museum) is directly across the street from the eastern shore of beautiful Green Lake. The romantic Parkview Suite is the pièce de résistance, with a full view of the park, and pale green walls that play off the green of the leaves just outside the windows. The Cascade has a very limited view of the lake, but it has funky red walls and a gas fireplace to make up for it. All rooms have private baths with jetted tubs and heated tile floors. Owners Blayne and Julie McAfterty have put a lot of thought into everything: a public computer with Internet is available in the living room. A communal minibar in the hall dispenses complimentary sodas and water. Bookshelves in the upstairs hallway have an extensive DVD collection of Oscar-winning Best Pictures (along with a few guilty-pleasure action movies and some kids' favorites). To keep things interesting, the full breakfast alternates between savory (an omelet for example) and sweet (such as French toast with fresh seasonal fruit). **Pros:** Views of and access to Green Lake, thoughtful amenities, can accommodate kids. **Cons:** Far from downtown, immediate neighborhood doesn't have much of interest. ⊠ *7630 E. Green Lake Dr. N, Green Lake, 98103* ☎ *206/729–8700 or 866/355–8700* ⊕ *www.greenlakeguesthouse.com* ⊷ *4 rooms* ⬡ *In-room: no phone, DVD, Wi-Fi. In-hotel: no elevator, public Internet, public Wi-Fi, no kids under 4, no-smoking rooms* ⊟ *DC, MC, V* ⊚| *BP.*

UNIVERSITY DISTRICT

$$–$$$ 🏨 **Hotel Deca.** Within blocks of UW, this 1931 property has been restored to its original art deco elegance. Guest rooms are individually decorated and have bright gem colors and bold details. Beds have floor-to-ceiling headboards done in vibrant colors and fabrics, and some rooms have fireplaces that look like they're encased in giant stainless-steel picture frames. Sky Level rooms have great views of the Cascades and the skyline to boot. The elegant District Lounge restaurant serves a mix of tasty comfort dishes, snacks, and upscale Pacific Northwest cuisine with Mediterranean influences. **Pros:** Trendiest hotel in the U District, convenient to main thoroughfare and to UW, high-tech amenities. **Cons:** Small bathrooms, expensive for the area, disappointing

Where to Stay in the U-District

room service and breakfast options. ⊠*4507 Brooklyn Ave. NE, University District, 98105* ☎*206/634–2000 or 800/899–0251* ⊕*www.hoteldeca.com* ⤢*158 rooms* ⟨*In-room: Wi-Fi. In-hotel: restaurant, room service, bar, gym, laundry service, concierge, public Wi-Fi, parking (no fee), no-smoking rooms* ⊟*AE, D, DC, MC, V* ⦿*CP.*

$–$$ 🏠 **Chambered Nautilus.** A vivid red door fronts this Georgian Revival home, which overlooks an ivy-covered hillside. In the large living room, a fireplace flickers onto classic Oriental rugs, free guest computer, and sideboard stocked with cookies and tea. Bedrooms have down comforters and such attractive extras as sleigh beds, fireplaces, and private porches. Among the best quarters are the Scallop Chamber, trimmed in khaki and green; the Rose Chamber, with its vivid floral motifs; and the Sunrise Chamber, with its yellow walls and blue-and-white bedding. Three-course breakfasts might include roasted pears with caramel sauce or individual crustless quiches in ramekins. **Pros:** Attractive rooms and living room, extras like robes and handmade soaps, great breakfast. **Cons:** Steep stairs, property is attractive but it's close to university housing. ⊠*5005 22nd Ave. NE, University District, 98105* ☎*206/522–2536* ⊕*www.chamberednautilus.com* ⤢*6 rooms* ⟨*In-room: Wi-Fi. In-hotel: no elevator, public Internet, public Wi-Fi, no kids under 8, no-smoking rooms* ⊟*AE, MC, V* ⦿*BP.*

NIGHTLIFE

Every neighborhood has a little bit of everything, save for dance clubs, which are in short supply and mostly concentrated in Pioneer Square and Belltown. The number of bars in each neighborhood increases greatly if you take into account all of the great restaurants that also have thriving bar scenes.

Downtown is a great place for anyone looking to dress up a bit and hit swanky hotel bars, classy lounges, and wine bars where you don't have to be under the age of 30 to fit in. Belltown is the trendiest part of town. It's a madhouse on weekends and most places have a distinct meat market vibe and a youngish, moneyed crowd that tends to get very, very drunk. That said, there are some lovely spaces here, a few of which stay relatively low-key even during the Saturday-night crush, as well as some quirky old neighborhood dives left over from Belltown's former life. Capitol Hill has a lot of music venues and bars and is one of the city's liveliest areas at night. The Hill is also the center of the city's gay and lesbian community, with the majority of gay bars and dance clubs along Pike, Pine, and Broadway. Fremont has quite a few bars lining its main commercial drag of N. 36th Street, including a few spots for live music. Unfortunately, Fremont sometimes suffers from a Doctor Jekyll and Mr. Hyde syndrome. During the week, almost any of its simple bars are fine places to grab a quiet drink with a friend. On weekends, the neighborhood does on occasion transform into an extended frat party and almost no place is tolerable.

Ballard is quickly eclipsing Capitol Hill in popularity. There are at least half a dozen bars on Ballard Avenue alone. The neighborhood has quickly evolved from a few pubs full of old salts to a thriving nightlife district that has equal parts average-Joe bars, hipster haunts, music spots, wine bars, and Belltown-style lounges.

BARS & LOUNGES

DOWNTOWN & BELLTOWN

Black Bottle (⊠ *2600 1st Ave., Belltown* ☎ *206/441–1500* ⊕ *www.black-bottleseattle.com*) is a deliberate attempt at a gastropub and therefore it serves a carefully selected, reasonably priced, and uniformly delicious small-plates menu (as opposed to the overly heavy or overly ambitious menus found in so many upscale bars). The interior is simple—just a few black chairs and tables, and wood floors—but sleek. Because it's on the fringe of Belltown, it gets crowded on weekends, but it's less of a see-and-be-seen scene and more of a place for good friends to gather. There's a limited selection of beers on tap, but the wine list is good.

Oliver's (⊠ *405 Olive Way, Downtown* ☎ *206/623-8700* ⊕ *www.mayflowerpark.com*), in the Mayflower Park Hotel, is famous for its martinis. In fact, having a cocktail here is like having afternoon tea in some parts of the world. Wing chairs, low tables, and lots of natural light make it easy to relax after a hectic day.

Purple Café and Wine Bar (⊠ *1225 4th Ave., Downtown* ☎ *206/829–2280* ⊕ *www.thepurplecafe.com*) is certainly the biggest wine bar in the city and possibly its most dramatic—despite the cavernous qual-

NIGHTLIFE KNOW-HOW

THE CITY THAT GOES TO SLEEP EARLY

With very few exceptions, bars and clubs close at 2 AM. This means that last call can come as early as 1:30 AM, which depending on where you're from may be the time you're used to *starting* your evening.

THE SMOKE WON'T GET IN YOUR EYES

An expanded smoking ban was overwhelmingly approved by Washington State voters in 2005. You cannot smoke in restaurants, bars, or clubs (the ban covers all public places and workplaces).

GETTING AROUND

Program the numbers for the city's cab companies (⇨ Seattle Essentials) into your cell phone. Unless you have a designated driver or are not venturing too far from your hotel, you will need them. Expect long waits for pickups on Saturday nights. Though you'll probably be able to hail cabs on the street in the deader sections of Downtown—making a restaurant–wine bar type of trip easy enough to manage—you'll have trouble finding empty cabs in Capitol Hill, Belltown, and in the northern neighborhoods.

Unfortunately, drunk driving is a fact of life, as so many people rely on their cars to get around and public transportation becomes even less frequent late at night.

Parking in Belltown is an absolute nightmare on weekend nights. The neighborhood has ample pay lots, but even those fill up.

GOOD NEWS FOR CLUB-HOPPERS

Many Pioneer Square clubs participate in a "joint cover" pricing scheme; you pay a onetime cover charge at the first club you hit, get your hand stamped, and then are allowed into all other participating venues for free (you'll still have to pay exorbitant prices for drinks everywhere, though). If you don't know where to start, Doc Maynard's on 1st Avenue and Yesler Way usually has the info.

INFORMATION OVERLOAD

The Stranger and *Seattle Weekly* give detailed music, art, and nightlife listings, as well as hot tips and suggestions for the week's events. Friday editions of the *Seattle Times* and the *Seattle Post-Intelligencer* include weekend pullout sections detailing arts and entertainment events.

ity of the space and floor-to-ceiling windows, all eyes are immediately drawn to the 20-foot tower ringed by a spiral staircase that holds thousands of bottles. There are full lunch and dinner menus (American and Pacific Northwest fare), as well as tasting menus. The place does look and function more like a restaurant than a bar, but there are two actual bars to belly up to, and on busy weekend nights it's there where you'll get the better service. Though Purple is surprisingly unpretentious for a place in the financial district, it's sophisticated enough that you'll want to dress up a bit.

★ **Rendezvous** (✉ 2232 2nd Ave., Belltown ☎ 206/441–5823 ⊕ *www.jewelboxtheater.com*) has been around since 1924, starting out as an elite screening room for film stars and moguls. It weathered some rough times as a porn theater and a much-loved dive bar, but it's been spruced up just enough to suit the new wave of wealthy locals without alienating everyone else. An old-time feel and the great calendar of events at the bar's Jewelbox Theater (live music, film, burlesque shows) sets it apart from the neighborhood's string of cookie-cutter trendy spots.

Shorty's (⊠ *2222 2nd Ave., Belltown* ☎ *206/441–5449* ⊕ *www.shortydog.com*) may be one of the dingiest bars in Belltown, but it's a bright spot in a neighborhood where most bars serve $10 drinks. Along with a come-as-you-are atmosphere, you'll get pinball machines and video games, cheap beer and hot dogs, and lots of no-frills fun.

Umi Sake House (⊠ *2230 1st Ave., Belltown* ☎ *206/374–8717* ⊕ *www.umisakehouse.com*) offers a great selection of sake and sake-based cocktails in a space designed to look like someone shoehorned a real *izakaya* (a sake house that also serves substantial snacks) into a Belltown building—there's even an enclosed patio, which they refer to as the "porch," and a tatami room that can be reserved for larger parties. The sushi is good and there's a very long happy hour offered at one of the bar areas. Despite its chic interior, Umi is less of a meat market than some Belltown spots—unless you're here late on a Friday or Saturday night.

★ **Vessel** (⊠ *1312 5th Ave., Downtown* ☎ *206/652–5222* ⊕ *www.vesselseattle.com*) is the place to go if you've saved up some cash in anticipation of spending one night sampling intricate and inventive cocktails. The specialty drinks are outstanding here and you're bound to find a few concoctions that you won't find anywhere else. Service can be a bit slow on crowded weekends, but just spend the time eyeing the attractive bi-level space, which is supermodern without being a caricature of itself. The staircase leading to the mezzanine is backlighted in the type of unnatural yellow color you'd expect to find in a cocktail with 10 ingredients—it's a surprisingly nice touch. This is a sophisticated place (leave the sport sandals at home) that knows it doesn't have to trade on pretension—it's all about the drinks.

> **WORD OF MOUTH**
>
> "Best cocktails in seattle can be had at Vessel and at Zig Zag- neither have music but if you sit at the bar and engage the bartenders you will have a great time."
>
> –Stormygirl

Virginia Inn (⊠ *1937 1st Ave., Downtown* ☎ *206/728–1937*) brings Pike Place Market tourists, office workers, and Belltown residents together. It's an institution, really, the kind of place where crowds spill out onto the patio on warm summer evenings. Skip the food, which is overpriced and can be hit or miss, and cross your fingers in the hopes of getting good service—the waitstaff can sometimes demonstrate puzzling amounts of attitude.

W Hotel Bar (⊠ *1112 4th Ave., Downtown* ☎ *206/264–6000*) allows you to enjoy the hotel's signature design style even if you haven't booked a room here. You will certainly feel fabulous sipping a well-poured—if pricey—martini among the city's wealthy and beautiful. There's a bar menu that will give you a taste of the hotel's restaurant, Earth and Ocean.

★ **Zig Zag Cafe** (✉*1501 Western Ave., Downtown* ☎*206/625–1146* ⊕*www.zigzagcafe.net*) gives Oliver's a run for its money when it comes to pouring perfect martinis and is much more eclectic and laid-back than its competitor. A mixed crowd of mostly locals hunts out this unique spot at the bottom of the Market on the Hillclimb. The Zig Zag is friendly, retro without being obnoxiously ironic, and serves up tasty, simple food and the occasional live music show to boot.

QUEEN ANNE & SEATTLE CENTER

Bricco Della Regina Anna (✉*1525 Queen Anne Ave. N, Upper Queen Anne* ☎*206/285–4900* ⊕*www.briccoseattle.com*) is a lovely candlelit wine bar that serves a small menu of Italian snacks and entrées that change nightly. The wine list ranges all over the map, but Italian and Northwest wines are particularly well represented. Though it can get crowded on weekends, this place is unfailingly low key, despite the fact that it's popular with the moneyed Upper Queen Anne set.

The **Sitting Room** (✉*108 W. Roy St., Queen Anne* ☎*206/285–2830* ⊕*www.the-sitting-room.com*) has a European-café vibe, excellent mixed drinks, and the hearts of residents of both the lower and upper parts of Queen Anne. It's quite an accomplishment to get those two very different demographics to agree on anything, but this sweet, relaxed little spot has done it with its eclectic, mismatched (but not shabby) furniture; zinc bar; sexy, dim lighting; and friendly staff.

The **Spectator** (✉*529 Queen Anne Ave. N, Lower Queen Anne* ☎*206/599–4263* ⊕*www.thespectatorsports.com*) stands out in an area that has quite a few nondescript pubs and sports bars meant to catch pre- or postgame Sonics fans. Watch the NBA, NHL, and NFL on 15 high-definition, flat-screen TVs from comfy red leather booths. The bar also shows international broadcasts of important soccer, rugby, and cricket matches. There's a pool table and video games to keep you busy during commercials or half-times. The Spectator is about as chic and pleasant as a place with 15 TVs showing NASCAR can possibly be.

CAPITOL HILL

★ At **Licorous** (✉*928 12th Ave., Capitol Hill* ☎*206/325–6947* ⊕*www.licorous.com*) you might spend more time staring at the striking molded-tin ceiling than perusing the room for a potential date. This attractive bar has provided something that the Hill has been missing for a long time: a hip, well-designed space that attracts a true mix of the neighborhood's residents—one where everyone can feel like a grown-up and enjoy a low-key evening sipping tasty specialty cocktails. The small plates are pretty tasty, too.

★ **Linda's Tavern** (✉*707 E. Pine St., Capitol Hill* ☎*206/325–1220*) is one of the Hill's iconic dives—and not just because it was allegedly the last place Kurt Cobain was seen alive. The interior has a vaguely Western theme, but the patrons are pure Capitol Hill indie-rockers and hipsters. The bartenders are friendly, the burgers are good (brunch is even better), and the always-packed patio is one of the liveliest places to grab a happy-hour drink.

Poco Wine Room (✉*1408 E. Pine St., Capitol Hill* ☎*206/322–9463* ⊕*www.pocowineroom.com*) deserves accolades just for taking one of the least interesting architectural spaces out there—the oddly proportioned retail space of a condo complex—and making it into a sophisticated parallel universe where a friendly crowd lounges on couches and crowds around two small bars to enjoy a competent menu of artisan Northwest wines. A selection of subtle fruit wines is a nice surprise.

FREMONT

Brouwer's (⊠*400 N 35th St., Fremont* ☎*206/267–2437* ⊕*www.brou werscafe.com*) is a Belgian-beer lovers heaven—even if it looks more like a trendy Gothic dungeon than a place with white clouds and harp-bearing angels. A converted warehouse provides an ample venue for a top selection of suds provided by the owners of Seattle's best specialty-beer shop, Bottleworks. There are plenty of German and American beers on offer, too, as well as English, Czech, and Polish selections. A menu of sandwiches, frites, and Belgian specialties help to lay a foundation before imbibing (remember that Belgian beers have a higher alcohol content). Before settling on a seat downstairs, check out the balcony and the cozy parlor room.

BALLARD

★ The **People's Pub** (⊠*5429 Ballard Ave. NW, Ballard* ☎*206/783–6521*) is a Ballard institution and a great representative of what locals love about this unpretentious neighborhood. The pub (a dining room and a separate bar in the back) isn't much to look at—just a lot of wood paneling, simple wood tables and chairs, and some unfortunate floral upholstery—but it has a great selection of German beers and draws a true cross section of the neighborhood's denizens from hipsters to old-school fishermen.

Portalis (⊠*5205 Ballard Ave. NW, Ballard* ☎*206/783–2007* ⊕*www. portaliswines.com*) attracts serious wine drinkers who gather around communal tables and at the long bar to sample wines from around the world in this cozy, brick-lined bar. It's a full-service retail shop as well, so you can pick up a few bottles to take home. Though it's a bit stuffy for Ballard, it's a nice alternative to the frenetic scene on the upper part of Ballard Avenue.

★ If you manage to score a table at **Sambar** (⊠*425 NW Market St., Ballard* ☎*206/781–4883*), a teeny-tiny bar attached to French restaurant Le Gourmand, you probably won't leave for hours—there's nothing else like it in Seattle. Though it claims to have French flair, the only thing that cries corner café is its small size. The interior is modern in a way that would look pretentious and stark if translated into a bigger space. Excellent cocktails are mixed with panache and made with premium liquors—just try to walk a straight line out the door when you're done. A small menu offers delicious bites from Le Gourmand, from fresh salads to guilty pleasures like the *croque monsieur* and rich desserts. The crowd is mixed and different every night; soccer moms, young professionals, and Ballard residents who are either too cool or not cool enough for the hipster joints on Ballard Avenue all show up here. A small patio adds some additional and highly coveted seating in summer.

BREWPUBS

Elysian Brewing Company (⊠ *1221 E. Pike St., Capitol Hill* ☎ *206/860–1920* ⊕ *www.elysianbrewing.com*), a large, industrial-looking space with a brewery in back, lets you sample house concoctions at the copper-stamped upstairs bar or in the downstairs lounge. It's a perennial favorite of Seattleites and Capitol Hill residents and a good alternative to the hipster haunts and swanky lounges in the area. The winter and fall seasonal ales are particularly good. There's another branch in Wallingford near Green Lake on N. 55th and Meridien, but it's a bit off the beaten path unless you're staying in the area.

Pyramid Alehouse (⊠ *1201 1st Ave. S, Downtown* ☎ *206/682–3377* ⊕ *www.pyramidbrew.com*), a loud festive spot south of Pioneer Square and across from Safeco Field, brews the varied Pyramid line, including a top-notch Hefeweizen and an apricot ale that tastes much better than it sounds. Madhouse doesn't even begin to describe this place during games at Safeco Field, so if you're looking for quiet and immediate seating, make sure your visit doesn't coincide with one. The brewery offers tours daily.

Six Arms (⊠ *300 E. Pike St., Capitol Hill* ☎ *206/223–1698* ⊕ *www.mcmenamins.com*), named for its six-armed Indian dancer logo, is a spacious, popular, two-story brewpub with 17 house and craft beers on tap. Two that stand out are the medium-bodied Hammerhead, and the dark Terminator Stout. As you head back to the restrooms, note the fermenting tanks painted with amusing murals.

GAY & LESBIAN SPOTS

Most bars are male oriented, though they welcome mixed crowds who respect the clubs and their patrons. Many establishments are on Capitol Hill.

Girl4Girl (☎ *206/628–3151 Showbox SoDo's info line* ⊕ *www.girl4girlseattle.com*) organizes the largest lesbian dance parties and events in the Pacific Northwest. The party has changed venues several times over the years, but the Showbox SoDo south of Downtown seems to be its current haunt. Events generally take place on the third or fourth Saturday of every month. Expect a lot of dancing and drinking, and the odd burlesque performance. The crowd is often very young, but all are welcome.

Madison Pub (⊠ *1315 E. Madison St., Capitol Hill* ☎ *206/325–6537* ⊕ *www.madisonpub.com*) is a laid-back place to grab a drink—leave your hair gel and dancing shoes at home. Regulars shoot pool, hang out with groups of friends, and chat up the friendly bartenders. This is the antithesis of the scenester spots like Purr.

Neighbours (⊠ *1509 Broadway, Capitol Hill* ☎ *206/324–5358* ⊕ *www.neighbours.com*) is an institution thanks in part to its drag shows, great theme DJ nights, and relaxed atmosphere (everyone, including the straightest of the straights, seems to feel welcome here). The place is packed Thursday through Saturday. The Tuesday night '80s party is popular, too.

Re-Bar (⊠ *1114 Howell St., Capitol Hill* ☎ *206/233–9873* ⊕ *www.rebarseattle.com*) is a bar, theater, dance club, and art space that is extremely friendly to all persuasions—straight, gay, lesbian, transgender, whatever. A loyal following enjoys cabaret shows, weekend stage performances, and great DJs. The place has a reputation for playing good house music, but there are many different theme nights, including a rock-and-roll karaoke. Every fourth Saturday of the month Re-Bar hosts Cherry (⊕ *www.cherryseattle.com*), a popular lesbian dance party.

R Place (✉ *619 E. Pine St., Capitol Hill* ☎*206/322–8828* ⊕*www.rplace seattle.com*) has all its bases covered—the bottom floor is a sports bar; the second floor has pool tables, pinball, and video games; and the top floor is a full-blown dance club.

The Wildrose (✉*1021 E. Pike St., Capitol Hill* ☎*206/324–9210* ⊕ *wwww.thewildrosebar.com*) is Seattle's only dedicated lesbian bar, so expect a mob nearly every night. The crowd at weeknight karaoke is fun and good-natured, cheering for pretty much anyone. Weekends are raucous, so grab a window table early and settle in for perpetual ladies' night.

MUSIC

FOLK & COUNTRY

You might actually hear an Irish accent or two at **Conor Byrne Pub** (✉*1540 Ballard Ave. NW, Ballard* ☎*206/784–3640* ⊕*www.conor byrnepub.com*), along with live folk, roots, alt country, bluegrass, and traditional Irish music. There's live music almost every night of the week and great beer (including the obligatory Guinness on tap) at this laid-back pub.

Tractor Tavern (✉*5213 Ballard Ave. NW, Ballard* ☎*206/789–3599* ⊕*www.tractortavern.com*) is Seattle's top spot to catch local and national acts that specialize in roots music and alternative country. The large, dimly lighted hall has all the right touches—wagon-wheel fixtures, exposed-brick walls, and a cheery staff. The sound system is outstanding.

JAZZ, BLUES & R&B

Dimitriou's Jazz Alley (✉*2033 6th Ave., Downtown* ☎*206/441–9729* ⊕*www.jazzalley.com*) is where Seattleites dress up to see nationally known jazz artists. The cabaret-style theater, where intimate tables for two surround the stage, runs shows nightly except Monday. Those with reservations for cocktails or dinner, served during the first set, receive priority seating and $2 off the combined meal-and-show ticket.

Egan's Jam House (✉*1707 N.W. Market St., Ballard* ☎*206/789–1621* ⊕*www.ballardjamhouse.com*) has provided Seattle with a gift—another club devoted solely to jazz that's a neighborhood spot rather than an overpriced tourist trap. This small club and restaurant is devoted to jazz education for local high-schoolers during the day and performances from local and touring acts in the evenings.

Tula's (⊠*2214 2nd Ave., Belltown* ☎*206/443–4221* ⊕*www.tulas. com*) is less of a production (and expense) than Dimitriou's but still manages to offer a similar lineup of more-traditional favorites as well as top-notch local and national acts. The intimate space hosts weekly Latin jazz and Big Band jazz jams and often showcases vocal artists.

ROCK

Neumo's (⊠*925 E. Pike St., Capitol Hill* ☎*206/709–9467* ⊕*www. neumos.com*) was one of the grunge era's iconic clubs (when it was Moe's), and it has managed to reclaim its status as a staple of the Seattle rock scene, despite being closed for a six-year stretch. And it is a great rock venue—sight lines and acoustics are excellent, and the roster of cutting-edge indie rock bands is the best in the city.

Showbox (⊠*1426 1st Ave., Downtown* ☎*206/628–3151* ⊕*www. showboxonline.com*), near Pike Place Market, presents locally and nationally acclaimed artists. This is a great place to see some pretty big-name acts—the acoustics are decent, the venue's small enough so that you don't feel like you're miles away from the performers, and the bar areas flanking the main floor provide some relief if you don't want to join the crush in front of the stage.

The **Triple Door** (⊠*216 Union St., Downtown* ☎*206/838–4333* ⊕*www.thetripledoor.net*) has been referred to (perhaps not kindly) as a rock club for thirty- and fortysomethings. While it's true that you'll see more world music and jazz here than alternative music, and the half-moon booths that make up the majority of the seating in the main room are more cabaret than rock, The Triple Door has an interesting lineup that often appeals to younger patrons, too.

THE ARTS

Tickets for high-profile performances range from $11 to $125; fringe-theater plays and performance-art events range from $5 to $25. Many alternative theaters host "pay-what-you-can" evenings. The Seattle Symphony offers half-price tickets to seniors and students one hour before scheduled performances.

DANCE

On the Boards (⊠*100 W. Roy St., Queen Anne* ☎*206/217–9888* ⊕*www.ontheboards.org*) presents contemporary and cutting-edge dance performances, as well as theater, music, and multimedia events. The main subscription series runs from October through May, but events are scheduled nearly every weekend year-round.

Pacific Northwest Ballet (⊠*McCaw Hall at Seattle Center, Mercer St. at 3rd Ave., Queen Anne* ☎*206/441–2424* ⊕*www.pnb.org*), the resident Seattle company and school, has an elegant home at the Seattle Center. The season, which runs September through June, has traditionally included a mix of classic and international productions (think *Swan Lake* and *Carmina Burana*); however, Peter Boal, a well-known former New York City Ballet principal dancer, shook things up a bit when he took the reins as artistic director in 2006, and the lineup now includes works from celebrated contemporary choreographers like Christopher Wheeldon. Fans of *Swan Lake* and *The Nutcracker* can rest assured that those timeless productions are still part of the company's repertoire.

FILM

★ Seattle has several wonderful film festivals; the **Seattle International Film Festival** (☎*206/633–7151* ⊕*www.seattlefilm.com*) is the biggest one, taking place over several weeks from mid-May to mid-June. Though some highly anticipated events sell out, last-minute and day-of tickets are usually available.

If you're tired of 40-ounce Cokes and $10 popcorn with neon-color butter and wish that moviegoing could be a little more dignified, check
★ out **Central Cinema** (⊠*1411 21st Ave., Central District* ☎*206/686–6684* ⊕*www.central-cinema.com*). The first few rows of this charming, friendly little theater consist of diner-style booths—before the movie starts a waiter takes orders for delicious pizzas, salads, and snacks (including real popcorn with inventive toppings like curry or dill); your food is delivered unobtrusively during the first few minutes of the movie. Wash it down with a normal-size soda, a cup of coffee, or better yet a glass of wine or beer. You won't find first-run films here, but the theater shows a great mix of favorites (*Hairspray* and *E.T.*) and local indie and experimental films.

★ **Cinerama** (⊠*2100 4th Ave., Belltown* ☎*206/441–3080* ⊕*www.cinerama.com*), a 1963 cinema scooped up and restored by billionaire Paul Allen, seamlessly blends the luxury of the theater with state-of-the-art technology. Behind the main, standard-size movie screen sits an enormous, 30-foot by 90-foot restored curved panel—one of only three in the world—used to screen old three-strip films like *How the West Was Won*, as well as 70-millimeter presentations of *2001: Space Odyssey*. The sight lines throughout are amazing. Rear-window captioning, assistive listening devices, audio narration, wheelchair access, and other amenities ensure that everyone has an outstanding experience.

Grand Illusion Cinema (⊠*1403 N.E. 50th St., at University Way, University District* ☎*206/523–3935* ⊕*www.grandillusioncinema.org*), Seattle's longest-running independent movie house, was a tiny screening room in the 1930s. It's still tiny, but it's an outstanding and unique home for independent and art films that feels as comfortable as a home theater.

★ The **Northwest Film Forum** (⊠*1515 12th Ave., Capitol Hill* ☎*206/267–5380* ⊕*www.nwfilmforum.org*) is the cornerstone of the city's independent film scene. Its hip headquarters has two screening rooms that show everything from classics like *East of Eden* to cult hits to experimental films and documentaries.

MUSIC

Seattle Opera (⊠*McCaw Hall at Seattle Center, Mercer St. at 3rd Ave., Queen Anne* ☎*206/389–7676* ⊕*www.seattleopera.org*), whose home is the beautiful Marion Oliver McCaw Hall, stages such productions as *Carmine, Ariadne auf Naxos,* and *The Girl of the Golden West* from

August through May. Evening-event guests are treated to a light show from 30-foot hanging scrims above an outdoor piazza. Extra women's bathrooms and a soundproof baby "crying room" make the programs comfortable and family-friendly.

Fodor's Choice **Seattle Symphony** (✉*Benaroya Hall, 1203 2nd Ave., at University St.,*
★ *Downtown* ☎*206/215–4747* ⊕*www.seattlesymphony.org*) performs under the direction of Gerard Schwartz from September through June in stunning, acoustically superior Benaroya Hall. This exciting symphony has been nominated for numerous Grammy Awards and is well regarded nationally and internationally.

READINGS & LECTURES

★ **Elliot Bay Book Co.** (✉*101 S. Main St., Pioneer Square* ☎*206/624–6600* ⊕*www.elliottbaybook.com*) presents a popular series of renowned local, national, and international author readings in a cozy, basement room next to a café. Events are free, but tickets are often required.

Christian Scientists occupied the Roman-revival-style **Town Hall** (✉*1119 8th Ave., Downtown* ☎*206/652–4255* ⊕*www.townhallseattle.org*) for decades and attending lectures here does feel a bit like going to church, though the folks sharing the pews with you are liable to be among Seattle's most secular. Town Hall hosts scores of events in its spacious yet intimate Great Hall, chief among them talks and panel discussions with leading politicians, authors, scientists, and academics.

THEATERS

5th Avenue Theatre (✉*1308 5th Ave., Downtown* ☎*206/625–1900* ⊕*www.5thavenue.org*) opened in 1926 as a silent-movie house and vaudeville stage, complete with a giant pipe organ and ushers who dressed as cowboys and pirates. Today the chinoiserie landmark has its own theater company, which stages lavish productions October–May. At other times it hosts concerts, lectures, and films. It's worth a peek—it's one of the most beautiful venues in the world.

Intiman Theatre (✉*201 Mercer St., Queen Anne* ☎*206/269–1900* ⊕*www.intiman.org*), at the Seattle Center, presents important contemporary works and classics of the world stage from May through November in its 485-seat space.

Seattle Children's Theatre (✉*Charlotte Martin Theatre at Seattle Center, 2nd Ave. N and Thomas St., Queen Anne* ☎*206/441–3322* ⊕*www. sct.org*), stages top-notch productions of new works as well as adaptations from classic children's literature. After the show, actors come out to answer questions and explain how the tricks are done.

Seattle Repertory Theater (✉*155 Mercer St., Queen Anne* ☎*206/443–2222* ⊕*www.seattlerep.org*) brings new and classic plays to life, split between Seattle Center's Bagley Wright and Leo K. theaters during its September-through-April season. You can preorder a boxed dinner from the Café at the Rep before the show, or linger afterward over coffee and dessert.

SPORTS & THE OUTDOORS

BASEBALL

The **Seattle Mariners** play in the West Division of the American League, and their home is **Safeco Field** (⊠*1st Ave. S and Atlantic St., Sodo* ☎*206/346–4000* ⊕*seattle.mariners.mlb.com*), a retractable-roof stadium where there really isn't a bad seat in the house. You can purchase tickets through Ticketmaster; online or by phone from Safeco Field (to be picked up at the Will Call); in person at Safeco's box office (no surcharges), which is open daily 10–6; or from the Mariners team store at 4th Avenue and Stewart Street in Downtown. The cheap seats cost $7; the best seats cost $38–$55.

BASKETBALL

The men's NBA season runs from November to April. The **Seattle SuperSonics,** known simply as the Sonics, play at **Key Arena** (⊠*Seattle Center, 1st Ave. N and Mercer St., Queen Anne* ☎*206/283–3865, 800/462–2849 NBA* ⊕*www.nba.com/sonics*). Tickets range from $10 to $200 for courtside seating. You can buy tickets online, at the box office, or by calling the NBA toll-free number.

BEACHES

The general number for information on all city beaches is 206/684–4075. The City of Seattle's Web site, www.seattle.gov/parks, also has details on all parks within city limits, as well as detailed directions on how to reach them by car.

FodorśChoice ★ **Alki Beach** (⊠*1702 Alki Ave. SW, West Seattle*). In summer, cars inch along Alki Avenue, seeking a coveted parking space, all the passengers heading for this 2½-mi stretch of sand that has views of both the Seattle skyline and the Olympic Mountains. It's something of a California beach scene (except for the water temperature), with in-line skaters, joggers, and cyclists sharing the walkway and sun-loving singles playing volleyball and flirting. Year-round, families come to build sand castles, beachcomb, and fly kites; in winter, storm-watchers come to see the crashing waves. Facilities include drinking water, grills, picnic tables, phones, and restrooms; restaurants line the street across from the beach. To get here from Downtown, take either I–5 south or Highway 99 south to the West Seattle Bridge and exit onto Harbor Avenue Southwest, turning right at the stoplight.

Golden Gardens Park (⊠*8498 Seaview Pl. NW, near N.W. 85th St., Ballard*). Puget Sound waters are bone-chilling cold, but that doesn't stop folks from jumping in to cool off. Besides brave swimmers, who congregate on the small strip of sand between the parking lot and the canteen, this park is packed with sunbathers in summer. In other seasons, beachcombers explore during low tide, and groups gather around bonfires to socialize and watch the sun go down. The park has drinking water, grills, picnic tables, phones, and restrooms. It also has two wetlands, a short loop trail, and a rugged coast with breathtaking views. From Downtown, take Elliott Avenue N, which becomes 15th Avenue W, and cross the Ballard Bridge. Turn left to head west on Market Street and follow signs to the Ballard Locks; continue about another mile to the park. Note that even though the park has two dedicated parking lots, these quickly fill up on weekends, so be prepared to circle. On weekdays the swimming beach gets packed with school and summer camp groups; go early or late in the day if you don't want to be surrounded by screaming kids.

Green Lake (✉ *7201 E. Greenlake Dr. N, Green Lake*) is best known for its ever-lively jogging path, but this beauty of a lake also has two small beach areas from which it's possible to swim. The West Beach is on the northwestern corner of the lake by N. 76th Street; the East Beach is directly across the lake on its east side around N.E. 72nd Street. Both beaches have diving boards, swimming rafts, and lifeguards in summer, but not much in terms of actual sand.

Madrona Park (✉ *853 Lake Washington Blvd., Madrona*). Several beach parks and green spaces front the lake along Lake Washington Boulevard; Madrona Park is one of the largest. Young swimmers stay in the roped-in area while teens and adults swim out to a floating raft with a diving board. Runners and in-line skaters follow the mile-long trail along the shore. Kids clamber about the sculpted-sand garden and climb on rocks and logs. Grassy areas encourage picnicking; there are grills, picnic tables, phones, restrooms, and showers. A barbecue stand is open seasonally. From Downtown, go east on Yesler Way about 2 mi to 32nd Avenue. Turn left onto Lake Dell Avenue and then right; go to Lake Washington Boulevard and take a left.

★ **Matthews Beach Park** (✉ *Sand Point Way NE and N.E. 93rd St., Sand Point*). On warm summer days the parking lot and nearby streets overflow with people visiting Seattle's largest freshwater swimming beach. The Burke-Gilman Trail, popular with cyclists and runners, travels through the park. Picnic areas, basketball hoops, and a big playground round out the amenities. From Downtown, take I–5 north and get off at the Lake City Way Northeast exit. Stay on Lake City Way for about 1½ mi. Turn right on to Northeast 95th Street, right onto Sand Point Way Northeast, and left onto Northeast 93rd Street.

Fodor's Choice **Sand Point Magnuson Park** (✉ *Bordered by N.E. 65th and 74th Sts., Sand*
★ *Point Way NE, and Lake Washington, entrances at 65th St. and 74th St., Sand Point* ☎ *206/684–4946*). As it was once an airport, it's not surprising that this 200-acre park northeast of the University District (U-District) is flat and open. The paved trails are wonderful for cycling, in-line skating, and pushing a stroller. Many kids have learned to ride their two-wheelers here; quite a few more have spent time on the large playground. Leashed dogs are welcome on the trails; a large off-leash area includes one of the few public beaches where pooches can swim. Farther south, on the mile-long shore, there's a swimming beach, a seasonal wading pool, and a boat launch. The park also has tennis courts, sports fields, and a terrific kite-flying hill. Be sure to look for the unique public art. *The Fin Project: From Swords to Plowshares* uses submarine fins to depict a pod of orca whales. *No Appointment Necessary* has

two bright red chairs extended into the sky. *The Sound Garden* (at the neighboring National Oceanic and Atmospheric Administration campus) has steel pipes that give off sounds when the wind blows for an art display that you can hear as well as see. From Downtown, take I–5 north to the Northeast 65th Street exit, turn right and continue east to Sand Point Way Northeast.

BICYCLING

The city-maintained Burke-Gilman Trail follows an abandoned railroad line 12 mi along Seattle's waterfront from Lake Washington almost to Salmon Bay. Discovery Park is a very tranquil place to tool around in. Myrtle Edwards Park, north of Pier 70, has a two-lane path for bicycling and running. The islands of the Puget Sound are also easily explored by bike (there are rental places by the ferry terminals), though be forewarned that Bainbridge has some tough hills.

King County has more than 100 mi of paved and nearly 70 mi of unpaved routes including the Sammamish River, Interurban, Green River, Cedar River, Snoqualmie Valley, and Soos Creek trails. For more information contact the King County Parks and Recreation office.

The **Bicycle Alliance of Washington** (☎206/224–9252 ⊕*www.bicycle alliance.org*), the state's largest cycling advocacy group, is a great source for information. The **Cascade Bicycle Club** (☎206/522–2453 ⊕*www.cascade.org*) organizes more than 1,000 rides annually for recreational and hard-core bikers. Of its major events the most famous is the Seattle-to-Portland Bicycle Classic. It offers daily rides in Seattle and the Eastside that range from "superstrenuous" to leisurely all-ages jaunts, like easy passes through the Japanese Garden at the Washington Park Arboretum. Check out the Web site for a complete list of rides and contact information. The **Seattle Bicycle Program** (☎206/684–7583 ⊕*www.seattle.gov/transportation/bikeprogram.htm*) was responsible for the creation of the city's multiuse trails (aka bike routes) as well as pedestrian paths and roads with wide shoulders—things, in other words, that benefit bicyclists. The agency's Web site has downloadable route maps; you can also call the number above to request a printed version of the Seattle Bicycling Guide Map.

RENTALS

Gregg's Greenlake Cycle (✉*7007 Woodlawn Ave. NE, Green Lake* ☎206/523–1822 ⊕*www.greggscycles.com*). On Green Lake's northern end, this Seattle institution has been in business since 1932. It sells and rents mountain bikes, standard road touring bikes, and hybrids; helmets and locks are included with each rental. Gregg's is close to the Burke-Gilman Trail and across the street from the Green Lake Trail. Rental fees range from $20 to $50 for the day, $25 to $75 overnight, and $60 to $135 per week. Gregg's also rents in-line skates, jogging strollers, snowboarding equipment, and snowshoes.

BOATING & KAYAKING

★ **Agua Verde Paddle Club and Cafe** (✉ *1303 N.E. Boat St., University District* ☎ *206/545–8570* ⊕ *www.aguaverde.com*). Start out by renting a kayak and paddling along either the Lake Union shoreline, with its hodgepodge of funky-to-fabulous houseboats and dramatic Downtown vistas, or Union Bay on Lake Washington, with its marshes and cattails. Afterward, take in the lakefront as you wash down some Tex-Mex food with a margarita. Kayaks are available March through October and are rented by the hour—$15 for singles, $18 for doubles. The third and fourth hours are free on weekdays; fourth hours are free on weekends.

★ **Center for Wooden Boats** (✉ *1010 Valley St., Lake Union* ☎ *206/382–2628* ⊕ *www.cwb.org*). Seattle's free maritime heritage museum also rents classic wooden rowboats and sailboats for short trips around Lake Union. Rowboats, pedal boats, and canoes are $15 an hour on weekdays and $25 an hour on weekends. Sloops and catboats cost $20–$45 an hour, depending on the type and size of the vessel. There's a $10 skills-check fee. Free half-hour guided sails and steamboat rides are offered on Sunday from 2 to 3 (arrive an hour early).

Green Lake Boat Rental (✉ *7351 W. Green Lake Way N, Green Lake* ☎ *206/527–0171*) is the source for canoes, paddleboats, sailboats, kayaks, sailboards, and rowboats to ply Green Lake's calm waters. On beautiful summer afternoons, however, be prepared to spend most of your time negotiating other traffic on the water as well as in the parking lot. Fees are $10 an hour for paddleboats, single kayaks, and rowboats; $12 an hour for double kayaks; and $14 an hour for sailboats and sailboards. Don't confuse this place with the Green Lake Small Craft Center, which offers sailing programs but no rentals.

Moss Bay Rowing and Kayak Center (✉ *1001 Fairview Ave. N, Lake Union* ☎ *206/682–2031* ⊕ *www.mossbay.net*). Moss Bay rents a variety of rowing craft—including Whitehall pulling boats, wherries, and sliding-seat rowboats. Single kayaks rent for $12 per hour, doubles go for $17. You can also rent kayaks to take with you on trips outside the city; daily rates are $55 for singles and $75 for doubles, weekly rates are $235 for singles and $315 for doubles. You can rent rowing shells or sailboats for $25–$35 depending on the type of craft; there is an additional $10 skills-check fee for renting these types of vessels. The center offers rowing and sailing lessons daily for $65 for a onetime private lesson; two or four lesson series cost $100 or $200 respectively. Lastly, the center also offers daily 2½-hour sailing tours of Lake Union as well as guided kayaking tours; prices start at $45 per person.

Northwest Outdoor Center (✉ *2100 Westlake Ave. N, Lake Union* ☎ *206/281–9694* ⊕ *www.nwoc.com*). This center on Lake Union's west side rents one- or two-person kayaks (it also has a few triples) by the hour or day, including equipment and basic or advanced instruction. The hourly rate is $12 for a single and $17 for a double, with daily maximums of $60 and $80, respectively. Third and fourth hours are free during the week; a fourth hour is free on weekends. If you want to find your own water, NWOC offers "to-go" kayaks; the rate for a single is $65 first day, plus $35 each additional day. Doubles cost $85 the first day and $45 for each day thereafter. In summer, reserve least three days ahead. NWOC also runs guided trips to the Nisqually Delta and Chuckanut Bay for $70 per person. Sunset tours to Golden Gardens Park ($40 per person) and moonlight tours of Portage Bay ($30 per person) are other options. Every May there are two overnight whale-watching trips to the San Juan Islands for $325 per person.

Waterfront Activities Center (⊠ *3800 Montlake Blvd. NE, University District* ☎ *206/543–9433*). This center behind UW's Husky Stadium rents three-person canoes and four-person rowboats for $7.50 an hour February through October. You can tour the Lake Washington shoreline or take the Montlake Cut portion of the ship canal and explore Lake Union. You can also row to nearby Foster Island and visit the Washington Park Arboretum.

FOOTBALL

The **Seattle Seahawks** play in the $430 million, state-of-the-art **Quest Field** (⊠ *800 Occidental Ave., Sodo* ☎ *425/827–9777* ⊕ *www.seahawks.com*). Single-game tickets go on sale in July or August and all home games sell out quickly. Tickets are expensive, with the cheapest seats in the 300 section (where you actually get a really good view of the field) starting at $42. Note that traffic and parking are both nightmares on game days; try to take public transportation if possible.

HIKING

Washington State has so many beautiful trails, if there was ever a state sport, hiking should be it. There are enough trails in Mt. Rainier National Park alone to keep you busy (and awestruck) for months. If hiking is a high priority for you, and if you have more than a few days in town, your best bet is to grab a hiking book or check out the site www.cooltrails.com, rent a car, and head out to the Olympics or east to the Cascades (⇨ Chapter 4, Washington for more information on the major parks in the area). If you have to stay close to the city, don't despair, there are many beautiful walks within town and many gratifying hikes only an hour away.

Within Seattle city limits, the best trails can be found in Discovery and Seward parks and at the Washington Park Arboretum. Following the Burke-Gilman Trail from Fremont to its midway point at Matthews Beach Park (north of the U-District) would take several hours and cover more than 7 mi. You'll get a good glimpse of all sides of Seattle as the trail winds through both urban areas and leafier residential areas; the first part of the walk takes you right along the Lake Washington Ship

OUTSIDE SEATTLE

Cougar Mountain Regional Wildland Park. This spectacular park in the "Issaquah Alps" has more than 36 mi of hiking trails and 12 mi of bridle trails within its 3,000-plus acres. The Indian Trail, believed to date back 8,000 years, was part of a trade route that Native Americans used to reach North Bend and the Cascades. Thick pine forests rise to spectacular mountaintop views; there are waterfalls, deep caves, and the remnants of a former mining town. Look for deer, black bears, bobcats, bald eagles, and pileated woodpeckers, among many other woodland creatures. ⊠ *18201 S.E. Cougar Mountain Dr., Issaquah* ⊹ *From Downtown Seattle take I-90 east; follow signs to park beyond Issaquah* ⊙ *Daily 8 AM–dusk.*

★ **Larrabee State Park.** A favorite spot of the hippies and college students that call Bellingham home, Larrabee has two lakes, a coastline with tidal pools, and 15 mi of hiking trails. The Interurban Trail, which parallels an old railway line, is perfect for leisurely strolls or trail running. Head up Chuckanut Mountain to reach the lakes and to get great views of the San Juan Islands. ⊹ *Take I-5 north to Exit 231. Turn right onto Chuckanut Dr. and follow that road to park entrance.*

Mt. Si. A good place to cut your teeth before setting out on more-ambitious hikes or a good place to just witness the local hiking and trail-running communities in all their weird and wonderful splendor, Mt. Si offers a moderately challenging hike with views of a valley (slightly marred by the suburbs) and the Olympic Mountains in the distance. The main trail to Haystack Basin is 8 mi round-trip, but there are several obvious places to rest or turn around if you'd like to keep the hike to 3 or 4 mi. Note that serenity is in short supply here—this is an extremely popular trail thanks to its proximity to Seattle. ⊹ *Take I-90 east to Exit 31 (toward North Bend). Turn onto North Bend Way and then make a left onto Mt. Si Rd. and follow that road to trailhead parking lot.*

ROCK CLIMBING

The mountains of Washington have cut the teeth (among other body parts) of many a world-class climber. So it's only natural that there are several places to get in some practice.

REI (⊠ *222 Yale Ave. N, Downtown* ☎ *206/223–1944* ⊕ *www.rei.com*). Every day around 200 people have a go at REI's Pinnacle, a 65-foot indoor climbing rock. Climbing hours are Monday 10–6, Wednesday–Saturday 10–9, and Sunday 10–5. The cost is $15 including equipment. Although reservations are a good idea, you can also schedule a climb in person. The wait can be anywhere from 30 minutes to four hours, but it's rare that you don't get to climb on the very day you sign up. Adult climbing classes ($25) are held on Tuesday nights at 6:15 PM and kids' climbing classes ($15) are held on Sunday at 5:30 PM.

★ **Schurman Rock** (⊠ *Camp Long, 5200 35th Ave. SW, West Seattle* ☎ *206/ 684–7434* ⊕ *www.ci.seattle.wa.us/parks/environment/camplong.htm*). The nation's first man-made climbing rock was designed in the 1930s by local climbing expert Clark Schurman. Generations of climbers have practiced here, from beginners to rescue teams to such legendary mountaineers as Jim Whittaker, the first American to conquer Mt. Everest. Don't expect something grandiose—the rock is only 25 feet high. It's open for climbs Tuesday–Saturday 10–6.

Stone Gardens Rock Gym (⊠ *2839 N.W. Market St., Ballard* ☎ *206/781–9828* ⊕ *www.stonegardens.com*). Beyond the trying-it-out phase? Head here and take a stab at the bouldering routes and top-rope faces. Although there's plenty to challenge the advanced climber, the mellow vibe is a big plus for families, part-timers, and the aspiring novice-to-intermediate crowd. The cost is $15; renting a full equipment package of shoes, harness, and chalk bag costs $9. There are "Climbing 101" classes most weekday evenings for $45.

RUNNING

The roughly 3-mi trail that rings picturesque Green Lake seems custom-made for running—and walking, bicycling, rollerblading, fishing, lounging on the grass, and feeding the waterfowl. Seward Park has a more-secluded, less-used 3-mi loop where the park juts out into Lake Washington in southeast Seattle. At least one pair of bald eagles is known to nest in the park, so it's not unusual for a trip around the loop to include spotting an eagle *and* Mt. Rainier.

Other good running locales are the Burke-Gilman Trail, the reservoir at Capitol Hill's Volunteer Park, and at Myrtle Edwards Park, north of Pier 70 Downtown. Discovery Park in Magnolia has a 3-mi trail that takes you "off-roading" through patches of woods and meadows, and along bluffs.

■TIP➔ **If you need a good pair of running shoes, check out Super Jock 'n Jill on East Greenlake Drive and 72nd Street. Staff members are extremely knowledgeable, and they'll even let you take each pair you try on out for a test run to ensure proper fit.**

SHOPPING

As appropriate for a city that can at times feel like a small town, most of Seattle's best stores are cute neighborhood boutiques; however, the city also has quite a few malls and we defy you to name a major national store that isn't represented in the 5th Avenue shopping district.

DOWNTOWN

ANTIQUES & COLLECTIBLES

Antiques at Pike Place. Well stocked with vintage objects of all styles from dozens of vendors, this is the kind of antiques shop that's fun for everyone to browse in—there are plenty of small, affordable treasures to take home, from jewelry to vases to clocks to ceramic pieces. ⊠ *92 Stewart St., Downtown* ☎ *206/441–9643* ⊕ *www.antiquesat pikeplace.com.*

Big People Toys. The Madison Street store offers 18th- and 19th-century Asian antiques focusing on furniture from China. You'll find the standard lacquered trunks and small boxes and carved wooden pieces, but what will really get your attention is the stunning collection of insects under glass. ✉ *90 Madison St. , Downtown* ☎ *206/749–9016* ⊕ *www. bigpeopletoys.com.*

★ **Honeychurch Antiques.** Known for its high standards of quality and service, this striking gallery has several rooms of Asian art, artifacts, and furniture ranging from museum-grade antiques to early-20th-century decorative pieces. The owners also oversee Glenn Richards, which has a similar focus and equally impressive collection of Asian antiques. It's three blocks south of Honeychurch, around the corner on Denny Avenue. ✉ *411 Westlake Ave. N, Downtown* ☎ *206/622–1204* ⊕ *www. honeychurch.com.*

BOOKS

Left Bank Books. The bookstore for activists, Left Bank has progressive (often antiestablishment) political and social books covering everything from environmental issues to race relations to gay and lesbian rights. It's a not-for-profit shop, owned and operated by its staff. ✉ *92 Pike St., Downtown* ☎ *206/622–0195* ⊕ *www.leftbankbooks.com.*

★ **Peter Miller Architectural & Design Books and Supplies.** A floor-to-ceiling stock of architecture, art, and graphic design books in this urbane store attracts a stylish clientele. Sleek notebooks, bags and portfolios, drawing tools, and gifts are on hand for the discerning designer or businessperson, including Le Corbusier stencils. ✉ *1930 1st Ave. , Downtown* ☎ *206/441–4114* ⊕ *www.petermiller.com.*

CLOTHING

Alhambra. The interior at this pricey boutique may be Moorish-inspired, but the clothes are strictly now (and slightly European). If you need a party dress, you should definitely take a look here, though you'll also find sophisticated separates casual enough for the office or for brunch. The clothing here appeals to a wide age range—the connective thread is the emphasis on fine fabrics and detailing. ✉ *101 Pine St., Downtown* ☎ *206/621–9571* ⊕ *www.alhambranet.com.*

Baby and Co. Taking style inspiration directly from the major fashion houses of Europe and Japan, this longtime Seattle favorite dresses women in esoteric fashions by Girbaud, Ishiko, and Lilith. You'll pay a lot for the privilege of being ahead of the trends. ✉ *1936 1st Ave., Downtown* ☎ *206/448–4077.*

Butch Blum. The attentive staff at this decidedly upscale retailer for men and women gives expert guidance on cultured creations by Giorgio Armani, Ermenegildo Zegna, Yohji Yamamoto, and Jil Sander—just to drop a few names. ✉ *1408 5th Ave., Downtown* ☎ *206/622–5760* ⊕ *www.butchblum.com.*

Isadora's Antique Clothing. It may look like every other vintage store, but Isadora's has built up quite a reputation for its excellent-quality vintage apparel (much of it from big-name designers like Dior and Halston), outrageous party dresses, and vintage and estate jewelry. ✉ *1915 1st St., Downtown* ☎ *206/441–7711* ⊕ *www.isadoras.com.*

★ **Mario's of Seattle.** Known for fabulous service and designer labels, this high-end boutique treats every client like a superstar. Men shop the ground floor for Armani, Zegna, and Dolce & Gabbana; women ascend the ornate staircase for Prada, Vera Wang, and Marc Jacobs. A freestanding Hugo Boss boutique sells the sharpest tuxedos in town. ⊠*1513 6th Ave., Downtown* ☎*206/223–1461* ⊕*www.marios.com.*

★ **Tulip.** This sweet boutique is all about flirtatious clothing that has a much longer shelf life (and more dignity) than the trends-of-the-moment goods populating most of the Downtown stores. Even if you don't find anything, you'll be glad you stepped off busy 1st Avenue to browse in this lovely space—with soothing earth tones, a few pieces of Indonesian furniture, and a supremely laid-back vibe, Tulip feels more like a spa than a store. ⊠*1201 1st Ave., Downtown* ☎*206/223–1790* ⊕*www.tulip-seattle.com.*

DEPARTMENT STORES

★ **Nordstrom.** Seattle's own local retail giant sells good-quality clothing, accessories, cosmetics, jewelry, and lots of shoes—in keeping with its roots in footwear—including many hard-to-find sizes. Deservedly renowned for its customer service, the busy Downtown flagship has a concierge desk and valet parking. ■TIP➔ **The Nordstrom Rack store at 1st Avenue and Spring Street by Pike Place Market has great deals on marked-down items; new merchandise arrives every Tuesday.** ⊠*500 Pine St., Downtown* ☎*206/628–2111.*

FOOTWEAR

A Mano. Ped, a superpopular shoe store closed and morphed into … another shoe store. Like its predecessor, A Mano sells high-quality shoes from all over the world, many of them handmade, along with some jewelry from local designers and other accessories. The space is still lovely: colorful handbags hang on exposed-brick walls and patrons can sit on comfy emerald-green couches while trying things on. ⊠*1115 1st Ave., Downtown* ☎*206/292–1767* ⊕*www.shopamano.com.*

John Fluevog. You'll find the store's own brand of fun, funky boots, chunky leather shoes, and urbanized wooden sandals here in men's and women's styles. ⊠*205 Pine St., Downtown* ☎*206/441–1065* ⊕*www.fluevog.com.*

GIFTS & HOME DECOR

★ **Great Jones Home.** Though refurbished vintage furniture is one of the store's specialties, most shoppers come to Great Jones Home to browse through the stylish housewares (French candles, dishes, bath products) in this spacious, skylighted store. One whitewashed wall is devoted to imported fabrics. ⊠*1921 2nd Ave., Downtown* ☎*206/448–9405* ⊕*www.greatjoneshome.com.*

★ **Peter Miller Details.** Streamlined Alessi housewares and brightly printed Marimekko bags are part of the well-edited stock of indispensable *objets* for home and office in this lifestyle gallery. ⊠*1924 1st Ave., Downtown* ☎*206/441–4114* ⊕*www.petermiller.com.*

♺ **Schmancy.** At first glance, the toys here seem a little too hip for kids under the age of 20. After all, not many kids would want to foster stuffed animals that come with not only their own names but their own psychiatric disorders: Kroko the crocodile clutches his pillow as he fights off paranoid hallucinations. But not all the figurines and toys in this tiny, adorable store are so troubled—the plush cupcakes and donuts seem very content. ✉1932 2nd Ave., Downtown ☎206/728–8008 ⊕www.schmancytoys.com.

Watson Kennedy Fine Living. This jewel box of a store in the courtyard of the Inn at the Market stocks luxurious bath products and aromatic gifts. The sister store on 1st Avenue and Madison Street has vintage furniture, tableware, gourmet olive oil, and its own line of beeswax candles. ✉86 Pine St., Downtown ☎206/443–6281 ⊕www.watsonkennedy.com.

Velocity Art & Design. Velocity's showroom has a little bit of everything: furniture, bedding, lighting, accessories, and artwork from local artists. It all follows a mid-century esthetic, whether a piece is an overt homage to an icon of the area or just coyly retro new creation from one of today's hippest designers. Prices are high, but so is the quality of the selection. ✉251 Yale Ave., Downtown ☎206/749–9575 ⊕www.velocityartanddesign.com.

OUTDOOR CLOTHING & EQUIPMENT

North Face. You can't swing a salmon in this town without hitting a North Face jacket. North Face must be doing something right, because they seem to provide the garments of choice for residents who don't believe in umbrellas. Besides the ubiquitous slickers, you'll find plenty of outdoor equipment. ✉1023 1st Ave., Downtown ☎206/622–4111 ⊕www.thenorthface.com.

Fodor's Choice
★

REI. REI (for the record, Recreational Equipment, Inc., but nobody calls it that) is Seattle's sports-equipment mecca. The enormous flagship store has an incredible selection of outdoor gear and its own 65-foot climbing wall. The staff is extremely knowledgeable and there always seems to be enough help on hand even when the store is busy. You can try things out on the mountain-bike test trail or in the simulated rain booth. ■TIP➜ REI also rents gear such as tents, sleeping bags, and backpacks in case you don't want to lug all your camping stuff across the country. ✉222 Yale Ave. N, Downtown ☎206/223–1944 ⊕www.rei.com.

WINE & SPECIALTY FOODS

★ **Pike & Western Wine Shop.** Pike & Western is one of the two best wineshops in the city (the other is McCarthy & Schiering in Queen Anne). It has a comprehensive stock of wines from the Pacific Northwest, California, Italy, and France—and expert advice from friendly salespeople to guide your choice. ✉1934 Pike Pl., Downtown ☎206/441–1307 ⊕www.pikeandwestern.com.

The Tasting Room. A handful of Washington State boutique wineries are represented at this tasting room and wineshop. Most of the wines featured are handcrafted and/or reserve vintages. At the northern end of Post Alley, this quiet, tucked-away shop is a great place to sequester yourself from the mania of the market and try a few bottles you probably won't find in any other wineshop. ✉1924 Post Alley, Downtown ☎206/770–9463 ⊕www.winesofwashington.com.

BELLTOWN

CLOTHING

Karan Dannenberg Clothier. Though the clothes here aren't cheap, this is one of the most egalitarian boutiques in Seattle. Dannenberg stocks sophisticated, modern clothing, but doesn't bow to useless trends, meaning that items will last more than one season. She also stocks a lot of plus sizes, something you don't see in many boutiques. Belltown party girls can find the perfect pair of jeans and executives can find classy work-appropriate clothes. The store also stocks glamorous formal wear. ⊠*2232 1st Ave., Belltown* ☎*206/441–3442.*

Kuhlman. This tiny store on the same ultrahip block as the Ace Hotel has a careful selection of urban street wear that includes hard-to-find designers—it's sophisticated while still maintaining an edge. If you've got some time, Kuhlman is best known for creating unique custom jeans, pants, and jackets, often from superb European and Japanese fabrics. ⊠*2419 1st Ave., Belltown* ☎*206/441–1999.*

Monica Gutweis. Gutweis herself makes each one-of-a-kind garment in this tiny gallery; her fabrics and detailing have earned her a cult following. If you want to let your inner rock star out without letting go of your dignity, come to this store. Gutweis is a little bit Goth, a little bit punk, and not one bit pretentious; therefore, her pieces are dramatic, but never impractical. She also stocks jewelry and accessories from other local designers. ⊠*2405 1st Ave., Belltown* ☎*206/956–4620.*

FOOTWEAR

★ **J. Gilbert Footwear.** Wrap your feet in comfort and European styling by designers Thierry Rabotin, Anyi Lu, and Taryn Rose. Along with limited-edition deluxe cowboy boots, you'll find glove-soft leather jackets and chic, casual clothing. ⊠*2025 1st Ave., Belltown* ☎*206/441–1182* ⊕*www.jgilbertfootwear.com.*

PIONEER SQUARE

Many pay lots in the neighborhood participate in the "Parking Around the Square" program, which works with local businesses to offer shoppers validated parking; the Web site www.pioneersquare.org lists the lots and stores that offer it.

ANTIQUES & COLLECTIBLES

Chidori Asian Antiques. So packed full of stuff it looks more like a curio shop than a high-end antique seller, Chidori offers high-quality Asian antiques, pre-Columbian and primitive art, and antiquities from all over the world. ⊠*108 S. Jackson St., Pioneer Square* ☎*206/343–7736* w *www.chidoriasianart.com.*

Flury & Company. View one of the largest collections of vintage photographs by Edward Curtis, along with Native American antiques, traditional carvings, baskets, jewelry, and tools in a historic space that's as interesting as the store's wares. ⊠*322 1st Ave., Pioneer Square* ☎*206/587–0260* ⊕*www.fluryco.com.*

Jean Williams Antiques. Eighteenth- and 19th-century English and French furniture is arranged formally in an elegant space. This is the polar opposite of exploring cluttered Asian antiques stores—less an adventure and more a serious appointment with your checkbook. ⊠*115 S. Jackson St., Pioneer Square* 🕾*206/622–1110* ⊕*www.jeanwilliams antiques.com.*

★ **Kagedo Japanese Art and Antiques.** The finest quality Japanese antiques and works by modern masters are on display in this influential gallery. Among the treasures are intricately carved *okimono* (miniature figures rendered in wood, ivory, or bronze), stone garden ornaments, studio basketry, and textiles. The gallery itself is worth a look—it's beautifully laid out, and includes a small rock garden and rice-paper screens that cover the storefront's picture windows. ⊠*520 1st Ave. S, Pioneer Square* 🕾*206/467–9077* ⊕*www.kagedo.com.*

Laguna. Watch your step as you navigate through this colorful, crowded shop; it's wall-to-wall collectible 20th-century American dinnerware, art pottery, vintage linens, tiles, and garden pieces. ⊠*116 S. Washington St., Pioneer Square* 🕾*206/682–6162* ⊕*www.lagunapottery.com.*

BOOKS & MUSIC

★ **Bud's Jazz Records.** Bud's is a Seattle institution (it's over 20 years old), and the store almost makes up for the fact that the city doesn't have a great jazz scene. A narrow set of stairs leads to a tightly packed underground store that sells just jazz (equal parts vinyl and CDs) and lots of it, including hard-to-find recordings. And there's always something good playing on the sound system, making this a great place for a leisurely browse. ⊠*102 S. Jackson St., Pioneer Square* 🕾*206/628–0045.*

Fodor'sChoice **Elliott Bay Book Company.** Many Seattleites consider this enormous independent bookstore the literary heart of the city. More than 150,000 titles are arranged on rustic wooden shelves in a labyrinth of brick-lined rooms. A side room contains used books—about 22,000 of them—on all subjects; some are signed first editions. The store is well known for its popular lectures and readings by local and international authors. As you enter, check out the great selection of Pacific Northwest history books and fiction titles by local authors, complete with handwritten recommendation cards from staff members. ■ TIP➔ **The café in the basement is one of neighborhood's best options for lunch or a quick bite.** ⊠*101 S. Main St., Pioneer Square* 🕾*206/624–6600* ⊕*www.elliott baybook.com.*

CLOTHING

Betty Blue. Big-ticket designer labels at deep discount prices are snapped up quickly at this boutique. You'll find last season's runway creations by Prada, Stella McCartney, Jil Sander, Michael Kors, Balenciaga, and many others. The store carries men's clothing, too. ⊠*608 2nd Ave., Pioneer Square* 🕾*206/442–6888* ⊕*www.shopbettyblue.com.*

Ragazzi's Flying Shuttle. For older women who want to add some whimsy and color to their wardrobe without veering into crazy cat-lady territory, Ragazzi's offers locally crafted, handwoven clothing in bold colors, as well as chunky, get-noticed jewelry. ⊠*607 1st Ave., Pioneer Square* 🕾*206/343–9762.*

Violette. The owner of this lovely little boutique has a penchant for vintage and accordingly, many of pieces sold here are made with vintage fabrics or affect a vintage style. Clothes are fresh, functional, and girlie in a good way—just like the best fashions from the '40s and '50s. The store also carries handbags and some home-decor items. ✉602 *2nd Ave., Pioneer Square* ☎206/652–8991 ⊕*www.violetteboutique. blogspot.com.*

GIFTS & HOME DECOR

Glass House Studio. Seattle's oldest glassblowing studio and gallery lets you watch fearless artisans at work in the "hot shop." Studio pieces and other works on display are for sale. ✉*311 Occidental Ave. S, Pioneer Square* ☎206/682–9939 ⊕*www.glasshouse-studio.com.*

Northwest Fine Woodworking. More than 20 fine Northwest craftspeople are represented in this large, handsome showroom. Even if you're not in the market for new furniture, stop in for a reminder of how much personality wood pieces can have when they're not mass-produced. The store also carries gifts like chess sets and ornate handcrafted kaleidoscopes and more-practical household items like wooden bowls and utensils. ✉*101 S. Jackson St., Pioneer Square* ☎206/625–0542 ⊕*www.nwfinewoodworking.com.*

CAPITOL HILL

BOOKS & MUSIC

Bailey/Coy Books. Handwritten recommendations guide you through a thoughtful selection of diverse topics; there's a substantial section of gay and lesbian literature. ✉*414 Broadway Ave. E, Capitol Hill* ☎206/323–8842 ⊕ *baileycoybooks.com.*

Twice Sold Tales. This excellent used-book store has more shelf space than most and the best sleeping-cat-to-customer ratio in the city. As only a Capitol Hill business could afford to do, the shop stays open until 2 AM on Friday, with 20% discounts offered between 11 PM and closing. ✉*905 E. John St., Capitol Hill* ☎206/324–2421.

Wall of Sound. World-music enthusiasts who can't bear to listen to another Putumayo release will love this small, neatly organized boutique. From Japanese avant-rock to the latest club hits of Ghana to local artists warping folk music into something palatable, if it's obscure, experimental, and good, you'll find it here. ✉*315 E. Pine St., Capitol Hill* ☎206/441–9880 ⊕*www.wosound.com.*

CLOTHING

Atlas Clothing. Atlas is loaded with previously appreciated shirts, jackets, and tees; stacks of new and vintage denim; must-have sneakers from the '70s and '80s; and tons of accessories. This is not over-the-top costume vintage; visit Red Light for that. ✉*1515 Broadway, Capitol Hill* ☎206/329–4460.

Juniper. Slightly off the beaten path in the eastern neighborhood of Madrona—you'll have to drive here from Capitol Hill—this sleek boutique offers high-priced "haute green" clothing and accessories from designers as diverse as American Apparel and Anna Cohen, a Portland-based designer and current darling of green fashion. Sustainable materials are turned into sophisticated fashions—if you can't believe that bamboo can be made into a dress, head here. ⊠*3314 E. Spring St., Madrona* ☎*206/838–7496* ⊕*www.juniperinmadrona.com.*

★ **Le Frock.** It may look like just another overcrowded consignment shop, but Le Frock is Seattle's favorite vintage store. Among the racks, you'll find plenty of labels, and the store has a good shoe selection as well. Prices are reasonable and there are frequent sales. ⊠*317 E. Pine St., Capitol Hill* ☎*206/623–5339* ⊕*www.lefrockonline.com.*

Pretty Parlor. You'd better like pink if you're going to step into this boutique. Being a fan of tutus and lace doesn't hurt either, though the parlor's mix of vintage, used, and new clothes isn't nearly as precious as its interior. The creative, one-off pieces from local designers are usually the best things in stock, though the used and vintage sections often have outrageous party dresses that are fun to try on even if you have nowhere to wear them. Jewelry, handbags, shoes, and hats round out the store and there's even a competent selection of men's clothes. ⊠*119 Summit Ave. E, Capitol Hill* ☎*206/405–2883* ⊕*www.pretty parlor.com.*

★ **Red Light Clothing Exchange.** Nostalgia rules in this cavernous space filled with well-organized, good-quality vintage clothing. Fantasy outfits from decades past are arranged by era or by genre. There's plenty of denim, leather, and disco threads alongside cowboy boots and evening wear. There's a smaller branch in the University District. ⊠*312 Broadway E, Capitol Hill* ☎*206/329–2200* ⊕*www.redlightvintage.com.*

FOOTWEAR

Capitol 1524. Savvy "sneakerheads" come here to buy limited-edition Nikes, Pumas, Adidas, and New Balance kicks and reissued styles from the 1980s. Vintage shoes are also on sale at premium prices. This is one of the few stores in the neighborhood where you'll hear hip-hop playing instead of indie rock. ⊠*1524 E. Olive Way, Capitol Hill* ☎*206/322–2305* ⊕*www.capitol1524.com.*

GIFTS & HOME DECOR

Area 51. Anything might materialize in this 6,000-square-foot industrial space, from Eames replicas to kitschy coffee mugs, but it will all look like it's straight out of a hipster's handbook to the design trends of the 1960s and '70s. ⊠*401 E. Pine St., Capitol Hill* ☎*206/568–4782.*

Kobo. On the most dignified offshoot of the Broadway shopping district is this lovely store, selling artisan crafts from studios in Japan and in the Northwest. You'll find a similar stock here as in the International District branch: tasteful home wares, cute but functional gifts, and the odd piece of furniture. After a long day of looking at retro and ironic items, this place will cleanse your palate. ⊠*814 E. Roy St., Capitol Hill* ☎*206/726–0704* ⊕*www.koboseattle.com.*

Square Room. The Square Room sells furniture, objets d'art, jewelry, and home accessories that are hip but never gimmicky. The art here often imitates nature and many of the store's wares are made from either ecofriendly or recycled materials. The two owners often contribute their own artwork to the mix. ⊠*910 E. Pike St., Capitol Hill* ☎*206/329–1214* ⊕*www.squareroom.us.*

ANTIQUES & COLLECTIBLES

Fremont Antique Mall. Decades of popular American culture are stuffed into every conceivable corner of this bi-level space. The clothing selection might not look that impressive, but it sometimes yields incredible finds. The dishes, furniture, toys, and other cool stuff are fun to look through whether you're a serious collector or just an innocent bystander. It's easy to walk right past this place—look carefully for the door and then proceed down the flight of stairs. ✉ *3419 Fremont Pl. N, Fremont* ☎ *206/548–9140.*

CLOTHING

Flit. In spite of its name, this tiny new boutique seems to have a solid head on its shoulders. The selection, which includes denim, some outerwear, and gorgeous casual dresses, is cohesive and modern but still practical—clothing for women who want to stand out, but not too far out. Some of the brands you'll regularly find here are Odyn, Voom, and the classiest pieces from the Triple Five Soul line. Prices can be high, but they can also sometimes be surprisingly reasonable. ✉ *3526 Fremont Pl. N, Fremont* ☎ *206/547–2177* ⊕ *http://flitboutique.blogspot.com.*

Impulse. At first it looks like this stark basement space doesn't have much of a selection, but as you make your way around the racks, you notice how each piece flows effortlessly into the next, and how each selection is impeccable. You'll find some denim and footwear here, but you'll find better elsewhere; Impulse excels at sophisticated slacks, skirts, dresses, and outerwear that often seem subdued or basic until you notice an interesting seam line here or a hand-stitched detail there. You'll find some big names here, too, like Alice Roi and Vivienne Westwood. ✉ *621 N. 36th St., Fremont* ☎ *206/545–4854* ⊕ *www.impulseseattle.com.*

★ **Les Amis.** The best-looking boutique in Fremont, Les Amis is like a pop-up from a little girl's storybook set in a French country cottage. The over-35 set will breathe a sigh of relief when they see that the racks are not just filled with low-rise jeans but with sophisticated dresses, gorgeous handknits, and the makings of great work outfits. Younger fashionistas come here, too, to snap up unique summer skirts and ultrasoft T-shirts. Everyone seems to love the lingerie collection. Les Amis carries some top designers such as Lulu Guinness and Nanette Lepore; accordingly, this is the most expensive store in Fremont. You know prices are high when even the bargain bin discounts don't seem like a good deal. ✉ *3420 Evanston Ave. N, Fremont* ☎ *206/632–2877* ⊕ *www.lesamis-inc.com.*

GIFTS & HOME DECOR

Bitters Co. Textiles, linens, tableware, and jewelry—whose organic forms speak of the human touch—fill this unique general store. There are handcrafted goods from Guatemala, Indonesia, and the Philippines, and an in-house line of tables made from reclaimed Douglas fir. ✉ *513 N. 36th St., Fremont* ☎ *206/632–0886* ⊕ *www.bittersco.com.*

Burnt Sugar. Look for the store on the corner with the rocket on the roof: that's where you'll find a funky mélange of handbags, greeting cards, soaps, candles, jewelry, toys, and other eclectic baubles you never knew you needed. There's a makeup counter, and half the store is devoted to a small but cool selection of men's and women's shoes. ✉ *601 N. 35th St., Fremont* ☎ *206/545–0699.*

Frank & Dunya. Named after the owners' dogs, this cheerful shop sells colorful, locally crafted art. Gift items range from hand-painted switch-plate covers and elaborate night lights to pillowcases and coffee mugs. Although there's a lot of kitsch here, the paintings, prints, and mixed-media pieces displayed on the far wall are less whimsical and often very good. ✉ *3418 Fremont Ave. N, Fremont* ☎ *206/547–6760.*

BALLARD

BOOKS & MUSIC

★ **Sonic Boom Records** Though now something of a minichain (there are branches in Ballard and Capitol Hill), Sonic Boom is an independent shop through and through. It carries a little bit of everything, but the emphasis is definitely on indie rock. Handwritten recommendation cards from the staff help you find local artists and the best new releases from independent Northwest labels. The store has listening stations as well. Sonic Boom recently expanded: the vaunted "vinyl annex" was brought street level into an adjacent space, which also includes books, gifts, and other indie paraphernalia. ✉ *2209 NW Market St.* ☎ *206/297–2666* ⊕ *www.sonicboomrecords.com.*

CLOTHING & ACCESSORIES

☾ **Clover.** This precious store has unusual and high-quality toys, games, and children's clothes that you won't find at Toys "R" Us and The Gap. However, unlike Toys "R" Us, the space isn't exactly conducive to playing in the aisles, so you might want to make sure the kids have burned off some energy before taking them here. ✉ *5335 Ballard Ave. NW, Ballard* ☎ *206/782–0715* ⊕ *www.clovertoys.com.*

Olivine. Olivine is like a mini–department store: you'll find everything from evening wear to footwear to lingerie to bath products and makeup in one airy space. The clientele is mostly young, but some of the items are sophisticated enough for women who don't want to dress like college students. The prices are somewhat high, though competitive for the brands on offer. Service, unfortunately, is bad—not unfriendly, just completely disinterested. ✉ *5344 Ballard Ave. NW, Ballard* ☎ *206/706–4188* ⊕ *www.olivine.net.*

★ **Velouria.** The owner of Velouria, Tess de Luna, is a designer herself. She adds the best of her line to the racks, along with unique creations from independent West Coast designers. Overall, the clothes have a crafty, DIY feel—lots of appliqués and deliberately off-kilter hems and seams—but some of the separates would work well in any wardrobe. Even if you can't rock the hipster look, pop in to this friendly little store to check out the handbags, wallets, and jewelry. ✉ *2205 N.W. Market St., Ballard* ☎ *206/788–0330* ⊕ *http://shopvelouria.tripod.com.*

FOOTWEAR

re-souL. Stocking cool but comfortable shoes from Paul Smith, Palladium, and Roberto de Carlo, as well as its own line, this hip space offers a small selection of boots, sneaks, and high heels for real humans at reasonable (or at least competitive) prices. In keeping with the "little bit of everything" trend so popular with Seattle boutiques, re-souL also sells great jewelry pieces, as well as a few CDs and the odd piece of furniture. They carry both men's and women's shoes and accessories. ✉*5319 Ballard Ave., Ballard* ☎*206/789–7312* ⊕*www.resoul.com.*

GIFTS & HOME ACCESSORIES

★ **Archie McPhee.** Leave it to Seattle to have a novelty store that sells gag gifts that are subversive and often wickedly funny. Barista action figures, demon rubber duckies, and homicidal unicorns share the shelves with more-sedate items like rubber bouncing balls in all sizes and colors, bandages adorned with T-bone steaks or ninjas, and tiki-theme glasses and coasters. ✉*2428 N.W. Market St., Ballard* ☎*206/297–0240* ⊕*www.mcphee.com.*

Venue. Venue is the chic version of the Made In Washington stores: it only stocks goods made by designers from within the city's borders (some of whom have their studios in the sleek bi-level space), but you won't find anything resembling a tacky souvenir here. Artisan chocolates, custom handbags, hand-painted silk pillows, and prints and photographs are just a few examples of the gift items being produced right under our noses. ✉*5408 22nd Ave., Ballard* ☎*206/789–3335* ⊕*www.venueballard.com.*

WINE

Portalis. This sophisticated little wine bar is also a full shop that sells nearly 400 wines, with origins that span the globe, including a few choice Pacific Northwest bottles. They offer tastings every Sunday from noon to 3 PM. ✉*5205 Ballard Ave. NW, Ballard* ☎*206/783–2007* ⊕*www.portaliswines.com.*

SEATTLE ESSENTIALS

BY AIR

Seattle is a hub for regional air service, air service to Alaska, Hawaii, and Canada, as well as for some carriers to Asia. It's also a convenient North American gateway for flights originating in Australia, New Zealand, and the South Pacific. But it's a long westbound flight to Seattle from Europe. Such flights usually stop in New York; Washington, D.C.; Boston; or Chicago after crossing the Atlantic. The major gateway is Seattle–Tacoma International Airport (SEA), known locally as Sea-Tac.

Airport Information **Boeing Field** (☎*206/296–7380* ⊕*www.metrokc.gov/airport).* **Seattle–Tacoma International Airport** (☎*206/433–5388* ⊕*www.portseattle.org/seatac).*

GROUND TRANSPORTATION

Sea-Tac is about 15 mi south of Downtown on I-5 (from the airport, follow the signs to I-5 North, and take the Seneca Street Exit for Downtown). Although it can take as little as 30 minutes to ride between Downtown and the airport, if you're traveling during either rush hour, it's best to allow at least an hour for the trip in case of traffic snarls.

Metered cabs cost around $30 (not including tip) between the airport and Downtown, though some taxi companies offer a flat rate to Sea-Tac from select Downtown hotels. Expect to pay $35–$40 to Capitol Hill, Queen Anne, or the neighborhoods directly north of the canal. Seattle has a small cab fleet, so expect long waits if a lot of flights arrive at the same time, especially late at night.

Shuttle Express has the only 24-hour door-to-door shared van service. Rates vary depending on destination, number of people in your party, and how many bags you have, but a one-way trip to the Downtown hotel area for one adult with two bags is around $27. You can make arrangements at the Shuttle Express counter upon arrival or make advance reservations online or by phone. For trips to the airport, make reservations at least 24 hours in advance.

Gray Line Downtown Airporter offers shuttle service to select Downtown hotels for $10.25 one- way or $17 round-trip. The last shuttle leaves Sea-Tac at 11 PM. Express Car and Atlas Towncar have limo service to and from the airport. The fare is $45 to Downtown and can be shared by up to four passengers.

Your least-expensive transportation option ($1.50–$2; cash only, exact change in bills or coins) is a Metro Transit city bus. If you don't have a lot of luggage, this is a fantastic option for reaching Downtown cheaply. You can catch a bus outside the baggage claim areas for the 30- to 45-minute ride into town. Take Express Tunnel Bus 194 or regular Bus 174. Metro Transit's Web site has a great trip planner that provides door-to-door itineraries, explaining any connections you may have to make if you're not staying Downtown; representatives can also help you plan your trip over the phone.

Contacts Atlas Towncar (☎ 888/646–0606 or 206/860–7777 ⊕ www.atlastown car.com). **Gray Line Airport Express** (☎ 800/426–7532 recorded schedule info, 206/626–6088 ⊕ www.graylineseattle.com). **Metro Transit** (☎ 206/553–3000 ⊕ http://transit.metrokc.gov). **Shuttle Express/Express Car** (☎ 425/981–7000 ⊕ www.shuttleexpress.com).

BY BUS

Most buses, which are wheelchair-accessible, run until around midnight or 1 AM; some run all night, though in many cases taking a cab late at night is a much better solution than dealing with sporadic bus service. The visitor center at the Washington State Convention and Trade Center has maps and schedules or you can call **Metro Transit** directly. Better yet, if you have Internet access, you can make use of Metro Transit's excellent trip planner feature. You simply type in your starting and ending addresses and the approximate time you want to start your trip or arrive at your destination and you'll get three or four options and detailed information on bus stop locations.

Between 6 AM and 7 PM, city buses are free within the Metro Bus Ride Free Area, bounded by Battery Street to the north, 6th Avenue to the east (and over to 9th Avenue near the convention center), S. Jackson Street to the south, and the waterfront to the west; you'll pay as you disembark if you ride out of this area. Throughout King County, both one-zone fares and two-zone fares at off-peak times are $1.50; during peak hours (6 AM–9 AM and 3 PM–6 PM), one-zone fares are $1.75 and two-zone fares $2. Unless you travel outside the city limits, you'll pay one-zone fares. Onboard fare collection boxes have prices posted on them. ■TIP➔**The $5 King County Visitor Pass is a bargain if you're doing a lot of touring.** Valid for one day, it includes rides on King, Pierce, and Snohomish county buses, the waterfront trolley, and the Elliott Bay Water Taxi. You can purchase passes online or at Metro offices. Transfers between most lines are free; if you think you'll need one, make sure you ask the driver for a transfer slip when you get on the bus.

Fares for city buses are collected in cash or by prepaid tickets and passes *as you board* the bus heading into Downtown, and *as you exit the bus* on the way out of Downtown. Fare boxes accept both coins and bills, but drivers won't make change, so don't board the bus with a $5 bill and a hapless grin. You can only buy bus passes at Metro offices or online, not on the vehicle; cash, debit cards, MasterCard, and Visa are accepted at all offices.

City Bus Information **Metropolitan Transit** (☎*800/542-7876 or 206/553-3000, 206/287-8463 for automated schedule line* ⊕*transit.metrokc.gov*).

BY CAR
The best advice about driving in Seattle is to avoid driving during rush hour whenever possible. The worst tangles are on I–5 and I–90, and any street Downtown that has a major on or off ramp to I–5. The Fremont Bridge and the 15th Avenue Bridge also get tied up. Aurora Avenue/99 gets very busy but often moves quickly enough. Other than that, you should find driving around Seattle a lot less anxiety-inducing than driving around other major cities.

PARKING
Parking is a headache and a half in Seattle. Street parking is only guaranteed in the quietest residential areas—even leafy parts of Capitol Hill are crammed full of cars all hours of the day. The city has a good share of pay lots and garages in the central core of the city, but even the pay lots can fill up on weekend nights, particularly in Belltown and Capitol Hill. Metered street parking exists in Downtown Seattle and the commercial stretches of Capitol Hill, but consider yourself lucky if you manage to snag a spot. Meters are $1.50 per hour and although there are a few old-style coin-only meters left here and there, most pay stations are electronic and take either coins or debit and credit cards. You get a printed sticker noting the time your parking is up, which you affix to the curbside passenger window. Street parking is free Sunday, holidays, and after 6 PM weekdays and Saturday.

Pay lots are the next price tier up, though Downtown they are often just as expensive as garages. Rates vary greatly, but expect to pay at least $5 or $6 for a few hours in Capitol Hill and $8 or $9 for the same amount of time in Downtown or Belltown. Garage rates begin at $3 an hour and cap off between $15 and $25 for the day.

Important: No matter where you park, always lock your car and never leave valuables in your vehicle. The city has plenty of problems with break-ins. Don't be fooled by the laid-back suburban feel of some of the residential areas—they all experience waves of car theft and vandalism.

BY FERRY

Ferries are a major part of Seattle's transportation network, and they're the only way to reach such points as Vashon Island and the San Juans. Ferries also transport thousands of commuters a day from Bainbridge Island, Bremerton, and other outer towns to their jobs in the city. For visitors, ferries are one of the best ways to get a feel for the region and its ties to the sea. You'll also get outstanding views of the skyline and the elusive Mt. Rainier from the ferry to Bainbridge.

Information **Clipper Navigation** (☎ *800/888–2535 in U.S., 250/382–8100 in Victoria, 206/448–5000 in Seattle* ⊕ *www.victoriaclipper.com*). **Elliott Bay Water Taxi** (☎ *800/542–7876 in WA, 206/553–3000* ⊕ *http://transit.metrokc.gov/tops/ oto/water_taxi.html*). **Washington State Ferries** (☎ *800/843–3779 automated line in WA and BC, 888/808–7977, 206/464–6400* ⊕ *www.wsdot.wa.gov/ferries*).

BY MONORAIL

The Seattle monorail is a quick, convenient link for tourists that travels an extremely short route between the Seattle Center and Downtown's Westlake Mall, located at 4th Avenue and Pike Street. Making the 1-mi journey in just 2 minutes, the monorail departs both points every 10 minutes from 11 AM to 9 PM daily. The round-trip fare is $4; children age four and under ride free. During weekends, Seattle Sonics basketball games, and the Folklife, Bite of Seattle, and Bumbershoot festivals—which all take place at the Seattle Center—you can park in the Macy's garage at 3rd Avenue and Stewart Street, take the monorail, and present your monorail ticket stub when you return for discounted parking rates of $5 on Friday and Saturday and $4 on Sunday and Monday.

Information **Seattle Center Monorail** (☎ *206/905–2620* ⊕ *www.seattlemono rail.com*).

BY STREETCAR

The Waterfront Streetcar line of vintage 1920s-era trolleys from Melbourne, Australia, runs 1.6 mi south along Alaska Way from Pier 70, past the Washington State Ferries terminal at Piers 50 and 52, turning inland on Main Street, and passing through Pioneer Square before ending on South Jackson Street in the International District. It runs at about 20-minute intervals daily from 7 AM to 9 or 10 PM (less often and for fewer hours in winter). The fare is $1.25 from 9 to 3 and after 6, $1.50 during peak commuting hours. The stations and streetcars are wheelchair accessible. At this writing, construction on a new station has slightly disrupted streetcar service—the service still exists, but the trolleys have been replaced by green-and-beige buses clearly marked WATERFRONT STREETCAR LINE. The route is slightly different, so consult Metro Transit for updated schedule information.

A new streetcar system is under construction, and the first section, which travels from South Lake Union down Westlake Avenue to the Westlake Center, began service in late 2007. Jokingly referred to as the S.L.U.T. (South Lake Union Trolley, get it?) by many locals, the streetcar is basically another version of the monorail a few paces east. Service runs daily from 6 am to 9 pm Monday through Thursday, 6 am to 11 pm Friday and Saturday, and 10 am to 7 pm Sunday. The fare is $1.50.

Information **Metropolitan Transit** (☎ 206/553–3000, 206/287–8463 for automated schedule line ⊕ transit.metrokc.gov).**South Lake Union Streetcar** (☎ 206/553–3000 ⊕ www.seattlestreetcar.com).

BY TAXI

Seattle has a pretty small taxi fleet; taking a cab is not a major form of transportation in the city. Most people only take cabs to and from the airport and when they go out partying on weekends. You'll often be able to hail cabs on the street in Downtown, but anywhere else, you'll have to call. Expect long waits on Friday and Saturday nights.

Rides generally run about $2 per mile, and unless you're going a very short distance, the average cost of a cab ride in the city is $10–$12. The meter drop alone is $2.50 and you'll pay 50¢ per minute stuck in traffic. Soaring gas prices may add a surcharge of $1 to the total. The nice thing about Seattle metered cabs is that they almost always accept credit cards and an automated system calls you on your cell phone to let you know that your cab has arrived. All cab companies listed below charge the same rates.

Metered cabs are not the best way to visit the Eastside or any destination far outside the city—if you get stuck in traffic, you'll pay dearly for it. Ask your hotel for car service quotes concerning short side trips outside city limits.

Taxi Companies **Orange Cab** (☎ 206/522–8800). **Red Top Cab** (☎ 206/789–4949). **Yellow Cab** (☎ 206/622–6500).

TOUR OPTIONS

BOAT

Argosy Cruises sails around Elliott Bay (1 hour, from Pier 55, $15–$19), the Ballard Locks (2½ hours, from Pier 56, $28–$36), and offers a cruise between Lake Union and Lake Washington (2 hours, from AGC Marina in South Lake Union, $22–$28). Let's Go Sailing permits passengers to take the helm, trim the sails, or simply enjoy the ride aboard the *Obsession* or the SC70 *Neptune's Car,* both 70-foot ocean racers. Three 1½-hour excursions ($25) depart daily from Pier 54. A 2½-hour sunset cruise ($40) is also available. Passengers can bring their own food on board.

BUS

Gray Line of Seattle operates bus and boat tours, including a 3½-hour City Sights ($34) that includes many sights, lunch in Pike Place Market, and admission to the Space Needle observation deck. The hop-on, hop-off double-decker buses ($19) that do one-hour-long loops of the city core from the Seattle Center to Pioneer Square are the best bet for travelers who want to experience the city from outside of a bus, too. They also do day trips to Mt. Rainier and Mt. St. Helens, though note that these tours only stop at scenic lookouts and visitor centers—you won't actually have the chance to do any hiking or exploring in either park.

ORIENTATION

For $40, Show Me Seattle takes up to 14 people in vans on three-hour day tours of the major sights. Though they bill the tour as Seattle "as the natives see it," this is an extremely touristy program that makes stops at places like the flagship Eddie Bauer store and the first Starbucks, and the *Sleepless in Seattle* floating home (what year is it, again?). The tour is comprehensive—it takes in the views at Kerry Park in Queen Anne and heads above the canal to see Fremont, Ballard, and Green Lake—but don't expect this tour to be any more authentic than the others. For $45, Seattle Tours also has similar day tours of the city in vans, with stops for picture taking. The Seattle Skyscrapers Tour visits all the major buildings of Downtown in about two hours for $12.

SELF-GUIDED

One way to tour Seattle at your own pace is with the Go Seattle Card, which provides admission to more than 30 of the city's top attractions. The credit-card-style ticket comes with a map and guidebook, and then you're off to explore the Space Needle, Museum of Flight, and other famous sights. Slightly discounted cards are available for children, students, and seniors, and if you're not up for a one-day whirlwind sweep through the city, they also come in two-, three-, five-, and seven-day increments. But before you buy one, think seriously about how many admissions costs you'll encounter each day—the cards start at $55 for one day of sightseeing and jump to $79 for two days and $99 for three days. Unless you're doing a lot of hopping around between museums and major sights like the Space Needle, it may not be that great a deal.

WALKING

Chinatown Discovery Tours offers 1½-hour walking tours of the neighborhood that may include a presentation at the affiliated Wing Luke Asian Museum; tickets are $16.95–$27.95, depending on the number of people in your group. Seattle Walking Tours creates customized, 2½-hour itineraries that cover specific areas of the city. These cost $15 per person for a minimum of three guests.

Tour Companies **Argosy Cruises** (☎ 800/642–7816 or 206/623–1445 ⊕ www. argosycruises.com). **Chinatown Discovery Tours** (☎ 206/623–5124). **Go Seattle Card** (⊕ www.goseattlecard.com). **Gray Line of Seattle** (☎ 800/426–7532 or 206/624–5077 ⊕ graylineseattle.com). **Kenmore Air** (☎ 866/435–9524 or 425/486–1257 ⊕ www.kenmoreair.com). **Let's Go Sailing** (☎ 800/831–3274 or 206/624–3931 ⊕ www.sailingseattle.com). **Seattle Flight** (☎ 206/767–5234

⊕ *www.seattleflight.com*). **Seattle Seaplanes** (☎ *800/637–5553 or 206/329–9638* ⊕ *www.seattleseaplanes.com*). **Seattle Skyscrapers Tour** (☎ *206/667–9184*). **Seattle Tours** (☎ *206/768–1234* ⊕ *www.seattlecitytours.com*). **Seattle Walking Tours** (☎ *425/885–3173* ⊕ *www.seattlewalkingtours.com/walk_tour.htm*). **Show Me Seattle** (☎ *206/633–2489* ⊕ *www.showmeseattle.com*).

VISITOR INFORMATION

The Seattle Convention and Visitor's Bureau is really pulling out all the stops these days. Not only have they coined a new cringe-worthy yet oddly appropriate tagline for Seattle—"Metronatural"—but they have rebranded their visitor center as the "Citywide Concierge Center." The service, which has an office in the Washington State Trade and Convention Center on Pike Street (between 7th and 8th avenues) can help you plan all aspects of your trip from securing events tickets to making accommodations and restaurant reservations to arranging ground transportation and other services. They're set up to accept drop-ins (open weekdays 9–1 and 2–5) and you can also contact them before your trip with questions and requests.

Contacts **Seattle Convention and Visitor's Bureau** (☎ *206/461–5840 or 206/461–5888* ⊕ *www.visitseattle.org*).

Washington

WORD OF MOUTH

"San Juan Island has the most amenities and choices of places to stay. The town of Friday Harbor is self-contained and walkable for just about everything. Also, if you are biking, it is pretty flat. Orcas is another good choice, but it is much hillier and has more limited choices for accommodations or activities."

—ALF

"Visited Sequim for the lavender fields. Had origianlly wanted to go for the Lavender Festival, but all lodging in the entire area was booked nearly a year in advance, so we went the week prior. Worked out just fine."

—Dayle

LONG BEFORE OUTDOOR ADVENTURES WERE popular in the rest of the country, they were a way of life for Washington residents. In this state you're never far from natural attractions: saltwater sounds, wind-swept beaches, purling rivers, alpine peaks, majestic canyons, and rolling hills. The southern shore's sandy strands and calm bays contrast with the Olympic Peninsula's rugged sea cliffs. The coastal rain forests and the moist slopes of the Cascade Mountains are robed in moss and bedecked with ferns; the music of waterfalls and songbirds enlivens the deepest woods. East of the Cascades, mighty rivers flow through steep-walled coulees, while eagles and curlews drift above wildflowers and sagebrush, grasslands and wheat fields. Here ponds and lakes attract ducks, geese, and sandpipers; sandhill cranes stalk through irrigated fields bordering dry steppe.

The Salish Sea, a multifingered saltwater inlet, meanders inland, south to the state capital of Olympia and north to the Canadian waters of the Inland Passage. Large cities and busy ports—Seattle, Tacoma, Everett, and Bellingham—border these inland waters. The islands of southern Puget Sound, the Kitsap Peninsula, and the San Juan archipelago divide the Salish Sea into inlets and tidal passages. From these labyrinthine shores, where villages have sheltered moorages for pleasure boats, rise Mt. Rainier, the Olympic Mountains, Mt. Baker, and the North Cascades.

The mountains put on the most spectacular display of wildflowers in spring and summer. Flowering plums and cherries, dogwoods, rhododendrons, azaleas, and peonies light up the landscape with the colors of an impressionist palette. In winter skiers rush to the area's slopes, from Mt. Baker in the north to White Pass in the south. Winthrop, Leavenworth, and other small, friendly towns of the glaciated valleys east of the mountains are popular with cross-country skiers. Two great rivers, the Columbia and the Snake, flow through the arid steppes of the Columbia Plateau, greening a patchwork quilt of fields and fruit orchards. The flow of these rivers is interrupted by dams, of which Grand Coulee Dam is the mightiest. The warm beaches of Lake Chelan, a deep inland fjord, draw Seattleites pining for the sun.

Bathed in constant radiance, vegetables and fruits thrive in the deep, fertile soils of the Yakima and Walla Walla valleys, beneath slopes covered with vineyards. Vast fields of wheat and barley gild the flanks of the Palouse and Horse Heaven Hills. Spokane, Washington's second-largest city, rules as the "Capital of the Inland Empire," a mountainous region of pastures and forests.

EXPLORING WASHINGTON

The Cascade Range divides Washington into western and eastern halves, which differ considerably in climate and topography. Western ecosystems vary from coastal areas to moist forests; eastern ecosystems range from pine woods to dry grass-and-brush steppes, from deep river valleys to lakes and marshes. Curiously, the hot-summer "dry" east side has more wetlands and marshes than the cool-summer "wet" west side

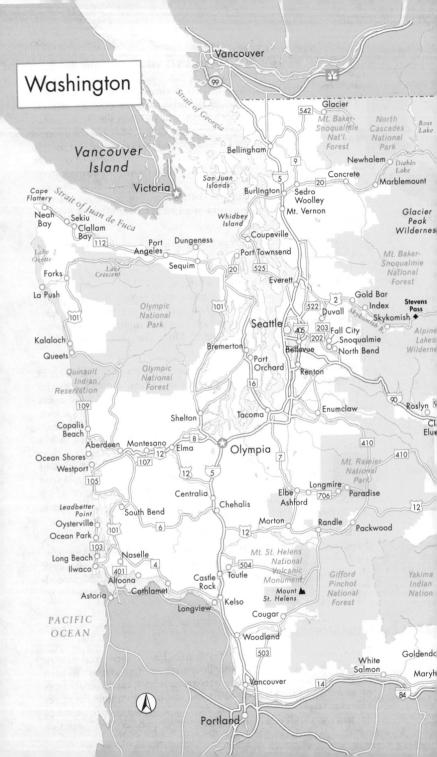

BRITISH COLUMBIA
CANADA
UNITED STATES
IDAHO
OREGON
Okanogan National Forest
Colville National Forest
Colville Indian Reservation
Spokane Indian Reservation
Wenatchee National Forest
Umatilla National Forest
Washington Pass
Sun Lakes State Park
Ginkgo Petrified Forest State Park
Chewuch R.
Lake Chelan
Columbia River
Franklin D. Roosevelt Lake
Banks Lake
Lake Wenatchee
Potholes Res.
Snake R.
Tonasket
Republic
Colville
Winthrop
Twisp
Okanogan
Stehekin
Carlton
Chewelah
Newport
Methow
Brewster
Grand Coulee
Coulee Dam
Chelan
Wilbur
Coeur d'Alene
Spokane
Leavenworth
Davenport
Cashmere
Wenatchee
Ephrata
Sprague
Moses Lake
Ritzville
Ellensburg
Othello
Colfax
Washtucna
Pullman
Yakima
Pomeroy
Wapato
Zillah
Toppenish
Dayton
Richland
Pasco
Kennewick
Prosser
Walla Walla
Pendleton
20
21
25
195
155
231
291
174
97
2
17
28
90
10
26
395
82
221
12
14
84
0
40 miles
0
40 kilometers

IF YOU LIKE

BEACHES

The southwestern coast's long, surf-tossed sands are popular with hikers, kite flyers, bird-watchers, and surfers; however, the waves are very rough and the water is cold—making swimming almost impossible for most people. In season, folks come here by the thousands to dig for tasty razor clams. The Olympic Peninsula's beaches are rocky, though there are a few sandy coves tucked between the headlands. The muddy shores of the Salish Sea are popular with clam diggers probing for the hard-shelled mollusks. Sandy beaches are scarce, even in the San Juan Islands. More often than not, the glacier-cut rocks drop straight into the water. But tide pools teeming with sea slugs, crabs, anemones, and tiny fish hold a fascination all their own. Bird-watching is great along all of the shores. California gray whales migrate close to the beaches of the outer shore and frequently visit the sheltered waters of the Salish Sea. Sea kayaking is very popular, and most waterfront towns have kayak rentals.

FORESTS

Forests in western Washington are dense and overgrown with ferns, mosses, and other vegetation. This is true of the rain forests of the southwest coast and the Olympic Peninsula as well as the forests on the western slopes of the Cascades. Trees in the alpine areas are often gnarled and bent by snow and wind into fascinating shapes. Forests east of the Cascades are sunny and contain stands of ponderosa pine. In spring the forest floor is covered with wildflowers, as are the steppes of the Columbia Plateau. From the San Juan Islands south, and on the mainland from Tacoma south, prairies are dotted with stands of Oregon white oak and evergreens.

LAKES & RIVERS

It's best to visit eastern Washington's lakes and coulees between April and mid-October, when the weather is at its best. Lake Chelan, Moses Lake, and the Columbia River Gorge are very popular during the height of the travel season. The scenic, central Okanogan highlands and the southeastern Blue Mountains are uncrowded year-round. The state's turbulent mountain streams and rivers are popular with rafters and white-water kayakers. The 160-mi Cascadia Marine Trail, which is completely navigable by kayak, traces part of a trading route used by early Native Americans to get from Olympia to Point Roberts on the Canadian border.

of the state. Both sections have alpine fells, which on the east side have two timberlines: one on the upper slopes (where forests are restricted by the heavy snows and frosts of an alpine climate), and another on the lower slopes (where tree growth is limited by lack of moisture).

ABOUT THE RESTAURANTS

Washington's abundant seafood shows up on menus throughout the state, and spicy yet subtle flavors testify to strong Asian influences. Tender halibut, sweet Dungeness crab, plump oysters, and delicate mussels are as popular as the ubiquitous salmon. Coastal forests are rich in wild mushrooms, and the inland valleys are famed for their beef and lamb in addition to their wines. In autumn the mountains produce a bountiful harvest of wild berries; in fact, almost every region of the state grows great berries, as well as vegetables and apples. This bounty translates, in the hands of the state's many skilled chefs, into fine cuisine.

ABOUT THE HOTELS

There's a good mix of expensive and moderately priced properties throughout the state. Some of Washington's best lodgings are in bed-and-breakfasts (B&Bs) or small inns surrounded by breathtaking natural beauty. They're often equipped with hot tubs and in-room fireplaces that take the edge off the crisp coastal or wintry inland air. A vast B&B network is operated by the state tourism board, and you can request a brochure or research your options online. For budget travelers, there are youth hostels, inexpensive chain hotels, and campsites.

	WHAT IT COSTS				
	¢	$	$$	$$$	$$$$
RESTAURANTS	under $10	$10–$20	$20–$30	$30–$40	over $40
HOTELS	under $100	$100–$150	$150–$200	$200–$250	over $250

Restaurant prices are per person, for a main course at dinner. Hotel prices are for two people in a standard double room in high season, excluding tax.

TIMING

Summer is the best time for hiking mountain trails and enjoying coastal beaches. Skies are often clear and temperatures mild; July and August can be downright hot. Spring is often overcast and wet, but it's the time to catch the gorgeous Skagit Valley tulip fields in full bloom. Leavenworth and other mountain towns can be as busy in summer with hikers as they are with skiers in winter. Coastal towns are packed on summer weekends. Note that some inns and restaurants close from late fall through spring—be sure to call ahead. Washington's major cities, however, are lively year-round.

SEATTLE ENVIRONS

Updated by
Holly S. Smith

Seattle and its surrounding suburbs form a metropolis that stretches from Arlington in the north to Olympia in the south, and from Snoqualmie Falls in the east to the western edge of the Kitsap Peninsula. This 100-mi-long, 40-mi-wide, roughly formed megacity is fragmented into slim inlets and forested islands by Puget Sound. Only one set of spans, the Tacoma Narrows suspension bridge and its newly minted twin, connect the mainland to the Kitsap Peninsula; car and passenger ferries are the alternative. The region is further subdivided by Lake Washington, separating Seattle from the Eastside, which you can cross on the Evergreen Point and Mercer Island floating bridges. A third floating bridge crosses the Hood Canal near Port Gamble, connecting the Kitsap and Olympic peninsulas.

Although many of western Washington's business, social, and cultural interests are in Seattle, a day's drive around the area makes it clear that the suburbs are very separate communities. All are framed by miles of

GREAT ITINERARIES

IF YOU HAVE 4 DAYS

Tour the northern section of the Olympic Peninsula, visit one of the coastal islands, and roam through a bit of the Cascade Range. On the first day, head from Seattle to Port Townsend, a seaside town with Victorian buildings. Explore shops and galleries, have lunch, and then take the ferry to Whidbey Island, passing through Deception Pass State Park en route to Anacortes. Take a late-afternoon ferry to the San Juan Islands, disembarking on hilly Orcas Island, the more touristy San Juan Island, or quiet Lopez Island. Whichever island you choose, you'll need two full days. On the fourth day, catch an early ferry back to the mainland and head—via Everett and U.S. 2—out on a loop through the North Cascades. Have lunch in Bavarian–style Leavenworth, before crossing Snoqualmie summit via U.S. 97 and I-90. Pass through Cle Elum, and consider stopping in the small, picturesque town of Roslyn for dinner. From here it's less than two hours back to Seattle.

IF YOU HAVE 7 DAYS

Spend two days exploring the Seattle area, including an afternoon ferry trip to Bainbridge Island. On Day 3, drive southeast to Mt. Rainier National Park and spend the night. On Day 4 drive to Yakima, then make a long southeastern loop through Pasco and Walla Walla on your way to Spokane. Spend the night, then use Day 5 to look around the city. On Day 6, start out early for Moses Lake; then travel northwest along U.S. 2 to explore the apple fields of Wenatchee and Leavenworth. Spend the night, then make a side trip north to Lake Chelan before returning to Seattle.

pristine wilderness, and a short drive away from parks and beaches where seals, sea lions, and gray whales patrol the coastlines; wild ducks and geese invade inland marshes; and deer, black bears, and cougars wander through the mountainous woodlands.

BAINBRIDGE ISLAND

9 mi northwest of Seattle by ferry.

The 35-minute ferry ride to Bainbridge Island from downtown Seattle provides superb views of the city skyline and surrounding mountains. The inexpensive ferry trip is a classic Northwest experience, and Bainbridge's small-town vibe and scenic countryside are simply charming. From the ferry terminal, you can walk to Winslow and wander around its clutch of small antiques shops, art galleries, bookstores, and cafés. Visitors are free to use the yellow bicycles around the ferry dock.

A five-minute drive from the ferry dock is the small, family-owned **Bainbridge Island Vineyard and Winery,** established in 1977. It's the only winery in the Puget Sound region to have its own vineyards, and it's open for tastings and picnicking Friday through Sunday from noon to 5. Free vineyard tours take place Sundays at 2. ✉*8989 E. Day Rd.* ☎*206/842–9463* ⊕*www.bainbridgevineyards.com.*

TOP 5

1. Take a Ride: Hop on the Seattle—Bainbridge ferry for spectacular views of Puget Sound and its islands. The panorama of downtown is unbeatable! Tip: Try a sunset return.

2. Wander a While: Stroll through the charming ferry-stop village of Winslow, with its cafés, bookshops, wineries, and waterfront restaurants.

3. Explore Outdoors: Head to Point Defiance Park in Tacoma to venture through forest paths, along drift-wood beach scenes, and around the collection of exotic zoo creatures.

4. Go Navy: The Bremerton waterfront opens the U.S. Turner Joy, the Naval Museum, and other maritime attractions.

5. Cruise the Docks: Rent a kayak to explore Puget Sound's charming seaside communities of Poulsbo or Gig Harbor.

★ The 150-acre **Bloedel Reserve** has fine Japanese gardens, a bird refuge, a moss garden, and other gardens planted with island flora. A French Renaissance–style mansion is surrounded by 2 mi of trails and ponds dotted with trumpeter swans. Dazzling rhododendrons and azaleas bloom in spring, and Japanese maples colorfully signal autumn's arrival. Note that reservations are essential, picnicking is not permitted, and payment is cash only. ⊠ *7571 N.E. Dolphin Dr., 6 mi north of Winslow, via Hwy. 305* ☎ *206/842–7631* ⊕ *www.bloedelreserve. org* ⊠ *$10* ⊘ *Wed.–Sun. 10–4.*

☺ In town, the **Kids' Discovery Museum** has a revolving calendar of exciting programs and exhibits. On tap regularly are puppet shows, art classes, cooking demos, Native American arts and crafts, and a host of musical, sports, and science activities. ⊠ *305 Madison Ave. N, Suite C* ☎ *206/855–4650* ⊕ *www.kidimu.org* ⊠ *$5* ⊘ *Tues.–Sat. 10–4, Sun. noon–4.*

WHERE TO EAT

$$–$$$ ✕ **Four Swallows.** The elegant white farmhouse, pristine in architecture and rambling in style, is the setting for one of the Seattle-area's top dining experiences. Warm colors cover the walls, and mirrors reflect chunky wood tables and banquettes adorned with gleaming silver and glass. Top-rate service delivers a changing menu of seasonal Northwest and Italian-inspired dishes, many of which highlight locally caught seafood and fresh market produce. Linger over a fine regional wine, or a seasonal dessert with plump berries or pungent mint flavorings. ⊠ *481 Madison Ave. E,* ☎ *206/842–3397* ⊛ *Reservations essential* ▭ *AE, D, MC, V* ⊘ *Closed Sun. and Mon. No lunch*.

$–$$ ✕ **Café Nola.** Tucked into a cozy brickfront building next to the bay, this casually upscale spot is the place to nosh on stepped-up Northwest fare. Seasoned with an international array of ingredients, dishes range from savory Seattle-style cioppino to chili-braised short ribs, rosemary-crusted halibut, and pumpkin ravioli. The waitstaff is friendly and very casual, but chattiness and crowds can make service slow. On fine days,

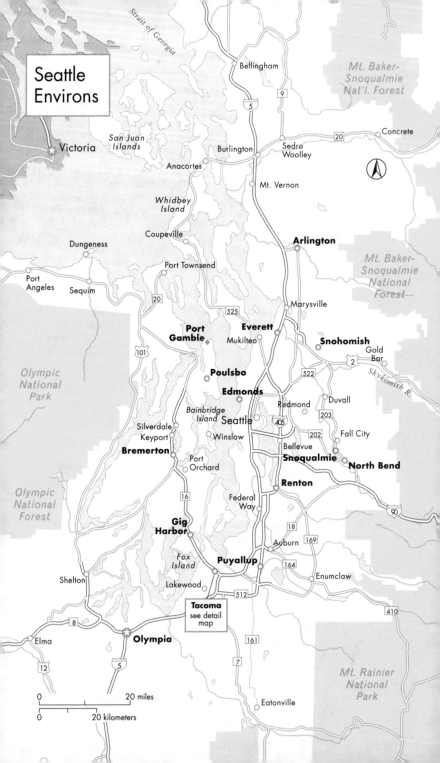

Seattle
Environs

Strait of Georgia

Bellingham
9
5

San Juan
Islands

Victoria

Burlington
Sedro
Woolley

20
Concrete

Anacortes
Mt. Vernon

Whidbey
Island

Coupeville

Dungeness

Port Townsend

Arlington

Port
Angeles
Sequim

20
Mt. Baker-
Snoqualmie
Nat'l. Forest

Mt. Baker-
Snoqualmie
National
Forest

525
Marysville

Everett

101

Port
Gamble
Mukilteo

Snohomish
Gold
Bar

2
Skykomish R.

Poulsbo

522

Olympic
National
Park

Edmonds

Redmond
Duvall

203

Bainbridge
Island
Seattle
405

202
Fall City

Silverdale
Keyport

Winslow

Bellevue

Bremerton

Port
Orchard

Snoqualmie
North Bend

Renton

90

Olympic
National
Forest

16

Federal
Way

18

Gig
Harbor

Auburn
169

Fox
Island

Puyallup
164
Enumclaw

Shelton

Lakewood

512

410

Tacoma
see detail
map

Elma

8

161

Olympia

7

12

5

Mt. Rainier
National
Park

Eatonville

0   20 miles

0   20 kilometers

take an umbrella table on the deck; frosty nights bring out the warmth of the summer hues inside. ⊠*101 Winslow Way E*, ☎*206/842–3822* ⊟*AE, D, MC, V.*

¢–$ ✕**Harbor Public House.** An 1881 estate home overlooking Eagle Harbor was renovated to create this casual restaurant at Winslow's public marina. Top-notch fish-and-chips, key-lime chicken, steak pitas, and pub burgers are typical fare, as are key-lime pie and root-

WORD OF MOUTH

"A ferry ride to Bainbridge Island offers great views of the Seattle skyline, and, on a clear day, Mt. Rainier, the Olympic Mountains, and the Cascades. On Bainbridge Island, walk to Cafe Nola in downtown Winslow for a good lunch."

–happytrailstoyou

beer floats. This is where the pleasure-boating crowds come to dine in a relaxed, waterfront setting. Things get raucous during open-mike sessions, held the first Tuesday night of the month. ⊠*231 Parfitt Way, Winslow* ☎*206/842–0969* ⊟*AE, DC, MC, V.*

$$–$$$$ 🏨 **Eagle Harbor Inn.** This elegant small hotel, set a half-block between the marina and downtown Winslow, is a quiet haven surrounding a court-yard garden. French country–style rooms are elegant, done in muted colors, and have harbor and village views. Suites have vaulted ceilings and marble bathrooms, while spacious, fully equipped town houses come with gourmet kitchens. ■**TIP**➜ You can often join the hosts for area cruises on their colorful electric boat. **Pros:** Small, country-home ambience. **Cons:** Some traffic and tourist noise. ⊠*291 Madison Ave. S, 98110* ☎*206/842–1446* 📠*206/780–1715* ⊕*www.theeagleharborinn. com* ⥱*3 rooms, 2 suites, 4 town houses* ⅋*In-room: kitchens (some). In-hotel: VCRs, dial-up, Wi-Fi, boating, bicycles* ⊟*AE, D, MC, V.*

¢–$$ 🏨 **Island Country Inn.** One of a high-quality chain of Northwest hotels, the inn mixes contemporary styles with country comforts. Elegant rooms, done in the colors of the surrounding forest and sunsets, have such amenities as data ports and down pillows. Deluxe rooms have kitchen appliances and terry robes; the master suite has a gas fireplace, VCR, and CD player. There's no restaurant, but a sumptuous, self-serve breakfast—with goodies like do-it-yourself Belgian waffles—is set up each morning in the dining room. **Pros:** Modern comforts. **Cons:** Smallish rooms, standard decor. ⊠*920 Hildebrand La., Bainbridge 98110* ☎*206/842–6861 or 800/842–8429* 📠*206/842–9808* ⊕*www. bainbridgelodging.com/inns* ⥱*39 rooms, 6 suites* ⅋*In-room: kitchen (some). In-hotel: refrigerator (some), VCR (some), dial-up, Wi-Fi, pool, some pets allowed* 🍽*CP* ⊟*AE, D, DC, MC, V.*

¢–$$ 🏨 **Waterfall Gardens.** Waterfalls and spring-fed ponds are threaded
★ throughout the wooded, 5-acre property. Luxury suites, each with private entrance, occupy two homes: one before a tumbling stream and magnificent cedars, the other surrounded by ponds and deep forest. Nature park–style landscaping provides meandering paths and quiet sitting areas, and the owners can organize lawn games and cheery group bonfires. Although breakfast isn't provided, you're welcome to bring your own goodies, and even to raid the organic vegetable garden in summer. **Pros:** Exquisite setting. **Cons:** Cash or check only.

✉ *7269 N.E. Bergman Rd., Bainbridge 98110* ☏ *206/842–1434* ⊕ *www.waterfall-gardens.com* ⇔ *4 suites* ⚭ *In-room: kitchen. In-hotel: refrigerator, no-smoking rooms* ▭ *No credit cards.*

POULSBO

12 mi northwest of Winslow.

Velkommen til Poulsbo (*pauls*-bo), an endlessly charming village on lovely Liberty Bay. Soon after it was settled by Norwegians in the 1880s, shops and bakeries sprang up along Front Street, as did a cod-drying facility to produce the Norwegian delicacy called lutefisk. Although it's no longer made here, lutefisk is still served at holiday feasts. Front Street is crammed with authentic Norwegian bakeries, eclectic Scandinavian craft shops, small boutiques and bookstores, and art galleries. Norwegian flags flutter from the eaves of the town's chalet-style buildings. Grassy Liberty Bay Park is fronted by a network of slender docks where seals and otters pop in and out of the waves. One of the town's biggest events is the annual May Viking Festival, complete with Viking tents and weapons, costumed locals, and a lively parade.

ℭ Right along the shoreline and the edge of Liberty Bay Park, the **Marine Science Center** is raised above the water and jam-packed with exhibits of local sea creatures. An inter-tidal touch tank lets kids feel anemones, sea urchins, and starfish, while other displays house crabs, jellyfish, and plants. Puppets, puzzles, murals, and videos help youngsters learn more about what they see. Don't miss the giant Pacific octopus in a 2,000-gallon tank beneath the center. A small gift shop fronts the building, and the museum provides special activities during Poulsbo festivals. ✉ *18743 Front St. NE* ☏ *360/779–5549* ☉ *Tues.–Sun. 11–4.*

WHERE TO EAT

¢–$ ✕ **J.J.'s Fish House.** Rain-worn wood, saltwater scents, and the sounds of the bay accompany this classic waterfront family restaurant. Scenes of seagulls and kayakers meandering along the shoreline accompany delicious fish-and-chips, crispy crab cakes, and pungent clam chowder, but juicy burgers, tasty pastas, and big salads are also offered. Service is as casual as the ambience, and the noise level is loud in evenings and on weekends, but it's a fun, friendly neighborhood spot to savor while in town. ✉ *18881 Front St.,* ☏ *360/779–6609* ▭ *AE, D, MC, V.*

¢ ✕ **Sluys.** Rhyme it with "pies" and you'll sound like a local when you enter the town's most famous bakery. Gorgeous Norwegian pastries, braided bread, and *lefse* (traditional Norwegian round, flat bread) line the shelves. Kids often beg for one of the decorated cookies or frosted doughnuts displayed at eye level. There's only strong coffee and milk to drink, and there are no seats, but you can grab a bench along busy Front Street or take your goodies to the waterfront at Liberty Bay Park. ✉ *18924 Front St.* ☏ *360/779–2798* ▭ *MC, V.*

¢ ✕ **Wild Horse BBQ.** Step into the Old West, amid barn-style decor lined with rodeo photos, to grab some of the tastiest grilled grub in the area. Specialties include pulled pork, meaty sandwiches, and tangy ribs and chicken. Save room to top off with homemade pie, such as the mouth-puckering sour cherry, or the ultra-indulgent bourbon pecan. You'll find the place tucked into the Poulsbo Village Shopping Center. ✉ *19472-B 7th Ave. NE,* ☎ *360/697–1459* ▤ *AE, D, MC, V* ⊘ *Closed Sun.*

$–$$ ▦**Manor Farm Inn.** A classic white clapboard home built in 1886, Manor Farm Inn is the heart of a 25-acre farm. White walls, rough-hewn beams, and wide windows generate tranquillity in the spacious guest quarters, which are appointed with French country antiques. Two rooms have wood-burning fireplaces, and one is a loft. Each morning a four-course breakfast awaits in the charming "Rabbit Hutch," decorated with a collection of lagormorphs; afterward you can stroll by the pond or visit the barn and chicken coop. **Pros:** Real country feel, fun setting. **Cons:** Few amenities. The inn also hosts and caters for special group events. ✉ *26069 Big Valley Rd. NE, 98370* ☎ *360/779–4628* 🖷 *360/779–4876* ⊕ *www.manorfarminn.com* ⇨ *7 rooms* ⚭ *In-room: no phone. In-hotel: no TV, restaurant, bicycles, no-smoking rooms, no kids, no elevator* ▤ *AE, MC, V* ⦿ *BP.*

$ ▦**The Poulsbo Inn.** At this lodge-style inn, large rooms come painted in forest greens and browns and with polished timber furnishings. Roomier suites have kitchens. The massive breakfast buffet includes do-it-yourself Belgian waffles, hot sausages and gravy poured over biscuits, and a variety of fruits and fresh breads. The inn is close to the main Kitsap Peninsula sights. **Pros:** Inexpensive, convenient locale. **Cons:** Cheapy motel style. ✉ *18680 Hwy. 305 NE, 98370* ☎ *360/779–3921 or 800/597–5151* 🖷 *360/779–9737* ⊕ *www.poulsboinn.com* ⇨ *85 rooms, 12 suites* ⚭ *In-room: refrigerator. In-hotel: pool, spa, gym, laundry facilities, no elevator* ▤ *AE, MC, V* ⦿ *BP.*

PORT GAMBLE

6 mi northeast of Poulsbo.

Residents from the opposite side of America founded Port Gamble around a sawmill in 1853; hence its New England–style architecture mimicking founder Capt. William Talbot's hometown of East Machias, Maine. Its setting amid the Kitsap Peninsula's tall stands of timber brought in great profits, but the mill was later destroyed by fire, and much of the forest has disappeared. Today many of the houses in this quiet town are on the National Register of Historic Places. A walk will take you past the 1870 St. Paul's Episcopal Church as well as the Thompson House, thought to be the state's oldest continuously lived-in home.

Altogether, the settlement is a burgeoning tourist attraction gathered into a compact clutch of small shops and businesses. Every Sunday from April to October is the Sunday Market, where you can browse stalls of antiques, local crafts, produce, and flowers. Live music provides a background to the scene.

On Saturday at the **Dauntless Bookstore** (✉ *4790 Hwy. 104 NE* ☎ *360/297–4043* ⊕ *www.dauntlessbooks.com*)—a charming red house built of former ship parts—families come to the Children's Annex for weekly story times and crafts programs. Note that it's open daily 10 to 5 in summer, but closed Monday and Tuesday October through May.

The town also stages three major summertime festivals: the Arts & Crafts Fair, the Medieval Faire, and the Civil War reenactment performances. The latter takes place each June in the hills beyond Port Gamble, along Highway 104. This is also an excellent hiking area, with numerous back-country trails tracing the edges of the battlefield grounds. These tracks, some former service roads, cut through miles of thick woodlands and old-growth forests that surround the town and the edges of the water.

☺ Beneath the General Store, the Smithsonian-designed **Port Gamble Historic Museum** takes you through the region's timber heyday. Highlights include artifacts from the Pope and Talbot Timber Company, which built the town, and realistic ship's quarters. Above the General Store, the **Of Sea and Shore Museum** houses more than 25,000 shells. Kids love the weird bug exhibit. Stop at the kitschy General Store for a cheap souvenir and a huge ice-cream cone. ⊠ *1 Rainier Ave.* ☎ *360/297–8074* ⊕ *www.portgamble.com* ⊠ *Historic Museum $2.50, Shell Museum free* ☉ *May–Sept. daily 9:30–5; Oct.–Apr., by appointment.*

WHERE TO STAY & EAT

¢–$ ✕ **Tea Room at Port Gamble.** The sunny yellow exterior of this colonial home provides a lovely front for this elegant spot. Sip specials like cream tea with scones and cream, or take chocolate high tea with finger sandwiches and chocolate fondue. The adjacent Candy Shoppe whips up homemade dark and white chocolate truffles, as well as a variety of molded chocolate candies. Hint: Ask for free samples! ⊠ *32279 N.E. Rainier Ave.* ☎ *360/297–4225* ⊟ *MC, V.*

BREMERTON

18 mi southwest of Seattle by ferry, 68 mi southwest of Seattle by road, 25 mi southwest of Port Gamble by road.

Nearly surrounded by water, and with one of the largest Navy bases on the West Coast, Bremerton is a green city of colorful residential homes fronted by a wide bay lined with massive warships. Attractions center on the waterfront, with its gardens, fountains, and Seattle ferry docks. Downtown is a burgeoning business area on its own, however, with the western Charlestown neighborhood a rapidly expanding hub of art galleries and restaurants. Ten miles to the north, Keyport is a center for torpedo research, and nearby Bangor is home to a fleet of nuclear submarines.

The waterfront expanse of the **Bremerton Marina,** lining the glistening blue bay between the warships and ferry docks, is the place to walk, bicycle, picnic, run through fountains in summer, and watch a mass of sailboats and military craft pass through the calm waters. It's an especially good place for spotting the host of birds and marine life around the docks. ⊠ *Off Washington Ave.*

☺ The **USS** *Turner Joy* Navy destroyer, along the marine near the ferry docks, is open for self-guided tours. Walk through the narrow passages to view the cafeteria, medical office, barbershop, prison cell, cramped bunk rooms, and captain's quarters. ✉*300 Washington Beach Ave.* ☎*360/792–2457* ☛*$8* ☺*May–Oct., daily 10–5; Nov.–Apr., Fri–Sun. 10–4.*

The **Naval Memorial Museum of the Pacific** right on the waterfront and near the ferry terminal, brings American naval history to life through war photos, ship models, historic displays, and American and Japanese war artifacts. ✉*251 1st St.* ☎*360/479–7447* ☛*Free* ☺*Mon.–Sat. 10–4, Sun. 1–4.*

The small **Kitsap County Historical Society Museum** has pioneer artifacts, nautical items, and a collection of old photographs. The staff plans such special children's events as costume dress-up sessions and treasure hunts for the first Friday of the month, when the museum is open late in conjunction with the town's monthly Art Walk. ✉*280 4th St.* ☎*360/479–6226* ⊕*www.kitsaphistory.org* ☛*$2* ☺*Tues.–Sat. 9–5, 1st Fri. of month 9–8.*

☺ The **Naval Undersea Museum**, a 15-minute drive north of Bremerton, is fronted by a can't-miss sight: the 88-ton *Trieste II* submarine, which dove to the deepest spot in the ocean (the Marianas Trench) in 1960. In the main building are torpedoes, diving equipment, model submarines, and mines. ✉*610 Dowell St., Keyport* ☎*360/396–4148* ⊕*www.key portmuseum.cnrnw.navy.mil* ☛*Free* ☺*June–Sept., daily 10–4; closed Tues. Oct.–May.*

WHERE TO STAY & EAT

$–$$ ✗**Boat Shed.** At this deliberately rustic waterfront restaurant diners share a casual, seaside camaraderie as they slurp up clam chowder, steamed clams, and mussels. Sailors, who enjoy free boat moorage, arrive early for the famed Sunday brunch. ✉*101 Shore Dr.* ☎*360/377–2600* ▬*AE, MC, V.*

$–$$ ✗**Yacht Club Broiler.** With lovely views of Dyes Inlet (where gray whales are occasionally spotted), this simple but elegant family restaurant specializes in fresh, flavorful seafood. For those who prefer meat, top sirloin combos are a good bet. In warm weather you can dine outside on the deck or on an adjacent grassy knoll. ✉*9226 Bayshore Dr. NW, Silverdale* ☎*360/698–1601* ▬*AE, D, MC, V.*

¢–$ 🏨**Oyster Bay Inn.** This hotel sits at the lower curve of Oyster Bay, just outside of Bremerton but seemingly on an isle of its own. Panoramic views of the water are the highlight of the comfortable rooms, and you can see the bay up close on a stroll through the surrounding gardens and woods. The elegant restaurant is a lively spot to feast on seafood, steaks, and fancy pastas. Afterward head to the adjacent lounge, which has a piano bar. **Pros:** Locale quiet but convenient. **Cons:** Motel-style exterior. ✉*4412 Kitsap Way, 98312* ☎*360/377–5510 or 800/393–3862* ⊕*www.oysterbayinn.com* ☛*62 rooms, 10 suites, 1 chalet* ☺*In-room: kitchen (some). In-hotel: refrigerator, restaurant, bar, gym, some pets allowed, no elevator* ▬*AE, D, DC, MC, V* ⏹*CP.*

¢ ⬚ **Flagship Inn.** Although it's a budget spot, rooms here have private balconies overlooking Oyster Bay and the Olympic Mountains. It's close to everything, rooms have a microwave, refrigerator, and VCR, and there's even a free video library for rainy evenings. Free tea, coffee, fruit, and cookies are available all day. ⊠*4320 Kitsap Way, 98312* ☎*360/479–6566 or 800/447–9396* 🖷*360/479–6745* ⊕*www.flag ship-inn.com* ⟲*29 rooms* ♿*In-room: kitchen. In-hotel: refrigerator, VCR, dial-up, Wi-Fi, pool, some pets allowed, no elevator* ⊟*AE, D, DC, MC, V* ⦿*CP.*

GIG HARBOR

23 mi southeast of Bremerton.

One of the most picturesque and accessible waterfront cities on Puget Sound, Gig Harbor has a neat, circular bay dotted with sailboats and fronted by hills of evergreens and million-dollar homes. Expect spectacular views all along the town's winding 2-mi bayside walkway, which is intermittently lined by boat docks, kitschy shops, cozy cafés, and broad expanses of open water.

The bay was a storm refuge for the 1841 survey team of Captain Charles Wilkes, who named the area after his small gig (boat). A decade later Croatian and Scandinavian immigrants put their fishing, lumber, and boat-building skills to profitable use, and the town still has strong seafaring traditions. By the 1880s, steamboats carried passengers and goods between the harbor and Tacoma, and auto ferries plied the narrows between the cities by 1917.

The town winds around the waterfront, centering at the crossroads of Harborview Drive and Pioneer Way, where shops, art galleries, and restaurants often attract more foot traffic than vehicles. From here, Harborview makes a long, gentle curve around the bay toward the renovated Finholm Market building, which has shops, docks, a restaurant, kayak rentals, and more views. A Gig Harbor Historical Society self-guided walk brochure covers 49 sights (see if you can spot the 16 metal salmon sculptures, designed by local artists, placed in front of sights around town).

Along the waterfront is **Jersich Park,** where the Fisherman's Memorial statue commemorates the town's sea-loving founders. The long public dock slopes right out into the bay, toward a sunny sitting spot where you can watch pleasure boats sliding in and out of the docks and kayakers practicing their paddling.

The **Gig Harbor Museum** has an excellent collection of exhibits describing the city's maritime history, as well as photo archives, video programs, and a research library focusing on the area's pioneer and Native American ancestors. The facilities include a one-room, early-20th-century schoolhouse and a 65-foot, 1950s purse seiner, a type of fishing vessel from the community's famous seafaring fleets. News clippings and videos about "Galloping Gertie," the original bridge, are particularly eerie. The staff also stages major historic activities for the area, including a four-hour history cruise each summer ($60) and twice-yearly Harbor Heritage kayak outings from the city docks to locales around Puget Sound ($25 per person). ⊠*Harborview Dr.* ☎*253/858–6722* ⊕*www. gigharbormuseum.org* ☜*$2* ⊙*Tues.–Sat. 10–4.*

Surrounding Gig Harbor, pine forests and open woods alternate with rolling pastures; it's enjoyable scenery (even on rainy days) during the 10-minute drive to **Fox Island.** Crossing the Fox Island Bridge over Echo Bay, you'll see stunning views of the Olympic Mountains to the right and the Tanglewood Lighthouse against a backdrop of Mt. Rainier to the left. **Tanglewood Island,** the small drop of forest on which the Tanglewood lighthouse sits, was once an Indian burial ground known as Grav Island. At low tide the boat ramp and boulder-strewn beach next to the bridge are scattered with stranded saltwater creatures.

The **Fox Island Historical Museum** displays island pioneer memorabilia in an authentic log cabin. Pioneer-days children's activities, such as Maypole dances, memory boxes, and old-fashioned Valentine crafts, are scheduled the first Saturday of every month, and the local farmer's market runs summer Wednesdays. ⊠*1017 9th Ave.* ☎*253/549–2461* ☜*$1* ⊙*Wed. 11–3 and Sat. 1–4.*

Kopachuk State Park, a 10-minute drive from Gig Harbor, is a wonderful beachcombing area at low tide. Indian tribes once fished and clammed here, and you can still see people trolling the shallow waters or digging deep for razor clams in season. Children and dogs alike delight in discovering huge Dungeness crabs, sea stars, and sand dollars. Picnic tables and walking trails are interspersed throughout the steep, forested hills, and the campground is always full in summer. ⊠*11101 56th St. NW* ☎*253/265–3606* ☜*Free* ⊙*Daily 6* AM*–10* PM.

WHERE TO EAT

$–$$$ ✕**Brix 25.** Simple seafood dishes and classic European fare are beautifully presented in this cozy, glass-fronted setting at the base of Harborview Drive and the Gig Harbor bay. Lunches run the gourmet gamut from spring rolls, salads, sandwiches, soups, and chowders to full-blown grilled steaks and fish. Dinners are formal affairs that focus on seafood and light meats accompanied by fresh local greens. Tempting desserts include an array of sugary cakes, sorbets, and cobblers, and there's a fine wine to match every course. Seasonal events include chef-hosted, multicourse dinners. ⊠*7707 Pioneer Way* ☎*253/858–6626* ⊕*www.harborbrix.com* ▭*AE, D, MC, V* ⊙*No lunch weekends.*

$$ ✕**Green Turtle.** The unassuming exterior belies a dining room surrounded by a mural of an azure underwater world, one that includes a huge sea turtle. Wraparound windows show off the bayside setting, as does the front deck. Eclectic Northwest cuisine is beautifully presented in such dishes as halibut cheeks and filet mignon. It's difficult to leave without succumbing to crêpes suzette topped with vanilla ice cream and warm orange liqueur. ⊠*2905 Harborview Dr.* ☎*206/851–3167* ▭*AE, MC, V* ⊙*Closed Mon. No lunch weekends.*

$–$$ ✕**Anthony's HomePort.** Here you're encircled by wide windows overlooking boats slipping through sparkling blue waters. Fine Northwest wines match mains like alder-planked salmon, red-broth cioppino, and ginger soy tuna with homemade pineapple chutney. Dine downstairs in the more casual Shoreline Room and you'll get the same pretty views without the wait (although the menu is lighter). In warm weather you can eat outside on the deck, and boat moorage is free. ⊠*8827 N. Harborview Dr.* ☎*253/853–6353* ⊟*AE, D, DC, MC, V* ⊘*No lunch weekdays.*

¢–$ ✕**El Pueblito.** The mariachi music, cilantro and chili pepper scents from the kitchen, and a waitstaff that chats in Spanish are reminiscent of a compact cantina south of the border. Huge portions of better-than-average Mexican dishes and frothy margaritas are served amid much gaiety. The adjacent bar is a lively late-night hangout on weekends. ⊠*3226 Harborview Dr.* ☎*253/858–9077* ⊟*AE, D, MC, V.*

¢–$ ✕**The Thai Hut.** Drop into this little Southeast Asian haven across from the bay and dig into some of the Northwest's best Thai food. Close-set tables and a cozy space make for family-friendly camaraderie as heaping plates of noodles, rice dishes, and curries steam through the two rooms. A narrow front deck looks out to water views, but can be noisy with traffic. Weekend waits can be long—but carry-out tastes just as good! ⊠*4116 Harborview Dr.* ☎*253/858–8523* ⊟*MC, V.*

WHERE TO STAY

$–$$ 🏨**Inn at Gig Harbor.** The city's largest hotel has a multicolor exterior that makes it seem more like a mansion than a member of the Heritage chain. Upstairs from the large, stone fireplace foyer are elegantly decorated rooms; many have Mt. Rainier views, and suites have a fireplaces or jetted tub. The Heritage restaurant serves classic American fare with Northwest flair. Browse through the little shop, which is jam-packed with good-quality regional crafts and treats. The inn is a major base for business travelers driving into Seattle, Tacoma, and Bremerton. **Pros:** Lodge-style ambience, professional staff. **Cons:** no pool. ⊠*3211 56th St. NW* ☎*253/858–1111 or 800/795–9980* 🖷*253/851–5402* ⊕*www. innatgigharbor.com* ⊄*52 rooms, 12 suites* ◿*In-room: refrigerators (some), dial-up. In-hotel: Wi-Fi, restaurant, room service, gym, laundry service, airport shuttle* ⊟*AE, D, DC, MC, V* ⫯❶*CP.*

¢–$$ 🏨**Maritime Inn.** On a hill across from Jersich Park and the docks, this boutique hotel combines class and comfort with water views. Individually decorated and themed rooms include the Captain's Room, the Canterwood Golf Room, and the Victorian Room. All have fireplaces, and several have decks. Cottages along the back of the hill afford privacy and quiet; streetside rooms are noisy but have excellent views. **Pros:** Right on the waterfront street. **Cons:** front rooms absorb traffic noise. ⊠*3112 Harborview Dr.* ☎*253/858–1818* ⊕*www.maritimeinn. com* ⊄*15 rooms* ◿*In-room: dial-up. In-hotel: no elevator* ⊟*AE, D, DC, MC, V.*

$ 🏨**Beachside Bed & Breakfast.** You're right on the beach, surrounded by blossoming gardens, at this waterfront gem on Fox Island. The sunny suite's feminine, English-style touches—lacy curtains, floral couches, and frilly bedspread—are tempered by the masculinity of the beamed ceiling, enormous brick fireplace, and bold maritime accents. Step onto the deck and you're inspired to stroll on the pebbled sand, dip into the hot tub, or take a boat cruise or kayak run from the deepwater moorage. A bountiful basket of homemade goodies awaits you each morning. **Pros:** Like your own private island getaway. **Cons:** A 15-minute drive from town. ⊠*679 Kamus Dr.* ☏*253/549–2524* ⊕*www. beachsidebb.com* ⌁*1 suite* ⌂*In-room: kitchen. In-hotel: refrigerator, VCR, beachfront, no kids under 12, no elevator* ▭*No credit cards* ❏*CP.*

NIGHTLIFE

Java & Clay Cafe (⊠*3210 Harborview Dr.* ☏*253/851–3277*), a pottery painting shop, is fronted by a coffee room that hosts acoustic guitar players on weekends around 7:30. It's a dive, but the unheated bar and wide deck at the **Hy-Iu-Hee-Hee** (⊠*4309 Burnham Dr.* ☏*253/851–7885*) tavern are packed nightly with locals wanting cheap drinks, dart and pool games, and big portions of bar food. The legendary **Tide's Tavern** (⊠*2925 Harborview Dr.* ☏*253/858–3982*), right on the water in a weather-worn building that housed the town's original general store, has been the local hot spot for 21-and-over drinks, darts, and live music since the 1930s.

TACOMA

❶–⓯ *25 mi southeast of Gig Harbor, 34 mi southwest of Seattle.*

Tacoma is coming into its own, having in the last decade blossomed into a very livable city that has good museums, an edgy arts scene, and attractive old suburbs. It's a broad, hilly city whose clean-cut waterfront stretches west from the busy port, past the city and Puget Sound islands to the cliff-lined Tacoma Narrows. Renovated 19th-century homes, pretty beaches, and parks pocket the outskirts, and a young population gives the city a spirited character. The Tacoma Dome, that wooden, blue-and-gray half-sphere stadium visible along I–5, hosts international expos, sporting events, and famous entertainers in its 28,000-seat arena. The city's convenient setting provides easy access to Seattle and Canada to the north; the small town of Auburn to the northeast; Mt. Rainier to the southeast; Olympia to the south; and the Kitsap and Olympic peninsulas to the west.

Tacoma was the first Puget Sound port connected by train to the East, and its economy was once based on the railroad. Old photos show tall-masted windjammers loading at the City Waterway, whose storage sheds were promoted by local boosters as the "longest warehouse under one continuous roof in the world." The city's shipping industry certainly weathered the tests of time, as Tacoma is the largest container port in the Northwest.

WHAT TO SEE

❺ Broadway Center for the Performing Arts. Cultural activity in Tacoma centers on this complex of performance spaces. The famous theater architect B. Marcus Pritica designed the **Pantages** (⊠*901 Broadway* ☏*253/591–5890* ⊕*www.broadwaycenter.org*), a 1918 Greco-Roman–influenced music hall with classical figures, ornate columns, arches, and

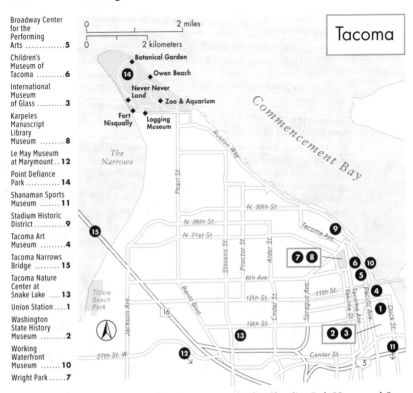

reliefs. W. C. Fields, Mae West, Charlie Chaplin, Bob Hope, and Stan Laurel all performed here. The Tacoma Symphony and BalleTacoma perform at the Pantages, which also presents touring shows. Adjacent to the Pantages, the contemporary **Theatre on the Square** (⊠ *Broadway between 10th and 11th Sts.* ☎ *253/591–5890*) is the home of the Tacoma Actors Guild, one of Washington's largest professional theater companies. In its early days, the **Rialto Theater** (⊠ *301 S. 9th St.* ☎ *253/591–5890* ⊕ *www.rialtotheater.com*) presented vaudeville performances and silent films. The Tacoma Youth Symphony now performs in the 1918 structure.

❻ **Children's Museum of Tacoma.** Fun activities for little ones take place in
🕐 spacious exhibits. The Learning Lounge has touchable, movable pieces; Becka's Clubhouse has hands-on art; and New Digs goes from simple gardening to cooking. Older kids have fun on the climbing wall and at the cultural displays. Families get in free on the first Friday of the month. ⊠ *936 Broadway Ave.* ☎ *253/627–6031* ⊕ *www.childrens museumoftacoma.org* ⊠ *$6* ☉ *Mon.–Sat. 10–5, Sun. noon–5.*

❸ **International Museum of Glass.** The showpiece of this spectacular, 2-acre
Fodor'sChoice combination of delicate and creative exhibits is the 500-foot-long Chi-
★ huly Bridge of Glass, a tunnel of glorious color and light that stretches above I–705. Cross it to reach the building grounds, which sit above

the bay and next to a shallow reflecting pool dotted with large modern-art sculptures. Inside, you can wander with the crowds through the quiet, light-filled galleries, take a seat in the theater-like Hot Shop to watch glass-blowing artists, or try your own hand at arts and crafts in the studio. You'll also find a souvenir shop and café. ⊠*1801 E. Dock St.* ☎*253/284–4750* ⊕*www.museumofglass.org* ⊡*$10* ⊗*Mon.–Sat. 10–5, Sun. noon–5.*

⑧ Karpeles Manuscript Library Museum. Housed in the former American Legion hall and across from Wright Park, the museum showcases rare and unpublished letters and documents by those who have shaped history. Themes of temporary exhibits have included the War of 1812 and Einstein's theory of relativity. ⊠*407 S. G St.* ☎*253/383–2575* ⊕*www.rain.org/~karpeles/* ⊡*Free* ⊗*Tues.–Sun. 10–4.*

⑫ The Le May Museum at Marymount. Harold Le May was the ultimate collector of vintage cars; his collection is in the *Guinness Book of World Records* as the largest privately owned collection in the world. Highlights include a LaSalle, a Pierce-Arrow, a Packard, and a Tucker, along with fire engines, antique buses, and old-fashioned trucks. About 400 of the top models are on display; a new building, scheduled to open in 2009, will house the full 4,000-vehicle collection. ⊠*423 152nd St. E* ☎*253/779–8490 or 877/902–8490* ⊕*www.lemaymuseum.org* ⊡*Tours $15* ⊗*Tues.–Sat. 10–5, last tour at 3.*

⑭ Point Defiance Park. Jutting into Commencement Bay, this hilly, 698-acre ⟳ park surrounds Five Mile Drive with lush picnicking fields and patches ★ of forest. Hiking trails, bike paths, and numerous gardens draw crowds year-round, particularly during summer festivals such as the Taste of Tacoma, in June. The park begins at the north end of Pearl Street as you drive toward the Point Defiance Ferry Terminal, where vehicles depart for Vashon Island just across the Sound. A one-way road branches off the ferry lane, past a lake and picnic area, a rose garden, and a Japanese garden, finally winding down to the beach.

One of the Northwest's finest collections of regional and international species is the winding and hilly **Point Defiance Zoo and Aquarium.** Tigers, elephants, tapirs, and gibbons inhabit the Southeast Asian area, where paw-print trails lead between lookouts so even the smallest tots can spot animals. The aquarium is also fun to explore, with its glass-walled, floor-to-ceiling shark tank; seahorse room; touch-tank marine area; and open-topped, two-level Pacific Northwest reef display. Other areas house such cold-weather creatures as beluga whales, wolves, polar bears, and penguins. Thirty-minute animal shows, run two to four times daily, let five different creatures show off their skills. The fantastic playground area has friendly farm animals running between the slides, and seasonal special events include a Halloween trick-or-treat night and the famous nightly Zoolights holiday displays around Christmas. ⊠*Point Defiance Park: 5400 N. Pearl St.* ☎*253/305–1000* ⊕*www. pdza.org* ⊡*Park free, zoo $10* ⊗*Park daily dawn–dusk; zoo Apr.– Memorial Day, daily 9–5; Memorial Day–Labor Day, 9–6; Labor Day– 1st weekend Nov., 9–5; 1st weekend Nov.–Apr., 9:30–4.* On Five Mile

Drive, the **Rhododendron Species Botanical Garden** is a 22-acre expanse of more than 10,000 plants—some 2,000 varieties of 450 species—which bloom in succession. It's one of the finest rhododendron collections in the world. ⊠*2525 S. 336th St.* ☎*253/927–6960* ⊕*www.rhody garden.org* ▭*$3.50* ⊙*Mar.–May., Fri.–Wed. 10–4; June–Feb., Sat.–Wed. 11–4.* A half-mile past the gardens is **Owen Beach,** a driftwood-strewn stretch of pebbly sand near the ferry dock and a wonderful place for beachcombing and sailboat-watching. Kayak rentals and concessions are available in summer. Continue around the looping drive, which offers occasional views of the narrows. Cruise slowly to take in the scenes—and watch out for joggers and bikers. Near the drive's end, the 15-acre **Camp Six Logging Museum** (☎*253/752–0047*) has restored bunkhouses, hand tools, and other equipment illustrating the history of steam logging from 1880 to 1950. From here you can take a short ride through the woods on a steam train. The fare is $4, and the train runs every half hour on weekends between noon and 6:30. The museum is free, and open Wednesday to Friday 10 to 5, weekends 10 to 7. West of the Camp Six Logging Museum is **Ft. Nisqually** (☎*253/591–5339* ⊕*www.fortnisqually.org*), a restored Hudson's Bay Trading Post. A British outpost on the Nisqually Delta in the 1830s, it was moved to Point Defiance in 1935. The compound houses a trading post, granary, blacksmith's shop, bakery, and officers' quarters. Docents dress in 1850s attire and demonstrate pioneer skills like weaving and loading a rifle. Queen Victoria's birthday in August is a big event, and eerie candlelight tours run throughout October. It's open daily 11 to 5 Memorial Day–Labor Day, and Wednesday to Sunday 11–4 the rest of the year; admission is $4.**Never Never Land,**a children's fantasy world of sculptured storybook characters, is across the parking lot from Ft. Nisqually.

⑪ **Shanaman Sports Museum.** Housed on the lower level of the atmospheric wooden Tacoma Dome, the museum highlights the accomplishments of local athletes. All sports are represented, from baseball, basketball, football, soccer, and tennis to gymnastics and volleyball. You must either hold a Tacoma Dome event ticket or make a tour by appointment. ⊠*2727 E. D St.* ☎*253/627–5857* ⊕*www.tacomasportsmuseum.com* ▭*Free* ⊙*Open during events or by appointment.*

⑨ **Stadium Historic District.** Several of the Victorian homes in this charming neighborhood, high on a hill overlooking Commencement Bay, have been converted to bed-and-breakfast inns. Stadium High School at 111 North E Street is in an elaborate château-style structure built in 1891 as a luxury hotel for the Northern Pacific Railroad. The building was converted into a high school after a 1906 fire.

④ **Tacoma Art Museum.** Adorned in glass and steel, this Antoine Predock masterpiece wraps around a beautiful garden. Inside you'll find paintings, ceramics, sculptures, and other creations dating from the 18th century to the present. Look for the many glass sculptures by Dale Chihuly—especially the magnificent, flame-color *Mille Fiori* (Thousand Flowers) glass garden. ⊠*1701 Pacific Ave.* ☎*253/272–4258* ⊕*www.*

tacomaartmuseum.org ✉$7.50, free on 3rd Thurs. of month ⊗Tues.–Sat. 10–5, Sun. noon–5, plus Mon. 10–5 Memorial Day–Labor Day.

⑮ The Tacoma Narrows Bridge. A mile-wide waterway is the boundary between the Tacoma hills and the rugged bluffs of the Kitsap Peninsula. From the twin bridges that span it, the view plunges hundreds of feet down to roiling green waters, which are often busy with barge traffic or obscured by fog. The original bridge, "Galloping Gertie," famously twisted itself to death and broke in half during a storm in 1940. Today its mint-green replacement and a sister bridge opened in 2007 top the world's largest man-made reef and is a popular dive site. Note: The $3 toll is for eastbound cars only; westbound it's free from Tacoma into Gig Harbor. ✉*Part of Hwy. 16.*

⑬ Tacoma Nature Center at Snake Lake. Fifty-four acres of marshland, evergreen forest, and shallow lake break up the urban sprawl of west Tacoma and shelter 25 species of mammals and more than 100 species of birds. The lake has nesting pairs of wood ducks, rare elsewhere in western Washington, and the interpretive center is a fun place for kids to look at small creatures, take walks and nature quizzes, and dress up in animal costumes. ✉*1919 S. Tyler St.* ☎*253/591–6439* ⊕*www.tacomaparks.com* ✉*Free* ⊗*Center Tues.–Fri. 8–5, Sat. 10–4; trails daily dawn–dusk.*

❶ Union Station. This heirloom dates from 1911, when Tacoma was the western terminus of the Northern Pacific Railroad. Built by Reed and Stem, architects of New York City's Grand Central Terminal, the copper-domed, beaux arts–style depot shows the influence of the Roman Pantheon and Italian baroque style. The station houses federal district courts, but its rotunda contains a gorgeous exhibit of glass sculptures by Dale Chihuly. Hint: Since it's a highly guarded government facility, be prepared to walk through a metal detector and show photo ID. ✉*1717 Pacific Ave.* ☎*253/572–9310* ✉*Free* ⊗*Weekdays 8–5.*

❷ Washington State History Museum. Adjacent to Union Station, and with the same opulent architecture, Washington's official history museum presents interactive exhibits and multimedia installations about the exploration and settlement of the state. Some rooms are filled with Native American, Eskimo, and pioneer artifacts, while others display logging and railroad memorabilia. The upstairs gallery has rotating exhibits, and summer programs are staged in the outdoor amphitheater. ✉*1911 Pacific Ave.* ☎*253/272–3500* ⊕*www.wshs.org* ✉*$8* ⊗*Mon.–Wed., Fri., and Sat. 10–5, Thurs. 10–8.*

❿ Working Waterfront Museum. With its beautiful setting right along the Thea Foss waterfront, the turn-of-the-20th-century, wharf-style structure is easily reached along a walk by the bay. Inside the enormous timber building, displays trace the history of Tacoma's brisk shipping business. Extensive exhibits cover boat-making, importing and exporting, and the development of the waterfront. Photos and relics round out the exhibits, and children's activities are staged monthly. Note: Currently under renovations, the museum will be open for Tall Ships in June 2008, and will open for good early 2009. ✉*705 Dock St.*

4

*☎253/272–2750 ⊕www.wwfrontmuseum.org ⊠$3 ☉Mid-Apr.–
mid-Oct., weekdays 9–5, weekends noon–5; mid-Oct.–mid-Apr., daily
noon–4.*

❼ Wright Park. The chief attraction at this 28-acre park, which is on the
National Register of Historic Places, is the glass-dome **W.W. Seymour
Botanical Conservatory** (⊠316 S. G St. ☎253/591–5330), a Victorian-style greenhouse (one of only three such structures on the West
Coast) with exotic flora. ⊠Between 6th and Division Sts., Yakima
and Tacoma Aves. ☎253/591–5331 ⊠Free ☉Park daily dawn–dusk,
conservatory daily 8:30–4:20.

WHERE TO EAT

$$–$$$ ✕**Sea Grill.** Infused with the light-and-shadows blues of the ocean,
this restaurant brings just-fresh seafood away from the water and into
downtown. Framed by a glasslike circular bar, the elegant dining room
is highlighted by layered copper chandeliers, tables topped in creamy
white linens, and a waitstaff that whisks dishes to you in a dash. The
food here is first-class, from such appetizers as crispy sesame oysters
and white-asparagus salad to mains such as Hawaiian yellowfin tuna in
mango salsa, and smoked black cod. Catch the buzz of the city's summer energy by dining out on the patio. ⊠1498 Pacific Ave., Suite 300
☎253/272–5656 ⊕www.the-seagrill.com ⊟AE, D, MC, V ☉No
lunch.

$–$$ ✕**The Cliff House Restaurant.** For an unforgettable scene, witness the
ocean panorama from the Rainier Room when there's a full moon.
Comfortable, curved banquettes with floral upholstery provide the best
positioning, but the cozier tables tucked in between offer more intimacy.
When the succulent steaks, seafood, and wild game are served, your
attention is turned away from the views. Memorable entrées include
oven-roasted New Zealand lamb rack and jumbo prawns stuffed with
Dungeness crabmeat. The casual bistro Guido's Downstairs has the
same scenery but a lighter menu. ⊠6300 Marine View Dr. ☎253/927–
0400 ⊕www.cliffhouserestaurant.com ⊟AE, D, DC, MC, V.

$–$$ ✕**Indochine** The elegant, pan-Asian conglomeration of sounds, scents,
and sights takes place in a sleekly modern, yet darkly cozy space.
Black-leather seats, curving banquettes, and steely metal accents set
off plush red curtains and pavilion tables. The taste-dazzling array of
Thai, Chinese, Indian, and Japanese cuisines includes curries, stir-fries,
soups, and seafood. Standouts include coconut and galangal chicken
soup, and the Oceans Five seafood and cilantro, served over vegetables. ⊠1924 Pacific Ave. ☎253/272–8200 ⊟MC, V ☉Closed Sun.
⊠31254 Pacific Hwy. S, Federal Way ☎253/946–3992.

$–$$ ✕**Lobster Shop.** Built on stilts above the Dash Point tide flats, this former grocery store and beachside soda fountain is now an elite, two-story seafood spot with panoramic bay views. Start with a house
martini (always a double) or a taste of Washington wine, and perhaps
coconut–macadamia nut prawns or lobster bisque. Move on to crab
cakes, potato-crusted ling cod, or pasta with wild-mushroom cream
sauce. Finish with white-chocolate banana-bread pudding—or the
Ghirardelli's chocolate brownie tower. Twilight meals, served before

5:30, provide a mix of courses at a reduced price. ✉*6912 Soundview Dr. NE, off Dash Point Rd.* ☎*253/927–1513* ✉*4013 Ruston Way* ☎*253/759–2165* ▤*AE, DC, MC, V* ◷*No lunch.*

$ ✕**Engine House No. 9.** The 1907 brick building once housed the horse-drawn fire-engine brigade, and today the structure is on the National Register of Historic Places. It's now a pub-style restaurant that's filled with firehouse memorabilia. The hearty, offbeat, Americanized ethnic fare (Thai chicken, soft tacos, pizza, and pasta) have made it a hit. The adjacent brewery, which serves microbrews and regional wines, is packed on weekends. ✉*611 N. Pine St.* ☎*253/272–3435* ▤*AE, MC, V.*

$ ✕**21 Commerce.** "Unwind and dine" is the theme at this chic warehouse space–cum–martini bar, where you can choose from 21 terrific offbeat bar drinks plus food. In fact, the number 21 says it all. The 21 martini styles draw in after-work and weekend crowds, and a nearly over-whelming array of 21 appetizers and mains often keeps diners noshing and chatting until after midnight. Entrées blend Asian, European, and Northwest flavors and seasonings in such offerings as fish-and-chips and three-cheese ravioli in rosemary cream sauce. ✉*Commerce St., at 21st St.* ☎*253/272–6278* ⊕*www.21martinis.com* ▤*AE, MC, V* ◷*Closed Sun. and Mon. No lunch.*

¢–$ ✕**Steamers.** A backdrop of deep-blue Narrows bay and the saltwater-soaked timber ruins of the old Tacoma ferry terminal surround this popular little shack, where fresh-caught seafood is served up in a clap-board, dockside-tavern environment. Specials are jotted in chalk in the entry; the bar-style ordering area often has a line out the door; and the close-set tables are usually jam-packed from noon until closing. Portions lean toward the miniscule, but everything is simple, straight-forward, and down-home Northwest, from the creamy clam chow-der and hot beer-battered fish to the grilled salmon. ✉*8802 6th Ave.* ☎*253/565–4532* ⊜*Reservations not accepted* ▤*MC, V.*

¢ ✕**Pastrami's.** East Coast transplants love this New York–style deli in Tacoma's theater district. A meeting place for much of the city's work-force, Pastrami's serves kosher and vegetarian items, French onion soup, and hot pastrami on rye. You can build your own sandwich or just order an espresso drink at the dark, curving bar. ✉*Rhodes Bldg., 950 Broadway* ☎*253/779–0645* ⊜*Reservations not accepted* ▤*AE, MC, V* ◷*Closed weekends. No dinner.*

WHERE TO STAY

$$$$ ▦**Thornewood Castle Inn and Gardens Bed & Breakfast.** Spread over four lush acres along beautiful American Lake, this 27,000-square-foot, Gothic Tudor–style mansion built in 1908 has hosted two American presidents: William Howard Taft and Theodore Roosevelt. Among the exquisite details inside are medieval stained-glass windows, gleaming wood floors, large mirrors, antiques, fireplaces, and hot tubs. From the lakeside patio and sunken garden you can meditate on the spectacular sunsets. The inn is 12 mi south of Tacoma. **Pros:** Castlelike ambience, lively events. **Cons:** Iffy Internet access. ✉*8601 N. Thorne La. SW, Lakewood 98498* ☎*253/589–9052* ⊟*253/584–4497* ⊕*www.thorne woodcastle.com* ⇆*2 rooms, 5 suites, 1 apartment* ☍*In-room: micro-*

wave, refrigerator. In-hotel: VCR, beachfront, Wi-Fi, no kids under 12, no elevator ⊟AE, D, MC, V ⫯⊚⫯BP.

$$$–$$$$ ⚏ **Hotel Murano.** Named for the Italian island where some of the world's best glass is created, this big hotel with an intimate ambience centers around exhibits by world-famous glass artists. Bold colors and sleek metals infuse public spaces with style and energy, and each floor exhibits a different glass artist's pieces. Rooms are done in black and white with fiery accents; each has high thread-count linens, iPod docks, and a flat-screen TV. The stark, chrome-and-glass restaurant sits spectacularly above glass creations in the hotel atrium. **Pros:** Boutique feel, luxury amenities, top-flight service. **Cons:** No pool, lots of breakables. ⊠*1320 Broadway Plaza, 98402* ☎*253/238–8000 or 888/862–3255* 📠*253/591–4105* ⊕*www.hotelmuranotacoma.com* ⧟*319 rooms, 10 suites* &*In-room: Wi-Fi. In-hotel: restaurant, bar, spa* ⊟AE, D, DC, MC, V.

$$$–$$$$ ⚏ **Silver Cloud Inn.** Tacoma's only waterfront hotel juts right out into the bay along picturesque Ruston Way and the historic Old Town area. Views are of the forested surroundings and the boardwalk marina area stretching along either side. Rooms are elegant, extra-comfortable, and functional, each with a microwave, refrigerator, high-speed Internet connection, and glossy bay vistas. Suites feel like rooms in a posh mansion, with plush carpets, overstuffed chairs, fireplaces, and corner hot tubs that hang out over the water. On Tuesday evening the hotel hosts free wine-and-cheese receptions. **Pros:** Waterside locale, Ruston Way walking paths and restaurants. **Cons:** Summer traffic, compact rooms. ⊠*2317 N. Ruston Way, 98402* ☎*253/272–1300 or 866/820–8448* 📠*253/274–9176* ⊕*www.silvercloud.com* ⧟*90 rooms* &*In-room: refrigerator. In-hotel: room service, gym, laundry facilities, laundry service, Wi-Fi* ⊟AE, D, MC, V ⫯⊚⫯CP.

$–$$$ ⚏ **Chinaberry Hill.** Original fixtures and stained-glass windows are among the grace notes in this 1889 Queen Anne–style B&B in the Stadium Historic District. Suites have shining wood floors, antique feather beds dressed in fine-quality linens, and ornate desks; three have a hot tub. The two-story Catchpenny Cottage carriage house, which sleeps six, has a claw-foot tub and memorabilia from its horse-and-buggy days. A guest kitchen stocks complimentary drinks, cookies, and popcorn. **Pros:** Wraparound porch with vast bay views. **Cons:** Creaks and quirks of a century-old mansion. ⊠*302 Tacoma Ave. N, 98403* ☎*253/272–1282* 📠*253/272–1335* ⊕*www.chinaberryhill.com* ⧟*4 suites, 1 cottage* &*In-room: VCR. In hotel: Wi-Fi, no elevator* ⊟AE, D, MC, V ⫯⊚⫯BP.

$–$$ ⚏ **Green Cape Cod Bed & Breakfast.** Built in 1929, this house stands in a residential neighborhood only blocks from the historic Proctor shopping district. Three rooms with frilly linens and beautiful antiques provide the full scale of pampering with down comforters, soft robes, and bedside Almond Roca candy, a Northwest specialty. Guests receive passes to the downtown YMCA. **Pros:** Cozy, frilly rooms. **Cons:** Must drive to all Tacoma attractions. ⊠*2711 N. Warner St., 98407* ☎*253/752–1977 or 888/752–1977* 📠*253/756–9886* ⊕*www.greencapecod.com*

⇥3 *rooms* ⚃*In-room: no phone. In-hotel: dial-up, laundry service, no kids under 10, no elevator* ☰*AE, MC, V* ⦶*BP.*

$ ⊡**DeVoe Mansion Bed and Breakfast.** On 1½ beautiful acres, this 1911 colonial-style mansion fronted with tall white columns is a national and state historic site. Rooms, which are named after suffragettes, have such antiques as an oak sleigh bed with claw feet. **Pros:** Old-fashioned fun, lavish breakfasts. **Cons:** Streetside locale, away from main attractions. ⊠*208 E. 133rd St., 98445* ☎*253/539–3991 or 888/539–3991* ⎙*253/539–8539* ⊕*www.devoemansion.com* ⇥*4 rooms* ⚃*In-room: VCR. In-hotel: no kids under 12, no-smoking rooms, no elevator* ☰*AE, D, MC, V* ⦶*BP.*

NIGHTLIFE

BARS & LOUNGES **The Loft** (⊠*2106 Pacific Ave.* ☎*253/404–0540* ⊕*www.loftlive.com*) is a groovy, renovated-warehouse-style hangout for cool thirtysomethings.

Sea Grill (⊠*1498 Pacific Ave.* ☎*253/272–5656* ⊕*www.the-seagrill. com*), with its expansive, circular bar done in the iridescent hues of the ocean, is open daily—and it's the best place in town for a perfect mai tai. **Six Olives** (⊠*2708 6th Ave.* ☎*253/272–5574* ⊕*www.sixolives lounge.com*) has a selection of innovative martini drinks Wednesday through Saturday, including the famous Eve at the Apple. Live jazz plays Friday and Saturday.

On the Ruston Way waterfront, the enormous **Ram Grill & Big Horn Brewery** (⊠*3001 Ruston Way* ☎*253/756–7886*)—a wood-paneled restaurant, bar, and brewery complex—is a fun, loud, ever-packed nightspot popular with the post-college crowd. There's a live DJ and dancing every Tuesday, Thursday, and Sunday. Dark, intimate **Shenanigans** (⊠*3017 Ruston Way* ☎*253/752–8811*), with gorgeous waterfront views, has a chic bar, excellent Northwest cuisine, and a line of sleek, cozy window booths.

Jazzbones (⊠*2803 6th Ave.* ☎*253/396–9169* ⊕*www.jazzbones.com*) is a classy no-cover, no-smoking, no-fuss, just-great-music joint on the Sixth Avenue strip, with live jazz on stage every night.

The **Swiss** (⊠*1904 S. Jefferson Ave.* ☎*253/572–2821*) has microbrews on tap, pool tables, and bands on stage Thursday through Saturday ($10 cover). Monday brings free admission for live blues night, and there's karaoke on Wednesday. The music varies from night to night at the **Vault** (⊠*1025 Pacific Ave.* ☎*253/572–3145*), a popular dance club.

SPORTS & THE OUTDOORS

Wild Waves/ Enchanted Village, the only amusement park near Seattle, has a few moderately sized roller coasters and other rides. From Thanksgiving through New Year's the park shimmers with a nightly drive-through holiday light show. The **Wild Waves** section is the Northwest's largest water park, with giant slides, a 24,000-square-foot wave pool, and Splash Central, for younger children. Tickets get you into all pools and rides. Note: It's expensive and cash only, plus no outside food or drinks are allowed—but there's parking on the side streets, and discount coupons are available at local grocery and drug stores. ⊠*36201 Enchanted Pkwy. S* ☎*253/925–8000* ⊕*www.wildwaves.com* ☒ *Wild Waves: $35* ⊙*June, weekdays 9:30–4, weekends 10–6; July–Labor Day., daily 10–8; Oct., Fri. and Sat. 5 PM–11 PM, Sun. 5 PM–9 PM.*

HORSE
RACING

Emerald Downs is a Thoroughbred horse-racing stadium, with music festivals, and picnics staged on summer weekends. Races are run every half hour Thursday–Monday, and free tours (which also include free track admission) take place Thursday at 10 and Saturday at 10:30 ⊠*2300 Emerald Downs Dr., Auburn* ☎*253/288–7000 or 888/931–8400* ⊕*www.emeralddowns.com* ☒*$4* ⊙*Mid-Apr.–mid-Sept., Wed.–Fri. 6 PM first post; weekends 1 PM first post.*

SCUBA DIVING

Tacoma Lighthouse Diving Center (⊠*2502 Pacific Ave.* ☎*800/777–3843* is a full-service dive operation with lessons, equipment, and regional trips. **Tacoma Underwater Sports** (⊠*9606 40th Ave. SW, Lakewood* ☎*253/588–6634 or 800/252–7177*), the area's largest scuba center sells and rents gear, plans trips, and has branches and repair facilities throughout Puget Sound. Open weekdays 10 to 7, weekends 9 to 6.

SHOPPING

Antique Row (⊠*Broadway Ave. at St. Helen's St., between 7th and 9th Sts.*) contains upscale antiques stores and boutiques selling collectibles and 1950s paraphernalia. A farmers' market is held here every Thursday in summer. **Freighthouse Square Public Market** (⊠*25th and D Sts* ☎*253/305–0678* ⊕*www.freighthousesquare.com*) is a former railroad warehouse filled with gift shops, offbeat boutiques, and ethnic food stalls. It's open Monday through Saturday 10–7, and Sunday noon–5 The **Proctor District** (⊡*Box 7291, Tacoma* ☎*253/370–1748* ⊕*www.proctorbusinessdistrict.com*) is a gathering of upscale boutiques, restaurants, and specialty shops. The **Tacoma Mall** (⊠*4502 S. Steele, of Tacoma Mall Blvd. and I–5* ☎*253/475–4565* ⊕*www.tacomamall.com*) area, 1½ mi south of the Tacoma Dome, is a massive indoor-outdoor complex of department stores, specialty shops, and restaurants.

PUYALLUP

10 mi southeast of Tacoma.

Set before the towering forests and snowfields of Mt. Rainier is Puyallup (pyoo-*al*-lup), one of western Washington's oldest towns. Founder Ezra Meeker came west on the Oregon Trail in 1806–07, and he returned East at age 76 in hopes of prodding President Theodore Roosevelt to mark the trail before its route was forgotten. He caused quite a stir when he rode his ox-drawn covered wagon down Broadway in New York City, but he continued on to the White House and received the president's endorsement.

Today the Puyallup Fair attracts all of western Washington to its carnival rides, performers, produce, and animals. The annual event is held at the fairgrounds on the northwest end of town each September. The Spring Fair and Daffodil Festival (known as "The Little Puyallup") is another beloved event that takes place each April.

Puyallup is centered around **Pioneer Park,** where you'll find the large local library, a playground with swings, a big round wading pool open on summer weekdays, and an amphitheater for summer concerts. The lovely, tree-framed pavilion, set on the corner, exhibits local arts and hosts community events. The popular **Puyallup Main Street Farmers' Market,** open May through August on Saturday from 9 to 2 and through September from 10 to 2, sets up next to the park. ⊠ *107 N. Meridian* ☎ *253/841–5518 pavilion, 253/840–2631 market* ⊕ *www. puyallupmainstreet.com.*

The downtown area is quickly developing into a satellite attraction to Seattle all its own, with monthly arts events and a collection of boutiques and kitschy shops. The *Traces* brochure, available at merchants around town, takes you on a walk past all the major historic sites.

Puyallup's Outdoor Gallery (☎ *253/840–6015* ⊕ *www.artsdowntown. org*), presented by the Arts Downtown program, shows off dozens of rotating sculptures around the city via self-guided tours. Monthly Art Walks, held on first Saturdays, provide a look into all the new local galleries, and the semi-annual Art and Wine Walks bring Puget Sound residents southeast to explore the top creative projects of this offbeat community.

The city's developing **Antique Shopping District,** with two-dozen cozy little walk-between stores lining the streets, is one of the largest in the region. More than 400 separate vendors are scattered around the area, and the sidewalks are often crowded on summer weekends. Events and openings are guided by the Puyallup Antique District Association. ⊠ *101 S. Meridian* ☎ *253/845–4471.*

☾ ★ The **Pioneer Farm Museum and Ohop Indian Village,** 23 mi south of Puyallup, provides a look at pioneer and Native American life. Kids can learn how to hunt and fish in a realistic Indian village, grind grain, milk a cow, churn butter, and do other old-fashioned chores. A trading post shows the commodities of earlier eras. One-hour pioneer farm tours take place 11:15 to 4; Ohop Indian Village tours are at 1 and 2:30 from Memorial Day to Labor Day. ⊠ *Hwy. 7 off Ohop Valley Rd.* ☎ *360/832–6300* ⊕ *www.pioneerfarmmuseum.org* ⊠ *Farm $7.50, village $7, combined tour $13.50* ☾ *Memorial Day–Labor Day, Fri.– Sun. 11:15–4; Sept.–mid-Nov., weekends 11–4.*

☾ ★ **Northwest Trek,** a spectacular wildlife park 35 mi south of Puyallup, is devoted to native creatures of the Pacific Northwest. Walking paths wind through natural surroundings—so natural that in 1998 a cougar entered the park and started snacking on the deer (it was finally trapped and relocated to the North Cascades). See beavers, otters, and wolverines; get close to wolves, foxes, coyotes; and observe several species of big cats and bears in wild environments. Admission includes a 55-minute tram ride through fields of wandering moose, elk, bison, and mountain goats. Note: Hours vary slightly by month, so check for specific times. ⊠ *11610 Trek Dr. E, Eatonville* ☎ *360/832–6117* ⊕ *www.nwtrek.org* ⊠ *$13.50* ☾ *Memorial Day–Labor Day, daily 9:30–6; Labor Day–Memorial Day, weekends 9:30–4.*

Another early pioneer settlement is Enumclaw (ee-num-claw), 14 mi southeast, which was founded in the 1850s and through stages grew as a railroad, lumber, and dairy town. The name is taken from a nearby peak, which—depending on which legend you believe—means either "Thundering Mountain" or "Abode of Evil Spirits" in the Salish language. The town is the site of the annual King County Fair, which has amusement rides, rodeos, and logging shows.

WHERE TO STAY & EAT

$–$$$ ✗ **Decateruba's Market Grill & Bar.** This posh spot overlooks the greenery of Pioneer Park, just a minute's stroll from the city library. Inside it's elegant and comfortable, with exposed-brick walls, gleaming wood floors, and sleek, autumn colors. Food captures Northwest and Mediterranean styles, with entrées like pancetta-wrapped scallops, cioppino, and dried fruit–stuffed pork loin. Service is friendly, but sometimes hurried on weekends. ⊠ 328 S. Meridian ☎ 253/848–2523 ▭ AE, MC, V.

¢–$ ✗ **Powerhouse Brewery and Restaurant.** The interior of what was once a railroad powerhouse is adorned with glass insulators and high-voltage signs. A dozen brews are served—six brewed on the premises and six from a sister brewery. The pub fare includes salads, pizzas, burgers, sandwiches, and pastas. ⊠ 504 E. Main Ave. ☎ 253/845–1370 ▭ V.

¢–$ 🛏 **Hedman House.** The coziest accommodation in town is small and delightful, with wood accents, antiques, and handmade crafts throughout the house, from the comfortable living areas to the two guest rooms. April's Room provides a brass-bed–centered little nook with old-fashioned touches; Sharon's Room is a larger space for a king or two twin beds. A full breakfast, served in the dining room, highlights home cooking and fresh local produce. ⊠ 502 9th St. SW, 98371 ☎ 253/848–2248 or 866/433–6267 ⊕ www.hedmanhouse.com ➷ 2 rooms ♿ In-hotel: no-smoking rooms, no kids ▭ MC, V ⊙ BP.

OLYMPIA

33 mi southwest of Puyallup.

Olympia has been the capital of Washington since 1853, the beginning of city and state. It is small for the capital city of a major state, but that makes it all the more pleasant to visit. The old and charming downtown area is compact and easy on the feet, stretching between Capitol Lake and the gathering of austere government buildings to the south, the shipping and yacht docks around glistening Budd Inlet to the west, the colorful market area capping the north end of town, and I-5 running along the eastern edge. There are little unexpected surprises all through town, from pretty little half-block parks and blossoming miniature gardens to clutches of Thai and Vietnamese restaurants and antiques shops. The imposing state capitol, finished in 1928, is set above the south end of town like a fortress, framed by a skirt of granite steps. The monumental 287-foot-high dome is the fourth largest masonry dome in the world (only St. Peter's in Rome, St. Paul's in London, and the national capitol in the other Washington are larger).

Capitol Lake, a broad, flat expanse of shallow brown water, was formed in 1951 by damming the mouth of the Deschutes River. The former mud flats are now covered with some 30 feet of water; salmon can be seen ascending the fish ladders in autumn. Surrounded by parks, the lake serves as a magnificent reflecting pool for the capitol building. Head across the street and a block east of the main lake parking lot to find a gathering of squirting summertime fountains that make a perfect cooling-off spot on hot afternoons.

The Hands On Children's Museum is a fun little corner spot just a block north of the Capitol Campus where children can touch, build, and play with all sorts of crafts and exhibits. Fifty-plus interactive stations include an art studio and a special gallery for kids 4 and under. During the city's First Friday art walks the museum is open late and stages special programs and events. ⊠ *106 11th Ave. SW* ☎ *360/956–0818* ⊕ *www.hocm.org* ☞ *$7.95 ages 2 and over, $4.95 ages 12–23 months; half-price 3–5 on school weekdays; free 5–9 on first Fri. of the month* ☉ *Mon.–Sat. 10–5, Sun. noon–5.*

Percival Landing Waterfront Park, framing nearly an acre of landscaped desert gardens and bird-watching areas, stretches along a 1½-mi boardwalk through a beachy section of the Ellis Cove coastline. To the south are yachts bobbing in the water at the wooden docks and the waterfront Anthony's restaurant; to the north are the shipyards and cargo cranes; and to the east is the market. In the center is an open space with an outdoor stage for summer shows, music, and festivals. You can see it all from three stories up by climbing the winding steps of the timber viewing tower, where open benches invite visitors to relax and enjoy the city views. ⊠ *4th Ave. to Thurston Ave.* ☎ *360/753–8380* ☞ *Free* ☉ *Daily dawn–dusk.*

The **Olympia Farmers' Market** is a neat, clean, and well-run expanse of covered fruit, vegetable, pastry, and craft stalls at the north end of town. Much of the produce is organic, and you'll find all sorts of oddities such as ostrich eggs, button magnets, and glass sculptures. With a dozen tiny ethnic eateries tucked in between the vendors, it's also a terrific place to grab a bite and then walk over to the waterfront area. ⊠ *700 N. Capitol Way* ☎ *360/352–9096* ⊕ *www.olympiafarmers market.com* ☞ *Free* ☉ *Apr.–Oct., Thurs.–Sun. 10–3; Nov. and Dec., weekends 10–3.*

The **Yashiro Japanese Garden,** a symbol of the sister-city relationship of Olympia and Yashiro, Japan, opened in 1989. Within it are a waterfall, a bamboo grove, a koi pond, and stone lanterns. ⊠ *1010 Plum St.* ☎ *No phone* ☞ *Free* ☉ *Daily dawn–dusk.*

Priest Point Park is a beautiful section of protected shoreline and wetlands. Thick swaths of forest and glistening bay views are the main attractions, with picnic areas and playgrounds filling in the open spaces. The 3-mi **Ellis Cove Trail,** with interpretive stations, bridges, and nature settings, runs right through the Priest Point Park area and around the Olympia coast. ⊠ *East Bay Dr.* ☎ *360/753–8380.*

The Olympic Flight Museum, housed in a hangar at the Olympic Regional Airport south of town, brings to life an ever-changing collection of vintage aircraft. Important pieces include a colorful P-51 Mustang, a sleek F-104 Starfighter, and a serious-looking AH-1 Cobra helicopter. On the annual schedule are winter lectures, weekly tours, monthly flights, and the Gathering of Warbirds event each June. The shop sells a model of just about everything you see on-site. ⊠ *7637 A Old Hwy. 99 SE* ☎ *360/705–3925* ⊕ *www.olympicflightmuseum.com* 🎫 *$5* ⊙ *May–Sept., daily 11–5; Oct.–Apr., Tues.–Sun. 11–5.*

☾ **Wolf Haven International** is an 80-acre sanctuary dedicated to wolf conservation. One-hour guided walking tours show how wolves are raised, rehabilitated, and released into the wild. In summer the facility hosts a so-called Howl-In (reservations essential), with tours, musicians performing around a campfire, and howling with the wolves. On the first Thursday of the month there's "Dinner at Dusk" with the wolves, and you can spend the final hour on your own in the sanctuary every last Sunday. ⊠ *3111 Offut Lake Rd., Tenino* ✛ *from Olympia, take I–5 south to Exit 99 and follow signs east for 7 mi* ☎ *800/448–9653* ⊕ *www.wolfhaven.org* 🎫 *Daily tours $8, Howl-Ins $15* ⊙ *May–Sept., Wed.–Mon. 10–5; Apr. and Oct., Wed.–Mon. 10–4; Nov.–Mar., Sat. 10–4, Sun. noon–3.*

WHERE TO STAY & EAT

$–$$$ ✗ **Falls Terrace.** An elegant, multilevel restaurant in front of the Olympia Brewery, Falls Terrace offers unobstructed views of Tumwater Falls. Steaks, burgers, and seafood are as fancy as the food gets. There is dining on the deck, but you have to be over 21. Inside is the place to be for a family Sunday brunch. ⊠ *106 S. Deschutes Way* ☎ *360/943–7830* ▤ *AE, D, DC, MC, V.*

$–$$ ✗ **Mercato.** Tucked into a glitzy, glass-front office building on a sunny corner across from the Farmers' Market, the aptly named restaurant brings an Italian countryside ambience to this relaxed neighborhood. Tables line up against sponge-painted gold walls decorated with a series of Patés Baroni posters, with tiny stained-glass lamps lighting the scene. Specialties include the *piadina* sandwiches, slices of warmed flatbread slathered with such cold fillings as smoked duck on spinach vinaigrette. ⊠ *111 Market St. NE* ☎ *360/528–3663* ▤ *AE, D, MC, V.*

$–$$ ▦ **Phoenix Inn Suites.** This polished accommodation is nestled right up to Budd Inlet and just a couple of blocks from the Farmers' Market. The lobby is filled with gray-blue and lavender hues, crystal chandeliers, and gilt-framed paintings, and rooms follow suit with plush fabrics in deep charcoals, golds, and beiges. Splashy bonuses include corner jetted tubs, chaise lounges, and jump-right-to-it service. Extra touches include complimentary bottled water, coffee, and tea, free weekday newspapers, and fresh-baked cookies served every evening. **Pros:** Big place for a small capital, lots of amenities, indoor pool open 24 hours. **Cons:** Pedestrian hotel appearance. ⊠ *415 Capitol Way N, 98501* ☎ *360/570–0555 or 877/570–0555* 🖷 *360/570–1200* ⊕ *www.phoenixinnsuites.com* ⇝ *102 suites* ⌕ *In-room: refrigerator, Wi-Fi.*

In-hotel: dial-up, restaurant, pool, spa, gym, laundry facilities ⊟*AE, D, DC, MC, V* ⎮○⎮*CP.*

$–$$ ⊞ **Swantown Inn.** Antiques and lace ornament every room of this stylish, peak-roofed Victorian inn, built as a mansion in 1893 and then used as a boarding house. Resting high above fragrant gardens and landscaped lawns, the rooms have views of the capitol and the inn's breezy gazebo. The Astoria Suite has a four-poster bed and a two-person hot tub; the smaller Columbia Room has a claw-foot tub. Though the setting is old-fashioned, the inn is wired throughout for high-speed Internet, and guests are treated to a three-course, internationally plucked breakfast with such delicacies as German pancakes and New Orleans French toast. **Pros:** 19th-century feel, but modern business-friendly. **Cons:** Slightly spooky exterior ⊠*1431 11th Ave. SE, 98501* ☎*360/753–9123 or 877/753–9123* ⊕*www.swantowninn.com* ⇖*3 rooms, 1 suite* ⚒*In-room: no phone. In-hotel: no TV, Ethernet, dial-up, Wi-Fi, no kids under 9, no elevator* ⊟*MC, V* ⎮○⎮*BP.*

NORTH BEND

40 mi northeast of Puyallap.

This truck stop gets its name from a bend in the Snoqualmie River, which here turns toward Canada. The gorgeous surrounding scenery is dominated by 4,420-foot Mt. Washington, 4,788-foot Mt. Tenerife, and 4,167-foot Mt. Si. Named for early settler Josiah "Si" Merrit, Mt. Si has a steep, four-hour trail that in summer provides views of the Cascade and Olympic peaks down to Puget Sound and Seattle. In winter, however, these mountains corner the rains: North Bend is one of the wettest places in western Washington, with an annual precipitation often exceeding 100 inches.

Scenes from the TV show *Twin Peaks*—notably the stunning opening waterfall sequence—were shot in North Bend, though most of the work was done in studios in Seattle. This is the last town on I–90 for gassing up before Snoqualmie Pass.

The **Snoqualmie Valley Historical Museum** focuses on life centuries ago, with Native American tools, crafts, and attire as well as pioneer artifacts. The timber industry is another focus. ⊠*320 Bendego Blvd. S* ☎*425/888–3200* ⊕*www.snoqualmievalleymuseum.org* ⇖*$1* ⊗*Apr.–Oct. and 1st 2 wks of Dec., Thurs.–Sun. 1–5; Nov. and mid-Dec.–Mar., by appointment.*

WHERE TO STAY & EAT

$–$$ ✕ **Robertiello's.** Pictures of Venice add a European touch to the intimate dining room of the McGrath Hotel, built in 1922. Tastes are true to Italy: try the meaty traditional lasagna, or penne *sovietiche* (pasta and prawns in a spicy mascarpone-cream-cheese sauce). For dessert there's homemade tiramisu and several types of cheesecake. The flower-bedecked patio is perfect for summertime meals. The bar in the firelit McGrath Room is backed by a fresco from the building's early years.

101 W. N. Bend Way ☎*425/888–1803* ▭*AE, D, MC, V* ☺*Closed Mon. No lunch Tues.–Fri.*

$ 🏠 **Roaring River Bed & Breakfast.** Tucked amid 2½ acres above the Snoqualmie River, this secluded B&B has unbeatable mountain and wilderness views. Rooms with wainscoting and fireplaces have private entrances and decks. The Mountain View Room has a whirlpool tub; the Bear-Iris Room has a featherbed and a two-person Japanese soaking tub. Herb's Place is a hunting cabin with a kitchen and loft, and the Rock and Rose Room has its own sauna—behind a giant boulder. Homemade goodies are delivered to your room each morning. ✉*46715 S.E. 129th St., 98045* ☎*425/888–4834 or 877/627–4647* ⊕*www.theroaringriver.com* 🛏*5 rooms* ♿*In-room: no a/c. In-hotel: Wi-Fi, no phone, no kids under 12, no elevator* ▭*AE, D, MC, V* ⋈*BP.*

SNOQUALMIE

3 mi northwest of North Bend.

Spring and summer snowmelt turn the Snoqualmie (sno-*qual*-mie) River into a thundering torrent at Snoqualmie Falls, the sweeping cascades that provided the backdrop for the *Twin Peaks* opening montage. The water pours over a 268-foot rock ledge (100 feet higher than Niagara Falls) to a 65-foot-deep pool. These cascades, considered sacred by the Native Americans, are Snoqualmie's biggest attraction. A 2-acre park and observation platform afford views of the falls and the surrounding area. The 3-mi round-trip River Trail winds through trees and over open slopes to the base of the cascade.

WHERE TO STAY & EAT

¢ ✗ **Snoqualmie Falls Candy Factory.** An Old West–style storefront leads to this combination candy store, gift shop, and soda fountain serving quick-cooked American burgers, hot dogs, and sandwiches. Homemade caramel corn, saltwater taffy, and nut brittles in pretty packages make great treats and souvenirs. The downtown Snoqualmie location attracts crowds during local railroad events. ✉*8102 Railroad Ave. SE* ☎*425/888–0439 or 800/636–2263* ▭*AE, MC, V.*

$$$–$$$$ 🏠 **Salish Lodge.** The stunning, chalet-style lodge sits right over Sno-
Fodor$Choice qualmie Falls. Eight rooms have gorgeous views of the cascades, while
★ others have a river panorama. All the luxurious quarters have featherbeds, fireplaces, whirlpool baths, terry robes, and window seats or balconies. The world-famous spa offers relaxing and purifying treatments after a day of kayaking, golfing, or hiking. The elegant Dining Room restaurant serves such eclectic delicacies as wild Scottish partridge, herb-crusted John Dory fillet, and potato-wrapped elk loin; weekend brunches are elaborate. In the cozy and more casual Attic bistro, you can still sample fine Northwest wines and views of the falls beneath the eaves. Note that if you pay an extra $15 nightly resort fee, you'll have such privileges as valet service, 24-hour Wi-Fi, and unlimited access to the soaking pool, sauna, and fitness facilities. ✉*6501 Railroad Ave. SE, 98065* ☎*206/888–2556* 📠*425/888–2420* ⊕*www.salishlodge.com*

🛏81 rooms, 4 suites ⚙In-room: VCR (some). In-hotel: Wi-Fi (some), 2 restaurants, room service, bar, gym, spa, concierge, laundry service, refrigerator ☐AE, D, DC, MC, V.

SPORTS & THE OUTDOORS

Fodor'sChoice
★

⟲ **The Summit at Snoqualmie,** 53 mi east of Seattle, combines the Alpental, Summit West, Summit East, and Summit Central ski areas along Snoqualmie Pass. Spread over nearly 2,000 acres at elevations of up to 5,400 feet, the facilities include 65 ski trails, 22 chairlifts, and two half-pipes. Those seeking tamer pursuits can head to the Summit Nordic Center, with groomed trails and a tubing area. Shops, restaurants, lodges, and ski schools are connected by shuttle vans; there's even child care. For a different take on the mountains, head up to the pass after dinner; this is the world's largest night-skiing area. Tickets, which let you ski and play at any of the above areas, are $41–$51, depending on the time of day. Ski and snowboard rental packages run $29–$35. Inner-tube rentals, including lighted rope tows, are $10. ☒*From Seattle, take I–90 east to Alpental Rd.* ☎425/434–7669, 425/236–1600 snow conditions ⊕www.summit-at-snoqualmie.com ☉Oct.–Apr.

EDMONDS

45 mi northwest of Snoqualmie, 15 mi north of Seattle.

Charming Edmonds has a waterfront lined by more than a mile of boutiques and restaurants, seaside parks and attractions, and a string of broad, windswept beaches. Just beyond is the small but lively downtown area, where you can wander into chic cafés and wine shops, peruse attractive antiques stores and chic galleries, and browse the colorful Summer Market, which runs Saturday 9 to 3 from May to September. The Third Thursday Art Walk shows off the work of local artists, and a host of events and festivals takes place year-round. On the east side of Puget Sound, Edmonds is also the gateway to the Kitsap Peninsula, as ferries from here connect with Kingston.

The lower level of the **Edmonds Historical Museum** is the place to find out about local legends and traditions; temporary exhibits upstairs often have a patriotic theme. The museum's Summer Garden Market sells handmade and hand-grown items on Saturday from 9 to 3 from May through September. ☒*118 5th Ave. N* ☎425/774–0900 ⊕*www. historicedmonds.org* ☜$2 ☉*Wed.–Sun. 1–4.*

The **Edmonds Underwater Park** (☎425/771–0230), perhaps the best-known dive site in Puget Sound besides the Narrows Bridge area, has 27 acres of sunken structures and developed dive trails. It's immediately north of the ferry landing at the foot of Main Street. Dive outfitters in town have lessons, equipment rentals, and underwater tours of the park. The adjacent Brackett's Landing Park has trails, picnic areas, and restrooms.

The **Olympic Beach** fishing pier attracts anglers all year. Today the park is dedicated to such Olympic athletes and champions as figure skater Roslyn Summers, and it's an excellent spot to watch the sun set behind

Whidbey Island and the Olympic Mountains. ⊠*Railroad Ave. at Dayton St.* ☎*No phone.*

WHERE TO EAT

$–$$$ ✕**Arnie's in Edmonds.** Sitting directly across from the sound, the dining room has views of the water. The restaurant's specialty, seafood, means that the menu is constantly changing according to what's in season. One famous dish is Prawns Undecided, which consists of prawns prepared in three different ways—stuffed with crab, roasted with garlic, and coated in a beer batter and fried. Sunday-morning brunches, which last until 2, draw local crowds. ⊠*300 Admiral Way* ☎*425/771–5688* ☐*AE, MC, V.*

$–$$ ✕**Girardi's Osteria Italiana.** Coming here is like walking into an elegant yet comfortable Italian kitchen, where every space beneath the high, peaked ceiling glows with warm country colors and muted light. Small tables, set with gleaming glass and white linens, are set along polished-wood floors and tucked in near exposed-brick walls. The menu is an induction to the Italian dining experience, with such entrées as *anitra della casa* (pan-seared duck breast on herb polenta) and *vitello del capitano* (veal medallions in a Madeira wine sauce). Come Monday for half-price bottled wines, and look for seasonal wine-tasting dinners following specific regions of Italy. ⊠*504 5th Ave. S* ☎*425/673–5278* ☐*AE, D, MC, V* ⊙*No lunch Fri.–Mon.*

¢–$ ✕**Olives Café & Wine Bar.** Northwest wines are the focus of this chic, gallery-style spot. With the restaurant's selection of 40-plus local labels, you could come here to just sip and smile. However, if you delve into the menu, you'll find eclectic meals to complement every bouquet. Lunch specialties include excellent grilled panini and over-stuffed sandwiches as well as rich soups and tangy salads. Dinners surge forward into perfectly shareable antipasti and tapas that draw gourmands from all over the region. A chef's menu appears on Friday and Saturday evenings, and box lunches are available daily. Note that on Monday and Tuesday wines are half-price. ⊠*107 5th Ave. N, Suite 103* ☎*425/771–5757* ⊕*www.olivescafewinebar.com* ☐*AE, MC, V* ⊙*Closed Sun., and Mon. in winter.*

WHERE TO STAY

$–$$ 🏨**Edmonds Harbor Inn & Suites.** In the midst of downtown Edmonds, this luxurious, country-style inn has comfortable mint-and-mauve rooms with such homey touches as natural soaps and feather pillows. Some rooms have a fireplace, kitchen, and oversize bathtub. A day pass to the health club behind the inn costs just $5. **Pros:** Proximity to the waterfront, and only 1½ blocks from the Kingston ferry terminal. **Cons:** No beach views. ⊠*130 W. Dayton St., 98020* ☎*425/771–5021 or 800/441–8033* 🖷*425/672–2880* ⊕*www.nwcountryinns.com/edmonds* ⇆*92 rooms* ⚬*In-room: kitchen (some). In-hotel: refrigerator (some), VCR (some), laundry facilities, laundry service, no-smoking rooms, some pets allowed, Wi-Fi* ☐*AE, D, MC, V* ⫿⃝*CP.*

$ 🏨**The Inn at Third & Dayton.** Each of the accommodations inside this two-story Craftsman home takes on a different theme: the nationally flavored Americana Room; the relaxing Nostalgia Room; the tropical Palm Room; the Asian-tinged Pagoda Room; and the woodsy Lodge

Room. Guests are treated not only to multicourse breakfasts but also to the inn's famous caramel apples and endless candy bowl of gourmet goodies. Soak up the local scene on the patio, or hike two blocks northwest to the waterfront. ⊠ *202 3rd Ave., at Dayton St., 98020* ☎ *425/361–8999* ⊕ *www.innonthird.com* ⥱ *5 rooms* ⚷ *In-room: no phone. In-hotel: no TV, Wi-Fi, airport shuttle, no kids under 9, no elevator* ⊟*MC, V* ⧡*BP.*

EVERETT

19 mi north of Edmonds.

Everett is the county seat of Snohomish County. Much of this industrial town sits high on a bluff above Port Gardner Bay and the Snohomish River. The waterfront was once lined by so many lumber, pulp, and shingle mills that Everett proudly called itself "the city of smokestacks." Downtown Everett has many elegant old commercial buildings dating from the period when John D. Rockefeller heavily invested in the fledgling town, hoping to profit from the nearby Monte Cristo mines—which turned out to be a flop. Another scheme failed when James J. Hill made Everett the western terminus of the Great Northern Railroad, hoping to turn it into Puget Sound's most important port. Everett is best known for the Boeing Aircraft plant and for having the second-largest Puget Sound port (Seattle has the largest). The naval station here is home to the U.S.S. *Abraham Lincoln* aircraft carrier and a support flotilla of destroyers and frigates.

The pleasant waterfront suburb of Mukilteo, about 5 mi southeast of Everett, is the main departure point for ferries to Clinton, on Whidbey Island. The old lighthouse and waterfront park are fun to explore. An important Indian treaty was signed in 1855 at nearby Point Elliott.

Marysville, 6 mi north of Everett, was set up as a trading post in 1877. Pioneers exchanged goods with the Snohomish Indians who once occupied southeastern Whidbey Island and the lower Snohomish Valley. Settlers drained and diked the lowlands, raised dairy cows, planted strawberry fields, cleared the forests, and in no time a thriving community was established. Marysville kept to itself for a century, until the I–5 freeway was built; today it's a thriving community and the home of the popular Tulalip (Too-*lay*-lip) Casino.

☾ ★ **Jetty Island** is a 2-mi-long, sand-fringed offshore haven full of wildlife and outdoor opportunities. Seasonal programs include guided walks, bonfires, and mid-summer Jetty Island Days festivities. A free ferry provides round-trip transport; group tours (book first) run daily at 10:45 and 3:30. ⊠ *Ferry departures 10 St., at W. Marine View Dr.* ☎ *425/257–8324* ⊕ *www.ci.everett.wa.us* ⊠*Free* ☾ *Ferry departures on the half-hour 10–5:25 Mon.–Sat., 11–5:25 Sun.*

★ The **Future of Flight Aviation Center,** a 73,000-square-foot facility at Snohomish County Airport's Paine Field, blends a sparkling, state-of-the-art Aviation Gallery and conference area with the modern Boeing Tour Center. Both provide a fascinating, in-depth look into the history of flight from the perspective of Boeing, one of the world's most powerful and innovative aircraft manufacturers. Exhibits cover the development of flight technology through displays and interactive exhibits. The gallery houses numerous vintage and futuristic sorts of aircraft. A large theater, café, and gift shop are also on-site. ⊠ *8415 Paine Field Blvd.* ☎ *425/438–8100 or 888/467–4777* ⊕ *www.painefield.com* 🖃 *$9* ☉ *Daily 9:30–5:30.*

★ The 11-story, 62-acre **Boeing Everett Facility,** where Boeing 747s and 767s are built, is one of the world's largest buildings. It's second only to Canada's West Edmonton Mall—and so big that it often creates its own weather system inside. You can watch planes in production on one-hour tours introduced by a short video. Note that there are no bathroom breaks on the tour, and no purses, cameras, videos, or children under 50 inches tall are permitted. You can reserve tickets by credit card over the Internet and phone a day in advance. If you want to buy same-day tickets at the door, note that sales start at 8:30. ⊠ *8415 Paine Field Blvd., at Hwy. 526 W* ☎ *206/544–1264, 800/464–1476 reservations* ⊕ *www.boeing.com* 🖃 *$15; advance reservations $2.50* ☉ *Daily 8:30–5:30, tours hourly 9–3.*

The **Museum of Flight Restoration Center** is where vintage planes are restored by a volunteer staff who simply love bringing vintage aircraft back to life. You can wander among the mix of delicate and behemoth planes on a leisurely, self-guided tour at Paine Field. ⊠ *2909 100th St. SW, Bldg. C-72* ☎ *425/745–5150* 🖃 *Free* ☉ *Tues.–Thurs. 8–4, Sat. 9–5.*

Ⓒ The **Imagine Children's Museum** is on a pioneer homestead built in the 1800s. Interactive exhibits and crafts are part of the fun; wee ones will love the magic school bus as well. ⊠ *1502 Wall St.* ☎ *425/258–1006* ⊕ *www.imaginecm.org* 🖃 *$5* ☉ *Thurs. and Fri. 10–5:30, Tues., Wed., and Sat. 10–4, Sun. 11–5.*

WHERE TO STAY & EAT

$–$$$ ✕**Anthony's Homeport.** Tucked into chic Marina Village, this elegant waterfront restaurant has large windows opening to a panorama of Port Gardner Bay. In summer, sunsets appear to ooze into the water. The specials, which change daily, might include meaty Dungeness crab, wild Chinook salmon, and other sea creatures caught just offshore. Desserts are fabulous, especially those crafted from Washington's succulent berries and fruits. ⊠ *1726 W. Marine View Dr.* ☎ *425/252–3333* 🖃 *AE, MC, V.*

$–$$ ✕**Alligator Soul.** The Louisiana cooking is straight from the bayou, and always receives rave reviews. It's a fun, noisy place where plates come piled high with thick smoked ribs, shrimp-packed gumbo, or fried green tomato salad. Spicy corn relish and hot barbecue sauce let you ratchet up the heat. Live music is on tap Friday and Saturday nights. ⊠ *3121 Broadway Ave.* ☎ *425/259–6311* 🖃 *MC, V* ☉ *Closed Mon.*

¢   ✕**The Sisters.** This funky breakfast and lunch café in Everett Public Market is as popular now as it was a decade ago. Perhaps that's because the blueberry or pecan hot cakes, rich soups, and overflowing sandwiches are as good as ever. Eye-opening espresso drinks start the morning; homemade ice cream is a perfect end to the afternoon. ✉*2804 Grand St.* ☎*425/252–0480* ☐*MC, V* ✪*Closed Sun. No dinner.*

$–$$$$ ⊞**Inn at Port Gardner.** Stroll along the marina and you'll encounter this grey, warehouse-style structure, which wraps around a cozy, modern hotel. Public spaces are done in summery colors and enhanced by modern art pieces, while the lobby is warmed by a fireplace. Rooms are contemporary, each with a DVD player and Wi-Fi; Marina View quarters add a water panorama from big glass windows or a French-door patio, and Harbor View suites have a kitchenette, fireplace, and soaking tub. All guests receive free gym passes and a bountiful breakfast basket. **Pros:** Right on the waterfront. **Cons:** No pool or restaurant. ✉*1700 W. Marine Dr., 98201* ☎*425/252–6779 or 888/252–6779* ⊕*www. innatportgardner.com* ➥*27 rooms, 6 suites* ☒ *In-hotel: Wi-Fi* ☐*AE, D, MC, V* ⦿*CP.*

$ ⊞**Gaylord House.** Down a lane lined by shady maples, this Craftsman welcomes visitors to relax in the creaky rockers on its wide front porch. Themed guest rooms, filled with antiques and original art, include the Sunrise Mediterranean room; the nautical Commodore's Quarters; and the Victorian-style Lady Anne's Chamber. An exquisite breakfast is included, there's a bottomless cookie jar, and you can book ahead for equally exquisite high teas or dinners, when the table is set with fine china, sterling silver, and crystal. **Pros:** Well-stocked library, host piano concerts. **Cons:** Not a lot of elbow room. ✉*3301 Grand Ave., 98201* ☎*425/339–9153 or 888/507–7177* 🖷*425/303–9713* ⊕*www. gaylordhouse.com* ➥*5 rooms* ☒*In-room: VCR. In-hotel: Wi-Fi, no elevator, no kids under 12* ☐*MC, V* ⦿*BP.*

SNOHOMISH

10 mi southeast of Everett.

Snohomish is an undeniably quaint and quiet residential town. First Street is the center of the historic district, where elegant 19th-century buildings now house shops, restaurants, and small inns. Dutch Colonial–style homes, English-style cottages, and gingerbread Queen Annes are close-set along the narrow lanes. Not surprisingly, the town is the self-proclaimed "Antiques Capital of the Northwest," with more than 400 stores, shops, and vendors selling old treasures.

A string of former logging and mining towns lines Highway 2 southeast of Snohomish. Sultan, at the confluence of the Sultan and Skykomish rivers, was founded as a gold-mining settlement, and some folks still pan the river. Gold Bar, a rough mining camp in the 1800s, is now a quiet resort town. Follow signs on First Street to the 2-mi trail winding uphill to 250-foot Wallace Falls, one of the highest waterfalls in the northern Cascades. East of Skykomish, U.S. 2 crosses the Cascade crest along 4,061-foot-high Stevens Pass; farther east is the faux-Bavarian village of Leavenworth. Wenatchee, the orchard-filled apple capital of Washington, sits even closer to the sunrise in a valley at the confluence of the Wenatchee and Columbia rivers.

Old Snohomish Village is a gathering of six authentic log cabins, including a blacksmith shop and a general store with items from a century ago on the shelves. ✉ *2nd St. at Pine St.* ☎ *360/568–5235* ⊕ *www.old snohomishvillage.com* 🖃 *$2* ⊗ *Memorial Day–Labor Day, Wed.–Sun. noon–4.*

⟳ **The Serpentarium** provides a room full of well-cared-for reptiles, all up
★ close in clear glass displays. Hold 10 different types of snakes, watch a giant snapping turtle swimming for lunch, gaze at a worldly collection of lizards, and eye an albino alligator. The world's 10 most deadliest snakes—plus a two-headed turtle, a five-legged frog, and other oddities—are also on exhibit. Kids will love it! The site is the home zoo of the Northwest's famous Reptile Man, an icon who brings his scaly friends to events all around the region. ✉ *Hwy. 2, 2 mi east of Monroe* ☎ *360/ 805–5300* ⊕ *www.reptileman.com* 🖃 *$5* ⊗ *Daily 10–6.*

SPORTS & THE OUTDOORS

Following a former mountain train route, the **Centennial Trail** (✉ *Pine St. at Maple Ave.*) is a paved, 8-mi, walking, blading, biking, and horse-back-riding path that leads all the way to Lake Stevens.

A very snowy ski area (with avalanche danger and periodic closures in winter), **Stevens Pass** ranges in elevation from 3,800 feet to 5,800 feet; the vertical drop is 1,800 feet. There are 10 chair lifts. This popular ski area has limited parking, so arrive early or risk being turned away. ✉ *U.S. 2 at the pass* ☎ *360/634–1645* ⊕ *www.stevenspass.com* 🖃 *$55* ⊗ *Nov.–mid-Mar., Thurs.–Mon. 9 AM–10 PM, Tues. and Wed 9 AM–4 PM; mid-Mar.–Apr., daily 9–4.*

SEATTLE ENVIRONS ESSENTIALS

BY AIR

Seattle-Tacoma International Airport (Sea-Tac), 15 mi south of Seattle, is the hub for the Seattle environs. Regional airports include Bellingham International Airport, the hub between northwestern Washington and Canada; Friday Harbor, the San Juan Islands airport; Oak Harbor, Whidbey Island's flight center; and Fairchild International in Port Angeles, serving the Olympic Peninsula and Vancouver Island. The Tacoma Narrows Airport in Gig Harbor connects the Kitsap Peninsula with Sea-Tac.

Allegiant has direct flights between Bellingham and Las Vegas. Horizon Air flies between Bellingham, Port Angeles, and Sea-Tac airports. United Express also connects Bellingham with Sea-Tac. San Juan Airlines flies between Bellingham, Anacortes, and San Juan, Orcas, and Lopez islands.

Contacts **Bellingham International** (✉ *1801 Roeder Ave., Bellingham* ☎ *360/626–2500* ⊕ *www.portofbellingham.com*). **Fairchild International** (✉ *1402 Airport Rd., Port Angeles* ☎ *360/457–1138* ⊕ *www.portofpa.com/airports*). **Friday Harbor** (✉ *San Juan Island* ☎ *360/378–2688* ⊕ *www.portfridayharbor. org/airport*). **Horizon Air** (☎ *800/547–9308* ⊕ *www.horizonair.com*). **Oak Harbor** (✉ *Whidbey Island* ☎ *800/359–3220*). **San Juan Airlines** (☎ *800/874–4434*

⊕ www.sanjuanairlines.com). **Sea-Tac Airport** (⊠ *17801 Pacific Hwy. S, [Hwy. 99]* ☎ *206/433-5388* ⊕ *www.seatac.org*). **Tacoma Narrows Airport** (⊠ *1202 26th Ave., Gig Harbor* ☎ *253/853-5844*). **United Express** (☎ *800/241-6522* ⊕ *www.ual.com*).

AIRPORT TRANSFERS

Shuttle Express provides scheduled ride-share service hourly from Sea-Tac Airport to all Washington zip codes. Bremerton–Kitsap Airporter shuttles passengers from Sea-Tac to points in Tacoma, Bremerton, Port Orchard, and Gig Harbor ($12–$20, double for round-trip). The Capital Aeroporter connects Sea-Tac with Olympia ($26 one-way, $45 round-trip). Olympic Bus Lines and Pennco have shuttles from Port Angeles and the Olympic Peninsula to Sea-Tac. The Bellair Airporter makes 10 round-trips daily between Sea-Tac and Bellingham ($34 one-way, $60 round-trip), with stops in Blaine, the Alaska Ferry, Marysville, Arlington, Mount Vernon, LaConner, Anacortes, San Juan Ferries, and Whidbey Island; the shuttle also runs east from Sea-Tac through Cle Elum and Ellensburg on the way to Yakima ($26–42). Quick as Air Coachlines takes passengers to Canada.

Contacts Bellair Airporter (☎ *866/235-5247* ⊕ *www.airporter.com*). **Bremerton–Kitsap Airporter** (☎ *800/562-7948* ⊕ *www.kitsapairporter.com*). **Capital Aeroporter** (☎ *360/754-7113 or 800/962-3579* ⊕ *www.capair.com*). **Olympic Bus Lines** (☎ *360/417-0700 or 800/457-4492* ⊕ *www.olympicbuslines.com*). **Pennco** (☎ *360/452-5104 or 888/673-6626*). **Quick as Air** (☎ *800/665-2122, 604/244-3744 in Canada* ⊕ *www.quickcoach.com*). **Shuttle Express** (☎ *425/981-7000* ⊕ *www.shuttleexpress.com*).

BY BOAT & FERRY

Washington State Ferries ply Puget Sound, including from Seattle to Bainbridge Island, Port Orchard (via Vashon Island), and Bremerton; between Edmonds and Kingston on the Key Peninsula, between Mukilteo and Clinton, on Whidbey Island, and between Port Townsend and Keystone, also on Whidbey. You can get updated ferry information on the company's Web site. Passenger ferries between Bremerton and Port Orchard are operated in summer by Kitsap Transit.

Contacts Kitsap Transit (⊠ *Bremerton* ☎ *360/383-2877*). **Washington State Ferries** (☎ *206/464-6400, 888/808-7977, 800/843-3779 automated line in WA and BC* ⊕ *www.wsdot.wa.gov/ferries*).

BY BUS

Greyhound Lines and Northwestern Trailways cover Washington and the Pacific Northwest. From Seattle, Greyhound connects Tacoma (45 minutes, $7.25–$8), Olympia (1 hour and 45 minutes, $12–$14), and Everett (1 hour and 45 minutes, $8.25). Northwestern Trailways also has daily buses from Seattle south through Tacoma ($7.25) and north through Everett ($8). Olympic Bus Lines runs between Port Angeles, Sequim, and Seattle. Pierce Transit provides bus service around Tacoma.

Bus Information Greyhound Lines (☎ *800/231-2222* ⊕ *www.greyhound.com*). **Northwestern Trailways** (☎ *800/366-3830* ⊕ *www.northwesterntrailways.com*). **Olympic Bus Lines** (☎ *800/457-4492* ⊕ *www.olympicbuslines.com*). **Pierce County Transit** (☎ *253/581-8000* ⊕ *www.piercetransit.org*).

BY CAR

Interstate 5 runs south from the Canadian border through Seattle, Tacoma, and Olympia to Oregon and California. Interstate 90 begins in Seattle and runs east through North Bend all the way to Idaho. Highway 2 meanders east, parallel to I–90, from Everett to Spokane. Highways 7 and 167 connect the Tacoma area with the Puyallup suburbs and towns around Mt. Rainier. U.S. 101 begins northwest of Olympia and traces the coast of the Olympic Peninsula.

BY TRAIN

Amtrak has service within Washington and to Canada, Oregon, California, and the East. Sounder Trains (commuters) leave Tacoma between 5 AM and 7:20 AM, as well as at 4:45 PM with stops in Puyallup, Sumner, Auburn, Kent, and Tukwila on the way to Seattle. Southbound trains leave Seattle for the reverse route between 3:35 and 5:55 PM. Cost is $4.75 one-way, $9.50 roundtrip.

Contacts **Amtrak** (☎ 800/872-7245 ⊕ www.amtrak.com). **Sounder Trains** (☎ 206/398-5000 or 888/889-6368 ⊕ www.soundtransit.org).

EMERGENCIES

Hospitals **Providence Medical Center** (⊠ 1321 Colby Ave., Everett ☎ 425/258-7123). **Providence St. Peter Hospital** (⊠ 413 Lilly Rd. NE, Olympia ☎ 360/491-9480). **Mary Bridge Children's Hospital** (⊠ 317 Martin Luther King Jr. Way, Tacoma ☎ 253/403-1400). **Tacoma General Hospital** (⊠ 315 Martin Luther King Jr. Way, Tacoma ☎ 253/403-1000).

TOUR OPTIONS

Argosy Cruises operates daily sightseeing, lunch and dinner, and charter tours around Puget Sound. Tacoma Walking Tours takes groups around the major city sights and historic areas; prior reservations are required. Two-hour Dale Chihuly Tours ($10) explore the famous local artist's works at the Art Museum, in Union Station, and through the Bridge of Glass Tuesday through Saturday at 10 and 2; reservations must be made 14 days prior. Wavetrek organizes white-water rafting, kayaking, and climbing trips, and children's adventure activities in the North Cascades.

Contacts **Argosy Cruises** (⊠ Pier 55, Seattle ☎ 206/623-4252 or 800/642-7816 ⊕ www.argosycruises.com). **Dale Chihuly Tours** (☎ 253/272-4258 Ext. 5001). **Tacoma Walking Tours** (⊠ 1911 Pacific Ave., Tacoma ☎ 253/209-6873). **Wavetrek** (⊡ Box 236, Index ☎ 360/793-1705 or 800/543-7971 ⊕ www.wavetrek.com).

VISITOR INFORMATION

Marysville/Tulalip Visitor Information Center (⊠ Off I-5, Exit 199, Marysville ☎ 360/653-2634 ⊕ snohomish.org). **Snohomish Chamber of Commerce** (⊠ 127 Ave. A, Snohomish ☎ 360/568-2526 ⊕ www.cityofsnohomish.com). **Snohomish County Tourism Bureau** (⊠ 101 128th St. SE, Suite 5000, Everett ☎ 888/338-0976 ⊠ 19921 Poplar Way, Lynnwood ☎ 425/776-3977 ⊠ 26625 Hwy. 99 N, Stanwood ☎ 360/629-6164 ⊕ www.snohomish.org). **State Capitol Visitor Information Center** (⊠ 14th St. and S. Capitol Way, Olympia ☎ 360/586-3460 ⊕ www.ci.olympia.wa.us). **Tacoma Regional Convention & Visitors Bureau** (⊠ 1001 Pacific Ave., Suite 400, Tacoma ☎ 253/627-2836 or 800/272-2662 ⊕ www.tpctourism.org).

NORTHWESTERN WASHINGTON

Updated by
Holly S. Smith

In the northwestern lowlands between the Snohomish River and the Canadian border you're never far from saltwater or mountains. Three rivers lazily wind through valleys covered in meadows and woods: the Stillaguamish, the Skagit, and the Nooksack. Rocky hills, which once were islands, have been joined to the mainland by the alluvial deposits of the streams, making for a rather flat landscape in places. Such former islands rise as hills above Burlington, La Conner, and Mount Vernon. A few rocky islands still rise offshore, though their proximity to the land almost makes them peninsulas: Fidalgo Island is separated from the mainland by a slough; Guemes and Lummi Island by a narrow passage. Despite its name, Samish Island is a peninsula.

All of this makes for a varied and beautiful landscape, especially since the flats are a patchwork of green pastures and vegetable fields highlighted in spring by acres of colorful tulips, and the moraine uplands and rocky outcroppings are covered with evergreen forest. White-water creeks gush from the mountains, and placid streams meander through the lowlands, providing havens for ducks, geese, and blue herons. In winter the low-lying flats are white with snow geese and swans.

Most of the towns and villages of this region are built along saltwater bays or on the banks of navigable rivers, because the swampy terrain, overgrown by tall trees, meant travel for the first settlers was feasible only by water. Today, with logging in decline, dairy and berry farming are the mainstays of local economies, though Bellingham and Mount Vernon also have some light industry. But increasingly the small towns and villages of western Washington have begun to market their real asset: the region's natural beauty.

The North Cascades look like a different world, and they are. Some geologists believe that they once were a Pacific Ocean island that drifted eastward and bumped into the North American continent, or, as geologists like to say, "docked," since the experts don't consider these attachments permanent.

Rising from valley floors that are only a few feet above sea level, 4,000-foot peaks crowd out the sky. Farther east the peaks top 9,000 feet. Some, like Mt. Shuksan, glow with blue glacial ice; others are marked by white streaks of cascading creeks. In summer the hanging valleys are densely covered with wildflowers; in autumn they glow red and yellow with the fall foliage of huckleberry, mountain ash, and aspen. In winter these mountains have the greatest measured snowfall on earth—more than 80 feet in the high places of the western slopes. Because of the depth of the glaciated valleys, these mountains are uncommonly accessible by roads and short, albeit steep, hiking trails. Passes are low, in the 3,000- to 5,000-foot range, making crossing feasible even at the height of winter.

While the Cascade Range in general is of volcanic origin, the North Cascades have only two prominent volcanic peaks, both more than 10,000 feet tall. Glacier Peak is almost hidden amid tall nonvolcanic mountains, but Mt. Baker, to the north, stands west of the main range and can be seen from far out to sea. This is the ultimate hiking and backpacking country, but it also has good fishing, quiet streams and lakes for boating, and shady trails for taking refreshing strolls.

WHIDBEY ISLAND

The ferry makes a 3 mi trip from Mukilteo (5 mi south of Everett) across Possession Sound to Clinton, on Whidbey Island.

From the air, Whidbey Island looks like a languid dragon, a blend of low pastoral hills, evergreen and oak forests, meadows of wildflowers, sandy beaches, and dramatic, precarious bluffs. To the north, Fidalgo Island tops Whidbey's 60-mi-long, 8-mi-wide expanse, which is second in size only to New York State's Long Island. This is a place for taking slow drives and bicycle rides, for viewing sunsets over the water, and for boating or kayaking along the protected shorelines of Saratoga Passage, Holmes Harbor, Penn Cove, and Skagit Bay. The ferry trip here across Possession Sound from Port Townsend provides views of gulls, terns, sailboats, and the occasional orca or bald eagle.

TOP 5
1. The Bavarian-style mountain village of Leavenworth
2. The North Cascades Highway for sweeping valley views and surprising wildlife sightings.
3. The Snohomish Railway for a chug-along tour of the Cascades.
4. Enjoy the summery serenity of a Lake Diablo boat tour.
5. The Serpentarium in Monroe for a look at some of the world's most deadly and unusual reptiles.

The best beaches are on the west side, where wooded and wildflower-bedecked bluffs drop steeply to sand or surf, which can cover the beaches at high tide and can be rough on this exposed shore. Both beaches and bluffs have great views of the shipping lanes and the Olympic Mountains. Maxwelton Beach, with its sand, driftwood, and great views across Admiralty Inlet to the Olympic Mountains, is popular with the locals. Possession Point includes a park, a beach, and a boat launch. West of Coupeville, Ft. Ebey State Park has a sandy spread; West Beach is a stormy patch north of the fort with mounds of driftwood.

LANGLEY
7 mi north of Clinton.

The village of Langley is above a 50-foot-high bluff overlooking Saratoga Passage, which separates Whidbey from Camano Island. A grassy terrace just above the beach is a great place for viewing birds that are on the water or in the air. On a clear day you can see Mt. Baker in the distance. Upscale boutiques selling art, glass, jewelry, and clothing line First and Second streets in the heart of town.

The **South Whidbey Historical Society Museum** (⊠*312 2nd St.* ☎*360/7303367*), in a former one-room schoolhouse that was once the home of Langley founder Jacob Anthes, displays Victrolas, farm tools, kitchen

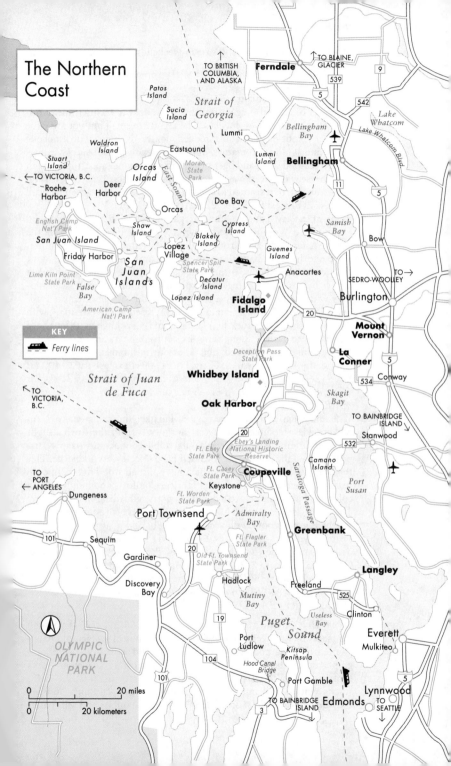

The Northern Coast

KEY

Ferry lines

Strait of Georgia

Strait of Juan de Fuca

Puget Sound

Saratoga Passage

OLYMPIC NATIONAL PARK

Patos Island
Sucia Island
Waldron Island
Stuart Island
← TO VICTORIA, B.C.
Roche Harbor
English Camp Nat'l Park
San Juan Island
Friday Harbor
Lime Kiln Point State Park
False Bay
American Camp Nat'l Park
San Juan Islands
Deer Harbor
Orcas Island
Eastsound
Moran State Park
East Sound
Orcas
Doe Bay
Shaw Island
Lopez Village
Blakely Island
Cypress Island
Spencer Spit State Park
Decatur Island
Lopez Island

TO BRITISH COLUMBIA, AND ALASKA

Ferndale
↑ TO BLAINE, GLACIER
9
5
539
542
Lake Whatcom
Lake Whatcom Blvd.
Lummi
Bellingham Bay
Bellingham
Lummi Island
11
5
Samish Bay
Bow
Guemes Island
Anacortes
SEDRO-WOOLLEY
TO →
Fidalgo Island
20
Burlington
Mount Vernon
La Conner
5
534
Conway
Skagit Bay
Deception Pass State Park

Whidbey Island

Oak Harbor

TO BAINBRIDGE ISLAND
Stanwood
532
Camano Island
Port Susan

20
Ft. Ebey State Park
Ebey's Landing National Historic Reserve
Ft. Casey State Park
Coupeville
Keystone

Saratoga Passage

TO PORT ANGELES ←
Dungeness
101
Sequim
Gardiner
Discovery Bay
Ft. Worden State Park
Port Townsend
Admiralty Bay
Ft. Flagler State Park
Old Ft. Townsend State Park
20
Hadlock
Mutiny Bay
19
Port Ludlow
104
Hood Canal Bridge
101
Port Gamble
Kitsap Peninsula
TO BAINBRIDGE ISLAND
3
Edmonds

Greenbank
Langley
Freeland
525
Clinton
Useless Bay
Everett
Mulkiteo
5
Lynnwood
TO SEATTLE
↓

0   20 miles
0   20 kilometers

utensils, and antique toys. It's open weekends 1 to 4 and by appointment, with admission by donation.

WHERE TO STAY & EAT

$ ✕**Café Langley.** Terra-cotta tile floors, antique oak tables, and the aroma of garlic, basil, and oregano set the mood at this Mediterranean restaurant with Northwest touches. The tables are small but not too close together. Exotic dishes include smoked mozzarella ravioli with artichoke hearts and sun-dried tomatoes, doused in creamy garlic sauce; Mediterranean seafood stew; and tiger prawns in white wine sauce, topped with feta cheese. For Northwest fare, try the Dungeness crab cakes, Penn Cove mussels, or a seafood salad. Green or Greek salads accompany all entrées. ✉*113 1st St.* ☎*360/221–3090* ▤*AE, MC, V.*

$$$$ ▥**Inn at Langley.** Langley's most elegant inn, this concrete-and-wood
Fodor's Choice   Frank Lloyd Wright–inspired structure perches on a bluff above the
★   beach. Asian-style guest rooms, all with a jetted tub facing the fireplace and balcony, have dramatic marine and mountain views. Stark yet comfortable rooms, turned out in plain white walls, rough-hewn timber beams, and soaring, floor-to-ceiling windows, contrast beautifully with the lush landscape; larger suites and cottages are also available. The Chef's Kitchen restaurant ($$$$, reservations essential), with its double-sided river-rock fireplace and full-view kitchen, is set above a pretty herb garden. Sumptuous six-course dinners are served Friday through Sunday year-round, plus Thursday in summer. **Pros:** Exquisite setting, top food and wines. **Cons:** Prices reflect exclusivity. ✉*400 1st St., 98260* ☎*360/221–3033* ⊕*www.innatlangley.com* ⇲*26 rooms* ⚐*In-room: refrigerator. In-hotel: restaurant, spa, Wi-Fi, no elevator* ▤*AE, D, MC, V* ⦿*CP.*

$$ ▥**Saratoga Inn.** Settled at the edge of Langley, this cedar-shake, Nantucket-style accommodation is a short walk from the town's shops and restaurants. Wood-shingle siding, gabled roofs, and wraparound porches lend the inn a neatly blended Euro–Northwest ambience. This theme extends to the interior, which has polished wood floors, smooth stone fireplaces, and lots of plaid fabrics. Comforts abound, from rich colors and plush carpets to a complimentary teddy bear in every room. The carriage house, which has a deck as well as a bedroom with a king-size bed, a bathroom with a claw-foot tub, and a sitting area with a sleep sofa, offers more privacy. Included in the price are breakfast and a daily wine reception with hors d'oeuvres. **Pros:** Crisp, upscale elegance. **Cons:** No facilities. ✉*201 Cascade Ave., 98260* ☎*360/221–5801 or 800/698–2910* ⊟*360/221–5804* ⊕*www.saratogainnwhidbeyisland. com* ⇲*15 rooms, 1 carriage house* ⚐*In-room: no a/c. In-hotel: Wi-Fi, no elevator* ▤*AE, D, MC, V* ⦿*BP.*

SHOPPING   At **Blackfish Gallerio** (✉*111 Anthes Ave.* ☎*360/221–1274*) you can see pieces by Kathleen Miller, who produces enamel jewelry and hand-painted clothing and accessories; and Donald Miller, whose photographs depict the land and people of the Northwest, as well as works by other regional artists. The **Cottage** (✉*210 1st St.* ☎*360/221–4747*) stocks vintage and imported men's and women's clothing. **Karlson/ Gray Gallery** (✉*302 1st St.* ☎*360/221–2978*) exhibits and sells paintings and sculpture by established and emerging artists in a variety of mediums.

Meet glass and jewelry artist Gwenn Knight at her gallery, the **Glass Knight** (⌧*214 1st St.* ☎*360/221–6283*), which also exhibits work by other Northwest artists. The **Museo** (⌧*215 1st St.* ☎*360/221–7737*), a gallery and gift shop, carries contemporary art by recognized and emerging artists.

GREENBANK
15 mi northwest of Langley

Fodor's Choice ★ **Greenbank Farm,** about halfway up Whidbey Island, comprises 125 acres of loganberry fields encircled by views of the Olympic and Cascade ranges. You can't miss the huge, chestnut-color, two-story barn with the wine vat out front, the centerpiece to this picturesque property. Volunteers harvest the loganberries—which are a cross between blackberries and raspberries—and turn them into rich jams and loganberry wine–filled chocolates. Greenbank's signature loganberry dinner and dessert wines, as well as two dozen or so boutique labels, can be sampled daily in the Greenbank Tasting Room. The adjacent Whidbey Pies Café creates gourmet confections, which disappear quickly as visitors head for the scattered picnic tables, twisted mountain trails, and shimmering pond. Besides wildlife, be on the lookout for the herd of fluffy alpacas raised on site by the Whidbey Island Alpacas company. The 1904 barn, which once housed a winery, is now a community center for farmers' markets, concerts, flea markets, and other events, including the famous Loganberry Festival each July.

⌧*657 Wonn Rd.* ☎*360/678–7700* ⊕*www.greenbankfarm.com* ⌦*Free* ☉*June–Sept., daily 10–5; Oct.–Apr., weekdays 11–4, weekends 10–5; May, weekdays 11–5, weekends 10–5.*

The 53-acre **Meerkerk Rhododendron Gardens** contain 1,500 native and hybrid species of rhododendrons and more than 100,000 spring bulbs on 10 acres of display gardens with numerous walking trails and ponds. The flowers are in full bloom in April and May. Summer flowers and fall color provide interest later in the year. The 43 remaining acres are kept wild as a nature preserve. ⌧*3531 Meerkerk La.* ☎*360/678–1912* ⊕*www.meerkerkgardens.org* ⌦*$5* ☉*Daily 9–4.*

WHERE TO STAY

$$–$$$$ ★ 🖫**Guest House Cottages.** Surrounded by 25 forested acres, each of these private log cabins, resembling cedar-sided barns with towering stone chimneys, comes with a feather bed, hot tub, country antiques, a kitchen and fireplace, fresh flowers, CD and DVD players, and robes. The Cabin and the Tennessee and Kentucky cottages are built like classic log cabins; the Carriage House has stained-glass windows and a private deck; and the Farm Guest House is done in a blend of country and colonial styles. The log cabin–style Lodge has comfortable Northwest-style furnishings set around a soaring river-rock fireplace. Rates include a country-style breakfast the first two days of your stay, and winter brings three-nights-for-the-price-of-two specials. **Pros:** Rustic

charm with modern conveniences. **Cons:** Can be rough around the edges. ✉24371 Hwy. 525, 98253 ☎360/678–3115 or 800/997–3115 ⊕www.guesthouselogcottages.com ⇆6 units ⚬In-room: no phone. In-hotel: kitchen, VCR, pool, gym, no kids under 16 ☰No credit cards.

COUPEVILLE

★ *On the south shore of Penn Cove, 15 mi north of Greenbank.*

Restored Victorian houses grace many of the streets in quiet Coupeville, Washington's second-oldest city. It also has one of the largest national historic districts in the state, and has been used for filming movies depicting 19th-century New England villages. Stores above the waterfront have maintained their old-fashioned character. Captain Thomas Coupe founded the town in 1852. His house was built the following year, and other houses and commercial buildings were built in the late 1800s. Even though Coupeville is the Island County seat, the town has a laid-back, almost 19th-century air.

☾ The **Island County Historical Museum** has exhibits on Whidbey's fishing, timber, and agricultural industries, and conducts tours and walks. The square-timber **Alexander Blockhouse** outside dates from the Puget Sound Indian War of 1855. Note the squared logs and dovetailed joints of the corners—no overlapping log ends. This construction technique was favored by many western Washington pioneers. ✉908 N.W. Alexander St. ☎360/678–3310 ✎$3 ☾Oct.–June, Mon.–Sat. 10–4, Sun. 11–4; other months until 5.

☾ **Ebey's Landing National Historic Reserve** encompasses a sand-and-cobble beach, bluffs with dramatic views down the Strait of Juan de Fuca, two state parks, and several (privately held) pioneer farms homesteaded in the early 1850s. The reserve, the first and largest of its kind, holds nearly 100 nationally registered historic structures, most of them from the 19th century. Miles of trails lead along the beach and through the woods. Cedar Gulch, south of the main entrance to Ft. Ebey, has a lovely picnic area in a wooded ravine above the beach.

Ft. Casey State Park, on a bluff overlooking the Strait of Juan de Fuca and the Port Townsend ferry landing, was one of three forts built after 1890 to protect the entrance to Admiralty Inlet. Look for the concrete gun emplacement and a couple of 8-inch "disappearing" guns. The Admiralty Head Lighthouse Interpretive Center is north of the gunnery emplacements. There are also grassy picnic sites, rocky fishing spots, and a boat launch. ✉2 mi west of Hwy. 20 ☎360/678–4519 ⊕www.parks.wa.gov ✎Free ☾Park daily 8 AM–sunset, Lighthouse daily 11–5. In late May **Ft. Ebey State Park,** a 25-square-mi National Historical Reserve just off the Keystone ferry docks, blazes with native rhododendrons. West of Coupeville on Point Partridge, it has 22 acres of beach, campsites in the woods, trails to the headlands, World War II gun emplacements, wildflower meadows, spectacular views down Juan de Fuca Strait, and a boggy pond. ✉3 mi west of Hwy. 20 ☎360/678–6084 or 800/233–0321 ⊕www.parks.wa.gov ✎Free, parking $5 ☾Daily dawn–dusk.

WHERE TO STAY & EAT

$–$$ ✕**Christopher's on Whidbey.** A warm and casual spot in the waterfront district, this home-style restaurant is furnished eclectically and has tables set with linens, fresh flowers, and candles. The contemporary Northwest menu features local oysters and mussels, and such flavorful fare as raspberry-barbecued salmon, bacon-wrapped pork tenderloin with mushrooms, lamb stew, and grilled ahi—all prepared with a light touch. The wine list is extensive. ⊠*105 N.W. Coveland St.* ☏*360/678–5480* ▤*AE, MC, V.*

¢–$$ ✕**The Oystercatcher.** The town's top seafood spot turns out sophisticated dinners from a modest little storefront shop along the main street. Once you dine here you're hooked—and you'll never tire of coming back to see what's on the menu, as the owner turns out four unique sets of meals twice monthly. Although the emphasis is on seafood, dishes start from basic fish, fowl, meat, and vegetarian themes, then blossom into artfully arranged fare. ⊠*901 Grace St. NW* ☏*360/678–0683* ▤*AE, MC, V* ⊗*Closed Mon. and Tues. No lunch.*

$–$$$ ▥**Captain Whidbey Inn.** Almost a century old, this venerable madrona lodge on a wooded promontory offers a special kind of hospitality and charm now rarely found. Gleaming fir-paneled rooms and suites, which have pedestal sinks but share bathrooms, are furnished with antiques and modern amenities; quarters on the north side have views of Penn Cove. More luxurious Lagoon Rooms, in a separate cedar motel, overlook a quiet, marshy expanse. A cluster of small, one-bedroom cabins have stone fireplaces, private baths, and share a hot tub, while the two-bedroom cottages each have a fireplace, private hot tub, and kitchen. **Pros:** Quiet and private. **Cons:** Shared baths. ⊠*2073 W. Captain Whidbey Inn Rd., off Madrona Way, 98239* ☏*360/678–4097 or 800/366–4097* ⊕*www.captainwhidbey.com* ➟*23 rooms, 2 suites, 4 cabins, 3 cottages* △*In-room: no a/c (some). In-hotel: no phone (some), no TV (some), restaurant, bar, beachfront, no elevator* ▤*AE, D, MC, V.*

¢–$ ▥**Anchorage Inn.** The exterior of this reproduction Victorian has fanciful details such as gables, dormer windows, and a tower. Inside, hardwood floors, reproduction furniture, and antiques harmonize with the Victorian theme. There are splendid views of Penn Cove from each room. The two-bedroom Calista Cottage is perfect for families. **Pros:** Steps away from historic Coupeville, great water views. **Cons:** Often booked weeks in advance. ⊠*807 N. Main St., 98239* ☏*360/678–5581 or 877/230–1313* ⊕*www.anchorage-inn.com* ➟*6 rooms, 1 suite* △*In-room: no a/c. In-hotel: VCR, dial-up, Wi-Fi., bicycles, no kids under 11, no elevator* ▤*D, MC, V* ⊠|*BP.*

$ ▥**Compass Rose Bed and Breakfast.** Inside this 1890 Queen Anne Victorian, five minutes from the Keystone spit, awaits a veritable museum of art, artifacts, and antiques. The proprietor's naval career carried him and his wife to all corners of the globe, from which they have collected the inn's unique adornments. Upstairs, the rooms share a parlor with a TV; in the morning, the downstairs dining room is laid out with a spread of eggs Benedict, wild-rice pancakes, and baked apples. The innkeepers' friendliness makes stays here all the more enjoyable and interesting. **Pros:**

Old-fashioned elegance. **Cons:** Very small. ✉ *508 S. Main St., 98239* ☎☎ *360/678–5318* ☎ *800/237–3881* ⊕ *www.compassrosebandb.com* ⤳ *2 rooms* ⅄ *In-room: no a/c. In-hotel: no phone, no TV, no-smoking rooms* ⊟ *No credit cards* ⭘*BP.*

10 mi north of Coupeville.

Oak Harbor, now a flat spread of modernity inlaid with strip malls and gas stations, takes its name from a more noble past: the majestic Oregon oaks that grow above the bay. Dutch and Irish immigrants settled the town in the mid-1800s; several windmills in town were built by descendants of the Dutch as symbols of their heritage. The marina, at the east side of the bay, has a picnic area with views of Saratoga Passage and the entrance of Penn Cove.

☺ **Deception Pass State Park** has 19 mi of rocky shore and beaches, three ★ freshwater lakes, and more than 38 mi of forest and meadow trails. The park occupies the northernmost point of Whidbey Island and the southernmost tip of Fidalgo Island, on both sides of the Deception Pass Bridge. Park on Canoe Island and walk across the bridge for views of two dramatic saltwater gorges, whose tidal whirlpools have been known to swallow large logs. ✉ *Hwy. 20, 7 mi north of Oak Harbor* ☎ *360/675–2417* ⤳ *Park free, campsite fees vary* ☉ *Apr.–Sept., daily 6:30* AM*–dusk; Oct.–Mar., daily 8* AM*–dusk.*

¢–$$ 🖫 **Coachman Inn.** Three modern motel buildings comprise this modern, chain-style accommodation with a few surprises. Each room is done up differently, accented with light-wood trim and polished tile floors. The pool and hot tub, child-friendly facilities, and low prices year-round make this a favorite of families. **Pros:** Comfortable, low-key, modern. **Cons:** Traffic and family noises. ✉ *32959 Hwy. 20, 98277* ☎ *360/675–0727 or 800/635–0043* 🖷 *360/675–1419* ⊕ *www.the coachmaninn.com* ⤳ *103 rooms* ⅄ *In-room: kitchen (some), Wi-Fi. In-hotel: refrigerator (some), pool, spa, gym, laundry facilities* ⊟ *AE, D, DC, MC, V* ⭘*CP.*

FIDALGO ISLAND

15 mi north of Oak Harbor.

The Deception Pass Bridge links Whidbey to Fidalgo (fee-*dal*-go) Island. From the bridge it's just a short drive to Anacortes, Fidalgo's main town and the terminus for ferries to the San Juan Islands. Anacortes has some well-preserved brick buildings along the waterfront, several well-maintained old commercial edifices downtown, and many beautiful older homes off the main drag.

The frequently changing exhibits at the **Anacortes Historical Museum** (✉ *1305 8th St., Anacortes* ☎ *360/293–1915* ⊕ *www.anacorteshistory museum.org*) focus on the cultural heritage of Fidalgo and nearby Guemes Island. The gallery is open 1 to 5 Thursday through Monday; the research library is open Monday, Thursday, and Friday 1 to 5.

West of Anacortes, near the ferry landing, **Washington Park** has dense forests, sunny meadows, trails, and a boat launch. A narrow, 2-mi loop road takes cars, cyclists, and hikers on a winding route through the woods and to overlooks of islands and saltwater. You can picnic or camp under tall trees near the shore. Beaches, picnic areas, and a playground complete the family-friendly environment. ⊠*6300 Sunset Ave.* ☎*360/293–1927* ✉*Free, camping $12–$15* ⊙*Daily dawn–dusk.*

WHERE TO EAT

$–$$ ✕ **Randy's Pier 61.** The simple dining room has a blue-and-white nautical theme, and waterfront tables look across the channel to the San Juans. Specialties include seafood gumbo, crab-stuffed prawns, and a beautifully flavored apples-and-almond salmon. The Sunday brunch buffet is a sumptuous hot-and-cold spread that draws crowds. ⊠*Pier 61, Anacortes* ☎*360/293–5108* ▭*AE, D, MC, V.*

¢–$ ✕ **Rockfish Grill.** It's a comfortable family restaurant that's affiliated with the Anacortes Brewery. Both establishments are in a restored 1929 building that has seen many uses, including saloon, ice-cream parlor, and plumbing shop. Note the mahogany back bar; it was crafted in Pennsylvania and once graced the Skagit Saloon. The food is simple but tasty pub fare: wood-fired pizzas and salmon, grilled steak, and pasta dishes as well as sandwiches, burgers, and fish-and-chips. Beers range from pilsner to amber ale, porter, stout, and seasonal brews. ⊠*320 Commercial Ave., Anacortes* ☎*360/588–1720* ⊕*www.anacortesrockfish.com* ▭*MC, V.*

¢ ✕ **Gere-A-Deli.** This bright, glass-front sandwich place in a brick corner building is Anacortes' favorite lunch hangout. Twenty-foot ceilings and antique signs surround the bustling daily crowds, who nosh on big sandwiches, steaming soups, and crisp salads. Winners include Grandma McPhee's meatloaf, and Grandma Gere's famous bumbleberry cobbler. Join the first-Friday art walk and stop in for home-style dinners, too. ⊠*502 Commercial Ave., Anacortes* ☎*360/293–7383* ▭*AE, MC, V.*

SHOPPING

Compass Wines (⊠*1405 Commercial Ave., Anacortes* ☎*360/293–6500* ⊕*www.compasswines.com*) is one of the state's premier wine shops, with lots of hard-to-find vintages from small wineries whose annual releases sell out quickly. Besides wines, the shop purveys artisan cheeses, provisions yachts and charter boats, and assembles delectable lunch baskets of imported specialties.

LA CONNER

14 mi southeast of Anacortes, 68 mi north of Seattle.

Morris Graves, Kenneth Callahan, Guy Anderson, Mark Tobey, and other painters set up shop in La Conner in the 1940s, and the village on the Swinomish Channel (Slough) has been a haven for artists ever since. In recent years the community has become increasingly popular as a weekend escape for Seattle residents, because it can be reached after a short drive but seems far away.

La Conner has several historic buildings near the waterfront or a short walk up the hill—use the stairs leading up the bluff, or go around and walk up one of the sloping streets—as well as several good shops and restaurants. In summer the village becomes congested with people and cars, and parking can be hard to find. The flat land around La Conner makes for easy bicycling along levees and through the tulip fields.

The **Museum of Northwest Art** presents the works of regional creative minds past and present. Soaring spaces, circular exhibit rooms, a glass gallery, and a broad spiral staircase add to the free-form feeling of the displays. The small shop sells examples of what you see in the exhibits. ⊠ *121 S. 1st St.* ☎ *360/466–4446* ⊕ *www.museumofnwart.org* ⌲ *$5* ⊙ *Daily 10–5.*

The hilltop **Skagit County Historical Museum** surveys domestic life in early Skagit County and Northwest Coastal Indian history. ⊠ *501 4th St.* ☎ *360/466–3365* ⌲ *$4* ⊙ *Tues.–Sun. 11–5.*

★ **Roozengaarde,** a 1,200-acre estate established by the Roozen family and Washington Bulb Company in 1985, is the world's largest family-owned tulip-, daffodil-, and iris-growing business. Fifteen acres of greenhouses are filled with multicolored blossoms, and more than 200,000 bulbs are planted in the show gardens each fall. The Skagit Valley Tulip Festival, held in April, is the main event, when the flowers pop up in neat, brilliant rows across the flat land, attracting thousands of sightseers. The garden and store are open year-round, and the staff and Web site are full of helpful advice for both novice and experienced gardeners. ⊠ *1587 Beaver Marsh Rd.* ☎ *360/4248531 or 866/488-5477* ⊕ *www.tulips.com* ⌲ *Free* ⊙ *Mon.–Sat. 9–6, Sun. 11–4.*

WHERE TO STAY & EAT

$-$$ ✕ **Kerstin's.** The intimate dining room overlooks the channel. The menu, which changes seasonally, includes portobello mushrooms roasted with pesto, pan-braised fresh king salmon, pork tenderloin, rib-eye steak with Indonesian spices, halibut, and lamb shank with port wine sauce. The oysters baked in garlic-cilantro butter and finished with Parmesan are particularly popular. ⊠ *505 S. 1st St.* ☎ *360/466–9111* ▭ *AE, DC, MC, V* ⊙ *Closed Tues. No lunch Sun.–Wed. mid-Oct.–mid-Apr.*

¢ ✕ **Calico Cupboard.** A local favorite, this storefront bakery-café turns out some of the best pastries in Skagit County. Lunches focus on fresh, gourmet salads, soups, and burgers; you can also order big "breakfast for lunch" combos. No seats? Buy picnic goodies at the take-out counter. ⊠ *720 S. 1st St.* ☎ *360/466–4451* ▭ *MC, V* ⊙ *No dinner.*

FodorśChoice ★

$-$$$ ▦ **La Conner Country Inn.** The multistory waterfront hotel is split into two sections: a large country inn, and an understated lodge overlooking the narrow Swinomish Channel. Rooms, done in subdued gray tones with wooden trim, have a gas fireplace, flat-screen TV, DVD player, and a private balcony or patio. Twelve inn rooms have whirlpool baths. The lodge hosts weekend wine receptions and movie gatherings, and massage services are available in the privacy of your room. Nell Thorn's is a pub-style restaurant that serves hearty Northwest fare, organic seasonings, and fine wines. **Pros:** Big stone fireplace, rustic charm wrapped around sleek modern amenities. **Cons:** Overpriced catering services and meeting equipment. ⊠*207 S. 2nd St., 98257* ☎*360/466–3101* ⊕*www.laconnerlodging.com* ➫*28 rooms, 17 suites* &*In-hotel: Wi-Fi, no elevator* ⊟*AE, D, DC, MC, V.*

$–$$ ☷**Wild Iris.** The garden-laced exterior is a sprawling model of a Victorian-style inn, and the elegantly decorated interior begins with a river-rock fireplace. Spacious rooms have soft, colorful fabrics and polished wood accents; suites have CD players, robes, fireplaces, whirlpool spa tubs, and private decks or balconies. Breakfast is served in the large, restaurant-style dining room. ⊠*121 Maple Ave., 98257* ☎*360/466–1400 or 800/477–1400* ⊕*www.wildiris.com* ➫*4 rooms, 12 suites* &*In-room: no a/c. In-hotel: DVD, dial-up, Wi-Fi, no elevator* ⊟*AE, MC, V* ⍾*BP.*

¢–$ ☷**Heron.** A replica Victorian structure with a stone living-room fireplace houses this cozy bed-and-breakfast. Spacious rooms focus on country simplicities, and it's just steps from the door into town. Mornings bring scrumptious homemade muffins, breads, and hot breakfasts in the formal dining room. The on-site Watergrass Day Spa provides organic treatments, and massage services are available there or in your room. ⊠*117 Maple Ave., 98257* ☎*360/466–4626* ⊟*360/466–3254* ⊕*www.theheron.com* ➫*8 rooms, 3 suites* &*In-room: no a/c. In-hotel: spa, Wi-Fi, some pets allowed, no elevator* ⊟*MC, V* ⍾*BP.*

MOUNT VERNON

11 mi northeast of La Conner.

This attractive riverfront town is the county seat of Skagit County and was founded in 1871. After a giant log jam on the lower Skagit was cleared, steamers began churning up the river, and Mount Vernon soon became the major commercial center of the Skagit Valley, a position it has never relinquished. More recently, Mount Vernon was named Best Small City in the U.S. by *The New Rating Guide to Life in America's Small Cities.*

The city is surrounded by dairy pastures, vegetable fields, and bulb farms, and is famous for its annual Tulip Festival in April, when thousands of people visit to admire the floral exuberance. Rising above downtown and the river, 972-foot-high Little Mountain is a city park with a view. It used to be an island until the mudflats were filled in by Skagit River silt. Glacial striations in rocks near the top of the mountain, dating from the last continental glaciation (10,000–20,000 years ago), were made when the mountain (and all of the Puget Sound region) was covered by some 3,500 feet of ice.

Atop Little Mountain at the southeastern edge of town, 480-acre **Little Mountain Park** has great views of the Skagit Valley (especially in March and April, when the daffodils and tulips are in full bloom), the San Juan Islands, and the distant Olympic Mountains. ⊠*Blackburn Rd. W* ☎*360/336–6213* ⊠*Free* ☉*Daily dawn–dusk.*

Adjoining the small waterfront community of the same name, **Bay View State Park** has a campground in the woods and picnic tables on the low grassy bluff above the bay. Canoers and kayakers take note: Padilla Bay runs almost dry at low tide, when water is restricted to a few creek-like tidal channels. ⊠ *10905 Bay View-Edison Rd.* ☎ *360/757–0227* ⊕ *www.parks.wa.gov* ⊠ *$5 day use, $17–$23 camping* ☉ *Daily 8 AM–dusk.*

At **Padilla Bay National Estuarine Reserve,** the Breazeale Interpretive Center has great birding: there are black brant geese, raptors, peregrine falcons, and bald eagles. Trails lead into the woods and to a rocky beach, with more good bird-watching opportunities. The 2¼-mi Padilla Bay Trail starts at the south end of Bayview; look for signs directing you to the parking area, which is away from the water off the east side of the road. ⊠ *10441 Bayview-Edison Rd.* ☎ *360/428–1558* ⊠ *Free* ☉ *Wed.–Sun. 10–5.*

WHERE TO EAT

$–$$ ✕ **Il Grainaio.** Tucked deep into the town's historic Old Grainery, amid
★   displays of century-old farming equipment, is this cozy and rustic Italian restaurant. Dark-wood floors, small tables, and lanternlike lighting give it the authentic ambience of a local trattoria. The waitstaff is quick and knowledgeable, turning out enormous pasta bowls, seafood salads, and pan-fried eggplant or salmon with flair. Excellent wines garnish the tables, and desserts are simple and rich. Slip in early on weekends, when dinners bustle with groups. ⊠ *100 E. Montgomery St.,* ☎ *360/419–0674* ⊟ *AE, MC, V.*

BELLINGHAM

29 mi northeast of Mount Vernon.

The fishing port and college community of Bellingham is transforming itself from a grungy blue-collar area to the arts, retirement, and pleasure-boating capital of Washington's northwest corner. Downtown has cafés, specialty shops, and galleries, and the waterfront, once dominated by lumber mills and shipyards, is slowly being converted into a string of parks with connecting trails. College students and professors from Western Washington University make up a sizable part of the town's population and contribute to its laid-back intellectual climate. The lushly green bayfront, creeks meandering through town, and Lakes Whatcom and Padden attract wildlife like deer, raccoons, river otters, beavers, ducks, geese, herons, bald eagles, and the occasional cougar.

The four-building **Whatcom Museum of History and Art** has as its centerpiece Bellingham's 1892 former city hall, a redbrick structure converted into a museum in 1940. Victorian clothing, toys, games, and clocks are on display, and there are art exhibits as well. The other buildings in the complex include a natural-history gallery and photo archive, a children's museum, and a gift shop. ⊠ *121 Prospect St.* ☎ *360/676–6981* ⊕ *www.whatcommuseum.org* ⊠ *Free, children's museum $2* ☉ *Tues.–*

Sun. noon–5; gallery by appointment; children's museum Thurs.–Sat.
10–5, Tues., Wed., Sun. noon–5.

Ⓒ The **Maritime Heritage Park,** down a flight of stairs behind the Whatcom Museum, pays tribute to Bellingham's fishing industry. Self-guided
Marine Heritage Center tours take you through a salmon's life cycle,
winding past hatcheries, aquarium tanks, and fish ladders. A boardwalk route from Holly Street leads to the ponds and a waterfall, where
Bellingham was founded in 1852. Note that salmon runs occur annually around September and October. ✉*1600 C St.* ☎*360/676–6806*
🖂*Free* ☉*Daily dawn–dusk.*

Ⓒ A good place to fish, lounge, picnic, or walk is the **Squalicum Harbor**
Marina, which holds more than 1,900 commercial and pleasure boats.
Pete Zuanich Park, at the end of the spit, has a telescope for close-up
views of the water and a marine-life center with touch tanks. ✉*Roeder*
Ave. and Coho Way ☎*360/676–2542.*

The only public access in Bellingham to 14-mi-long Lake Whatcom is
at its north end, in **Bloedel Donovan Park.** Locals swim in the sheltered
waters of a cove, but you might find the water too cold. If so, spend
some time trying to spot beavers, river otters, ducks, great blue herons, and yellow pond lilies at Scudder Pond, which is another 100 feet
west (reached by trail from a parking area at Northshore and Ala-
bama). ✉*2214 Electric Ave.* ☎*360/676–6985* 🖂*Parking $3* ☉*Daily*
dawn–dusk.

Fairhaven, the historic district just shy of 3 mi south of Bellingham and
at the beginning of Chuckanut Drive (Highway 11), was an independent city until 1903, and still retains its distinct identity as an intellectual and artistic center. The beautifully restored 1890s redbrick
buildings of the Old Fairhaven District, especially on Harris Avenue
between 10th and 12th streets, house restaurants, galleries, and specialty boutiques.

The **Bellingham Cruise Terminal** (✉*355 Harris Ave.* ☎*360/676–2500*),
a massive brick building surrounded by gardens, dispatches daily ferries
to the San Juan Islands, Victoria, and Alaska. There's terrific wildlife-
watching right off the docks and adjacent shoreline, where sea lions,
otters, and gray whales frolic out in the water as great blue herons,
cormorants, and harlequin ducks bob on the surface.**Fairhaven Marine**
Park, a long, sandy beach at the foot of Harris Street a few blocks
south, is the place to launch sea kayaks. A rough trail runs south from
the park along the railroad tracks to shingle beaches and rocky headlands, where you'll find clams, summer blackberries, and splendid
views of Lummi Island.

★ Highway 11, also known as **Chuckanut Drive,** was once the only highway heading south from Bellingham. The drive begins in Fairhaven,
reaches the flat farmlands of the Samish Valley near the village of Bow,
and joins up with I–5 at Burlington, in Skagit County; the full loop
can be made in a couple of hours. For a dozen miles this 23-mi road
winds along the cliffs above beautiful Chuckanut and Samish bays. It

twists its way past the sheer sandstone face of Chuckanut Mountain and crosses creeks with waterfalls. Turnouts are framed by gnarled madrona trees and pines and offer great views of the San Juan Islands. Bald eagles cruise along the cliffs or hang out on top of tall firs. Drive carefully: the cliffs are so steep in places that rock slides are common; note that the road washes out once or twice each winter.

Larrabee State Park, south of Chuckanut Bay along the Whatcom–Skagit county line, is one of the state's most scenic and popular parks. It straddles a rocky shore that has quiet, sandy coves and runs high up along the slopes of Chuckanut Mountain. Even though the mountain has been logged repeatedly, some of it is still wilderness. Miles of trails lead through ferny fir and maple forests to hidden lakes, caves, and cliff-top lookouts from which you can see all the way to the San Juan Islands. At the shore there's a sheltered boat launch; you can go crabbing here or watch the birds—and the occasional harbor seal—that perch on the offshore rocks. The area west of Chuckanut Drive has picnic tables as well as tent and RV sites with hookups, which are open all year. ⊠ *245 Chuckanut Dr.* ☎ *360/676–2093* ⊠ *$5* ☉ *Daily dawn–dusk.*

WHERE TO EAT

$$$
★
✕ **Oyster Bar.** Above the shore on a steep, wooded bluff, this intimate restaurant in the village of Bow is regionally famous for what is probably the best marine view from any Washington restaurant. People come here to dine and watch the sun set over the islands to the west or to watch the full moon reflect off the waters of Samish Bay. The menu changes regularly, so it's hard to predict what you might find, but the oyster bar, seafood dishes, wild game, and pastas never disappoint—and there are fine wines to complement every dish. ⊠ *2578 Chuckanut Dr., Bow* ☎ *360/766–6185* ▭ *AE, MC, V.*

$–$$$
✕ **Big Fat Fish Company.** Have a fish craving? Head to this spacious, brewpub-style restaurant for everything from panfried trout to cedar-planked salmon and sea bass Wellington. A lot of other fishy items round out the menu: king crab legs, scallops in truffle butter, and rich seafood cioppino. The sushi is spot-on, too; novices can try the sample platter. Aquaphobia? Dig into a rib eye with wild mushrooms, or the Big Fat Kobe Burger. Service is casual and fun, although weekends often bring long waits. ⊠ *1304 12th St.* ☎ *360/733–2284* ▭ *AE, D, MC, V.*

$$
✕ **Nimbus.** Downtown Fairhaven's upscale star is this small, posh spot rising 14 stories above the boutique neighborhood. Seasonal menus enhance fresh Washington produce, with delicacies including an apple-cider pork belly and caramelized sea scallops combination, and homemade melted leek ravioli. If you can't decide, go for the exquisite five-course tasting menu. After-hours tidbits, served until midnight, offer truffle fries, wild mushroom cannoli, and heirloom tomato soup. Service for all meals is professionally crisp, yet still relaxed and amiable. ⊠ *118 N. Commercial St., 14th fl.* ☎ *360/676–1307* ▭ *AE, MC, V* ☉ *Closed Sun. No lunch.*

$–$$
✕ **Chuckanut Manor.** The old-fashioned, glassed-in dining room and bar overlook the mouth of the Samish River, Samish Bay, and the mudflats,

where great blue herons hang out. It's a popular spot for sunset- and bird-watching: bird feeders outside the bar's picture windows attract finches, chickadees, red-winged blackbirds, and other songbirds. Occasionally bald eagles can be seen gliding past. Besides the view, folks come here for traditional American fare with an emphasis on steak and fresh seafood. ⊠ *3056 Chuckanut Dr., Bow* ☎ *360/766–6191* ☐ *AE, DC, MC, V.*

WHERE TO STAY

$$–$$$$ ⊡ **Schnauzer Crossing.** Meticulously maintained gardens surround this contemporary B&B in a peaceful residential neighborhood overlooking Lake Whatcom. The original 1920s house was extended in the 1970s; the modern living room has extremely high ceilings. The guest room has a lake view, while the large suite has a glass-enclosed atrium and fireplace. A cottage unit, whose cost may leave you expecting something more lavish, has a kitchen and a gas fireplace. Friendly owners Donna and Vermont McAllister serve such ample, unusual breakfast dishes as triple sec French toast. **Pros:** Luscious food. **Cons:** Expect dog noise. ⊠ *4421 Lakeway Dr., 98226* ☎ *360/733–0055 or 800/562–2808* ☐ *360/734–2808* ⊕ *www.schnauzercrossing.com* ⬦ *1 room, 1 suite, 1 cottage* ☐ *D, MC, V* ⦿ *BP.*

$$$ ⊡ **Chrysalis Inn and Spa at the Pier.** The facade, which rises above the waterfront, is gray and stark, but in the lobby warm wood predominates. On sunny days you can see far across Bellingham Bay; on cloudy days, you can stare into the blaze of the big main fireplace. Rooms also have fireplaces, as well as double baths, window seats, and such amenities as coffeemakers, irons, hair dryers, and CD players. Artwork enlivens the walls of the modern Fino Wine Bar ($–$$$), and picture windows frame the bay. You can sample European and Pacific Northwest wines at the long back bar or dine on Mediterranean-inspired fare at white linen–clad tables. **Pros:** Utterly relaxing. **Cons:** Adjacent railway. ⊠ *804 10th St., 98225* ☎ *360/756–1005 or 888/808–0005* ⊕ *www.thechrysalisinn.com* ⬦ *34 rooms, 9 suites* ⬥ *In-room: refrigerator. In-hotel: VCR, dial-up, restaurant, bar, spa, Wi-Fi, no elevator* ☐ *AE, D, DC, MC, V* ⦿ *CP.*

$$$ ⊡ **Hotel Bellwether.** Bellingham's original waterfront hotel overlooks
★ the entrance to bustling Squalicum Harbor. Its luxuriously appointed rooms are augmented by a lighthouse suite ensconced in its own tower. Rooms have gas fireplaces and private balconies for lounging and dining. The pleasant Harborside Bistro and comfortable bar have grand views across Bellingham Bay to Lummi Island. There's also an adjacent spa and boutique shopping area. **Pros:** beautiful bay views, large private dock. **Cons:** hub for groups, small pets in public areas ⊠ *1 Bellwether Way, Squalicum Harbor Marina, 98225* ☎ *360/392–3100 or 877/411–1200* ☐ *360/392–3101* ⊕ *www.hotelbellwether.com* ⬦ *50 rooms, 15 suites, 1 lighthouse suite* ⬥ *In-hotel: restaurant, bar, gym, dock, bicycles, Wi-Fi, no elevator* ☐ *AE, D, DC, MC, V.*

NIGHTLIFE & THE ARTS

Boundary Bay Brewery & Bistro (⊠*1107 Railroad Ave.* ☎*360/647–5593*), a warehouse turned classy brewery, pours five beers, serves some of Bellingham's best food, and displays eclectic local art. **Mt. Baker Theatre** (⊠*104 N. Commercial St.* ☎*360/734–6080*), a restored vaudeville-era theater, has a 110-foot-tall Moorish tower and a lobby fashioned after a Spanish galleon. Home to the Whatcom Symphony Orchestra, it's also a venue for movies and touring performers. Take a 45-minute tour of the facility every first Saturday at 10:15, 11:15, and 12:15. The mellowest place in Bellingham for a beer is the **Up and Up** (⊠*1234 N. State St.* ☎*360/733–9739*).

SPORTS & THE OUTDOORS

CLIMBING The **American Alpine Institute** (⊠*1613 12th St.* ☎*360/671–1570* ⊕*www. americanalpineinstitute.com*) is a prestigious mountain- and rock-climbing school.

WHALE-WATCHING **Island Mariner Cruises** (⊠*5 Squalicum Harbor Loop* ☎*360/734–8866* ⊕*www.orcawatch.com*) conducts whale-watching and nature cruises to the Queen Charlotte Islands and Alaska, and sunset cruises around Bellingham Bay. **Victoria/San Juan Cruises** (⊠*355 Harris Ave., inside Bellingham Cruise Terminal* ☎*360/738–8099 or 800/443–4552* ⊕*www.whales.com*) sails to Victoria, British Columbia, and the San Juan Islands on daylong or overnight trips. Under the right conditions, the views of whales and sunsets cannot be beat.

FERNDALE

10 mi north of Bellingham.

On the Nooksack River and amid dairy farms, Ferndale is a pleasant town that has burst its seams in recent years as urban sprawl arrived. It has the best views of Mt. Baker in the county.

In **Pioneer Park** you can wander through log buildings from the 1870s—including Whatcom County's first church—that have been restored and converted into museums. Note the beautifully "squared" cedar logs, a western Washington pioneer building technique. Highlights include summer tours, an old-time Settlers Picnic at the end of July, and Old-Fashioned Christmas festivities. ⊠*2004 Cherry St.* ☎*360/384–0792* 🎟*Free* ⊙*May–Sept., Tues.–Sun. 11:30–4:30.*

🅒 **Hovander Homestead Park**, a pioneer farm, is now a national historic site with a Victorian-era farmhouse, barnyard animals, a water tower, vegetable gardens, and antique farm equipment. Surrounding it are 60 acres of walking trails and picnic grounds, and there's access to fishing in the Nooksack River. ⊠*5299 Nielsen Ave.* ☎*360/384–3444* 🎟*Free* ⊙*Park daily dawn–dusk; Hovander House weekends 1–4:30 in May, Thurs.–Sun. noon–4:30 June–Labor Day.*

The **Tennant Lake Natural History Interpretive Center,** within an early home-stead, has exhibits and information about nature walks. An observation tower allows for bird-watching from an eagle's perspective, and the elevated boardwalk takes you right through the marshes. The lake is part of a 624-acre habitat where bald eagles, ducks, beavers, muskrats, and other wildlife can be seen. The Fragrance Garden, an herb- and flower-laden pathway, is lined with interpretive signs in English and Braille. ⊠ *5236 Nielsen Rd.* ☎ *360/384–3444* ☒ *Free* ☉ *Daily dawn–dusk.*

GLACIER

41 mi northeast of Ferndale.

The canyon village of Glacier, just outside the Mt. Baker–Snoqualmie National Forest boundary, has a few shops, cafés, and lodgings. Highway 542 winds east from Glacier into the forest through an increasingly steep-walled canyon. It passes 170-foot-high Nooksack Falls, about 5 mi east of Glacier, and travels up the north fork of the Nooksack River and the slopes of Mt. Baker to a ski area, which is bright with huckleberry patches and wildflowers in summer.

Mt. Baker–Snoqualmie National Forest is a vast area including much of the mountain and forest land around North Cascades National Park. The region has many trails, but because the snowline is quite low in Washington State, the upper ridges and mountains are covered by snow much of the year. This makes for a short hiking, climbing, and mountain-biking season, usually from mid-July to mid-September or October—but winter brings skiing and snowmobiling. The wildflower season is also short but spectacular; expect fall color by late August and early September. The 10,778-foot-high, snow-covered volcanic dome of **Mt. Baker** is visible from much of Whatcom County and from as far north as Vancouver and as far south as Seattle ⊠ *2934 Wetmore Rd., Everett* ☎ *360/783–6000 or 800/627–0062* ⊕ *www.fs.fed.us/r6/mbs* ☒ *$5* ☉ *Daily 24 hrs.*

WHERE TO STAY

$$ ☐ **The Inn at Mt. Baker.** Nestled into the upper Cascades, this stately country home offers airy spaces with vaulted ceilings—and sweeping mountain panoramas from every angle. Each bedroom, named for an area gold mine or peak, has down-soft beds, a rocking chair, and big views. Guests relax in the reading room, TV lounge, or on the patio, and there's an on-call massage therapist. Big breakfasts in the sunny dining room feature upside-down peach pancakes, potato pancakes, and homemade granola. **Pros:** Easy to find, European-style luxuries. **Cons:** Simple room decor can seem sparse. ⊠ *Hwy. 542, milepost 28, 98244* ☎ *360/599–1776* 🖷 *360/599–3000* ⊕ *www.theinnatmt baker.com* ⇌ *5 rooms* ⚲ *In-hotel: hot tub, no elevator* ☰ *AE, MC, V* ⏏❘ *BP.*

$ ☐ **The Logs at Canyon Creek.** This comfortable back-country resort, set on a creek and surrounded by forest, is a haven for deer, eagles, and other wildlife. Rustic two-bedroom cabins have a full kitchen, plus a living room with a rock fireplace—your wood is even provided. Cedar chalet vacation homes have two or three bedrooms and come fully equipped with such amenities as DVD players, dishwashers, and claw-

foot tubs. The property is open year-round, but rates plummet September through June, when you can stay two nights and get a third night free Sunday through Thursday. **Pros:** Your home in the woods, great ski access. **Cons:** A long drive from civilization. ⊠*7577 Canyon View Dr., 98244* ☎*360/599–2711* ⊕*www.thelogs.com* ⇆*5 cabins, 3 vacations homes* ⚐*In-room: no a/c. In-hotel: no phone, kitchen, no TV, no elevator* ⊟*MC, V.*

¢ 🏨**Kale House Bed & Breakfast.** The charming home gleams with polished wood and large windows, which look out to knobby apple trees and a weeping willow. The pastel main-floor bedroom has a private bath, while the bright, two-room second-floor suite has a unique cupboard sleeping nook. Public spaces include the cozy dining room, the comfortable fireplace lounge, and a gift shop and gallery. **Pros:** Small and inviting. **Cons:** No services or amenities. ⊠*201 Kale St, Everson 98247* ☎*360/966–7027* ⊕*www.bbonline.com/wa/kale* ⇆*2 rooms* ⚐*In-hotel: no elevator* ⊟*MC, V* ⒪*BP.*

SPORTS & THE OUTDOORS

At the **Mt. Baker Ski Area** you can snowboard and ski downhill or cross-country from roughly November to the end of April. The area set a world snowfall record in winter 1998–99. Ski and snowboard equipment are available to rent. ⊠*Hwy. 542, Mt. Baker* ☎*360/734–6771, 360/671–0211 snow reports* ⊕*www.mtbakerskiarea.com* ☒*Lift ticket weekdays $33.90, weekends and holidays $41.32.*

SEDRO-WOOLLEY

42 mi southwest of Glacier, 9 mi northeast of Mount Vernon.

On its way east from I–5, Highway 20 skirts Burlington and Sedro-Woolley, the latter a former mill and logging town now considered "The Gateway to the Cascades." Fronted by a huge black steam engine, the settlement has a bit of an old downtown and a smattering of Tar Heel culture, as it was settled by pioneer loggers and farmers from North Carolina. It also has an institute that arranges trips into the North Cascades National Park and a nearby park headquarters.

The steam-powered **Lake Whatcom Railway** makes short jaunts through the woods 11 mi north of Sedro-Woolley. Excursions run all summer and during special events, such as the December Christmas train rides with Santa. During peak weekends, tours depart around 9:30, noon, and 2:30, and children pay half-price. Note that the schedule changes seasonally. ⊠*Hwy. 9, in Wickersham* ☎*360/595–2218* ⊕*www.lake whatcomrailway.com* ☒*$14* ⓧ*Call for hrs.*

MARBLEMOUNT

40 mi east of Sedro-Woolley.

Like Sedro-Woolley, Marblemount is a former logging town now depending on outdoor recreation for its fortunes. Anglers, campers, hikers, bird-watchers, and hunters come and go from the town's collection of motels, cafés, and stores, while day-trippers head in for sips at the area's small wineries. It's also a good base for exploring North Cascades National Park.

WHERE TO EAT

$–$$ ✕ **Buffalo Run Restaurant.** A clean and simple, one-room highway stop, the restaurant has blackboard specials of buffalo, venison, elk, and ostrich (and a few veggie dishes). Buffalo heads and Old West memorabilia hang from the dining room's walls; a patio provides seating next to a garden outside. ✉ 60084 Hwy. 20 ☎ 360/873–2461 ▭ AE, D, MC, V ☾ Closed Wed. Oct.–Apr.

WINTHROP

87 mi east of Marblemount, 128 mi east of Sedro-Woolley.

Before the cowboys came, the Methow Valley was a favorite gathering place for Indian tribes, who dug the plentiful and nutritious bulbs and hunted deer while their horses fattened on the tall native grasses. For wayward pioneers who came later, the cool, glacier-fed streams provided welcome relief on hot summer days, and the rich fields were a starting point for vast crops and orchards. The 1800s saw the burgeoning riverside settlement of Winthrop grow into a cattle-ranching town, whose residents inspired some of Owen Wister's colorful characters in his novel *The Virginian*. Today Winthrop, in the center of the Methow Valley, still retains its Wild West character throughout the business district, where many of the original, turn-of-the-20th-century buildings still stand.

Getting to town through the Washington countryside is a picturesque drive, with endless vistas of golden meadows, neatly sewn crop fields, and rustic old barn frames. In winter the land is a crisp blanket of glittering frost; in summer little fruit-and-vegetable stands pop up along the back roads. Massive tangles of blackberry bushes produce kumquat-size fruit you can eat right off the vines, and the pungent aroma of apples pervades the breezes in autumn. Flat roads, small towns, incredible views, and plenty of camp spots make this the perfect weekend wandering territory by bike, car, or motorcycle.

WHERE TO EAT

¢–$ ✕ **Duck Brand Cantina, Bakery and Hotel.** The former 19th-century saloon still stands in roadhouse style, with comfortable frontier decor, antique signs and knickknacks, and rustic touches enhancing the Old West atmosphere inside. The draws are good, square meals at reasonable prices, and the globe-trotting menu runs the gamut from breakfast omelets and burritos to pastas and sandwiches. Steaks, grilled chicken, and stir-fries are the dinner specials; fresh margaritas and 12 microbrews are on hand to refresh your palate. Six rooms, each with a bed and TV, provide a rest for the weary traveler. ✉ 248 Riverside Ave. ☎ 509/996–2192 ⊕ www.methow.com/duck ▭ AE, D, DC, MC, V.

Continued on page 403

North Cascades National Park

Countless snow-clad mountain spires dwarf narrow glacial valleys in this 505,000-acre expanse of the North Cascades, which actually encompasses three diverse natural areas. North Cascades National Park is the core of the region, flanked by Lake Chelan National Recreation Area to the south and Ross Lake National Recreation Area to the north; all are part of the Stephen T. Mather Wilderness Area. This is an utterly spectacular gathering of snowy peaks, glacial meadows, plunging canyons, and cold, deep-blue lakes. Traditionally the lands of several Native American tribes, it's fitting that it's still a completely wild—and wildlife-filled—stretch of earth that is all but inaccessible most of the year.

WELCOME TO NORTH CASCADES

TOP REASONS TO GO

★ **Pure wilderness:** Nearly 400 mi of mountain and meadow trails immerse hikers in pristine natural panoramas, with sure sightings of bald eagles, deer, elk, and other wildlife.

★ **Majestic glaciers:** The North Cascades are home to 318 moving ice masses, more than half of the glaciers in the United States.

★ **Splendid flora:** A bright palette of flowers blankets the hillsides in midsummer, while October's colors paint the landscape in vibrant autumn hues.

★ **Thrilling boat rides:** Lake Chelan, Lake Ross, and the Stehekin River are the starting points for kayaking, white-water rafting, and ferry trips.

★ **19th-century history:** Delve into the state's farming, lumber, and logging pasts in clapboard towns and homesteads around the park.

1 North Unit. The park's creek-cut northern wilderness, centered on snowy Mount Challenger, stretches north from Highway 20 over the Picket Range toward the Canadian border. It's an endless landscape of pine-topped peaks and ridges, hemmed in by sinewy Ross Lake to the east and the western slopes of the Mt. Baker Ski Area.

2 South Unit. Hike the South Unit's lake-filled mountain foothills in summer, where you'll take in a panorama of blue skies and flower-filled meadows. Waterfalls and wildlife are abundant here.

3 Ross Lake National Recreation Area. Drawing a thick line from British Columbia all the way down to the North cascades Scenic Highway, placid Ross Lake is edged with pretty bays that draw swimmers and boaters.

4 Lake Chelan National Recreation Area. Ferries steam between small waterfront towns along this pristine waterway, while kayakers and hikers follow quiet trails along its edges. This is one of the Northwest's most popular summer escapes, where simple country life, nature-bound activities, and rustic accommodations all focus on the pleasures of the outdoors.

WASHINGTON

GETTING ORIENTED

The park rises upward from the massive Cascade ranges seen northeast of Seattle, widening in a swath of snow-covered peaks all the way to the Canadian border. The broad Skagit River and many large creeks cut through the valleys; most end in the long arm of Lake Chelan in the south or in the snakelike expanse of Ross Lake at the park's northern edge. Picturesque 19th-century settlements are tucked into the folds of the slopes, notably Stehekin and Winthrop to the east, Chelan to the south, and Marblemount and Sedro-Woolley, west of the park along Highway 20. Even in summer, valleys can start the day shrouded in fog; it's best to drive the highway west-to-east during the afternoon. A morning start is a good choice coming the other way. The most sensational scenery, however, is reached by hiking to one of the high park passes or mountain lookouts.

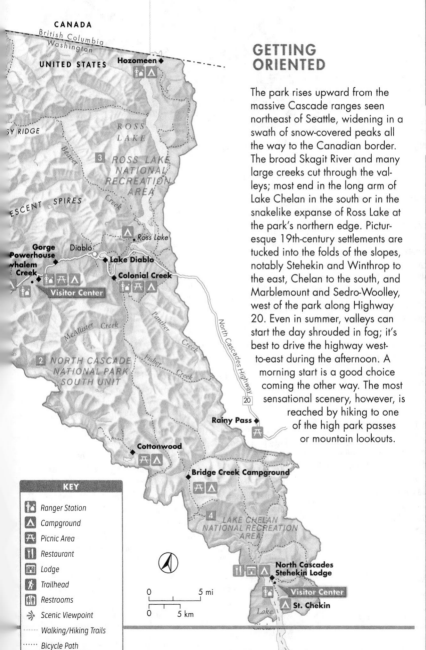

CANADA
British Columbia
Washington

UNITED STATES
Hozomeen ◆

SY RIDGE

ROSS LAKE

3 ROSS LAKE NATIONAL RECREATION AREA

Beaver Creek

ESCENT SPIRES

Ross Lake

Gorge Powerhouse Diablo
whalem Creek
● Lake Diablo
● Colonial Creek
Visitor Center

McAllister Creek

Panther Creek

North Cascades Highway

Fisher Creek

2 NORTH CASCADE NATIONAL PARK SOUTH UNIT

20

Rainy Pass ◆

Cottonwood

Bridge Creek Campground

4 LAKE CHELAN NATIONAL RECREATION AREA

KEY

- 🏠 Ranger Station
- △ Campground
- 🏕 Picnic Area
- 🍴 Restaurant
- 🏨 Lodge
- 🥾 Trailhead
- 🚻 Restrooms
- ⛰ Scenic Viewpoint
- --- Walking/Hiking Trails
- ⋯⋯ Bicycle Path

North Cascades Stehekin Lodge
Visitor Center
St. Chekin

Lake Chelan

0   5 mi
0   5 km

NOTH CASCADES NATIONAL PARK PLANNER

When to Go

The spectacular, craggy peaks of the North Cascades—often likened to the Alps—are breathtaking in any season. **Summer is short and glorious in the high country, extending from snowmelt (late May to July, depending on the elevation and the amount of snow) to early September. This is peak season for the North Cascades,** especially along the alpine stretches of Route 20; weekends and holidays can be crowded. The North Cascades Highway is a popular autumn drive in September and October, when the changing leaves (on larches, the only conifer that sheds its leaves, as well as aspen, vine maple, huckleberry, and cottonwood) put on a colorful show. The lowland forest areas, such as the complex around Newhalem, can be visited almost any time of year. These can be wonderfully quiet in early spring or late autumn on mild, rainy days, when you can experience the weather that makes the old-growth forest possible. Snow closes the North Cascades Highway November through mid-April; exact dates depend on snow conditions.

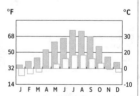

Flora & Fauna

Bald eagles are present year-round along the Skagit River and the various lakes—although in December, hundreds flock to the Skagit to feed on a rare winter salmon run; they remain through January. Black bears are often seen in spring and early summer along the roadsides in the high country, feeding on new green growth. Deer and elk can often be seen in early morning and late evening, grazing and browsing at the forest's edge. Other mountain residents include beaver, marmots, pika, otters, skunks, opossums, and smaller mammals, as well as forest and field birds.

Getting There & Around

Highway 20, the North Cascades Highway, splits the park's north and south sections. The gravel Cascade River Road, which runs southeast from Marblemount, splits off Highway 20; Sibley Creek/Hidden Lake Road (USFS 1540) breaks off Cascade River Road to the Cascade Pass trailhead. Thornton Creek Road is another rough four-wheel-drive track. For the Ross Lake area in the north, the unpaved Hozomeen Road (Silver–Skagit Rd.) provides access between Hope, British Columbia; Silver Lake; and Skagit Valley provincial parks. From Stehekin, the Stehekin Valley Road continues to High Bridge, Car Wash Falls, Bridge Creek, and Cottonwood campgrounds—although seasonal floods may cause washouts. Note that a day trip isn't nearly enough to make a thorough exploration of the park: roads are narrow and closed from October to June, many sights are off the beaten path, and the scenery is so spectacular that, once you're in it, you won't want to hurry through anyway.

SCENIC DRIVES

By Holly
S. Smith

★ **North Cascades Highway.** Also known as Highway 20, this classic scenic route first winds through the green pastures and woods of the upper Skagit Valley, the mountains looming in the distance. Beyond Concrete, a former cement-manufacturing town, the highway climbs into the mountains, passes the Ross and Diablo dams, and traverses Ross Lake National Recreation Area. Here several pullouts offer great views of the lake and the surrounding snowcapped peaks. From June to September, the meadows are covered with wildflowers, and from late September through October, the mountain slopes flame with fall foliage. The pinnacle point of this stretch is 5,477-foot-high Washington Pass: look east, to where the road descends quickly into a series of hairpin curves between Early Winters Creek and the Methow Valley. Remember, this section of the highway is closed from roughly November to April, depending on snowfall. From the Methow Valley, Highway 153 takes the scenic route along the Methow River's apple, nectarine, and peach orchards to Pateros, on the Columbia River; from here, you can continue east to Grand Coulee or south to Lake Chelan.

WHAT TO SEE

HISTORIC SITES

Buckner Homestead. Founded in 1912, this pioneer farm includes an apple orchard, farmhouse, barn, and many ranch buildings, which are slowly being restored by the National Park Service. ⊠ *Stehekin Valley Rd., 3½ mi from Stehekin Landing, Stehekin* ☎ *360/854–7635 Ext. 340 then press 14* ☉ *June–Sept., daily 9–5.*

Diablo Dam. Since 1918, Seattle City Light has brought hydroelectric power to the area. Today, Skagit Tours runs 2½-hour excursions across Diablo Dam by motor coach, followed by a boat cruise of Diablo Lake. Purchase snacks at the Skagit General Store or bring a picnic lunch. ⊠ *Milepost 120, Hwy. 20, Newhalem* ☎ *206/684–3030* ⊠ *$55* ☉ *Tours July and Aug., Fri.–Sun. at 12:30; June and Sept., weekends at 12:30.*

SCENIC STOPS

Gorge Powerhouse/Ladder Creek Falls and Rock Gardens. A powerhouse is a powerhouse, but the rock gardens overlooking Ladder Creek Falls, 7 mi west of Diablo, are beautiful and inspiring. ⊠ *Rte. 20, 2 mi east of North Cascades Visitor Center, Newhalem* ☎ *206/684–3030* ⊠ *Free* ☉ *Daily May–Sept.*

Fodor'sChoice **Stehekin.** One of the most beautiful and secluded valleys in the Pacific ★ Northwest, Stehekin was homesteaded by hardy souls in the late 19th century. The small community, set at the northwest end of Lake Chelan, is accessible only by boat, floatplane, or trail. Year-round residents, who have intermittent outside communications, boat-delivered supplies, and just two dozen cars between them, enjoy a wilderness lifestyle—and only around 200 visitors make the trek here during the peak summer season.

VISITOR CENTERS

Chelan Ranger Station. The base for the Chelan National Recreation Area and Wenatchee National Forest has an information desk and a shop selling regional maps and books. ⊠ *Foot of Lake Chelan, Chelan* ☎ *360/854–7200* ☾ *Mon.–Sat. 7:45–4:30.*

Glacier Public Service Center. This office doubles as a headquarters for the Mt. Baker–Snoqualmie National Forest; it has maps, a book and souvenir shop, and a permits desk. The center is also right on the way to some of the park's main trailheads. ⊠ *10091 Mt. Baker Hwy., east of Glacier* ☎ *360/854–7200* ☾ *Mid-Mar.–mid-Oct., daily 8:30–4:30; 3 weekends past Thanksgiving 9–3.*

Golden West Visitor Center. Rangers here offer guidance on hiking, camping, and other activities, as well as audiovisual and children's programs and bike tours. There's also an arts and crafts gallery. Maps and concise displays explain the complicated ecology of the valley, which encompasses in its length virtually every ecosystem in the Northwest. Access is by floatplane, ferry, or trail only. ⊠ *Stehekin Valley Rd., ¼ mi north of Stehekin Landing, Stehekin* ☎ *360/854–7365* ☾ *Mid-Mar.–mid-Oct., daily 8:30–5.*

North Cascades Institute. Come here for information on park hiking, wildlife watching, horseback riding, climbing, boat rentals, and fishing, as well as classroom education and hands-on nature experiences. Guided tours staged from the center include mountain climbs, pack-train excursions, and float trips on the Skagit and Stehekin rivers. There's even a research library, a dock on Lake Diablo, an amphitheater, and overnight lodging. ⊠ *Rte. 810, at Rte. 20* ☎ *360/854–7365* ⊕ *www.ncascades.org.*

North Cascades National Park Headquarters Information Station. This is the park's major administrative center, and the place to pick up passes, permits, and information about current conditions. ⊠ *810 Rte. 20, Sedro-Woolley* ☎ *360/854–7200 Ext. 515* ☾ *Memorial Day–Oct., daily 8–4:30; Nov.–Memorial Day, weekdays 8–4:30.*

North Cascades Visitor Center. The main visitor facility for the park complex has extensive displays on surrounding landscape. Learn about the history and value of old-growth trees, the many creatures that depend on the rain forest ecology, and the effects of human activity on the ecosystem. Park rangers conduct guided hikes and junior ranger programs; check bulletin boards for schedules. ⊠ *Milepost 20, N. Cascades Hwy., Newhalem* ☎ *206/386–4495 Ext. 11* ☾ *Daily 9–5.*

Marblemount Ranger Station. The main stop to secure backcountry and climbing permits for North Cascades National Park and the Lake Chelan and Ross Lake recreational areas, this office has maps, a bookshop, and wilderness displays. Note that if you arrive after hours, there's a permit and climbing register outside. ⊠ *Ranger Station Rd., off Milepost 105, N. Cascades Hwy., Marblemount* ☎ *360/854–7245* ☾ *July–Labor Day, Sun.–Thurs. 7–6, Fri. and Sat. 7 AM–8 PM; mid-May–mid–June and Sept., Sun.–Thurs. 8–4:30, Fri. and Sat. 7–6.*

SPORTS & THE OUTDOORS

BICYCLING

Mountain bikes are permitted on all highways, unpaved back roads, and a few designated tracks around the park; however, you can't take a bike on any footpaths. Ranger stations have details on the best places to ride in each season, as well as notes on spots that are closed due to weather, mud, or other environmental factors. Note that it's $15 round-trip to bring your own bike on the Lake Chelan ferry.

OUTFITTERS & EXPEDITIONS
Discovery Bikes. You can rent mountain bikes and book breakfast rides to Stehekin Valley Ranch at a self-serve rack in front of the Courtney Log Office in Stehekin for $5 per hour, $15 a day; helmets are provided. ☎*No phone* ⊕*www.stehekindiscovery.com.*

North Cascades Stehekin Lodge. Bikes rent for $5 per hour or $40 per day, and seasonal trips can be arranged. ☎*509/682–4494* ⊕*www.stehekin.com.*

BOATING

The boundaries of North Cascades National Park touch two long and sinewy expanses: Lake Chelan in the far south, and Ross Lake, which runs toward the Canadian border. Boat ramps, some with speed- and sailboat, paddleboat, kayak, and canoe rentals, are situated all around Lake Chelan, and passenger ferries cross between towns and campgrounds. Hozomeen, accessible via a 39-mi dirt road from Canada, is the boating base for Ross Lake; the site has a large boat ramp, and a boat taxi makes drops at campgrounds all around the shoreline. Diablo Lake, in the center of the park, also has a ramp at Colonial Creek. Gorge Lake has a public ramp near the town of Diablo.

OUTFITTERS & EXPEDITIONS
Skagit Tours. Diablo Lake excursions include transportation from Seattle. ☎*206/684–3030, 206/233–2709 tour reservations* ⊕*www.skagittours.com.*

HIKING

⚠ **Black bears are often sighted along trails in the summer; do not approach them!** Back away carefully, and report sightings to the Golden West Visitor Center. Cougars, which are shy of humans and well aware of their presence, are rarely sighted in this region. Still, keep kids close and don't let them run ahead too far or lag behind on a trail. If you do spot a cougar, pick up children, have the whole group stand close together, and make yourself look as large as possible.

EASY
Happy Creek Forest Walk. Old-growth forests are the focus of this kid-friendly boardwalk route, which loops just mi through the trees right off the North Cascades Highway. Interpretive signs provide details about flora along the way. ⊠*Milepost 135, Hwy. 20.*

Rainy Pass. An easy and accessible 1-mi paved trail leads to Rainy Lake, a waterfall, and glacier-view platform. ⊠*Hwy. 20, 38 mi east of visitor center at Newhalem.*

Rock Shelter Trail. This short trail—partly boardwalk—leads to a campsite used 1,400 years ago by Native Americans; interpretive signs tell the history of human presence in the region. ⊠*Off Hwy. 20.*

★ **Skagit River Loop.** Take this flat and easy, 1⁴/₅-mi, wheelchair-accessible trail down through stands of huge, old-growth firs and cedars toward the Skagit River. ⊠*Near North Cascades Visitor Center.*

Sterling Munro Trail. Starting from the North Cascades Headquarters and Information Station, this popular introductory stroll follows a board-walk path to a lookout above the forested Picket Range peaks. ⊠*810 Hwy. 20.*

★ **Trail of the Cedars.** Only ½ mi long, this trail winds its way through one of the finest surviving stands of old-growth Western Red Cedar in Washington. Some of the trees on the path are more than 1,000 years old. ⊠*Near North Cascades Visitor Center.*

MODERATE   **Cascade Pass.** The draws of this extremely popular 3²/₃-mi, four-hour
Fodor'sChoice trail are stunning panoramas from the great mountain divide. Dozens
★   of peaks line the horizon as you make your way up the fairly flat, hairpin-turn track, the scene fronted by a blanket of alpine wildflow-ers from July to mid-August. Arrive before noon if you want a park-ing spot at the trailhead. ⊠*End of Cascade River Rd., 14 mi from Marblemount.*

Diablo Lake Trail. You can explore nearly 4 mi of waterside terrain on this moderate route, which is accessed from the Sourdough Creek park-ing lot. An excellent alternative for parties with small hikers is to take the Seattle City Light Ferry one way. ⊠*Milepost 135, Hwy. 20.*

DIFFICULT   **Thornton Lakes Trail.** A 5-mi climb into an alpine basin with two pretty lakes, this steep and strenuous hike takes about 5–6 hours round-trip. ⊠*Hwy. 20, 3 mi west of Newhalem.*

OUTFITTERS & **Alpine Ascents.** The Seattle company makes North Cascades National
EXPEDITIONS Park one of its prime excursions. ☎206/378–1927 ⊕*www.alpineas-cents.com.*

American Alpine Institute. Based in Bellingham, WA, the organization conducts training trips and guided tours of the park, as well as the Index and Leavenworth areas. ☎360/671–1505 ⊕*www.aai.cc.*

Pacific Crest Trail Association. The National Pacific Crest Hiking Track stretches from the western Canadian border all the way down to Mexico, passing through North Cascades National Park and Lake Chelan National Recreation Area along the way. The organization provides maps, route advice, and tour suggestions. ☎916/349–2109 ⊕*www.pcta.org.*

Pacific Northwest Trail Association. Some 60 mi of the magnificent Pacific Northwest Trail, which links Glacier National Park in Montana to Cape Alava on the Washington coast of Olympic National Park, passes right through North Cascades National Park and the Ross Lake National Recreation Area. Sights along the way include Ross Lake, Big Beaver Trail, and the Whatcom and Hannegan passes. The managing association has all sorts of resources, including advice on tours and independent travel. ☎877/854–9415 ⊕*www.pnt.org.*

OUTFITTERS & **Cascade Corrals.** This company organizes 2 ½-hour horseback trips to
EXPEDITIONS Coon Lake. Costs depend on experience, and English- and Western-

style riding lessons are also available. Reservations are taken at the Stehekin Log Officekiosk. ☎509/682–7742 ⊕*www.cascadecorrals.com* ☎*$40–$50 ⊙Mid-June–mid.-Sept, daily at 8:30 and 2:30.*

KAYAKING

The park's twisted waterways link remote areas with some of the most pristine and secluded mountain scenes on the continent. Bring your own kayak and you can launch from any boat ramp or beach; otherwise, companies in nearby towns and Seattle suburbs offer kayak and canoe rentals, portage, and tours. The upper basin of Lake Chelan and Ross Lakeare two well-known kayaking expanses, but dozens of smaller lakes and creeks are between them. The Stehekin River also provides many kayaking possibilities.

Ross Lake Resort. The resort rents kayaks for $37 to $48 a day and offers portage service for exploring Ross Lake. If you bring your own kayak, a drop-off/pick-up water-taxi service is available. ☎206/386–4437.

Stehekin Adventure Company. Book a two-hour trip along the lake's upper estuary and western shoreline for $35, or hire a kayak for $10–$15 an hour. Make reservations at the Stehekin Log Office. ⟁*Box 36, Stehekin* ☎*509/682–4677* ☎*Tour $30 ⊙Apr.–mid-Oct. tours daily at 10, rentals 8–5.*

RAFTING

June through August is the park's white-water season, and rafting trips run through the lower section of the Stehekin River. Along the way you'll take in views of cottonwood and pine forests, glimpses of Yawning Glacier on Magic Mountain, and placid vistas of Lake Chelan.

Stehekin Valley Ranch. Guided trips on the class III Stehekin River leave from here. ⊠*Stehekin Valley Rd., 3½ mi from Stehekin Landing, Stehekin* ☎*509/682–4677 or 800/536–0745* ☎*$35–$75 ⊙June–Sept.*

Wildwater River Tours. Half- and full-day rafting excursions take on the Skagit and Skykomish rivers, plus eight more waterways throughout Washington. Prices run $69–$84 and include transportation and a picnic. ⟁*Box 3623, Federal Way* ☎*253/939–3337.*

WINTER SPORTS

Mt. Baker, just off the park's far northwest corner, is one of the Northwest's premier skiing, snowboarding, and snowshoeing regions—the area set a U.S. record for most snow in a single season during the winter of 1998–99 (1,140 inches). The Mt. Baker Highway (Route 542) cuts through the slopes toward several major ski sites; main access is 17 mi east of the town of Glacier, and the season runs roughly from November to April. Salmon Ridge, 46 mi east of Bellingham at exit 255, has groomed trails and parking.

Stehekin is another base for winter sports. The Stehekin Valley alone has 20 mi of trails; some of the most popular are around Buckner Orchard, Coon Lake, and the Courtney Ranch (Cascade Corrals).

OUTFITTERS &   **Mt. Baker.** Off the park's northwest corner, this is the closest winter-
EXPEDITIONS   sports area, with facilities for downhill and Nordic skiing, snowboard-

ing, and other recreational ventures. The main base is the town of Glacier, 17 mi west of the slopes. Equipment, lodgings, restaurants, and tourist services are on-site. ✉*Mt. Baker Hwy. 542, 62 mi east of Bellingham* ☎*360/734–6771, 360/671–0211 for snow reports* ⊕*www.mtbaker.us* ✉*All-day lift ticket weekends and holidays $44, weekdays $37* ☺*Fri.–Sun. mid-Nov.–mid-Mar.*

Gwyn Howat, Business Office & Marketing Manager Silver Bay Inn Resort. The resort rents ski and snowshoe equipment, and puts on winter bonfires and other events for day-trippers and guests. ☎*509/682–2212 or 800/555–7781* ⊕*www.silverbayinn.com.*

Stehekin Valley Lodge. This well-known winter-sports base offers equipment rentals, tours, and activities. ☎*509/682–4677 or 800/536–0745* ⊕*www.courtneycountry.com.*

NEARBY TOWNS

Heading into North Cascades National Park from Seattle on Interstate 5 to Highway 2, **Sedro-Woolley** is the first main hub you'll encounter. Surrounded by farmlands, it's a pretty spot to stop and has basic visitor services like hotels, gas stations, and groceries. It's also home to the North Cascades National Park Headquarters. From here, it's about 40 mi to the park's western edges. Along the way, you still have a chance to stop for supplies in **Concrete**, about 20 mi from the park along Highway 2. **Marblemount** is 10 mi further east, about 12 mi west of the North Cascades Visitor Center. Its growing collection of motels, cafés, and tour outfitters draw outdoor enthusiasts each summer. The park's base town, though, is **Newhalem**, tucked right along the highway between the north and south regions. This is the place to explore the visitor center and its surrounding trails, view exhibits, and pick up maps, permits, and tour information.

Winthrop is about a 6-mi drive east of Washington Pass. This is also an outdoor-recreation base, offering activities that range from cross-country skiing to hiking, mountain biking, and white-water rafting. The resort town of **Chelan**, lakeside about 40 mi due south of Winthrop along Highway 153, is a serene summer getaway. Boating and swimming are the main activities, but it's also an access point for other small villages and campgrounds along the shoreline. **Stehekin**, at the lake's northern end, is a favorite tourist stop for its remoteness—without road connections, your only options for getting here are by boat, floatplane, or trail. A regular ferry runs between Chelan and Stehekin year-round. For more information on nearby towns, *see* town listings in this chapter.

AREA ACTIVITIES

EDUCATIONAL OFFERINGS

Skagit River Bald Eagle Interpretive Center (✉*52804 Rockport Rd., Rockport* ☎*509/853–7626* ⊕*www.skagiteagle.org*) schedules monthly programs, including lectures, classes, workshops, and performances. This is also the site of the annual Upper Skagit Bald Eagle Festival. From

December to February you can tour the on-site Fish Hatchery, which houses all five species of Northwest salmon. The facility is open 10 to 4 Friday through Sunday, Monday holidays, and daily the same hours December 26 to 31; free guided tours run weekends at 10:30, 11:30, 1:30, and 2:30.

WHERE TO EAT

There are no formal restaurants in North Cascades National Park, just a lakeside café at the North Cascades Environmental Learning Center. The only other place to eat out is in Stehekin, at the **Stehekin Valley Ranch** dining room or the **Stehekin Pastry Company** *(⇨ Where to Eat in Chelan)*; both serve simple, hearty, country-style meals and sweets. Towns within a few hours of the park on either side all have a few small eateries, and some lodgings have small dining rooms. Don't expect fancy decor or gourmet frills—just friendly service and generally delicious homemade stews, roasts, grilled fare, soups, salads, and baked goods.

PICNIC AREAS Developed picnic areas at Rainy Pass (Route 20, 38 mi east of the park visitor center) and Washington Pass (Route 20, 42 mi east of the visitor center) each have a half-dozen picnic tables, drinking water, and pit toilets. The vistas of surrounding peaks are sensational at these two overlooks. More picnic facilities are located near the visitor center in Newhalem and at Colonial Creek Campground 10 mi east of the visitor center on Highway 20.

WHERE TO STAY

Accommodations in North Cascades National Park are rustic, cozy, and comfortable. Options range from plush Stehekin lodges and homey cabin rentals to spartan Learning Center bunks and campgrounds. Expect to pay roughly $50 to $200 per night, depending on the rental size and the season—you'll be out of luck if you don't book at least three months in advance, or even a year in advance for popular accommodations in summer. Outside the park, you'll find numerous resorts, motels, bed-and-breakfasts, and even overnight boat rentals. *(⇨ Hotel and restaurant recommendations in Chelan, Marblemount, Sedro-Woolley, and Winthrop.)*

CAMPING

Tent campers can choose between forest sites, riverside spots, lake grounds, or meadow spreads encircled by mountains. Note that many campsites, particularly those around Stehekin, are completely remote and without road access anywhere—so you'll have to walk, boat, ride a horse, or take a floatplane to reach them. Most don't accept reservations, and spots fill up quickly May through September. If there's no ranger on-site, you'll often sign in yourself—be sure to always check in at a ranger station before you set out overnight. Note that some areas are occasionally closed due to flooding, forest fires, or other factors. Outside the park, each town has several managed camping spots, which can be at a formal campgrounds or in the side yard of a motel.

$ ⚠ **Ross Lake National Recreation Area.** The National Park Service maintains three upper Skagit Valley campgrounds near Newhalem. ☎360/854–7200 ⌫Reservations not accepted ▭No credit cards.

Joyce Brown, Information Receptionist, North Cascades National Park Service Complex ⚠ **Colonial Creek Campground.** In a valley setting amid old-growth forest, this campground is close to Route 20 services and Diablo Lake. A boat ramp affords easy access to the lake, and several hiking trails begin at the campground. ✉10 mi east of Newhalem on Rte. 20 ⇆130 tent sites, 32 RV sites ♿Flush toilets, dump station, drinking water, fire grates, picnic tables ⊙Mid-May–Sept. ⚠ **Goodell Creek Campground.** This forested site lies across the Skagit River from Newhalem Creek Campground, near the North Cascades Visitor Center. It's more primitive than Newhalem Creek, with pit toilets and no programs. No water is available in winter. ✉Rte. 20, ½ mi west of park visitor center turnoff ☎360/873–4590 ⇆21 tent sites ♿Pit toilets, drinking water, fire grates, picnic tables ⚠ **Newhalem Creek Campground.** With three loops, a small amphitheater, a playground, and a regular slate of ranger programs in summer, Newhalem Creek is the main North Cascades park complex campground. Perched on a bench above the Skagit River, in old-growth forest, it's adjacent to the North Cascades Visitor Center, and close to several forest and river trails. ✉Rte. 20, along the access road to the park's main visitor center ☎360/873–4590 ⇆111 RV sites ♿Flush toilets, dump station, drinking water, fire grates, picnic tables, public telephone, play area, ranger station ⊙Mid-May–mid-Oct.

¢ ⚠ **Lake Chelan National Recreation Area.** Many backcountry camping areas are accessible via park shuttles or boat. All require a free backcountry permit; 12 boat-in sites also require a $5 per day dock fee. Everything you bring must be hung on bear wires, so rethink those big coolers. Purple Point, the most popular campground due to its quick access to Stehekin Landing, has just seven tent sites, bear boxes, and nearby road access. Note that group requests must be made in writing. ✉Stehekin Landing, NPS, Box 7, Stehekin, WA ☎360/854–7200 ⊕www.nps.gov/noca/focus/focus5.htm ⇆63 tent sites ♿Pit toilets, drinking water, bear boxes ⌫Reservations not accepted ▭No credit cards.

NORTH CASCADES ESSENTIALS

ACCESSIBILITY

Visitor centers along North Cascades Highway, including the main facility in Newhalem, are open to those with mobility impairments. Accessible hikes along the highway include Sterling Munro, River Loop, and Rock Shelter, three short trails into lowland old-growth forest, all at Mile 120 along Route 20 near Newhalem; and the Happy Creek Forest Trail at Mile 134.

ADMISSION FEES

A Northwest Forest Pass, required for use of various park and National Forest facilities, such as trailheads, is $5 per vehicle for one calendar day or $30 for one year. A free wilderness permit is required for all overnight stays in the backcountry; these are available in person only. Dock permits for boat-in campgrounds are also $5 per day. Passes and permits are sold at visitor centers and ranger stations around the park area.

ADMISSION HOURS

The park never closes, but access is limited by snow in winter. Route 20 (North Cascades Highway), the major access to the park, is partially closed from mid-November to mid-April.

ATMS/BANKS

There are no ATMs in the park. Marblemount, Winthrop, and Chelan have banks with 24-hour ATMs.

AUTOMOBILE SERVICE STATIONS

No gas or service stations are between Marblemount and Mazama.

LOST & FOUND

The park's lost and found is at the visitor center in Newhalem.

POST OFFICES

There are no post offices in the park.

Contacts **Marblemount Post Office** (⊠ *60096 Rte. 20, Marblemount* ☎ *360/873-2125*)

PUBLIC TELEPHONES & RESTROOMS

Public telephones and restrooms are found at the North Cascades Visitor Center and Skagit Information Center in Newhalem; and at the Golden West Visitor Center and North Cascades Stehekin Lodge in Stehekin.

TRANSPORTATION

Contacts **Chelan Air** (✉ *Box W, Chelan 98816* ☎ *509/682-5555* ⊕ *www.chelanairways.com* ✉ *$159 round-trip*). Brick Wellman, Pilot (office manager, floor sweeper, etc.). **Lake Chelan Boat Company** (⊠ *1418 W. Woodin Ave., Chelan* ☎ *509/682-4584, 509/682-4444 info line* ⊕ *www.ladyofthelake.com* ✉ *$38–$102*). **Mountain Transporter** (☎ *509/996-8294 or 866/638-4691* ⊕ *www.mountaintransporter.com*). **Stehekin Adventures Shuttle Bus** (☎ *360/854-7200* ⊕ *www.nps.gov/noca/focus/focus.htm* ✉ *$5 one way* ▤ *No credit cards* ⊙ *Mid-May–mid-Oct.*). **Stehekin Pastry Company** (☎ *No phone* ⊕ *www.stehekinvalley.com/pastryco.htm* ✉ *$1* ▤ *No credit cards* ⊙ *Mid-May–mid-Oct.*).

VISITOR INFORMATION

Contacts **North Cascades National Park Headquarters and Information Station** (⊠ *810 Rte. 20, Sedro-Woolley, WA 98284* ☎ *360/854-7200* ⊕ *www.nps.gov/noca*).

¢–$ ╳**Heenan's Burnt Finger Bar-B-Q & Steak House.** Slow-smoked, meaty ribs and chicken generously slathered in tangy sauce are the specialties of this regional favorite. Sidled up to the Methow River, the restaurant provides sweeping views of the water, the valley, and the farmlands beyond. There's something for everyone, including milder sauces for kids and salads or vegetarian chilies for non–meat eaters. It's a spot for relaxing, either in the cozy, rustic dining rooms or outside by the grill. The dance floor opens on weekends, and summers bring cowboys playing guitars or Native American flute music. ☒*716 Hwy. 20 S.* ☎*509/996–8221* ▭*MC, V.*

¢–$ ╳**Winthrop Brewery.** The long, one-room pub sits between the town's main street and the river, and the garlicky aromas of bar food and pizzas entice from a block away. Small wood tables line one wall; the bar occupies the other. While you're waiting for big burgers, fish-and-chips, or chicken Caesar salad, sip your Grizzly Pie Honey Rye or Hop-Along Red Ale and have a look at the action-hero pictures (Clint, Mel, John Wayne included) and the arsenal of hunting equipment. Tip: The seasoned fries are the best in the Northwest. ☒*155 Riverside Ave.* ☎*360/996–3183.*

¢ ╳**Sheri's Sweet Shoppe.** Tucked into this Wild West–style clapboard building is a haven of treats for all ages: myriad candy bins, jars stuffed with lollipops and licorice, boxes of chocolate, and an endless arrangement of trinkets. The homemade ice cream might be slightly more nutritious, but it tastes just as vibrantly sinful. Shady tables on the patio provide respite for grownups—and saddle-topped stools for the kids. ☒*Main St.* ☎*509/996–3834* ▭*No credit cards.*

WHERE TO STAY

$$$–$$$$ ▦**Sun Mountain Lodge.** A hilltop location gives guests panoramic views of the Cascade Mountains and Methow Valley; some rooms face Mt. Gardner or Mt. Robinson. Accommodations mirror the lodge-style elegance of the main building; many have a fireplace, kitchen facilities, CD player, and a private deck. Luxury cabins are off-site, 1½ mi below on the Patterson lakefront. Miles of hiking, horseback-riding, and ski trails are nearby; afterward, you can indulge your sore muscles at the spa. The conference center is a hub for business away from the grind. The restaurant ($$–$$$$), with snowy mountain views from every table, serves Northwest fare and has a private wine cellar. **Pros:** Magnificent lodgings and facilities, many activities. **Cons:** Not always family-friendly. ☒*604 Patterson Lake Rd., Winthrop* ☎*509/996–2211 or 800/572–0493* ☐*509/996–3133* ⊕*www.sunmountainlodge. com* ⇱*98 rooms, 17 cabins* ♿*In-room: kitchen (some), refrigerator (some), no TV. In-hotel: restaurant, room service, bar, tennis court, pools, spa, bicycles, Wi-Fi, children's programs (ages 4–10)* ▭*AE, DC, MC, V.*

$$$ ▦**Freestone Inn.** At the heart of a 120-acre farm amid more than 2 mil-
★ lion acres of forest, this rustic resort embraces luxury in a pioneer-style setting. The massive log-cabin main building holds simple, spacious guest rooms, each done in Northwest colors and enhanced with a gas fireplace, hot tub, and balcony. Several spacious lodges stand lakeside, and wood-paneled cabins snuggle up to Early Winters Creek; some

have stone fireplaces, others have wrought-iron fireplaces and decks over the water. The inn houses a vast library, a Great Room with a three-story fireplace, and a restaurant serving Northwest cuisine. Jack's Hut Adventure Center organizes everything from hot-air balloon trips and mountaineering expeditions to sleigh rides and children's activities. Note that this is also one of the Northwest's top heli-skiing bases. **Pros:** Beautiful setting, myriad activities, very family-friendly, close to Winthrop. **Cons:** A bit off the beaten path. ⊠*31 Early Winters Dr., Mazama* ☎*509/996–3906 or 800/639–3809* 🖷*509/996–3907* ⊕*www.freestoneinn.com* ↩*21 rooms, 15 cabins, 5 lodges* ♦*In-room: no a/c (some), kitchen (some), refrigerator, VCR, dial-up. In-hotel: restaurant, pool, bicycles, some pets allowed, no elevator* ▤*AE, MC, V.*

¢   🖳**Virginian Resort.** Named for the Owen Wister novel detailing stories of the lives of the area's homesteaders, this tranquil clutch of log buildings on the Methow River provides accommodations in a pristine backcountry setting. Small, simple, no-frills rooms have timber beams and wood paneling; some have kitchens or look out to the river. Cozy cabins are scattered around the lawn, with picnic tables outside. The rustic Virginian Restaurant (¢–$$), full of curio cupboards and antique farming implements, serves American fare near the crackling fireplace. To get here, look for the covered wagon about a mile outside of Winthrop. ⊠*808 N. Cascades Hwy.,* ☎*509/996–2535 or 800/854–2834* 🖷*509/999–2468* ⊕*www.virginian-resort.com* ↩*37 rooms* ♦*In-room: no a/c. In-hotel: no phone, kitchen, no TV (some), restaurant, pool, some pets allowed, no elevator* ▤*MC, V* ☉*Closed Oct.–Apr.*

CHELAN

61 mi south of Winthrop.

Long before the first American settlers arrived at the long, narrow lake, Chelan (sha-*lan*) was the site of a Chelan Indian winter village. The Indians would range far and wide on their horses in spring and summer, following the newly sprouting grass from the river bottoms into the mountains; in winter they converged in permanent villages to feast, perform sacred rituals, and wait out the cold weather and snow. During the winter 1879–80, Chelan served briefly as an army post, but the troops were soon transferred to Ft. Spokane. American settlers arrived in the 1880s.

Today Chelan serves as the favorite beach resort of western Washingtonians. In summer Lake Chelan is one of the hottest places in Washington, with temperatures often soaring above 100°F. The mountains surrounding the 55-mi-long fjordlike lake rise from a height of about 4,000 feet near Chelan to 8,000 and 9,000 feet near the town of Stehekin, at the head of the lake. There is no road circling the lake, so the only way to see the whole thing is by boat or floatplane. Several resorts line the lake's eastern (and warmer) shore. Its northwestern end, at Stehekin, just penetrates North Cascades National Park. South of the lake, 9,511-foot Bonanza Peak is the tallest nonvolcanic peak in Washington.

Lake Chelan State Park, right on the lake and 9 mi west of Chelan on the opposite (less crowded) shore, is a favorite hangout for folks from the cool west side of the Cascades who want to soak up some sun. There are docks, a boat ramp, RV sites with full hookups, and lots of campsites for those who prefer a less "citified" approach to camping. ⊠*U.S. 97A, west to South Shore Dr. or Navarre Coulee Rd.* ☎*800/452–5687* ⊕*www.parks. wa.gov* ⊠*$5* ⊗*Memorial Day–Labor Day, daily 6:30* AM*–10* PM*; Labor Day–Memorial Day, weekends 8–5.*

Directly north of Lake Chelan State Park, **Twenty-Five Mile Creek State Park** also abuts the lake's eastern shore. It has many of the same facilities as the park in Chelan, as well as a swimming pool. Because it's the more remote of the two, it's often less crowded. ⊠*South Shore Dr.* ☎*509/687–3610 or 800/452–5687* ⊕*www.parks.wa.gov* ⊠*$5* ⊗*Apr.–Sept., daily dawn–dusk.*

Lake Chelan Boat Company (⊠*1418 W. Woodin Ave., Chelan* ☎*509/682–4584* ⊕*www.ladyofthelake.com*) connects Chelan to Stehekin and stops at lakeside campgrounds along the way. The *Lady of the Lake* departs from Chelan at 8:30, returning at 6, twice daily June through September and once daily the rest of the year; tickets are $39 round-trip, half price for those 2 to 11. The company's speedy catamaran, *Lady Express,* also runs between Stehekin, Holden Village, the national park, and Lake Chelan; tickets are $59. Connections run daily June to October; Monday, Wednesday, Friday, and Sunday November to mid-March; daily through April, and weekends in May.

In one of the most beautiful and secluded valleys in the Pacific Northwest, **Stehekin** was homesteaded by hardy souls in the late 19th century. It's not really a town but rather a small community at the north end of Lake Chelan. There's no road; access is by boat or floatplane or on foot. A few facilities serve about 200 summer visitors. Year-round residents enjoy a wilderness lifestyle—there are barely two dozen cars in the whole valley, outside communication is iffy, especially in winter, and supplies arrive once or twice a week by boat.

Buckner Homestead. Founded in 1912, this pioneer farm includes an apple orchard, farmhouse, barn, and many ranch buildings, which are slowly being restored by the National Park Service. ⊠*Stehekin Valley Rd., 3½ mi from Stehekin Landing, Stehekin* ☎*360/854–7635 Ext. 340 then press 14* ⊗*June–Sept., daily 9–5.*

Rangers at the **Purple Point Information Center** offer guidance on hiking and camping and information about the national parks and recreation areas. This is a good place to pick up permits and passes. Maps and concise displays explain the complicated ecology of the valley, which encompasses in its length virtually every ecosystem in the Northwest. Hours vary in spring and fall. ⊠*Stehekin Valley Rd., ¼ mi north of Stehekin Landing, Stehekin* ☎*360/856–5700 Ext. 340 then press 14* ⊗*Mid-Mar.–mid-Oct., daily 8:30–5.*

¢–$$ ✕**Stehekin Valley Ranch.** The rustic log ranch house is a tourist favor-ite, where meaty dinner buffets are eaten at long, polished log tables. Entrées include steak, ribs, hamburgers, salad, beans, and dessert. Breakfast is served for riders on the early Discovery Bikes tour, and lunch is guests-only. Note: Dinner is served 5:30 to 6:30; make reser-vations at the Stehekin Landing kiosk, and catch the round-trip shuttle ($3) at the landing. The friendly owners and upbeat crowds make this a fun and nourishing experience for all ages. ⊠*Stehekin Valley Rd., 9 mi north of Stehekin Landing, Stehekin* ☎*509/682–4677 or 800/536–0745* ▤*MC, V* ☉*Closed Oct.–June.*

¢ ✕**Stehekin Pastry Company.** Enter this lawn-framed timber chalet and you're is immersed in the tantalizing aromas of a European bakery. Glassed-in display cases are filled with trays of homemade baked goods, and the pungent espresso is eye-opening. Sit down at a window-side table and dig into an over-filled sandwich or rich bowl of soup—and you'll never taste a better slice of pie, with fruit fresh-picked from local orchards. Although it's outside of town, the shop is conveniently en route to Rainbow Falls and adjacent to the Norwegian Fjord Horses stables, which also makes it a popular ice-cream stop for summertime sightseers. ⊠*Stehekin Valley Rd., about 2 mi from Stehekin Land-ing, on way to Rainbow Falls, Stehekin* ☎*509/682–4677* ▤*No credit cards* ☉*Closed mid-Oct.–June.*

¢ ✕**Ship 'n' Shore Drive/Boat In.** The casual "dining room" here consists of dockside picnic tables, where hamburgers, hot dogs, and seafood baskets are local favorites. On hot days kids line up for sweets. When it's open, it's like the ice cream truck is driving down the street, with hoardes of hungry patrons clamoring for the next order. ⊠*1230 W. Woodin Ave., Chelan* ☎*509/682–5125* ☉*Closed Labor Day–Memo-rial Day.*

$$$–$$$$ ▦**Campbell's Resort.** Open for more than a century, this sand-color apartment-style resort sits on landscaped grounds alongside Lake Chelan. Every room has cooking facilities and a balcony or patio with lake views. Two-bedroom cabins with a kitchen and porch are on the east side of the property, near the marina. The elegant House Café ($–$$), with hardwood walls and a nautical feel, serves Northwest fare and wines in an elegant atmosphere; the second-floor Pub and Veranda, with views over the lake, dishes out simpler meals. The parklike, fam-ily-friendly setting includes pristine beaches, picnic areas, barbecues, and lots of room to romp. **Pros:** Lots of activity, but also tranquil spaces. **Cons:** Kicks into typical vacation-condo mode in high season. ⊠*104 W. Woodin Ave., Chelan* ☎*509/682–2561 or 800/553–8225* ☏*509/682–2177* ⊕*www.campbellsresort.com* ⇨*168 rooms, 2 cot-tages* ⌂*In-room: kitchen (some), refrigerator, dial-up, Wi-Fi. In-hotel: restaurant, bar, 2 pools, gym, 2 spas, children's summer programs (ages 4–15)* ▤*AE, MC, V.*

$$ ▦**Stehekin Landing Resort.** The setting is a ranch-style motel stretched out right in front of the water, where simple rooms are comfortable and inexpensive. There's also the large, four-bedroom Lake House, which

has a laundry and hot tub. Fine Northwest fare is served in the restaurant, the area's only dining venue set before a full panorama of Lake Chelan. Fly-in/fly-out day trips are popular, and year-round seasonal packages combine accommodations, boat fare across Lake Chelan, a bus tour, mainland parking, and sports equipment. **Pros:** Central location, good prices, helpful management. **Cons:** Bustling with crowds in summer. ⊠ *At Stehekin Landing* ⌂ *Box 457, Stehekin Landing, Chelan* ☎ *509/682–4494* ⊕ *www.stehekinlanding.com* ⏎ *27 rooms, 1 house* ⌂ *In-room: no a/c, no phone, kitchen (some), no TV. In-hotel: restaurant, no elevator* ═ *D, MC, V.*

SPORTS & THE OUTDOORS

On a scenic half-day raft trip you can traverse the lower section of the Stehekin River, which winds through cottonwood and pine forest, from Yawning Glacier on the slopes of Magic Mountain southeast to Lake Chelan. From June through September guided trips on Class III waters leave from the **Stehekin Valley Ranch** (⊠ *Stehekin Valley Rd., 3½ mi from Stehekin Landing, Stehekin* ☎ *509/682–4677 or 800/536–0745*). Trip prices are $35–$75.

Mountain bikers also make their way into this rugged terrain. **North Cascades Stehekin Lodge** (☎ *509/682–4494* ⊕ *www.stehekin.com*) rents bikes for $5 per hour or $40 per day, and organizes seasonal trips.

WENATCHEE

39 mi southwest of Chelan.

Wenatchee (we-*nat*-chee), the county seat of Chelan County, is an attractive city in a shallow valley at the confluence of the Wenatchee and Columbia rivers. Surrounded by orchards, Wenatchee is known as the "Apple Capital of Washington." Downtown has many old commercial buildings as well as apple-packing houses where visitors can buy locally grown apples by the case (at about half the price charged in supermarkets). The paved Apple Valley Recreation Loop Trail runs on both sides of the Columbia River. It crosses the river on bridges at the northern and southern ends of town and connects several riverfront parks. The Wenatchee section is lighted until midnight.

The town was built on an ancient Wenatchi Indian village, which may have been occupied as long ago as 11,000 years, as recent archaeological finds of Clovis hunter artifacts suggest. (The Clovis hunters, also known as Paleo-Indians, were members of the oldest tribes known to have inhabited North America.)

The **Wenatchee Valley Museum & Cultural Center** has displays of local Indian and pioneer artifacts, as well as Northwest artist exhibits. ⊠ *127 S. Mission St.* ☎ *509/888–6240* ⊕ *www.wenatcheewa.gov* ⏎ *$5* ⊙ *Tues.–Sat. 10–4.*

Rocky Reach Dam has a museum and visitors center as well as picnic tables and elaborately landscaped grounds. The Gallery of the Columbia has the pilothouse of the late-19th-century Columbia River steamer

Bridgeport, replicas of Indian dwellings, and Indian, logger, and railroad workers' tools. The Gallery of Electricity has exhibits explaining why dams are good for you. ⊠ *U.S. 97A N, about 10 mi north of Wenatchee* ☎ *509/663–7522 or 509/663–8121* ⌨ *Free* ⊙ *Park, daily dawn–dusk. Museum, daily 8:30–5. Visitor center, daily 8:30–5:30.*

Okanogan-Wenatchee National Forest, a pine forest, covers 2.2 million acres, from the eastern slopes of the Cascades to the crest of the Wenatchee Mountains and north to Lake Chelan. Camping, hiking, boating, fishing, hunting, and picnicking are popular activities. ⊠ *215 Melody La., Wenatchee* ☎ *509/662–4335* ⊕ *www.fs.fed.us/r6/ wenatchee* ⌨ *$5 daily parking pass, or $30 Northwest Forest Pass* ⊙ *Daily 24 hrs.*

WHERE TO STAY & EAT

$–$$ ✕ **The Windmill.** The comfortable old roadhouse, gamely topped by a windmill, opened in 1937. Here it's all about home-style food, particularly steak: famous entrées include whiskey pepper steak (peppercoated New York strip sautéed, flamed with whiskey, and finished with mushrooms in a rich demi-glace) and the marinated tenderloin chunks. Seafood isn't overlooked, though; try the charbroiled salmon coated with apple brandy barbecue sauce. Save room for fresh-baked pies and regional wines. ⊠ *1501 N. Wenatchee Ave.* ☎ *509/665–9529* ⌨ *Reservations not accepted* ⊟ *AE, DC, MC, V* ⊙ *No lunch.*

$ ⌂ **Coast Wenatchee Center Hotel.** A skywalk links this hotel to a convention center. Although it tends to attract business travelers, the Coast Wenatchee has enough facilities and amenities to appeal to vacationing families. Rooms are tidy and comfortable, and suites have a kitchenette. The ninth-floor restaurant serves a blend of American and European fare from breakfast until late. You can walk from the hotel to the riverfront park and downtown. **Pros:** Convenient access to local sights and activities. **Cons:** Standard hotel atmosphere. ⊠ *201 N. Wenatchee Ave.,* ☎ *509/662–1234* ⊟ *509/662–0782* ⊕ *www. coasthotels.com* ⇆ *147 rooms* ⌂ *In-room: dial-up. In-hotel: Wi-Fi (some), restaurant, bar, pools, spa, airport shuttle, some pets allowed* ⊟ *AE, D, DC, MC, V.*

$ ⌂ **Warm Springs Inn Bed & Breakfast.** Roses planted along the driveway lead you to this 1917 mansion amid 10 acres of gardens and trees. The rooms, some of which look out onto the Wenatchee River, are filled with a tasteful selection of art and antiques. The Chandelier Suite is the largest, bedecked with the glittering namesake lamp and complete with a private bath and attached twin bedroom. The Garden Room, done in pastel yellows and blues, has a four-poster bed and a shower. The River Room and the Autumn Leaf Room, both on the lower level, share a hot tub and have private entrances along a riverside deck. Larger extended-stay apartments and a cottage are also available. **Pros:** charming, quiet setting. **Cons:** wedding bookings fill rooms far in advance. ⊠ *1611 Love La.,* ☎ *509/662–8365 or 800/543–3645* ⊟ *509/663– 5997* ⊕ *www.warmspringsinn.com* ⇆ *6 rooms* ⌂ *In-room: no a/c. In-hotel: no phone., some pets allowed, no kids under 10, no elevator* ⊟ *AE, D, MC, V* ⍟ *BP.*

SPORTS & THE OUTDOORS

Four lifts, 33 downhill runs, powder snow, and some 30 mi of marked cross-country trails make **Mission Ridge Ski Area** one of Washington's most popular ski areas. There's a 2,100-foot vertical drop, and the snowmaker scatters whiteness from the top to bottom slopes during the season. Snowboarding is allowed. Lift tickets cost $42 per day, but look for deals like the Bomber Card, which gives you discounted and direct lift access for $59. (Note: The pass takes its name from the Bomber Bowl, a ski run where a B-52 bomber crashed on the slopes during World War II.) ⊠*7500 Mission Ridge Rd.* ☎*509/663–6543, 800/374–1693 snow conditions* ⊕*www.missionridge.com* ☉*Dec.–Apr., Thurs.–Mon. 9–4.*

CASHMERE

11 mi northwest of Wenatchee.

Surrounded by snow-capped mountain peaks, Cashmere is one of Washington's oldest towns, founded by Oblate missionaries back in 1853, when the Wenatchi and their vast herds of horses still roamed free over the bunch grasslands of the region. Some of the great Wenatchi leaders are buried in the mission cemetery. Today Cashmere is the apple, apricot, and pear capital of the Wenatchee Valley.

Aplets and Cotlets/Liberty Orchards Co., Inc. was founded by two Armenian brothers who escaped the massacres of Armenians by Turks early in the 20th century, settled in this peaceful valley, and became orchardists. When a marketing crisis hit the orchards in the 1920s, the brothers remembered dried-fruit confections from their homeland, re-created them, and named them aplets (made from apples) and cotlets (made from apricots). Sales took off almost immediately, and today aplets and cotlets are known as the combination that made Cashmere famous. Free samples are offered during the 15-minute tour of the plant. ⊠*117 Mission St.* ☎*509/782–2191* ⊕*www.libertyorchards.com* ☜*Free* ☉*Daily 8–5:30, tours every 20 min.*

The **Chelan County Historical Museum and Pioneer Village** has an excellent collection of Indian artifacts, as well as 20 pre-1900 Chelan County buildings that were reassembled here and furnished with period furniture and other historic objects. ⊠*600 Cotlets Way* ☎*509/782–3230* ☜*$4.50* ☉*Mar.–Oct. 1, daily 9:30–4:30; Nov.–Dec. 21, Fri.–Sun. 11–3.*

LEAVENWORTH

11 mi northwest of Cashmere, 134 mi east of Seattle.

Leavenworth is one of Seattle's favorite weekend getaways, and it's easy to see why: the charming (if occasionally *too* cute) Bavarian-style village, home to good restaurants and attractive lodgings, is a hub for some of the Northwest's best skiing, hiking, rock climbing, rafting, canoeing, and snowshoeing.

A railroad and mining center for many years, Leavenworth fell on hard times around the 1960s, and civic leaders, looking for ways to capitalize on the town's setting in the heart of the Central Cascade Range, convinced shopkeepers and other businesspeople to maintain a gingerbread-Bavarian architectural style in their buildings. Today, even the Safeway supermarket and the Chevron gas station carry out the theme. Restaurants prepare Bavarian-influenced dishes, candy shops sell Swiss-style chocolates, and stores and boutiques stock music boxes, dollhouses, and other Bavarian items.

Settled into the 19th-century, barn-style Big Haus, the **Leavenworth Upper Valley Museum** (⊠ *347 Division St.* ☎ *509/548–0728*) invokes pioneer days in the Cascades. The riverside grounds were once Arabian stallion-grazing terrain, and Audubon programs take advantage of plentiful bird sightings. Exhibits highlight the lives and times of the Field family, local Native American tribes, and other prominent residents of Leavenworth and the Upper Wenatchee Valley. The gallery is open 11 to 5 Thursday through Sunday and holiday Mondays; admission is by donation. The **Nutcracker Museum** (⊠ *735 Front St.* ☎ *509/548–4573 or 800/892–3989*), which contains more than 5,000 kinds of antique and modern nutcrackers, is housed in the Nussknacker House, a shop selling nutcrackers and other knickknacks. The store is open daily 10 to 6, the museum 2 to 5 daily May through October, and weekends November through April. Admission is $2.50.

Icicle Junction is an amusement arcade in the wilderness replete with miniature golf, a rock wall, a movie theater, and other activities. ⊠ *565 Hwy. 2, at Icicle Rd.* ☎ *509/5482400 or 800/558–2438* ⊕ *www. iciclejunction.com* ☉ *Park, Mon.–Thurs. noon–9, Fri.–Sun. 10–9. Train, weekdays noon–5, weekends 10–6.*

At the **National Fish Hatchery,** Chinook salmon are released into the river in the hope they will return someday to spawn and keep the species alive while still providing fish to catch. Even if nothing's spawning, the view of millions of eggs in the nursery or thousands of small, four-inch "fries" wriggling in the aquarium is something to see. ⊠ *12790 Fish Hatchery Rd.* ☎ *509/548–7641* ⊡ *Free* ☉ *Daily 8–4.*

The **Marlin Handbell Ringers** (☎ *509/548–4319* ⊕ *www.marlinhandbells. com*) keep alive an 18th-century English tradition that evolved into a musical form. Eleven ringers play 108 bells covering 5½ chromatic octaves. The bells are rung as part of the town's Christmas festivities and also in early May.

WHERE TO EAT

$–$$ ✕ **Andreas Keller German Restaurant.** Merry "oompah" music bubbles out from marching accordion players at this fun-focused dining hub, where the theme is "Germany without the Passport." Laughing crowds lap up strong, cold brews and feast on a selection of brat-, knack-, weiss-, and mettwursts, polish sausage, and wienerschnitzel, all nestled into heaping sides of sauerkraut, tangy German potato salad, and thick, dark rye bread. Get a taste of it all with the sampler plate—and save room for the knockout apple strudel. Note that service can be slow at times, so just sit back and enjoy the ambience. ⊠*829 Front St.* ☎*509/548–6000* ▤*AE, D MC, V.*

$–$$ ✕**Cafe Mozart.** This café looks like the upstairs apartments of a cen-
★ tral European town house: it captures the essence of Gemütlichkeit (coziness) in the way the small dining rooms are decorated and the curtains are cut, as well as with the authentic aromas that drift from the kitchen. The food is superb, with ingredients blending together beautifully. Menu highlights include slow-roasted duck with pear and raspberry confiture, pork medallions accompanied by flavorful red cabbage, and chicken breast topped with Black Forest ham and melted Gouda cheese. A harpist plays during weekend dinners. ⊠*829 Front St.* ☎*509/548–0600* ▤*AE, D, MC, V.*

WHERE TO STAY

$$$–$$$$ ⊡**Run of the River.** This intimate, relaxed mountain inn stands on the
★ banks of the Icicle River near Leavenworth, placing the rustic rooms with timber furnishings close to nature. The largest, the Tumwater Suite, has two wood stoves, a loft, and a private deck overlooking the river's cascading torrents. Other rooms have views of the Pinnacles (a dramatic rock formation), an aspen grove, meadows (where deer browse), or Icicle and Tumwater canyons. Ravenwood Lodge is a spacious, chalet-style luxury retreat complete with a full kitchen, river-rock fireplace, and loft bedroom. Cushy bathrobes, a fireplace, a jetted tub, a DVD player, and an old-fashioned typewriter are in every room. **Pros:** Close to town, abundant healthy breakfasts, lots of outdoor activities. **Cons:** Not for techno-enthusiasts. ⊠*9308 E. Leavenworth Rd.,* ☎*509/548–7171 or 800/288–6491* 🖷*509/548–7547* ⊕*www.runoftheriver.com* ➟*6 rooms, 1 lodge* ♿*In-hotel: Wi-Fi, no kids under 16* ▤*AE, D, MC, V* ⏐◎⏐*BP.*

$–$$$ ⊡**Mountain Home Lodge.** This contemporary mountain inn, built of sturdy cedar and redwood, sits amid a 20-acre alpine meadow with breathtaking Cascade Mountains views. Peeled-pine and vine-maple furniture fill the rooms, which also contain handmade quilts, binoculars, robes, and port wine; self-contained cabins are also available. Forty miles of trails thread through the property, and sports options range from hiking and skiing to tennis and horseshoes. Winter rates include all meals, plus Sno-Cat transportation from the parking lot below. **Pros:** Pristine luxury, high-quality sports and activities. **Cons:** Tough winter transport. ⊠*Mountain Home Rd., 3 mi south of Leavenworth,* ☎*509/548–7077 or 800/414–2378* 🖷*509/548–5008* ⊕*www.mthome.com* ➟*10 rooms, 2 cabins* ♿*In-room: no a/c. In-hotel: Wi-Fi, no phone, no TV, tennis courts, pool, spa, no kids under 16, no elevator* ▤*D, MC, V* ⏐◎⏐*BP.*

¢–$$ ⊡**Haus Rohrbach.** Unobstructed views at this alpine-style B&B take in the village and the valley. Some rooms have king-size beds, balconies, and separate sitting areas. Two suites also have coffeemakers and other amenities. The full breakfast typically includes Dutch babies (a sweet, fluffy omelet) or sourdough pancakes and sausage. ⊠*12882 Ranger Rd.,* ☎*509/548–7024 or 800/548–4477* 🖷*509/548–5038* ⊕*www.hausrohrbach.com* ➟*5 rooms, 5 suites* ♿*In-room: no a/c. In-hotel:*

no phone, refrigerator (some), no TV (some), pool, no elevator $\boxminus$ *AE, D, DC, MC, V* †◎│*BP.*

SPORTS & THE OUTDOORS

GOLF   **Leavenworth Golf Club** ($\boxtimes$ *9101 Icicle Rd.* ☎*509/548–7267*) has an 18-hole, par-71 course. The greens fee is $20, plus $20 for an optional cart.

HIKING   The Leavenworth Ranger District has more than 320 mi of scenic trails, among them Hatchery Creek, Icicle Ridge, the Enchantments, Tumwater Canyon, Fourth of July Creek, Snow Lake, Stuart Lake, and Chatter Creek. Both of the following sell the Northwest Forest pass ($5 day pass; $30 annual pass), which is required year-round for parking at trailheads and for camping in the upper Chiwawa Valley. The **Lake Wenatchee Ranger Station** ($\boxtimes$ *22976 Hwy. 207* ☎*509/763–3101*) provides updates on trails and fire closures. Contact the **Leavenworth Ranger District** ($\boxtimes$ *600 Sherburne St.* ☎*509/782–1413*) for information on area hikes.

HORSEBACK   Rent horses by the hour, or take daylong rides (including lunch) or
RIDING   overnight pack trips ($26–$100) at **Eagle Creek Ranch** ($\boxtimes$ *7951 Eagle Creek Rd.* ☎*509/548–7798*). **Icicle Outfitters & Guides** ($\boxtimes$ *7373 Icicle Rd.* ☎*800/497–3912* ⊕*www.icicleoutfitters.com*) has 2- to 4-mi trail rides ($24–$42 per person), daylong rides ($130), and overnight pack trips ($300–650). **Mountain Springs Lodge** ($\boxtimes$ *19115 Chiwawa Loop Rd.* ☎*509/763–2713 or 800/858–2276* ⊕*www.mtsprings.com*) offers horseback rides from 40 minutes to all day ($16–$150) long, as well as daytime sleigh rides ($16), moonlight dinner sleigh rides ($45), and snowmobile tours one to four hours long ($55–$150).

SKIING   More than 20 mi of cross-country ski trails lace the Leavenworth area. In winter enjoy a Nordic ski jump, snowboarding, tubing, and really great downhill and cross-country skiing at **Leavenworth Ski Hill** ($\boxtimes$ *Ski Hill Dr.* ☎*509/548–5807* ⊕*www.skileavenworth.com*). In summer enjoy the wildflowers or view the Leavenworth Summer Theatre's production of *The Sound of Music*. The ski hill is 1 mi north of downtown Leavenworth. The Play All Day Pass is $12; there's also a Nordic Day Pass ($8), an Alpine Day Pass ($10), and a Tubing Pass ($7).

Stevens Pass ($\boxtimes$ *Summit Stevens Pass, U.S. 2, Skykomish* ☎*360/973–2441 or 360/634–1645* ⊕*www.stevenspass.com*) has snowboarding and cross-country skiing as well as 36 major downhill runs and slopes for skiers of every level. Lift tickets cost $44.

WHITE-WATER   Rafting is popular from March to July; the prime high-country runoff
RAFTING   occurs in May and June. The Wenatchee River, which runs through Leavenworth, is considered one of the best white-water rivers in the state—a Class III on the International Canoeing Association scale.

Alpine Adventures (☎*206/323–1220 or 800/723–8386* ⊕*www.alpine adventures.com*) conducts challenging white-water and relaxing river floats through spectacular scenery. An all-day Wenatchee River drift costs $75 (lunch included); a half-day drift is $50 (no lunch). The Methow River drift is $80. **Blue Sky Outfitters** (☎*509/682–8026*

⊕*www.blueskyoutfitters.com*) makes half- and full-day rafting trips on the Methow and Wenatchee rivers.

Osprey Rafting Co. (⊠*Icicle Rd.* ☎*509/548–6800 or 800/743–6269* ⊕*www.ospreyrafting.com*) offers 4½-hour trips on the Wenatchee River for $65, which includes wet suits and booties, transportation, and lunch; a $50, two-hour trip includes gear and transportation but no lunch.

NORTHWESTERN WASHINGTON ESSENTIALS

BY AIR

In this part of the state there are too few flights going to too few places. Of the region's many airports, only Pangborn Memorial in East Wenatchee and Bellingham International have commercial flights (on Horizon Air); the rest only serve charter planes. Thanks to this limited service—as well as to prohibitive fares—it's best to fly into Seattle and rent a car to head north.

Horizon Air has service to Bellingham International Airport and Wenatchee's Pangborn Memorial Airport. Kenmore Air can arrange charter floatplanes to Whidbey Island from Seattle. San Juan Airlines links the mainland towns with Friday Harbor, Lopez Village, and Orcas Island in the San Juan Islands. On-demand (and very expensive) service between Chelan and Stehekin is available by charter floatplane through Chelan Airways; the scenic flight takes about 45 minutes.

Contacts Anacortes Airport (⊠*4000 Airport Rd., Anacortes* ☎*360/293–4691*). **Bellingham International Airport** (⊠*4255 Mitchell Way, Bakerview Exit off I–5, Bellingham* ☎*360/671–5674*). **Chelan Air** (✏*Box W, Chelan 98816* ☎*509/682–5555* ⊕*www.chelanairways.com* ✉*$159 round-trip*). **Horizon Air** (☎*800/547–9308* ⊕*www.horizonair.com*). **Kenmore Air** (☎*206/486–1257 or 800/543–9595* ⊕*www.kenmoreair.com*). **Lake Chelan Airport** (⊠*32 Airport Way, Chelan* ☎*509/682–5976*). **Pangborn Memorial Airport** (⊠*1 Pangborn Dr., East Wenatchee* ☎*509/884–4912*). **Skagit Regional Airport** (⊠*15400 Airport Dr., Burlington* ☎*360/757–0011*). **San Juan Airlines** (☎*800/874–4434* ⊕*www. sanjuanairlines.com*).

AIRPORTS & TRANSFERS **Contacts A Cab N Courier** (⊠*Wenatchee* ☎*509/886–4222*). **Airporter** (⊠*Bellingham* ☎*866/235–5247* ⊕*www.airporter.com*). **Taxi Services** (⊠*Bellingham* ☎*360/733–8294*).

BY BOAT & FERRY

Victoria/San Juan Cruises sends *Island Commuter* ferries from the Bellingham Cruise Terminal to Friday Harbor and Victoria from May through September. There's a whale-watching-only option ($39), or you can continue on to Victoria, where you'll spend five hours and enjoy a buffet on the way back ($79).

Washington State Ferries connect Mukilteo (20 mi north of Seattle off I–5 at Exit 189) with Clinton, at the south end of Whidbey Island. Walk-on passengers pay only for the westward leg of the trip. Ferries leave roughly every half hour, more erratically off-season. Ferries also run from Port Townsend, at the tip of the Olympic Peninsula, to Keystone, at Whidbey's midpoint. The ride is 20 minutes one-way.

Contacts **Victoria/San Juan Cruises** (☎ 360/738–8099 or 800/443–4552 ⊕ www.islandcommuter.com). **Washington State Ferries** (☎ 206/464–6400 ⊕ www.wsdot.wa.gov/ferries).

BY BUS

Greyhound has daily service to Mount Vernon and Bellingham from Seattle and Vancouver. It also serves Stevens Pass, Leavenworth, Cashmere, and Wenatchee from Everett and Spokane. (Note, though, that you can't buy tickets at Cashmere and Stevens Pass.) Valley Shuttles vans provide access to Stehekin Valley Road. In mid-May there's service to the lower Stehekin Valley; come June you can get a lift to the upper valley. In July the shuttles serve Cascade Pass's east trailhead (near Marblehead) and other destinations within 20 mi of the Stehekin boat dock. Reservations are strongly recommended.

Many communities throughout the region have bus service. Island Transit buses on Whidbey Island are free. Link Transit buses in the Wenatchee area cost 50¢ to $1 (payable in cash), depending on how far you travel. Rates also vary in Whatcom County. To ride buses in Skagit County you have to buy a pass (available at local stores); four trips will cost you $2; $5 buys 10 trips.

Contacts **Greyhound** (☎ 360/733–5251 or 800/231–2222 ⊕ www.greyhound. com). **Island Transit** (☎ 800/240–8747 ⊕ www.islandtransit.org). **Link Transit** (☎ 509/662–1155 ⊕ www.linktransit.com). **Skagit Transit** (☎ 360/757–4433 or 360/299–2424 ⊕ www.skat.org). **Valley Shuttles** (☎ 360/856–5700 Ext. 340 then press 14 ⊕ www.nps.gov/noca/focus/focus.htm). **WTA/Whatcom Transportation Authority** (☎ 360/376–7433 ⊕ www.ridewta.com).

BY CAR

You can reach Whidbey Island by heading north from Seattle or south from the Canadian border on I–5, west on Highway 20 onto Fidalgo Island, and south across Deception Pass Bridge. Interstate 5 is the main north–south route through western Whatcom and Skagit counties. Highway 542 winds east from Bellingham to Mt. Baker. Highway 20 heads east from Burlington to Sedro-Woolley and continues on through the North Cascades to the Methow and Okanogan valleys, and across the northeastern mountains to the Idaho state line near Newport.

Snow falls in the mountains from October or November until as late as May, and makes driving extremely hazardous. Highway 20 is usually closed (because of avalanche danger) from November through April. Stevens Pass faces intermittent closures for avalanche control (the avalanches are dislodged with howitzer shells; snow sliding onto the highway is cleared by plows). Every few winters it snows in the lowlands as well. Although the snow never lasts for more than a few days, snow tires and even chains may be required for driving even on I–5. If snow melt (which can occur at any time during the winter) coincides with heavy rain, lowland roads may flood. If the highways are closed for more than a few hours, local shelters aid stranded motorists.

BY TRAIN

Amtrak's *Empire Builder,* which runs from Chicago to Seattle, stops in Wenatchee. The company's *Cascades* train, which runs from Seattle to Vancouver, BC, stops in Mount Vernon and Bellingham.

Contacts **Amtrak** (☎ *800/872–7245* ⊕ *www.amtrak.com*).

EMERGENCIES

Hospitals **Central Washington Hospital** (✉ *1201 S. Miller St., Wenatchee* ☎ *509/665–6046*). **Island Hospital** (✉ *1211 24th St., Anacortes* ☎ *360/299–1300*). **Lake Chelan Community Hospital** (✉ *137 Chelan Manson Hwy., Chelan* ☎ *509/682–2531*). **Skagit Valley Hospital** (✉ *1415 E. Kincaid St., Mount Vernon* ☎ *360/424–4111*). **St. Joseph's Hospital** (✉ *2901 Squalicum Pkwy., Bellingham* ☎ *360/734–5400*). **United General Hospital** (✉ *2000 Hospital Dr., Sedro-Woolley* ☎ *360/856–6021*). **Whidbey General Hospital** (✉ *101 N. Main St., Coupeville* ☎ *360/321–5151*).

24-Hour Pharmacies **Walgreens** (✉ *909 17th St., Anacortes* ☎ *360/299–2816* ✉ *4090 Meridian St., Bellingham* ☎ *360/734–0229*).

TOUR OPTIONS

Apple Country Tours has farm tours, and the Cascade Foothills Farmland Association has mapped out a driving tour of local orchards and vineyards. The *Lady of the Lake* Boat Company takes you up the lake on narrated cruises. Upper Lake Chelan tours are arranged by the *Lady of the Lake II* folks; options include a Stehekin Valley bike tour and a bus trip (including lunch) to Rainbow Falls and the High Bridge Gorge.

On Rainbow Falls tours, operators use an old school bus to take you 3½ mi up-valley to the 312-foot cascade. There are also stops at an old schoolhouse and a bakery. The driver, who narrates the tour, is an inexhaustible source of local lore. Tours are offered year-round—even in winter when the falls are frozen.

Contacts **Apple Country Tours** (☎ *866/459–9614* ⊕ *www.washingtonapple country.com*). **Cascade Foothills Farmland Association** (✉ *125 Easy St., Wenatchee* ☎ *509/663–5159* ⊕ *www.visitwashingtonfarms.com*). **Lake Chelan Tour Boat** (✉ *Chelan* ☎ *509/682–8287*). **Upper Lake Chelan Tours** (✉ *Chelan* ☎ *509/682–4584* ⊕ *www.ladyofthelake.com*).

VISITOR INFORMATION

Contacts **Anacortes Chamber of Commerce** (✉ *819 Commercial Ave., Suite G, Anacortes* ☎ *360/293–7911* ⊕ *www.anacortes.org*). **Bellingham/Whatcom County Convention and Visitors Bureau** (✉ *904 Potter St., Bellingham 98229* ☎ *360/671–3990 or 800/487–2032* ⊕ *www.bellingham.org*). **Cashmere Chamber of Commerce** (✉ *204 Cottage Ave., Cashmere* ☎ *509/782–7404* ⊕ *www.cash merechamber.com*). **Central Whidbey Chamber of Commerce** (✉ *107 S. Main St., Coupeville* ☎ *360/678–5434* ⊕ *www.whidbeychamber.com*). **Greater Oak Harbor Chamber of Commerce** (✉ *32630 Hwy. 20, Oak Harbor* ☎ *360/675–3535* ⊕ *www. oakharborchamber.org*). **La Conner Chamber of Commerce** (✉ *606 Morris St., La Conner* ☎ *360/466–4778* ⊕ *www.laconnerchamber.com*). **Lake Chelan Chamber of Commerce** (✉ *102 E. Johnson Ave., Chelan 98816* ☎ *800/424–3526* ⊕ *www. lakechelan.com*). **Langley/South Whidbey Chamber of Commerce** (✉ *208*

Anthes St., Langley ☎ *360/221–6765* ⊕ *www.southwhidbeychamber.com).* **Leavenworth Chamber of Commerce** (✉ *894 U.S. 2, Leavenworth* ☎ *509/548–5807* ⊕ *www.leavenworth.org).* **Mount Vernon Chamber of Commerce** (✉ *105 E. Kincaid, Suite 101, Mount Vernon* ☎ *360/428–8547* ⊕ *www.mtvernonchamber. com).* **North Cascades Chamber of Commerce** (✉ *59831 Rte. 20, Marblemount* ☎ *360/873–2106* ⊕ *www.marblemount.com).* **North Cascades National Park** (✉ *2105 Hwy. 20, Sedro-Woolley* ☎ *360/856–5700).* **Sedro-Woolley Chamber of Commerce** (✉ *714-B Metcalf St., Sedro-Woolley 98284* ☎ *360/855–1841* ⊕ *www. sedro-woolley.com).* **Wenatchee Chamber of Commerce** (✉ *116 N. Wenatchee Ave., Wenatchee* ☎ *509/663–2116 or 800/572–7753* ⊕ *www.wenatcheevalley.org).* **Winthrop Chamber of Commerce** (✉ *202 Hwy. 20, Winthrop* ☎ *509/996–2125 or 888/463–8469* ⊕ *www.winthropwashington.com).*

THE SAN JUAN ISLANDS

Updated by
Holly S. Smith

The coastal waters of the Pacific Northwest, between mainland Washington and Vancouver Island, contain hundreds of islands, some little more than sandbars, others rising 3,000 feet. Among these, the San Juans are considered by many to be the loveliest. There are 176 named islands in the San Juan archipelago, although these and large rocks around them amount to 743 at low tide and 428 at high tide. Sixty are populated (though most have only a house or two), and 10 are state marine parks, some of which are accessible only to kayakers navigating the Cascadia Marine Trail.

This small archipelago of rock and glacial till derives its singular

> **TOP 5**
>
> 1. A seaplane ride into Friday Harbor is a thrilling adventure.
>
> 2. Head to Orcas Island for pristine San Juan views atop the ridges of Moran State Park.
>
> 3. Rent a bike to cycle the long, sloping country roads of Lopez Island.
>
> 4. Pick your own bouquets in the fields of San Juan Island.
>
> 5. Hike the coastal rocks at Lime Kiln Point lighthouse and take a whale-spotting tour, where sightings are guaranteed.

beauty from dramatic cliffs, lush seaside meadows, gnarled trees, and multicolor wildflowers clinging to seemingly barren rock. The islands have valleys and mountains where eagles soar, and forests and leafy glens where the tiny island deer browse. Even a species of prickly pear cactus (*Opuntia fragilis*) grows here. Beaches can be of sand or shingle, but all are scenic and invite beachcombers and kayakers to explore them. The islands are visited by ducks and swans, herons and hawks, otters and whales. Offshore, seals haul out on sandbanks and orcas patrol the deep channels. Since the late 1990s, gray whales have begun to summer here, instead of heading north to their arctic breeding grounds; an occasional minke or humpback whale can also be seen frolicking in the kelp.

Ferries stop at the four largest islands: Lopez, Shaw, Orcas, and San Juan; others, many privately owned, can be reached by commuter ferries from Bellingham and Port Townsend. Seaplanes owned by local airlines regularly splash down near the public waterfronts and resort bays around San Juan, Orcas, and Lopez, while charters touch down in private waters away from the crowds. Lopez, Orcas, and San Juan support a little fishing and farming, but tourism generates by far the largest revenues. Serene, well-appointed inns cater to visitors, and creative chefs operate small restaurants, serving food as contemporary as anything in Seattle. Each island maintains a distinct character, though all share in the archipelago's blessings of serene farmlands, unspoiled coves, blue-green or gray tidal waters, and radiant light. The area receives approximately 250 days of sunshine a year. Nevertheless, the islands stay cool in summer (around 70°F) and get outright cold in winter, when temperatures can hover at the freezing point.

LOPEZ ISLAND

45 minutes by ferry from Anacortes.

Known affectionately as "Slow-pez," the island closest to the mainland is a broad, bay-encircled bit of terrain amid sparkling blue seas, a place where cabinlike homes are tucked into the woods, and boats are moored quietly in lonely coves. Of the three San Juan islands with overnight accommodations, Lopez has the smallest population (approximately 1,800), and with its old orchards, weathered barns, and rolling green pastures, it's the most rustic. Gently sloping roads cut wide curves through golden farmlands and trace the edges of pebbly beaches, while peaceful trails wind through thick patches of forest. Sweeping country views make Lopez a favorite year-round biking locale, and except for the long hill up from the ferry docks, most roads and designated bike paths are easy enough for novices to negotiate.

The only settlement is Lopez Village, really just a cluster of cafés and boutique shops, as well as a summer market and outdoor theater, visitor-information center, and grocery store. Other attractions—such as seasonal berry-picking farms, small wineries, kitschy galleries, intimate restaurants, and isolated B&Bs—are scattered around the island.

Spencer Spit State Park is on former Native American clamming, crabbing, and fishing grounds. The spit is a stop along the Cascadia Marine Trail for kayakers, and it's a good place for summer camping. It's also one of the few Washington beaches onto which cars are allowed to drive. ⊠ *2 mi northeast of Lopez Village via Port Stanley Rd.* ☎ *360/468–2251* 🖃 *Free* ☾ *Apr.–Oct., daily 8–dusk.*

A quiet forest trail along beautiful **Shark Reef** leads to an isolated headland jutting out above the bay. The sounds of raucous barks and squeals mean you're nearly there, and eventually you may see throngs of seals and seagulls on the rocky islets across from the point. Bring binoculars to spot bald eagles in the trees as you walk, and to view sea otters frolicking in the waves near the shore. The trail starts at the Shark Reef Road parking lot south of Lopez Village, and it's a 15-minute walk to

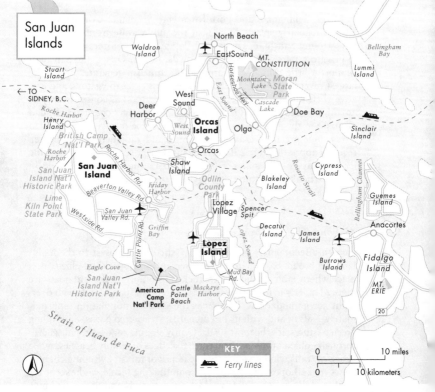

San Juan Islands

the headland. ⊠ *Off Shark Reef Rd., 2 mi south of Lopez Island Airport* ☎ *360/856–3500 or 800/527–3305* ▣ *Free* ⊙ *Daily.*

Lopez Island Vineyard is spread over 6 acres about 1 mi north of Lopez Village. The winery produces chardonnay, merlot, and cabernet sauvignon–merlot blends, as well as sweeter wines, such as those made from raspberries, blackberries, and other local fruits. The tasting room has regular hours in summer, but you can schedule a sampling session off-season. ⊠ *724 Fisherman Bay Rd.* ☎ *360/468–3644* ⊕ *www.lopez islandvineyards.com* ▣ *Free; tasting $3* ⊙ *May, June, and Sept., Fri. and Sat. 10–5; July and Aug., Wed.–Sat. 10–5; Apr., Oct.–mid-Dec., Sat. 10–5.*

WHERE TO STAY & EAT

$–$$$ ✕ **Bay Café.** Boats dock right outside this pretty waterside mansion at the entrance to Fisherman Bay. In winter sunlight streams into the window-framed dining room; in summer you can relax on the wraparound porch before a sunset panorama. The three-course dinner menu includes such delicacies as seafood tapas, basil- and goat cheese–stuffed prawns with saffron rice, and sea scallops with sun-dried tomatoes. Homemade sorbet and a fine crème caramel are among the desserts. ⊠ *Lopez Village* ☎ *360/468–3700* ▤ *AE, DC, MC, V* ⊙ *Closed Mon.–Wed. Oct.–May. No lunch.*

¢–$ ✕**Holly B's Bakery.** Tucked into a small, cabinlike strip of businesses
★   set back from the water, this cozy, wood-paneled dining room is the
highlight of daytime dining in the village. Fresh-cooked pastries and
big homemade breakfasts are the draw. Sunny summer mornings bring
diners out onto the patio, where kids play and parents relax. Pick up a
copy of Holly's famous cookbook and re-create some of her delicious
samplings at home. ⊠*Lopez Plaza* ☎*360/468–2133* ⊕*www.hollybs
bakery.com* ▭*No credit cards* ☉*Closed Dec.–Mar. No dinner.*

$$ ⌗**Edenwild.** This large Victorian-style farmhouse, surrounded by gar-
dens and framed by Fisherman Bay, looks as if it's at least a century old,
but it actually dates from 1988. Large rooms, each painted or papered
in different pastel shades, are furnished with simple antiques; some
have claw-foot tubs and brick fireplaces. The sunny dining room is a
cheery breakfast spot. In summer you can sip tea on the wraparound
ground-floor veranda or relax with a book on the garden patio. **Pros:**
Quiet country charm; quaint, cozy rooms. **Cons:** A long trip to get
here. ⊠*132 Lopez Village Rd., Lopez Village* ☎*360/468–3238 or
800/606–0662* ⎙*360/468–4080* ⊕*www.edenwildinn.com* ⇨*8 rooms*
⌂*In-hotel: no kids under 12, no elevator* ▭*MC, V* ⏲*BP.*

$–$$ ⌗**Mackaye Harbor Inn.** This white former sea captain's house, built
★   in 1904, rises two stories above the beach and rocks at the south-
ern end of Lopez Island. Rooms have golden-oak and brass details
and wicker furniture; three have views of Mackaye Harbor. Breakfast
includes Scandinavian specialties like Finnish pancakes; tea, coffee, and
chocolates are served in the evening. Rooms are simple, with colorful coverlets. The Rose Room is done all in pink. The Harbor Suite
has a private bath, deck, and fireplace. Kayaks are available for rent,
and mountain bikes are complimentary. ⊠*949 McKaye Harbor Rd.,
Lopez Village* ☎*360/468–2253 or 888/314–6140* ⎙*360/468–3293*
⊕*www.mackayeharborinn.com* ⇨*4 rooms, 2 with bath, 1 suite* ⌂*In-
room: kitchen (some). In-hotel: beachfront, bicycles, Wi-Fi, no elevator*
▭*MC, V* ⏲*BP.*

SPORTS & THE OUTDOORS

BICYCLING   Mountain-bike rental rates start at around $5 an hour and $25 a day;
tandem, recumbent, and electric bikes are $13 to $20 an hour or $42
to $65 per day. Helmets are $1 extra. Children's bike trailers and additional equipment are usually available. Reservations are recommended,
particularly in summer.

The Bike Shop on Lopez (⊠*Lopez Village* ☎*360/468–3497*) makes free
deliveries to the ferry docks or your hotel. **Cycle San Juans** (⊠*Hwy. 1*
☎*360/468–3251*) offers rentals and tours under the slogan "Cycle
with bald Lopezian to discover island curiosities." **Lopez Bicycle Works**
(⊠*2847 Fisherman Bay Rd.* ☎*360/468–2847* ⊕*www.lopezbicycle
works.com*), open May through September at the marina, can bring
bicycles to your door or the ferry.

BOATING &   **Harmony Charters** (☎*360/468–3310* ⊕*www.interisland.net/countess*)
SAILING   maintains a 65-foot yacht for lunch ($65) and dinner ($75) cruises,
as well as for trips to British Columbia and Alaska ($325 per person
per day). Prices include crew, food, sports equipment, utensils, and

linens. **Kismet Sailing Charters** (☎ *360/468–2435* ⊕ *www.rockisland. com/~sailkismet*) makes three-day cruises ($195 per person per day) and custom charter trips in a skippered 36-foot yacht.

SEA KAYAKING   **Elakah! Expeditions** (☎ *360/734–7270 or 800/434–7270* ⊕ *www.elakah. com*), a family-run sea-kayaking company, leads kayaking clinics on Lopez and two- to five-day trips ($225 to $495) around the San Juans. Specialty trips, such as those for women only, are also organized. **Lopez Kayaks** (☎ *360/468–2847* ⊕ *www.lopezkayaks.com*), open May to October at Fisherman Bay, offers a four-hour tour of the southern end of Lopez for $75 and a two-hour sunset tour for $35. Kayak rentals start at $15 an hour or $40 per day, and the company can deliver kayaks to any point on the island.

SHOPPING

The main cluster of shops is in Lopez Village, though you'll find a few dozen small, independent studios scattered around the island.

The **Chimera Gallery** (✉ *Village Rd.* ☎ *360/468–3265*), a local artists' cooperative, exhibits and sells crafts, jewelry, and fine art. **Fish Bay Mercantile** (✉ *Lopez Rd.* ☎ *360/468–2126*) is a fun, quirky gallery full of hand-carved wooden masks and furnishings, handwoven shawls and blankets, handmade jewelry, and scenic paintings by island artists—plus quirky international stuff like the Hindu lunchbox collection. **Grayling Gallery** (✉ *3630 Hummel Lake Rd.* ☎ *360/468–2779*) displays the paintings, prints, sculptures, and pottery works of nearly a dozen Lopez Island artists. **Islehaven Books** (✉ *Village Rd.* ☎ *360/468– 2132*), which is supervised in part by the owner's pack of five Russian wolfhounds, is stocked with publications on San Juan Islands history and activities, as well as books about the Pacific Northwest. There's also a good selection of mysteries, literary novels, children's books, and craft kits, plus greeting cards, art prints, and maps. Many of the items sold here are the works of local writers, artists, and photographers. **Tsunami Books** (✉ *Village Rd.* ☎ *360/468–3763*), in the Watertower, carries out-of-print, antiquarian, and used books, as well as music. You can even swap the bestseller you just finished for another book or perhaps a tape of '70s tunes.

ORCAS ISLAND

75 minutes by ferry from Anacortes.

Roads on flower blossom–shape Orcas Island, the largest of the San Juans, sweep through wide valleys and rise to gorgeous hilltop views. Spanish explorers set foot here in 1791, and the island is named for their ship—not for the black-and-white whales that frolic in the surrounding waters. The island was also the home of Native American tribes, whose history is reflected in such places as Pole Pass, where the Lummi people used kelp and cedar-bark nets to catch ducks, and Massacre Bay, where in 1858 a tribe from southeast Alaska attacked a Lummi fishing village.

Today farmers, anglers, artists, retirees, and summer-home owners make up the population of about 4,000. Houses are spaced far apart, and towns typically have just one major road running through them. Resorts dotting the island's edges are evidence of the thriving local tourism industry. Orcas is a favorite place for weekend getaways from the Seattle area any time of the year, as well as one of the state's top settings for summer weddings.

EastSound, the main town, lies at the head of the East Sound channel, which nearly divides the island in two. Small shops here sell jewelry, pottery, and crafts by local artisans. Along Prune Alley are a handful of stores and restaurants.

☺ **The Funhouse** is a huge, nonprofit activity center and museum for families. Interactive exhibits on age, hearing, kinetics, and video production, among other subjects, are all educational. Kids can explore an arts-and-crafts yurt, a climbing wall, a library, Internet stations, and a big metal "Jupiter" tree fort. Sports activities include indoor pitching cages and games, as well as an outdoor playground. Kids and adults can also take classes on music, theater, digital film, and poetry. Free programs for preteens and teenagers run Friday and Saturday nights (hint to mom and dad, who might want to enjoy dinner alone). ⊠*30 Pea Patch La., Eastsound* ☎*360/376-7177* ⊕*www.thefunhouse. org* ⊠*$7* ☉*Sept.–June, weekdays 3–5:30, Sat. 11–5; July and Aug., Mon.–Sat. 11–5.*

★ **Moran State Park** comprises 5,000 acres of hilly, old-growth forests dotted with sparkling lakes, in the middle of which rises 2,400-foot-high Mt. Constitution, the tallest peak in the San Juans. A drive to the summit affords exhilarating views of the islands, the Cascades, the Olympics, and Vancouver Island. You can explore the terrain along 14 hiking trails and choose from among 151 campsites if you'd like to stay longer. ⊠*Star Rte. 22. Head northeast from Eastsound on Horseshoe Hwy. and follow signs* ⓓ*Box 22, Eastsound 98245* ☎*360/376–2326, 800/226–7688 reservations* ⊠*Camping $10–$19 per night.*

WHERE TO EAT

$$–$$$ ✕**Christina's.** Copper-top tables and paintings by island artists enhance
Fodor's Choice this cozy bayside spot. The seasonal menu focuses on local seafood,
★ paired with fresh herbs and served with vegetables. Look for delicacies like spring greens with fennel and Samish Bay cheese; roast chicken with mushroom bread pudding; and curry coconut fish stew. Fine views of the East Sound make for a romantic dinner on the rooftop terrace or the enclosed porch. An excellent wine list and a bevy of rich desserts complement every meal. ⊠*310 N. Beach Rd., Eastsound 98245* ☎*360/376–4904* ⊟*AE, DC, MC, V* ☉*Closed Mon.–Wed. Oct.–mid-June and 1st 3 wks Nov. No lunch.*

$–$$ ✕**Bilbo's Festivo.** Stucco walls, colorful tiles, and wood benches reflect this restaurant's Tex-Mex inclinations. And the food here is improbably healthy. The fresh, delectable burritos, enchiladas, and chalupas are lard-free. There's also fabulous homemade guacamole and locally grown organic salad greens. In summer the patio is a pleasurable place to kick back with fresh-grilled lunch plates and icy margaritas. ⊠*N. Beach Rd. and A St., Eastsound* ☎*360/376–4728* ▭*AE, MC, V* ⊘*No lunch weekends Oct.–May.*

$$$–$$$$ 🏨 **Rosario Spa & Resort.** Shipbuilding magnate Robert Moran built this Mediterranean-style mansion on Cascade Bay in 1906. It's now on the National Register of Historic Places and worth a visit even if you're not staying here. The house has retained its original Mission-style furniture and numerous antiques; its centerpiece, an Aeolian organ with 1,972 pipes, is used for summer concerts in the ballroom. Some of the rooms are compact and basic; others are luxurious suites with outdoor decks, Jacuzzis, gas fireplaces, and kitchens. You can hike, kayak, and scuba dive nearby or stay in for a day of pampering in the downstairs Avanyu Spa. From your room you can watch seaplanes splash down in the bay and fishing and sailboat charters come into the marina. With prior notice, a Rosario shuttle will meet you at the ferry dock and take you to the hotel. **Pros:** Big, busy, lots of activities. **Cons:** Some rooms appear well used, dining service can be slow. ⊠*1400 Rosario Rd., Eastsound 98245* ☎*360/376–2222 or 800/562–8820* ⊕*www.rosarioresort.com* ⇖*111 rooms, 5 suites* ⏢*In-room: kitchen (some). In-hotel: Wi-Fi, 2 restaurants, bar, tennis courts, pools, gym, spa, concierge, Internet* ▭*AE, DC, MC, V.*

$$$–$$$$ 🏨 **Spring Bay Inn.** Two former park rangers run this woodland B&B
Fodor'sChoice   at the edge of private Spring Bay. All rooms have water views, wood-
★   burning fireplaces, feather beds, and sitting areas; one room has an outdoor hot tub. Mornings begin with coffee, muffins, and croissants outside your door—fortification for the free, two-hour kayaking trip around the island's craggy edges, or for hiking the trails that meander through the property. Afterward, there's an enormous complimentary brunch. Winter is for group bookings only, with a gourmet dinner option available. One of the owners is also a minister who can perform marriage ceremonies along the inn's forested bluffs. **Pros:** Spectacular location, free kayaking. **Cons:** Often booked far in advance. ⊠*Obstruction Pass Trailhead Rd. off Obstruction Pass Rd., Olga 98279* ☎*360/376–5531* 🖷*360/376–2193* ⊕*www.springbayinn.com* ⇖*5 rooms* ⏢*In-room: refrigerator. In-hotel: beachfront, spa, Internet, no elevator* ▭*D, MC, V* ⫶⊙⫶*BP.*

$–$$$ 🏨 **Turtleback Farm Inn.** Eighty acres of meadow, forest, and farmland in the shadow of Turtleback Mountain surround this forest-green inn. Rooms are divided between the carefully restored late-19th-century green-clapboard farmhouse and the newer cedar Orchard House. All are well-lit, with hardwood floors, wood trim, and colorful curtains and quilts, some of which are made from the fleece of resident sheep. The inn is a favorite place for local weddings. Breakfast is in the dining room or on the deck overlooking the valley. The Elopement package includes a minister, flowers, champagne, photos, and more. **Pros:** Comfort and elegance. **Cons:** A bumpy drive here. ⊠*1981 Crow Valley Rd., Eastsound 98245* ☎*360/376–4914 or 800/376–4914* 🖷*360/376–5329* ⊕*www.turtlebackinn.com* ⇖*11 rooms* ⏢*In-hotel: bar, no elevator* ▭*MC, V* ⫶⊙⫶*BP.*

SPORTS & THE OUTDOORS

BICYCLES &
MOPEDS

Mountain bikes rent for about $30 per day or $100 per week, including a helmet; tandem, recumbent, and electric bikes rent for about $50 per day. Most biking centers also rent strollers, children's bikes, and child trailers. Mopeds rent for $20 to $30 per hour or $60 to $70 per day. It's recommended that you reserve bikes and mopeds, especially in summer.

The Boardwalk (⊠*Orcas Village* ☎*360/376–2791* ⊕*www.orcasisland boardwalk.com*), at the ferry landing, rents road and mountain bikes. **Dolphin Bay Bicycles** (⊠*Orcas Village* ☎*360/376–3093* ⊕*www.rockis land.com/~dolphin*), at the Orcas ferry landing, rents road, mountain, and BMX bicycles for children and adults. They also organize guided bike tours of the San Juan Islands. **Key Moped Rental** (⊠*Eastsound* ☎*360/376–2474*) rents mopeds May through October. **Susie's Mopeds** (⊠*Eastsound* ☎*360/376–5266 or 800/532–0087*) rents mopeds June through September. **Wildlife Cycles** (⊠*Eastsound* ☎*360/376–4708* ⊕*www.wildlifecycles.com*) rents bikes and can recommend routes all over the island.

BOATING &
SAILING

Amante Sail Tours (⊠*Deer Harbor* ☎*360/376–4231*) offers half-day sailing trips for up to six people for $35 per person. **Deer Harbor Charters** (⊠*Deer Harbor* ☎*360/376–5989* ⊕*www.deerharborcharters. com*) has several small sailboats making half-day cruises around the San Juans for $45 to $75 per person. Outboards and skiffs are also available, as is fishing gear. **Lieber Haven Marina Resort** (⊠*Obstruction Pass* ☎*360/376–2472* ⊕*www.lieberhavenresort.com*) rents sailboats, motorboats, and kayaks June through September.

Sharon L. Charters (⊠*West Sound* ☎*360/376–4305*) has a 28-foot wooden vessel for six that costs $50 per person per day. **West Beach Resort** (⊠*3 mi west of Eastsound* ☎*360/376–2240 or 800/937–8224* ⊕*www.westbeachresort.com*) rents motorized boats, kayaks and canoes, and fishing gear.

SEA KAYAKING

All equipment is usually included in a rental package or tour. One-hour trips cost around $25; three-hour tours, about $45; day tours, $95 to $120; and multiday tours, about $100 per day.

Crescent Beach Kayaks (⊠*Eastsound* ☎*360/376–2464*) caters to families with free instruction and kayak rentals. **Orcas Outdoors Sea Kayak Tours** (⊠*Orcas Village* ☎*360/376–2222* ⊕*www.orcasoutdoors.com*) has one- and three-hour journeys, as well as day trips and rentals; a second branch is based at the Outlook Inn in Eastsound. **Osprey Tours** (⊠*Eastsound* ☎*360/376–3677 or 800/529–2567* ⊕*www.osprey tours.com*) uses handcrafted wooden Aleutian-style kayaks for half-day, full-day, and overnight tours of the islands. **Shearwater Adventures** (⊠*Eastsound* ☎*360/376–4699* ⊕*www.shearwaterkayaks.com*) holds kayaking classes and runs three-hour, day, and overnight tours from Rosario, Deer Harbor, and Doe Bay resorts. **Spring Bay Inn** (⊠*Obstruction Pass Trailhead Rd. off Obstruction Pass Rd., Olga* ☎*360/376–5531* ⊕*www.springbayinn.com*) arranges daily kayaking tours. **West**

Beach Kayaks (⊠ *West Beach* ☎ *360/376–2240 or 877/937–8224*) has half-day guided tours of the island in summer.

SCUBA DIVING **Island Dive & Water Sports** (⊠ *Rosario Resort, Eastsound* ☎ *360/376–7615* ⊕ *www.divesanjuan.com*) has a dive shop with rentals and offers a complete program of services, including instruction and charter trips. Two custom dive boats make two-tank dives for $75 with gear; resort packages are available. **West Beach Resort** (⊠ *West Beach* ☎ *360/376–2240 or 877/937–8224*) is a popular dive spot where you can fill your own tanks.

WHALE-
WATCHING
Cruises, which run about four hours, are scheduled daily in summer and once or twice weekly at other times. The cost is around $50 per person, and boats hold 20 to 40 people. Wear warm clothing, bring a snack, and have your camera ready to catch unexpected orca jumps and passes.

Deer Harbor Charters (☎ *360/376–5989 or 800/544–5758*) has whale-watching cruises around the island straits. **Eclipse Charters** (☎ *360/376–4663 or 800/376–6566* ⊕ *www.orcasislandwhales.com*) searches around Orcas Island for whale pods and other wildlife. **Whale Spirit Adventures** (⊠ *West Sound Marina* ☎ *360/376–5052 or 800/376–8018* ⊕ *www.whalespirit.com*) offers whale-sighting tours to the accompaniment of new-age chanting or flutes.

SAN JUAN ISLAND

45 minutes by ferry from Orcas Island, 75 minutes by ferry from Anacortes.

Lummi Indians were the first settlers on San Juan, with encampments along the north end of the island. North-end beaches were especially busy during the annual salmon migration, when hundreds of tribal members would gather along the shoreline to fish, cook, and exchange news. Many of the Lummi tribe were killed by smallpox and other imported diseases in the 18th and 19th centuries; in fact, Smallpox Bay was where tribal members plunged into the icy water to cool the fevers that came with the disease. The 18th century brought explorers from England and Spain, but the island remained sparsely populated until the mid-1800s. From the 1880s Friday Harbor and its newspaper were controlled by lime-company owner and Republican bigwig John S. McMillin, who virtually ran San Juan Island as a personal fiefdom from 1886 until his death in 1936.

The town's main street, rising from the harbor and ferry landing up the slopes of a modest hill, is packed with snazzy cafés, boutique shops, tour kiosks, and real estate offices. Spread in front of it all are views of the marina, where an open pavilion houses a huge tank of saltwater creatures and is tiled with a bright undersea mural. This is the departure point for kayaking journeys and summertime wildlife-watching excursions as well as the landing point for regional seaplanes and ferries from Seattle, Port Townsend, and Port Angeles (via Sidney, BC). Warm weather draws visitors in the thousands, as the island is a piece of near-pristine Northwest wilderness that's completely accessible by public transport and bicycle.

♺ A stairwell painted with a life-size, lifelike underwater mural leads you to the **Whale Museum.** Here you'll find a variety of whale bones and skeletons, as well as costumes, recordings, and videos of underwater creatures. Head around to the back of the first-floor shop to view maps of the latest orca pod trackings in the area. ⊠*62 1st St. N* ☎*360/378–4710* ⊕*www.whale-museum.org* ⊠*$6* ⊙*June–Sept., daily 10–6; Oct.–May, Thurs.–Mon. 10–5.*

The **San Juan Historical Museum,** in an old farmhouse, presents island life at the turn of the 20th century through historic photography, documents, and buildings. ⊠*405 Price St.* ☎*360/378–3949* ⊕*www. sjmuseum.org* ⊠*$4* ⊙*Oct.–Apr., Tues.–Thurs. 10–2; May–Sept., Tues.–Thurs. and weekends 2–4.*

♺ To watch whales cavorting in Haro Strait, head to **Lime Kiln Point State**
★ **Park,** on San Juan's western side 6 mi from Friday Harbor. A rocky coastal trail leads to lookout points and a little white lighthouse, built in 1914. April through August is the best whale-sighting season, but a resident pod of orcas regularly cruises past the point. Stop in at the summer-only Interpretive Center to learn about park history, view an intertidal zone exhibit, and find orca and marine mammal facts at interactive computer stations. ⊠*6158 Lighthouse Rd.* ☎*360/378–2044* ⊠*Free* ⊙*Daily 8 AM–10 PM; Interpretive Center Memorial Day–Labor Day, daily 10–6; lighthouse tours–Memorial Day–Labor Day, Thurs. and Sat. 7 PM–dusk, plus once in Dec. 1 PM–dusk.*

♺ **San Juan Island National Historic Park** commemorates the Pig War, in
★ which the United States and Great Britain nearly went to war over their respective claims on the San Juan Islands. The dispute began in 1859 when an American settler killed a British soldier's pig, and escalated until roughly 500 American soldiers and 2,200 British soldiers with five warships were poised for battle. Fortunately, no blood was spilled and the disagreement was finally settled in 1872 in the Americans' favor, with Emperor William I of Germany as arbitrator.

The park comprises two separate areas on opposite sides of the island. English Camp, in a sheltered cove of Garrison Bay on the northern end, includes a blockhouse, a commissary, and barracks. American Camp, on the southern end, stretches along driftwood-strewn beaches; come on summer evenings to view thousands of rabbits nibbling in the fields. There's also a visitor center and the remains of fortifications. From June to August you can take guided hikes and see reenactments of 1860s-era military life. ⊠*American Camp 6 mi southeast of Friday Harbor; English Camp 9 mi northwest of Friday Harbor; Park Headquarters, 125 Spring St., Friday Harbor* ☎*360/468–3663* ⊕*www.nps.gov/sajh.*

♺ The **Wescott Bay Institute/Sculpture Park** is a 19-acre open-air art gallery
★ within the spectacular Westcott Bay Reserve. Stroll along winding trails to view more than 80 sculptures spread amid freshwater and saltwater wetlands, open woods, blossoming fields, and rugged terrain. The park

is also a haven for more than 120 species of birds. Art workshops and events are scheduled throughout the year in the tented area. ⊠ *Westcott Dr. off Roche Harbor Rd.* ☎ *360/370–5050* ⊕ *www.wbay.org* 🆓 *Free* ⊙ *Daily dawn–dusk.*

It's hard to believe that fashionable **Roche Harbor** at the northern end of San Juan Island was once the most important producer of builder's lime on the West Coast. In 1882 John S. McMillin gained control of the lime company and expanded production. But even in its heyday as a limestone quarrying village, Roche Harbor was known for abundant flowers and welcoming accommodations. McMillin transformed a bunkhouse into private lodgings for his invited guests, who included such notables as Teddy Roosevelt. The guesthouse is now the Hotel de Haro, which displays period photographs and artifacts in its lobby. The staff has maps of the old quarry, kilns, and the Mausoleum, an eerie Greek-inspired memorial to McMillin.

McMillin's heirs operated the quarries and plant until 1956, when they sold the company to the Tarte family. Although the old lime kilns still stand below the bluff, the company town has become a resort. Locals say it took two years for the limestone dust to wash off the trees around the harbor. McMillin's former home is now a restaurant, and workers' cottages have been transformed into comfortable visitors' lodgings. With its rose gardens, cobblestone waterfront, and well-manicured lawns, Roche Harbor retains the flavor of its days as a hangout for McMillin's powerful friends—especially since the sheltered harbor is very popular with well-to-do pleasure boaters.

C **Krystal Acres Alpaca Farm,** an enormous swath of farmland on the west side of the island, is dotted with more than alpacas from South America. Many are less than two years old, and you can take a self-guided walking tour to see them up close. Alpacas are smaller than their well-known cousins, llamas, and have thicker hair, which is sheared here once a year. In the big barn, the shop displays exquisite, high-quality clothing and crafts, all handmade from alpaca fibers. ⊠ *152 Blazing Tree Rd., Friday Harbor* ☎ *360/378–6125* ⊕ *www.krystalacres.com* 🆓 *Free* ⊙ *May–Dec., daily 10–5; Jan.–Apr. weekends 10–5.*

C At **Pelindaba Lavender Farm,** a spectacular 20-acre valley is smothered with rows of fragrant purple-and-gold lavender blossoms. The oils are distilled for use in therapeutic, botanical, and household products, all created on site, as are an array of gorgeous craft items and decorations. Be sure and try the delicious lavender-infused ice cream, lemonade, tea, or baked goods—all of which are delicious. You can also indulge in a variety of exquisite lavender massages and therapies at the day spa in Friday Harbor. ⊠ *33 Hawthorn La., at Wold Rd., Friday Harbor* ☎ *360/378–4248 or 866/819–1911* ⊕ *www.pelindaba.com* 🆓 *Free* ⊙ *May–Oct., daily 10–5.*

WHERE TO EAT

$$–$$$ ✕ **Duck Soup Inn.** Blossoming vines thread over the cedar-shingled walls
FodorśChoice of this restaurant next to pristine pond views. Inside, island-inspired
★   paintings and a flagstone fireplace are the background for creative

meals served at comfortable booths. Everything is made from scratch daily, including sourdough bruschetta and ice cream. You might start with twice-baked corn soufflé, or perhaps coconut-crusted calamari. For a second course, consider fish piccatal or wild blackberry prawns. Vegetarian options and child portions are available. Northwest, California, and European wines are also on hand. Hint: If you like what you taste—and who doesn't?—the owner–chef offers hands-on cooking classes. ⊠*50 Duck Soup La.* ☎*360/378–4878* ⊕*www.ducksoup inn.com* ▭*MC, V* ⊗*Closed Nov.–Mar., Mon.–Thurs. Apr.–mid-May, Mon.–Wed. mid-May–mid-June, Mon. and Tues. mid- to late June, Mon. July–mid-Sept., Mon. and Tues. last 2 wks Sept., Mon.–Wed. 1st wk Oct., and Mon.–Thurs. last 2 wks Oct. No lunch.*

$–$$$ ✕**Downrigger's.** Ferries glide across the bay right in front of the dining-room windows at this waterfront restaurant. Polished wood floors, warm colors, and salmon decorations provide a classy yet comfortable setting for enjoying fresh seafood, blended fruit drinks, and local wines. Unusual choices include the Asian-spiced prawns, a banana-leaf–wrapped seafood pocket, and Cuban pork stew. Weekend breakfasts are popular, and meals are served outside on the deck in warm weather. ⊠*10 Front St., Friday Harbor* ☎*360/378–2700* ⊕*www. downriggerssanjuan.com* ▭*AE, MC, V.*

$ ✕**Front Street Ale House.** This dark, woodsy English-style ale house across from the water serves pub-style fish-and-chips, roast beef with bubble and squeak (grilled cabbage and mashed potatoes) and shepherd's pie. Less pubby choices include sesame chicken, a prawn curry noodle bowl, big burgers, and "ass-kicking chili." A draft from the adjacent San Juan Brewing Company is the perfect accompaniment (try the Pig War Stout or Royal Marine Pale Ale), or choose the beer sampler with five shot glass–size samples. The second-floor Top Side area has a dance floor and great harbor views. ⊠*1 Front St., Friday Harbor* ☎*360/378–2337* ⊕*www.sanjuanbrewing.com* ⌦*Reservations not accepted* ▭*AE, MC, V.*

¢ ✕**Blue Dolphin Cafe.** The best-known breakfast spot in town might be tiny, but the portions that emerge from the kitchen would satisfy the hungriest sailor. Stacks of pancakes, big egg scrambles, crisp bacon, and tender sausages are turned out with astonishing speed, often in carry-out boxes for travelers rushing to make the next ferry. Side dishes and sandwiches turn up at lunchtime, but the whole operation shuts down mid-afternoon. ⊠*1st St.* ☎*360/378–6116* ⌦*Reservations not accepted* ▭*No credit cards* ⊗*No dinner.*

WHERE TO STAY

$$$–$$$$ ⊞**Friday Harbor House.** This contemporary hotel takes advantage of
★ its bluff-top location with floor-to-ceiling windows that overlook the marina, ferry landing, and San Juan Channel below. Sleek, modern wood furnishings and fabrics in beige hues fill the rooms, all of which have fireplaces, deep jetted tubs, and at least partial views of the water. The elegant restaurant serves seasonal meals and special wine-tasting dinners, often to a backdrop of glowing sunsets in summer. **Pros:** Central, walkable spot close to ferry; great rooms for low prices off-season. **Cons:** Tourist hubbub can ruin mood of island serenity. ⊠*130 West*

St., Friday Harbor 98250 ☎*360/378–8455* 🖷*360/378–8453* ⊕*www.fridayharborhouse.com* 🖙*26 rooms, 3 suites* ⚷*In-room: refrigerator. In-hotel: dial-up, restaurant* ▤*AE, D, MC, V* ⦿|*CP.*

$–$$$$ 🛏 **Bird Rock Hotel.** One of the first hotels in the San Juan Islands, this 1891 bunkhouse is now a comfortable, boutique-style B&B. Rooms are individually decorated with a mix of antique furnishings and modern amenities, and styles range from simple economy spaces to deluxe suites. Some budget rooms even have a vaulted ceiling, balcony or patio, and water views, while suites might have a fireplace, wet bar, two-person jetted tub, or private outdoor hot tub. **Pros:** Stylish rooms, convenient locale. **Cons:** No pool or activities. ✉*35 1st St., Friday Harbor 98250* ☎*360/352–2632 or 800/352–2632* 🖷*360/378–2881* ⊕*www.friday-harbor.com* 🖙*7 rooms, 4 with bath, 8 suites* ⚷*In-room: no a/c. In-hotel: no phone, kitchen (some), refrigerator (some), VCR (some), Wi-Fi, Ethernet, airport shuttle* ▤*MC, V* ⦿|*CP.*

¢–$$$ 🛏 **Elements Hotel & Spa.** Divided into Earth and Sky spaces, the large rooms have glossy floors, comforting contemporary colors, and perks like iPod docking radios. Sun Places, under the sloping eaves, have a private deck, and compact Water Places have a jetted tub. Apartment-style Sea Suites have full kitchens, and the luxurious Wind Place is a two-bedroom home. The adjacent Lavender Day Spa provides a full range of beauty and health treatments; guests have free use of the pool and fitness facilities. **Pros:** Upscale style at reasonable rates, relaxing ambience. **Cons:** Can seem a little "New Age-y" for practical travelers. ✉*410 Spring St., Friday Harbor 98250* ☎*360/378–4000 or 800/793–4756* 🖷*360/378–4351* ⊕*www.hotelelements.com* 🖙*72 rooms* ⚷*In-room: kitchens (some), refrigerators, microwaves. In-hotel: pool, spa, sauna, gym, bike rental, Wi-Fi* ▤*MC, V.*

$–$$ 🛏 **Kirkhouse Bed and Breakfast.** Steel magnate Peter Kirk had this Crafts-
Fodor'sChoice   man bungalow built as a summer home in 1907. Rooms are all differ-
★   ently decorated: the Garden Room has a botanical motif and French doors leading outside, the sunny Trellis Room has both a jetted Jacuzzi and an antique claw-foot tub, and the Veranda Room has polished woodwork and a fireplace. You may take breakfast in the parlor—or have it in bed, served on antique Limoges china. Bountiful wicker-basket picnics, with all the trimmings, can be prepared for a day's excursion. **Pros:** Award-winning breakfast granola, tasty house coffee. **Cons:** No water views, a five-block walk from the ferry. ✉*595 Park St., Friday Harbor 98250* ☎*360/378–3757 or 800/639–2762* 🖷*360/378–8543* ⊕*www.kirkhouse.net* 🖙*4 rooms* ⚷*In-room: DVD, no a/c. In-hotel: Wi-Fi, no phone, airport shuttle, no elevator, no kids under 10* ▤*MC, V* ⦿|*BP.*

$–$$ 🛏 **Roche Harbor Resort.** First a log trading post built in 1845, and later an 1880s lime-industry complex, including hotel, homes, and offices, this sprawling resort is still centered around the lime deposits that made John S. McMillin his fortune in the late 19th century. Rooms are filled with notable antiques, like the claw-foot tub where actor John Wayne used to soak. Luxury suites in the separate McMillin House have fireplaces, heated bathroom floors, and panoramic water views from a private veranda. The beachside Company Town Cottages, once the homes of lime company employees, have rustic exteriors but modern interiors. Elsewhere are contemporary condos with fireplaces; some have lofts and water views. Walking trails thread through the resplendent gardens and the old lime quarries. The resort is a very popular boating base, as it's an official entry point to Canada, 15 mi to the north. **Pros:** Variety of accommodations and prices, lots of things to do. **Cons:** Can be noisy in summer. ⊠ *4950 Reuben Memorial Dr., Roche Harbor 98250* ✛ *10 mi northwest of Friday Harbor off Roche Harbor Rd.* ☎ *360/378–2155 or 800/451–8910* ☐ *360/378–6809* ⊕ *www. rocheharbor.com* ➡ *16 rooms without bath, 14 suites, 9 cottages, 20 condos* ⧖ *In-room: no a/c (some). In-hotel: no phone (some), kitchen (some), refrigerator (some), VCR (some), no TV (some), restaurant, tennis court, pool* ☐ *AE, MC, V.*

SPORTS & THE OUTDOORS

BEACHES **American Camp** (⊠ *6 mi southeast of Friday Harbor* ☎ *360/468–3663*), part of San Juan Island National Historical Park, has 6 mi of public beach on the southern end of the island. **San Juan County Park** (⊠ *380 Westside Rd. N, Friday Harbor* ☎ *360/378–2992*) has a wide gravel beachfront where orcas often frolic in summer, plus grassy lawns with picnic tables and a small campground.

BICYCLES & MOPEDS You can rent classic, mountain, and BMX bikes for $30 per day or $100 per week. Prices include a helmet, although fits aren't always exact. Tandem, recumbent, and electric bikes rent for about $50 per day. Strollers, children's bikes, and child trailers are usually available as well. You can rent mopeds for $20 to $30 per hour or $60 to $70 per day. Make sure to reserve bikes and mopeds a few days ahead in summer.

Island Bicycles (⊠ *380 Argyle St., Friday Harbor* ☎ *360/378–4941*) is a full-service shop that rents bikes. **Island Scooter & Bike Rental** (⊠ *Friday Harbor* ☎ *360/378–8811*) has bicycles and scooters for rent. **Susie's Mopeds** (⊠ *Friday Harbor* ☎ *360/378–5244 or 800/532–0087* ⊕ *www. susiesmopeds.com* ⊠ *Roche Harbor*) rents mopeds July through Labor Day at Roche Harbor and March through October in Friday Harbor.

BOATING Fees for moorage at private docks are $8 per night for boats under 26 feet long and $11 per night for larger vessels. Moorage buoys are $5 a night. Fees are paid in cash on site, while annual permits ($50–$80) are available from shops in Friday Harbor. At public docks, high-season moorage rates are 70¢–$1.35 per foot (of vessel) per night.

Port of Friday Harbor (☎ *360/378–2688* ⊕ *www.portfridayharbor.org*) provides marina services including guest moorage, vessel assistance and repair, bareboat and skippered charters; overnight accommodations; and whale-watching and wildlife cruises. **Roche Harbor Marina** (☎ *360/378–2155 or 800/451–8910* ⊕ *www.rocheharbor.com*) has a fuel dock, pool, grocery, and other guest services. **Snug Harbor Resort Marina** (☎ *360/378–4762*) provides marina services and van service to and from Friday Harbor, including ferry and airport shuttle service, and rents small powerboats.

CHARTERS   Charter sailboat cruises start at about $225 per day and run up to $400 per day for deluxe vessels. Charter powerboat trips start at about $150 per day. Extra costs for overnight cruises may include skipper fees ($150–$175), meals ($10–$15 per person daily), preboarding fees ($50–$100), spinnaker hire ($80–$100 per week), crab traps ($4–$6 each), sleeping bags ($13–$17), blanket sets ($15–$25), and towels ($6–$10).

ABC Yacht Charters (☎800/426–2313 ⊕*www.abcyachtcharters.com*) offers three-day and weeklong full-service sailboat and powerboat charters. **Amante Sail Tours** (☎360/376–4321) leads morning and afternoon sails for two to six guests. **Cap'n Howard's Sailing Charters** (☎360/378–3958 or 877/346–7245) hires out full-size vessels for sailing excursions around the islands. **Harmony Sailing Charters** (☎360/468–3310 ⊕*www. interisland.net/countess*) conducts daylong and multiday sailboat charters throughout the San Juan Islands and the Pacific Northwest. **Kismet Sailing Charters** (☎360/468–2435 ⊕*www.rockisland.com/~sailkismet*) leads overnight excursions through the San Juans and southwest Canada on a 36-foot-long customized yacht.

SCUBA DIVING   **Island Dive & Water Sports** (✉*Friday Harbor* ☎360/378–2772), at the waterfront, is a full-service dive shop with classes, equipment, airfills, and charters. Single-tank dives cost $55 and two-tank dives cost $75, with gear included. Overnight adventure packages with two days of diving start at $200.

SEA KAYAKING   Many kayakers bring their own vessels to the San Juans. If you're a beginner or didn't bring a kayak, you'll find rentals in Friday Harbor, as well as outfitters providing classes and tours. Be sure to make reservations for service in summer. One-hour trips start at $25, three-hour tours run about $45, day tours cost $90–$125, and overnight tours cost $80–$100 per day with meals. Equipment is always included.

Crystal Seas Kayaking (☎360/378–7899 or 888/625–7245 ⊕*www.crys talseas.com*) combines sea kayaking and sailing trips. **Doe Bay Resort** (☎360/376–2291) conducts guided kayak tours. **A Leisure Kayak Rentals** (☎360/378–5992 or 800/836–8224) will shuttle you from the ferry to the start of your kayaking class; hourly, daily, and overnight tours are also scheduled. **San Juan Kayak Expeditions** (☎360/378–4436) runs kayaking and camping tours in two-person kayaks. **San Juan Safaris** (☎360/378–1323 or 800/450–6858 ⊕*www.sanjuansafaris. com*) makes numerous kayaking trips around the islands. **Sea Quest** (☎360/378–5767 or 888/589–4253 ⊕*www.sea-quest-kayak.com*) conducts kayak ecotours.

WHALE-WATCHING   Tour companies have offices near the docks at Friday Harbor or in Roche Harbor, and hotels can help you with bookings. Whale-watching expeditions run three to four hours and cost around $50 per person. **Salish Sea Charters** (☎360/378–8555 or 877/560–5711 ⊕*www.salish sea.com*) has three tours per day from April through September that get you right up next to the orcas. **San Juan Excursions** (☎360/378–6636 or 800/809–4253 ⊕*www.watchwhales.com*) makes whale-watching cruises around the islands. **Western Prince Cruises** (☎360/378–5315 or

800/757–6722 ⊕*www.orcawhalewatch.com*) operates a four-hour narrated whale-watching tour.

SHOPPING

Friday Harbor is the main shopping area, with dozens of shops selling a variety of art, crafts, and clothing created by islanders, as well as a bounty of island-grown produce. Many farms, bed-and-breakfasts, resorts, and restaurants around the island also have a shop on-site. For ideas on what's available around the island, and where to buy, contact the **San Juan Islands' Artist Community Online** (☎*360/378–8274* ⊕*www. sanjuanartistcommunity.com*). From May to September, the **San Juan Island Farmers Market** (⊠*2nd St., Friday Harbor* ☎*360/378–5240* ⊕*www.sanjuanisland.org*) fills a parking lot two blocks northwest of town on Saturdays from 10 to 5.

Boardwalk Bookstore (⊠*5 Spring St., Friday Harbor* ☎*360/378–2787*) has a good collection of popular and classic literature. **Dan Levin** (⊠*50 1st St., Friday Harbor* ☎*360/378–2051*) stocks original jewelry. **Napier Sculpture Gallery** (⊠*232 A St., Friday Harbor* ☎*360/378–2221*) exhibits metal sculptures. **Pelindaba Lavender Farm** (☎*360/378–4248* ⊕*www.pelindaba.com*) brings many of the island farm's handmade lavender products to town. **Rainshadow Arts** (⊠*20 1st St., Friday Harbor* ☎*360/378–1371* ⊕*www.rainshadow-arts.com*) displays Pacific Northwest art and crafts: baskets, pottery, watercolors, sculpture, and photographs. **Waterworks Gallery** (⊠*315 Argyle St., Friday Harbor* ☎*360/378–3060* ⊕*www.waterworksgallery.com*) represents eclectic contemporary artists.

San Juan Vineyards (⊠*2000 Roche Harbor Rd.* ☎*360/378–9463 or 888/983–9463*), 3 mi north of Friday Harbor, has a winery, tasting room, and gift shop, and organizes such events as May barrel tastings, "Bottling Day" in July, volunteer grape-harvesting in October, and winter wine classes and tastings. Visit **Westcott Bay Sea Farms** (⊠*904 Westcott Dr., off Roche Harbor Rd.* ☎*360/378–2489*), a rustic oyster farm tucked into a small bay 2 mi south of Roche Harbor, for some of the tasty oysters, especially November through April.

THE SAN JUAN ISLANDS ESSENTIALS

AIR TRAVEL

Port of Friday Harbor is the main San Juan Islands airport, although there are also small airports on Lopez, Shaw, and Orcas islands. Seaplanes land on the waterfront at Friday Harbor and Roche Harbor on San Juan Island, Rosario Resort and West Sound on Orcas Island, and Fisherman Bay on Lopez Island. San Juan Islands flights are linked with mainland airports at Anacortes, Bellingham, Port Angeles, and Seattle-Tacoma International (Sea-Tac).

The small propeller jets and seaplanes of Island Air and San Juan Airlines hop among the San Juans. Kenmore Air has seaplane flights from Seattle to all the main islands. Northwest Seaplanes has seaplane service from Renton to San Juan, Orcas, and Lopez islands. Sound Flight also connects the islands with Renton. Rose Air takes passengers from Portland, Oregon, to the San Juans. All these airlines have charter and sightseeing flights.

Contacts **Island Air** (☎360/378-2376 or 888/378-2376 ⊕www.rockisland. com/~islandair). **Kenmore Air** (☎206/486-1257 or 800/543-9595 ⊕www. kenmoreair.com). **Northwest Seaplanes** (☎425/277-1590 or 800/690-0086 ⊕www.nwseaplanes.com). **Port of Friday Harbor Airport** (✉72 Airport Circle Dr., San Juan Island ☎360/378-4724 ⊕www.portfridayharbor.org/airport). **Port of Lopez Airport** (☎360/468-2131). **Port of Orcas Airport** (☎360/376-5285). **Rose Air** (☎503/675-7673 ⊕www.roseair.com). **San Juan Airlines** (☎800/690-0086 ⊕www.sanjuanairlines.com). **Sound Flight** (☎425/254-8063 or 866/921-3474 ⊕www.soundflight.net).

AIRPORTS & TRANSFERS There are taxis on Lopez, Orcas, and San Juan islands. Most hotels and B&Bs have complimentary airport pick-up and drop-off services.

Contacts **Bob's Taxi & Tours** (✉San Juan Island ☎360/378-6777 or 877/482-9426). **Island Taxi** (✉Orcas Island ☎360/376-8294). **San Juan Taxi** (✉San Juan Island ☎360/378-3550).

BY BOAT & FERRY

Washington State ferries depart from Anacortes, about 76 mi north of Seattle, to the San Juan Islands. Sunny weekends and summer months mean long lines of cars at ferry terminals all around the San Juan Islands. No reservations are accepted (except for the Sidney–Anacortes run from mid-May through September). Passengers and bicycles load first, and loading stops two minutes before sailing time.

The Mosquito Fleet connects Everett to Friday Harbor daily from early July through Labor Day, Thursday through Sunday in September, and weekends in October for $39.50. Humpback Hauling makes runs between the islands in summer for $95. The *San Juan Islands Shuttle Express* takes passengers from Bellingham to Orcas Island and Friday Harbor for $65 one-way. The *San Juan Island Commuter* has daily scheduled service for $35 one-way to 16 islands in the San Juans, including four islands that are state parks. The ferry also carries kayaks, bicycles, and camping equipment. April through October, the *P.S. Express* passenger-only ferry cruises daily from Port Townsend to Friday Harbor for $53 one-way. You can reach Victoria, British Columbia, from Seattle via Friday Harbor on the *Victoria Clipper* for $73 round-trip. The *Victoria Express* runs from Friday Harbor to Victoria for $53, continuing on to Port Angeles on the Olympic Peninsula.

Contacts **Humpback Hauling** (☎360/317-7433). **Mosquito Fleet** (☎425/252-6800 or 800/325-6722 ⊕www.whalewatching.com). **P.S. Express** (☎360/385-5288 ⊕www.pugetsoundexpress.com). **San Juan Island Commuter** (✉Bellingham Cruise Terminal, aka Alaska Ferry Terminal, 355 Harris Ave., No. 104, Bellingham ☎360/734-8180 or 888/734-8180). **San Juan Islands Shuttle Express** (✉Bellingham Cruise Terminal, aka Alaska Ferry Terminal, 355 Harris Ave., No. 105, Bellingham ☎360/671-1137 or 888/373-8522). **Victoria Clipper** (☎206/448-5000 or 800/888-2535 ⊕www.victoriaclipper.com). **Victoria Express** (☎360/452-8088 ⊕www.victoriaexpress.com). **Washington State Ferries** (☎206/464-6400, 800/843-3779 in WA ⊕www.wsdot.wa.gov/ferries).

BY BUS

On San Juan Island, San Juan Transit & Tours shuttle bus operates a schedule from mid-May to mid-September. Hop on at Friday Harbor, the main town, to get to all the island's significant points and parks, including the San Juan Vineyards, Pelindaba Lavender Farm, Lime Kiln Point State Park, and Snug and Roche harbor resorts. Tickets are $5, or $10 for a day pass.

Contacts **San Juan Transit & Tours** (☎ 360/378–8887 or 800/887–8387 ⊕ www. sanjuantransit.com).

BY CAR

To reach the San Juan Islands from Seattle, head north on I–5 to Exit 230, then follow signs west on Highway 20 to the ferry terminal in Anacortes. Be prepared for long auto lines at all hours between May and September, and weather delays throughout the year. Many accommodations arrange pick-up at their island's docks, which costs less and allows you to walk on the ferry immediately. Island roads have one or two lanes, but most of the main thoroughfares are paved. However, beware the distractions of sweeping water views, and be on the lookout for deer and rabbits.

There are few car-rental agencies on the islands. Angie's is the only office on Lopez. M&W is the only agency on Orcas, and they also have an office on San Juan Island. Island Petroleum Services rents cars on Orcas from June through September. Susan's Mopeds rents cars and mopeds on Orcas Island from June through September, as well as on San Juan Island at Friday Harbor from March through October and at Roche Harbor from July through Labor Day. Summer rates run $50 to $70 per day.

Local Agencies **Angie's Cab Courier** (✉ Lopez Island ☎ 360/468–2227). **Island Petroleum Services** (✉ Orcas Island ☎ 360/376–3883). **M&W Rental Cars** (✉ San Juan Island ☎ 360/378–2794 or 800/323–6037 ⊕ www.sanjuanauto. com). **Susan's Mopeds** (✉ San Juan Island ☎ 360/378–5244 or 800/532–0087 ⊕ www.susiesmopeds.com).

EMERGENCIES

Fire, Medical, Police (☎ 911).

Doctors & Dentists **Inter-Island Medical Clinic** (✉ 550 Spring St., Friday Harbor ✛ San Juan Island ☎ 360/378–2141). **Lopez Island Medical Clinic** (✉ 10 Washburn La. ☎ 360/468–2245). **Orcas Island Medical Clinic** (✉ 1269 Dove La. ☎ 360/376–2561).

Pharmacies **Friday Harbor Drug** (✉ 210 Spring St. ☎ 360/378–4421). **Lopez Island Pharmacy** (✉ Lopez Village ☎ 360/4680–2616). **Ray's Pharmacy** (✉ Eastsound ✛ Orcas Island ☎ 360/376–2230 or 360/376–3693).

TOUR OPTIONS

Numerous travel and tour agencies operate in the San Juan Islands. Walking tours of Friday Harbor, local parks, and island wineries are offered in addition to outdoor adventure and nature tours. Popular tours are those by air, speedboat, sea kayak, bicycle, and trail.

Krystal Acres Alpaca Farm can arrange group tours of their scenic farm and the largest alpaca herd in the San Juans. The San Juan Nature Institute, Skylark, and Wescott Bay have nature tours on San Juan and other islands. Tortas & Hare covers Orcas Island. Bob's and San Juan Sightseeing can show you San Juan Island, while Island Girl has one-hour walking tours of Friday Harbor, and Soul of the San Juans offers historic tours. San Juan Transit & Tours runs narrated walking tours of Friday Harbor, as well as a bus tour of the island for $15.

Contacts Bob's Taxi & Tours (⊠ *398 Spring St., San Juan Island* ☎ *360/378–6777 or 877/481–9417*). **Krystal Acres Alpaca Farm** (⊠ *152 Blazing Tree Rd., Friday Harbor* ✛ *San Juan Island* ☎ *360/378–6125* ⊕ *www.krystalacres.com*). **San Juan Nature Institute** (⌂ *Box 3110, San Juan Island 98250* ☎ *360/378–3646*). **San Juan Sightseeing** (⌂ *Box 2809, Friday Harbor, San Juan Island 98250* ☎ *360/378–8887 or 800/887–8387*). **San Juan Transit & Tours** (☎ *360/378–8887 or 800/887–8387* ⊕ *www.sanjuantransit.com*). **Skylark Nature Tours** (⊠ *5163 Roche Harbor Rd., San Juan Island* ☎ *360/378–3068*). **Soul of the San Juans** (⊠ *San Juan Island* ☎ *360/378–2942 or 800/874–4434*). **Tortas & Hare Excursions** (⊠ *Orcas Island* ☎ *360/376–2464*).

THE OLYMPIC PENINSULA

Updated by
Holly S. Smith

Wilderness covers much of the rugged Olympic Peninsula, the westernmost corner of the continental United States. Its heart of craggy mountains and a 60-mi stretch of its ocean shore are safeguarded in Olympic National Park, 95% of which is designated wilderness land. Several thousand acres more are protected in Olympic National Forest, five wilderness areas, and seven Indian reservations.

This is a landscape whose primeval ecosystem has remained in large part intact, and it's a land of almost incredible variety. The rain forest of the western river valleys soaks up 140 to 167 inches of precipitation per year, while the dry slopes of the northeastern peninsula, in the so-called "rain shadow" of the mountains, generally receive fewer than 16 inches. With some of the wettest and driest climates in the coastal Pacific Northwest, the peninsula supports a great diversity of plants and animals.

At its southwestern corner, the peninsula is defined by Grays Harbor, Washington's second largest estuary and one of only eight natural harbors between Mexico and Canada. The harbor is named for discoverer and fur trader Robert Gray, who in 1792 became the first European-American to enter the harbor. Two long, forested sand spits separate and protect Grays Harbor from the fury of the Pacific Ocean.

Although rugged terrain and a lack of roads make much of the Olympic Peninsula's interior accessible only to backpackers, the 300-mi-long outer loop of U.S. 101 provides fabulous views over ocean, rain forest, and mountains. Side roads provide excellent opportunities for exploring remote villages, beaches, and valleys. The following section describes a clockwise journey, primarily via U.S. 101, beginning and ending in Olympia.

MONTESANO

30 mi west of Olympia.

Montesano was settled in 1852 at the confluence of the Chehalis, Satsop, and Wynoochee rivers. Log-toting team boats churned through the river passages from 1859 until railroad tracks arrived in 1885. When the town was incorporated in 1870, its population had reached about 1,500. The *Vidette,* which published its first issue in 1883, is still going strong, chronicling the times since Montesano became the Grays Harbor County seat in 1886. The town has a historic district with several buildings dating from the late 19th and early 20th centuries.

> ### TOP 5
>
> 1. The Makah Museum in Neah Bay for authentic scenes of early life in the Northwest.
>
> 2. The expansive beach scenes at Ocean Shores offer glimpses into the underwater world.
>
> 3. Head to Westport for explorations of coastal boating history.
>
> 4. Drive to the top of Hurricane Ridge for spectacular summer hikes and winter snowsports.
>
> 5. Ruby Beach for heart-stopping vistas of rugged, ocean-carved rock formations.

In 1900 Frederick Weyerhaeuser and 15 partners began the Weyerhaeuser timber company with 900,000 acres of Washington forestland. Forty years later the company purchased 200,000 acres near Montesano and established the Clemons Tree Farm, the world's first. Today the Weyerhaeuser Company ships paper and lumber worldwide and is one of Washington's most profitable firms, and Montesano dubs itself the "Home of the Tree Farm."

The enormous, sandstone **Grays Harbor County courthouse** seems exceptionally grand for such a small town, but it was entirely appropriate at the time it was built, between 1909 and 1912, when Montesano was a prosperous railroad boomtown. Its clock tower soars above the classical, pillared entrance. The lobby has a marble staircase flanked by murals depicting Robert Gray in 1792, discovering the harbor that bears his name, and Territorial Governor Isaac Stevens negotiating with Native Americans at Cosmopolis in 1855. The murals inaccurately depict native people wearing feather headdresses and standing in front of tepees (neither was used by the local Chehalis). Information packets for self-guided tours around town are available in the room to the right of the Commissioner's Office. ⊠*102 W. Broadway* ☎*360/249–3441* ⊠*Free* ⊙ *Weekdays 8–5.*

WHERE TO STAY & EAT

¢–$ ✕**Savory Faire.** Homemade sandwiches, salads, soups, and quiches are on order in the French-style café. The home-baked breads and desserts, including gooey cinnamon rolls and amaretto bread pudding, are famous around the peninsula. Come for the monthly Friday-evening wine tastings, from 5:30 to 8, to sample a full range of Northwest vintages accompanied by tapas. ⊠*135 S. Main St.* ☎*360/249–3701* ⊟*D, MC, V* ⊙*No dinner.*

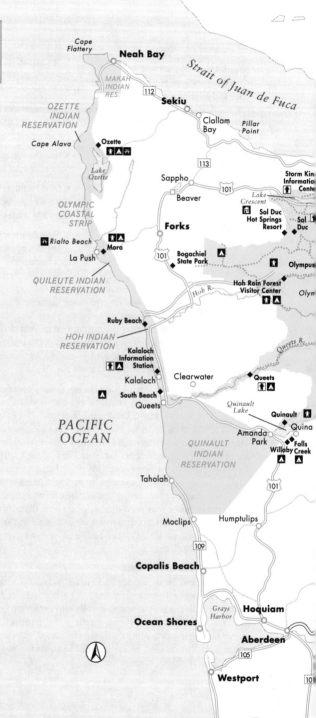

Olympic Peninsula

Cape Flattery

Neah Bay

Strait of Juan de Fuca

MAKAH INDIAN RES.

112

Sekiu

Clallam Bay

Pillar Point

OZETTE INDIAN RESERVATION

113

Storm Kin Information Cente

Lake Crescent

Sappho

101

Beaver

Sol Duc Hot Springs Resort

Sol Duc

Cape Alava

Ozette

Lake Ozette

OLYMPIC COASTAL STRIP

Forks

Bogachiel State Park

Olympus

Rialto Beach

101

Mora

Hoh Rain Forest Visitor Center

Olym

La Push

QUILEUTE INDIAN RESERVATION

Hoh R.

Ruby Beach

HOH INDIAN RESERVATION

Queets R.

Kalaloch Information Station

Queets

Kalaloch

Clearwater

Quinault Lake

Quinault

Quina

South Beach

Queets

Amanda Park

PACIFIC OCEAN

QUINAULT INDIAN RESERVATION

Falls Creek

Willaby

Taholah

101

Moclips

Humptulips

109

Copalis Beach

Grays Harbor

Hoquiam

Ocean Shores

Aberdeen

105

Westport

101

KEY

— Highway
— Minor Road
-- Unpaved Road
····· Trail
▲ Campground
🔺 Picnic Area
🚹 Ranger Station

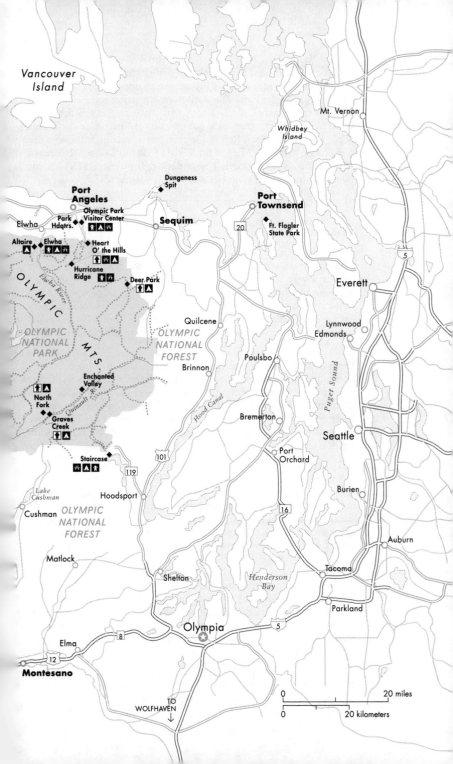

¢–$ 🖼Abel House. This 1908 white-stucco-and-stone manor house, now a B&B, is surrounded by a lovely English garden. Pastel walls, wood trim, and handmade quilts distinguish the country-style rooms, one of which has a private bath. The third-floor recreation room can be converted into an extra children's bedroom. You can relax in the sitting room before the fireplace, pick out tunes on the piano, or shoot pool in the game room. **Pros:** Relaxed setting, free afternoon tea. **Cons:** Just one private bath. ✉*117 Fleet St. S, 98563* ☎*360/249–6002* ⊕*www. abelhouse.com* ⇱*4 rooms, 1 with bath* ⌕*In-room: DVD/VCR, no phone. In-hotel: no TV, no elevator* ▭*AE, MC, V* ¶❘*BP.*

ABERDEEN

6 mi west of Montesano.

The pretty town of Aberdeen, on Grays Harbor at the mouth of the Chehalis River, was settled in 1867 by farmers. Some of the earliest residents were Scottish immigrants who named it after their own city set along a harbor at the mouth of a river. Growth and prosperity came to the town after Scotsman George R. Hume started a salmon cannery here in 1878 and the town's first sawmill was built in 1884. Soon tall ships crowded the narrow harbor to load lumber, and waterfront bars were busy with sailors and lumberjacks.

Early homesteaders found the cleared forest land too soggy to support anything except cranberries, which still thrive in the bogs. Other farmers turned to cultivating oysters in the shallow harbor bays. In 1903 most of Aberdeen's buildings, made of wood and surrounded by streets of sawdust, burned down during a dry spell. These were replaced with stone and brick buildings, many of which still stand in the downtown area.

Aberdeen is known for its lovely harbor, spread glittering and gray along the west edge of town, where the bay bobs with sailboats and speed cruisers. Vast swaths of lumberyards are broken up by towering cranes, which transport the massive timbers onto immense metal barges. Forested hills serve as a backdrop to town, promising a picturesque entry into the Olympic Peninsula to the north. The town is also dotted with the classic, century-old mansions built by shipping and timber barons of the 20th century, and the "Aberdeen Walking Tour" brochure ($4) provides a self-guided look at more than four dozen of the largest and most beautiful homes. The contemporary Walk of Fame tour follows the local highlights from some of the town's best-known former residents, including Bill Boeing and Kurt Cobain. For a general look at the lay of Aberdeen, take the 1½-mi-long, paved **Morrison Riverfront Park Walk** to the 40-foot-wide Compass Rose mosaic, inlaid at the confluence of the Wishkah and Chehalis rivers.

★   Tall, billowing white sails in the harbor mark the presence of the *Lady Washington,* a replica of the 1750s coastal freighter from Boston, which in 1792, under the command of famous explorer Captain Robert Gray, was the first American vessel to reach the northwest American coast.

The Olympic Peninsula > **439**

The replica was famously converted into the multimasted HMS *Interceptor* sloop for the 2002 Disney movie *Pirates of the Caribbean*. Its main base is the Grays Harbor Historic Seaport, but you'll find the vessel at local coastal towns throughout the region, where it's open for self-guided tours. Three-hour cruises include the hands-on "Adventure Sail" and a mock "Battle Sail" war between two vessels, and if you're at least 18 you can volunteer as a deckhand for multiday trips. The free **Seaport Learning Center,** a 214-acre site spread across the harbor and surrounding wetlands, runs tours on two historic longboats, and schedules monthly boatbuilding, rope-climbing, and marine-trade programs for families and students. ✉️ *712 Hagara St.* ☎️ *360/532–8611 or 800/200–5239* ⊕ *www.ladywashington.org* 🖃 *Tours by donation, sailings $55–$60* ⊙ *Tours weekdays 4–5, Sat. 10–1, sailings weekends 2–5.*

WHERE TO STAY & EAT

$-$$ ✕ **Bridges.** This café takes its name not from its location between the Wishkah and Chehalis river spans but from owner Sonny Bridges, who's been running local restaurants for more than 30 years. This classy, pastel-hue place has excellent seafood and huge steaks. ✉️ *112 N. G St.* ☎️ *360/532–6563* ▭ *AE, D, DC, MC, V* ⊙ *No lunch Sun.*

$ ✕ **Billy's.** This bar and grill used to be the most popular saloon and brothel in town, and the restaurant has a collection of prints recalling those bawdy days. Even the establishment's name was taken from the saloon's notorious original owner, Billy Ghol. It's said his ghost haunts the premises. Standard fare includes burgers and salads, but you can go exotic with grilled yak. ✉️ *322 E. Heron St.* ☎️ *360/533–7144* ▭ *AE, DC, MC, V.*

$-$$ 🏠 **A Harbor View Inn.** You can see the harbor from every room in this 1905 Victorian mansion. Hand-stenciled walls surround the elegant parlors, where three fireplaces warm the air on cool autumn evenings. Sun rooms bring in the light to help a variety of plants flourish. Take the ballroom staircase to the old-fashioned rooms, where handmade quilts cover the antique beds. ✉️ *11 W. 11th St., 98520* ☎️ *360/533–7996 or 877/533–7996* 🖷 *360/533–0433* ⊕ *www.aharborview.com* 🛏 *4 rooms* ♿ *In-room: no phone. In-hotel: dial-up, Wi-Fi, no kids under 8, no elevator* ▭ *AE, MC, V* ⴼ*BP.*

$ 🏠 **Guest House International Suites and Inn.** Three stories high and overlooking the Wishkah River, this peaked-roof inn looks more like a mansion than a chain hotel. Rooms, all with VCRs and kitchenettes, are spacious and bright, with shades of cream and blue. Larger suites have fireplaces and Jacuzzis. The Wishkah Mall and the city center are just steps away. **Pros:** Modern, neat, efficient. **Cons:** Unimaginative motel decor. ✉️ *701 E. Heron St., 98520* ☎️ *360/537–7460 or 800/214–8378* 🖷 *360/537–7462* ⊕ *www.guesthouse.net* 🛏 *75 rooms, 12 suites* ♿ *In-room: kitchen. In-hotel: refrigerator, VCR, dial-up, Wi-Fi, pool, gym, laundry facilities, laundry service, public Internet, some pets allowed* ▭ *AE, D, MC, V* ⴼ*CP.*

WESTPORT

15 mi southwest of Aberdeen.

Westport is a bayfront fishing village on the southern spit that helps protect the entrance to Grays Harbor from the fury of the Pacific Ocean. Numerous charter companies based here offer salmon, ling-cod, rockfish, and albacore fishing trips, as well as whale-watching tours. If you're not taking a cruise, you can stand on Westport's beach to look for gray whales migrating southward in November and December, toward their breeding grounds in Baja California, and northward in April and May, toward their feeding grounds in the Bering Sea. The serene beach is perfect for walking, surfing, or kite-flying—although it's too dangerous for swimming and too cold for sunbathing. In winter it's one of the best spots on the coast to watch oncoming storms.

Westport's **Harbor Walkway** is a 2-mi-long paved promenade that winds along the sandy beach. ⊠*Ocean Ave. between Grays Harbor Lighthouse and West Haven State Park.*

☼ **Westport Aquarium** has exhibits of local marine life, including a wolf eel, an octopus, and a dog shark. Touch tanks let you feel shells, starfish, anemones, and other sea creatures. You can even hand-feed two live seals. ⊠*321 Harbor St.* ☎*360/268–0471* ☑*$5* ☉*May–Sept., Mon.–Thurs. and Sun. 10–6, Fri. and Sat. 10–8; Oct.–Apr., weekends 10–6 and by appointment.*

In a former Coast Guard station, the **Westport Maritime Museum** displays historic photos, equipment, clothing, and other relics from the life-saving service and such local industries as fishing, logging, and cranberry farming. Among the exhibits is a collection of sea-mammal bones, and the 17-foot-tall Destruction Island Lens, a lighthouse beacon that was built in 1888 and weighs almost six tons. The octagonal **Grays Harbor Lighthouse**, a 107-foot structure built in 1898, is the tallest on the Washington coast. It stands near the museum and adjacent to Westport Light State Park, a day-use area with picnic tables and a beach. A tour of the lighthouse base is included with museum admission; if you want to climb to the top, it's $4. ⊠*2201 Westhaven Dr.* ☎*360/268–0078* ⊕*www.westportwa.com/museum* ☑*$4 museum, lighthouse base free* ☉*Apr.–Sept., daily 10–4; Oct.–Mar., Fri.–Mon. noon–4; lighthouse closed Dec. and Jan.*

WHERE TO STAY & EAT

¢–$ ✕ **The Fogcutter Café.** Only a few steps from the lighthouse, this eatery is a favorite of beach strollers. Big breakfasts are the specialty, with an assortment of tasty scrambled and fried fixings. High-stacked sandwiches are also available, and home-baked pastries, some made with local cranberries, are the perfect endings. ⊠*1155 W. Ocean Ave.* ☎*360/268–6097* ⊟*D, MC, V* ☉*No dinner.*

¢–$$ ⊞ **Harbor Resort.** Right on the ocean, this two-story hotel offers prime views of seals, seabirds, and even whales. Cottages, all overlooking the bay, have soaring cathedral ceilings, plus fans, full kitchens, fireplaces, and bay windows with water views. Even the standard rooms have kitchenettes and decks looking out to sea. The two-story house can be rented separately by floor. *✉861 Neddie Rose Dr., 98595 ☎360/268–0169 🖷360/268–0338 🌐www.harborresort.com 🛏7 rooms, 7 cottages, 1 house ♿In-room: kitchen (some). In-hotel: refrigerator (some), some pets allowed, no elevator 💳AE, D, MC, V.*

HOQUIAM

10 mi west of Aberdeen.

Hoquiam (pronounced *hoh*-quee-ahm) is a historic lumber town near Aberdeen and the mouth of the Hoquiam River. Both river and town were named for the Chehalis word meaning "hungry for wood." The town was settled in the mid-19th century, around the same time as Aberdeen, and is now a major Grays Harbor port for cargo and fishing vessels. Its industries include canneries and manufacturers of wood products and machine tools.

4

In fall and spring, **Grays Harbor National Wildlife Refuge** is a perfect place to observe the multitude of migrating shorebirds that visit the area. Keep your binoculars handy as you stroll along the 1,800-foot-long boardwalk, and make sure to stop at the visitor center's shop and bookstore. To get here from Hoquiam, drive west on Highway 109 to Pawlson Road, then turn left and continue to Airport Way, where you make a right toward the refuge. *✉Airport Way ☎360/753–9467 🌐www.fws.gov/graysharbor 🎟$3 🕓Park: daily dawn–dusk; visitor center: Wed.–Sun. 9–4.*

The Polson Museum, in a 26-room mansion built in 1924, is filled with artifacts and mementos relating to Grays Harbor's past. You can walk through the remodeled dining room, kitchen, and living room, where an exhibit traces the history of tall ships in the Pacific Northwest. Upstairs is the logging exhibit, with a replica Little Hoquiam Railroad; a period-costume room; and the Polson children's room and doll house. Outside you can wander the riverside grounds, which have exotic trees and a rose garden. *✉1611 Riverside Ave. ☎🖷360/533–5862 🌐www.polsonmuseum.org 🎟$4 🕓Jan.–Aug., Wed.–Sat. 11–4, Sun. noon–4; late Dec.–Mar., weekends noon–4.*

WHERE TO STAY

$–$$ **Hoquiam's Castle Bed & Breakfast.** A registered National Historic Site, this imposing, 10,000-square-foot Victorian mansion was built in 1887 by lumber baron Robert Lytle. Three floors and 28 rooms are filled with exquisite antique and reproduction furnishings, including crystal chandeliers, Tiffany-style lamps, stained-glass windows, and canopy beds. The charming bedrooms overlook the town and harbor, and dinner and breakfast are included. Nonguests can take a 45-minute tour, scheduled by appointment, for $6; guests receive a free guided walk-through. *✉515 Chenault Ave., 98550 ☎360/533–2005 🌐www.hoquiamscastle.com 🛏4 rooms ♿In-room: no a/c. In-hotel: no phone, no TV, no kids under 12, no elevator 💳AE, D, MC, V 🍽BP.*

OCEAN SHORES

18 mi west of Hoquiam, 4 mi northwest of Westport.

Ocean Shores, a long stretch of resorts, restaurants, shops, and attractions, sits on the northern spit that encloses Grays Harbor. The whole area was planned by housing developers in the 1960s, and with its broad, flat white beach, shallow surf, and sunset panoramas, it's been a favorite seaside getaway since. Come summer, dune buggies and go-karts buzz up and down the sand road, weaving around clusters of horses trotting tourists over the dunes. Colorful kites flap overhead, dogs romp in the waves, and tide pools are filled with huge orange Dungeness crabs, live sand dollars, and delicate snails, to the delight of small children. It's no tropical haven, however, as summer can bring chilly breezes, and the water never warms up much for swimming—hence jackets are mandatory even in July. A fog of sea mist often blows in during the late afternoon, and in winter massive thunderstorms billow onto land directly before the line of coastal hotels. An indoor pool and in-room fireplace are coveted amenities year-round in this cool climate, and well worth the added expense.

The **Ocean Shores Interpretive Center,** a great stormy-day educational spot for families, highlights the seaside environment, local history, and Native American traditions. Displays include dried local wildflowers, a rock identification table, Native American basketry, and a model of the Quinault River's Chow Chow Bridge. Reproduction seabirds, whale bones, and a vast shell collection let you examine the shoreline wildlife up close. ⊠ *1033 Catala Ave. SE* 🕾 *360/289–4617* ⊕ *www. oceanshoresinterpretivecenter.com* 🖃 *Free* ☉ *May–Sept., daily 11–4; Nov.–Mar., Sat. 11–4, Sun. 11–2.*

WHERE TO EAT

$–$$ ✕ **Alec's by the Sea.** Some of the region's best seafood is served at this elegant restaurant conveniently set between town and beach. The best dishes are made with creatures caught locally, such as razor clams and Willapa Bay oysters. For a light meal, try the garlic bread served with bouillabaisse, or one of the salads. Steaks and burgers are also on the menu. ⊠ *131 E. Chance a la Mer Blvd.* 🕾 *360/289–4026* 🖃 *AE, D, MC, V.*

$–$$ ✕ **Mike's Seafood.** Wander through the small, roadside seafood shop
★   to see what's cooking before you sit down in the adjacent restaurant. Everything served is fresh-caught, and salmon is smoked on the premises. Italian specialties round out the menu—one of the best ways to sample it all is in the tomato-based cioppino. ⊠ *830 Point Brown Ave. NE* 🕾 *360/289–0532* 🖃 *AE, D, MC, V.*

¢–$ ✕ **Mariah's Restaurant.** You can walk to this restaurant at the Polynesian Resort from the adjacent beach. The focus is on local seafood, with appetizers like Dungeness crab dip spread on baguettes, and main courses like grilled salmon and steamed shellfish. The prime rib is just as popular as the seafood. Sunday breakfasts are a sumptuous buffet of brunch items and mains. ⊠ *615 Ocean Shores Blvd. NW* 🕾 *360/289–3315* 🖃 *AE, D, DC, MC, V* ☉ *No lunch Mon.–Sat.*

$-$$ 🏨 **Quinault Beach Resort & Casino.** A half mile of dunes and wild beach
★ grasses separates this enormous resort from the crowds. Shades of
green, gray, and gold appear throughout the rooms, which all have
10-foot ceilings, gas fireplaces, and twin bathroom sinks. Enormous
suites have sea vistas, corner jetted tubs, and plasma TVs. The full-
service spa has private sauna and Jacuzzi rooms and an ocean-view
patio. Surrounded by 200 acres of protected wetlands, there's plenty
of room to swim, hike, and watch for wildlife. **Pros:** Grand rooms
for low rates, upscale setting. **Cons:** Gambling crowds can be rowdy.
⊠ *78 Hwy. 115, 98569* ☎ *360/289–9466 or 888/461–2214* ⊕ *www.
quinaultbeachresort.com* ⇆ *150 rooms, 9 suites* ⌂ *In-room: kitchen
(some). In-hotel: refrigerator, VCR, dial-up, Wi-Fi, restaurant, room
service, bar, pool, gym, spa, beachfront, laundry service, Wi-Fi, refrigerator* ⊟ *AE, D, DC, MC, V.*

$-$$ 🏨 **Shilo Inn.** Framed by a Pacific Ocean seascape to the west and a
dune-covered state park to the south, this all-suites hotel welcomes
guests resort-style. The lower floor opens into an expanse of elegant
lounging areas, each dotted with hand-carved models of international
sailing vessels and life-size marble sea creatures—and it's all backed
by a 3,000-gallon aquarium that looks into the pool. Large, modern
accommodations are like apartments, each with a living area, fireplace, and a balcony overlooking the beach. A five-minute walk takes
you to the surf, local shops, and outdoor activities. The restaurant
and lounge serves a mix of American fare and fine Northwest cuisine.
Pros: Great location, attractive lobby, lots of amenities. **Cons:** Lots
of tourists, families, and groups make hallways noisy late and early.
⊠ *707 Ocean Shores Blvd., 98569* ☎ *360/289–4600 or 800/222–2244*
🖷 *360/289–0355* ⊕ *www.shiloinns.com* ⇆ *113 suites* ⌂ *In-room:
kitchen. In-hotel: Ethernet, dial-up, Wi-Fi, restaurant, bar, pool, gym,
laundry facilities, airport shuttle* ⊟ *AE, DC, MC, V.*

$ 🏨 **Floating Feather Inn.** This pretty white house, surrounded by a white
picket fence and fronted by a fountain, is on the Grand Canal and
near the marina at the south end of town. The foyer opens into the
lobby, warmed by a fireplace, and a few steps farther is a waterside sunroom. Each guest room is individually decorated and comes with plush
robes and a down comforter. The Wood Duck Suite has a deck, while
another room has two twin-size trundle beds and canal views. The
rate includes breakfast, which is also available to nonguests Thursday
through Sunday. The restaurant serves innovative dinners Thursday
through Sunday as well. **Pros:** Water views, child- and pet-friendly, on-
site restaurant. **Cons:** Just one room booked per family, no matter how
many people. ⊠ *982 Point Brown Ave. SE, 98569* ☎ *360/289–2490 or
888/257–0894* 🖷 *360/289–9291* ⊕ *www.floatingfeatherinn.com* ⇆ *4
rooms, 1 cottage* ⌂ *In-room: no a/c. In-hotel: no phone, DVD, VCR,
restaurant, no-smoking rooms, some pets allowed* ⊟ *AE, DC, MC, V*
⍾ *BP.*

¢-$ 🏨 **Discovery Inn Condos.** The connected apartments that make up this
complex overlook either the ocean or the property's private dock. Studios have modern furnishings and most have kitchenettes and pull-out
sofas. One-bedroom units have fireplaces and full kitchens. In the cen-

ter of the complex are a pool, game room, and glassed-in hot tub with water views. The beach, Damon Point bird sanctuary, and Westport ferry dock are a 15-minute walk south. ⊠*1031 Discovery Ave. SE, 98569* ☎*360/289–3371* ⊕*www.oceanshores.org/lodging* ⇆*16 studios, 8 1-bedroom units* ♿*In-room: kitchen (some). In-hotel: pool, some pets allowed* ☰*AE, DC, MC, V.*

COPALIS BEACH

3 mi north of Ocean Shores.

A Native American village for several thousand years, this small coastal town at the mouth of the Copalis (pronounced coh-*pah*-liss) River was settled by European-Americans in the 1890s. The beach here is known locally for its innumerable razor clams, which can be gathered by the thousands each summer, and for its watchtowers, built between 1870 and 1903 to spot and stalk sea otters—the animals are now protected by Washington state law. The first oil well in the state was dug here in 1901, but it proved to be unproductive. However, some geologists still claim that the continental shelf off the Olympic Peninsula holds major oil reserves.

You can hike or ride horses at **Griffiths-Priday Ocean State Park,** a 364-acre marine park stretching more than a mile along both the Pacific Ocean and the Copalis River. A boardwalk crosses low dunes to the broad, flat beach. The Copalis Spit section of the park is a designated wildlife refuge for thousands of snowy plover and other bird life. ⊠*3119 Hwy. 109* ☎*360/902–8844* ☒*$5* ⊙*Daily dawn–dusk.*

Pacific Beach State Park, between Copalis Beach and the town of Moclips, is a lovely spot for walking, surf-perch fishing, and razor-clam digging. There's also excellent fishing for sea-run cutthroat trout in the Moclips River—but be careful not to trespass onto Indian land, as the Quinault Reservation starts north of the river. The park has developed tent and RV sites, as well as a few primitive beachfront campsites. ⊠*Hwy. 109 S, 5 mi north of Copalis Beach* ☎*360/289–3553* ☒*$5* ⊙*Daily dawn–dusk.*

Moclips, 8 mi north of Copalis Beach, is a small, windswept beach town at the edge of the Quinault Reservation. Storm watchers, beachcombers, clammers, and surfers head to the string of magnificent, surf-tossed sands that begin here and run north along Highway 109. The highway ends 8 mi north of Moclips at Taholah in the reservation; note that only tribal members are allowed to leave the main road. Nonmembers must contact the tribal office for permission to go onto Quinault land, including the beach.

Museum of the North Beach houses artifacts and mementos, such as turn-of-the-20th-century newspaper clippings and an old gas pump, from the communities of Copalis Beach, Ocean Shores, and Moclips, among others, as well as crafts from the nearby Quinault Indian Nation. ⊠*4658 Hwy. 109* ☎*360/276–4441* ⊕*www.moclips.org* ☒*Free* ⊙*May–Sept., Fri.–Mon. 11–4; Oct.–Apr., weekends 11–4.* The **Quinault Pride**

Fish House, famous for its environmentally conscious practices, harvests seafood from Quinault tribal lands. Come around sunrise for the top catches, which are gone by 9 AM. Other goods include canned and smoked salmon and steelhead, plus Quinault arts and crafts. If you're overwhelmed with the choices, get one of the gift packs, which combine a range of ocean delicacies. Sales proceeds benefit the Quinault Indian Nation. The fish house is open weekdays 8 to 3. ⊠*100 Quinault, Taholah* ☎*360/276–4431.*

WHERE TO STAY & EAT

¢ ✕**Green Lantern Tavern.** The Copalis River flows beside this rustic, cedar shake–covered local favorite, in business since the 1930s. Huge picture windows show off ocean views, and the flowery outdoor beer garden attracts beachgoers in summer. Although clams are the specialty—witness the 10-foot-long clam-digging shovel in the corner—breakfasts, BLTs, grilled cheese, and fish are also on the menu. You must be 21 to enter. ⊠*3119 Hwy. 109* ☎*360/289–2297* ▤*No credit cards.*

¢–$ ☷**Iron Springs Resort.** Rustic wood cabins scattered along the beach and through the forest make up this isolated, 100-acre accommodation. Each cabin is outfitted in country colors, timber furnishings, and a fireplace. You're steps from the ocean and coastal trails, which together attract a mix of surfers, divers, boaters, and hikers. Don't miss the free fresh cinnamon rolls dished up by the owner each morning, or the tasty clam chowder on offer during cold evenings. ⊠*3707 Hwy. 109, 3 mi north of Copalis Beach, 98535* ☎*360/276–4230* 🖷*360/276–4365* ⊕*www.ironspringsresort.com* ⇄*29cottages* ⌂*In-room: no phone. In-hotel: kitchen, no TV, pool, beachfront, some pets allowed, no elevator* ▤*AE, DC, MC, V.*

¢–$ ☷**Sandpiper Beach Resort.** This resort is on a secluded beach 3 mi south of Moclips. The clean, contemporary studios and one-, two-, and three-bedroom suites each have a fireplace, a kitchen, exposed wood ceilings, and sliding glass doors leading to a porch overlooking the ocean. Little extras include heated towel bars, and there's housekeeping service every third day. No restaurant is on-site, but you're within walking distance of local cafés. ⊠*4159 Hwy. 109, Pacific Beach 98571* ☎*360/276–4580 or 800/567–4737* ⊕*www.sandpiper-resort.com* ⇄*31 units* ⌂*In-room: no a/c. In-hotel: no phone, kitchen, refrigerator, no TV, beachfront, some pets allowed, no elevator* ▤*MC, V.*

EN ROUTE **Ruby Beach,** named for the rosy fragments of garnet that color its sands, is one of the peninsula's most beautiful stretches of coastline. A short trail leads to the wave-beaten sands, where sea stacks, caves, tidal pools, and bony driftwood make it a favorite place of beachcombers, artists, and photographers. It's 15 mi south of Forks, off U.S. 101.

FORKS

99 mi north of Copalis Beach.

The former logging town of Forks is named for two nearby river junctions: the Bogachiel and Calawah rivers merge west of town, and a few miles farther they are joined by the Soleduck to form the Quileute

River, which empties into the Pacific at the Native American village of La Push. Forks is a small, quiet gateway town for Olympic National Park's Hoh River valley unit. The surrounding countryside is exceptionally green, with an annual precipitation of more than 100 inches.

The **Big Cedar,** thought to be the world's largest cedar tree, stands 178 feet tall and is 19 feet 5 inches in diameter. Area loggers left it standing when they realized just how enormous it really was. The tree is off Nolan Creek Road. From U.S. 101, turn right onto Highway N1000 for 1.3 mi, then turn right onto N1100 for 2.4 mi. Turn right again onto N1112 for 0.4 mi, and then turn right once more for 0.1 mi.

WHERE TO STAY & EAT

$–$$ ✕ **Smoke House Restaurant.** Rough-panel walls give a rustic appeal to the dining room of this two-story Forks favorite. Successful surf-and-turf specials remain unchanged since the place opened as a smokehouse in 1975. Smoked salmon is a top-seller, but the steaks and prime rib are also delicious. Burgers, fries, and milk shakes will please the kids. ⊠*193161 U.S. 101* ☎*360/374–6258* ▤*D, MC, V.*

$ ✕ **Forks Coffee Shop.** This modest restaurant on the highway in downtown Forks serves terrific, home-style, classic American fare. From 5 AM onward you can dig into giant pancakes and Sol Duc scrambles (eggs, sausage, hash browns, and veggies tumbled together). At lunch there's a choice of soups, salads, and hot and cold sandwiches, which the waitstaff will bag for pick-up if you're on the run. Dinner specials come with free trips to the salad bar and include entrées like baby back ribs and grilled Hood Canal oysters. Top off the meal with a home-baked treat, like a slice of flaky-crust pie made with locally grown marionberries, blueberries, strawberries, cherries, or apples. ⊠*U.S. 101* ☎*360/374–6769* ⊕*www.forkscoffeeshop.com* ▤*D, DC, MC, V.*

$–$$ ⊞ **Miller Tree Inn Bed and Breakfast.** Built as a farmhouse in 1916, this pale yellow B&B is still bordered on two sides by pastures. Numerous windows make the rooms bright, cheerful places to relax amid antiques, knickknacks, and quilts. Premier rooms have king-size beds, gas fireplaces, and hot tubs for two. A separate apartment has a private entrance and kitchenette. One parlor has a library and piano, the other has games. In summer, lemonade and cookies are served on the lawn or the wide front porch. From October through April, nearby rivers offer prime salmon and steelhead fishing. ⊠*654 E. Division St., 98331* ☎*360/374–6806 or 800/943–6563* ⊟*360/374–6807* ⊕*www.miller treeinn.com* ⊅*6 rooms, 1 apartment* ⟳*In-room: no a/c. In-hotel: no phone, kitchen, Wi-Fi, spa, VCR (some), no TV (some), no kids under 7, some pets allowed, no elevator* ▤*DC, MC, V* ⟦⟧*BP.*

¢–$$ ⊞ **Manitou Lodge.** If seclusion is what you seek, turn off your cell phone (they're useless here) and visit this cedar lodge in the rain forest, which bills itself as the westernmost B&B in the continental United States. The cathedral-size main room has a towering stone fireplace, a tall bookcase, and multiple couches. Five lodge rooms of varying sizes and two suites in the adjacent cottage have cedar paneling, handmade quilts, driftwood headboards, and oak furnishings; the large Sacagawea room even has a fireplace. A small, rustic cabin is available from May through October. Afternoon cookies and coffee are served in the dining room. ✉813 Kilmer Rd., 98331 ☎360/374–6295 📠360/374–7495 ⊕www.manitoulodge.com ➱8 rooms, 1 suites, 2 cabins, 2 campsites ♿In-room: no a/c. In-hotel: no phone, no TV, Ethernet, Wi-Fi, no kids under 5, no elevator ▭AE, D, DC, MC, V ❘⊚❘BP.

SEKIU

28 mi northwest of Forks.

The village of Sekiu (pronounced *see*-kyu) rests on the peninsula's northern shore, a rocky and roiling stretch of coastline inhabited for centuries by the Makah (ma-*kah*), Ozette, and S'Klallum tribes. White settlers moved to Sekiu after a salmon cannery opened near the fishing grounds in 1870. Logging became the mainstay of the local economy in the early 1900s. Both industries shut down when resources became overexploited, and now Sekiu is a scenic vacation town known for excellent fishing and scuba diving. As the twisted two-lane road rises and dips along the rugged edge of the land, the forest often yields to a panorama of surf-thrashing, boulder-strewn beaches, with distant views of mountainous Vancouver Island. Autumn attracts fishing pros to the Sekiu River for cutthroat trout and steelhead, and the town jetty is a base for sports divers.

On the former site of an Indian fishing village, the 33-acre **Clallam Bay Spit** brings beachcombers, fishers, and divers. The 4-acre Pillar Point Fishing Camp to the east has campsites and a boat ramp. Dress warmly: Pysht Bay takes its name from a S'Klallam term meaning "where the wind blows from all directions." ✉Off Hwy. 112 at Clallum Bay and Pysht Bay ⊘Daily.

WHERE TO STAY & EAT

¢–$$ ✗**Breakwater Restaurant.** This restaurant above the Strait of San Juan de Fuca claims to be the most northwesterly dining establishment in the continental United States. Look for seafood, of course, served by a friendly and accommodating staff. Chicken dishes, burgers, steaks, and breakfasts fill out the menu. While you wait for your food, enjoy the collection of "Messy Palate" locally painted works hung along the walls. ✉Hwy. 112, Clallam Bay ☎360/963–2428 ▭MC, V.

¢–$ ▦**Winter Summer Inn.** The late-1800s home is the community's oldest, and its walls are appropriately adorned with American antiques and works by local artists. The master suite has a full kitchen and private deck, and the Quilt Room has a Jacuzzi. You can see panoramas of the Clallam River and Strait of Juan de Fuca from all around the inn. **Pros:** Central to upper Olympic Peninsula sights, stunning water views. **Cons:** Two rooms have private half-bath but share the shower. ✉16651 Hwy. 112, Clallam Bay 98326 ☎360/963–2264 ⊕www.wintersummerinn.com ➱3 rooms, 1 suite ♿In-room: no a/c. In-hotel: kitchen (some), refrigerator (some), no TV (some), no kids under 12, no elevator ▭AE, D, MC, V ❘⊚❘BP.

NEAH BAY

15 mi northwest of Sekiu.

One of the oldest villages in Washington, Neah (pronounced *nee*-ah) Bay is surrounded by the Makah Indian Reservation at the northwestern tip of the Olympic Peninsula. Today it's still a quiet, seldom-visited seaside settlement of one-story homes, espresso stands, and bait shops stretched along about a mile of gravelly coastal road, which parallels the glistening, boat-filled bay. Stroll along the docks to watch boot-clad fishermen and shaggy canines motoring out on warped and barnacled vessels, and peer into the oil-stained water for views of anemones, shell-fish, and sea lions. The rocky bulkhead rises behind the marina; look beyond that to view sunsets and Cape Flattery, the northwesternmost point in the contiguous United States.

Explorer James Cook named the cape in 1778 when his ship missed the fog-smothered Strait of Juan de Fuca and landed here instead. In 1792 Spanish mariners established a short-lived fort here, which was the first European settlement in what is now Washington State. The local Makah tribe is more closely related to the Nootka of Vancouver Island, just across the water, than to any Washington tribe. Like their ancestors, they embark on whale hunts by canoe, although fleets of kayaks skimming through the calm bay are all you're likely to see during your visit.

🌀
Fodor'sChoice
★
The outstanding **Makah Cultural and Research Center** displays thousands of Makah art pieces and artifacts, many eons old. Done in low lights and rich timbers, the space is divided into an easy route of intriguing exhibits. The centerpiece is a full-size cedar longhouse, complete with hand-woven baskets, fur skins, cat-tail wool, grass mats on the bed planks, and a background of tribal music. Another section houses full-size whaling and seal-hunting canoes and weapons. Other areas show games, clothing, crafts, and relics from the ancient Ozette Village mudslide. The small shop stocks a collection of locally made art pieces, books, and crafts; plan to spend some time looking around. This is as well-done a museum as you'd find in any major city, and should be a stop on any itinerary in the region. ⊠*1880 Bayview Ave.* ☎*360/645–2711* ⊕*www.makah.com* 🖻*$5* ⊗*Daily 10–5.*

At the **Makah National Fish Hatchery** you can view Chinook salmon as they make their way over fish ladders to the hatchery's spawning area. Spawning months are October and November, and the salmon are released in late April. Smaller numbers of coho and chum salmon and steelhead trout also populate the hatchery. From Neah Bay, follow signs south for 7 mi. ⊠*897 Hatchery Rd.* ☎*360/645–2521* 🖻*Free* ⊗*Daily 7:30–4.*

WHERE TO STAY & EAT

$
★
✕ **Warm House.** Fresh-caught seafood and hearty breakfast-style fare stock the menu of this attractive and popular waterfront café. The indoor dining room is cozy, and there are picnic tables outside. A specialty is the traditional salmon bake, with fish cooked on cedar planks

in a fire pit. These meals, which run $19 per person, must be booked a week in advance for a minimum of four people. ✉ *1471 Bay View Ave.* ☎*360/645–2924* ▤*MC, V* ⊗*No lunch.*

$$ ▣**King Fisher Inn.** The three-story, sky-gray chalet above the Strait of Juan de Fuca is decked out in Northwest style, trimmed with timber and a fringe of colorful flowers. Each room comes with fluffy robes, and a breakfast buffet is included. One unique focus of the inn is quilting, and you can view many local creations in the gallery; quilting classes and workshops run autumn through winter. Note that a two-night minimum stay is required on weekends. **Pros:** Chairlift service up to rooms, full meal plan for groups. **Cons:** Scrapbooking and meeting groups can disrupt serene atmosphere. ✉*1562 Hwy. 112, 98357* ☎*360/645–2150 or 888/622–8216* ⊕*www.kingfisherenterprises.com* ⤶*4 rooms* ♿*In-room: VCR. In-hotel: laundry facilities, no kids under 12, no elevator* ▤*AE, MC, V* ⦿*BP.*

PORT ANGELES

65 mi east of Neah Bay.

Sprawling along the hills above the deep-blue Strait of San Juan de Fuca, Port Angeles is the crux of the Olympic Peninsula's air, sea, and land links. The town is capped off at the water's edge by a gathering of glittering hotels, restaurants, shops, and attractions, all set around the modern marina and the bone-white swath of Hollywood Beach. With a population of about 19,000, the town is the largest on the Olympic Peninsula and a major gateway to Olympic National Park. Summer foot traffic is shoulder-to-shoulder downtown with hopefuls rushing to ferries, vacationers strolling the waterfront, and locals relaxing at outdoor cafés.

It didn't start out this way, though, as the seasonal crowds have only been a phenomenon since the 1950s. The area was first settled by the Hoh, Makah, Quileute, Quinault, and S'Klallam tribes, and others had little reason to visit until a Greek pilot named Apostolos Valerianus—aka Juan de Fuca—sailed into the strait in 1610. In 1791 Spanish explorer Juan Francisco de Eliza followed him and named the Puerto de Nuestra Señora de Los Angeles, or Port of Our Lady of the Angels. George Vancouver shortened the name to Port Angeles in 1792, and the site was settled by pioneers in 1856. In the century that followed, Port Angeles became a timber-mill town, a military base, and a key regional fishing port.

☺ The **Fiero Marine Life Center,** at the corner of the marina and Hollywood Beach, is brightly painted with an array of life-size ocean murals. Meander along the boardwalk overlooking the bay, then step inside to see just what's down in those waters. A variety of touch and display tanks along the walls house octopus, scallops, rockfish, and anemones, and volunteers are on hand to answer questions. ✉*Port Angeles City Pier, Railroad St. at Lincoln St.* ☎*360/417–6254* ⊕*www.olypen.com/ feirolab* ▣*Summer $3; free off-season* ⊗*Memorial Day–Labor Day, Tues.–Sun 10–5; otherwise weekends noon–4.*

The **Museum of the Clallam Historical Society** preserves the region's past in a handsome 1919 building. Downstairs, historic photos and artifacts illustrate the lifestyles and history of the town's Native American and Anglo communities; rotating temporary exhibits are featured upstairs. ⊠207 S. Lincoln St. 🕾360/452–6779 📧Donations accepted ⊗ Wed.–Sat. 1–4.

Ediz Hook, at the western end of Port Angeles, is a long natural sand spit that protects the harbor from big waves and storms. The Hook is a fine place to take a walk along the water and watch shore and seabirds, and to spot the occasional seal, orca, or gray whale. From downtown, take Front Street west and follow it as it meanders past the shuttered lumber mill.

The small, sophisticated **Port Angeles Fine Arts Center** is inside the former home of the late artist and publisher Esther Barrows Webster, one of Port Angeles's most energetic and cultured citizens. Outdoor sculpture and trees surround the center, which has panoramas of the city and harbor. Exhibitions emphasize the works in various mediums of emerging and well-established Pacific Northwest artists. ⊠1203 W. Lauridsen Blvd. 🕾360/417–4590 ⊕www.pafac.org 📧Free ⊗Indoor exhibits Mar.–Nov., Wed.–Sun. 11–5, otherwise 11–4. Outdoor exhibits daily dawn–dusk.

WHERE TO EAT

$$–$$$ ✕**C'est Si Bon.** Far more Euro-savvy than is typical on the Olympic Pen-
Fodor'sChoice insula, this first-rate restaurant stands out for its decor as well as for its
★ food. The fanciful dining room is done up in bold red hues, with crisp white linens, huge oil paintings, and glittering chandeliers; the spacious solarium takes an equally formal approach. The changing menu specials highlights homemade onion soup, Cornish hen, filet mignon, and lobster tail. The wine list is superb, with French, Australian, and Northwest choices to pair with everything. The friendly, knowledgeable owners are happy to chat or answer questions about their cuisine creations, and the waitstaff is well trained. ⊠23 Cedar Park Rd., Port Angeles 🕾360/452–8888 ⚑Reservations essential ▤AE, DC, MC, V ⊗Closed Mon. No lunch.

$–$$ ✕**The Bushwhacker.** More than three decades of excellent surf-and-turf keep the locals coming back to this Northwest-style restaurant just east of the city. It's a big, friendly place where families gather to dig into huge cuts of meat or seafood dishes. Other tasty fare includes jam-packed seafood fettucine, and stout bread-bowl Guinness stew topped with garlic mashed potatoes. A salad and soup bar comes with every meal—but save room for decadent desserts like triple berry cobbler and peanut-butter pie. ⊠1527 E. 1st St. 🕾360/457–4113 ⊕www.bushwhackerpa.com ▤AE, MC, V.

$–$$ ✕**Crab House.** This waterfront restaurant, linked to the Red Lion Inn in front of the Port Angeles Pier, is one of the region's most famous spots for fresh local seafood. Crab is the specialty, of course, and it shows up in a tasty variety of dishes, including crab hash, crab bisque, crab cakes, and crab-stuffed fish specials. Windows surrounding the elegant dining room let you view the serene gray waters where much of what's on the menu is caught daily. ⊠*221 N. Lincoln St.* ☎*360/457–0424* ⊕*www. pacrabhouse.com* ⊟*AE, D, DC, V* ☉*No lunch.*

$–$$ ✕**Dupuis Restaurant.** Flower-filled gardens surround this little log cabin,
★ painted a cheery yellow and blue and trimmed with bright flower boxes. One of the dining rooms was a tavern in the 1920s, and today close-set tables in the elegant main dining room are lit by small chandeliers. Grilled local fish, steamed crabs and oysters, seafood sautés, and a selection of continental choices, like cheese-topped French onion soup, round out the menu. It's a dress-up dinner spot that's a highlight of a trip to the region. Hint: The owner will open the restaurant during lunch and off days for groups of 10 or more. ⊠*256861 U.S. 101* ☎*360/457–8033* ⊟*AE, D, MC, V* ☉*Closed Tues. in winter. No lunch.*

WHERE TO STAY

$$–$$$$ ⊡**Colette's Bed & Breakfast.** A contemporary mansion curving around 10
Fodor'sChoice acres of gorgeous waterfront property, this B&B offers more space, ser-
★ vice, and luxury than any other property in the area. Leather sofas and chairs and a river-rock fireplace make the front room a lovely spot to watch the water through expansive 20-foot windows. The suites, which have such names as Iris, Azalea, and Cedar, also overlook the water and have fireplaces, balconies, private entrances, CD and DVD players, and two-person Jacuzzi tubs. A specially made outdoor fireplace means you can enjoy the deck even in winter. Multicourse gourmet breakfasts include espresso-based drinks and fresh fruit, hors d'oeuvres and wine, and nightly chocolates are special highlights. **Pros:** Exquisite rooms, magnificent ocean views. **Cons:** Slippery floors. ⊠*339 Finn Hall Rd., 10 mi east of town, Port Angeles 98362* ☎*360/457–9197 or 877/457– 9777* ⊕*www.colettes.com* ➫*5 suites* △*In-room: refrigerator, VCR. In-hotel: restaurant, no kids under 16, no elevator* ⊟*MC, V* ⍩*BP.*

$$–$$$$ ⊡**Domaine Madeleine.** This luxury B&B, surrounded by acres of gardens on a bluff above the Strait of Juan de Fuca, is breathtaking from first sight. Rooms, all with private entrances, are decorated with either impressionist or Asian accents and overlook water and mountain views. Four rooms have a hot tub, and three also have a kitchenette, with gas fireplaces, designer robes, CD players, and VCRs. The living room, set aside for private use with bookings of the Renoir Room, has a 14-foot-tall basalt fireplace, antique Asian furnishings, and a harpsichord. For breakfast, expect a five-course gourmet affair with fresh baguettes, chicken crepes, and seafood omelets. **Pros:** Sweeping views, a serene waterfall in the woodland gardens, firepit cheer on wintry nights. **Cons:** The drive from city attractions. ⊠*146 Wildflower La., 8 mi east of Port Angeles, 98362* ☎*360/457–4174 or 888/811–8376* ⊟*360/457–3037* ⊕*www.domainemadeleine.com* ➫*5 rooms* △*In-room: refrigerator (some). In-hotel: VCR, no kids under 12, no elevator* ⊟*AE, D, DC, MC, V* ⍩*BP.*

$$–$$$ ⊡**BJ's Garden Gate.** A gingerbread-style porch fronts this waterfront
★ Victorian home on three acres of landscaped grounds. Exquisitely appointed guest rooms include Victoria's Repose, which has a finely carved half-tester English oak bed and a balcony with a private two-person hot tub. All rooms have fireplaces, hot tubs, CD players and

VCRs, plus panoramic water views through floor-to-ceiling glass windows. Antiques are artfully arranged throughout the living and dining rooms, which have expansive views of the strait. Gorgeous flower gardens, which have been featured in national commercials, help make this an ideal romantic getaway. ⌧*397 Monterra Dr., 98362* ☎*360/452–2322 or 800/880–1332* ⊕*www.bjgarden.com* ⊲*5 rooms* ⌖*In-room: VCR. In-hotel: Ethernet, dial-up, Wi-Fi, no kids under 18, no elevator* ⊟*MC, V* ⏅*BP.*

¢–$$ 　🖼**Five Sea Suns Bed & Breakfast.** The clever name of this cozy 1926
★ 　 inn refers to its rooms, each elegantly appointed in the theme of a time of year: the four seasons plus an Indian summer. If you stay in Lente (spring), you can enjoy a breezy balcony. Na Zomer (Indian summer) is in a separate carriage house. The B&B overlooks the mountains and the bay, which you can view from the pond-side pergola and award-winning gardens. In the morning, coffee is served in a silver tea set in your room. **Pros:** Garden setting is steps from town; the owner's home-baked chocolate-chip cookies. **Cons:** No modern communications perks. ⌧*1006 S. Lincoln St., 98362* ☎*360/452–8248 or 800/708–0777* ☒*360/417–0465* ⊕*www.seasuns.com* ⊲*5 rooms* ⌖*In-room: no a/c. In-hotel: no phone, no TV (some), airport shuttle, no kids under 12, no elevator* ⊟*AE, D, MC, V* ⏅*BP.*

SEQUIM

17 mi east of Port Angeles on U.S. 101.

Sequim (pronounced *skwim*), incorporated in 1913, is a pleasant farming and mill town between the northern foothills of the Olympic Mountains and the southeastern stretch of the Strait of Juan de Fuca. With neat, quiet blocks and lovely views, it's also a popular place to retire. A few miles to the north is the shallow and fertile Dungeness Valley. Though it has some of the lowest rainfall in western Washington, fragrant purple lavender flourishes in local fields.

You'll find lavender and other local produce in abundance at the Saturday **Open Aire Market** (⌧*Cedar St., between Seal St. and 2nd Ave.* ☎*360/683–4855* ⊕*www.sequimopenairemarket.com*), a tented affair with lots of color and live music, open from 9 to 3 between mid-May and mid-October

The **Original Sequim Farmers Market** (⌧*Washington St.* ☎*No phone*), an event for those who like to get up and go, takes place April to October on Saturdays from 7:30 am to 10 am at the west edge of town.

In 1977 12,000-year-old mastodon remains were discovered near Sequim. You can view the bones of these Ice Age creatures, plus a beautiful wall mural, at the **Sequim-Dungeness Museum.** There are also exhibits on Captain Vancouver's explorations, the early Klallam Indians, and the area's pioneer towns. Temporary exhibits examine regional topics like earthquakes. ⌧*175 W. Cedar St.* ☎*360/683–8110* ⊕*www. sequimmuseum.org* ⌧*Free* ⏰*Tues.–Sun. 10–3:30.*

Continued on page 471

Olympic National Park

One of the country's most fascinating environments lies at its far northwestern corner, within the heart-shape Olympic Peninsula. Edged on all sides by water, the elegant snowcapped and forested landscape is remote and pristine. The endless sharpened ridges of the towering Olympic Mountains are visible for 50 mi inland. Big lakes cut pockets of blue in the rugged blanket of pine forests, and hot springs gurgle up from the foothills. Along the coast the sights are even more amazing: wave-sculpted boulders, tidal pools teeming with sea life, and tree-topped sea stacks.

WELCOME TO OLYMPIC

TOP REASONS TO GO

★ **Exotic rain forest:** A rain forest in the Pacific Northwest? Olympic National Park is one of a few places in the world with this unique temperate landscape.

★ **Beachcombing:** Miles of spectacular, rugged coastline dotted with tidal pools, sea stacks, and driftwood hem the edges of the Olympic Peninsula.

★ **Nature's hot tubs:** Take a relaxing dip in the wooded heart of the park at the Sol Duc hot springs, a series of geothermal mineral pools.

★ **Lofty vistas:** The Olympics have plenty of peaks you can climb—or you just drive up to Hurricane Ridge for endless views over the ranges.

★ **A sense of history:** The first evidence of humans on the Olympic Peninsula dates back 12,000 years. Today, eight tribes still have traditional ties to lands in Olympic National Park, and there are ample opportunities for exploring Native American history in and around the region.

1 **Coastal Olympic.**
Here the Pacific smashes endlessly into the rugged coastline, carving out some of the park's most memorable scenes in the massive, rocky sea stacks and islets just offshore. Back from the water are beaches and tide pools full of starfish, crabs, and anemones.

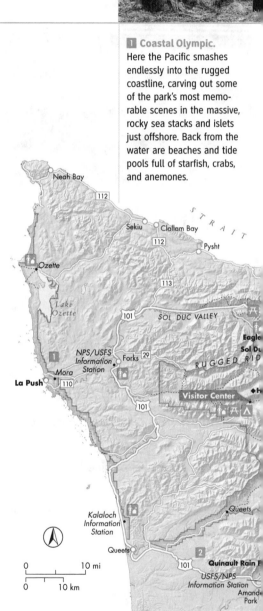

2 **The rain forest.** Centered on the Hoh, Queets, and Quinault river valleys, this is the region's most unique landscape. Fog-shrouded Douglas firs and Sitka spruces, some more than 300 feet tall, huddle in this moist, pine-carpeted area, shading fern- and moss-draped cedars, maples, and alders.

3 **The mountains.** Craggy gray peaks and snow-covered summits dominate the skyline. Low-level foliage and wildflower meadows make for excellent hiking in the plateaus. Even on the sunniest days, temperatures are brisk. Some roads are closed in winter months.

4 **Alpine meadows.** In midsummer, the swathe of colors is like a Monet canvas spread over the landscape, and wildlife teems within the honeyed flowers. Trails are never prettier, and views are crisp and vast.

WASHINGTON

GETTING ORIENTED

The Olympic peninsula's elegant snowcapped and forested landscape is edged on all sides by water: to the north, the Strait of Juan de Fuca separates the United States from Canada, while a network of Puget Sound bays laces the east, the Chehalis River meanders along the southern end, and the massive gray Pacific Ocean guards the west side.

4

OLYMPIC NATIONAL PARK

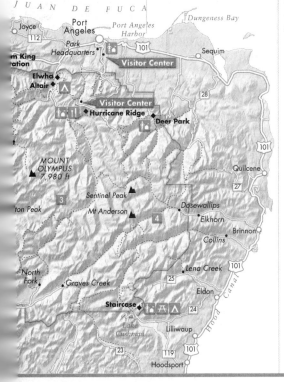

JUAN DE FUCA

Joyce
112
Port Angeles
Park Headquarters
Port Angeles Harbor
101
Dungeness Bay
Sequim
n King ation
Visitor Center
Elwha
Altair
28
Visitor Center
Hurricane Ridge
Deer Park
101
MOUNT OLYMPUS 7,980 ft
Quilcene
27
ton Peak
Sentinel Peak
Mt Anderson
4
Dosewallips
Elkhorn
Brinnon
Collins
North Fork
Graves Creek
25
Lena Creek
101
Eldon
Hood Canal
Staircase
24
Lake Cushman
Lilliwaup
23
119
101
Hoodsport

OLYMPIC NATIONAL PARK PLANNER

When to Go

Summer, with its long stretches of sun-filled days, is prime touring time for Olympic National Park, perfect for taking in sweeping mountain-top vistas and dazzling Northwestern beaches. **June through September are peak months,** when more than 75% of park visitors stream into the area; popular stops like Hurricane Ridge, the Hoh Rain Forest, Lake Crescent, and Ruby Beach are bustling by 10 AM.

Late spring and early autumn are also good bets for clear weather; any time between April and October, and you'll have a chance of blue skies. Between Thanksgiving and Easter, it's a toss-up as to which days will turn out fair; prepare for heavy clouds, rain showers, and chilly temperatures, then hope for the best.

That said, winter is a great time to visit if you enjoy isolation. Locals are usually the only hardy souls exploring the park's winter scenes, except for weekend skiers heading to the snowfields around Hurricane Ridge. Many visitor facilities have limited hours or are closed from October to April.

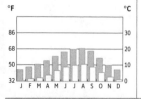

Getting There & Around

U.S. 101 essentially encircles the main section of Olympic National Park, and a number of roads lead from the highway into the park's mountains and toward its beaches. You can reach U.S. 101 via Interstate 5 at Olympia, via Route 12 at Aberdeen, or via Route 104 from the Washington State ferry terminals at Bainbridge or Kingston. The ferries are the most direct route to the Olympic area from Seattle; call **Washington State Ferries** (☎800/843–3779 or 206/464—6400, www.wsdot.wa.gov/ferries) for information. You can enter the park at a number of points, though access roads do not penetrate far, since the park is 95% wilderness. The best way to get around and to see many of the park's key sites is on foot.

Grays Harbor Transit (☎360/532–2770 or 800/562–9730 ⊕www.ghtransit.com) runs free daily buses between Forks and Amanda Park, to the south on the west end of Lake Quinault. **West Jefferson Transit** (☎800/371–0497 ⊕www.jeffersontransit.com) also runs daily buses (50¢) between Forks and Amanda Park, as well as to the east side of Jefferson County.

Good Reads

Robert L. Wood's **Olympic Mountain Trail Guide** is useful for planning hikes and longer excursions. Stephen Whitney's **A Field Guide to the Cascades and Olympics** is an excellent trailside reference, covering more than 500 plant and animal species found in the park.

The park's newspaper, the *Bugler*, is a seasonal guide for activities and opportunities in Olympic National Park. You can pick these up at the visitor centers. A handy mail-order catalog of books and maps about the park is available from the **Northwest Interpretive Association (NWIA).** ✉ 164 S. Jackson St., Seattle ☎ 206/220–4140 or 877/874–6775 ⊕ http://nwpubliclands.org.

SCENIC DRIVES

Updated by Holly S. Smith

★ **Port Angeles Visitor Center to Hurricane Ridge.** Climbing steeply—from thick fir forests in the foothills and subalpine meadow below the ridge, to sweeping upper alpine meadows—this is the premier scenic drive in Olympic National Park. At the summit, the visitor center at Hurricane Ridge has some truly spectacular views of the heart of the mountains and across the Strait of Juan de Fuca. (Backpackers note wryly that you have to hike a long way in other parts of the park to get the kinds of views you can drive to here.) Hurricane Ridge also has an uncommonly fine display of wildflowers in spring and summer.

WHAT TO SEE

Most of the park's attractions are found either far off Highway 101 or down trails that require hikes of 15 minutes or longer. West coast beaches are linked to the highway by downhill trails; the number of cars parked alongside the road at the start of the paths indicate how crowded the beach will be.

HISTORIC SITES

La Push. At the mouth of Quileute River, La Push is the tribal center of the Quileute Indians. In fact, the town's name is a variation on the French *la bouche,* which means "the mouth." Offshore rock spires known as sea stacks dot the coast here, and you may catch a glimpse of bald eagles nesting in the nearby cliffs. ✉ *Rte. 110, 14 mi west of Forks.*

★ **Lake Ozette.** The third-largest glacial impoundment in Washington anchors the coastal strip of Olympic National Park at its north end. The small town of Ozette, home to a coastal tribe, is the trailhead for two of the park's better one-day hikes. Both 3-mi trails lead over boardwalks through swampy wetland and coastal old-growth forest to the ocean shore and uncrowded beaches. ✉ *At end of Hoko-Ozette Rd., 26 mi southwest of Hwy. 112 near Sekiu* ☎ *360/963–2725.*

SCENIC STOPS

Fodor'sChoice
★ **Hoh River Rain Forest.** South of Forks, an 18-mi spur road links Highway 101 with this unique temperate rain forest, where spruce and hemlock trees soar to heights of more than 200 feet. Alders and big-leaf maples are so densely covered with mosses they look more like shaggy prehistoric animals than trees, and elk browse in shaded glens. Be prepared for precipitation: the region receives 140 inches or more each year (that's 12 feet and up). ✉ *From Hwy. 101, at about 20 mi north of Kalaloch, turn onto Upper Hoh Rd. 18 mi east to Hoh Rain Forest Visitor Center* ☎ *360/374–6925.*

Fodor'sChoice
★ **Hurricane Ridge.** The panoramic view from this 5,200-foot-high ridge encompasses the Olympic range, the Strait of Juan de Fuca, and Vancouver Island. Guided tours are given in summer along the many paved and unpaved trails, where wildflowers and wildlife such as deer and marmots flourish. ✉ *Hurricane Ridge Rd., 17 mi south of Port Angeles* ☎ *360/565–3130* ☉ *Visitor center daily 10–5.*

OLYMPIC IN ONE DAY

Start out early from **Lake Quinault Lodge,** in the park's southwest corner, and drive a half hour into the Quinault Valley via **South Shore Road.** Tackle the forested **Graves Creek Nature Trail,** then head up **North Shore Road** to the Quinault Rain Forest Interpretive Trail. Next, head back to Highway 101 and drive to **Ruby Beach,** where a shoreline walk presents a breathtaking scene of sea stacks and sparkling, pink-hued sands.

Forks, and its **Timber Museum,** are your next stop; have lunch here, then drive 20 minutes to the beach at **La Push.** Next, head to **Lake Crescent,** around the corner to the northeast, where you can rent a boat, take a swim, or enjoy a water-side picnic. Drive through **Port Angeles** to **Hurricane Ridge Road,** an hour's drive to the top if there aren't too many visitors. At the ridge, explore the visitor center or hike the 3-mi loop to 5,757-foot **Hurricane Hill,** where you can see over the entire park north to Vancouver Island and south past Mt. Olympus.

Kalaloch. With a lodge, a huge campground, miles of coastline, and easy access from the highway, this is another popular spot. Keen-eyed beachcombers may spot sea otters just offshore; they were reintroduced here in 1970. ⊠ *156954 Hwy. 101, 32 mi northwest of Lake Quinault, Forks* ☎ *360/962–2283.*

Lake Crescent. Visitors see Lake Crescent as Highway 101 winds along its southern shore, giving way to gorgeous views of azure waters rippling in a basin formed by Tuscan-like hills. In the evening, low bands of clouds caught between the surrounding mountains often linger over its reflective surface. ⊠ *Hwy. 101, 16 mi west of Port Angeles and 28 mi east of Forks* ☎ *360/928–3380.*

★ **Lake Quinault.** This glimmering lake, 4½ mi long and 300 feet deep, is the first landmark you'll reach when driving the west-side loop of U.S. 101. The rain forest is densest here, with moss-draped maples and alders, and towering spruce, fir, and hemlock. Enchanted Valley, high up near the Quinault River's source, is a deeply glaciated valley that's closer to the Hood Canal than to the Pacific Ocean. A scenic loop drive circles the lake and travels around a section of the Quinault River. ⊠ *Hwy. 101, 38 mi north of Hoquiam* ☎ *360/288–2444* ⊙ *Ranger station May–Sept., daily 8–5.*

Second and Third Beaches. During low tide, the pools here brim with life, and you can walk out to some sea stacks. Gray whales play offshore during their annual spring migration, and most of the year the waves are great for surfing and kayaking (bring a wet suit). ⊠ *Hwy. 101, 32 mi north of Lake Quinault* ☎ *360/374–5460.*

Sol Duc. Sol Duc Valley is one of those magical, serene places where all the Northwest's virtues seem at hand—lush lowland forests, a sparkling river, salmon runs, and quiet hiking trails. Here, the popular Sol Duc Hot Springs area includes three sulfuric pools ranging in temperature from 98°F to 104°F. ⊠*Sol Duc Rd. south of U.S. 101, 1 mi past the west end of Lake Crescent* ☎*360/374–6925.*

Staircase. Unlike the forests of the park's south and west sides, Douglas fir is the dominant tree on the east slope of the Olympic Mountains. Fire has played an important role in creating the majestic forest here, as the Staircase Ranger Station explains in interpretive exhibits. Note that the area is closed November through April. ⊠*At end of Rte. 119, 15 mi from U.S. 101 at Hoodsport* ☎*360/877–5569.*

VISITOR CENTERS

Wilderness Information Center. The office has park maps and brochures; they also provide permits and rent bear-proof containers. ⊠*551 S. Forks Ave., Forks* ☎*360/374–7566* ⊕*www.nps.gov/olym* ⊗*June–Aug., Sat.–Wed. 9:30–5, Thurs. and Fri. 8:30–6; Sept.–May, daily 9–4.*

Hoh Rain Forest Visitor Center. Pick up park maps and pamphlets, permits, and activities lists in this busy, woodsy chalet; there's also a shop and exhibits on natural history. Several short interpretive trails and longer wilderness treks start from here. ⊠*Upper Hoh Rd., Forks* ☎*360/374–6925* ⊕*www.nps.gov/olym* ⊗*Sept.–June, daily 9–4; July and Aug., daily 9–6:30.*

Hurricane Ridge Visitor Center. The upper level of this visitor center has exhibits, a gift shop, and a café; the lower level has open seating and nice views. Guided walks and programs start in late June, and you can also get details on the surrounding Winter Use Area ski and sledding slopes. ⊠*Hurricane Ridge Rd., Port Angeles* ☎*360/565–3131* ⊕*www.nps.gov/olym* ⊗*Memorial Day–Labor Day, daily 9–7; Dec.–Apr., Fri.–Sun. 9–4.*

Olympic National Park Visitor Center. This modern, well-organized facility, staffed by park rangers, provides everything: maps, trail brochures, campground advice, listings of wildlife sightings, educational programs and exhibits, information on road and trail closures, and weather forecasts. ⊠*3002 Mount Angeles Rd., Port Angeles98362* ☎*360/565–3130* ⊕*www.nps.gov/olym* ⊗*May–Sept., daily 9–4; Oct.–Apr., weekdays 10–4, weekends 9–4.*

South Shore Quinault Ranger Station. This office at the Lake Quinault Lodge has maps, campground information, and program listings. ⊠*S. Shore Lake Quinault Rd., Lake Quinault* ⊕*www.nps.gov/olym* ⊗*Memorial Day–Labor Day, weekdays 8–4:30, weekends 9–4.*

Wilderness Information Center (WIC). Located behind Olympic National Park Visitor Center, this facility provides all the information you'll need for a trip in the park, including trail conditions, safety tips, and weather bulletins. The office also issues camping permits, takes campground reservations, and rents bear-proof food canisters for $3. ⊠*3002 Mount Angeles Rd., Port Angeles* ☎*360/565–3100* ⊕*www.nps.gov/olym* ⊗*Late June–Labor Day, Sun.–Thurs. 7:30–6, Fri. and Sat. 7:30–7; otherwise weekdays 8–4:30.*

SPORTS & THE OUTDOORS

BEACHCOMBING

★ The wild, pebble- and shell-strewn Pacific coast teems with tide pools and clawed creatures. Crabs, sand dollars, anemones, starfish, and all sorts of shellfish are exposed at low tide, when flat beaches can stretch out for hundreds of yards. Note that the most easily accessible sand-strolling spots are Rialto; Ruby; First and Second near Mora and La Push; and beaches No. 2 and No. 4 in the Kalaloch stretch.

The Wilderness Act and the park's code of ethics strongly encourage visitors to leave all natural materials where they are for others to enjoy.

BICYCLING

The rough gravel car tracks to some of the park's remote sites were meant for four-wheel-drive vehicles, but can double as mountain-bike routes. The Quinault Valley, Queets River, Hoh River, and Sol Duc River roads have bike paths through old-growth forest. Graves Creek Road, in the southwest, is a mountain-bike path; Lake Crescent's north side is also edged by the bike-friendly Spruce Railroad Trail. More bike trails run through the adjacent Olympic National Forest. Note that Highway 101 has heavy traffic and isn't recommended for cycling, although the western side has broad roads with beautiful scenery and can be biked off-season. Bikes are not permitted on foot trails. *For bike rentals and guides,* ⇨ *Outfitters & Expeditions box.*

CLIMBING

At 7,980 feet, Mt. Olympus is the highest peak in the park and the most popular climb in the region. To attempt the summit, participants must register at the Glacier Meadows Ranger Station. Mt. Constance, the third-highest Olympic summit at 7,743 feet, has a well-traversed climbing route that requires technical experience; reservations are recommended for the Lake Constance stop, which is limited to 20 campers. Mt. Deception is a third possibility, though tricky snows have caused several fatalities and injuries in the last decade. Climbing season runs late June through September. Note that crevasse skills and self-rescue experience are highly recommended. Climbers must register with park officials and purchase wilderness permits before setting out. The best resource for climbing advice is the Wilderness Information Center in Port Angeles. *For guides and equipment,* ⇨ *Outfitters & Expeditions box.*

FISHING

Lake Crescent is home to cutthroat and rainbow trout, as well as petite kokanee salmon; Lake Cushman, Lake Quinault, and Ozette Lake have trout, salmon, and steelhead; and Lake Mills has three trout varieties. As for rivers, the Bogachiel and Queets have steelhead salmon in season. The glacier-fed Hoh River is home to chinook salmon April to November, and coho salmon from August through November; the Sol Duc River offers all five species of salmon, plus cutthroat and steelhead trout. Rainbow trout are also found in the Dosewallips, Elwha, and Skykomish rivers. Other places to go after salmon and trout include the

OUTFITTERS & EXPEDITIONS

BICYCLING

Bicycle Adventures (☎ *360/786–0989 or 800/443–6060* ⊕ *www.bicycleadventures.com*), an Olympia bike tour outfit, stages trips in and around the park area, including up Hurricane Ridge. **Mike's Bikes** (✉ *150 W. Sequim Bay Rd., Sequim* ☎ *360/681–3868* ⊕ *www.mikes-bikes.net*), a bike, gear, and repair shop, is a great resource for handmade trail maps and advice on routes around the Olympic Peninsula. **Sound Bike & Kayak** (✉ *120 E. Front St., Port Angeles* ☎ *360/457–1240* ⊕ *www.soundbikeskayaks.com*) rents and sells biking equipment.

CLIMBING

Alpine Ascents (✉ *121 Mercer St., Seattle* ☎ *206/378–1927* ⊕ *www.alpineascents.com*) leads tours of the Olympic ranges. **Mountain Madness** (✉ *3018 S.W. Charlestown St., Seattle* ☎ *206/937–8389* ⊕ *www.mountainmadness.com*) offers adventures to summits around the Olympic Peninsula.

FISHING

Bob's Piscatorial Pursuits (☎ *866/347–4232* ⊕ *www.piscatorialpursuits.com*), based in Forks, offers year-round fishing trips around Olympic. **Kalaloch Lodge** (✉ *157151 U.S. 101, Forks* ☎ *360/962–2271 or 866/525–2562* ⊕ *www.visitkalaloch.com*) organizes guided fishing expeditions around the Olympic Peninsula.

HIKING

Peak 6 (✉ *4883 Upper Hoh Rd., Forks* ☎ *360/374–5254*) sells hiking and camping gear. **Timberline Adventures** (☎ *800/417–2453* ⊕ *www.timbertours.com*) offers excursions around the Olympic Peninsula.

KAYAKINGM, CANOEING & RAFTING

Blue Sky Outfitters (✉ *3500 Harbor Ave. SW* ☎ *206/938–4030* ⊕ *www.blueskyoutfitters.com*), in Seattle, organizes whitewater trips in the area.

Fairholm General Store (✉ *U.S. 101, Fairholm* ☎ *360/928–3020*) rents rowboats and canoes on Lake Crescent for $10 to $45. It's at the lake's west end, 27 mi west of Port Angeles. **Lake Crescent Lodge** (✉ *416 Lake Crescent Rd.* ☎ *360/928–3211*) rents rowboats for $9 per hour.

Log Cabin Resort (✉ *Piedmont Rd., off U.S. 101* ☎ *360/928–3325*), 17 mi west of Port Angeles, has boat rentals for $49 per day. The dock provides easy access to Lake Crescent's northeast section. **Olympic Raft and Kayak** (☎ *360/452–5268 or 888/452–1443* ⊕ *www.raftandkayak.com*), based in Port Angeles, makes sea kayak runs offshore of Port Angeles and rafting trips along the Elway and Hoh rivers.

Peak 6 (✉ *5763 Upper Hoh Rd., Forks* ☎ *360/374–9288*), an adventure store on the way to the Hoh Rain Forest Visitor Center, rents kayaks ($11–$29), leads kayak trips along the Olympic Discovery Trail between Sequim and Port Angeles, and mounts river rafting expeditions along the Quileute River ($44–$69).

Rain Forest Paddlers (✉ *4882 Upper Hoh Rd., Forks* ☎ *360/374–5254 or 866/457–8398* ⊕ *www.rainforestpaddlers.com*), at Harbor Café, rents vessels and takes kayakers out on the Quileute River.

Duckabush, Quillayute, Quinault, and Salmon rivers. A Washington state punch card is required during salmon-spawning months; general fishing regulations vary throughout the park. Licenses are available from sporting goods and outdoor supply stores. *For guides and equipment,* ⇨ *Outfitters & Expeditions box.*

HIKING

Caution for coastal tracks: Know your tides, or you might be trapped by high water. Tide tables are available at all visitor centers and ranger stations. Remember that a wilderness permit is required for all overnight backcountry visits. *For guides,* ⇨ *Outfitters & Expeditions box.*

EASY **Hoh Valley Trail.** Leaving from the Hoh Visitor Center, this rain forest jaunt takes you into the Hoh Valley, wending its way alongside the river, through moss-draped maple and alder trees, and past open meadows where elk roam in winter. ⊠ *Hoh Visitor Center, 18 mi east of U.S. 101.*

FodorsChoice
★

Hurricane Ridge Trail. A ¼-mi alpine loop, most of it wheelchair-accessible, leads through wildflower meadows overlooking numerous vistas of the interior Olympic peaks to the south and a panorama of the Strait of Juan de Fuca to the north. ⊠ *Hurricane Ridge Rd., 17 mi south of Port Angeles.*

MODERATE **Boulder Creek Trail.** The 5-mi round-trip walk up Boulder Creek leads to a half-dozen hot spring pools of varying temperatures. ⊠ *End of Elwha River Rd., 4 mi south of Altair Campground.*

Cape Alva Trail. Beginning at Ozette, this 3-mi trail leads from the forest to wave-tossed headlands. ⊠ *End of Hoko-Ozette Rd., 26 mi south of Hwy. 112, west of Sekiu.*

Graves Creek Trail. This 6-mi-long moderately strenuous trail climbs from lowland rain forest to alpine territory at Sundown Pass. Due to spring floods, a fjord halfway up is often impassable in May and June. ⊠ *End of S. Quinault Valley Rd., 23 mi east of U.S. 101.*

Sol Duc Trail. The 1½-mi gravel path off Sol Duc Road winds through thick Douglas fir forests toward the thundering, three-chute Sol Duc Falls. Just 1/10 mi from the road, below a wooden platform over the Sol Duc River, you'll come across the 70-foot Salmon Cascades. In late summer and autumn, thousands of salmon negotiate 50 mi or more of treacherous waters to reach the cascades and the tamer pools near Sol Duc Hot Springs. The popular 6-mi **Lovers Lane Loop Trail** links the Sol Duc falls with the hot springs. You can continue up from the falls 5 mi to the **Appleton Pass Trail**, at 3,100 feet. From there you can hike on to the 8½-mi mark, where views at the High Divide are from 5,050 feet. ⊠ *Sol Duc Rd., 11 mi south of U.S. 101.*

DIFFICULT **High Divide Trail.** A 9-mi hike in the park's high country defines this route, which includes some strenuous climbing on its last 4 mi before topping out at a small alpine lake. A return loop along High Divide wends its way an extra mile through alpine territory, with sensational views of Olympic peaks. This trail is only for dedicated, properly equipped hikers who are in good shape. ⊠*End of Sol Duc River Rd., 13 mi south of U.S. 101.*

KAYAKING & CANOEING

Lake Crescent, a serene expanse of teal-color waters surrounded by thick, deep-green forests, is one of the park's best boating areas. Note that the west end is for swimming only; no speedboats are allowed here.

Lake Quinault has boating access from a gravel ramp on the north shore. From U.S. 101, take a right on North Shore Road, another right on Hemlock Way, and a left on Lakeview Drive. There are plank ramps at Falls Creek and Willoughby campgrounds on South Shore Drive, $^1/_{10}$ mi and $1^1/_5$ mi past the Quinault Ranger Station, respectively.

Lake Ozette, with just one access road, is a good place for overnight trips. Only experienced canoe and kayak handlers should travel far from the put-in, since fierce storms occasionally strike—even in summer. *For equipment and guides,* ⇨*Outfitters & Expeditions box.*

RAFTING

Olympic has excellent rafting rivers, with Class II to Class V rapids. The Elwha River is a popular place to paddle, with some exciting turns. The Hoh is better for those who like a smooth, easy float. *For guides,* ⇨*Outfitters & Expeditions box.*

WINTER SPORTS

Hurricane Ridge is the central spot for winter sports. Miles of downhill and Nordic ski tracks are open late December through March, and a ski lift, tow ropes, and ski school are open 10 to 4 weekends and holidays. Tubing areas for adults and children are open Friday through Sunday across from Hurricane Ridge Lodge. *For equipment and guides,* ⇨*Outfitters & Expeditions box.*

NEARBY TOWNS

Although most Olympic Peninsula towns have evolved from their exclusive reliance on timber, **Forks,** outside the national park's northwest tip, remains one of the region's logging capitals. Washington State's wettest town (100 inches or more of rain a year), it's a small, friendly place with just 3,500 residents and a modicum of visitor facilities. **Port Angeles,** a town of 19,000, now focuses on its status as the main gateway to Olympic National Park and Victoria, BC. Set below the Strait of Juan de Fuca and looking north to Vancouver Island, it's an enviably scenic site filled with attractive, Craftsman-style homes. The Pacific Northwest has its very own "Banana Belt" in the waterfront community of **Sequim,** 15 mi east of Port Angeles along Highway 101. The town of 6,000 is in the rain shadow of the Olympics and receives only 16 inches of rain per year (compared to the 40 inches that drench the Hoh Rain Forest just 40 mi away). For more information on nearby towns, *see* town listings in this chapter.

WHERE TO EAT

The major resorts are your best bets for eating out in the park. Each has a main restaurant, café, and/or kiosk, as well as casually upscale dinner service, with regional seafood, meat, and produce complemented by a range of microbrews and good Washington and international wines. Reservations are either recommended or required.

All Olympic National Park campgrounds have adjacent picnic areas with tables, some shelters, and restrooms, but no cooking facilities. The same is true for major visitor centers, such as Hoh Rain Forest. Drinking water is available at ranger stations, interpretive centers, and inside campgrounds.

$$-$$$$ ✕**Lake Crescent Lodge.** Part of the original 1916 lodge, the fir-paneled
★ dining room overlooks the lake; you also won't find a better spot for a view of the sunset. Entrées include crab cakes, grilled salmon, halibut fish-and-chips, classic American steaks, and elk ribs. A good Northwest wine list complements the menu. Note that meals are only offered during set hours. ⊠*416 Lake Crescent Rd., Port Angeles* ☎*360/928– 3211* ⚱*Reservations essential* ▤*AE, D, DC, MC, V* ⊘*Closed mid-Oct.–May.*

$$-$$$ ✕**Kaloloch Lodge.** A tranquil country setting and ocean views create
★ the perfect backdrop for savoring local dinner specialties like cedar-planked salmon, fresh shellfish, wild mushrooms, and well-aged beef. Note that seating is every half hour after 5, and reservations are recommended. Hearty breakfasts and sandwich-style lunches are more casual. ⊠*157151 Hwy. 101, Kalaloch* ☎*360/962–2271 or 866/525– 2562* ▤*AE, MC, V.*

$$-$$$ ✕**The Roosevelt Room at Lake Quinault Lodge.** The region's bounty plays
Fodor'sChoice a starring role at this destination restaurant inside the Lake Quinault
★ Lodge. The flavorful Pacific Northwest cuisine here is much better than it has to be, given the lodge's fairly captive audience. The atmosphere is low-key and friendly for a dining room in such a stately setting, with servers extending warm greetings and happily sharing their recommendations. It's fine to venture in wearing hiking boots and shorts during the day, and jeans are acceptable in the evening. Come for hearty breakfasts like the signature sweet potato pancakes or housemade biscuits with sausage gravy. Fuel up for an afternoon hike with chowder made from locally harvested clams, a juicy burger, or a thick deli sandwich. At dinnertime, relax with a glass of Washington wine as you preruse the menu. For a fantastic starter, don't miss the sauteed rain forest mushrooms, finished with white wine and cream. As an entrée, try the slow-roasted salmon cooked on a cedar plank, or pan-sauteed lemon trout with roasted vegetables. Dinnertime entrées are well priced, with most entrees in the low $20s. There are separate kids menus for breakfast and lunch. ⊠*South Shore Rd., Box 7,* ☎*360/288--2900 or 800/562– 6672* ⚱*Reservations essential* ▤*AE, D, MC, V.*

$-$$$ ✕**The Springs Restaurant.** The main Sol Duc Hot Springs Resort restaurant is a rustic, fir-and-cedar paneled dining room surrounded by trees. Breakfast buffets are turned out daily 7:30 to 10½while dinner is served daily between 5:30 and 9 (lunch and snacks are available at the Poolside Deli or Espresso Hut). Evening choices include Northwest seafood and game highlighted by fresh-picked fruits and vegetables. ✉ *12076 Sol Duc Rd., at U.S. 101, Port Angeles* ☎ *360/327–3583* 🚮 *AE, D, MC, V* ⊗ *Closed mid-Oct.–mid-May.*

PICNIC AREAS **East Beach Picnic Area.** Set on a grassy meadow overlooking Lake Crescent, this popular swimming spot has six picnic tables and vault toilets. ✉ *Hwy. 101, 17 mi west of Port Angeles, at far east end of Lake Crescent.*

La Poel Picnic Area. Tall firs lean over a tiny gravel beach at this small picnic area, which has five picnic tables and a splendid view of Pyramid Mountain across Lake Crescent. ✉ *Hwy. 101, 22 mi west of Port Angeles.*

North Shore Picnic Area. This site lies beneath Pyramid Mountain along the north shore of Lake Crescent; a steep trail leads from the eight-table picnic ground to the mountain top. ✉ *North Shore Rd., 3 mi east of Fairholm.*

Rialto Beach Picnic Area. Relatively secluded at the end of the road from Forks, this is one of the premier day-use areas in the park's Pacific coast segment. This site has 12 picnic tables, fire grills, and vault toilets. ✉ *Rte. 110, 14 mi west of Forks.*

WHERE TO STAY

Major park resorts run from good to terrific, with generally comfortable rooms, excellent facilities, and easy access to trails, beaches, and activity centers. Midsize accommodations, like Sol Duc Hot Springs Resort, are often shockingly rustic—but remember, you're here for the park, not for the rooms.

Note that only a few campgrounds take reservations; if you can't book in advance, you'll have to arrive early to get a place. Each site usually has a picnic table and grill or fire pit, and most campgrounds have water, toilets, and garbage containers; for hookups, showers, and laundry facilities, you'll have to head into the towns. Firewood is available from camp concessions, but if there's no store you can collect dead wood within 1 mi of your campsite. Dogs are allowed in campgrounds, but not on trails or in the backcountry. Trailers should be 21 feet long or less (15 feet or less at Queets Campground). There's a camping limit of two weeks.

If you have a backcountry pass, you can camp virtually anywhere throughout the park's forests and shores. Overnight wilderness permits are $5—plus $2 per person per night—and are available at visitor centers and ranger stations. Note that when you camp in the backcountry, you must choose a site at least ½ mi inside the park boundary.

$$–$$$$ 🏨 **Kalaloch Lodge.** A two-story cedar lodge overlooking the Pacific, Kalaloch has cozy rooms with sea views. The surrounding log cabins have a fireplace or woodstove, knotty-pine furnishings, earth-tone fabrics, and kitchenettes; waterfront cottages have deep couches

and picture windows overlooking the sea. The restaurant's ($$–$$$) menu changes seasonally, but usually includes local oysters, crab, and salmon. **Pros:** Real "Northwest" feel, beachside locale. **Cons:** Dead after dark. ☒ *157151 U.S. 101, Forks 98331* ☎ *360/962–2271 or 866/525–2562* 🖷 *360/962–3391* ⊕ *www.visitwashingtonparks.com* 🖙 *10 lodge rooms, 6 motel rooms, 3 motel suites, 44 cabins* 🖘 *In-room: no phone, kitchen, no TV. In-hotel: restaurant, bar, some pets allowed, no elevator* ☰ *AE, MC, V.*

★
$$–$$$$

🏨 **Lake Crescent Lodge.** Deep in the forest at the foot of Mt. Storm King, this comfortable 1916 lodge has a wraparound veranda, and picture windows that frame the lake's sapphire waters. Rooms in the rustic Roosevelt Cottage have polished wood floors, stone fireplaces, and lake views, while Tavern Cottage quarters resemble modern motel rooms. The historic lodge has second-floor rooms with shared baths. The lodge's fir-paneled dining room ($$–$$$$) overlooks the lake, and the adjacent lounge is often crowded with campers. Seafood dishes like grilled salmon or steamed Quilcene oysters highlight the restaurant menu; reservations are required. Note that although the dining room and shops are closed in winter, the Roosevelt Cottage is open weekends Thanksgiving through April. **Pros:** Tranquil lakeside setting, good rates. **Cons:** Set restaurant times can be inconvenient; no laundry. ☒ *416 Lake Crescent Rd., Port Angeles 98363* ☎ *360/928–3211* 🖷 *360/928–3253* ⊕ *www.lakecrescentlodge.com* 🖙 *30 motel rooms, 17 cabins, 5 lodge rooms with shared bath* 🖘 *In-room: no phone, no TV. In-hotel: restaurant* ☰ *AE, DC, MC, V* ☯ *Closed mid-Oct.–Mother's Day.*

$$–$$$

🏨 **Lake Quinault Lodge.** On a lovely glacial lake in Olympic National Forest, this beautiful early-20th-century lodge complex is nestled between the lakeshore and a hillside of hiking trails that snake through the spectacular old-growth forest. The Great Room, outfitted with a towering brick fireplace, leather couches, and a handful of card tables, is where guests gather in the evenings to play cards and board games. There are several room-types available, ranging from lodge rooms with antique stylings like claw-foot tubs; lakeside rooms with generic modern décor and private balconies; and boathouse rooms with a more rustic summer camp feel. The lively Great Room, with a service bar, is a good place to unwind after a day outdoors, as is the full-service spa. The restaurant ($$–$$$) serves upscale Northwest cuisine, like slow-roasted salmon with roasted vegetables. **Pros:** Stately ambience; magical, somewhat isolated location; many activities and amenities. **Cons:** No kids' dinner menu; no restaurants or bars nearby. ☒ *South Shore Rd., Box 7, Quinault 98575* ☎ *360/288–2900 or 800/562–6672* 🖷 *360/288–2901* ⊕ *www.visitlakequinault.com* 🖙 *91 rooms* 🖘 *In-room: no phone, VCR (some), no TV (some). In-hotel: restaurant, bar, pool, some pets allowed, no elevator* ☰ *AE, D, MC, V.*

$–$$

🏨 **Log Cabin Resort.** This rustic hotel has an idyllic setting at the northeast end of Lake Crescent. Settle into one of the A-frame chalet units, standard cabins, "camping cabins" (wooden tents with shared bathroom), motel units, or RV sites, which include full hookups. Some rooms have full kitchens. Some units are on the lake. You can rent paddleboats or kayaks to use by the day. **Pros:** Lovely waterside setting. **Cons:** Pricey for what you get. ⊠*3183 E. Beach Rd., Port Angeles 98363* ☎*360/928–3325* ⊕*www.logcabinresort.net* ↪*28 units, 4 cabins, 40 RV sites* ♻*In-room: no a/c, no phone, no TV. In-hotel: restaurant, laundry facilities, Wi-Fi, no elevator* ⊟*D, MC, V* ⊘*Closed Oct.–Apr.*

$$ ⚠**Lake Quinault Rain Forest Resort Village Campground.** Stretching along the south shore of Lake Quinault, this gathering of campsites, suites, and cabins has many recreation facilities, including beach access, ball fields, and horseshoe pits—and the world's largest Sitka spruce tree. Salmon House restaurant, specializing in seafood, is also on-site. ⊠*3½ mi east of U.S. 101, South Shore Rd., Lake Quinault* ☎*360/288–2535 or 800/255–6936* ⊕*www.rainforestresort.com* ↪*31 sites* ♻*Flush toilets, full hookups, drinking water, showers, grills, picnic tables, electricity, public telephone, general store, gift shop* ⊟*AE, D, MC, V* ⊘*Apr.–Oct.*

$–$$ ⚠**Kalaloch Campground.** Kalaloch is the biggest and most popular Olympic campground, and it's open all year. Its vantage of the Pacific is unmatched on the park's coastal stretch—although the campsites themselves are set back in the spruce fringe. ⊠*U.S. 101, ½ mi north of Kalaloch Information Station, Olympic National Park* ☎*360/962–2271 or 800/896–3826* ↪*30 sites* ♻*Flush toilets, dump station, drinking water, fire grates, public telephone, ranger station* ⊟*AE, D, MC, V* ⊘*Year-round.*

$ ⚠**Altair Campground.** This small campground sits amid an old-growth forest by the river in the rather narrow Elwha River Valley. The 3-mi West Elwha Trail leads downstream from the campground. ⊠*Elwha River Rd., 8 mi south of U.S. 101, Olympic National Park* ☎*No phone* ↪*30 sites* ♻*Flush toilets, drinking water, fire grates* ⊘*Apr.–Oct.*

$ ⚠**Deer Park Campground.** At 5,400 feet, this is the park's only drive-to alpine campground. The part-gravel access road is steep and winding; RVs are prohibited. ⊠*Deer Park (Blue Mountain) Rd., 21 mi south of U.S. 101, Olympic National Park* ☎*No phone* ↪*14 sites* ♻*Pit toilets, drinking water, fire grates* ⊘*May–Sept.*

$ ⚠**Dosewallips Campground.** This small, remote campground lies beneath Mt. Constance in old-growth forest along the river. The long gravel access road is not suitable for RVs. ⊠*Dosewallips River Rd., 15 mi west of Brinnon, Olympic National Park* ☎*No phone* ↪*30 sites* ♻*Pit toilets, fire grates* ⊟*MC, V* ⊘*May–Oct.*

$ ⚠**Elwha Campground.** The larger of the Elwha Valley's two campgrounds, this is one of Olympic's year-round facilities. Two campsite loops lie in an old-growth forest. ⊠*Elwha River Rd., 7 mi south of U.S. 101, Olympic National Park* ☎*No phone* ↪*40 sites* ♻*Pit toilets, drinking water (summer only), fire grates, public telephone, ranger station* ⊟*MC, V* ⊘*Year-round.*

$ ★ ⚠**Fairholme Campground.** One of just three lakeside campgrounds in the park, Fairholm is near the Lake Crescent Resort. There is an on-site boat launch. ⊠*U.S. 101, 28 mi west of Port Angeles, on west end of Lake Crescent, Olympic National Park* ☎*No phone* ↪*88 sites*

&. *Flush toilets, dump station, drinking water, fire grates, public telephone, swimming (lake)* ⊙ *Apr.–Oct.*

$ &. **Graves Creek Campground.** At the junction of its namesake creek and the east fork of the Quinault, this campground lies deep in an old-growth rain forest. The access road includes an 11-mi stretch of gravel that is prone to washouts. Nearby is the Graves Creek trailhead, the start of one of the park's best alpine day hikes. ⊠*S. Quinault Valley Rd., 22 mi east of U.S. 101, Olympic National Park* ☎*No phone* ⌦*30 sites* &. *Pit toilets, drinking water, fire grates, ranger station* ⊙ *Apr.–Oct.*

$ &. **Heart O' the Hills Campground.** At the foot of Hurricane Ridge in a grove of tall firs, this popular year-round campground offers a regular slate of summer programs. The trade-off is a distinct lack of peace and quiet. ⊠*Hurricane Ridge Rd., 4 mi south of main park visitor center in Port Angeles, Olympic National Park* ☎*No phone* ⌦*105 sites* &. *Flush toilets, drinking water, fire grates, public telephone, ranger station* ⊙ *Year-round.*

$ &. **Hoh Campground.** Crowds flock to this rain-forest site, near the Hoh Visitor Center under a canopy of moss-draped maples and towering spruce trees. ⊠*Hoh River Rd., 17 mi east of U.S. 101, Olympic National Park* ☎*No phone* ⌦*88 sites* &. *Flush toilets, dump station, drinking water, fire grates, public telephone, ranger station* ▤*MC, V* ⊙ *Year-round.*

$ &. **July Creek Campground.** This walk-in campground overlooks Lake Quinault and the rugged mountains beyond. Lake access is less than 100 yards away. ⊠*North Shore Rd., 3 mi east of U.S. 101, Port Angeles* ☎*No phone* ⌦*28 sites* &. *Pit toilets, drinking water (no water in winter), fire grates, swimming (lake)* ⊙ *Apr.–Oct.*

$ &. **Mora Campground.** Along the Quillayute estuary, this campground
★ doubles as a popular staging point for hikes northward along the coast's wilderness stretch. ⊠*Rte. 110, 13 mi west of Forks, Olympic National Park* ☎*No phone* ⌦*94 sites (1 walk-in)* &. *Flush toilets, dump station, drinking water, fire grates, public telephone, ranger station* ⊙ *Year-round.*

$ &. **North Fork Campground.** The park's smallest campground is for self-sufficient travelers who want to enjoy the rain forest in peace. It's deep, wet woods here; RVs are not advised. ⊠*N. Quinault Valley Rd., 19 mi east of U.S. 101, Olympic National Park* ☎*No phone* ⌦*7 sites* &. *Pit toilets, fire grates, ranger station* ⊙ *May–Sept.*

$ &. **Ozette Campground.** Hikers heading to Cape Alava, a scenic promontory that is the westernmost point in the lower 48 states, use this lakeshore campground as a jumping-off point. There's a boat launch and a small beach. ⊠*Hoko-Ozette Rd., 26 mi south of Hwy. 112, Olympic National Park* ☎*No phone* ⌦*15 sites* &. *Pit toilets, fire grates, ranger station* ▤*MC, V* ⊙ *Year-round, but call ahead in winter.*

$ &. **Queets Campground.** Set amid lush old-growth forests in the southwestern corner of the park near Olympic's largest Douglas fir tree, this campground is not suitable for camp trailers or RVs. ⊠*Queets River Rd., 12 mi east of U.S. 101, Olympic National Park* ☎*No phone* ⌦*20 sites* &. *Pit toilets, fire grates, ranger station* ⊙ *Apr.–Oct.*

$ 🏕 **Sol Duc Campground.** Sol Duc resembles virtually all Olympic campgrounds save one distinguishing feature—the famed hot springs are a short walk away. ✉ *Sol Duc Rd., 11 mi south of U.S. 101, Olympic National Park* ☎ *360/327–3534* 🛏 *82 sites* ♿ *Flush toilets, dump station, drinking water, fire grates, public telephone, ranger station, swimming (hot springs)* ⊘ *May–Oct.*

$ 🏕 **South Beach Campground.** The first campground travelers reach as they enter the park's coastal stretch from the south, this is basically an overflow campground for the more popular and better-equipped Kalaloch a few miles north. There is no water. ✉ *2 mi south of Kalaloch Information Station at the southern boundary of the park, U.S. 101, Olympic National Park* ☎ *No phone* 🛏 *50 sites* ♿ *Pit toilets, fire grates* ▭ *No credit cards* ⊘ *Apr.–Oct.*

$ 🏕 **Staircase Campground.** In deep woods away from the river, this campground is a popular jumping-off point for hikes into the Skokomish River Valley and the Olympic high country. ✉ *Rte. 119, 16 mi northwest of U.S. 101, Olympic National Park* ☎ *No phone* 🛏 *56 sites* ♿ *Flush toilets, drinking water, fire grates, public telephone, ranger station* ⊘ *Year-round.*

OLYMPIC ESSENTIALS

ACCESSIBILITY
There are wheelchair-accessible facilities—including trails, campgrounds, and visitor centers—throughout the park; contact visitor centers for more information.

ADMISSION FEES
Seven-day vehicle admission fee is $10, plus $5 for each individual; an annual family pass is $30. Parking at Ozette, the trailhead for one of the park's most popular hikes, is $1 per day.

ADMISSION HOURS
Six park entrances are open 24/7; gate kiosk hours (for buying passes) vary widely according to season and location, but most are staffed during daylight hours. Olympic National Park is located in the Pacific time zone.

ATMS/BANKS
Contacts **Bank of America** (✉ *481 S. Forks Ave., Forks* ☎ *360/374–2261* ✉ *134 W. 8th St., Port Angeles* ☎ *360/457–2747* ✉ *102 E. Front St., Port Angeles* ☎ *360/457–2737* ⊕ *www.bankofamerica.com*). **Washington Mutual Bank** (✉ *101 W. Front St., Port Angeles* ☎ *360/452–8981* ✉ *680 W. Washington St., Sequim* ☎ *360/683–7242* ⊕ *www.wamu.com*).

AUTOMOBILE SERVICE STATIONS
Contacts **Fairholm General Store** (✉ *416 Lake Crescent Rd., Lake Crescent* ☎ *360/928–3020*). **Port Angeles Chevron** (✉ *402 Marine Dr., Port Angeles* ☎ *360/457–6350*).

EMERGENCIES

For all park emergencies, dial 911. Rangers are on duty during daylight hours at Port Angeles Visitor Center, Hoh Rain Forest Visitor Center, and Hurricane Ridge Visitor Center. Other ranger stations are staffed daily in summer, staff levels permitting; off-season schedules vary.

POST OFFICES

Contacts **Forks Post Office** (✉ *61 S. Spartan Ave., Forks 98331* ☎ *360/374–6303*). **Port Angeles Post Office** (✉ *424 E. 1st Ave., Port Angeles 98362* ☎ *360/452–9275*).

PUBLIC TELEPHONES

Public phones are at the Olympic National Park Visitor Center, Hoh River Rain Forest Visitor Center, and the lodging properties within the park—Lake Crescent, Kalaloch, and Sol Duc Hot Springs. Fairholm General Store also has a phone. Note that there is no cell phone reception in wilderness areas.

RESTROOMS

Visitor centers, interpretive centers, and ranger stations within the park have public restroom facilities, as do picnic grounds, campgrounds, and the lodging properties within the park: Lake Quinault, Lake Crescent, Kalaloch, and Sol Duc Hot Springs.

VISITOR INFORMATION

Contacts **Olympic National Park** (✉ *600 E. Park Ave., Port Angeles, WA 98362* ☎ *360/565–3130* ⊕ *www.nps.gov/olym*).

Jamestown S'Klallam Village, on the beach near the mouth of the Dungeness River, has been occupied by the S'Klallam tribe for thousands of years. The tribe, whose name means "strong people," was driven to the Skokomish Reservation on Hood Canal after the signing of the Treaty of Point No Point in 1855. However, in 1874, tribal leader James Balch and some 130 S'Klallam together purchased 210 acres where the town is today. S'Klallam members have lived here ever since. One gallery along the highway sells locally made artwork; another is a mile west at the casino. ✉ *1033 Old Blyn Hwy., off U.S. 101, 7 mi east of Sequim* ☎ *360/683–1109* ⊕ *www.jamestowntribe.org.*

Fodor'sChoice
★ **Dungeness Spit,** curving 5½ mi into the Straight of San Juan de Fuca, is the longest natural sand spit in the United States and a wild, beautiful section of shoreline. Visitors arrive by the thousands in summer, though you never feel crowded along the seemingly endless, driftwood-strewn, wave-pummeled section of sand. At high tide the thread of pebble-strewn whiteness might be only 50 feet wide, and it's completely covered when storms brew up turbulent waters. More than 30,000 migratory waterfowl stop here each spring and fall, but you'll see plenty of bird life any time of year. The entire spit is part of the Dungeness National Wildlife Refuge. At the end of the Dungeness Spit is the tall, white **Dungeness Lighthouse** (☎ *360/683–9166* ⊕ *www.new dungenesslighthouse.com*), in operation since 1867 and saved from closure in 1994. Tours are available, but access is limited to those who can hike the 5 mi out to the end of the spit, or kayak up to the beach. Volunteers staff the lighthouse around the clock. ✉ *Kitchen Rd., 3 mi north from U.S. 101, 4 mi west of Sequim* ☎ *360/457–8451 wildlife refuge, 360/683–5847 campground* 🖃 *$3 per family* ☉ *Wildlife refuge daily dawn–dusk.*

★ **Railroad Bridge Park,** set along a beautifully serene, 25-acre stretch of the Dungeness River, is centered on a lacy ironwork bridge that was once part of the coastal line between Port Angeles and Port Townsend. Today the park shelters a pristine river environment. The River Walk hike-and-bike path leads from the River Center educational facility, on the banks of the Dungeness, into the woods, and a horseback track links Runnion Road with the waterway. In summer families picnic at the River Shed pavilion, students participate in science programs at the Dungeness River Audubon Society office, and locals come to watch performances at the River Stage amphitheater. Free guided bird walks run every Wednesday morning from 8:30 to 10:15, and summer float trips are organized along the Elwha River ($50). You'll find the park 2 mi west of town, and a five-minute drive from the coast. ✉ *2151 Hendrickson Rd.* ☎ *360/681–4076* ⊕ *www.dunge*

WORD OF MOUTH

"Without knowing if there was actually a bridge in Railroad Bridge Park we ventured a short distance off the highway in Sequim. There is a bridge. First used in 1915, it is now part of a footpath. It was worth going to see the bridge as well as the lovely countryside with red & yellow fall foliage."

–April

nessrivercenter.org ✉*Free* ☉*Park, daily dawn–dusk. Audubon office Tues.–Sat. 10–4, Sun. noon–4.*

The 200-acre **Olympic Game Farm**—part zoo, part safari—is Sequim's biggest attraction after the Dungeness Spit. For years the farm's exclusive client was Walt Disney Studios, and many of the bears here are former movie stars. On the drive-through tour, be prepared to see large animals like buffalo surround your car (and lick your windows). You'll view leopards, pumas, and small indigenous animals on the walk-through. Facilities also include an aquarium, a studio barn with movie sets, a snack kiosk, and a gift shop. You can drive through the park at any time of year; one-hour guided walking tours are offered June–September between 11 and 2 on weekdays, 10 and 4 on Saturday, and 10 and 3 on Sunday. ✉*1423 Ward Rd.* ☎*360/683–4295 or 800/778–4295* ⊕*www.olygamefarm.com* ✉*Drive-through tour $9, walking tour $10, combined tour $15* ☉*May–Sept., weekdays 9–5, weekends 9–6; Oct.–Apr., daily 9–3.*

WHERE TO EAT

$ ✕**Café Provencé.** The greenhouse-enclosed restaurant, overlooking
★ Sequim and the Strait of Juan de Fuca, serves French-country cuisine with Northwestern Mediterranean flavorings. Carefully crafted soups, salads, and sandwiches are served up at lunch, but the main event is dinner, with such entrées as white-bean cassoulet and roast chicken Provençal. Finish with a delicacy like crêpes Suzette and chocolate mousse, or a smooth dessert wine. Tip: The sumptuous Sunday brunch buffet runs 10 to 3, when the regular dinner menu is served. ✉*1345 S. Sequim Ave.* ☎*360/683–4541* ▭*AE, D, DC, MC, V.*

¢–$ ✕**Oak Table Café.** Pancakes, waffles, and omelets are made using creative techniques at this breakfast and lunch restaurant. Eggs Nicole, for instance, is a medley of sautéed mushrooms, onions, spinach, and scrambled eggs served over an open-face croissant and covered with hollandaise sauce. You can get breakfast all day, or opt for the lunch menu, which includes burgers, salads, and sandwiches. ✉*292 W. Bell St.* ☎*360/683–2179* ▭*AE, D, DC, MC, V* ☉*No dinner.*

WHERE TO STAY

$–$$$ 🛏**Red Caboose Getaway.** Vintage metal railcars form the centerpiece
Fodor'sChoice of this bed-and-breakfast, where you get to sleep in a luxury train,
★ each decorated with a different famous theme. Track 1 is the Casey Jones, outfitted with the original conductor's desk and intercom; Track 2 holds the bright-red Orient Express, a cozy, wood-infused space with two-person whirlpool bath; Track 3 is the family-size Circus Caboose, with a boat-shape jetted tub and two extra bunks; and Track 4 captures an Old West theme with desert decor and an antique claw-foot bathtub. The gleaming Silver Eagle restaurant, in an elegant 1937 Zephyr dining car, turns out hot, four-course breakfasts on china and crystal. ✉*24 Old Coyote Way, 98382* ☎*360/683–7350* 📠*360/683–7364* ⊕*www.redcaboosegetaway.com* �*4 suites* ⌂*In-room: kitchen. In-hotel: VCR, restaurant, no kids under 12, no elevator* ▭*AE, MC, V.*

$–$$ 🛏**Greywolf Inn Groveland Cottage B&B.** On a 5-acre hilltop overlooking
★ the town and bay, this country retreat among the trees is right on the

Olympic Discovery Trail. A gazebo, Japanese-style hot tub, and warm front room encourage convivial gatherings. Berry bushes and occasionally elk dot the 5 acres of wild grounds. Room themes are inspired by diverse places and cultures like the south of France, the African savanna, and Bavaria. One room has a fireplace, another has a featherbed, and two have magnificent views. The glass-enclosed dining room and deck overlook a meadow. Cozy rooms are done in country style and filled with antiques; there's also a rustic 19th-century bungalow. The pastoral setting is a favorite for weddings. **Pros:** Pretty garden setting, inexpensive. **Cons:** Decor too frilly for some. ⊠ *395 Keeler Rd., 4861 Sequim–Dungeness Way, Sequim 98392* ☎ *360/683–5889 or 800/914–9653* ⊕ *www.greywolfinn* ⇖ *5 rooms* ⚬ *In-room: no phone, Wi-Fi. In-hotel: restaurant, Wi-Fi, no kids under 16, no elevator* ⊟ *AE, D, MC, V* ⧖ *BP.*

¢–$$ ⊞ **Toad Hall Bed and Breakfast.** Kenneth Grahame's *Wind in the Willows* inspired the decorations in this B&B. Suites have mahogany furnishings and views of the garden and mountains. You may take your afternoon tea in the lounge or on the wraparound porch. Aromatherapy products are left in the bathrooms, and you're welcome to pick a bouquet from the fragrant lavender plants in the garden. ⊠ *12 Jesslyn La., 98382* ☎ *360/681–2534* ⇖ *3 suites* ⚬ *In-room: no phone. In-hotel: refrigerator, VCR, no-smoking rooms, no kids* ⊟ *MC, V* ⧖ *BP.*

PORT TOWNSEND

31 mi east of Sequim.

A Victorian-era city with a restored waterfront historic district, Port Townsend is the most picturesque gateway to the Olympic Peninsula. You could easily spend a weekend exploring its art galleries, shops, and trendy restaurants.

Settled in 1851, and fondly dubbed the "City of Dreams," Port Townsend was laid out with two separate urban quarters: Watertown, on the waterfront, catered to sailors, while uptown, on the plateau above the bluffs, was where Watertown merchants and other permanent citizens lived and raised their families. Today the city has a strong community of writers, musicians, painters, and other artists, and the waterfront is where you'll find chic stores and seafood restaurants. Handsomely restored brick buildings from the 1888–90 railroad boom line the bay, and the crowd of impressive yachts beyond attest to the town's status as one of the state's premier sailing spots. At the east edge of town, the Point Hudson Maritime District is a beach-side educational area with historic walks, traditional wooden boatbuilding demonstrations, and historic exhibits.

Fodor'sChoice
★   The **Northwest Maritime Center** opens the myriad traditions and trades of the Pacific Northwest's seafaring history to the public, specifically citing the importance of Port Townsend as one of only three Victorian-era seaports on the country's register of National Historic Sites. It's the core of the Point Hudson district and the center of operations for the

Wooden Boat Foundation, which stages the annual Wooden Boat Festival early each September. The center has interactive exhibits, hands-on sailing and boatbuilding crafts, a wood shop, and a pilot house where you can test navigational tools. The boardwalk, pier, and sandy beach that front the buildings are laced with marine life, and are the perfect points to launch a kayak or watch sloops and schooners gliding along the coast. ⊠ *914 Washington St., Suite 3* ☎ *360/379–2629* ⊕ *www.nwmaritime.org* ⊠ *Free* ☉ *Weekdays 10–5, weekends 9–6.*

The 1892 City Hall building, where Jack London briefly languished in jail on his way to the Klondike, contains the **Jefferson County Historical Museum**. Here you'll find four floors of Native American artifacts, photos of the Olympic Peninsula, and exhibits chronicling Port Townsend's past. ⊠ *540 Water St.* ☎ *360/385–1003* ⊕ *www.jchsmuseum.org* ⊠ *$4* ☉ *Daily 11–4.*

The **Fire Bell Tower,** set high along the bayside bluffs, is recognizable by its pyramid shape. Built in 1890, it was once the key alert center for local volunteer firemen, and a century later it's considered one of the state's most valuable historic buildings. Inside are firefighting equipment and regional artifacts from pioneer days, including a 19th-century horse-drawn hearse. You can reach the tower by climbing the stairs at Tyler Street. ⊠ *Jefferson St.* ☎ *360/385–1003* ⊠ *$3* ☉ *By appointment with Jefferson Co. Historical Society.*

☾ The manicured grounds of 443-acre **Fort Worden State Park** include a row of restored Victorian officers' houses, a World War II balloon hangar, and a sandy beach that leads to the Point Wilson Lighthouse. The fort, which was built on Point Wilson in 1896, 17 years after the lighthouse, hosts art events, kayaking tours, camping, and outdoor activities. ⊠ *200 Battery Way* ☎ *360/385–4730* ⊕ *www.parks.wa.gov* ⊠ *Free* ☉ *Daily dawn–dusk.*

The **Port Townsend Marine Science Center,** along the seafront at Fort Worden State Park, is divided into two sections. The actual Science Center, set at the end of a long pier and within a former World War II military storage facility, houses numerous aquarium displays, as well as touch tanks of starfish, crabs, and anemones. The separate, on-shore Natural History Exhibit Center is filled with displays following the region's geography and marine ecology. Beach walks, nature camps, cruises, and day camps run throughout the summer, and there's a Low Tide Festival each July. ⊠ *520 Battery Way* ☎ *360/385–5582 or 800/566–3932* ⊕ *www.ptmsc.org* ⊠ *$3 each bldg., $5 combined ticket* ☉ *Marine Science Center: Sept.–mid-June, weekends noon–4; June–mid-Sept., Wed.–Mon. noon–5; Natural History Exhibit Center: Sept.–mid-June, weekdays noon–5; June–mid-Sept., Wed.–Mon. 11–5.*

A gazebo is all that remains of the original fort, but 377 acres of forest and meadow land makes **Old Fort Townsend State Park** a lovely place for hiking, picnicking, and camping. ⊠ *1370 Old Ft. Townsend Rd.* ☎ *360/385–3595 or 800/233–0321* ⊠ *Free* ☉ *Mid-Apr.–Sept., daily 6:30–dusk.*

Alongside the highway next to the bay sits **Discovery Bay Railroad Park**, marked by four brightly colored vintage rail cars. Grab a hot dog, burger, sugared ice-cream cone, or a half-pound of candy, then take it out to the water-view deck to relax before views of passing sailboats and kayaks. You'll find it—in fact, you can't miss it—a few miles before the Hood Canal Bridge on the way to Port Townsend. ⊠ *282023 Hwy. 101, Port Townsend* ☎ *360/379–1903.*

WHERE TO EAT

$–$$ ✕ **The Belmont.** The town's only remaining 1880s saloon is tucked into the line of brickfront buildings along the busy main street. Tall windows let in the light and afford broad harbor views, which make a perfect backdrop to the innovative seafood and Northwest dishes. Dig into scallops carbonara, or try crisp crostini with warmed Dungeness crab and artichoke dip. The second floor is a hotel with Victorian furnishings to match the history and architecture; three of the four rooms have lofts with second queen beds. ⊠ *925 Water St.* ☎ *360/385–3007* ▤ *AE, D, DC, MC, V.*

$–$$ ✕ **Fountain Café.** This funky, art- and knickknack-filled café is a town favorite. Although it's known for sumptuous vegetarian dishes and delicate warm salads, you'll find tender steaks, baked apple chicken, and other hearty choices on the rotating menu as well. Delicious seafood entrées appear nightly, along with a selection of Northwest beers and wines. ⊠ *920 Washington St.* ☎ *360/385–1364* ▤ *MC, V.*

$–$$ ✕ **T's Restaurant.** Italian cuisine is the focus of this rustic local favorite, which is decked out in white linen and fresh local flowers. The aroma of fresh-baked breads leads you into a comfortable dining room filled with fragrant seasonings of pungent garlic, sweet basil, crumbled oregano, and spicy tomato. Handsome wood furnishings and ochre walls provide the background for pasta and seafood, including pan-roasted wild sea scallops and ginger and scallion-crusted wild salmon. Vegetarian dishes also offered, like rigotoni Gorgonzola, doused in rich garlic and cream sauce and dotted with basil. Fine wines and espresso round out the menu. ⊠ *2330 Washington St.* ☎ *360/385–0700* ⊕ *www. ts-restaurant.com* ▤ *AE, D, MC, V* ☉ *Closed Tues.*

$–$$ ✕ **Silverwater Cafe.** On the first floor of the 1889 Elks' Lodge building—with its high ceilings, polished floors, brick walls, and timber accents—this restaurant matches elegant surroundings to a sophisticated menu. Start with sesame ahi, or crab cakes with mozzarella, tomato, and basil, then make a light meal of hickory-smoked chicken with brandy and apples, or jumbo prawns with cilantro-ginger-lime butter. Save room for such dessert delicacies as Northwest blackberry pie, raspberry white-chocolate cheesecake, and the signature coconut flan—caramel-topped custard with a wisp of coconut flavoring. ⊠ *237 Taylor St.* ☎ *360/385–6448* ⊕ *www.silverwatercafe.com* ▤ *MC, V* ☉ *No lunch Sun.*

¢–$ ✕ **Salal Café.** Informal and bright, the restaurant is especially beloved for its ample, all-day breakfasts. Try to get a table in the glassed-in solarium, where you can brunch in style facing a plant-filled courtyard. After 11:30, lunch items appear, mixing sandwiches and soups with fresh salads and vegetarian options. The town's top-rated Elevated Ice

4

Cream is the perfect dessert. Note that the restaurant closes at 2. ⊠*634 Water St.* ☎*360/385–6532* ☐*MC, V* ☉*No dinner.*

WHERE TO STAY

$–$$$ ⌂**James House.** This white three-story Victorian, built in 1889, occupies a prime position on the bluff overlooking Port Townsend's waterfront. Cozy top-floor rooms beneath the eaves have wonderful views but small baths. The second floor has spacious rooms and the splendid Bridal Suite. On the ground floor are two more spacious suites, and behind the house is the original Gardener's Cottage. Rooms have dark cherry, oak, or wicker furnishings, colorful rugs, and plush armchairs. Breakfasts are served in the formal dining room, as are fresh-baked cookies and complimentary sherry in the evening. The adjacent Bungalow on a Bluff, a contemporary-style, free-standing home, has a wood-burning fireplace, Jacuzzi, and sweeping bay views. **Pros:** Ocean views, 19th-century elegance. **Cons:** Some minor creaks, squeaks, cracks, and drafts. ⊠*1238 Washington St., 98368* ☎*360/385–1238 or 800/385–1238* 🖷*360/379–5551* ⊕*www.jameshouse.com* ⤡*7 rooms, 3 suites, 1 cottage, 1 bungalow* ⌕*In-room: dial-up. In-hotel: Wi-Fi, no elevator* ☐*AE, D, MC, V* ⍟*BP.*

$–$$$ ⌂**Bishop Victorian Guest Suites.** Once an office building and warehouse, ★ this brick-front inn abounds with elegant 19th-century living spaces and thoughtful service. One- and two-bedroom suites are adorned with lush fabrics, antique furnishings, and authentic brass and glass features, and each has a fireplace and pull-out couch. Some quarters even have a large bathtub, and most have spectacular garden, mountain, or water views. The in-house gallery exhibits the works of local artists, and the gorgeous backyard Victorian gardens and a gazebo are a favorite wedding site. A breakfast basket and passes to a nearby athletic club are included. **Pros:** The chance to meet area artists and celebrities. **Cons:** No amenities on-site. ⊠*714 Washington St., 98368* ☎*360/385–6122 or 800/824–4738* 🖷*360/379–1840* ⊕*www.bishopvictorian.com* ⤡*16 suites* ⌕*In-room: no a/c. In-hotel: kitchen, refrigerator, DVD, VCR, dial-up, Wi-Fi, no-smoking rooms, some pets allowed* ☐*AE, D, MC, V* ⍟*CP.*

$–$$ ⌂**Ann Starrett Mansion.** Gables, turrets, and gingerbread trim decorate Fodor'sChoice this glorious 1889 mansion, a gift from a wealthy contractor to his ★ young bride. You can climb the three-tiered hanging spiral staircase to a 70-foot-high cupola tower, where outdoor murals and red stained-glass windows catch the first light of each changing season. Each guest room is unique and beautifully decorated with American antiques. Two separate cottages have more modern furnishings and facilities. **Pros:** Seasonal decorations, tours for nonguests. **Cons:** Can bustle with non-stop activities during high seasons. ⊠*744 Clay St., 98368* ☎*360/385–3205 or 800/321–0644* 🖷*360/385–2976* ⊕*www.starrettmansion.com* ⤡*8 rooms, 2 cottages* ⌕*In-room: no a/c. In-hotel: kitchen (some), no elevator* ☐*AE, MC, V.*

$–$$ ⌂**Manresa Castle.** An immense imposing stone structure, this mansion was built in 1892 for Port Townsend businessman and mayor Charles Eisenbeis and his wife Kate. Later tenants included Jesuit priests, who named the castle after the town in Spain where their order was founded.

A hotel since the late 1960s, the castle retains its Victorian character, although it's been renovated to offer modern amenities. Rooms have wood trim and furniture, patterned wallpaper, and lace curtains covering tall windows. The austere, period dining room ($–$$; closed Monday) serves rack of lamb, beef tournedos, and osso buco, plus a lavish Sunday brunch. Make time for a round in the Edwardian-style cocktail lounge, set around the bar from San Francisco's old Savoy Hotel. ⊠ *7th and Sheridan Sts., 98368* 🕾 *360/385–5750 or 800/732–1281* 🖷 *360/385–5883* ⊕ *www.manresacastle.com* ⇨ *30 rooms, 9 suites* ⌂ *In-room: no a/c. In-hotel: restaurant, bar, Wi-Fi* ⊟ *D, MC, V* ⦿ *CP.*

$ 🖾 **Palace Hotel.** Built in 1889, this is one of the most famous buildings in town, a former bordello. Walk inside and you're surrounded by cream walls, mint-color woodwork, and complete 19th-century grandeur. A half-level up, the mezzanine lounge has a balcony overlooking the entryway scene, and a circular mural decorating the soaring ceiling. Rooms, named for the ladies who used to work here, are light-filled and packed with elegant period furnishings like hand-carved dressers and big claw-foot baths. The Miss Ruby has graceful, arched windows and a kitchenette; Miss Rose has a whirlpool tub; and Miss Marie is a corner suite with a fireplace. Local events are often hosted in the hotel's other two lobbies. October through February a free continental breakfast is delivered to your door. **Pros:** Fun and funky architectural layout. **Cons:** Some shabbiness might detract from charm. ⊠ *1004 Water St., 98368* 🕾 *360/385–0773 or 800/962–0741* 🖷 *360/946–5287* ⊕ *www.palacehotelpt.com* ⇨ *19 rooms, 17 with bath* ⌂ *In-room: refrigerators. In-hotel: Wi-Fi* ⊟ *AE, D, MC, V.*

$ 🖾 **Tides Inn.** The multistory, peak-roofed inn resembles a classic San Francisco mansion, and its setting next to the ferry docks makes it one of the town's most popular accommodations. A slim brown beach and blue bay front the property, which includes two separate sections; a wing of small, basic, budget rooms, and an expanse of spacious condo-style digs with kitchenettes, jetted tubs, and private decks right over the water. All rooms are done in light Northwest hues with wood trimmings. Note to movie buffs: scenes from *An Officer and a Gentleman* were filmed here. **Pros:** Beach locale, choice of rooms and prices. **Cons:** Need to book far in advance in high season. ⊠ *1807 Water St., 98368* 🕾 *360/385–0595 or 800/822–8696* 🖷 *360/385–7378* ⊕ *www.tides-inn.com* ⇨ *22 rooms, 21 suites* ⌂ *In-room: kitchen (some). In-hotel: refrigerator (some), dial-up, beachfront, laundry facilities, no elevator* ⊟ *AE, D, DC, MC, V* ⦿ *CP.*

¢–$$ 🖾 **Port Townsend Inn.** Set midway along a bluff about a half-mile east of downtown, the two-story inn blends hotel-style elegance with small-town charm and tourist conveniences. Rooms are large and light-filled, lined with front and back windows to catch the constant ocean breeze, and done in cream and sea colors. This is also Port Townsend's only accommodation with an indoor pool and hot tub. There are bay views from most rooms, and it's a five-minute stroll to town and the ferry docks. **Pros:** Pool, modern comforts. **Cons:** Hot tub sometimes on the fritz, central location heightens traffic sounds. ⊠ *2020 Wash-*

ington St., 98368 ☎*360/385–2211 or 800/216–4985* 📠*360/385–7443* ⊕*www.porttownsendinn.com* 📲*36 rooms* ⚙*In-room: kitchen (some). In-hotel: kitchen, refrigerator, pool, no elevator* ☰*AE, D, MC, V* ⦿*CP.*

¢–$$ 🏛**Quimper Inn.** The stately, white, colonnaded 1888 Georgian-style home is a retreat for those who love books. Suites are stuffed with tomes, including the favorite Library Room, which has a rolling ladder so you can reach the top shelves. Two rooms share a bath; two others have claw-foot tubs. A broad walking porch overlooks Admiralty Inlet. You'll find candlelight and music in the dining room, and a fireplace in the living room. **Pros:** Great book collection, captivating views. **Cons:** Noises sometimes transfer between guest quarters. ✉*1306 Franklin St., 98368* ☎*360/385–1060 or 800/557–1060* 📠*360/385–2688* ⊕*www.quimperinn.com* 📲*4 rooms* ⚙*In-room: no phone. In-hotel: no TV, no kids under 12, no elevator* ☰*MC, V* ⦿*BP.*

NIGHTLIFE & THE ARTS

NIGHTLIFE **Back Alley** (✉*923 Washington St.* ☎*360/385–2914*), a favorite with locals, hosts rock-and-roll bands on weekends. Secluded **Sirens** (✉*832 Water St.* ☎*360/379–0776*) overlooks the water from the third floor and books rock, blues, and jazz acts on weekends. The large old **Town Tavern** (✉*639 Water St.* ☎*360/385–4706*) has live music—from jazz to blues to rock—on weekends.

Centrum (🖃*Box 1158, 98368* ☎*360/385–3102 or 800/733–3608* ⊕*www.centrum.org*), a creative-arts coalition combining the efforts of Washington's arts, educational, and parks departments, makes its base in a white colonial-style building at Fort Worden State Park. The organization schedules theater performances, writers' conferences, multimedia workshops, and music festivals throughout the year at venues around Port Townsend.

SPORTS & THE OUTDOORS

BICYCLING The nearest place to go biking is Fort Worden State Park, but you can range as far afield as Fort Flagler, the lower Dungeness trails (no bikes are allowed on the spit itself), or across the water to Whidbey Island.

P.T. Cyclery (✉*100 Tyler St.* ☎*360/385–6470*) rents mountain bikes and can advise you on where to start your journey.

BOAT CRUISE **P.S. Express** (✉*431 Water St.* ☎*360/385–5288* ⊕*www.pugetsound express.com*) has run summer speedboat connections between Port Townsend and Friday Harbor for more than 20 years. The round trips costs $52.50. May through September, boats depart from Port Townsend at 8:30, arriving in Friday Harbor at noon; the return trip departs from Friday Harbor at 3:30 and arrives back in Port Townsend at 5:30. Whale-watching trips from Friday Harbor depart at 12:15 and cost $25.

KAYAKING **Kayak Port Townsend** (✉*435 Water St.* ☎*360/385–6240*) conducts guided kayak tours from April to September. Tours cost $40 for three hours or $80 for a full day with lunch. You can also rent single and double kayaks for $15 and $25 per hour, respectively. **PT Outdoors**

(✉*10178 Water St.* ☎*360/379–3608 or 888/754–8598*) offers kayaking classes and guided trips. Waterfront tours are $35; two- to three-hour early-bird tours, sunset tours, and half-day tours are $40; full-day tours are $70. Single kayaks and rowboats rent for $15 per hour; double kayaks rent for $25 per hour.

SCUBA DIVING   The **Port Townsend Dive Shop** (✉*2200 Washington St.* ☎*360/379–3635* ⊕*www.ptdive.com*) makes seasonal charter trips to river and ocean sites around the peninsula. South of Port Townsend, the waterfront **Hood Sport 'n Dive** (✉*27001 U.S. 101, Hoodsport* ☎*360/877–6818*) has scuba equipment rentals and sales—and you can test your gear before you buy it. **Mike's Diving Center** (✉*22270 U.S. 101, Shelton* ☎*360/877–9568*) rents and sells gear for Hood Canal trips.

SHOPPING

Port Townsend is packed with art galleries, New Age-y book and gift shops, and pseudo-hippie clothing boutiques, especially along Water Street and its offshoots. The Fountain District, along Washington and Taylor streets a block west of the water, brims with charming clothing boutiques and craft shops. More stores are uptown on Lawrence Street near an enclave of Victorian houses.

North by Northwest Gallery (✉*18 Water St.* ☎*360/385–0955*) specializes in Eskimo and Native American art, artifacts, jewelry, and clothing. **Russell Jaqua Gallery** (✉*21 Taylor St.* ☎*360/385–5262*) exhibits metalworks. **William James Bookseller** (✉*829 Water St.* ☎*360/385–7313*) stocks used and out-of-print books in all fields, with an emphasis on nautical, regional history, and theology titles. For a little bit of everything—including arts, crafts, furnishings, bath items, books, and antiques—head to the **Perfect Season** (✉*918 Water St.* ☎*360/385–9265*).

In the Fountain District, **All Things Lavender** (✉*230 Taylor St.* ☎*360/379–2573*) brings a wealth of fragrant bath, bedroom, and food items in from Sequim's famous lavender farms. **Simply Charming** (✉*234 Taylor St.* ☎*360/379–2977*) is filled with locally created home furnishings and decorations. The **Twisted Ewe** (✉*919 Washington St.* ☎*360/379–9273*) presents finely spun wool and high-quality implements for knitting and weaving. Three dozen dealers at the two-story **Port Townsend Antique Mall** (✉*802 Washington St.* ☎*360/385–2590*) sell merchandise ranging from pricey Victorian collectors' items to cheap flea-market kitsch.

Sport Townsend (✉*1044 Water St.* ☎*360/379–9711*) is stocked with high-quality outdoor gear, including backpacks, hiking boots, camping supplies, and boating and fishing equipment. Winter sports gear is also sold here, including downhill and cross-country ski accessories, cold-weather clothing, and snowshoes.

THE OLYMPIC PENINSULA ESSENTIALS

BY AIR

Port Angeles is the major northern gateway to the Olympic Peninsula, while Olympia is the major entry point in the south. San Juan Airlines connects Port Angeles with Boeing Field, near Seattle, where passengers make the 15-minute trip to Sea-Tac Airport via a free shuttle bus. Big Sky Airlines connects Olympia with Spokane.

Fairchild International Airport, the largest on the Olympic Peninsula, is 6 mi southwest of Port Angeles off U.S. 101 (take Airport Rd. north from U.S. 101). Jefferson County Airport, a small charter-flight base, is 4 mi southwest of Port Townsend off Highway 19.

Contacts **Fairchild International Airport** (⊠ *1404 Fairchild International Airport Rd.* ☎ *360/457–1138).* **Jefferson County International Airport** (⊠ *310 Airport Rd.* ☎ *360/385–0656).* **Kenmore Air** (☎ *425/486–1257 or 800/543–9595).* **San Juan Airlines** (☎ *425/277–1590 or 800/874–4434* ⊕ *www.sanjuanairlines.com).*

AIRPORTS & TRANSFERS   Olympic Bus Lines, a Greyhound affiliate, transports passengers twice daily from Port Angeles and Sequim to Sea-Tac Airport ($49) and downtown Seattle ($39). Pennco also has service from the Olympic Peninsula to Seattle.

Contacts **Olympic** (☎ *360/417–0700 or 800/457–4492* ⊕ *www.olympicbuslines. com).* **Pennco** (☎ *360/452–5104).*

BY BOAT & FERRY

Washington State Ferries charge $9.50 per vehicle from Port Townsend to Keystone; it's $2.08 each way if you walk on. From Port Angeles you can reach Victoria, British Columbia, on the *Victoria Express* passenger ferry, which makes the one-hour trip ($25) two to four times daily from mid-May to mid-October. The boat then continues on 2½ hours longer to Friday Harbor, on San Juan Island. Or, take your car on the M.V. *Coho*, operated by Black Ball Transport, which makes 1½-hour Port Angeles–Victoria crossings four times daily from mid-May through mid-October and twice daily the rest of the year (except when it's docked for maintenance, from mid-January through mid-March). Rates are $33 per car and driver, $8.50 per passenger, and $3.75 per bike. The *Victoria Express* departs from the Landing Mall terminal, while the *Coho* departs from the ferry terminal at the foot of Laurel Street.

Contacts **Black Ball Transport** (☎ *360/457–4491 in Port Angeles, 250/386–2202 in Victoria* ⊕ *www.ferrytoVictoria.com).* **Victoria Express** (☎ *360/452–8088 in Port Angeles, 250/361–9144 in Victoria* ⊕ *www.victoriaexpress.com).* **Washington State Ferries** (⊠ *Colman Dock, Pier 52, Downtown, Seattle* ☎ *206/464–6400, 888/808–7977, 800/843–3779 automated line in WA and BC* ⊕ *www.wsdot. wa.gov/ferries).*

BY BUS

Traveling by bus is slow going on the Olympic Peninsula. Clallam Transit covers the northeastern side of the peninsula, including Port Angeles to Sequim, Forks, and La Push. Jefferson Transit makes connections between Port Angeles, Bremerton, Silverdale, Poulsbo, and Seattle. Olympic Bus Lines connects Seattle, Sea-Tac Airport, and Edmonds with Port Angeles, Sequim, Port Townsend, and the Hood Canal Bridge.

Contacts **Clallam Transit** (☎ *360/452–4511 or 800/858–3747* ⊕ *www. clallamtransit.com*). **Jefferson Transit** (☎ *360/385–4777 or 800/833–6388* ⊕ *www.jeffersontransit.com*). **Olympic Bus Lines** (☎ *360/417–0700 or 800/457– 4492* ⊕ *www.olympicbuslines.com*).

BY CAR

U.S. 101, the main thoroughfare around the Olympic Peninsula, is a two-lane, well-paved highway. Rural back roads are blacktop or gravel, and tend to have potholes and get washed out during rains. In winter, landslides and wet weather frequently close roads. Highway 112 heads west from U.S. 101 at Port Angeles to Neah Bay. Highway 113 winds north from U.S. 101 at Sappho to Highway 112. Highway 110 travels west from U.S. 101 at Forks to La Push. Highway 109 leads west from U.S. 101 at Hoquiam to Copalis Beach, Moclips, and Taholah. Highway 8 heads west from Olympia and connects with U.S. 12, which travels west to Aberdeen.

EMERGENCIES

Hospitals **Forks Community Hospital** (✉ *520 Bogachiel Way, Forks* ☎ *360/374– 6271* ⊕ *www.forkshospital.org*). **Grays Harbor Community Hospital** (✉ *915 Anderson Dr., Aberdeen* ☎ *360/537–5000*). **Jefferson General Hospital** (✉ *834 Sheridan St., Port Townsend* ☎ *360/385–2200 or 800/244–9912* ⊕ *www.jgh.org*). **Mason General Hospital** (✉ *901 Mt. View Dr., Bldg. 1, Shelton* ☎ *360/426–1611*). **Olympic Memorial Hospital** (✉ *929 Caroline St., Port Angeles* ☎ *360/417–7000* ⊕ *www.olympicmedical.org*).

TOUR OPTIONS

BOATING & DIVING TOURS   Kayak tours generally run for two to three hours and cost $30 to $40; full-day excursions with lunch cost between $70 and $100. Boat tours and whale-watching tours usually last three to five hours and cost $30 to $60. Scuba-diving tours, including equipment, are in the $50 to $75 range for a two-tank dive.

Curley's Resort & Dive Center in Sekiu is a regional scuba shop. Also in Sekiu, Puffin Adventures organizes boating, kayaking, fishing, and scuba-diving trips in the region. Extreme Adventures runs two-hour and overnight float trips on the Hoh River. Olympic Adventures runs kayak trips on the Port Townsend waterfront and around the Strait of San Juan de Fuca. Olympic Raft & Kayak conducts white-water and scenic float trips on the Hoh and Elwha rivers. Sound Dive Center has scuba certification classes, dive equipment, and tours around the region.

Contacts **Curley's Resort & Dive Center** (✉ *291 Front St., Sekiu* ☎ *360/963–2281 or 800/542–9680* ⊕ *www.curleysresort.com*). **Extreme Adventures** (⌂ *Box 1991, Forks* ☎ *360/374–8747*). **Olympic Adventures** (✉ *1001 Water St., Port Townsend* ☎ *360/379–7611*). **Olympic Outdoor** (✉ *773 Pt. Brown Ave. NW, Port Townsend* ☎ *360/289–3736*). **Olympic Raft & Kayak** (✉ *123 Lake Aldwell Rd.,*

Port Angeles ☎ 360/452–1443 ⊕ www.raftandkayak.com). **Puffin Adventures** (☎ 360/640–1998 ⊕ www.puffinchartertours.com). **Sound Dive Center** (✉ 625 E. Front St., Port Angeles ☎ 360/457–3749 ⊕ www.sounddive.com).

HIKING & WALKING TOURS
Guided Historical Tours conducts two- to three-hour walking tours of Port Townsend for $10 to $20. Olympic Van Tours and Bus Lines, based in Port Angeles, offers guided day and multiday tours of Olympic National Park and shuttle service for backpackers to all national park trail heads. Van tours of Olympic National Park and the surrounding area range from half-day to full-day trips; costs range from $40 to $75. John Monk's Guide Service leads hiking and fishing tours around Washington's coastal rivers. Peak Six Tours, in Forks, provides gear and information for hiking, biking, camping, climbing, and sightseeing on the Olympic Peninsula. Guided hikes cost about $50 per day.

Contacts **Guided Historical Tours** (✉ 820 Tyler St., Port Townsend ☎ 360/385–1967). **John Monk's Guide Service** (⌂ Box 1012, Forks ☎ 360/374–5817). **Olympic Van Tours and Bus Lines** (☎ 360/452–3858 or 888/457–3500). **Peak Six Tours** (✉ 4883 Upper Hoh Rd., Forks ☎ 360/374–5254).

VISITOR INFORMATION

Information **Clallam Bay/Sekiu Chamber of Commerce** (⌂ Box 355, Clallam Bay 98326 ☎ 360/963–2339 ⊕ www.sekiu.com). **Forks Chamber of Commerce** (✉ 1411 S. Forks Ave., Forks 98331 ☎ 360/374–2531 or 800/443–6757 ⊕ www.forkswa.com). **Grays Harbor Chamber of Commerce** (✉ 506 Duffy St., Aberdeen 98520 ☎ 360/532–1924 ⊕ www.graysharbor.org). **Montesano Chamber of Commerce** (✉ 128 Brumfield Ave., Montesano 98563 ☎ 360/249–5522 ⊕ www.montesano-wa.com). **North Olympic Peninsula Visitor and Convention Bureau** (✉ Port of Port Angeles, 338 W. 1st St., Suite 104, Port Angeles 98362 ☎ 360/452–8552 or 800/942–4042 ⊕ www.olympicpeninsula.org). **Northwest Interpretive Association** (✉ 3002 Mt. Angeles Rd., Port Angeles 98104 ☎ 360/565–3195 ⊕ www.nwpubliclands.com). **Ocean Shores Information Center** (✉ 120 Chance a la Mer, Ocean Shores 98569 ☎ 360/289–2451 or 800/762–3224 ⊕ www.oceanshores.org). **Olympic National Forest** (✉ 1835 Blacklake Blvd., Olympia 98512 ☎ 360/956–2400). **Olympic National Park** (✉ 1835 Blacklake Blvd., Olympia 98512 ☎ 360/956–4501). **Port Angeles Chamber of Commerce** (✉ 121 E. Railroad Ave., 98362 ☎ 360/452–2363). **Port Townsend Chamber of Commerce and Visitor Information Center** (✉ 2437 Sims Way, Port Townsend 98368 ☎ 360/385–7869 or 888/365–6978 ⊕ www.ptguide.com). **Sequim Chamber of Commerce** (✉ 1192 E. Washington St., Sequim 98382 ☎ 360/683–6197 or 800/737–8462 ⊕ www. sequimchamber.com). **Washington Coast Chamber of Commerce** (✉ 2272 Hwy. 109, Box 562, Ocean City 98569 ☎ 360/289–4552 ⊕ www.washingtoncoastchamber.org). **Westport-Grayland Chamber of Commerce** (✉ 2985 S. Montesano, Westport 98595 ☎ 360/268–9422 or 800/345–6223 ⊕ www.westportgrayland-chamber.org).

VISITOR INFORMATION

Contacts **Lopez Island Chamber of Commerce** (⌂ Box 102, Washington 98261 ☎ 360/468–4664 or 877/433–2789 ⊕ www.lopezisland.com). **Orcas Island Chamber of Commerce** (⌂ Box 252, Eastsound 98245 ☎ 360/376–2273 ⊕ www.orcasisland.org).

San Juan Island Chamber of Commerce (Box 98, Friday Harbor 98250 360/378–5244 www.sanjuanisland.org). **San Juan Islands Visitors Bureau** (Box 98, Friday Harbor 98250 360/468–3701 or 888/468–3701 www. guidetosanjuans.com).

SOUTHWESTERN WASHINGTON

Updated by Shelley Arenas

With volcanic peaks to the northeast, the Columbia River Gorge to the southeast, and sandy beaches along the Pacific shore, southwestern Washington offers ample opportunity for exploration and adventure. It's also home to one of the most famous sections of the Lewis and Clark Trail: it was near Long Beach, after making their way west through the Columbia River Gorge, that Meriwether Lewis and William Clark first saw the Pacific Ocean.

Along much of Washington's southern coast, mountains are separated from ocean by wide beaches and broad inlets, which, in turn, are protected by sandy spits. The exception is Cape Disappointment at the mouth of the Columbia River. There are depressions in the sand that hold bogs, many of which are planted with cranberries. The mainland margins of the inlets and the banks of the lower Columbia are swampy and cut by channels into marshy islands. This area is as close to Louisiana bayou country as the Northwest comes. A few islands even have their own breed of swamp dwellers—fishermen and oyster growers, who live on house barges tied to the shore. This part of the coast is also very wet, and several of the lowland rivers are bordered by rain forest.

TOP 5
1. At Cape Disappointment State Park, visitors can follow in the footsteps of Lewis and Clark.
2. Maryhill Museum has a fascinating art collection, interesting history, and unique location.
3. Fort Vancouver National Historic Site is a place to take a step back in time.
4. Mt. St. Helens National Volcanic Monument showcases the devastating power of volcanoes.
5. The beach town of Long Beach with its fun museums.

A long, sandy spit known as the Long Beach Peninsula stretches north from the rocky knobs at Cape Disappointment, shielding Willapa Bay, Washington's southernmost estuary, from the ocean's fury and creating an ideal stretch of sand for the peninsula's resort communities. One of every six U.S. oysters is grown in Willapa Bay. When you add the oysters grown in Grays Harbor, the Hood Canal, Samish Bay, and southern Puget Sound, you'll understand why Washington is the number one of the top oyster-producing states. Follow the signs for a scenic drive around the peninsula. The trip along Highway 100 follows headlands for the only panoramic views along the otherwise flat peninsula.

The Cascade Mountains south of Snoqualmie Pass are more heavily eroded than those to the north and generally not as high. But a few peaks do top 7,000 feet, and two volcanic peaks are taller than any of the state's northern mountains. Mt. Adams is more than 12,000 feet high, and Mt. Rainier rises to more than 14,000 feet. The third of the southern peaks, Mt. St. Helens, blew its top in 1980, and is now little more than 8,000 feet tall.

The southern lowlands are part of a long trough that runs from the Georgia Strait in southern British Columbia to Oregon's southern Willamette Valley. The area is bordered in the west by the low hills of the coast ranges, to the east by the foothills of the Cascades, to the north by Puget Sound, and to the south by the Columbia. The region is bisected by two rivers: the Chehalis in the north, and the Cowlitz, which flows west from the southern slopes of Mt. Rainier, then turns south to the Columbia.

Vancouver, Washington, just across the Columbia River from Portland, Oregon, is the state's fourth-largest city and by far the region's most populated area. The city has experienced a renaissance and has a large farmers' market, several waterfront restaurants, and an urban park surrounded by shops, eateries, and condominiums.

Cut thousands of feet deep, the Columbia River Gorge travels through the basalt ridges of the Cascades. West of the Cascade crest, there's one timberline; east of the crest there's an upper timberline in the alpine zone, like that of western Washington's mountains; and a lower timberline, where the land becomes too dry to support trees, and grasses or steppe scrub take over. This is most visible as you follow the Columbia River east through the gorge and rain forests give way to the Columbia Plateau.

The rushing waters of the untamed, wild Columbia River encountered by American and British explorers gave their name to the bordering mountains. The Native Americans of the Pacific Northwest knew the wild river and its cascades well and came here to harvest salmon, to trade, and to socialize. The river was dammed long ago, but even in this captive state it's still exceptionally beautiful.

LONG BEACH PENINSULA

Town of Ilwaco is 169 mi southwest of Seattle, 106 mi northwest of Portland, Oregon.

The seas are so turbulent beneath the cliffs of Cape Disappointment, where the mighty Columbia River meets the stormy waters of the Pacific Ocean, that several explorers, from James Cook to George Vancouver, mistook the river's mouth for surf breaking on a wild shore. Many ships have crossed (and many have come to grief) here since American sea captain Robert Gray sailed into the river on May 11, 1792, and named it after his ship.

Long Beach Peninsula stretches north from Cape Disappointment, protecting Willapa Bay from the ocean. The peninsula has vast stretches of sand dunes, friendly beach towns, dank cranberry bogs, and forests and meadows. Willapa Bay was once known as Shoalwater Bay because it runs almost dry at low tide. It's a prime oyster habitat, producing more of the creatures than any other estuary in the country.

The 28-mi-long, uninterrupted stretch of sand that runs along the peninsula's ocean shore is a great place to beachcomb. Don't even think about swimming here, however. Though surfers in wetsuits brave the waves in some areas, the water is too cold and the surf too rough for most people; hypothermia, shifting sands underfoot, and tremendous undertows account for several drownings each year.

The peninsula is a great place to hike, bike, and bird-watch. Lakes and marshes attract migrating birds, among them trumpeter swans. Long Island, in southeastern Willapa Bay, has a stand of old-growth red cedar trees, home to spotted owls, marbled murrelets (a western seabird), elks, and black bears. The island is accessible only by private boat (the boat ramp is on the bay's eastern shore).

CHINOOK
172 mi southwest of Seattle, 99 mi northwest of Portland, OR.

The pleasant Columbia River fishing village of Chinook (*shi*-nook) takes its name from the tribe that once controlled the river from its mouth to Celilo Falls. The same group encountered Lewis and Clark during their stay on the Pacific coast. Chinook is a great base from which to explore the lower Columbia River by boat.

Ft. Columbia State Park and Interpretive Center blends so well into a rocky knob above the river that it's all but invisible from land or water (U.S. 101 passes underneath, via tunnel). The 1902 bastions offer great views of the river's mouth and of the river flowing past the foot of the cliff. In spring the slopes are fragrant with wildflowers. The interpretive center has displays on barracks life and Chinook Indian culture. Two historic buildings on the property are available for vacation rental. ⊠*U.S. 101, 2 mi east of Chinook* ☎*360/642-3078 or 888/226-7688* *Free* ⊘*Memorial Day–Sept., Wed.–Sun. 10–5 (subject to change, depending on volunteer staffing).*

ILWACO
13 mi west of Chinook.

Ilwaco (ill-*wah*-co) has been a fishing port for thousands of years, first as a Native American village and later as an American settlement. A 3-mi scenic loop winds past Ft. Canby State Park to North Head Lighthouse and through the town. The colorful harbor is a great place for watching gulls and boats. Lewis and Clark camped here before moving their winter base to the Oregon coast at Ft. Clatsop.

The dioramas and miniatures of Long Beach towns at the **Ilwaco Heritage Museum** illustrate the history of southwestern Washington. Displays cover Native Americans; the influx of traders, missionaries, and pioneers; and the contemporary workers of the fishing, agriculture, and forest industries. The original Ilwaco Freight Depot and a Pullman car from the Clamshell Railroad highlights rail history. ⊠*115 S.E. Lake St., off U.S. 101 98624* ☎*360/642-3446* ⊕*www.ilwaco-heritagemuseum.org*

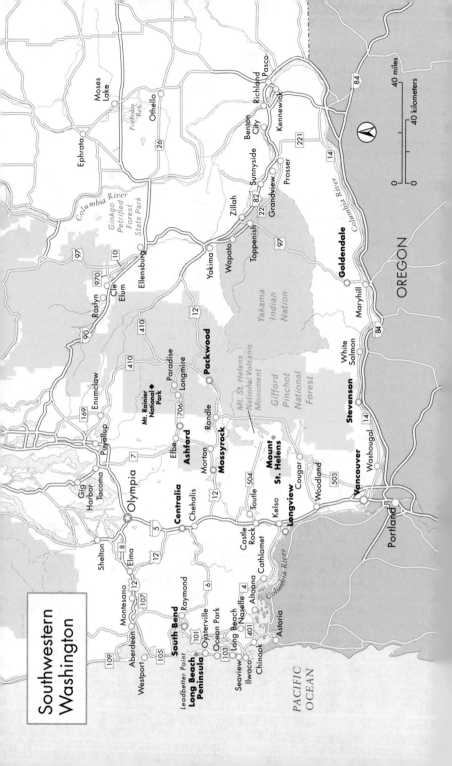

Southwestern Washington

PACIFIC OCEAN

OREGON

Westport

Aberdeen
109

Montesano
Elma
Shelton
8
12
107
105
Raymond
South Bend
101
Oysterville
Ocean Park
103
Long Beach
Leadbetter Point
Long Beach Peninsula
Seaview
Ilwaco
401
Chinook
Naselle
4
Altoona
Astoria
Cathlamet

Gig Harbor
Tacoma
Puyallup
Olympia
169
Enumclaw
7
Elbe
Ashford
706
Mt. Rainier National Park
Paradise
Longmire
410
410
Morton
Randle
Packwood
12
Mossyrock
Centralia
Chehalis
12
5
Castle Rock
Toutle
504
Mount St. Helens
Mt. St. Helens National Volcanic Monument
Cougar
Kelso
Longview
Woodland
503
Vancouver
Washougal
14
Stevenson
White Salmon
Gifford Pinchot National Forest

Portland

90
Roslyn
Cle Elum
970
10
Ellensburg
97
97
Columbia River
Ginkgo Petrified Forest State Park
Ephrata
Moses Lake
Othello
Potholes Res.
26

12
Yakima
Wapato
Toppenish
Zillah
97
22
82
Sunnyside
Grandview
Prosser
221
Yakama Indian Nation

Benton City
Richland
Kennewick
Pasco
84
14
Goldendale
Maryhill
84
Columbia River

OREGON

N

0   40 miles
0   40 kilometers

✉$5 ⊙ *Mon.–Sat. 10–4, Sun. noon–4; closed New Year's, Thanksgiving, Christmas.*

☾ The 1,700-acre **Cape Disappointment State Park (formerly Ft. Canby)** was an
★ active military installation until 1957. Emplacements for the guns that
once guarded the Columbia's mouth remain, some of them hidden by
dense vegetation. Trails lead to stunning beaches. Be on the lookout
for deer eagles on the cliffs. All of the park's 240 campsites have stoves
and tables; some have water, sewer, and electric hookups. The park also
has three lightkeepers' residences (houses) available for rent, as well as
14 yurts and three cabins.

Exhibits at the park's **Lewis & Clark Interpretive Center** tell the tale
of the duo's 8,000-mi round-trip expedition. Displays include artwork, journal entries, and other items that elaborate on the Corps of
Discovery, which left Wood River, Illinois, in 1803; arrived at Cape
Disappointment in 1805; and got back to Illinois in 1807. ✉*Robert
Gray Dr., 2½ mi southwest of Ilwaco off U.S. 101* ☎*360/642–3029
or 360/642–3078* ⊕*www.parks.wa.gov* ✉*Interpretive center $5, park
admission free, campsites $19–$31* ⊙*Park: daily dawn–dusk. Interpretive center: daily 10–5.*

Cape Disappointment was named in 1788 by Captain John Meares, an
English fur trader who had been unable to find the Northwest Passage.
This rocky cape and treacherous sandbar—the so-called graveyard of
the Pacific—has been the scourge of sailors since the 1800s. More than
250 ships have sunk after running aground on its ever-shifting sands.
A ½-mi-long path from the Lewis & Clark Interpretive Center in Cape
Disappointment State Park leads to the Cape Disappointment Lighthouse. Built in 1856, it's the oldest lighthouse on the west coast still
in use.

The **U.S. Coast Guard Station Cape Disappointment** (☎*360/642–2384*) is
the northwest coast's largest search-and-rescue station. The rough conditions of the Columbia River provide plenty of lessons for the students
of the on-site National Motor Life Boat School. The only institution of
its kind, the school teaches elite rescue crews from around the world
advanced skills in navigation, mechanics, firefighting, and lifesaving.
The observation platform on the north jetty in Cape Disappointment
State Park is a good place to watch the motor lifeboats. If you call
ahead, you can arrange an informal tour.

★ **North Head Lighthouse** was built in 1899 to help skippers sailing from
the north who couldn't see the Cape Disappointment Lighthouse. Stand
high on a bluff above the pounding surf here, amid the windswept
trees, for superb views of the Long Beach Peninsula. Lodging is available in the Lighthouse Keepers' Residence. ✉*From Cape Disappointment follow Spur 100 Rd. for 2 mi* ☎*360/642–3078* ⊕*www.parks.
wa.gov* ✉*$2.50* ⊙*Apr.–Sept., daily 10–5; Oct.–Mar., 11–3, weekends
only, hrs subject to volunteer availability.*

WHERE TO STAY & EAT

$-$$ ✕ **Doogers.** Locals will urge you to eat here—listen to them. The place serves seafood from 11 AM to 9 PM in winter, and until 10 in summer. The ample portions come with potatoes, shrimp-topped salad, and garlic toast. Clam chowder and fish and chips are popular lunch choices. ⊠900 Pacific Hwy. S ☎360/642–4224 ⊟AE, D, MC, V.

$-$$ ✕ **The Port Bistro.** Since opening in spring 2006, Larry Piaskowy and
Fodor's Choice   Jennifer Williams's restaurant has received rave reviews from critics,
★   local diners, and tourists alike. The emphasis is on locally grown products, so the menu changes with the season. Staples include the Bistro Burger, handformed of Montana range natural beef on a housemade bun, available at lunch. Dinner offerings include Willapa Bay oysters and clams, in such dishes as gumbo and bouillabaisse, and fish, beef, free-range chicken, and vegetarian options. The clam chowder is a year-round favorite. ⊠235 Howerton, 98624 ☎360/642–8447 ⊟AE, MC, V ⊗Closed Tues.; also closed 2–5 pm daily.

$$$-$$$$ 🛏 **China Beach Retreat.** Between the port of Ilwaco and Ft. Canby State
★   Park, this secluded B&B is surrounded by wetlands and has wonderful views of Baker's Bay and the mouth of the Columbia River. Each of the three rooms has antiques and original art. The Audobon Cottage opened in late 2006, and offers a secluded, romantic experience in nature, with a river-view outdoor soaking tub for two. Decorated with stained glass, rare woods, and period antiques, the cottage also has a flat-screen TV, microwave, small refrigerator, and wireless Internet. **Pros:** Secluded, back-to-nature setting, new cottage is very nice. **Cons:** Rooms need updating according to some guests, no a/c, breakfast is not on-site but at nearby sister property, Shelburne Inn. ⊠222 Robert Gray Dr., 98624 ☎360/642–5660 ⊕www.chinabeachretreat.com ↪3 rooms, 1 cottage ⚘In-room: no a/c. In-hotel: no phone, no TV (except cottage), no kids under 16, no-smoking rooms ⊟AE, MC, V ⍟BP.

SPORTS & THE   Gray whales pass the Long Beach Peninsula twice a year: December–
OUTDOORS   February, on their migration from the Arctic to their winter breeding grounds in Californian and Mexican waters, and March–May, on the return trip north. The view from the North Head Lighthouse is spectacular. The best time for sightings is in the morning, when the water is calm and overcast conditions reduce the glare. Look on the horizon for a whale blow—the vapor, water, or condensation that spouts into the air when the whale exhales. If you spot one blow, you're likely to see others: whales often make several shorter, shallow dives before a longer dive that can last as long as 10 minutes.

The fish that swim in the waters near Ilwaco include salmon, rock cod, lingcod, flounder, perch, sea bass, and sturgeon. Charters generally cost from $90 to $200 per person. Free fishing guides are available from the **Port of Ilwaco** (☎360/642–3143 ⊕www.portofilwaco.com).

SEAVIEW
3 mi north of Ilwaco.

Seaview, an unincorporated town, has 750 year-round residents and several homes that date from the 1800s. The Shelburne Inn, built in 1896, is on the National Register of Historic Places. In 1892 U.S. Senator Henry Winslow Corbett built what's now the Sou'wester Lodge.

WHERE TO STAY & EAT

$–$$
★
✕**42nd Street Cafe.** Chef Cheri Walker's fare is inspired, original, and reasonably priced. Oysters are baked with spinach, Parmesan cheese, cream, bacon, brandy, fennel, and cracker crumbs; charbroiled albacore tuna is served with hoisin sauce and sesame guacamole; and baked spice-rubbed sturgeon comes with a salad of wild rice, dried cranberries, apples, and carrots with a bacon vinaigrette. Try the Dungeness crab beignets for a tempting Northwest treat. The excellent wine list has Pacific Northwest labels. ⊠*Hwy. 103 and 42nd Pl., 98644* ☎*360/642–2323* ⊕*www.42ndstreetcafe.com* ⊟*MC, V.*

$–$$
Fodor'sChoice
★
⚏**Shelburne Inn.** A white picket fence surrounds rose and other gardens as well as an 1896 Victorian that's home to Washington's oldest continuously run hotel. Fresh flowers, antiques, fine-art prints, and original works adorn guest rooms, a few of which have decks or balconies. The Shoalwater Restaurant ($$–$$$) has a dark wooden interior and a contemporary American menu dominated by seafood dishes. Homemade pastries and specialty desserts feature fresh local ingredients. The cozy Heron & Beaver Pub serves lighter fare. **Pros:** Excellent breakfast, historic appeal as state's oldest hotel, attentive service. **Cons:** Like many B&Bs, there are no in-room phones or TVs; some rooms are rather small. ⊠*Hwy. 103 and N. 45th St., 98644* ☎*360/642–2442 (inn), 360/642–4142* ⊟*360/642–8904* ⊕*www.theshelburneinn.com* ⌨*15 rooms, 2 suites* ⚬*In-room: no a/c, no phone, no TV. In-hotel: Wi-Fi, restaurant, bar, no-smoking rooms, public Wi-Fi* ⊟*AE, D, DC, MC, V* ⍐*BP.*

¢–$$
⚏**Sou'wester Lodge.** A stay at the Sou'wester is a bohemian experience. Proprietors Len and Miriam Atkins came to Seaview from South Africa, by way of Israel and Chicago, and they're always up for a stimulating conversation. The lodge was built in 1892 as the summer retreat for Henry Winslow Corbett, a Portland banker, timber baron, shipping and railroad magnate, and U.S. senator. Soirees and chamber music concerts are sometimes held in the parlor. Guest rooms are eclectic. Beach cottages and the classic mobile-home units just behind the beach have cooking

> **WORD OF MOUTH**
>
> "Second the Shelburne Inn; we stayed a night there last year. Decent restaurant (for the area) on the property too. If it's not available, they'll probably direct you to China Beach, a sister property, located overlooking the water just outside of Ilwaco. We drove by; I'd stay there, too. In either case, spend a few hours at Cape Disappointment State Park. In particular, I'd recommend the North Lighthouse, and the Interpretive Center overlooking the mouth of the Columbia River."
>
> –Beachbum

facilities; you're also welcome to make breakfast in the homey kitchen. **Pros:** Very unique lodgings, interesting history, involved and attentive owners. **Cons:** Not for luxury-seekers, some rooms don't have private baths. ⊠*Beach Access Rd., Box 102, 98644* ☎*360/642–2542* ⊕*www.souwesterlodge.com* ⇱*3 rooms without bath, 6 suites, 4 cottages, 12 trailers* &*In-hotel: beachfront* ▤*D, MC, V.*

LONG BEACH
½ mi north of Seaview.

Long Beach bears a striking resemblance to Brooklyn's Coney Island in the 1950s. Along its main drag, which stretches southwest from 10th Street to Bolstadt Street, you'll find everything from cotton candy and hot dogs to go-carts and bumper cars.

☺ The ½-mi-long **Long Beach Boardwalk** runs through the dunes parallel
★ to the beach and is a great place for strolling, bird-watching, or just sitting and listening to the wind and the roar of the surf. It's ¼ mi west of downtown.

☺ Created to memorialize Lewis and Clark's explorations here in 1805–
★ 06, the 8-mi **Discovery Trail** traces the explorers' moccasin steps from Ilwaco to north Long Beach. ☎*800/451–2542* 🖳*360/642–3900* ⊕*www.funbeach.com.*

Each August Long Beach hosts the Washington State International Kite Festival; the community is also home to the Northwest Stunt Kite Championships, a competition held each June. At the **World Kite Museum and Hall of Fame,** the only U.S. museum focused solely on kites and kiting, you can view an array of kites and learn about kite making and history. ⊠*303 Sid Snyder Dr. SW* ☎*360/642–4020* ⊕*www. worldkitemuseum.com/* 🖾*$5* ☉*May–Sept., daily 11–5; Oct.–Apr., Fri.–Tues. 11–5.*

☺ If you've got kids in your group, or simply an appreciation of oddities, be sure to visit the quirky **Marsh's Free Museum.** Best known for "Jake the Alligator Man," Marsh's is filled with plenty of other curiousities like real shrunken heads, skeletons, and an 8-legged lamb. ⊠*400 S. Pacific, 98631* ☎*360/642–2188* ⊕*www.marshsfreemuseum.com* 🖾*Free* ☉*Daily 9–6, later in summer.*

At the **Cranberry Museum** learn about the 100-plus-year history of cranberries in this area, take a self-guided walking tour through the bogs, try some cranberry tea, and buy cranberry products to take home. ⊠*2907 Pioneer Rd., 98631* ☎*360/642–5553* ⊕*www.cranberrymuseum.com* 🖾*Free* ☉*Apr.–mid-Dec., daily 10–5.*

OCEAN PARK
9 mi north of Long Beach.

Ocean Park is the commercial center of the peninsula's quieter north end. It was founded as a camp for the Methodist Episcopal Church of Portland in 1883. Although the law that prohibited the establishment of saloons and gambling houses no longer exists, the deeds for some homes still state that the properties will be forfeited if alcohol is bought on the premises.

The **Taylor Hotel,** built in 1892 on Bay Avenue, houses retail businesses and is the only structure from the early days that's open to the public.

WHERE TO STAY

$$–$$$ ⭐ 🏠 **Caswell's on the Bay B&B.** From the outside, this B&B with a wraparound porch looks like an old Victorian house. But inside it's clearly a modern creation, with high ceilings and enormous windows looking onto Willapa Bay and the Long Island wildlife sanctuary. Antiques-furnished guest rooms have sitting areas and waterside or garden views. Featherbeds, robes, pressed linens, and full concierge service are among the indulgences. **Pros:** Pleasant setting in nature, rooms are spacious and inn is relatively new, wonderful gourmet breakfasts. **Cons:** Though Victorian in style, the B&B was built in the mid-90s; still, period antiques add some historical authenticity. ✉25204 Sandridge Rd., 98640 ☎360/665–6535 🖷360/665–6500 ⊕www.caswellsinn.com ➘5 rooms, 1 suite 🚼In-room: no a/c. In-hotel: no phone, no-smoking rooms ▭AE, D, MC, V 🍴BP.

$–$$ ⭐ 🏠 **Klipsan Beach Cottages.** Built in the 1940s, this row of waterfront cottages is a favorite for family getaways. An adjacent A-frame house is available for large groups. The cottages face the sea, and a trail makes short work of getting to the beach. Full kitchens and fireplaces or woodstoves—as well as plenty of (free) firewood—are among the amenities. **Pros:** Family-friendly, quiet beach cottage ambience, nicely kept up. **Cons:** Not too exciting for people who don't love nature, cottages are close to each other. ✉22617 Pacific Way, 98640 ☎360/665–4888 🖷360/665–3580 ⊕www.klipsanbeachcottages.com ➘8 cottages, 1 house 🚼In-room: no a/c, no phone, Wi-Fi (some). In-hotel: kitchen, refrigerator ▭MC, V.

OYSTERVILLE

6 mi north of Nahcotta.

Oysterville is a 19th-century waterfront village, with houses set in gardens or surrounded by greenswards. Signs posted on the fence of each building tell when it was built and who lived in it. You can tour the restored Oysterville Church (pick up a free historical map here), a schoolhouse, a tannery, and the home of the mayor. The town, established in 1854, got out of the oyster business after a decline in the late 19th century. Although the native shellfish were harvested to extinction, they have been successfully replaced with the Pacific oyster, a Japanese variety that has become thoroughly naturalized.

WILDLIFE-HERITAGE SCULPTURE CORRIDOR

In and around the town of Raymond (5 mi northeast of South Bend), look for life-size steel sculptures that depict the heritage of the area—including wildlife, Native Americans, and loggers. In the 1990s the locally designed sculptures were added to the landscape along Highway 101, Highway 6, and in the town of Raymond. If you find one you love, you can buy a replica from the **Raymond Chamber of Commerce** (☎ *360/942–5419*).

4

✪ Three miles north of Oysterville (take Sandridge Road to the left and
★ follow the signs) is **Leadbetter State Park,** a wildlife refuge at Long Beach
Peninsula's northernmost tip and a great spot for bird-watching. Black
brants, sandpipers, turnstones, yellowlegs, sanderlings, and knots are
among the 100 species biologists have recorded here. The dune area at
the very end of the point is closed from April to August to protect the
nesting snowy plover. From the parking lot, a ½-mi-long paved wheelchair-accessible path leads to the ocean and a 2½-mi loop trail winds
through the dunes along the ocean and Willapa Bay. Several trails along
the loop lead to isolated patches of coast. These trails flood in winter,
often becoming impassable swamps, so pay attention to the warning
signs. ⊠ *Off Stackpole Rd.* ☎ *360/642–3078* 🎫 *Free* ☉ *Dawn–dusk.*

CENTRALIA

60 mi east of South Bend.

Centralia (sen-*trail*-ya) was founded by George Washington, a freed
slave from Virginia, who faced serious discrimination in several states
and territories before settling here in 1852. The town has a well-maintained historic business district. In a park just off I–5 stand the Borst
Blockhouse (built during the 1855–56 Indian Wars) and the elegant
Borst farmhouse. Centralia is an antiques-hunter's paradise, with 350
dealers in 11 malls. It's also known for its 17 murals depicting the
region's history. Pick up a brochure about the murals at the Centralia
Train Depot. Six miles to the south is the sister city of Chehalis (sha-
hay-liss), where there's a historical museum and the Chehalis–Centralia
Steam Train.

Constructed during the Indian Wars, **Ft. Borst** was later used for grain
storage. Standing within a 100-acre park, the Borst Home is a Greek
Revival mansion, built in 1857. ⊠ *Borst Park, 2500 Bryden Ave.* W
☎ *360/330–7688* 🎫 *$2* ☉ *Thanksgiving–Christmas and Memorial
Day–Labor Day, weekends 1–4.*

The small **Lewis County Historical Museum** has regional pioneer memorabilia, some Chehalis Indian art, and a collection of children's dolls
and toys. ⊠ *599 N.W. Front Way, Chehalis 98532* ☎ *360/748–0831*
⊕ *www.lewiscountymuseum.org* 🎫 *$2* ☉ *Tues.–Sat. 9–5, also Sun.
1–5 in summer.*

✪ Through scenic landscapes and over covered bridges, the authentic
engines of the **Chehalis–Centralia Steam Train** will carry you on rails originally laid for logging. The line runs through farmland and rolling hills,
and crosses several wooden bridges. The 12-mi round-trip ride (departing at 1 and 3 on weekends) costs $10; the 18-mi ride (departing at 5
PM on Saturday) is $13. Call for dinner train and special event sched-
ules and pricing. ⊠ *1945 S. Market Blvd., Chehalis* ☎ *360/748–9593*
⊕ *www.steamtrainride.com* ☉ *Memorial Day–Labor Day, weekends.*

✪ The wooded, 125-acre **Rainbow Falls State Park** is en route to the coast.
Along the way are several shallow waterfalls cascading down shelves
of rock. The park, which opened in 1935, has towering old-growth

forest and 3,400 feet of freshwater shoreline along the Chehalis River. Another popular feature is the fuchsia garden, with 40 varieties of the blooming shrubs. ⊠ *Hwy. 6, 17 mi west of Chehalis* ☎ *360/291–3767 or 800/233–0321* ⊕ *www.parks.wa.gov* ☒ *$19–$25 camping fee* ⊙ *Daily dawn–dusk.*

WHERE TO STAY & EAT

$–$$ ✕ **Mary McCrank's Dinner House.** It's an elegant yet cozy farmhouse restaurant that opened in 1928 as the Dutch Mill Inn and was acquired by namesake Mary McCrank in 1935. There are armchairs in the waiting parlor and fireplaces in some of the dining rooms. The chicken-and-dumplings Sunday night special is sublime; so are the dessert pies. You can buy the restaurant's signature jams, syrups, and sauces. ⊠ *2923 Jackson Hwy., 98532* ☎ *360/748–3662* ⊟ *AE, D, MC, V* ⊙ *Closed Mon.*

¢ 🏨 **McMenamins Olympic Club Hotel & Theater.** When it opened in 1908, the
★ Olympic Club was an exclusive gentlemen's resort. It's now owned by the Portland, Oregon, microbrewery moguls the McMenamin brothers, and it houses a restaurant, a bar, and a pool hall. The Tiffany chandeliers, the card room, and various signs (one reading WOMEN'S PATRONAGE NOT SOLICITED hangs above the entrance) remain almost as they were when the club first opened. The restaurant ($) serves up burgers, sandwiches, pastas, steak, fish, and signature chicken wings. The club not only brews its own beer but also bottles its own wine and distills its own spirits. The hotel has 27 European-style rooms with bathrooms down the hall. Some rooms have bunk beds, others are queen and king rooms. Hotel guests receive free movie passes to the house theater. **Pros:** restored historical facility complete with its own theater, inexpensive rates, and restaurant. **Cons:** Rooms are comfortable but nearby train tracks may prove too noisy for light sleepers; shared bathrooms; small rooms. ⊠ *112 N. Tower Ave., 98531* ☎ *360/736–5164 or 866/736–5164* ⊕ *www.mcmenamins.com* ♿ *In-room: no phone. In-hotel: no TV, restaurant, no elevator* ⊟ *AE, D, DC, MC, V.*

MOSSYROCK

35 mi southeast of Centralia.

Mossyrock is a charming small town nestled between two large lakes—Riffe and Mayfield—that were created by dams in the 1960s. The area is a haven for camping, fishing, and boating; two lakefront parks are owned and operated by Tacoma Power (which generates power from the dams and stocks the lakes with fish). At Mayfield Lake there are also a state park and a privately owned marina and resort. The town has the only movie theater in the area playing first-run movies, the Mossy G, housed in a 1930s-era brick building that is also home to a café, pizza place, and offices.

★ Just outside of town, fields of tulips and other flowers grown at the **DeGoede Bulb Farm** provide a colorful backdrop along Highway 12. Stroll through the manicured show gardens year-round. ⊠ *409 Moss-*

yrock Rd. W, 98564 ☎*360/983–9000* ✉*Free* ☉*Closed most Sun. except Apr.–June, Nov.–Dec; also closed Mon. in Jan.*

Fish, camp, and boat at **Mossyrock Park,** on Riffe Lake, just a few miles east of town. The lake is stocked with cutthroat, rainbow and brown trout, coho salmon, steelhead, and bass. ✉*202 Ajlune Rd., 98564* ☎*360/983–3900* ✉*Parking $5 (summer weekends and holidays); camping $14–$25* ☉*Closed Dec. 20–Jan 1.*

Mayfield Lake Park has a handy boat launch right off Highway 12, 4 mi west of Mossyrock. Camping spots are especially scenic, with lake views, forest settings, and even lakefront spots. Fish for trout, bass, and coho salmon. ✉*180 Beach Rd., 98564* ☎*360/983–3900* ✉*Parking $5 (summer weekends and holidays); camping $25–$27* ☉*Mid-Apr.–mid-Oct.*

Ike Kinswa State Park is on the north side of Mayfield Lake, about 4 mi from Mossyrock. The park is named after a Cowlitz Indian; the Cowlitz tribe lived in this area and their burial grounds are nearby. There's year-round camping, two boat ramps, and hiking trails. ✉*873 Harmony Rd.* ☎*360/983–3402* ⊕*www.parks.wa.gov* ✉*Camping $19–$25* ☉*Summer, daily 6:30–dusk; winter, daily 8:30–dusk.*

WHERE TO STAY

$ 🏨**Lake Mayfield Resort and Marina.** The resort has a variety of accommodations, from studios to large units that sleep 8. There are also two rustic cabins (no bathrooms), RV hookups, tent campsites, and even a private camping island. Playgrounds and picnic areas make this a family-friendly place. At this writing, a two-level lakeside restaurant was due to open. **Pros:** Good variety of lodgings, accommodating to groups and families. **Cons:** No pool; resort is open year-round but it's mainly a place to visit in summer. ✉*350 Hadaller Rd., 98564* ☎*360/985–2357* ⊕*www.lakemayfield.com* ⇌*20 rooms, 3 cabins* ⌂*In-room: kitchen (some), refrigerator (some), DVD/VCR. In-hotel: restaurant, some pets, no smoking, beachfront, water sports* ▤*AE, MC, V.*

ASHFORD

36 mi northeast of Mossyrock.

Ashford sits astride an ancient trans-Cascades trail used by the Yakama Indians to trade with the people of western Washington. The town began as a logging railway terminal; today the village provides access to the Nisqually (Longmire) entrance to Mt. Rainier National Park, and caters to 2 million annual visitors with lodges, restaurants, groceries, and gift shops along Highway 706.

☯ In Elbe, 11 mi west of Ashford, **Mt. Rainier Scenic Railroad** has a historic
★ train depot. However, due to 2006 storms that damaged the Nisqually River bridge tracks, the train's departure point was moved in 2007 to the town of Mineral, about a 15-minute drive south. A return to the Elbe route is planned eventually, but a date had not been set at the time of this writing. The steam train takes riders on a 12-mi trip from

Mineral Lake through the foothills of Mt. Rainier. A longer 18-mi route goes over trestles to the logging town of Morton and back. The three-hour *Snowball Express* runs December weekends and includes an on-board Santa. ⊠*Hwy. 7, Elbe* ☎*360/569–2599 or 888/783–2611* ⊕*www.mrsr.com* ⊠*$16–$18* ⊙*Memorial Day–July 4, Labor Day–end of Sept. and Dec., weekends; July 4–Labor Day, daily.*

WHERE TO STAY & EAT

¢ ╳**Scaleburgers.** What started as a state weigh station in 1939 has been converted into a popular restaurant serving hamburgers, fries, milk shakes, and ice cream made from only the finest ingredients. You eat outside on tables overlooking the hills and scenic railroad. The restaurant is 11 mi west of Ashford. ⊠*54109 Mountain Hwy. E, Elbe* ☎*360/569–2247* ☰*No credit cards.*

$$ ⛺**Alexander's Country Inn.** Serving guests since 1912, Alexander's offers ★ premier lodging just a mile from Mt. Rainier. Antiques and fine linens lend the main building romance. There are also two adjacent guest houses. Rates include a hearty breakfast and evening wine, and access to the hot tub and media room. A day spa is available for massage treatments. The cozy restaurant ($–$$; closed weekdays in winter except dinners for guests), the best place in town for lunch or dinner, serves fresh fish and pasta dishes; bread and desserts are baked on the premises. Box lunches are available for picnics. **Pros:** Popular restaurant, guest houses are roomy for families and groups. **Cons:** Some rooms/facilities show their age, day spa is small (massage only), "private" bathrooms are across hall from bedroom. ⊠*37515 Hwy. 706 E, 4 mi east of Ashford, Ashford 98304* ☎*360/569–2300 or 800/654–7615, 360/569–2323 restaurant* ☎*360/569–2323 or 800/654–7615* ⊕*www. alexanderscountryinn.com* ⊲*12 rooms, 2 3-bedroom houses* ⌂*In-room: no phone (some), no TV (some), kitchen (some), Wi-Fi. In-hotel: restaurant, spa, Wi-Fi, no elevator* ☰*MC, V* ⏏*BP.*

¢–$ ⛺**Whittaker's Bunkhouse.** This 1912 motel once housed loggers and mill workers. In those days it was referred to as "the place to stop on the way to the top." In the early 1990s famed climber Lou Whittaker bought and renovated the facility. Today it's a comfortable hostelry, with inexpensive bunk spaces (available May–September) as well as large private rooms. **Pros:** Inexpensive, convenient, historical draw for mountain buffs. **Cons:** No frills except Wi-Fi, very basic rooms, some shared bathrooms. ⊠*30205 Hwy. 706 E, Ashford 98304* ☎*360/569–2439* ⊕*www.whittakersbunkhouse.com* ⊲*18 private rooms, bunk room has 14 beds* ⌂*In-room: no TV. In-hotel: restaurant, Wi-Fi* ☰*MC, V.*

PACKWOOD

25 mi southeast of Ashford via Skate Creek Rd. (closed in winter).

Packwood is a pretty mountain village on U.S. 12, below White Pass. It's a great base for exploring wilderness areas, since it's between Mt. Rainier and Mt. St. Helens.

★ **Goat Rocks Wilderness,** the crags in Gifford Pinchot National Forest, south of Mt. Rainier, are aptly named: you often see mountain goats in this 105,600-acre alpine area, especially when you hike into the back-country. Goat Lake is a particularly good spot for viewing these elusive beasts. You can see the goats without backpacking by traveling along certain forest roads; ask for exact routes and directions in Packwood or ask a forest ranger. Note that many trails and roads in the forest were damaged by the floods and wind storm of 2006; call or visit the Web site for current conditions. ⊠ *Forest headquarters: 10600 N.E. 51st St. Circle, Vancouver* ☎ *360/891–5000* ⊕ *www.fs.fed.us/gpnf.*

WHERE TO STAY

¢–$ 🏨 **Mountain View Lodge.** Just east of the town of Packwood, this conve-nient, quiet motel is 40 mi from both Mt. Rainier and Mt. St. Helens, and 17 mi from White Pass Ski Resort. Rooms have pine paneling and some have log furniture. Family suites have fireplaces and sleep six. There's also a year-round hot tub, seasonal outdoor pool, and pic-nic area. **Pros:** Roomy accommodations, some with kitchens, close to ski resort, pleasant and helpful owners. **Cons:** No restaurant on-site. ⊠ *13163 U.S. Hwy. 12, 98361* ☎ *360/494–5555 or 877/277–7192* ⊕ *www.mtvlodge.com* 🛏 *23* rooms ♿ *In-room: kitchen (some). In-hotel: pool, some pets allowed, no smoking* ⊟ *AE, D, MC, V* ⫟*EP.*

¢–$ 🏨 **Cowlitz River Lodge.** You can't beat the location of this comfortable two-story family motel: it's just off the highway in Packwood, the gate-way to Mt. Rainier National Park *and* the Mt. St. Helens National Vol-canic Monument. A lodgelike construction and a large stone fireplace in the great room add some character—a good thing, since guest rooms have standard motel furniture and bedding. The hot tub is popular with skiers returning from a day at nearby White Pass Ski Area. **Pros:** Con-venient location, helpful manager. **Cons:** No pool, no restaurant, rooms are basic motel style. ⊠ *13069 U.S. 12, 98361* ☎ *360/494–4444 or 888/305–2185* 📠 *360/494–2075* ⊕ *www.escapetothemountains.com* 🛏 *31* rooms ♿ *In-room: dial-up. In-hotel: laundry facilities, Wi-Fi, no elevator* ⊟ *AE, MC, V* ⫟*CP.*

MT. ST. HELENS

☾   *51 mi southwest of Packwood.*

★   On March 8, 2005, Mt. St. Helens came to life again, sending a 36,000-foot plume of steam and ash into the air. Since then, the mountain has been in a state of dome-building activity. Severe flooding in November 2006 damaged many trails and roads in the area; not all had reopened at the time of this writing. Call for updates (☎ 360/449–7800) on Mt. St. Helens activity and closures.

It was once a premier camping destination, with a Mt. Fuji–like cone and pristine forest. But the May 18, 1980, eruption blew off its top and stripped its slopes of forest. The 8,365-foot-high mountain, formerly 9,665 feet high, is one of a string of volcanic Cascade Range peaks that runs from British Columbia's Mt. Garibaldi south to California's Mt. Lassen. The string includes such notable peaks as Mt. Baker and Mt. Rainier to the north, Mt. Adams to the east, Mt. Hood in Oregon, and Mt. Shasta in California. Most people travel to Mt. St. Helens via the

Continued on page 513

Mount Rainier National Park

Its snowy slopes often veiled in clouds, even when the surrounding forests and fields are bathed in sunlight, the massive, 14,411-foot volcano of Mt. Rainier is the centerpiece of its namesake park. The impressive landmark, part of the Cascades chain and the fifth-highest peak in the lower 48 states, draws more than 2 million visitors a year to its spectacular scenery and high-adventure activities.

The mountain holds the largest glacial system in the contiguous United States, with more than two dozen major glaciers. On the lower slopes you'll find silent forests made up of cathedral-like groves of Douglas fir, Western hemlock, and Western red cedar, some more than 1,000 years old. Water and lush greenery are everywhere in the park, and dozens of thundering waterfalls, accessible from the road or by a short hike, fill the air with mist.

WELCOME TO MOUNT RAINIER

TOP REASONS TO GO

★ **The mountain:** Some say Mt. Rainier is the most magical mountain in America. At 14,411 feet, it is a popular peak for climbing, with more than 10,000 attempts per year—half of which are successful.

★ **The glaciers:** About 35 square mi of glaciers and snowfields encircle Mt. Rainier, including Carbon Glacier and Emmons Glacier, the largest glaciers by volume and area, respectively, in the continental United States.

★ **The wildflowers:** More than 100 species of wildflowers bloom in the high meadows of the national park; the display dazzles from midsummer until the snow flies.

★ **Fabulous hiking:** Mt. Rainier has more than 240 mi of maintained trails that provide access to old-growth forest, river valleys, lakes, subalpine meadows, and rugged ridges.

★ **Unencumbered wilderness:** Mount Rainier National Park is one of those rare places with the ability to nurture and deeply inspire the human spirit.

1 Longmire. The Nisqually Gate in the southwest corner of the park was Mount Rainier's original entrance, and highlights of this area include the Longmire Historic District, Christine Falls, Glacier Bridge, and Narada Falls.

2 Paradise. Located 11 mi from Longmire on the south side of the park, Paradise has become Mount Rainier's most popular destination. Famous for its wildflower meadows in summer and its Nordic skiing in winter, there are also a number of good trails here. Be sure to visit the Jackson Memorial Visitor Center, Paradise Inn, and the Paradise Ranger Station.

3 Ohanapecosh. As you approach the park from the southeast, the first stop will be Ohanapecosh. When you're here, check out the Ohanapecosh Visitor Center, the Grove of Patriarchs, and Tipsoo Lake.

KEY

	Ranger Station
▲	Campground
⊼	Picnic Area
⁑	Restaurant
▦	Lodge
⚡	Trailhead
⚥	Restrooms
⇘	Scenic Viewpoint
-----	Walking/Hiking Trails
⋯⋯	Bicycle Path

4 Sunrise/White River.
The east side of the park is easy to visit in summer if you enter from the east side, but it's a long drive from the southwest entrance. Plan to see White River Wilderness Information Center, White River Ranger Station, White River Campground, and Sunrise, the highest point you can drive to in the park and the site of the Sunrise Visitor Center and Sunrise Day Lodge.

5 Carbon River/Mowich Lake. Before entering the northwest corner of the park, pay your entrance fees and pick up park brochures at the Wilderness Information Center in downtown Wilkeson. Don't miss the temperate forest near Carbon River entrance station, Carbon Glacier, and Mowich Lake.

GETTING ORIENTED

Mt. Rainier is the focal point of this 337-square-mi national park. The Nisqually entrance brings you into the southwest corner of the park, where you'll find the historic Longmire District. The most popular destination in the park, Paradise, is located in the park's southern region, and Ohanapecosh, the Grove of Patriarchs, and Tipsoo Lae are in the southeastern corner. Mount Rainier National Park's eastern and northern areas are dominated by wilderness.

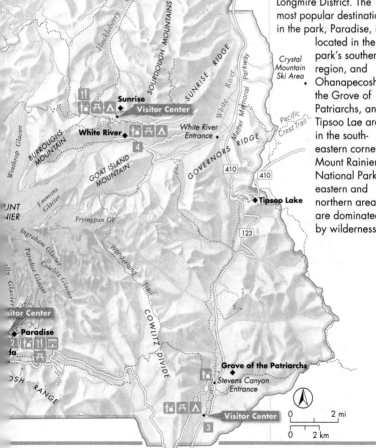

4

MOUNT RAINIER NATIONAL PARK

MOUNT RAINIER NATIONAL PARK PLANNER

When to Go

Crowds are heaviest in July, August, and September, when the parking lots at Paradise and Sunrise often fill before noon. During this period campsites are reserved months in advance, and other lodgings are reserved as much as a year ahead. Washington's rare periods of clear winter weather bring lots of residents up to Paradise for cross-country skiing.

Rainier is the Puget Sound's weather vane: if you can see it, the weather is going to be fine. Visitors are most likely to see the summit in July, August, and September. True to its name, Paradise is often sunny during periods when the lowlands are under a cloud layer. The other nine months of the year, Rainier's summit gathers lenticular clouds whenever a Pacific storm approaches, and once it vanishes from view, not only is it impossible to see the peak, it's time to haul out rain gear.

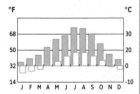

Getting There & Around

More than 2 million people visit Mount Rainier National Park each year to experience the majesty of nature by hiking, camping, picnicking, skiing, and joining guided interpretive programs. Park roads are narrow and winding, with maximum speeds of 35 mph in most places, and you have to watch for pedestrians, cyclists, and wildlife. Parking can be very difficult to find during the peak summer season, especially at Paradise, Sunrise, the Grove of Patriarchs, and at the trailheads between Longmire and Paradise; it's best to arrive early in the day if you plan to visit these sites.

The major roads that reach Mount Rainier National Park—highways 410, 706, and 123—are paved and well-maintained state highways. The Nisqually entrance is on Highway 706, 14 mi east of Route 7; the Ohanapecosh entrance is on Route 123, 5 mi north of U.S. 12; and the White River entrance is on Route 410, 3 mi north of the Chinook and Cayuse passes.

As these highways reach Rainier, they become mountain roads and wind up and down many steep slopes—cautious driving is essential. Vehicles hauling large loads should gear down, especially on downhill sections. Even drivers of passenger cars should take care not to overheat brakes by constant use. Because they traverse the shoulders of a mountain with tempestuous weather, these roads are subject to storms any time of year—even in midsummer—and are almost always being repaired in summer from winter damage and washouts. Expect to encounter road-work delays several times if you are circumnavigating the mountain.

The side roads that wind their way into the park's western slope are all narrower, unpaved, and subject to frequent flooding and washouts. All but Carbon River Road and Highway 706 to Paradise are closed by snow in winter. During this time, however, Carbon River Road tends to flood near the park boundary. (Route 410 is open to the Crystal Mountain access road entrance.) Cayuse Pass usually opens in late April; the Westside Road, Paradise Valley Road, and Stevens Canyon Road usually open in May; Chinook Pass, Mowich Lake Road, and White River Road open in late May; and Sunrise Road opens in late June. All these dates are subject to weather fluctuations.

SCENIC DRIVES

By Holly S. Smith

★ **Chinook Pass Road.** Route 410 (the highway to Yakima) follows the eastern edge of the park to Chinook Pass, where it climbs the steep, 5,432-foot pass via a series of switchbacks. At its top, you'll see broad views of Rainier and the east slope of the Cascades.

★ **Mowich Lake Road.** In the northwest corner of the park, this 24-mi mountain road begins in Wilkeson and heads up the Rainier foothills to Mowich Lake, traversing beautiful mountain meadows along the way. Mowich Lake is a pleasant spot for a picnic; there's also a peaceful walk-in campground.

Paradise Road. This 9-mi stretch of Highway 706 winds its way up the mountain's southwest flank from Longmire to Paradise, taking you from lowland forest to the ever-expanding vistas of the mountain above. Visit on a weekday if possible, especially in peak summer months, when the road is packed with cars. The route is open year-round.

Route 123 and Stevens Canyon Road. At Chinook Pass you can pick up Route 123 and head south to its junction with Stevens Canyon Road. Take this road west to its junction with the Paradise–Nisqually entrance road, which runs west through Longmire and exits the park at Nisqually. The route winds among valley-floor rain forest and uphill slopes; vistas of Puget Sound and the Cascade Range appear at numerous points along the way.

Sunrise Road. This popular (read: crowded) scenic road carves its way 11 mi up Sunrise Ridge from the White River Valley on the northeast side of the park. As you top the ridge there are sweeping views of the surrounding lowlands. The road is open late June to October.

WHAT TO SEE

HISTORIC SITES

National Park Inn. Even if you don't plan to stay overnight, stop by to observe the architecture of this 1917 inn, which is listed on the National Register of Historic Places. While you're here, relax in front of the fireplace in the lounge, shop at the gift shop, or dine at the restaurant. ⊠ *Longmire Visitor Complex, Hwy. 706, 6 mi east of Nisqually entrance, Longmire 98304* ☎ *360/569–2411.*

SCENIC STOPS

Christine Falls. These two tiered falls were named in honor of Christine Louise Van Trump, who climbed to the 10,000-foot level on Mt. Rainier in 1889 at the age of nine, despite having a crippling nervous-system disorder. ⊠ *Next to Hwy. 706, about 2½ mi east of Cougar Rock Campground.*

Fodor'sChoice

★ **Grove of the Patriarchs.** Protected from the periodic fires that swept through the surrounding areas, this small island of 1,000-year-old trees is one of Mount Rainier National Park's most memorable features. A 1½-mi loop trail heads through the old-growth forest of Doug-

MOUNT RAINIER IN ONE DAY

The best way to get a complete overview of Mt. Rainier in a day or less is to enter via Nisqually and begin your tour by browsing in **Longmire Museum.** When you're done, get to know the environment in and around Longmire Meadow and the overgrown ruins of Longmire Springs Hotel on the ½-mi **Trail of the Shadows** nature loop.

From Longmire, Highway 706 E climbs northeast into the mountains toward Paradise. Take a moment to explore gorgeous **Christine Falls,** just north of the road 1½ mi past Cougar Rock Campground, and **Narada Falls,** 3 mi farther on; both are spanned by graceful stone footbridges. Fantastic mountain views, alpine meadows crosshatched with

nature trails, a welcoming lodge and restaurant, the **Jackson Memorial Visitor Center,** and the rustic new **Mt. Rainier Visitor Center** combine to make lofty Paradise the primary goal of most park visitors. One outstanding (but challenging) way to explore the high country is to hike the 5-mi round-trip **Skyline Trail** to Panorama Point, which rewards you with stunning 360-degree views.

Continue eastward on Highway 706 E for 21 mi and leave your car to explore the incomparable, thousand-year-old **Grove of the Patriarchs.** Afterward, turn your car north toward White River and **Sunrise Visitor Center,** where you can watch the alpenglow fade from Mt. Rainier's domed summit.

las fir, cedar, and hemlock. ✉ *Rte. 123, west of the Stevens Canyon entrance.*

★ **Narada Falls.** A steep but short trail leads to the viewing area for these spectacular 168-foot falls, which expand to a width of 75 feet during peak flow times. In winter the frozen falls are popular with ice climbers. ✉ *Along Hwy. 706, 1 mi west of turnoff for Paradise, 6 mi east of Cougar Rock Campground.*

☾ **Tipsoo Lake.** The short, pleasant trail that circles the lake here—ideal for families—provides breathtaking views. Enjoy the subalpine wildflower meadows during the summer months; in early fall there is an abundant supply of huckleberries. ✉ *Off Cayuse Pass east on Hwy. 410.*

VISITOR CENTERS

Mt. Rainier National Park Visitor Center. The park's newest facility has rustic, ecologically friendly architecture and numerous exhibits on the mountain's geology, flora, fauna, and history. A casual restaurant and bookshop are also housed within, and the base is a starting point for several major trails. ✉ *Hwy. 706 E, 19 mi. east of the Nisqually park entrance* ☎ *360/569–2211* ✉ *Free* ☉ *Memorial Day–Labor Day, daily 7–7; Sept.–mid-Oct., daily 10–6, otherwise weekends and holidays 10–5.*

Jackson Memorial Visitor Center. High on the mountain's southern flank, this center houses exhibits on geology, mountaineering, glaciology, winter storms, and alpine ecology; multimedia programs repeat at half-hour intervals. Note that it will close for good in fall 2008. ⊠ *Hwy. 706 E, 19 mi. east of Nisqually park entrance* ☎ *360/569–2211 Ext. 2328* ⊗ *May–mid-Oct., daily 9–5; Nov.–Apr., weekends and holidays 10–5.*

★ **Longmire Museum and Visitor Center.** Glass cases inside this museum preserve plants and animals from the park—including a large, friendly-looking stuffed cougar—and historical photographs and geographical displays provide a worthwhile overview of the park's history. The visitor center, next door to the museum, has some perfunctory exhibits on the surrounding forest and its inhabitants, as well as pamphlets and information about park activities. ⊠ *Hwy. 706, 17 mi east of Ashford* ☎ *360/569–2211 Ext. 3314* ⊡ *Free* ⊗ *June–mid-Oct. daily 9–5, otherwise 9–4.*

Ohanapecosh Visitor Center. Learn about the region's dense old-growth forests through interpretive displays and videos at this visitor center, located near the Grove of the Patriarchs. ⊠ *Rte. 123, 11 mi north of Packwood* ☎ *360/569–6046* ⊗ *Late May–mid-Oct., daily 9–5.*

Sunrise Visitor Center. Exhibits at this center explain the region's sparser alpine and subalpine ecology. A network of nearby loop trails leads you through alpine meadows and forest to overlooks that afford broad views of the Cascades and Rainier. Evening programs are offered at White River Campground on Thursday through Saturday nights in summer. ⊠ *Sunrise Rd., 15 mi from the White River park entrance* ☎ *360/663–2425* ⊗ *Early July–Labor Day, daily 9–5.*

SPORTS & THE OUTDOORS

BIRD-WATCHING

★ Watch for kestrels, red-tailed hawks, and, occasionally, golden eagles on snags in the lowland forests. Also present at Rainier, but rarely seen, are great horned owls, spotted owls, and screech owls. Iridescent rufous hummingbirds flit from blossom to blossom in the drowsy summer lowlands, and sprightly water ouzels flutter in the many forest creeks. Raucous Steller's jays and gray jays scold passersby from trees, often darting boldly down to steal morsels from unguarded picnic tables. At higher elevations, look for the pure white plumage of the white-tailed ptarmigan as it hunts for seeds and insects in winter. Waxwings, vireos, nuthatches, sapsuckers, warblers, flycatchers, larks, thrushes, siskins, tanagers, and finches are common throughout the park.

OUTFITTERS & EXPEDITIONS

HIKING

Rainier Mountaineering Inc.
Reserve a private hiking guide through this mountaineering outfitter. ⊠ *30027 Hwy. 706 E, Ashford* ☎ *888/892–5462 or 360/569–2227* ⊕ *www.rmiguides.com.*

Whittaker Mountaineering. This retail outfitter rents hiking gear and outdoor equipment, and can arrange for private guides. ⊠ *30027 Hwy. 706 E, Ashford* ☎ *360/569–2142 or 800/238–5756* ⊕ *www.whittaker-mountaineering.com.*

MOUNTAIN CLIMBING

Rainier Mountaineering Inc. The highly regarded concessionaire teaches the fundamentals of mountaineering at one-day classes held from mid-May through late September; participants are evaluated on their fitness for the climb and must be able to withstand a 16-mi round-trip hike with a 9,000-foot gain in elevation. ⊠ *30027 Hwy. 706 E, Ashford* ☎ *888/892–5462 or 360/569–2227* ⊕ *www.rmiguides.com* ⌂ *$805 (3-day summit climb package).*

Whittaker Mountaineering. This all-purpose Rainier Base Camp outfitter rents climbing equipment. ⊠ *30027 Hwy. 706 E, Ashford* ☎ *800/238–5756 or 360/569–2142* ⊕ *www.whittakermountaineering.com.*

SKIING & SNOWSHOEING

Paradise Ski Area. Here you can cross-country ski or, in the Snowplay Area north of the upper parking lot at Paradise, sled using inner tubes and plastic disk sleds from December to April. Check with rangers for any restrictions. ⊠ *Accessible from Nisqually entrance at park's*

southwest corner and from Stevens Canyon entrance at park's southeast corner (summer only) ☎ *360/569–2211* ⊕ *www.nps.gov/mora* ⊙ *May–mid-Oct., daily, dawn–dusk; mid-Oct.–Apr., weekends dawn–dusk.*

Rainier Mountaineering Inc. This mountaineering outfitter offers winter ski programs and seminars; they also arrange private cross-country skiing and snowshoeing guides. ⊠ *30027 Hwy. 706 E, Ashford* ☎ *888/892–5462 or 360/569–2227* ⊕ *www.rmiguides.com.*

Rainier Ski Touring Center. This company rents cross-country ski equipment and provides lessons from mid-December through Easter. ⊠ *Hwy. 706, 10 mi east of Nisqually entrance, Longmire* ⊕ *www.mashell.com/~mtrretail/Skiing.htm* ☎ *360/569–2411 weekdays*

Snowshoe Walks. Park rangers lead snowshoe walks from the Visitor Center at Paradise Saturdays at noon and 2. Snowshoes are provided, even for kids, and trails cover 1¼ mi in about two hours. Check park publications for exact dates. ⊠ *1 mi north of Ohanapecosh on Rte. 123, at high point of Hwy. 706* ☎ *360/569–2211 Ext. 2328* ⌂ *$1 donation* ⊙ *Late Dec.–Apr., weekends and holidays.*

Ed Strass, 360/569–2902 **Whittaker Mountaineering.** Rent outdoor equipment, skis, snowshoes, and snowboards through this outfitter, which also arranges for private cross-country skiing guides. ⊠ *30027 Hwy. 706 E, Ashford* ☎ *800/238–5756 or 360/569–2142* ⊕ *www.whittakermountaineering.com.*

BOATING

Nonmotorized boating is permitted on all lakes inside the park except Frozen, Ghost, Reflection, and Tipsoo lakes. Mowich Lake, in the northwest corner of the park, is the only lake easily accessible to canoes and kayaks. There are no boat rentals inside the park.

HIKING

★ Although the mountain can seem remarkably benign on calm summer days, hiking Rainier is not a city-park stroll. Dozens of hikers and trekkers annually lose their way and must be rescued—and lives are lost on the mountain each year. Weather that approaches cyclonic levels can appear quite suddenly, any month of the year. With the possible exception of the short loop hikes listed below, all visitors venturing far from vehicle access points should carry day packs with warm clothing, food, and other emergency supplies.

EASY **Nisqually Vista Trail.** Equally popular in summer and winter, this trail is a 1¼-mi round-trip through subalpine meadows to an overlook point for Nisqually Glacier. The gradually sloping path is a favorite venue for cross-country skiers in winter; in summer, listen for the shrill alarm calls of the area's marmots. ⊠ *Jackson Memorial Visitor Center, Rte. 123, 1 mi north of Ohanapecosh, at high point of Hwy. 706.*

Sourdough Ridge Self-Guiding Trail. The mile-long loop of this easy trail takes you through the delicate subalpine meadows near the Sunrise Visitor Center. A gradual climb to the ridgetop yields magnificent views of Mt. Rainier and the more distant volcanic cones of Mts. Baker, Adams, Glacier, and Hood. ⊠ *Sunrise Visitor Center, Sunrise Rd., 15 mi from White River park entrance.*

Trail of the Shadows. This ½-mi trek is notable for its glimpses of meadowland ecology, its colorful soda springs (don't drink the water), James Longmire's old homestead cabin, and the foundation of the old Longmire Springs Hotel, which was destroyed by fire around 1900. ⊠ *Hwy. 706, 10 mi east of Nisqually entrance.*

MODERATE
Fodor's Choice
★

Skyline Trail. This 5-mi loop, one of the highest trails in the park, beckons day-trippers with a vista of alpine ridges and, in summer, meadows filled with brilliant flowers and birds. At 6,800 feet, Panorama Point, the spine of the Cascade Range, spreads away to the east, and Nisqually Glacier grumbles its way downslope. ⊠ *Jackson Memorial Visitor Center, Rte. 123, 1 mi north of Ohanapecosh at high point of Hwy. 706.*

Van Trump Park Trail. You gain an exhilarating 2,200 feet on this trail while hiking through a vast expanse of meadow with views of the southern Puget Sound. The 5-mi trail provides good footing, and the average hiker can make it up in three to four hours. ⊠ *Hwy. 706 at Christine Falls, 4⁴⁄₁₀ mi east of Longmire.*

DIFFICULT
★

Burroughs Mountain Trail. Starting at the south side of the Sunrise parking area, this three-hour, 7-mi round-trip hike offers spectacular views of the peak named in honor of naturalist and essayist John Burroughs. The challenging trail passes Shadow Lake before climbing to an overlook of the White River and Emmon's Glacier. As you continue on, you'll reach First Burroughs Mountain and Second Burroughs Mountain. This area on the northeast slope of Mt. Rainier has some of the most accessible tundra in the Cascades, and you can observe the delicate slow-growing plants that survive in this harsh environment. Note: early-season hiking on this trail can be particularly hazardous due to snow and ice on the steep mountain slopes; check trail conditions before starting out.

Fodor's Choice
★   **Wonderland Trail.** All other Mt. Rainier hikes pale in comparison to this stunning 93-mi trek, which completely encircles the mountain. The trail passes through all the major life zones of the park, from the old-growth forests of the lowlands to the alpine meadows and goat-haunted glaciers of the highlands. Be sure to pick up a mountain-goat sighting card from a ranger station or information center to help in the park's ongoing effort to learn more about these elusive animals. Wonderland is a rugged trail; elevation gains and losses totaling 3,500 feet are common in a day's hike, which averages 8 mi. Most hikers start out from either Longmire or Sunrise and take 10–14 days to cover the 93-mi route. Snow lingers on the high passes well into June (sometimes July), and you can count on rain any time of the year. Campsites are wilderness trailside areas with pit toilets and water that must be purified before drinking. Only hardy, well-equipped, and experienced wilderness trekkers should attempt this trip, but those who do will be amply rewarded. Wilderness permits are required, and reservations are strongly recommended. ⚠ **Parts of the Wonderland Trail were severely damaged in the Nov. 2006 floods, and some sections may remain closed in 2007. Be sure to check with one of the park's visitor centers for the trail's current status.** ✉ *Longmire Visitor Center, Hwy. 706, 17 mi east of Ashford; Sunrise Visitor Center, Sunrise Rd., 15 mi west of White River park entrance.*

For information on tours and equipment, see Outfitters & Expeditions box.

MOUNTAIN CLIMBING

★   Climbing Mt. Rainier is not for amateurs; each year, climbers die on the mountain, and many climbers become lost and must be rescued. Near-catastrophic weather can appear quite suddenly, any month of the year. If you're experienced in technical, high-elevation snow, rock, and ice-field adventuring, Mt. Rainier can be a memorable experience. Experienced climbers can fill out a climbing card at the Paradise, White River, or Carbon River ranger stations and lead their own groups of two or more. Climbers must register with a ranger before leaving and check out upon return. A $30 annual climbing fee applies to anyone venturing above 10,000 feet or onto one of Rainier's glaciers. During peak season it is recommended that you make a climbing reservation in advance. The reservation fee is $20 per group, and reservations are taken by fax beginning on April 1 on a first-come first-served basis. For more information on climbing Mt. Rainier or for a reservation form and fax number, visit the park's Web site ⊕*www.nps.gov/mora/climb/climb.htm. For information on tours and equipment, see Outfitters & Expeditions box.*

SKIING

Mt. Rainier is a major Nordic ski center. Although trails are not groomed, those around Paradise are extremely popular. If you want to ski with fewer people, try the trails in and around the Ohanapecosh–Stevens Canyon area, which are just as beautiful and, because of their more easterly exposure, slightly less subject to the rains that can douse the Longmire side, even in the dead of winter. You should never ski on the plowed main roads, especially in the Paradise area—the snowplow operator can't see you. No rentals are available on the eastern side of the park. *For information on tours and equipment, see Outfitters & Expeditions box.*

SNOWSHOEING

★ Deep snows make Mt. Rainier a snowshoeing Mecca. The network of trails in the Paradise area makes it the best choice for snowshoers. The park's east side roads, routes 123 and 410, are unplowed and provide another good snowshoeing venue, although you must share the main parts of the road with snowmobilers. *For information on tours and equipment, see Outfitters & Expeditions box.*

EDUCATIONAL OFFERINGS

Fodor'sChoice **Gray Line Bus Tours.** This company conducts sightseeing tours of Seat-
★ tle, and one-day and longer tours from Seattle to Mount Rainier and Olympic national parks, Mt. St. Helens, the North Cascades, and the Washington Wine Country (Yakima Valley). ✉*4500 Marginal Way SW, Seattle* ☎*206/624–5077 or 800/426–7532* ⊕*www.graylineofseattle.com* ✆*Call for prices and schedules.*

★ **Ancient Forest Walks.** Park naturalists help visitors learn to identify different rain-forest trees and plants on forest walks. For exact schedules, consult bulletin boards at visitor centers, ranger stations, and campgrounds. ✉*Ohanapecosh Visitor Center: Rte. 123, 11 mi north of Packwood* ☎*360/569–6046* ✆*Free* ☽*June–Sept., hrs and days vary according to staffing schedules.*

NEARBY TOWNS

Ashford sits astride an ancient trail across the Cascades used by the Yakama Indians to trade with the coastal tribes of western Washington. The town began as a logging railway terminal; today, it's the main gateway to Mount Rainier—and the only year-round access point to the park—catering to visitors with lodges, restaurants, groceries, and gift shops. Surrounded by Cascade peaks, **Packwood** is a pretty mountain village on U.S. 12, below White Pass. Between Mt. Rainier and Mt. St. Helens, it's a perfect jumping-off point for exploring local wilderness areas. For more information on nearby towns, *see* town listings in this chapter.

WHERE TO EAT

Only a few restaurants are inside the park; a few others worth checking out lie beyond its borders (*See Where to Eat in Ashford and Packwood*). Mt. Rainier's picnic areas are justly famous, especially in summer, when wildflowers fill the meadows and friendly yellow pine chipmunks dart hopefully about in search of handouts. Note that en route to Mt. St. Helens there's no food, even at visitor centers, past milepost 27.

$–$$$
★

✕ **Paradise Inn.** Where else can you get a decent Sunday brunch in a historic heavy-timbered lodge halfway up a mountain? Tall, many-paned windows provide terrific views of Rainier, and the warm glow of native wood permeates the large dining room. The lunch menu is simple and healthy—grilled salmon, salads—and for dinner, there's nothing like a hearty plate of the inn's signature bourbon buffalo meat loaf. Service is leisurely and friendly, so you can just relax and enjoy the woodsy ambience. ⊠ *Paradise* ☎ *360/569–2413* ⚓ *Reservations not accepted* ▭ *AE, D, MC, V* ⊘ *Closed Oct.–late May.*

$–$$
★

✕ **National Park Inn.** Photos of Mt. Rainier taken by some of the Northwest's top photographers adorn the walls of this inn's large dining room, a bonus on the many days the mountain refuses to show itself. Breakfasts feature fresh, home-baked goods like cinnamon rolls with cream-cheese frosting. Other meals are simple but tasty: maple hazelnut chicken, tenderloin tip stir-fry, and grilled red snapper with black bean sauce and corn relish. Tip: You can only make same-day dinner reservations to secure an evening seat. ⊠ *Longmire* ☎ *360/569–2411* ▭ *AE, D, MC, V.*

¢
☾

✕ **Jackson Memorial Visitor Center.** Cafeteria-style grill fare such as hot dogs, hamburgers, and soft drinks are on the menu daily. Tucked amid the exhibit and viewing levels of the lodgelike interior, the dining room is very casual, convivial, and often noisy with tour groups. Note: The facility closes for good in October 2008. ⊠ *Rte. 123, 1 mi north of Ohanapecosh at high point of Hwy. 706* ☎ *360/569–2211* ▭ *No credit cards* ⊘ *Closed weekdays early Oct.–Apr.*

¢
☾

✕ **Sunshine Day Lodge & Visitor Center.** A cafeteria and grill at this visitor center serves inexpensive hamburgers, chili, hot dogs, and snacks from early July to early September. It's a busy, family-style spot usually bustling with hikers and day tourists. ⊠ *Sunrise Rd., 15 mi from White River park entrance* ☎ *360/663–2425* ▭ *No credit cards* ⊘ *Closed early Sept.–early July.*

PICNIC AREAS   All Mt. Rainier picnic areas are open July through September only.

Carbon River Picnic Ground. You'll find a half-dozen tables in the woods, near the park's northwest boundary. ⊠ *Carbon River Rd., 1½ mi east of park entrance.*

Paradise Picnic Area. This site has great views on clear days. After picnicking at Paradise, you can take an easy hike to one of the many waterfalls in the area—Sluiskin, Myrtle, or Narada, to name a few. ⊠ *Hwy. 706, 11 mi east of Longmire.*

Sunrise Picnic Area. Set in an alpine meadow that's filled with wildflowers in July and August, this picnic area provides expansive views of the mountain and surrounding ranges in good weather. ⊠*Sunrise Rd., 11 mi west of White River entrance.*

WHERE TO STAY

The two national park lodges, at Longmire and Paradise, ooze history and charm. However, reservations are key—and make them up to a year in advance for summer months.Dozens of motels and cabin complexes are also near the park entrances, but most are plain and pricey. Camping is the way to go here.

The four drive-in campgrounds, which have some 700 sites, are at Cougar Rock, Ipsut Creek, Ohanapecosh, and White River. None have hot water or RV hookups; showers are available at Jackson Memorial Visitor Center.

For backcountry camping, you must obtain a free wilderness permit at one of the visitor centers. Primitive sites are spaced at 7- to 8-mi intervals along the Wonderland Trail. A copy of *Wilderness Trip Planner: A Hiker's Guide to the Wilderness of Mount Rainier National Park*, available from any of the park's visitor centers or through the superintendent's office, is an invaluable guide if you're planning backcountry stays. Reservations for specific wilderness campsites are available by fax or letter from May 1 to September 30 for $20; for details, call the Wilderness Information Center at 360/569–4453.

$–$$
★
National Park Inn. Surrounded by soaring pines, this cabin-style country lodging is the only park accommodation open year-round. Walk into a cozy room with alarge stone fireplace, where you can warm up and dry off mittens in winter, then head up to cedar-paneled rooms with wrought-iron lamps and antique bentwood headboards. Simple American fare is served in the restaurant ($–$$). Note: The inn is operated as a B&B from November through April. **Pros:** Comfortable, cozy, great backcountry ambience. Hallways can be noisy and cold; bathrooms can be busy. ⊠*Longmire Visitor Complex, Hwy. 706, 10 mi east of Nisqually entrance, Longmire 98304* ☎*360/569–2275* ⊟*360/569–2770* ⊕*www.rainier.guestservices.com* ⇆*25 rooms, 8 with bath* ⚒*In-room: no a/c, no phone, no TV. In-hotel: restaurant, no elevator* ☐*AE, D, MC, V.*

$–$$
Fodor's Choice
★
Paradise Inn. Towering above the Mt. Rainier slopes, this solid gray edifice, built in 1917, rises from the forests like a castle in the midst of the Alps. Inside, carved Alaskan cedar logs, burnished parquet floors, stone fireplaces, and Indian rugs are part of the rugged, mountain-style decor, which also highlights furnishings by German carpenter Hans Fraehnke. Glorious mountain views are all around, including from the full-service dining room ($–$$$) and snack bar. The inn is 19 mi inside the park's southwest entrance. **Pros:** Beautiful building, convenient locale, lots of history. **Cons:** Few modern amenities, can feel damp and drafty. ⊠*Hwy. 706, Paradise* ✐*c/o Mount Rainier Guest Services, Box 108 Ashford 98304* ☎*360/569–2275* ⊟*360/569–2770* ⊕*www.*

guestservices.com/rainier ⇌*120 rooms, 90 with bath* 🚻 *In-room: no phone, no TV. In-hotel: restaurant, bar, no elevator* 🚭*AE, D, MC, V* ⊘*Closed Oct.–mid-May.*

🏕**Cougar Rock Campground.** A secluded, heavily wooded campground with an amphitheater, Cougar Rock is one of the first to fill up. You can reserve group sites for $3 per person, per night, with a minimum of 12 people per group. Reservations are accepted for summer only. ✉*2½ mi north of Longmire* ☎*301/722–1257* ⊕*reservations.nps.gov* ⇌*173 sites* 🚻*Flush toilets, dump station, drinking water, fire grates, ranger station* 🚭*AE, D, MC, V* ⊘*Closed mid-Oct.–Apr.*

★   🏕**Ohanapecosh Campground.** This lush, green campground in the park's southeast corner has a visitor center, amphitheater, and self-guided trail. It's one of the first campgrounds to open. Reservations are accepted for summer only. ✉*Ohanapecosh Visitor Center, Hwy. 123, 1½ mi north of park boundary* ☎*301/722–1257* ⊕*reservations.nps.gov* ⇌*184 sites* 🚻*Flush toilets, dump station, drinking water, fire grates, ranger station* 🚭*AE, D, MC, V* ⊘*Closed late-Oct.–Apr.*

🏕**White River Campground.** At an elevation of 4,400 feet, White River is one of the park's highest and least-wooded campgrounds. Here you can enjoy campfire programs, self-guided trails, and partial views of Mt. Rainier's summit. ✉*5 mi west of White River entrance* ☎*360/569–2211* ⇌*112 sites* 🚻*Flush toilets, dump station, drinking water, fire grates, ranger station* 🚭*AE, D, MC, V* 🚫*Reservations not accepted* ⊘*Closed mid-Sept.–early June.*

🏕**Ipsut Creek Campground.** The quietest park campground is also the most difficult to reach. It's in the park's northwest corner, amid a wet, green, and rugged wilderness; many self-guided trails are nearby. The campground is theoretically open year-round, though the gravel Carbon River Road that leads to it is subject to flooding and potential closure at any time. Reservations aren't accepted here. ✉*Carbon River Rd., 4 mi east of Carbon River entrance* ☎*360/569–2211* ⇌*30 sites* 🚻*Pit toilets, running water (nonpotable), fire grates* 🚭*AE, D, MC, V.*

★   🏕**Mowich Lake Campground.** This is Rainier's only lakeside campground. Located at 4,959 feet, it's also peaceful and secluded. Note that the campground is accessible only by 5 mi of convoluted gravel roads, which are subject to weather damage and potential closure at any time. ✉*Mowich Lake Rd., 6 mi east of park boundary* ☎*360/568–2211* ⇌*30 sites* 🚻*Pit toilets, running water (nonpotable), fire grates, picnic tables, ranger station* 🚫*Reservations not accepted* ⊘*Closed Nov.–mid July.*

MOUNT RAINIER ESSENTIALS

ACCESSIBILITY

The only trail in the park that is fully accessible to those with impaired mobility is Kautz Creek Trail, a ½-mi boardwalk that leads to a splendid view of the mountain. Parts of the Trail of the Shadows at Longmire and the Grove of the Patriarchs at Ohanapecosh are also accessible. Campgrounds at Cougar Rock, Ohanapecosh, and Sunshine Point have several accessible sites. All main visitor centers, as well as National Park Inn at Longmire, are accessible.

ADMISSION FEES & PERMITS

The entrance fee is $15 per vehicle, which covers everyone in the vehicle for seven days; motorcycles and bicycles pay $5. Annual passes are available for $30. Climbing permits are $30 per person per climb or glacier trek. Wilderness camping permits, which must be obtained for all backcountry trips, are free, but advance reservations are highly recommended and cost $20 per party.

ADMISSION HOURS

Mt. Rainier National Park is open 24 hours a day year-round, but with limited access in winter. Gates at Nisqually (Longmire) are open 24 hours a day year-round, but may only be staffed during the day. The Carbon River Ranger Station is open 24 hours a day year-round; the White River Ranger Station is open 24 hours a day from June through September; and the Stevens Canyon entrance by Ohanapecosh is open 24 hours a day from late May to late September. Hours for the new Mt. Rainier Visitor Center, slated to open in October 2008, are late Memorial Day to Labor Day 7–7 daily, 10 to 6 daily September through mid-October, and 10–5 weekends and holidays the rest of the year; Jackson Memorial Visitor Center will have the same hours until October 2008, when it will close for good Sunrise Visitor Center is open daily 9–5, and the Longmire Museum is open daily 9–5 year-round.

ATMS/BANKS

There are no ATMs in the park. Numerous ATMs are available at stores, gas stations, and bank branches in Ashford, Packwood, and Eatonville. In Ashford there are ATMs at Ashford Valley Grocery and Suver's General Store.

Contacts **Venture Bank** (⊠ *121 Washington Ave. N, Eatonville* ☎ *360/832–7200*). **Key Bank** (⊠ *101 Center St. E, Eatonville* ☎ *360/832–6125*).

AUTOMOBILE SERVICE STATIONS

Gas and automotive services are not available in Mount Rainier National Park. Ashford and Packwood, with several stations each, are the closest outlets.

Contacts **Mill Town Shell** (⊠ *360 Center St. S, Eatonville* ☎ *360/832–6476*).

EMERGENCIES

For all park emergencies, dial 911.

LOST & FOUND

The park's lost and found is located at the park headquarters office in Ashford. You can call or visit in person to see if your missing item has been found, or fill out a form, and park staff will call you when your item is recovered.

Contacts **Lost and Found** (⊠ *55210 238th Ave E, Ashford 98304* ☎ *360/569–2211 Ext. 2334*).

POST OFFICES

Contacts **The National Park Inn Post Office** (⊠ *Longmire Visitor Complex, Hwy. 706 E, 10 mi east of Nisqually entrance, Longmire 98304* ☎ *No phone*).

Paradise Inn Post Office (⊠ *Jackson Memorial Visitor Center, Paradise 98304* ☎ *No phone*).

PUBLIC TELEPHONES & RESTROOMS

Public telephones and restrooms are located at all park visitor centers (Sunrise, Ohanapecosh, and Paradise), at the National Park Inn at Longmire, and at Paradise Inn at Paradise.

SHOPS & GROCERS

Contacts **General Store at the National Park Inn** (⊠ *Longmire Visitor Complex, Longmire* ☎ *360/569–2411*). **Plaza Market** (⊠ *203 Center St., Eatonville* ☎ *360/832–6151*).

VISITOR INFORMATION

Contacts **Mount Rainier National Park** ⊠ *Tahoma Woods, Star Rte., Ashford, WA 98304* ☎ *360/569–2211* ⊕ *www.nps.gov/mora*.

Spirit Lake Memorial Highway (Highway 504), whose predecessor was destroyed in a matter of minutes in 1980. This highway has unparalleled views of the mountain and the Toutle River Valley.

The U.S. Forest Service operates the Mt. St. Helens National Volcanic Monument. A Northwest Forest Pass is required to park at trailheads, visitor centers, and other forest facilities. The pass costs $5 per vehicle per day and can be purchased at visitor centers, Ape's Headquarters, and Cascade Peaks Restaurant and Gift Shop on Forest Road 99.

Climbing is limited to the south side of the mountain. Permits are required; the fee is $22 per person. On the east side of the mountain are two bare-bones visitor centers, Windy Ridge and Ape Cave. On the south side of the mountain there's a center at Lava Canyon. The two centers along Highway 504 on the forest's west side—Mt. St. Helens Visitor Center (at Silver Lake), and Johnston Ridge Observatory—are open daily in summer. Silver Lake is open from 9 to 6 in summer and 9 to 4 in winter; Johnston Ridge operates from 10 to 6 in summer and is closed from October until May.

Castle Rock's location on I–5 at the Spirit Lake Highway makes it a major point of entry for the Mt. St. Helens National Monument. The site takes its name from a tree-covered knob that once stood on the bank of the Cowlitz River and served as a landmark for Hudson's Bay Company trappers and traders. The landscape changed dramatically when the 1980 eruption filled the Toutle and Cowlitz Rivers with volcanic mush.

The **Mount St. Helens Visitors Center at Silver Lake** (⊠ *Hwy. 504, 5 mi east of I–5, Silver Lake* ☎ *360/274–0962* ⊕ *www.parks.wa.gov/mount sthelens.asp*) is owned and operated by the Washington State Parks Commission. It doesn't have great views of the mountain, but it has a walk-through volcano and interactive exhibits documenting the eruption. Theater presentations run twice an hour.

☾ **Weyerhauser/Hoffstadt Bluff Visitors Center** (⊠ *Hwy. 504, 27 mi east of I–*
★ *5* ☎ *360/274–7750* ⊕ *www.mt-st-helens.com*), run by Cowlitz County, has a full-service restaurant and gift shop with plenty of Mt. St. Helens souvenirs. The center also has picnic areas; a helicopter-tour operator; hiking trails; and the Memorial Grove, which honors the 57 people who lost their lives during the 1980 eruption. Admission is free.

☾ The **Johnston Ridge Observatory** (⊠ *Hwy. 504, 53 mi east of I–5*
★ ☎ *360/274–2140* ⊕ *www.fs.fed.us/gpnf/mshnvm/*) in the heart of the blast zone has spectacular views of the crater and lava dome. Exhibits here interpret the geology of Mt. St. Helens and explain how scientists monitor an active volcano.

VANCOUVER

19 mi south of Woodland.

This sprawling river town started as a Hudson's Bay Company fort and trading depot in 1824, and soon became *the* frontier metropolis of the

Pacific Northwest. The U.S. Army built a fort on the bluff above the Hudson's Bay post in 1846. Today the National Park Service maintains and runs the reconstructed Ft. Vancouver, and the fort as well as the Officers' Row complex are part of the larger Ft. Vancouver National Historic Reserve.

Downtown Vancouver has several historic buildings, and Esther Short Park, in the center of town, is surrounded by the new Hilton Vancouver Washington and Vancouver Conference Center, shops, and restaurants, and has gardens, a playground, fountains, and an amphitheater. On summer weekends the park hosts concerts. The nearby Vancouver Farmers' Market is the region's largest. The market moved into a permanent year-round indoor location adjacent to the park in the lower level of Esther Short Commons in fall 2005. The Columbia River waterfront district is another hot spot for dining, shopping, and strolling, along the paved Renaissance Trail.

In the 1909 Carnegie Library, the **Clark County Historical Museum** displays Native American artifacts, items from the Hudson's Bay Company, an 1890 country store, and a 1900 doctor's office. The museum also has a research library of local and regional history. ⊠ *1511 Main St.* ☎ *360/993–5679* 🖨 *360/993–5683* ⊕ *www.cchmuseum.org* 💲*$4* ⊘ *Tues.–Sat. 11–4.*

The 10 officers' houses and duplexes of **Officers' Row** line former parade grounds and were built between 1867 and 1906. Ulysses S. Grant lived in the 1849 log building now bearing his name when he was quartermaster of Vancouver Barracks from 1852 to 1853. Today the Grant House is home to the Restaurant at the Historic Reserve. The Marshall House, named for George C. Marshall, who served as commanding officer at Vancouver Barracks from 1936 to 1938, is open to the public. All the homes along the main boulevard have been restored and are part of the Ft. Vancouver National Historic Reserve. Picnic areas line the parade grounds. ⊠ *750 Anderson St.* ☎ *360/693–3103* ⊕ *www. vnhrt.org* 💲*Free* ⊘ *Weekdays 9–5.*

☾ The fort of the **Ft. Vancouver National Historic Site**—with squared-log
★ buildings, an encircling palisade, and corner bastions—was established here by the Hudson's Bay Company in 1825. In summer, rangers dress in period costume and provide cultural demonstrations. ⊠ *1501 E. Evergreen Blvd.* ☎ *360/696–7655* ⊕ *www.nps.gov/fova* 💲*$5 families, $3 individuals* ⊘ *Daily 9–4 winter; 9–5 summer.*

☾ The **Pearson Air Museum** has vintage aircraft in working order. Displays rotate; more than a dozen planes are on view at a time. Planes include a 1953 Cessna 170 that flew around the world in 1956-57, a 1913 Voisin III (1 of just 3 in the world), and a 1941 DeHavilland Tiger Moth. Kids love the hands-on displays (and the gift shop). Pearson is the West's oldest continuously operating airfield. ⊠ *1115 E. 5th St.* ☎ *360/694–7026* 🖨 *360/694-0824* ⊕ *www.pearsonairmuseum.org* 💲*$8* ⊘ *Weds.–Sat. 10–5; also open Tues. noon–5, Memorial Day–Labor Day.*

♻ Bike, skate, jog, or stroll the 4-mi **Columbia Waterfront Renaissance Trail**
★ that follows the Columbia River, passing restaurants and shops along
the way. Visit the old apple tree, which was planted in 1826, and stop
to enjoy the vistas. The trail passes by the Captain (George) Vancouver
Monument and a plaza dedicated to Ilchee, a Chinook Indian chief's
daughter. ⊠*115 Columbia Way* ☎*360/619–1111.*

Gifford Pinchot National Forest, stretching from Mt. St. Helens east to Mt.
Adams and north to Mt. Rainier, is one of Washington's oldest forests.
It's named for the first chief of the forest service. ⊠*Forest headquarters:
10600 N.E. 51st Circle, accessible via Hwy. 14, Hwy. 25, or Hwy. 503*
☎*360/891–5000* ⊕*www.fs.fed.us/gpnf* ⊠*Free* ⊙ *Weekdays 8–5.*

WHERE TO STAY & EAT

¢–$$$ ✕**Beaches Restaurant.** This restaurant is on the water and has gorgeous
★ views up and down the river. The menu includes pastas, fresh fish,
wood-fired-oven pizzas, steak, and salads, all prepared in the open
kitchen. In summer the restaurant gets really lively, with beach-volley-
ball matches and outdoor dining. Check out a beach cruiser bicycle and
go for a ride along the waterfront while waiting for a table. Kids are
especially welcome here; for $5.95 their meal also includes a bucket of
beach toys to play with while waiting, a prize from the Treasure chest,
and a visit to the sundae bar. The popular happy hour happens daily
4–6 pm and again after the dining room closes (starting at 9 pm Sunday
and Monday, 10 pm Tuesday–Saturday). ⊠*1919 S.E. Columbia River
Dr.* ☎*360/699–1592 or 503/222–9947* ⊟*AE, D, DC, MC, V.*

¢–$ ✕**Puffin Cafe.** Just 16 mi east of Vancouver is a funky little restaurant
hidden among the docks of the Port of Camas–Washougal Marina.
Locals flock here for festive open-air dining or a quick bite after they
haul in their pleasure boats. Coconut shrimp, zesty fish tacos, and other
Caribbean-style offerings are served in ample portions. ⊠*14 S. A St.,
Washougal* ☎*360/335–1522* ⊟*MC, V.*

$ 🏨**Heathman Lodge.** Amenities and facilities here—from the ultra-com-
★ fortable mattresses to the outstanding food in Hudson's Bar & Grill
($–$$)—make you feel spoiled. The alpine-style lodge, with massive
hand-hewn logs, is central—five minutes from Westfield Shoppingtown,
Vancouver's only mall—yet seems very secluded once you come inside.
Goat cheese and herb-stuffed Draper Valley chicken breast with wild-rice
pancakes, and stuffed cedar-plank salmon over roasted-shallot whipped
potatoes and wilted spinach are among the signature offerings at Hudson's, where chef Mark Hosak is in charge. **Pros:** Sincerely attentive service; roomy accommodations, especially the suites; lodge theme is warm,
rustic, and unique. **Cons:** The rumble of traffic can sometimes be heard
from the rooms closest to the freeway, not the greatest in-room coffee.
⊠*7801 N.W. Greenwood Dr., 98662* ☎*360/254–3100 or 888/475–
3100* 🖷*360/254–6100* ⊕*www.heathmanlodge.com* ⇋*121 rooms, 21
suites* ⚅*In-room: refrigerator, Wi-Fi. In-hotel: restaurant, room service,
pool, gym, Wi-Fi* ⊟*AE, D, DC, MC, V.*

$–$$ 🏨**Hilton Vancouver Washington and Vancouver Conference Center.** Opened
Fodor'sChoice in June 2005, this hotel and conference center is the crown jewel of
★ Vancouver's redeveloped downtown. The property is owned by the

City of Vancouver and operated by Hilton. The elegant, contemporary interior is done in sage, pimento, and butternut hues and has an urban glow. The hotel restaurant, Gray's At The Park Bistro & Bar ($–$$), serves Pacific Northwest cuisine and reservations are generally required. Tantalizing selections include Painted Hills natural beef, the hefty 24-ounce porterhouse steak, and wild Pacific king salmon. Baked onion soup is a signature item. **Pros:** New and very clean; good service; across street from Esther Short Park and near seasonal farmers' market and beachfront restaurants. **Cons:** More than 200 rooms, lots of business guests and conferences, some areas nearby seem unsafe for walking. ⊠ *301 W. 6th St., 98660* ☎ *360/993–4500* 📠 *360/993–4484* ⊕ *www.hilton.com* 🛏 *226 rooms, 10 suites* ⚹ *In-room: Wi-Fi. In-hotel: Wi-Fi, restaurant, room service, pool, gym, parking (fee)* ▤ *AE, D, DC, MC, V.*

STEVENSON

49 mi east of Vancouver.

The Skamania County seat, Stevenson is a hillside village overlooking the Columbia River Gorge. For dining and lodging recommendations in Stevenson, *see Oregon chapter.*

An interpretive center in town has interesting displays of Native American artifacts, as well a replica of a fish wheel, a mechanical contraption that automatically scooped salmon from the river (they were outlawed in 1935 because they were too efficient and took too many fish).

★ The rock in **Beacon Rock State Park,** the world's second-largest monolith, was named by Lewis and Clark and is actually the core of an ancient volcano. At this landmark along the Columbia River, the explorers first noticed tidal influences in the river. The 4,650-acre park has camping and a lengthy shoreline. You can climb the rock via a steep trail for amazing views of the Columbia River Gorge. Trails lead from the campground to stunning waterfalls and the top of Hamilton Mountain. ⊠ *Hwy. 14, 35 mi east of Vancouver* ☎ *888/226–7688* ⊕ *www. parks.wa.gov* 🎫 *Free* ⊙ *May–Sept., daily 8 AM–10 PM; Oct.–Apr., daily 8–5.*

ひ   The **Columbia Gorge Interpretive Center** is dwarfed by the dramatic basalt
Fodor'sChoice   cliffs that rise behind it. It's on the north bank of the Columbia River
★   Gorge, 1 mi east of Bridge of the Gods on Highway 14. Exhibits illustrate the region's geology and history. Among the many artifacts are a Native American pit house, a fish wheel, and dip nets used for hunting salmon. Other items pertain to Lewis and Clark and other explorers, missionaries, pioneers, and soldiers who have passed through the gorge. ⊠ *990 S.W. Rock Creek Dr.* ☎ *509/427–8211 or 800/991–2338* 🎫 *$6* ⊙ *Daily 10–5.*

GOLDENDALE

78 mi northeast of Stevenson.

The seat of Klickitat County and a commercial center for ranchers and farmers, Goldendale was settled in 1872 and is a down-to-earth town with many old clapboard houses. Goldendale Observatory State Park, 1½ mi north of town via Columbus Avenue, has the nation's largest public telescope.

The **Klickitat County Historical Museum** is small but delightful, thanks to its local Native American and pioneer artifacts. ⊠*127 W. Broadway 98620* ☎*509/773–4303* ☜*$3* ⊙*Apr.–Oct., daily 9–5; Nov.–Mar., by appointment.*

The 12,276-foot-tall **Mt. Adams,** northwest of Goldendale, is enclosed by a wilderness area and by the Yakama Indian Reservation. Camping and hiking are permitted in the latter only by permission of the tribe. Call the tribe's Forestry Development Program or the Mt. Adams Ranger Station for information. ⊠*Between Yakima Valley and Columbia Gorge* ☎*509/395–3400 ranger station, 509/865–5121 Ext. 657 Forestry Development Program* ☜*$5/per vehicle forest pass (year-round); $10/day climbing pass (req. June–Sept. only)* ⊙*Year-round.*

☾ **Goldendale Observatory,** the nation's largest public observatory, has a 24½-inch reflecting telescope. The night sky here is gorgeous, unaffected by light pollution. ⊠*1602 Observatory Dr., 98620* ☎*509/773–3141* ⊕*www.perr.com/gosp.html* ☜*Free* ⊙*Apr.–Sept., Wed.–Sun. 2–5 and 8–midnight; Oct.–Mar., Fri.–Sun. 2–5 and 7–10.*

Fodor'sChoice ★ **Maryhill Museum of Art.** Rising from the bare hills of the Columbia Plateau, castlelike Maryhill is an oddity—a Flemish château–style museum built in the 1920s by railroad magnate Sam Hill. In 1926 Hill invited Queen Marie of Romania to dedicate the museum, which was still unfinished. The queen, who was grateful for Hill's generous aid to Romania after World War I, agreed and arrived to enthusiastic crowds who came for the dedication. The museum houses, among other objects, Rodin sculptures, Native American artifacts, and an extensive collection of chess sets. Peacocks stroll the manicured grounds, which overlook the Columbia River. ■TIP➔ **Take time for the 2-mi drive east on Hwy 14 to see the Stonehenge replica that Hill built to honor area soldiers that were killed in WWI.** ⊠*35 Maryhill Museum Dr., 98620* ☎*509/773–3733* ⊕*www.maryhillmuseum.org* ☜*$7* ⊙*Mid-Mar.–mid-Nov., daily 9–5.*

The **Maryhill Winery** has quickly become one of the most-visited tasting rooms in Washington State. Wines produced here are grown at the estate vineyards. Spectacular views of the Columbia River Gorge and Mt. Hood in the distance, free music on summer weekends, and a concert series at the river-facing amphitheater add to the appeal. ⊠*9774 Hwy. 14, 98620* ☎*877/627–9445* ⊕*www.maryhillwinery. com* ☜*Free* ⊙*Daily 10–6.*

You can fish, hike, windsurf, and rock climb at **Columbia Hills State Park,** about 20 mi southwest of Goldendale. The Horsethief Lake section of the park is a national historic site, famous for its petroglyphs; there are tours of them from April to October, Friday and Saturday at 10 AM. You must make reservations. ⊠*Hwy. 14, Milepost 85* ☎*509/767– 1159* ⊕*www.parks.wa.gov* ⊠*Free* ☉*Apr.–Oct., daily 6:30–dusk.*

WHERE TO STAY & EAT

¢ ✕**St. John's Bakery, Coffee & Gifts.** Run by Greek Orthodox nuns at St. John's Monastery, this small coffee shop is definitely worth a stop if you're traveling on Highway 97 north of Goldendale (10 mi north at mp 24). Traditional Greek deli and bakery items are on the menu, including gyros, moussaka, spanakopita, and baklava. A gift shop carries religious items and candles, soaps, and lotions made by the sisters. ⊠*2378 Hwy. 97, 98620* ☎*509/773–6650* ▭*MC* ☉*Closed Sun.*

¢ ⏢**Quality Inn and Suites.** Formerly the Farvue Motel, this two-story motel is just a block off Highway 97. Many of the rooms have great views of Mt. Hood and Mt. Adams. There's a coffee shop on-site and a McDonald's across the parking lot. The outdoor pool is popular on hot summer days. **Pros:** Convenient location, nice mountain views from second level, pool. **Cons:** No luxury here, just basic chain motel rooms and amenities. ⊠*808 E. Simcoe Dr., 98620* ☎*509/773–5881* ⊕*www.choicehotels.com* ⟿*48* rooms ⏣*In-room: refrigerator, Wi-Fi. In-hotel: restaurant, pool, no-smoking rooms, no elevator* ▭*AE, D, DC, MC, V* ⏏*EP.*

SOUTHWESTERN WASHINGTON ESSENTIALS

BY AIR

Getting to the northern and southern portions of Southwestern Washington by air is no problem, but traveling to the mountains, coast, and Columbia River Gorge requires considerable road travel.

Contacts Portland International Airport (⊠*N.E. Airport Way at I–205* ☎*877/739–4636* ⊕*www.portlandairportpdx.com*). **Sea-Tac International Airport** (⊠*International Blvd. and Pacific Hwy. S* ☎*206/431–4444* ⊕*www. portseattle.org*).

AIRPORTS &TRANSFERS If you're planning to visit the Long Beach Peninsula, Mt. St. Helens National Volcanic Monument, and places near the Columbia River Gorge, you're better off flying into Portland International Airport (PDX) in Oregon, 10 mi south of Vancouver, Washington. For visits to Mt. Rainier National Park, it's best to fly into Seattle-Tacoma International Airport (Sea-Tac), a larger airport with more carriers.

Driving is the best way to get from the airports to your Southwestern Washington destination. At Portland's airport, car-rental agencies are on the first floor of the parking garage. At Sea-Tac the agencies have counters in the baggage claim area.

BY CAR

Much of Southwestern Washington is rural, with very little traffic congestion. The exceptions are Vancouver, due to its proximity to Portland, Oregon, and Mt. Rainier National Park, which experiences heavy summer traffic at the main visitor centers. You can avoid traffic problems by traveling to Rainier on weekdays and staying off the roads around Vancouver during morning and evening rush hours. Note, though, that that there are bound to be traffic jams along I–5 any night there's a concert at the amphitheater just north of Vancouver.

U.S. 101 curves around the southern part of the Long Beach Peninsula. Highway 103 travels north through the peninsula. From I–5 north of Kelso, take Highway 4 west through Longview to Highway 401. Turn south if you're going to Chinook or Ilwaco, or continue on Highway 4 to U.S. 101 if you're going to Seaview, Long Beach, and points north. The stretch of U.S. 101 along Willapa Bay's rocky eastern shore, south of the Naselle River estuary, is scenic. From Olympia, take U.S. 101 west; continue west on Highway 8 and U.S. 12. At Montesano turn south onto Highway 107, which will take you to U.S. 101; turn left (south) onto U.S. 101 at the junction.

Highway 504 is the main road through the Mt. St. Helens National Volcanic Monument. The Castle Rock Exit (No. 49) off I–5 is just outside the monument's western entrance. Follow Highway 504 into the park. You can access the park from the north by taking Forest Service Road 25 south from U.S. 12 at the town of Randle. Forest Service Road 25 connects with Forest Service Road 90, which heads north from the town of Cougar. These two roads are closed by snow in winter.

Highway 14 through the Columbia River Gorge is a narrow, winding, two-lane road that skirts steep drop-offs and overlooks as you head east to Goldendale. As it's the only east–west route on the Washington side of the river, backups behind slow trucks and RVs are common. Travel through the gorge in winter can be particularly treacherous, owing to strong winds and icy conditions.

EMERGENCIES

Hospitals **Ocean Beach Hospital and Clinics** (⊠ *174 1st Ave. N, Ilwaco* ⊕ *www. oceanbeachhospital.org* ☎ *360/642–3181*). **St. John Medical Center** (⊠ *1615 Delaware St., Longview* ☎ *360/414–2000 or 800/438–7562*). **Southwest Washington Medical Center** (⊠ *400 N.E. Mother Joseph Pl., Vancouver* ☎ *360/256–2000*).

Legacy Salmon Creek Hospital (⊠ *2211 N.E. 139th St., Vancouver* ☎ *360/487–1000*).

VISITOR INFORMATION

Contacts **Destination Packwood Association** (⌂ *Box 64, Packwood 98361* ☎ *360/494–2223* ⊕ *www.destinationpackwood.com*). **East Lewis County Chamber of Commerce** (⊠ *118 State St.* ⌂ *Box 562, Mossyrock 98564* ☎ *360/983–3778* ⊕ *www.eastlewiscountychamber.com*). **Greater Goldendale Area Chamber of Commerce** (⊠ *903 E. Broadway St., Goldendale 98620* ☎ *509/773–3400* ⊕ *www. goldendalechamber.org*). **Greater Vancouver Chamber of Commerce** (⊠ *1101 Broadway St., Suite 120, Vancouver 98660* ☎ *360/694–2588* ⊕ *www.vancouverusa.*

com). **Long Beach Peninsula Visitors Bureau** (✉ U.S. 101 and Hwy. 103, 3914 Pacific Way 🏠 Box 562, Long Beach 98631 ☎ 360/642–2400 or 800/451–2542 ⊕ www.funbeach.com). **Longview Area Chamber of Commerce** (✉ 1563 Olympia Way, Longview 98632 ☎ 360/423–8400 ⊕ www.kelsolongviewchamber.org). **Mt. St. Helens National Volcanic Monument** (☎ 360/449–7800 ⊕ www.fs.fed.us/gpnf/mshnvm). **Skamania County Chamber of Commerce** (✉ 167 N.W. 2nd Ave., Hwy. 14, Stevenson 98648 ☎ 509/427–8911 or 800/989–9178 ⊕ www.skamania. org). **Southwest Washington Visitor and Convention Bureau** (✉ 101 East 8th St., Suite 240, Vancouver 98660 ☎ 360/750–1553 or 800/600–0800 ⊕ www.south westwashington.com). **Tourism Lewis County** (✉ 500 N.W. Chamber of Commerce Way, Chehalis 98532 ☎ 800/525–3323 ⊕ www.tourlewiscounty.com).

YAKIMA RIVER VALLEY

Updated by
Rob Phillips

The Yakima River binds a region of great contrasts. Snow-capped volcanic peaks and golden hills overlook a natural grass steppe turned green by irrigation. Famed throughout the world for its apples and cherries, its wine and hops, this fertile landscape is also the ancestral home of the Yakama people from whom it takes its name.

The river flows southeasterly from its source in the Cascade Mountains near Snoqualmie Pass. Between the college town of Ellensburg, at the heart of the Kittitas Valley, and Yakima, the region's largest city, the river cuts steep canyons through serried, sagebrush-covered ridges before merging with the Naches River. Then it breaks through Union Gap to enter its fecund namesake, the broad Yakima Valley. Some 200 mi from its birthplace, the river makes one final bend around vineyard-rich Red Mountain before joining the Columbia at the Tri-Cities.

Mount Rainier stands west of the Cascade crest but is often more readily seen east of the mountains, where the air is clear and clouds are few. South of Rainier is the broad-shouldered Mt. Adams, the sacred mountain of the Yakama people. The 12,276-foot-tall mountain marks the western boundary of their reservation, second largest in the Pacific Northwest. Here wild horses run free through the Horse Heaven Hills, as they have for centuries. Deer and elk roam the evergreen forests, eagles and curlews soar overhead.

Orchards and vineyards dominate Yakima Valley's agricultural landscape. Cattle and sheep ranching initially drove the economy; apples and other produce came with the first irrigation schemes in the 1890s. The annual asparagus harvest begins in April, followed by spring cherries; apricots and peaches ripen in early to mid-summer. Exported throughout the world for the brewing of beer, hops are ready by late August; travelers may see the bushy vines spiraling up fields of twine. The apple harvest runs from late summer through October.

The valley's real fame rests on its wines, however, which have a growing reputation as among the best in the world. Concord grapes were first planted here in the 1960s, and they still take up large tracts of land. But *vinifera* grapes, the noble grapes of Europe, now dominate the local wine industry. Merlot and white burgundies boosted the region, and syrah is often regarded as the grape of the future. There are fine cabernets, grenaches, Rieslings, chardonnays, gewürztraminers, sémillons, sauvignon blancs, chenin blancs, and muscats, as well as such lesser known varietals as sangioveses, nebbiolos, and lembergers.

Yakima Valley wineries range in size from small backyard cellars to large commercial operations. Barrels are tapped and the main wine-tasting season begins in late April and runs to the end of the fall harvest in November. Most wineries are easily reached from I–82. Winery hours vary in winter, when you should call ahead before visiting. The Yakima Valley Winery Association (⊕ *www.wineyakimavalley. org*) publishes a map-brochure that lists wineries with tasting-room hours. Most are owned and managed by unpretentious enthusiasts, and their cellar masters are often on hand to answer questions.

> **TOP 5**
>
> Inn at Suncadia: A beautiful resort-lodge for golfers, hikers, skiers, or just about anybody looking to get out and play.
>
> Red Horse Drive In: More than a hamburger joint, it's a restaurant and museum all in one.
>
> Yakima Valley Museum: One of the finest museums in the state, with plenty of history of the real West.
>
> Piety Flats Winery: Not stuffy or stodgy, a fun visit for the whole family.
>
> Desert Winds Winery: Food, gifts, novelty items, oh, and some great wines, too!

CLE ELUM

86 mi southeast of Seattle.

A former railroad, coal, and logging town, Cle Elum (pronounced "klee *ell*-um") now caters to travelers stopping for a breath of air before or after tackling Snoqualmie Pass.

The **Cle Elum Bakery** (⊠ *501 E. 1st St.* ☏ *509/674–2233*) has been doing business from the very same spot since 1906.

Across from the bakery is **Owens Meats** (⊠ *502 E. 1st St.* ☏ *509/674–2530*); established in 1889 this marvelous smokehouse has been run by the Owens family since 1937.

Roslyn, a former coal-mining town just 3 mi northwest of Cle Elum, is famous as the stand-in for the Alaskan village of Cicely on the 1990s TV program *Northern Exposure*. A map locating sites associated with filming is available from the city offices at First Street and Pennsylvania Avenue. Roslyn is also notable for its 28 ethnic cemeteries. Established by communities of miners in the late 19th and early 20th centuries, they are clustered on a hillside west of town.

WHERE TO STAY & EAT

$ ✕**MaMa Vallone's Steak House and Inn.** Set in a building constructed in 1906, the upscale but rustic Western look makes the perfect decor for this cozy and informal restaurant that once was a boarding house for

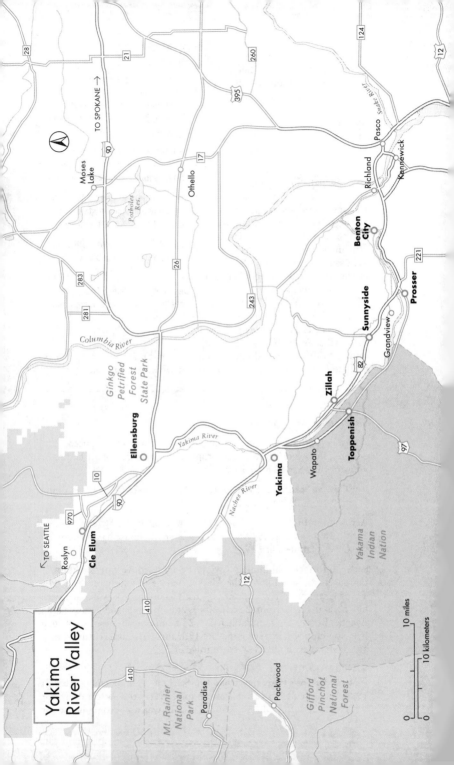

unmarried miners. Guests dine on antique tables, and the works of several local artists hang on the walls. Pasta dishes such as the tomato-based *fagioli* (soup with vegetables and beans) and *bagna calda* (a bath of olive oil, garlic, anchovies, and butter for dredging vegetables and meat) attract diners from as far away as Seattle. ✉️*302 W. 1st St.* ☎️*509/674–5174* 🍴*AE, DC, MC, V* ⊘*No lunch.*

$$–$$$$ 🏨**The Inn at Suncadia.** Situated in the middle of one of the region's premier golf courses (Prospector), this great stone-and-wood lodge blends beautifully with the mountain and forest surroundings. Gas fireplaces lend a rustic warmth to the luxurious rooms, and the Gas Lamp Grille restaurant serves fresh Pacific Northwestern fare. **Pros:** Intimate mountain-retreat environment. Golfing, fly-fishing, cross-country skiing, and hiking just minutes away. **Cons:** Costs can quickly add up for a family visit. ✉️*3320 Suncadia Trail, Cle Elum 98922* ☎️*509/649–6405, 866/904–6300* 🌐*www.suncadia.com* 🛏️*18 rooms,* ⚒️*In-room: phone, Ethernet, Wi-Fi, refrigerator. In hotel: restaurant, pool, gym* 🍴*AE, MC, V.*

¢–$ 🏨**Iron Horse Inn Bed and Breakfast.** What was once a boarding house for rail workers (1909–74) is now a comfortable country inn owned by the daughter and son-in-law of a one-time lodger. Rooms are named for former crewmen and are full of railroad memorabilia. Four adjacent cabooses have been transformed into guest quarters complete with microwaves and refrigerators. **Pros:** Unique lodging experience. **Cons:** Some sharing of bathrooms. ✉️*526 Marie Ave., South Cle Elum 98943* ☎️*509/674–5939, 800/228–9246 in WA and OR* 🌐*www.ironhorse-innbb.com* 🛏️*12 rooms, 9 with private bath* ⚒️*In-room: no phone. In-hotel: refrigerator (some), no TV (some), no elevator* 🍴*MC, V* 🍽️*BP.*

¢ 🏨**Aster Inn.** A quirky, circa-1918 antiques shop doubles as the office for this charming motel, which wraps around a central garden and picnic area. Grapevines drape the doors to each of the cozy rooms, some of which have brass beds and claw-foot tubs. **Pros:** Affordable and close to downtown. **Cons:** Old building and rooms. ✉️*521 E. 1st St., 98922* ☎️*509/674–2551 or 800/616–9722* 🌐*www.asterinn.com* 🛏️*10 rooms* ⚒️*In-room: kitchen. In-hotel: refrigerator, no elevator* 🍴*AE, D, MC, V.*

ELLENSBURG

24 mi southeast of Cle Elum.

This university and college town is one of the state's friendliest and most easygoing places. "Modern" Ellensburg had its origin in a July 4 fire that engulfed the original city in 1889. Almost overnight, Victorian brick buildings rose from the ashes; many still stand, though their functions have changed. Stroll downtown to discover art galleries, comfortable cafés, secondhand-book and -record stores, an old-fashioned hardware store, and one antiques shop after another.

Central Washington's single biggest event is the Ellensburg Rodeo, held Labor Day weekend. On the national circuit since the 1920s, the rodeo has a year-round headquarters on Main Street where you can buy tickets and souvenirs. You can also get a bird's-eye view of the rodeo grounds from Reed Park, in the 500 block of North Alder Street.

★   The **Clymer Museum of Art** has the largest collection of works by painter John Clymer (1907–89). The Ellensburg native was one of the most widely published illustrators of the American West, focusing his oils and watercolors on wildlife and traditional lifestyles. ⊠*416 N. Pearl St.* ☎*509/962–6416* ⊕*www.clymermuseum.com* 🖾*Free* ⊙*Weekdays 10–5, weekends noon–4.*

Gallery One, in the 1889 Stewart Building, is a community art center with rotating shows by regional artists, a fine gift shop, and art classes. ⊠*408 N. Pearl St.* ☎*509/925–2670* 🖾*Free* ⊙*Tues.–Sat. 11–5.*

The six-room **Kittitas County Museum** has one of the state's better pioneer artifact collections, ranging from Indian basketry to early-20th-century carriages. ⊠*114 E. 3rd Ave.* ☎*509/925–3778* 🖾*Free* ⊙*Mon.–Sat. 10–4.*

☾   **Dick and Jane's Spot,** nestled in suburbia, is the area's most peculiar attraction. The home of artists Dick Elliott and Jane Orleman is a continuously growing whimsical sculpture, a collage of 20,000 bottle caps, 1,500 bicycle reflectors, and other bits. Their masterpiece stands on private property near downtown, but it's still possible to see the recycled creation from several angles; sign the guestbook mounted on the surrounding fence. ⊠*101 N. Pearl St.* ☎*509/925–3224* ⊕*www. reflectorart.com.*

Olmstead Place State Park is an original pioneer farm built in 1875. A ²/₃-mi interpretive trail links eight buildings, including a barn and schoolhouse, on a 217-acre working farm. ⊠*N. Ferguson Rd., ½ mi south of Kittitas Hwy., 4 mi east of Ellensburg* ☎*509/925–1943* ⊕*www.parks.wa.gov* 🖾*Free, parking $5* ⊙*Apr.–Oct., 6:30 AM–dusk; Nov.–Mar., 8 AM–dusk.*

Ginkgo and Wanapum State Parks, 28 mi east of Ellensburg on the Columbia River, are separated by I–90. Ginkgo Petrified Forest State Park preserves a fossil forest of ginkgos and other trees. A 3-mi-long trail leads from the interpretive center. Wanapum State Park, 3 mi south, has camping and river access for boaters. ⊠*I–90 east to Exit 136, Vantage* ☎*509/856–2700* ⊕*www.parks.wa.gov* 🖾*Free; parking $5, camping $17* ⊙*Apr.–Sept., 6:30 AM–dusk, Oct.–Mar., 8 AM–dusk.*

Indian and pioneer artifacts are exhibited at the **Wanapum Dam Visitor Center,** which also has displays on modern hydroelectric power. ⊠*Hwy. 243 S* ☎*509/932–3571 Ext. 2571* 🖾*Free* ⊙*Weekdays 8:30–4:30, weekends 9–5.*

WHERE TO STAY & EAT

$–$$ ✕**Starlight Lounge & Dining Room.** Like a speakeasy with flair, the Starlight is really three separate establishments: a fine restaurant, a college pool hall, and a martini-and-cigar bar (with an extensive martini menu). All nestled within Ellensburg's most prominent structure, the turreted 1889 Davidson Building. Chef Jordan Lawson builds a variety of hearty dishes around certified Angus beef. ⊠*402 N. Pearl St.* ☏*509/962–6100* ▤*AE, D, MC, V.*

$ ✕**Pearl's on Pearl.** A smoke-free wine bar and bistro in the 1889 Geddis Building, Pearl's has live music several nights a week. The menu changes every few months on the whim of chef Cinda Kohler. Expect anything from Kohler's signature contemporary American dishes to theme meals featuring Mediterranean, Caribbean, French Provincial, New American, or Cajun cuisine. ⊠*311 N. Pearl St.* ☏*509/962–8899* ▤*AE, MC, V* ⊗ *No lunch.*

¢–$$ ✕**Valley Cafe.** Meals at this vintage art deco eatery consist of Mediter-
★ ranean bistro-style salads, pastas, and other plates. Featured dinner entrées include rack of lamb, seared ahi tuna, and chicken marsala. An impressive wine list offers dozens of Yakima Valley options. Owner Greg Beach also owns the wine shop next door. ⊠*105 W. 3rd Ave.* ☏*509/925–3050* ▤*AE, D, DC, MC, V.*

¢ ✕**Red Horse Drive-In.** Step back in time to a 1930s-era service station. Now, however, the service at this refurbished Mobile Oil station includes specialty sandwiches, shakes, and more. While you wait for your burger and fries, check out the hundreds of old metal signs and advertisements that enhance the vintage appeal of this classic burger joint. ⊠*1518 W. University Way* ☏*509/925–1956* ▤*MC, V.*

¢–$ ▥**Inn at Goose Creek.** Each room of this modern house—sparse from the outside, elegant within—has its own theme. The Homespun Room contains an assortment of black Shaker-style furniture, plain walls, and (like all the rooms) a handmade rug. The Timber Creek Lodge Room appeals to fishing enthusiasts. **Pros:** Close to the freeway and amenities; rooms have the feel of a bed and breakfast. **Cons:** Although the rooms are very quiet, lots of car traffic. ⊠*1720 Canyon Rd., 98926* ☏*509/962–8030 or 800/533–0822* 🖷*509/962–8031* ⊕*www.innat-goosecreek.com* ⟿*10 rooms* ♿*In-room: refrigerator. In-hotel: VCR, Wi-Fi, no elevator* ▤*AE, MC, V* ⊙I*CP.*

YAKIMA

38 mi south of Ellensburg.

The gateway to Washington wine country is sunny Yakima (pronounced *yak*-imah), with about 72,000 people. Spread along the west bank of the Yakima River just south of its confluence with the Naches, it's a bustling community with lovely parklands and a downtown on the cusp of revitalization. Downtown street improvements with period lighting, trees, and planters are all but complete, creating a fresh new "old" feel that is inviting to both residents and visitors alike.

The town was settled in the late 1850s as a ranching center where Ahtanum Creek joins the Yakima River, on the site of earlier Yakama tribal villages at present-day Union Gap. When the North Pacific Railroad established its terminal 4 mi north in 1884, most of the town picked up and moved.

Yakima's Mission-style Northern Pacific Depot (1912) is the highlight of its historic North Front Street. Other old buildings face the depot; behind it, colorful Track 29 Mall is in old rail cars. Four blocks east is the ornate Capitol Theatre, built in 1920. The former vaudeville and silent-movie hall is now a performing arts center. Opposite is Millennium Plaza, a public art installation that celebrates the importance of water to the Yakima Valley. Residents and visitors alike enjoy year-round natural beauty in the heart of Yakima, thanks to the city's ongoing restoration and preservation of the Yakima Greenway. The natural area stretches from Selah Gap to Union Gap, and west along the Naches River. The greenway includes more than 10 mi of paved pathway that connects parks, trails, and adjacent protected natural areas.

The **Yakima Valley Museum** documents Yakama, pioneer, and 20th-century history in exhibits ranging from horse-drawn vehicles to a "neon garden" of street signs. Highlights include a fully operating 1930s soda fountain and a model of Yakima native and Supreme Court Justice William O. Douglas's Washington, D.C. office. ⊠*2105 Tieton Dr.* ☎*509/248–0747* ⊕*www.yakimavalleymuseum.org* ⊠*$5* ⊗*Mon.– Sat. 10–5, Sun. 11–5.*

The **McAllister Museum of Aviation** (⊠*2008 S. 16th Ave.* ☎*509/457– 4933* ⊕*www.mcallistermuseum.org*) is on the site of a pioneering flight school. The museum is open Thursday and Friday 10–4 and Saturday 9–4. Donations are accepted.

The **Yakima Area Arboretum,** on the west bank of the Yakima River at Highway 24 and I–82, adjoins the 10-mi-long Yakima Greenway, a paved path that links a series of riverfront parks. A Japanese garden and a wetland trail are the arboretum's highlights. ⊠*1401 Arboretum Dr., off Nob Hill Blvd.* ☎*509/248–7337* ⊕*www.ahtrees.org* ⊠*Free* ⊗*Daily dawn–dusk.*

Sagelands Vineyard, 7 mi southeast of Yakima, produces cabernet sauvignon, merlot, and chardonnay. The main building has a huge stone fireplace and a commanding view of the upper valley. ⊠*71 Gangl Rd., Exit 40 off I–82, Wapato* ☎*509/877–2112* ⊕*www.sagelandsvineyard. com* ⊗*Mar.–Oct., daily 10–5; Nov.–Feb., daily noon–4.*

WHERE TO EAT

$–$$ ✕**Greystone Restaurant.** The 1899 Lund Building has come a long way since its days as a sheep-ranchers' hotel, saloon, and brothel. Beneath the pressed-tin ceiling and between the gray stone walls, the same creative steak-and-seafood menu is served in the dining room and bistro bar. Specialties include a scrumptious muscovy duck breast with julienne of apples or short ribs braised in a Yakima Valley syrah and mushrooms. ⊠*5 N. Front St., at Yakima Ave.* ☎*509/248–9801* ⊕*www. greystonerestaurant.com* ⊟*AE, MC, V* ⊗*Closed Sun. Open for lunch weekdays.*

¢–$ ✕**Barrel House.** A former miners' tavern one block east of the depot, Barrel House is now Yakima's leading wine bar. Chef Tim Schroeder's menu favorites include hand-cut New York steak with Barrel House roasted veal reduction and the broiled scallops au gratin. ⊠*22 N.*

1st St. ☎*509/453–3769* ⊕*www.thebarrelhouse.net* ▤*AE, MC, V* ⊗*Closed Sun. and Mon.*

¢–$ ✕**Santiago's.** Elegant and charming, Jar and Deb Arcand's skylit estab-
★ lishment puts a new spin on Mexican dishes. For chili verde, chunks of
pork loin are slow-cooked in jalapeno sauce; the Yakima apple pork
mole is prepared with chocolate and cinnamon. ⊠*111 E. Yakima Ave.*
☎*509/453–1644* ⊕*www.santiagos.org* ⚲*Reservations accepted for 5*
or more ▤*MC, V* ⊗*Closed Sun. No lunch Sat.*

WHERE TO STAY

$–$$$ 🏨**Birchfield Manor.** The valley's only luxury accommodation is on a
Fodor'sChoice plateau just outside Yakima surrounded by corn and cattle. The Old
★ Manor House contains the restaurant and five upstairs rooms. Rooms
in a newer cottage are more private and have such amenities as steam-
sauna showers and gas fireplaces. Chef-owner Brad Masset oversees the
continental-style restaurant ($$$–$$$$, no lunch; one seating Thursday
and Friday, two seatings Saturday; reservations essential), often assisted
by his father Will, a European-trained chef who established the inn in
1978, and his brother Greg, a local vintner. The limited prix-fixe menu
changes seasonally. The wine cellar has an excellent selection of local
and imported vintages. Pros: A unique experience for this region. Cons:
A little difficult to find. ⊠*2018 Birchfield Rd., just south of Hwy. 24,*
98901 ☎*509/452–1960 or 800/375–3420* 🖷*509/452–2334* ⊕*www.*
birchfieldmanor.com ⤶*11 rooms* ⚘*In-room: no phone (some). In-*
hotel: VCR (some), no TV (some), Wi-Fi, restaurant, pool, no-smoking
rooms ▤*AE, DC, MC, V* ⍾*BP.*

$ 🏨**Hilton Garden Inn.** Modern, spacious, and comfortable rooms make
this hotel in the heart of downtown Yakima one of the city's finest
upscale lodgings. With an atypical lobby that is more akin to a New
York town house, it combines elegance and simplicity. A two-sided gas
fireplace near the open-air restaurant, just adjacent to the lobby, offers
guests a comfy place to read a book or check e-mails. Close to bou-
tiques, downtown wineries, restaurants, and the Capitol Theatre. Full-
service restaurant allows guests to stay in if desired. Pros: One block
from the convention center and within walking distance of dozens of
shops. Cons: In the midst of the concrete jungle. ⊠*402 E. Yakima Ave.*
Yakima, 98901 ☎*509/454–1111* ⊕*www.yakima.stayhgi.com* ⤶*111*
rooms (3 suites), ⚘*In-room: Ethernet, Wi-Fi, refrigerator. In-hotel:*
pool, elevator, laundry service, room service ▤*AE, MC, V.*

SHOPPING

Johnson Orchards (⊠*4906 Summitview Ave.* ☎*509/966–7479*) has
been growing fruit—including cherries, peaches, apples, and pears—
since 1904.

Central Washington's largest shopping center, **Valley Mall** (⊠*2529 Main*
St., Union Gap ☎*509/453–8233*) has three major department stores:
Sears, Macy's, and Gottschalks.

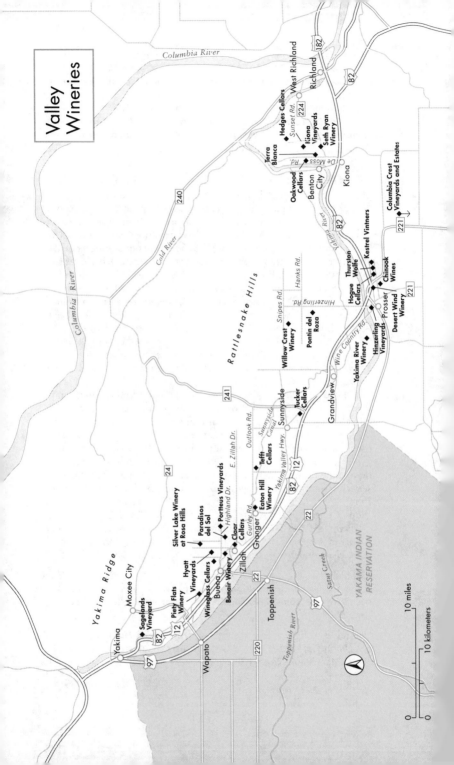

Valley Wineries

Columbia River

182
West Richland
Richland
82
224
Hedges Cellars
Sunset Rd.
Kiona Vineyards
Seth Ryan Winery
Terra Blanca
De Moss Rd.
Oakwood Cellars
Benton City
Kiona
Yakima River
82
Columbia Crest Vineyards and Estates
221
Kestrel Vintners
Cold River
Hanks Rd.
Thurston Wolfe
Chinook Wines
Rattlesnake Hills
Hinzerling Rd.
Hogue Cellars
Prosser
240
Willow Crest Winery
Pontin del Roza
Desert Wind Winery
Yakima River Winery
Hinzerling Vineyards
221
Wine Country Rd.
241
Snipes Rd.
Grandview
Tucker Cellars
Sunnyside
Yakima Valley Hwy.
12
82
Outlook Rd.
Tefft Cellars
E. Zillah Dr.
24
Porteus Vineyards
Highland Dr.
Sunnyside Canal
Silver Lake Winery at Rosa Hills
Claar Cellars
Eaton Hill Winery
Gurley Rd.
Paradisos del Sol
Granger
22
Yakima Ridge
Hyatt Vineyards
Zillah
Moxee City
Piety Flats Winery
Wineglass Cellars
Bonair Winery
Bueta
Sagelands Vineyard
97
82
12
Toppenish
97
YAKAMA INDIAN RESERVATION
Yakima
Wapato
22
220
Status Creek
Toppenish River

10 miles
10 kilometers
0
0

TOPPENISH

17 mi southeast of Yakima.

An intriguing small town with a rustic Old West sensibility, Toppenish—which lies within the Yakama Indian Reservation—blends history and culture, art and agriculture. You can't miss the 70 colorful murals that adorn the facades and exterior walls of businesses and homes: commissioned since 1989 by the Toppenish Mural Association, done in a variety of styles by regional artists, they commemorate the town's history and Western spirit. Tours in a horse-drawn covered wagon leave from the association's office on Toppenish Avenue.

⚛ The Yakima Valley grows 75% of the nation's hops and 25% of the
★ world's. The industry's story is well told at the **American Hop Museum** (⊢*22 S. B St.* ☎*509/865–4677* ⊕*www.americanhopmuseum.com*). Exhibits describe the history, growing process, and unique biology of the plant, a primary ingredient in beer. It's open Wednesday through Saturday10–4 and Sunday 11–4 from early May until late September. Admission is $3.

★ The **Yakama Nation Cultural Center** (⊢*Buster Dr. at U.S. 97* ☎*509/865– 2800* ⊕*www.yakamamuseum.com*) has a fascinating museum of tribal history and culture, including costumes, basketry, beadwork, and reconstructions of traditional lodges. Tribal dances and other cultural events are often staged in the Heritage Theater; the six-building complex also includes a gift shop, library, and restaurant. The center is open daily 8–5; admission is $5.

Ft. Simcoe Historical State Park. The residential quarters of an 1856 army fort 30 mi west of Toppenish look like a Victorian summer retreat. Exhibits focus on relations between the Yakama tribe—in the heart of whose reservation the fort stands—and American settlers. ⊢*5150 Ft. Simcoe Rd.* ☎*509/874–2372* ⊕*www.parks.wa.gov* ⊢*Free* ☀*Apr.–Sept., daily 6:30* AM*–dusk; Oct.–Mar., weekends and holidays 8* AM*–dusk.*

ZILLAH

5 mi northeast of Toppenish.

The south-facing slopes above Zillah, a tiny town named after the daughter of a railroad manager, are covered with orchards and vineyards. Several wineries are in or near the community; more are near Granger, 6 mi southeast.

Piety Flats Winery Located just off 1–82 (Exit 44) this former mercantile (circa 1911) and fruit stand is now a winery and tasting room. Offering syrah, merlot, Mercantile Red, and more, the winery also offers a number of other Yakima Valley specialty foods and items. ⊢*2560 Donald-Wapato Rd.* ☎*509/877–3115* ⊕*www.pietyflatswinery.com* ☀*Mar.–Nov., daily 10–5; Dec.–Feb., Fri.–Sun. 10–4:30.*

Bonair Winery is run by the Puryear family, who after years of amateur wine making in California began commercial production in their native Yakima Valley. They make cabernets, cabernet francs, chardonnays, malbecs, merlots, and riesling as well as medieval-style mead. ☒ *500 S. Bonair Rd.* ☎ *509/829–6027* ⊕ *www.bonairwine.com* ⊗ *Mar. 1–Oct. 31, daily 10–6; Nov.–Dec., 10–5; Jan.–Feb., weekends noon–5.*

Claar Cellars has one of the highest visitor rates of any Yakima Valley winery by virtue of its location: right off I–82 at Exit 52. The family-owned estate produces merlot, cabernet, chardonnay, sauvignon blanc, and dessert wines from vineyards in the White Bluffs region. ☒ *1001 Vintage Valley Pkwy.* ☎ *509/829–6810* ⊕ *www.claarcellars. com* ⊗ *Apr.–Nov., daily 10–6; Dec.–Mar., daily 11–5.*

Eaton Hill Winery, in the restored Rinehold Cannery building, produces cabernet, merlot, chardonnay, Riesling, sémillon, and various sweeter and fortified wines. ☒ *530 Gurley Rd., off Yakima Valley Hwy., Granger* ☎ *509/854–2220* ⊗ *Feb.–Nov., daily 10–5; closed Dec. and Jan.*

Horizon's Edge Winery takes its name from its tasting room's view of the Yakima Valley, Mt. Adams, and Mt. Rainier. The winery makes sparkling wine, chardonnay, pinot noir, merlot, cabernet sauvignon, and muscat canelli. ☒ *4530 E. Zillah Dr., east of Yakima Valley Hwy.* ☎ *509/829–6401* ⊗ *June–Nov., daily 11–5; Mar.–June, Fri.–Mon. 11–5.*

An estate vineyard on 97 acres, **Hyatt Vineyards** specializes in chardonnay, fume blanc, merlot, syrah, cabernet, and late-harvest Riesling. ☒ *2020 Gilbert Rd., off Bonair Rd.* ☎ *509/829–6333* ⊕ *www.hyattvineyards.com* ⊗ *Apr.–Nov., daily 11–5; Dec., Feb. and Mar., daily 11–4:30.*

European-style gardens adjoin the **Maison de Padgett Winery,** a small family operation producing hand-crafted wines. ☒ *2231 Roza Dr., at Highland Dr.* ☎ *509/829–6794* ⊗ *Mar.–Nov., Thurs.–Mon. 11–5; Dec.–Feb., by appointment.*

Paradisos del Sol is another family-owned winery, a labor of love for industry veteran Paul Vandenberg. Specialties are gewürztraminer, Riesling, cabernet, and a lemberger-cabernet blend designed especially for pizza. ☒ *3230 Highland Dr.* ☎ *509/829–9000* ⊕ *www.paradisosdelsol.com* ⊗ *Daily 11–6.*

The **Portteus Vineyards** are beloved by red-wine drinkers. Production is limited to cabernet sauvignon and franc, merlot, syrah, zinfandel, and port—as well as a robust chardonnay. Grapes are grown at 1,440-foot elevation on 47 acres above Zillah. ☒ *5201 Highland Dr.* ☎ *509/829–6970* ⊕ *www.portteus.com* ⊗ *Daily 10–5.*

★ On the expansive grounds at **Silver Lake at Roza Hills,** bands serenade picnickers on summer weekends. Large windows afford views of the cabernets, merlots, chardonnays, Rieslings, and other vintages in production. ☒ *1500 Vintage Rd., off Highland Dr.* ☎ *509/829–6235*

⊕*www.silverlakewinery.com* ⊘*Apr.–Nov., daily 10–5; Dec.–Mar., Thurs.–Mon. 11–4.*

Tefft Cellars was an old Concord grape vineyard replanted in the late 1980s with *vinifera*. Today it produces cabernet, merlot, syrah, sangiovese, pinot grigio, pinot meunier, and late-harvest dessert wines. The owners' original three-bedroom house, adjacent to the winery, is now the Outlook Inn. ✉*1320 Independence Rd. via Gurley Rd., Outlook* ☎*509/837–7651* ⊕*www.tefftcellars.com* ⊘*Feb.–Dec., daily 10–5; Jan., by appointment.*

An unusual collection of antique wine glasses has given its name to **Wineglass Cellars.** The winery produces limited lots of merlot, cabernet sauvignon, zinfandel, sangiovese, chardonnay, and port. ✉*206 N. Bonair Rd.* ☎*509/829–3011* ⊕*www.wineglasscellars.com* ⊘*Mid-Feb.–Nov., Thurs.–Sun. 10:30–5.*

WHERE TO STAY & EAT

¢–$ ✕**El Porton.** Authentic, yet inexpensive, Mexican fare is what you get at El Porton. Savory seafood dishes such as *mariscos al mojo de ajo—* sautéed prawns with mushrooms and garlic—are a favorite. Traditional items such as beef or chicken burritos and enchiladas served up in a variety of Mexican styles round out the menu. ✉*905 Vintage Valley Pkwy. Exit 52 Just off I–82.* ☎*509/829–9100* ⌔*Reservations not accepted* ▭*MC, V.*

¢–$ ▦**Comfort Inn–Zillah.** Just a few steps from Claar Cellars off I–82, this clean and modern hotel is a favorite of winery visitors. Kids love the free cookies and milk served each evening. **Pros:** right on the freeway and the only motel within miles. **Cons:** potential freeway traffic noise ✉*911 Vintage Valley Pkwy., 98953* ☎*509/829–3399 or 800/501–5433* ▤*509/829–3428* ⊕*www.comfortinnzillah.com* ⇘*40 rooms* △*In room: refrigerator, . In-hotel: pool, laundry facilities, some pets allowed, Wi-Fi, no elevator* ▭*AE, D, MC, V* ��*CP.*

SUNNYSIDE

14 mi southeast of Zillah.

The largest community in the lower Yakima Valley and the hometown of astronaut Bonnie Dunbar, Sunnyside runs along the sunny southern slopes of the Rattlesnake Hills.

Tucker Cellars adjoins a fruit and produce market just off the Yakima Valley Highway, about 4 mi east of Sunnyside. It produces gewürztraminer, chenin blanc, riesling, chardonnay, and pinot noir. ✉*70 Ray Rd.* ☎*509/837–8701* ⊕*www.tuckercellars.com* ⊘*10–5 year-round.*

⟳ South of I–82, the **Darigold Dairy Fair** allows self-guided tours of its large automated cheesemaking factory. There's also an expansive gift shop, and an ice-cream bar and deli. ✉*400 Alexander Rd.* ☎*509/837–4321* ⊘*Mon.–Sat. 8–6, Sun. 10–6.*

WHERE TO STAY & EAT

$-$$ ✕**Dykstra House.** In a wine valley with few upscale restaurants, this
★ 1914 Craftsman house in quiet Grandview (6 mi southeast of Sunnyside) has held its own for nearly two decades. Breads are made
from hand-ground wheat grown locally. Lunch, which is quite a bit
less expensive than dinner, features salads, sandwiches, and daily specials. Casual Friday night dinners are Italian; grand Saturday night
dinners revolve around chicken, beef, or fish. Local beers and wines
are served. ✉ *114 Birch Ave., Grandview* ☎ *509/882-2082* ⌨ *Reservations essential* 🟰 *AE, D, DC, MC, V* ☯ *Closed Sun. and Mon. No
dinner Tues.–Thurs.*

¢ ✕**El Conquistador.** The bright, lively colors and clean, modern-Mexican
decor belies the aging facade of this quaint eatery. The menu ranges
from burritos, fajitas, and enchiladas mole to shrimp sautéed with
green peppers and onions and served with a tangy salsa. Egg dishes are
also on the menu, as are some unique Mexican salads and soups. Handcrafted clay masks on the walls add a festive flair. ✉ *612 E. Edison Ave.*
☎ *509/839-2880* 🟰 *AE, D, DC, MC, V.*

¢–$ ▦**Sunnyside Inn Bed & Breakfast.** Built in 1919 as a doctor's residence
and office, this two-house inn, remodeled in 2007, is larger than the
usual B&B. Eight rooms have whirlpool tubs; several have small sun-
rooms and all have private entrances. Breakfast consists of breads,
pastries, meats, and a griddle entrée. Families are welcome. **Pros:** In
the heart of wine country, offering a short drive to several different
wineries. **Cons:** Immediate surroundings are not the most appealing.
✉ *800–804 E. Edison Ave., 98944* ☎ *509/839-5557 or 800/221-4195*
🖷 *509/839-3520* ⊕ *www.sunnysideinn.com* ➦ *12 rooms* ⌂ *In room:
cable TV, private baths.* 🟰 *AE, MC, V* ❏ *BP.*

PROSSER

13 mi southeast of Sunnyside.

On the south bank of the Yakima River, Prosser feels like small-town
America of the 1950s. The seat of Benton County since 1905, it has
a 1926 courthouse and a charming museum in City Park. In 2005,
Prosser's Horse Heaven Hills, on the Columbia River's north slope,
became Washington's seventh federally recognized wine region.

Desert Wind Winery has an expansive tasting room housed in an elegant
Southwestern-style building with a vast patio overlooking the Yakima
River. You'll delight in sémillon, barbera, Ruah Bare Naked Viognier,
and various other unique wine selections Just off I-82, the winery also
includes a small restaurant, a shop with Yakima Valley food products,
and gift items. ✉ *2258 Wine Country Rd.* ☎ *800/437-2313* ⊕ *www.
desertwindvineyard.com* ☯ *May–Sept. 10, Oct.–Apr. 11–5.*

Chinook Wines, a small house winery, is run by Kay Simon and Clay
Mackey, vintners known for their merlot, chardonnay, and sauvi-
gnon blanc. ✉ *Wittkopf Loop at Wine Country Rd.* ☎ *509/786-2725*
☯ *May–Oct., weekends noon–5.*

★ **Hinzerling Vineyards** specializes in dessert and appetizer wines including port, sherry, and muscat. Vintner Mike Wallace is one of the state's wine pioneers: he planted his first Prosser-area vines in 1972, and established the small winery in 1976. ✉ *1520 Sheridan Rd. at Wine Country Rd.* ☎ *509/786–2163* ⊕ *www.hinzerling.com* ☉ *Apr.–Dec. 24, Mon.– Sat. 11–5, Sun. 11–3; Dec. 26–Mar., Mon.–Sat. 11–4.*

Hogue Cellars is a large commercial winery. The gift shop carries the winery's famous pickled beans and asparagus as well as cabernet sauvignon, merlot, chenin blanc, rieslings, and pinot grigio, among other wines. ✉ *2800 Lee Rd., in Prosser Wine and Food Park* ☎ *509/786– 4557* ⊕ *www.hoguecellars.com* ☉ *Daily 10–5.*

Kestrel Vintners has one the oldest vineyards, having been planted in 1973. Winemaker Flint Nelson focuses on cabernets, merlots, and syrahs, among others ✉ *2890 Lee Rd., in Prosser Wine and Food Park* ☎ *509/786–2675* ⊕ *www.kestrelwines.com* ☉ *Daily 10–5.*

Pontin del Roza is named for its owners, the Pontin family, and the grape-friendly slopes irrigated by the Roza Canal. Here you'll find Italian-style sangioveses and pinot grigios as well as rieslings, chenin blancs, chardonnays, sauvignon blancs, and cabernet sauvignons, syrahs, and merlots. ✉ *35502 N. Hinzerling Rd., 3½ mi north of Prosser* ☎ *509/786–4449* ☉ *Daily 10–5.*

At **Thurston Wolfe,** look for Wade Wolfe's unusual blends—a white pinot gris-viognier, for instance, and a red mix of zinfandel, syrah, lemberger, and turiga. The zinfandel is excellent. ✉ *2880 Lee Rd., in Prosser Wine and Food Park* ☎ *509/786–3313* ☉ *Apr.–early Dec., Thurs.–Sun. 11–5.*

VineHeart is a boutique winery that offers a buttery riesling, a raspberry-toned sémillon, a lemberger, and a sangiovese, as well as zinfandel, cabernet sauvignon, and syrah. ✉ *44209 N. McDonald Rd., 7 mi northeast of Prosser* ☎ *509/973–2993* ⊕ *www.vineheart.com* ☉ *Thurs.–Mon. 10–5.*

David Minick's tiny **Willow Crest Winery**—which indeed has a draping willow tree at its entrance—produces award-winning syrah as well as cabernet franc and pinot gris. ✉ *135701 Snipes Rd., 6 mi north of Prosser* ☎ *509/786–7999* ⊕ *www.willowcrestwinery.com* ☉ *Apr.– Nov., weekends 10–5.*

Yakima River Winery, specializing in barrel-aged reds and a memorable port along with a new variety petit vedot, was established by John and Louise Rauner in 1977. ✉ *143302 N. River Rd., 1½ mi south of Wine Country Rd.* ☎ *509/786–2805* ☉ *Daily 9–5.*

WHERE TO STAY & EAT

¢–$$ ✕**Blue Goose.** Here you'll find many different robust country breakfast items; later, indulge in Granny Smith chicken salad, veal parmagiana, or a big steak-and-lobster dinner. Casual and friendly, it's just off Wine Country Road in downtown Prosser. There's a small menu for kids. ✉ *306 7th St.* ☎ *509/786–1774* ▭ *AE, MC, V.*

$–$$ ⬚ **Inn at Horse Heaven.** Just off I–82 beneath its namesake hills, this handsome property has a lobby where you can choose a book from a small library and relax beside the fireplace. Kids will love the indoor pool in the winter and the outdoor pool in the summer. **Pros:** Close to several wineries and several restaurants. **Cons:** No frills here, just your basic motel. ⊠ *259 Merlot Dr., 99350* ☎ *509/786–7977 or 800/688–7192* 🖷 *509/786–7236* ⊕ *www.innathorseheaven.com* 📪 *85 rooms* ⛭ *In-room: kitchen, Wi-Fi. In-hotel: refrigerator, pool, laundry facilities, no-smoking rooms* ⊟ *AE, D, DC, MC, V* ⭕ *CP.*

¢   ⬚ **Vintners Inn.** You'll think you have time-warped back to the turn of the 20th century when you arrive at this 1905 Queen Anne that has been remodeled into a farmhouse-style B&B. Located next to the Hinzerling Winery, it offers two cozy rooms that may remind you of the comfort of Grandma's. Five-course prix-fixe dinners ($$$–$$$$; by reservation only) are served boarding-house style on Friday and Saturday nights. ⊠ *1520 Sheridan Ave., 99350* ☎ *509/786–2163 or 800/727–6702* ⊕ *www.hinzerling.com* 📪 *2 rooms* ⛭ *In-room: no phone, no TV. In-hotel: bar, no elevator, some pets allowed, no kids under 18* ⊟ *AE, MC, V* ⭕ *BP.*

BENTON CITY

16 mi east of Prosser.

The Yakima River zigzags north, making a giant bend around Red Mountain and the West Richland district before pouring into the Columbia River. Benton City—which, with a mere 3,000 residents, is hardly a city—is on a bluff west of the river and facing vineyard-cloaked Red Mountain. High-carbonate soil, a location in a unique high-pressure pocket, and geographical anomalies have led to this district being given its own appellation. You can access the wineries from Highway 224.

★   At **Blackwood Canyon Vintners** winemaker Michael Taylor Moore freely admits he's pushing the edge. Meticulously crafting wines by hand, he shuns modern filters, pumps, and even sulfites, and carefully avoids pesticides. Chardonnays, sémillons, merlots, cabernets, and late-harvest wines age *sur lies* (on their sediment), for as many as eight years before release. ⊠ *53258 N. Sunset Rd.* ☎ *509/588–6249* ⊙ *Daily 10–6.*

★   Robust reds designed to age are the specialty of **Hedges Cellars,** whose spectacular hillside château dominates upper Red Mountain. The estate blends cabernet sauvignon, cabernet franc, merlot, syrah, and reserve blends are superb. ⊠ *53511 N. Sunset Rd.* ☎ *509/588–3155* ⊕ *www.hedgesfamilyestate.com* ⊙ *Apr.–Dec., weekends noon–4.*

John Williams of **Kiona Vineyards Winery** planted the first grapes on Red Mountain in 1975, made his first wines in 1980, and produced the first commercial lemberger, a light German red, in the United States. Today Williams's newly constructed 10,000-square-foot tasting room features 180-degree views of Red Mountain and the Rattlesnake Hills. Kiona also produces premium Riesling, chenin blanc, chardonnay, cabernet sauvignon, merlot, syrah, sangiovese, and dessert wines. ⊠*44612 Sunset Rd.* ☎*509/588–6716* ⊙*Daily noon–5.*

Tiny **Oakwood Cellars** produces lemberger, merlot, cabernet sauvignon, Estate blanc, and Riesling. The boutique winery is on the west slope of Red Mountain overlooking the Yakima River. ⊠*40504 N. Demoss Rd.* ☎*509/588–5332* ⊕*www.oakwoodcellars.com* ⊙*Mar.–Nov., Fri.–Sun. noon–5.*

Picnickers enjoy the grounds at **Seth Ryan Winery** on lower Red Mountain. The boutique winery produces German-style gewürztraminer and Rieslings, plus chardonnay, merlot, and cabernets sauvignon and franc. ⊠*35306 Sunset Rd.* ☎*509/588–6780* ⊕*www.sethryan.com* ⊙*Tues.– Sat. noon–5.*

Named for the calcium carbonate in its soil, **Terra Blanca**, "white earth" in Latin, nonetheless is a specialist in red wines. Specialties are syrah, merlot, cabernet sauvignon, malbec, dessert wines, and chardonnay. ⊠*34715 N. Demoss Rd.* ☎*509/588–6082* ⊕*www.terrablanca.com* ⊙*Daily 11–6.*

YAKIMA RIVER VALLEY ESSENTIALS

BY AIR

Although major airlines serve the region's two airports, most people fly into Seattle or Portland, Oregon, and drive to the area. Horizon Airlines has several nonstops daily between Sea-Tac and Yakima, a 45-minute flight. Tri-Cities Airport has a similar schedule from Seattle, a 60-minute trip, with additional nonstop connections to Denver, Portland, and Salt Lake City. Both Yakima and the Tri-Cities are served by Delta and Horizon. The Tri-Cities is also served by United

Contacts Delta (☎*800/221–1212* ⊕*www.delta.com*). **Horizon Air** (☎*800/547– 9308* ⊕*www.horizonair.com*). **Tri-Cities Airport** (⊠*3601 N. 20th Ave., Pasco* ☎*509/547–6352*). **United** (☎*800/241–6522* ⊕*www.ual.com*). **Yakima Air Terminal** (⊠*2300 W. Washington Ave.* ☎*509/575–6150*).

AIRPORTS & TRANSFERS Yakima Air Terminal is 4 mi southeast of downtown Yakima. Tri-Cities Airport is more convenient to Grandview, Prosser, and Benton City. Taxis and public transit are available at both airports. (In Yakima, several cab companies or Yakima City Transit can provide transportation to hotels.) The Airporter Shuttle offers shuttle services from Sea-Tac airport (between Seattle and Tacoma) and Seattle Amtrak to Yakima ($37 in either direction), with stops in downtown Seattle, Cle Elum ($26), and Ellensburg ($31).

Contacts Airporter Shuttle (☎*866/235–5247*). **Diamond Cab** (☎*509/453– 3113*). **Yakima City Transit** (☎*509/575–6175*).

BY BUS

Greyhound Lines runs to and from Seattle on several routes. Its I–90 route passes through Ellensburg ($44 round-trip) three times daily from Seattle en route to Spokane and points east. It also travels along

U.S. 97 south from Ellensburg through Yakima ($50) and Toppenish ($62) once a day before cutting away from the Yakima Valley. Its I–82 route offers two more daily trips to Ellensburg, Yakima, and Toppenish, proceeding through Sunnyside ($62) and Prosser ($70) en route to the Tri-Cities.

Yakima is the only city in the region with a public transportation system. Yakima City Transit buses operate weekdays 6 AM to 6:45 PM and Saturday from 8:45 to 6:45 at half-hour intervals on nine routes. The one-way fare is 50¢.

Bus Information Greyhound Lines (☎ 800/229–9424 ⊕ www.greyhound.com). **Yakima City Transit** (☎ 509/575–6175 ⊕ www.ci.yakima.wa.us/services/transit).

BY CAR

The region has a single interstate, though it has two different numbers. I–90 links Seattle to Cle Elum and Ellensburg before heading east toward Spokane. I–82 branches south off I–90 just east of Ellensburg, and runs through the Yakima Valley to the so-called Tri-Cities (Richland, Pasco, and Kennewick). U.S. 97 is the primary link from Ellensburg north (Wenatchee, Canada's Okanagan Valley) and from Yakima south toward central Oregon.

From just north of Yakima, Highway 410 passes Mt. Rainer on the north, connecting with Highway 164 and I–5 south of Seattle; U.S. 12 passes Mt. Rainer on the south. Both routes offer spectacular alpine scenery but occasionally hazardous driving conditions. A major section of Highway 410 is closed by winter snow.

If you're touring wineries, be sure to stop at the Yakima Valley Visitor Information Center (Exit 34 off I–82) to pick up a wine-tour brochure and map of more than 30 wineries. Most are within a few miles of the freeway and there are directional signs.

The Yakima Valley Highway is a reliable, off-the-beaten-track alternative to I–82 for wine-country visits; but it can be slow, especially through towns, or if farm machinery is on the road. Because of unmarked turns and other potential hazards, it's wise to stick to the freeway after dark. Gas stations in towns, and at major freeway intersections, are typically open well after dark.

EMERGENCIES

Hospitals Providence Yakima Medical Center (✉ 110 S. 9th Ave., Yakima ☎ 509/575–5000). **Yakima Valley Memorial Hospital** (✉ 2811 Tieton Dr., Yakima ☎ 509/249–5219).

TOUR OPTIONS

Lifelong residents run Yakima Valley Tours' custom agricultural, historical, wine-tasting, and adventure-sports tours. Accent! Tours has informative trips to area wineries. Bus companies such as A & A Motorcoach, and limo services, including Moonlit Rides, conduct charter tours of the Yakima area.

Contacts A & A Motorcoach (✉ 2410 S. 26th Ave., Yakima ☎ 509/575–3676 ⊕ www.aamotorcoach.com). **Accent! Tours** (✉ 1001 W. Yakima Ave., Yakima

☎ *509/575–3949* ⊕ *www.accenttours.com*). **Moonlit Ride Limousine** (✉ *3908 River Rd., Yakima* ☎ *509/575–6846* ⊕ *www.moonlitride.com*). **Yakima Valley Tours** (✉ *551 N. Holt Rd., Mabton* ☎ *509/985-8628 or 509/840-4777* ⊕ *www. yakimavalleytours.com*).

VISITOR INFORMATION

Contacts **Cle Elum/Roslyn Chamber of Commerce** (✉ *401 W. 1st St., Cle Elum* ☎ *509/674–5958* ⊕ *www.cleelumroslyn.org*). **Ellensburg Chamber of Commerce** (✉ *609 N. Main St.* ☎ *509/925–3183 or 888/925–2204* ⊕ *www. ellensburg-chamber.com*). **Prosser Chamber of Commerce** (✉ *1230 Bennett Ave.* ☎ *509/786–3177 or 800/408–1517* ⊕ *www.prosserchamber.org*). **Sunnyside Chamber of Commerce** (✉ *230 E. Edison.* ☎ *509/837–5939 or 800/457–8089* ⊕ *www.sunnysidechamber.com*). **Toppenish Chamber of Commerce** (✉ *5A S. Toppenish Ave.* ☎ *509/865–3262 or 800/863–6375* ⊕ *www.toppenish.net*). **Yakima Valley Visitor Information Center** (✉ *101 Fair Ave., Exit 34 off I–82* ☎ *509/573–3388 or 800/221–0751* ⊕ *www.visityakima.com*). **Wine Yakima Valley Association** (☎ *800/258–7270* ⊕ *www.wineyakimavalley.com*).

EASTERN WASHINGTON

Updated by
Shelley Arenas

The Columbia Plateau was created by a series of lava flows that were later deeply cut by glacial floods. Because its soil is mostly made up of alluvial deposits and windblown silt (known to geologists as loess), it's very fertile. But little annual rainfall means that its vast central section—more than 30,000 square mi from the foothills of the Cascades and the northeastern mountains east to Idaho and south to Oregon—has no forests. In fact, except for a few scattered pine trees in the north, oaks in the southwest, and willows and cottonwoods along creeks and rivers, it has no trees.

This treeless expanse is part of an even larger steppe and desert region that runs north into Canada and south to California and the Sea of Cortez. There is water, however, carried from the mountains by the great Columbia and Snake rivers and their tributaries. Irrigation provides the region's cities with shrubs, trees, and flowers, and its fields bear a great variety of crops: asparagus, potatoes, apples, peaches, alfalfa, sweet corn, wheat, lentils, and much more. This bounty of agriculture makes the region prosperous and provides funds for symphony halls and opera houses, theaters, art museums, and universities.

Southeast of the Columbia Plateau lies a region of rolling hills and fields. Farmers of the Palouse region and of the foothills of the Blue Mountains don't need to irrigate their fields, as rain here produces record crops of wheat, lentils, and peas. It's a blessed landscape, flowing green and golden under the sun in waves of loam. The region is not only fertile, it is historically significant as well. The Lewis and Clark expedition passed through the Palouse in 1805, and Walla Walla was one of the earliest settlements in the inland Northwest.

The northeastern mountains, from the Okanogan to the Pend Oreille Valley, consist of granite peaks, glaciated cliffs, grassy uplands, and sunlit forests. Few Washingtonians seem to know about this region's attractions, however. Even at the height of the summer its roads and trails are rarely crowded.

The hidden jewel of these mountains is the Sanpoil River Valley, which is a miniature Yosemite Valley, with vertical rock walls rising 2,000–3,000 feet straight from the river, their height accentuated by the narrowness of the canyon. The valley has no amenities and is still in the possession of its original owners, the Indians of the Colville Reservation, who have preserved its beauty. These wild highlands have few visitor facilities. Towns in the Okanogan Valley and the regional metropolis of Spokane, on the fringes of the region, offer more services.

TOP 5

1. The Davenport Hotel blends the very best of yesteryear with high-tech touches.

2. The Northwest Museum of Arts and Culture has an excellent Native American collection and displays of Spokane's history.

3. Walla Walla, for its notable wines and fine restaurants and lodgings.

4. The unique and free laser-light show at Grand Coulee Dam every summer night .

5. Spokane's Riverfront Park has family-friendly fun year-round.

RICHLAND

202 mi southeast of Seattle, 145 mi southwest of Spokane.

Richland is the northernmost of the three municipalities along the bank of the Columbia River known as the Tri-Cities (the others are Pasco and Kennewick). Founded in the 1880s, Richland was a pleasant farming village until 1942, when the federal government built a nuclear reactor on the nearby Hanford Nuclear Reservation. The Hanford site was instrumental in the building of the Tri-Cities and still plays a major role in the area's economy. In recent years this has also become a major wine producing area. You can find more than 60 wineries within a 50-mi radius, many with tasting rooms.

The **Barnard Griffin Winery and Tasting Room** is next to Highway 182. Rob and Deborah Griffin offer a variety of fine wines, including excellent merlot and cabernet. ⊠ *878 Tulip La., 99352* ☎ *509/627–0266* ⊕ *www.barnardgriffin.com* ⊙ *Daily 10–6.*

Next door to Barnard Griffin Winery and Tasting Room, **Bookwalter Winery** produces eight varieties, from sweet Johannesburg Riesling to a classic merlot. Live music plays Wednesday–Saturday evenings year-round and Sunday afternoons in summer. The lounge features a changing variety of artisan cheeses, antipasto plates, other light fare, and desserts. ⊠ *894 Tulip La., 99352* ☎ *509/627–5000* ⊕ *www.bookwalterwines.com* ⊙ *Summer, Mon. and Tues. 10–10, Wed.–Sat. 10 AM–11 PM, Sun. 10–6; winter, Sun.–Tues. 10–6, Wed.–Sat. 10–10.*

☾ The **CREHST Museum** *(Columbia River Exhibition of History, Science, and Technology)* has educational exhibits, some of which are hands-on. Displays show the area's development from prehistoric times to

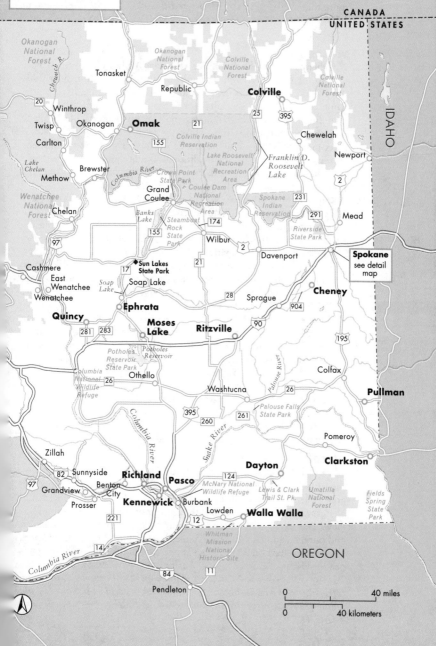

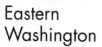

Eastern Washington

BRITISH COLUMBIA

CANADA
UNITED STATES

Okanogan National Forest

Chewuch R.

Tonasket

Okanogan National Forest

Republic

Colville National Forest

Colville

Colville National Forest

20

Winthrop

Twisp

Okanogan

Omak

155

Chewelah

Newport

2

Carlton

Lake Chelan

Brewster

Columbia River

Crown Point State Park

Grand Coulee

Coulee Dam National Recreation Area

Lake Roosevelt National Recreation Area

Franklin D. Roosevelt Lake

Spokane Indian Reservation

231

Methow

Colville Indian Reservation

Wenatchee National Forest

Chelan

Banks Lake

Steamboat Rock State Park

155

174

Wilbur

2

Davenport

291

Riverside State Park

Mead

97

Cashmere

East Wenatchee

Wenatchee

17

♦Sun Lakes State Park

Soap Lake

Soap Lake

21

28

Sprague

Cheney

904

Spokane
see detail map

Quincy

281 283

Ephrata

Moses Lake

Ritzville

90

195

Potholes Reservoir State Park

Potholes Reservoir

Colfax

Columbia National Wildlife Refuge

26

Othello

Washtucna

26

Pullman

395

260

261

Palouse River

Palouse Falls State Park

Pomeroy

Clarkston

Zillah

82

Sunnyside

Benton City

Richland

Pasco

124

Dayton

Lewis & Clark Trail St. Pk.

Umatilla National Forest

Fields Spring State Park

97

Grandview

Prosser

Kennewick

Burbank

Lowden

Walla Walla

McNary National Wildlife Refuge

221

12

Whitman Mission National Historic Site

14

OREGON

Columbia River

84

11

Pendleton

0   40 miles

0   40 kilometers

IDAHO

the nuclear age. The outdoor Boomers on Wheels exhibit depicts local trailer life in the 1940s, when the Hanford Construction Camp was the largest trailer camp in the world. A Lewis and Clark exhibit tells the story of the famous explorers and their expedition through the area more than 200 years ago. ⊠*95 Lee Blvd.99352* ☎*509/943–9000 or 877/789–9935* ⊕*www.crehst.org* ☜*$3.50* ☉*Mon.–Sat. 10–5, Sun. noon–5.*

WHERE TO EAT

$-$$$ ✕**Anthony's at Columbia Point.** For years the Anthony's chain has been known for fine waterfront dining in western Washington; since 2004 the Tri-Cities has had its own Anthony's on the Columbia River waterfront. Seafood is the specialty—even the appetizers are fish-focused, including fresh garlic herb mussels and Hawaiian ahi nachos. Willapa Bay oysters, Dungeness crab—whole, in fettuccine, or in crab cakes—alder-planked salmon, and Fishermen's cioppino are a few of the many entrée offerings. Anthony's traditional Sunday-night crab feeds and weekday sunset four-course dinners are also popular. ⊠*550 Columbia Point Dr., 99352* ☎*509/946–3474* ▭*AE, D, DC, MC, V.*

$-$$ ✕**Katya's Bistro & Wine Bar.** Since opening in 2005, Katya's has become a favorite of both locals and tourists, who come to enjoy the skillful efforts of executive chef Jimmy McBryar, previously with Bin 20, Anthony's, and the former Sundance Grill. Select from nearly 200 regional wines to accompany such dishes as osso bucco, lamb chops, wild salmon, lasagna, and several steak and chicken choices. Ukrainian items include borscht and dumplings called *pelmini*. Live music plays on Wednesday and Saturday. ⊠*430 George Washington Way, 99352* ☎*509/946–7777* ▭*MC, V* ☉*No.*

$-$$ ✕**Monterosso's Italian Restaurant.** In a refurbished railroad dining car, this small and charming Italian restaurant is fun for the whole family, but it's also suitable for a romantic meal. It's known for its tortellini and chicken marsala; also try the homemade tiramisu and cheesecake. ⊠*1026 Lee Blvd.99352* ☎*509/946–4525* ▭*AE, D, DC, MC, V* ☉*Closed Sun. No lunch.*

$ ✕**Atomic Ale Brewpub and Eatery.** The staff is friendly at this small, casual brewpub, which serves mainly house-brewed beers. The delicious pizzas are cooked in a wood-fired oven; soups, sandwiches, and salads are also fine. ⊠*1015 Lee Blvd.* ☎*509/946–5465* ▭*AE, D, MC, V.*

WHERE TO STAY

$ ▦**Red Lion Hotel Richland Hanford House.** Richland's Red Lion overlooks the Columbia River and is near many major Hanford contractors and government facilities. The hotel borders a greenbelt riverfront park and has easy access to trails along the levee; ask for a room with a river view. The Edgewater restaurant features steak, salmon, salads, pasta, and burgers, and an early-bird dinner special 5–6. **Pros:** Nice location, some rooms have views of river. **Cons:** Older hotel, some say the rooms need updating. ⊠*802 George Washington Way, 99352* ☎*509/946–7611* 🖷*509/943–8564* ⊕*www.redlion.com* ⥅*149 rooms* ⟐*In-room: refrigerator, Wi-Fi. In-hotel: restaurant, room service, bar, pool, gym, laundry service, airport shuttle, no-smoking rooms, some pets allowed* ▭*AE, D, DC, MC, V.*

¢–$ Shilo Inn Rivershore. Bordering the Columbia River above the mouth of the Yakima, the Shilo Inn has easy access to riverside trails and parks. Rooms have coffeemakers, microwaves, irons, and ironing boards. In O'Callahan's Restaurant and Lounge ($–$$), enjoy the view from inside or out on the deck as you indulge in prime rib, halibut-and-chips, pastas, or salads. ⊠*50 Comstock St., 99352* ☎*509/946–4661* ⊜*509/943–6741* ⊕*www.shiloinns.com* ⊅*151 rooms, 13 suites* ⧖*In-room: kitchen (some), Wi-Fi. In-hotel: restaurant, room service, bar, pool, gym, no elevator, laundry facilities, airport shuttle, no-smoking rooms, some pets allowed* ⊟*AE, D, DC, MC, V* ⦿*BP.*

PASCO

4

10 mi east of Richland.

Tree-shaded Pasco, a college town and the Franklin County seat, is an oasis of green on the Columbia River near a site where the Lewis and Clark expedition made camp in 1805. The city began as a railroad switchyard and now has a busy container port. The neoclassical Franklin County Courthouse (1907) is worth a visit for its fine marble interior.

The Pasco Basin has first-rate vineyards and wineries and some of the state's most fertile land. You can purchase the regional bounty at the farmers' market, held downtown every Wednesday and Saturday morning during the growing season.

Franklin County Historical Museum is home to numerous items illustrating local history, including artifacts from Native American tribes. Revolving exhibits have featured the Lewis and Clark expedition, the railroad, and World War II. ⊠*305 N. 4th Ave.* ☎*509/547–3714* ⊕*www. franklincountyhistoricalsociety.org* ⊠*Donations accepted* ⊗*Tues.– Fri. noon–4.*

Just off Highway 182, **Gordon Brothers Family Vineyards** produces some of the region's most acclaimed wines. Try the chardonnay, merlot, or cabernet sauvignon. All wines are grown in their south-facing vineyard along the Snake River. ⊠*671 Levey Rd.* ☎*509/547–6331* ⊕*www. gordonwines.com* ⊠*Free* ⊗*Open by appointment.*

Preston Estate Vineyards is one of the Pasco Basin's oldest wineries. The tasting room has great views of surrounding fields. ⊠*502 E. Vineyard Dr., 99301* ☎*509/545–1990* ⊕*www.prestonwines.com* ⊠*Free* ⊗*Daily 10–5:30.*

Sacajawea State Park, at the confluence of the Snake and Columbia rivers, occupies the site of Ainsworth, a railroad town that flourished from 1879 to 1884. It's named for the Shoshoni Indian woman who guided the Lewis and Clark expedition over the Rocky Mountains and down the Snake River. The 284-acre day-use park has an interpretive center and a large display of Native American tools. A beach, boat launch, picnic area, and children's playground round out the facilities; sand dunes, marshes, and ponds are great for watching wildlife. ⊠*Off U.S.*

12, 5 mi southeast of Pasco ☎509/545–2361 ⬛*Free* ☉*Apr.–Oct.,
6:30 AM–dusk.*

WHERE TO STAY & EAT

$–$$$ ✕**Bin 20 Steak and Seafood Restaurant.** Formerly the Vineyard Steak-
house, Bin 20 opened as a wine bar and still carries over 118 kinds
of wine, most from Washington state. In 2007 it expanded beyond
the wine focus to become a full-fledged steak and seafood restaurant.
On Saturday nights live piano accompanies the dinner hours. ⬛*2525
N. 20th St., 99301* ☎509/544–3939 ▭*AE, D, DC, MC, V* ☉*No
lunch.*

$ 📺**Red Lion Hotel Pasco.** This large, full-service hotel is loaded with ame-
nities, including in-room coffeemakers, irons, and ironing boards; many
rooms have microwaves, too. It's four blocks from the airport. ⬛*2525
N. 20th St., 99301* ☎509/547–0701 🖨509/547–4278 ⊕*www.redlion.
com* ⬏*279 rooms, 10 suites* ⬙*In-room: refrigerator (some), Wi-Fi.
In-hotel: 2 restaurants, room service, bar, pool, gym, airport shuttle,
no-smoking rooms, some pets allowed* ▭*AE, D, DC, MC, V.*

KENNEWICK

3 mi southwest of Pasco, directly across the Columbia River.

In its 100-year history, Kennewick (*ken-uh-wick*) evolved from a rail-
road town to a farm-supply center and then to a bedroom community
for Hanford workers and a food-processing capital for the Columbia
Basin. The name Kennewick translates as "grassy place," and Native
Americans had winter villages here long before Lewis and Clark passed
through. Arrowheads and other artifacts aside, the 9,000-year-old skel-
eton of Kennewick Man has been studied by scientists at the University
of Washington to determine if its features are American Indian or, as
some claim, Caucasian.

One of Washington's great parks, 3-mi-long, riverfront **Columbia Park**
has boat ramps, a golf course, a picnic area, and tennis courts. In sum-
mer, hydroplane races are held here. ⬛*U.S. 12 west to Lake Wallula*
☎509/585–4293.

The entire entryway of the **East Benton County Historical Museum** is made
of petrified wood. Photographs, agricultural displays, and a large
collection of arrowheads interpret area history. ⬛*205 Keewaydin
Dr., 99336* ☎509/582–7704 ⊕*www.ebchs.org* ⬛*$2* ☉*Tues.–Sat.
noon–4.*

At 103 feet, the single-lift locks at the **Ice Harbor Lock and Dam,** located
about 12 mi southeast of Kennewick, are among the world's highest.
⬛*2339 Ice Harbor Dr., Burbank 99323* ☎509/547–7781 ⬛*Free*
☉*Visitor center open Apr.–Sept., daily 9–5; dam is open year-round.*

On a hill above Kennewick, **Badger Mountain Vineyard** offers a beautiful
view of the valley and wine made without pesticides or preservatives.
In 2004 Badger Mountain scored highest among 30 wines on *Wine and
Health* magazine's "Health Score Index." ⬛*1106 S. Jurupa St., 99338*

☎509/627–4986 or 800/643–9463 ⊕*www.badgermtnvineyard.com* ✉*Free* ⊙*Daily 10–5.*

For those who prefer beer to wine, 7,000-square-foot **Ice Harbor Brewing Company** has a tasting room, gift shop, and a pub with an antique bar. ✉*206 N. Benton St.99336* ☎*509/582–5340 or 888/701–2350* 🖷*509/545–0571* ⊕*www.iceharbor.com* ✉*Free* ⊙*Mon.–Wed. 11–9, Thurs. 11–10, Fri. and Sat. 11–11, Sun. noon–6.*

In winter, **McNary National Wildlife Refuge** is a resting and feeding area for up to 100,000 migrating Canada geese, mallards, and American wigeons. But its 3,629 acres of water and marsh, croplands, grasslands, trees, and shrubs are most enjoyable in spring and summer, when there is no hunting. A self-guided 2-mi trail winds through the marshes, and a cabinlike blind hidden in the reeds allows you to watch ducks, geese, grebes, and yellow-headed blackbirds up close. With luck you may also spot long-billed curlews and white pelicans. ✉*64 Maple Rd., Burbank 99323* ✛*¼ mi east of U.S. 12, south of Snake River Bridge* ☎*509/547–4942* ✉*Free* ⊙*Daily 24 hrs.*

WHERE TO STAY & EAT

$-$$$ ✕ **The Cedars.** Right on the edge of the Columbia River, Cedars has beautiful views and a 200-foot dock for boaters coming to dine. The menu includes top-quality steaks, pasta, poultry, and wild salmon, and the extensive wine list features many local labels. ✉*355 Clover Island Dr.* ☎*509/582–2143* ▤*AE, D, DC, MC, V* ⊙*No lunch.*

$ 🛏 **Red Lion Columbia Center.** Talk about convenience: it's next to a regional shopping mall and a block from the convention center. Enjoy dining in the skylight Cavanaugh's Landing restaurant, which offers an extensive Sunday buffet brunch, and visit the lounge for karaoke on weekend nights. ✉*1101 N. Columbia Center Blvd., 99336* ☎*509/783–0611 or 800/733–5466* 🖷*509/735–3087* ⊕*www.redlion. com* ⇋*162 rooms, 9 suites* ⬥*In-room: refrigerators, Wi-Fi. In-hotel: restaurant, room service, bar, pool, gym, no elevator, airport shuttle, no-smoking rooms, some pets allowed* ▤*AE, D, DC, MC, V.*

WALLA WALLA

52 mi southeast of Kennewick.

Walla Walla, founded in the 1850s on the site of a Nez Perce village, was Washington's first metropolis. As late as the 1880s its population was larger than that of Seattle. Walla Walla occupies a lush green valley below the rugged Blue Mountains. Its beautiful downtown boasts old residences, green parks, and the campus of Whitman College, Washington's oldest institution of higher learning.

A successful downtown restoration has earned Walla Walla high praise. The heart of downtown, at 2nd and Main streets, looks as pretty as it did 50 years ago, with beautifully maintained old buildings and newer structures designed to fit in. Residents and visitors come here to visit shops, wineries, cafés, and restaurants.

West of town, the green Walla Walla Valley—famous for asparagus, sweet onions, cherries, and wheat—has emerged as Washington's premier viticultural region. Tall grain elevators mark Lowden, a few miles west of Walla Walla, a wheat hamlet that now has several wineries.

Planted with native and exotic flowers and trees, **Pioneer Park** (⊠ *E. Alder St. and Division St., 99362*) is a shady, turn-of-the-20th-century park with a fine aviary. It was originally landscaped by sons of Frederick Law Olmsted, who designed New York City's Central Park.

Large, tree-lined lawns surround the many beautiful 19th-century stone and brick structures of the **Whitman College** (⊠ *345 Boyer Ave., 99362* ☎ *509/527–5111*) campus. The school began as a seminary in 1859 and became a college in 1883.

WORD OF MOUTH

"Walla Walla Valley is one of Eastern Washington's best kept secrets. It has scenic beauty, great wines, surprising restaurants, and at least one fine hotel, the recently restored Whitman. The Inn at Abeja is positively splendid. . . . Standout restaurants in Walla Walla include Grapefields and Whitehouse-Crawford. Also check out Dayton, WA for its great historic homes and two completely out of place restaurants considering the tiny town, the regionally famous Patit Creek restaurant (French), and the historic Weinhard Cafe."

–Sgorces

Waterbrook Winery hides in a converted warehouse just south of Lowden, but the tasting room of the Valley's largest winery is in downtown Walla Walla. Waterbrook is best known for chardonnay, sauvignon blanc, and viognier. ⊠ *31 E. Main St., 99362* ☎ *509/522–1262* ⊕ *www.waterbrook.com* ۞ *Daily 10:30–4:30.*

Canoe Ridge Vineyards, owned by the Chalone Wine Group, produces merlot, cabernet, chardonnay, and other wines. A tasting room and vineyard tours are offered. ⊠ *1102 W. Cherry St.* ☎ *509/527–0885* ⊕ *www.canoeridgevineyard.com* ۞ *Feb.–Nov., daily 11–5; Dec. and Jan., daily 11–4.*

At **Seven Hills Winery,** owner Casey McClellan makes well-balanced merlot, cabernet sauvignon, and syrah. The winery is in Walla Walla's historic Whitehouse-Crawford building. ⊠ *212 N. 3rd Ave., 99362* ☎ *509/529–7198 or 877/777–7870* ⊕ *www.sevenhillswinery.com* ۞ *Thurs.–Sat. 11–4, and by appointment.*

☾ ★ **Whitman Mission National Historic Site,** 7 mi west of Walla Walla, is a reconstruction of Waiilatpu Mission, a Presbyterian outpost established on Cayuse Indian lands in 1836. The park preserves the foundations of the mission buildings, a short segment of the Oregon Trail, and, on a nearby hill, the graveyard where the Native American victims of an 1847 measles epidemic and subsequent uprising are buried. ⊠ *328 Whitman Mission Rd. 99362* ☎ *509/522–6360, 509/522–6357* *or 509/529–2761* ⊕*www.nps.gov/whmi* ⊠*$3* ☉*Daily dawn—dusk; visitor center open 8–6 summer, 8–4:30 winter.*

☺ **Ft. Walla Walla Museum,** a few miles west of Walla Walla, occupies a museum building. Before the U.S. Army established Ft. Walla Walla at this site, five fur-trader forts bearing that name were built near Wallula, above the mouth of the Walla Walla River. All of them were destroyed by flood waters. ⊠*755 Myra Rd., at Dalles Military Rd., 99362* ☎*509/525–7703* ⊕*www.fortwallawallamuseum.org* ⊠*$7* ☉*Apr.–Oct., daily 10–5.*

Lovers of fine wines make pilgrimages to **Woodward Canyon Winery,** 12 mi west of Walla Walla, for the superb cabernet sauvignon, merlot, and chardonnay. The winery occasionally produces other varietals. ⊠*11920 W. U.S. 12, Lowden 99360* ☎*509/525–4129* ⊕*www.woodwardcanyon.com* ☉*Daily 10–5.*

A few blocks from Woodward Canyon Winery is **L'Ecole N. 41.** Housed in the lower floors of a former schoolhouse, the winery produces outstanding sémillon and merlot, among other wines. ⊠*41 Lowden School Rd., Lowden 99360* ☎*509/525–0940* ⊕*www.lecole.com* ☉*Daily 10–5.*

About a mile east of L'Ecole N. 41 is **Three Rivers Winery.** Just off U.S. 12 and surrounded by vineyards, the winery is home to premium cabernet sauvignon, merlot, sangiovese, and syrah. It also has a nice tasting room, a gift shop, summer concerts, and a 3-hole golf course. ⊠*5641 W. U.S. 12, 99362* ☎*509/526–9463* ⊕*www.threeriverswinery.com* ☉*Daily 10–6.*

WHERE TO EAT

$–$$$ ✕**Whitehouse-Crawford Restaurant.** In a former wood-planing mill, this
★ restaurant has gained a reputation for quality and excellence. Local is the watchword here, where hamburgers are made with beef from the Thundering Hooves Farm in nearby Touchet. Try the smoked trout and warm spinach salad and save room for the twice-baked chocolate cake. The extensive wine list features many Walla Walla Valley winemakers. ⊠*55 W. Cherry St.* ☎*509/525–2222* ⊟*AE, MC, V* ☉*Closed Mon. and Tues. No lunch.*

$$ ✕**CreekTown Café.** About seven blocks off Main Street, the intimate
★ CreekTown Café is one of the town's hidden gems. The emphasis is on local ingredients, and the menu changes seasonally. The sweet onion soup is a favorite with locals in the summer. Seared prawns and scallops and crab cannelloni are year-round house favorites.Try the desserts with fresh fruit from local growers. All desserts are made in-house. Patio seating is available in summer. ⊠*1129 S. 2nd Ave.* ☎*509/522–4777* ⊟*AE, D, MC, V* ☉*Closed Sun. and Mon.*

$–$$ ✕**Grapefields.** This popular café and wine shop with 14 tables is known
★ for its homemade bread pudding, quiche, and chicken coconut curry soup. The French-influenced menu includes pasta, seafood, lamb, and beef (the boeuf bourguignon is noteworthy). The extensive wine list includes 15 varieties that you can order by the glass. ⊠*4 E. Main St.* ☎*509/522–3993* ⊟*AE, MC, V* ☉*Closed Mon. No dinner Sun.*

WHERE TO STAY

$$$–$$$$ 🏠 **Inn at Abeja.** Twenty-five acres of gardens and vineyards surround
Fodor'sChoice   a turn-of-the-20th-century farm with guest cottages and suites. Each
★   accommodation has board games, books, and magazines, binocular+s
(to better enjoy the bucolic views), CD players, and satellite TV. Break-
fast can be delivered to your room or served in the small barn. It's a
short drive to both downtown Walla Walla and valley wineries. **Pros:**
Beautiful grounds, high-end, very spacious accommodations with
kitchens, private tours of the winery on-site. **Cons:** Not open year-
round, secluded. ⊠*2014 Mill Creek Rd., 99362* ☎*509/522–1234*
⊕*www.abeja.net/inn* ⇨*3 cottages, 2 suites* ⊘*In-room: kitchen, dial-
up (some), DVD. In-hotel: no-smoking rooms, some pets allowed, no
kids under 13, no elevator* ☐*MC, V* �🍴*BP.*

$–$$ 🏠 **Green Gables Inn.** One block from the Whitman Campus, this 1909
Arts and Crafts–style mansion sits among flowering plants and shrubs
on a quaint, tree-lined street. Charming guest rooms, their names
derived from Lucy Maud Montgomery's *Anne of Green Gables,* are
individually decorated with Victorian antiques. The Idlewild contains
a fireplace and private deck, while French doors in Dryad's Bubble
lead to a small, private balcony. **Pros:** Mini-fridges in rooms are a nice
touch, pretty setting, good room amenities for a B&B. **Cons:** New ownership so there may be changes (hopefully positive). ⊠*922 Bonsella
St., 99362* ☎*509/525–5501* ⊕*www.greengablesinn.com* ⇨*5 rooms*
⊘*In-room: refrigerator, VCR, Wi-Fi. In-hotel: no kids under 12, no
elevator, no-smoking rooms* ☐*AE, D, MC, V* �🍴*BP.*

$–$$ 🏠 **Inn at Blackberry Creek.** Blackberry Creek runs through the backyard
of this secluded but centrally located inn. Built in 1906, the Kentucky
farmhouse–style home sits on a 1½-acre lot in a residential area near
the city park. Renoir's Studio has a private hot tub for two. **Pros:** Wonderful breakfast with several choices, rooms are very well-stocked with
lots of extras, hosts are warm and friendly. **Cons:** Very popular but
only 3 rooms, so book ahead for special wine event weekends. ⊠*1126
Pleasant St., 99362* ☎*509/522–5233 or 877/522–5233* ⊕*www.innat-
blackberrycreek.com* ⇨*3 rooms* ⊘*In-room: refrigerator, DVD, VCR,
Wi-Fi. In-hotel: no kids under 12, no-smoking rooms, no elevator, Ethernet* ☐*AE, D, MC, V* �🍴*BP.*

$–$$ 🏠 **Marcus Whitman Hotel.** Since its restoration this 1928 hotel has
★   become *the* landmark in downtown Walla Walla. The hotel has standard and deluxe rooms as well as two-room parlor suites and spa
suites. Most guest quarters, which are adorned with Renaissance-style
Italian furnishings, have king beds. The Marc restaurant has fine dining, with views of the Blue Mountains and the valley. You can sample
local wines at the Vineyard Wine Bar. **Pros:** Range of accommodations
to choose from, convenient restaurant and wine bar. **Cons:** Rooms
in new wing are standard motel style, some guests have complained
about noise especially in new section, no pool. ⊠*6 W. Rose St., 99362*
☎*509/525–2200 or 866/826–9422* 🖶*509/524–1747* ⊕*www.marcus-
whitmanhotel.com* ⇨*127 rooms, 16 suites* ⊘*In-room: refrigerator
(some), DVD (some), Ethernet (some), Wi-Fi (some). In-hotel: restau-*

rant, bar, gym, some pets allowed, airport shuttle, no-smoking rooms
⊟*AE, D, DC, MC, V.*

DAYTON

31 mi northeast of Walla Walla.

The tree-shaded county seat of Columbia County is the kind of Currier & Ives place many people conjure up when they imagine the best qualities of rural America. This tidy town has 117 buildings listed on the National Register of Historic Places, including the state's oldest railroad depot and courthouse.

At Washington's oldest standing depot, the **Dayton Historical Depot Society** houses exhibits illustrating the history of Dayton and surrounding communities. ⊠*222 E. Commercial St.* ☎*509/382–2026* ⊕*www.daytonhistoricdepot.org* ⊡*$3* ⊙*May–Oct., Wed. and Thurs. 11–5, Fri. and Sat. 10–5, Sun. 1–4; early Nov.–Apr., Wed.–Sat. 11–4.*

OFF THE BEATEN PATH

Palouse Falls State Park. Just north of its confluence with the Snake River, the Palouse River gushes over a basalt cliff higher than Niagara Falls and drops 198 feet into a steep-walled basin. Those who are sure-footed can hike to an overlook above the falls, which are at their fastest during spring runoff in March. Just downstream from the falls at the Marmes Rock Shelter, remains of the earliest-known inhabitants of North America, dating back 10,000 years, were discovered by archaeologists. The park has 10 primitive campsites. ⊠*U.S. 12, 50 mi north of Dayton* ☎*360/902–8844 or 888/226–7688* ⊡*Campsites $12* ⊙*Park daily summer 6:30 AM–dusk, winter 8 AM–dusk; campsites mid-Mar.–mid-Sept.*

WHERE TO STAY & EAT

$$–$$$ ✕**Patit Creek Restaurant.** The chef turns out inspired beef, duck, and
★ lamb dishes at this small café, which has been a favorite southeastern Washington eatery for more than 25 years. Portobello mushroom saltimbocca is favorite vegetarian option. Not only can the food be truly sublime, but the service is also excellent. The wine list is short but has some rare Walla Walla Valley vintages. ⊠*725 E. Dayton Ave., 99328* ☎*509/382–2625* ⊟*MC, V* ⊙*Closed Sun.–Tues. No lunch Sat.*

$ ✕**Weinhard Café.** The past seems to echo through this restaurant, which is near the Weinhard Hotel and in what was once a pharmacy. Try a panini sandwich for lunch; for dinner, the rib-eye steak with potato thyme gratin and wild mushrooms—is a good bet. The blackberry cobbler and lemon coconut pie are dessert favorites. The menu changes frequently to highlight seasonal specialties. ⊠*258 E. Main St., 99328* ☎*509/382–1681* ⊟*MC, V* ⊙*Closed Sun. and Mon.*

¢–$ ▦**Purple House Bed and Breakfast.** This Italianate-style house was built in 1882 by a pioneer physician. Today European art and Chinese collectibles adorn the interior. Bedrooms are individually appointed with a tasteful selection of Victorian antiques. Afternoon pastries and tea are presented in the parlor. The master suite on main floor is wheelchair accessible. **Pros:** Elegant furnishings, much historical appeal, on-site pool. **Cons:** Some rooms have shared baths, advanced reservations (like most smaller B&Bs) are generally necessary. ✉ *415 E. Clay St., 99328* 📠*509/382–3159 or 800/486–2574* ⊕*www.purplehousebnb.com* ➥*2 rooms, 1 suite, 1 cottage* ♿*In-room: Ethernet. In-hotel: pool, no kids under 16, no-smoking rooms, some pets allowed* ☰*MC, V* ⦿*BP.*

¢–$ 🖭 **Weinhard Hotel.** Step back into the Old West at this hotel, which
★ was built as a saloon and lodge in the late 1800s by the nephew of beer baron Henry Weinhard. Rooms have modern amenities but period antiques; fruit baskets and bouquets of flowers are thoughtful touches. An Internet coffeehouse was added in 2005. Enjoy sparkling cider and live music at weekend evening socials; catch a breeze in the pleasant rooftop garden. **Pros:** weekend live music is fun; rooms reflect the history of the era but have modern features. **Cons:** some rooms face highway and can be noisy, some guests have complained about the front desk service. ✉*235 E. Main St., 99328* 📠*509/382–4032* 🖨*509/382–2640* ⊕*www.weinhard.com* ➥*15 rooms* ♿*In-room: dial-up (some), VCR (some), Wi-Fi (some). In-hotel: public Wi-Fi, no elevator, no-smoking rooms, some pets allowed* ☰*D, MC, V* ⦿*CP.*

CLARKSTON

58 mi northeast of Dayton.

This former ferry town was founded in 1862 as a way station for travelers heading to the Idaho goldfields. It is the twin city of Lewiston, Idaho, across the river. Clarkston is surrounded by grass-covered hills—green in spring and gold in summer. Along the river a pleasant walkway, the Greenbelt, and Swallows Park invite visitors to explore. You can walk all the way downriver to Asotin, about 5 mi south of town. Swallow Rock is dotted with the jug-shape mud nests of cliff swallows. Clarkston has a symphony orchestra, a civic theater, and art galleries.

The **Valley Art Center** has rotating exhibits of watercolors, oils, and other mediums by local artists, and sells bronze castings, pottery, and glasses. ✉*842 6th St., 99403* 📞*509/758–8331* 🎟*Free* ⦿ *Weekdays 9–3.*

The small **Asotin County Museum,** in the county seat of Asotin, 5 mi south of Clarkston, preserves a few old buildings moved from nearby communities, including a log cabin with blacksmith's forge. The museum itself was the first funeral home in the city. There's a very good collection of local branding irons (a rustler's dream) and old carriages. ✉*215 Filmore St., Asotin 99402* 📞*509/243–4659* 🎟*$2 suggested donation* ⦿*Tues.–Sat. noon–4 and by appointment.*

Fields Spring State Park is partially on Puffer Butte, 30 mi south of Clarkston and in the Blue Mountains. The views are great, and the bird-watching is rewarding year-round. In spring there are spectacular wildflower displays. Primitive camping is allowed; there are also two tepees that can be rented, and two group rental facilities. ✉*Hwy. 129* 📞*509/256–3332* ⊕*www.parks.wa.gov* 🎟*Free; tent campsites*

$12; tepee rentals $20 ⊙ *Summer, daily 6:30* AM–*dusk; winter, daily 8* AM–*dusk.*

WHERE TO STAY

$ 🏠 **Cliff House Bed and Breakfast.** On a bluff above the Snake River 7 mi west of Clarkston, Cliff House has views up and down the river valley. Snag a hammock on the wraparound deck surrounding the house and watch barges and ships pass by, or relax in the outdoor hot tub. A Native American motif dominates one room, while an imposing river view beautifies the other. A common room and outdoor enclosed gazebo are available for extra sleeping spaces for larger groups. **Pros:** gorgeous setting, hot tub is pleasant amenity, flexible for accommodating groups. **Cons:** only 2 rooms, no credit cards. ⊠ *1227 Westlake Dr., 99403* ☎ *509/758–1267* ⊕ *www.cliffhouseclarkston.com* 🛏 *2 rooms* ♿ *In-room: no phone, DVD (some). In-hotel: dial-up, no-smoking rooms* ▭ *No credit cards* ⦿ *BP.*

PULLMAN

33 mi northwest of Clarkston.

This funky, liberal town—home of Washington State University—is in the heart of the rather conservative Palouse agricultural district. The town's freewheeling style can perhaps be explained by the fact that most of the students come from elsewhere in Washington.

The Palouse River, whose upper course flows though the town, is an exception among Washington rivers: because of the high erosion rate of the light Palouse loess soils it usually runs muddy, almost like a gruel during floods (most Washington Rivers run clear, even after major storms). The 198-foot-high Palouse Falls farther downstream, near Washtucna, dramatically drop as a thin sheet of water into a steep box canyon.

Opened in 1892 as the state's agriculture school, **Washington State University** today sprawls almost all the way to the Idaho state line. To park on campus, pick up a parking pass in the Security Building on Wilson Road. ⊠ *1 S.E. Stadium Way* ☎ *509/335–4527* 🖨 *509/335–9113* ⊕ *www.wsu.edu* 🎟 *Free* ⊙ *Daily.*

On weekdays between 9:30 and 4:30, you can pop into **Ferdinand's** (⊠ *S. Fairway La.* ☎ *509/335–2141*), a soda fountain–cheese shop in the food-science building, to buy Aged Cougar Gold, a cheddar-type cheese in a can. The small **Museum of Art** (⊠ *WSU Fine Arts Center, Wilson Rd. and Stadium Way* ☎ *509/335–1910*) has lectures, as well as exhibitions that might include turned-wood art, Native American art, or landscaping displays. It's open Monday–Wednesday, Friday and Saturday 10–4, Thursday 10–7; admission is free. The **Charles R. Conner Museum of Zoology** (⊠ *Science Hall* ☎ *509/335–3515*) has the finest collection of stuffed birds and mammals and preserved invertebrates in the Pacific Northwest. It's open daily 8–5, and there's no admission fee.

Steptoe Butte State Park is named after an army officer who lost a battle in 1858 against Native Americans at nearby Rosalia. The lieutenant colonel and other survivors snuck away at night—a retreat historians think was permitted by the Indians. The park has picnic tables but no water. ⊠*32 mi north of Pullman via U.S. 195* ☎*360/902–8844* ⊕*www.parks.wa.gov* ⊠*Free* ☉*Daily 6–6.*

Kamiak Butte County Park has a 3,360-foot-tall butte that's part of a mountain chain that was here long before the lava flows of the Columbia basin erupted millions of years ago. Ten miles north of Pullman, the park has great views of the Palouse hills and Idaho's snow-capped peaks to the east, as well as nine primitive campsites, a picnic area, and a 1-mi trail to the top of the butte. ⊠*Hwy. 272 to Rd. 5100 to Rd. 6710* ☎*509/397–6238* ⊠*$2* ☉*Daily dawn–dusk.*

WHERE TO STAY & EAT

¢   ✕ **Basilio's Italian Café.** In the heart of downtown, Basilio's serves up such classics as pasta, lasagna, and chicken parmigiana in addition to an assortment of sandwiches. Gaze at scenic downtown from the sidewalk seating area. ⊠*337 E. Main St., 99163* ☎*509/334–7663* ☐*MC, V.*

¢   ✕ **Sella's Calzone and Pastas.** Made daily from scratch, the calzones are always fresh at this cozy storefront. The most popular is the Coug (pepperoni, mushrooms, and black olives), followed by Gourmet (artichoke hearts, sundried tomatoes, pesto sauce, and mozzarella). Pizzas, sandwiches, pastas, and salads are also served. ⊠*1115 E. Main St., 99163* ☎*509/334–1895* ☐*MC, V.*

¢–$ ⊞ **Churchyard Inn.** Registered as a national and state historic site, this 1905 Flemish-style inn, 15 mi southeast of Pullman in Uniontown, was once a parish house for the adjacent church, and then a convent, before becoming a B&B in 1995. Kids are sometime sallowed; ask in advance. And book well in advance during WSU games/events. **Pros:** Welcoming and helpful innkeeper, interesting history, quiet and scenic. **Cons:** No a/c or TVs in rooms. ⊠*206 St. Boniface St., Uniontown 99179* ☎*509/229–3200 or 800/227–2804* ☐*509/229–3213* ⊕*www.churchyardinn.com* ⊶*6 rooms* ♿*In-room: no a/c, no TV, Wi-Fi. In-hotel: no elevator, no-smoking rooms* ☐*AE, D, MC, V* ☉◯*BP.*

SPOKANE

❶–❿ *75 mi north of Pullman, 282 mi east of Seattle.*

Washington's second-largest city, Spokane (spo-*can,* not spo-*cane*) takes its name from the Spokan tribe of Salish Indians. It translates as "Children of the Sun," a fitting name for this sunny city. It's also a city of flowers and trees, public gardens, parks, and museums. Known as the "Capital of the Inland Empire," Spokane is the cultural and financial center of the inland Northwest.

Spokane began as a Native American village at a roaring waterfall where each autumn salmon ascended in great numbers. American settlers built a sawmill at the falls in 1873. Several railroads arrived after 1881, and Spokane soon became the transportation hub of eastern

Washington. In 1885 Spokane built the first hydroelectric plant west of the Mississippi. Downtown boomed after the fire of 1889, as the city grew rich from mining ventures in Washington, Idaho, and Montana, and from shipping to the south the wheat grown on the Palouse hills.

Until they were cleared away for the 1974 World's Fair, bridges and railroad trestles hid Spokane's magnificent falls from view. Today they form the heart of downtown's Riverfront Park, and the city rises from the falls in a series of broad terraces to the valley's rim. Urban parks are among Spokane's assets. The dry, hot summers here make it easy to plan golf, fishing, and hiking excursions; long, snowy winters provide nearly six months to enjoy skiing, snowboarding, and sledding.

WHAT TO SEE

4

⑩ Arbor Crest Wine Cellars. The eclectic mansion of Royal Riblet, the inventor of a square-wheel tractor and the poles that hold up ski lifts, was built in 1924. Sample complimentary Arbor Crest wines, enjoy the striking view of the Spokane River below, or meander through the impeccably kept grounds (the house isn't open to tours). Enjoy Sunday evening concerts (5:30 PM–sunset) for $5 from June through October. ⊠ *4705 N. Fruithill Rd., 99217* ☎ *509/927–9463* ⊕ *www.arborcrest. com* ☑ *Free* ☉ *Daily noon–5.*

❺ Caterina Winery. Featuring wines that have won both national and international awards, this is also one of Washington's few downtown wineries. It's in the Broadview Building, formerly home to Carnation Dairy, across the river from Riverfront Park. The wine bar hosts live music Friday and Saturday nights. ⊠ *905 N. Washington St., 99201* ☎ *509/328–5069* ⊕ *www.caterinawinery.com* ☑ *Free* ☉ *Mon.–Sat. noon–5; Thurs.–Sat. 8 PM–11 PM.*

❻ Cathedral of St. John the Evangelist. An architectural masterpiece, the church
★ was constructed with sandstone from Tacoma and Boise and limestone from Indiana. It's considered one of America's most important and beautiful Gothic cathedrals. The cathedral's renowned 49-bell carillon has attracted international guest musicians. Free concerts are held on Thursday evenings in July; bring a picnic to enjoy on the lawn. ⊠ *127 E. 12th Ave., 99202* ☎ *509/838–4277* ⊕ *www.stjohns-cathedral.org* ☑ *Free* ☉ *Tours Mon., Tues., Thurs., Sat. noon–3.*

❽ Cat Tales Zoological Park. Among the large cats living at this zoo are
☾ lions, tigers, ligers (a combination of lion and tiger), leopards, puma, and lynx. Guided tours give background on the animals. There's also a petting zoo. ⊠ *N. 17020 Newport Hwy., 12 mi north of I–90, Mead 99021* ☎ *509/238–4126* ⊕ *www.cattales.org* ☑ *$6* ☉ *May–Sept., Tues.–Sun. 10–6; Oct.–Apr., Tues.–Sun. 10–4.*

❶ Finch Arboretum. This mile-long green patch along Garden Springs Creek has an extensive botanical garden with more than 2,000 labeled trees, shrubs, and flowers. Follow the walking tour on well-manicured paths along the creek, or follow your whim—depending on the season— through flowering rhododendrons, hibiscus, magnolias, dogwoods,

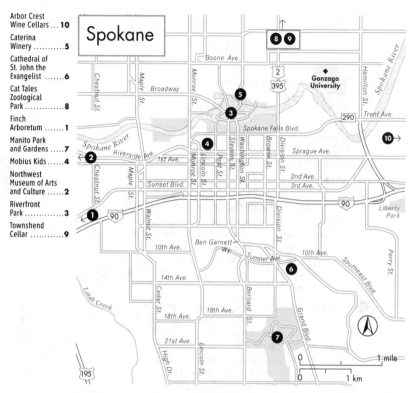

hydrangeas, and more. ⊠ *3404 W. Woodland Blvd., off Sunset Blvd.
99204* ☎ *509/624–4832* ⌑ *Free* ⊙ *Daily dawn–dusk.*

❼ Manito Park and Gardens. A pleasant place to stroll in summer, this 90-
acre park has a formal Renaissance-style garden, conservatory, Japanese
Fodor's Choice garden, duck pond, and rose and perennial gardens. Snowy winters find
★ its hills full of sledders and its frozen pond packed with skaters. ⊠ *S.
Grand Blvd. between 17th and 25th Aves.* ☎ *509/363–5422* ⌑ *Free*
⊙ *Daily, summer–4 AM–11 PM; winter 5 AM–10 PM; Japanese garden
Apr.–Oct., 8 AM to ½ hr before dusk.*

❹ Mobius Kids. Spokane's Children's Museum re-opened in 2005 with a
new name and a new location. The 16,000-square-foot museum is on
the first floor of River Park Square and has seven interactive galleries
for hands-on learning. Exhibits include a Safety Town with a fire truck
and medical area, an art studio, a science exhibit called Geotopica, and
a Filipino village with home, market, and boat. A 75,000-square-foot
Mobius Science Center is currently being developed as well, with 2010
projected as the opening date. ⊠ *808 W. Main St., 99201* ☎ *509/624–
5437* ⊕ *www.mobiusspokane.org* ⌑ *$5.75* ⊙ *Mon.–Sat. 10–5, Sun.
11–5.*

🔄 ❷ **Northwest Museum of Arts and Culture.** What is affectionately referred to
FodorśChoice as the MAC is in an impressive six-level glass-and-wood structure. The
★ museum has an audiovisual display and artifacts that trace Spokane's
history as well as a fine Native American collection that includes baskets and beadwork of the Plateau Indians. The MAC also hosts several
traveling exhibits each year. Wander the adjacent Victorian, the Campbell House, to admire the interior or view mining-era exhibits; guided
tours are available by reservation only. ✉ *2316 W. 1st Ave., 99201*
☎ *509/456–3931* ⊕ *www.northwestmuseum.org* 💲 *$7* ⊙ *Tues.–Sun.*
11–5, 1st Fri. until 8.

🔄 ❸ **Riverfront Park.** The 100-acre park is what remains of Spokane's Expo
★ '74. Sprawling across several islands in the Spokane River, near the falls,
the park was developed from old railroad yards. One of the modernist
buildings houses an IMAX theater, a skating rink, and an exhibition
space. The opera house occupies the former Washington State pavilion.
The stone clock tower of the former Great Northern Railroad Station,
built in 1902, stands in sharp architectural contrast to the Expo '74
building. A children's train chugs around the park in summer, and a
1909 carousel, hand-carved by master builder Charles I. D. Looff, is a
local landmark. Another icon here is the giant red slide shaped like a
Radio Flyer wagon. ✉ *507 N. Howard St., 99201* ☎ *509/625–6600 or*
800/336–7275 ⊕ *www.spokaneriverfrontpark.com* 💲 *Park: free. Fees*
for some attractions. Summer and winter day passes for seasonal activi-
ties: $13–$16. ⊙ *Park, daily 4* AM*–midnight. Attractions, hrs vary.*

❾ **Townshend Cellar.** A drive to the Green Bluff countryside about 13 mi
northeast of downtown leads wine lovers to this small winery and its
tasting room. Open since 1998, it's already won awards for its cabernet
sauvignon, and also makes merlot, chardonnay, syrah, port, gewürztraminer, and chenin blanc. Berries from nearby Idaho are used in
huckleberry port, blush, and sparkling wine. ✉ *16112 N. Greenbluff*
Rd., via N. Division and U.S. 2 N, Colbert 99005 ☎ *509/238–1400*
⊕ *www.townshendcellar.com* 💲 *Free* ⊙ *Open Fri.–Sun. noon–6 and*
by appointment.

WHERE TO EAT

$–$$$ ✕ **Luna.** You'll find inventive approaches to classics here, including
★ pork, chicken, salmon, and lamb. The menu highlights fresh ingredi-
ents grown in the restaurant's garden and changes seasonally. Sunday
brunch has such treats as scrambled-egg salad with field greens and
smoked bacon and French toast with caramelized bananas. Monthly
Sunday night prix-fixe dinners ($25) feature ethnic cuisines. Luna is
especially known for its extensive wine list, with more than 900 vin-
tages, and now has a wine bar as well. The rose terrace and courtyard
are open in summer. ✉ *5620 S. Perry St., 99223* ☎ *509/448–2383*
▭ *AE, D, MC, V.*

$–$$ ✕ **Latah Bistro.** Tucked into a strip mall in south Spokane near Qual-
★ chan Golf Course, Dave and Heather Dupree's neighborhood restau-
rant serves an eclectic menu that changes frequently and includes pasta,
duck, pork, beef, shrimp, and ahi tuna. Pizzas, including the aromatic
g.a.s.p. pizza (garlic, artichoke hearts, sundried tomatoes and pesto)

are baked in a wood-burning oven. Try the rosemary cashew-crusted halibut with chive cream sauce and basmati rice, and be sure and save room for dessert, which is a real treat. On Monday, bottles of wine are half off; Thursday martinis are half-price. Enjoy live music on Wednesday. ⊠ *4241 S. Cheney-Spokane Rd., 99224* ☎ *509/838–8338* ☐ *AE, D, MC, V* ⊗ *No lunch Sun.*

$–$$ ✕ **Milford's Fish House.** This brick and terra-cotta tile structure was built in 1925, and the terrazzo floor and tin ceiling are relics of that era. The interior's exposed brick walls and wood details, lit by candles, create a romantic environment in which to enjoy the wide array of seafood dishes and steaks. Everything is fresh here, and it is hard to predict what the menu will include, but you might find such items as tuna, shark, cod, salmon, snapper, mahimahi, clams, and prawns. Pan-fried oysters are a house specialty. ⊠ *719 N. Monroe St., 99201* ☎ *509/326–7251* ☐ *D, MC, V* ⊗ *No lunch.*

$–$$ ✕ **Mizuna Restaurant.** Fresh flowers and redbrick walls lend both color
★   and charm to this downtown eatery. Local produce is the inspiration for such scrumptious vegetarian fare as white cheddar and apple salad and fresh papparadelle pasta with wild mushrooms. Natural Harris Ranch steak is served with olive-oil whipped Yukon golds, seasonal veggies, and honey and thyme–roasted shallots and figs; vegetarians can substitute the beef with grilled field roast. Tofu can be substituted for meat on several other entrées. The wine bar has tastings, and highlights Northwest wines with a five-course winemakers' dinner several times a year. The patio is open for outdoor dining May–September, with live music on the weekends. ⊠ *214 N. Howard St., 99201* ☎ *509/747– 2004* ☐ *AE, D, MC, V* ⊗ *No lunch weekends.*

$–$$ ✕ **Niko's Greek Restaurant and Wine Bar.** Sunlight streaming through the large storefront windows renders the dining room bright and cheerful. Lamb is the specialty here, served in a variety of ways including curried, grilled with rosemary, and grilled on skewers in a marinade of lemon, garlic, and white wine. There are several vegetarian dishes, including feta fettuccine and spanakopita. Niko's boasts the largest wine list in the inland Northwest—more than 1,200 choices. ⊠ *725 W. Riverside Ave., 99201* ☎ *509/624–7444* ☐ *AE, D, MC, V* ⊗ *No lunch.*

$–$$ ✕ **Rock City Grill.** This upbeat restaurant, which is close to Riverfront Park, has excellent pastas and gourmet wood-fired pizzas. Expect some kidding around from the outgoing staff, who will make sure your soft drinks and lemonades never go empty. Save room for such desserts as Snickers pie or tiramisu for two. If you love peanut sauce, take some home; it's available by the bottle. ⊠ *808 W. Main St., 99201* ☎ *509/455–4400* ☐ *AE, D, DC, MC, V.*

$ ✕ **Catacombs.** Catacombs wins accolades for its unique setting and
★   menu. The underground restaurant is in the former boiler room of the Montvale Hotel. Modeling his creation on pubs and underground restaurants he's visited on his travels, owner Rob Brewster has incorporated stone walls, iron chandeliers, lots of brick, and wall tapestries. Try a thin-crust pizza or one of the European specialties, such as Hungarian goulash. For dessert, pretend you're camping and roast s'mores

at your table. ✉*10 S. Monroe St., 99201* ☎*509/838–4610* ▭*AE, D, MC, V* ⊘*No lunch weekends.*

¢–$ ✗**Elk Public House.** This eatery in the relaxed Browne's Addition neighborhood, west of downtown, serves pub food such as lamb sandwiches, pastas, salads, and many vegetarian dishes, together with 18 microbrews, most from the Northwest. A copper bar stands along one wall, in front of a mirror, giving the interior a saloonlike appearance. ✉*1931 W. Pacific Ave., 99201* ☎*509/363–1973* ⌂*Reservations not accepted* ▭*MC, V.*

¢–$ ✗**Europa Pizzaria and Bakery.** The name might fool you: pizza occupies only part of the menu, which also includes lots of homemade pastas, calzones, and salads. Candles on the tables, murals, exposed brick, and wood beams give a European flavor to the dining room and adjacent pub. A 2006 redesign added elegant granite tables. ✉*125 S. Wall St., 99201* ☎*509/455–4051* ▭*AE, D, MC, V.*

¢–$ ✗**Steelhead Bar & Grill.** This casual, pub-style eatery is popular for its convenient downtown location and affordable prices. Housed in one of Spokane's many older brick buildings, the interior design has an urban contemporary vibe, with lots of burnished metal artwork by local artists. About a dozen beers are on tap, but this is a place the whole family can enjoy; there's a decent kids' menu with the usual favorites. Sandwiches and burgers make this a handy place for lunch; kebabs, steak, and halibut-and-chips are heartier fare for dinner. ✉*218 N. Howard, 99201* ☎*509/747–1303* ⌂*Reservations not accepted* ▭*AE, D, DC, MC, V.*

¢ ✗**Mary Lou's Milk Bottle.** Built in 1933, this restaurant is shaped like a gigantic milk bottle. The focus is on burgers, though some Greek dishes are also served. Since 1978 the eatery has been selling homemade ice cream. ✉*802 W. Garland Ave., 99205* ☎*509/325–1772* ▭*No credit cards* ⊘*Closed Sun.*

WHERE TO STAY

$$$–$$$$ ⊡**The Davenport Hotel & Tower.** Elegant rooms in the main hotel have
Fodor'sChoice   hand-carved mahogany furniture and fine Irish linens as well as high-
★   speed Internet access and flat-screen TVs. Though the sleeping areas are not huge, the marble bathrooms, with big soaking tubs and separate showers, are spacious and inviting. You can dine in the restaurant or in the Peacock Lounge, which serves light fare and has a cigar room. On the lobby level are an espresso bar, candy and flower shops, and an art gallery. The 21-floor Tower building opened in 2007, more than doubling the number of rooms and making the Davenport the fourth largest hotel in Washington. The contemporary style rooms have 32-inch flat-screen LCD TVs and marble showers and vanities. The Safari Grill restaurant in the new Tower serves breakfast, lunch, dinner, and a late-night menu. **Pros:** Bathrooms exude luxury, hotel's historical restoration is a marvel to see, abundant resort-like amenities and experienced service. **Cons:** Hotel can sometimes seem too big, Wi-Fi access can be spotty (Ethernet cables available for back-up). ✉*10 S. Post St., 99201* ☎*509/455–8888 or 800/899–1482* 🖷*509/624–4455* ⊕*www.davenporthotel.com* ⬦*563 rooms, 48 suites* ⌂*In-room: safe,*

Ethernet, Wi-Fi. In-hotel: 3 restaurants, room service, bars, pools, gym, spa, laundry service, concierge, airport shuttle, parking (fee), no-smoking rooms, some pets allowed ⊟*AE, D, DC, MC, V.*

$-$$$$ ⛫**Coeur d'Alene Resort.** Each "premier" room at this lakeside high-rise, in
Fodor'sChoice   Idaho and just 31 mi east of Spokane, has either a balcony with terrific
★   views of the water or a fireplace. The lower-price rooms are standard motel fare but offer full access to the resort amenities, including indoor and outdoor pools, two Jacuzzis, steam and sauna room, and fitness center. The top-of-the-line restaurant, Beverly's, is known for its fine Northwest cuisine, superb wine cellar, and incomparable views. The golf course is famous for its unique floating green. Scenic boat cruises tour the lake April–October, and the Holiday Lights Cruise runs from the Friday after Thanksgiving through New Year's Day. **Pros:** Best rooms are worth the splurge, plenty of activities and amenities. **Cons:** Very big hotel, crowded during high season, some guests have complained about maintenance and cleanliness issues in the standard rooms. ⊠*115 S. 2nd St., Exit 11 off I–90, Coeur d'Alene, ID 83814* ☎*208/765–4000 or 800/688–5253* 🖷*208/664–7276* ⊕*www.cdaresort.com* 📞*326 rooms, 11 suites* ♿*In-room: refrigerators, Ethernet (some), Wi-Fi (some). In-hotel: 4 restaurants, golf course, tennis courts, pools, gym, spa, beachfront, water sports, laundry service, concierge, airport shuttle, parking (fee), some pets allowed, no-smoking rooms* ⊟*AE, D, DC, MC, V.*

$$ ⛫**Hotel Lusso.** Italian marble tile ornaments the floor, archways, and
★   fountains of this hotel's elegant lobby. Guest rooms are appointed with European furnishings and many modern amenities. Each evening the hotel hosts a wine and champagne social. **Pros:** Small and intimate, luxurious rooms. **Cons:** Service can be inconsistent, near the bus station, no recreational facilities. ⊠*N. 1 Post St., 99201* ☎*509/747–9750* 🖷*509/747–9751* ⊕*www.hotellusso.com* 📞*36 rooms, 12 suites* ♿*In-room: Wi-Fi. In-hotel: restaurant, room service, bar, concierge, laundry service, airport shuttle, parking (fee), no-smoking rooms* ⊟*AE, D, DC, MC, V* ⊺⊙⍭*CP.*

$ ⛫**Angelica's Bed and Breakfast.** On a tree-lined residential street, this 1907 brick mansion is a paradigm of Victorian elegance, with polished wood floors, lace curtains, beautiful antique furniture, and period lighting. Each individually appointed room has its own charm: Jessica, for example, has a tile fireplace and view of the trees. Five- and seven-course meals are available through on-site culinary services. ⊠*1321 W. 9th Ave., 99204* ☎*509/324–8428* ⊕*www.angelicasbedandbreakfast. com* 📞*4 rooms* ♿*In-room: no phone, no TV (some). In-hotel: public Wi-Fi, no elevator, no-smoking rooms* ⊟*AE, MC, V* ⊺⊙⍭*BP.*

$ ⛫**Red Lion Hotel at the Park.** This hotel is adjacent to Riverfront Park and just a two-block walk from the downtown shopping district. All floors in the main building open onto an atrium lobby; more guest rooms are in two newer wings. Bathrooms were recently upgraded with granite counters and multi-spray shower heads. In summer, cool off in the swimming lagoon's waterfalls and waterslide. An indoor pool, hot tub, and sauna are open year-round. ⊠*303 W. North River*

Dr., 99201 ☎*509/326–8000 or 800/733–5466* 🖷*509/325–7329* ⊕*www.redlion.com* 🗬*400 rooms, 25 suites* ♿*In-room: refrigerator (some), Wi-Fi. In-hotel: 3 restaurants, room service, bar, pools, gym, concierge, executive floor, airport shuttle, parking (no fee), some pets allowed, no-smoking rooms* ▭*AE, D, DC, MC, V.*

$ 🏨**Red Lion River Inn.** East of Riverfront Park in the heart of downtown, this hotel overlooks the Spokane River. The Inn strives for a resort-like atmosphere, with tennis, volleyball, and basketball courts, horseshoes, a Jacuzzi, and two outdoor pools. In summer, enjoy views of the river from the patio while eating at Ripples Riverside Grill restaurant. ✉*N. 700 Division St., 99202* ☎*509/326–5577 or 800/733–5466* 🖷*509/326–1120* ⊕*www.redlion.com* 🗬*245 rooms, 2 suites* ♿*In-room: Wi-Fi. In-hotel: restaurant, room service, bar, tennis courts, pools, gym, laundry services, airport shuttle, parking (no fee), no-smoking rooms, some pets allowed* ▭*AE, D, DC, MC, V* ⦿*EP.*

¢–$ 🏨**Marianna Stolz House.** Across from Gonzaga University on a tree-lined street, this B&B is an American foursquare home built in 1908. Listed on Spokane's historical register, it's decorated with leaded-glass china cabinets, Renaissance Revival armchairs, and original dark-fir woodwork. ✉*427 E. Indiana Ave., 99207* ☎*509/483–4316 or 800/978–6587* 🖷*509/483–6773* ⊕*www.mariannastoltzhouse.com* 🗬*4 rooms, 2 with bath* ♿*In-room: no phone, Wi-Fi. In-hotel: no-smoking rooms* ▭*AE, D, MC, V* ⦿*BP.*

NIGHTLIFE & THE ARTS

NIGHTLIFE At the **Blue Spark** (✉*15 S. Howard St.* ☎*509/838–5787*) the '80s are still trendy, as evidenced by the music and decor. It's known for great service, great drinks, and a party atmosphere. Check out Monday open-mike night. **The Big Easy Concert House** (✉*919 W. Sprague* ☎*509/244–3279*) hosts top national acts in its 1,500-seat venue. On Thursday and Saturday it's a happening dance club for ages 18 and up.

Downstairs at **Dempsey's Brass Rail** (✉*909 W. 1st St.* ☎*509/747–5362*) is Spokane's most popular gay bar and restaurant; upstairs it's a dance club popular with the local college crowd, both gay and straight. There's a cover on weekends and dancing until 4 AM, a daily happy hour, and karaoke Monday and Wednesday nights. If chilling out with light jazz and a good meal is more your style, check out **Ella's Supper Club** (✉*1017 W. 1st St.* ☎*509/747–8243*), housed in Spokane's former Odd Fellows Hall, across the street from the restored Fox Theater. Ella's is open Tuesday–Saturday with live music ($1 cover charge).

THE ARTS **Interplayers Ensemble**(✉*174 S. Howard St.* ☎*509/455–7529*) is a professional theater company whose season runs September–May. The 200-seat **Spokane Civic Theatre** (✉*1020 N. Howard St.* ☎*509/325—2507 or 800/446–9576*) presents musicals and dramas on two stages August–June.

The **Spokane Symphony** (✉*818 W. Riverside Ave.* ☎*509/624–1200*) plays classical and pops concerts from September to May in the newly restored historic Fox Theater, presents special events such as the *Nut-*

cracker at the INB Performing Arts Center, gives free outdoor concerts at city parks in summer, and performs chamber music in the elegant Davenport Hotel.

SPORTS & THE OUTDOORS

CLIMBING You can get a taste of rock climbing on the indoor wall at **Mountain Gear** (⊠*2002 N. Division St.* ☎*509/325–9000 or 800/829–2009*). A three-hour class costs $20; rent climbing shoes for $6 a day. At **Wild Walls** (⊠*202 W. 2nd Ave.* ☎*509/455–9596*), a single climb up the Big Wall costs $5; there are also classes for ages 10 and up, a women's climbing night, and special rates for college students.

> ### A THEATER IS REBORN
>
> Built in 1931, the Fox Theater was an impressive art deco–style venue where generations of Spokanites made memories. In 2000, after years of neglect, it was slated for the wrecking ball when civic- and culture-minded citizens came to the rescue. The Spokane Symphony Orchestra purchased it and began raising funds from public and private sources to restore it and make it the orchestra's permanent home. In November 2007 the Fox reopened with 1,600 seats and a new name–Martin Woldson Theater at The Fox–in honor of the inaugural donor's father.

GOLF **Hangman Valley** (⊠*2210 E. Hang-*
★ *man Valley Rd.* ☎*509/448–1212*), an 18-hole, par-72 course, has greens fees of $18/residents, $24/nonresidents. **Indian Canyon** (⊠*4304 W. West Dr.* ☎*509/747–5353*), an 18-hole course on the slope of a basalt canyon, has great views of North Spokane and Mt. Spokane. The greens fees are $25 weekdays, $27 weekends. **Liberty Lake** (⊠*24403 E. Sprague Ave., Liberty Lake* ☎*509/255–6233*) is near MeadowWood, so avid golfers can visit both and play 36 holes. The greens fees are $18/residents, $24/nonresidents. **MeadowWood** (⊠*24501 E. Valleyway Ave., Liberty Lake* ☎*509/255–9539*) is Spokane's newest golf course. A Scottish-style course, it has been ranked in Washington's top 10. Greens fees are $18/residents, $24/nonresidents.

HIKING The hills around Spokane are laced with trails, almost all of which connect with 37-mi-long Centennial Trail, which winds along the Spokane River. Beginning in Nine Mile Falls, northwest of Spokane, the well-marked trail ends in Idaho. Maps are available at the visitor center at 201 West Main Street. Northwest of downtown at Riverside State Park, a paved trail leads through a 17-million-year-old fossil forest in Deep Creek Canyon. From there it's easy to get to the western end of the Centennial Trail by crossing the suspension bridge at the day-use parking lot; trails heading both left and right will lead to the Centennial.

SKIING **49° North** (⊠*U.S. 395, Chewelah* ☎*509/935–6649 or 866/376–4949* ⊕*www.ski49n.com*), an hour north of Spokane in the Colville National Forest, is a 1,200-acre family-oriented resort. Lift tickets cost $39–$43; snowboards and ski package rentals are about $30. **Mt. Spokane** (⊠*29500 N. Mt. Spokane Park Dr., Mead* ☎*509/238–2220* ⊕*www. mtspokane.com*), 23 mi northeast of Spokane, is a modest downhill resort with a 2,000-foot drop and 10 mi of groomed cross-country ski trails. Snowshoeing is also an option. There's night skiing Wednesday–

Saturday. Lift tickets cost $34–$39. A state Sno-Park permit, available at the resort, is required.

SHOPPING

When the **Flour Mill** (✉ *621 W. Mallon Ave.*) was built in 1895, it was a huge technical innovation. Today it's home to shops, restaurants, and offices. The mill sits virtually atop the falls, north of the river.

Upscale **RiverPark Square** (✉ *808 W. Main St.* ⊕ *www.riverparksquare. com*) has Nordstrom, Talbots, Williams-Sonoma, Restoration Hardware, Pottery Barn, and other national retailers—more than 30 stores in all. Several restaurants are here or nearby, and there's a 20-screen movie theater.

4

MOSES LAKE

45 mi west of Ritzville.

The natural lake from which this sprawling town takes its name seems to be an anomaly in the dry landscape of east-central Washington. But ever since the Columbia Basin Project took shape, there's been water everywhere. Approaching Moses Lake from the west on I–90 you'll pass lushly green irrigated fields; to the east lie vast stretches of wheat. The lakes of this region have more shorebirds than Washington's ocean beaches. Potholes Reservoir is an artificial lake that supports as much wildlife as does the Columbia Wildlife Refuge. The Winchester Wasteway, west of Moses Lake, is a great place to paddle a kayak or canoe and watch birds as you glide along the reedy banks. The airfield north of town was once a major Air Force base and now serves as a training facility for airline pilots.

Claw-shaped, 38-foot-deep, 18-mi-long **Moses Lake** is filled by Crab Creek—which originates in the hills west of Spokane—with three side branches known as Parker Horn, Lewis Horn, and Pelican Horn. The city sprawls over the peninsulas formed by these "horns" and can therefore be a bit difficult to get around. This is the state's second largest lake. ✉ *Hwy. 17, off I–90.*

Fossils collected all over North America, including prehistoric land and marine animals, are exhibited at the **Moses Lake Museum and Art Center.** One gallery also has visual-arts displays. ✉ *228 W. 3rd Ave.* ☎ *509/766–9395* ✉ *Free* ☉ *Tues.–Sat. 11–5.*

☾ Cool off from the hot central Washington sunshine at the **Surf 'n** ★ **Slide Water Park.** In addition to the Olympic-sized pool, there are two 200-foot water slides, a tube slide, a "baby octopus" slide, and diving boards. ✉ *McCosh Park, 4th and Cedar* ☎ *509/766–9246* ✉ *$7* ☉ *Mid-June–mid-Aug., Mon.–Thurs. 11–6:30, Fri. and Sat. 11–7; Memorial Day–mid-June and mid-Aug.–Labor Day, weekdays 4–8, weekends 11–7.*

Reed-lined **Winchester Wasteway,** a slough west of Moses Lake and off I–90, carries excess irrigation waters south toward the Columbia. It's a good place for watching waterfowl, rails, songbirds, muskrats, and beavers. ⊠ *Dodson Rd. S* ☎ *509/754–4624* 🎫 *$11 parking permit* ⊙ *Daily 24 hrs.*

Potholes Reservoir is an artificial lake in a natural depression carved by the huge Spokane Floods. Its waters are contained by O'Sullivan Dam, one of the country's largest earth-filled dams. ⊠ *Hwy. 17 to Hwy. 170* ☎ *509/754–4624* 🎫 *$11 parking permit* ⊙ *Daily–24 hrs.*

Potholes State Park is 20 mi southwest of Moses Lake on the west side of O'Sullivan Dam. Camping and boating, as well as fishing for trout, perch, and walleye, are popular diversions. ⊠ *Hwy. 17 to Hwy. 170* ☎ *360/902–8844 or 888/226–7688* ⊕ *www.parks.wa.gov* 🎫 *$19–$26 for camping* ⊙ *Summer, daily 6:30–dusk; winter, daily 8–dusk.*

Columbia National Wildlife Refuge attracts a great number of birds: hawks, falcons, golden eagles, ducks, sandhill cranes, herons, American avocets, black-necked stilts, and yellow-headed and red-winged blackbirds. The refuge is also home to beavers, muskrats, badgers, and coyotes. It's 8 mi northwest of the town of Othello, about 20 mi southeast of Moses Lake. ⊠ *Refuge headquarters at 735 E. Main St., Othello* ☎ *509/488–2668* ⊕ *http://pacific.fws.gov/refuges/field/wa_columbia. htm* 🎫 *Free* ⊙ *Daily dawn–dusk; office open Mon.–Thurs. 7–4:30, Fri. 7–3:30.*

QUINCY

34 mi northwest of Moses Lake.

On the fences along I–90 to George and north on Highway 281 to Quincy, crop identification signs highlight what the Quincy Valley is known for: agriculture. From Thanksgiving to New Year's Eve, these same fields are filled with Christmas motion-light displays, powered by electricity from farmers' irrigation lines—a delightful sight for highway travelers in the dark winter nights. Agriculture hasn't always been king in this area. Though the rich soils attracted many settlers after the railroad made the region accessible in the early 1900s, several serious droughts proved that Mother Nature could not be relied on to water the crops consistently. In the mid-1930s the federal government began to assist with irrigation plans and by the early 1950s the first systems were in place.

Today the area has 200,000 irrigable acres growing corn, alfalfa, wheat, potatoes, seed, apples, and more. An annual Farmer Consumer Awareness Day is held the second Saturday of September, with farm tours, entertainment, food, arts and crafts, and plenty of fresh produce. Tourism is also growing here, with visitors from across the state and beyond coming to summer concerts at the Gorge Amphitheatre, touring wineries between Quincy and Wenatchee, and hiking and climbing near the Columbia River.

The 20,000-seat **Gorge Amphitheatre** has won accolades as best outdoor concert venue due to its fine acoustics and stunning setting overlooking the Columbia River, a setting compared to the Grand Canyon's. Set in one of the sunniest parts of the state, the concert season runs from May to September. Concertgoers often overnight at the adjacent campground or at motels and hotels in Quincy, Moses Lake, and Ellensburg. ⊠*754 Silica Rd. NW, George* ☏*206/628–0888 tickets* ⊕*www.hob. com/venues/concerts/gorge.*

WHERE TO STAY

$$–$$$$
Fodor'sChoice
★

🏨 **Cave B Inn at Sagecliffe.** Washington's first destination winery resort is built on (and into) ancient basalt cliffs 900 feet above the Columbia River. The 15 cliff houses, cavern (with 12 rooms), and inn (with three rooms, restaurant, meeting rooms, and spacious lobby) all were designed to blend into the natural environment. The buildings' exterior walls are made of precast concrete embedded with rocks taken from the land. The inn's restaurant, Tendrils ($$–$$$), highlights local produce and Northwest beef and seafood, complemented by the wines produced on-site. Guests can tour the Cave B Estate Winery to taste and learn about the wine-making process. A pleasant spa offers an array of treatments. The outdoor pool is open seasonally, and a golf course is set to open in 2009. Cave B Inn is the first step in a grand plan of owners Vince and Carol Bryan, who want to create a cultural village retreat on this and adjacent land, featuring performances by theater groups and musicians, artists-in-residence, and classes for all ages. ⊠*344 Silica Rd. NW, 98851* ☏*509/785–2283 or 888/785–2283* 🖷*509/785–3670* ⊕*www.cavebinn.com* ⚒ *In-room: refrigerator, Ethernet, Wi-Fi, DVD. In-hotel: restaurant, room service, gym, pool, spa, no-smoking rooms, some pets allowed* ▭*AE, MC, V.*

COULEE DAM NATIONAL RECREATION AREA

60 mi northeast of Ephrata, 239 mi northeast of Seattle, 87 mi northwest of Spokane.

Grand Coulee Dam is the one of the world's largest concrete structures. At almost a mile long, it justly deserves the moniker of Eighth Technological Wonder of the World. Beginning in 1932, 9,000 men excavated 45 million cubic yards of rock and soil and dammed the Grand Coulee, a gorge created by the Columbia River, with 12 million cubic yards of concrete—enough to build a sidewalk the length of the equator. By the time the dam was completed in 1941, 77 men had perished and 11 towns were submerged under the newly formed Roosevelt Lake. The waters backed up behind the dam turned eastern Washington's arid soil into fertile farming land, but not without consequence: salmon fishing stations that were a source of food and spiritual identity for Native Americans were destroyed. Half the dam was built on the Colville Indian Reservation on the north shore of the Columbia; the Colville tribes later received restitution in excess of $75 million from the U.S. government.

In 1946 most of Roosevelt Lake and the grassy and pine woodland hills surrounding it were designated the Coulee Dam National Recreation Area. Crown Point Vista, about 5 mi west of Grand Coulee on Highway 174, may have the best vantage for photographs of the dam, Roosevelt Lake, Rufus Woods Lake (below the dam), and the town of Coulee Dam.

After nightfall from Memorial Day through September, the dam is transformed into an unlikely entertainment complex by an extravagant, free laser-light show. With 300-foot eagles flying across the white water that flows over the dam, the show is spectacular, if hokey. The audio portion is broadcast on 90.1 FM. Show up early to get a good seat. The show starts at 10 PM Memorial Day–July, 9:30 PM in August, and 8:30 PM in September.

  The **Coulee Dam National Recreation Area Visitors Arrival Center** has colorful displays about the dam, a 13-minute film on the site's geology and the dam's construction, and information about the laser-light show. The U.S. Bureau of Reclamation, which oversees operation and maintenance of the dam, conducts tours year-round, weather and maintenance schedules permitting. You can also pick up a self-guided historical walking tour that will take you from the visitors center through the old part of town, across the bridge, and into the old engineers' town. ⊠ *Hwy. 155 north of Grand Coulee* ☎ *509/633–9265, 509/633–3074, or 509/633–3838* ⊕ *www.grandcouleedam.org* ⎙ *Free* ⊙ *Late May– July, daily 8:30 AM–11 PM; Aug., daily 8:30 AM–10:30 PM; Sept., daily 8:30 AM–9:30 PM; Oct. and Nov. and Feb.–late May, 9–5.*

The **Lake Roosevelt National Recreation Area** contains the 150-mi-long lake created by the Columbia River when it was backed up by Grand Coulee Dam. Several Native American villages, historic sites, and towns lie beneath the waters. ⊠ *1008 Crest Dr., headquarters address* ☎ *509/633–9441* ⊕ *www.nps.gov/laro* ⎙ *Free day use; camping $10 May–Sept., $5 Oct.–Apr.* ⊙ *Daily dawn–dusk.*

At **Steamboat Rock State Park** a 2,200-foot-high flat-topped lava butte rises 1,000 feet above Banks Lake, the 31-mi-long irrigation reservoir filled with water from Lake Roosevelt by giant pumps and siphons. Water is distributed from the south end of the lake throughout the Columbia Basin. The state park has campsites and is popular with boaters and anglers. ⊠ *Hwy. 155, 16 mi north of Coulee City* ☎ *360/902– 8844 or 888/226–7688* ⊕ *www.parks.wa.gov* ⎙ *Camping $17–$26* ⊙ *Daily 6:30–dusk.*

Sun Lakes State Park is a high point in the coulee. Campgrounds, picnic areas, and a state-run golf course attract visitors year-round; in summer the lakes bristle with boaters. From the bluffs on U.S. 2, west of the dam, you can get a great view over this enormous canyon. To the north, the banks of the lake are hemmed in by cliffs. At Dry Falls, the upstream erosion of the canyon caused by the floods stops. Below Dry Falls, steep, barren cliffs—some 1,000 feet tall—rise from green meadows, marshes, and blue lakes bordered by trees. Most of the water is irrigation water seeping through the porous rock, but the effect is no less spectacular. Eagles and ravens soar along the cliffs, while songbirds, ducks, and geese hang out in the bottomlands.

South of the Sun Lakes, the landscape turns even wilder. The coulee narrows and the cliffs often look like they are on fire, an illusion created by the bold patterns of orange and yellow lichens. The waters of the lakes change, too. The deep blue waters of the small lakes below Dry Falls are replaced by lapis lazuli in the Sun Lakes and turn milky farther south. Presentations at the park's interpretive center at Dry Falls survey the area's geology, and an excellent film describes the great floods. ⊠ *From Grand Coulee Dam take Hwy. 155 south, U.S. 2 east, and Hwy. 17 south* ☎ *360/902–8844 or 888/226–7688* ⊕ *www.parks. wa.gov* ⊠ *$17–$24 camping* ⊙ *Daily 6:30–dusk.*

Highway 155 passes through the **Colville Indian Reservation,** one of the largest reservations in Washington, with about 7,700 enrolled members of the Colville Confederated Tribes. This was the final home for Chief Joseph and the Nez Perce, who fought a series of fierce battles with the U.S. Army in the 1870s after the U.S. government enforced a treaty that many present-day historians agree was fraudulent. Chief Joseph lived on the Colville reservation until his death in 1904. There's a memorial to him off Highway 155 east of the town of Nespelem, 17 mi north of the dam; four blocks away (two east and two north) is his grave. You can drive through the reservation's undeveloped landscape, and except for a few highway signs you'll feel like you've time-traveled to pioneer days. For a better understanding of frontier history, visit the **Colville Confederated Tribes Museum and Gift Shop** (⊠ *512 Mead Way, ½ mi north of Grand Coulee Dam via Hwy. 155, Coulee Dam* ☎ *509/633–0751* ⊠ *Free* ⊙ *Apr.–Dec., Mon.–Sat. 10–6*).

WHERE TO STAY & EAT

¢–$$ ✕**Melody Restaurant.** This casual, family-friendly spot with excellent views of Grand Coulee Dam prepares sandwiches, steaks, seafood, and pasta, and is open for breakfast. ⊠ *512 River Dr., Coulee Dam 99116* ☎ *509/633–1151* ⊟ *AE, D, MC, V.*

¢ ✕**Flo's Cafe.** One mile south of the dam, this diner dishes up heaps of local color along with loggers' food: biscuits and gravy, corned-beef hash, hamburgers, chicken-fried steak, and chef's salads. Flo's is open for breakfast but closes at 1. ⊠ *316 Spokane Way, Grand Coulee 99133* ☎ *509/633–3216* ⊟ *No credit cards* ⊙ ⊘ *losed Tues. No dinner.*

$ 🏨**Columbia River Inn.** The spacious, brightly colored rooms all have private decks at this inn across the street from Grand Coulee Dam, with easy access to hiking trails and fishing. The sauna and hot tub are useful amenities after a day of active recreation. ⊠ *10 Lincoln St., Coulee Dam 99116* ☎ *509/633–2100 or 800/633–6421* 🖷 *509/633–2633* ⊕ *www.columbiariverinn.com* ⇦ *35 rooms* △ *In-room: refrigerator, kitchen (some), Wi-Fi. In-hotel: pool, gym, no elevator, laundry facilities, no-smoking rooms* ⊟ *AE, D, MC, V.*

¢ 🏨**Coulee House Motel.** This motel with "the best dam view in town" (someone had to say it) has modern rooms decorated in earth tones.

The gift shop is open daily and well stocked with souvenirs. ✉*110 Roosevelt Ave., Coulee Dam99116* ☎*509/633–1101 or 800/715–7767* 🖶*509/633–1416* ⊕*www.couleehouse.com* 🛏*61 rooms* ⌂*In-room: kitchen (some), refrigerator, DVD (some), ethernet, Wi-Fi. In-hotel: Ethernet, pool, gym, no elevator, laundry facilities, some pets allowed, no-smoking rooms* ▤*AE, D, DC, MC, V.*

EASTERN WASHINGTON ESSENTIALS

BY AIR

Spokane International Airport is the main hub for air travel in eastern Washington. Smaller airports include Pullman, Tri-Cities, Walla Walla, and Lewiston, Idaho (across the border from Clarkston). Spokane International Airport is served by the airlines listed below, including Horizon, which also serves the smaller regional airports. Tri-Cities is served by Delta and United Express.

Contacts **Alaska Airlines** (☎*800/426–0333* ⊕*www.alaskair.com*). **Delta** (☎*800/221–1212* ⊕*www.delta.com*). **ExpressJet** (☎*888/958–9538* ⊕*www. expressjet.com*). **Frontier Airlines** (☎*800/432–1359* ⊕*www.frontierairlines.com*). **Horizon** (☎*800/547–9308* ⊕*www.horizonair.com*). **Lewiston-Nez Perce County Airport** (✉*406 Burrell Ave., Lewiston* ☎*208/746–7962* ⊕*www.lcairport.net*). **Northwest** (☎*800/225–2525* ⊕*www.nwa.com*). **Pullman-Moscow Regional Airport** (✉*3200 Airport Complex N, Pullman* ☎*509/338–3223* ⊕*www.pullman wa.gov/airport/*). **Southwest** (☎*800/435–9792* ⊕*www.southwest.com*). **Spokane International Airport** (✉*9000 W. Airport Dr., Spokane* ☎*509/455–6455* ⊕*www. spokaneairports.net*). **Tri-Cities Airport** (✉*3601 N. 20th, Pasco* ☎*509/547–6352* ⊕*www.portofpasco.org*). **United** (☎*800/241–6522* ⊕*www.united.com*). **US Airways** (☎*800/428–4322* ⊕*www.americawest.com*).

Walla Walla Regional Airport (✉*45 Terminal Loop Rd., Walla Walla* ☎*509/525–3100* ⊕*www.wallawallaairport.com*).

AIRPORTS & TRANSFERS Many hotels offer a free airport shuttle service. Spokane Transit runs about hourly, 6–6 daily, and costs $1. Wheatland Express has shuttle service between the Spokane Airport and Pullman and Moscow, Idaho. Reservations are recommended; the cost is $39 one-way. TransX Taxi and Yellow Cab are two companies that serve the Spokane area. Metered fares run $1.80–$2.30 a mile. A taxi ride from the Spokane airport to downtown costs about $$16–$20.

Contacts **TransX Taxi** (☎*509/536–1666*). **Spokane Transit Authority** (☎*509/456–7277*). **Wheatland Express** (☎*509/334–2200 or 800/334–2207*). **Yellow Cab** (☎*509/624–4321*).

BY BUS

Greyhound Lines runs daily to Spokane from Seattle (5–6½ hours) and Portland (8–13 hours). The line serves Ephrata, Moses Lake, Okanogan, Omak, Pasco, Pullman, Quincy, and Ritzville. Spokane has an extensive local bus system. The fare is $1; exact change or a token is required. Pick up schedules, maps, and tokens at the bus depot or the Plaza, the major downtown transfer point.

Contacts **The Plaza** (✉ *701 W. Riverside Ave.* ☎ *509/456–7277* ⊕ *www. spokanetransit.com*). **Greyhound Lines** (✉ *221 W. 1st Ave., in Amtrak station* ☎ *509/624–5251* ⊕ *www.greyhound.com*).

BY CAR

Spokane can be reached by I–90 from the east or west. U.S. 395 runs north from Spokane to Colville and the Canadian border. U.S. 195 traverses southeastern Washington to Pullman. Leave U.S. 195 at Colfax, heading southwest on Highway 26 and then 127, and finally U.S. 12 to Dayton and Walla Walla. South of I–90, U.S. 395 leads to the Tri-Cities from the east; the Tri-Cities can also be accessed via I–82 from the west. Gas stations along the main highways cater to truckers and some are open 24 hours.

Downtown Spokane is laid out along a true grid: streets run north–south, avenues east–west; many are one-way. Spokane's heaviest traffic is on I–90 between Spokane and Spokane Valley on weekday evenings. Metered parking is available on city streets; there are also several downtown lots.

BY TRAIN

Amtrak's *Empire Builder* runs daily between Spokane and Seattle and between Spokane and Portland, stopping at points in between (including Ephrata and Pasco). Reservations are recommended. Round-trip fares vary depending on season; $85 is a typical fare between Seattle and Spokane.

Contacts **Amtrak** (☎ *800/872–7245* ⊕ *www.amtrak.com*).

EMERGENCIES

Hospitals **Deaconess Medical Center** (✉ *800 W. 5th Ave., Spokane* ☎ *509/458–5800*). **Kennewick General Hospital** (✉ *900 S. Auburn St., Kennewick* ☎ *509/586–6111*). **Pullman Regional Hospital** (✉ *835 S.E. Bishop Blvd., Pullman* ☎ *509/332–2541*). **Samaritan Hospital** (✉ *801 E. Wheeler Rd., Moses Lake* ☎ *509/765–5606*). **Sacred Heart Medical Center** (✉ *101 W. 8th Ave., Spokane* ☎ *509/474–3131*). **Walla Walla General Hospital** (✉ *1025 S. 2nd Ave., Walla Walla* ☎ *509/525–0480*).

VISITOR INFORMATION

Contacts **Clarkston Chamber of Commerce** (✉ *502 Bridge St., 99403* ☎ *509/758–7712 or 800/933–2128* ⊕ *www.clarkstonchamber.org*). **Colville Chamber of Commerce** (✉ *121 E. Astor Ave., 99114* ☎ *509/684–5973* ⊕ *www. colville.com*). **Ephrata Chamber of Commerce** (✉ *90 Alder St. NW, 98823* ☎ *509/754–4656* ⊕ *www.ephratawachamber.com*). **Grand Coulee Dam Area Chamber of Commerce** (✉ *306 Midway, Grand Coulee 99133* ☎ *800/268–5332 or 509/268–5332* ⊕ *www.grandcouleedam.org*). **Moses Lake Area Chamber of Commerce** (✉ *324 S. Pioneer Way, Moses Lake 98837* ☎ *509/765–7888 or 800/992–6234* ⊕ *www.moseslake.com*). **Pullman Chamber of Commerce** (✉ *415 N. Grand Ave.* ☎ *509/334–3565 or 800/365–6948* ⊕ *www.pullmanchamber.com*). **Spokane Area Visitors Information** (✉ *201 W. Main St., 99201* ☎ *509/747–3230 or 888/776–5263* ⊕ *www.visitspokane.com*). **Tri-Cities Visitor and Convention**

Bureau (✉ *6951 W. Grandridge Blvd., Kennewick 99302* ☎ *509/735-8486 or 800/254-5824* ⊕ *www.visittri-cities.com*). **Walla Walla Valley Chamber of Commerce** (✉ *29 E. Sumach St., 99362* ☎ *509/525-0850 or 877/998-4748* ⊕ *www. wwvchamber.com*). **West Plains Chamber of Commerce** (✉ *201 1st St., Cheney 99004* ☎ *509/235-8480 or 509/299-8480* ⊕ *westplainschamber.org*).

Vancouver & Victoria

WORD OF MOUTH

"Vancouver is situated in a gorgeous setting. You need at least one full day in Vancouver. On the other hand, it has so much to offer that you could spend a week there."

—Judy_In_Calgary

"The Inner Harbor in Victoria is where 90% of the tourist attractions are located. It's very tiny physically—you can walk its entirety in one morning—so having a car is pointless. If you wish to see Butchart Gardens . . . you can take public transit, or hop on one of the many tour buses that organize packaged trips there."

—Carmanah

Updated by
Chris McBeath

VANCOUVER IS A YOUNG CITY, even by North American standards, but what it lacks in history, it makes up for with natural beauty and a multicultural vitality that has the readers of *Condé Nast Traveler* (those arbiters of taste) consistently rating it as one of the world's top cities.

The mountains and seascape make Vancouver an outdoor playground for hiking, skiing, kayaking, cycling, and sailing—and so much more—while the cuisine and arts scenes are equally diverse, reflecting the makeup of Vancouver's ethnic (predominantly Asian) mosaic. And despite all this vibrancy, the city exudes an easy West Coast style that can make New York or London feel edgy and claustrophobic to some.

More than 8 million visitors each year come to this, Canada's third-largest metropolitan area, and thousands more are expected as the city gears up to meet the challenges of co-hosting (with Whistler) the Olympic and Paralympic Winter Games in 2010. Because of its peninsula location, traffic flow is a contentious issue, and the construction of new rapid-transit lines and Olympic sites through to 2009 can make getting around by car these days pretty frustrating. Thankfully, Vancouver is deliciously walkable, especially in the downtown core, and the congestion and construction cranes needn't get in the way of enjoying the city and its people.

The mild climate, exquisite natural scenery, and relaxed outdoor lifestyle keep attracting new residents, and the number of visitors is increasing for the same reasons. People often get their first glimpse of Vancouver when catching an Alaskan cruise, and many return at some point to spend more time here.

VANCOUVER

The heart of Vancouver is the city's downtown core: it includes the main business district between Robson Street and the harborfront, Stanley Park, Yaletown, and the West End. Elsewhere in the city you'll find other places of interest: the North Shore across Burrard Inlet; Granville Island, south of downtown across English Bay in the West End and the suburb of Richmond, south of the city near the airport.

DOWNTOWN & GASTOWN

Numbers in the margin correspond to the Downtown Vancouver map.

Museums and buildings of architectural and historical significance are the primary sightseeing draws in this part of downtown Vancouver, but there's also plenty of fine shopping. The intersection of Granville and Georgia streets is considered the city's epicenter, though it's somewhat disrupted at the moment by the construction of the new SkyTrain line.

TOP REASONS TO GO

STANLEY PARK
The views, the activities, the natural wilderness beauty here are quintessential Vancouver.

Museum of Anthropology at UBC.

The phenomenal collection of art and cultural artifacts, and the incredible setting make this Vancouver's must-see museum.

THE SEABUS
The trip across Burrard Inlet is the cheapest cruise around, and offers some of the neatest photo angles of Vancouver's working harbor.

KITSILANO BEACHES
Follow the coastline road to the University of British Columbia and you'll travel past a magnificent array of beaches, from grass-edged shores to windswept stretches of sand, to cliff-side coves so private that clothing is optional.

KAYAKING INTO INDIAN ARM
Barely 30 minutes from downtown, the fjordic landscape is stunning (*see* Vancouver Outdoors, *especially* Takaya Tours, *for more info*).

5

The east side of downtown gives way to Gastown, which is touted as an up-and-coming hip neighborhood but is still really geared to tourists, with quaint cobblestone streets, Victorian era–styled streetlamps, and a plethora of souvenir shops from tacky to tasteful. Nevertheless, Vancouverites hold it dear to their hearts.

When Gastown, along with Chinatown, was declared a historic district in 1971, it became the focus of a huge revitalization effort. Warehouses that once lined the shorefront (note some of the "wavy" shapes of the buildings), were remodeled to house boutiques, cafés, loft apartments, and souvenir shops.

MAIN ATTRACTIONS

❸ The Bill Reid Gallery of Northwest Coast Art. Vancouver's new aboriginal art gallery, named after one of B.C.'s preeminent artists, Bill Reid (1920–98), is set to open May 10, 2008. Reid's legacy of works includes wood carvings, jewelry, print, and sculpture. ⊠*639 Hornby St., Downtown* ☎*604/682–3455* ⊕*www.billreidgallery.com.*

❹ Canada Place. When Vancouver hosted the Expo '86 world's fair, this former cargo pier was transformed into the Canadian pavilion. Extending four city blocks (about a mile and a half) north into Burrard Inlet, the complex mimics the style and size of a luxury ocean liner, with exterior promenades and open deck space. The Teflon-coated fiberglass roof, shaped like five sails (the material was invented by NASA and once used in astronaut spacesuits!), has become a Vancouver skyline landmark. Home to Vancouver's main cruise-ship terminal, Canada Place can accommodate up to four luxury liners at once. It's also home to the luxurious **Pan Pacific Hotel** and the **Vancouver Convention and Exhibition Centre** (☎*604/647–7390*) ⊠*999 Canada Place Way, Downtown* ☎*604/775–7200* ⊕*www.canadaplace.ca.*

OFF THE BEATEN PATH

Vancouver Art Gallery. Painter Emily Carr's haunting evocations of the British Columbian hinterland are among the attractions at Western Canada's largest art gallery. Carr (1871–1945), a grocer's daughter from Victoria, fell in love with the wilderness around her and shocked middle-class Victorian society by running off to paint it. Her work accentuates the mysticism and the danger of B.C.'s wilderness and records the diminishing presence of native cultures during that era (there's something of a renaissance now). The gallery, which also hosts touring historical and contemporary exhibitions, is housed in a 1911 courthouse that Canadian architect Arthur Erickson redesigned in the early 1980s as part of the Robson Square redevelopment. ⊠ *750 Hornby St., Downtown* ☎ *604/662–4719* ⊕ *www.vanartgallery. bc.ca* 🖾 *C$19.50; higher for some exhibits; by donation Thurs. 5–9* ☺ *Mon.–Wed. and Fri.–Sun. 10–5:30, Tues. and Thurs. 10–9.*

❺ Vancouver Lookout! The lookout looks like a flying saucer stuck atop a high-rise and at 553 feet high, it affords one of the best views of Vancouver. A glass elevator whizzes you up 50 stories to the circular observation deck. On a clear day you can see Vancouver Island and Mt. Baker in Washington State. The top-floor restaurant makes one complete revolution per hour; the elevator ride up is free for diners. ■ TIP➔ **Tickets are good all day, so you can visit in daytime and return for another look after dark.** ⊠ *555 W. Hastings St., Downtown* ☎ *604/689–0421* ⊕ *www.vancouverlookout.com* 🖾 *C$13* ☺ *May–Sept., daily 8:30 AM–10:30 PM; Oct.–Apr., daily 9–9.*

ALSO WORTH SEEING

❷ Christ Church Cathedral. The oldest church in Vancouver was built between 1889 and 1895. Constructed in the Gothic style, this Anglican church looks like the parish church of an English village from the outside, though underneath its sandstone-clad exterior it's made of Douglas fir from what is now south Vancouver. ⊠ *690 Burrard St., Downtown* ☎ *604/682–3848* ⊕ *www.cathedral.vancouver.bc.ca* ☺ *Weekdays 10–4. Services Sun. at 8 AM, 10:30 AM, and 9:30 PM; weekdays at 12:10 PM.*

❻ Steam clock. An underground steam system, which also heats many local buildings, supplies the world's first steam clock—possibly Vancouver's most-photographed attraction. On the quarter hour a steam whistle rings out the Westminster chimes, and on the hour a huge cloud of steam spews from the apparatus. ⊠ *Water and Cambie Sts., Gastown.*

CHINATOWN

Vancouver's Chinatown, declared a historic district in 1971, is one of the oldest and largest in North America. Many Chinese immigrants came to British Columbia during the 1850s seeking their fortunes in the Cariboo gold rush that inspired them to name the place Gum-shan, or Gold Mountain. Thousands more arrived in the 1880s, recruited as laborers to build the Canadian Pacific Railway.

Today, however, Chinatown is a vital neighborhood and although a large percentage of Vancouver's Chinese community has shifted to suburban Richmond, there's still a wonderful buzz of authenticity in the open-front markets, bakeries, and herbalist and import shops.

MAIN ATTRACTION

❾ Dr. Sun Yat-Sen Classical Chinese Garden. The first authentic Ming Dynasty–style garden outside China, this small garden was built in 1986 by 52 artisans from Suzhou, China. It incorporates design elements and traditional materials from several of Suzhou's centuries-old private gardens. No power tools, screws, or nails were used in the construction. Guided tours (45 minutes long), included in the ticket price, are conducted on the hour between mid-June and the end of August (call ahead for off-season tour times); they are valuable for understanding the philosophy and symbolism that are central to the garden's design. ⊠ *578 Carrall St., Chinatown* ☎ *604/662–3207* ⊕ *www.vancouverchinesegarden.com* ⌨ *C$8.75* ⊗ *May–mid-June and Sept., daily 10–6; mid-June–Aug., daily 9:30–7; Oct., daily 10–4:30; Nov.–Apr., Tues.–Sun. 10–4:30.*

Fodor'sChoice ★

ALSO WORTH SEEING

❿ Chinese Cultural Centre Museum and Archives. This Ming Dynasty–style facility is dedicated to promoting an understanding of Chinese-Canadian history and culture. A compelling permanent exhibit on the first floor traces the history of Chinese Canadians in British Columbia. The art gallery upstairs hosts traveling exhibits by Chinese and Canadian artists. Across the street is the Chinatown Memorial Monument, commemorating the Chinese-Canadian community's contribution to the city, province, and country. ⊠ *555 Columbia St., Chinatown* ☎ *604/658–8880* ⊕ *www.cccvan.com* ⌨ *C$4, Tues. by donation* ⊗ *Tues.– Sun. 11–5.*

❼ Vancouver Chinatown Millennium Gate. This four-pillar, three-story high, brightly painted arch spanning Pender Street was erected in 2002 to mark the millennium and commemorate the Chinese community's role in Vancouver's history.

YALETOWN & FALSE CREEK

In 1985–86 the provincial government cleaned up a derelict industrial site on the north shore of False Creek, built a world's fair, and invited everyone; 20 million people showed up at Expo '86. Now the site of the fair has become one of the largest urban-redevelopment projects in North America as well as the site for the upcoming Winter Olympics Athlete's Village.

Tucked into the forest of green-glass condo towers is the old warehouse district of Yaletown. It's one of the city's most fashionable neighborhoods, and the Victorian-brick loading docks have become terraces for cappuccino bars.

Numbers in the margin correspond to the Vancouver map.

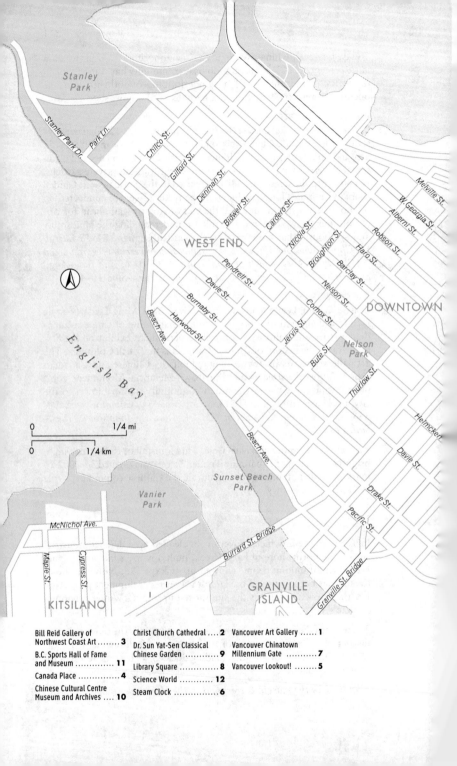

Stanley
Park

Stanley Park Dr.

Park Ln.

Chilco St.

Gilford St.

Denman St.

Bidwell St.

Cardero St.

Nicola St.

Broughton St.

Haro St.

Robson St.

Alberni St.

W. Georgia St.

Melville St.

WEST END

Pendrell St.

Davie St.

Barclay St.

Nelson St.

Cornox St.

Jervis St.

Bute St.

Nelson
Park

DOWNTOWN

Burnaby St.

Harwood St.

Beach Ave.

Thurlow St.

Helmcken

English Bay

0   1/4 mi

0   1/4 km

Beach Ave.

Davie St.

Drake St.

Sunset Beach
Park

Pacific St.

Vanier
Park

McNichol Ave.

Maple St.

Cypress St.

Burrard St. Bridge

GRANVILLE
ISLAND

Granville St. Bridge

KITSILANO

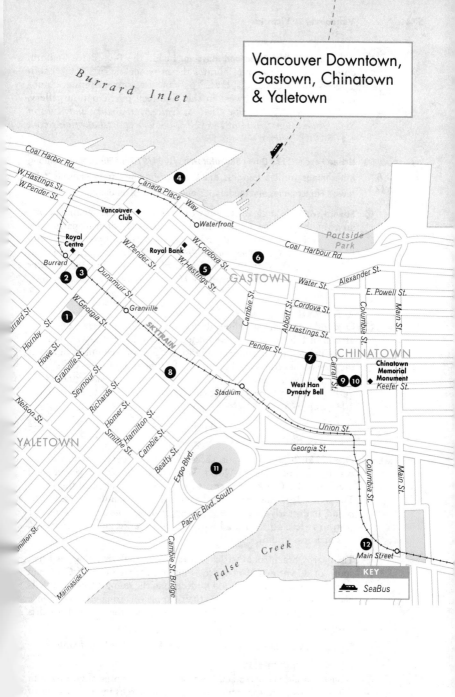

Vancouver Downtown, Gastown, Chinatown & Yaletown

Burrard Inlet

Coal Harbor Rd.

W. Hastings St.

W. Pender St.

Canada Place Way

4

Vancouver Club

Waterfront

Royal Centre

Royal Bank

W. Pender St.

Burrard

2 **3**

Dunsmuir St.

W. Cordova St.

W. Hastings St.

5

GASTOWN

Coal Harbour Rd.

Portside Park

Water St.

Alexander St.

6

E. Powell St.

W. Georgia St.

Granville

1

Cambie St.

Cordova St.

Abbott St.

Hastings St.

Columbia St.

Main St.

CHINATOWN

Hornby St.

Howe St.

Granville St.

Seymour St.

SKYTRAIN

Pender St.

7

Carrall St.

Chinatown Memorial Monument

Keefer St.

8

West Han Dynasty Bell

9 **10**

Richards St.

Homer St.

Hamilton St.

Stadium

Smithe St.

Cambie St.

Beatty St.

YALETOWN

Nelson St.

Union St.

Georgia St.

Columbia St.

Main St.

11

Expo Blvd.

Pacific Blvd. South

Hamilton St.

Cambie St. Bridge

Marinaside Ct.

False

Creek

12

Main Street

KEY

⛴ SeaBus

MAIN ATTRACTIONS

⑪ **B.C. Sports Hall of Fame and Museum.** Inside the B.C. Place Stadium
complex, this museum celebrates the province's sports achievers in
a series of historical displays. You can test your sprinting, climbing, and throwing prowess in the high-tech participation gallery.
⊠*B.C. Place, 777 Pacific Blvd. S, Gate A, at Beatty and Robson
Sts., Downtown* ☎*604/687–5520* ⊕*www.bcsportshalloffame.com*
⊠*C$10* ☉*Daily 10–5.*

**NEED A
BREAK?**　　**Urban Fare** (⊠*177 Davie St., Yaletown* ☎*604/975-7550*) supplies, among
other things, truffles, foie gras, and bread air-freighted from France to Yaletown's Francophiles and foodies. It's open daily 6 AM–midnight.

⑫ **Science World.** In a gigantic, shiny dome built over the Omnimax theater, this hands-on science center encourages children to participate
in interactive exhibits and demonstrations. ⊠*1455 Québec St., False
Creek* ☎*604/443-7443 or 604/443–7440* ⊕*www.scienceworld.
bc.ca* ⊠*Science World C$16, Science World and Omnimax theater
C$18.75* ☉*July–Labor Day, daily 10–6; Sept.–June, weekdays 10–5,
weekends 10–6.*

ALSO WORTH SEEING

❽ **Library Square.** The spiraling library building, open plazas, and lofty
atrium of Library Square, completed in the mid-1990s, were built to
evoke images of the Colosseum in Rome. A high-tech public library is
the core of the structure; the outer edge of the spiral houses cafés and a
handful of boutiques. ⊠*350 W. Georgia St., Downtown* ☎*604/331-
3600* ⊕*www.vpl.vancouver.bc.ca* ☉*Mon.–Thurs. 10–9, Fri. and Sat.
10–6, Sun. 1–5.*

GRANVILLE ISLAND & KITSILANO

Fodor'sChoice　One of North America's most successful urban-redevelopment schemes
★　was just a sandbar until World War I, when the federal government
dredged False Creek for access to the sawmills that lined the shore.
The sludge from the creek was heaped onto the sandbar to create the
island. In the early '70s, the federal government came up with a creative
plan to redevelop the island with a public market, marine activities,
and artisans' studios.

The nearby beachfront district of Kitsilano (popularly known as Kits),
south of downtown Vancouver, is among the trendiest of Canadian
neighborhoods. After a period of decline in the mid-20th century, Kits
became a haven for hippies and their yuppie offspring who have since
restored many of the wood-frame houses, and the neighborhood is
once again chic.

Numbers in the margin correspond to the Granville Island map.

MAIN ATTRACTIONS

❶ **Granville Island Public Market.** Because no chain stores are allowed in
★　this 50,000-square-foot building, each shop here is unique. Dozens of
stalls sell locally grown produce direct from the farm; others sell crafts,

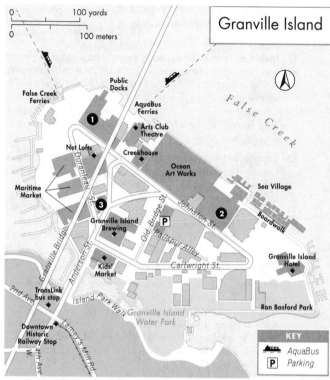

chocolates, cheese, fish, meat, flowers, and exotic foods. On Thursday in summer, market gardeners sell fruit and vegetables from trucks outside. At the north end of the market you can pick up a snack, lunch, or coffee at one of the many food stalls. ☒*1689 Johnston St., Granville Island* ☎*604/666–6477* ⊕*www.granvilleisland.com* ☉*Daily 9–7.*

☾ **Kitsilano Beach.** Picnic sites, a playground, tennis courts, beach volleyball, a restaurant, take-out concessions, Vancouver's biggest outdoor pool, and some fine people-watching can all be found at Kits Beach. ☒*2305 Cornwall Ave., Kitsilano* ☎*604/731–0011 pool (summer only)* ⊕*www.vancouver.ca/parks/* ☒*Beach free, pool C$4.85* ☉*Pool: late May–mid-June, weekdays noon–8:45, weekends 10–8:45; mid-June–Labor Day, weekdays 7 AM–8:45 PM, weekends 10–8:45; Labor Day–mid-Sept., weekdays 7 AM–7:15 PM, weekends 10–7:15.*

☾ **H. R. MacMillan Space Centre.** The interactive exhibits and high-tech learning systems at this museum include a Virtual Voyages ride, where visitors can take a simulated space journey (definitely not for those afraid of flying); GroundStation Canada, showcasing Canada's achievements in space; and the Cosmic Courtyard, full of hands-on space-oriented exhibits including a moon rock and a computer program that shows what you would look like as an alien. ☒*Vanier Park, 1100 Chestnut*

St., Kitsilano ☎*604/738–7827* ⊕*www.hrmacmillanspacecentre.com* ☜*C$15* ⊙*July and Aug., daily 10–5; Sept.–June, Tues.–Sun. 10–5.*

ALSO WORTH SEEING

② **Emily Carr Institute of Art and Design.** The institute's three main buildings—tin-plated structures formerly used for industrial purposes—were renovated in the 1970s. The **Charles H. Scott Gallery** to the right of the main entrance hosts contemporary exhibitions in various media. Two other galleries showcase student work. ⊠*1399 Johnston St., Granville Island* ☎*604/844–3811* ⊕*www.eciad.ca* ☜*Free* ⊙*Weekdays noon–5, weekends 10–5.*

③ **Granville Island Museums.** This is two museums under one roof: the collection of the **Model Ships Museum** includes exquisitely detailed early-20th-century military and working vessels, notably a 13-foot replica of the HMS *Hood,* the British Royal Navy ship that was sunk by the German warship *Bismarck* in 1941, and a model of the *Hunley,* an 1863 Confederate submarine that was the first to sink a surface vessel. ⊠*1502 Duranleau St., Granville Island* ☎*604/683–1939* ⊕*www.granvilleislandmuseums.com* ☜*Both museums C$7.50* ⊙*Mid-May–mid-Oct., daily 10–5:30; mid-Oct.–mid-May, Tues.–Sun. 10–5:30.*

☾ **Vancouver Museum.** Vancouver's short but funky history comes to life at this seaside museum. The war-years gallery remembers some poignant episodes involving the Japanese internment, as well as local stories of the war effort. The 1950s Gallery boasts a 1955 Ford Fairlane Victoria and a Seeburg select-o-matic jukebox. ⊠*Vanier Park, 1100 Chestnut St., Kitsilano* ☎*604/736–4431* ⊕*www.vanmuseum.bc.ca* ☜*C$10* ⊙*June–Sept., Fri.–Wed. 10–5, Thurs. 10–9; Oct.–June, Tues., Wed., and Fri.–Sun. 10–5, Thurs. 10–9.*

STANLEY PARK

Fodor's Choice ★ A 1,000-acre wilderness park, only blocks from the downtown section of a major city, is a rare treasure. And it's all thanks to the Americans—sort of! In the 1860s, because of a threat of American invasion, this oceanfront peninsula was designated a military reserve, though it was never needed. When the City of Vancouver was incorporated in 1886, the council's first act was to request the land be set aside as a park. Permission was granted two years later and the grounds were named Stanley Park after Lord Stanley, then governor general of Canada.

Stanley Park is, perhaps, the single most prized possession of Vancouverites, who make use of it fervently to cycle, walk, jog, rollerblade, play cricket and tennis, and enjoy outdoor art shows and theater performances alongside attractions such as the renowned aquarium.

The free **Stanley Park Shuttle** (☎*604/257–8400* ⊕*www.vancouver.ca/parks/*) operates mid-June to mid-September between 10 AM and 6:30 PM, providing frequent (every 15 minutes) transportation to 15 major park sights. Pick it up on Pipeline Road, near the Georgia Street park entrance, or at any of the stops in the park.

For information about guided nature walks in the park, contact the **Lost Lagoon Nature House** (☎604/257–8544 ⊕ *www.stanleyparkecology.ca*) on the south shore of Lost Lagoon, at the foot of Alberni Street. They operate May to September, Tuesday through Sunday, 9–4:30.

WHAT TO SEE

Miniature Railway and Children's Farmyard. A child-size steam train takes kids and adults on a ride through the woods. Next door is a farmyard full of critters, including goats, rabbits, and pigs. At Christmastime, an elaborate light display illuminates the route, and Halloween displays draw crowds throughout October. ■ TIP→ **A family ticket gets everyone in for the child's rate.** ⊠ *Off Pipeline Rd., Stanley Park* ☎604/257–8531 ⬛*Each site C$5.50, C$2.75 for adults accompanying children* ⊙*Feb.–May, weekends only 11–4, weather permitting; June–Sept., daily 10:30–5; call for holiday and off-season hrs.*

NEED A BREAK?

Stanley's Park Bar and Grill (☎*604/602–3088*), in a 1911 manor house, is a family-friendly verandah serving burgers, wraps, soups, and salads. It overlooks the Rose Garden and is very near the Children's Farmyard and Malkin Ball, where outdoor theater and concerts are held in summer. There's also a gift and souvenir shop here.

Prospect Point. At 211 feet, Prospect Point is the highest point in the park and provides striking views of the Lions Gate Bridge (watch for cruise ships passing below), the North Shore, and Burrard Inlet. There's also a year-round souvenir shop, a snack bar with terrific ice cream, and a restaurant (May–September only). From the seawall, you can see where cormorants build their seaweed nests along the cliff ledges.

Second Beach. The 50-meter pool, which has lifeguards and waterslides, is a popular spot in summer. The sandy beach has a playground and covered picnic areas. If you like romantic beachside sunsets, this is one for the books. ☎604/257–8371 *summer only* ⊕*www.vancouver.ca/ parks/* ⬛*Beach free, pool C$4.85* ⊙*Pool mid-May–mid-June, weekdays noon–8:45, weekends 10–8:45; mid-June–late July, daily 10–8:45; late July–Labor Day, Mon., Wed., Fri. 7 AM–8:45 PM, Tues., Thurs., and weekends 10–8:45.*

Totem poles. Totem poles are an important art form among native peoples along British Columbia's coast. These eight poles, all carved in the latter half of the 20th century, include replicas of poles originally brought to the park from the north coast in the 1920s, as well as poles carved specifically for the park by First Nations artists. The several styles of poles represent a cross section of B.C. native groups, including the Kwakwaka'wakw, Haida, and Nisga'a. An information center near the site has a snack bar, a gift shop, and information about B.C.'s First Nations.

Vancouver Aquarium Marine Science Centre. Massive pools with windows below water level let you come face to face with beluga whales, sea otters, sea lions, dolphins, and harbor seals at this research and educational facility. In the Amazon rain-forest gallery you can walk through a jungle populated with piranhas, caimans, and tropical birds, and in summer, you'll be surrounded by hundreds of free-flying butterflies. Other displays, many with hands-on features for kids, show the underwater life of coastal British Columbia and the Canadian Arctic. A Tropic Zone is home to exotic freshwater and saltwater life, including clownfish, moray eels, and black-tip reef sharks. Beluga whale, sea lion, and dolphin shows, as well as dive shows (where divers swim with aquatic life, including sharks) are held daily. For an extra fee, you can help the trainers feed and train otters, belugas, and sea lions. ■TIP→The quietest time to visit is before 11 AM or after 2:30 PM. ☎604/659–3474 ⊕www.vanaqua.org ☜C$19.95 ۞July–Labor Day, daily 9:30–7; Labor Day–June, daily 9:30–5:30.

GREATER VANCOUVER

Some of Vancouver's best gardens, natural sights, and museums, including the renowned Museum of Anthropology on the campus of the University of British Columbia, are south of downtown Vancouver. In the other direction, cross the Lions Gate Bridge—also known as the Second Narrows Bridge—over Burrard Inlet, or hop onto the SeaBus, and you'll be on the north shore, where the districts of West Vancouver and North Vancouver are found.

MAIN ATTRACTIONS

Fodor'sChoice ★

Capilano Suspension Bridge. At Vancouver's oldest tourist attraction (the original bridge was built in 1889), you can get a taste of rain-forest scenery and test your mettle on the swaying, 450-foot cedar-plank suspension bridge that hangs 230 feet above the rushing Capilano River. Across the bridge is the Treetops Adventure, where you can walk along 650 feet of cable bridges suspended among the trees; there's also a scenic pathway along the canyon's edge, appropriately called Cliff Hanger Walk. Without crossing the bridge, you can enjoy the site's viewing decks, nature trails, totem park, and carving center (where you can watch First Nations carvers at work), as well as history and forestry exhibits, a massive gift shop in the original 1911 teahouse, and a restaurant. May through October, guides in 19th-century costumes conduct free tours on themes related to history, nature, or ecology, while fiddle bands, First Nations dancers, and other entertainers keep things lively. ⊠3735 Capilano Rd., North Vancouver ☎604/985–7474 ⊕www.capbridge.com ☜Mid-May–Oct. C$26.95, Nov.–mid-May C$23.95, plus C$3 for parking ۞May–Labor Day, daily 8:30–8; Nov.–Apr., daily 9–5; Sept., Oct., and Apr.–mid-May call for hrs.

Grouse Mountain. North America's largest aerial tramway, the **Skyride** is a great way to take in the city, sea, and mountain vistas (be sure to pick a clear day or evening). The Skyride makes the 2-km (1-mi) climb to the peak of Grouse Mountain every 15 minutes. Once at the top you can watch a half-hour video presentation at the Theatre in the Sky (it's included with your Skyride ticket). Other free mountaintop activities include, in summer, lumberjack shows, chairlift rides, walking tours, hiking, falconry demonstrations, and a chance to visit the grizzly bears and grey wolves in the mountain's wildlife refuge. For an extra fee you can also try tandem paragliding, or take a helicopter tour. In winter you can ski, snowshoe, snowboard, ice-skate on a mountaintop pond, or take Sno-Cat-drawn sleigh rides. A stone-and-cedar lodge is home to a café, a pub-style bistro, and a high-end restaurant, all with expansive city views. ⊠ *6400 Nancy Greene Way, North Vancouver* 🕾 *604/980–9311* ⊕ *www.grousemountain.com* 🖃 *Skyride and most activities C$32.95* ⊘ *Daily 9 AM–10 PM.*

Fodor'sChoice ★ **Museum of Anthropology.** Part of the University of British Columbia, the MOA has one of the world's leading collections of Northwest Coast First Nations' art. The Great Hall displays dramatic cedar poles, bent-wood boxes, and canoes adorned with traditional Northwest Coast painted designs. On clear days, the gallery's 50-foot-tall windows reveal a striking backdrop of mountains and sea. Another highlight is the work of the late Bill Reid, one of Canada's most respected Haida artists. In *The Raven and the First Men* (1980), carved in yellow cedar, he tells a Haida story of creation. Reid's gold-and-silver jewelry work is also on display, as are exquisite carvings of gold, silver, and argillite (a black shale found on Haida Gwaii, also known as the Queen Charlotte Islands) by other First Nations artists. Arthur Erickson designed the cliff-top structure that houses the MOA, which also has a book and fine-art shop and a summertime café. ⊠ *University of British Columbia, 6393 N.W. Marine Dr., Point Grey* 🕾 *604/822–5087* ⊕ *www.moa.ubc.ca* 🖃 *C$9, free Tues. 5–9* ⊘ *Memorial Day–Labor Day, Tues. 10–9, Wed.–Mon. 10–5; Labor Day–Memorial Day, Tues. 11–9, Wed.–Sun. 11–5.*

ALSO WORTH SEEING

ⓒ **Queen Elizabeth Park.** At the highest point in the city, offering 360-degree views of downtown, this 52-hectare (130-acre) park has lavish sunken gardens (set in a former stone quarry), a rose garden, and an abundance of grassy picnicking spots. In the **Bloedel Floral Conservatory** you can see tropical and desert plants and 100 species of free-flying tropical birds in a glass triodetic dome—the perfect place to be on a rainy day. ⊠ *Cambie St. and 33rd Ave., Cambie Corridor* 🕾 *604/257–8570* ⊕ *www.vancouver.ca/parks/* 🖃 *Conservatory C$4.50* ⊘ *Apr.–Sept., weekdays 9–8, weekends 10–9; Oct.–Mar., daily 10–5.*

VanDusen Botanical Garden. An Elizabethan maze, a formal rose garden, a meditation garden, and a collection of Canadian heritage plants are among the many themed displays at this 55-acre site. The collections include flora from every continent and many rare and endangered species. The new Phyllis Bentall Garden area features hybrid water lilies and carnivorous plants (a hit with kids). ⊠ *5251 Oak St., at W. 37th Ave., Shaughnessy* 🕾 *604/878–9274 garden, 604/261–0011 restaurant* ⊕ *www.vandusengarden.org* 🖃 *C$8.25 Apr.–Sept., C$6 Oct.–Mar.* ⊘ *June–Aug., daily 10–9; Sept.–May, daily (call for hrs).*

WHERE TO EAT

Updated by
Carolyn B.
Heller

From inventive downtown bistros to waterfront seafood palaces, to Asian restaurants that rival those in Asia, Vancouver has a diverse array of gastronomical options. Many cutting-edge establishments are defining and perfecting Modern Canadian fare, which incorporates Pacific Northwest seafood—notably salmon and halibut—and locally grown produce, often accompanied by British Columbia wines.

British Columbia's wine industry is enjoying great popularity, and many restaurants feature wines from the province's 100-plus wineries. Most B.C. wines come from the Okanagan Valley in the province's interior, but Vancouver Island is another main wine-producing area. Merlot, pinot noir, pinot gris, and chardonnay are among the major varieties; also look for ice wine, a dessert wine made from grapes that are picked while they are frozen on the vines.

WHAT IT COSTS IN CANADIAN DOLLARS				
	¢	$	$$	$$$	$$$$
AT DINNER	under C$8	C$8–C$12	C$13–C$20	C$21–C$30	over C$30

Restaurant prices are per person for a main course at dinner.

DOWNTOWN VANCOUVER

BELGIAN

$$–$$$ ✕ **Chambar.** Who would have predicted that a hip Belgian eatery in a high-ceiling space on a dreary block between Downtown and Gastown would take Vancouver by storm? A young, smartly dressed crowd hangs out at the bar sipping Belgian beer or funky cocktails such as the "Kissy Suzuki" (vodka infused with jasmine tea and blended with sake, blueberry, and passionfruit), working up their appetites for chef Nico Schuermans's creative cooking, in which classic Belgian dishes are reinvented with flavors from North Africa and beyond. He might rub duck breast with ginger and sumac and serve it with Moroccan-flavored rice pilaf, while *moules* (mussels) might be sauced with smoked chilies, cilantro, and coconut cream. Unusual? Perhaps. Delicious? Definitely. ✉ *562 Beatty St., Downtown* ☎ *604/879–7119* ▤ *AE, MC, V* ☾ *Closed Sun. No lunch.*

CAFÉ

¢–$ ✕ **Sciué.** Inspired by the street foods of Rome, this cafeteria-style Italian bakery–café (pronounced "Shoe-eh") starts off the day serving espresso drinks and pastries, then moves on to panini, soups, and pastas. One specialty is the pane romano, essentially a thick-crust pizza, which is sold by weight. There can be lines out the door at noontime, so try to visit early or late (they close at 8 PM weeknights, 6 PM Saturday). ✉ *110–800 W. Pender St., Downtown* ☎ *604/602–7263* ◢ *Reservations not accepted* ▤ *MC, V* ☾ *Closed Sun. No dinner Sat.*

$–$$ ✕ **Salt Tasting Room.** If your idea of a perfect lunch or light supper revolves around fine cured meats, artisanal cheeses, and a glass of wine from a wide-ranging list, find your way to this sleek, spare space in a decidedly unsleek Gastown lane. The restaurant has no kitchen and simply assembles its first-quality provisions, perhaps meaty *bunder-fleisch* (cured beef), smoked pork chops, or B.C.-made Camembert, with accompanying condiments, into artfully composed grazers' delights—more like an upscale picnic than a full meal. There's no sign out front, so look for the salt-shaker flag in Blood Alley, which is off Abbott Street, half a block south of Water Street. ⊠*45 Blood Alley, Gastown* ☎*604/633–1912* ⊟*AE, MC, V.*

ITALIAN

$$$$ ✕ **Il Giardino di Umberto.** The vine-draped terrace with a wood-burning
★ oven or any of the four terra-cotta-tiled rooms inside are attractive places to enjoy this long-established restaurateur's traditional Tuscan cuisine. The frequently changing menu includes a variety of pasta dishes, osso buco Milanese with saffron risotto, grilled salmon with saffron and fennel vinaigrette, and roast reindeer loin with a pink-peppercorn sauce. Dine here with someone special. ⊠*1382 Hornby St., Downtown* ☎*604/669–2422* ⊟*AE, DC, MC, V* ⊗*Closed Sun. No lunch Sat.*

JAPANESE

$–$$ ✕ **Hapa Izakaya.** *Izakayas* are Japanese pubs that serve tapas-style small
★ plates designed for sharing, and they've sprouted up all over Vancouver. One of the best places to sample the izakaya phenomenon is at this sleek pair of pubs popular with festive groups of twenty- and thirtysomethings. Try the mackerel (cooked tableside—with a blowtorch—and served with hot mustard), udon noodles coated with briny cod roe, or the Korean-style stone bowl filled with rice, pork, and vegetables. Sake or Japanese beer are the drinks of choice. If you're dining alone, sit at the counter facing the open kitchen to watch the action. The Robson branch is in the city center; the Kitsilano branch is one block from Kits Beach. ⊠*1479 Robson St., West End* ☎*604/689–4272* ⊟*AE, MC, V* ⊗*No lunch* ⊠*1516 Yew St., Kitsilano* ☎*604/738–4272* ⊟*AE, MC, V* ⊗*No lunch.*

¢–$ ✕ **Kintaro Ramen.** If your only experience with ramen is instant noodles, get thee to this authentic Japanese soup joint. With thin, fresh egg noodles and homemade broth (it's a meat stock, so vegetarians are explicitly not invited), a bowl of noodle soup here is cheap, filling, and ever so tasty. Expect long lines, but you can use the waiting time to decide between lean or fatty pork and miso or soy stock: once you're inside the barebones storefront, the harried staff doesn't tolerate any dithering. ⊠*788 Denman St., West End* ☎*604/682–7568* ⚄*Reservations not accepted* ⊟*No credit cards* ⊗*Closed Mon.*

MEDITERRANEAN

$$–$$$$ ✕ **Provence Marinaside.** This airy, modern Mediterranean-style eatery on Yaletown's waterfront presents French and Italian takes on seafood, including a delicious bouillabaisse and lush, garlicky wild prawns, though the rack of lamb and an extensive antipasti selection are also popular. The marina-view patio makes a sunny breakfast or lunch spot, and the take-out counter is a great place to put together a picnic. Under

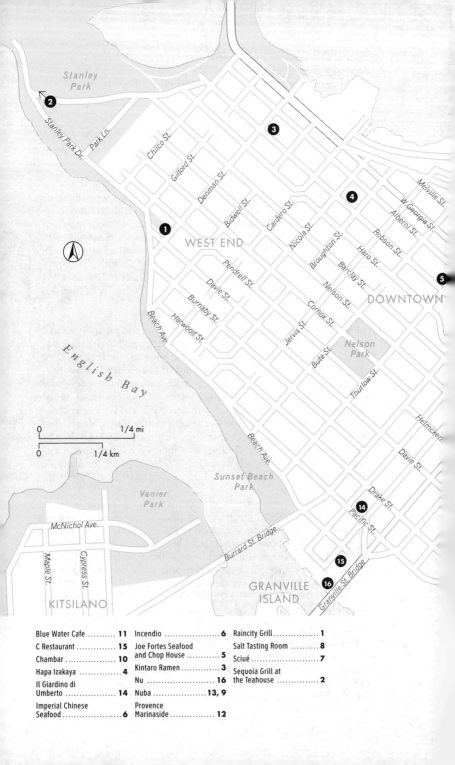

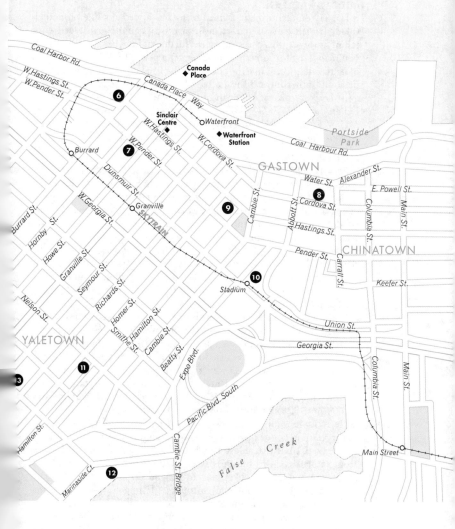

Where to Eat in
Downtown Vancouver

the same ownership, the **Provence Mediterranean Grill** (⊠*4473 W. 10th Ave., Point Grey* ☎*604/222–1980)* serves a similar menu to West Side denizens. ⊠*1177 Marinaside Crescent, at foot of Davie St., Yaletown* ☎*604/681–4144* ⊟*AE, DC, MC, V.*

MIDDLE EASTERN

¢–$ ✕**Nuba.** You could make a meal of meze—appetizers like tabbouleh salad, *labneh* (spiced yogurt dip), or crispy cauliflower served with tahini sauce—at this cheap and cheerful duo of Lebanese restaurants. If you're looking for something heartier, try a plate of *mjadra,* a spicy mix of lentils and rice. While they do serve chicken kebabs, lamb *kafta* (patties), and other meat dishes, most of the menu is vegetarian-friendly, and there are plenty of vegan options as well. ⊠*1206 Seymour St., Downtown* ☎*778/371–3266* ⌁*Reservations not accepted* ⊟*AE, MC, V* ⊠*322 W. Hastings St., Gastown* ☎*604/688–1655* ⌁*Reservations not accepted* ⊟*AE, MC, V* ☉*Closed weekends.*

MODERN CANADIAN

$$$–$$$$ ✕**Raincity Grill.** One of the best places to try British Columbian food and
★   wine is this pretty candlelit bistro overlooking English Bay. The menu, which owner Harry Kambolis likes to call "stubbornly regional," changes seasonally and relies almost completely on local and regional products, from salmon and shellfish to game and fresh organic vegetables. Vegetarian selections are always on the menu, and the exclusively Pacific Northwest and Californian wine list has at least 40 choices by the glass. The prix-fixe early dinner (C$30), served from 5 to 6 PM is a steal; reservations are required for these early dinners and recommended other times. ⊠*1193 Denman St., West End* ☎*604/685–7337* ⊟*AE, DC, MC, V.*

$$$–$$$$ ✕**Sequoia Grill at the Teahouse.** The former officers' mess in Stanley Park is perfectly poised for watching sunsets over the water. The Pacific Northwest menu is not especially innovative, but it includes such specialties as spinach and pear salad, and mushrooms stuffed with crab and mascarpone cheese, as well as seasonally changing treatments of B.C. salmon, ahi tuna, and rack of lamb. In summer you can dine on the patio. ⊠*7501 Stanley Park Dr., Ferguson Point, Stanley Park* ☎*604/669–3281 or 800/280–9893* ⊟*AE, MC, V.*

$$–$$$ ✕**Nu.** With its wall of windows overlooking False Creek, this contemporary dining room boasts lovely water views. The name is French for "naked," but that doesn't refer to the patrons' attire (which runs from smart-casual to business suits) or the room's decor (chic Euro style, from the funky bucket seats to the gilded brass ceiling). Instead, it represents the restaurant's philosophy of letting good-quality ingredients shine. You could linger over a cocktail and light bites, perhaps cute mini-burgers or a goat-cheese soufflé, but don't overlook the far more innovative dishes, such as the luxurious seafood salad, the "all-night braised" pork belly paired with yam dumplings, and the caramelized lamb cheeks served with artichokes and saffron-scented couscous. ⊠*1661 Granville St., Yaletown* ☎*604/646–4668* ⊟*AE, MC, V.*

PIZZA

$$ ✕**Incendio.** The hand-flipped thin-crust pizzas, with delicious toppings including gorgonzola, chicken, fresh spinach, and sun-dried tomatoes, and the mix-and-match pastas and sauces (try the hot smoked-duck sausage, artichoke, and tomato combination or the spicy *puttanesca* with anchovies, capers, and olives) draw crowds to this Gastown eatery. The room, in a circa-1900 heritage building, with exposed brick, local artwork, and big curved windows, has plenty of atmosphere. There's a second location in Kitsilano. ✉*103 Columbia St., Gastown* ☎*604/688–8694* ▤*AE, MC, V* ✉*2118 Burrard St., Kitsilano* ☎*604/736–2220* ▤*AE, MC, V* ⊘*No lunch weekends.*

SEAFOOD

$$$$ ✕**Blue Water Cafe.** Executive chef Frank Pabst features both popular
★ and lesser-known local seafood at this fashionable restaurant; he even offers an appetizer called "Unsung Heroes," which might include such frequently overlooked varieties as mackerel, sardines, and herring. Halibut, which could be paired with roasted cauliflower, or buttery sablefish caramelized with a sake-soy glaze, are both excellent options. Ask the staff to recommend wine pairings from the B.C.-focused list. There's a good selection of raw oysters, too, and sushi chef Yoshihiro ("Yoshi") Tabo turns out both classic and new creations. You could dress up a bit, whether you dine in the candlelit interior with exposed beams and brick or outside on the former loading dock that's now an attractive terrace. ✉*1095 Hamilton St., Yaletown* ☎*604/688–8078* ▤*AE, DC, MC, V.*

$$$$ ✕**C Restaurant.** Save your pennies, fish fans—dishes such as pickled
FodorśChoice sablefish served with mustard sorbet and minty cucumber soup or tuna
★ grilled ultrarare and dressed with an octopus vinaigrette have established this spot as Vancouver's most innovative seafood restaurant. Start with shucked oysters from the raw bar or perhaps the lavender-cured halibut. The 6-course (C$98 per person) and 10-course (C$130 per person) tasting menus with optional wine pairings highlight regional seafood; executive chef Robert Clark is an active promoter of British Columbia's bounty. Both the ultramodern interior and the waterside patio overlook False Creek, but dine before dark to enjoy the view. ✉*2–1600 Howe St., Downtown* ☎*604/681–1164* ▤*AE, DC, MC, V* ⊘*No lunch weekends or Oct.–Apr.*

GREATER VANCOUVER

ASIAN

$–$$ ✕**The Flying Tiger.** Inspired by the street foods of Asia, this laid-back lounge and eatery has a menu that roams from the Philippines to Thailand to Singapore and beyond. Start with a creative cocktail, perhaps the Dragon Slayer (dragon fruit–infused vodka mixed with pomegranate liqueur and fresh lime soda), or a glass of B.C. wine, before sampling a range of small plates, including crisp panko-crusted squid, petite pancakes heaped with duck confit and fresh herbs, or smoked halibut paired with green-papaya salad. Dishes are designed to share, so it's fun with a group. ⊠*2958 W. 4th Ave., Kitsilano* ☎*604/737–7529* ⊟*AE, MC, V* ☾*No lunch.*

ECLECTIC

$$ ✕ **Bin 942.** High-energy murals, low lights, and up-tempo (sometimes loud) music draw crowds to this tiny tapas bar. The real star here, though, is the food. From the scallop and tiger-prawn tournedos to the beef tenderloin phyllo Wellington, the chef creates some of the most eclectic small plates in town. Fun is also part of the deal: the chocolate fruit fondue, for example, is designed for two and comes with a paintbrush. Food is served until 1:30 AM (until midnight on Sunday), and the excellent, affordable, wines are all available by the glass. ⊠*1521 W. Broadway, South Granville* ☎*604/734–9421* ☜*Reservations not accepted* ⊟*MC, V* ☾*No lunch.*

$ ✕ **Stella's Tap and Tapas Bar.** If you're looking for a bite and a brew while browsing on Commercial Drive, join the locals at this comfortable hangout with burnished wide-plank floors and stone walls. Belgian beers are featured, so be sure to check the "fresh sheet" for current offerings. The menu of eclectic small plates rambles the world, from fried tofu with a sweet soy-sambal sauce, to a grilled veggie antipasto, or a trio of Pacific salmon, so you can pick and choose according to your mood. At midday, the kitchen turns out less exotic but still worthy sandwiches and salads. ⊠*1191 Commercial Dr., East Side* ☎*604/254–2437* ⊟*MC, V.*

FRENCH

$$$–$$$$ ✕ **Lumière.** Although celebrity chef Robert Feenie is no longer associated
Fodor'sChoice   with this long-acclaimed restaurant, Dale MacKay, formerly of Gordon
★   Ramsay's Maze Restaurant in New York, has taken on the chef's toque. MacKay has retained this sophisticated contemporary French dining room's carefully choreographed, frequently changing multicourse set menus. Whether you choose seafood, vegetarian, or the elaborate 12-course signature menu, expect to spend more than C$100 per person, not including wine, for these creative takes on French cuisine, using regionally sourced organic produce. Although the main dining room offers only a prix-fixe option, you can sample the chef's other creations at the à la carte (and somewhat less pricey) tasting bar. ⊠*2551 W. Broadway, Kitsilano* ☎*604/739–8185* ☜*Reservations essential* ⊟*AE, DC, MC, V* ☾*Closed Mon. No lunch.*

INDIAN

$$$ ✕ **Vij's.** Vikram Vij, the genial proprietor of Vancouver's most innovative Indian restaurant, uses local ingredients to create exciting takes on South Asian cuisine. The dishes, such as lamb "popsicles" in a creamy fenugreek-scented curry, or black-eyed peas served on a pilaf of brown basmati rice and vegetables, are far from traditional but are spiced beautifully. Mr. Vij circulates through the room, which is decorated with Indian antiques and whimsical elephant-pattern lanterns, greeting guests and suggesting dishes or cocktail pairings. Expect to cool your heels at the bar sipping chai or a cold beer while you wait for a table (lineups of an hour or more are not uncommon), but if you like creative Indian fare, it's worth it. ⊠*1480 W. 11th Ave., South Gran-*

ville ☎ *604/736–6664* ✍ *Reservations not accepted* ▭ *AE, DC, MC, V* ☽ *No lunch.*

ITALIAN

$$$–$$$$ ✕ **Quattro on Fourth.** Central Italian cuisine shines at this family-run favorite. The signature Spaghetti Quattro comes with hot chilies, minced chicken, black beans, olive oil, and generous lashings of garlic. Mains include Cornish hen grilled with herbs, garlic, and spicy peppers; rack of lamb with a fig and Dijon demi-glace; and pistachio-crusted black cod with roasted sweet-pepper sauce. Mahogany tables, chandeliers, candlelight, and a hand-painted floor glow indoors; a patio beckons in summer. The cellar has 400 wine varieties and an extensive grappa selection. The same owners also run the similar **Gusto di Quattro** (✉ *1 Lonsdale Ave., next to Lonsdale Quay, North Vancouver* ☎ *604/924–4444*) a quick SeaBus ride across the harbor from downtown. ✉ *2611 W. 4th Ave., Kitsilano* ☎ *604/734–4444* ▭ *AE, DC, MC, V* ☽ *No lunch.*

JAPANESE

$$$–$$$$ ✕ **Tojo's.** Hidekazu Tojo is a sushi-making legend in Vancouver, with ★ thousands of special preparations stored in his creative mind. Though the restaurant relocated to a striking modern space in an open high-ceilinged room, complete with a separate sake lounge, Tojo's sushi bar remains a convivial ringside seat for watching the creation of edible art. The best way to experience Tojo's creativity is to reserve a spot at the sushi bar and order *omakase* (chef's choice); chef Tojo will keep offering you wildly more adventurous fare, both raw and cooked, until you cry uncle. Budget a minimum of C$50 per person (before drinks) for the omakase option; tabs topping C$100 per person are routine. ✉ *1133 W. Broadway, Fairview* ☎ *604/872–8050* ▭ *AE, DC, MC, V* ✍ *Reservations essential* ☽ *Closed Sun. No lunch.*

MODERN CANADIAN

$$$$ ✕ **Bishop's.** Before "local" and "seasonal" were all the rage, this highly ★ regarded room was serving West Coast cuisine with an emphasis on organic, regional produce. The menu changes weekly, but highlights have included such starters as duck liver terrine and mains like steamed smoked sablefish, Dungeness crab cakes, and locally raised lamb. All are beautifully presented and impeccably served with suggestions from Bishop's extensive local wine list. The split-level room displays elaborate flower arrangements and selections from owner John Bishop's art collection. ✉ *2183 W. 4th Ave., Kitsilano* ☎ *604/738–2025* ▭ *AE, DC, MC, V* ☽ *Closed 1st wk in Jan. No lunch.*

$$$$ ✕ **West.** Contemporary regional cuisine is the theme at this chic restau-
Fodor's Choice rant, one of the city's most innovative dining rooms. Among the kitch-
★ en's creations are fresh tomato jelly with Thai basil, Dungeness crab, and avocado; sablefish with butternut squash puree and white asparagus; and braised pork cheeks served with baby carrots and candied shallots. There's an extensive selection of cheeses and decadent desserts that might include a chocolate-coconut devil's food cake or poached peaches paired with maple ice cream, brioche cinnamon toast, and melted brie. Marble floors, high ceilings, and warm caramel leather set

into red walls make the space feel simultaneously energetic and cozy. Elaborate multicourse tasting menus and a good-value (C$49) early-evening set menu, served before 6 PM, mean plenty of dining options. ⊠ *2881 Granville St., South Granville* ☎ *604/738–8938* ⊟ *AE, DC, MC, V* ⊘ *No lunch weekends.*

$$–$$$ ✕ **Cru.** "Small plates and big glasses" is the motto of this tapas- and
★ wine-focused restaurant, stylishly outfitted with tan banquettes and romantic low lighting. More than 35 wines by the glass (plus more by the bottle) complement the inventive designed-to-share dishes. There's a wonderfully crispy duck confit served on a frisée salad with warm bacon dressing, hearty wine-braised short ribs matched with macaroni 'n cheese, and an assortment of cheeses from B.C., Québec, and beyond. Save room for dessert, perhaps the decadent bittersweet chocolate torte or the goat-cheese cake with sour-cherry compote. If you prefer, you can order a three-course prix-fixe meal for C$38. ⊠ *1459 W. Broadway, South Granville* ☎ *604/677–4111* ⊟ *AE, MC, V* ⊘ *No lunch.*

SEAFOOD

$ ✕ **Go Fish.** If the weather's fine, head for this seafood stand on the docks
★ near Granville Island. It's owned by Gord Martin, of Bin 941/942 fame, so it's not your ordinary chippie. The menu is short—highlights include fish-and-chips, grilled salmon or tuna sandwiches, and oyster po' boys—but the quality is first-rate, and the accompanying Asian-flavored slaw leaves ordinary cole slaw in the dust. There are just a few (outdoor) tables, so go early or be prepared to wait. To get here, walk along the waterfront path from Granville Island; by car, drive east from Burrard on 1st Avenue until it ends at the docks. ⊠ *1505 W. 1st Ave., Fisherman's Wharf, Kitsilano* ☎ *604/730–5039* ⊟ *MC, V* ⊘ *Closed Mon. and Tues. No dinner.*

WHERE TO STAY

Updated by
Chris McBeath

Accommodations in Vancouver range from luxurious waterfront hotels to neighborhood B&Bs, chain hotels (both luxury and budget), basic European-style pensions, and backpackers' hostels. There are also many top-quality choices that epitomize countryside—within a 30-minute drive of the downtown core.

Although the city is quite compact, each area has its distinct character and accommodation options. All our recommendations are within easy reach of transit that will take you to the major attractions, though if you choose to stay outside of the downtown core, a car will still be the easiest way to tour neighborhoods on the West Side or North Shore.

WHAT IT COSTS IN CANADIAN DOLLARS				
¢	$	$$	$$$	$$$$
HOTELS	under C$75	C$75–C$125	C$126–C$175	C$176–C$250	over C$250

Hotel prices are for two people in a standard double room in high season, excluding tax.

DOWNTOWN

$$$$ ☷ **Fairmont Hotel Vancouver.** The copper roof of this 1939 château-style hotel dominates Vancouver's skyline, and the hotel itself is considered the city's gracious grand dame. Guest rooms vary in size, but even the standard rooms have an atmosphere of prestige, with high ceilings, lush draperies, and 19th-century-style mahogany furniture. Two friendly dogs (Mavis and Boe) are on hand for petting and walking, and the full-service spa here was Canada's first to cater to men, with bigscreen TVs, wireless Internet, and black-leather pedicure chairs. Rooms on the Fairmont Gold floor have access to extra services, including a private lounge and a special concierge. **Pros:** The male-oriented spa, great location for shopping, the architecture. **Cons:** Regal size makes it a shade impersonal, diversity of "standard" room sizes can be irritating for guests expecting a room similar to the one they stayed in before. ✉ *900 W. Georgia St., Downtown, V6C 2W6* ☎ *604/684–3131* 📠 *604/662–1929* ⊕ *www.fairmont.com* ⇨ *556 rooms, 37 suites* ♨ *In-room: refrigerator (some), Ethernet. In-hotel: 2 restaurants, room service, bar, pool, gym, spa, concierge, laundry service, executive floor, parking (fee), no-smoking rooms, some pets allowed, public Wi-Fi* 🖃 *AE, D, DC, MC, V.*

$$$$ ☷ **Four Seasons.** This 29-story downtown luxury hotel is famous for pampering guests. The lobby, which connects to the Pacific Centre shopping mall, is lavish, with an atrium-style lounge. Standard rooms, with understated color schemes, marble bathroom fixtures, and tall windows with city views, are spacious and traditionally furnished, as are the even more spacious corner rooms with sitting areas. Service at the Four Seasons is top-notch and the many amenities include free evening limousine service. Regular visitors may be saddened to learn that the superlative, long-time signature restaurant is gone, but the new Yew restaurant + bar, serving regional cuisine, is set to takes its place. **Pros:** Premier location for shopping, Four Seasons service standards. **Cons:** No on-site spa. ✉ *791 W. Georgia St., vehicle entrance on Howe St., Downtown, V6C 2T4* ☎ *604/689–9333* 📠 *604/684–4555* ⊕ *www.fourseasons.com* ⇨ *306 rooms, 66 suites* ♨ *In-room: refrigerator, safe, Ethernet. In-hotel: public Wi-Fi, 2 restaurants, room service, bar, pool, gym, concierge, laundry service, parking (fee), no-smoking rooms, some pets allowed* 🖃 *AE, DC, MC, V.*

$$$$ ☷ **Loden Hotel.** Vancouver's newest hotel, this ultra-sophisticated boutique inn has all manner of high-tech amenities such as in-room iPod stations and oversized LCD TV screens. Floor-to-ceiling windows fill the spacious guest rooms with natural light—and if you slide open the bathroom half-wall you can enjoy the views from the soaker tub. The Voya restaurant has a sophisticated West Coast menu and a cosmopolitan 1940s design with lots of mirrors and crystal chandeliers. The glitter continues on the outside, where the reflective glass covering the building creates the illusion that it's constructed entirely of mirrors. **Pros:** It's the happening hotel of the moment. **Cons:** It's the happening hotel of the moment. ✉ *1177 Melville St., Downtown, V6E 0A3* ☎ *604/669–5060 or 877/225–6336* 📠 *604/662–8904* ⊕ *www. lodenvancouver.com* ⇨ *70 rooms, 7 suites* ♨ *In-room: refrigerator,*

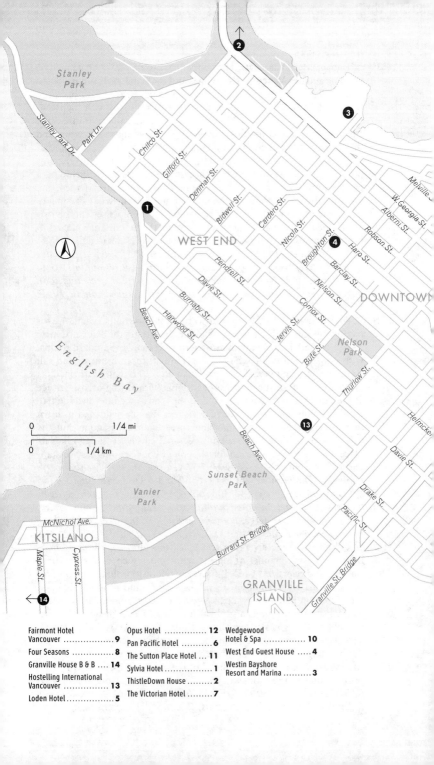

Where to Stay in Downtown Vancouver

Burrard Inlet

Coal Harbor Rd.

W. Hastings St.
W. Pender St.

Canada Place Way

Canada Place

6

Sinclair Centre

W. Hastings St.

W. Pender St.

Burrard

Waterfront

W. Cordova St.

♦ **Waterfront Station**

Coal Harbour Rd.

5

GASTOWN

Water St. Alexander St.

E. Powell St.

Dunsmuir St.

Cambie St.

Abbott St.

Cordova St.

Columbia St.

Main St.

9

W. Georgia St.

8

Granville

SKYTRAIN

7

Hastings St.

CHINATOWN

1

Burrard St.

10

Hornby St.

Pender St.

Carrall St.

Keefer St.

Howe St.

Granville St.

Seymour St.

Richards St.

Stadium

Nelson St.

Union St.

YALETOWN

Smithe St.

Cambie St.

Beatty St.

Georgia St.

Homer St.

Expo Blvd.

Main St.

Columbia St.

Hamilton St.

12

Hamilton St.

Pacific Blvd. South

Creek

Cambie St. Bridge

Main Street

Marinaside Ct.

False

Portside Park

safe, Ethernet, Wi-Fi. In-hotel: restaurant, bar, room service, spa, gym, concierge, laundry service, parking (fee), no-smoking rooms, some pets allowed, public Wi-Fi ⊟AE, D, DC, MC, V.

$$$$ ⊡ **Pan Pacific Hotel.** A centerpiece of waterfront Canada Place, the luxu-
★ rious Pan Pacific shares a complex with the Vancouver Convention and Exhibition Centre and Vancouver's main cruise-ship terminal. Rooms are large and modern with maplewood throughout, marble vanities, Italian linens, and stunning ocean, mountain, or skyline views, all of which have been enjoyed by a star-studded list of royals, celebs, and well-heeled newsmakers. The high-end suites, some with private steam room, sauna, or baby-grand piano, are popular with visiting VIPs. The 26-room Roman bath–theme Spa Utopia and Salon is a sumptuous experience, and the health and fitness center is state-of-the-art. If you're staying over a Friday or Saturday night, Puccini and pasta were never as good as at the Italian Opera Buffet in the main dining room. **Pros:** The harbor views are only an elevator ride to the cruise-ship terminal (a real plus for heavy baggage transfers), the "go the extra mile" service attitude. **Cons:** Next door to waterfront construction the atrium is open to the convention center's main lobby so the hotel foyer, lounge, and entrance fills with delegates bearing conference badges talking shop, nabbing the best seats in the house, and vying for taxis. ⊠*999 Canada Pl., Downtown, V6C 3B5* ☎*604/662–8111, 800/663–1515 in Canada, 800/937–1515 in U.S.* ⊟*604/685–8690* ⊕*www.panpacific. com* ⊷*465 rooms, 39 suites* ⌂*In-room: refrigerator, safe, kitchen (some), Ethernet, dial-up, Wi-Fi. In-hotel: 2 restaurants, room service, bar, pool, gym, spa, concierge, laundry service, parking (fee), no-smoking rooms, some pets allowed, public Wi-Fi* ⊟AE, DC, MC, V.

$$$$ ⊡ **The Sutton Place Hotel.** More like an exclusive European guesthouse
★ than a large modern hotel, the rooms here are furnished in a Parisian style with soft neutrals and lush fabrics, and the service is gracious and attentive. The full spa (also open to nonguests) has a wide menu. La Grande Résidence (part of Sutton Place), an apartment hotel suitable for stays of at least a week, is next door, at 855 Burrard. The hotel's new wine boutique carries a number of hard-to-find specialty labels from all over the world. The Fleuri restaurant serves Continental cuisine and is particularly noted for its late-night chocolate buffet. **Pros:** Classy, terrific lounge bar for romantic trysts, the chocolate buffet is diet decadence, the spa. **Cons:** The wide-open, nondescript corridor joining restaurant and lounge couldn't be further from the hotel's discreet style: in other words, your tryst better not be clandestine! ⊠*845 Burrard St., Downtown, V6Z 2K6* ☎*604/682–5511 or 800/961–7555* ⊟*604/682–5513* ⊕*www.suttonplace.com* ⊷*350 rooms, 46 suites, 164 apartments* ⌂*In-room: refrigerator, safe, DVD, Ethernet, Wi-Fi. In-hotel: restaurant, room service, bar, pool, gym, spa, concierge, laundry service, parking (fee), no-smoking rooms, some pets allowed, public Wi-Fi* ⊟AE, D, DC, MC, V.

$$$$ ⊡ **Wedgewood Hotel & Spa.** The small, lavish Wedgewood has just
Fodor's Choice earned membership to the exclusive Relais & Châteaux Group, and
★ is run by an owner who cares fervently about her guests. The lobby and guest rooms display a flair for old-world Italian luster with origi-

nal artwork and antiques selected by the proprietor on her European travels. Guest rooms are capacious, and each has a balcony. The four penthouse suites have fireplaces, luxury spa bathrooms, and private garden terraces. All the extra touches are here, too: afternoon ice delivery, dark-out drapes, CD players, robes, and a morning newspaper. The turndown service includes homemade cookies and bottled water. The sophisticated Bacchus restaurant and lounge ($$$–$$$$) is in the lobby; it's also a terrific pit-stop for afternoon tea after shopping along Robson Street. The tiny but luxurious on-site spa is very popular—book ahead for an appointment. **Pros:** Personalized and attentive service, boutique atmosphere, afternoon tea with flair, great location close to top shops, spa. **Cons:** The small size means it gets booked quickly. ⊠ *845 Hornby St., Downtown, V6Z 1V1* ☎ *604/689–7777 or 800/663–0666* 🖷 *604/608–5348* ⊕ *www.wedgewoodhotel.com* ⤴ *41 rooms, 43 suites* ⏦ *In-room: refrigerator, safe, Ethernet, Wi-Fi. In-hotel: restaurant, room service, bar, gym, spa, laundry facilities, laundry service, parking (fee), no-smoking rooms, public Wi-Fi* ⊟ *AE, D, DC, MC, V.*

$–$$
Fodor's Choice
★
The Victorian Hotel. Budget hotels can be beautiful, as attested by the gleaming hardwood floors, high ceilings, and chandeliers at this prettily restored 1898 European-style pension. This is one of Vancouver's best-value accommodations, and guest rooms in the two connecting three-story buildings have down duvets, oriental rugs atop hardwood floors, lush draperies, and period furniture; a few have bay windows or mountain views. Some of the private bathrooms are outfitted with marble tiles and granite countertops (though some have a shower and no tub). Even the shared baths are spotlessly clean and nicely appointed. With three queen beds, room #15 is a good choice for families. **Pros:** Great location for the price, helpful staff, clean, comfortable. **Cons:** Location near the "rummy part of town" a few blocks east. It's relatively safe (honest), but common sense says you would probably take a cab to the door after midnight rather than walk. ⊠ *514 Homer St., Downtown, V6B 2V6* ☎ *877/681–6369 or 604/681–6369* 🖷 *604/681–8776* ⊕ *www.victorianhotel.ca* ⤴ *39 rooms, 18 with bath* ⏦ *In-room: no a/c, refrigerator (some). In-hotel: no elevator, laundry service, parking (fee), no-smoking rooms, public Wi-Fi* ⊟ *MC, V* ⏹ *CP.*

¢–$
Hostelling International Vancouver. Vancouver has three Hostelling International locations: a former hotel in the downtown core, above a boisterous bar; a big hostel set in parkland at Jericho Beach in Kitsilano; and a smaller building in a residential neighborhood near English Bay. Each has private rooms for two to four people; bunks in men's, women's, and coed dorms (with bedding and lockers); a shared kitchen, a TV lounge, and a range of free or low-cost tours and activities. The central hostel has rooms with private baths and TVs and is the pricier location; the Jericho, with the cheapest rates, is open only in the summer. **Pros:** Great staff, cheap and clean but you get what you pay for. **Cons:** Not for the fussy traveler, lots of students, dorm accommodations can be noisy with snorers and night owls who come in late. ⊠ *HI Vancouver Central, 1025 Granville St., Downtown, V6Z 1L4* ☎ *604/685–5335 or 888/203–8333* 🖷 *604/685–5351* ⊕ *www.hihostels.ca* ⤴ *36 rooms, 26*

with bath; 41 4-bed dorm rooms ⌂*In-room: no a/c (some), no phone, no TV (some), Ethernet. In-hotel: bar, laundry facilities, public Internet, public Wi-Fi, no-smoking rooms* ▭*MC, V* 🍴*CP* ✉*HI Vancouver Downtown, 1114 Burnaby St., West End, V6E 1P1* ☎*604/684–4565 or 888/203–4302* 📠*604/684–4540* 🌐*www.hihostels.ca* ⇆*23 rooms, 44 4-bed dorm rooms* ⌂*In-room: no a/c, no phone, no TV. In-hotel: bicycles, laundry facilities, public Internet, public Wi-Fi, parking (no fee), no-smoking rooms* ▭*MC, V* 🍴*CP* ✉*HI Vancouver Jericho Beach, 1515 Discovery St., Kitsilano, V6R 4K5* ☎*604/224–3208 or 888/203–4303* 📠*604/224–4852* 🌐*www.hihostels.ca* ⇆*10 rooms, 9 14-bed dorm rooms* ⌂*In-room: no a/c, no phone, no TV. In-hotel: bicycles, laundry facilities, public Internet, parking (fee), no-smoking rooms* ▭*MC, V* ⏲*Closed Oct.–Apr.*

NORTH VANCOUVER

$$–$$$$ ★ **ThistleDown House.** This 1920 Arts and Crafts house with its private, sunny garden, is handy to North Shore hiking and skiing, but just 15 to 30 minutes from downtown. Furnished with a low-key, eclectic arrangement of antiques, art deco touches, local art, and treasures gathered on the hosts' travels, each room has its own charm: Under the Apple Tree, with its private patio, gas fireplace, and air-jet tub, is a romantic choice; Mulberry Peek, an octagonal tower room, has four walls of windows and a private balcony; Pages, the former library, has a cast-iron pedestal tub and book-lined walls. **Pros:** Personal style of genuine hospitality, attention to detail, free afternoon tea. **Cons:** Away from the crowds; need a car to get here and to explore. ✉*3910 Capilano Rd., North Vancouver, V7R 4J2* ☎*604/986–7173 or 888/633–7173* 📠*604/980–2939* 🌐*www.thistle-down.com* ⇆*6 rooms* ⌂*In-room: no a/c, no phone. In-hotel: no elevator, laundry service, public Internet, public Wi-Fi, parking (no fee), no kids under 12, no-smoking rooms* ▭*MC, V* ⏲*Closed Dec. and Jan.* 🍴*BP.*

WEST END

$$$$ ★ **Westin Bayshore Resort and Marina.** Perched on Coal Harbour beside Stanley Park, the Bayshore has a picturesque marina on its doorstep as well as impressive harbor and mountain views. Most rooms take full advantage of this, with floor-to-ceiling windows that open to a railing or a step-out balcony. Interiors are cheery and comfortable, with rich modern blue-and-gold fabrics, plush armchairs, and comfortable beds. The only downtown resort hotel, the Bayshore is also rich with recreational facilities, including fishing charters, sightseeing cruises, and poolside yoga. Vancouver's Seawall Walk connects the resort to Stanley Park and the Vancouver Convention and Exhibition Centre. **Pros:** Resort amenities within minutes of downtown, the doormen still dress up as Beefeaters, fabulous water views, Stanley Park your next-door neighbor. **Cons:** Away from the downtown core; the posh new conference space sees a lot of business travelers, which might put families off, and vice versa; the spacious lobby is rather impersonal; tower rooms are a fair walk from registration. ✉*1601 Bayshore Dr., off Cardero St., West End, V6G 2V4* ☎*604/682–3377* 📠*604/687–3102* 🌐*www.westinbayshore.com* ⇆*482 rooms, 28 suites* ⌂*In-room: refrigerator, safe (some), Ether-*

net, Wi-Fi (some). In-hotel: 2 restaurants, room service, bar, pools, gym, concierge, laundry service, parking (fee), no-smoking rooms, some pets allowed, public Wi-Fi ⊟*AE, D, DC, MC, V.*

$$–$$$$ 🖭**West End Guest House.** This Victorian B&B, built in 1906, is painted the deep pink of the fragrant "Painted Lady" variety of Sweet Pea flower that dates back to the 18th century—and the guesthouse is just as charming inside with a gracious front parlor, cozy fireplace, and early 1900s furniture. Most of the handsome rooms are furnished with antiques; two larger rooms have gas fireplaces and two have brass beds. All the bathrooms have been recently renovated, and each has a mural of one of the heritage homes in the surrounding residential neighborhood. The inn is a two-minute walk from Robson Street and five minutes from Stanley Park. The owners also have a suite in a modern building next door; it's ideal for families and couples looking for weekly lets. **Pros:** Great heritage interior, quiet residential location, free use of mountain bikes, private patio garden. **Cons:** Furnishings a bit precious. ⊠*1362 Haro St., West End, V6E 1G2* ☎*604/681–2889 or 888/546–3327* 🖷*604/688–8812* ⊕*www.westendguesthouse.com* ➾*8 rooms* ⏃*In-room: no a/c, DVD (some), VCR (some), Wi-Fi. In-hotel: no elevator, bicycles, public Internet, public Wi-Fi, parking (no fee), no-smoking rooms* ⊟*AE, D, DC, MC, V* �‖⃝*BP.*

$–$$$ 🖭**Sylvia Hotel.** To stay at the Sylvia in June through August, you must
★   book six months to a year ahead: this Virginia-creeper-covered 1912 building is popular because of its low rates and near-perfect location: about 25 feet from the beach on scenic English Bay, 200 feet from Stanley Park, and a 20-minute walk from Robson Street. The rooms and apartment-style suites vary from tiny to spacious. Many of the basic but comfortable rooms are large enough to sleep four and all have windows that open. The restaurant and bar are popular and its tenure on English Bay has made it a nostalgic haunt for Vancouverites. **Pros:** Beachfront location, close to restaurants, a good place to mingle with the locals. **Cons:** Older building, parking can be difficult if the lot is full, the 15-minute walk to the downtown core is slightly uphill. ⊠*1154 Gilford St., West End, V6G 2P6* ☎*604/681–9321* 🖷*604/682–3551* ⊕*www.sylviahotel.com* ➾*97 rooms, 22 suites* ⏃*In-room: no a/c, kitchen (some), dial-up, Wi-Fi. In-hotel: restaurant, room service, bar, laundry service, public Internet, parking (fee), no-smoking rooms, some pets allowed* ⊟*AE, DC, MC, V.*

WEST SIDE

$$$ 🖭**Granville House B&B.** At the edge of posh Shaughnessy, this Tudor-revival house exudes a peaceful elegance that belies its address on one of Vancouver's busiest thoroughfares. Triple glazing, radiant floor heat, and electronic locks (which allow you to check-in in advance since there are no keys to exchange) are some of the finishing touches. Trade your shoes for plush slippers (provided) in the front hall and head to one of the five king-size rooms, each with a sitting area and appointed with luxurious linens, spa robes, and amenities made locally on Salt Spring Island. There's a self-serve refreshment/coffee bar in the inviting modern lounge; continental breakfast includes one hot dish. **Pros:** New, on the main drag into/out of town, customized/independent style of check-in. **Cons:** Granville Street is very busy, everything at this B&B is so new that you might feel hesitant to dirty the linens! ⊠ *5050 Granville St., Shaughnessy, V6M 3B4* ☎ *604/307–2300 or 604/733–2963* ⊕ *www.granvillebb.com* ⤷ *4 rooms* ♿ *In-room: refrigerator, Wi-Fi. In-hotel: no elevator, laundry service, parking (no fee), no-smoking rooms, public Wi-Fi* ⊟ *AE, DC, MC, V* ❑ *BP.*

YALETOWN

$$$$ ▦ **Opus Hotel.** The design team had a good time with this boutique
★   hotel, creating fictitious characters and designing rooms for each. Billy's room is fun and offbeat, with pop art and lime-green accents. Dede's room boasts leopard skin, velveteen, and faux-fur accents, while Bob and Carol's place has softer edges and golden tones. Amenities are fun, too: look for mini-oxygen canisters in the bathrooms—a whiff'll clear your head if you have a hangover, and it'll stimulate blood flow for other pursuits. An interesting note: the nighttime reading by your bed is a hotel murder mystery written by the General Manager himself! Most rooms have a full wall of windows, lots of natural light, and views of the city or the Japanese garden in the courtyard. Two rooms have private access to the garden; seventh-floor rooms have balconies. Other perks include dog-walking if you've brought Fido along, personal shopping, and free car service anywhere downtown. **Pros:** The central Yaletown location; the hotel is funky and hip the lobby bar is a fashionable meeting spot. **Cons:** Renovated heritage building has no views surrounding neighborhood is mostly high-rises trendy nightspots nearby can be noisy at night. ⊠ *322 Davie St., Yaletown, V6B 5Z6* ☎ *604/642–6787 or 866/642–6787* ☎ *604/642–6780* ⊕ *www.opushotel.com* ⤷ *85 rooms, 11 suites* ♿ *In-room: refrigerator, safe, DVD (some), VCR (some), Ethernet, Wi-Fi. In-hotel: restaurant, room service, bar, gym, concierge, laundry service, parking (fee), no-smoking rooms, some pets allowed, public Wi-Fi, bicycles* ⊟ *AE, DC, MC, V.*

NIGHTLIFE

Updated by
Celeste Moure

With easy access to the sea and mountains, it's no surprise that Vancouver is such an outdoorsy kind of town but once the sun goes down, the city's dwellers trade in their kayaks, hiking shoes, and North Face windbreakers for something decidedly more chic. There's plenty to choose from in just about every neighborhood: hipster Gastown is the place to go for swanky clubs and trendy wine bars while the gay-friendly West End is all about bumpin' and grindin' in retro bars and clubs. A posh crowd of glitterati flocks to Yaletown's brewpubs and stylish lounges. Meanwhile, Kitsilano (the Venice Beach of Vancouver) attracts a laid-back bunch who like to sip beer and frilly cocktails on cool bar patios with killer views.

BARS, PUBS & LOUNGES

Afterglow. Typically packed by 10 PM, this Yaletown lounge, tucked behind Glowbal restaurant, gets its radiance from the fuchsia lighting on pink-and-white brick walls (or maybe the fake tans and hairspray have something to do with it). It's a great place to lounge on comfy sofas, sip colorful martinis, and practice the art of see-and-be-seen. ⊠*1082 Hamilton St., Yaletown* ☏*604/602–0835.*

Bridges. This Vancouver landmark near the Public Market has the city's biggest marina-side deck and a cozy nautical-theme pub. ⊠*1696 Duranleau St., Granville Island* ☏*604/687–4400.*

Fodor'sChoice **Chill Winston.** Decked out with plush black leather sofas, exposed wood
★ beams, warm lighting, and a view of Gastown's lively square, this restaurant-cum-lounge attracts a well-heeled crowd of jetsetters and urban dwellers. ⊠*3 Alexander St., Gastown* ☏*604/288–9575.*

Fodor'sChoice **Fountainhead Pub.** With one of the largest streetside patios in downtown,
★ you can do as the locals do here: sit back, down a few beers and watch the passersby. ⊠*1025 Davie St., West End* ☏*604/687–2222.*

SOMA. Recently reopened in a new location, this stylish café-cum-wine-bar showcases a nice selection of B.C. and New World wines to complement tasty salads, cheeses, and artisanal meats. A free Wi-Fi password is available upon request. ⊠*151 E. 8th Ave., Mount Pleasant/SoMa* ☏*604/630–7502.*

★ **The Whip Gallery.** It's a bit out of the way but this lofty space with exposed brick and Douglas fir–beamed ceiling attracts a hip crowd (they wear a lot of black). There's a bar, atrium, and mezzanine with a DJ. Order what's on tap (Storm Brewing, R&B, Unibroue) or choose from one of seven deadly sin martinis. ⊠*209 East 6th Ave., at Main St., East Vancouver* ☏*604/874–4687.*

COMEDY CLUBS

Vancouver TheatreSports League. A hilarious improv troupe performs four nights a week to an enthusiastic crowd at the New Revue Stage on Granville Island. ⊠*Granville Island* ☏*604/738–7013.*

GAY NIGHTLIFE

★ **1181.** This new addition to the gayborhood is all about stylish interior design—plush sofas, glass coffee tables, wood-paneled ceiling—and fancy cocktails (think caipirinhas and mojitos). It gets particularly crowded on Saturday, when a DJ spins behind the bar. ⊠*1181 Davie St., West End* ☏*604/687–3991.*

Lick. Vancouver's most popular lesbian dance bar sizzles as girls who like girls dance to kick-ass electronic, hip-hop, and drum-and-bass beats. A quiet chill-out area in front offers respite from the noise and heat. Two other dance clubs, **Honey** and **Lotus,** at the same site, are open to all. ⊠*455 Abbott St., Gastown* ☏*604/685–7777.*

MUSIC CLUBS

Caprice. R&B and Top 40 play to a Britney and Paris wannabe crowd at this two-level former movie theater with a restaurant and lounge. Tag along with a hooked-up local or expect to wait in line, like, forever. ⊠*967 Granville St., Downtown* ☏*604/681–2114.*

Cellar Restaurant and Jazz Club. This is the top venue for jazz in Vancouver and the club calendar features a who's who of the Canadian jazz scene. ⊠*3611 W. Broadway, Kitsilano* ☏*604/738–1959.*

★ **ginger sixty-two.** This dark, moody '60s-inspired lounge—with its plush carpets, comfy sofas, and black-and-white retro films projected on the wall—attracts a crowd of beautiful locals and the occasional VIP dressed to the nines. When internationally renowned DJs come to town, this is where they spin. Be prepared to spend at least an hour waiting in line before setting foot inside. ✉ *1219 Granville St., Downtown* ☎ *604/688–5494.*

THE ARTS

From performing arts to theater, classical music, dance, and a thriving gallery scene, there's much for an art lover to choose from in Vancouver.

CLASSICAL MUSIC

OPERA **Vancouver Opera.** The city's opera company stages four productions a year, from October through May, at the Queen Elizabeth Theatre. ☎ *604/682–2871.*

ORCHESTRAS **Vancouver Symphony Orchestra.** The resident company at the **Orpheum Theatre** presents classical and popular music performances to a wide variety of audiences. ✉ *601 Smithe St., Downtown* ☎ *604/876–3434.*

DANCE

Ballet British Columbia. Innovative ballet and timeless classics by internationally acclaimed choreographers are presented by this company; most performances are at the Queen Elizabeth Theatre. ☎ *604/732–5003.*

Scotiabank Dance Centre. The hub of dance in British Columbia, this striking building with an art deco facade has performances, studio showings, and other types of events by national and international artists. ✉ *677 Davie St., Downtown* ☎ *604/606–6400.*

THEATER

Arts Club Theatre Company. This company operates two theaters. The **Arts Club Granville Island Stage** (✉ *1585 Johnston St., Granville Island* ☎ *604/687–1644*) is an intimate venue and a good place to catch works by local playwrights. The **Stanley Industrial Alliance Stage** (✉ *2750 Granville St.*) is a lavish former movie palace staging works by such perennial favorites as William Shakespeare and Noel Coward. Both operate year-round. **Theatre Under the Stars.** Family-friendly musicals like *The Sound of Music* and *Kiss Me Kate* are the draw at Malkin Bowl, an outdoor amphitheater in Stanley Park, during July and August. You can watch the show from the lawn, or from the Rose Garden Tea House as part of a dinner–theater package. ☎ *604/687–0174.*

Vancouver Playhouse. The leading venue in Vancouver for mainstream theater is in the same complex as the Queen Elizabeth Theatre. ✉ *649 Cambie St., Downtown* ☎ *604/665–3050.*

VANCOUVER OUTDOORS

Updated
by Alison
Appelbe

Blessed with a mild climate, fabulous natural setting, and excellent public facilities, it's not surprising that Vancouverites are an outdoorsy lot. It's not uncommon for locals to commute to work by foot or bike and, after-hours, they're as likely to hit the water, trails, ski slopes, or beach volleyball courts as the bars or nightclubs.

Exceptional for North American cities, the downtown peninsula is almost entirely encircled by a seawall along which you can walk, in-line skate, cycle, or otherwise propel yourself. Indeed, it's so popular that it qualifies as a, albeit unofficial, national treasure. There are places along the route where you can hire a bike, Rollerblades, canoe, or kayak, or simply go for a swim or play tennis. Top-rated skiing, snowboarding, mountain biking, fishing, diving, and golf are just minutes away.

The **Mountain Equipment Co-op** is something of a local institution, a veritable outdoors-lovers emporium with every kind of gear imaginable, as well as rentals, books and maps, and information from people in the know. ✉ *130 W. Broadway, Fairview* ☎ *604/872–7858.*

BEACHES

Fodor'sChoice
★ **Kitsilano Beach.** To the west of the south end of the Burrard Bridge, this is the city's busiest beach—in-line skaters, volleyball games, and sleek young people are ever present. Facilities include a playground, restaurant and concession stand, and tennis courts. **Kitsilano Pool** is also here: at 137 meters (445 feet), it's the longest pool in Canada and one of the few heated salt-water pools in the world. ✉ *2305 Cornwall Ave., Kitsilano* ☎ *604/731–0011* ◷ *Late May–mid-Sept.*

Stanley Park beaches. There are several beaches accessed from Stanley Park Drive in Stanley Park. **Second Beach** has a playground, a small sandy area, and a large heated pool with a slide. **Third Beach** has a larger stretch of sand, fairly warm water, and great sunset views. It's a popular evening picnic spot.

West End beaches.English Bay, the city's best known beach, lies just to the east of the south entrance to Stanley Park, at the foot of Denman Street. A waterslide, street performers, and artists keep things interesting all summer. Farther along Beach Drive, **Sunset Beach** is too close to the downtown core for clean, safe swimming, but is a great spot for an evening stroll. You can catch a ferry to Granville Island here, or swim at the **Vancouver Aquatic Centre** (✉ *1050 Beach Ave.* ☎ *604/665–3424*), a public indoor pool and fitness center.

CYCLING

Fodor'sChoice
★ The most popular recreational route, much of it off-road, is the **Seaside route.** It runs about 32 km (20 mi) from the seawall in Coal Harbour, around Stanley Park and False Creek, through Kitsilano to Spanish Banks. For detailed route descriptions and a downloadable map check out ⊕ *www.city.vancouver.bc.ca.*

BIKE RENTALS Most bike-rental outlets also rent Rollerblades and jogging strollers.

Bayshore Bicycles. If you're starting your bike ride near Stanley Park, try this friendly store. It has a range of bikes and Rollerblades as well as baby joggers and bike trailers. ✉ *745 Denman St., West End* ☎ *604/688–2453.*

Reckless Bike Stores. This outfit rents bikes on the Yaletown section of the bike path. To explore the Granville Island and Kitsilano area, a better bet might be their Kitsilano branch. ✉ *110 Davie St., Yaletown* ☎ *604/648–2600* ✉ *1810 Fir St., at 2nd Ave., Kitsilano* ☎ *604/731–2420.*

MOUNTAIN
BIKING

Lower Seymour Conservation Reserve. Nestled into the precipitous North Shore Mountains, this reserve has 25 km (15.5 mi) of challenging rain-forest trails. ⊠*End of Lillooet Rd., North Vancouver* ☎*604/432–6286.*

MOUNTAIN
BIKE RENTALS

Cove Bike Shop. In the village of Deep Cove on Indian Arm, the Cove Bike Shop pioneered the design and construction of mountain bikes for this punishing terrain and continues to market them worldwide. Given huge insurance costs, it's also the only bike shop that rents them. Bikes of all types and sizes are available March through October. ⊠*4310 Gallant Ave., North Vancouver* ☎*604/929–2222 or 604/985–2222.*

ECOTOURS & WILDLIFE VIEWING

Sewell's Marina Horseshoe Bay. This long-time marina at the foot of Howe Sound runs year-round two-hour ecotours of the surrounding marine and coastal mountain habitat. Sightings range from seals to soaring eagles. High-speed rigid inflatable hulls are used. ⊠*6409 Bay St., Horseshoe Bay* ☎*604/921–3474.*

BIRD- &
EAGLE-
WATCHING

Between mid-November and mid-February, the world's largest concentration of bald eagles gathers to feed on salmon at **Brackendale Eagles' Park** (⊠*Government Rd. off Hwy. 99, Brackendale*), about an hour north of Vancouver.

George C. Reifel Bird Sanctuary. More than 260 species of migratory birds visit this 850-acre site on Westham Island, about an hour south of Vancouver. A seasonal highlight is the arrival of an estimated 80,000 Lesser Snow Geese in the late fall. ⊠*5191 Robertson Rd., Ladner* ☎*604/946–6980* 💲*C$4* 🕙*Daily 9–4.*

WHALE-
WATCHING

Between April and October pods of Orca whales travel through the Strait of Georgia, near Vancouver. The area is also home to harbor seals, elephant seals, bald eagles, minke whales, porpoises, and a wealth of birdlife.

Wild Whales Vancouver. Boats leave Granville Island in search of Orca pods in Georgia Strait, traveling as far as Victoria. Rates are C$109 for a three- to seven-hour trip in either an open or glass-domed boat. Each boat leaves once daily, April through October, conditions permitting. ☎*604/699–2011.*

GOLF

Vancouver-area golf courses offer challenging golf with great scenery. Most are open year-round.

The Vancouver Park Board operates three public courses, all located on the city's south-facing slope. The most celebrated is the 18-hole, par-72, 6,700-yard **Fraserview Golf Course** (⊠*7800 Vivian Dr., South Vancouver* ☎*604/257–6923, 604/280–1818 advance bookings*), where facilities include a driving range and a new club house. The greens fee is C$55–C$58. The other two, both 18 holes and with slightly lower greens fees, are **Langara Golf Course** (⊠*6706 Alberta St.* ☎*604/713–1816*) and **McCleary Golf Course** (⊠*7188 Macdonald St.* ☎*604/257–8191*).

Fodor'sChoice
★

Westwood Plateau Golf and Country Club. Westwood is a well-manicured, 18-hole, par-72 course located just east of the city; it's closed November through March. The greens fee, which includes a cart, is C$169 and the club also has a restaurant open seasonally. The 9-hole **Academy Course** nearby (604/941–4236) is open year-round. ✉ *3251 Plateau Blvd., Coquitlam* ☎ *604/552–0777 or 800/580–0785.*

HIKING

Fodor'sChoice ★ **Capilano River Regional Park.** This small but spectacular park is where you'll find the Capilano River canyon, several old-growth fir trees approaching 61 meters (200 feet), a salmon hatchery open to the public, and the Cleveland Dam, as well as 26 km (16 mi) of hiking trails. It's at the end of Capilano Park Road, off Capilano Road, North Vancouver. ☎ *604/224–5739.*

★ **Grouse Grind.** Vancouver's most famous, or infamous, hiking route, the Grind is a 2.9-km (1.8-mi) climb straight up Grouse Mountain. Thousands do it annually (indeed, it's so popular the name is trademarked), but climbers are advised to be in "excellent physical condition." Those that aren't will suffer (though live to tell about it); it's not for children. The route is open daily, 6:30 AM to 7:30 PM, from spring through autumn (conditions permitting). There is no charge for the climb, but you are charged a small fee (C$5) to ride down the Grouse Mountain Skyride (gondola). A round-trip ticket costs C$32.95. Eco-walks are led along the paths accessed from the Skyride. ✉ *6400 Nancy Greene Way, North Vancouver* ☎ *604/980–9311 Grouse Mountain, 604/432–6200 Metro Vancouver (formerly GVRD).*

★ **Lighthouse Park.** This 75-hectare (185-acre) wilderness park wraps around Point Atkinson and its historic lighthouse (of the same name), where Howe Sound meets Burrard Inlet in the municipality of West Vancouver. A bank of soaring granite (popular for picnicking) shapes the foreshore, while the interior is an undulating terrain of mostly Douglas fir, rich undergrowth, birds, and other wildlife. Trails, from easy to challenging, wend throughout. A trail map is downloadable at the municipal Web site. ✉ *Beacon La. off Marine Dr., West Vancouver.*

Fodor'sChoice ★ **Stanley Park.** Stanley Park is well suited for moderate walking and easy hiking. The most obvious and arguably most picturesque route is the 8.8-km (5.5-mi) seawall around its perimeter, but this 1,000-acre park also offers 27 km (16.7 mi) of interior trails through the coniferous forest, including a few small patches of original forest, or old growth. The interior paths are wide and well maintained; here you'll experience something of the true rain forest and spot some of the birds and small mammals that inhabit it. You can download a trail map at the Park Board Web site. ☎ *604/257–8400.*

GUIDED HIKES **Rockwood Adventures.** This company offers guided walks of rain-forest or coastal terrain including Lighthouse Park, Lynn Canyon, and Capilano Canyon, and Bowen Island in Howe Sound (including a short flight). They also offer walking tours of Vancouver's Chinatown. ☎ *604/980–7749 or 888/236–6606.*

5

SKIING & SNOWBOARDING

CROSS-
COUNTRY
Cypress Mountain. This private operator within Cypress Provincial Park maintains 19 km (10 mi) of cross-country or "nordic" trails into the undulating, lake-dotted landscape of Hollyburn Mountain. There is a charge for their use. There are also 10 km (6 mi) dedicated to snowshoeing. ⊠ *Cypress Bowl Rd., West Vancouver* ⊹ *Exit 8 off Hwy. 1 westbound* ☎ *604/419–7669.*

DOWNHILL
SKIING &
Cypress Mountain. The most recent of three North Shore commercial ski destinations, Cypress is nonetheless well equipped, and will be more so with the completion of freestyle skiing and snowboarding venues being built for the 2010 Winter Olympics. Facilities include 5 quad or double chairs, 38 downhill runs, and a vertical drop of 1,750 feet. The mountain also has a snow-tubing area and snowshoe tours. ⊠ *Cypress Bowl Rd., West Vancouver* ⊹ *Exit 8 off Hwy. 1 westbound* ☎ *604/419–7669.*

Grouse Mountain. Reached by gondola (with an entrance fee) from the upper reaches of North Vancouver, much of the Grouse Mountain resort inhabits a slope overlooking the city. While views are fine on a clear day, at night (the area is known for its night-skiing) they're spectacular. Facilities include 2 quad chairs, 26 skiing and snowboarding runs, and several all-level freestyle-terrain parks. The vertical drop is 1,210 feet. There's a choice of upscale and casual dining in a good-looking stone-and-timber lodge. ⊠ *6400 Nancy Greene Way, North Vancouver* ☎ *604/980–9311, 604/986–6262 snow report.*

Mt. Seymour. Described as a full-service winter activity area, the Mt. Seymour resort sprawls over 200 acres accessed from eastern North Vancouver. With three chairs for varying abilities; a beginner's rope tow, equipment rentals, and lessons; and toboggan and tubing runs, it's a popular destination for families. Snowboarding is particularly popular. The eateries aren't fancy. ⊠ *1700 Mt. Seymour Rd., North Vancouver* ☎ *604/986–2261, 604/718–7771 snow report.*

WATER SPORTS

BOATING &
SAILING
With an almost limitless number and variety of waterways—from Indian Arm near Vancouver, up Howe Sound and the Sunshine Coast, across Georgia Strait to the Gulf Islands, and on to Vancouver Island, southwestern British Columbia is a boater's paradise. And much of this territory has easy access to marine and public services.

Cooper Boating charters sailboats and cabin cruisers, with or without instructing skippers. ⊠ *1620 Duranleau St., Granville Island* ☎ *604/687–4110 or 888/999–6419.*

CANOEING &
KAYAKING
Kayaking—sea-going and river kayaking—has become something of a lifestyle in Vancouver. While many sea kayakers start out (or remain) in False Creek, others venture into the open ocean and up and down the Pacific Coast. You can white-water kayak or canoe down the Capilano River and several other North Vancouver rivers. And paddling in a traditional, sea-going aboriginal-built canoe is an increasingly popular way to experience the maritime landscape.

Ecomarine Ocean Kayak Centre. Lessons and rentals are offered year-round from Granville Island, and from early May to early September at Jericho Beach and English Bay. ✉ *1668 Duranleau St., Granville Island* ☎ *604/689–7575 or 888/425–2925* ✉ *English Bay* ☎ *604/685–2925* ✉ *Jericho Beach* ☎ *604/222–3565.*

★ **Takaya Tours.** A trip with Takaya is a unique experience: you can paddle a 45-foot Salish ocean-going canoe while First Nations guides relay local legends, sing traditional songs, and point out ancient village sites. The two-hour tours cost C\$54 and leave from Cates Park in North Vancouver, and Belcarra Park in Port Moody. They also have trips up Indian Arm on motorized kayaks. Reservations are essential. ☎ *604/904–7410.*

SHOPPING

Updated by Chris McBeath

Unlike many cities where suburban malls have taken over, Vancouver is full of individual boutiques and specialty shops. Antiques stores, ethnic markets, art galleries, gourmet-food shops, and high-fashion outlets abound, and both Asian and First Nations influences in crafts, home furnishings, and foods are quite prevalent.

Stretching from Burrard to Bute, **Robson Street** is the city's main fashion-shopping and people-watching artery. The Gap and Banana Republic have their flagship stores here, as do Canadian fashion outlets Club Monaco and Roots. Souvenir shops and cafés fill the gaps. One block north of Robson, **Alberni Street** is geared to the higher-income visitor and is where you'll find duty-free shopping. At the stores in and around Alberni, and around Burrard, you'll find names such as Tiffany & Co., Louis Vuitton, Gucci, Coach, Hermés, and Betsey Johnson. Treasure hunters like the 300 block of **West Cordova Street** in **Gastown**, where offbeat shops sell curios, vintage clothing, and locally designed clothes. Bustling **Chinatown**—centered on Pender and Main streets—is full of Chinese bakeries, restaurants, herbalists, tea merchants, and import shops. Frequently described as Vancouver's SoHo, **Yaletown** on the north bank of False Creek is home to boutiques, home stores, and restaurants—many in converted warehouses—that cater to a trendy, moneyed crowd. On the south side of False Creek, **Granville Island** has a lively food market and a wealth of galleries, crafts shops, and artisans' studios. It gets so busy, especially on the weekends, that the crowds can detract from the pleasure of the place you're best off getting there before 11 AM.

DEPARTMENT STORES & SHOPPING CENTERS

The Hudson Bay Co. A Canadian institution (even though it's now owned by Americans), the Bay was founded as part of the fur trade in the 17th century. A whole department sells the signature tri-color Bay blankets and other Canadiana. ✉ *674 Granville St., at Georgia St., Downtown* ☎ *604/681–6211.*

Chinatown Night Market. Chinatown is at its liveliest when stalls set up shop selling food, T-shirts, and "do I really need this?" bits 'n bobs. It's open from late May to mid-September, 6:30 PM to 11 PM, Friday through Sunday. It's fun to wander. ⊠*Keefer St., between Columbia and Gore Sts., Chinatown* ☎*604/682–8998.*

Pacific Centre Mall. Filling three city blocks in the heart of downtown, this mall has mostly mid-price, mainstream clothing shops on the lower level; chicer, pricier items can be found on the upper floor. There are several street-level entrances as well as access via Holt Renfrew, the Hudson's Bay, and Sears department stores—worth knowing about on rainy days. ⊠*700 W. Georgia St., Downtown* ☎*604/688–7236.*

SPECIALTY STORES

ART & CRAFTS GALLERIES

Granville Island is a must-do destination for crafts aficionados. Stroll Railspur Alley (off Old Bridge Street), which is lined with working artists' studios; the Net Loft building opposite the Public Market also has several galleries. In the West End, Gallery Row along Granville Street between 5th and 15th avenues is home to about a dozen high-end contemporary-art galleries.

★ **Coastal Peoples Fine Arts Gallery.** The beautiful books and postcards make affordable souvenirs though you could well be tempted by the impressive collection of First Nations jewelry, ceremonial masks, prints, and carvings. ⊠*1024 Mainland St., Yaletown* ☎*604/685–9298.*

Craft House. Run by the Crafts Association of B.C., this tiny house contains a veritable smorgasbord of works by local artisans. ⊠*1386 Cartwright St., Granville Island* ☎*604/687–7270.*

Fodor'sChoice ★ **Hill's Native Art.** This highly respected store has Vancouver's largest selection of First Nations art. If you think the main level is impressive, try going upstairs where the collector-quality stuff is. ⊠*165 Water St., Gastown* ☎*604/685–4249.*

Inuit Gallery of Vancouver. In addition to quality Inuit art like the signature carvings in soapstone and antler, there's also an excellent collection of Northwest Coast Native art such as baskets, totems, bentwood boxes, and masks. ⊠*206 Cambie St., Gastown* ☎*888/615–8399 or 604/688–7323.*

★ **Robert Held Art Glass.** Held is an award-winning glassblower whose work is known worldwide. Located two blocks west of South Granville, you can watch glassblowers in action here, then browse the retail area crammed with one-of-a-kind vases, paperweights, bowls, ornaments, and perfume bottles. Tours are available, too. ⊠*2130 Pine St., between 5th and 6th Aves., South Granville* ☎*604/737–0020.*

CLOTHES

Fodor'sChoice ★ **Holt Renfrew.** Already high on the ritzy scale, Holts recently refurbished their image and their location: it's the very swanky showcase for international high fashion and accessories for men and women. Think Prada, Dolce & Gabbana, and other designer labels. ⊠*Pacific Centre, 737 Dunsmuir St., Downtown* ☎*604/681–3121.*

★ **Leone.** Marble alcoves in an elegantly palatial store set the scene for men's and women's fashions by Jil Sander, Versace, Yves Saint Laurent, Rive Gauche, Dior, Miu Miu, and others. On the lower level is

L-2 Leone, where you'll find edgier fashions and an Italian café. ⊠*350 Howe St., in Sinclair Centre Downtown* ☎*604/685–9327.*

★ **Lululemon Athletica.** This is a real Vancouver success story: everyone from power-yoga devotees to soccer moms covet the fashionable well-constructed workout wear with the stylized "A" insignia. Nike "swoosh" be warned. ⊠*1148 Robson St., West End* ☎*604/681–3118* ⊠*2113 W. 4th Ave., Kitsilano* ☎*604/732–6111* ⊠*Metropolis at Metrotown Centre, Burnaby* ☎*604/430–4659.*

Patricia Fieldwalker. Julia Roberts, Christie Turlington, Kathleen Turner, and Demi Moore have Patricia's lingerie, lounge, and resort wear close to their skin. It sells under the Arabesque label. This is a factory direct showroom. ⊠*302–343 Railway St., East Vancouver* ☎*604/689–1210.*

Roots. For outdoorsy clothes that double as souvenirs (many sport maple-leaf logos), check out these Canadian-made sweatshirts, leather jackets, and other comfy casuals. An interesting note: Roots outfits the Canadian Olympic team. ⊠*1001 Robson St., West End* ☎*604/683–4305.*

FOOD

Fodor'sChoice **Granville Island Public Market.** All your senses will be exhilarated, though
★ most especially your taste buds. Stalls are packed with fresh produce, meats, just-caught fish, baked goods, and prepared foods from exotic cheeses and handmade fudge to frothy cappuccinos. If the sun is out, dine on your purchases out on the decks. At the **Salmon Shop** (☎*604/669–3474*), you can pick up fresh or smoked salmon vacuum-packed and wrapped for travel. ⊠*1689 Johnston St., Granville Island* ☎*604/666–5784.*

★ **Les Amis du Fromage.** If you love cheese, don't miss the mind-boggling array of selections from B.C., the rest of Canada, France, and elsewhere at this shop of delicacies. The extremely knowledgeable mother-and-daughter owners, Alice and Allison Spurrell, and their staff encourage you to taste before you buy. Yum. ⊠*1752 W. 2nd Ave., Kitsilano* ☎*604/732–4218.*

Meinhardt Fine Foods. Pick up fixings for an elegant picnic or find a gift for a foodie friend at this sophisticated neighborhood groceteria. The same owners run a deli-style coffee shop next door; good for sandwiches, wraps, and pastries to eat in or take out. ⊠*3002 Granville St., South Granville* ☎*604/732–4405.*

JEWELRY

Birks. In a neoclassical building that was the former headquarters of the Canadian Imperial Bank of Commerce, this Canada-wide chain has been a national institution since 1879. An impressive staircase connects the main level to the mezzanine floor—descending, it feels as if you're royalty. ⊠*698 W. Hastings St., Downtown* ☎*604/669–3333.*

SHOES

Dayton Boot Company. These biker boots have a worldwide, cultlike following because they're that enduringly good, and hip, too. Celebrities like Kurt Russell, Harry Connick Jr., Cindy Crawford, and Sharon Stone are wearers. ⊠*2250 E. Hastings St., East Side* ☎*604/255–6671.*

VANCOUVER ESSENTIALS

BY AIR

The major airport is Vancouver International Airport (YVR), located in the suburb of Richmond about 16 km (10 mi) south of downtown Vancouver.

There are many options for getting downtown from Vancouver International Airport, a drive of about 20 to 45 minutes, depending on traffic. If you're driving, go over the Arthur Laing Bridge and north on Granville Street (also signposted as Highway 99). Signs direct you to Vancouver City Centre.

The Vancouver Airporter Service bus leaves the international- and domestic-arrivals levels of the terminal building approximately every half hour, stopping at major downtown hotels. The first departure from the airport is 8:30 AM, and the service runs until 9:45 PM. The fare is C$13.50 one-way and C$21 round-trip.

Taxi stands are in front of the terminal building on domestic- and international-arrivals levels. The taxi fare to downtown is about C$30; it's probably the fastest way to downtown. Area cab companies include Black Top and Yellow.

In November 2009 the Canada Line train will offer high-speed service between the airport and downtown.

Contacts **Black Top Cabs** (☎ *604/681–2181*). **TransLink** (☎ *604/953–3333* ⊕ *www.translink.bc.ca*). **Vancouver Airporter Service** (☎ *604/946–8866 or 800/668–3141* ⊕ *www.yvrairporter.com*). **Vancouver International Airport** (☎ *604/207–7077* ⊕ *www.yvr.ca*). **Yellow Cab** (☎ *604/681–1111*).

BY BOAT & FERRY

The British Columbia (BC) Ferry Corporation operates one of the largest ferry fleets in the world, serving about 40 ports of call on B.C.'s west coast. The ferries carry all vehicles as well as bicycles and foot passengers.

Reservations are optional on services between Vancouver and Vancouver Island and on most sailings between Vancouver and the Southern Gulf Islands. Most other services do not accept reservations and load vehicles on a first-come, first-served basis.

BC Ferries operates two major ferry terminals outside Vancouver. From Tsawwassen to the south (an hour's drive from downtown), ferries sail to Swartz Bay near Victoria, to Nanaimo on Vancouver Island, and to the Gulf Islands (the small islands between the mainland and Vancouver Island). From Horseshoe Bay (45 minutes north of downtown), ferries sail to the Sunshine Coast and to Nanaimo on Vancouver Island. Vehicle reservations on Vancouver to Victoria and Nanaimo routes are optional and cost C$15 to C$17.50 in addition to the fare. There's no extra charge for reservations on Gulf Island routes.

The SeaBus is a 400-passenger commuter ferry that crosses Burrard Inlet from Waterfront Station downtown to the foot of Lonsdale Avenue in North Vancouver. Leaving every 15 to 30 minutes, the bus takes 13 minutes and costs the same as the TransLink bus. With a transfer, connection can be made to any TransLink bus or SkyTrain.

Aquabus Ferries connect several stations on False Creek, including Science World, Plaza of Nations, Granville Island, Stamp's Landing, Spyglass Place, Yaletown, and the Hornby Street dock. Some Aquabus ferries take bicycles, and the company also operates two historic wooden boats on some runs.

False Creek Ferries provides foot-passenger service between the Aquatic Centre on Beach Avenue, Granville Island, Science World, Stamp's Landing, and Vanier Park.

False Creek and Aquabus ferries are not part of the TransLink system, so bus transfers aren't accepted.

Contacts **Aquabus Ferries** (☎ *604/689–5858* ⊕ *www.theaquabus.com*). **BC Ferries** (☎ *250/386–3431, 888/223–3779 in B.C., Alberta, and Washington state* ⊕ *www.bcferries.com*). **False Creek Ferries** (☎ *604/684–7781* ⊕ *www.granvil leislandferries.bc.ca*). **SeaBus** (☎ *604/953–3333* ⊕ *www.translink.bc.ca*).

BUS & RAPID TRANSIT TRAVEL WITHIN VANCOUVER

TransLink buses provide regular service throughout Vancouver and its suburbs. Exact change is needed to ride TransLink buses: each cash fare offers up to 90 minutes of travel, and fares are based on zones: 1 zone (C$2.50), 2 zones (C$3.75), or 3 zones (C$5).

A rapid-transit system called SkyTrain travels underground downtown and is elevated for the rest of its route to Coquitlam and Surrey. The system has two lines: the Expo Line and the Millennium Line.

Contacts **SkyTrain** (☎ *604/953–3333* ⊕ *www.translink.bc.ca*). **Translink** (⊕ *www. translink.bc.ca*).

BY CAR

If you plan to spend most or all your time in downtown Vancouver, you won't need a car: parking can be difficult to secure and most attractions are within walking distance or a short cab or bus ride away. If you do want to rent a car, rates in Vancouver begin at about C$40 a day or C$230 a week, usually including unlimited mileage. Some companies located near Vancouver International Airport offer free customer pick-up and drop-off at the airport, enabling you to avoid the latter fee. Vancouver's airport and downtown locations usually have the best selection.

Local Vancouver Agencies **Lo-Cost Rent A Car** (☎ *888/556–2678* ⊕ *www. locost.com*).

BY TAXI

It can be difficult to hail a cab in Vancouver, especially when it's raining. Unless you're near a hotel, you'll have better luck calling a taxi service. Try Black Top or Yellow.

Contacts **Black Top Cabs** (☎ *604/681–2181*). **Yellow Cab** (☎ *604/681–1111*).

BY TRAIN

Amtrak has service from Seattle to Vancouver, providing connections between Amtrak's U.S.-wide network and VIA Rail's Canadian routes. In B.C. VIA Rail has two routes: Vancouver to Jasper, and Jasper to Prince Rupert with an overnight stop in Prince George. Rocky Mountaineer Vacations operates a variety of spectacular all-daylight rail trips between the Canadian Rockies and the west coast. All trains offer a smoke-free environment.

Reservations are essential on the Rocky Mountaineer and highly recommended on Amtrak and VIA routes. There's no extra charge for reservations on any of the train services listed.

Information **Rocky Mountaineer Vacations** (☎ *800/665–7245* ⊕ *www.rocky mountaineer.com*). **VIA Rail Canada** (☎ *888/842–7245* ⊕ *www.viarail.ca*).

VISITOR INFORMATION

Contacts **Downtown Ambassadors** (☎ *604/689–4357* ⊕ *www.downtownvan couver.net*). **Granville Island Information Services** (☎ *604/666–5784* ⊕ *www. granvilleisland.com*). **Vancouver Tourist InfoCentre** (☎ *604/683–2000* ⊕ *www. tourismvancouver.com*).

VICTORIA

Updated by Alison Appelbe & Sue Kernaghan

What's not to love about Victoria? The capital of a province whose license plates brazenly label it "The Best Place on Earth" is a walkable, livable seaside town of fragrant gardens, waterfront paths, engaging museums, and beautifully restored 19th-century architecture. In summer, the Inner Harbour—Victoria's social and cultural center—buzzes with visiting yachts, horse-and-carriage rides, street entertainers, and excursion boats heading out to visit pods of friendly, local whales. Yes, it's touristy, but Victoria's good looks, gracious pace, and manageable size are instantly beguiling, especially if you look past the somewhat cheesy mimes and caricature artists, and stand back to admire the mountains and ocean beyond.

At the southern tip of Vancouver Island, forming the western point of a triangle with Seattle and Vancouver, Victoria dips slightly below the 49th parallel. That puts it farther south than most of Canada, giving it the mildest climate in the country, with virtually no snow and less than half the rain of Vancouver.

The city's geography, or at least its place names, can cause confusion. Just to clarify: the city of Victoria is on Vancouver Island (not Victoria Island). The city of Vancouver is on the British Columbia mainland, not on Vancouver Island, or on Victoria Island (which isn't in British Columbia but rather way up north, spanning parts of Nunavut and the Northwest Territories).

These days, however, Victorians prefer to celebrate their combined indigenous, Asian, and European heritage, and the city's stunning wilderness backdrop. Locals do often venture out for afternoon tea (although typically in a rather informal sense of the tradition), but they're just as likely to nosh on dim sum or tapas. Decades-old shops sell imported linens and tweeds, but newer upstarts offer local designs in hemp and organic cotton. And let's not forget that fabric prevalent among locals: Gortex. The outdoors are ever present here. You can hike, bike, kayak, sail, or whale-watch straight from the city center, and forests, beaches, offshore islands, and wilderness parklands lie just minutes away.

EXPLORING VICTORIA

Exploring Victoria is easy. A walk around downtown, starting with the museums and architectural sights of the Inner Harbour, followed by a stroll up Government Street to the historic areas of Chinatown and Old Town, covers most of the key attractions, though seeing every little interesting thing along the way could easily take two days.

5

DOWNTOWN VICTORIA

Numbers in the text correspond to numbers in the margin and on the Downtown Victoria map.

WHAT TO SEE

❹ **Beacon Hill Park.** The southern lawns and waterfront path of this 154-acre park afford great views of the Olympic Mountains and the Strait of Juan de Fuca. Also here are ponds, jogging and walking paths, abundant flowers and gardens, a petting zoo, a putting green, and a cricket pitch. ⊠ *East of Douglas St., south of Southgate St., Downtown* ☎ *250/361–0600 City of Victoria Parks Division, 250/381–2532 children's farmyard, 250/389–0444 Victoria Film Festival* ⊕ *www.victoria.ca.*

❾ **Chinatown.** Chinese immigrants built much of the Canadian Pacific Railway in the 19th century, and their influence still marks the region. Victoria's Chinatown, founded in 1858, is the oldest and most intact such district in Canada ⊠ *Fisgard St. between Government and Store Sts. Chinatown.*

❸ **Emily Carr House.** One of Canada's most celebrated artists and a respected writer, Emily Carr (1871–1945) was born and raised in this very proper wooden Victorian house before she abandoned her middle-class life to live in, and paint, the wilds of British Columbia. Carr's own descriptions, from her autobiography *Book of Small,* were used to restore the house. Catch, if you can, one of the days when an actress playing Carr tells stories of her life. Art work on display includes work by modern-day B.C. artists and reproductions of Carr's work. You'll need to visit the Art Gallery of Greater Victoria or the Vancouver Art Gallery to see Carr originals. ⊠ *207 Government St., James Bay* ☎ *250/383–5843* ⊕ *www.emilycarr.com* ▣ *C$5; C$10 for actress performances and other special events* ⊙ *May and Sept., Tues.–Sat. 11–4; July and Aug., daily 11–4; Oct.–Apr. by arrangement or during special events.*

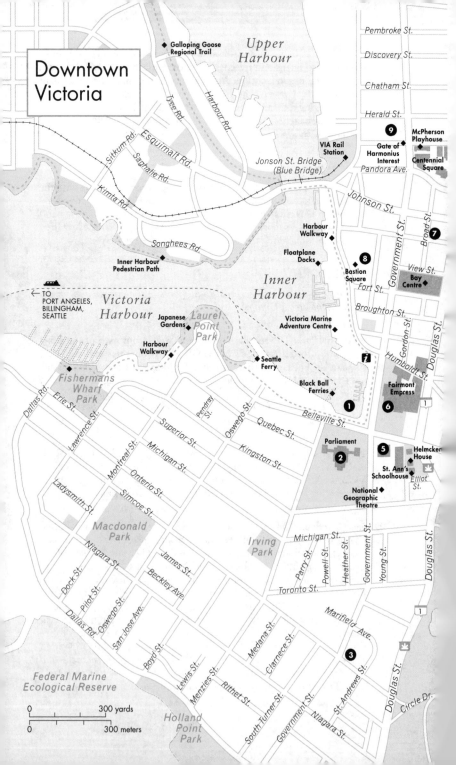

Downtown Victoria

Upper Harbour

Pembroke St.

Discovery St.

Chatham St.

Herald St.

9 Gate of Harmonius Interest

McPherson Playhouse

Centennial Square

Pandora Ave.

Galloping Goose Regional Trail

Tyee Rd.

Harbour Rd.

Esquimalt Rd.

Sitkum Rd.

Saghalle Rd.

Kimta Rd.

VIA Rail Station

Jonson St. Bridge (Blue Bridge)

Johnson St.

Songhees Rd.

Harbour Walkway

7

Broad St.

Government St.

View St.

Inner Harbour

Floatplane Docks

Bastion Square **8**

Fort St.

Bay Centre

Inner Harbour Pedestrian Path

Broughton St.

Gordon St.

Douglas St.

TO PORT ANGELES, BILLINGHAM, SEATTLE

Victoria Harbour

Japanese Gardens

Laurel Point Park

Victoria Marine Adventure Centre

Humboldt St.

i

Harbour Walkway

Seattle Ferry

Black Ball Ferries

Belleville St.

1

Fairmont Empress **6**

1

Fishermans Wharf Park

Dallas Rd.

Erie St.

Lawrence St.

Pendray St.

Oswego St.

Quebec St.

Superior St.

Kingston St.

Parliament **2**

5 Helmcker House

St. Ann's Schoolhouse

Elliot St.

Montreal St.

Michigan St.

Ontario St.

Simcoe St.

National Geographic Theatre

Ladysmith St.

Macdonald Park

Niagara St.

James St.

Beckley Ave.

Irving Park

Michigan St.

Parry St.

Powell St.

Heather St.

Government St.

Young St.

Douglas St.

Toronto St.

Dock St.

Pilot St.

Oswego St.

San Jose Ave.

Dallas Rd.

Boyd St.

Lewis St.

Menzies St.

Medana St.

South Turner St.

Clarnece St.

Rithet St.

Government St.

3

Marifield Ave.

St. Andrews St.

1

Niagara St.

Circle Dr.

Douglas St.

Federal Marine Ecological Reserve

Holland Point Park

| 0 | 300 yards |
| 0 | 300 meters |

Central Park

Royal Athletic Park

Pembroke St.

Green St.

Caledonia Ave.

Caledonia Ave.

Herald St.

North St.

Park St.

Fisgard St.

Balmoral St.

Cormorant St.

City Hall

Mason St.

Pandora Ave.

Rudlin St.

Johnson St.

Yates St.

Blanshard St.

Quadra St.

View St.

Cook St.

Fort St.

Broughton St.

Meares St.

Pioneer Square

Courtney St.

Rockland Ave.

Rockland Ave.

Burdett Ave.

Burdett Ave.

Bridge Park

Fairfield Rd.

McClure St.

Humbold St.

Collinson

Richardson St.

Vancouver St.

Theatre Inconnu

Fairfield Rd.

Academy St.

Quadra St.

Southgate St.

Fairfield Rd.

Arbutus Way

Pakington St.

Southgate St.

Cook St.

Heywood Ave.

Vancouver St.

Pendergast St.

Linden Ave.

Beacon Hill

Sutlej St.

Oliphant St.

KEY

Park Blvd.

🛈 Tourist information

🚢 Ferry

---- Pedestrian trail

Children's Farm

Leonard St.

5

VICTORIA'S HISTORY

Vancouver didn't even exist in 1843 when Victoria, then called Fort Victoria, was founded as the westernmost trading post of the British-owned Hudson's Bay Company. It was the first European settlement on Vancouver Island, and in 1868, it became the capital of British Columbia.

The British weren't here alone, of course. The local First Nations people—the Songhees, the Saanich, and the Sooke—had already lived in the areas for thousands of years before anyone else arrived. Their art and culture—which are currently experiencing a renaissance after decades of enforced decline—are visible throughout southern Vancouver Island. You can see this in private and public galleries, in the totems at Thunderbird Park, in the striking collections at the Royal British Columbia Museum, and at the Quw'utsun'Cultural and Conference Centre in nearby Duncan.

Spanish explorers were the first foreigners to explore the area, although they left little more than place names (Galiano Island and Cordova Bay, for example). The thousands of Chinese immigrants drawn by the gold rushes of the late 19th century had a much greater impact, founding Canada's oldest Chinatown and adding an Asian influence that's still quite pronounced in Victoria's multicultural mix.

Despite its role as the provincial capital, Victoria was largely bypassed, economically, by Vancouver throughout the 20th century. This, as it turns out, was all to the good, helping to preserve Victoria's historic downtown and keeping the city free of skyscrapers and freeways. For much of the 20th century, Victoria was marketed to tourists as "The Most British City in Canada," and it still boasts more than its share of Anglo-theme pubs, tea shops, and double-decker buses.

6 **Fairmont Empress.** Opened in 1908 by the Canadian Pacific Railway, the Empress is one of the grand château-style railroad hotels that grace many Canadian cities and is a symbol of the city. ⊠ *721 Government St., entrance at Belleville and Government, Downtown* ☎ *250/384–8111, 250/389–2727 tea reservations* ⊕ *www.fairmont.com/empress* ⊠ *Free, afternoon tea C$55 July and Aug., C$38–C$49 Sept.–June.*

7 **Legacy Art Gallery and Café.** Victoria's newest art gallery opened in 2007 to display some of the 1,600 paintings, sculptures, and antiques collected by the late Michael Williams, the owner of Swans Hotel. Rotating exhibits in the 3,000-square-foot space comprise mostly Canadian works, including many by First Nations artists, but international painters are represented, too. ⊠ *630 Yates St., Downtown* ☎ *250/381–7670* ⊕ *www.maltwood.uvic.ca/legacy_gallery/home.htm* ⊠ *Free* ⊙ *Wed.–Sun. 10–7:30.*

8 **Maritime Museum of British Columbia.** The model ships, Royal Navy charts, photographs, uniforms, and ship bells at this museum, in Victoria's original courthouse, chronicle the province's seafaring history. ⊠ *28 Bastion Sq., Downtown* ☎ *250/385–4222* ⊕ *www.mmbc.bc.ca* ⊠ *C$8* ⊙ *Daily 9:30–4:30.*

❶ Pacific Undersea Gardens. If you want an up-close look at a wolf eel or an octopus, you might check out this underwater sea-life display, housed in and under a barge floating in the Inner Harbour. ✉ *490 Belleville St.* ☎ *250/382–5717* ⊕ *www.pacificunderseagardens.com* ☜ *C$9.50* ⊙ *Apr.–June, daily 10–6; July and Aug., daily 9–8; Sept.– Mar., daily 10–5.*

❷ Parliament Buildings. Officially the British Columbia Provincial Legislative Assembly Buildings, these massive stone structures are more popularly referred to as the Parliament Buildings. Designed by Francis Rattenbury (who also designed the Fairmont Empress Hotel) when he was just 25 years old and completed in 1898, they dominate the Inner Harbour. Free, informative half-hour tours run every 20 minutes during the summer, and hourly in the off-season; they're obligatory on summer weekends (mid-May until Labor Day) and optional the rest of the time. ✉ *501 Belleville St., Downtown* ☎ *250/387–3046* ⊕ *www.leg.bc.ca* ☜ *Free* ⊙ *Mid-May–early Sept., weekdays 9–5, weekends 9–7; early Sept.–mid-May, weekdays 9–5 (last tour an hr before closing).*

❺ Royal British Columbia Museum. This excellent museum, one of Victoria's leading attractions, traces several thousand years of British Columbian history. Its First Peoples Gallery, home to a genuine Kwakwaka'wakw big house and a dramatically displayed collection of masks and other artifacts, is especially strong. Also on-site is an IMAX theater showing *National Geographic* films on a six-story-high screen. ✉ *675 Belleville St., Downtown* ☎ *250/356–7226 or 888/447–7977* ⊕ *www.royalbc museum.bc.ca* ☜ *C$14, IMAX theater C$10.50, combination ticket C$22.50. Rates may be higher during special-exhibit periods* ⊙ *Museum: Mid-Oct.–June, daily 9–5; July–mid-Oct., daily 9–6 (open until 10 PM most Fri. and Sat. early June–mid-Oct.). Theater: daily 10–8; call for show times.*

FodorsChoice ★

OAK BAY, ROCKLAND & FAIRFIELD

The winding shady streets of Victoria's older residential areas—roughly bordered by Cook Street, Fort Street, and the seaside—are lined with beautifully preserved Victorian and Edwardian homes. These include many stunning old mansions now operating as B&Bs, and Victoria's most elaborate folly: Craigdarroch Castle. Among the lavish waterfront homes are plenty of public parks and beaches offering views across Juan de Fuca Strait to the Olympic Mountains of Washington State.

A car or a bike is handy, but not essential, for exploring this area. For a nice drive or cycling excursion, follow Scenic Marine Drive (also signposted as the Seaside Touring Route for cyclists) along Dallas Road. No wheels? Big Bus, Gray Line, and other tour companies offer Oak Bay and Marine Drive tours.

Art Gallery of Greater Victoria. Attached to an 1889 mansion, this modern building houses one of Canada's largest collections of Chinese and Japanese artifacts. The Japanese garden between the buildings is home to the only authentic Shinto shrine in North America. The gallery, which is a few blocks west of Craigdarroch Castle, off Fort Street, displays a permanent exhibition of works by well-known Canadian artist Emily Carr and regularly changing exhibits of Asian and historical and contemporary Western art. Major touring exhibitions include an Andy Warhol exhibit set for summer 2008. ✉*1040 Moss St., Rockland* ☎*250/384–4101* ⊕*www.aggv.bc.ca* ▣*C$12* ☉*Mon.–Wed., Fri.–Sun. 10–5, Thurs. 10–9.*

Craigdarroch Castle. This resplendent mansion complete with turrets and Gothic rooflines was built as the home of one of British Columbia's wealthiest men, coal baron Robert Dunsmuir, who died in 1889, just a few months before the castle's completion. Converted into a museum depicting life in the late 1800s, the castle's 39 rooms have ornate Victorian furnishings, stained-glass windows, carved woodwork, displays of the Dunsmuir daughters' party dresses, and a beautifully restored painted ceiling in the drawing room. ✉*1050 Joan Crescent, Rockland* ☎*250/592–5323* ⊕*www.thecastle.ca* ▣*C$11.75* ☉*Mid-June–early Sept., daily 9–7:30; early Sept.–mid-June, daily 10–5.*

THE BUTCHART GARDENS

30 km (18 mi) north of Victoria on Hwy. 17.

☙ **The Butchart Gardens.** This stunning
Fodor'sChoice 55-acre garden and National His-
★ toric Site has been drawing visitors since it was planted in a limestone quarry in 1904. Seven hundred varieties of flowers grow in the site's Japanese, Italian, rose, and sunken gardens. Highlights include the view over the ivy-draped and flower-filled former quarry, the dramatic 21-meter-high (70-foot-high) Ross Fountain, and the formal and intricate Italian garden, complete with a gelato stand. The Butchart Gardens Express Shuttle, run by Grey Line West, runs half-hourly service between downtown Victoria and the Butchart Gardens during peak season. The C$39 round-trip fare includes admission to the gardens. ✉*800 Benvenuto Ave., Brentwood Bay* ☎*250/652–5256 or 866/652–4422* ⊕*www.butchartgardens.com* ▣*Mid-June–late Sept. C$25, discounted rates rest of yr* ☉*Mid-June–Labor Day, daily 9 AM–10:30 PM; Sept.–mid-June, daily 9 AM–dusk; call for exact times.*

> **WORD OF MOUTH**
>
> "Butchart Gardens—beautiful place!! We took the Evening Illuminations tour with Grey Line and got to see the Gardens right before sunset and on into the late night . . . Seeing the Gardens lit up at night was unique."
>
> —globetrotterxyz

WHERE TO EAT

Victoria is said to have the second-highest number of restaurants per capita in North America (after San Francisco); this fact, and the glorious pantry that is Vancouver Island, keeps prices down (at least compared to Vancouver) and standards up. Wild salmon, locally made cheeses, Pacific oysters, organic vegetables, local microbrews, and even wines from the island's new farm gate wineries (The B.C. government allows very small wineries to sell their wines "at the farm gate") are tastes to watch for.

Afternoon tea is a Victoria tradition, as is good coffee—despite the Starbucks invasion, there are plenty of fun and funky local caffeine purveyors around town.

DOWNTOWN

ASIAN

$$ ✕**The Mint.** Ever wondered what a Nepalese night club might look like? Well, this subterranean space is as close as it gets, with good, affordable Nepalese and Tibetan dishes, from the traditional—chilies and chicken, spicy lamb curry, and Tibetan dumplings—to the less strictly Himalayan, such as *nan* pizzas and cheese plates. Local vegans swear by the nut burgers and almond-cashew pesto pasta. ⊠*1414 Douglas St., Downtown* ☎*250/386–6468* ⊟*AE, MC, V* ⊘*No lunch.*

$–$$ ✕**The Noodle Box.** Noodles, whether Indonesian-style with peanut
★ sauce, thick Japanese Udon in teriyaki, or Thai-style chow mein, are piled straight from steaming woks in the open kitchen to bowls or cardboard take-out boxes at this local answer to fast-food. Malaysian, Singapore, and Cambodian-style curries tempt those who like it hot. The brick, rose, and lime walls keep things modern and high energy. ⊠*818 Douglas St., Downtown* ☎*250/384–1314* ⚲*Reservations not accepted* ⊟*AE, MC, V* ⊠*626 Fisgard St., Downtown* ☎*250/360– 1312* ⚲*Reservations not accepted* ⊟*AE, MC, V.*

CAFÉS

¢–$ ✕**Blue Carrot Café.** Tucked off to the north side of Bastion Square, this family-run spot with a few tables on the cobbles outside keeps local office workers in wholesome omelet and benny breakfasts and affordable soup, sandwich, wrap, and burger lunches. Everything, including the Blue Carrot Cake, is homemade: Mom does most of the baking, but grandma makes the chocolate cake. Local art lines the walls. ⊠*18B Bastion Sq., Downtown* ☎*250/381–8722* ⚲*Reservations not accepted* ⊟*MC, V* ⊘*Closed Sun. Oct.–Mar. No dinner.*

CANADIAN

$$$$ ✕**Empress Room.** Candlelight dances on tapestried walls beneath a
★ carved mahogany ceiling at the Fairmont Empress hotel's flagship restaurant where one of the two gracious rooms has an expansive harbour view. The classically influenced Pacific Northwest menu changes frequently, but might start with seared Pacific sea scallops or risotto with local morels, and move to such mains as veal tenderloin with foie gras; local wild salmon; or mustard-crusted rack of lamb. The vegetarian and seafood fare on the spa menu is also tempting. Service is discreet and attentive, and there are more than 800 labels on the wine list. ⊠*Fairmont Empress, 721 Government St., Downtown* ☎*250/389– 2727* ⚲*Reservations not accepted* ⊟*AE, D, DC, MC, V.*

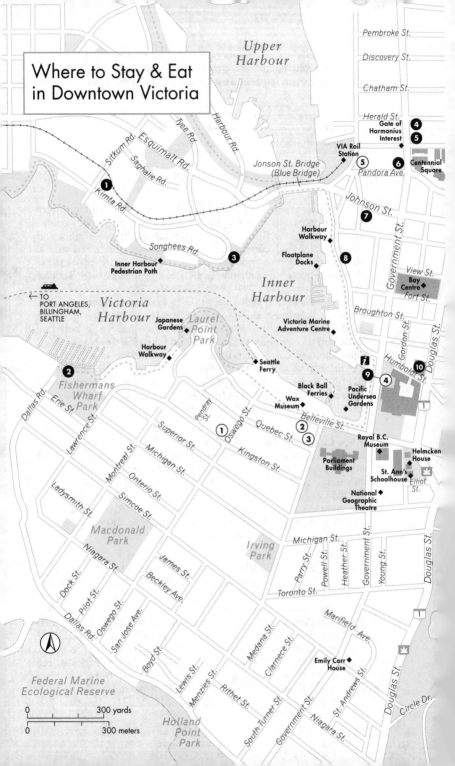

Where to Stay & Eat in Downtown Victoria

Upper Harbour

Pembroke St.

Discovery St.

Chatham St.

Herald St.

Gate of Harmonius Interest **4**

5

VIA Rail Station **5**

Pandora Ave.

6 Centennial Square

Tyee Rd.

Harbour Rd.

Jonson St. Bridge (Blue Bridge)

Esquimalt Rd.

Sitkum Rd.

Saghalie Rd.

Kimta Rd.

1

Johnson St.

7

Songhees Rd.

3

Harbour Walkway

Floatplane Docks **8**

Government St.

View St.

Bay Centre

Fort St.

Inner Harbour Pedestrian Path

Inner Harbour

Victoria Marine Adventure Centre

Broughton St.

Gordon St.

Douglas St.

← TO PORT ANGELES, BILLINGHAM, SEATTLE

Victoria Harbour

Japanese Gardens

Laurel Point Park

Humboldt St.

10

Harbour Walkway

Seattle Ferry

7

9 **4**

Pacific Undersea Gardens

2

Fishermans Wharf Park

Black Ball Ferries

Wax Museum

Belleville St.

Dallas Rd.

Erie St.

Lawrence St.

Pendray St.

Oswego St.

Superior St.

Quebec St.

1

2 **3**

Royal B.C. Museum

Helmcken House

Montreal St.

Michigan St.

Kingston St.

Parliament Buildings

St. Ann's Schoolhouse

Elliot St.

Ladysmith St.

Onterio St.

Simcoe St.

National Geographic Theatre

Macdonald Park

Niagara St.

James St.

Irving Park

Michigan St.

Dock St.

Pilot St.

Beckley Ave.

Parry St.

Powell St.

Heather St.

Government St.

Young St.

Douglas St.

San Jose Ave.

Oswego St.

Dallas Rd.

Toronto St.

Marifield Ave.

Boyd St.

Lewis St.

Menzies St.

Medana St.

Clarnece St.

Rithet St.

South Turner St.

Emily Carr House

St. Andrews St.

Government St.

Niagara St.

Douglas St.

Circle Dr.

Federal Marine Ecological Reserve

0   300 yards

0   300 meters

Holland Point Park

KEY

1 Restaurants

(1) Hotels

🛈 Tourist information

🚢 Ferry

---- Pedestrian trail

$$$ ✕ **Cafe Brio.** "Charming, comfortable, and hip with walls of art—all
★ backed by city's best chef and kitchen," is how one fodors.com user
describes this bustling Italian villa–style room. The frequently chang-
ing menu highlights regional, organic fare and favorites include braised
beef short ribs, local wild salmon in season, Cowichan Bay duck breast,
local lamb, and housemade charcuterie. Virtually everything, including
the bread, pasta, and desserts, as well as some of the cheeses, is made
in-house—even the butter is hand churned. ✉ *944 Fort St., Downtown*
☎ *250/383–0009 or 866/270–5461* ▭ *AE, MC, V* ⊘ *No lunch.*

$–$$ ✕ **Spinnakers Gastro Brewpub.** Victoria's longest menu of hand-crafted
★ beer is just one reason to trek over the Johnson Street Bridge or hop a
Harbour Ferry to this Vic West waterfront pub. Canada's oldest licensed
brewpub, Spinnakers relies almost exclusively on locally sourced ingredients for its top-notch casual fare. Opt for the pubby adults-only tap-
room, with its glassed-in waterfront deck, double-sided fireplace, and
plethora of paraphernalia-filled rooms; or dine in the all-ages waterfront restaurant. Either way you can enjoy such high-end pub grub as
mussels steamed in ale, brewery grain-fed beef burgers, wild salmon
fettucine, or fish-and-chips with kennebec fries. ✉ *308 Catherine St.,
Downtown* ☎ *250/386–2739 or 877/838–2739* ⚘ *Reservations not
accepted* ▭ *AE, MC, V.*

CHINESE

$–$$ ✕ **J&J Won Ton Noodle House.** Lunchtime queues attest to the popular-
ity of the fresh house-made noodles and won tons at this pan-Chinese
spot on antique row. The lines move fast, though, thanks to the efficient
service. Szechuan and Shanghai specialties, from shrimp noodle soup to
beef with hot chili bean sauce, dominate the long menu, but Singapore-
style noodles and Malaysian chow mein appear, too. ✉ *1012 Fort St.,
Downtown* ☎ *250/383-0680* ▭ *MC, V* ⊘ *Closed Sun. and Mon.*

FRENCH

$$–$$$ ✕ **Brasserie L'école.** The French country cooking shines at this informal
★ Chinatown bistro and the historic room—once a schoolhouse for the
Chinese community—evokes a timeless brasserie, from the white linens
and patina-rich fir floors to the chalkboards above the slate bar listing
the day's oyster and mussel options. Sean Brennan, one of the city's
better-known chefs, works with local farmers and fishers to source the
best seasonal, local, and organic ingredients. The menu changes daily
but lists such classic bistro fare as duck confit, steak frites, and trout
with chorizo and almonds. The wine list is primarily French and if you
order two glasses they'll open any bottle in the house. ✉ *1715 Government St., Downtown* ☎ *250/475–6260* ▭ *AE, MC, V* ⊘ *Closed Sun.
and Mon. No lunch.*

ITALIAN

$$–$$$$ ✕ **Il Terrazzo.** A charming redbrick terrace edged with potted greenery
★ and warmed by fireplaces and overhead heaters makes Il Terrazzo—
tucked away off Waddington Alley near Market Square and not visible
from the street—the locals' choice for romantic alfresco dining. The
menu changes frequently, but starters might include a salad of shred-
ded duck confit and baby spinach, or a dish of roasted artichoke and

tiger prawns. Thin-crust pizzas and such traditional Northern Italian mains as Dijon-crusted rack of lamb and osso buco with wild mushrooms come piping hot from the restaurant's wood oven. ⊠*555 Johnson St., off Waddington Alley (½ block east of Wharf St.), Downtown* ☏*250/361–0028* ⊟*AE, DC, MC, V* ⊗*No lunch Sun.*

SEAFOOD

$$$ – $$$$ ⨯**Lure Seafood Restaurant and Bar.** Walls of windows embrace Inner Harbour views at the Delta Victoria Ocean Pointe Resort's flagship restaurant. Seafood-loving locals and hotel guests book windowside tables at sunset to watch the lights come on across the water: the large, comfortable, but bland room with upholstered chairs and beige walls doesn't even try to compete with the view. The food puts on a good show, though, with elaborate presentations of locally sourced fare. Sooke trout, wild salmon, and B.C. halibut top a menu that also encompasses Cowichan Valley duck and coriander-crusted lamb loin. ⊠*45 Songhees Rd., Downtown* ☏*250/360–5873* ⊟*AE, D, DC, MC, V.*

$-$$ ⨯**Barb's Place.** Funky Barb's, a tin-roofed take-out shack, floats on the quay at Fisherman's Wharf, west of the Inner Harbour off St. Lawrence Street. Halibut, salmon, oysters, mussels, crab, burgers, and chowder are all prepared fresh on the premises. The picnic tables on the wharf provide a front-row view of interesting vessels, including a paddle wheeler, houseboats, and some vintage fishing boats, or you can carry your food to the grassy park nearby. Ferries sail to Fisherman's Wharf from the Inner Harbour. ⊠*Fisherman's Wharf, St. Lawrence St., Downtown* ☏*250/384–6515* ⊟*AE, MC, V* ⊗*Closed Nov.–Feb.*

OAK BAY & ROCKLAND

CANADIAN

$$$ ⨯**Paprika Bistro.** Local farmers and fishers and the owners' own garden
★ provide most of the ingredients at this intimate neighborhood bistro where chef George Szasz, together with his wife, Linda, create seasonal menus. He combines his classical French training with some ideas from his Hungarian grandmother and the results might be Cortes Island mussels, a spot prawn bisque, and house-made charcuterie, followed by duck-leg confit with balsamic glaze, organic beef tenderloin with shallot confit, or just-caught local fish. Three small rooms with brocade booths and local art on paprika-and-lemon walls are warm, romantic, and informal. The same owners also run **Stage,** a small-plates and wine bar. ⊠*2524 Estevan Ave., Oak Bay and Rockland* ☏*250/592–7424* ⊟*AE, MC, V* ⊗ ⊗*Closed Sun. No lunch* ⊠*1307 Gladstone Ave.* ☏*250/388–4222* ⊟*AE, MC, V* ⊗ *Closed Sun. No lunch.*

WHERE TO STAY

Victoria has a vast range of accommodation, with what seems like whole neighborhoods dedicated to hotels. Options range from city resorts and full-service business hotels to mid-price tour-group haunts, family-friendly motels, and backpacker hostels, but the city is especially known for its lavish B&Bs in beautifully restored Victorian and Edwardian mansions.

DOWNTOWN

$$$$ ✕⊞ **The Fairmont Empress.** A hundred years old in 2008, this ivy-draped harborside château and city landmark has aged gracefully, with top-notch service and sympathetically restored Edwardian decor. The 176 different room configurations include standard and harbor-view rooms with 11-foot ceilings, crisp white duvets, and fresh floral drapes. Turret rooms with Jacuzzi tubs are a little-known romantic option. State-of-the-art gym equipment, pillow-top beds, Wi-Fi, and flat-screen TVs are all planned for 2008. The hotel is a tourist attraction, but a guests-only lobby separates hotel guests from the throng. **Pros:** Central location, historic ambience, great spa and restaurant. **Cons:** Small-to-average-size rooms and bathrooms, tourists in the public areas, pricey. ✉ *721 Government St., Downtown, V8W 1W5* ☎ *250/384–8111 or 800/257–7544* 🖷 *250/381–5959* ⊕ *www.fairmont.com/empress* ⤵ *436 rooms, 41 suites* ✆ *In-room: no a/c (some), refrigerator, DVD (some), Ethernet (some), Wi-Fi. In-hotel: 2 restaurants, room service, bar, pool, gym, spa, laundry service, concierge, executive floor, public Internet, parking (fee), some pets allowed, no-smoking rooms* ▤ *AE, D, DC, MC, V.*

$$$$ ⊞ **The Oswego Hotel.** Victoria's hip quotient went up a notch with the ★   2007 opening of this chic all-suites hotel. Just in from the water in quiet but handy James Bay, the unassuming brick building is home to 80 sleek, modern suites. The look—black and white offset with soft neutrals, natural stone floors and countertops, and a wall of windows—is airy, modern, and comfortable with just a touch of West Coast. Full kitchens and balconies, many with sea views, encourage hanging out. The inviting lobby and terrace doubles as a casual bistro ($$). **Pros:** Stylish, quiet, friendly staff, free local calls. **Cons:** Murphy beds in the studios, 10-minute walk to town center, no pool. ✉ *500 Oswego St., Downtown, V8V 5C1* ☎ *250/294–7500 or 877/767–9346* 🖷 *250/294–7509* ⊕ *www.oswegovictoria.com* ⤵ *16 studio, 49 1-bedroom suites, 15 2-bedroom suites* ✆ *In-room: no a/c, kitchen, Ethernet, Wi-Fi. In-hotel: restaurant, bar, gym, laundry facilities, laundry service, public Internet, parking (fee), some pets allowed, no-smoking rooms* ▤ *AE, MC, V* �†⊙∣ *CP.*

$$$–$$$$ ⊞ **Hotel Grand Pacific.** The city's best health club (with yoga classes, ★   an ozone pool, squash courts, and state-of-the-art equipment) and a prime Inner Harbour location appeal to savvy business, government, and leisure regulars, including Seattleites stepping off the ferry across the street. Feng Shui design elements apply throughout, lending a calm energy to the gleaming marble lobby. Rooms are large and surprisingly quiet, with duvets, deep soaker tubs, floor-to-ceiling windows, and a muted, mainstream decor. Upper-floor rooms have views of the harbor, the Parliament Buildings, or distant mountains, which you can admire from your private covered balcony big enough to sit out on. Watch for local politicos plotting in the lounge. Pros: Great health club, prime location, balconies and views. **Cons:** Standard hotel decor, markup on local calls. ✉ *463 Belleville St., Downtown, V8V 1X3* ☎ *250/386–*

0450 or 800/663–7550 🖷*250/380–4475* ⊕*www.hotelgrandpacific. com* 🛏*258 rooms, 46 suites* ♿*In-room: safe, refrigerator, DVD (some), VCR (some), Ethernet. In-hotel: 3 restaurants, room service, bar, pool, gym, spa, laundry service, concierge, public Internet, public Wi-Fi, parking (fee), some pets allowed, no-smoking rooms* ▤*AE, D, MC, V.*

$$$ 🏨**Swans Suite Hotel.** This 1913 former warehouse in Victoria's old town is one of the city's most attractive boutique hotels. The studios and one- and two-bedroom suites, all with full kitchens, are roomy, comfortable, and stylish with rich earth tones, exposed beams, and pieces from the late owner's extensive art collection. **Pros:** Big beautiful suites with kitchens, great for families and groups, close to shopping and dining. **Cons:** Tiny lobby, pub noise on lower floors, uneven service, off-site parking. ⊠*506 Pandora Ave., Downtown, V8W 1N6* ☎*250/361–3310 or 800/668–7926* 🖷*250/361–3491* ⊕*www.swans hotel.com* 🛏*30 suites* ♿*In-room: no a/c, kitchen, DVD, VCR, Wi-Fi. In-hotel: restaurant, room service, bar, laundry facilities, laundry service, public Wi-Fi, parking (fee), no-smoking rooms* ▤*AE, D, DC, MC, V* ⦿*CP.*

$$–$$$ 🏨**Royal Scot Suite Hotel.** Large suites, great rates, a handy location, and friendly staff (some in kilts) keep families, seniors, and bus tours coming back to this well-run James Bay hotel—the games room, pool table, hot tub, laundry room, and even a small grocery store on-site make this an especially good choice. The decor is ordinary, but it's clean, freshly upholstered, and well maintained. The grounds, including a restaurant courtyard, are prettily landscaped with flower beds and hanging baskets, and a shuttle service saves the five-minute walk to the town center. **Pros:** Great for kids, good value, quiet neighborhood lots of facilities. **Cons:** Few low-cost dining options in immediate area. ⊠*425 Quebec St., Downtown, V8V 1W7* ☎*250/388–5463 or 800/663–7515* 🖷*250/388–5452* ⊕*www.royalscot.com* 🛏*30 rooms, 146 suites* ♿ ✎*n-room: no a/c, safe, kitchen (some), refrigerator, VCR (some), Ethernet. In-hotel: restaurant, room service, bar, pool, gym, laundry facilities, laundry service, public Internet, parking (no fee), no-smoking rooms* ▤*AE, D, DC, MC, V.*

OAK BAY & ROCKLAND

$$–$$$ 🏨**Abbeymoore Manor Bed & Breakfast Inn.** This 1912 mansion has the
★ wide verandas, dark wainscoting, and high ceilings of its era but the attitude is informal, from the helpful hosts to the free snacks and coffee on tap all day. Two modern, one-bedroom suites on the ground floor have kitchens while five upper-level rooms have charm with such period details as claw-foot tubs or sleigh beds, and verandas or antique-tile fireplaces. The Penthouse Suite has a full kitchen and private entrance. Multicourse breakfasts are served family style or at tables for two in the sunroom or on the patio. **Pros:** Good value, friendly hosts. **Cons:** Not central. ⊠*1470 Rockland Ave., Rockland, V8S 1W2* ☎*250/370– 1470 or 888/801–1811* ⊕*www.abbeymoore.com* 🛏*5 rooms, 3 suites* ♿*In-room: no a/c, no phone (some), kitchen (some), DVD (some), VCR (some), no TV (some), Wi-Fi. In-hotel: no elevator, public Inter-*

5

net, parking (no fee), some pets allowed, no kids under 12, no-smoking rooms ☐*MC, V* ⱓ*IBP.*

$ ⅏**Craigmyle Guest House.** Affordable and historic, this four-story manor near Craigdarroch Castle has been a guesthouse since 1913. A large, welcoming common room is replete with Victoriana and original stained glass; a traditional English breakfast is served in the garden-view dining room. Rooms are cozy with floral bedspreads and wallpaper; all have private baths though in some cases the baths are across the hall. Two-room units and a guest kitchen appeal to families, and single rooms are offered at a single rate (C$65). A one-bedroom suite, remodeled in 2006, has modern furnishings, a jetted tub, and a rain-forest shower; it's the only unit with a phone, TV, and kitchenette. **Pros:** Affordable, atmospheric, family and single friendly. **Cons:** A bit removed from downtown, parking lot not available until evening. ✉*1037 Craigdarroch Rd., V8S 2A5* ☎*250/595–5411 or 888/595–5411* ☐*250/370–5276* ⊕*www.BandBvictoria.com* ⬚*16 rooms, 1 suite* ♿*In-room: no a/c, no phone, no TV, Wi-Fi. In-hotel: no elevator, parking (no fee), no-smoking rooms* ☐*AE, MC, V* ⱓ*IBP.*

NIGHTLIFE & THE ARTS

NIGHTLIFE

Victoria's nightlife is low-key and casual, with many wonderful pubs, but a limited choice of nightclubs. Several of Victoria's trendier restaurants double as lounges, offering cocktails and small plates well into the night.

BARS & CLUBS **Bengal Lounge.** Deep leather sofas and a Bengal tiger skin help to re-create the days of the British Raj at this iconic lounge in the Fairmont Empress Hotel. Martinis and a curry buffet are the draws through the week. On Friday and Saturday nights a jazz combo takes the stage. ✉*721 Government St., Downtown* ☎*250/384–8111* ⊕*www.fairmont.com/empress.*

Irish Times Pub. Stout on tap, live Celtic music nightly, and a menu of fish-and-chips, shepherd's pie, and Irish stew draw tourists and locals to this former bank building on Victoria's main shopping strip. ✉*1200 Government St.* ☎*250/383–7775.*

Steamers. This downtown bar has live bands every night, ranging from blues to zydeco. ✉*570 Yates St., Downtown* ☎*250/381–4340.*

Temple. DJs, martinis, and a trendy small-plates menu draw a fashionable late-evening crowd to this downtown restaurant, where a sandstone fireplace warms the cool modernist space. ✉*525 Fort St, Downtown* ☎*250/383–2313.*

THE ARTS

MUSIC **Summer in the Square.** Free jazz, classical, and folk concerts; cultural events; and more run all summer at Centennial Square, next to City Hall at Pandora and Douglas streets. ☎*250/361–0388* ⊕*www.victoria.ca/2007summerinthesquare.*

Victoria Symphony. The Royal Theatre and the University Centre Auditorium are the venues for regular season concerts. Watch, too, for **Symphony Splash** on the first Sunday in August, when the Victoria Symphony plays a free concert from a barge in the Inner Harbour. *Sym-*

phony Information: ☎*250/385–6515.* **Royal Theatre** ✉*805 Brough-ton St., Downtown* ☎*250/386–6121.* **University Centre Auditorium** ✉*Finnerty Rd., University of Victoria Campus* ☎*250/721–8480.*

OPERA **Pacific Opera Victoria.** Three productions a year are performed at the Royal Theatre. ☎*250/385–0222* ⊕*www.pov.bc.ca.*

Theatre Inconnu. Victoria's oldest alternative theater company, housed in a venue across the street from the Belfry Theatre, offers a range of performances at affordable ticket prices. ✉*1923 Fernwood Rd., Oak Bay and Rockland* ☎*250/360–0234* ⊕*www.theatreinconnu.com.*

The Victoria Fringe Festival. Each August a vast menu of offbeat, original, and intriguing performances takes over several venues around town; it's the last stop on a nationwide circuit of fringe-theater events attract-ing performers—and fans—from around the world. ☎*250/507–2663* ⊕*www.victoriafringe.com.*

SPORTS & THE OUTDOORS

BEACHES

Cadboro Gyro Park. A sandy beach backed by a grassy park with a play area draws families to this sheltered bay, accessible via the Scenic Marine Drive. ✉*Off Cadboro Bay Rd., Oak Bay and Rockland.*

Cordova Bay. A long stretch of sand is the draw at this beach, just north of Mount Douglas Park on the Scenic Marine Drive. ✉*Off Cordova Bay Rd., Sidney and Saanich Peninsula.*

Juan de Fuca Provincial Park. West of Sooke, this coastal wilderness park comprises a long string of beaches. Tossed with driftwood and backed with old-growth forest, these beaches are wild and beautiful with few services. French Beach and China Beach have campgrounds. French and Sombrio beaches attract surfers; Botanical Beach, near Port Ren-frew, has a wonderful array of sea life at low tide. ✉*Off Hwy. 14, Sooke and West Coast.*

BIKING

BIKE ROUTES **The Seaside Touring Route.** Starting at Victoria's Via Rail Station on John-son Street, this 11-km (7-mi) route was designed specifically for visitors and takes in most of the city's key sights.

BIKE RENTALS **Cycle BC Rentals.** Bicycles, scooters, and motorbikes are for rent at two & TOURS downtown locations. ✉*747 Douglas St., Downtown* ☎*250/380–2453* ✉*950 Wharf St., Downtown* ☎*250/385–2453.*

GOLF

Olympic View Golf Club. The distant peaks of the Olympic mountains are the backdrop to this bucolic par-72 course, home to 2 waterfalls and 12 lakes. The first B.C. course played by Tiger Woods, it's about 20 minutes west of downtown Victoria in the suburb of Colwood. ✉*643 Latoria Rd., West Shore and Malahat* ☎*250/474–3673* ⊕*www.olym picviewgolf.com.*

5

HIKING & WALKING

Island Adventure Tours. This company offers guided day hikes in East Sooke Regional Park and Juan de Fuca Marine Park, including hotel pickup in Victoria and a picnic lunch. They also offer equipment and transport for self-guided multiday hikes along the Juan de Fuca Marine Trail. ☎*250/812–7103 or 866/812–7103* ⊕*www.islandadventure tours.com.*

★ **Juan de Fuca Marine Trail.** This tough 47-km (30-mi) coastal hike begins at China Beach, near the village of Jordan River, about 48 km (29 mi) west of Victoria. There are three other trailheads, each with a parking lot, at Sombrio Beach, Parkinson Creek, and Botanical Beach (which is 5 km [3 mi] southeast of Port Renfrew), allowing hikers to tackle the trail in day hike sections. ⊠*Off Hwy. 14, between Jordan River (southeast end) and Port Renfrew (northwest end)* ☎*800/689–9025 camping reservations* ⊕*www.env.gov.bc.ca/bcparks.*

SHOPPING

Shopping in Victoria is easy: virtually everything can be found in the downtown area on or near Government Street stretching north from the Fairmont Empress hotel. Victoria stores specializing in English imports are plentiful, though Canadian-made goods are usually a better buy.

SHOPPING DISTRICTS & MALLS

Antique Row. Fort Street between Blanshard and Cook streets is home to dozens of antiques, curio, and collectibles shops.

Lower Johnson Street. This row of candy-color Victorian shop-fronts between Government and Store streets is Victoria's hub for independent fashion-designer boutiques. Storefronts—some closet-size—are filled with local designers' wares, funky boutiques, and no fewer than three shops selling ecologically friendly clothes of hemp and organic cotton. ⊠*Johnson St. between Government and Store Sts., Downtown.*

Market Square. During the late 19th century, this three-level square, built like an old courtyard, originally provided everything a sailor, miner, or lumberjack could want. It's lined with independent shops selling toys, imports, gifts, souvenirs, jewelry, local art, and even homemade dog treats. ⊠*560 Johnson St., Downtown* ☎*250/386–2441.*

Victoria Bay Centre. Downtown Victoria's main department store and mall has about 100 boutiques and restaurants. ⊠*1 Victoria Bay Centre, at Government and Fort Sts., Downtown* ☎*250/952–5680.*

SPECIALTY STORES

Artisan Wine Shop. This offshoot of Okanagan winery Mission Hill Family Estate replicates a visit to the winery with a video show and tasting bar. The focus is Okanagan wine, but staff are knowledgeable about Vancouver Island producers as well. ⊠*1007 Government St.* ☎*250/384–9994.*

Cowichan Trading Co., Ltd. First Nations jewelry, art, moccasins, and Cowichan sweaters are the focus at this long-established outlet. ⊠*1328 Government St., Downtown* ☎*250/383–0321.*

Irish Linen Stores. Since 1917 this tiny shop has kept Victorians in fine linen, lace, and hand-embroidered items. ✉*1019 Government St., Downtown* ☎*250/383–6812.*

Murchie's. You can choose from more than 40 varieties of tea, to sip here or take home, plus blended coffees, tarts, and cakes. ✉*1110 Government St., Downtown* ☎*250/383–3112.*

STREET MARKETS

Victorians seem to relish any excuse to head outdoors, which may explain the recent boom in outdoor crafts-, farmers', and other open-air markets around town.

Bastion Square Public Market. Crafts vendors and entertainers congregate in this historic square throughout the summer. ✉*Bastion Square, off Government St., Downtown* ☎*250/885–1387* ⊕*www.bastionsquare.ca.*

James Bay Market. Organic food, local produce, crafts, and live music draw shoppers to this summer Saturday market just south of the Inner Harbour. ✉*Superior and Menzies Sts., Downtown* ☎*250/381–5323* ⊕*www.jamesbaymarket.com.*

Inner Harbour Night Market. Local handmade arts and crafts feature at this harbor-side night market, held Friday and Saturday evenings in summer. ✉*Ship Point Pier, Downtown* ☎*250/413–6828* ⊕*www.victoriaharbour.org.*

VICTORIA ESSENTIALS

To research prices, get advice from other travelers, and book travel arrangements, visit www.fodors.com.

BY AIR

Victoria International Airport is 25 km (15 mi) north of downtown Victoria, off Highway 17. It's served by Horizon, Pacific Coastal, Skywest Airlines, and WestJet airlines. Air Canada and its regional service, Air Canada Jazz, provide frequent airport-to-airport service from Vancouver to Victoria. Flights take about 25 minutes.

Contacts & Local Airlines **Airporter** (☎*250/386–2525 or 877/386–2525* ⊕*www.victoriaairporter.com*). **BC Transit** (☎*250/382–6161* ⊕*www.bctransit.com*).

BY BOAT & FERRY

FROM THE B.C. MAINLAND — BC Ferries operates daily service between Tsawwassen, about an hour south of Vancouver, and Swartz Bay, at the end of Highway 17 (the Patricia Bay Highway), about 30 minutes north of downtown Victoria. Sailing time is about 1½ hours.

BC Transit buses meet the ferries at both ends, but if you're traveling without a car, the easiest option is to take a Pacific Coach Lines bus.

FROM WASHINGTON STATE — Black Ball Transport operates the *MV Coho,* a car ferry, daily year-round between Port Angeles, Washington and Victoria's Inner Habour. The car and passenger fare is US$44; bikes are carried for US$5.50.

The *Victoria Clipper* runs daily year-round passenger-only service between downtown Seattle and downtown Victoria. Sailings take about three hours, and the one-way fare from mid-May to late September is US$79; bicycles are carried for an extra US$10.

Boat & Ferry Information **BC Ferries** (☎ 250/386–3431, 888/223–3779 in B.C. ⊕ www.bcferries.com). **Black Ball Transport** (☎ 250/386–2202 or 360/457–4491 ⊕ www.ferrytovictoria.com). *Victoria Clipper* (☎ 206/448–5000 in Seattle, 250/382–8100 in Victoria, 800/888–2535 elsewhere ⊕ www.clippervacations.com/). **Victoria Express** (☎ 360/452–8088 or 250/361–9144 ⊕ www.victoriaexpress. com). **Victoria Harbour Ferries** (☎ 250/708–0201 ⊕ www.victoriaharbourferry. com). **Victoria San Juan Cruises** (☎ 360/738–8099 or 800/443–4552 ⊕ www. whales.com). **Washington State Ferries** (☎ 206/464–6400 or 888/808–7977 ⊕ www.wsdot.wa.gov/ferries).

BY BUS

Pacific Coach Lines operates frequent daily service between downtown Vancouver and downtown Victoria. The bus travels on the ferry, so transfers are seamless. BC Transit serves Victoria and the surrounding areas, including the Swartz Bay ferry terminal, Victoria International Airport, Butchart Gardens, Sidney, and Sooke.

Bus Information **BC Transit** (☎ Victoria: 250/382–6161. Duncan Transit: 250/746–9899 ⊕ www.bctransit.com). **Pacific Coach Lines** (☎ 604/662–8074 in Vancouver, 250/385–4411 in Victoria, 800/661–1725 elsewhere ⊕ www.pacificcoach.com).

VISITOR INFORMATION

Tourist Information **Tourism Cowichan** (☎ 250/746–1099 or 888/303–3337 ⊕ www.visit.cowichan.net). **Galiano Island Travel InfoCentre** (☎ 250/539–2233 ⊕ www.galianoisland.com). **Hello BC** (☎ 800/435–5622 ⊕ www.hellobc.com). **Salt Spring Island Visitor Information Centre** (☎ 250/537–5252 or 866/216–2936 ⊕ www.saltspringtoday.com). **Sooke Region Museum and Visitor InfoCentre** (☎ 250/642—6351 or 866/888-4748 ⊕ www.sooke.museum.bc.ca/srm). **Tourism Vancouver Island** (☎ 888/655–3483 ⊕ www.SeeTheIslands.com). **Tourism Victoria Visitor InfoCentre** (✉ 812 Wharf St. ☎ 250/953–2033 or 800/663–3883 ⊕ www.tourismvictoria.com).

Pacific Northwest Essentials

PLANNING TOOLS, EXPERT INSIGHT, GREAT CONTACTS

There are planners and there are those who, excuse the pun, fly by the seat of their pants. We happily place ourselves among the planners. Our writers and editors try to anticipate all the issues you may face before and during any journey, and then they do their research. This section is the product of their efforts. Use it to get excited about your trip to Pacific Northwest, to inform your travel planning, or to guide you on the road should the seat of your pants start to feel threadbare.

GETTING STARTED

We're really proud of our Web site: Fodors.com is a great place to begin any journey. Scan Travel Wire for suggested itineraries, travel deals, restaurant and hotel openings, and other up-to-the-minute info. Check out Booking to research prices and book plane tickets, hotel rooms, rental cars, and vacation packages. Head to Talk for on-the-ground pointers from travelers who frequent our message boards. You can also link to loads of other travel-related resources.

▌ RESOURCES

ONLINE TRAVEL TOOLS

The Oregon Coast Visitors Association provides information on coastal towns as well as a helpful FAQ on driving tours and beach etiquette at ⊕*www.visittheoregoncoast.com*. The Columbia River Gorge Visitors Association web site, ⊕*www.crgva.org*, has tons of links to help you find outfitters, events, and accommodations in Oregon's most-popular recreation area. Before you head to Mt. Hood to hike or ski, go to ⊕*www.mthoodterritory.com* to find everything from driving tour maps to agritourism suggestions. Oregon's wine country is a big attraction, and the Willamette Valley Visitor's Association does a good job of cataloging the state's sizable number of wineries by region or by experience at ⊕*www.oregonwinecountry.org*.

Washington's Olympic Peninsula is the state's top attraction outside of Seattle; for information on the towns surrounding Olympic National Park, check out ⊕*www.olympicpeninsula.org* or go to ⊕*www.nps.gov/olym* for detailed information on the park from the National Park Service. Get an overview of Washington wine country, along with a full list of wineries at ⊕*www.washingtonwine.org*. The National Park Service has the best site dedicated to the North Cascades

recreation area at ⊕*www.nps.gov/noca*; if you're planning a driving tour of the region, check out ⊕*www.cascadeloop.com*.

If you're eager to get outdoors, gorp.com has information on adventure travel in Oregon and Washington—everything from weekend city escape ideas to the logistics of camping in old fire lookouts.

If you plan to explore beyond Vancouver and Victoria, check out ⊕*www.hellobc.com* for information on British Columbia's many attractions, the most popular of which is Whistler (⊕ *www.tourismwhistler.com*).

All About the Pacific Northwest Go Northwest (⊕ www.gonorthwest.com). Northwest.com (⊕ www.northwest.com). NWCoast.com (⊕ www.nwcoast.com). U.S. Forest Service–Pacific Northwest Region (⊕ www.fs.fed.us/r6/).

Currency Conversion Google (⊕ www.google.com). Oanda.com (⊕ www.oanda.com) XE.com (⊕ www.xe.com).

Safety Transportation Security Administration (TSA ⊕ www.tsa.gov).

Weather Accuweather.com (⊕ www.accuweather.com) is an independent weather-forecasting service with good coverage of hurricanes. Weather.com (⊕ www.weather.com) is the Web site for the Weather Channel.

VISITOR INFORMATION

British Columbia Tourism Vancouver Island (✉ 203–335 Wesley St., Nanaimo ☎ 250/754–3500 ⊕ www.tourismvictoria.com). Tourism Victoria (⊕ www.tourismvictoria.com). Vancouver Tourist InfoCentre (✉ Plaza Level, 200 Burrard St., Vancouver V6C 3L6 ☎ 604/683–2000 ⊕ www.tourismvancouver.com).

Oregon Oregon Tourism Commission (✉ Jantzen Beach State Welcome Center, 12348 N. Center Ave., Portland 97217 ☎ 503/289–7535 or 800/547–7842 ⊕ www.

traveloregon.com).**Portland Oregon Visitors Association** (✉ *1000 S.W. Broadway, Suite 2300, Portland 97205* ☎ *503/275–9750 or 800/962–3700* ⊕ *www.travelportland.com*).

Washington **Seattle Convention and Visitor's Bureau** (✉ *520 Pike St., Suite 1300, Seattle 98101* ☎ *206/461–5840 or 206/461–5888* ⊕ *www.visitseattle.org*). **Washington State Tourism** (✉ *101 General Administration Bldg., Olympia 98504* ☎ *800/544–1800* ⊕ *www.experiencewashington.com*).

▌ THINGS TO CONSIDER

GEAR

It's all about the layers here, as there's no other way to keep up with the weather, which can morph from cold and overcast to warm and sunny and back again in the course of a few hours, especially in spring and early fall. Summer days are warm and more consistent, but evenings can cool off substantially. Bring an umbrella or raincoat for unpredictable fall and winter weather. Hikers will want to bring rain gear and a hat with them, even if they're visiting in summer; insect repellent is also a good idea if you'll be hiking along mountain trails or beaches.

PASSPORTS

As of January 2007 all people traveling by air between the United States and Canada are required to present a passport to enter or reenter the United States. To enter Canada (or more precisely, to reenter the U.S. from Canada) by land or sea you need to present one of the following: 1) passport, 2) a government-issue photo ID and a certified copy of your birth certificate, or 3) a U.S. Passport Card—sort of a "passport lite" that is only valid for land or sea crossings from Canada, Mexico, Caribbean, or Bermuda—which they're already taking applications for and will be available by spring 2008.

For more information on border crossings see By Car under Transportation

U.S. passports are valid for 10 years. You must apply in person if you're getting a passport for the first time; if your previous passport was lost, stolen, or damaged; or if your previous passport has expired and was issued more than 15 years ago or when you were under 16. All children under 18 must appear in person to apply for or renew a passport. Both parents must accompany any child under 14 (or send a notarized statement with their permission) and provide proof of their relationship to the child.

The cost to apply for a new passport is $97 for adults, $82 for children under 16; renewals are $67. Allow at least six weeks, sometimes longer for processing, both for first-time passports and renewals. For an expediting fee of $60 you can reduce this time to about two weeks. If your trip is less than two weeks away, you can get a passport even more rapidly by going to a passport office with the necessary documentation. Private expediters can get things done in as little as 48 hours, but charge hefty fees for their services.

U.S. Passport Information **U.S. Department of State** (☎ *877/487–2778* ⊕ *www.travel.state.gov/passport*).

Canadian Passports **Passport Office** (✉ *To mail in applications: 70 Cremazie St., Gatineau, Québec J8Y 3P2* ☎ *819/994–3500 or 800/567–6868* ⊕ *www.ppt.gc.ca*).

U.S. Passport & Visa Expediters **A. Briggs Passport & Visa Expeditors** (☎ *800/806–0581 or 202/338–0111* ⊕ *www.abriggs.com*). **American Passport Express** (☎ *800/455–5166 or 800/841–6778* ⊕ *www.americanpassport.com*). **Passport Express** (☎ *800/362–8196* ⊕ *www.passportexpress.com*). **Travel Document Systems** (☎ *800/874–5100 or 202/638–3800* ⊕ *www.traveldocs.com*). **Travel the World Visas** (☎ *866/886–8472 or 301/495–7700* ⊕ *www.world-visa.com*).

BOOKING YOUR TRIP

▌ ONLINE

You really have to shop around. A travel wholesaler such as Hotels.com or Hotel-Club.net can be a source of good rates, as can discounters such as Hotwire or Priceline, particularly if you can bid for your hotel room or airfare. Indeed, such sites sometimes have deals that are unavailable elsewhere. They do, however, tend to work only with hotel chains (which makes them just plain useless for getting hotel reservations outside of major cities) or big airlines (so that often leaves out upstarts like jetBlue and some foreign carriers like Air India).

▌**TIP→** To be absolutely sure everything was processed correctly, confirm reservations made through online travel agents, discounters, and wholesalers directly with your hotel before leaving home.

▌ WITH A TRAVEL AGENT

A knowledgeable brick-and-mortar travel agent can be a godsend if you're booking a cruise, a package trip that's not available to you directly, an air pass, or a complicated itinerary including several overseas flights. What's more, travel agents that specialize in a destination may have exclusive access to certain deals and insider information on things such as charter flights. Agents who specialize in types of travelers (senior citizens, gays and lesbians, naturists) or types of trips (cruises, luxury travel, safaris) can also be invaluable.

▌**TIP→** Remember that Expedia, Travelocity, and Orbitz are travel agents, not just booking engines. To resolve any problems with a reservation made through these companies, contact them first.

The Pacific Northwest is a do-it-yourself region in spirit, and you'll find it's fairly easy to book all travel on your own, especially if you're using the major cities of Seattle, Portland, and Vancouver as bases. Help from a travel agent may be warranted if your itinerary requires a lot of ferry travel (Seattle to the San Juan Islands and up to Victoria, for example) or if you know your agent can get you great deals on car rentals (one of the more-expensive components of any Northwest trip). Just be sure to do some prior research on hotel options—especially in Seattle, tour groups and cruise-ship passengers tend to get stuck in the most dismal of downtown's lodgings.

Agent Resources American Society of Travel Agents (☎ 703/739–2782 ⊕ www.travelsense.org).

Pacific Northwest Travel Agents Pacific Northwest Journeys (☎ 800/935–9730 or 206/935–9730 ⊕ www.pnwjourneys.com).

▌ ACCOMMODATIONS

The lodgings we list are the cream of the crop in each price category. We always list the facilities that are available, but we don't specify whether they cost extra; when pricing accommodations, always ask what's included and what costs extra. Properties are assigned price categories based on the range between their least and most expensive standard double rooms at high season (excluding holidays).

All prices are for a standard double room in high season, based on the European Plan (EP) and excluding tax and service charges. Seattle room tax: 15.8%. Elsewhere in WA: ranges from 10% to 16%. Portland room tax: 11.5%. Elsewhere in Oregon: ranges from 6 to 10%. Vancouver room tax: 10%. Elsewhere in BC: 8%.

Most hotels and other lodgings require you to give your credit-card details before they will confirm your reservation. If you don't feel comfortable e-

Online Booking Resources

AGGREGATORS

Kayak	www.kayak.com	looks at cruises and vacation packages.
Mobissimo	www.mobissimo.com	examines airfare, hotels, cars, and tons of activities.
Qixo	www.qixo.com	compares cruises, vacation packages, and even travel insurance.
Sidestep	www.sidestep.com	compares vacation packages and lists travel deals and some activities.
Travelgrove	www.travelgrove.com	compares cruises and vacation packages and lets you search by themes.

BOOKING ENGINES

Cheap Tickets	www.cheaptickets.com	discounter.
Expedia	www.expedia.com	large online agency that charges a booking fee for airline tickets.
Hotwire	www.hotwire.com	discounter.
lastminute.com	www.lastminute.com	specializes in last-minute travel; the main site is for the U.K., but it has a link to a U.S. site.
Luxury Link	www.luxurylink.com	has auctions (surprisingly good deals) as well as offers on the high-end side of travel.
Onetravel.com	www.onetravel.com	discounter for hotels, car rentals, airfares, and packages.
Orbitz	www.orbitz.com	charges a booking fee for airline tickets, but gives a clear breakdown of fees and taxes before you book.
Priceline.com	www.priceline.com	discounter that also allows bidding.
Travel.com	www.travel.com	allows you to compare its rates with those of other booking engines.
Travelocity	www.travelocity.com	charges a booking fee for airline tickets, but promises good problem resolution.

ONLINE ACCOMMODATIONS

Hotelbook.com	www.hotelbook.com	focuses on independent hotels worldwide.
Hotel Club	www.hotelclub.net	good for major cities and some resort areas.
Hotels.com	www.hotels.com	big Expedia-owned wholesaler that offers rooms in hotels all over the world.
Quikbook	www.quikbook.com	offers "pay when you stay" reservations that allow you to settle your bill when you check out, not when you book; best for trips to U.S. and Canadian cities."

OTHER RESOURCES

Bidding For Travel	www.biddingfortravel.com	good place to figure out what you can get and for how much before you start bidding on, say, Priceline.

mailing this information, ask if you can fax it (some places even prefer faxes). However you book, get confirmation in writing and have a copy of it handy when you check in.

■TIP➜ Assume that hotels operate on the European Plan (**EP**, no meals) unless we specify that they use the Breakfast Plan (**BP**, with full breakfast), Continental Plan (**CP**, continental breakfast), Full American Plan (**FAP**, all meals), Modified American Plan (**MAP**, breakfast and dinner) or are all-inclusive (**AI**, all meals and most activities).

BED & BREAKFASTS

The Pacific Northwest is known for its vast range of bed-and-breakfast options, which are found everywhere from busy urban areas to casual country farms and coastal retreats. Many B&Bs here provide full gourmet breakfasts, and some have kitchens that guests can use. Other popular amenities to ask about are fireplaces, jetted bathtubs, outdoor hot tubs, and area activities.

The regional B&B organizations listed below can provide information on reputable establishments. Note that before leaving the United Kingdom, you can book a B&B through American Bed & Breakfast, Inter-Bed Network.

Reservation Services **American Bed & Breakfast Association** (⊕ www.abba.com). **American Bed & Breakfast, Inter-Bed Network** (✉ 31 Ernest Rd., Colchester, EssexCO7 9LQ ☎ 0206/223162). **BBCanada.com** (⊕ www.bbcanada.com). **Bed & Breakfast. com** (☎ 512/322–2710 or 800/462–2632 ⊕ www.bedandbreakfast.com) also sends out an online newsletter. **Bed & Breakfast Inns Online** (☎ 615/868–1946 or 800/215–7365 ⊕ www.bbonline.com). **British Columbia Bed & Breakfasts** (⊕ www.bcbbonly.com). **BnB Finder.com** (☎ 212/432–7693 or 888/547–8226 ⊕ www.bnbfinder.com). **The Canadian Bed & Breakfast Guide** (☎ 877/213–0089 or 905/262–4597 ⊕ www.canadianbandbguide.ca). **Oregon Bed & Breakfast Guild** (☎ 800/944–6196 ⊕ www.obbg.org). **Wash-**

ington Bed & Breakfast Guild (☎ 800/647–2918 ⊕ www.wbbg.com). **Western Canada Bed & Breakfast Innkeepers Association** (⊕ www.wcbbia.com).

CAMPING

Oregon, Washington, and British Columbia have excellent government-run campgrounds found throughout each state. A few accept advance camping reservations, but most do not. Privately operated campgrounds sometimes have extra amenities such as laundry rooms and swimming pools. For more information, contact the state or provincial tourism department.

Campground Reservations **British Columbia Lodgings & Campground Association** (⊕ www.camping.bc.ca). **Discover Camping (British Columbia)** (☎ 800/689–9025 ⊕ www.discovercamping.ca). **Oregon Parks and Recreation Dept.** (☎ 800/452–5687 reservations ⊕ www.oregon.gov/oprd/parks). **Washington State Parks and Recreation Commission** (☎ 888/226–7688 reservations ⊕ www.parks.wa.gov/reserve.asp).

HOTELS

When booking a room, always call the hotel's local toll-free number (if one is available) rather than the central reservations number—you'll often get a better price. Deals can often be found at hotel Web sites. Always ask about special packages or corporate rates. Many properties offer special weekend rates, sometimes up to 50% off regular prices. However, these deals are usually not extended during peak summer months, when hotels are normally full. All hotels listed have private bath unless otherwise noted.

▌ AIRLINE TICKETS

The least expensive airfares to the Pacific Northwest are often priced for round-trip travel and usually must be purchased in advance. Airlines generally allow you to change your return date for a fee; most low-fare tickets, however, are nonrefundable. America West sometimes offers specials deals and packages around the region. Air Canada is the only airline that offers a regional flight pass, which covers 10 one-way trips between cities in the western United States and western Canada. The pass is nontransferable, so it only makes sense if you're planning to do a lot of flying or make multiple trips to the region within a year.

You can also save money on your car rental (a must for most Pacific Northwest itineraries) by booking a fly/drive package through your airline. Many airlines offer deals on rental cars if you book through them.

▌ RENTAL CARS

▌TIP➔ Make sure that a confirmed reservation guarantees you a car. Agencies sometimes overbook, particularly for busy weekends and holiday periods.

Unless you only visit Seattle, Portland, and Vancouver, you will need to rent a car for at least part of your trip. It's possible to get around the big cities by public transportation and taxis, but once you go outside city limits, your options are limited. National lines like Greyhound do provide service between major towns, and Amtrak has limited service between Washington and Oregon (allowing you to get from, say, Seattle to Portland, by train), but it is nearly impossible to get to and around the major recreation areas and national parks of each state without

your own wheels. For example, there is no public transportation from Seattle to Mt Rainier National Park.

Rates in Seattle begin at $23 a day ($126 per week) for an economy car. This does not include the 18.5% tax. The tax on rentals at Sea-Tac Airport is a whopping 30%, so try to rent from a downtown branch. Rates in Portland begin at $30 a day and $138 a week, not including the 12.5% tax. Rates in Vancouver begin at about C$32 a day or C$196 a week, usually including unlimited mileage.

Car rentals in British Columbia also incur a 15% sales tax, a C$1.50-per-day social services tax, and a vehicle licensing fee of C$1.18 per day. An additional 17% Concession Recovery Fee, charged by the airport authority for retail space in the terminal, is levied at airport locations.

All the major agencies are represented in the region. If you're planning to cross the U.S.–Canadian border with your rental car, discuss it with the agency to see what's involved.

In the Pacific Northwest you must be 21 to rent a car. Car seats are compulsory for children under four years *and* 40 pounds; older children are required to sit in booster seats until they are eight years old *and* 80 pounds. (In British Columbia, children up to 40 pounds or 18 kilos in weight must use a child seat.) In the United States nonresidents need a reservation voucher, passport, driver's license, and insurance for each driver.

CAR-RENTAL INSURANCE

Everyone who rents a car wonders whether the insurance that the rental companies offer is worth the expense. No one—including us—has a simple answer. It all depends on how much regular insurance you have, how comfortable you are with risk, and whether or not money is an issue.

If you own a car and carry comprehensive car insurance for both collision and lia-

Car Rental Resources

AUTOMOBILE ASSOCIATIONS		
U.S.: American Automobile Association (AAA)	315/797–5000	www.aaa.com; most contact with the organization is through state and regional members.
National Automobile Club	650/294–7000	www.thenac.com; membership is open to California residents only.
LOCAL AGENCIES		
In Seattle		
Ace ExtraCar	800/227–5397 or 206/246–7844	www.bnm.com/extra.htm.
Advantage	800/777–5500	www.arac.com.
Best Rent-A-Car	206/784–2378	www.bestrent-a-car.com.
Express Rent-A-Car	866/443–6825	www.expressrentacar.com.
MAJOR AGENCIES		
Alamo	800/462–5266	www.alamo.com.
Avis	800/331–1212	www.avis.com.
Budget	800/527–0700	www.budget.com.
Hertz	800/654–3131	www.hertz.com.
National Car Rental	800/227–7368	www.nationalcar.com.

bility, your personal auto insurance will probably cover a rental, but read your policy's fine print to be sure. If you don't have auto insurance, then you should probably buy the collision- or loss-damage waiver (CDW or LDW) from the rental company. This eliminates your liability for damage to the car.

Some credit cards offer CDW coverage, but it's usually supplemental to your own insurance and rarely covers SUVs, minivans, luxury models, and the like. If your coverage is secondary, you may still be liable for loss-of-use costs from the car-rental company (again, read the fine print). But no credit-card insurance is valid unless you use that card for *all* transactions, from reserving to paying the final bill.

■ TIP→ **Diners Club offers primary CDW coverage on all rentals reserved and paid for with the card. This means that Diners Club's company—not your own car insurance—pays in case of an accident. It** *doesn't* **mean that your car-insurance company won't raise your rates once it discovers you had an accident.**

You may also be offered supplemental liability coverage; the car-rental company is required to carry a minimal level of liability coverage insuring all renters, but it's rarely enough to cover claims in a really serious accident if you're at fault. Your own auto-insurance policy will protect you if you own a car; if you don't, you have to decide whether you are willing to take the risk.

U.S. rental companies sell CDWs and LDWs for about $15 to $25 a day; supplemental liability is usually more than $10 a day. The car-rental company may offer you all sorts of other policies, but they're rarely worth the cost. Personal accident insurance, which is basic hospitalization coverage, is an especially egregious rip-off if you already have health insurance.

■TIP→ **You can decline the insurance from the rental company and purchase it through a third-party provider such as Travel Guard (www.travelguard.com)—$9 per day for $35,000 of coverage. That's sometimes just under half the price of the CDW offered by some car-rental companies.**

▌CRUISES

Seattle's cruise industry welcomes some of the world's largest ships to its docks on Elliott Bay.

Vancouver is the major embarkation point for Alaska cruises, and virtually all Alaska-bound cruise ships call there; some also call at Victoria and Prince Rupert.

Cruise Lines International Association is the official trade organization of the cruise industry, and its Web site is a good starting point if you don't have a specific carrier in mind.

CRUISE LINES

American Safari Cruises (✉ *3826 18th Ave. W, Seattle, WA 98119* ☎ *888/862–8881* ⊕ *www.amsafari.com*). **Bluewater Adventures** (✉ *3–252 E. 1st St., North Vancouver V7L 1B3BC* ☎ *604/980–3800 or 888/877–1770* ⊕ *www.bluewateradventures. ca*). **Carnival Cruise Line** (☎ *305/599–2600 or 800/227–6482* ⊕ *www.carnival.com*). **Celebrity Cruises** (☎ *800/647–2251* ⊕ *www. celebrity.com*). **Clipper Cruise Lines** (✉ *11969 Westline Industrial Dr., St. Louis, MO 63146-3220* ☎ *314/655–6700 or 800/456–8100* ⊕ *www.clippercruise.com*). **Cruise Lines International Association** (☎ *754/224–2200* ⊕ *www.cruising.org*). **Cruise West** (✉ *2301 5th Ave., Suite 401, Seattle, WA98121-1438* ☎ *888/851–8133* ⊕ *www.cruisewest.com*). **Holland America Line** (☎ *206/281–3535 or 877/932–4259* ⊕ *www.hollandamerica. com*). **Majestic America** (☎ *800/434–1232* ⊕ *www.majesticamericaline.com*). **Norwegian Cruise Line** (☎ *305/436–4000 or 800/327–7030* ⊕ *www.ncl.com*). **Princess Cruises** (☎ *661/753–0000 or 800/774–6237* ⊕ *www. princess.com*). **Regent Seven Seas Cruises** (☎ *877/505–5370* ⊕ *www.rssc.com*). **Royal Caribbean International** (☎ *305/539–6000 or 800/327–6700* ⊕ *www.royalcaribbean.com*). **Seabourn Cruise Line** (☎ *305/463–3000 or 800/929–9391* ⊕ *www.seabourn.com*). **Silversea Cruises** (☎ *954/522–4477 or 800/722–9955* ⊕ *www.silversea.com*).

TRANSPORTATION

You'll need a car to get around all but the major cities of the Pacific Northwest. Although a car will also grant you more freedom to explore the outer areas of Portland, Seattle, and Vancouver, these three cities have adequate public transportation and taxi fleets. This is not the case in most other towns in the region, so even if bus or train service exists between two points, you may need a car to get around once you reach your new destination.

I–5 is the major north-south conduit of the region, offering a straight shot at high speeds—when there aren't traffic snarls, of course—from Oregon's southern tip all the way up to the Canadian border. Seattle and Portland are both along I–5 and Vancouver is right across the border from where it ends. This makes driving between the major hubs an easy option, though it's also possible to travel between them by train or bus, which may be preferable—I–5 isn't very scenic, so it doesn't make for a very inspiring road trip.

U.S. 101, on the other hand, is one of the main attractions of the region. It starts in Washington west of Olympia, makes a very wide loop around Olympic National Park and then heads through Oregon, hugging the coast almost the whole way down. Most of the road is incredibly scenic—the loveliest stretches are in northern and central Oregon—but this is not a very convenient way to traverse either state. Make sure you want to commit to the coastal drive, which may be slow going in some parts, before getting on 101—it takes some time to work your way over from I–5, so jumping back and forth between the two isn't an option.

The Cascade Range cuts through the middle of Washington and Oregon, which means east-west journeys often meander over mountain passes and can be either simply beautiful (summer) or beautiful and treacherous (winter). I–90 is the main

east-west artery in Washington, connecting Seattle with Spokane, but Highway 20, which passes through the North Cascades National Park, is more scenic. I–84 is Oregon's major east-west artery; not far east of Portland it enters the Columbia River Gorge. U.S. 26 parallels I–84 a bit before dipping south toward Mt. Hood.

TRAVEL TIMES FROM SEATTLE BY CAR	
Portland	3–3½ hours
Vancouver	2½–3 hours
Victoria	2½ –3 hrs drive to Vancouver; 1½ hrs ferry ride from Vancouver
Mt. Rainier National Park (Paradise or Longmire entrances)	2½ hours
North Cascades National Park	2½–3½ hrs
Olympic National Park	2½ hrs to Port Angeles; 1 hr from Port Angeles to Hurricane Ridge
Mt. St. Helens	3–3½ hours
Yakima Valley	2–2½ hours

TRAVEL TIMES FROM PORTLAND BY CAR	
Crater Lake National Park	4½–5 hours
Columbia River Gorge/Mt. Hood	1½ hours
Willamette Valley	1½–2 hours

▌ BY AIR

▌TIP→ Ask the local tourist board about hotel and local transportation packages that include tickets to major museum exhibits or other special events.

It takes about 5 hours to fly nonstop to Seattle or Portland from New York, 4 hours from Chicago, and 2½ hours from Los Angeles. Flights from New York to Vancouver take about 6 hours nonstop; from Chicago, 4½ hours nonstop; and from Los Angeles, 3 hours nonstop. Flying from Seattle to Portland takes just under an hour; flying from Portland to Vancouver takes an hour and 15 minutes.

■TIP→ **If you travel frequently, look into the TSA's Registered Traveler program. The program, which is still being tested in several U.S. airports, is designed to cut down on gridlock at security checkpoints by allowing prescreened travelers to pass quickly through kiosks that scan an iris and/or a fingerprint. How sci-fi is that?**

Airlines & Airports **Airline and Airport Links.com** (⊕ *www.airlineandairportlinks.com*) has links to many of the world's airlines and airports.

Airline Security Issues **Transportation Security Administration** (⊕ *www.tsa.gov*) has answers for almost every question that might come up.

AIRPORTS

The main gateways to the Pacific Northwest are Portland International Airport (PDX), Sea-Tac International Airport (SEA), and Vancouver International Airport (YVR).

■TIP→ **Long layovers don't have to be only about sitting around or shopping. These days they can be about burning off vacation calories. Check out** ⊕*www.airportgyms. com* **for lists of health clubs that are in or near many U.S. and Canadian airports.**

Airport Information **Portland International Airport (PDX)** (✉ *N.E. Airport Way at I-205* ☎ *877/739-4636* ⊕ *www.flypdx. com*). **Sea-Tac International Airport (SEA)** (☎ *206/433-5388* ⊕ *www.seatac.org*). **Vancouver International Airport (YVR)** (☎ *604/207-7077* ⊕ *www.yvr.ca*).

GROUND TRANSPORTATION

See the Essentials sections in the Portland, Seattle, and Vancouver & Victoria

chapters for information about airport transfers to the center of each city.

FLIGHTS

Many international carriers serve the Pacific Northwest, including Air France, British Airways, Cathay Pacific (Vancouver), Japan Airlines (Vancouver), KLM, Lufthansa, and Qantas. Vancouver has the most connections with international cities. U.S. carriers serving the area include Alaska Airlines, Continental, Delta, Northwest, and United. American Airlines has frequent flights to Seattle and Vancouver. JetBlue has daily flights from New York's JFK airport to both Seattle and Portland. As of spring 2008 Virgin America will have daily flights to Seattle from San Francisco and Los Angeles. USAirways flies from Portland and Seattle to Las Vegas, Phoenix, Charlotte, and Philadelphia, and from Vancouver to Las Vegas and Phoenix. Big Sky, Frontier Airlines, Horizon Air, and United Express provide frequent service between cities in Washington, Oregon, Idaho, Montana, and California. Southwest Airlines has frequent service to Seattle and Portland from cities in California, Nevada, Idaho, and Utah, as well as some other parts of the country. The major regional carrier in western Canada is Air Canada (and its subsidiary, Air Canada Jazz), which has flights from Seattle and Portland to Vancouver and Victoria.

Airline Contacts **Air Canada/Air Canada Jazz** (☎ *888/247-2262* ⊕ *www.aircanada. com or www.flyjazz.ca*). **Alaska Airlines** (☎ *800/252-7522 or 206/433-3100* ⊕ *www.alaskaair.com*). **American Airlines** (☎ *800/433-7300* ⊕ *www.aa.com*). **Big Sky** (☎ *8001/237-7788* ⊕ *www.bigskyair. com*). **British Airways** (☎ *800/247-9297* ⊕ *www.britishairways.com*). **Cathay Pacific** (☎ *800/233-2742 in U.S., 800/268-6868 in Canada* ⊕ *www.cathaypacific.com*). **Continental Airlines** (☎ *800/523-3273 for U.S. and Mexico reservations, 800/231-0856 for international reservations* ⊕ *www.continental. com*). **Delta Airlines** (☎ *800/221-1212 for*

U.S. reservations, 800/241–4141 for international reservations ⊕ www.delta.com). **Frontier** (☎ 800/432–1359 ⊕ www.frontierairlines.com). **Helijet** (☎ 800/665–4354 ⊕ www.helijet.com). **Horizon Air** (☎ 800/547–9308 ⊕ www.alaskaair.com). **Japan Airlines** (☎ 800/525–3663 ⊕ www.japanair.com). **jetBlue** (☎ 800/538–2583 ⊕ www.jetblue.com). **Kenmore Air** (☎ 800/543–9595 ⊕ www.kenmoreair.com). **Lufthansa** (☎ 800/399–5838, 800/645–3880 in U.S., 800/563–5954 in Canada ⊕ www.lufthansa.com). **Northwest Airlines** (☎ 800/225–2525 ⊕ www.nwa.com). **Qantas** (☎ 800/227–4500 ⊕ www.qantas.com). **Southwest Airlines** (☎ 800/435–9792 ⊕ www.southwest.com). **United Airlines** (☎ 800/864–8331 for U.S. reservations, 800/538–2929 for international reservations ⊕ www.united.com). **US Airways** (☎ 800/428–4322 for U.S. and Canada reservations, 800/622–1015 for international reservations ⊕ www.usairways.com). **Virgin America** (☎ 877/359–8474 ⊕ www.virginamerica.com).

▌ BY BOAT

Ferries play an important part in the transportation network of the Pacific Northwest. Some are the sole connection to islands in Puget Sound and to small towns and islands along the west coast of British Columbia. Each day ferries transport thousands of commuters to and from work in the coastal cities. Always comfortable, convenient, and surrounded by spectacular views, ferries are also one of the best ways for you to get a feel for the region and its ties to the sea.

The best times for travel are 9–3 and after 7 PM on weekdays. In July and August you may have to wait hours to take a car aboard one of the popular ferries, such as those to the San Juan Islands. Walk-on space is always available; if possible, leave your car behind. Reservations aren't taken for domestic routes.

WASHINGTON & OREGON

Washington State Ferries carries millions of passengers and vehicles each year on 10 routes between 20 points on Puget Sound, the San Juan Islands, and Sidney, British Columbia. Onboard services vary depending on the size of the ferry, but many ships have a cafeteria, vending machines, newspaper and tourist-information kiosks, arcade games, and restrooms with family facilities. There are discounted fares in off-peak months, as well as monthly passenger-only passes for those planning more than 16 round-trips in 30 days.

Argosy cruising vessels make sightseeing, dinner, weekend brunch, and special-event cruises around Elliott Bay, Lake Union, Lake Washington, the Ballard Locks, and other Seattle waterways. Black Ball Transport's MV *Coho* makes daily crossings year-round from Port Angeles to Victoria. The *Coho* can carry 800 passengers and 100 cars across the Strait of Juan de Fuca in 1½ hours. Reservations aren't accepted. Clipper Vacations operates the passenger-only *Victoria Clipper* jet catamaran between Seattle, the San Juan Islands, and Victoria. The Puget Island Ferry crosses from Westport, Oregon, to Puget Island, near Cathlamet, Washington.

From Portland the *Portland Spirit, Willamette Star,* and *Crystal Dolphin* make sightseeing and dinner cruises on the Willamette and Columbia Rivers. America West also uses paddle-wheel boats for overnight historic tours along the Columbia and Snake rivers. Departing from Cascade Locks, Oregon (45 minutes east of Portland), the sternwheeler *Columbia Gorge* cruises the Columbia Gorge and the Willamette River (December only). To view the rich wildlife along the edge of the Columbia River, you can take an ecologically focused cruise or an estuary tour, both of which depart from Astoria, Oregon.

BRITISH COLUMBIA

British Columbia Ferries operates passenger and vehicle service between the mainland and Victoria and elsewhere. Most ferries take reservations.

Information **Argosy Cruises** (☎ 206/623–
1445 or 800/642-7816 ⊕ www.argosycruises.
com). **Black Ball Transport** (☎ 250/386-2202
in Victoria, 360/457-4491 in Port Angeles
⊕ www.cohoferry.com). **British Columbia Ferries** (☎ 250/386-3431 in Victoria,
888/223-3779 ⊕ www.bcferries.bc.ca). **Clipper Vacations** (☎ 250/382-8100 in Victoria,
206/448-5000 in Seattle, 800/888-2535 in
U.S. ⊕ www. clippervacations.com). Columbia
Gorge (☎ 503/224-3900 or 800/224-3901
⊕ www.sternwheeler.com). Portland Spirit
(☎ 503/224-3900 or 800/224-3901 ⊕ www.
portlandspirit.com). **Puget Island Ferry**
(☎ 360/795-3301 ⊕ www.co.wahkiakum.
wa.us/depts/pw). **Washington State Ferries**
(☎ 206/464-6400, 800/843-3779 automated
information line, 888/808-7977 ⊕ www.wsdot.
wa.gov/ferries).

▌ BY BUS

Greyhound and Northwestern Trailways
buses travel to and within the region.
Experience Oregon in Eugene operates
charter bus services and scheduled sightseeing tours that last from a few hours
to several days. People Mover travels on
Highway 26 between Bend and John Day.
Greyhound serves most towns in British
Columbia and provides frequent service
on popular runs. Quick Shuttle runs
buses from Sea-Tac airport and downtown Seattle to various Vancouver spots
and hotels.

Gray Line, which operates from Portland,
Seattle, Vancouver, and Victoria, schedules a variety of popular bus tours and
overnight packages around the Pacific
Northwest. The company also has daily
service from Seattle to the Washington State Ferry terminal in Anacortes.
Pacific Coach Lines runs multiple daily
buses between Vancouver and Victoria,
including a ferry ride across the Strait
of Georgia. The company also has connections from Vancouver to Vancouver
International Airport and the cruise ship
terminal, and operates numerous package
tours around British Columbia.

Greyhound's domestic and international
Discovery Passes allow unlimited bus
travel in North America—including Canada and Mexico—for periods of 7 to 60
days.

Bus Information **Experience Oregon**
(☎ 541/342-2662 or 888/342-2662
⊕ www.experienceoregon.com). **Gray Line**
(☎ 503/684-3322, 888/684-3322 in Portland ⊕ www.grayline.com ☎ 206/624-5077,
800/426-7532 in Seattle ⊕ www.grayline-
seattle.com ☎ 800/667-0882 in Vancouver
☎ 250/388-6539, 800/663-8390 in Victoria
⊕ www.graylinewest.com). **Greyhound
Lines** (☎ 800/231-2222 in U.S. ⊕ www.
greyhound.com ☎ 800/661-8747 in Canada
⊕ www.greyhound.ca). **Northwestern
Trailways** (☎ 800/366-3830 ⊕ www.north
westerntrailways.com). **Pacific Coach Lines**
(☎ 800/661-1725 in U.S., 604/662-7575 in
Vancouver ⊕ www.pacificcoach.com). **People
Mover** (☎ 541/575-2370). **Quick Shuttle**
(☎ 800/665-2122 in U.S., 604/940-4428 in
Vancouver ⊕ www.quickcoach.com).

▌ BY CAR

Driver's licenses from other countries are
valid in the United States and Canada.
International driving permits (IDPs)—
available from the American and Canadian automobile associations and, in
the United Kingdom, from the Automobile Association and Royal Automobile
Club—are a good idea. Valid only in conjunction with your regular driver's license,
these permits are universally recognized;
having one may save you a problem with
local authorities.

Bookstores, gas stations, convenience
stores, and rest stops sell maps (about
$5) and multiregion road atlases (about
$12). Along larger highways, roadside
stops with restrooms, fast-food restaurants, and sundries stores are well spaced.
Police and tow trucks patrol major highways and lend assistance.

BORDER CROSSING

You will need a valid passport to cross the border (⇨ Passports under Things to Consider). In addition, drivers must carry owner registration and proof of insurance coverage, which is compulsory in Canada. The Canadian Non-Resident Inter-Provincial Motor Vehicle Liability Insurance Card, available from any U.S. insurance company, is accepted as evidence of financial responsibility in Canada. If you are driving a car that is not registered in your name, carry a letter from the owner that authorizes your use of the vehicle.

The main entry point into British Columbia from the United States by car is on I–5 at Blaine, Washington, 48 km (30 mi) south of Vancouver. Three highways enter British Columbia from the east: Highway 1, or the Trans-Canada Highway; Highway 3, or the Crowsnest Highway, which crosses southern British Columbia; and Highway 16, the Yellowhead Highway, which runs through northern British Columbia from the Rocky Mountains to Prince Rupert. From Alaska and the Yukon, take the Alaska Highway (from Fairbanks) or the Klondike Highway (from Skagway or Dawson City).

Border-crossing procedures are usually quick and simple. Every British Columbia border crossing is open 24 hours (except the one at Aldergrove, which is open from 8 AM to midnight). The I–5 border crossing at Blaine, Washington (also known as the Douglas, or Peace Arch, border crossing), is one of the busiest border crossings between the United States and Canada. Listen to local radio traffic reports for information about wait times.

GASOLINE

Gas stations are plentiful in major metropolitan areas and along major highways like I–5. Most stay open late, except in rural areas, where Sunday hours are limited and where you may drive long stretches without a refueling opportunity. This is particularly true in Oregon, where you are not allowed to pump your own gas, and therefore won't be able to find an automated pump in an emergency.

■ TIP → Keep an eye on the gauge when traveling to national parks and off-the-beaten-path trails, particularly if you'll be heading down Forest Service roads. A good rule of thumb is to fill up before you get off (or too far away from) a major highway like I-5 or I-90. Making a wide loop around Olympic National Park can burn a lot of fuel, and there are very few towns between Port Angeles to the north and Aberdeen to the south. The eastern stretches of Washington and Oregon can be virtually empty, so always fill up before you exit major highways.

ROAD CONDITIONS

Winter driving can present challenges. In coastal areas the mild, damp climate contributes to frequently wet roadways. Snowfalls generally occur only once or twice a year, but when snow does fall, traffic grinds to a halt and roadways become treacherous and stay that way until the snow melts.

Tire chains, studs, or snow tires are essential equipment for winter travel in mountain areas. If you're planning to drive into high elevations, be sure to check the weather forecast beforehand. Even the main-highway mountain passes can close because of snow conditions. In winter state and provincial highway departments operate snow advisory telephone lines that give pass conditions.

For more information about traffic conditions in Portland, Seattle, and Vancouver, see the Essentials sections in the individual chapters.

ROADSIDE EMERGENCIES

Contacts For **police, ambulance,** or **other emergencies** dial 911. **Oregon State Police** (☎ *503/378-3720 or 800/452-7888*).

▌ BY TRAIN

Amtrak, the U.S. passenger rail system, has daily service to the Pacific Northwest from the Midwest and California. The *Empire Builder* takes a northern route through Minnesota and Montana from Chicago to Spokane, from which separate legs continue to Seattle and Portland. The *Coast Starlight* begins in Los Angeles; makes stops throughout California, western Oregon, and Washington; and terminates in Seattle.

Amtrak's *Cascades* trains travel between Seattle and Vancouver and between Seattle, Portland, and Eugene. The trip from Seattle to Portland takes roughly 3½ hours and costs $28–$44 for a coach seat; this is a pleasant alternative to a mind-numbing drive down I–5. The trip from Seattle to Vancouver takes roughly 4 hours and costs $39. The *Empire Builder* travels between Portland and Spokane (7 hours, $75), with part of the route running through the Columbia River gorge. From Portland to Eugene, it's a 3-hour trip; the cost is $21–$35.

■TIP➜ Book Amtrak tickets at least a few days in advance, especially if you're traveling between Seattle and Portland on the weekend.

VIA Rail has train service from Victoria along the coast of Vancouver Island. The line terminates at Courtenay (4½ hours from Victoria); the fare for this journey is $28.

Information Amtrak (☎ 800/872-7245 ⊕ www.amtrak.com). **VIA Rail Canada** (☎ 888/842-7245 ⊕ www.viarail.ca).

ON THE GROUND

▌ COMMUNICATIONS

INTERNET

The Pacific Northwest is well wired, and it's difficult to find a hotel in a major city that doesn't offer either Ethernet connections or Wi-Fi, or both. (Whether those services are free, however, is another issue.)

Coffeehouses almost always have reliable Wi-Fi and the service is often free (assuming, of course, that you at least buy a cup of coffee); a few have a communal computer or two if you didn't bring the laptop, but often your best bet for dedicated computer stations is either your hotel's business center or public library branches.

For a list of wired coffee shops in Seattle or Portland, check out ⊕*http://seattle.wifimug.org/* and ⊕*http://portland.wifimug.org*. For more Portland hot spots, check out ⊕*www.wifipdx.com*; ⊕*www.seattle.gov/html/citizen/wifi.htm* has a list of additional free Wi-Fi hot spots in Seattle. Some highway rest stops in Washington have Wi-Fi (some fees may apply—check out ⊕*www.wsdot.wa.gov/biz/restareas/wifi.htm* for a handy map of these locations. Both ⊕*www.wififreespot.com* and ⊕*www.jwire.com* list Oregon hot spots.

Contacts **Cybercafes** (⊕ www.cybercafes.com) lists more than 4,000 Internet cafés worldwide.

▌ CUSTOMS & DUTIES

You're always allowed to bring goods of a certain value back home without having to pay any duty or import tax. But there's a limit on the amount of tobacco and liquor you can bring back duty-free, and some countries have separate limits for perfumes; for exact figures, check with your customs department. The values of so-called "duty-free" goods are included in these amounts. When you shop abroad, save all your receipts, as customs inspectors may ask to see them as well as the items you purchased. If the total value of your goods is more than the duty-free limit, you'll have to pay a tax (most often a flat percentage) on the value of everything beyond that limit.

Information in Canada **Canada Border Services Agency** (☎ 204/983–3500 or 800/461–9999 ⊕ www.cbsa-asfc.gc.ca).

U.S. Information **U.S. Customs and Border Protection** (⊕ www.cbp.gov).

▌ EATING OUT

Pacific Northwest cuisine highlights regional seafood and locally grown, organic produce, often prepared in styles that reflect an Asian influence (Seattle, Victoria, and Vancouver have large Asian populations) or incorporate European (often French or Italian) influences. *See also Cuisines of the Pacific Northwest at the beginning of this book.*

All the region's major cities have top-rated, nationally renowned dining spots, though Seattle's booming restaurant scene has gotten the most national attention. Outside of major cities or hippie enclaves, you'll find more chain restaurants and your options won't be as exciting; however, farm stands are plentiful in the rural areas and are definitely worth a stop. Coffee, of course, is a staple of the Seattle experience, and it's important throughout the state—no matter how small a town is, it's bound to have at least one espresso joint, usually in a converted Photomat booth. Oregon also has good grounds.

The restaurants we list are the cream of the crop in each price category.

MEALS & MEALTIMES

Unless otherwise noted, the restaurants listed in this guide are open daily for lunch and dinner.

PAYING

Credit cards—Visa and MasterCard, in particular—are widely accepted in most restaurants, especially in Seattle, Portland, and Vancouver. Debit cards are widely accepted in coffeehouses, delis, and grocery stores.

WINES, BEER & SPIRITS

Both Oregon and Washington have thriving wineries—restaurants in Seattle take their wine lists very seriously. Most of Washington's wineries are east of the Cascades in the south-central part of the state, but you'll find a few close to Seattle as well. Oregon's wineries mostly lie in the valleys between the southern Cascades and the coast. The Washington State Wine Commission (⊕*www.washington wine.org*) and the Oregon Wine Board (⊕*www.oregonwine.org*) both maintain Web sites with facts, history, and information on local wineries. British Columbia winemaking has become increasingly prominent. The British Columbia Wine Institute's Web site (⊕*www.winebc.com*) has facts and information on individual wineries.

Oregon has more than 60 microbreweries, and Washington has no shortage of excellent local microbrews. Both states have festivals and events celebrating their brews—Seattle's Fremont neighborhood has its own Oktoberfest. The Web site for the Washington Brewers Guild (⊕*www.washingtonbeer.com*) has info on breweries in the state and events throughout the Pacific Northwest. The Oregon Brewers Guild (⊕*www.oregon beer.org*) also has links to breweries and information on events.

You must be 21 to buy alcohol in Washington and Oregon. The legal drinking age in British Columbia is 19.

∎ HOURS OF OPERATION

In Washington and Oregon, store hours can be erratic, a testament to the laid-back nature of the region. Major department stores or shops in the busy downtown areas of Seattle and Portland generally follow the 10-to-6 rule, but you should always phone ahead if you have your heart set on visiting a smaller shop. Never assume a store is open on Sunday, even in the major cities; many smaller shops have truncated Saturday hours as well. To make matters more confusing, most smaller stores close one day during the week (usually Monday or Tuesday, but it varies), and some stores don't open until 11 AM, noon, or even 1 PM. Thankfully, coffeehouses tend to keep regular and long hours, so you'll have no problem finding one to kill time in if you have to wait for a store to open.

Note that bars in Washington and Oregon close at 2 AM, with last call coming as early as 1:30.

∎ MONEY

Meals in the Pacific Northwest are generally a little less expensive than in other major North American regions. Portland is by far the cheapest of the major cities in all respects; Vancouver is the most expensive. Prices for first-class hotel rooms in Seattle, Portland, Vancouver, and Victoria are high in summer ($250–$400), though the same rooms become surprisingly affordable in low season ($100 to $200 a night). Unless you're willing to stay in rundown motels, the cheapest rooms you'll find inside the major cities start at $75–$90 a night. Though you'll get some great deals on food and other on-the-ground expenses (fewer sights charge prohibitive fees), you'll find that some urban "necessities," like taxi rides, are frustratingly expensive.

Debit cards and major credit cards are accepted almost everywhere—some cafes will even let you charge a single cup of coffee—so don't worry about carrying around wads of cash. In the major cities it's a good idea to keep handy a few small bills and coins for parking meters.

ITEM	AVERAGE COST
Cup of Coffee	$1.50
Glass of Wine	$6–$9
Glass of Beer	$4–$6
Sandwich	$5–$8
One-Mile Taxi Ride in Capital City	$4.50 all cities
Museum Admission	$10–$15

Prices throughout this guide are given for adults. Substantially reduced fees are almost always available for children, students, and senior citizens.

■**TIP→ Banks never have every foreign currency on hand, and it may take as long as a week to order. If you're planning to exchange funds before leaving home, don't wait until the last minute.**

ATMS & BANKS

Several major U.S. banks, like Citibank and HSBC, have branches in British Columbia. ATMs are plentiful there (most take any card with the Cirrus or Plus network logo) and throughout the Pacific Northwest, as are vendors who accept debit cards that have the Visa or MasterCard logos.

■**TIP→ PIN numbers with more than four digits are not recognized at ATMs in many countries. If yours has five or more, remember to change it before you leave.**

ATM Locations Plus (☎800/843-7587).

CREDIT CARDS

Throughout this guide, the following abbreviations are used: **AE,** American Express; **D,** Discover; **DC,** Diners Club; **MC,** MasterCard; and **V,** Visa.

Reporting Lost Cards American Express (☎800/528-4800 in the U.S. or 336/393-

1111 collect from abroad ⊕www.american express.com). **Diners Club** (☎800/234-6377 in the U.S. or 303/799-1504 collect from abroad ⊕www.dinersclub.com). **Discover** (☎800/347-2683 in the U.S. or 801/902-3100 collect from abroad ⊕www.discovercard.com). **MasterCard** (☎800/627-8372 in the U.S. or 636/722-7111 collect from abroad ⊕www.mastercard.com). **Visa** (☎800/847-2911 in the U.S. or 410/581-9994 collect from abroad ⊕www.visa.com).

CURRENCY & EXCHANGE

The units of currency in Canada are the Canadian dollar (C$) and the cent, in almost the same denominations as U.S. currency ($5, $10, $20, 1¢, 5¢, 10¢, 25¢, etc.). The C$1 and C$2 bill are no longer used; they have been replaced by C$1 and C$2 coins (known as a "loonie," because of the loon that appears on the coin, and a "toonie," respectively). Check with a bank or other financial institution for the current rate. A good way to be sure you're getting the best exchange rate is by using your credit card or ATM/debit card. The issuing bank will convert your bill at the current rate.

■**TIP→ Even if a currency-exchange booth has a sign promising no commission, rest assured that there's some kind of huge, hidden fee. (Oh . . . that's right. The sign didn't say no *fee*.) And as for rates, you're almost always better off getting foreign currency at an ATM or exchanging money at a bank.**

▮ SAFETY

The most dangerous element of the Northwest is the great outdoors. Don't hike alone, and make sure you bring enough water plus basic first-aid items. If you're not an experienced hiker, stick to tourist-friendly spots like the more accessible parts of the national parks; if you have to drive 30 miles down a Forest Service road to reach a trail, it's possible you might be the only one hiking on it.

▌ TAXES

Oregon has no sales tax, although many cities and counties levy a tax on lodging and services. Room taxes, for example, vary 6%–9½%. The state retail sales tax in Washington is 6.5%, but there are also local taxes that can raise the total tax to 11.5%, depending on the goods or service and the municipality; Seattle's retail sales tax is 8.9%. A Goods and Services Tax (GST) of 5% applies on virtually every transaction in Canada except for the purchase of basic groceries.

In addition to the GST, British Columbia levies a sales tax of 7% on most items (although services, accommodation, groceries, children's clothes, and restaurant meals are exempt). Hotel rooms are subject to an 8% tax (in addition to the GST), and some municipalities levy an additional 2%. Wine, beer, and spirits purchased in bars and restaurants are subject to a 10% tax. Some restaurants build this into the price of the beverage, but others add it to the bill.

You can get a GST refund on purchases taken out of the country and on short-term accommodations of less than one month, but not on food, drink, tobacco, car or motor-home rentals, or transportation; rebate forms, which must be submitted within a year of leaving Canada, may be obtained from certain retailers, duty-free shops, customs officials, or from the Canada Customs and Revenue Agency. Instant cash rebates up to a maximum of C$500 are provided by some duty-free shops when you leave Canada, and most provinces do not tax goods that are shipped directly by the vendor to the purchaser's home. Always save your original receipts from stores and hotels (not just credit-card receipts), and be sure the name and address of the establishment are shown on the receipt. Original receipts are not returned. For you to be eligible for a refund, your receipts must total at least C$200, and each individual receipt for goods must show a minimum purchase of C$50 before tax. Some agencies in Vancouver and Whistler offer on-the-spot cash GST refunds. Although they charge a commission of about 20%, some visitors may find it worth it for the convenience, especially as Canadian Government checks may be difficult to cash in some countries. *See the shopping sections of individual chapters for locations.*

Information **Canada Customs and Revenue Agency** (✉ *Visitor Rebate Program, Summerside Tax Centre, 275 Pope Rd., Suite 104, Summerside PEC1N 6C6* ☎ *902/432–5608, 800/668–4748 in Canada* ⊕ *www.ccra-adrc.gc.ca*).

INDEX

PHOTO CREDITS

8, *Jim Lundgren/age fotostock.* 9 (left), *Jean Carter/age fotostock.* 9 (right), *Bruno Perousse/age fotostock.* 10, *Alan Kearney/viestiphoto.com.* 11, *Richard Cummins/viestiphoto.com.* 13 (left), *Ross Geredien/viestiphoto.com.* 13 (right), *Alan Kearney/viestiphoto.com.* 14, *Sylvain Grandadam/age fotostock.* 15 (left), *Greg Vaughn/Alamy.* 15 (right), *Eugene Bochkarev/Shutterstock.* 183 (top) and 184 (center), *Charles A. Blakeslee/age fotostock.* 183 (bottom), *SuperStock/age fotostock.* 184 (top), *William Blackel/age fotostock.* 184 (bottom), *Corey Rich/Aurora Photos.* 185, *Chris Howes/Wild Places Photography/Alamy.* 389 (top and bottom), *Alan Kearney/age fotostock.* 390 (top), *Don Geyer/Alamy.* 390 (bottom), *Washington State Tourism.* 392, *QT Luong/terragalleria.com.* 453 (top), *Washington State Tourism.* 453 (bottom), *David A. Barnes/Alamy.* 454-55, *Washington State Tourism.* 497 (top), *SuperStock/age fotostock.* 497 (bottom), *Cornforth Images/Alamy.* 498, *Washington State Tourism.*

ABOUT OUR WRITERS

Alison Appelbe is a Vancouver-based freelance writer and photographer. She frequently writes about her native city of Vancouver and the province of British Columbia. Her work appears in mostly print publications in Canada, the United States, Australia, and occasionally Europe.

Shelley Arenas, who covered eastern and southwestern Washington, grew up in Spokane and has lived in the Seattle area all of her adult life. She also does volunteer community development work in southwest Washington and enjoys exploring every part of the Pacific Northwest. She is a freelance writer, technical editor, and web designer who has contributed to several Fodor's books, co-authored a guidebook to Seattle for families, and writes for regional publications, including *Seattle Woman* magazine.

One winter vacation many years ago, former Fodor's editor Carissa Bluestone peered at the Emerald City through a thick veil of rain and fell in love with the place immediately. She made many return trips and soon decided to ditch New York for the Northwest. Now a freelance editor and writer, she makes the rounds of the northern neighborhoods' coffeehouses while working on a variety of book projects that have ranged in subject matter from travel (including updating stints on *Fodor's Seattle* and *Fodor's Mexico*) to sustainability to martial arts.

Kimberly Gadette's writings encompass travel, film, politics, sports, dating and dogs (though it's funny, dogs seldom date). Her first novel, *So Much for Love*, is debuting this year. Aside from her ongoing movie column, "The Screen Savor" with www.livepdx.com, she's been published more than 300 times in the last three years, in publications from the West Coast to the East, from *The Oregonian* to the *Boston Globe*. Though no one's ever asked to see it, she has an MFA from UCLA.

Carolyn B. Heller, who updated the Vancouver Dining, has been enthusiastically exploring—and eating—her way across her adopted city of Vancouver since she relocated there in 2003. Her travel and food articles have appeared in publications ranging from the *Boston Globe* and the *Los Angeles Times*, to *FamilyFun* magazine and *Travelers' Tales Paris*, and she's contributed to more than 25 Fodor's guides for destinations from New England to New Zealand.

Vancouver-born freelance writer Sue Kernaghan has written about British Columbia for dozens of publications throughout North America and the U.K. A fourth-generation British Columbian, she has contributed to several editions of *Fodor's Guide to Vancouver & British Columbia*, as well as to *Fodor's Alaska, Great Canadian Vacations, Healthy Escapes,* and *Escape to Nature Without Roughing It*. She lives on Salt Spring Island with her partner and small son.

An award-winning, freelance travel writer, Chris McBeath's more than 25 years in tourism have given her an insider's eye as to what makes a great vacation experience. Whether routing through backcountry, or discovering a hidden-away inn, Chris has combined history, insight, and anecdotes into her research for this book, and of her home, British Columbia.

Janna Mock-Lopez is a Beaverton-based writer enamored by the spirit, beauty and vitality of Portland, Oregon and the Northwest. She is also a writer and publisher of *Portland Family* magazine which distributes over 40,000 copies locally each month.

After a decade living in L.A., Celeste Moure recently traded traffic and smog for a slice of Vancouver heaven: crisp mountain air, fresh powder, and old-growth forests. Her work has appeared in *Condé Nast Traveler, Outside, Spin,* and various other publications.

Portland-based writer Deston Nokes enjoys escaping the Oregon clouds to write about compelling cultures and provocative people. Raised in a family of journalists, he grew up traveling, having lived in Old San Juan, Buenos Aires and along the eastern seaboard. Deston specializes in Hawaiian, Pacific Northwest, Caribbean and Latin American travel, and his two teenage kids often come along for the ride.

Freelance writer and columnist Rob Phillips was raised in the Yakima Valley and has lived in Central Washington for nearly 50 years. Since becoming a professional writer in 1986, Rob has written for dozens of different publications, mostly on outdoor subjects. His award-winning Northwest Outdoors column appears every Thursday in the *Yakima Herald-Republic.*

As a Fodor's writer and editor for more than a decade, Holly S. Smith has covered the world from Indonesia and Australia to Oregon and Peru. *Fodor's Pacific Northwest* gave her a chance to work closer to her Puget Sound island home, from where she had fun exploring the Seattle Environs, San Juan Islands, Olympic Peninsula, and Northwestern Washington with her three children. Holly, who completely enjoys her freelance career, has also written for *The Seattle Times*, the *International Examiner*, Oxford University Press, the Sierra Club, and other publishers.